THE LONG ARM OF LEE

THE

Long Arm of Lee

THE HISTORY OF THE ARTILLERY OF

THE ARMY OF NORTHERN VIRGINIA

———— ◆ ————

JENNINGS CROPPER WISE

With a foreword by L. VAN LOAN NAISAWALD

New York
OXFORD UNIVERSITY PRESS
1959

The Long Arm of Lee was first published in 1915
by J. P. Bell Company, Inc., Lynchburg, Virginia

DEDICATED

TO THE MEMORY

OF

MY FATHER

JOHN SERGEANT WISE

FOREWORD

For forty-odd years Jennings Wise's *The Long Arm of Lee* has stood as the only published account of Civil War artillery. While this work treats only one segment of that arm—the field batteries of Lee's Army of Northern Virginia—it has been much sought after by students of that war in general, and it has also served as a source book for those wishing to study in some detail the techniques, tactics, and organization of Civil War artillery.

Any student of that conflict must realize that while countless volumes have been written on personalities, on grand strategy, on specific campaigns, and on individual units, the role of the field batteries has, with this exception, been relegated to generalizations and broad collective terminology.

Every student of this war knows that the infantry of both sides, and the cavalry as well, used regiments as the basis of their organization. They know, too, that both sides fought their armies by brigades, by divisions, and by army corps. But what about the artillery? How were they organized; what system was used in assigning batteries? Did they fight as individual units; were they attached to commands as the needs dictated; did they have their own chain of command? What problems of commands, administration, and supply were unique to this arm? The answers to these and countless other questions, as they pertain to Lee's artillery, are covered by Colonel Wise.

With the study of this war once more undergoing a vigorous revival, it is only fitting that *The Long Arm of Lee* be reprinted as a valuable contribution to the literature of this field. In conjunction with the forthcoming study of the Federal artillery entitled *Grape and Canister,* these two works should fill a vast gap in any reader's Civil War library.

Colonel Wise was one of those fortunate persons who had the opportunity to talk with many survivors of

Lee's 'long arm,' and from them he gained much valuable information, as well as the increased enthusiasm to tell their story in detail—a story that had been completely neglected.

As background he gives a short history of the development of the artillery arm in the United States from Colonial days to the outbreak of the Civil War. But in contrast to writing the history of an army which has been in existence for some time, with a nucleus of units, of trained personnel, and of matériel, Colonel Wise was faced with the added task of explaining how the Confederacy built and, almost simultaneously, sent its armies to war.

Few nations have ever entered a war of national survival as poorly equipped to wage such a struggle as did the Confederacy. With virtually no heavy industry and only a handful of obsolete cannon in the State arsenals, it was a major accomplishment to provide adequate field artillery for its armies. While never equaling the Federals in gun strength, they did succeed in building and maintaining an artillery arm which in morale, dash, and determination was every bit equal to the Federals.

Appropriately then, Wise's first fifty pages are devoted to the creation of the Confederate Bureau of Ordnance: this is one of the most valuable portions of his work. The author explains how the Confederacy built its military house from the most austere and meager beginnings, which was particularly so in the case of the artillery. The Federals had the solid core of, first four, and then five, full Regular Army regiments of artillery, totaling almost sixty batteries, around which to build their organization; the South had no such base, the only organized artillery unit of any size in the Confederacy being the militia unit of New Orleans known as the Washington Artillery Battalion. Beyond this there were only scattered militia companies in varying stages of training, armament, and size.

It was one thing to have a body calling itself an artillery unit, but it was still another to find a trained cadre, and to equip it with usable and effective cannon. No small problem either was the procurement of saddles, bridles, and traces. Colonel Wise tells how the South got its artillery officers, with the few West Pointers too valuable to waste as individual battery commanders. He shows how by tremendous personal efforts on the part of General W. N. Pendleton, subsequently Lee's chief of artillery, and Colonel Josiah Gorgas of the Confederate Ordnance Bureau, the South overcame the initial lack of artillery matériel and equipment.

It is unfortunate that Wise did not go into greater detail in covering the ordnance and ammunition used by the South and explain certain terminology. For example, in speaking of 12-pounder howitzers he fails to clarify that this term did not mean a weapon capable of high angle fire, but a light type of field piece originally designed to shoot frangible projectiles such as shell—the forerunner of modern high explosive—and case shot or shrapnel as it was later called. The howitzer was found to be less desirable and less durable than the heavier and longer range field guns, though the Confederates would continue to use them for reasons of necessity.

When one reads this account it will become obvious that the artillery of the Confederacy attracted a particularly high caliber group of young officers. Led by the brilliant E. Porter Alexander, the foresight and leadership of these men enabled Lee's 'long arm' to neutralize much of the quantitative superiority of their opponents. As a result the tactical organization of the artillery of the Army of Northern Virginia was for the first part of the war continually one step ahead of the Federals.

The author chose to treat his subject on a relatively high level of command, dealing to a great extent with high command problems and theory; only occasionally does he dip down to the story of the individual battery. Nevertheless, one cannot help but become familiar, as the pages go by, with many of Lee's colorful and legendary battery commanders—the famous John Pelham, scholarly looking Willie Pegram, handsome Tom Carter, horse artilleryman Preston Chew, and many others. On top of these the tremendous ability of the senior commanders—Porter Alexander, Armistead Long, Stapleton Crutchfield, Henry Cabell, to name a few—cannot help but shine through the cloud of their lack of guns and of over-all military strength.

Since Colonel Wise's subject is the artillery of only the Army of Northern Virginia, it is natural that the bulk of his research was centered on that army, with minor attention devoted to the Union opposition, and as such, some of Wise's figures as they relate to Federal detail are subject to question.

Some of the errors in Union data which have been noted are as follows:

p. 72, l. 28. The gun strength of the five Union batteries which crossed Bull Run was 24 pieces not 25.

p. 132, ll. 23-27. There were only three Regular batteries—Griffin's, Ricketts', and Arnold's. In addition, there was the 2d Rhode Island Battery, plus 2 12-pounder boat howitzers dragged by men of the 71st New York Infantry, a total of 24 pieces. Of this number 10 were 10-pounder Parrott rifles, 8 were 13-pounder James rifles, 4 were 12-pounder howitzers, and 2 were 6-pounder guns. None of these weapons was considered "heavy."

p. 136, l. 8. There was no New York battery *per se* on the field, though there was the cannon company of the 71st New York with the two boat howitzers.

p. 207. The engagement in front of Beaver Dam Creek was fought on the afternoon of June 26, 1862, not on the 27th, and is commonly called the Battle of Mechanicsville. Porter did not withdraw under the fire of his artillery, but rather during the night and morning of 26-27 June. Two Regular batteries were lightly engaged early in the morning of the 27th in covering Porter's rear.

p. 208. Porter employed 6, possibly 7 batteries at Mechanicsville, not massed but distributed along 2500 yards of front.

p. 216, ll. 37-38. The battery seized by the Confederates was not

Randolph's Battery E, 1st Rhode Island Light Artillery, but Randolph's Regular Battery E, 1st US Artillery.

p. 222, l. 35. Colonel Hunt was Chief of the Artillery Reserve at this time, with Barry still holding the title of Chief of Artillery, Army of the Potomac. While actually Hunt was now functioning as the artillery chief, he was not promoted officially to this slot until September 5, 1862.

p. 230, l. 20. There is no firm evidence corroborating the statement that at Malvern Hill Hunt massed the artillery's fire and deliberately ordered the shifting of this mass from target to target. It may have seemed the case to the Confederates since they were able to get so few batteries into action at the same time to oppose the Federals; as each isolated battery came in view it was fair game for every blue gunner who could bring his piece to bear.

p. 266, l. 1. The date should be August 29th.

p. 296, l. 2. Wise's estimate of 275 guns for McClellan appears to be too low; it was closer to 298 pieces.

p. 298, l. 16. The same point holds here.

p. 305, ll. 3, 5. The name of Captain Joseph M. Knap is misspelled.

p. 383, l. 1. Initially two Pennsylvania and one Regular battery engaged Pelham. A third Pennsylvania battery crossed the river and joined the engagement sometime later.

p. 442, l. 3. More recent studies give Hooker's gun strength as slightly higher, 411-419 pieces.

p. 453, l. 13. The total of Andrews' battalion should apparently read 11 pieces.

p. 479, l. 28. Captain Wiedrich's name is misspelled.

p. 480, l. 6. The 3-inch ordnance rifles were not Rodmans.

p. 487, l. 12. Captain Huntington was not the division chief of artillery, but assumed command when the chief, Captain Puttkammer, was absent.

p. 489, ll. 10-17. Recent research into the Federal gun strength confronting Jackson at Fairview and Hazel Grove indicates that a total of at least 64 guns were in action.

p. 507, l. 23. Confederate accounts state that they seized four pieces of this unit which was Huntington's Ohio battery. They admit retiring shortly thereafter, leaving one piece behind, and Huntington reports the loss of only three guns.

p. 575, l. 14.

also

p. 576, l. 10. In an official report Hunt gives the army's gun strength as of June 30th 1863, at 69 batteries and 362 guns. Of this total, at least two batteries of 4 guns each did not accompany the army past Westminster, Md. In his account in *Battles and Leaders* General Hunt says he had 65 batteries with 370 guns at Gettysburg, but this appears a bit too high in total guns.

p. 619, l. 11. The total number of Union batteries on the field during the day was 11, but the most that were engaged at any one time was 9.

p. 645, ll. 18-19. These weapons were either 24-pounder howitzers or 20-pounder Parrotts; there was no such weapon as a 24-pounder Parrott.

p. 670, l. 15. Captain Rorty's name is misspelled.

p. 715, l. 12. The 3-inch iron rifles were neither Dahlgrens nor Rodmans.

L. VAN LOAN NAISAWALD

Manassas, Virginia
July 1958

TABLE OF CONTENTS

Part I

PAGE

Preface   15

CHAPTER

I   EARLY ORDNANCE WORK AND STATUS OF ORDNANCE IN 1861   23

II   ORGANIZATION OF THE BUREAU OF ORDNANCE AND ITS EARLY OPERATIONS   34

III   ORGANIZATIONS AND OPERATIONS   52

IV   ORIGINAL ARMAMENT OF THE ARMY OF NORTHERN VIRGINIA   61

Part II

I   THE ARTILLERY OF THE EARLY DAYS   85

II   THE VIRGINIA MILITARY INSTITUTE AS A SCHOOL OF ARMS   95

III   THE FIELD ARTILLERY OF THE CONFEDERATE STATES OF AMERICA   107

IV   THE VIRGINIA VOLUNTEERS   112

V   ACTIVE OPERATIONS COMMENCE: BIG BETHEL AND GAINESVILLE   118

VI   BLACKBURN'S FORD AND FIRST MANASSAS   127

VII   WINTER OF 1861-62   140

VIII   TACTICS AND EARLY INSTRUCTION   149

IX   FEDERAL ORGANIZATION AND TACTICAL CONCEPTS   156

X   THE HORSE ARTILLERY AND THE VALLEY CAMPAIGN   162

XI   THE PENINSULA CAMPAIGN   176

XII   GENERAL LEE ASSUMES COMMAND—REORGANIZATION—BEGINNING OF THE SEVEN DAYS   197

XIII   GAINES' MILL   210

XIV   SAVAGE'S STATION AND FRAZIER'S FARM   215

CHAPTER		PAGE
XV	MALVERN HILL	221
XVI	CEDAR MOUNTAIN	241
XVII	GAINESVILLE AND GROVETON	255
XVIII	SECOND MANASSAS	266
XIX	THE MARYLAND INVASION—HARPER'S FERRY AND SOUTH MOUNTAIN	277
XX	REORGANIZATION, FROM SHARPSBURG TO FREDERICKSBURG	327
XXI	FREDERICKSBURG	357
XXII	THE WINTER OF 1862-63—KELLYSVILLE AND THE DEATH OF PELHAM, "THE GALLANT, THE INCOMPARABLE"—REORGANIZATION AGAIN	409
XXIII	THE BATTLE OF CHANCELLORSVILLE—PRELIMINARY DISPOSITIONS	442
XXIV	CHANCELLORSVILLE—MAY 1ST	458
XXV	CHANCELLORSVILLE—MAY 2D—JACKSON'S ATTACK	466
XXVI	CHANCELLORSVILLE—SUNDAY, MAY 3D	505
XXVII	CHANCELLORSVILLE, CONTINUED—FREDERICKSBURG AND SALEM CHURCH—MAY 3D	515
XXVIII	CHANCELLORSVILLE—MAY 4	530
XXIX	PREPARATION FOR THE SECOND MARYLAND INVASION—DEATH OF JACKSON—BRANDY STATION	556
XXX	FROM FREDERICKSBURG TO GETTYSBURG	598
XXXI	GETTYSBURG—JULY 1	616
XXXII	GETTYSBURG—JULY 2	635
XXXIII	GETTYSBURG—JULY 3	660
XXXIV	GETTYSBURG—THE RETREAT	695
XXXV	REORGANIZATION AFTER GETTYSBURG—THE WINTER OF 1863-64	706
XXXVI	THE ARTILLERY COMMANDERS OF THE ARMY COMPARED	742
XXXVII	THE WILDERNESS	760
XXXVIII	SPOTSYLVANIA	775
XXXIX	THE NORTH ANNA	799
XL	COLD HARBOR	812
XLI	COLD HARBOR TO PETERSBURG	834

TABLE OF CONTENTS

CHAPTER		PAGE
XLII	PETERSBURG—THE SIEGE COMMENCES	842
XLIII	THE TRENCHES IN JULY	847
XLIV	THE CRATER	859
XLV	THE SECOND CORPS IN THE VALLEY	876
XLVI	PETERSBURG—THE WINTER OF 1864	895
XLVII	THE BEGINNING OF THE END—1865	919
XLVIII	"LE DEBACLE"	928
	General Index	959
	Battery Index	980
	Battalion Index	992

PUBLISHER'S NOTE: This book was originally issued in two separate volumes, with Volume I ending on page 496, and Volume II beginning on page 505.

PREFACE

THIS work has been written in my first year as Commandant of the Corps of Cadets of the Virginia Military Institute. Its writing, therefore, has been attended by many interruptions incident to my military and academic duties. Convinced that the Field Artillery of the Army of Northern Virginia has received too little attention on the part of the historian, I have for years projected such a work as this. In fact, writers on the Civil War have almost as if intentionally ignored the subject, referring but casually to the gunner's part in the great tragedy. Their failure to discuss this subject has no doubt been due to a feeling of uncertainty whenever they sought to enter upon what they conceived to be a more or less special domain. Nor was this sentiment uncommon to the participants themselves. The reports of the various commanders engaged in the war are generally vague in matters pertaining to the artillery. Not failing in tribute to the gunners, they have failed to record any definite information concerning the artillery.

The result is that to-day he who enters into an investigation of more than the most casual character finds himself involved in a game of historical dominoes, with many of the pieces lacking. I will illustrate my point by saying that even Maj. H. B. McClellan, Chief of Staff of the Cavalry Corps, in his history of Stuart's campaigns avoids the mention of the horse batteries on certain occasions as if by design. Yet these batteries were as much a part of Stuart's command as the cavalry troops themselves. He does not even include them in the organization of the cavalry, which he gives in an otherwise most valuable work.

More often than not, the corps, division, and brigade returns include the artillery personnel in the strength of the infantry, and rarely are the names of the batteries, or the number of guns engaged, specified. Over such details is merely thrown the cloak of the mysterious word "artillery," as if that should suffice for the curious.

While little in the way of service statistics is to be obtained from the survivors, I have secured many clues from the veteran soldiers of my acquaintance, who have often assisted me to make the mask of time less inscrutable.

Originally, I had intended to treat the subject in three distinct parts,—that is, the Bureau of Ordnance, its resources, operations, and organization; the organization, material and personnel of the Field Artillery, and the tactics of the arm. But almost immediately after beginning the work I concluded that the two last sub-divisions should be combined for the sake of brevity, as well as on account of the difficulty of treating them separately, which would have at least entailed much repetition.

Once, in the literary enthusiasm of youth, I gathered together a number of my speeches and papers, and, having them printed, I distributed copies of the pamphlet among my friends. But, as is usually the case, vanity betrayed me, for some of these pamphlets fell into the hands of able critics, who quite frequently attacked my comparisons between the Confederate and Federal artillerymen, despite my repeated denials that "odious comparisons" were intended to be drawn. My Northern friends simply declared that comparisons were inherently odious, and that I could not make them otherwise. I learned my lesson, and in this work I have endeavored to avoid anything that even savored of a comparison, except in matters of material, organization, equipment, and tangible things in general, believing that history would best be subserved by presenting the facts and allowing each reader to draw his own conclusions.

To me the record of Lee's artillery, or his "long arm," has been one of surpassing interest. Each chapter, as it unfolded itself, seemed more and more in need of a stronger pen than mine. Yet I feel that if I have failed to draw the proper inferences from the tangle of avail-

able facts, the proof that I have erred will at least disclose the truth, and I will, therefore, have been indirectly responsible for a better account than my own.

The story of the gunners of Lee's army has always
appealed with peculiar force to my imagination, by
reason of the lasting repute so many juniors, from the
standpoints of both age and rank in the service, acquired.
Every Southern child has heard, in terms of praise and
tenderest affection, the story of Pegram, the youthful
colonel; of the one-armed Haskell; of Latimer, the
boy major; of Breathed; of Caskie; of Jimmie Thomson and Preston Chew. And lives there a son of the
Southland who has not heard of Pelham, "the Gallant,"
so named by the lips of Lee himself? It seems almost
invidious to mention these few and to omit the names of
their peers. *Ab uno disce omnes.*

While the cherished deeds of the Confederate artillery subalterns are in no wise comparable, according to
a strict standard of military accomplishment, with the
achievements of such soldiers as Longstreet, the Hills,
Ewell, Mahone, Gordon, and many others of like mold,
yet, in the South at least, of the two, the personal recollection of many of the juniors is the more lastingly
tender, and the general interest in them grows greater
with each year, by reason of the heroic traditions that
cluster about their youthful memories.

Undoubtedly there was something in the spiritual
composition of these boyish soldiers, a mixture of dash
and conviction, not akin to mere bravado, but more like
divine faith, which made them unconquerable. Living,
they possessed that quality electric, more spirituelle than
physical, which gave temper to their steel and made
their thrusts the keener. Dead, there survives in connection with their memory that elusive influence which,
lingering, when appealed to, makes brave men of
cowards.

It may be suggested that a sympathetic note in the
scale of sentiment is struck by the heroes of defeat. But
no, the luster of which I write is not the shimmer of

pathos. It was while living and victorious that they touched the souls of their people and laid the foundation for that everlasting renown which depends not for its freshness upon the written pages of history,—in which their names are scarcely mentioned.

Amid the cherished traditions and in close association with the companions of Pelham and Pegram and the others of whom I write, I have found an inspiration at least to·essay the task of recording some of their heroisms, tarrying now and then to point out the transcendent quality of their valor. And from the pages of the numerous books,—many of them professional works, bearing the autographs of Lee, and Johnston, and Pendleton, and Cocke, and Crozet, and Mercer, and Bomford, and Mordecai, and Gilham, and many others,—to which I have had the privilege of access, I have drawn another inspiration; that is, to be just to the noblest foe an army ever had, to a foe who, after all, whether the equal or the superior, was but the brother of the artilleryman whose history I have sought to record in more collected form than it has hitherto existed.

Should the narrative seem to ignore the part played by the other arms of the service, it must be recalled that this work professes to be but a history of the Field Artillery. In undertaking such a specialized work there is always grave danger that the writer may be charged with undue partiality, that his enthusiasm for his particular subject may be at the expense of others. But, in this case, the author can only deny any intent to laud the Field Artillery by disparaging its sister arms, and he has not failed to point out its faults as well as its virtues. There is glory enough for all, and he recognizes the fact that, in the last analysis, the artillery, however important and valiant its services may have been, was in 1861-65, as it always will be, but the auxiliary arm of the infantry, and that the exploits of the Field Artillery of the Army of Northern Virginia depended upon and were made possible by what was perhaps one of the most superb bodies of foot soldiers war has yet produced.

To Gens. Thomas T. Munford and Scott Shipp, Col. R. Preston Chew, Maj. R. W. Hunter, Capts. William T. Poague, W. Gordon McCabe, William W. Chamberlaine, J. J. Shoemaker, and Judge George L. Christian, all of whom were intimates of and soldiers under "Stonewall" Jackson, and all of whom, except the first, served with his artillery, I am much indebted for aid. And to Capt. James Power Smith,—who was one of Jackson's gunners, and who to-day is the sole surviving member of his staff, and with whom I had the honor to serve on the staff of the First Battalion Field Artillery Virginia Volunteers for several years,—I am also deeply grateful for much information. To Col. R. T. Kerlin, Professor of English, Virginia Military Institute, I desire to express my thanks for his interest and advice.

To Col. J. V. Bidgood, Virginia's efficient Secretary of Military Records, I am also indebted for much assistance. His untiring industry and splendid system has made available for the student a vast amount of historical material which is a priceless asset of the State. There are few who know the real nature and extent of his labor and the results he has attained.

The portraits illustrating this work have been collected with great labor. Many of them have never before been published. Of many of the famous Confederate artillery officers no pictures are to be had.

The author is conscious of the fact that maps showing the topography and positions of the battlefields described in the text would add greatly to the value of the book, but it has been found impracticable to include them. The use of the series of maps published in connection with the Rebellion Records is recommended to military students.

In conclusion, I desire to call particular attention to the part the Virginia Military Institute played in furnishing officers to the Confederacy as a whole, and to the Army of Northern Virginia in particular, and the direct influence it exerted upon the greatness of "Stonewall" Jackson. JENNINGS C. WISE.

Lexington, Virginia,
   July 1, 1914.

PART I

CONFEDERATE BUREAU OF ORDNANCE

ITS ORGANIZATION, PERSONNEL, MATERIAL, AND RE-
SOURCES, WITH AN ACCOUNT OF THE ORIGINAL
ARMAMENT OF THE ARTILLERY OF
THE ARMY OF NORTHERN
VIRGINIA

THE LONG ARM OF LEE

CHAPTER I

EARLY ORDNANCE WORK AND STATUS OF ORDNANCE IN 1861

IN the nature of things a study of the artillery of the Army of Northern Virginia involves an investigation of the system under which the material therefor was provided and the resources from which it was drawn. Hence we find ourselves at the very outset face to face with the Ordnance Department, its organization, and its personnel, in addition to the material resources at its command.

Military critics, passing judgment after the event, seldom prosecute their investigations beyond an inquiry into the actual movements of the troops and the battle orders of the commanders. The war chest, the weather conditions, and such things as material and equipment frequently escape their attention entirely. Public opinion, that bogie of military men, is generally totally ignored. The move that would have surely resulted in success, had it been made, is unfalteringly pointed out, and woe to the general who failed to execute it, no matter what the obstacles in his path may have been. There stands the height which, crowned with a hundred guns, could have changed history. The fact that it was on the particular day of the battle beyond human ability to place those guns on that hill, or that, even if they had been there, a sufficient supply of ammunition was lacking, due to some influence beyond the control of the general commanding,—such things as these enter not into the calculations of the critics a century later.

The logicians of war alone appreciate the skill and the labor which others must have brought to the aid of Cæsar. They know that an army moves on its belly, and that its thrusts are no keener than the weapons it wields. And it is well, in studying Lee's artillery, to commence with a proper appreciation of the limitations which circumstances imposed upon its employment. Any layman must know that the artillery is dependent upon the Ordnance Department for material, equipment, and stores, and that however efficient the artillery personnel may be its effectiveness bears a direct relation to the efficiency of that agency which provides it with the machinery of war. Ordinarily, as in the case of Germany in 1866 and 1870, and of the Balkan States in their present struggle with Turkey, material and equipment are manufactured, stored, and issued in advance by a well-organized corps of experts.

Few instances are recorded where a belligerent has actually created the very factories for the fabrication of its arms and munitions of war after the outbreak of hostilities with a powerful adversary. This was true, however, in the case of the Confederate States of America, although it has been frequently charged and very successfully disproved that Mr. Davis and Mr. Floyd used their office while Secretary of War of the United States to transfer arms and military supplies from the North to Southern arsenals where they might be more readily seized in the event of secession.

The condition of his ordnance and ordnance supplies, as well as his Medical, Commissary, and Quartermaster Departments, undoubtedly made impossible Johnston's immediate advance upon Washington after Bull Run.

Had the Confederate Bureau of Ordnance been created *de novo,* we might begin our study with the year 1861, but since it was the offspring of an old system, we must look further back in order to appreciate the character of the foundation upon which it was raised.

At the very outbreak of the War of American Independence Congress appointed a committee to consider ways and means to supply the Colonies with ammunition and military stores, a most important provision, since

Great Britain had prohibited the shipment of such things to America and was in a most advantageous position to enforce the restriction. This, then, was the inception of the American system for the supply of munitions of war, for the mother country had very wisely created no plants for their manufacture in the colonial wilderness.

The recommendations of the committee led to the appointment, in 1776, of a Commissioner of Artillery Stores, in coöperation with whom the business of procuring material and ammunition was conducted by a secret committee of the Board of War. This and various subsequent provisions,—quite inadequate, as shown by experience,—were relied upon until the War of 1812, when, in May of that year, the Ordnance Department was created by Act of Congress. After having passed through various legislative vicissitudes, as an independent bureau of the War Department, it was abolished by Act of March 2, 1821, and merged in the Artillery. The President was authorized to select such artillery officers as might be necessary for ordnance work, and to each regiment of artillery one supernumerary captain was attached for ordnance duty. When assigned to such duty these officers were subject to the direct orders of the War Department only, a provision almost tantamount to preserving the independence of the bureau, yet hampering it in the interest of economy with an organization soon found to be impracticable. As a result of eleven years of bitter experience the Ordnance Department was organized on an independent footing by the Act of April 5, 1832.

Following the reorganization of the system, the War Department, in 1834, during the incumbency of Lewis Cass, sought to define the duties of ordnance officers and regulate their operations. Hitherto the loosely organized system had relied solely upon civilian contractors for the supply of material, but definite regulations were now prescribed for its production, and it was provided that there should be established as many arsenals of construction as the public service might require, not exceeding six in number. It was directed that four of the arsenals should be erected at Washington, Watervliet, Pittsburg, and Fort Monroe, respectively, and upon their completion the fabrication and issue of ordnance stores should commence under the direction of the Colonel or Chief of Ordnance with headquarters at the national capital. In addition to the corps of ordnance officers proper, it was provided that lieutenants of artillery should be detailed to the Ordnance Department, for not more than four years, to engage in the manufacture of gun carriages and artillery equipment.

The regulations published in 1834 were followed in 1841 by a manual prepared by Col. George Bomford, Chief of Ordnance, and again by a similar work in 1850, revised in 1861 under the immediate direction of Maj. Laidley. Meanwhile the regulations for the department were being amplified and enforced, in which work Capt. Alfred Mordecai, of Virginia, and Col. Benjamin Huger, of South Carolina, took an important part as assistants of Col. Talcott, the Chief.

By the year 1852 there had been established twenty-seven ordnance stations in the United States, of which number there were three in Virginia,—one being at Harper's Ferry, one at Old Point Comfort, and the Bellona Arsenal in Chesterfield County, near Richmond.

The labor of Southern officers had largely contributed to the development of the Ordnance Department, and upon the outbreak of the war the Confederacy secured the services of many efficient men, who created much out of little. Under the direction of the Chief of Ordnance, C. S. A., a manual was immediately prepared fully setting forth the material and equipment adopted for use by the Confederacy. Practically no differences existed between that of the two services, except as to the shape of certain pieces of ordnance, more particularly with respect to rifled field guns, columbiads, and the rifled mountain pieces.

The various regulations and manuals published during the period 1834-1860 contain the history of the development of ordnance up to the Civil War and set forth fully the character of the artillery material in use in this country in 1860. These works are also referred to because they are descriptive of the school of training through which many of the Confederate officers had passed. The foregoing paragraphs briefly describe the foundation upon which the Confederate Bureau of Ordnance was based, and in the upbuilding of which a number of former United States officers took important parts. And now, before going further in our investigation, it will be well to examine the stage of development of field ordnance in 1861.

The classification of ordnance shown in the manual of 1861 includes no field pieces except 6- and 12-pounder bronze guns, 12-pounder bronze mountain howitzers, and 12-, 24-, and 32-pounder bronze field howitzers, which were all smooth-bore pieces. The new system of rifling is not referred to in the work and it will be shown later that its status in the United States Army was entirely unofficial until late in 1861. There had been much experimenting going on since 1850, but the fact remains that field ordnance as prescribed in the official manuals at the beginning and end of the decade was identical. With the outbreak of the war, however, iron field ordnance was cast, and in 1862 there were in use 3-inch iron rifled guns, the old bronze pieces, 12-pounder bronze Napoleons, the various old types of bronze howitzers, and 12-pounder iron howitzers, the last-named having been added in 1861. The 32-pounder bronze howitzer had become obsolete for use in the field. Both armies purchased foreign guns of various types, but although they were used they were not prescribed as regulation ordnance for manufacture in this country. The Confederates had developed by 1862 a 2.25-inch bronze mountain rifle which does not appear to have been in use in the Northern Army.

It would be impracticable to discuss here the great
variety of ordnance that was used during the war.
Officially, at least, a great deal of it was unknown to the
Ordnance Department and formed no part, as has been
said before, of the regulation material. The development of ordnance in the United States Army, with the
exception of a 3-inch rifle, seems to have been left
entirely in the hands of private persons, the war giving
an impetus to the manufacture of all kinds of artillery
material. Some conception of the armament of the time
may be had from a report of the field artillery material
of Rosecrans' army in 1863, in which it is stated there
were thirty-two 6-pounder smooth-bores, twenty-four
12-pounder howitzers, eight 12-pounder light Napoleons, twenty-one James rifles, thirty-four 10-pounder
Parrotts, two 12-pounder and two 6-pounder Wiard
steel guns, two 16-pounder Parrotts, and four 3-inch
rifled ordnance guns. This assortment is typical of the
Confederate material of the time.

Rifling as adapted to the use of field ordnance was
little known to our ordnance experts at the time and
was scarcely more familiar to those of Europe.

William Greener, C. E., in a treatise on Rifles, Cannon, and Sporting Arms, published in London in 1858,
points out that gun barrels were grooved first in Vienna
about 1498 for the purpose of providing space for the
foul residue produced by discharge, thus diminishing
friction in reloading. Within twenty years of this time
the grooves were given a twist, and some of the bullets
had projections to fit the grooves. This was not
practicable, however, so the shape of the bullets was
changed, and it passed through various stages from being egg-shaped to practically the present form. These
rifles were unsuccessful, due to the fact that there was
too much of what was then called windage,—gas escaping by the bullet. In 1836 Greener produced the perfect expansive bullet,—that is, a bullet which upon
discharge would expand and fill the rifling,—although
Capt. Norton, an English officer, had invented an ex-

plosive detonating lead shell in 1822, which incidentally only partly accomplished the same purpose on account of its inability to resist the compression due to the explosion. It is interesting to note that the principles of the invention of Greener were adopted by the English about 1848 under the name of Miniè rifle, Capt. Miniè having proposed practically the same things that were previously rejected when proposed by Greener.

Scoffern, in his New Recourses of Warfare, published in London, in 1859, discusses rifling of small arms and cannon. He credits Sir William Armstrong with the development of the English gun which bore his name, into a rifled, breech-loading piece, and he gives details of its construction. He also describes the Swedish or Wahrendorff breech-loading rifled cannon which was displayed in the Crystal Palace Exhibition of 1851. This model was never successful, however, because the cross section at the breech was not strong enough to withstand the shock of the explosion. In addition to these he mentions the fact that Cavalli, of the Sardinian service, accomplished the act of breech-loading, but he does not give details.

Just as our ordnance officers paid little heed to what was transpiring in military circles abroad, so the Europeans ignored our development of the new system until after the Seven Weeks' War of 1866. Napoleon and the Prussians had both been experimenting with rifling as early as 1857, but in the case of the latter the novelty found much opposition. In England the Lancaster gun, with two grooves, was considered by many decidedly unsatisfactory, if not a failure, and the Armstrong gun was but in the experimental stage at the time, though its invention had attracted much notice. The Cavalli breech-loading rifle gun was not well adapted to use in the field and was considered entirely too complicated for service.

The views of American experts concerning these guns are fully set forth in Gibbon's "Artillerist's Manual," published August 14, 1859, in which the author, though stationed at West Point, fails to refer to Parrott.

Napoleon went so far, however, in 1858, as to order his S. B. guns rifled, under the bastard system known as the "Lahitte System," which continued in general use in France until 1870. The French had also developed a rifled 30-pounder, more or less unsuited to field use, although it was employed in Italy in 1859 with results as to range and accuracy which gave great impetus to the system on the continent. This seems to be the first instance of the use of a rifled gun on the field of battle. Hohenlohe tells us that before the termination of the War between France and Germany the Prussian authorities had given orders to construct three hundred rifled 6-pounders and a number of 4-pounders. But no convincing results were obtained by the Prussians with their new field guns in the war with the Danes in 1864, though some satisfaction was obtained with rifled siege guns at Düppel. The prevailing opinion in Prussia in 1866 as to rifled field pieces is evidenced by the fact that, despite the American experiences during the preceding five years, one-fourth of the Prussian guns were smooth-bores, this number being considered necessary on account of their supposed superiority with case and shrapnel for close fighting. The satisfaction obtained with their rifled guns in the Austrian War was by no means universal among the Prussians. In fact, there was much disappointment, a result due more to the poor tactical handling of the artillery than to the material, though this fact had not then been generally perceived. One soldier at least there was in Prussia, who, like Jackson, as we shall see, never faltered in his conviction that rifled field pieces had come to stay. The sturdy Von Hindersen, Inspector General of Artillery, made up his mind as to their superiority and by that persistence for which he was noted gradually overbore all opposition to a complete armament with the new piece, a condition, however, which did not obtain until 1870. In the meantime, England had obtained results with a rifled gun in China in 1860.

In America, as early as 1855 experiments were made at Fortress Monroe with a grooved gun, but no satisfactory results had been obtained. This, in brief, was the status of rifled ordnance just prior to the outbreak of the war.

The smooth-bore system which prevailed in this country was of its kind unexcelled elsewhere. The Rodman heavy guns were marvels of their day and the process developed by the inventor for the manipulation of the iron in their casting placed American ordnance experts well to the front in the estimation of the military world. As to field material, the increased use and improvement of the 3-inch rifle sustained the reputation of the American Artillery acquired by reason of its advances in heavy armament, though Europe has been loath to accord to America the credit due the latter for the development of the rifled piece, a development which was eminently practical as opposed to the theoretical or experimental state of the various foreign systems of rifling of the time.

The introduction of rifled field pieces in this country and the events and influences leading up thereto will be considered later at length.

The claims to important inventions and discoveries are generally conflicting, and this is eminently true of revolutionary ones. In a discussion of the artillery material of the Civil War it is proper that the Confederacy should be given credit for its part in the invention of machine guns and breech-loaders. Before entering upon the general treatment of Confederate ordnance operations the subject of these guns will be briefly disposed of.

Attempts to construct multiple firing guns may be traced back to the earlier part of the seventeenth century, and small complicated guns of this character made by the Chinese have been found bearing dates as early as 1607. It was not until the introduction of fixed ammunition about 1860, however, that their successful construction was realized. Dr. Reed of Alabama perfected a shell for rifled guns about this time. During the Civil War a great variety of breech-loaders and machine guns, generally ineffective, made their appearance, the invention of the first practicable machine gun being commonly attributed to Dr. R. J. Gatling, of Hartford County, North Carolina. During the war he perfected the revolving gun which now bears his name. The first six which he made were destroyed in his factory by fire. Afterward he had twelve made which were first used in actual service by Gen Butler on the James River. It was not until 1866 that the improved Gatling gun was adopted by the United States Ordnance Department. The use of this gun on the battlefield was antedated by that of a machine gun manufactured at the Richmond Tredegar Works, the first year of the war, the inventor being Capt. R. S. Williams, C. S. A., of Covington, Ky. The gun was a 1-pounder steel breech-loader with a barrel about four feet long, and a bore of two inches. It was mounted on a two-wheeled carriage similar to that of a boat howitzer and was drawn by one horse in shafts. It was operated by a lever attached to a revolving cam shaft which rotated a cylinder, above which was an ammunition hopper. The cartridges were fired by a sliding hammer which automatically struck the percussion caps at each revolution of the cylinder. The gun had a range of about 2,000 yards. Its first test in action was on May 31, 1862, at the battle of Seven Pines under the direction of the inventor himself, who accompanied Pickett's Brigade. The results obtained were so satisfactory that the Confederate Government had six of the guns made which comprised the material of Williams', later Schoolfield's Battery, of the Western Army. A graphic account of their effect in the battle of Blue Springs, East Tennessee, October 10, 1863, is given by Capt. T. T. Allen of the 7th Ohio Cavalry.*

*Confederate Veteran, November, 1908, p. 581. Also Ibid., February, 1909, p. 65.

These breech-loading machine guns, probably the first used in war, were discarded according to Capt. T. M. Freeman, of Houston, Tex., Giltner's Brigade, because when firing the breech expanded and failed to relock.

Officers captured by Pickett's Division at Gettysburg asked many questions about the strange rapid-fire gun used by the Confederates at Seven Pines, showing that not only was the use of such a gun novel to them, but that it had made a lasting impression by its noise and the uncanny screech of its spike-like bolts. The subsequent reputation acquired by Williams' Battery in Tennessee and Kentucky undoubtedly attracted the attention of Dr. Gatling, who lived nearby in Cincinnati, Ohio, then a man beyond military age, and already distinguished as the inventor of a steamplow and many other valuable machines. It is not at all impossible that the Gatling gun is the outgrowth of Capt. Williams' revolving gun, which certainly made its appearance on the battlefield before the former did. One of the Williams' guns is now in possession of the United States War Department and has been extensively exhibited.

CHAPTER II

One of the most serious problems confronting Mr.
Davis upon assuming office as Chief Executive of the
Confederate States of America, was the supply of
arms and munitions of war, and for this reason it was
one of the first to receive his attention. In no branch
of the new service were the needs so pressing and the
means relatively so inadequate to supply them, as in
the matter of ordnance and ordnance stores. Thousands were clammering in vain for arms wherewith to
defend their country.

The selection of an officer to organize the Bureau of
Ordnance was a wise one, the choice falling upon Capt.
Josiah Gorgas, but recently resigned from the Ordnance
Department of the United States Army, in response to
the call of the South, though he himself was a native of
Pennsylvania. The record which this man made as
Chief of Ordnance, C. S. A.,* is indeed a remarkable
one, and had it not been for such ability and energy as
he displayed in the administration of his department,
the Confederacy could never have maintained armies in
the field as long as it did. It is not too much to say that
General Gorgas was himself in large measure the
ordnance department, and for this reason a brief sketch
of his career is not thought to be inappropriate.†

Born in Dauphin County, Pa., July 1, 1818, he was
graduated at West Point sixth in the Class of 1841, and
was assigned to the Ordnance Department, in which he
served until April, 1861. Soon after entering the
Army, he secured leave of absence for the purpose of
studying his profession abroad, returning for more

---

*Appointed. Special Orders No. 17, A. G. O., April 8, 1861, Series IV, Vol. I,
Rebellion Records, p. 211.
†He created the Ordnance Department of nothing.—Joseph E. Johnston.

active service in the Mexican War and distinguishing himself in the siege of Vera Cruz. During the years following, he was assigned to duty at various arsenals throughout the country, among them the Mt. Vernon arsenal in Alabama, where in 1853 he married the daughter of ex-Governor Gayle of Mobile. Promoted captain in 1855, he was transferred to Maine and again to Charleston, S. C., in 1860, but was on duty in Pennsylvania at the time of his resignation. There seems to be little doubt that the Department recognized his great abilities, and sought to retain his services by ordering him from Charleston to his native State at the critical hour, for the influence of his Southern wife and associates had done much to fix his allegiance to the South.

When Col. Gorgas was appointed Chief of the Bureau of Ordnance he at once looked to the several sources of supply for the ordnance material demanded of him from all sides. First the supply in possession of the various States, whether purchased or seized by them, must be husbanded and immediate steps taken in order to prevent its waste and loss, forming as it did the sole reliance of the Confederacy at the outset. Second, while ordnance plants were being created to supply future needs, prompt purchases would have to be made abroad to supplement the present supply of the States. From these sources the troops of the South must secure their armament.

Fully appreciating the material poverty of the country, Col. Gorgas at once sent an efficient officer to Europe, in order to avail himself of that source of supply, having become thoroughly familiar with the foreign markets during a year of travel abroad.

He next set about locating arsenals, powder mills, lead and copper mines, and preparing elaborate and skillful plans for the collection and distribution of the armament of the Confederacy. Not only did he devise and secure the creation of the Bureau of Foreign Supplies, and the Mining and Niter Bureau, but he did much for the establishment of a blockade-running service. His insistent views in regard to the governmental control of the cotton and tobacco crops, if adopted in time, would no doubt have prevented the early dissolution of the Confederate currency system. The power to select officers of ability as assistants was a striking characteristic of this energetic, modest man, so little known to the general public.*

When Gen. Gorgas assumed office in April, 1861, the Confederacy was without a single arsenal, laboratory or powder mill of any capacity, the United States War Department having depleted rather than over-stocked the small depots located in the South. In the entire South, there was but one plant available as a cannon foundry and rolling mill. Fortunately for the Army of Northern Virginia, that one, The Richmond Tredegar Works, was located in Virginia.†

By an act approved March 16, 1861, the Confederate Government appropriated $110,000.00 for the purchase of ordnance and ordnance stores, followed in May by a larger appropriation amounting to $4,440,000.00, directing that out of the latter sum were to be purchased 16 field batteries of 6 pieces each, with harness implements and ammunition. Of the general appropriation of $5,700,000.00 for the public defense made in August, an apportionment of $3,500,000.00 was made to the Bureau of Ordnance, all available funds thereof having

---

*In the spring of 1865, Gen. Gorgas returned to his adopted state, Alabama, and became Superintendent of the Briarfield Iron Works, soon after accepting appointment as Vice-Chancellor University of the South, at Sewanee, Tenn., and becoming President of the University of Alabama in 1877. He died May 15, 1883, having resigned his high office after a brief tenure, on account of ill health, serving until his death as Librarian of the University. Mr. Davis pays no higher tribute to any of his officers than to this unimpeachable man.

It is interesting to know that the son of this distinguished Confederate officer is Col. W. C. Gorgas, U. S. Medical Corps, whose work as Chief Sanitary Officer of the Panama Canal Zone has attracted the attention of the world.

†The Tredegar Works possessed at this time the maximum capacity for the production of rails of 8,000 tons a year.

The noble manner in which the South accepted defeat and set about the upbuilding of its institutions was in a great measure due to the influence of a very large number of ex-officers, who connected themselves with schools and colleges, and to a host of others who set an example from the pulpit. Nearly every Southern institution of learning was headed by gallant Confederates who commanded the highest respect, and the church was largely in the hands of ex-soldiers, who led their people to accept with humility the outcome of the war as the decree of the Almighty. Lee, Pendleton, Alexander, Maury, Brooke, Randolph, McKim, Gorgas, Mallet, Carter, and McCabe are but a few soldiers who occupied prominent positions in the educational and ecclesiastical walks of life after the war.

been exhausted before the following December. The necessity of a new appropriation of $2,340,000 that month and of $2,660,000.00 the following February, at the instance of Gen. Gorgas, gives some idea of the activity of his department. There were further appropriations on April 3 and 17 of $11,000,000,00 and $200,000.00, respectively.

In September, 1861, the Chief of Ordnance reported that in addition to a small number of 12-pounder iron howitzers in storage, outstanding contracts existed for the supply of one hundred and thirty-five 6-pounder gun carriages and caissons, one hundred and thirty-one 3-inch rifled guns, eighty-one 12-pounder and forty 24-pounder iron howitzers, a number of howitzer carriages, and a few 6-pounder brass guns. There was only one government plant engaged in the manufacture of field gun carriages at this time, and that had a capacity of but one carriage a week, though arrangements for the enlargement of this, the Baton Rouge arsenal, were being completed.

Upon the formation of the Confederate Government, Mr. Davis had placed Caleb Huse as Foreign Purchasing Agent, under the direction of the Chief of Ordnance. Visiting England at once, this agent met the inventors of the Armstrong and Blakely guns, but, failing to secure any material there, repaired to the continent where he purchased in Austria 12 field batteries and 4 batteries of S. B. guns, which he ordered to be converted. This material together with a small quantity of French harness, shell, powder, friction-tubes, and some forge and battery wagons, was shipped from Hamburg, but not until March, 1862.

In April, the Chief of Ordnance reported a total of 35 field pieces of all descriptions, as taken over with the forts which fell into the hands of the Confederacy, stating that only four 6-pounders, two 12-pounder howitzers, and six 6-pounder steel rifled pieces had been ordered in addition to 27,518 rounds of field artillery ammunition.

A report of May, 1861, shows that practically no field artillery material had been seized with the government depots, though ammunition sufficient for 60 field guns was found in the Baton Rouge arsenal.*

From the foregoing facts, we must conclude that such ordnance as was issued to the field artillery up to the fall of 1861 was on hand before the outbreak of the war, with the possible exception of a few small purchases in Mexico immediately thereafter, and it is not conceivable that the armies in Virginia received any great amount from outside of the State until the regular manufacture of ordnance began the following year.

Before examining the resources of Virginia, however, let us see what was done to organize the Bureau of Ordnance of the Confederacy.

The Act of March 6, 1861, providing for the establishment and organization of the Army, charged the Artillery Corps with all ordnance duties, but, in addition, authorized such staff departments to be continued as were already established.

The Act of February 21 created the War Department, as a bureau of which, though attached to the Artillery Corps, the Bureau of Ordnance was formed, it, with the Engineer Bureau, being originally in charge of Gen. Gorgas as Acting Chief, with the rank of Major of Artillery.†

Under this organization of the bureau, in connection with the Artillery, its operations were not satisfactory, since the artillery officers performing ordnance duties were not directly subject to the control of the Chief of Ordnance, leading to the recommendation on the latter's part the following March that a new organization be given the department, to be styled the Bureau of Artillery and Ordnance and to consist of 1 colonel, 1 lieutenant-colonel, 4 majors and 12 captains (to be nominated by the President), and as many lieutenants

---

*The Washington Artillery secured 6 old S. B. guns and a considerable amount of obsolete ordnance equipment from the Baton Rouge arsenal.

†Relieved from duty as Chief of Engineer Bureau, and superseded by Maj. Daniel Leadbetter, S. O., No. 114, A. G. O., August 3, 1861.

detailed from the Army for such time as the service might require.*

The views of the Chief were partially adopted, and definite regulations for the new organization prescribed soon after.†

It was now provided that all officers assigned to ordnance duty with troops in the field should report direct to the head of the Bureau, and in the case where an ordnance officer was not assigned by the Bureau, corps, division and brigade commanders were to designate their own ordnance officers, to be known as Chiefs of Ordnance, Division and Brigade Ordnance Officers, respectively. The Chief of Ordnance of an army, or of a corps, held the rank of major, and the division and brigade officers, the rank of captain of artillery in the regular army. These officers were ordered to be selected by a test for special fitness, were attached to the staffs of their respective commands, and when once appointed, were forbidden to be changed without authority of the Chief of Ordnance. The Division and Brigade Ordnance Officers made monthly returns to the Chief Ordnance Officer of their corps or army, and only in extraordinary cases were they authorized to contract for supplies. Every regimental commander was required to appoint an ordnance sergeant. Full instructions for ordnance officers in the field were issued by the Secretary of War May 20, 1862,‡ the collection of captured arms being dealt with in detail.

The exertions of the Bureau of Ordnance during the first year overcame difficulties thought to be insuperable. "During the harassments of war, while holding our own in the field defiantly and successfully against a powerful enemy; crippled by a depreciated currency; throttled by a blockade that deprived us of nearly all the means of getting material or workmen; obliged to

---

*See letter, Chief of Ordnance, *Rebellion Records,* Series IV, Vol. I, p. 990, March 12, 1862.
†G. O. No. 24, A. G. O., April 16, 1862, Ibid., p. 1065.
‡*Rebellion Records,* Series IV, Vol. I, p. 1124.

send almost every able-bodied man to the field; unable to use the slave labor, with which we were abundantly supplied, except in the most unskilled departments of production; hampered by want of transportation even of the commonest supplies of food; with no stock on hand, even of articles such as steel, copper, leather, iron, which we must have to build up our establishments—against all these obstacles, in spite of all these deficiencies, we persevered at home as determinedly as did our troops in the field, against a more tangible opposition; and in that short period created (first two years of the war), almost literally out of the ground, foundries and rolling mills at Selma, Richmond, Atlanta, and Macon; smelting works at Petersburg, chemical works at Charlotte, N. C.; a powder mill far superior to any in the United States and unsurpassed by any across the ocean; and a chain of arsenals, armories, and laboratories equal in their capacity and their improved appointments to the best of those in the United States, stretching link by link from Virginia to Alabama."

The foregoing words of the Chief of Ordnance do not exaggerate, and give a vivid impression of the conditions in the South at the opening of the war. It is all but impossible to believe so much could be accomplished in a purely agricultural region, almost wholly devoid of factories, industrial machinery, manufacturing materials and skilled labor. The fact remains, however, that in the spring of 1862, one year after the fall of Sumter, the following plants were in operation:

Fayetteville Arsenal and Armory, Fayetteville, N. C.; Richmond Armory and Richmond Arsenal, Richmond, Va.; Charleston Arsenal, Charleston, S. C.; Augusta Arsenal, Augusta, Ga.; Confederate Powder Mills, Augusta, Ga.; Savannah Depot, Savannah, Ga.; Montgomery Depot, Montgomery, Ala.; Mount Vernon Arsenal, Mount Vernon, Ala.; Baton Rouge Arsenal, Baton Rouge, La.; Texas Arsenal, San Antonio, Texas; Little Rock Arsenal, Little Rock, Ark.;

Memphis Depot, Memphis, Tenn.; Nashville Arsenal, Nashville, Tenn.; New Orleans Depot, New Orleans, La. Eight of these were in successful operation before the first summer of the war.

The idea is prevalent that the Confederacy acquired by seizure from the United States Government the machinery and plants with which the manufacture of arms was undertaken, in addition to an enormous supply of ordnance and ordnance stores. This is a most erroneous belief. On the contrary, practically no serviceable artillery material or ammunition was thus acquired, as shown by the reports of the Chief of Ordnance. What little powder was stored in the Southern States before the war was a relic of Mexican days, except about 60,000 pounds of old cannon powder captured at Norfolk and several other points. There were absolutely no batteries of field artillery at the arsenals and forts, only a few old iron guns mounted on Gribeauval carriages fabricated in 1762. The volunteer batteries of the States, however, did possess some serviceable guns, but practically no harness, saddles, bridles, blankets, or other artillery equipment.

The United States arsenals within the limits of the Confederacy had for years been employed as mere depots, the only one possessing machines other than foot lathes being that at Fayetteville, N. C. Not a gun nor a gun carriage, and except during the Mexican war, scarcely a round of ammunition, had for 50 years been manufactured in the South. The only foundry at which a cannon had ever been cast was the Richmond Tredegar Works, and copper, so necessary for field artillery purposes, was just being obtained in East Tennessee. Not a single rolling-mill for bar iron existed south of Richmond, and the few small blast furnaces in operation were located in the border States of Virginia and Tennessee.

The manufacture of field guns was from the first confined almost entirely to the Richmond Tredegar Works, a few pieces only being cast in New Orleans and Nashville, while in Rome, Ga., a very limited number of three-inch iron rifled guns were made.

Gun carriages and field artillery equipment for the army in Virginia were also wholly supplied by the Richmond arsenal, while that at Augusta produced much of the same material for the troops in the South and West.

It has been shown that not only was there no powder for the field artillery on hand in the South before the war, but that no mills of any but the smallest capacity existed in the South for its manufacture, notwithstanding the original plans for the armament of that arm contemplated the placing in the field of 300 guns, with 200 rounds of ammunition for each piece. It became immediately necessary, therefore, to provide not less than 175,000 pounds of powder for the batteries alone. Efforts to satisfy this demand were first made by agents in the North, but only a few orders were filled before the attack on Sumter, when all shipments ceased. It then became necessary to undertake the erection of government powder mills.

Before June 1, 1861, niter had been secured in Northern Alabama, and in Tennessee, and sulphur in Louisiana, into which state a considerable supply had been imported for use in the manufacture of sugar. This supply was supplemented by that furnished under a contract with Doctor Ullmann, of Talapoosa, Ala., who undertook to deliver from 1,000 to 2,000 pounds a day. Efforts were also made to secure the product from the reduction of iron pyrites by private contractors in Alabama and Louisiana, and in the end this was the source from which the necessary sulphur was obtained.

For the third ingredient of powder, viz., charcoal, recourse was had chiefly to cotton-wood from the banks of the Savannah River, in which locality it was abundant and gave an excellent product.

There were 2 small private powder mills in Tennessee, 2 in South Carolina, 1 in North Carolina, and a little stamping-mill in New Orleans. Contracts were immediately made to take over all the powder these plants could produce and they were offered every encouragement to continue and increase their outputs. Messrs. Bowen & Co., of Pendleton, S. C., and J. M. Ostendorff & Co., of Walhalla, S. C., together, accepted contracts for 300 pounds of powder a day. S. D. Morgan, of Nashville, Tenn., also immediately undertook to furnish a considerable supply. An order for 250 tons was accepted by C. D. Yale, of Virginia, the price named being forty cents per pound. Foreign orders were placed for 2,500,000 pounds, and negotiations were opened for the immediate purchase of 650,-000 pounds in Mexico. Gen. Davis, who in the meantime had secured a small supply of sulphur and saltpetre, began the manufacture of powder near Lewisburg, Va., for the immediate use of the troops.* Such was the condition up to August, 1861.

In the meantime, Georgia had imported about 250,-000 pounds of niter, and before the battle of Bull Run the Government had gathered from all sources a supply of about 200,000 pounds of artillery powder. The construction of a great government powder mill at Augusta, Ga., was placed in charge of Gen. G. W. Rains, a North Carolinian, at the time engaged in the manufacture of machinery in New York, in which industry he possessed wide experience.† Only inquiring how he could serve the Confederacy best, this officer immediately repaired to Augusta and undertook the seemingly impossible task assigned him, soon producing a supply of powder of unexcelled quality, due to the skill with which the niter, secured from various sources, was purified.

The immediate demands for saltpetre were satisfied by contracts. In May, Messrs. Leonard and Riddle, of Montgomery, Ala., undertook to furnish 60,000 pounds from local sources. Colonel Hindman, of

*Rebellion Records, Series IV, Vol. I, p. 555.
†George Washington Rains, of North Carolina, graduated from the U. S. M. A. in 1838, was first assigned to the Engineers and then transferred to the Artillery. He served with distinguished gallantry in the Mexican War, and received various brevets, resigning from the Army in 1856.

Arkansas, contracted to furnish 100,000 pounds, and Richard Ross, of Memphis, agreed to secure a like amount from the caves in East Tennessee. In Northern Alabama, a section rich in saltpetre, Messrs. Nelson and Davis, S. D. Bowen & Co., and William Worley, were the principal contractors, and they controlled an output of about 1,000 pounds per day, the weekly yield of the East Tennessee beds being about four tons, a supply of 8,000 to 10,000 pounds being already on hand for sale there. The contract price offered by the Bureau of Ordnance for saltpetre at this time was twenty-five cents per pound, the market price ranging from twenty-two to thirty cents.*

Later on, after the supply of saltpetre in the caves was exhausted, resort was had to tobacco houses, damp cellars and to artificial beds in which human urine was largely used for the lixiviation of the earth. The principal beds were established in Columbia, S. C., Charleston, Savannah, Augusta, Mobile, Selma, and Richmond. Thus the inferior imported powder, in the manufacture of which a poor grade of niter was generally used, the quality depending upon the not too scrupulous honesty of the foreign shippers, had no longer to be relied upon as at first.

Upon the recommendation of the Chief of Ordnance, the Mining and Niter Bureau was created early in 1862. The corps of officers authorized for the Niter Bureau consisted of one Superintendent of the rank of a major of artillery, and four assistants and eight subordinates, with the rank of captains and lieutenants of artillery, respectively.† The officers of the corps were authorized to impress free negroes to work the caves.

Some idea of the efficiency of the Niter Bureau may be derived from the fact that before the close of 1864, a supply of 2,800,000 feet of nitrous earth was on hand, of which a large proportion was capable of yielding 1½ pounds of niter per foot. Within a year after the pro-

---

*Rebellion Records. Series IV, Vol. II, p. 556.
†Act approved April 11, 1862. *Rebellion Records,* Series IV, Vol. I, p. 1054.

duction of the niter was undertaken, the government resources supplied more than half the annual consumption, and at the close of the war, the central laboratory, then about completed at Macon, Ga., in charge of the Superintendent of Laboratories, Col. Jno. W. Mallet, a celebrated chemist and an officer of remarkable energy and ability, coöperating with the Augusta Mills, would have been able to supply the ammunition for an army of 300,000 combatants.* This fact seems almost beyond belief, yet it must be added that the complete mechanical equipment of the powder mills, including the enormous rollers, was made in the South in spite of the almost entire absence of machine shops and factories at the beginning of the war. Due entirely to Generals Gorgas and Rains, Colonels St. John and Mallet, after the fall of 1862, when the powder mills were completed, no requisition of an army in the field was ever dishonored. What higher tribute can be paid these men than the statement of this fact?

So extensive and complete were the Augusta Powder Mills and the Macon Laboratories, that more than mere mention of them should be made. The site selected for the former was a large piece of land on the

*As I write these lines, November 8, 1912, the news of Col. Mallet's death yesterday, at the University of Virginia, where he lived in retirement, is received. Born in Dublin, Ireland, in 1832, of English parents, Dr. Mallet obtained his doctorate at the University of Göttingen, and after graduating from the University of Dublin, in 1853, came to this country in the same year, becoming professor of chemistry at the University of Alabama in 1855. There he accomplished, in 1856, the first important work in physical chemistry performed in this country, the determination of the atomic weight of lithium, the lightest metallic element known. This work firmly established his reputation as a chemist of the first rank; and when, during the civil war, the Confederate Government found need for chemists to direct the manufacture of explosives, Dr. Mallet, at that time a member of Gen. Rodes' staff, was transferred to the artillery arm of the service and placed in supervision of the manufacture of ammunition. His distinguished service to the cause led the government to promote him to the rank of lieutenant-colonel.

After the war Dr. Mallet went back to the classroom as professor of chemistry in the medical department of the University of Louisiana. In 1868 he came to the University of Virginia. In 1880 he was chosen by the National Board of Health to consider and report upon the proper analytical methods to be used in the analysis of drinking waters. So well was this work done that it introduced him to a new field of usefulness. He became famous as an expert upon sanitary water supply. Not only was his advice eagerly sought far and wide in the planning of such supplies, but he was very frequently called upon as an expert witness in legal cases involving chemical questions, in all parts of the country. Indeed, his reputation as an expert witness was but little less extensive than his fame as a scientist.

In 1885 Dr. Mallet went to the University of Texas as Chairman of the Faculty, and then to Jefferson Medical College, in Philadelphia, but returned to the University of Virginia in 1885 as head of the School of Chemistry. He was retired on the Carnegie Foundation four years ago.

canal near Augusta, work on the plant commencing in
September, 1861. The largest pieces of the machinery,
including the heavy incorporating rollers and pans,
were made at the Richmond Tredegar Works, while
the innumerable small parts were made wherever the
necessary equipment for their fabrication could be
found.

Powder was actually turned out as early as April,
1862. "The statement may seem startling in view of
the difficulties under which this establishment was built
up, but it is no exaggeration to say that it was amongst
the finest and most efficient powder mills in the world
at the time, if not the very best in existence."*

The erection of a central ordnance laboratory for the
production of standard ammunition, including that for
the field artillery, was decided upon in September, 1862.
A tract of about 145 acres, near the city of Macon, was
immediately purchased and enclosed, a branch track run
out from the Macon and Western Railroad, and the
erection of the plant begun by Col. Mallet. The line
of the three main buildings, connected with each other,
had a frontage of about 1,200 feet, the middle building
being about 600 feet long. In addition to this great
structure, there were over 40 other buildings. All of
the bricks for their construction were made in a great
yard near Macon, opened and conducted by the ordnance
officers in charge of the work. Orders were sent to
England for a large and various assortment of special
machinery, including several large steam engines, to
furnish the motive power, much of which had reached
Bermuda when the blockade service was practically
destroyed near the close of the war.

Not only were these plants able to contribute their
outputs to the armies in the field, but the ordnance
officers conducting them were able, in spite of the greatest difficulties, to make many improvements in the
various machines and processes. One of the most notable of these was the method of steaming the mixed

*See article in *University of Virginia Alumni Bulletin*, April, 1910, on "Work
of Confederate Bureau of Ordnance," by Col. J. W. Mallet.

materials for gunpowder just before incorporation in the cylinder mills, which was invented and introduced by Col. Rains, not only very largely increasing the capacity of the plants, but greatly improving the quality of the powder. As another example of the skill of the officers of the ammunition laboratories, may be mentioned the casting of shells with polygonal cavities, securing the bursting of the projectile into a determinate number of pieces. It was in these laboratories that the Reed shell with the soft metal base cup for taking the rifling was brought to so practical a state of perfection that it has been little improved upon since, being the very first satisfactory projectile for rifled guns. Many ingenious devices for the ignition of time fuzes for use in rifled guns were also invented in these shops.

From the saltpetre secured as before described, nitric acid could be made, which, with mercury and copper, was necessary in the manufacture of percussion caps and friction primers. The mercury was imported from Mexico, but after the fall of Vicksburg, no adequate supply was available. The ordnance chemists, however, discovered a mixture of chloral potash and sulphuret of antimony which they used in place of fulminate of mercury, the necessary supply of copper being obtained by collecting all the turpentine and apple brandy stills in the country, which were shipped to Richmond, there to be cut up and rolled into strips.

There had been established at Ducktown, Tenn., before the close of the war, a small plant for the smelting and rolling of copper, though on no great scale. A moderate amount of sheet copper was found at Cleveland, Tenn., already manufactured from the Ducktown ores.

Great trouble from the first was experienced in securing the necessary leather for artillery saddles, harness, and equipment. A comparatively small amount could be purchased abroad, and the principal government leather shops at Montgomery were unable to procure a sufficient supply of raw material to fill the tremendous demands of the various armies. The production of this and the Richmond factory was supplemented by means of small contracts placed in the rural districts, especially in the Valley of Virginia, where old men were induced to devote their energies to the fabrication of harness, and other horse equipment. In order to economize the insufficient quantity of leather available, due to the early elimination of the Texas and Mexican supplies, bridle reins and saddle skirts were made of cotton cloth stitched in three or four layers. The tannery industry was encouraged by exemptions from military duty in the field, and a premium was put upon the saving and curing of hides throughout the South.

The friction resulting from the scramble for leather by the Quartermaster Department, and the ordnance agents was, as might have been expected under the circumstances, the cause of frequent War Department orders, endeavoring to regulate the activities of the two interests.

The home resources were supplemented by extensive foreign purchases of leather from time to time. Before the close of the year 1863 harness shops had been established in Clarksville, Va.

In view of the scarcity of leather and the absolute lack of india-rubber, a process was developed for the treatment of the cotton cloth used in the fabrication of blankets, equipments, etc. Linseed oil answered best for making the drying oil, and when the necessary supply could no longer be imported, a fishery was established on the Cape Fear River where it was made.

Country blacksmiths, wheelwrights and carriage builders were perforce generally exempted and subsidized to make horseshoes, gun carriages, transport wagons, etc., The metal for the smiths was precariously obtained, the small individual outputs of these wayside mechanics being gathered by districts. During the year ending September 30, 1863, tremendous efforts were made by the government to supplement the supply of horseshoes procurable through contracts, and of the 266,951 pounds of shoes issued during the foregoing period, nearly half were fabricated in the arsenals.

To provide the metals required in the manufacture of cannon, projectiles, and metallic articles, was a task of tremendous proportions. To supervise and direct this work the Mining Bureau was created, conjointly with the Niter Bureau; Col. St. John, being assigned to the administration of this important organization, assisted the Bureau of Ordnance with distinguished ability.

At the outset, lead had been purchased abroad, much in Mexico, and early in the spring a contract was made for the delivery of 500 tons at Columbia, and a like amount at San Antonio, Tex., the price being seven cents per pound. But this supply was by no means sufficient.

One of the first steps taken by the Chief had been the erection of a small smelting plant in Petersburg, which was in full operation before the summer of 1862.

Every encouragement was now given by government contracts to stimulate the mining and smelting of ores, and much ingenuity and great labor were expended in providing the necessary metals. The Virginia lead mines at Wytheville supplied the bulk of the lead, having an output of from thirty to forty tons a month. There was also a small lead mine operated in Davidson, N. C. To supplement this inadequate supply, the country was literally scoured from end to end, piping, window weights, roofs, cistern linings and utensils of all kinds contributing to meet the demand. Lead and tin in small quantities were also imported from abroad, especially from the West Indies. Under the able direction of Dr. Pigott, formerly of Baltimore, the lead from Wytheville and several other points, as well as the promiscuous supply of scrap, was reduced in the Petersburg plant where some progress in desilverization by the Pattison process was made. The several tons of enriched lead set aside, however, had to be melted up for bullets before cupellation.

Most important of all were the results obtained in the development of the iron ores of the South in 1862, and the following year, especially in Alabama where the foundation for the present vast iron industry was laid. The Mining Bureau both by the labor of its own officers and subsidized contractors opened mines, erected furnaces and rolling-mills, and turned out an immense quantity of iron of superior quality. Scrap was collected from all available sources, and battlefields were carefully gleaned for metals which commanded a price at any of the arsenals.*

This sketch of the Confederate Bureau of Ordnance, however brief, would be utterly incomplete without fuller reference to the Richmond Tredegar Works than has hitherto been made. Prominent in the surrounding landscape of Virginia's Capital City, to-day as in 1861, are the slated roofs and tall chimneys of this plant, rising above the white foam of the rapids. The ominous clouds of smoke by day and the lurid flashes of fire by night, which shoot upward from this island haunt of Vulcan, comport well with the turbulence of the James at this point, the restless waters bounding among the great boulders in the river bed to the very furnace doors. And, as one gazes downward from the height of Gamble's Hill, the site of the great Confederate Hospitals, upon the massive plant, hissing and seething in midstream; the great Dunlop Flour Mills of war-time fame silhouetted against the horizon beyond; Hollywood, the magnificent city of the dead, nearer at hand, an awful consciousness clutches the mind that here indeed life, strife, woe, and death met together, here where the heart of the Confederacy beat the strongest and is now enshrined.

So potent a factor was the firm of Jos. R. Anderson & Co., the proprietors of the Tredegar Works, in the aggressive power of the Southern armies, that it acknowledged no superior among the government plants. When the war began, its foundry was the only

*For early measures to provide supplies of powder, lead, sulphur, saltpetre, etc., see *Rebellion Records*, Series IV, Vol. I, pp. 555, 557.

one capable of casting heavy guns, and its shops continued the only rolling-mill of great capacity, in the South. Initiated into ordnance work as an adjunct of the nearby Bellona Arsenal of the United States Government, its experience was at once turned to account by the Confederate authorities, and even to this day, large projectiles are there manufactured for the united country. Adding to its utility by enlarging its plant, and by importations of costly machinery through the blockade, for which purpose it employed its own ship, in spite of great loss by fire, Jos. R. Anderson & Co. continued operations throughout the war as the strong arm of the Bureau of Ordnance, while the senior partner led his brigade in the field. It was here that the famous 7-inch rifled Brooke gun was first cast, tested and perfected; that most of the heavy guns for coast defense, with their projectiles, were made; that the plates for the first iron clads were rolled and the shells for the first torpedoes were made. Operating mines, mills, and pork packeries, in various sections of the South; obtaining coal and metal at a time when industry was almost at a standstill elsewhere; with a brigade of its own employees, in spite of the closest conscription, organized, armed, and drilled by its own officers, and, on several occasions led against the common enemy to repel raids; no wonder when provisions became scarce the agents of the "Works" proceeded with those of the Government commissary, *pari-passu.**

---

*An interesting anecdote illustrative of the importance of the Tredegar Works is here borrowed from Mr. T. C. DeLeon, author of "Belles, Beaux, and Brains of the '60's," and "Four Years in Rebel Capitals."

A special train was crossing the bridge *en route* for Petersburg at a time when transportation was rare. A huge negro, blacker than the soot upon his face, sat placidly upon the platform of the rear car.

"What are you doing here?" was asked by the officer in charge.

"Ridin' t' Petersburg," was the placid reply.

"Have you paid your fare?"

"Don' got none to pay, boss. Rides on'r pass, I does!"

"Work for the government?" this rather impatiently.

Ebo rolled his eyes, with an expression of deep disgust, as he responded grandly:

"No—sah! Fur t'uther consarn!"

CHAPTER III

ORGANIZATION AND OPERATIONS

HAVING familiarized ourselves somewhat with its material development, let us now examine the conditions with respect to the personnel and organization of the Bureau of Ordnance, which continued to be merely a bureau of the War Department instead of possessing the character of a distinct department of the Army. There were, of course, grave disadvantages incident to such an organization; yet, in spite of this defect and a great deficiency in the number of ordnance officers, the work had been efficiently conducted during the early part of the war, far more so with the available resources than could reasonably have been expected.

As soon as Congress was thoroughly awake to the seriousness of the war it became far easier to secure the needed appropriations for ordnance material, and increases in the corps of officers, whose staff duties were no longer viewed in the light of departmental sinecures.

By Act of April 21, 1862, Congress authorized the appointment of 80 officers of artillery in the Provisional Army for ordnance duties, prescribing that from this number there should be one lieutenant-colonel appointed for each command composed of more than one army corps; a major for each army corps composed of more than one division; the others to have the rank of captain and first lieutenant in such proportion as the President might prescribe. This increase proving inadequate the corps was again enlarged by Act of September 16, 1862, authorizing the President to appoint 70 officers of artillery in the Provisional Army for ordnance duties. Having secured this increase the Adjutant-General, in order that capable men only might be detailed to the Corps, announced certain educational requisites to their appointment and created an examining board composed of Col. T. S. Rhett, Col. W. LeRoy Broun,

Maj. S. Stansbury, and Capt. Benj. Sloan, who were directed to visit the various armies in the field, and examine candidates who had made application for appointment to the army commanders through their chiefs of ordnance. Notice of examinations was required to be published in the *Richmond Enquirer*. It was provided that no candidate could be commissioned captain unless proficient in the subjects of algebra, trigonometry, mechanics, and chemistry. Meantime, Brig.-Gen. Benj. Huger, formerly of the United States Ordnance Corps, had been appointed Inspector General of Artillery and Ordnance, and enjoined to enforce the regulations of the branches of the service subject to his inspections. Orders were also published providing for a waiting list of those who might pass the examinations for whom no vacancy existed, the successful candidates to be given rank according to merit when finally appointed, and examination for promotion was also prescribed. Notice of examinations to be held were to be printed in the *Richmond Enquirer,* and applications to stand the same were directed to be made to army commanders through their chiefs of ordnance.* The test applied to candidates proved so exacting that the Corps contained many vacancies as late as January, 1863. The artillery officers authorized to be appointed in the Provisional Army were in addition to those of the Regular Army detailed to ordnance duty by the War Department and those in the Provisional Army and Volunteer Corps so detailed, and those of the Mining and Niter Bureau, appointed by Congress.†

In August, 1863, the officers appointed from the Provisional Army were distributed as follows: 4 lieutenant-colonels, 9 majors, 65 captains, 40 first lieutenants and 32 second lieutenants, there being 150 commissions authorized, two assistants not above the rank of captain being allowed the Chief of Ordnance of

---

*G. O. Nos. 68, 70, 71, A. & I. G. O., September 17, September 23, September 26, 1862. The general educational requirements were a good English education, knowledge of elementary mathematics, and familiarity with the Ordnance Manual published by the Bureau.

†G. O. No. 71, A. & I. G. O., September 26, 1862.

an army, and one not above the rank of first lieutenant the chief of ordnance of a department. Ordnance officers on duty in the field were now assigned, lieutenant-colonels to armies, majors to army corps, captains to departments and divisions, and lieutenants to brigades.*

Shortly after this redistribution, it was held by the Adjutant-General that "Chiefs of Ordnance" of armies and departments were to be assigned by the department only, and that they no longer formed a part of the personal staffs of commanding generals,† subject to appointment by them, when no officer was designated for ordnance duties with their commands as had hitherto been authorized.

The Chief of the Bureau now holding the rank of lieutenant-colonel, recommended to the Secretary of War November 15, 1863, in view of the fact that the officers of the Regular Confederate Army on ordnance duty, with temporary rank dependent upon the duties assigned them from time to time, were entirely distinct from the provisional organization, the rank of the officers of which was fixed by law, that a law creating a permanent ordnance department be enacted. Not only did this long-neglected measure seem necessary to him for the proper administration of ordnance affairs, but it would, he very rightly claimed, give character and recognition to ordnance officers as belonging to a distinct branch of the service, the members of the Corps being promoted in their own branch in accordance with seniority and efficiency.

Becoming curious as to the expenditure of the ordnance appropriations, Congress passed a resolution September 10, 1862, calling upon the President for full information with respect to the disbursements of the War Department for arms, etc. In the report of the Chief of the Bureau, of January 7, 1863, in reply to this resolution, a complete and interesting statement of the number and character of the small arms and equip-

*Compare this reassignment with the distribution originally made.
†G. O. No. 84, A. & I. G. O., June 15, 1863.

ments fabricated, issued, and on hand, up to September 1, 1862, showing the cost of production thereof, is given. In this report, however, nothing concerning artillery material appears. Up to this time practically all such material had been purchased abroad, but very little as has been shown, before the summer of 1862.* Major Huse of the Artillery, commissioned in April, 1861, to purchase abroad on account of the Bureau of Ordnance, had been more successful in assisting the Quartermaster Department than the former, and for his trouble became involved in difficulties with the latter. On his own responsibility he had purchased and shipped to the Quartermaster-General large supplies of blankets, clothing, shoes, and cloth, prompted, as he said, by a knowledge of the nakedness of the Confederate soldiers. His strenuous efforts to secure ordnance material were rewarded during the winter of 1862 and 1863, and before February of the latter year he had purchased 129 pieces of ordnance, as follows: fifty-four 6-pounder S. B. bronze guns; 18 S. B. bronze howitzers; carriages and caissons for same; 6 rifled 2.10-inch Blakely guns complete with 18,000 rounds of ammunition therefor; 2,000 fuses; 3 rifled 8-inch Blakely guns with 680 shells for same; twelve 12-pounder rifled steel guns with a large supply of ammunition therefor; 32 bronze rifled Austrian pieces, or 4 batteries complete with 10,000 rounds of shrapnel; 2 bronze rifles with 200 shells therefor; 756 rounds of shrapnel; 9,820 wooden fuses; 4 steel 9-pounder rifles with 1,008 shell and fuses; 220 sets of harness with spare parts, at a total cost of nearly half a million dollars. In addition to the foregoing, he had secured a large quantity of leather, 57,000 pounds of saltpetre, 80,900 friction tubes, 286 ingots of tin, and 931 pigs of lead. Other purchases before November, 1863, brought the number of foreign field pieces issued to date up to 193, the field artillery ordnance having been produced with these exceptions in the arsenals and workshops of the Confederacy.

*Letter of Maj. Huse, *Rebellion Records*, Series IV, Vol. II, p. 227.

In a paper written after the war, Gen. Gorgas states that the principal issues of the Richmond Arsenal alone, during the period from July 1, 1861, to January 1, 1865, including the work done for this plant by the Richmond Tredegar Works, embraced the following field artillery material and equipment:*

    1,396 field pieces (including captured guns repaired),
    1,375 gun carriages,
      875 caissons,
      152 forges,
    6,852 sets artillery harness,
 921,441 rounds of field, seige and sea coast ammunition.
1,456,190 friction primers,
1,110,966 fuses,
  17,423 port fires,
   3,985 rockets,
  69,418 saddles, artillery and cavalry,
  85,139 bridles,
  75,639 halters,
  56,624 pairs of spurs,
  42,285 horse brushes,
  56,903 curry combs.

The casual reader may weary with such figures as have been here given, but it is the knowledge of such details that gives the serious investigator food for reflection and a true grasp of his subject.

Such importations as were made by the Bureau were transported by its own fleet of four steamers, and a number of smaller vessels subsidized for blockade running. The blockade service, in charge of Maj. T. L. Bayne, assumed great importance at the very beginning of the war. Agencies were established at Bermuda, Nassau, and Havana, and gradually the purchase was made of a number of steamers specially suited to blockade running. The fleet proper, consisting of the *R. E. Lee, Lady Davis, Eugenia,* and *Stag,* all fine

---

*Report Chief of Ordnance, November 15, 1863.

vessels for their day, carried out the cotton apportioned the Bureau of Ordnance, in lieu of drafts or specie, to be sold in foreign markets, the proceeds being applied to the account of purchases from foreign houses. Such was the method enforced by the depreciation of the currency, adding finance on a large scale to the cares and duties of the ordnance officers.

In November, 1863, there were 5,090 persons, of whom two-thirds were non-conscripts, disabled soldiers, boys, women, or slaves, employed in the arsenals and shops of the Bureau of Ordnance, the various establishments, and their superintendents being as follows:

Richmond Arsenal, Lieut.-Col. W. L. Brown;
Richmond Armory, and Clarksville Harness Shops, Supt. W. S. Downer;
Danville Depot, Capt. E. S. Hutter;
Lynchburg Depot, Capt. C. T. Getty;
Fayetteville Arsenal and Armory, Maj. F. L. Childs;
Salisbury Foundry, Capt. A. C. Brenizer;
Charleston Arsenal, Maj. T. J. Trezevant;
Augusta Arsenal, Foundry and Powder Mills, Col. G. W. Rains;
Atlanta Arsenal, Col. M. H. Wright;
Macon Arsenal, Lieut.-Col. R. M. Cuyler;
Macon Laboratory, Col. J. W. Mallet;
Macon Armory, Supt. J. H. Burton;
Montgomery Arsenal, Maj. C. G. Wagner;
Columbus Arsenal, Maj. F. C. Humphreys;
Selma Arsenal, Lieut.-Col. J. L. White.

Their capacity was so augmented that during the year ending September 30, 1863, 677 field pieces, with carriages, caissons, and battery equipment complete, 251 extra carriages, caissons, store and forge wagons, 4,221 sets of harness and 318,197 rounds of field artillery ammunition were issued to the troops in the field.*

*Superintendents of Armories, with pay and allowances of a major of artillery, were authorized by Act of Congress of August 21, 1861. So, also, a number of storekeepers of ordnance, by acts of May 16 and August 21, 1861, the same to have pay and allowance of captain of infantry.

Each of these plants met with peculiar problems demanding ready solution, the labor question being generally foremost. Careful search had to be made for trained mechanics among the troops in the field, details for ordnance service being made only on proper evidence that the applicant was really a mechanic, in order that mere evasion of active duty in the field might not be encouraged. Some attempts were made to import mechanics from Europe, but with practically no success. Every effort was made to convert unskilled into skilled labor by teaching on the part of the few who were already themselves trained. Some of the more competent operators accomplished remarkable results in constructing with but poor appliances special machinery for ordnance purposes. Then there was the grave danger of unfaithful servants who by their treachery might wreck the plants or cause irreparable loss.

To guard the larger mills and arsenals, the operators were generally organized for purposes of defense. The battalion of the Tredegar Works has been mentioned. The powder mills in Augusta were also able to muster a battalion and a field battery as well. At the Macon plants there were two companies of infantry and a section of guns ready at all times, being called out on three occasions to repel attacks. These forces were quite efficient, including among their men many detailed soldiers. Thus, on a number of occasions, they were able to save the plants for which they were the sole guard, and which were naturally a much coveted prize for the raiding parties of the enemy.

Many discouragements in the way of irreparable losses of plants with costly machinery, both by capture and fire were experienced by the Bureau of Ordnance during the period of its phenomenal upbuilding. The arsenals and shops which it had first commanded in Missouri, Arkansas, Texas, Mississippi, Kentucky, Tennessee, Louisiana, and Florida, had not only been gradually cut off by the encroachments of the enemy, but the supplies of raw material from these States had in large measure become unavailable, and in no department of government activity could the slow but steady contraction of Confederate territory have been more forcefully realized. Yet, to the end, the loss of a mammoth plant, erected—created, it might better be said—with so much toil, and in spite of infinite difficulties, only served to inspire the ordnance officers to greater exertions, building, ever rebuilding, as they were, a house of cards upon a foundation of hope. Time and destiny put a period to hope, it is true, but not before the Confederate Bureau of Ordnance had written into history the story of the unexcelled genius of its officers.

The Confederate Bureau of Ordnance, however, did not depend solely upon foreign credits and the creative genius of its own officers, for throughout the war the Federal Ordnance Department proved a prolific source of supply. Seldom has one belligerent so extensively equipped itself, with arms and munitions of war at the expense of its adversary, as did the South in the War of Secession. Nor is this fact in any way discreditable to the Federal Army. It was the outgrowth of that strange inventor, Necessity. Opportunity for the capture of ordnance materials and military stores frequently dictated and controlled campaigns to a degree unknown to pure strategy. Risks, which would have ordinarily appeared foolhardy, were taken because of the possible reward, which success held out in the shape of warm clothing, full haversacks, and new arms. In fact, it is no exaggeration to say that the Confederate military policy was essentially one of material necessity. Of this fact, the unusual frequency of orders concerning, and the completeness of the system for, the collection, preservation and repair of captured arms and munitions, are sufficient evidence. The premium set upon captured property accounts for the large amount of such material thus obtained and reissued to the Confederate troops. Towards the close of the war, the Northern armies practically disarmed the

South, yet the material taken was no better then, and generally not so good as their own; hence there was no reason for its distribution for use among the captors.

To follow the history of the Bureau of Ordnance through the declining days of the Confederacy would be unfruitful. It would be an account of lack of funds, material poverty, absolute bankruptcy in fact, when every possible makeshift was employed to keep arms and ammunition in the hands of the fighting line. Yet, at no time, however pressing the want of food, clothes, forage, harness, and equipment, was there ever a lack of field guns and powder. The roads from Petersburg to Appomattox were blocked with guns, which the available teams could scarcely draw. One thing no carper could well say—"The army surrendered for lack of ordnance."

CHAPTER IV

ORIGINAL ARMAMENT OF THE ARMY OF
NORTHERN VIRGINIA

WERE the account of the Confederate ordnance resources to close here, well might it be said that no light has been thrown upon the initial armament of the troops in Virginia. "Whence came the guns at Bull Run, at Malvern Hill," the reader naturally inquires. And the answer lies in the preparedness of Virginia, such as her armament was. To the Old Dominion, the mother of states and of presidents, who though struggling to the last to render secession unnecessary, yet, through the foresight of her statesmen was armed against a contingency which to many appeared inevitable, is almost entirely due the credit. And, so, when the flood-tide of circumstances, of political rancor, of sectional bitterness, or to whatever may be attributed the fateful plunge, washed Virginia up against the bulwarks of the Union, she was able to place in the hands of her sons and those who flocked to her borders, arms with which to strike for the principles to which, in the fullness of her conscience, she had finally elected to adhere.

An examination of the early Codes of Virginia will show that the militia of the State received constant attention from the Legislature, having a very complete organization on paper. As early as 1792, the force was declared to consist of 5 divisions and 26 brigades, the entire territory being divided into regimental districts.* While the militia existed merely in the law, volunteer companies were encouraged by ample provisions as to arms, equipment, pay, and quarters, being attached to and forming a part of the district commands existing on paper. The volunteer artillery companies were assigned to the paper regiments of artillery, there being

---

*The number of brigades was later increased to twenty-eight.

one for each division. Hence the law contemplated the organization of 5 regiments of artillery in the event of the militia being called into actual service. In 1849, the governor was authorized to issue 4 guns to the volunteer artillery companies in Richmond, Norfolk, Petersburg, Fredericksburg, Portsmouth, Wheeling, Alexandria, Lynchburg, and Winchester, these being light batteries; but not more than 2 guns were to be furnished or provided for issue to other companies, presumably heavy batteries, which were liable to service as light artillery under the Act of 1833-34. The organization, discipline, and equipment of the artillery were required to conform to that of the United States. That the volunteers had no effective organization, even as late as 1859, is evidenced by the fact that the State appropriations for its maintenance, including the salary of the Adjutant-General ($1,500.00), aggregated only $5,800.00, a small company known as the public guard and employed as a garrison for the State arsenal and penitentiary being maintained at an additional expense of about $25,000.00. For the rapid and efficient organization of its troops, the State depended upon the Military Institute which it maintained at Lexington, as at present, for the careful and thorough training of its future officers.

While little was done for the armament of the State, the serious aspect of the impending storm in 1859 made its impression upon the Legislature, and, on January 21, an elaborate measure was passed carrying an appropriation of $500,000.00 for the purchase of arms, equipment, etc., and authorizing the appointment of 3 commissioners to secure the same as quickly as possible.

So active was the commission appointed by the Governor, that additional appropriations aggregating $106,-000.00 were made in March, the armory in Richmond having already been put in thorough condition, and steps taken to secure the newest machinery, implements and material for its operation. The commission was furthermore directed to purchase the patent rights of "newly invented arms," wherever the same could be secured, and the armament procured was to be distributed for the immediate use in the more exposed parts of the State. These were drastic measures and clearly show what was in the minds of the people of Virginia, the anticipation having been forced upon them by the country's attitude towards the Harper's Ferry incident.*

The Commission for the Public Defense consisted of Col. Philip St. George Cocke, Capt. George W. Randolph, and Col. Francis H. Smith, the first and third being graduates of West Point, and the second of Annapolis. Col. Cocke, afterwards a Confederate general, was at the time president of the Board of Visitors, and Colonel, afterwards Gen. Smith, was the Superintendent of the Virginia Military Institute. These able men, whose military training qualified them to grasp the true situation, at once determined to visit the various arsenals of the country, and open negotiations with the foremost manufacturers of arms in America and abroad. They were accompanied by the Chief Executive of the State, John Letcher, afterwards famous as the energetic war governor. Their tour embraced visits to Springfield, Harper's Ferry, and the West Point Foundry, at Cold Spring, on the Hudson. While at the last-named place, they were invited by Capt. R. P. Parrott, one of the proprietors, a retired army officer and personal friend of Gen. Smith, to witness a series of experiments he was conducting with his new rifled field piece. The Ordnance Department of the Army had been slow to grasp the importance of Parrott's invention, just as it had declared the percussion cap interesting, but only as a toy, not many years before, and Parrott had, up to this time, failed to secure the adoption of his gun.†

But the Virginians did not hesitate. The effect of the fire of Parrott's ordnance witnessed from behind

*See Act passed March 28, 1860, Chap. 29, Acts of Assembly, 1859-60.
†It was not until November 1, 1860, that an experimental board recommended the conversion of fifty per cent of the guns at the forts and arsenals, but even then little attention was paid to rifled field pieces.

epaulments, convinced the commission of its superiority over anything they had seen, and Gen. Smith was instructed to invite the inventor to send 1 gun and 100 shells to the Virginia Military Institute to be tested by Maj. Thomas J. Jackson, Instructor of Artillery.* The suggestion was promptly complied with, the gun was given a fair trial in July by the artillery class, and the results obtained by the cadets, as embodied in Maj. Jackson's report, led to the purchase by the commission of 12 rifled field pieces, with a large supply of shells therefor. These guns were first used, and with great effect, at the Battle of Bethel, and the reputation they there acquired led to the general introduction of the Parrott field piece into the artillery of both armies.†

Jackson had at once grasped the situation. Being an artillery expert, he appreciated the great possibility of rifled field pieces. The results he had obtained with the Parrott gun on the Institute range were startling, to him as well as to all those who had been accustomed to smooth-bore guns, the greatest range of which was from 1,800 to 2,000 paces. Even when firing at 1,000 paces, the results with the old guns had been so doubtful that gunners generally, as Hohenlohe said, acted on the proverb, "The first shot is for the devil, the second for God, and only the third for the King,"—that is to say, that at such a range only one shot in three would hit a target 6 feet high and 50 yards wide.

Jackson could have been little influenced by such rumors concerning rifled ordnance as may have sifted across the Atlantic before his own trial of the Parrott gun. His nature was not one which allowed him to be influenced by less than the most tangible knowledge or experience. That the Americans knew little of European progress with rifling is again borne out by the fact that Gen. Johnston, though frantic in his efforts to secure ordnance for his field artillery, wrote his Chief of Artillery, in Richmond,‡ after the battle of

---

*The famous "Stonewall" Jackson. The gun was received July 5, 1860.
†During the Civil War the West Point foundry furnished the United States Government with 1,200 guns and 3,000,000 projectiles.
‡Col. William N. Pendleton, later Chief of Artillery, A. N. V.

Bull Run, "Do not fail to urge the making of 12-pounder howitzers. I have faith in them. Let them send guns and equipments and leave us to organize. I enclose a requisition for equipment of a battery of rifles, which cannot be filled here (Manassas). Will you see if the authorities in Richmond can do it? *Do not, however, let them prefer it to the fitting out of field batteries of smooth-bore guns."* And on the 10th of August, he wrote to President Davis urging an increase of the artillery arm, to be armed and equipped by borrowing material from the States, or by casting guns, especially in Richmond, adding a particular request for 12-pounder howitzers. Though thoroughly aware of the value of artillery, attributing the success of the great Napoleon to its proper use, Gen. Johnston had not yet realized the value of rifled ordnance.

In the light of the present day, it seems strange that so great a soldier, especially distinguished for his ability as an organizer, and for his military learning, should have failed to appreciate the lessons of Bethel, emphasized by current report. *Masked batteries* and *rifled guns* were subjects of common talk among the soldiery, and especially in the press of the time. McDowell's men had heard so much of these terrible things, that they marched into Virginia imagining them to crown every crest. The explanation lies in the fact that Johnston's experience had not so far brought him into personal familiarity with the new invention, already well known to Jackson and Pendleton, both of whom had first-hand knowledge of the new gun through personal experience with it in Lexington the previous year. Having staked his professional reputation, as it were, in his favorable report of the Parrott invention, Jackson was, of course, only confirmed in his views by the events of Bethel, and when Pendleton became Chief of Artillery of Johnston's army, he was soon able to enforce his views as to the new arm and overcome the prejudices of his commanding general.

The United States War Department was not ignorant of the tests made of Parrott's gun in Lexington, and the subsequent report of its own board of ordnance and artillery officers was in its hands. Already it had received exaggerated accounts of the effect of rifled pieces at Bethel. Now came to its ears the story of Hainesville, confirming the sudden reversal of opinion and reassuring the authorities that no mistake had been made in providing McDowell with a large number of rifled pieces for his impending invasion of Virginia.

As to the sudden popularity of the new gun in the Confederate Army, it is only necessary to refer, by way of explanation, to the fact that the influence of Jackson extended throughout the South, hundreds of his pupils holding important offices in the Confederate armies, each one of them, we may be sure, hanging upon the words of their former tutor in arms, by this time become a "martial divinity" in their eyes.

Though not a field gun, the story of the 200-pounder Parrott rifle, known as the "Swamp Angel," used by the Federals during the bombardment of Sumter, had gone the rounds, being eagerly devoured by all, as was every incident connected with this first act of the war.* Then, too, Col. Olmstead in his defense of Fort Pulaski, had used two 4.5-inch Blakely rifles imported from England by the State of Georgia, their employment having attracted much attention.

Before dismissing the subject of rifled guns, one more fact may be cited as evidence that American development of the system was substantially independent of foreign experience. While all powers, whether the fact was known to each other or not, were experiencing the utmost difficulty in securing a satisfactory shell for rifled ordnance, due to the uncertainty of motion of the projectile, and the consequent jamming in the bore, Dr. Reed, of Alabama, invented a projectile which

---

*The "Swamp Angel" is now mounted as a monument in Trenton, N. J. See account of its use, *Battles and Leaders of the Civil War*, Vol. IV, pp. 72, 73, 74. Ibid., Vol. II, pp. 9, 10, 11.

solved the problem. His method was the attachment
of a wrought iron band to the base of an elongated projectile, the explosion of the powder forcing the soft
metal into the grooves, a device which is still universally
employed. The effect of such an invention was far-
reaching and led directly to the subsequent improvement in the rifling itself. The Confederate ordnance
officers rapidly perfected the Reed projectile, practically unknown until 1860, and soon thereafter followed
the making of the first Brooke gun, the invention of
Capt. John Mercer Brooke, Chief of Ordnance and
Hydrography, C. S. N., this distinguished scientist having resigned his commission in the United States Navy
in answer to the call of his native State.*

In a report rendered by the Adjutant-General of
Virginia, to the Governor, dated December 15, 1860, it
is stated that in addition to the 5 divisional artillery regiments of the militia, there were 26 companies of volunteer artillery fully recruited and organized. Of this
number 11 were armed with 6-pounder field guns, there
being 24 pieces in all, with full equipment, including
artillery sabers, and one with six 12-pounder howitzers,
with horse artillery sabers, the 12 field batteries thus
armed being fully horsed, the personnel of the artillery
aggregating 1,066. In addition to the field material
issued to the volunteer batteries, there were the following pieces of ordnance on hand: issued to militia, 44; in
depot for immediate issue, 8; at the Virginia Military
Institute, 15; in the Richmond Armory, 229; or a total
of 296, of which number 77 were bronze, and 219 iron
field guns or howitzers. There were 62 gun carriages,
40 caissons, 38 sets of harness, 703 artillery swords, 90
musketoons, and 50,000 pounds of artillery powder on
hand in the State depots. The foregoing, with a few

---

*John M. Brooke, a graduate of Annapolis, had accompanied Perry on his
initial visit to Japan. Not only did he invent the gun which to-day retains his
name, but he designed and built the iron-clad *Merrimac*. He also had charge of
the Confederate experiments, with submarine boats, and contributed much to the
development of the torpedo, first employed in war under his direction. He was
also noted for many valuable inventions of deep-sea sounding apparatus. He
contributed much to science, especially, as a Confederate officer, to the science
of war. From 1866 to 1899 he occupied the chair of Physics and Astronomy at
the Virginia Military Institute, where he died in 1904, at a very advanced age,
as Professor Emeritus.

additional small items, may fairly be taken to represent the resources of the field artillery of Virginia at the outbreak of the war, a large portion of which had been purchased by the commissioners whose expenditures up to June, 1861, had been $1,737,950.49 for the Army, and $100,748.49 for the Naval force of the State.*

We have seen to what extent the Confederacy as a whole enriched itself at the expense of the Federal Government in arms and munitions of war. Now let us inquire what Virginia's record was in this respect.

While the State Convention was in session, debating whether or not Virginia should secede from the Union, it was rumored abroad that the United States Ordnance Department contemplated the immediate removal of a large number of heavy guns from the Bellona Foundry, near Richmond, to Fortress Monroe. The guns were made by Dr. Junius L. Archer, under a contract with the Federal Government, the consideration being $20,-896.47. A joint resolution was passed by the Convention directing the seizure of the guns, and it was ordered that Archer should be paid out of the State Treasury the unpaid balance on his contract of about $8,000.00, and the United States the remaining part of the consideration or about $12,000.00, which had already been paid to the contractor. This action on the part of Virginia could hardly be characterized as other than commendable; if anything, it was overconscientious.

Early in April, the Commandant of the Harper's Ferry Arsénal, in the belief that Virginia troops were approaching to seize it, destroyed the plant with its entire contents. Writing to army headquarters in Washington, Lieut. Jones, who applied the torch, April 18, stated: "The steps I have taken to destroy the arsenal, which contains nearly 15,000 stand of arms, are so complete that I can conceive of nothing that will prevent their entire destruction." Again on the 19th—"In three

*Between the date of secession and the following November, the State appropriations for defense aggregated $6,000,000.00. Series IV, Vol. I, p. 938, *Rebellion Records;* also see p. 391.

minutes, or less, both the arsenal buildings containing nearly 15,000 arms, together with the carpenter's shop, which was at the end of a long and connected series of workshops of the Armory proper, were in a complete blaze. There is every reason for believing that the destruction was complete." And on the 22d, he again wrote: "They also report that the fire in the workshops was arrested, but that the arsenal building containing the arms, together with their contents, were [*sic*] completely demolished, and that it is probable not a single gun was saved from them." That the demolition was more or less complete is amply testified to by the congratulatory letter of even date from the Secretary of War to Lieut. Jones, for the success of his work.* Yet, the State troops arrested the conflagration in time to save much of the machinery for the manufacture of small arms, which was later removed to the Fayetteville Arsenal, in North Carolina.†

Coincident with the partial destruction of the Harper's Ferry Arsenal was the evacuation of the Norfolk Navy Yard attended with a similar attempt at destruction, the value of the property lost being estimated at several millions of dollars. From the charred remains of the government plants within her boundaries, Virginia was able to glean little of value. The only Federal property she succeeded in seizing intact, before becoming a belligerent with belligerent rights, she undertook to pay for.

In January, 1861, nearly a million dollars were appropriated by the Legislature for the purchase of arms, in addition to the sums previously placed at the disposal of the commission.

Charles Dimmock, of Massachusetts, a graduate of West Point in the Class of 1817, and a former artillery officer, was appointed Chief of Ordnance of Virginia, with the rank of colonel, and immediately set about the work of securing arms and equipment for the State troops.‡

*The total appraised value of arsenal and stores, $1,207,668 to $1,470,513.
†Turned over to the Confederate States Government for use elsewhere.
‡Col. Dimmock died in October, 1863.

Col. Dimmock at once undertook the erection of plants, for the manufacture of ammunition, and by June was able to turn over to the Confederate States a small amount of powder and a laboratory with machines, fixtures, and workmen, of a daily capacity of 75,000 rounds of ammunition. Gen. Lee in command of the Virginia forces, had foreseen from the first that the resources of the State would be called upon for the arming and equipment of the troops sent to Virginia from other quarters, and had done all in his power to assist the Chief of Ordnance in preparing to meet the demand. As early as May, Virginia was called upon by the central government to supply its troops with arms, ammunition, and every variety of equipment. Before the middle of June, over 20 field batteries had been armed, mounted and equipped, and a total of 115 field guns provided for the troops of Virginia and of other States. Field ordnance had even been sent to Missouri. Of heavy ordnance, 40 guns, including 32-pounders, 12- and 6-pounder howitzers, and 8-inch and 9-inch columbiads, had been mounted in permanent batteries for the defense of the James River; 30 similar guns were in position at the mouth of the York; 12 on Aquia Creek; 4 on the Rappahannock; 85 in and about Norfolk; 19 on the Nansemond River; 19 in Hampton Roads, and arrangements had been completed for mounting 60 heavy guns in the lines about Richmond, and a large number in the chains of works extending around Norfolk, across the Peninusula at Yorktown, at Drewry's Bluff, and at Jamestown Island.*

Between June and November of 1861, an immense amount of material was issued to Confederate troops by the State Ordnance Officer, including 15,000 muskets with bayonets, 1,700 sabers, 147 field pieces, including both guns and howitzers, 82 caissons, harness, shells, percussion caps, fuses, miscellaneous supplies, and 97,-450 pounds of powder. In July the Harper's Ferry Arsenal as reconstructed by the State, with all its ma-

*Rebellion Records, Series I, Vol. II, pp. 928, 929.

chinery, was transferred to the Confederate Government, the State forces having been mustered into the Confederate service in June.

About this time, Gov. Brown of Georgia, originally having secured a supply of about 100,000 pounds of powder, was pressing the Confederate Government for the return of the 39,000 pounds previously loaned for use at Savannah and Fort Pulaski, defenses within the borders of his own State.*

Other than the guns brought to Virginia by the gallant battalion of four companies from Louisiana, the Washington Artillery, the most minute investigation fails to disclose that the State was assisted in any respect, in the armament of the artillery with the troops who met the first and second invasions of the common enemy and hurled them back.† Fortunate indeed it was for her sisters that Virginia held the most advanced post.

In the battle of Bull Run, the Army of the Potomac had 8 light batteries available on the field, with a total armament of 27 guns, or an average of about 3 guns to the battery. But 17 of these guns were engaged. The Army of the Shenandoah had 5 batteries, each with 4 guns engaged. Therefore, the Confederates had a total of 47 guns available, most of which were old smooth-bore 6-pounders. Some guns of this pattern had been reamed out to give a larger bore and rifled with three grooves after the manner of Parrott by Col. Dimmock, but the real Parrott rifles which had been purchased by the State were at the time with Magruder at Yorktown. After the battle the Confederate batteries were able to equip with the captured material, which is stated by Gen. Johnston to have consisted of 28 pieces of artillery, with 64 artillery horses and harness. According to an itemized account made at the time by

*Rebellion Records, Series IV, Vol. I, pp. 368, 406.
†The battalion arrived in Virginia with six 6-pounder guns, two 12-pounder howitzers, and one 6-pounder rifled gun, its armament being completed in Richmond. It was superbly appointed as to equipment, but possessed material for only about 2 batteries on its arrival. The battalion had six 6-pounder, four 12-pounder howitzers, and three 6-pounder rifles at Manassas.

Col. Pendleton, Chief of Artillery, he received the following captured material July 23, 1861:

1 30-pounder Parrott rifled gun,
9 10-pounder Parrott rifled guns,
9 12-pounder brass rifled guns,
3 12-pounder brass howitzers,
2 12-pounder boat howitzers,
3 6-pounder brass smooth-bore guns,
34 caissons, more or less complete with spare parts,
4 battery wagons,
6 battery forges,
24 horses,
34 sets harness and spare pieces.

In a return of captures made by the ordnance officer of Johnston's Staff, Capt. E. P. Alexander, the field artillery material, etc., captured at Bull Run is itemized as follows:

1 30-pounder Parrott, with 300 rounds,
9 10-pounder Parrotts, with 900 rounds,
3 6-pounder brass guns, with 600 rounds,
3 12-pounder brass howitzers, with 300 rounds,
2 12-pounder boat howitzers, with 200 rounds,
9 James rifles, with 900 rounds,
37 caissons, 6 forges, 4 battery wagons, splendidly equipped, 64 artillery horses with harness.

McDowell's 11 batteries had a total of 49 guns, a fact which shows an average battery armament of more than 4 pieces. Five Federal batteries, with 25 guns, crossed Bull Run. Most of these guns were rifled pieces, and none escaped, at least 2 additional ones being captured after the battle.

The guns captured at Manassas were promptly refitted by Col. Pendleton, Johnston's Chief of Artillery, and Col. E. P. Alexander, who the day after the battle had been appointed Chief of Ordnance, Army of the Potomac, the armies of the Shenandoah and the Po-

tomac being later consolidated under the name of the
Army of Northern Virginia, in command of Gen.
Jos. E. Johnston.

Col. Alexander was a wise choice for the position
assigned him.   A graduate of the United States Military Academy of the Class of 1857, he had served
with distinction in the Corps of Engineers until the
outbreak of the war, when he resigned his commission
as second lieutenant, having served under Albert
Sidney Johnston in the Mormon war, in the Indian
campaigns of Oregon, and at West Point, where he
was on duty for a year as Commandant of the Corps,
and Assistant Instructor of Engineering.   In 1859 he
was placed in charge of artillery target practice at the
Academy.   While there, he also assisted Capt. Myer
in the development of his wig-wag signal system with
torches and flags.   He had also been a member of a
board of officers, who conducted experiments with the
new breech-loading rifles, a number of which were being offered the War Department.   He, therefore,
brought to the Army of Northern Virginia a knowledge
of the new ordnance possessed by few others in the
country.   Arriving in Richmond, June 1, 1861, after
a long and eventful journey from Washington Territory, where he had been on duty, he was at once appointed Captain of Engineers by President Davis, who
recalled the young officer's appearance before the committee of the Senate, to which he had demonstrated the
Myer system the previous year, and was directed to
start a factory in Richmond for the manufacture of
signal apparatus and to perfect plans for introducing
into the Army the system with which he was so familiar.
While on this duty at the Capital Capt. Alexander was
directed to organize 5 batteries of artillery into a battalion and to prepare them for the field.   This work he
undertook with marked ability, being himself responsible for the battalion formation, hitherto unknown to the
service.   His whole training and experience had been
along the lines of organization, and as he subsequently

stated, "It would have been a decided step in advance had we inaugurated, so soon, a battalion organization of several batteries. We came to it about a year later, but meanwhile our batteries had been isolated and attached to infantry brigades. So they fought singly, and in such small units artillery can do little."*

While accomplishing great results in the task assigned him, early in July Capt. Alexander was attached to the staff of Gen. Beauregard, and ordered to install the signal system for use in the great battle, then foreseen by all. Capt. Alexander's system of communications during the battle and the days preceding it, was of great value to the generals in command, he himself transmitting the first definite intelligence of McDowell's line of advance.†

The absence of such a staff officer was sorely felt on the Peninsula in the subsequent campaign, where all worked in the dark. What might have been the outcome had the abilities of Alexander been employed by Lee and Jackson in that campaign is interestingly problematical. But this is true of the whole war in which military information was precariously obtained, staff duties being illy defined, and in which no efficient system of gaining intelligence was generally made use of.

The foregoing remarks concerning this officer, somewhat lengthy it may seem, have been indulged in, for the purpose of showing what manner of men had to do with the early equipment and organization of the Confederate artillery. Each one with whom we meet, whether Gorgas, St. John, Mallet, Jackson, Pendleton, or Alexander, possesses character and abilities of high order, a fact which is a tribute to the directing hands. Remarkable results were obtained simply because extraordinary men produced them.

Reverting to the Army of Northern Virginia, it will be recalled that the Chief of Artillery was sent to Rich-

---

*Memoirs of a Confederate, Alexander, p. 14. We shall see later that Gen. Alexander had been the first in the Confederacy to grasp this great fact. True, the Washington Artillery had a battalion organization, but it was employed in battery formation at first.

†Alexander had familiarized himself with the terrain of a large territory in a manner quite unknown to the military service at the time.

mond, after Bull Run, to "rustle" material, as the saying is in the service. The efforts of Johnston, aided by Pendleton and Alexander, to increase and equip the artillery were unremitting. In a letter to his wife, dated July 22, Pendleton wrote from Richmond, "Have had a great deal to do here pushing up artillery preparations. Will have several batteries at Manassas next week, and several others the week after, etc. Several difficulties obstruct the way. Want of tin to make brass; only one good foundry here, deficiency of hands, etc.; and not least of all, no suitable head in the War Department. Still, by hook or by crook, we get along. And, I trust our force, artillery and all, will be strong for the work to be done. The Lincoln dynasty will press the war, I am persuaded, to the bitter end. . . . My duties about harness, etc., may take me to Staunton and Lynchburg. . . . I long to be back in the brigade again. All this equipping work is the plague of my life, but it must be done, however disagreeable."

Gen. Johnston wrote to him about this time:

"COLONEL—I received duly your note in relation to additional artillery for this army, and asking if you should continue to attend to that service or return.

"The duty to which you have been attending is, I think, the most important to which you can attend. I beg you, therefore, to devote yourself to it until we have reason to believe another action imminent when, of course, you will be necessary in the field. Do not fail to urge the making of 12-pounder howitzers, etc. . . ."*

Pendleton's duties at this time were not enviable ones and it was fortunate for the artillery that a minister of the gospel, with the patience of his calling, was assigned to the task allotted him. Equipments for the batteries were almost more difficult to supply than guns. So many skilled mechanics had gone into active service that workmen enough to operate the larger establishments were scarcely to be found. These establishments were, therefore, unable to undertake large contracts for furnishing the needed artillery supplies.

---

*Remainder of this letter calling for S. B. guns in preference to rifled pieces has been hereinbefore quoted, p. 65.

To contract for them by the dozen or score wherever blacksmiths, wheelwrights, harness makers, and tinners could be found, was the only solution. This was accordingly done throughout the small towns and villages of the Shenandoah Valley and Piedmont country. From them, with the aid of capable workmen here and there, relieved from active service for the purpose, the necessary equipments were procured. Col. Pendleton, whose influence in the pulpit was very great, even preached sermons arousing the people to redouble their efforts in behalf of the army, stirring the spirit of the people to assist as best they might. Old men and boys wrought at the forge and carpenter's bench, while women made tents, uniforms, knapsacks, blankets, bandages, and similar articles.

To visit the small contractors and encourage them in their work, and, wherever it was possible, enlist the efforts of others, was also part of Col. Pendleton's business. For this purpose, it was necessary to see the cannon founders and other operators in Lynchburg, and the harness makers in Staunton. Passing from one place to another in September, from the pulpit, he persuaded his neighbors in Lexington to make for him harness, canteens, and other small but necessary articles.

The want of ammunition for the artillery was even more pressing than that of larger and better guns. Such, indeed, was the absolute scarcity of it in the army at Manassas, that had McClellan been allowed to advance during the late summer and autumn, no sustained resistance could have been made by Johnston. Referring to his deficiencies in respect to ammunition, the latter has stated that until about the middle of August, he had only half enough for a battle,* and on August 24, the ordnance officer of his army telegraphed Pendleton: "Our cannon ammunition is all exhausted except 6-pounder." Again on August 27, "Most of the very small stock of ammunition on hand when you left has been issued, and, in fact, I may say that the

---

*Johnston's Narrative, pp. 60, 61.

stock is entirely exhausted. . . . If the Army had to take the field just now, the scarcity of ammunition would be alarming." As late as September 14, Pendleton was informed by the ordnance officer with the Army that the necessary shrapnel, shell, and cartridges for the artillery had not been received.* Yet, the failure of Gen. Johnston to advance upon and seize Washington during the summer of 1861 has been frequently charged against him as an inexcusable blunder. All through the summer he had continued with the utmost persistence to urge the forwarding of the necessary artillery material and equipment, the government making strenuous efforts, spurred by Pendleton's presence, to fulfill the ordnance requisitions.

On September 5, Mr. Davis wrote Gen. Johnston: "Every effort shall be made to furnish you the howitzers you want. Col. Pendleton will give you details. . . . My means are short of the wants of each division of the wide frontier I am laboring to protect."†

But, in spite of all efforts, the exigencies continued great and pressing. On October 27, the Acting-Secretary of War,‡ writing to Gov. Letcher of Virginia, mentioned the fact that Gen. Johnston was constantly asking for powder and howitzers, and requested the State to turn over to the Army all of both in its possession.

Pendleton's range of duties constantly increased as his efficiency became more apparent. Before his return to the Army early in October, he had even been called upon to provide men as well as guns for the batteries, and for the cavalry. Confidence in his ability to comply with any demands made upon him seems to have been almost unlimited. At last, however, his trying labors in Richmond came to an end and he returned to Manassas, where he took up the more congenial work of perfecting the organization of his command, assisted and advised by his old friend, Gen.

---

*See *Memoirs of William Nelson Pendleton,* p. 158.
†*Rebellion Records,* Series I, Vol. V, p. 830.
‡Hon. J. P. Benjamin.

Jackson, whose tent he shared, and preaching to his men while he worked. On October 19, he wrote that his artillery corps consisted of 600 men, 450 horses, and 28 pieces of ordnance, more guns being expected*

Some idea of the labor performed by the Chief of Artillery and the ordnance officers with the Army may be had from the results obtained by the end of November. At this time, there were 15 batteries assigned to brigades, in addition to the reserve artillery, of which 8 batteries with about 40 pieces were in command of Maj. Walton, and 9 under the direct command of the Chief of Artillery, with 44 pieces and more batteries on the way to join.†

Whence had come the vast amount of material, not less than 150 pieces of ordnance alone, required for this force? The total number of guns in the hands of the army after Bull Run, including those captured, was less than 60. The following statement of material secured by him, made out August 17, by Col. Pendleton, before his return to the Army, answers the question, a statement from which we see again that the Bureau of Ordnance, C. S. A., had not as yet begun to supply the armament.‡

"STATEMENT OF GUNS, CARRIAGES, CAISSONS, ETC., ORDERED

CARRIAGES AND CAISSONS

Talbott & Bro., Richmond, Va., thirty 6-pounder carriages; no caissons. Ten will be completed in a few days, and 10 each three months till the order is finished.

Philip Rham, Richmond, Va., fourteen 6-pounder carriages, and caissons. Four of each delivered, 4 will be ready in 10 days, and the remaining 6 in three weeks.

J. R. Cato, three 6-pounder carriages, and caissons.

I. & J. Van Pelt, Petersburg, Va., twenty-five 6-pounder carriages, and caissons.

Tappy & Lumsden, Petersburg, Va., twenty-five 6-pounder carriages, and caissons, and five 24-pounder carriages.

---

*Pendleton's son, A. S. Pendleton (Sandie), later one of Jackson's aides, and his nephew, John Page, were on his own personal staff.
†*Rebellion Records,* Series I, Vol. V, pp. 1029, 1032. *Memoirs of W. N. Pendleton,* pp. 165, 168, 169.
‡*Memoirs of W. N. Pendleton,* pp. 168, 169.

Ettenger & Edmond, Richmond Va., sixteen 6-pounder carriages, and caissons. Deliveries of 4 of each will be made every two weeks.

H. M. Smith, Richmond, Va., ten 6-pounder carriages, and caissons.

B. F. Harris, Charlottesville, Va., six 6-pounder carriages, and caissons.

J. R. Anderson & Co., Richmond, Va., twenty-four 12-pounder carriages, and caissons.

Philip Rham, six 12-pounder carriages, and caissons, completed in six weeks.

Rice & Wright, Florence, Ala., forty 24-pounder carriages, and caissons.

J. R. Anderson & Co., sixty 24-pounder carriages, and caissons. No limbers.

GUNS

Anderson & Co., thirty-four 12-pounder howitzers, forty-eight 3-inch iron rifled guns, sixty 6-pounder carriages, and caissons, twenty-four 6-pounder iron guns.

Noble Bros. & Co., Rome, Ga., six 6-pounder brass guns, fifty 3-inch iron rifled guns.

Rice & Wright, Florence, Ala., forty 24-pounder howitzers.

J. L. Archer, Black Heath, Chesterfield County, Va., forty 12-pounder howitzers.

F. B. Deane, Jr., & Son, Lynchburg, Va., forty 12-pounder howitzers.

J. L. Archer, eighty 3-inch iron rifled guns.

RECAPITULATION

6-pounder brass guns	6		
6-pounder iron guns	24	30	
3-inch iron rifled guns		178	
12-pounder howitzers		104	312
6-pounder carriages			219
6-pounder caissons			189
24-pounder carriages, complete			45
24-pounder carriages, no limbers			40

HARNESS

Messrs. Cottrell & Co., Richmond, unlimited order. Contracted through Maj. Smith, New Orleans, 400 sets of harness."

The foregoing detailed statement is given in full because it illustrates better than anything else could what were the material resources from which the artillery equipment in 1861 was drawn. It also evidences the tremendous energy of Johnston's Chief of Artillery. When it is contemplated that many of the manufacturers had probably never seen a gun before they were called upon to make them, that before undertaking the fabrication of these strange articles it was necessary to install machinery and equipment for their making, that detailed drawings of all the parts had to be carefully prepared and furnished them, the accomplishment seems all the more remarkable. It also serves to call our attention to the changes in material and equipment of recent years. Many of the old firms enumerated above are still in successful operation. Long may they continue so. But the fact remains that they could no more turn out modern quick firing guns with their intricate steel carriages, and caissons, than they could manufacture heavenly bodies.

In November, 1860, we have seen that the United States Board of Ordnance officers recommended the conversion of half the heavy ordnance after the James system into rifled pieces.* But the attempt proved a failure, and was soon abandoned. The United States bought various types of rifled pieces when war became imminent, having unlimited means at its disposal. Less than one year after the receipt of Parrott's trial gun by Jackson at the Virginia Military Institute, we find Pendleton actually manufacturing 178 of them, at three different plants, and these in two different States. Johnston had surely been converted.

This brings us down to the winter of 1861 and 1862, when the organization of the Confederate Ordnance Department had become effective and when artillerymen no longer had to "rustle" for themselves, except for horses and harness. The Artillery, Army of Northern Virginia, has been armed and equipped. Henceforth its requisitions are filled either by the proper department to the best of its ability, or upon the field

---

*Report of this board submitted November 1, 1860, pursuant to S. O. No. 144, A. G. O., 1860.

of battle from the plunder of the enemy. Though it
was at all times inferior in the quantity and quality of
its material and lighter in metal, yet the brains and the
industry of the men behind the guns, whether begrimed
with the soot of the foundry or the smoke of the battlefield, enabled it to maintain for four terrible years of
almost constant warfare a contest then unparalleled in
history.

The weapon we have examined. Now let us pass on
to the men who wielded it, first inquiring who they
were, and then how they bore themselves.

PART II

The Field Artillery of the Army of Northern Virginia

Its Foundation, Organization, Personnel, and Tactics

CHAPTER I

THE ARTILLERY OF THE EARLY DAYS

In the first part of this work, an endeavor has been made to give the student of the Civil War a conception of the means which enabled the Confederate Government to place artillery in the field. In the treatment of ordnance operations it was not always easy, nor in many instances possible, for the writer to refrain from infringing upon the present subject. The line of demarkation between ordnance operations and material is at best indefinite, and the patience of the reader is craved when repetition perforce occurs, the excuse being offered that historical continuity will be preserved, even though at times its attainment may entail the tedium incident to a seeming literary defect.

Again, it seems necessary, in order to establish the status of field artillery in the United States and its development prior to the outbreak of the Civil War, to begin with the Revolutionary Period.*

Although American artillery dates from the French and Indian Wars, at which time colonial companies were formed in a number of the large cities, the only artillery organization which seems to have existed in the South, prior to the Revolutionary War, was that of Charleston, S. C. The organization of the early colonial Artillery naturally followed very closely that of the Royal Artillery, with which it was associated.

The first regiment arrayed against the Crown was raised by the Colony of Massachusetts, and adopted by the Continental Congress. It consisted of 10 companies, with a greater number of field officers than was

---

*The facts given in the following brief outline of the Artillery, from 1775 to 1859, were extracted almost entirely from Lieut. William E. Birkhimer's *Historical Sketch of the United States Artillery;* the first four volumes of *United States Ordnance Reports,* kindly presented the writer by the present Ordnance Office, through Capt. Oliver L. Spaulding, U. S. F. A.; *Military Policy of the United States,* Upton; *Historical Register United States Army,* etc.; and *The Late War,* Thompson. Citations will not be given from these, as the sources are available to all.

prescribed by the British regulations, and was commanded by Col. Richard Gridley, a retired British officer, under whose advice it was organized. Passing through various reorganizations, this regiment, together with a Rhode Island battery and two batteries from New York, constituted the entire artillery force of the colonial army until after the disastrous Long Island campaign in the summer of 1776. At this time the Corps of Artillery consisted of about 600 officers and men, of which a large number were with the army in the North, there being 88 authorized battalions of infantry. From the latter, Washington and Gates had each been forced to draft about 600 men for the service of the guns.

When Congress resolved to reorganize the Army, the committee in charge called upon the senior artillery officer, Col. Knox, to submit his recommendations. Laying great stress upon the gross disproportion of artillery to infantry, and the almost utter lack of the former, amongst other things that this able officer urged was the creation of arsenals and cannon-foundries, an ordnance bureau for their conduct, and an *academy on the same plan as that at Woolwich, where the whole theory and practice of fortification and gunnery might be taught;* claiming that to the British school the enemy was indebted for their superiority in artillery to all who had opposed them. Knox, then, we are justified in believing, was the first American artillerist to advocate the scientific study of gunnery, and was in a sense the father of the present excellent system of theoretical and practical instruction, though it has taken over a century to grasp the full meaning of his recommendation.

"There ought to be a respectable body of artillery established which shall be equal to all the services of the war. In proportion to every 1,000 men of the marching regiments, there ought to be one company of 60 men, including officers. This number will be found to be small when the various contingencies of the artillery

shall be considered. Supposing, then, the army consist
of 80 battalions of 726 men each, making nearly 60,000
men, the number of artillery requisite will be 3,360.
These may be thrown into two or three battalions, as
may be thought best."

The foregoing words were written by Knox near a
century and a half ago! Well might they be pondered
to-day by Congress! These recommendations made
more impression upon the Government at that time than
similar ones do now, and it was at once decided to raise
5 battalions of artillery, and the British—not the
French system, as is thought by some—was adhered to
by Knox in their organization. Many French officers
trained in the school of Gribeauval, it is true, sought
service in the American Artillery, but they found at its
head a man whose views obtained in preference to their
own.*

The artillery force contemplated was intended to
supply artillery to all the armies in the field, and the 5
battalions authorized were quickly raised, one of them
being converted into an artificer regiment, the forerunner of an ordnance organization.† Pursuant to the
resolution of Congress, November 26, 1776, one of the
artillery battalions embracing 2 companies or batteries
was raised by Gen. Charles Lee, in Virginia, the field
officers being Col. Charles Harrison, Lieut.-Col. Edward Carrington, and Maj. Christian Holman.

While the 5 battalions raised by Knox were considered to constitute the regular artillery, the colonies
had begun to organize companies, as a rule, however,
for State defense only, most of them being heavy or
coast artillery. The Provincial Congress of South
Carolina, in November, 1775, put on foot an artillery
battalion of 3 companies of 100 men each, and this
organization, in command of Lieut.-Col. Owen Roberts,
was taken into continental pay. And, in 1777, a number of Georgia batteries, in command of a French officer, Maj. Roman de Lisle, were turned over to the

---

*See *Military Policy of United States*, p. 29.
†The terms regiment and battalion were used synonymously.

Federal government.* These southern batteries were not subject to service, however, beyond the limits of their States. They were paid by Congress for the sole reason that the States were unable to maintain them; over them the Chief of Artillery exercised no control.

In November, 1778, another reorganization of the Army followed while Washington lay at Valley Forge. For the first time the organization of the various artillery regiments was placed on a uniform basis, the same number of officers and men being assigned to each. The Virginia regiment, now designated the First, was thus increased to 12 batteries by attaching to it two companies from Maryland.† Due to the reduction in the number of its officers, and to inexperienced hands, the Artillery, in common with the rest of the Army, did not thrive during the next few years. Consequently again in 1780 its reorganization was undertaken. It was finally decided to retain the 4 line regiments but to reduce them to 10 companies of 65 enlisted men and 6 officers each, the regimental field and staff consisting of 7 officers.‡ In accordance with the original plan, the First Regiment was again assigned to Virginia. Soon being placed under Gates, it suffered severely at Camden, and in consequence never rejoined the main army, the fragments of the organization remaining in Georgia and the Carolinas until the end of the war. It was not, therefore, at Yorktown; the Second, or New York regiment, and the Fourth, or Pennsylvania regiment, composed the entire force of artillery at that memorable siege.§

Promotion in the continental Artillery was regimental, the power of appointing officers being retained by the States. During the period after peace had been declared, when Congress was making every effort to re-

---

*The famous Chatham Artillery of Savannah had its origin in one of these batteries.
†Before the reorganization the regiment had already been increased to 10 companies.
‡See *Military Policy of the United States*, p. 48.
§The Fourth Regiment served a short time in the South with the First. Except this and the service at Yorktown, the Second and Third served wholly in the North.

duce the Army to a peace footing, the Artillery as it had
existed practically dissolved by reason of the expiration
of enlistments, etc.   Certain duties, however, connected
with the incompleted transfer of property by the
British in the Northwest, necessitated the retention in
service of a battalion consisting of 138 officers and men
drawn entirely from the old Second and Third Regiments.   With this exception, the old organizations were
disbanded as Federal troops, many of the batteries continuing to exist as State militia.   In 1784, even the
small battalion which had been continued in the service was discharged, leaving one New York and one
Pennsylvania battery as the only artillery force in the
Federal Army, it being united with some Maryland
infantry of the line to form a mondescript regiment,
known as the "First American."

It was not until October 20, 1786, when the Army was
increased to 2,040 enlisted men, including those of the
"First American," that Knox, then become Secretary
of War, was able to organize a separate battalion
of artillery under a major in which the present artillery
organization as a separate arm of the service originated.
The personnel of the new artillery battalion was entirely Northern.   After frequent changes in its organization, including one merging it with the Engineer Corps,
the Artillery as a separate corps of 3 battalions was increased in 1808 (one being a light regiment of 10
batteries.)   Many distinguished Frenchmen had served
of late in the Engineer and Artillery Corps, but a
distinctly American character was now enforced upon
the Artillery.   It was some time before the regiment
could be properly equipped as light artillery, due to the
extremes of the economists, but finally the result was accomplished.   Winfield Scott, afterwards commander-
in-chief, and a Virginian, stood second on the list of
captains of this the first properly-equipped American
regiment of light artillery.   Among its original officers
were other Southern men, afterwards distinguished.
The several batteries of the regiment recruited in the

South were soon after their formation concentrated at New Orleans, pending the settlement of the difficulties with Great Britain. But instead of trouble being averted, war became a fact, and January 11, 1812, two provisional artillery regiments were authorized by the measure increasing the Army, each regiment having 10 companies, to be known as the Second and Third Regiments, respectively, the old or regular regiment, being designated the First.

Capt. George Izard, of South Carolina, formerly of the older regiment, became Colonel, and Capt. Winfield Scott, and Francis K. Huger, of South Carolina, Lieutenant-Colonels of the Second Regiment. Like Scott, Izard rose to be a general officer. Educated in the best military schools of France, he had no superior as an educated and practical officer in America, being much relied upon as an organizer by the War Department. When he was promoted in 1813, he was succeeded by Lieut.-Col. Scott in command of the Second. Capt. George Armistead, of Virginia, had been made a major in the Third. In 1814, Scott also became a brigadier-general.

The status of the Artillery as fixed by the Act of 1814, was that of a corps of 12 battalions, in the formation of which Izard had been most influential. The light artillery was left as organized in 1808, however, and so also by the Act of 1815, fixing the military peace establishment. In the latter year, the territory of the United States was divided into military departments, five in the North and four in the South, the line of division being roughly that passing east and west through the capital. In the attempt to maintain an artillery equipoise in the two great divisions, the light artillery and 4 battalions or half of the Corps of Artillery was assigned to the North, and the other 4 battalions to the South. This distribution obtained until the artillery organization as a corps was abolished in 1821, when 4 regiments of artillery were created, of 9 companies each, only one company of each being designated to be equipped as light artillery, the old light regiment being broken up with the Corps. This organization continued until the exigencies of the Seminole War, in 1837, caused an increase of one company in each regiment, and in the company strength from 42 to 58 men. The Mexican War again brought an increase of 2 companies to a regiment, 4 additional companies to be equipped as light batteries, the latter provision resulting from the brilliant service of the field batteries in the Rio Grande campaign, where they astonished not only the country, but the Army itself, by their power and efficiency.

The artillery organization of 1847 was maintained substantially unchanged until the Civil War, in spite of many efforts to alter it. Failing to overcome Gen. Scott's opposition to changes in organization, although such men as Bomford, Talcott, and Mordecai had favored them, it was next sought, and successfully, to establish systematic courses of instruction for the Artillery, among them a School of Fire at Fortress Monroe, which has continued to this day.

Such had been the career of the American Artillery up to the year 1861. To be found in its personnel during the period from the Mexican to the Civil War were an entirely disproportionate number of Southern officers, who had not only received professional training in the service of the Regular Artillery, but many of whom had received extensive experience in the Ordnance Department.[*]

It must not be thought, however, that the militia had played no part in the education of artillery officers during the wars of the Republic, for the Continental troops during the Revolution and the Regulars subsequent thereto were largely supplemented by the militia on all occasions.[†] In 1792, Congress, seeking to organize the militia, provided that each State should maintain at least one company of artillery, and a number of South-

---

[*] Artillery officers of the line were regularly detailed to the Ordnance Department in the old service, as in the Confederate Army. As shown in Part I, Gen. Gorgas, Chief of Ordnance, C. S. A., came from the United States Ordnance Department.

[†] To what extent, see *Military Policy of United States,* Upton.

ern artillery organizations gained experience in the
War of 1812.* Included in the force of 10,000 militia,
which assembled on the Virginia coast to defend Norfolk against Cockburn and Warren, in 1814, was the
Portsmouth Light Artillery, a previously organized
battery.† The Chatham Artillery, of Georgia, also
saw service in the War of 1812, in the more Southern
quarter, as did the Charleston Battery. In 1828, two
other famous militia batteries, the Norfolk Light
Artillery Blues, and the Fayette Artillery, of Richmond, were organized in Virginia.‡ Out of their early
experiences arose traditions which still permeate the
spirit of these corps, while they have ever been valuable
military assets to the Commonwealths boasting their
allegiance. The *esprit de corps* of these old batteries
was not only a military but a social factor during the
critical period of our country. The proud records
which they had established, and their traditions, generated in many a youthful Southern breast the martial
spirit and the love of the service which, in large measure,
made the Confederacy possible. Who that has mingled
with the men of these gallant commands can put a
period to the influence which their *ante-bellum* existence exerted upon the naturally martial spirit of the
South?

The popularity of the artillery service in the South
from the earliest times is well attested by the fact that
of the 25,295 volunteer and militia artillerymen who
were called out to supplement the corps of 12 depleted
regular battalions of artillery, in the War of 1812, an
overwhelming proportion of the officers and men came
from that territory which afterwards comprised the
Confederate and the border States.§

*Of the 49,187 militia called into service at the beginning of this war,
Massachusetts furnished 208 men and Connecticut none, these States declining
to assist in the general defense. Maryland, Virginia, Delaware, and North
Carolina furnished 66,376 militia in 1813.
†In 1861 this was the oldest artillery company in the South, and took the
field under command of Capt. Cary F. Grimes, winning great distinction.
‡The Norfolk Blues Battery was known as Vickery's or Grandy's Battery in
the Civil War. From it was organized Huger's Battery.
§*Military Policy of United States,* Upton, p. 138; and *Historical Register
United States Army,* Heitman.

While the volunteers and militia which served in the
Mexican War were largely drawn from southern territory, the only artillery organizations from that quarter
which served as such, were the "Native American Artillery," and a French battery of New Orleans, known
as the "Orleans Artillery." Organized in 1838, the
"Native American Artillery" was commanded by Capt.,
afterwards Gen., E. L. Tracy, being attached to the
Washington regiment of New Orleans in 1841. This
regiment was a mixed command modeled after the
"First American," being composed of infantry, cavalry,
and artillery. In command of Col. Persifer F. Smith,
the Washington Regiment became the crack corps of
the State. The army of occupation dispatched to
Corpus Christi, July 26, 1845, was entirely lacking in
artillery, the regular mounted batteries not having yet
arrived from the North. Gen. Taylor, therefore, called
upon Gen. Gaines, commanding the Department of the
South, for a force of "skilled volunteer artillerists." All
the volunteer batteries in the South responded with
alacrity, but two were deemed sufficient, and the
"Native American," with its six 6-pounder bronze guns.
and Capt. Bercier's Orleans (French) Battery, were
selected. These two batteries were placed under command of Maj. Golly of the "Orleans Artillery," and
embarked at Jackson Barracks, New Orleans, August
22, 1845, for the front. At the expiration of three
months' service on the Texas frontier, the regular
mounted batteries having arrived in the meantime, the
Louisiana batteries were ordered home. When on May
9, 1846, Gen. Gaines made another call upon the State
for volunteer infantry, Capt. Henry Forno, having become Lieutenant-Colonel of the Washington Regiment,
the Native American again responded under its new
Captain, Isaac F. Stockton, serving as Company A
(infantry). The regiment, now in command of
Col. J. B. Walton, was the first of the six Louisiana
infantry regiments to volunteer, all of which were dis-

charged from the United States service July 21, 1846, their services having been accepted only for six months.

Reorganized in 1852, the "Native American" Battery became theWashington Artillery, Col. J. B. Walton becoming its Captain in 1857.* At the outbreak of the Civil War there was not a finer organization of citizen soldiery in America. So great was its prestige and influence in the South that, immediately expanding to a battalion of 4 companies, one equipped as a battery, it was ordered to Richmond in time to be fully armed and to participate in the first great encounter of the Civil War.†

So much for the status of artillery in the South at the outbreak of the war. The outlook, while not bright, was, as has been shown, comparatively satisfactory. It would have been quite impossible to begin the study of the Confederate Artillery without at least the foregoing knowledge of its resources of personnel, of the school of experience in which many of its officers had been trained, and of the model after which it was organized.

---

*In Camp and Battle with the Washington Artillery, Owen. Also see historical sketch in the Washington Artillery Souvenir, p. 30.

†Much of the equipment of the battery, including six 6-pounder guns, with ammunition for same, was obtained by the command when it seized the Baton Rouge Arsenal, April 11, 1861.

CHAPTER II

EVEN before officers of the Old Army were invited by the various States to resign and enter their service, and before the Confederate States government offered them offices in the new military establishment, resignations had begun to pour in upon the War Department in Washington. Exactly how many of these officers entered the Southern Artillery it is difficult to determine. Of the 821 graduates of West Point in the United States Army at the close of 1860, 184 resigned and entered the armies of the South, and of the 313 graduates in civil life at the time 99 did the same. The Confederacy thus obtained a total of 283 trained officers, 8 of whom attained the rank of general, 15 that of lieutenant-general, 48 that of major-general, and 11 that of brigadier-general in the Confederacy, leaving but 101 who were given lower rank, and it is fair to assume that most of these became field or staff officers. We know that there were but 4 officers with rank above that of colonel in Lee's Artillery—Pendleton, Alexander, Walker, and Long—three of whom were West Pointers, but few of his artillery field officers and battery commanders were graduates of the United States Military Academy. All the more, then, since the Artillery was not largely officered by former United States officers, are we astounded at the comparative efficiency of its personnel, and constrained to inquire whence came that gallant corps which handled the guns.

The answer is plain, though no historian as yet has ever sought it. The results obtained by Lee's Artillery were not accidental, nor did they flow from the inherent quality of Southerners as artillerymen. Artillery is a science, as pointed out by Gen. Knox during the Revolution, as understood by the founders of Woolwich, and as perceived by the "Grand Monarch" centuries ago.

War may produce, now and then, a great natural soldier.
Such men as Forrest are exceptions, however. They
become noted, not because they have had no military
training, but for the very reason that they are born with
qualities for the development of which in others study
and experience are required. Too often we hear the
Southern orator refer in eloquent words to the leaders
of that division which recoiled only after reaching the
fire-wreathed muzzles of Cemetery Ridge, as typifying the inherent martial character of Virginia's sons.
At heart, it is true, they were soldiers, but by no means
adventitiously so. They were trained soldiers, educated
in advance for the service of their country, in a school
of arms second to none in this country, that which stood
upon the Hudson not excepted. Nearly every field
officer who participated in Pickett's charge was an
élève of the Virginia Military Institute, and a former
pupil of the distinguished soldier William Gilham, and
of the immortal Jackson himself. In order to grasp the
full meaning of this assertion, it is necessary to examine
the character of that school.

In 1836, J. T. L. Preston, Esq., conceived the idea
of substituting for the company maintained by the
State for garrisoning the western arsenal in Lexington,
a corps of cadets, who in addition to the duties of an
armed guard should pursue a course of scientific and
military instruction. Pursuant to this proposal, the
Virginia Military Institute, since generally styled "The
West Point of the Confederacy," was established by
Act of the General Assembly, March, 1839, the first
corps being mustered into the State service the following November. The President of the first Board of
Visitors, one who had much to do with the original
organization of the school, was Col. Claudius Crozet, a
Frenchman by birth, a graduate of the great Polytechnic School of Paris, and a distinguished veteran of
Napoleon's Grand Army. Before accepting the appointment as Chief Engineer of Virginia, in which
office he designed, and put into effect the scheme of her

physical development, he had for some years occupied the chair of Engineering at the Unites States Military Academy. With scientific attainments of the highest order, and an intimate knowledge of the distinctive organization of West Point, to the upbuilding of which in company with Bernard he had contributed much, he was well fitted to assist in the organization of a school of arms in Virginia. Other members of the Board with military experience were Capt. John F. Wiley, a maimed veteran of the Canadian campaign of 1812, Gen. Bernard Peyton, Gen. Peter C. Johnston, Gen. Thomas H. Botts, and James McDowell, afterwards Governor of Virginia. To these must be added Col. John T. L. Preston, who had originated the enterprise, and who for thirty years was one of the professors of the school. Soon followed the appointment of Gen. W. H. Richardson, Adjutant-General of Virginia at the outbreak of the Civil War, and the veteran soldier William Ligon, vice Peyton and Wiley.

At the outset, it was provided that a certain number of cadets should be appointed by State authority, and the number has since been increased to about 60. Frequent visits were paid the school in its early days by such distinguished scholars as Professors Bartlett, Church, Mahan, and Hardie, of the United States Military Academy. Thus it was moulded closely after the national school. Some idea of its character from the first may be had from a knowledge of the careers of the sixteen cadets who composed the first class to graduate.* Of these, John B. Strange, after a distinguished career as Principal of the Norfolk Academy, was killed at Boonsboro, Md., while in command of a Virginia regiment. William Forbes, a professor in a college in Texas, was killed at Second Manassas while commanding a Tennessee regiment. J. H. Jameson died with the rank of Captain C. S. A., while a prisoner of war. Col. Edmund Pendleton was wounded while in command of a Louisiana regiment; Gen. Wyatt

*July 4, 1842.

Elliott commanded a Virginia regiment in the War, served in the State Legislature, and became Rector of the University of Virginia; C. P. Dyerle died before the war while an Assistant Surgeon, U. S. A.; O. M. Knight held the rank of Surgeon in the Confederate Army; William D. Fair became a member of the Senate of California; and Capt. James Marshall commanded a cavalry troop in the Confederate Army.

The military instruction of the school during the first few years of its existence had been solely in the hands of its Superintendent, Col. Francis H. Smith, a distinguished graduate of West Point. With the advice and assistance of the brilliant Crozet, his was the master mind which laid the foundation upon which all its success was based, and by him the school in its formative period was given its character as a real school of arms. Its educational aims were never lost sight of by this illustrious man, nor were the distinctive purposes to which it owed its origin. First, last, and all the time, a cadet must be a soldier, which in the Superintendent's mind was not a requisite in conflict with the education of useful citizens.

We hear much of Jackson as the military genius of the school. Undoubtedly he did much in the preparation of a corps of officers for the Confederacy, but he was not appointed Professor of Natural and Experimental Philosophy until March 21, 1851, and his military duties were restricted to artillery instruction. Long before this great soldier took up his work in Lexington, Lieut. William Gilham, a distinguished graduate of West Point, who had gained distinction in the army of Gen. Taylor, in the battles of Palo Alto, and Resaca de la Palma, had been appointed Commandant.*

As a military instructor and drillmaster, Maj. Gilham had no superior. Quick, accurate, and self-possessed, he had a magnetic power of command, which in the opinion of many made the drill of his battalion of cadets superior even to that of the West Point corps.

---

*Appointed in 1846 as Major and Commandant, and head of the Department of Physical Science.

He also excelled as a teacher, having been three years assistant to Prof. Bartlett at the National Academy. So celebrated had Gilham become as an organizer and tactician that his manual of instruction for the volunteers and militia, including the three arms, was adopted by the Confederate Government in preference to all other works of the kind.

Before 1861, the Corps numbered over 200 cadets, and in April of that year it was ordered to Richmond in command of Maj. Jackson, its members to be assigned to duty as drillmasters for the volunteers then assembling at Camp Lee. Soon the Corps dissolved by the appointment of the cadets as officers throughout the Army. But their work had been well done and their drill squads formed the army which overthrew McDowell at Bull Run. The cadets not only drilled the green companies of volunteers, but they were largely responsible for the equipment and organization of the troops, including the batteries, furnishing a large proportion of the staff officers for the Army, a number of them taking part in the battle of Bull Run before they were commissioned.* Though their work has not attracted due notice from the historian, it was well appreciated by Lincoln, who, when asked by a United States Senator in the early part of the war, why he had not put an end to the rebellion, is said to have answered that there was a certain military school in Virginia which made it impossible. Certainly no one can estimate the value of the service which the school rendered the Confederacy at this time in welding the raw levies into shape, and furnishing to the Army as a whole a nucleus of trained and educated young officers.

But so apparent to the Confederacy was the need of the institution as a training school for its officers that immediate steps were taken by the State to reopen it after the first crisis had passed, and in 1862 its regular work was resumed. Upon its parade ground were marshalled the scions of nearly every distinguished family

---

*Three were killed in this battle: Moore, Moffett, and Norris.

of the South, from Texas to Maryland, from Missouri to Florida, then as to-day; nor were these youths content to bide the time of graduation. The wounded officers ordered back to the Institute to drill and instruct the Corps filled their boyish breasts with such ardor, and such a longing for active service, that the problem arose how to keep them in hand. Many deserted to face the enemy. Hundreds who never graduated flocked to the combatant forces in the field. Nor were those who remained deprived of all chance of seeing active service, the Corps being repeatedly called upon for duty in the Valley of Virginia, and on the various defensive lines of the State. Already, in 1859, the Corps had been ordered by Gov. Wise to Harper's Ferry, as a part of the State force present at the execution of John Brown.* After the reorganization of the Corps in 1862, it was sent to the support of Jackson at McDowell, and took part in the pursuit of Fremont's Army as far as Franklin. Then came in 1864 the battle of New Market, in which the cadets saved the day for Breckinridge by a superb charge, unsurpassed for gallantry in the annals of war, losing 57 of their number, including 9 killed, a loss of 20 per cent of those engaged.†

The Institute was completely demolished by Gen. D. H. Hunter, the following month, June, 1864, when the Corps was assigned to duty with the cavalry command of Gen. John McCausland, who fell back before the invader upon Lynchburg, at which point the Federal force was checked and driven off. Ordered to Richmond, the Corps soon found itself on the Richmond lines before Grant, being dispersed only when the Capital of the Confederacy was evacuated, not to be assembled until the fall of 1865. The Corps organization had been throughout that of a battalion of infantry of 4 companies, and a battery of artillery.‡

---

*For a graphic description of the event, by Col. Preston, see *History of the Virginia Military Institute,* Wise.

†In addition to the 5 cadets killed on the field of battle, 4 died within a month from wounds received.

‡Only 1 section of cadet artillery took part in the Battle of New Market.

Besides the most thorough instruction in the art of war, embracing all arms, practical artillery instruction under Jackson had been given for nearly a decade, not less than 600 cadets having been instructed in this time in the theory and practice of gunnery.

At the outbreak of the war, every inducement was offered graduates of West Point to enter the Confederate Army, 182 attaining the rank of general officer during the first year of their service. Up to June, 1861, there had been 554 graduates of the Institute, and 1,210 matriculates who had served one year or more as cadets. Of this number, there were not more than 1,100 available for military service, and three-fourths of these were under 30 and half under 25 years of age, for the school had been in existence but 22 years.* West Pointers were naturally preferred to Institute men by the authorities in order to reward them for resigning from the United States Army. But at the time of the reorganization of the Army, Institute men won the recognition due them, the efficient military organization of the school with its distinctive scientific courses of instruction being then fully appreciated.

We have seen that West Point sent a total of but 283 officers to the Southern armies. Statistics are instructive, if dry at times, but in this case they will enable us to estimate the comparative influence of the two schools upon the military career of the Confederacy. While the records of the Institute are not complete as to the matriculates up to 1861, they show that the school produced 3 major-generals, 17 brigadier-generals, 92 colonels, 64 lieutenant-colonels, 107 majors, and over 300 captains, besides a host of junior officers. This list, incomplete as it is, comprises a total of 20 general officers, and 263 field officers, an overwhelming proportion of whom served in the Army of Northern Virginia. Among the generals were such men as Mahone, Rodes, Wharton, Echols, R. L. Walker, Colston, J. R. Jones, Garland, Lane, McCausland, and Munford,

*The number of graduates during the decade 1851-1861 was double that of the preceding 10 years; the proportion of matriculates much larger.

most of whom were mere youths.* Among the field-officers were Col. Walter H. Taylor, Gen. Lee's Adjutant-General, Col. Edwin J. Harvie, Gen. Johnston's Inspector-General, Col. Briscoe G. Baldwin, who succeeded Gen. Alexander as Chief of Ordnance, A. N. V., Cols. Thomas H. Carter, Stapleton Crutchfield, and R. Preston Chew, Chiefs of Artillery of Jackson's, Early's, and Stuart's commands, respectively, and Col. A. R. H. Ranson, Assistant Chief of Ordnance, C. S. A. Gen. R. Lindsay Walker, of the Class of 1845, was Chief of Artillery of Hill's Corps.

The Institute furnished 1 brigadier-general, Carrington, 1 colonel, 2 lieutenant-colonels, 3 majors, and 2 lieutenants to the Northern Army, all save one of the officers being from the western part of the State, now West Virginia.

In the Mexican War, an incomplete list shows that one of her graduates was a major, 2 were captains, and 15 or more were lieutenants, 3 of whom were killed in action. The school had then been in existence but seven years.

Since 1865, the school has furnished nearly 200 officers to the United States Army, Navy, and Marine Corps, there being in 1912 over 100 holding commissions in the Army alone. The average number commissioned each year since 1898 is 12.

In the Spanish-American War, the Southern volunteers included many Institute men, a very incomplete list showing 6 colonels, 2 lieutenant-colonels, 9 majors, and more than 100 officers of junior rank.

In the National Guard of the country, imperfect records show that there have been 2 major-generals, 7 brigadier-generals, 20 colonels, 10 lieutenant-colonels, 12 majors, more than 100 captains, 12 State adjutant-generals, 2 inspector-generals, 1 surgeon-general, and 1 judge-advocate-general. These figures are up to

*Among the other generals were Payne, Terry, Terrill, J. A. Walker, Slaughter, Rives, Fry, Elliott, Bass, Vaughan, Penn, and A. C. Jones.

1909. An immense number have since joined the organized militia, due to the increasing interest of the country therein.

From the foregoing we see that whether the remark attributed to Lincoln is authentic or not, well might it have been founded upon fact. We are also able to see the gross fallacy of the current belief that West Pointers and untrained civilians, with a few exceptions, led the men of Lee's Army. While the enlisted men were citizen soldiers, the Confederacy owed more than can ever be determined to the Virginia Military Institute, and the pupils of Smith, Crozet, Gilham, and Jackson.* Particularly was this true of the artillery of that army in which Carter, Crutchfield, Latimer, Chew, Nelson, Barton, Shields, Rouse, Baldwin, Ranson, Thomson, Carpenter, Ford, Harman, Keiter, Ker, Macon, Otey, Rogers, Selden, Porter, Truehart, Thornton, Waddey, Stanard, Moorman, Flowerree, Hutter, Lynch, Oliver, Cutshaw, Paris, Cunningham, Reverley, the Browns, Smiths, and Johnstons were a few of the field officers and battery commanders among the graduates of the school, who attained distinction in the service of the guns.

Before dismissing the subject of the influence of the Virginia Military Institute upon the success of the Confederate arms, it would seem proper here to mention what, to the writer, has always explained, in great measure at least, the wonderful performances of Jackson's troops. One frequently finds the historian alluding to the ability of Jackson to exact greater sacrifices from his officers and men than is customary, and endeavoring to analyze the character of the man in order to arrive at the reason for this exceptional power on his part. That he possessed a remarkable character and unusual ability to command is unquestioned. Indirectly these traits explain his success, but there is a more direct ex-

---

*In the Superintendent's Report of 1863, an incomplete list of losses in service among the Alumni of the Institute appears as follows : Officers killed, 86 ; wounded 85 ; total. 171, including 4 general officers, 36 colonels, 22 lieutenant-colonels, 41 majors, and 94 officers of lesser rank. Can West Point show such a record up to this time?

planation. Stonewall Jackson, besides being inherently great, had the good fortune to exercise command over, and to be associated with armies the very backbone of which consisted of young men who had but recently borne the relation to him of the pupil to a beloved tutor. The full import of this fact becomes more apparent when it is recalled that nearly 300 field officers alone in the Army of Northern Virginia, distributed among the three arms, besides not less than an equal number of junior officers, had for varying periods been closely associated with him, and subjected to the influence of his personality before they were called upon to follow or coöperate with him upon the field of war. They were his children, his wards, and knew each and every whim of the leader, for whom only the highest respect was entertained. In him they reposed that sublime confidence which knows not reservation, content to rely upon the judgment of one who in the closest relations of life had never failed them in the past. Unconsciously, perhaps, but if so, then all the more thoroughly, they had absorbed his teachings, and become able to follow the habit of his mind. When his first successes crowned him with a halo of military glory they, who had already accorded him the fullest measure of confidence, enthroned him as the special object of their pride. From the very first Jackson's success was redolent of glory for a host of followers who held him up to the admiring world as their own tutelary genius. So far as they were concerned it was not an unfamiliar general whose orders bade them follow and suffer and die upon the field of battle. Their leader was Maj. Jackson, and they were cadets as of yesterday, each vying with the others to merit the favor of his approving eye. The stern, and occasionally harsh, drillmaster of former days had become a leader of acknowledged ability, and they had become the company, the battery, the battalion, the regimental, yea, the brigade leaders in such numbers as to leaven the entire army, and to transmit to the whole, receptive as it was, their own spirit of pride and devotion. Not only was this true, but to no one was it so well known as to Jackson himself. Conscious of the sincerity of his own purpose, confident of the power he held, and that no demand he might make would fail to elicit the fullest possible response from his men, in this spirit it was that at Chancellorsville, the supreme hour of his life, having given his commands, he viewed with pride the army which swept before him to execute his bidding, and, in the joy of a commander who felt the responsive throb of his army's pulse, exclaimed, "The Virginia Military Institute will be heard from to-day." The remark is capable of but one reasonable interpretation. Other constructions may be placed upon it, but the true one is that Jackson, surrounded by Rodes, Colston, Crutchfield, and Munford, all of whom had been his associates at the Institute, and closely scrutinizing the countenances of his men as they filed past him, saw in the faces of his youthful but seasoned field-officers something portentous of more than the usual *élan* of his troops; yes, from the eyes of the regimental, battalion, and company leaders, a host of whom he had guided to manhood's estate, bearing as they were the burden of his fame, flashed a mute assurance that nothing save death would deter them in executing his behest. And so, when smitten by fate at the hour of his greatest glory, it was not his officers alone who lamented his loss, but a multitude of his children, whose hearts were wrung with anguish as they gazed upon his fallen form. No mere loss of an heroic leader was this to an army, but a wound which tore the very heart strings of its men, many of them regarding the blow as prescient of the future.

Without desiring in any respect to detract from the fame of the man who, deprecating the advent of fratricidal strife, yet could throw away his scabbard, let us ask where in all the history of war was there another so fortunately circumstanced as was Jackson?*

---

*The following incident, illustrating the character of Jackson, is related on the authority of Gen. Henry T. Douglas: "After Lincoln's election, the papers were filled with discussions as to the probable outcome and the possibility of

It has been reiterated by such military philosophers as Bulow, Jomini, Willisen, Clausewitz, Moltke, Von der Goltz, Henderson, and Balck, that the moral force, is the preponderant one in war. The moral force which gives men the will-power to overcome all obstacles, to shrink from no danger, and to strive for victory at any cost, emanates in those sentiments which inspirit men to become courageous soldiers. "In a general way, these sentiments are, religious fanaticism, patriotism, enthusiasm for a commander, discipline, and, most of all, confidence resulting from experience."* The prestige of Jackson gave him complete moral ascendancy over his men, and that prestige was decidedly the outgrowth of an experience which many of his subordinates had gained with him, his officers comprising the psychological or suggestive medium by which the spirit of confidence in and enthusiasm for the commander was generated in his army. "The best obeyed commanders are neither the best instructed, the most intelligent, the most paternal, nor the most severe, but are those who have innate or acquired prestige. . . . It is because of it that his suggestions take on an irresistible power, that he is able to throw his soldiers against the enemy in an enthusiastic assault, and that he can stop with a gesture the first fugitives, transforming them into heroes."† The suggestions contained in the foregoing remarks about the personal power of Jackson as a soldier may be followed up with benefit by the military student. His circumstances as a leader were in a psychological sense fortuitous.

war between the sections, and the *New York Herald* was read with great interest. Ned Cunningham was an assistant professor to Maj. Jackson at the Institute, and he told me that one night he and Maj. Jackson were sitting in his section room absorbed in reading the papers. Neither had spoken for some time, when Ned put to Maj. Jackson this question: 'Major, would you like to see war?' He said Jackson stopped reading the paper and for five minutes hung down his head before replying. He then looked up, and. in a low and deliberate tone, said: 'Capt. Cunningham, as a Christian I wouldn't like to see war,' and then raising his voice until it rang out like a bugle call, with eye flashing and every fiber of his body filled with excitement, added, 'but as a soldier, sir, I would like to see war.' "

*Psychology of War, Eltinge, p. 64.
†Ibid., p. 70. For *Psychology of War* see *Études sur le Combat*, Dupicq; *Psychology du Combat de l'Infantere*, Louque; *Les Realites du Combat*, Daudignac; *Actual Experiences in Warfare*, Solaviev.

CHAPTER III

HAVING examined the experience which the South
had had in the service of artillery, and what material
there was for its officers, it is time to consider the steps
taken by the Confederate authorities for the organization of the artillery of the army in Virginia.

On December 28, 1860, the State of South Carolina
seceded from the United States of America, followed
in January, 1861, by Mississippi, Florida, Alabama,
Georgia, and Louisiana. The Congress of these States
assembled in Montgomery, Ala., February 4, 1861, and
ratified the Constitution of the Confederate States of
America four days later.

The only material of war possessed by this new
government was that held by the various States of the
Confederacy, and immediate military measures were
taken to provide for the public defense. On February
20 and 21 acts were passed providing for munitions of
war and establishing a War Department, respectively,
and on the 28th, one creating the Provisional Army,
C. S. A. This last Act authorized the President to take
charge of all military operations in the various States, to
provide for their common defense, to receive from the
States the arms and munitions, the forts, arsenals, etc.,
which they had seized from the United States, and such
other arms and munitions as they might desire to turn
over and make chargeable to the central government,
and to muster into the Confederate service such State
forces as might be tendered, or which might volunteer,
with the consent of their States, for a period of not less
than a year, unless sooner discharged. State forces accepted by the President were to be received with their
own officers, vacancies occurring thereafter to be filled by
appointment of the President, and the pay and allow-

ances of all were to be as prescribed for the Army of the Confederacy. March 6, another Act for the establishment and organization of the Confederate States of America was passed, declaring the military establishment to consist of a corps of artillery, 6 regiments of infantry, 1 regiment of cavalry and the staff departments already established by law.

The Corps of Artillery which, as in the old service, was charged with ordnance duties, was to consist of 1 colonel, 1 lieutenant-colonel, 10 majors, and 40 companies of artillery.*   The company organization was 1 captain, 2 first lieutenants, 1 second lieutenant, 4 sergeants, 4 corporals, 2 musicians, and 70 privates, or a total personnel of 3,072 for the Corps. Such portion of the force as the President deemed expedient was authorized to be equipped as light artillery with 6 pieces to a battery.

The monthly pay of the Artillery was fixed as follows: colonel, $210.00; lieutenant-colonel, $185.00; major, $150.00; captain, $130.00; first lieutenant, $90.00; second lieutenant, $80.00; adjutant (detailed from among first lieutenants), $10.00 in addition to pay of his grade. Officers of artillery serving in the light artillery, or performing ordnance duties, were to receive the pay of cavalry officers, which was the same as that of the Artillery for field-officers, but for captains, $140.00; first lieutenants, $100.00; and second lieutenants, $90.00. The monthly pay of enlisted men in the light artillery was declared to be the same as that for the cavalry, namely: sergeant-majors, $21.00; first sergeants, $20.00; sergeants, $17.00; corporals, musicians, farriers, artificers, blacksmiths, $13.00; privates, $12.00. The President was authorized to enlist as many master armorers, master carriage makers, master blacksmiths, artificers, and laborers for ordnance service as he might deem necessary, not exceeding 100 men in number, all of whom were to be attached to the Corps of Artillery. The master workmen were to receive

---

*Some of these were to be artificer companies.

$34.00 and the others $20.00, except artificers and ordinary laborers whose pay was fixed at $17.00 and $13.00 per month, respectively.

The Articles of War and Regulations for the Army of the United States were adopted *in toto,* with the exception that two slight changes were made in the former.

The following August an Act was passed increasing the Corps of Artillery to the extent of 1 lieutenant-colonel and 2 majors. But even this increase proved inadequate, for the limitations which had been imposed by law upon the number of field-officers in the Artillery rendered it impossible to reward conspicuous service by promotion or to take advantage of the abilities of certain artillery officers by placing them in positions of important command. While the act creating the Corps did not contemplate the organization of field batteries into battalions and regiments, which had not up to that time been united to form such large units, the regular practice being to assign individual batteries to brigades, yet, the President was empowered to so unite light batteries when tendered in separate companies, should he deem it advisable. This power on the part of the Commander-in-Chief was appealed to by the Secretary of War, in November, 1861,* and in order to remedy the defect arising out of the lack of authority for the appointment of officers to command the larger units, it was recommended that Congress should immediately pass an act providing for additional artillery officers in the Provisional Army, and the volunteer corps, not to exceed in number 1 brigadier-general for every 20 batteries, 1 colonel for every 10 batteries, 1 lieutenant-colonel for every 6 batteries, and 1 major for every 4 batteries, without reference to the number of batteries under the actual command of the officers so appointed. This wise recommendation was carefully considered, and soon the increase was authorized.† Again, the following spring, the Artillery Corps was increased by

---

*J. P. Benjamin to the President, November 30, 1861, *Rebellion Records,* Series IV, Vol. I, p. 761.
†Act approved January 22, 1862. *Rebellion Records,* Series IV, Vol. I, p. 867.

an act authorizing the appointment of 80 captains and first lieutenants in the Provisional Army for ordnance duties, a measure, which had great effect upon the line by relieving it of a burden of details.* But so extensive were the operations of the Bureau of Ordnance in its various branches of activity, that even this increase did not relieve the line of the onus of ordnance work, and the following fall the appointment of 70 additional artillery officers in the Provisional Army for ordnance duty was authorized.†

The fact that the appointment of brigadier-generals and additional field-officers in the Artillery Corps was authorized in January, 1862, does not mean that the field artillery was organized at that time into battalions, regiments, and brigades. This was not to come until after the disastrous lesson yet to be learned at Malvern Hill. Until that time batteries acted more or less independently with their brigades.

In 1861, a battery of light artillery of 6 guns consisted of 1 captain, 2 first lieutenants, 2 second lieutenants, 1 sergeant-major, or first sergeant, 1 quartermaster-sergeant, 6 sergeants, 12 corporals, 2 buglers, 1 guidon, 2 artificers, and from 64 to 125 privates. The organization of a battery of 4 guns was the same except that but 1 first lieutenant, 4 sergeants, and 8 corporals were prescribed therefor.‡ From the foregoing, it will be seen that the personnel of a light battery in 1862 was not dissimilar to that of the present day.

In the early part of the war, the material of a battery consisted of as many as 8 pieces, the company being divided into as many platoons as there were guns. Six pieces were considered to constitute the most desirable armament, four of which were ordinarily 6-pounder S. B. guns, and two of which were 12-pounder howitzers. As the 3-inch iron rifle made its appearance it was generally substituted for the 6-pounder guns. The regu-

*Act approved April 21, 1862. *Rebellion Records,* Series IV, Vol. I, p. 1080.
†Act approved September 16, 1862. *Rebellion Records,* Series IV, Vol. II, p. 198.
‡G. O. No. 81, A. & I. G. O., November 1, 1862, *Rebellion Records,* Series IV, Vol. II, p. 153.

lations as to the material of a battery, however, were perforce departed from and batteries possessing from 2 to 8 pieces were employed.* Each piece of a battery had its own caisson, which together constituted a platoon, and 2 platoons formed a section, the reverse of the present organization. To fully mount a light battery of 6 pieces with six-horse teams, 84 animals were required. The cannoneers being mounted, 149 horses were required to mount a horse artillery battery. These figures do not include the teams for forges and battery wagons.

It should be said here that the regulation complement of horses was seldom possessed by a battery, especially towards the close of the war when draught animals were no longer to be found on the farms. There was, of course, no adequate remount system in effect, and horses and mules for the mounted and transport services had to be impressed wherever found. Nothing became so tempting a prize to the Confederate artillerymen as the sleek teams of the enemy. With their capture in view, and in order to prevent their withdrawal from the field in the event of a successful issue of the fight, certain teams of a Confederate battery were so disposed in advance as to be available for the purpose of dashing with their riders in among the hostile teams, and securing them during the excitement.† This method was often successful, and caused the drivers of a battery to become as active in a combat as their gunners.

---

*In 1861 Carter's Battery was equipped with 2 S. B. bronze 6-pounders, one 12-pounder bronze howitzer, and one 3-inch iron rifle. The Washington Artillery when it arrived in Virginia, composed of 4 companies, was armed with 6 bronze 6-pounders, 2 bronze 12-pounder howitzers, and 1 iron 8-pounder rifle. The Letcher Artillery, a battery, fought until after Antietam with 2 bronze 6-pounder guns.

†G. O. No. 90, A. & I. G. O., November 11, 1862, *Rebellion Records,* Series IV, Vol. II, p. 194.

CHAPTER IV

THE VIRGINIA VOLUNTEERS

WE have examined the organization contemplated by the Confederate States Government. In the meantime the State of Virginia had not been idle in the organization of her field artillery.

Until April 21, 1861, the personnel of the volunteer artillery of Virginia which had been armed consisted of but 780 men, a large portion of whom comprised heavy batteries without guns.* The personnel of the militia regiments prescribed by law had not been mustered into the service. The organizations existed merely on paper, except as to the few volunteer companies which under the militia acts automatically attached to one of the five territorial or divisional artillery regiments. In the Fourth Regiment, for instance, the Fayette Artillery, of Richmond, was the only battery actually armed and equipped.†

In the First Regiment were two batteries, not however fully equipped as light batteries, the Portsmouth Light Artillery and the Norfolk Light Artillery Blues. These two batteries, the former with 4 S. B. iron 6-pounders, and the latter with 4 brass 12-pounder howitzers, were ordered out by the Governor April 19, 1861, and were therefore the first batteries in the field. The Portsmouth Battery, in command of Capt. Cary F. Grimes, was stationed at the Naval Hospital during the evacuation and burning of the Gosport Navy Yard by the Federal authorities, being sent to Hoffler's Creek in May as part of the Confederate force guarding the line from Craney Island to the mouth of the Nansemond River. The Norfolk Battery, in command of Capt.

---

*Rebellion Records, Series I, Vol. II, p. 940. There were also at this time but 3,350 cavalry and 7,920 infantry troops armed in the State, making a total armed force of 12,050.

†Letter of Col. T. H. Ellis to Gov. Letcher, Rebellion Records, Series IV, Vol. I, pp. 300, 301.

Jacob Vickery, was sent down the harbor to Craney Island on the morning of the 20th, to apprehend the Baltimore boat supposed to have on board a number of Federal marines for the Navy Yard. From this battery were created Huger's Battery, and Company H 16th Virginia Infantry, the latter being reorganized as a light battery March 26, 1862. In May of that year, when Norfolk was evacuated, these batteries were ordered to Petersburg, where they were rearmed, and then joined the Army of Northern Virginia, having had a number of experiences with Federal gunboats while on duty about Norfolk.*

On April 23, Robert E. Lee was appointed Major-General, Virginia Volunteers, and in *General Orders No. 1* of that date, assumed command of the military and naval forces of Virginia. On April 26, Maj.-Gen. Jos. E. Johnston, Virginia Volunteers, was assigned to the command of the forces gathering about Richmond, Maj.-Gen. Walter Gwynn, to the command of those about Norfolk, and on the 28th, Col. Thomas J. Jackson relieved Maj.-Gen. Kenton Harper, in command of the mobilization camp at Harper's Ferry.† These officers were directed to receive, and to muster into the service such organizations as might volunteer. Lieut.-Col. John McCausland was also sent to the Kanawha Valley, and specially directed to organize a light battery, for which the guns would be forthcoming.

At this time there was but one light battery, mounted and equipped as such, in the field, the Governor having ordered the newly raised Purcell Battery of Richmond, in command of Capt. Reuben Lindsay Walker, with its four 3-inch Parrott rifles, to Aquia Creek, early in the month. This battery was named after Mr. Purcell of Richmond who, when hostilities became imminent, had out of his own pocket equipped the battery. Its first

---

*Grimes' Battery was given 2 iron rifles, making 6 pieces in all, and the Norfolk Blues, now become Grandy's Battery, was given 2 3-inch iron rifles, 2 12-pounder brass howitzers, and 2 Napoleons.

For facts about Norfolk Light Artillery Blues, and Portsmouth Light Artillery, see *History of Norfolk County, Virginia, 1861-65*, Porter, pp. 38-247.

†See G. O. No. 3, S. O. Nos. 2 and 7, *Rebellion Records*, Series I, Vol. II, pp. 783, 787. Ibid., p. 788.

captain afterwards became Chief of Artillery, Hill's Corps, with rank of brigadier-general. Not having been formally mustered into the service of the State, it was now ordered back to Richmond to refit and recruit, its total personnel numbering but 40 men.

There were at this time three other light batteries being drilled and equipped in Richmond. The old Fayette Artillery of Richmond, with its 4 pieces, (it was named in honor of LaFayette, having had its origin about the time of his visit to America), was fully recruited by its Capt. H. C. Cabell.* The Richmond Howitzers, commanded by Capt. Geo. W. Randolph, a battery which had been raised and sent to Harper's Ferry just after the John Brown raid in 1859, had on its rolls 225 men, and Latham's Lynchburg Battery, with 4 pieces, had also reported for duty at the instruction grounds at Richmond.

Upon the suggestion of Capt. Alexander, Capt. Randolph took steps to organize a battalion with his surplus men, and on April 21, the First, Second, and Third Companies of Richmond Howitzers were mustered into the service of the State as a battalion, Randolph being appointed its major. The batteries were commanded by Capts. J. C. Shields, J. Thompson Brown, and R. C. Stanard, respectively.

There were now in the State 6 light batteries, in addition to the Cadet Battery, which had arrived in Richmond with the Corps from Lexington; the organization and instruction of these was assigned to Col. J. B. Magruder, but recently resigned from the old service. This officer had commanded the regular battery at the battle of Chapultapec, in which Jackson had served with such gallantry as a lieutenant. He was an accomplished artilleryman in every sense of the word, and well qualified to perform the duty assigned him. Immediate steps were taken by him to secure the 356 horses necessary to complete the complement of the light batteries, and the saddles, bridles, halters, picket ropes,

---

*He subsequently became colonel, and commanded a battalion of artillery in Longstreet's Corps.

girths, blankets, horseshoes, and forage, which the exigencies of the moment demanded. He also urged that 10 cadets be detailed to drill and instruct the batteries, and that as many former artillery officers of the service as could be spared should be ordered to report to him.* In response to the latter request, Capt. E. P. Alexander, of Georgia, who had been in the United States Engineer corps, was assigned to him for duty, and assisted by a large detail of cadets took charge of the drilling of the batteries.

Early in May, the Second and Third Companies of Richmond Howitzers, under Maj. Randolph, and Cabell's Battery, were ordered off to Yorktown with Magruder, leaving the entire work of organization to Alexander and the cadets.

There were at this time enough field pieces in the State, including thirteen 3-inch Parrott rifles, one of which was in possession of the cadet battery, to provide material for 20 batteries, though the necessary harness, caissons, and equipment were entirely lacking. A minimum of 1,000 horses was therefore needed in addition to those already provided in order to put the available guns in the field.

The Ordinance of Secession was passed April 17, 1861. Before May 1, not only had the Convention authorized a Provisional Army of 10,000 men, but arrangements were made to call out 50,000 volunteers if necessary, and on May 3 the call was made by proclamation of the Governor.†

That the Commander-in-Chief intended to take full advantage of the available field artillery material is evidenced by the fact that on the day this proclamation was issued he directed Gen. P. St. George Cocke, in command of the district comprised of the eighteen Piedmont counties, to raise 8 light batteries, urging Gen. Ruggles, in command of the Northern Neck section, to raise two.‡

---

*Magruder to Adjutant-General, April 29, 1861, *Rebellion Records,* Series I, Vol. II, pp. 789, 790.
†*Rebellion Records,* Series I, Vol. II, p. 797.
‡Letter of Gen. Lee to Gen. P. St. George Cocke, May 3, 1861, *Rebellion Records,* Series I, Vol. II, p. 797, and letter to Gen. Ruggles, May 4, 1861, Ibid., p. 803.

Col. Jackson, at Harper's Ferry, had already mustered into the service the Rockbridge Artillery, a battery armed with the four 6-pounder bronze cadet guns, from Lexington, but possessing no regular caissons or equipment.* He had also raised 2 companies of artillery for which he urged that horses, material, and equipment be sent, as well as 2 extra 12-pounder howitzers and caissons for the Rockbridge battery.† Occupying the heights along the Potomac, opposite the Point of Rocks, Berlin, and Shepherdstown, he was energetically endeavoring to secure heavy ordnance to defend his line, convinced that the enemy would be well provided therewith in addition to their field guns, some of which he thought would be long range rifled pieces.‡ Jackson's frequent references to rifled guns and his constant endeavor to secure them show plainly what his estimate of their value was even at this time.§

On May 7, the Inspector-General, Col. J. B. Baldwin, was authorized and directed to raise 6 batteries of light artillery, of 4 guns each, from among the Southside and James River Valley counties. Thus, at the very outset, provision was made for the raising and equipping of 25 or more light batteries.

Such ability had Gen. Lee shown in the organization and arming of the Virginia troops, and so confused had the Confederate War Department become with its various commanders, that on May 10, Gen. Lee was authorized to assume control of all Confederate States troops in Virginia.¶ Up to this time the contingents from the South, arriving in the State, had been under the sole command of their own individual leaders. Some of these troops had to be partly armed by the State of Virginia. This was true of the Washington Artillery, the gallant battalion of 4 companies from New Orleans, which arrived in Richmond June 4, with but six 6-

---

*These had not been taken to Richmond by the Cadet Battery, which now had iron pieces.
†*Rebellion Records*, Series I, Vol. II, pp. 793-809.
‡Ibid., pp. 823, 836.
§See references in Part I.
¶*Rebellion Records*, Series I, Vol. II, p. 827.

pounder bronze guns, two 12-pounder howitzers, and one 8-pounder rifled piece, and with a personnel of nearly 300 men in command of Maj. J. B. Walton, a veteran of the Mexican War.

The Act of May 10, 1861, authorized the President to muster into the service of the Confederate States any companies of light artillery, with such complement of officers as he might see fit, and encouragement of every kind was given the raising of batteries, for up to this time little had been accomplished in the organization of the light artillery.* There were but 6 light batteries actually mounted and on duty in the field, the two batteries of the Howitzer Battalion and Cabell's Battery, which had been sent to Yorktown; Walker's; Pendleton's, and Imboden's batteries which were with Jackson at Harper's Ferry. Most of the batteries which had been raised were yet without material, horses, and equipment.† Yet, the men were being well drilled and disciplined. Within the next 30 days, however, the army of 40,000 men which Virginia had placed in the field included 20 light batteries fully equipped and mounted, with 4 guns each, and a total personnel of near 2,500 men.‡ Up to this time, including a number sent to Missouri, and issued to troops from other States, Virginia had provided 115 pieces of field ordnance.

We are now prepared to understand to some extent what Virginia actually turned over to the Confederacy in the way of artillery material, equipment and personnel on June 8, 1861, when, by proclamation of the Governor, her entire force was legally transferred.

---

*Report of Inspector General, May 23, 1861, *Rebellion Records*, Series I, Vol. II, p. 868.
†Even the Richmond Howitzers were much disorganized by the necessity of using their horses for videttes, there being little cavalry with Magruder.
‡Ibid., pp. 885, 893.

CHAPTER V

ACTIVE OPERATIONS COMMENCE: BIG BETHEL AND
HAINESVILLE

ALREADY, on the 14th of May, at Gloucester Point, a section of Brown's Battery of the Howitzer Battalion, in an affair with the Federal gunboat "Yankee," had fired the first shot of the field artillery in Virginia. And, now, on the very day on which the Virginia troops were transferred to the Confederacy, it was to engage in a brush with the enemy on land. Being informed that a marauding party was operating along Back River, Magruder ordered a small detachment of infantry and one gun of Maj. Randolph's Battalion from the lines to drive the raiders off, a single howitzer shell sufficing to disperse the plunderers. Two days later, June 10, occurred the battle of Big Bethel, in which the artillery, armed with a 3-inch Parrott rifle and a number of 12-pounder howitzers, received its real baptism.

The Union force, consisting of between 2,500 and 3,500 men actually engaged, included a section of a regular battery with two 6-pounder S. B. guns, commanded by Lieut. John T. Greble.* The Confederate force engaged numbered about 1,200 men with 5 guns. Advancing boldly against the position which Maj. Randolph had prepared for his guns, the enemy were fired upon at 9:15 A. M., the fight opening with the discharge of a Parrott rifle. Greble promptly replied with his guns, but his fire was wild and ineffective, and was soon silenced by the more accurate rifles of the Confederates. About 11 o'clock a fresh Federal regiment arrived on the field, having dragged another gun with great labor from Hampton. With this piece Lieut. Greble heroically sought to stem the pursuit, but had fired not more than a dozen shots when he was killed and

---

*Battles and Leaders, Vol. II, p. 148, and Report of Gen. D. H. Hill, in "The Confederate Soldier in the Civil War," p. 36.

the gun abandoned, both it and the body of the young officer being gallantly rescued by Capt. Wilson and his company of the Second New York.

In this affair the effect of Randolph's guns was more startling, perhaps, than destructive, the Federal loss being only 18 killed and 53 wounded. But greatly exaggerated reports were at once circulated about the accuracy and power of the new Parrott rifle, which led to its more general introduction in the two armies. The fact remains, however, that Randolph's guns were well served, and whether by superiority in number or in other respects, had completely overwhelmed the regular battery opposed to them. This fact brought great prestige to the Confederate field artillery, and did much to arouse enthusiasm for, and create interest in, the "long arm."

The report of Maj. Randolph of the part played by his command in this engagement is so intensely interesting, and so full of information as to the defects of his artillery material, and so conclusive of the manner of handling the guns, as well as of the real effect of the fire of the new rifled field pieces, employed for the first time at Bethel, that it is given almost in full, especially as it was written almost immediately after the affair and before the facts could be unconsciously perverted by the trickery of time. To an artilleryman, nothing could be more interesting.

"Yorktown, June 12, 1861.

"Colonel—I have the honor to report that in the action of the 10th instant, the Howitzer battalion under my command fired 18 solid shot and 80 shells, spherical, case, and canister, and was injured in the following particulars: A lieutenant and 2 privates were wounded, one severely and 2 slightly; 5 horses and 3 mules were killed or disabled; the Parrott gun (iron rifled) had its linstock splintered, and a musket ball passed through the felloe of the left wheel; a musket ball pierced the corner plate and the partition of the limber chest of one of the howitzers, and lodged against a shell; two poles of caissons, one set of swinglebars, one large pointing ring, a chain for a rammer, and several priming wires were broken, and one of the howitzers was spiked by the breaking of a priming wire in its vent.

"As the position of the pieces was under your own observation, it is only necessary to state that the Parrott gun and one howitzer were posted in the battery immediately on the right of the road leading to Hampton; that a howitzer was placed in the battery erected on the right beyond the ravine, through which a passway was made for the purpose of withdrawing the piece if necessary; a howitzer was posted near the bridge; the rifled howitzer was placed on the left of the road behind the right of a redoubt erected by the North Carolina Regiment, and a howitzer was posted in the rear of the road leading from Halfway House, a howitzer having been previously sent to the Halfway House under the command of Lieut. Moseley.

"Early in the action, the howitzer in the battery on the right, having been spiked by the breaking of the priming wire, was withdrawn from the position, and the infantry supporting it fell back upon the church; but it was subsequently replaced by the howitzer of Lieut. Moseley, which arrived at a later period of the action.

"The ford on the left being threatened, the howitzer at the bridge was withdrawn and sent to that point, and the rifled howitzer was withdrawn from the left of the road and sent to assist in the protection of the rear. The same disposition was subsequently made of the howitzer at the main battery, situated immediately on the right of the road.

"The enemy came in sight on the road leading from Hampton a few minutes before 9 o'clock A. M., and their advance guard halted at a house on the roadside about 600 yards in front of our main battery. Fire, however, was not opened upon them for 10 or 15 minutes, when, from the number of bayonets visible in the road, we judged that a heavy column was within range. The action then commenced by a shot from the Parrott gun, aimed by myself, which struck the center of the road a short distance in front of their column, and probably did good execution in its ricochet. At no time could we see the bodies of the men in the column, and our fire was directed at their bayonets, their position being obscured by the shade of the woods on their right, and two small houses on their left and somewhat in advance of them. Our fire was immediately returned by a battery near the head of their column, but concealed by the woods and the houses so effectually that we only ascertained its position by the flash of the pieces. The fire was maintained on our side for some time by the 5 pieces posted in front of our position; but, as already stated, one of them being spiked and another withdrawn to protect the ford early in the action, the fire was continued with the 3 pieces, and at no time did we afterwards have more than 3 pieces playing upon the enemy. The fire on our part was deliberate, and was suspended whenever masses of the enemy were not within range, and the execution was good, as I afterwards ascertained by a personal inspection of the principal position of the enemy. The cannonade lasted with intervals of suspension from a few minutes before 9 o'clock A. M., until 1:30 o'clock P. M., and the fact that during this time but 98 shot were fired by us tends to show that the firing was not too rapid. The earthworks thrown up by the battalion were struck several times by the cannon shot of the enemy, but no injury was sustained. They fired upon us with shot, shell, spherical case, canister, and grape from 6- to 12-pounders, at a distance of about 600 yards, but the only injury received from their artillery was the loss of one mule.

"We found in front of our main battery, in and near the yard of the small house already mentioned, 5 killed and one mortally wounded by the fire of our artillery. We heard of 2 others killed at Crandall's, about a mile from us, and have reason to believe there were many others. The injury done to our artillery was from the fire of musketry on our left flank, the ground on that side between us and the enemy sinking down so as to expose us over the top of the breastwork erected by the North Carolina Regiment.

"After some intermission of the assault in front, apparently a reënforcement or reserve made its appearance on the Hampton road, and pressed forward towards the bridge carrying the United States flag near the head of the column. As the road had been clear for some time, and our flanks and rear had been threatened, the howitzer in the main battery had been sent to the rear, and our fire did not at first check them. I hurried a howitzer forward from the rear, loaded it with canister, and prepared to sweep the approach to the bridge, but the fire of the Parrott gun again drove them back. The howitzer brought from the Halfway House by Lieut. Moseley arriving most opportunely, I carried it to the battery on the right to replace the disabled piece. On getting there, I learned from the infantry that a small house in front was occupied by sharpshooters, and saw the body of a Carolinian lying 30 yards in front of the battery, who had been killed in a most gallant attempt to burn the house.

"I opened upon the house with shell for the purpose of burning it, and the battery of the enemy in the Hampton road, being on the line with it, and supposing probably that the fire was at them, immediately returned it with solid shot. This disclosed their position and enabled me to fire at the house and at their battery at the same time. After an exchange of 5 or 6 shots, a shell entered a window of the house, increased the fire already kindled until it soon broke out into a light blaze, and, as I have reason to believe, disabled one of the enemy's pieces. This was the last shot fired. They soon afterward retreated, and we saw no more of them.

"The action disclosed some serious defects in our ammunition and equipment, for which I earnestly recommend an immediate remedy. The shell of the Parrott gun have a fixed wooden fuse which cannot be extricated, the shortest being cut for four seconds. The consequence was that the shells burst far in the rear of the enemy and served merely as solid shot. Had they been plugged and uncut fuses furnished, I think that our fire would have been much more effective. The power and precision of the piece, demonstrated by the 30 rounds fired from it, render it very desirable that all of its advantages should be made available. I, therefore, respectfully suggest that the shell be hereafter furnished plugged and the fuses left uncut.

"It is reported to me that the Borman fuses used by one of the howitzers were defective, the shells cut for 5 seconds exploding as soon as those cut for 2.

"The caissons of the Navy howitzers were made by placing ammunition chests upon the running gear of common wagons, and the play of the front axles is so limited that the caisson cannot be turned in the ordinary roads of this part of the country, and wherever the road is ditched, or the woods impassable, it cannot be reversed. There is also great danger of breaking the poles in turning the caisson quickly, as was shown in the action of the 10th inst. I am aware that the expedient of using wagon bodies was resorted to in order to save time, but, as it might lead to great disaster, I recommend that their places be supplied as speedily as possible with those made in the usual way.

"The small size of the limber of the howitzer (Navy) renders it impossible to mount the men, and the pieces cannot move faster than the cannoneers can walk. In a recent skirmish with the enemy, in which we pursued them rapidly, we could only carry 2 men, and having gotten far ahead of the others we had to un-limber and fire with only 2 cannoneers at the piece. The piece having only 2 horses, and the carriages being very light, it is hazardous to mount any person on the limber. I, therefore, recommend that 4 horses be furnished to each Navy howitzer, one for the chief and the other three for the men usually mounted on the limber.

"We have succeeded since the action in unspiking the howitzer disabled by the breaking of the priming wire, but, from the inferior metal used in making our priming wires, we shall have to lay them aside altogether, and I must request that better ones be furnished. At present I can say nothing more of the conduct of the officers and men of the battalion than to express the high gratification afforded me by their courage, coolness, and precision, and to ask permission at a future time to call your attention to individual instances of gallantry and good conduct. I have requested the commandants of companies to furnish me with the names of such non-commissioned officers and privates as they think especially worthy of notice.

"I am happy at having an opportunity to render my acknowledgment to Col. Hill, the commandant of the North Carolina

Regiment, for the useful suggestions which his experience as an artillery officer enabled him to make to me during the action, and to bear testimony to the gallantry and discipline of that portion of his command with which I was associated The untiring industry of his regiment in intrenching our position enabled us to defeat the enemy, with a nominal loss on our side."*

In his report of the engagement, Gen. Magruder wrote: "Whilst it might appear invidious to speak particularly of any regiment or corps where all behaved so well, I am compelled to express my great appreciation of the skill and gallantry of Maj. Randolph and his Howitzer batteries," and D. H. Hill wrote: "I cannot close this too elaborate report without speaking in the highest terms of admiration of the Howitzer batteries, and their most accomplished commander, Maj. Randolph. He has no superior as an artillerist in any country, and his men displayed the utmost skill and coolness."† Neither Magruder nor Hill were ordinarily given to such expressions, both being officers of experience in the old service.

Before the first of July, the various forces assembled at Norfolk, Yorktown, Richmond, Harper's Ferry, and other points, had begun to show the results of the strenuous efforts which had been made to organize, arm and equip them, and some of the commands were attaining to a degree of mobility approaching effectiveness.

May 23, Col. Jackson was superseded in command at Harper's Ferry by Brig.-Gen. Joseph E. Johnston. The force there gathered, consisting of troops from many sections of the South, was promptly reorganized into brigades, as nearly as possible according to States, the whole assuming the name of the Army of the Shenandoah.‡ Col. Jackson, who was soon promoted to brigadier-general, was assigned November 4 to the command of the Virginia Brigade. To this brigade was

*Rebellion Records, Series I, Vol. II, pp. 98-101.
†Major George W. Randolph was a graduate of Annapolis, and had served in the U. S. Navy. He was soon appointed Colonel and Chief of Artillery on Magruder's staff; and later became Secretary of War, C. S. A.
‡The Army of the Shenandoah was really the Second Corps of the Army of the Potomac.

very naturally attached the Rockbridge Artillery from Lexington, in command of Capt. Pendleton, a graduate of West Point, who had for years been the Episcopal minister of his town, and an intimate friend of Jackson while the latter was a professor at the Virginia Military Institute.

About the time the Cadet Corps was ordered to Richmond to drill the troops gathering there, the Rockbridge Battery was raised and soon ordered to Harper's Ferry, being given the old bronze 6-pounder guns of the cadet battery, the Corps having taken with it other pieces, including the 3-inch Parrott rifle, with which Jackson had obtained such surprising results in Lexington the year before.* For caissons, the Rockbridge Battery constructed large chests on the running parts of hay wagons, the cadets having taken all the material of their battery except the guns.

The history of the cadet battery which had afforded instruction to so many artillery officers of the Confederate Army, and the guns which were now to be used in battle, is so full of interest that it should be given here.

In 1850, the Adjutant-General of the State ordered the Corps of Cadets to Richmond as the personal escort of President Taylor on the occasion of the laying of the corner-stone of the Washington Monument. So impressed was the old soldier with the bearing of the cadets, that he ordered a field battery of four 6-pounder guns and two 12-pounder howitzers to be cast of bronze, somewhat lighter than ordinary service pieces, with the arms of the State of Virginia thereon, and to be presented to the Cadet Corps. This beautiful battery, known as the "Cadet Battery," is still used for artillery instruction at the Institute. With it a large number of the Confederate artillery officers of note were trained between 1851 and 1861.

After Bull Run, the Rockbridge Artillery was issued rifled pieces captured in the battle, and the cadet guns were returned to Lexington. In the meantime, how-

*See Part I.

ever, the two 12-pounder howitzers of the battery had been issued to Milledge's Battery, one of which was later lost in the Potomac* on the retreat from Antietam. The remaining 5 pieces were captured by Gen. D. H. Hunter in June, 1864, when he destroyed the Institute, and were carried off by him as trophies of war, but were returned to the Corps completely remounted and refitted by Secretary Stanton, in 1865, upon the ardent solicitation of Gen. Smith, the Superintendent. This battery is now undoubtedly the oldest in actual use in the United States.

When on June 15, Johnston withdrew from Harper's Ferry to Winchester, he left Jackson at the front along the Baltimore & Ohio Railroad to observe Patterson's preparations. It was not long before the opposing forces came into contact near Martinsburg, and at Hainesville, a fight occurred on July 2. So well did Capt. Pendleton handle one of the old cadet guns that the reputation which had been acquired by the field batteries at Bethel, at once attached to the Rockbridge Artillery. In a letter to a home paper describing the affair, Pendleton wrote:

"Col. Jackson, with his staff, rode back to the point in the road occupied by my gun, and directed me to withdraw it further back to the rear, to a point better situated. Meantime, the enemy began to ply their artillery with vigor, firing around our little force a number of balls and shells. We, however, quietly took our position and awaited the best moment for opening fire with our single gun (the only one present). That moment arrived when I saw a body of horse, which seemed to be a squadron of cavalry about to charge on the turnpike about a half mile in front of our position. At that body I instantly had the gun directed, with careful instructions how it should be aimed. In another instant the messenger of death was speeding on its way. The effect was obvious and decided. Not a man or a horse remained standing in the road, nor did we see them again. . . . Our next shot was aimed with equal care at one of their cannon, in a field on the left of the road. The effect was scarcely less. The gunners scattered, and I am sure that gun fired no more. David Moore, of Lexington, fired our first gun, and J. L. Massie loaded it. The order from Richmond

*Its mate has been used as the evening gun at the Institute since 1865. For loss of the howitzer see Gen. Pendleton's report to Gen. Lee, September 24, 1862, *Memoirs of W. N. Pendleton,* p. 223. Also *Rebellion Records.*

promoting Col. Jackson to a brigadiership has just arrived. He richly deserves it. His part the day of the fight, as heretofore, was admirably performed. The enemy speak admiringly of our artillery firing of that morning; they ascribe it all to 4 rifled cannon, although we fired 8 shot from a common (smooth-bore) 6-pounder."

Thus it is seen that one of the cadet guns fired the first shot in the Valley, and, that the Federal troops were looking for the terrible rifled guns, of which they had recently heard so much, as well as for masked batteries, on every hillside, the press of the country echoing with terrifying accounts of these objects of the popular imagination.

CHAPTER VI

BLACKBURN'S FORD AND FIRST MANASSAS

In the meantime the troops which had been assembled and drilled at Richmond were ordered to Manassas Junction. At this point they were organized, June 20, into a corps of 6 brigades, and placed under Beauregard as commander of the 1st Corps or Army of the Potomac, independent of the 2d Corps or Army of the Shenandoah, in the Valley.

July 13 Capt. Pendleton was appointed Chief of Artillery of the Army of the Shenandoah, with rank of colonel, under authority of the original act creating the Artillery Corps of the Confederacy. He was thus from this time the senior artillery officer of the Army. His abilities as an organizer were well known to Gens. Johnston and Lee, and Mr. Davis, with all of whom he had been a cadet for several years at West Point.* His appointment, however, since he had held only the rank of captain, was not made without misgivings, for the gallant Maj. J. B. Walton, of Louisiana, had been mustered into the service with his battalion with the rank given him by his State, and it was feared lest this officer and his command might consider the elevation of Pendleton as a slight upon them† As stated before, this led to the recommendation on the part of the Secretary of War that additional field-officers in the Corps of Artillery be authorized by Congress, which was done the following January.

Upon being made Chief of Artillery, Col. Pendleton at once assigned the batteries of his corps to brigades as follows:

Pendleton's, or the Rockbridge Battery, 4 pieces, remained with the 1st or Jackson's Brigade; Alburtis'

---

*Memoirs of W. N. Pendleton, Lee, pp. 146, 147.
†See letter of Secretary of War to the President, November 30, 1861, Rebellion Records, Series IV, Vol. I, p. 761.

Wise Battery, 4 pieces, to the 2d or Bartow's Brigade; Imboden's Staunton Battery, 4 pieces, to the 3d or Bee's Brigade; and Groves' Culpeper Battery, 4 pieces, commanded by Lieut. Beckham, to the 4th or Elzey's Brigade. Later Stanard's Thomas Battery joined the 2d Corps.

The Artillery was not to wait long for a chance to test its metal, for on the 18th of July the Federal force resumed its slow advance, reaching Blackburn's Ford, where 2 guns of the Washington Artillery were brought into action against the enemy's cavalry, which promptly withdrew. In the meantime, Richardson's Brigade had gained close contact with Longstreet, who occupied the opposite bank of the stream. Both brigades withdrew in more or less disorder, and were rallied and led back with some difficulty, a few of Longstreet's men, after much wavering, finally crossing the stream and gaining a slight advantage over the enemy, who endeavored to withdraw. At this point a sharp artillery duel, lasting about forty-five minutes, occurred. The Federals engaged 8 guns, two 20-pounder and two 10-pounder Parrott rifles, two 6-pounder guns and two 12-pounder howitzers, which fired 415 rounds. Longstreet brought up 7 guns, four 6-pounders, and three of the converted rifles, which fired 310 rounds of the new Burton and Archer projectiles, all these pieces being from the Washington Artillery.* One of the brass 6-pounders soon became useless on account of an enlarged vent, and the new ammunition used by the rifles was entirely ineffective, although most favorable reports were made about it at the time by the inexperienced officers who conducted the fire.† During the first part of the duel both sides fired wildly, almost at random, neither being able to see much of the other on account of the screens of trees which the opposing guns had sought. But, after a pause, the Federal guns reopened

---

*In Camp and Battle with the Washington Artillery, Owen, pp. 27-28. Military Memoirs of a Confederate, Alexander, p. 24.
†The first competent test of these projectiles a few weeks later showed them to be worthless, and their manufacture was discontinued. They would not fly point foremost, but tumbled and had no range.

with better effect, having taken advantage of the lull to
better determine the position and range of Longstreet's
guns, and soon practically silenced them. Capt. Eshleman, commanding one of the batteries, was wounded
along with 4 enlisted men, another being killed, whereupon Capt. Squires, calling for reënforcements, was
ordered by Longstreet, who had no more artillery, to
withdraw the guns gradually, one at a time, covering
the movement by the fire of the pieces remaining in
position.

The Confederate Artillery was undoubtedly over-
matched in this affair, yet, at the very moment of its
withdrawal, the Federal batteries, which had suffered
a loss of but 2 killed and 2 wounded, ceased firing, allowing Capt. Squires the honor of the last shot. It was
this fact, perhaps, which gave credence to the report
that Longstreet's guns had prevailed and upon such a
belief Beauregard wrote in his official account of the
affair:

"Our artillery was manned and officered by those who, but
yesterday, were called from the civil avocations of a busy city.
They were matched with the picked artillery of the Federal
regular army,—Company E, Third Artillery, under Capt. Ayres,
with an armament, as their own chief of artillery admits, of two
10-pounder rifled Parrott guns, two 12-pounder Parrott rifled guns,
two 12-pounder howitzers, and two 6-pounder pieces, aided by two
20-pounder Parrott rifled guns of Company G, Fifth Artillery,
under Lieut. Benjamin. Thus matched, they drove their veteran
adversaries from the field, giving confidence in and promise of the
coming efficiency of this brilliant arm of the service."

From Beauregard's account one would hardly derive
a proper understanding of the comparative effect of the
fire of the batteries engaged in this opening duel, and it
is no disparagement to the Washington Artillery to say
that the report is an exaggeration, conscientious though
it may have been. Against such an armament as the
enemy possessed, the actual result was to be expected.
But Beauregard was quite correct in saying, "The
skill, the conduct and soldierly qualities of the Washington Artillery engaged were all that could be desired.

The officers and men attached to the 7 pieces already specified won for their battalion a distinction which, I feel assured, will never be tarnished, and which will ever serve to urge them and their corps to high endeavor."

In the 1st Corps, Maj. Walton, Acting Chief of Artillery, assigned his batteries on July 21 as follows, in which order they served at Bull Run:

First, or Bonham's Brigade, Shields' 1st Co. Richmond Howitzers, and Kemper's Alexandria Battery, of 4 and 2 pieces, respectively; 2d, or Ewell's Brigade, 1 battery of Washington Artillery, 4 pieces; 3d, or Jones' Brigade, 1 section Washington Artillery, 2 pieces; 4th, or Longstreet's Brigade, 1 section of Washington Artillery, 2 pieces; 5th, or Cocke's Brigade, Latham's Lynchburg Battery, 4 pieces; 6th, or Early's Brigade, 1 battery Washington Artillery, 3 pieces; 7th, or Evans' demi-brigade, Rogers' Loudoun Battery, 4 pieces; 1 battery of Washington Artillery held in reserve, a total of 27 pieces.*

In order to describe the part of the Confederate Artillery in the battle of Bull Run, it is not necessary to discuss the movements of the two armies leading up to the affair, but only to show in what manner the guns were employed. About 6 A. M., July 21, Tyler's Federal Division approached Evans' force holding the Stone Bridge, and opened fire with a 30-pounder Parrott rifle, soon followed by that of several other pieces from the hills about a half-mile north of the run, to which Evans made no reply. It not appearing that Tyler intended to advance immediately, Gens. Johnston and Beauregard, with their staffs, made a reconnaissance to the right in the direction of Mitchell's Ford about 8 A. M. About 8:45 A. M. Capt. Alexander, the signal officer, discovered by the reflection of the sun from a brass field gun the advance of a heavy flanking column on the left, at Sudley, 8 miles from his station, on the

*Beauregard's Report, *Rebellion Records,* Series I, Vol. II, pp. 440, 441, but see p. 480.

right of the Confederate line near McLean's Ford, and immediately informed Evans that his left was being turned about two miles from the bridge, and sent a prompt warning to Beauregard.* Leaving 4 companies in front of Tyler's Division behind the bridge, Evans immediately dispatched his remaining 6 companies to his left to oppose the flanking column of the enemy, and check it until reënforcements could be brought up, informing Gen. Cocke on his right of the movement. Bee's four regiments, Hampton's one, Jackson's five, with an average distance of three miles to go, were ordered from near the center of the line to proceed rapidly to the left in support of Evans. For the next half-hour while the turning column was resting at Sudley, Tyler merely endeavored to occupy the attention of Evans' pitifully weak force with a desultory cannonade. By 10 A. M. the column had entirely crossed the stream at Sudley, and soon its batteries opened a heavy fire on Evans' men, who, extending to their left, had come in contact with the Federal advance. The Federal batteries were briskly replied to by two guns of Rogers' Loudoun Battery, which Evans had sent forward, and with them the six companies of infantry succeeded in delaying the enemy for over an hour, whose first attack was made by a single regiment, thus giving the reënforcements time to cover the larger portion of the three miles. Had McDowell rushed forward even one of his brigades, and several of his fine regular batteries, his movement would undoubtedly have succeeded, for just at this junction the right of Evans' line which he had pushed out to the left to meet the column from Sudley, formed almost at right angles to the stream, was taken in flank by Sherman's and Keyes' brigades of Tyler's Division, assisted by their batteries. When this movement became apparent Holmes' and Early's brigades, with two regiments of Bonham's Brigade, and Walker's and Kemper's batter-

---

*See Beauregard's and Johnston's reports. Also see reference to Alexander's signal and ordnance work in Part I.

ies were at once put in motion towards the left.* The
fire of Tyler's batteries upon Evans and Bee increased,
and after a gallant stand the small force under their
command fell back upon the Warrenton Pike, parallel
to and about a mile in rear of their advanced line, where
it was partly rallied about Hampton's Regiment which
had reached that point. Here the remnants of Evans'
command, thus reënforced by the Hampton Legion,
with Kemper's two guns and Imboden's Battery, maintained the position along the Warrenton Pike, against
great odds, for two hours, finally being driven back to
the Henry House Hill, a short distance to the rear,
where another rally was made upon Jackson's Brigade,
which had just arrived and taken an excellent position
on the protected inner edge of the ridge, which had a
plateau-like top. Jackson had with ready perception
seen the advantage of such a position. In the meantime the remainder of Johnston's Army was arriving
from Winchester, and the two batteries brought upon
the field at this instant after tremendous exertion by Col.
Pendleton, Alburtis' and his own, were thrown into
position by Jackson on the line established by his
infantry to oppose the five regular batteries and the four
brigades of the enemy, which were rapidly advancing.
Thus, Jackson, with eight old 6-pounders, was face to
face with three regular and two finely equipped volunteer batteries, with 24 pieces, mostly heavy rifled guns.†
Imboden's Staunton Battery, the first of Pendleton's
Artillery to arrive upon the scene, having made an heroic
march from Winchester, and previously having gone
forward to the support of Evans and Bee, had been
terribly punished by the Federal Infantry, as well as
by the hostile batteries, and, rallying for a time on Jackson's line, had been ordered to the rear when its remaining few rounds were expended.‡

*Holmes' Brigade with Walker's Battery had joined the 1st Corps from
their previous positions east of Manassas Junction.
†Ricketts', Griffin's, Arnold's, R. I. Battery, and 71st New York Regiment
Battery. See Pendleton's reports to Johnston and Jackson, *Rebellion Records*,
Series I, Vol. II, Part I, pp. 35, 36, 37.
†*Battles and Leaders*, Imboden's account, Vol. I, p. 233.

While McDowell continued to bump his head against Jackson's stone-wall, on the Henry House Ridge, sending regiment after regiment to the assault, supported by the fire of Griffin's and Ricketts' batteries, the Confederate reënforcements were arriving in ever-increasing numbers, going into action always on the left of those which had preceded them, thus extending Jackson's original line. Failing to make a lodgment on the plateau with his infantry, McDowell now sent Griffin's and Ricketts' batteries in closer to take up the task of battering a way through at a decisive range. Nothing in war was ever more gallant than the efforts of these magnificent batteries, which, fearlessly advancing to within canister range of the Confederate lines, poured round after round into the enemy. Their infantry supports having been driven off by the freshly arrived regiments of Johnston's Army, the Federal batteries even then continued their fight.

This particular artillery fight, commencing about 3 P. M., had lasted for perhaps half an hour, when the 33d Virginia Regiment, commanded by Col. A. C. Cummings, boldly advanced from Jackson's left to take the guns. Griffin, in the act of opening upon it with a blizzard of canister at short range, was persuaded by Maj. Barry, Chief of McDowell's artillery, that the advancing men were Federal troops. Cummings' Regiment deliberately halted, and from a distance of but seventy yards fired a volley into Griffin's Battery, killing and wounding 40 of his men and 75 of his horses. Ricketts, whose battery was next to that of Griffin, was also wounded and captured, and one of his officers killed. Griffin managed to drag off three of his guns, but the other nine of the two batteries were left isolated between the two infantry lines. A terrific struggle now ensued, finally resulting in favor of the Confederates who turned a number of the captured guns against the retreating Federals.*

---

*Barry's Report, *Rebellion Records*, Series I, Vol. II, p. 345.

Meanwhile, Stanard's and Beckham's batteries had been coming up on the left of the guns with Pendleton, and assisted in hurling back the enemy. Upon the arrival of Kirby Smith's Brigade on the extreme Confederate left, the Federal lines began to waver, and when Beckham's Battery changed position, and opened a most demoralizing enfilade fire upon their flank from a well-chosen position, the resistance of the Federal Infantry, with which there were no longer any guns on their right to reply to Beckham, dissolved into a rout. Thus not only did Jackson and Pendleton exercise a great influence upon the battle at a most critical juncture, by the skillful disposition of the latter's batteries, in a position which nature herself could hardly have improved upon, but whether accidentally so or not, the fire of Beckham's guns, in the most effective manner possible—that is, from the immediate flank—was delivered upon the enemy at the psychological instant of the uncertainty incident to a check. Again evidence was given of a proper appreciation of field artillery when Kemper's and Walker's batteries, the latter just arrived with six 3-inch rifles, were ordered forward after the flight of the enemy set in to open upon the disordered masses retreating across Cub Run. The fire of Kemper's guns almost immediately wrecked a team on the bridge, causing an inextricable jam of guns, caissons, wagons, and ambulances, from which the panic-stricken drivers cut many of the teams. No guns could ever have been employed in a pursuit to better advantage, for at this point alone, 17 guns, including the immense 30-pounder Parrott rifle, with over 20 caissons, were captured and brought in by the Confederate Cavalry. Had the batteries on the Confederate right, which had not been engaged, been pushed forward to Centreville with proper infantry supports when the retreat commenced, and followed Kemper's example, there would be little indeed to criticise in the manner in which the Artillery as a whole was handled. Yet, this was not to be. Batteries in those days were tied to the apron strings of brigade commanders, and possessed little or no independence until after they had been set in motion. If Walton with his guns scattered to the four quarters, and for the most part idle, behind Ball's, Mitchell's, Blackburn's, and McLean's Fords, had but been a Hohenlohe with the organization and independence permitted the latter on such occasions, Centreville would have been the scene of glorious achievements for the Artillery, since rarely has a retreat presented such a helpless mass of humanity to the tender mercies of the pursuers, as blocked the roads at Centreville the evening of July 21, 1861. A Hohenlohe might have known of the true condition. It is quite certain, however, that the brigade commanders to whom Walton's guns were assigned did not know until too late to send their guns forward. Writing after the event, it is quite easy to point out how Walton should have assembled his fresh batteries, and galloped along one of the two available roads leading from the Confederate right to intercept the Federal retreat at Centreville. But a study of the conditions which actually existed the evening of July 21 will disclose the fact that not only was it impossible for him to do so because of the wide dispersion of his guns, but that far away from the actual scene of the conflict, he was even more ignorant of the opportunity than Johnston and Beauregard were.

The total personnel of the Artillery of the 2d Corps numbered 350, an average of 70 officers and men for each of the 5 batteries, and of Beauregard's army 533, or an average for each of his 8 batteries of about 67 officers and men. All of Johnston's batteries were engaged in the battle of Bull Run, but in the Army of the Potomac, or the 1st Corps, part of Rogers' Loudoun Battery, and some of the guns of the Washington Artillery, 10 in all, were not engaged; thus, there were engaged a total of 638 officers and men of the Artillery, with a total of 47 guns. With Beauregard's army were several companies of Pickens' heavy artillery, numbering 293 officers and men, who were also not engaged. The losses in Beauregard's artillery were: killed 2, wounded 8, total 10, and probably about the same for Johnston's batteries, or a grand total of losses for the Confederate Artillery of not more than 20.

The Federal batteries which crossed Bull Run were Ricketts', Griffin's, and Arnold's regular batteries, a Rhode Island and a New York Battery, with ten 10-pounder and eight 13-pounder rifled guns, four 12-pounder howitzers, and two 6-pounder smooth-bore guns, or a total of 24 pieces. In addition to these, Mc-Dowell had Hunt's, Carlisle's, Tidball's, Greene's, Ayres', and Edwards' regular batteries, or a grand total of 49 pieces, most of which were heavy rifled guns.* Of the Union guns, 27 in all were captured, with 37 caissons, 6 forges, 4 battery wagons, 64 artillery horses, with much harness, and nearly 5,000 rounds of field artillery ammunition.†

In his account of the battle Gen. E. P. Alexander states, with some degree of sarcasm, that McDowell should have had at least 100 guns, for, says he, "Artillery is the best arm against raw troops." But, if with 49 pieces only 24 could be brought up into effective range, it is not clear what Gen. Alexander's meaning is unless he was not satisfied with the number of guns captured. By such an increased train McDowell's road to Washington could have only been more effectually blocked, for he certainly could not have gotten so many guns on the field.

Most of the Confederate guns were 6-pounder S. B. pieces, or 12-pounder howitzers. There were a few old 6-pounders, which had been reamed out and rifled with three grooves after the Parrott system.‡

Thus, although the number of available guns in the two armies were about the same, Federal, 49; Con-

*Battles and Leaders, Vol. I, p. 195, Rebellion Records, Series I, Vol. II, p. 345.
†Rebellion Records, Series I, Vol. II, p. 571. Report of Capt. E. P. Alexander, Acting Ordnance Officer.
‡The 3-inch Parrott rifled guns, which had been purchased by the State of Virginia, were at Yorktown, with Magruder.

federate, 47; and although 37 of the latter were engaged
at close range, as opposed to 24 of the former, the
Federal Artillery had the advantage in weight of metal
in the proportion of at least three to one, besides a great
superiority in range.   Yet, it was the general belief in
the Army that the Confederate Artillery had again
more than proved a match for the regular batteries of
the United States.

"The efficiency of our infantry and cavalry might
have been expected from a patriotic people accustomed,
like ours, to the management of arms and horses, but
that of the artillery was little less than wonderful. They
were opposed to batteries far superior in the number,
range, and equipment of their guns, with educated officers and thoroughly instructed soldiers.   We had but
one educated artillerist, Col. Pendleton,—that model of
a Christian soldier,—yet they exhibited as much
superiority to the enemy in skill as in courage.   Their
fire was superior both in rapidity and precision." Thus
wrote Gen. Johnston in his report of the battle, and
Gen. Beauregard wrote that all the batteries displayed
"that marvellous capacity of our people as artillerists
which has made them, it would appear, at once the terror
and the admiration of the enemy."*   In his report of
the battle Jackson wrote: "Nobly did the artillery
maintain its position for hours against the enemy's admiring thousands.   Great praise is due Col. Pendleton
and the officers and men."†   Longstreet, in writing of
that portion of the Washington Artillery under his
command, said: "I am pleased to say that our young
artillerists proved themselves equal, if not superior, to
the boasted artillerists of the enemy."‡   Capt. Arnold
of McDowell's army stated in his report, in regard to
the part played by his battery: "During all this time
the battery was exposed to a severe and most accurate
artillery fire."§   And this officer's testimony with re-

---

*Rebellion Records, Series I, Vol. II, p. 494.
†Jackson's Report, Ibid., p. 481.
‡Longstreet's Report, Ibid., p. 462.
§See his report, Ibid., p. 416.

gard to the effectiveness of the fire of the Confederate guns is supported by all the Federal officers who participated in the fight.* But the Federal accounts of the artillery fire of the enemy are not over-trustworthy, for McDowell had himself instilled in them, as if by premeditation, a fear of the "long arm," altogether unwarranted by its actual power. Yet one of the greatest effects exerted by artillery in any battle is, after all, its moral effect, and in this particular manner it exercised a tremendous influence upon the Northern troops in the battle of Bull Run. McDowell's order of march was excellent with respect to the disposition of his troops but, as frequently pointed out, he spoiled the high morale he had created in his army by unwise caution which only sufficed to fill the minds of his men with fears. It "would not be pardonable in any commander to come upon a battery or breastwork without a knowledge of its position," cautioned the misled McDowell. These words were sufficient, and the mischief was done. His officers as well as his men advanced slowly, step by step, peering at each distant crest, and poking in every wayside thicket to locate the awful bugbear of the Press and of their own leader—"masked batteries." This direful term had originated in the Sumter episode—a battery having been constructed on the mainland behind a house which was demolished when the fire was ordered to be opened.† After that a masked battery figured in every affair even though but a skirmish. According to the pestilential swarm of press agents, which infested the safer places near the front, it was a masked battery which caused Butler's reverse at Big Bethel; and it was masked batteries which brought misfortune upon the Federal troops in various other instances.

The psychological effect upon his army resulting from McDowell's words was at best most adverse.

---

*Particularly interesting is Franklin's account, *Rebellion Records,* Series I, Vol. II., p. 406.
†*Memoirs of a Confederate,* Alexander, p. 21.

It has frequently been averred by military critics, and even by officers of professional repute who took part in the Bull Run campaign, both Confederate and Federal, that Johnston should have at once advanced and seized Washington after the overthrow of McDowell. The writer does not propose to discuss the general merits of this contention, but in so far as the Artillery is concerned, it seems necessary only to refer those supporting such a view to the records and correspondence of the hour.* Nor do I refer to the reports and statements of the generals in command, but to those of the ordnance officers occupying subordinate positions, and without responsibility for the movements of the Army as a whole. It would seem that if Johnston's guns were practically without ammunition as late as the middle of September he was hardly in position the night of July 21 to order an advance upon Washington, with a view to forcing his way through the outlying defenses, and laying siege to the National Capital.

*See Part I, as to armament and condition of artillery at this time.

CHAPTER VII

WINTER OF 1861-62

DURING the weeks immediately succeeding the victory at Manassas, Col Pendleton, who as Chief of Artillery of Johnston's army had displayed great ability as an artillerist, was temporarily appointed Chief of Ordnance to distribute the captured material and refit his batteries. But so destitute of ammunition and equipment was the Artillery found to be that it became necessary for him to repair to Richmond to beg, borrow, or secure in any way possible, the barest necessities for the batteries.* During his enforced absence Capt. E. P. Alexander, a most efficient officer, who had resigned from the Engineer Corps of the Old Army, and who had rendered splendid service as signal officer in the battle of Bull Run, was assigned to duty as acting Chief of Artillery.† Thus, while Pendleton with all but superhuman energy urged on the manufacture of material, ammunition, equipment and artillery stores of every kind in Richmond, and throughout the State, Alexander devoted his efforts to the better organization and discipline of the batteries already in the field, and to those which arrived from day to day.‡ The task assigned Pendleton was neither a simple nor a pleasant one, but before the end of October he was able to rejoin his command with the satisfaction of having accomplished the seemingly impossible.§

When Pendleton rejoined the Army of the Potomac, the artillery personnel consisted of 129 officers and 2,416 men, and with Loring in the Army of the Northwest, operating along the western frontier of Virginia, were 12 officers and 302 men besides a smaller number

---

*For the success of his efforts and the absolute lack of ammunition after the battle, see Part I.
†For sketch of Alexander, see Part I.
‡*Memoirs of W. N. Pendleton*, Lee, p. 154.
§For an intimate account of his labors in Richmond and elsewhere at this time, see *Memoirs of W. N. Pendleton*, Lee, pp. 154-167, and also Part I.

with Holmes in the Aquia District.* The personnel
of the main army was distributed as follows: 1st, or
Beauregard's Corps, 63 officers and 1,273 men; 2d, or
G. W. Smith's Corps, 27 officers and 480 men; artillery
reserve, 39 officers and 663 men.†

Before being assigned to duty as signal officer with
the Army in the field, Capt. Alexander had been engaged in the organization and drilling of the batteries in
Richmond in April, and had persistently advocated the
formation of battalions of light artillery of three or more
batteries, a suggestion entirely novel at the time. Had
he been allowed to remain on this duty longer, it is quite
probable his views would have obtained, but as it was,
he did succeed in inducing Magruder and Randolph to
create the Richmond Howitzer Battalion, of three companies. His influence being withdrawn, however, even
that battalion was divided, two of its batteries being assigned to the force at Yorktown, and one, Shields', to
Beauregard's Army. Thus, it was never employed as a
unit in accordance with Alexander's views. The Washington Artillery had arrived in Virginia with a battalion
formation of 4 batteries but it was at the very outset, as
has been shown, persistently split up into small, and
comparatively ineffective, detachments, conformable
with the prevailing custom of the time. The success
which had attended Pendleton in handling the Rockbridge, Alburtis', Imboden's, and Stanard's batteries,
in the movement from Winchester to Bull Run, and the
ability he had displayed to direct and control the massed
fire of at least three of these batteries in action, only
sufficed to call attention to the practicability of Alexander's ideas, and convinced Johnston that an artillery
reserve should be formed, though it was not for some
time that the true value of artillery masses was perceived.

When the winter of 1861-62 set in, Johnston withdrew his army to Centreville, and before January had

---

*Abstracts from Field Returns, *Rebellion Records,* Series I, Vol. V, pp.
932-933.
†For return dated December 1, see Series I, Vol. V, p. 974. There had been
little change.

reorganized his increased force into 4 divisions, two of 4 brigades each, and two of 5 each. These 18 brigades averaged about 4 regiments of 500 men each. Besides the main army, Jackson had a force in the Valley, and Holmes lay in observation behind Aquia Creek. The total effective strength of the Confederate forces, February 28, 1862, was 47,617, with 175 guns. The distribution of the batteries was, approximately, as follows:

FIRST DIVISION (Van Dorn)

Kemper's Alexandria (Va.) Battery, 1st or Bonham's Brigade.
Bondurant's Jeff Davis (Ala.) Battery, 2d or Early's Brigade.
Carter's King William (Va.) Battery, 3d or Rodes' Brigade.

SECOND DIVISON (G. W. Smith)

Alburtis' Wise (Va.) Battery, 1st or S. Jones' Brigade.
Thomas (Va.) Battery, 2d or Wilcox's Brigade.
Blodget's (Ga.) Battery, 3d or Toombs' Brigade.

THIRD DIVISION (Longstreet)

Rogers' Loudoun (Va.) Battery, 1st or Ewell's Brigade.
Stribling's Fauquier (Va.) Battery, 2d or D. R. Jones' Brigade.
Latham's Lynchburg (Va.) Battery, 3d or Cocke's Brigade.

FOURTH DIVISION (E. Kirby Smith)

Baltimore Light Artillery (Md.) Battery, 1st or Elzey's Brigade.
Courtney's Henrico (Va.) Battery, 2d or Trimble's Brigade.
Bowyer's Bedford (Va.) Battery, 3d or Taylor's Brigade.

WHITING'S DIVISION AT DUMFRIES

Imboden's Staunton (Va.) Battery, 1st or ————— Brigade.
Reilly's (N. C.) Detachment, 2d or Wigfall's Brigade.
Rives' (S. C.) Battery, 2d or Wigfall's Brigade.

HILL'S FORCE AT LEESBURG

Shields' Richmond Howitzer (Va.) Detachment, Griffin's Brigade.

HOLMES' FORCE AT AQUIA

Braxton's Fredericksburg (Va.) Battery, 1st or French's Brigade.
Cooke's Stafford (Va.) Battery, 2d or J. G. Walker's Brigade.
Walker's Purcell (Va.) Battery, 2d or J. G. Walker's Brigade.

JACKSON'S FORCE IN THE VALLEY

McLaughlin's Rockbridge (Va.) Battery, 1st or Garnett's Brigade.
Carpenter's Alleghany (Va.) Battery, 2d or Crittenden's Brigade.
Chew's Horse Artillery (Va.) Battery, Ashby's Cavalry.

RESERVE ARTILLERY WITH MAIN ARMY

(Col. Pendleton, Commanding)

Woolfolk's Ashland (Va.) Battery.
Cocke's Fluvanna (Va.) Battery.
Coleman's Morris Louisa (Va.) Battery.
Cutts' Sumter (Ga.) Battery.
Dance's Powhatan (Va.) Battery.
Hamilton's (Ga.) Battery.
Holman's Fluvanna (Va.) Battery.
Kirkpatrick's Amherst (Va.) Battery.
Lane's (Ga.) Battery.

(Maj. Walton, Commanding)

Squires' (La.) Battery, 1st Company, Washington Artillery.
Rosser's (La.) Battery, 2d Company, Washington Artillery.
Miller's (La.) Battery, 3d Company, Washington Artillery.
Eshleman's (La.) Battery, 4th Company, Washington Artillery.

From the foregoing schedule of assignments it will be seen that there were, before the close of 1861, not fewer than 35 batteries with the troops along the Potomac alone, 24 of which were raised in Virginia, and that 13 of these had been assigned to a reserve in two sections, commanded by Pendleton and Walton, respectively.[*]

About the first of March the aggregate present for duty of the field artillery personnel, was 2,967, including 146 officers, which gives an average strength for the 35 batteries present of about 85 men.

Just at this time the Federal Army had been reorganized by McClellan, his 5 corps together aggregating 185,420 men, with 465 field guns. Thus it is seen that the Federal Army had available nearly 3 guns for each one with Johnston's force, the disparity in per-

---

[*]*Rebellion Records*, Series I, Vol. V, p. 1086.

sonnel, horses, character of armament, ammunition and equipment being even greater. Indeed the odds in the latter respects were overwhelming, particularly as to ammunition, the Confederate Ordnance Department lacking throughout the war the material and skilled labor with which to make really reliable fuses and projectiles.

Before the close of 1861 Gen. Johnston had been much annoyed by the interference of the Secretary of War with matters affecting the organization of the Army. Mr. Benjamin had granted indiscriminately to officers, private soldiers, and even to' civilians, authority to raise troops of cavalry and batteries of artillery.* Many of the batteries thus raised were recruited from amongst the men of the infantry regiments, and while Johnston's objection on the ground that the field artillery arm already exceeded the European proportion was perhaps ill founded, yet, the creation of heavy batteries for local service away from the actual field of campaign, and to the detriment of the infantry, was a most injurious practice. "Fortunately," says Johnston, "the Ordnance Department was unable to arm and equip them; otherwise the Army would have been deprived of several regiments of excellent infantry, and encumbered with artillery that could not have been taken into battle without danger of capture, for want of infantry to protect it." The interference of the Secretary, so bitterly resented and complained of by Gen. Johnston, led to the organization of many light batteries which it would have been necessary to create later, if not at the time they actually were created. Yet, Gen. Johnston was much perplexed over the condition of the batteries already in the field, many of which still had four-horse teams, and, realizing their immobility, it is not strange that he desired the addition of no more to his army, in spite of the preponderance of the Federal guns.

*Johnston's Narrative, pp. 90, 91.

By special order the strength of the light artillery companies of Virginia militia was fixed in March at 150 men, rank and file, those containing over 120 men being entitled to an extra second lieutenant.*

We have seen that the Act of January 22, 1862, authorized the appointment of brigadier-generals, and additional field-officers in the field artillery arm. On the 27th the Secretary of War addressed the following letter to Gen. Johnston at Centreville:

"SIR—Congress has provided by law for the appointment of field officers of artillery in the provisional army in proportion to the number of guns in each command. You are respectfully requested to report as early as convenient the number of guns in each of the three armies under your command, and a list of the artillery officers in each army, in the order of their merit, so as to assist the President in doing justice to your meritorious subordinates by proper promotion. It would be agreeable to us to have a like list prepared separately by the commanders of each of the three armies in relation to the officers under his command, so as to compare the estimate made of their respective merits, and thus increase the probability of doing justice to all."

This communication evidences a worthy desire on the part of the appointing authority to increase the officers of the Artillery by judicious appointments in such numbers as to give the arm not only those needed, but officers of approved ability. Immediate steps were taken to make the appointments contemplated by Congress.

Early in March, it became certain that McClellan was preparing for a forward movement either by Fredericksburg or the Peninsula, and Johnston withdrew his army behind the Rappahannock, along which a line had been fortified.

The Artillery had been in cantonments about Culpeper during the winter, and the horses had been given a long rest, the men being drilled and instructed whenever the weather permitted. For the

*S. O. No. 2, A. G. O., Virginia, March 21, 1862, *Rebellion Records*, Series IV, Vol. I, p. 1011.

better mobilizing of the Army, Col. Pendleton's reserve corps was now ordered to abandon its cabins, and moved with the division of G. W. Smith to Warrenton, leaving the winter quarters March 8. The Artillery was in fine spirits when it reached Warrenton four days later where it lay for about a month, at the end of which time it was called upon to make various changes of position in the worst imaginable weather, finally arriving at Louisa Courthouse with Longstreet's Division. Here it was a serious problem to secure provender for the 750 animals of the Reserve Artillery.

April 10, Col. Pendleton received his well-earned promotion, his commission of brigadier-general of artillery bearing date of March 26. The news of this appointment was received with great favor throughout the Army, but there was undoubtedly jealously in some quarters.* Pendleton had entertained serious misgivings about his promotion over the gallant Maj. Walton who, himself, was too high and patriotic a soldier to be piqued by the advancement of the Virginian. Yet, a feeling existed among the men of the far South that favoritism had been too generally shown Virginians, though their resentment was in no sense directed against Pendleton.

To guard against the possibility of friction, it will be observed that the portion of the Reserve Artillery placed under Pendleton as Chief of Artillery, when he had previously been promoted from a captain to the rank of colonel, did not include the battalion of Maj. Walton.

The Reserve Artillery was now ordered to Richmond, where it arrived April 14, whence it was ordered to proceed two days later to Yorktown, Gen. Pendleton being sent on in advance by Gen. Johnston to confer with Gen. D. H. Hill in command, and to inspect the defences of the place. He reported at once that the

---

*Memoirs of W. N. Pendleton, p. 173. Also see Benjamin's letter to the President, November 30, 1861, Rebellion Records, Series IV, Vol. I, p. 761.

country was entirely unsuited for the use of field artillery, or large masses of men, and that with its armament it was impossible to hold Yorktown against the heavy rifled ordnance of the enemy.* On April 30, he wrote that Johnston's army would have to fall back to the neighborhood of Richmond before a land battle could be thought of. Pendleton, at the time, must have contemplated with misgivings the tremendous superiority of McClellan's artillery in numbers, material and general efficiency, yet his energies, in common with those of all his subordinates, were bent to the task of preparing his arm to meet its antagonist upon the best footing possible. New batteries continued to be added to the Army of Northern Virginia, to the equipment of which the Confederate Bureau of Ordnance was now contributing, and there were other conditions in favor of the Confederate Artillery. Not only was Jackson so playing upon the fears of Lincoln and Stanton that McClellan was continually being crippled, but the country through which the invader must pass was such that it would surely reduce the immense force of his artillery in large measure to the status of a train, which, blocking every road, would only add to the difficulties of his maneuvers. Pendleton at once perceived that for these reasons the numbers of the enemy, in so far as his artillery was concerned, would by the very nature of the field of operations be largely discounted.

To Lincoln and his cabinet, McClellan's movement to the Peninsula, in view of Jackson's activity in the Valley, seemed to uncover Washington. They feared an irruption of the Confederates, just as Lee's defensive strategy contemplated they would, which might expose the Federal Capital to capture. McClellan was, therefore, commanded to leave a force so disposed as to cover Washington and to protect it in any emergency. This he thought he had done when he left 63,000 men and 85 pieces of artillery distributed between the Valley, Warrenton, Manassas, and the lines about Washington. In

*Memoirs of W. N. Pendleton, Lee, p. 181.

addition to this force he had detached Blenker's Division of 10,000 men and 24 guns to join Fremont. But with fears greatly aroused by Jackson's attack at Kernstown, augmented by lack of confidence in McClellan, 75,000 men and 109 guns were not deemed sufficient to guard the Capital against the Army of the Valley, and McDowell's Corps of between 30,000 and 40,000 men was taken from McClellan and held between Washington and Richmond.*   Thus McClellan was deprived of about 200 of his 465 guns.

*Jackson's Valley Campaign, Allan, pp. 84-85.

CHAPTER VIII

Up to this time little has been said about the tactics of the Confederate Artillery, except to refer to Alexander's early conception of the organization of battalions. But the organization of the artillery reserve of the Army of Northern Virginia marks an event in its career which requires notice. Up to that point, there had been little attention bestowed upon the tactics of the arm, other than upon the mere drill of the battery and the evolutions of several when maneuvering together. Such was the scope of the treatise prepared by Capt. Stevens in 1792, the author having been an artillery officer in Lamb's continental regiment. Then appeared in 1809 a work called "The American Artillerist's Companion, or Elements of Artillery," by Col. Louis de Tousard, formerly of the British service, and later Colonel of the Second Continental Regiment of Artillery, and inspector of the Artillery of the United States. In 1800, Alexander Hamilton, Inspector-General, and Gen. Pinckney, had endeavored to formulate drill regulations for the Artillery, followed by Gen. James Wilkinson, in 1808, but nothing of permanent character had resulted from their efforts, so that other than a simple drill manual for horse, or flying artillery, as it was then called, written by Gen. Kosciusko, in Paris in 1800, and Tousard's work, there were no definite regulations for the arm when the War of 1812 was declared.

France at this time was generally recognized to be the school of highest artillery development, and in 1809, Capt. Winfield Scott had sought authority to repair thither for a study of its system upon which to base a comprehensive work, but his application was refused and no manual of instruction was adopted in the United States, until 1821, at which time a work by H. Lallemand, formerly a general in Napoleon's Imperial

Guard, known as a "Treatise on Artillery," was adopted. As the spirit of both Tousard's and Lallemand's works was essentially French, it will be well to gain some knowledge of the status of artillery and artillery tactics of the time in France.

The soldiers of the French Revolution had initiated many improvements in ordnance and artillery generally. The casting and boring of guns, the cleaning of saltpetre, and the preparation of powder, were much improved by the clever chemists and men of science of the Republic. The campaigns in the Alps led to the introduction of mountain guns, portable enough to be of real use in rough country, and Gribeauval's heavy gun carriages, and ammunition wagons were much simplified and improved for ordinary field use. On the whole, light and horse artillery material was brought up to a stage of perfection proportionate to that of the other arms of the service in which radical advances had been made since the days of Frederick the Great. Regimental guns were taken from the battalions and collected in batteries, and particular attention was paid to the artillery as a separate and not as a mere auxiliary arm. Prior to 1789, the French Artillery consisted of 7 regiments of foot artillery, with 6 companies of miners and artificers, but although Austria, Prussia and some other nations had introduced the horse batteries so dear to Frederick, the French had not done so.* The material of the field batteries consisted of 6-, 8-, and 12-pounder guns, and 6- and 8-pounder siege pieces. The whole field artillery arm was divided into regiments and companies. The guns of the foot regiments were mostly 4-pounders, and of these there were 1,200, which with the battery artillery made a disproportionate number of guns. But the object in this was to back up the courage of the ill-drilled and inexperienced conscripts by means

---

*The creation of horse artillery is generally attributed to Frederick the Great, a claim asserted by many countries; but, in an interesting article which appeared in the *Voyennui Sbornik*, translated for the *Journal of the Royal Artillery*, by Lieut. H. D. Ashby, R. F. A., and reprinted in the *Journal of the Military Service Institution* (American), July-August, 1912, p. 120, much evidence is adduced to prove that it was the conception of Peter the Great, of Russia.

of a heavy artillery fire. The creation of a large body of light infantry led to the production of lighter batteries, which might keep pace with the men; and in 1791, there were already two companies of this light artillery, each with two 8-pounder guns and two 6-inch howitzers, the men serving with them being carried along in wagons of peculiar construction. But soon the gunners were mounted, and thus the arm grew into horse artillery, an arm so well suited to the quick-acting French temperament that it at once assumed undue proportions.

When in 1793-94, the Army was reorganized, each half-brigade was given a battery of 6 guns, that is, the same number of two pieces to each battalion was retained. As, however, it was soon discovered that too much artillery on account of its comparative immobility retarded the movements of the Army without actual corresponding gain, the allowance was cut down to one gun for each brigade—a better proportion. The battalions were no longer hampered by each dragging its own gun, as had been largely done by the American troops in the War of Independence, since the guns were now consolidated into batteries capable of following the maneuvers of their respective brigades. Thus regimental guns gradually disappeared and batteries came into use, consisting of foot and horse artillery. In 1794, the French field artillery comprised 8 regiments of foot, and 8 regiments of horse artillery, 12 companies of artificers, and a battalion of pontoniers. The regiment of foot artillery had a staff and 20 companies; each company with a battery of 6 guns with 8 men per gun, having, also, supernumeraries for general service, a company thus aggregating 93 men. The mounted artillery regiment had a staff and 6 companies; each company was a battery of 6 guns, with 10 men per gun; a total of 60. This made 960 guns and 15,000 artillerymen in the foot, 280 guns and 3,000 artillerymen in the mounted artillery; a total of 1,248 guns and 18,000 men. In charge of the corps artillery were 228 general, staff, and superior officers, including those assigned to duty as inspectors.

The artillery had its own regulations and tactics, and in maneuver the field batteries possessed great mobility. Gunnery was scientifically studied and the schools, for which the foundation had been laid by Louis XIV, were greatly improved. With its many polytechnic schools, its military school at Chalons, and its regimental schools at La Fere, Besancon, Grenoble, Metz, Strasburg, Douay, Auxonne and Toulouse, where the several artillery regiments were stationed, the French system of instruction was advanced and thorough, ahead of that of any other country at the time.

But, it remained for the great master to teach the world the meaning of artillery, and how to employ it in battle. "A good infantry," said Napoleon, "is without doubt the backbone of the army, but if it had to fight long against superior artillery, it would be discouraged and disorganized."* And, so, possessing an unequalled ability to direct and control masses of men, he applied his principles to the tactical employment of his artillery, perceiving the great power of field guns, when the fire of a large number were used in combination. He had also learned that with the short range of the smooth-bore guns, it was practically impossible to change their position when once they had become engaged under fire, because of the vulnerability of a mounted battery, and the large target it presented while in motion.

He therefore created divisional artillery, thus securing his masses, and a reserve artillery which he was able to withhold until it could be thrown into action at the crisis to decide the issue. Writing to Eugene, he declared that "the artillery, like the other arms, must be collected in mass, if one wishes to attain a decisive result."†

Addressing Clarke in 1809 concerning the latter's green troops, he gave expression to his great belief in the artillery arm when he wrote: "Troops such as you have are just the kind which need most entrenchments,

*Dixhuit Notes, etc., XXXI, p. 395.
†C. N. to Eugene, Schönbrunn, 16 June, 1809, 5 P. M.

earthworks and artillery. The more inferior the quality of a body of troops, the more artillery it requires. There are some army corps with which I should require only one-third of the artillery which I need for other corps."*

After Lützen and Bautzen, he wrote, "It is the artillery of my guard which generally decides my battles, for as I have it always at hand, I can bring it to bear, whenever it becomes necessary.†

And, after the end of the campaign, he wrote, "Great battles are won by artillery."‡

Previous to the time of Gustavus, and his great artillery general, Torstenson, the number of guns per thousand men had varied from 1 to 5. Gustavus generally had 3, but at one time 6. In the Seven Years War, the average number was 4, though Frederick once increased it to 10 per thousand, endeavoring to compensate with additional guns for his losses in infantry. Napoleon rarely got more than 5 or 6 per thousand, though he possessed at one time the enormous total of 1,300 guns.

At Friedland, the French general, Senarmont, advanced his great line of guns to within 300 yards of the Russian Infantry and broke its front with a murderous storm of canister, and at Austerlitz, Wagram, and Gross-Görshen, the issue had been decided by Napoleon's masses of guns. Yet, it took the allies many years to perceive the cause of Napoleon's successes, employing as they did, against his great masses of artillery, individual batteries or small groups. It was not until 1813 that Blücher gave voice to the need of more guns with which to combat him. But while it took the allies time to learn the game, finally Napoleon was forced to exclaim angrily, when he saw their great masses on the field of Leipzig open fire upon him, "At last they have learned something."§

But, just as in the course of years the Napoleonic art had been learned by the world, so in a short time was

---

*C. N., Schönbrunn, 18 August.
†C. N. to Clarke, New Markt, 2 June.
‡C. N. to Eugene, St. Cloud, 20 November, 1813.
§Jomini's *Napoleon's Campaigns*.

it forgotten, and other than a knowledge of the minor tactics contained in the "Manual for the Artillery of the Garde Royale," little information as to the employment of field guns was possessed in America. This work had in 1826 been recommended to the Secretary of War by a board of officers of which Gen. Scott was president, being subsequently published under the title of "A System of Exercise and Instruction of Field Artillery, including Maneuvers of Light or Horse Artillery." By Act of Congress 5,000 copies of this work were authorized to be purchased and distributed for the use of the militia, the regular batteries retaining Lallemand's treatise as their manual. The next step was to send Lieut. Tyler of the regular service to Metz, in 1828, to translate the existing French manuals, but the old Gribeauval system becoming obsolete, Capt. Robert Anderson's translation of the French "Instruction for Field Artillery, Horse and Foot" appeared in 1839, and superseded all previously adopted works.* The manual of instruction employed during the Mexican War was that contained in Anderson's translation as revised by Maj. Ringold, in 1843, and adopted in 1845. These instructions, although excellent so far as they went, embraced little more than the manual of the piece and the maneuvers of a battery. The proper organization of artillery for, and its management in the field were merely touched upon. A new set of instructions going somewhat into the tactical employment of the arm, and also another translation from the French by Maj. Robert Anderson, entitled the "Evolutions of Field Batteries," and comprehending the school of a battalion of 3 or 4 batteries, appeared in 1860. This book was adopted by the Army and adhered to by the Federals during the entire Civil War. The Confederate States to a certain extent adhered to the same work, but a treatise entitled, "Manual of Instruction for the Volunteers and Militia of the Confederate States," by Col. William Gilham, Instructor of Tactics and Com-

---

*Major Anderson of Fort Sumter fame.

mandant of Cadets at the Virginia Military Institute, was given precedence over all others in so far as the school of the battery was concerned. This work was a most comprehensive manual of drill for the three arms, containing also the Articles of War of the Confederacy, and the regulations for military courts.*

But, as has been said before, in 1861 artillery was an arm consisting of so many individual batteries. The conception of field artillery at this time embraced nothing more than the evolutions of several battery units maneuvering together. Its tactical employment in accordance with Napoleonic principles was entirely forgotten, and indeed artillery tactics had reverted to the pre-Napoleonic stage of batteries, distributed throughout the army to brigades and even sections to regiments, simply by reason of the fact that there had never been enough artillery in this country at one time to attract the attention of our officers to the Napoleonic methods of employing large masses. This was not strange, but most natural. Indeed, the Prussians evidenced the same neglect in 1864, during their war with Denmark, and had to relearn the great principles of artillery masses from Austria, in 1866, Austria having been reminded of them in the French War of 1859. The Prussian lapse is far more inexplicable than that of the Americans in their civil conflict, for Prussia had maintained a large artillery arm for years.

We are now in position to grasp the true meaning of the formation of reserve artillery under Pendleton and Walton, and to appreciate the stand which Capt. Alexander had made early in 1861 for the organization of field artillery battalions to act as combat units. It was yet to be some time before the knowledge of "the way it should be done" was to enable the Confederate generals "to do it," and many hard knocks were to be received by the loosely organized and poorly handled Confederate field artillery until experience prevailed and added its dearly bought lessons.

*It had appeared in 1861 before the outbreak of the war as a semi-official publication of the United States Army.

CHAPTER IX

It will be well now to look more minutely at the artillery of McClellan's Army, so vastly superior in numbers, material and organization, in order that the inequality of the two armies in respect to this arm may be appreciated from the first.

Many of the Federal regiments which took the field in the spring of 1861 had batteries attached to them, true to the system of Gustavus and Frederick. As was to be expected, these batteries were found to be useless. When the Union Army marched to Manassas, the batteries not belonging to regiments, most of which were regular batteries, were assigned to brigades in accordance with the custom of the day. But, when McClellan undertook the reorganization of the defeated army in July, he inaugurated numerous imperative changes, many of which were innovations. Among the latter was his organization of the artillery. Perceiving the utter lack of artillery reserves, and that brigade commanders were not capable of supervising and directing artillery, of which they were generally quite ignorant, he set about the task before him of bringing order out of chaos. The force turned over to him July 27, 1861, consisted of 50,000 infantry, 1,000 cavalry, and 650 artillerymen manning 9 incomplete batteries, with an aggregate of but 30 guns. These figures should be borne in mind by all who are prone to question the ability of "Little Mac" as an organizer. Upon the foundation which he laid, single-handed, was erected the whole structure of Grant's success in Virginia. He gave the Army of the Potomac in its formative period the character, the cohesion, and indirectly, therefore, the stamina, which enabled it to withstand the severest punishments ever administered to an army ultimately victorious.

In the reorganization of the artillery the following radical and comprehensive regulations were promulgated by McClellan, largely proposed by Wm. F. Barry, his Chief of Artillery.

"1st. The proportion of artillery should be in the ratio of at least 2½ pieces to 1,000 men, to be expanded, if possible, to 3 pieces.

"2d. The field guns should be restricted to the systems of the United States Ordnance Department and of Parrott, the smoothbores (with the exception of a few howitzers for special service), to be exclusively the 12-pounder guns, model 1857, variously called the gun howitzer, light 12-pounder, or the Napoleon.

"3d. Each field battery to be composed, if practicable, of 6, and none to have less than 4, guns, those of each battery to be of uniform caliber.

4th. The field batteries to be assigned to divisions, and not to brigades, in the proportion of 4 to each division, one of which should be a regular battery, the rest volunteers; the captain of the regulars to command the artillery of the division. In the event of several divisions being united into an army corps, at least one-half of the divisional artillery to be withdrawn from the divisions and formed into a corps reserve.*

"5th. The reserve artillery of the whole army to consist of 100 guns, comprising besides a sufficient number of light mounted batteries, all the guns of position, and, until the cavalry be massed, all the horse artillery.

"6th. The amount of ammunition to accompany the field batteries to be not less than 400 rounds per gun.

"7th. A siege train of 50 pieces to be provided.†

"8th. Instruction in the theory and practice of gunnery, as well as the tactics of that arm, to be given to the officers and non-commissioned officers of the volunteer batteries, by the study of suitable books and by actual recitations in each division, under the direction of the regular officer commanding the divisional artillery.

"9th. Personal inspections, as frequent as circumstances will permit, to be made by the Chief of Artillery of the Army, to see to a strict observance of the established organization and drill, of the special regulations and orders issued from time to time, under authority of the commanding general, to note the improvement of officers and men of the volunteer batteries, and the actual fitness for field service of the whole, both regulars and volunteers."

*This contingency arose on the Peninsula in June, 1862. See subsequent mention.

†Subsequently expanded to 100 pieces at Yorktown, including 13-inch seacoast mortars and 100-pounder and 200-pounder Parrotts.

As early as August 21, Gen. Barry had urged Mc-Clellan to reorganize and increase the field artillery arm in the following words:

"To insure success, it is of vital importance that the army should have an overwhelming force of field artillery. To render this the more effective, the field batteries should, as far as possible, consist of regular troops."

While McClellan was not prepared to enlarge the regular establishment, he lost no time in increasing the general efficiency of the Army, by encouraging and directing his artillery officers. In his report, he wrote: "The creation of an adequate artillery establishment was a formidable undertaking, and had it not been that the country possessed in the regular service a body of accomplished and energetic artillery officers, the task would almost have been hopeless."

Assembling all the regular batteries he could secure for his army, when the 3 corps, or his 8 divisions embarked for the Peninsula, they were accompanied by 49 batteries aggregating 299 guns, of which 100, comprised of 18 batteries, were in the reserve. Of the 49 batteries, 20 were of the regular service and 14 of these were in the reserve. These figures do not include the guns of McDowell's 1st Corps, of which McClellan was soon deprived.*

The batteries of McClellan's Army were organized, equipped, and instructed in as exact accordance with the regulations he had prescribed, as a number of active and efficient officers, directed by a most capable chief, could cause them to be.

When the divisions were organized into corps for service on the Peninsula, corps commanders were ordered to create out of a half-part of their divisional batteries a corps reserve, in charge of a chief. This was done the first week of June.

The contemplated employment of field guns in masses as provided for by the organization of divisional,

---

*Historical Sketch of the Artillery of the United States Army, Birkhimer, p. 82.

corps, and reserve artillery in the Army of the Potomac, while a radical advance in tactics in one sense, was yet but a reversion to Napoleonic principles. It has been stated that the reason for the reserve was to withhold from committing to action all the guns, since once under fire they might not be shifted. By retaining in hand a large group, its massed fire might be suddenly hurled against any point, thereby bringing about a decision. The introduction of horse artillery made the very rapid concentration of guns at any point all the more possible.

Du Teil was the original exponent of increased mobility in field artillery, and the concentration of its fire.* "One must concentrate the bulk of the troops and a superior artillery on that point where one wishes to defeat the enemy, while one must deceive him in the other points. The artillery will gain superiority over the hostile artillery if it invariably concentrates its fire on the decisive points. The artillery must be increased against those points which decide the victory; thus it gives decisive results. When attacking a position, it is only a question of concentrating one's fire and efforts upon some of its weak points, in order to force the enemy to evacuate it. The moment when troops are to act is determined by the havoc which the artillery will have caused. If the redoubts are breached, the hostile troops demoralized and beaten, the victory which the artillery has prepared only depends then on the valour of the assailant, etc." The representative of these views had left the regiment la Fère shortly before young Bonaparte joined it, and du Teil's elder brother, in thorough accord with such views, was the Commandant of the Military School at Auxonne, where the young officer received his professional training.† Bonaparte, Senarmont, and Drouot, were therefore early impressed with the offensive possibilities of field artillery, and Napoleon, as Von Caemmerer says, thought of his guns when he exclaimed, "Le feu est tout, le reste n'est rien."

*The Development of Strategical Science, Von Caemmerer, p. 17.
†Von Caemmerer. See also L'Education Militaire de Napoleon, Colin.

Napoleon, then, was not so much the originator of artillery masses as the military executor of du Teil, as well as of Guibert and Bourcet. In his day the increased mobility of field guns over those of Frederick the Great, and the terrible power of case-shot preparation, together with the more judicious use of reserves, made it possible for him to shatter the resistance of the enemy.* But a vast change in conditions had come about with the introduction of the rifled gun.† Ranges so increased that no longer were field pieces finally committed when they first became engaged and the old reserve constantly tended to keep out of action guns which might better have been employed from the first. Superior ranges over the small arm not only enabled the guns to be retained in hand when pushed into action, but the increased range gave them a wider zone of efficiency, for without changing position rifled pieces were able to coöperate with others at distant points, in concentrating their fire on any given position of the enemy. Thus the effect of concentrated fire could be secured from dispersed groups as well as from great masses of guns.‡ Such conditions, rendering it unnecessary to hold back a great reserve group of guns, led to the change of name for the component groups of the reserve which now became known as corps, or divisional reserves.

"Many philosophers have said," wrote Prince Kraft, "What's in a name? But, you think with me on this subject, that the Army is not composed of philosophers. On the contrary, they are men, and thus human, and in the stress of battle, pay little attention to abstract principles. Names, gaudy uniforms, orders and an empty stomach, all things which a philosopher treats with contempt, play a decisive part in war. Thus the change of name by regulation was an act of far-reaching results. When the reserve artillery had been renamed corps artillery, every leader of troops and every

---

*Evolution of Infantry Tactics, Maude, pp. 118-120.
†Field Artillery with the Other Arms, May, pp. 60, 61, 62.
‡Letters on Field Artillery, Hohenlohe, p. 140.

staff officer was at once compelled to recognize that they were no longer to be held in reserve, but had become a part of the line of battle."

What the learned Prussian has written concerning the change in the tactical employment of field artillery in Germany, after the war of 1866, applies with great directness to conditions in America in 1862, but an admission cannot be found in his work that American experience had contributed to the Prussian knowledge. There are indications that Von Hindersin, the Inspector-General of Artillery, did take notice of our development of, and experience with, the new rifled piece in the Civil War. But the lessons of this war were not heeded by the Prussians until after they had received many reverses with their artillery in their struggle with Austria. The faulty employment of their guns through a continued adherence to the reserve formation led the Prussians into many snares in 1866, their antagonists having profited by their own experiences in 1859. But in their disregard of what had transpired in Virginia we find a striking admonition not to ignore what our neighbors may be able to teach us. That America had sounded the practical note of divisional artillery many years before it reverberated through the continent there can be little question, although the Austrians and Prussians had both in theory provided for divisional artillery. That Johnston totally ignored the tactical principles of Napoleon and the French, as displayed at Solferino, in 1859, with respect to artillery masses, is also beyond dispute.

It may be argued that the Americans were merely groping in the dark; that realizing that something was wrong somewhere, a change was necessary; that the fact that a reserve was maintained in addition to divisional groups indicates the imperfection of tactical ideas. Yet, the fact remains that new conditions which could only be thrown into relief by experience were promptly met and that nowhere do we find a practical guide for the radical changes effected by McClellan and Lee.

CHAPTER X

THE principle event in the field artillery arm of the Army during the fall of 1861, outside of the arrival of new batteries, including a number from Maryland, North and South Carolina, and Georgia, and the general activity in refitting and drilling, was the organization under special authority of the. Secretary of War, November 11, 1861, of a horse battery. This battery was created at the suggestion of Col. Ashby, commanding the cavalry with Jackson's Army in the Valley, who perceived the great value of guns possessing sufficient mobility to accompany his troopers, and its organization was the first step toward the formation of that wonderful horse artillery corps which, for the next four years under Pelham, Chew, Beckham, Breathed, Thomson, and others, astounded the world with its daring and deeds of valor.

Organized with an enlisted personnel of 33 men, its first officers were: Robert Preston Chew, Captain; Milton Rouse, First Lieutenant; James Thomson, Second Lieutenant; all young graduates of the Virginia Military Institute and former pupils of Jackson, to the fame of whose army they were now to contribute many laurels. Chew's Battery soon earned for itself a name and reputation second only to that of Ashby himself, and second to no other battery in the Confederate armies. The clatter of its horses' feet, the rumble of its guns upon the turnpike, the shriek of its shells, were sounds familiar to every resident of the Valley from the Potomac to Staunton, and it probably took part in more engagements than any other battery in the war, North or South. The membership of this celebrated command increased rapidly after its organization, up to April 9, 1865, when it surrendered 197 men. After the death

of Ashby and Jackson, Chew's Battery became a part
of Stuart's horse artillery battalion, of which in 1864
the gallant Chew became commander. The history of
the first horse battery is so inseparably interwoven with
that of Ashby, Jackson, and Stuart, that it cannot be
written apart from that of those famous soldiers and
their cavalry. In the minds of the men of the Army it
and Ashby's Cavalry "belonged to each other as by
natural affinity."

The armament of the battery from first to last consisted of 3 pieces; a Blakely imported British rifled
piece, which fired a percussion shell; a smooth-bore 12-
pounder howitzer; and a 3-inch iron rifle.

When Chew and his officers, mere beardless youths,
called upon Gen. Jackson, their former instructor, to
report for duty, the face of the stern soldier wore a
quizzical, though amused, expression,* as he said,
"Young men, now that you have your company, what
are you going to do with it?" The deeds of the battery
from then on were to be the answer, a reply which appealed far more to Jackson than words could have done.
Nothing in the history of artillery ever surpassed in
skill and courage the service of Ashby's horse battery
in the Valley campaign. Unlimbering on every hill, it
held the pursuers in check, and dashing to the front with
the foremost troopers it opened every fight; in pursuit
it was always on hand working havoc among the fleeing
foe. The remarks of Henderson regarding the unsurpassed character of Jackson's light horse under Ashby
apply to that portion of the latter's command known as
Chew's Battery.

Horse artillery had also been early recognized in the
Union Army as the associate of properly organized
cavalry, and about the time Chew's Battery was formed,
Company A, Second Regiment, Field Artillery, United
States Army, was equipped for that service at Wash-
ington. This and Chew's Battery were the first horse

---

*Chew was 19, Rouse 17, and Thomson 18 years old in November, 1861.
See Chew's address at the unveiling of Ezekiel's statue of Jackson, at the
Virginia Military Institute, June 19, 1912.

artillery in America since Bragg's company was dismounted at Sante Fé after the Mexican War.*

The force which was given Jackson in November 1861, with which to play upon the fears of the Washington Administration by threatening the Capital from the Valley, was indeed a small one, but by the first of the following year it had been largely increased. On January 10, he had with him McLaughlin's (Rockbridge) Battery, 6 guns; Waters' Battery, 4 guns; Carpenter's Alleghany Battery, 4 guns; Marye's Battery, 4 guns; Chew's Battery, 3 guns; or a total of 25 pieces, having lost Cutshaw's 2 guns at Romney on January 7.† Jackson's Chief of Artillery was at this time Maj. Daniel Truehart, an old cadet, with Lieut. Ed. Willis as his assistant, and his ordnance officer was Lieut. J. M. Garnett, who was succeeded by Lieut. H. H. Lee and the latter by Lieut. R. H. Meade.

When in February, 1862, Banks began his advance to seize Winchester, arriving at Martinsburg March 3, Jackson was instructed "to endeavor to employ the invaders in the Valley, but without exposing himself to the danger of defeat, by keeping so near the enemy as to prevent him from making any considerable detachment to reënforce McClellan, but not so near that he might be compelled to fight."‡ Jackson's force now consisted of 3,600 infantry, 600 cavalry, and the 6 batteries, with their 27 guns before mentioned, the artillery with a total personnel of 369.§

Banks had with him when he crossed the Potomac 38,000 men, including 2,000 cavalry, and 80 pieces of artillery, a large proportion of which were the most modern rifled guns, fully horsed and equipped.¶

In the great campaign which followed, the artillery, far inferior in equipment to that of the Federals in every respect, except as to personnel, was able by the daring

---

*Birkhimer, p. 70.
†Chew was with Ashby at the time.
‡*Johnston's Narrative*, p. 106.
§Henderson's *Stonewall Jackson*, p. 270; *Jackson's Valley Campaign*, Allan, p. 39.
¶Henderson's *Jackson*, p. 265.

and skill of its men successfully to oppose the enemy on almost every battlefield. The marching ability of the batteries, more often provided with four-horse teams than otherwise, was on a par with that of the wonderful infantry. "Whilst it is absolutely true that no soldiers ever marched with less to encumber them than the Confederates, it is no empty boast that none ever marched faster, or held out longer." "Fine feathers, though they may have their use, are hardly essential to efficiency in the field."*

In the Valley campaign there is little of a tactical nature to be considered concerning the light artillery. The batteries, though poorly armed, horsed, and equipped, were officered by bold, gallant, intelligent men, who did all which under the prevailing system could have been expected of them. The enlisted personnel, consisting largely of highly educated and socially superior volunteers, while not possessing the discipline of the men in the Northern batteries, surpassed the latter in individual efficiency. Of this, there can be little doubt, and to this fact must be largely attributed the ability of the Confederate gunners so successfully to oppose the highly efficient batteries of the Federal Army. The batteries of Jackson's army displayed the same endurance, tenacity, ability to stand punishment, and *élan* common to the rest of his troops. They were fought with few exceptions as batteries; massed fire when employed resulting from the accident of position, rather than from a preconceived plan. Jackson, an artilleryman himself, did much to scout the old idea that artillery was incapable of facing the fire of infantry. The practice of withdrawing the guns when infantry fire was opened upon them, so common in the armies of his opponents, received no sanction from him, and soon his gunners learned the fallacy of such tactics and took their punishment unflinchingly.

But, if no new principle of light artillery tactics developed, or no old forgotten ones were revived, in this

*Thus wrote Henderson of Jackson's troops, p. 273. In 48 marching days they covered 676 miles, an average of 14 miles per diem.

campaign, the same cannot be said of the horse artillery which introduced and adopted a maneuver in battle hitherto known to have been executed in but insolated cases, one of which was when Ramsey's horse battery at Fuentes de Onoro, finding itself cut off by French cavalry, limbered up, charged the enemy, and cut its way out. But this action, nor the charges of the mounted Prussian detachments of the horse artillery, which the gunners were trained to make to save their guns from capture, can be said to have constituted shock tactics for artillery. This new development in the Confederate artillery was the natural outgrowth of Ashby's reckless daring, and the courage of Capt. Chew. Born of an accident, as it were, when the practicability of the maneuver was perceived, the practice became more or less general in the Confederate horse artillery and was frequently repeated during the war as will be shown. The facts concerning the first instance of guns charging with the cavalry are given in the words of Col. R. Preston Chew himself, whose recollection of the incident is borne out by numerous authorities.*

"Gen. Jackson had assembled his army at Cedarville, on the road from Front Royal to Winchester, on the night of the 23d of May, 1862. On the 24th Gen. Ashby was ordered, with his cavalry, supported by a part of Taylor's Bridgade, to take Chew's Battery and two guns from the Rockbridge Artillery, and assail the enemy at Middletown on the Valley turnpike. His advance was stubbornly opposed by the Federal Infantry, but he succeeded in driving them back, and emerged into the open field near Middletown. Telling me to move with the cavalry, he charged the enemy's cavalry, from 2,000 to 2,500 strong, in the road at Middletown. Our guns charged with the cavalry, and when within a short distance, probably 100 yards from the turnpike, we unlimbered and opened on the Federals. There was a stone fence on either side of the road, and we caught them at a great disadvantage. . . . The enemy fled in every direction, and Ashby pursued them along the turnpike toward Newtown. When we came to a point called Crisman's, he reformed his cavalry, and telling me again to charge

*Col. Chew's statement is contained in a letter to the author, dated November 9, 1912. See also the *Laurel Brigade*, McDonald, pp. 60, 61; *Ashby and His Compeers*, Avirett; *Ashby and His Men*, Thomas.

with his troops, he assailed the enemy, who were drawn up upon the crest of a hill. We went at them with the same maneuver adopted at Middletown, and drove the enemy back in great confusion."*

In referring to the first charge of Ashby's cavalry, with Chew's guns, Jackson, in his official report, wrote: "In a few moments the turnpike, which just before had teemed with life, presented a most appalling spectacle of carnage and destruction. The road was literally obstructed with the mingled and confused mass of struggling and dying horses and riders. Amongst the survivors, the wildest confusion ensued, and they scattered in disorder in various directions, leaving some 200 prisoners in the hands of the Confederates."

Col. Chew recently gave the author a verbal and a more detailed account of the affair, stating that he was utterly amazed when Ashby told him to charge with the guns and that he hardly had time to consider the order before it was to be executed, the command and the time of execution being almost simultaneous. Forming behind a thin line of cavalry, the guns moved off at a gallop, the troopers passing to the flanks as the guns unlimbered and went into action. The enemy, unable to discern the guns at first, and seeing but a few troopers, were dumfounded when they perceived their peril and became panic stricken upon the first discharge of the "Blakely," and the bursting of a shell.

Writing of subsequent charges of the Horse Artillery, Col. Chew says:

"In 1864, when I commanded the Horse Artillery, we joined Rosser on the Cartharpin Road. He was engaged with Wilson's Division, cavalry, and, immediately after we joined him, we charged the enemy with his brigade. I carried Thomson's Battery into the charge with the cavalry, and, after Rosser had struck the head of their column, we threw the guns into position, and did fine execution. The next day at Rose's farm, when Stuart was in command, we went into the fight with the cavalry again. This was often done by the Horse Artillery in subsequent fights."†

*The incident as narrated is also declared to be correct by Col. W. T. Poague, who commanded the Rockbridge Battery at the time, and who is now an officer of the Virginia Military Institute with the author.
†Same personal letter hereinbefore referred to.

Such action on the part of horse artillery was as novel as it was effective, but it must be admitted its proper execution required extraordinary qualities. True, the chief duties of horse artillery, then as it now is and always has been, was to stay with the cavalry at all costs, and coöperate with it by preparing the road for its advance and retarding pursuers, but having prepared the road, it was never before contemplated that the gunners should accompany the troopers to the assault. The feats of Chew with his battery excelled even those of the horse gunner, Kostenetski, at Austerlitz, and more than fulfilled the maxim of Napoleon, that "Horse Artillery and Cavalry must be the complements, the one of the other"; and of Leer, that "Horse Artillery must be Cavalry with guns."

The Prussian Horse Artillery, of 1866, was considered by the greatest artillery authority on the continent to have done its full duty when it moved into position, perhaps the last 500 yards at a gallop, and silenced the enemy's guns in the artillery duel preceding the charge of its cavalry.* And, later, when rifled pieces were generally introduced into the horse batteries, it was not deemed necessary for them to approach as close to the enemy as before. In comparison with the Prussian ideas, Ashby's innovation was, to say the least, a radical one.

The limited scope of such a work as this is designed to be precludes the possibility of following in detail the performances of Jackson's gunners, which, while in innumerable instances quite remarkable, displayed few departures from the tactical principles of the time. For an intimate knowledge of officers, men, and conditions of the Artillery of the Army of the Valley, one must consult the numerous delightful works to be had, dealing with the minutia of the service.†

---

*Letters on Artillery, Hohenlohe, p. 144.
†Three Years in the Confederate Horse Artillery, Neese; The Story of a Cannoneer Under Stonewall Jackson, Moore; The Laurel Brigade, McDonald; Ashby and His Compeers, Avirett; Ashby and His Men, Thomas. For full and accurate accounts of Jackson's campaigns, see Jackson's Valley Campaign, Allan; and Stonewall Jackson, Henderson.

It is interesting, however, to note the comparative strength in personnel and guns of the artillery of Jackson and his various opponents.

At Kernstown, Jackson had with him 27 pieces of artillery, 18 of which only were engaged, while Shields had in command of Lieut.-Col. Philip Daum, Jenks' and Davis' brigade batteries, and Clark's regular battery, with a total of 24 guns. In this engagement, Carpenter's, McLaughlin's, and Waters' batteries, silenced the main body of the Federal guns and were withdrawn only as a result of Garnett's untimely retreat. The Confederate batteries on this occasion were divided between the two flanks of the infantry line, and the Federal batteries, 5 in number, occupied 5 quite distinct positions, and of course with the available lines of communication, were capable of little concert of action.

The massed fire of batteries contemplates more than proximity of position of guns. At Kernstown there was neither concentration of fire nor proximity of position, a number of the batteries on both sides merely having the same target. There is nothing to lead us to believe that the fire of the three batteries which Jackson placed on his right was even expected to be directed with any definite purpose, except to do the most harm possible to the enemy.

When Garnett fell back from his position near Jackson's main group of artillery on the right, a swarm of Federal skirmishers in the thickets fired upon the batteries, severely punishing them before they withdrew. In limbering up one of the 6-pounders was overturned, and as some of the enemy's infantry was already within 50 paces, the sergeant in charge cut loose the remaining three horses, the gun being abandoned to the enemy. Jackson had, therefore, lost three pieces of artillery, including the two guns captured from Cutshaw at Romney.

In the battle of Kernstown, the artillery personnel engaged was, Federal 608, and Confederate about 200.* The latter suffered a loss of 17 wounded and 1 missing, the former, killed 4, wounded 2.†

---

*For Federal strength, see *Rebellion Records*, Vol. XII, Part III, p. 4.
†*Stonewall Jackson*, Henderson, p. 262. *Battles and Leaders*, Vol. II, p. 299.

Soon after the battle of McDowell, in which there was no good opportunity to employ artillery, Gen. Jackson applied to have Lieut.-Col. Stapleton Crutchfield, of the 58th Virginia Infantry, assigned to him as Chief of Artillery. This officer had the previous Spring been assigned to duty as a major of the 9th Virginia Artillery, stationed at Craney Island near Norfolk, but not liking the monotony of coast defense duty, he had transferred to a more active branch. Crutchfield was just twenty-six years of age when he became Jackson's Chief of Artillery, but their relations were born of mutual confidence in one another. Not only had the young officer been a pupil of Jackson's at the Virginia Military Institute, graduating first in the Class of 1855, but he had served as an assistant professor of mathematics in the faculty of the school for six years with the man who was now to be his commander.

May 21, Jackson's force was largely increased by the union of his own division with that of Gen. Ewell, to which was attached Courtney's and Brockenbrough's batteries, the Army of the Valley now numbering about 1,600, including an artillery personnel of from 300 to 400.* The artillery with the Army at the time of the battle of Winchester was composed of the following batteries:

Poague's Battery, 6 guns; Carpenter's Battery, 4 guns; Cutshaw's Battery, 4 guns; Wooding's Battery, 4 guns; Caskie's Battery, 4 guns; Raine's Battery, 4 guns; Rice's Battery, 4 guns; Lusk's Battery, 4 guns; Courtney's Battery, 6 guns; Brockenbrough's Battery, 4 guns; Chew's Battery, 3 guns; total pieces of artillery, 47 guns.†

The Federal force at Strasburg, under Banks at this time, numbered between 6,000 and 7,000 men, including 3 batteries with a personnel of about 280 and an armament of ten 3-inch Parrott rifles, and six S. B. 6-

---

*Jackson's Valley Campaign, Allan, p. 93.
†Jackson's Valley Campaign, Allan, pp. 91, 92, 93, 108, 109, 111. Chew's Battery did not have four pieces as stated by Col. Allan. Poague's (Rockbridge) Battery, formerly commanded by Pendleton, then McLaughlin, had had 8 guns for some time, but 6 in May.

pounders. Jackson had captured the two 10-pounder Parrott rifles of Knapp's Battery at Front Royal, on the 22d of May, thus collecting the debt which the enemy owed him for the 3 guns he had lost.*

In the battle of Winchester, while the Confederates were greatly superior to Banks in artillery, as well as in infantry, 2 well-placed Federal batteries with rifled pieces, and a loss of but 2 killed, 14 wounded, and 12 missing, severely punished 3 batteries, Poague's, Carpenter's, and Cutshaw's, with which Jackson engaged them in a duel, the first alone losing 2 officers, 16 men, and 9 horses; the second, 1 officer, and 5 men. The Federal batteries were assisted to some extent by their skirmishers, who effectually harassed the Confederate gunners, but the great damage sustained by Poague's Battery was due to the fact that one of the Federal batteries skillfully changed position, supported by an infantry regiment, and enfiladed it. Yet, the fact remains that acting more or less together in their duel with Banks' guns, the three Confederate batteries almost entirely diverted the artillery fire of the enemy from the infantry, thus enabling Taylor's and Winder's men to charge home and win the day.

But the question naturally arises, if Banks had but 3 batteries and Jackson had 8, besides the two on the right with Ewell, and the horse battery off with Ashby, where were the five disengaged batteries? Surely they were not all being engaged by the remaining Federal battery of 6 pieces. It is quite plain now to see that with such a superiority in the number of guns, Jackson should not have allowed a few of his batteries to do all the work, but should have smothered the enemy's fire early in the day with the combined, or we should say, the simultaneous fire of every available gun, not only saving his batteries, but his infantry as well. The error committed by Jackson in this respect was one repeatedly committed by the Prussians in 1866, who did not under-

*Jackson's Valley Campaign, Allan, pp. 94, 109. These were Best's Battery, 6 guns; Cothran's Battery, 6 guns; and Hampton's Battery, 4 guns. Ibid., pp. 96, 98.

stand how to bring up their guns to the front, a lesson which the Austrians had learned in 1859, and applied throughout the war with disastrous results to their enemy. But, if the manner of the employment of his artillery was faulty in the engagement itself, the manner in which he caused two of his batteries to hang upon the heels of the retreating enemy is especially worthy of praise, the Potomac alone stopping the batteries which had suffered the most. Indeed, one is constantly surprised at the remarkable mobility and pertinacity of Poague's and Carpenter's batteries, which had won for themselves the name of the Stonewall Artillery, fitting companions of the Stonewall Brigade, acting on more than one occasion with Ashby's horse artillery.

The main difference between the artillery fire at Kernstown and Winchester, was in the range at which the guns fought in the two battles. At Kernstown, the opposing batteries certainly did not approach each other at any stage of the battle, nearer than one mile and much of their fire was delivered at a range of over 2,500 yards. On the other hand, at Winchester, the artillery duel between Poague's, Cutshaw's, and Carpenter's batteries, and the two Federal batteries, was conducted at a short range even for that period, not exceeding 800 yards in the main, and for some of the batteries as close as 500 yards. This sudden drawing together of the two artilleries was undoubtedly due more to the configuration of the terrain, than to any desire to develop the fire of the guns at a decisive range. Then, too, artilery positions were determined to a large extent by considerations for the supporting infantry, as well as for the guns, a feature which has become less important as the range of the latter has increased, since batteries with long range guns can secure great effect at distances which forbid the idea of a serious fire fight between infantry. In 1862, before infantry received its support from the guns, it had first to support them. Improved material, however, enabled the artillery to give the infantry effective support, more or less independently

of the position of the latter, and the batteries now are
expected to enter the zone of effective infantry fire only
after the opposing artillery has been silenced and their
own infantry has advanced to the assault, masking to a
large extent the fire of the guns which have helped them
forward. During this phase of the combat it is assumed
that either the infantry will divert the musketry fire of
the enemy from its guns, enabling the latter to move
up to a decisive range, or that if the defenders neglect
the assaulting infantry, the guns by receiving the fire
will make it all the easier for the assaulting infantry to
reach the position of the enemy. In either case, the
artillery will do its part, but the former will be the general result of the modern method of attack, when the
guns of the offense have obtained a superiority over
those of the defense.

In the battles of Port Republic and Cross Keys,
Crutchfield's artillery consisted of 6 batteries, Carpen-
ter's, Caskie's, Cutshaw's, Wooding's, Poague's, and
Carrington's, with a total personnel of about 300 men,
the last having joined since the battle of Winchester.
Only 5 batteries were actually engaged.* Ewell's Di-
vision had in addition to Brockenbrough's Baltimore
Battery, attached to the Maryland line under Steuart,
4 batteries, Latimer's Courtney, Lusk's, Raine's, and
Rice's. Thus, exclusive of Chew's Battery (under
Munford since Ashby's death), Jackson had 11 batteries
with a total personnel of about 600 men, and 48 guns.

In the two engagements the losses of the Confederate
Artillery were 8 killed, 29 wounded, and 9 missing, a
total of but 46.

Shields' Division at Port Republic had 16 guns, the
batteries being the same as at Winchester under Daum.
These batteries fought with great gallantry, losing 31
men, and 7 of their guns in hand-to-hand encounters
with the Confederate Infantry after having all but
routed the attackers before the latter were reënforced.
But if anything, they had by far the worst of the artillery

---

*Stonewall Jackson, Henderson, p. 474; Battles and Leaders, Vol. II, p. 301;
Jackson's Valley Campaign, Allan, p. 145, et seq.

fight proper, though they were most skillfully disposed, about half being placed on a wooded mountain side.

Fremont's artillery consisted of 10 batteries which, arriving with their supine leader, were overwhelmed by the Confederate guns, occupying as they did a most favorable position.

At Cross Keys, the batteries of Courtney, Lusk, Brockenbrough, and Raines, were massed in the center of Ewell's line and acted more in concert than artillery had hitherto done in the campaign. Their fire was well conducted, with all the advantages of position to which artillery is entitled by a prior selection for the defense of a given point.

At Port Republic, Wooding's, Poague's, and Carpenter's batteries, in position on the north bluff of the river, safe from infantry attack, the brigade being defended by Carrington's guns, exerted by a well-directed fire great influence upon the issue, raking the Federal Infantry with deadly effect, and playing upon Daum's guns whenever an opportunity to shift from the infantry was allowed them. The employment of the artillery at Port Republic and Cross Keys evidences a growing tendency on the part of Jackson to use his batteries, to a certain extent, in concert, instead of distributing them here and there on the battlefield with his brigades, and thereby dissipating the effect of their fire.

Early in the war, the Confederate Bureau of Ordnance had developed a 2.25-inch mountain rifle, which was transported in parts on the backs of mules, much after the present system of mountain artillery. There was also a 12-pounder mountain howitzer, of the model of 1841, in use in the service, though but few pieces of ordnance of this character were ever placed in the field. For occasional draught, when the roads permitted, the gun carriage was provided with a thill, which was attached to the same saddle that carried the pack.* A mule battery of 12-pounder mountain

---

*See pp. 9, 49, *Ordnance Manual*, C. S. A., 1863, and plate 6.

howitzers, in command of Maj. Imboden, reported to Jackson just before the action of Port Republic, but did not accomplish much in the way of results by reason of the conduct of the mules under fire. Their loads weighing about 300 pounds were so securely attached to them, that they resorted to the tactics of rolling on the ground to free themselves, and the gunners were principally occupied in holding down the recalcitrant mules, rather than delivering a fire upon the enemy.* But while the battery did not accomplish much from a military standpoint, it afforded rare amusement to the men of the Infantry. With the air of men seeking technical information, they would seriously inquire whether the mules or the guns were intended to go off first, and whether the gun was to fire the mule, or the mule the gun.† In the estimate of Jackson's artillery at Port Republic, Imboden's Battery was not included, for under the circumstances its guns could not be properly classed as effective ordnance.

In the Valley campaign the Confederate Artillery as a whole demonstrated its mobility beyond a question. It had been constantly engaged in fighting and marching for many days, pitted always against superior material. Yet, it had lost but 3 pieces, while the enemy lost 9. An unusual proportion of its officers subsequently attained higher rank, the experience they had gained in the Valley proving of great service to the Army as a whole.

---

*A 3-inch rifled Parrott gun which Imboden had brought with him was turned over to Poague's Battery at Port Republic.
†*Battles and Leaders,* Vol. II, p. 291, *et seq.; Stonewall Jackson,* Henderson, Vol. V., p. 465.

CHAPTER XI

THE PENINSULA CAMPAIGN

THE details of the movement of the Artillery down the Peninsula to Yorktown are simply those of monotonous marches day after day, through sand and mud, till men and beasts were exhausted. But, on this long and arduous march, the light batteries were well seasoned to work the character of which always tends to the elimination of surplus train, and the weaker element of the personnel. It was the first duty of· this kind which the Field Artillery, except that in the Valley, had been called upon to perform.

In front of Yorktown McClellan had established siege batteries, mounting 71 guns, including two 200-pounder, and five 100-pounder rifles, and a number of 13-inch mortars, with which to overwhelm Magruder's weak lines. On May 1, his batteries opened fire. To oppose the Federal land force, Magruder had mounted in his works about 15 nondescript pieces of ordnance, including a number of field guns, for which there were from 30 to 60 rounds of ammunition, according to the caliber of the pieces.* Desperate efforts were now made to transfer some of the heavier ordnance from the water batteries to the land side of the defenses.

The Army of the Peninsula, or the right wing of the Army of Northern Virginia, numbering 22,740 men of all arms, on April 23, 1862, included a field artillery personnel of 646, with 49 pieces, and a heavy artillery brigade of 697 men.† With such a deficiency of artillery, both as to men and material, Johnston never once contemplated risking siege operations at Yorktown, although on the 18th he had brought up the left wing and had reorganized his army, placing it in position behind the lines already established. The right of

---

*Rebellion Records, Series I, Vol. XI, Part III, pp. 438, 439, 447.
†Ibid., p. 460.

the position commencing at Dam No. 1, and extending
to the Warwick River, was assigned to Magruder;
Yorktown proper to D. H. Hill; the center to Longstreet; and the reserve to G. W. Smith. With the last
was the reserve artillery.*

May 2, the artillery, except the heavy guns, was
ordered to be quietly withdrawn from the lines after
sunset, and put in motion for Williamsburg,† and on
May 3, the entire Army began to retire before the
enemy up the Peninsula.

The artillery at this time was quite dependent upon
infantry supports, even on the march. Magruder's
battle orders, he himself having been an artilleryman,
prescribed that commanding officers should always
designate a sufficient force of infantry to protect the
guns in action, and that in all marches, whether to the
front or rear, the artillery should be placed at intervals
in the infantry columns. In marching on narrow roads,
brigade batteries were to be split up into sections, one
moving near the rear of the brigade to which its battery
belonged. If a column were attacked in retreat, the
practice was for the cavalry and infantry to leave the
road in order to allow the rear guns a clear field of fire,
and in the event the enemy's cavalry undertook to
charge the guns, the infantry formed a square, or
circle, about them at charge bayonets, firing when necessary.‡ Such dispositions were induced mainly by
the closeness of the country in which the Army of the
Peninsula was operating and were generally adhered
to in that section.

The retrograde movement of the Artillery from Yorktown was attended with the utmost difficulty and hardship. Execrable weather had rendered the roads all
but bottomless, and without the constant assistance of
the infantry commands, the gunners would have been
utterly unable to save their pieces from the mires and
later from the enemy. No march of artillery was ever,

*Rebellion Records, Series I, Vol. XI, Part III, p. 448, G. O. No. 1.
†Ibid., p. 489, General Order.
‡Ibid., p. 410, G. O. No. 168.

perhaps, made under more adverse conditions, for the route of the Army lay over roads which were delusions as highways. Horses for the additional guns taken from the Yorktown defenses were sadly lacking, and not even those of the cavalry, the personal property of the men themselves, were available for purposes of draught. Thus, the worn-out teams of the light batteries, already much reduced by the march of the preceding week, were called upon for the most unreasonable exertions. Sunday night, the 4th, the Reserve Artillery had reached Hickory Neck Church, and by the most tremendous efforts succeeded in reaching Barhamsville on the 5th. On that day occurred the fight at Williamsburg, in which nothing of special import concerning the artillery of either army took place, except that Hooker and Smith lost 12 pieces of artillery and young Capt. John Pelham of Stuart's horse battery greatly distinguished himself for daring. In this affair, a detaining engagement on the part of the Confederates for the purpose of saving their trains, the Confederate Artillery played a minor rôle and only the brigade batteries were present.

During the retreat, Gen. Rains, commanding the rear guard of Johnston's Army, had placed in the path of the pursuers an explosive shell which caused consternation among the enemy, and violent protests on the part of the Federal authorities. The actual result had been slight, however, yet, the practice led to an almost immediate investigation by Gen. Johnston.* In a communication, he took occasion to say: "It is the desire of the Major-General commanding that you put no shells or torpedoes behind you, as he does not recognize it as proper or effective method of war." On this communication were endorsed the following remarks:

"A shell which can be prepared and unprepared in a moment, and a sentinel to keep our own people off, are all that is wanted for our protection.

*Rebellion Records, Series I, Vol. XI, Part II, pp. 509, 510, 516.

"Our volunteers cannot be restrained from firing their guns when they ought not, and so frequent is this fault that the small report of a gun of a sentinel, as a rifle, for instance, is not heeded, and our troops liable to surprise and destruction, of which we have had three notable cases. A shell prepared would remedy this, for the advancing enemy would explode it, and that would lessen their force, demoralize their troops, and give us time with loud warning to prepare for the conflict. As it is, I am compelled to approximate to the same results—to send forward a picket of artillery, supported by infantry, which is liable to be cut off, and have our men killed or captured by such rigid philanthropy for the enemy, which I have myself possessed until lately.

"These shells give us decided advantage over the foe invading our soil, especially in frustrating night surprises, requiring but little powder for great results in checking advancing columns at all times.

"For their being proper for war, they are as much so as ambuscades, masked batteries, and mines. The enemy, I learn, intended to mine and blow up Redoubt No. 4, known as Ft. Magruder, at Yorktown; and if such means of killing by wholesale be proper, why should not smaller mines be used? Can we accord to them alone the privilege of using against us those vast supplies of gunpowder for which they have raked the world, by advantages derived from a navy much of which properly belongs to us? For their effectiveness, I refer to the enemy.

"Believing as I do the vast advantages to our country to be gained from this invention, I am unwilling to forego it, and beg leave to appeal direct to the War Department.

"I have the honor to be very respectfully, etc.,

"C. J. Rains,
"*Brigadier-General, Commanding Brigade
in the Field, near Richmond.*"

"Respectfully forwarded.

"In my opinion all means of destroying our brutal enemies are lawful and proper.

"D. H. Hill,
"*Major-General.*"

"HEADQUARTERS, DEPARTMENT OF NORTHERN VA.,

"NEAR CROSS ROADS, May 12, 1862.

"MAJ.-GEN. D. H. HILL.

"GENERAL—Gen. Johnston desires that you inquire into the enclosed report, taken from the *New York Herald,* to ascertain if there is any truth in the statement, to find out if there were any torpedoes placed, and, if so, when, where, and by whom.

"Most respectfully,

"Your obedient servant,

"A. P. MASON,

"*Asst. Adjutant-General.*

"P. S.—The works where the enemy say the torpedoes were placed were those at Yorktown."

(INCLOSURE)

"Torpedoes."

(Extract from Gen. McClellan's report):

"The rebels have been guilty of the most murderous and barbarous conduct in placing torpedoes within the abandoned works, near wells, and springs, and near flag staffs, magazines, and telegraph offices, in carpet-bags, barrels of flour, etc.

"We have not lost many men in this manner—some four or five killed and perhaps a dozen wounded. I shall make the prisoners move them at their own peril."

This letter was referred by Gen. Hill to Gen. Rains in much the same manner as in his indorsement before set forth, the latter being referred to the Secretary of War,* who returned the same with the following remarks:

INDORSEMENT

"Whether shells planted in roads or parapets, are contrary to usages of war depends upon the purpose with which they are used.

"It is not admissible in civilized warfare to take life with no other object than the destruction of life. Hence it is inadmissible to shoot sentinels and pickets, because nothing is attained but the destruction of life. It would be admissible, however, to shoot a general, because you not only take a life but deprive an army of its head.

---

*Major G. W. Randolph, formerly in command of the Richmond Howitzer Battalion.

"It is admissible to plant shells in a parapet to repel an assault, or in a road to check a pursuit, because the object is to save the work in one case, and the army in the other.

"It is not admissible to plant shells merely to destroy life and without other design than that of depriving your enemy of a few men, without materially injuring him.

"It is admissible to plant torpedoes in a river or harbor, because they drive off blockading or attacking fleets.

"As Gens. Rains and Longstreet differ in this matter, the inferior in rank should give way, or, if he prefers it, he may be assigned river defenses, where such things are clearly admissible.

"G. W. RANDOLPH."

In answer to the communication of May 12, referred to him by Gen. Hill, Gen. Rains wrote as follows:

"CAMP, REAR GUARD, May 14, 1862.

"MAJ.-GEN. HILL,
          "Commanding Third Division.

"GENERAL—Yours of yesterday is acknowledged, and in answer I beg leave to recall to your mind that my command was the first to leave Yorktown by your order, and consequently I know nothing of the location of torpedoes at the places mentioned, nor do I believe it, as wells, or springs of water, barrels of flour, carpet-bags, etc., are places incompatible with the invention.

"That invention is strictly mine, as well as the essential parts of Colt's weapons, for the use of which I have never been called to account.

"If it be required to know what use I have made of the invention, I answer I commanded at Yorktown for the last seven months, and when Gen. McClellan approached with his army of 100,000 men and opened his cannon upon us, I had but 2,500 in garrison, and our whole Army on the Peninsula under Maj.-Gen. Magruder amounted to but 9,300 effective men; then, at a salient angle, an accessible point of our works, as part of the defenses thereof, I had the land mined with the weapons alluded to, to destroy assailants and prevent escalade. Subsequently, with a similar view, they were placed at spots I never saw.

"And, again, when at Williamsburg we were ordered to turn upon our assailants and combat them, which we did successfully, most of us without food for forty-eight hours, having stood all night in the rain without fire or light, the second of our vigils, cold and drenched to the skin, we took up our line of march to the rear by order, and when physical endurance had been taxed to the utmost, at a place of mud slushes, where it was impossible for us to fight or bring a single cannon to bear, some six or seven miles this side of Williamsburg, my command forming the rear guard of the army, and the enemy advancing upon our wearied and scattered troops, firing his cannon along the road, some four small shells found abandoned by our artillery were hastily prepared by my efforts and put in the road near a tree felled across, mainly to have a moral effect in checking the advance of the enemy (for they were too small to do more), to save our sick, wounded, and enfeebled, who straggled in our rear.

"Finally, I conclude by stating that the enemy's vessels approached Yorktown April 6, 1862, and without a word of warning to innocent women and children, as at New Berne, N. C., my native place, they commenced to pitch into the town, at a distance of four miles, entirely beyond the range of our guns, massive beams of iron 18 feet long, and enormous shells (which they continued for a month), both by day and even at the hour of midnight, bursting with awful noise and scattering their death-dealing fragments among the innocent and unoffending; fiendish acts unknown among civilized nations, reversing the scriptural text that it is better for ninety-nine guilty persons to escape than for one innocent to suffer.

"Very respectfully, your obedient servant,

"C. J. RAINS,
"*Brigadier-General, Commanding Brigade, Rear Guard.*"

The merits of Rains' argument cannot be discussed here. The facts have been set forth in full merely to controvert the exaggerations emanating from Mc-Clellan, and it is suggested that the enforced removal of the torpedoes, mines, shells,—whatever they were—by prisoners of war as described by him in such merry vain was, perhaps, as great a breach of the rules of civilized warfare as the use of the objectionable explosives by the Confederates. The equitable principle that "he who comes into court must do so with clean hands" applies to military as well as to civil cases. The foregoing correspondence should forever acquit the Confederate authorities from the charge that they resorted to foul practice on this occasion, or failed to take immediate steps to discontinue a questionable practice, which to the minds of many was admissible in war.

May 7, the artillery train reached New Kent Court House, after resting the 6th while waiting for the Army to catch up. Meantime, Pendleton had heard of the movement of the enemy along the York River. On the

9th, the Army had reached the north bank of the
Chickahominy and had escaped the Peninsula trap, as
it was thought by all to be.* Thus we see that the Confederate Army had actually returned in the course of a
few days to the locality which Pendleton had hitherto
declared the only suitable point for successful resistance.

The *morale* of the Federal Army had been maintained
at a high pitch in spite of the weather conditions by
reason of the almost uninterrupted advance upon
Richmond, while that of Johnston's Army had most
certainly been depressed by the retrograde movement
and the exertions incident to the retreat. But the news
of Jackson's exploits at Cross Keys and Port Republic
now arrived to cheer the drooping spirits of the Confederates and counteract the influences mentioned, as
well as to increase McClellan's uncertainty due to the
constant interference with his movements by the timid
Administration in Washington. It is impossible even to
estimate the importance of such moral factors in the
game of war. To trace a campaign, without according
them much weight, is, as Clausewitz constantly points
out, but to mislead one's self. Indeed they supply the
reason for the delays as well as the motive for the
various moves, on the part of the opposing commanders.
They sharpen the edge of the weapon of the one, while
they dull that of the other adversary. It was under
the influence of just such conditions that McClellan and
Johnston were feeling for their openings in the impenetrable fastness of the Chickahominy Valley, the former
now in the mire, the latter with his feet on firmer
ground.

When the Army was reorganized at Yorktown, the
light batteries were disposed as follows:†

RIGHT OF POSITION (Magruder)

FIRST DIVISION (McLaws)

McLaws' Brigade—

Garrett's Williamsburg Battery_____	50 men
Young's Norfolk Battery _____	57 men

---

*Memoirs of W. N. Pendleton, Lee, p. 183.
†Rebellion Records, Series I. Vol. XI, Part III, pp. 479, 485, April 30, 1862.

Griffith's Brigade—

    Cosnahan's Peninsula Battery_____ 51 men
    McCarthy's Richmond Howitzer Battery_____ 103 men
    Manly's North Carolina Battery_____ 37 men
    Read's Georgia Battery_____ 72 men
    Sands' Henrico Battery_____ 80 men

Kershaw's Brigade—

    Kemper's Alexandria Battery_____ 77 men

Cobb's Brigade—

    Page's Morris Louisa Battery_____ 48 men

SECOND DIVISION (Toombs)

Toombs' and Semnes' Brigades, no batteries

FORCE AT WILLIAMSBURG (B. S. Ewell)

No light batteries, but 621 heavy artillerymen

CENTER OF POSITION (Longstreet)

A. P. Hill's Brigade—

    Rogers' Loudoun Battery_____ 62 men

R. H. Anderson's Brigade—

    Stribling's Fauquier Battery_____ 68 men

Colston's Brigade—

    No batteries _____ 00 men

Pickett's Brigade—

    Dearing's Lynchburg Battery_____ 60 men

Wilcox's Brigade—

    Stanard's Richmond Howitzer Battery_____ 60 men

Pryor's Brigade—

    Macon's Richmond Fayette Battery_____ 60 men

LEFT OF POSITION (D. H. Hill)

EARLY'S DIVISION

Early's Brigade—

    Jeff Davis Alabama Battery_____ 80 men

Rodes' Brigade—

    Carter's King William Battery_____ 80 men

RAINS' DIVISION

Rains' Brigade—
Nineteen Heavy Batteries----------------------- 1,151 men

Featherston's Brigade—
No batteries ----------------------------------- 00 men

Crump's Force at Gloucester Point—
Armistead's Mathews Battery------------------- 46 men
Battalion Heavy Artillery--------------------- 332 men

RESERVE (G. W. Smith)

WHITING'S DIVISION

Whiting's Brigade—
Imboden's Staunton Battery-------------------- 111 men
Reilly's North Carolina Battery--------------- 132 men

Hood's Brigade—
No batteries ----------------------------------- 00 men

Hampton's Brigade—
Moody's Louisiana Battery--------------------- 72 men

S. R. Anderson's Brigade—
Braxton's Fredericksburg Battery-------------- 50 men

Pettigrew's Brigade—
Andrews' 1st Maryland Battery----------------- 130 men

Cavalry Brigade—
Stuart Horse Artillery (1 battery, Capt. John
Pelham) ------------------------------------ 141 men

RESERVE ARTILLERY (Pendleton)

Pendleton's Corps (10 batteries), 36 pieces ⎫
Walton's Corps (Washington Artillery Battalion, ⎬ 1,050 men
4 batteries), 20 pieces ⎭

The foregoing figures are instructive. With the brigades were 23 light batteries, with a total personnel of 1,727, or with an average strength of 75 men. With the Reserve Artillery were 14 batteries.* Allowing each battery 75 men, the personnel of the Reserve Ar-

*Memoirs of W. N. Pendleton, Lee, pp. 184-5.

tillery numbered 1,050. The total field artillery personnel of the Army then numbered at this time 2,777, very unequally distributed among 37 batteries, with an average of 4 pieces each, or a total of 152 guns. There was absolutely no equality of distribution of guns, with respect to divisions and brigades. In Magruder's command consisting of 16,106 men, exclusive of heavy and light artillery personnel, there were 9 light batteries, or about 36 guns, a proportion of slightly over 2 guns per 1,000 men of the other arms, the field artillery personnel numbering 575. To the center, or Longstreet's command, numbering 13,506 men exclusive of a field artillery personnel of 310, were assigned 5 light batteries with about 20 guns, a proportion of less than 1.5 guns per 1,000 men. The left, or Hill's command, exclusive of 1,483 heavy, and 206 field, artillerymen numbered 10,945 men. With this portion of the Army were but 3 light batteries, or 12 guns, a proportion of about 1 gun per 1,000 men.* With the reserve division under G. W. Smith, were 5 field batteries with a total personnel of 520 and 20 guns. Smith's command, exclusive of his artillerymen, numbered 10,072 men. The proportion of guns was therefore about 2 per 1,000 men. Stuart's cavalry brigade numbered 1,148 men, and with it he had Capt. John Pelham's horse battery of 141 men and 8 pieces.† The proportion of horse guns to cavalry was, therefore, about 8 per 1,000 men. This battery was the second horse battery to be organized in the Army of Northern Virginia, and had been assigned to Stuart with his original brigade in December, 1861. It was always spoken of as the "Stuart Horse Artillery," a name given it at first to distinguish it from Ashby's or Chew's Battery in the Valley with Jackson. It was commanded after Pelham's death by the gallant Breathed.

Johnston's return of April 30, 1862, shows a total strength for his army, exclusive of the Reserve Artillery,

---

*Naturally a small proportion by reason of the fact that the command was largely assigned to fortifications, in which were mounted the heavy guns.
†See Pelham's Report of Battle of Williamsburg, *Rebellion Records.*

of 55,633 men. If from that number, 2,104 heavy artillerymen, 1,727 field artillerymen, and 1,289 men of
the cavalry brigade, including Pelham's Battery, be
deducted, or a total of 5,120, it appears that the infantry
force must have been 50,513. Since the total number
of his field guns, exclusive of those of the horse battery,
was 144, the general proportion of guns to infantry was
less than 3 per 1,000 men.

It is not so much for the strength of his field artillery
as for its loose distribution that fault is to be found with
Johnston, a condition which extended to the other arms
of his command, and which very justly led to constant
demands on the part of Mr. Davis, that the Army be
reorganized into divisions and brigades of some degree
of equality as to strength. Johnston, like McClellan,
is often referred to in handsome terms as a soldier of
marked ability for organization. This is undoubtedly
true of them both, and it is not the only point of simi-
larity between the two. But, the fact remains, that the
Army of Northern Virginia in April and May, 1862,
was very poorly hung together, a defect which became
sorely apparent in the jungle of the Peninsula, where
cohesion, of all things, was most to be desired. It must
be said, however, that its organization had been given
it at Yorktown for the specific work of defending the
lines at that point, the topography of which enforced
a distribution entirely unsuited to the subsequent retrograde movement. The conditions to be met in the
one case were entirely in opposition to those of the
other. But, if Johnston intended from the first to fall
back, as he invariably claimed, he should have foreseen
the needs of the future and organized with the certain
contingency of retreat before him. He had been advised from the first by Pendleton, if by no one else, that
a battle, if it were to be fought, must be undertaken near
Richmond, and the character of the terrain in that
quarter was well known to him. It was not until he
reached the Chickahominy that Johnston reorganized

his army into 4 divisions, giving it a somewhat more cohesive character. The artillery is now found distributed as follows:*

FIRST DIVISION (G. W. Smith)

Whiting's Brigade—
　　Imboden's Staunton Battery.

Hampton's Brigade—
　　Moody's Louisiana Battery.

Hood's Brigade—
　　No artillery.

Hatton's Brigade—
　　Braxton's Fredericksburg Battery.

Pettigrew's Brigade—
　　Andrews' 1st Maryland Battery.

Strength of division, 10,592.　Number of guns, 16.

SECOND DIVISION (Longstreet)

A. P. Hill's Brigade—
　　Rogers' Loudoun Battery.

Pickett's Brigade—
　　Dearing's Lynchburg Battery.

R. H. Anderson's Brigade—
　　Stribling's Fauquier Battery.

Colston's Brigade—
　　No artillery.

Wilcox's Brigade—
　　Stanard's Richmond Howitzer Battery.

Pryor's Brigade—
　　Macon's Richmond Fayette Artillery.

Strength of division, 13,816.　Number of guns, 20.

THIRD DIVISION (Magruder)

McLaws' Brigade—
　　Garrett's Williamsburg Battery.

Rebellion Records, Ibid., pp. 530, 533, May 21, 1862.

Cobb's Brigade—
  Page's Morris Louisa Battery.

Kershaw's Brigade—
  Kemper's Alexandria Battery.

Toombs' Brigade—
  No artillery.

Griffith's Brigade—
  McCarthy's Richmond Howitzer Battery.

D. R. Jones' Brigade—
  No artillery.

Strength of division, 15,920.   Number of guns, 16.

FOURTH DIVISION (D. H. Hill)

Early's Brigade—
  Jeff Davis Alabama Battery.

Rodes' Brigade—
  Carter's King William Battery.

Rains' Brigade—
  No artillery.

Crump's Brigade—
  Armistead's Mathews Battery.

Featherston's Brigade—
  No artillery.

Ward's Command—
  No artillery.

Strength of division, 11,151.   Number of guns, 12.

CAVALRY BRIGADE (Stuart)

  Pelham's Horse Battery.

Strength of brigade, 1,289.   Number of guns, 8.

RESERVE ARTILLERY (Pendleton)

Pendleton's Corps, 19 batteries, about 56 guns.
Walton's Battalion, Washington Artillery, 20 guns.
Cabell's Corps (attached to 3d Division).
Cosnahan's Peninsula Battery ⎫
Manly's North Carolina Battery ⎪
Read's Georgia Battery ⎬ 16 guns.
Sands' Henrico Battery ⎭

The foregoing assignment shows a total of 160 guns, bearing a proportion to the entire army strength of 53,688, of about 3 guns per 1,000 men. With the brigades were 64 guns, or a proportion of slightly over 1 gun per 1,000 men, supported by a reserve in 3 sections of 92 guns, and one battery of horse artillery.

Having become familiar with the relative strength of the artillery, it will prove interesting to examine the condition of other armies in this respect.

It has ever been impossible to establish dogmatically the proper proportion of field guns to the other arms, and strictly adhere thereto, for the question depends upon many considerations, such as the theater of operations, the composition of the enemy's forces, the special adaptability of the people of the country to one arm or another, and even upon the casualties in campaign. A comparison of the field armies of the past century will show that the number of guns has generally varied from 2 to 5 to 1,000 infantry, limits which have not been infrequently exceeded. It would appear that the common desire has been to provide from 3 to 4 guns for every 1,000 men of the other arms of the service, but in mountainous or heavy-wooded countries, where operations could only be conducted over a few poor roads, this proportion has quite generally been reduced. For instance, in Lombardy, in 1859, the French found it impossible, owing to the narrow roads and marshy fields, to get all their guns into action, although they had only 3 guns to 1,000 men.* Referring to conditions in the Wilderness Campaign, Gen. Grant wrote: "Artillery is very useful when it can be brought into action, but it is a very burdensome luxury where it cannot be used. Before leaving Spotsylvania, therefore, I sent back to the defenses of Washington over 100 pieces of artillery, with the horses and caissons. This relieved the road over which we were to march of more than 200 six-horse teams, and still left us more artillery than could be advantageously used."†

---

*Organization and Tactics, Wagner, p. 12.
†Memoirs, U. S. Grant, Vol. II, p. 241.

In Sherman's march to the sea, and in his subsequent campaign in the Carolinas, his artillery was reduced to 1 gun to every 1,000 men of the other arms, the reduction being induced by the character of the country, but made possible by the deficiency in the enemy's artillery. The broad and hard chaussées of France enabled the Germans in 1870 to maintain a proportion of 4 guns to 1,000 men, their artillery being always on hand when needed and rendering splendid service.

Due to the fact that losses are generally heavier in the infantry, no matter how efficient the service of the guns may be, the tendency is for the proportion of the latter to increase towards the end of a campaign. The personnel of the artillery may diminish in numbers, but the loss of guns is ordinarily slight. In the Franco-German War, notwithstanding the admirable recruiting methods of the Germans, their army corps were at times reduced to 15,000, or even as low as 7,000 men, while the number of guns remained unchanged. The increased proportion due to depletion is more desirable than otherwise, for an infantry weak in numbers, or in *morale* due to depressing losses, more than ever needs the support of a large and efficient artillery.

While, therefore, it is impossible definitely to fix the proportion of artillery to the other troops, it may be safely prescribed that guns with an army should be as many as there is prospect of being effectively employed on the field of battle.* Malvern Hill and Sedan bear witness that, under favorable circumstances, the fire of artillery may, almost alone, crush the enemy. But the fact should not be lost sight of that the terrible "circle of fire" was made possible by a gallant infantry.

In view of the dense character of the Peninsula country, and the entire absence of any but primitive roads, the available ones being few in number, we are forced to the conclusion that in point of numbers Johnston's, as well as McClellan's, artillery was more than adequate to the work at hand.

Organization and Tactics, Wagner, p. 14. The same is said by Hohenlohe.

Anticipating a great struggle about Richmond, Pendleton had been ordered to place the redoubts and batteries of the lines in condition for effective defense, in addition to his regular work with the field batteries. Much material had been lost during the month of May, and the deficit in the number of horses for the light batteries was appalling. There was little to be expected of field artillery maneuvers about the Chickahominy. All that could be done was to dispose such guns as the terrain permitted in earthworks, near the various crossings, or on the more commanding eminences of the swamps, in support of the infantry lines. The nature of the country was such as to permit McClellan slowly to move his heavy guns up into position, but yet to prevent their successful resistance by the lighter field pieces of his enemy. On one occasion, May 12, the Reserve Artillery had been brought upon the field several miles below Chickahominy bridge to support the infantry in a pending action, but its services were not called for.

On May 30, the battle of the next day, known as Seven Pines, or Fair Oaks, was planned. D. H. Hill had made a reconnaissance which disclosed McClellan's awkward position astride the Chickahominy. On that day the following note was addressed to Gen. Johnston by his Chief of Artillery:

"I venture to offer a suggestion based upon some information respecting the Chickahominy River. It is said to rise immediately after a rain like this, and to continue in flood some twenty-four hours. Would not this seem a providence to place all the Yankee force this side that stream, almost centainly in your power? Might not an active, sudden, and adequate movement of troops to-night and at dawn in the morning so overwhelm the divisions confronting Gen. Hill as to crush and capture them with next to certainty? I submit it with great deference. Your judgment will, I know, determine sagaciously on the subject."*

When this note was written, 7:30 P. M., Pendleton was at Oakwood Cemetery, in the northern environs of Richmond. Shortly after noon that day, Johnston in-

---

*Rebellion Records, Series I, Vol. XI, Part III, p. 685.

formed D. H. Hill that he would lead an attack upon
the enemy next morning.* But at that time the details
of the attack had not been worked out. This was done
by Johnston in conference with Longstreet some time
later in the day. Gen. Alexander states that the conference was prolonged by a violent storm, in which
probably over three inches of rain fell. Pendleton could
not have penned his note until after the rain commenced,
for he refers to the fact of its violent character. The
suggestion was undoubtedly received by Johnston
within two hours after it was written, that is before
10 P. M., and the influence it exerted upon the deliberations of Johnston and Longstreet, coming as it did from
one of Pendleton's character, must be estimated by the
reader. It is possible, of course, that McClellan's
situation at once suggested a similar plan to Johnston
and Longstreet. At any rate, the idea was clearly as
original with Pendleton as with them, a fact which testifies to the ready and accurate military perception of the
Chief of Artillery, who was destined to see the failure
of the plan, which appeared so simple to him. Before
dismissing this point, let us inquire if it is possible that,
receiving Pendleton's suggestion after Longstreet was
dismissed from the conference, Johnston sought to act
upon it, and that Longstreet's failure the next day to cooperate as expected was due to the late alteration of the
plan being imperfectly comprehended by him? This
suggestion is fruitful of many explanations.

The Reserve Artillery took no part in the battle of
Seven Pines, nor were the Confederate brigade
batteries employed with any degree of effect or intelligence. It must be borne in mind, however, that
the artillery had no organization competent to rapid
movements in such a country, no field officers to direct
its batteries, hither and thither in groups as needed, and
that the staff of the Chief of Artillery was entirely deficient in numbers as well as in experience with large
bodies of artillery. In the light of the time, there is

---

*Military Memoirs of a Confederate, Alexander, p. 74.

more to commend than to censure, for not only had the idea of a reserve taken firm root, but this reserve was being steadily increased from time to time, already containing half again as many guns as the total number with the brigades, a fact which to the unprejudiced mind was a presage of the future. Again, let the plea be advanced for a judgment based on conditions as they existed in 1862. Criticism after the event, and in the light of modern days, is of no value whatever, and only serves to muddle history. In his memoirs, a work of great military value, Gen. Alexander is given to this fault.* Writing of the battle of Seven Pines, he says: "Perhaps our greatest deficiency at this period was in the artillery service. None of our batteries were combined into battalions, but each infantry brigade had a battery attached to it. There were no field officers of artillery, charged with combining batteries and massing them to concentrate heavy fire upon important points. There was never greater need or better opportunity for this than in Johnston's battle of the 31st. The enemy had but two batteries, Kirby's and Brady's, and no more were available. They did not receive a single hostile cannon shot, and were able to devote their whole fire to our infantry lines, which in every instance seemed to be finally repulsed, only by heavy canister at close quarters.

"We had no lack of batteries. The roads were full of them, but there was no organization to make them effective. Both roads and open fields were in very miry condition, and all movements would have been slow, but a competent officer by doubling teams could have brought up the guns with little delay."

This last sentence contains rather a caustic criticism. It certainly reacts more on Johnston than on Pendleton, who held his reserve batteries at all times ready for use when called upon. But it is in no small measure a self-accusation, for who better than the Chief of Ordnance of an Army, and in this instance one of the acknow-

*Military Memoirs of a Confederate, E. P. Alexander, p. 90.

ledged authorities of the commanding officer's staff on all matters pertaining to artillery, was better able to employ the guns as they should have been employed? Magruder, equally as able an artilleryman as Alexander had shown himself to be, was in command of a division. Certainly it was not his office to advise Johnston about the employment of the auxiliary arm. Had Alexander really seen such opportunities at the time for the tactical employment of artillery masses, which we now know existed, then he himself as much as any other was to blame for the omissions he complains of. The guns were at hand. He should have urged their being ordered forward at the proper time. Certainly Johnston and Pendleton would not have opposed anything which when explained would so materially have contributed to the success of the Army and the credit of the Artillery. In his usual full and fair account of the Confederate military operations, Col. William Allan, makes no such criticism as does Alexander.*

After the disjointed affair of Seven Pines, every one began to seek for a scapegoat, and one was at last found in Huger. But earnest investigation and search disclosed many facts hitherto disregarded, among them the tactical neglect of the artillery.

Before closing this chapter an anecdote may well be included which throws an interesting light on the conditions of the time. On the retreat from Yorktown to Williamsburg Johnston ordered his cavalry to bring up the rear and help the cannoneers with their guns when necessary. A single piece of a certain battery had become stalled and the Gloucester troop undertook to assist in saving it. Meantime the Federals were streaming over a hill about half a mile distant and already hurrying to seize the gun. In the troop was a young Britisher who wore a monocle and who afforded his

---

*Lieut.-Col. William Allan, Chief Ordnance Officer, Second Corps A. N. V., author of *Chancellorsville, Stonewall Jackson's Valley Campaign*, and *The Army of Northern Virginia in 1862*, has contributed three of the most trustworthy military narratives yet written concerning the Civil War. He is invariably followed by Henderson in preference to all others, and much of Col. Henderson's greatest work is based on Col. Allan's writings.

comrades much amusement with his broad accent. Riding up to his troop commander he said:

"I beg pahdon, Capting, but may I enquire why we are staying here so long?"

"To save this gun," the Captain replied.

"What, that d—n thing," the Englishman enquired in a most puzzled manner.

"Certainly. We can't afford to leave it," said the officer.

"Pahdon me again," rejoined the gentleman with the monocle, "If I ask how much it is worth."

"I suppose about a thousand dollars," answered the Captain.

The Englishman readjusted his monocle in the most deliberate way, looked once more at the approaching enemy who were now popping at the troop, and turning to his officer, said in the most off-hand way:

"Well, Capting, let's move on, I'll give you my check for it at once."

Such were the conceptions of military service which were held by some of the gentry who served in the Confederate ranks at the beginning of the war. But it was not long before these pampered volunteers learned better and became as fine soldiers as ever bore a musket, strode a horse, or swabbed a gun.

CHAPTER XII

JUNE 1, 1862, Robert E. Lee assumed command of the Army of Northern Virginia, Gen. Johnston having been wounded that day. He immediately directed his Chief of Engineers to make a thorough examination of the country in the vicinity of the lines occupied by his army, with a view to ascertaining the best position in which a battle might be brought on, or the advance of the enemy resisted. The commanding points on the line selected were to be promptly prepared for occupation by the field batteries. This order was given June 3. "My object," explained Gen. Lee, "is to make use of every means in our power to strengthen ourselves and to enable us to fight the enemy to the best advantage."* June 5, Gen. Lee suggested the construction of a railroad battery consisting of plated cars and a heavy gun for the purpose of resisting the transportation by the enemy of heavy ordnance over the York River railway. And on the same date he urged that an imported Armstrong breech-loading piece be mounted on wheels and sent forward with a supply of projectiles.† There were at this time in the opinion of Gen. Lee a sufficient number of Parrott rifles with the Army. His main effort was to perfect the batteries already in the field, and the organization of the artillery as a whole, rather than to increase its numbers. Thus, on the 8th, he wrote the Secretary of War discouraging the organization of light batteries in Richmond, and suggesting that the horses and men available there be transferred to other branches of the service, since Beauregard was in no more need of field artillery than he himself was.‡

---

*Rebellion Records, Series I, Vol. XI, Part III, pp. 572, 573.
†Ibid., pp. 574, 575.
‡Ibid., p. 583, Lee states that Beauregard had already sent 150 surplus field pieces to the rear.

The point has now been reached when not only the numbers but the material of the field artillery seemed adequate to the commanding general. More than the necessary number of light batteries were available, and the Bureau of Ordnance was at last prepared to supply more guns than were actually needed in the field. But, as has been said, the artillery organization was most defective, and to the increase of its efficiency, Gen. Lee's attention was at once directed.

June 2, the day after taking command, he sent for Gen. Pendleton, with whom he had been a cadet at West Point, and requested him to continue as Chief of Artillery, and to make every effort to bring that arm of the service up to the fullest possible efficiency. The directions Gen. Lee gave his engineers the following day were significant of his determination to make more use of the guns.

Encouraged by his conference with his new commander, for whom he possessed profound admiration, Gen. Pendleton now set about the task of reorganization. One of the first measures was to complete his staff. His nephew, Dudley D. Pendleton, was appointed his adjutant-general, and George Peterkin, a son of a clerical brother, Bishop Peterkin, was assigned to duty on his staff as aide-de-camp. Edward P. Dandridge was appointed inspector of artillery, with Charles Hatcher, of Richmond, and Thomas N. Randolph, of Clarke County, Virginia, as volunteer aides. His original quartermasters, Maj. John Page, and Capt. William Meade; commissary, Maj. B. L. Wolffe; ordnance officer, Major John C. Barnwell; and medical officer, Dr. Isham Randolph Page, were retained.

With the assistance of a more complete staff, the Chief of Artillery at once undertook the reconnaissance of the Chickahominy lines, to determine upon suitable positions for his guns, in accordance with Gen. Lee's views.

Before the first week of June was over, Gen. Pendleton's reserve corps had been divided into 3 battalions under Col. Cutts, Maj. Richardson, and Maj. Nelson, respectively. With Walton's and Cabell's commands, the Reserve Artillery now consisted of 5 battalions. These battalions were, in the main, camped in different places in rear of the lines, but daily there was some popping away between these and the enemy's guns, a random practice, which resulted only in disclosing the position of the artillery, without accomplishing any material results.

The promptness with which Gen. Pendleton carried out Gen. Lee's instructions to render the artillery as effective as possible was most commendable. With increased independence of action and support, the Chief displayed marked abilities as an organizer, and at once put into effect reforms which his experience and general grasp of the situation enabled him to inaugurate. His letter book shows that as early as June 5 he drafted regulations for the more systematic administration of the artillery, which, being submitted to Gen. Lee, were approved.* Some of Pendleton's more radical ideas, in his own phrasing, were incorporated in *G. O. No. 71,* June 22, 1862, an order by which the new commander sought to overcome many defects in the Army. Those paragraphs relating to the artillery are here quoted:†

"4. The artillery of the army is necessarily so extensively diffused that it becomes essential for its due efficiency there should be in its administration rigid system.

"5. The Chief of Artillery in each division will have charge of all the batteries thereto attached, whether acting with brigades, or held in reserve. A battery duly assigned to a brigade will, until properly relieved, report to and be controlled by the brigade commander. It must also, however, report to and be inspected by the division Chief of Artillery, as he may require. When a brigade battery needs relief it will, when practicable, be made to change place with the division reserve. Should this be impracticable, application, authorized by the division commander, must be made to the army Chief of Artillery for temporary relief from the general reserve.

---

*This book is on file at Washington.
†*Rebellion Records,* Series I, Vol. XI, Part III, p. 612.

6. The army Chief of Artillery will have general charge of that branch of service and special direction of the general reserve. He will, under instructions from the commanding general, see that the batteries are kept in as efficient condition as practicable, and so distributed as to promise the best results. To this end, he will require from the several chiefs of artillery weekly returns exhibiting the condition of each battery, and where it is serving. He will, also, make to the commanding general a tri-monthly report of his entire charge."

These provisions, secured by the initiative of Pendleton alone, establish the claim that his tactical conceptions were well abreast of his time. Not only did he preserve the general army reserve, also possessed by the enemy, but he went further and provided for divisional reserves for the more immediate support of the brigade batteries, and even before the promulgation of Gen. Lee's order, he had organized his general reserve into battalion groups. The creation of this general reserve was a distinct tactical advance for the Confederates, who were by no means slow in profiting by the reforms of McClellan and Barry.

During the reorganization of the Artillery in June, 1862, it was found that many superfluous and quite inefficient heavy artillery companies were stationed in the various redoubts of the Richmond lines. To Pendleton was assigned the task of mustering them out, reducing their officers, and distributing the better men among the troops of the mobile army. A number of new light batteries were also broken up, and their men used to fill the ranks of the seasoned batteries. In the meantime, the divisional reserves had been assigned to position near the lines for use as prescribed in the order regulating the better employment of the Artillery. Anticipating the assault on McClellan's right, the reserve corps was so disposed as to aid in the operations on the north bank of the Chickahominy and to resist any approach of the enemy towards Richmond, also to provide support wherever it might be required.*

*General Lee's Report, *Rebellion Records*, Series I, Vol. XI, Part III. See also letter to Pendleton, Ibid., Part III, p. 686.

There was now a distinct effort on the part of the various division commanders to employ with better advantage the batteries assigned them and the conception of divisional groups for the support of the brigade batteries had taken firm root. On the 17th, Magruder had appointed Lieut.-Col. Stephen D. Lee, Acting Chief of Artillery, of the Right Wing, and had provided for his reserve.

At the beginning of the Seven Days fighting, the field pieces with the various brigades had been generally placed in entrenched positions along the infantry lines, the redoubts for the guns of the reserve battalions, being placed in their immediate rear, and further back the army reserve. It was hoped that with such a disposition of the guns any threatened point might be supported by a heavy fire of artillery, and that any advance of the lines which became expedient might be accompanied with the requisite artillery force.

The efficiency of the field artillery was yet far from satisfactory, as will appear from an analysis of the 14 batteries of Magruder's command.*

Yet, all of the batteries were rated as good by Col. Lee, except 3, which he urged should be sent to the reserve for repairs and refitting. The personnel of the batteries varied in strength from 26 to 121 men, the average personnel being 65 men and 3 officers. Thirteen of the batteries were armed with two 24-pounder and twelve 12-pounder Howitzers, two 24-pounder guns, three 1-pounder guns, six 6-pounder guns, two 6-pounder Parrotts and six 3-inch rifles, or 34 pieces in all, an average armament of less than 3 pieces. One battery had but 1 piece, others had 2, some 3, 4, 5, and 6 pieces. The number of horses varied from 93 to 15 per battery, with an average number of 53.†

Magruder's artillery, at this time, was composed of Carlton's Troup, Jordan's Bedford, Read's Pulaski (Ga.), Brown's Wise, Cosnahan's Peninsula, Lane's

---

*Ibid., p. 688.
†It will be recalled that 84 horses were prescribed for a battery of 6 pieces. Regulation strength, 150 men and 5 officers.

Georgia, Kemper's Alexandria, Page's Magruder, Richardson's James City, Ritter's Henrico, Woolfolk's Ashland, Young's Norfolk, Manly's North Carolina, and Moody's Louisiana batteries.

Longstreet's artillery with a total personnel of 1,600 men, of which number 395 were absent, consisted June 23, of Carter's King William, Nelson's Hanover, Hardaway's Jeff Davis, Clarke's, Peyton's Orange, Huger's Norfolk, Grimes' Portsmouth, Moseley's Richmond Howitzer, Turner's Goochland, Rogers' Loudoun, Stribling's Fauquier, Dearing's Lynchburg, Macon's Richmond Fayette, Anderson's Thomas, Coke's Williamsburg, Watson's, and Chapman's Dixie batteries, 17 in all, the average strength being 94 men.*

With Holmes there were, about this same time, 6 light batteries. According to the report of Col. Deshler, Chief of Artillery of Holmes' Division, French's Battery with 98 men, three 12-pounder howitzers, one Parrott rifle and two 3-inch iron rifles, was excellent in point of efficiency, but the other five, namely, Branch's, Brem's, E. Graham's, Grandy's, and Lloyd's, needed much drilling.† Of a personnel of 636 with an average strength of 106 men, but 440 were reported effective for the 6 batteries, the armament of which consisted of eight 6-pounders, thirteen 12-pounder howitzers, one Parrott rifle and nine 3-inch rifles, or a total of 31 pieces.

The foregoing figures give some idea of the armament and strength of the field batteries of the Army at the beginning of the Seven Days campaign, and will enable a fairly accurate estimate to be made of the total strength of the Artillery at that time.

Before this campaign commenced many changes were made in the disposition of the batteries, their assignments during that period being, approximately, as follows:

---

*Rebellion Records, Ibid., p. 615.
    †The last two joined after July 1. See Rebellion Records, Series I, Vol. XI, Part II, p. 912.

JACKSON'S COMMAND

Col. Stapleton Crutchfield, Chief of Artillery

WHITING'S DIVISION

Balthis' Staunton Battery,	Capt. W. L. Balthis.
Reilly's Rowan (N. C.) Battery,	Capt. James Reilly.

JACKSON'S DIVISION

Poague's 1st Rockbridge Battery,	Capt. William T. Poague.
Carpenter's Alleghany Battery,	Lieut. John C. Carpenter.
Caskie's Richmond Hampden Battery,	Capt. William H. Caskie.
Wooding's Danville Battery,	Capt. George W. Wooding.

EWELL'S DIVISION

Courtney's Henrico Battery,	Capt. A. R. Courtney.
Carrington's Charlottesville Battery,	Capt. J. McD. Carrington.
Brockenbrough's Baltimore Battery,	Capt. J. B. Brockenbrough.

D. H. HILL'S DIVISION

Maj. S. P. Pierson, Chief of Artillery

Carter's King William Battery,	Capt. Thomas H. Carter.
Hardaway's Alabama Battery,	Capt. R. A. Hardaway.
Jeff Davis Alabama Battery,	Capt. J. W. Bondurant.
Nelson's Hanover Battery,	Capt. George W. Nelson.

HILL'S RESERVE BATTALION (Temporarily attached)

Maj. Hilary P. Jones

Clarke's Long Island Battery,	Capt. P. H. Clarke.
Richmond Orange Battery,	Lieut. C. W. Fry.
Rhett's South Carolina Battery,	Capt. A. Burnett Rhett.

MAGRUDER'S COMMAND

JONES' DIVISION

Brown's Wise Battery,	Capt. James S. Brown.
Washington (S. C.) Battery,	Capt. James F. Hart.
Madison (La.) Battery,	Capt. George F. Moody.
Dabney's Richmond Battery,	Capt. W. J. Dabney.

McLAWS' DIVISION

Manly's North Carolina Battery,	Capt. Basil C. Manly.
Kemper's Alexandria Battery,	Capt. Del Kemper.

MAGRUDER'S DIVISION

Carlton's Troup (Ga.) Battery,	Capt. Henry H. Carlton.
1st Co. Richmond Howitzers,	Capt. E. S. McCarthy.

MAGRUDER'S RESERVE BATTALION

Lieut.-Col. Stephen D. Lee, Chief of Artillery

Pulaski George Battery,	Capt. J. P. W. Read.
James City Battery,	Capt. L. W. Richardson.
Magruder Battery,	Capt. T. Jeff Page, Jr.

LONGSTREET'S DIVISION

Rogers' Loudoun Battery,	Capt. Arthur L. Rogers.
Anderson's Thomas Battery,	Capt. Edwin J. Anderson.
Donaldsonville (La.) Battery,	Capt. Victor Maurin.
3d Co. Richmond Howitzers,	Capt. Benj. H. Smith, Jr.

LONGSTREET'S RESERVE BATTALION

Col. J. B. Walton, Chief of Artillery

1st Co. Washington Artillery,	Capt. Chas. W. Squires.
2d Co. Washington Artillery,	Capt. John B. Richardson.
3d Co. Washington Artillery,	Capt. M. B. Miller.
4th Co. Washington Artillery,	Capt. Joseph Norcom.
Dearing's Lynchburg Battery,	Capt. James Dearing.
Chapman's Dixie Battery,	Capt. W. H. Chapman.

HUGER'S DIVISION

Lieut.-Col. J. A. de Lagnel, Chief of Artillery

Grimes' Portsmouth Battery,	Capt. Carey F. Grimes.
Lynchburg Beauregard Battery,	Capt. M. N. Moorman.
Huger's Norfolk Battery,	Capt. Frank Huger.
Stribling's Fauquier Battery,	Capt. Robert M. Stribling.
Goochland Battery,	Capt. William H. Turner.

A. P. HILL'S (LIGHT DIVISION)

Maj. R. Lindsay Walker, Chief of Artillery
Maj. Lewis M. Coleman, Assistant Chief of Artillery

Andrews' 1st Maryland Battery,	Capt. R. Snowden Andrews.
Charleston (S. C.) German Battery,	Capt. Wm. K. Bachman.
Braxton's Fredericksburg Battery,	Capt. Carter M. Braxton.
Crenshaw's Richmond Battery,	Capt. William G. Crenshaw.
Davidson's Letcher Battery,	Capt. Greenlee Davidson.
Richmond Battery,	Capt. Marmaduke Johnson.
Masters' Battery (improvised siege),	Capt. L. Masters.
Pee Dee (S. C.) Battery,	Capt. D. G. McIntosh.
Pegram's Purcell Battery,	Capt. W. J. Pegram.

Holmes' Division

Col. James Deshler, Chief of Artillery

Branch's Petersburg Battery,	Capt. James R. Branch.
Brem's North Carolina Battery,	Capt. T. H. Brem.
French's Stafford Battery,	Capt. David A. French.
Graham's North Carolina Battery,	Capt. Edward Graham.

Wise's Legion

Andrews' Henry Battery,	Capt. W. C. Andrews.
Rives' Nelson Battery,	Capt. J. H. Rives.

Reserve Artillery, Army of Northern Virginia

Brig.-Gen. Wm. N. Pendleton, Chief of Artillery

First Virginia Artillery,	Col. J. Thompson Brown.
Williamsburg Battery,	Capt. John A. Coke.
Richmond Fayette Battery,	Lieut. William I. Clopton.
2d Co. Richmond Howitzers,	Capt. David Watson.
Jones' Battalion (temporarily attached to D. H. Hill's Division)	Maj. H. P. Jones.
Long Island Virginia Battery,	Capt. P. H. Clarke.
Orange Richmond Battery,	Lieut. C. W. Fry.
Rhett's South Carolina Battery,	Capt. A. Burnett Rhett.

First Battalion Artillery

Lieut.-Col. A. S. Cutts

"D" Bat'ry, Sumter (Ga.) Battalion,	Capt. James A. Blackshear.
"E" Bat'ry, Sumter (Ga.) Battalion,	Capt. John Lane.
"B" Bat'ry, Sumter (Ga.) Battalion,	Capt. John V. Price.
"A" Bat'ry, Sumter (Ga.) Battalion,	Capt. H. M. Ross.
Georgia Regular Battery,	Capt. S. P. Hamilton.

Second Battalion Artillery

Maj. Chas. Richardson

Ancell's 2d Fluvanna Battery,	Capt. John J. Ancell.
Milledge's Georgia Battery,	Capt. John Milledge, Jr.
Woolfolk's Ashland Battery,	Capt. Pichegru Woolfolk.

Third Battalion Artillery

Maj. William Nelson

Huckstep's 1st Fluvanna Battery,	Capt. Charles T. Huckstep.
Kirkpatrick's Amherst Battery,	Capt. Thomas J. Kirkpatrick.
Morris Louisa Virginia Battery,	Capt. R. C. M. Page.

Stuart Horse Artillery Battery,   Capt. John Pelham.
Chew's Battery,   Capt. R. Preston Chew.

An analysis of the foregoing organization of the Artillery shows a total of 45 batteries assigned to the brigades exclusive of the 6 batteries of Walton's Battalion attached to Longstreet's Division, and Lee's Battalion of 3 batteries attached to Magruder's command, both of which were organized as a reserve force. In the general reserve, we now find 5 battalions, four of 3, and one of 5 batteries, or a total of 17 batteries. With the Army then, there were not less than 71 batteries, including the horse artillery. Taking 75 men as the average effective strength of a battery, the total personnel must have numbered in the neighborhood of 5,500 men.

Between June 11 and 15, Stuart, with about 1,200 men, including a section of Pelham's horse battery with 2 guns, had performed a most remarkable exploit. Perhaps nothing that occurred during the early days of the war so awakened the Army to the possibilities of the more mobile guns as did this raid around McClellan, in which Pelham took part. But, while it was a brilliant feat, its results were adverse to Lee and far-reaching. It warned McClellan of a fatal opening on his right, through which other troops with more guns would soon endeavor to pass, and his change of base to Harrison's Landing was but the consequence of the cavalry exploit. Soon Jackson approached this very exposed point, accompanied by Col. Crutchfield and his artillery, as yet not organized in the new manner.

According to the general order of battle, *No. 75,* June 24, Jackson was to march from Ashland on the 25th, in the direction of Slash Church, encamping for the night west of the Central, or the present Chesapeake & Ohio Railroad, and to advance at 3 A. M. on the 26th, and turn Beaver Dam. A. P. Hill was to cross the river at Meadow Bridge when Jackson's advance beyond that point should be known and move directly upon Mechanicsville. As soon as the bridge at that point should be uncovered, Longstreet and D. H. Hill were to cross, the latter to proceed to the support of Jackson, and the former to that of A. P. Hill. The four commands were then to sweep down the north side of the Chickahominy River toward the York River Railroad, Jackson on the left in advance, Longstreet nearest the river and in the rear. Huger and Magruder were to hold their positions on the south side of the river, and on the right of the line, to observe the enemy and pursue in the event of his retreat. Stuart, with the cavalry and Pelham's horse battery, was to cover Jackson's left. A part of the Reserve Artillery under Pendleton himself was to support the movement on the north side, the remainder to be held in readiness for use whenever required.*

In the execution of this excellent plan, Jackson's arrival at the contemplated point on the 26th was delayed, but A. P. Hill crossed the river at Mechanicsville and attempted to turn the left of the enemy's position, being severely punished by musketry and artillery fire; yet, he drove the enemy from his intrenchments and forced him back about a mile to his works on the left bank of Beaver Dam, the strong character of the position preventing an assault that night. Hill had taken with him but 6 field batteries of 4 guns each.†

Before daylight on the 27th, the Federal batteries along Beaver Dam opened, and under cover of a brisk cannonade Porter's troops gradually withdrew to his lines at Gaines' Mill and Cold Harbor. On the Confederate side, A. P. Hill and Longstreet replied to the enemy's fire, and advanced their skirmishers to the borders of the stream. D. H. Hill was ordered to advance on the road from Mechanicsville to Bethesda Church, and turn the Federal right flank, while Jackson, having left his bivouac of the night before at Hundley's early in the morning, was moving south to gain their rear.‡ By the time Jackson was fairly across Beaver Dam, and D. H. Hill had gained the flank of Porter's former line, the bird had flown.

Rebellion Records, Series I, Vol. XI, Part III, pp. 490, 498.
†*From Manassas to Appomattox*, Longstreet, p. 123.
‡*The Army of Northern Virginia in 1862*, Allan, p. 84.

In this affair not over 8 Confederate brigade batteries were engaged. Of any employment of masses or of the new divisional reserve battalions as such, of any effort to prepare the way for the infantry attack in accordance with a previously well-defined schedule, there is no evidence. Coöperation, or "the need to do it," might have been understood; "how to do it" was still not known. Porter met the purely frontal attack of Pender's and Ripley's brigades, and 5 batteries, with a withering fire from his guns; he suffered little from those opposing him. Jackson's guns, so tardy in their arrival, did succeed in delivering their fire upon the head of Hill's column before the identity of the latter was discovered.

Porter had employed 6 of his 20 batteries, massed, losing but one, though forced to retire by Jackson's enveloping movement. Had the Confederate Artillery been properly handled, no such wholesale retirement of the Federal guns could have occurred in the face of not less than 19 hostile batteries. In fact, many of the 80 guns which Porter undoubtedly had should have been unable to retire had the Confederate Artillery, even without the support of Jackson's batteries, been properly employed. But, again, let us not blame the gunners. The pernicious brigade distribution destroyed their power at the outset to cope with Porter's masses. They were but victims of a system. The reserve battalions, just organized, were not brought into action for pure lack of experience in handling such large masses of artillery, not only on the part of the artillerymen, but on the part of Hill as well, whose attack was too headlong even to have permitted an artillery preparation, had the guns been on hand. The general who hurls his infantry columns upon the enemy's position at sight, simply chooses the precipitate assault in preference to the more deliberate attack with the artillery support which he might have elected, and if he neglects his guns, the artillery is not to blame.

The time had not yet come, nor ever will, when an artillery column can patrol the battlefield, undirected by the will of the commanding-general, or by the lieutenants to whom particular sections of the field have been assigned, and push its guns into action at the points which subsequent investigation will show to have been necessary and proper. Artillery officers must be conversant with the general design, and particular duties must be assigned them. The more definitely its mission is outlined in advance, the more definite will be the results which the artillery will attain. While an efficient artillery is the bone of an army, it is not like the cavalry, an arm of sudden movements, of rapidity of action, of improvisation, and especially is this so when it is in masses.

In the study of the earlier battles of the Civil War, the student must be deeply impressed by the nerve of the attacking infantry, which advanced to the assault practically without the support of artillery, the latter primarily designed to give the attack that solidity so characteristic of the arm. In the infantry, the human element dominates everything. "Its essential is solid character, unity of action, and mutual confidence. The man and the man alone makes the measure of these elements. All the power of the arm resides in the man himself."* To supplement the individualistic qualities of the foot-soldier a sufficient proportion of the "long arm" is essential. In the artillery, the part of the men is a secondary one. The reason for their being is the material about which the men are united, and they fight only by serving the guns. Within certain limits, losses in its personnel do not affect the fighting efficiency of a battery, the fire of which can continue undimished until a percentage of the gunners is lost, which occurring in the infantry would render the force of its blow harmless. Hence, the artillery is the "supporting arm par excellence." Its very nature makes it so. All the more remarkable then does the early power of the Confederate Infantry seem when it is recalled that not only did it fail to receive the moral support of artillery, but that it faced an enemy abundantly provided with such aid.

*Psychology of War, Eltinge, p. 92.

CHAPTER XIII

GAINES' MILL

WHEN the morning of the 27th was half gone, the four Confederate divisions were at last united about 3 miles from the new line of the enemy. That line was an arc of a circle about 2 miles in extent, behind Powhite Creek, covering the approaches to the bridge which connected the Federal right wing with the troops on the south side of the Chickahominy, to hold which Porter now had not less than 27,000 men and 20 batteries or 80 guns, 12 batteries being held in reserve. Naturally strong, it was rapidly strengthened with abattis and rifle pits, and before noon an excellent disposition of the defending force had been made, the guns having been adroitly placed along the commanding ground in groups between the divisions and brigades. Besides the division batteries, there were Robertson's and Tidball's excellent horse batteries from Hunt's reserve. One of these batteries was posted on the right of Sykes' Division, and the other on the extreme left of the line where it rested in the Valley against the river. The left flank in the bottom was heavily supported by pieces of position as well as field guns placed in batteries on the south side of the stream. The approach to the Federal position was generally over an open plain, about a quarter of a mile wide, affording a splendid field of fire for the defender's guns.

As soon as it had become evident that Porter was retiring from his position of the night before, Gen. Lee ordered A. P. Hill to follow and attack, while D. H. Hill was directed to unite with Jackson in operating against the flank and rear of the new line. The Confederate commanders on the south side were meantime ordered to keep up a vigorous demonstration with a view to preventing the reënforcing of Porter. Pressing on toward the York River Railroad, A. P. Hill en-

countered the enemy near New Cold Harbor about 2
P. M. and soon became hotly engaged. The arrival of
Jackson upon the field was now momentarily expected.
Longstreet, unexpectedly delayed, in order to repair
a bridge over Beaver Dam for the crossing of his artillery, had been expected to arrive as the effect of Jackson's threat became apparent. But again the plan miscarried. Jackson and Longstreet were both late in
coming up, and A. P. Hill, counting on their support,
launched his division against the centre and left of the
enemy's position, with little effective support from his
artillery, except on the part of Braxton's Battery,
which accompanied Archer's Brigade, maintaining a
desperate struggle for nearly 2 hours. Though it succeeded in reaching and piercing Porter's lines at a number of points, as was to be expected under such
conditions this gallant division was finally repulsed,
though not, however, until heavy reënforcements including 2 batteries had reached Porter's lines, nor until
it had been decimated by the almost undisturbed fire
of the batteries on the crest as well as on the south side
of the river.

Again we must pause to marvel at the prowess of this
infantry. Few of the men of this particular division
had been under fire before June 26.* Yet, on two con-
secutive days, it had made the most desperate frontal
assaults upon exceptionally strong artillery positions,
without the slightest preparation by its own guns. In
fact, such batteries as had attempted to deliver their fire
upon the enemy acted the rôle of infantry rather than
that of supporting guns. At Beaver Dam, Pegram's,
Andrews', McIntosh's, Johnson's, and Braxton's batteries had forced their way to as close quarters as possible, and at Gaines' Mill, Braxton's, Pegram's,
Johnson's, Crenshaw's, Pelham's, Brockenbrough's,
Carrington's, Courtney's, Bondurant's, and perhaps a
few other batteries had been engaged, but their fire

---

*General Lee's Report, *Rebellion Records,* Series I, Vol. XI, Part II, p. 492.

action had been entirely independent of each other, and entirely without unison with the infantry.

But, to resume. A number of Hill's brigades were broken and his division as a whole was forced to recoil from sheer lack of the necessary weight. Realizing the unsupported character of Hill's attack, Gen. Lee had ordered Longstreet, who had now come up, to make a diversion on Hill's right. In spite of the strength of the enemy's position in this quarter, as previously described, Longstreet determined at once to carry the heights by assault, and while his columns were deploying Whiting's Division of Jackson' force, which had lost its way, arrived on the field and formed on Longstreet's left. At the same time, D. H. Hill with the sole aid of Bondurant's Battery, soon overwhelmed and forced to retire, pushed his way to the front, Ewell coming up on his right. Jackson's other two brigades now filled the gap between Ewell and A. P. Hill. The position on the left was defended by Sykes' Division of regulars, supported by 18 guns, afterwards increased to 24. This portion of Porter's line was in some respects stronger than his right, for the field of fire for the guns widened towards the east of the position, to 1,000 yards or more of cornfields sloping from the opposing ridges to a thick swamp, in the bottom of which it was impossible to advance a battery. Crutchfield had to move to the extreme left with his artillery, 6 batteries of which forced their way through the dense thickets in the direction of Old Cold Harbor, and were able later to cover McGehee's Hill, raking Sykes' right, with a storm of shell.

Between 4 and 5 o'clock a general assault commenced which lasted about two hours in the face of a tremendous artillery fire. So rapidly were Porter's guns discharged, that his gunners had difficulty in loading the foul pieces, accomplished in some instances only by jamming the rammers against the trees.* Finally, after terrific losses, the Federal lines were carried, in-

*Letter from Porter to Longstreet.

cluding the artillery position, and 22 guns were taken
on the field. Night put an end to pursuit and daybreak
the 28th found the north bank clear of the enemy.

Why, is it asked, was the Confederate Artillery
totally neglected in this engagement as at Mechanicsville, especially when Porter had given such evidence
the day before of his ability to prepare his position for
defense? The same answer may be made. There was
no reconnaissance of the new position, no staff to discover its outlines in advance of an attack. A. P. Hill
before leaving one field of battle was ordered to follow
up the enemy and attack. Without hesitation, and with
undiminished ardor, he complied. As Longstreet and
Jackson came upon the field to the support of Hill, their
onrushing columns alone located the position of the enemy. The Artillery could not have preceded these columns upon the field. There was not time allowed it for
a duel nor was there time in which it might prepare for
the attack. Go forward with the attacking lines it must
or not at all, for once those lines were launched in their
headlong assaults the leaders had but one thought and
that to reach the position of their adversary. Thus in
large measure, the guns were masked from the first, and
at no time was their rôle more than a secondary one.

The better employment of his guns by Porter in these
two engagements in no wise argues a superior skill with
respect to artillery on his part. The effective use of his
artillery was due to his defensive attitude more than to
his skill as an artilleryman. Had the Confederates been
on the defensive, their artillery would no doubt have occupied the first line. Under such conditions, there is
nothing to do with the guns but mass them. It is on
the offensive that the massing of artillery requires
knowledge, coupled with skill and experience.

The errors of A. P. Hill with respect to his artillery
are attributable to A. P. Hill. When preparing for
operations on the north side of the Chickahominy, he
issued orders that but one battery would accompany each
of his 6 brigades, and that the rest of his batteries in-

cluding those of his reserve battalion would remain in the position previously prepared for them on the south side.* He did take the precaution of carrying with him 6 teams of spare horses for each of his batteries, but drew them, nevertheless, from his remaining batteries, thus crippling the latter for effective use.

*Rebellion Records, Series I, Vol. XI, Part III, p. 616, G. O. No. ——, June 24, 1862.

CHAPTER XIV

SAVAGE'S STATION AND FRAZIER'S FARM*

FROM the field of Gaines' Mill, long columns of dust rising above the forest to the south were descried by the Confederates on the morning of the 28th of June, and it soon became apparent that McClellan had abandoned his base on York River. That evening, after a reconnaissance of the cavalry, Lee rightly concluded that McClellan was falling back upon the James instead of retreating down the Peninsula.

While McClellan was much embarrassed by the necessity of moving his enormous trains and over 50 field batteries across the White Oak Swamp, and then past the front of Magruder's and Huger's lines, Lee was equally hindered by the dense character of the country, the lack of roads, and the destruction of the bridges across the river, by means of which Jackson, Longstreet, and A. P. Hill could pursue the enemy, their columns by necessity being widely separated.

The Federal movement was completed the night of the 28th, and the following morning saw the corps of Sumner and Heintzleman, and the division of Smith of Franklin's Corps, occupying a strong position covering Savage's Station, with Slocum's Division in reserve. In the meantime, Keyes was instructed to retire to the James and occupy a defensive position near Malvern Hill, the extreme left of the Federal line. Late in the afternoon Magruder gained contact with the enemy in position at Savage's Station, but was heavily repulsed without receiving support from Huger. Jackson, Longstreet, and Hill also failed to come up as contemplated.

During this disjointed attack, 3 Federal batteries, Hazzard's, Pettit's, and Osborn's, severely punished Magruder's Infantry. Later, Kershaw's Brigade with Kemper's Alexandria and Hart's South Carolina bat-

---

*Frazier's Farm also called Glendale.

teries came upon the field and pierced the enemy's center, creating some confusion until reënforcements reëstablished the line. Kershaw also made excellent use of a 32-pounder rifled gun under Lieut. Barry, which had been mounted on a railway car, protected with a sloping roof of iron plates. Magruder utterly failed to bring the remainder of his artillery into action, and succeeded in employing only a small portion of his infantry. Thus, McClellan was able by means of this rear guard action to withdraw the last of his trains from Savage's Station, and cover the retreat of his army during the night, though he had lost many prisoners and several batteries.

At nightfall, Jackson was still on the north side of the Chickahominy, Ewell's Division near Bottom's Bridge, and the others at Grape Vine, or Alexander's Bridge; Magruder lay in front of the Federal position at Savage's Station; Huger was at Brightwell's on the Charles City Road. Holmes had crossed to Drewry's Bluff on the north of the James; and Longstreet and A. P. Hill were on the Darbytown Road at Atlee's. Again Gen. Lee ordered his lieutenants to press forward from their positions in order to deliver to the enemy a decisive blow on the morrow.

The morning of the 30th, Longstreet, with Hill in support, moved forward and found a Federal division in position near Glendale. Bringing his artillery into action with most creditable decision, instead of rushing headlong upon the first position against which his column happened to bump, Longstreet now held his men in hand until Huger should come up on his left, and Jackson's guns should be heard at White Oak Swamp which he did not reach until about noon. But when Jackson's guns did open Longstreet was ordered to attack. The Federals holding their position until nightfall, made good their escape again, losing many prisoners, and 10 pieces of artillery including Randolph's Battery, but having inflicted heavy losses upon Longstreet in the sanguinary conflict. Huger failed

utterly to support Longstreet and hardly a man of
Jackson's Infantry pulled a trigger, Hill alone being
employed to assist Longstreet in repelling a determined
counter attack.   Holmes accomplished little in his
quarter.

While Longstreet employed his guns at Glendale, in
a manner approximating an artillery preparation, it
would seem that the opportunity given them was more
due to the necessity of his delay in the attack than to
any intention of sending his infantry forward after the
enemy had been shaken by the fire of artillery.

On the left the artillery performed with credit the
task assigned it, though the end for which it was used
and the delay incident thereto may be subject to
criticism.   Reaching the swamp about noon, Jackson
met with a determined effort on the part of the enemy
to prevent his junction with Longstreet.   The bridge
at the only crossing was destroyed, and the point was
commanded by two batteries of artillery with heavy
infantry supports.

The ground on the north bank of the swamp by no
means favored the action of guns.   To the right of the
road the slopes opposite the position of the enemy were
entirely open, but the crest was covered with a dense
forest, while on the left both the ridge and valley lay
beneath a heavy growth of pine.   The artillery of the
enemy occupied an excellent position on a crest opposite
Jackson's right, and below the guns which commanded
the crossing a thick growth on the south bank of the
stream was occupied by a swarm of sharpshooters.
Finding no ground for the deployment of his infantry,
Jackson determined to force a crossing with his guns.
Much time was consumed in cutting a road through the
woods on the right of the road by means of which his
batteries could gain the crest, but finally when Crutchfield's 28 guns, moving forward simultaneously, ready
shotted, opened fire on the enemy, the surprise was complete.   One of the Federal batteries which had already
driven the cavalry back, dispersed at once in confusion,

and the other soon disappeared. Whereupon Jackson ordered up 2 guns of Wooding's Battery to shell the belt of trees occupied by the skirmishers, who were also driven off. While he was engaged in repairing the bridge, 3 Federal batteries with infantry supports came up and drove off the working parties, and an artillery duel in which neither side could see the other continued throughout the afternoon, but Crutchfield's guns, mostly smooth-bore pieces, were quite unable to silence the Federal artillery of superior range and caliber.

Gen. Alexander is most critical of Jackson's failure to effect a crossing, claiming that even had the enemy been able to prevent it at the main bridge, a nearby ford was available. That that ford too was defended by artillery, there can be little doubt.* He asserts that Jackson's failure on this occasion to coöperate effectively with Longstreet was due to the same reluctance to bring his infantry into action which he had displayed ever since his arrival on the Peninsula.† "Here infantry alone could accomplish anything, but only cavalry and artillery were called upon. He could have crossed a brigade of infantry as well as Munford's Cavalry, and that brigade could have been the entering wedge which would split apart the Federal defense, and let in 13 brigades which followed. The bridge, whose destruction is mentioned, was not necessary to a crossing. It was only a high water bridge with a ford by it, which was preferably used except in freshets. Now the floor of the bridge, made of poles, had been thrown into the ford, but Munford's Cavalry got through without trouble, and the infantry could have swarmed across." This is a severe arraignment of Jackson. The feat which appears so simple to the critic certainly must have been attended with some elements of difficulty not mentioned. It is not in reason that so simple an undertaking would have been foregone by Jackson. Of the artillery, Gen. Alexander writes: "The cannonade, which was kept up during all the rest of the day, was

---

*Stonewall Jackson, Henderson, Vol. II, pp. 68, 69.
†Military Memoirs of a Confederate, Alexander, p. 147.

not only a delusion, but useless burning both of daylight and ammunition, for it was all random fire. The
Federal and Confederate artillery could not see each
other at all. They could scarcely see the high-floating
smoke clouds of each other's guns. They fired by
sound, at a distance of three-quarters of a mile, across
a tall dense wood, until they exhausted their ammunition. One Federal battery reported the expenditure
of 1,600 rounds. The noise was terrific, and some firing was kept up till 9 o'clock at night, but the casualties
on each side were naturally trifling. Only one Confederate battery, Rhett's, mentions any, and it reported
but 2 killed and 5 wounded."*

But, however correct the criticism may be as to the
faulty delays of Jackson, it is to be observed that his
guns were properly employed in the execution of the
work assigned them. Jackson encountered artillery in
position. Whether he should have maneuvered around
them or not is a consideration without the scope of this
work. When he did decide to silence them with his
own artillery, the attempt was made by the employment
of all his guns and here again we find evidence of his
growing tendency to make use of massed fire. The
very fact that he delayed, however unnecessary his
action may have been, in order to bring his entire artillery to the front, is significant in our investigation of
a better conception on his part of the use of artillery,
and in its employment we are alone concerned. One
thing is certain, Jackson sought to prepare a passage
for his infantry by the massed fire of his guns, even at
the cost of the time required for bringing his batteries
into position. A. P. Hill might have essayed a crossing
without such aid. Had he succeeded, his batteries would
have been blocking the roads far to the rear. Jackson
failed to cross in the proper way. On the other hand,
Hill might have crossed, but certainly not without tremendous loss to his command. On this point, Henderson says: "It is quite true, as a tactical principle, that

*Military Memoirs of a Confederate, Alexander, p. 148.

demonstrations, such as Jackson made with his artillery, are seldom to be relied upon to hold an enemy in position. When the first alarm has passed off, and the defending general becomes aware that nothing more than a fight is intended, he will act as did the Federals, and employ his reserves elsewhere. A vigorous attack is, almost invariably, the only means of keeping him to his ground. But, an attack which is certain to be repulsed, and to be repulsed in quick time, is even less effective than a demonstration. It may be the precursor of a decisive defeat."*

In conclusion, it may be remarked, that not only was the closest student of Jackson's campaigns who has yet contributed to military history thus convinced that Jackson could not have effected a crossing, his conviction being based upon an actual inspection of the terrain, but that Jackson's action on the 30th was in no wise a feint. It was a serious effort on the part of Jackson to attain that superiority of fire over the enemy which would permit his choked columns to pass through what amounted to a tactical defile. In the topographical features of the position, Jackson undoubtedly recognized many elements of danger for his command and sought in vain to overcome them.

---

*Stonewall Jackson, Vol. II, pp. 69, 70.

CHAPTER XV

MALVERN HILL

In connection with the history of warfare, one involuntarily thinks of Austerlitz, of Friedland, of Wagram, of Malvern Hill, of Gettysburg, of Königgratz, of Sedan, of Plevna, of Mukden, each in its own time, as typifying the great power of concentrated artillery fire. It is one of these, the great battle of Malvern Hill, now about to be considered, which Maj. May, R. H. A., states is as worthy to be remembered by gunners as is Friedland and Wagram.

About 10 P. M., June 30, Franklin, followed by Slocum, Heintzleman, and Sumner, fell back from the positions they had so stoutly maintained against Jackson and Longstreet, and by daylight had reached Malvern Hill overlooking the James River, at Turkey Bend, where Porter had been placed the day before, and where McClellan determined to make another stand.

The battlefield selected by McClellan is an elevated plateau rising to the height of 150 feet above the surrounding forests and embraced by the two branches of Western Run, and possessing nearly every requirement of a strong defensive position. The main branch of the stream gathers near the battlefield of the day before, and flows with a marshy course until it expands into the long milldam that supplies Carter's Mill. After passing this mill, it turn with a sinuous course at a sharp angle to the northwest, along the base of the bluff that constitutes the south end of Malvern Hill, and enters the James at Turkey Bend. Before entering the river, it receives a branch, which, rising about a mile further west, pursues a southeast course, parallel to the main branch and, skirting the western base of the hill, joins the main stream. Small tributaries drain the country to the north of the plateau between the two branches.

The open ground on the top of the hill is about 1½ miles in length by half a mile in breadth. Sloping gradually to the north, northwest and northeast, the hillsides were covered with wheat standing or in shock, to the edge of a wood some 800 yards or more from the commanding crest. The base of the hill, except to the east and southeast, was covered with a dense growth of trees, in the edge of which lay the marshy bed of a stream. Towards the southwest, and south, the plateau terminates in abrupt bluff-like hills, overlooking the river. To the southeast, it slopes away to the milldam bounding it on that side. On the left, or more open side of the upland, was an excellent artillery position, commanding a broad stretch of meadows, drained by a narrow stream and numerous ditches, capable of being flanked by fire from gunboats on the river. To Malvern Hill there were but three practicable approaches by land —the Quaker Road, from the north, the River Road from the west, and a track joining the Quaker Road from the northwest and connecting that road with the Long Bridge Road something over a mile from the summit.

Reconnaissance early on July 1 disclosed the fact that the Federal Army was drawn up in an arc on the summit of Malvern Hill, the center convex towards the north; the left wing extending southward to the bluffs above the river and facing west, the right wing curved back along the eastern side of the plateau, and facing east. A powerful artillery, posted just in rear of the crest, swept the wheat fields on the slopes, the guns capable of ranging well into the woods beyond. Behind the guns were stationed heavy masses of infantry, well under cover, with a strong line of skirmishers pushed down the hillside below the batteries.

Col. H. J. Hunt, McClellan's Chief of Artillery, had for some time been familiar with the striking features of the position, which once seen would not soon be forgotten by an artilleryman. Anticipating the battle, he had undertaken the posting of a number of his batteries on June 30, rearranging the artillery lines the following

morning. On the west side of the hill overlooking Warren, to whom had been assigned Martin's Battery of 12-
pounders, he had placed about 36 guns, some of long
range, to sweep the Low Meadow Valley. To these,
later in the day, were added the siege guns of the 1st
Connecticut Artillery under Col. Robert O. Tyler.
These guns were supported by Sykes' Division, the line
of which was extended in a northerly direction to the
Quaker Road by Morell's Division, with which were 7
batteries under Weeden and Griffin, the latter our gallant friend of Bull Run. Couch's Division extended the
line to the right almost as far as Western Run, and to
his right and rear were the troops of Heintzleman and
Sumner. Hunt's reserve artillery of 100 guns, complete in itself, and only a reserve in name, was held
closely in hand and from it batteries were sent to the
front line to replace those whose ammunition was exhausted, others being used to strengthen the line.*
Thus, we see that there was no question as to a sufficiency of guns, but simply one as to space for their
effective employment.

The setting was complete for a tremendous disaster,
the certainty of which to an attacking force unsupported
by a preponderance of artillery fire would have been pat-
ent to a novice who had become familiar with Porter's
position. But the same *élan* which had borne A. P.
Hill on at Beaver Dam and Gaines' Mill, now swept
forward the Confederate Army. But one man there
was in Lee's Army who forecasted the result. D. H.
Hill was familiar with the character of the new Federal
position, for a resident had described it to him, his in-
formant stating that "its commanding height, the difficulties of approach, its amphitheatrical form and ample
area, would enable McClellan to arrange his 350 field
guns, tier above tier, and sweep the plain in every
direction."† Meeting Gen. Lee early on the 1st, Hill
promptly apprised him of the substance of this report,

---

*Battles and Leaders, Vol. II, pp. 410, 411.
†Ibid., p. 391.

and remarked that "if Gen. McClellan is there in force, we had better let him alone," but Longstreet who was present, jocularly scoffed at the suggestion.

On rushed the Confederates and orders were immediately issued for an attack, Jackson having crossed White Oak Swamp early in the morning. Preparatory to the launching of his troops against the formidable Federal position, Gen. Lee, who was by no means well, directed Longstreet to reconnoiter the enemy's left. Jackson upon coming up had opposed a frontal attack, and advised an enveloping movement about the enemy's right. But Longstreet again took the lead, reporting that there was a good position for batteries opposite the Federal left from which the guns could sweep the field over to their right, and suggested that 60 pieces be stationed there for the purpose.* The open space along Jackson's front, also appeared to him to offer a field of fire for a hundred or more guns, and it was his opinion that Porter's batteries, under a cross fire from the two great Confederate groups, posted as he suggested, would be overwhelmed and the infantry thus enabled to make a successful assault.†

While Longstreet's conception was good, its execution for many reasons proved impossible. Lee ordered the attempt to be made.

The line of battle was formed about 4 o'clock with Jackson on the left, Whiting's Division extending beyond the Quaker Road, and D. H. Hill to its right. Ewell's and Jackson's own divisions were in reserve. About half a mile to the right of Hill's 5 brigades, came 2 of Huger's, 6 of Magruder's, and then 2 more of Huger's, including Ranson's detached from Holmes' Division, the latter occupying the extreme right near the River Road. Longstreet and A. P. Hill were in reserve on the Long Bridge Road, a mile or more to the rear of Magruder.

At the outset, warning was given by the enemy of what was to be expected, for heavy losses were inflicted

*Battles and Leaders, Vol. II, p. 403.
†From Manassas to Appomattox, p. 13.

by Hunt's guns upon D. H. Hill's Division while deploying in the woods.

The battle order sent about noon to Magruder, Huger, and D. H. Hill, with their 14 brigades, was remarkable. It consisted of the following words:

"July 1, 1862.

"Batteries have been established to rake the enemy's line. If it is broken, as is probable, Armistead, who can witness the effect of the fire, has been ordered to charge with a yell. Do the same. By order of Gen. Lee.

"R. H. CHILTON, *A. A. C.*"

Of one thing we are sure. When this order was penned, no batteries had been established to rake the enemy's line, nor was it possible to do so at any time during the day, in spite of the fact that the pioneers had made an unsuccessful effort to open a road by means of which guns could be brought up, and the evidence is that Gen. Pendleton did all in his power to overcome the insurmountable difficulties presented by the terrain. Holding well in hand his four reserve battalions in which were to be found the best material of the artillery, he sought in vain for an opening for their employment. His official report is as follows:

"Tuesday, July 1, was spent by me in seeking, for some time, the commanding general, that I might get orders, and, by reason of the intricacy of routes, failing in this, in examining positions near the two armies toward ascertaining what could be best done with a large artillery force, and especially whether any position could be reached whence our large guns could be used to good purpose. These endeavors had, of course, to be made again and again under the enemy's shells, yet no site was found from which the large guns could play upon the enemy without endangering our own troops, and no occasion was presented for bringing up the reserve artillery. Indeed, it seemed that not one-half of the division batteries were brought into action either Monday or Tuesday. To remain nearby, therefore, and await events and orders in readiness for whatever service might be called for, was all I could do."*

Rebellion Records, Series I, Vol. XI, Part II, p. 536.

Again we may feel sure of one thing, and that is, that Pendleton had not seen the Commanding-General the morning of the battle of Malvern Hill. In other words, Gen. Lee and Gen. Longstreet had decided to attack, the latter making the artillery reconnaissance, without the slightest consultation with the Chief of Artillery of the Army and the immediate commander of the reserve, from which, presumably, the large groups to be employed for the purposes of artillery preparation were to be drawn. And this in spite of the fact that upon the success of that preparation the entire action was to hinge. It could not have been that Pendleton was lost. His 5 battalions of not less than 17 batteries were literally blocking the few roads that existed in rear of the Army, not a brigade of which but had stumbled across them in winding its way from the direction of Glendale and White Oak Swamp. If there was one officer in the Army easy to find it was certainly the Chief of Artillery with his immense column of guns and trains. It is quite clear that Pendleton had no part in the conference before the battle, and we find the remarkable situation of a contemplated artillery duel, in which over 100 guns were to participate, unknown to the Chief of Artillery and the commander of those guns.

Referring to Gen. Pendleton, Alexander has this to say: "Pendleton graduated from West Point in 1830, one year after Lee. He resigned in 1833, and entered the ministry in 1837. In 1861, he returned to military life, and was appointed Chief of Artillery of the Army October, 1861, under Gen Johnston. His command did little during the Seven Days, and Col. Brown, commanding his largest battalion, in his report mentions the great superabundance of artillery, and the scanty use that was made of it."* Couched in these words is a direct accusation of his old chief. There is in them an intentional insinuation of incompetence, a practice to which many participants in the great Civil War have been too freely given. As a rule, such remarks only re-

*Military Memoirs of a Confederate, Alexander, pp. 158, 159.

act upon the author as they certainly do in this case, in a way to be shown later.

Again referring to that portion of Pendleton's report which has been cited, Alexander writes: "Between the lines one can but read a disappointing story. Pendleton did not find Lee all day long, nor did any orders from Lee find him. He implies that his reserve artillery was not expected to go in until all the division batteries were first engaged. The division batteries were not organized as battalions, and, acting separately, were easily overpowered when brought out one by one, in face of many guns, already in position. Pendleton's battalions, of from 3 to 6 batteries each, would have stood much better chances; and while there were not many places, there were two extensive ones, in either of which all of these battalions could have been used—Poindexter's field, and the position on Magruder's right, to which Lee made the pioneers open a road. As matters were, our whole reserve artillery stood idle all day."[*]

If General, then Col. Alexander, Chief of Ordnance, on Lee's staff at the battle of Malvern Hill, knew of such positions as those to which he refers a half century later; knew that a road had been cut to one of them, and then failed to find the Chief of Artillery with his 5 battalions, may the good God have mercy on his soul, for he knew what the majority of the generals did not know at the time, and yet let thousands of their men be sacrificed while he remained silent. With such information, it was his duty as a staff officer and one so closely affiliated with the artillery, to find the guns and guide them to the positions so obvious to him over the routes already blazed! The reserve battalions, the superabundance of artillery to which he alludes, could certainly have been found. A verbal order from Gen. Lee, transmitted by the initiative of Col. Alexander, for which initiative he was justly noted throughout his military career, would have brought them all galloping to the front, even had Gen. Pendleton been absent from his post as Alexander naïvely insinuates he was.

---

[*]*Military Memoirs of a Confederate*, Alexander, pp. 158.

That there is any inplication in the words of Pendleton, already quoted, that the reserve artillery was not
expected to become engaged until the divisional batteries had gone into action, is denied. Gen. Alexander's
conclusion is unwarranted. The obvious meaning of the
words referred to is that there was not space, due to the
dense character of the terrain and the lack of roads, in
which the divisional batteries, even acting individually,
could maneuver, and that since this was so, all the more
impossible was it for large masses of artillery to act.
Nor is there anything novel in Gen. Alexander's criticism of the artillery in the Seven Days campaign. Referring to Pendleton's report, dated July 26, 1862,
penned not less than fifty years before Alexander wrote
his book, we find the following remarks: "In conclusion, while gratefully recognizing that Divine favor
which crowned us with victory, I would commend to
the consideration of the commanding general what
seems to me to have been a serious error, with regard to
the use of artillery in these several fights—too little was
thrown into action at once; too much was left in the
rear unused.   One or two batteries brought into
position at a time to oppose a much larger artillery force
well posted must greatly suffer, if not ultimately yield,
under the concentrated fire.   This was in several
instances our experience.* We needed more guns taking part, alike for our own protection and for crippling
the enemy. With a powerful array opposed to his own,
we divide his attention, shake his nerves, make him shoot
at random, and more readily drive him from the field
worsted and alarmed. A main cause of this error in the
present case was no doubt a peculiar intricacy in the
country, from the prevalence of woods and swamps.
We could form little idea of positions, and were very
generally ignorant of those chosen by the enemy and
of the best modes of approaching them; nor were good
maps readily accessible by which in some measure to
supply this deficiency; hence a considerable degree of

---

*Beaver Dam, Gaines' Mill, Glendale, Malvern Hill.

perplexity, which nothing but careful reconnaissance, by skillful officers, experienced in such service, could have obviated, but being obviated, attack had been more coöperative, concentrated and effectual, the enemy's condition more crippled, and our success more triumphant, with less mourning in the land."

The man, who three weeks after Malvern Hill wrote this accurate, thorough, and terse resumé of the Confederate operations on the Peninsula, and of the erroneous tactical employment of field artillery in the campaign just over, is more entitled to credit than his critics of a half century later, for they show beyond dispute that the Chief of Artillery appreciated at the time the errors which had been committed. If the causes had not been beyond his control, in a measure at least, the Chief of Artillery would never have so placed himself on record.

The order for the attack was distributed, we have seen, about noon. Not only did it contain false information, in that it declared as a matter of fact supporting batteries to have been established, but it left the decision as to the proper time for the assault entirely in the hands of a brigade commander. Armistead commanded but one of the 14 brigades ordered to attack. Those brigades extended over a mile or more of shell-swept field, many of them entirely hidden from view in the dense thickets. In such circumstances it is difficult to conceive how any but a disjointed effort could result, even were Armistead competent to determine when the enemy had been effectively shaken. Not only was Armistead unable to decide upon the time at which the assault should be made, but he would have been equally unable to observe from his position the effect of the Confederate batteries, had they come into action as contemplated. But this fatal order, which should have been used by Buddecke and Von Kiesling in their works on Battle Orders to illustrate how not to write one, stood, with what results we shall see.

The difficult advance of Magruder's, Huger's, and D. H. Hill's brigades to the positions in line assigned them, at once disclosed the impossibility of executing the proposed plan, for it became apparent that the batteries not only could not be massed as contemplated, but that they could hardly force their way to the front through the swampy thickets. Yet, instead of abandoning so hopeless a plan, every prospect of its success, and every reason for its adoption, depending upon the massed fire of artillery, upon the unison of action of large groups of guns, which had never been attained by the Confederates, even in favorable country, the few batteries which could press through the thickets were ordered forward singly to their fate. Gallantly they essayed the task assigned them, and quickly they reaped the fruits of the error which committed them to so hopeless an undertaking, for as they unlimbered at the edge of the thicket they were swept from their positions by the concentrated fire of the Federal guns. From battery to battery, Hunt shifted the enormous sheaf of fire of more than 50 superior pieces, disabling four of Huger's and several of Jackson's batteries almost the instant they came into action. Those with Jackson which did manage to hold on in spite of the most terrible punishment not only acted without concert, but were entirely too few to make an impression, much less subdue the opposing batteries.

The manner in which, on this occasion, Hunt handled his superb battery of 60 pieces, together with a very similar performance at Gettysburg, the next year, show that he at any rate recalled the secret of Napoleon's success with artillery, and no doubt justifies the high encomium bestowed upon him by Col. Wagner, who declares that his "ability as an organizer and commander of artillery places him in the same rank with Lichtenstein, Senarmont, and Drouot.*"

On the Confederate side the batteries of Poague, Carpenter, Pegram, Davidson, Grimes, Balthis, Moor-

*Organization and Tactics, Wagner, p. 347.

man, and the few others which singly from time to time
took up the fight, while so ineffective against the artillery of the enemy that Gen. D. H. Hill described
their efforts as almost farcical, succeeded in driving
Sumner's infantry to the cover of the bluffs above the
river, Porter being ordered to follow, which he refused
to do. "How eloquent," writes Gen. Alexander, "is
this episode of what might have been the effect of bold
and energetic use, early in the day, not only of our
large artillery reserve, but of all our brigade and division batteries, brought in under their protection, as
might have been done under efficient management."
Again, we say, Col. Alexander of Gen. Lee's own staff,
should have contributed something besides a half
century of criticism. It was clearly, as has been shown,
within his power to do it at the battle of Malvern Hill.
According to his own words, the occasion was rife with
opportunities for an artilleryman. The commanding
general would have gladly permitted him to suggest the
way to accomplish that which the original plan had contemplated.

Realizing the inequality of the contest which the few
batteries that had succeeded in gaining position were
waging, and the ineffectiveness of their fire, Gen. Lee
himself, about 3 o'clock, abandoned his intention of assaulting with the infantry and so notified Longstreet,
who was in direct charge of the battle. Shortly before
this Gen. Lee, accompanied by Longstreet, had reconnoitered the enemy's right, passing along the entire
left of the Confederate position. Strange to say, even
before directing Longstreet to break off the fight,
neither he nor the latter, the originator of the contemplated artillery duel, now detected a practical position for the massing of the reserve batteries. Had the
developments of the Confederate position not been contrary to their original expectations, it seems reasonable
to suppose some concerted effort to bring up the reserve artillery would have been made by them, for

neither Lee nor Longstreet was given to vacillation or indecision on the field of battle, especially when once engaged.

While the generals were making their reconnaissance, the infantry became heavily engaged, and from then on, the various commands advancing by detachments, continued a spasmodic though desperate effort to carry the crest, all in vain. The field of Malvern Hill was the scene of unsurpassed heroism on the part of the Confederate troops, destined as they were by the attending circumstances to defeat. Let Porter describe the assault.

"The spasmodic, though sometimes formidable, attack of our antagonists, at different points along our whole front up to about 4 o'clock, were, presumably, demonstrations or feelers preparatory to their engaging in more serious work. An ominous silence, similar to that which had preceded the attack in force at Gaines' Mill, now intervened, until, at about 5:30 o'clock, the enemy opened upon both Morell and Couch with artillery from nearly the whole of his front, and soon after pressed forward his columns of infantry, first on one, then on the other, or on both.

"As if moved by a reckless disregard of life equal to that displayed at Gaines' Mill, with a determination to capture our army, or destroy it by driving us into the river, brigade after brigade rushed at our batteries, but the artillery of both Morell and Couch mowed them down with shrapnel, grape, and canister, while our infantry, withholding their fire until the enemy were in short range, scattered the remnants of their columns, sometimes following them up and capturing prisoners and colors."*

Every account of this battle, whether upon Northern or Southern authority, has for its main feature the overwhelming and irresistible artillery fire of Hunt's 50 field pieces, and 10 siege guns, which, continuing their fire until after 9 P. M., always concentrating on the most threatening points, completely overthrew in detail the 3 of Lee's 9 divisions, which were engaged, inflicting upon them a loss of not less than 5,000 men.† But in spite of their losses and the succession of mistakes, there seems to be little doubt that the Confederates came very

---

*Battles and Leaders, Vol. II, pp. 416, 417.
†Alexander says 5,965 ; Allan says a little over 5,000, so also does Henderson.

near winning the day. The most positive indications of this fact are to be found in Porter's account as well as in Hunt's report. The latter stating that 3 horse batteries and eight 32-pounder howitzers, were "brought up to the decisive point at the close of the day, thus bringing every gun of this large artillery force (artillery reserve of 100 pieces) into the most active and decisive use. Not a gun remained unemployed; not one could have been safely spared."*

Before 10 P. M. the great battle had become a matter of history, the Federal force was in full retreat to Harrison's Landing, the haven of which it reached before morning, and one-third of Lee's Army lay bleeding and exhausted before Malvern Hill, the awful sepulchre of victory, which for 6 of the past 7 days had attended the Confederate arms.

One episode of the pursuit the next morning alone concerns the artillery. At 9 A. M., Stuart's Cavalry had occupied Evelington Heights, overlooking and commanding the Federal position and camp at Harrison's Landing. These heights were peculiarly the position for the immediate occupation by Lee's artillery, a fact which the slightest forethought should have grasped. Dominating as they did the upper part of the peninsula which McClellan had occupied, thereby placing himself in a position in which the alternatives were further retreat down the river, or a frontal attack upon the heights, crowned with artillery they would have been impregnable. But, on the morning of the 3d, unable to resist the temptation, Stuart ordered Pelham, with one of his howitzers, for which little ammunition remained, to fire upon the enemy's camp below. "Judging from the great commotion and excitement below, it must have had considerable effect," wrote Stuart. Thus, by Stuart's horse-play, McClellan was at once apprised of his peril, and by causing the Federal general to immediately reoccupy Evelington Heights, Lee's last opportunity to force him to the offensive was sacrificed by Stuart.

---

*Rebellion Records, Series I, Vol. XI. Part II, p. 239.

One more incident in which the rôle of the Artillery was a leading one in connection with the Peninsula campaign remains to be mentioned. McClellan, as well as a number of his more ardent admirers, had, fortunately for the peace of their own minds, been able to find solace in the belief that in reaching Harrison's Landing, *via* the Seven Pines and Seven Days route, beset as it had been by so many dangers and the loss of some 20,-000 men, the Army of the Potomac was at last in a most advantageous position to threaten Richmond from the south side of the James. The contemplated route in that quarter was no doubt less circuitous than the one pursued from Hampton Roads to Westover. Whatever the proposed course may have been, preparatory thereto McClellan had for several weeks neglected to secure his army, confident in the ability of the gunboats to keep the opposite bank free of the enemy.

Late in the month of July, it was decided by Gen. Lee to bombard McClellan's camp and shipping by night from Coggin's Point, to which task an expeditionary force of artillery in command of Gen. Pendleton was assigned. The force of artillery designated for the work consisted of parts of Brown's Regiment and the battalions of Cutts and Nelson. Leaving Richmond with 32 field pieces, and 2 heavy rifles on siege carriages drawn by the teams of Milledge's Battery, Pendleton reached Petersburg the night of July 29, where he was joined by Gen. D. H. Hill with an infantry force and several batteries. After spending the next day and night in reconnoitering the south shore in the neighborhood of Coggin's Point, Hood's Point, and Claremont, Gen. Hill returned to Petersburg, leaving the expedition in charge of Gens. French and Pendleton. Having successfully kept the guns concealed from the observers in the Federal balloons, they were ordered on the night of the 31st into the positions which had been selected with great care for the various detachments. At 12:30, 41 of the 43 pieces which had been brought up opened fire simultaneously, firing from 20 to 30 rounds apiece,

the total expenditure being about 1,000 rounds, whereupon the guns were limbered and quietly moved to the
rear as previously directed, and proceeded to Petersburg after a slight rest.

The result of the enterprise was principally a great
excitement in the Federal camp, and 40 or 50 casualties
among the sleeping troops. A number of vessels were
also slightly injured. The Confederate casualties were
1 killed and 7 wounded.* The results obtained were
in no wise commensurate with the labor and risk incident to the undertaking and well illustrate the unfruitful character of such enterprises, however deliberately
planned and carefully executed. The range to the
shipping was some 600 to 800 yards; to the camp on the
opposite shore much greater, and owing to these facts
no great results should have been expected. The whole
affair was farcical, but while it served the purpose of
causing McClellan to grasp the strategic advantages of
a position astride the river, it also necessitated the construction of intrenchments about Petersburg, which in
1864 enabled Beauregard with a small force to ward
off Grant for three whole days until reënforcements
came to his support. The result, then, of Pendleton's expedition, was solely one which was not anticipated.†
This incident practically ended the Peninsula campaign.

The battles of the Seven Days cost the Confederates
20,000 men. The Federal loss was not more than 16,-
000, of which 10,000, about half wounded, were
prisoners. In addition to their loss in men, was that
of 52 guns, 35,000 rifles, and vast quantities of stores,
captured and destroyed. The loss of the Confederate
Artillery in material was slight, and in personnel, the
strength of which just after the battle of Malvern Hill
was 186 officers and 3,778, did not exceed 500.‡ In the
Reserve Artillery, the loss, as stated by Alexander, was
2 men, a figure at variance with the casualty return

*Rebellion Records, Series I, Vol. XI, Part II, pp. 944-6, Pendleton's Report.
†Gen. Alexander is much confused as to the character of the ordnance used
on this occasion as well as to dates. See his book, p. 171, and compare with
Official Records.
‡Rebellion Records, Series I, Vol. XI, Part II, p. 506, and Ibid., Part III,
pp. 645, 976.

which shows a loss of 8 killed and 30 wounded.* The
heaviest individual loss of any battery was that of Pegram's. Engaged in every battle of the Seven Days
campaign, the gallant Purcell Battery had suffered a
loss of 59 out of 80 men, and was able to man but a
single gun at the close of the battle of July 1. Johnson's, Davidson's, and Rhett's batteries were next in
order, with a loss of 19 men each. The loss in horses
suffered by the Artillery was especially great, many of
the batteries being almost dismounted.† But the damage done in this respect was soon remedied and was
more than compensated for by the fine rifled pieces
captured from the enemy, among which were listed 3
repeating guns.‡

It would be tedious and unfruitful to discuss in detail the individual movements of the various Confederate batteries engaged in the Seven Days campaign.
Enough facts have been given to show that the brigade batteries merely acted as best they could with the
commands to which they were attached, being called
upon to inflict such damage upon the enemy as they
might without any special time or assistance being given
them for the purpose. It was simply a case of blaze
away for the brigade batteries. Of the Reserve, Jones'
Battalion had alone accompanied a division in the
various egagements, eliciting from Gen. D. H. Hill, to
whom it was assigned, high praise. The other battalions of the Reserve and Brown's Regiment had endeavored with only slight success to render service, but
due more to a total ignorance of the tactical employment of such masses on the part of the division commanders than to anything else no opportunity was
afforded them to coöperate with the infantry and brigade batteries. On several occasions, however, while
hovering about the flanks or rear of the lines of battle,
in an entirely independent way, these battalions had

---

*Military Memoirs of a Confederate, Alexander, p. 174 ; and Official Casualty
Return, Rebellion Records, Series I, Vol. XI, Part II, p. 505, and also p. 973.
†Rebellion Records, Series I, Vol. XI, Part III, pp. 689-690.
‡Ibid., Part II, pp. 510-513. Also see a reference to revolving gun on p. 938,
no doubt one of those referred to in Part I of this work.

found openings, as in the case of Richardson's and Nelson's battalions at Gaines' Mill, and Golding's Farm.* The absence of the Reserve Artillery on the various battlefields of the Peninsula was as conspicuous as the presence of the splendid Federal batteries on all occasions, a result due in some degree to the artillery organization and experience of the two armies, but principally due to the fact that McClellan invariably defended selected and prepared positions, while Lee assailed them, as a rule, without previous reconnaissance and in the most headlong manner. The element of time requisite to the proper employment of field artillery in so difficult a country was lacking in every instance. The one case in which an artillery duel was attempted, that of Jackson at White Oak Bridge, incurring almost universal adverse criticism.

If the topography of the theater of operations during the Peninsula campaign be considered, with its dense covering of forest, its lack of all but the crudest highways, these facts alone, as Pendleton pointed out, would seem to account for the neglect of artillery masses on the part of the Confederates. But to repeat what has been said before, coupled with the adverse conditions of the terrain were even stronger influences which militated against the effective employment of the artillery, especially in masses. Lack of training and experience on the part of the division commanders, and the entire absence of trained staff officers, both in the infantry and artillery, from which resulted accidental contact with the enemy, precluded the deliberate use of artillery masses.

It is not so easy to overcome the enormous friction which must occur in war as it is to propound new theories. The novelty of reserve battalions of artillery, while readily accepted, was not, and could not have been expected to be, immediately adopted in practice. This will always be the case with tactical innovations, in all armies, at all times. Nothing is more natural in

*Pendleton's Report, *Rebellion Records*, Series I, Vol. XI, Part II, pp. 533-537.

green armies entirely lacking in anything approximating a tactical doctrine. It was true even in the Prussian Army of 1866, the leaders and staff of which were the carefully trained products of a school of thought, founded by Scharnhorst, tested by Napoleon, codified by Clausewitz, and put into more practical form by Gneisenau. But, in spite of their past experience, an experience which the Confederates had not had, in spite of all their training, the Prussians utterly failed in 1866 at Munchengratz, and Gitschin to bring up their reserve artillery, and at Nachod, Trautenau, and Sor, only succeeded in getting it into position very late in the day, not indeed until nightfall. In Austria, just as on the Peninsula, the long columns of reserve artillery with their ammunition trains were allowed to march in rear, the foremost gun following the hindmost combatant of the other arms. Thus it was that even a division marching alone when it gained contact with the enemy, more often than not unexpectedly, found its artillery reserve many miles to the rear. During the advance of the infantry the sight of the artillery columns filled the infantry officers with alarm, lest the roads might be blocked and the batteries were invariably side-tracked to make way for the foot columns. In both campaigns, orders were given from time to time tending to the more timely arrival of the artillery, but such orders when given suddenly, and when opposed to all previously existing principles, were very naturally rendered inoperative by that friction ever present with the movement of troops in the field.

It is not sufficient merely to wish and to order that masses of artillery be brought into action on time; it is necessary also to have learned and practiced the manner of doing it. The Prussians had partly learned the lesson before Königgrätz, and profited by it in 1870; the Confederates did not learn and practice it during the seven days terminating in the catastrophe of Malvern Hill. In his noted work on artillery, Prince Kraft devotes an entire chapter to the subject of "How it was that the artillery always came up at the right time," in the Franco-German War, and yet another, "How the Artillery saved itself," during that war. These chapters are merely complements of an unnamed one, "How the Artillery rarely came up at the right time," in the war of 1866. Most of Hohenlohe's deductions apply with peculiar force to the artillery operations on the Peninsula.

Before summing up the campaign, it should be said that Gen. Lee undoubtedly appreciated the many glaring defects of his army, yet was of great enough mind to recognize them as natural ones and not merely due to inefficiency on the part of his lieutenants. With respect to the Artillery, he knew that conditions and inexperience with the arm on the part of all was at the root of the trouble, and did not cast the blame upon the shoulders of its chief as Gen. Alexander has sought to do, for in his report he stated that Gen. Pendleton, Chief of Artillery, attended unceasingly to his duty.*

Finally, it may be said that the following conclusions, concerning the Peninsula campaign, seem to be justified by the facts:

1. The Confederate Army, especially with respect to the artillery, was poorly organized, and possessed but little cohesion among the divisional units; though slightly improved in this respect by Gen. Lee, who, in immediate contact with the enemy from the day he was assigned to command until the end of the campaign, had no opportunity to reorganize his forces.

2. The success of the Confederate arms was entirely due to the almost irresistible force of the infantry, the *morale* of which, in spite of the severest punishment, never waned.

3. In no general action during the campaign was anything approaching coöperation between the divisional units attained, a result due to the lack of a trained staff, sufficient cavalry, and the ignorance and almost entire neglect of reconnaissance duty.

Rebellion Records, Series I, Vol. XI, Part II, p. 498.

4. The artillery failed to perform the rôle of that arm by reason of inexperience on the part of divisional leaders, the impetuosity of their attacks, defective organization, the topographical features of the terrain, and comparatively inferior material and equipment.

5. Lee overthrew McClellan, not by superior tactical dispositions, which on the part of the Confederates were in the main inferior to, though of an entirely different character from those of the Federals, but by the sheer *élan* of his lion-hearted infantry, which, though unsupported by artillery, and poorly led from a tactical point of view, simply could not be stopped.

6. The superior tactical employment of artillery on the part of the Federals was due, not merely to a better organization, material, equipment, and ammunition, but in far greater measure to the defensive attitude it was invariably called upon to assume, thus minimizing those elements which kept the opposing artillery from the field.

7. The final situation of the two armies arose from the fact that without consideration of the tactical results which had been, or were to be attained, Lee, morally the stronger, always ordered his lieutenants forward to assail the enemy, while McClellan uniformly ordered his to retire to defensive positions, each in adherence to a strategic plan from which there was no departure after Lee took command.

CHAPTER XVI

CEDAR MOUNTAIN

WITH the close of the Peninsula campaign the Artillery of the Army of Northern Virginia may be said to have passed its formative period in which the great crisis of its youth had been Malvern Hill. The Army which had been united and fused in the fiery furnace of experience was now prepared to prosecute a greater career.

The salvation of the Artillery lay in the fact that in all matters connected with it, save in the undaunted courage of its officers and men, and the native talent they had displayed for the arm, grave defects were recognized to exist. A great effort was now made to increase its efficiency and to provide for its more adequate employment in battle. For its tactical neglect, the general consensus of opinion rested the blame on conditions. No one was particularly blamed at the time, though frequent harsh criticisms of individuals have since been made by those possessing belated sagacity.

Before the end of July a redistribution of the field batteries had been made and a number of new batteries had reported for duty in the field, among them Girardey's, and Crawford's or "C" Battery of the Sumter Battalion from Georgia, Joseph Graham's from North Carolina, Coit's from South Carolina, and Parker's Richmond, Fleet's Middlesex, Ruffin's Surry, Wyatt's Albemarle, Hupp's Salem, and Dance's Powhatan batteries of Virginia.

The Reserve Artillery was now organized as follows:

FIRST VIRGINIA LIGHT ARTILLERY REGIMENT

Col. J. Thompson Brown

1.	Williamsburg Battery,	Capt. J. A. Coke.
2.	Powhatan Battery,	Capt. Willis J. Dance.
3.	Salem Battery,	Capt. A. Hupp.
4.	Fayette Battery,	Capt. M. C. Macon.
5.	James City Battery,	Capt. L. W. Richardson.
6.	Henrico Battery,	Capt. W. B. Ritter.
7.	3d Richmond Howitzers,	Capt. B. H. Smith.
8.	2d Richmond Howitzers,	Capt. D. Watson.
9.	Albemarle Battery,	Capt. J. W. Wyatt.
10.	Fairfax Battery,	Capt. ·E. R. Young.

FIRST BATTALION RESERVE ARTILLERY

Lieut.-Col. A. S. Cutts

1.	"A" Battery, Sumter Battalion,	Capt. H. M. Ross.
2.	"B" Battery, Sumter Battalion,	Capt. J. V. Price.
3.	"C" Battery, Sumter Battalion,	Capt. C. P. Crawford.
4.	"D" Battery, Sumter Battalion,	Capt. J. A. Blackshear.
5.	"E" Battery, Sumter Battalion,	Capt. J. Lane.

SECOND BATTALION RESERVE ARTILLERY

Maj. Charles Richardson

1.	2d Fluvanna Battery,	Capt. J. J. Ancell.
2.	Georgia Battery,	Capt. John Milledge.
3.	Ashland Battery,	Capt. Pichegru Woolfolk.

THIRD BATTALION RESERVE ARTILLERY

Maj. William Nelson

1.	Charlottesville Battery,	Capt. Jas. McD. Carrington.
2.	1st Fluvanna Battery,	Capt. C. T. Huckstep.
3.	Amherst Battery,	Capt. Thomas J. Kirkpatrick.
4.	Morris Virginia Battery,	Capt. R. C. M. Page.

FOURTH BATTALION RESERVE ARTILLERY

Maj. Hilary P. Jones

1.	Long Island Battery,	Capt. P. H. Clarke.
2.	Richmond Orange Battery,	Capt. T. Jefferson Peyton.
3.	South Carolina Battery,	Capt. A. B. Rhett.
4.	Goochland Battery,	Capt. W. H. Turner.

This, indeed, was a powerful array which Gen. Pendleton had collected. With the 26 batteries of the reserve were not fewer than 100 guns, including much of the best material in the service. Among the guns captured from McClellan were many fine, serviceable pieces. In point of ordnance, the Confederate reserve now approached that of Hunt, but in discipline, mounts, and equipment, the artillery always fell far behind the Federal standard. The deficiencies in harness and equipment were now beginning to be made up to some extent by the Bureau of Ordnance, its manufacturing activities being in full swing by this time, thanks to the unremitting efforts of Col. Gorgas. Foreign importations of ordnance material and stores were also now being received and distributed to the Army by this energetic officer. Among the ordnance of the Army at this time was to be found a small number of Hotchkiss, Whitworth, Armstrong, and Blakely guns, purchased abroad by foreign agents, and brought in by the fleet of blockade runners operated by the Bureau of Ordnance. The Blakely field pieces were especially favored by the horse batteries.

In the lull succeeding the activities of June and July, strenuous efforts were also made by Pendleton to recruit the depleted batteries of the Army to full strength and to overcome the existing deficiencies with respect to their horses. It is probable, therefore, that the personnel of the reserve numbered 3,000 men or more by the middle of August, and that most of the batteries were well horsed, that is, with a sufficient number of four-horse teams, for the stringency in the South in the supply of remounts had not yet begun to pinch.

Another great stride forward occurred about this time in the enlargement and reorganization of the reserve ordnance train by Col. Alexander, Chief of Ordnance. While the service of ammunition supply on the Peninsula had been remarkably efficient, yet, for the contemplated increase in the activity of the artillery it did not appear adequate to its chief.

The batteries with the divisions were neither as strong in personnel, nor as well equipped and mounted as were those of the reserve at this time. For instance, on July 21, the 4 batteries with Early's and Trimble's brigades of Ewell's Division, namely, Johnson's Bedford (W. Va.), Brown's Chesapeake, the Manchester, and Latimer's Courtney batteries, possessed a personnel of but 222 men, present and absent, increased to 12 officers and 384 men by July 31. But of the latter number only 236 were present for duty, or an average of 3 officers and 56 effective men, and up to August 10, there had been no additions even to make up for the losses sustained, though the tri-monthly return for August 20 shows 14 officers and 276 men present, with an aggregate present and absent of 419. On paper, therefore, the individual battery strength was about 105 men, while in the field it was but 72. Since Ewell's Division had been ordered to take the field July 13 for active work, it is fair to assume that the figures of these batteries, if not typical, were rather above than below the average.*

G. O. No. 150, A. N. V., July 13, 1862, directed Jackson, with his own and Ewell's Division, to proceed to Louisa Court House and if possible to Gordonsville, to check the advance of Pope from the direction of Orange Court House. The same day Crutchfield assigned to Ewell Latimer's (Courtney's), Lusk's 2d Rockbridge, the 2d Baltimore or Brockenbrough's, and Rice's Star, batteries. On the 14th, in addition to Poague's 1st Rockbridge, Carpenter's Alleghany, and Caskie's Hampden batteries already with Jackson's Division, Balthis' Staunton, Brown's 4th Baltimore or Chesapeake, and J. R. Johnson's Bedford, batteries were attached to it. Maj. R. Snowden Andrews, and Maj. A. R. Courtney, former battery commanders, were promoted and assigned to the command of the artillery of Jackson's and Ewell's divisions, respectively. Carrington's Albemarle Battery was detached from

---

Rebellion Records, Series I, Vol. XII, Part III, pp. 964, 965, 966. Ibid., p. 915.

Ewell's Division and ordered to report for duty with the reserve. All of Jackson's batteries were to move with the infantry by train.*

Upon arriving at Gordonsville, July 19, Jackson at once perceived that his force of 12,000 was inadequate as opposed to Pope's 47,000 and called for reënforcements. A. P. Hill was consequently ordered to join him July 27, with 12,000 men, and Pegram's Purcell, Fleet's Middlesex, Braxton's Fredericksburg, and Latham's North Carolina or Branch, batteries. Lieut.-Col. Reuben Lindsay Walker commanded the artillery of the division.

Before the battle of Cedar Mountain, August 9, a number of changes were made in the assignment of the artillery. With the three divisions under Jackson which were present with him in that action were the following batteries:

FIRST DIVISION (Winder (K) Taliaferro)

Maj. R. Snowden Andrews, Chief of Artillery

1st Rockbridge Battery,	Capt. W. T. Poague.
Alleghany Battery,	Capt. Joseph Carpenter.
Hampden Battery,	Capt. W. H. Caskie.

SECOND (LIGHT) DIVISION (A. P. Hill)

Lieut.-Col. Reuben Lindsay Walker, Chief of Artillery

Purcell Battery,	Capt. W. J. Pegram.
Middlesex Battery,	Lieut. W. B. Hardy.
Fredericksburg Battery,	Capt. Carter M. Braxton.
Branch (N. C.) Battery,	Capt. A. C. Latham.

THIRD DIVISION (Ewell)

Maj. A. R. Courtney, Chief of Artillery

1st Md. or Andrews' Battery,	Capt. Wm. F. Dement.
4th Md. or Chesapeake Battery,	Capt. Wm. D. Brown.
La. Guard (Girardey's) Battery,	Capt. Louis E. D'Aquin.
Courtney's Henrico Battery,	Capt. J. W. Latimer.
Bedford Battery,	Capt. J. R. Johnson.

---

*Rebellion Records, Series I, Vol. XII, Part III, p. 915, and Vol. XI, Part III, p. 652. But compare with batteries enumerated in Vol. XII, Part III, p. 964.

Thus, with 23,750 men, Jackson had about 47 guns, or a proportion of 2 per 1,000 men of all arms. But, though small in numbers, his artillery was better organized than it had ever been before, that is in divisional masses, each commanded by an efficient officer, and all under the able Crutchfield, between whom and Jackson a perfect mutual confidence existed.

Jackson was now in his element. The sight of the Blue Ridge was to his soul like a tonic. Independence again roused him to emulate himself. No longer were his actions circumscribed by superior authority at which, whether intentionally or not, he ever chafed.

Released from the monotonous swamp-land of the Peninsula, the eagle had returned to his native hills where from familiar eyrie he might swoop upon the prey, or freely wheel from craggy peak to peak. No historian has yet satisfactorily explained the anomaly of Jackson's lethargy on the Peninsula. The very variance of the proffered solutions only serves to dissatisfy the student. Given this or that set of facts it can be explained. Taking them all together, again we become mystified. With his battery in Mexico, the young Jackson had in the independence of such a command won fame. As a professor in a subordinate position at the Virginia Military Institute, his initiative waned, and over his whole career in Lexington there hung a moody gloom, with only occasional flashes of his fiery soul, as when in his section room he expressed a soulful longing for war, and declared that if war must come, the South should throw away its scabbard. From the moment Jackson joined Lee near Richmond he was no longer the "Eagle of the Valley," but became a falcon, and, perched upon the wrist of a master, it seemed as if his wings were clipped. No longer did he swoop hither and thither glorying in his power. But, the hood removed, once more we discern the eagle-like character of his old self, for Jackson had become Jackson again. Some men are great when their efforts are directed by a guiding hand; the souls of others perish from dependence like wild animals in captivity.

On the 2d of August, while Jackson's command lay about Gordonsville, a brisk cavalry skirmish near Orange Courthouse gave warning that Pope's force must be struck promptly, if it were to be encountered in detail. August 7, therefore, the three divisions moved forward to gain contact with Banks, who had become separated from and was in advance of McDowell. The Federal Cavalry being driven back to Culpeper Courthouse, the Army crossed the Rapidan, Ewell's Division leading, early on the 8th. Continuing to press forward in spite of the many delays and misunderstandings which interefered with his plans, Jackson at last reached the vicinity of Cedar Run, where he gained contact with the Federal Infantry, disposed for the purpose of disputing his advance.

The Federal position lay behind a tributary stream running southward and joining Cedar Run near the eastern end of Slaughter Mountain, a range of hills running from northeast to southwest and overlooking the battlefield. The road from Orange, or the Culpeper Road, over which Banks and Jackson approached each other, crossed the tributary stream at right angles, the Federal position lying in an elevated wood to the west side of the latter. In front of the Federals lay an open and broken country, with a large wheatfield on the north side of the road, surrounded by woods, except along the highway. Farther to the north lay heavily-wooded high ground, but on the south side of the road was an open plateau of cornfields and pastures, gently ascending to the mountain. Ewell with Trimble's and Hays' brigades, Latimer's Courtney Battery, and a section of Johnson's Bedford Battery, under Lieut. Nathaniel Terry, was ordered forward about 1 o'clock, and occupied a commanding position on the northeast point of the mountain, completely overlooking the Federal left wing. Early's Brigade moved forward along the Culpeper Road and pressing back the enemy's cavalry, took up a position on the crest opposite the Federal center, perpendicular to the road and a little south of it, posting one 3-inch rifle from Brown's Chesapeake and 2 from Dement's 1st Maryland Battery on his right, near a clump of cedars just in advance of, and 2 of Dement's and 3 of D'Aquin's in rear of, Mrs. Crittenden's house. In Early's front was open pasture ground sloping gently downward, beyond which was a cornfield sloping upward to the Federal position; thus the ground at this point afforded an excellent field of fire for the guns on both sides. North of the Culpeper Road the wheatfield mentioned was just opposite the cornfield on the south side, but the country on the north side was much less open than to the south. To Early's immediate left was timber, which everywhere on the north side of the road extended up to the wheatfield. Winder, whose division had followed Ewell's, was directed to support Early. Advancing along the main road he placed Garnett's Brigade in the woods to the north facing the wheatfield with his right facing the road, near which 5 guns from Poague's, Carpenter's, and Caskie's batteries were posted, supported by Taliaferro's Brigade. Winder's own brigade was held in reserve. From left to right of the Confederate line the distance was probably 2 miles, a considerable gap intervening between Early and Ewell's other brigades. The 26 guns of Jackson's artillery which had been brought up were disposed in a crescent, the horns of which were to the rear, in 3 small groups; that of Maj. Andrews on the left with 5, that of Early in the center with 8, and that of Ewell on the right with 6 pieces, the range of the center group being perhaps 500, and the ranges of the others as much as 2,500 yards from the enemy's batteries.

In Banks' Corps, were 9 batteries well grouped about opposite Early. As soon as the latter took up his position, the Federal guns opened upon him, to which Dement and Brown at once replied, soon supported by Maj. Andrews' guns on the left and Latimer's on the right. The ensuing artillery duel continued with great vigor for about 2 hours. Gen. Winder was mortally wounded while directing the fire of his batteries. About 3 P. M. from Hill's divisional artillery, then in park in rear, Col. Walker was able to bring forward Pegram's Purcell, and Hardy's Middlesex batteries, to the support of those already in action, but found it impossible to bring up more guns before the action was over, due to the blocked condition of the roads in rear of the field. Thus the number of pieces engaged in this duel was finally about equal on the two sides.

Between 5 and 6 P. M. Banks, who, with his superior ordnance, had gotten somewhat the best of the artillery duel, advanced to the attack. His right, overlapping the Confederate left, threw the latter into confusion, routing Garnett's Brigade. Maj. Andrews ordering his batteries with those of A. P. Hill, which Walker had brought up, to change front, maintained a terrific fire from his guns upon the Federal Infantry, which had approached to within 300 yards before A. P. Hill's Division began to arrive upon the scene, and enabled the Confederates to repulse the assault and drive the Federals across Cedar Creek. By this time it was dark, but favored by a moon, almost full, two fresh brigades with Pegram's Purcell Battery undertook the pursuit, but were checked by Ricketts' Division, 3 of the batteries of which inflicted a loss of 2 killed and 14 wounded on Pegram's Battery alone. Pegram's action on this occasion was characteristically cool and gallant.*

In the whole affair, the loss of the Confederate Artillery was 2 killed and 28 wounded; that of the enemy was 7 killed, and 29 wounded, and 6 missing. In material, the Federal loss was the greater, involving, however, but one 12-pounder Napoleon.

Some idea of the severity of the artillery duel may be derived from the fact that Knapp's Pennsylvania Battery of six 10-pounder Parrotts reported an expenditure of 980 rounds during the day.

In this exceptionally bloody action on the part of the infantry, much less so, however, than it would have been

*Rebellion Records, Series I, Vol. XII, Part II, p. 171, Report of Major Davis Tillson, Chief of Artillery, 3d Army Corps.

had Jackson made the usual headlong assault on the Federal position, we again find him delaying until his better guns could be brought into action. While not all of his artillery was brought up, yet that employed was grouped in masses, small though they were, in order to secure from them the benefits of a cross fire on the Federal artillery. Jackson had undoubtedly learned the lesson that with long range guns concentrated fire did not necessarily require massed guns. Though Banks anticipated him in the infantry attack, yet the disposition of his guns had enabled Jackson, both on the right, between Early and Ewell, and on the extreme left, to assist his infantry with the canister of his batteries. In the battle of Cedar Mountain, in which the batteries were directed by divisional chiefs, is to be found by far the best tactical employment of field artillery up to that time exhibited by the Confederates, and in point of individual battery action in pursuit, nothing could have excelled the skill and dash displayed by Pegram, who, though severely punished, adroitly followed up the retreating infantry, working havoc in its ranks with his guns until they were silenced by the concentrated fire of 4 fresh batteries.

To Pegram belongs the credit of having been first to make Pope, with his entire staff, turn his back on the Army of Northern Virginia, a practice which he had boastingly declared was the great fault with his predecessor.*

We shall frequently meet with the name of William Johnston Pegram in this narrative from now on. As no officer of the Artillery of Lee's Army was more noted than he, some account of his career up to the time of which we write should here be given.†

"In October, 1860, he matriculated as a student in the University of Virginia, entering the School of Law.

---

*The disappearance of Pope, when a salvo from Pegram's Battery suddenly burst upon him as he arrived on the field, is an amusing incident in the career of that general.
†For complete sketch of his life see "The University Memorial," by the Rev. John L. Johnson. The sketch of Pegram is by W. Gordon McCabe, his brilliant adjutant and inseparable comrade.

He was then nineteen years old, reserved almost to shyness, grave and gracious in his manner, in which there was little of primness and much of the charm of an old-fashioned politeness. His apparent shyness was owing partly to his extreme near-sightedness, partly to the modesty of his nature. To those students who were not his intimates, but happened to meet him occasionally in the rooms of common friends, it was often a matter of wonder and remark how keen a sense of humor there was in this quiet, sober-looking lad, who assuredly yielded to no one in his thorough appreciation of the most delicate criticism.

"In the autumn of this year the students determined to organize two companies of infantry, and Pegram at once became an active promoter of the enterprise. He entered the first company formed, known as the 'Southern Guard,' and was appointed 1st Sergeant. He was then a capital infantry soldier, having been for two years a member of the famous 'Company F' of Richmond, and proved untiring in drilling his men. In 1861 came Lincoln's proclamation calling for 50,000 volunteers. From that moment books were little thought of in the University. All were eager to exchange gown for sword. Pegram at once left college and reported for duty with his old company, which had been ordered to Aquia Creek. With this company he remained but a short time. Sent as drillmaster to exercise the artillerymen of Walker in the infantry tactics, he was elected Lieutenant of the 'Purcell Battery.' It was as commander of this battery that he was destined to achieve his hard-won fame—a battery which was with him from the first battle of Manassas, through every general action in Virginia, to the trenches of Petersburg—which, always skillfully handled in the presence of the enemy, yet lost during its four years of service more than 200 men killed and wounded; and which he declared repeatedly when colonel that 'the Purcell men were the coolest and the most desperate men he ever saw in a tight place.' Lindsay Walker, afterwards

Brigadier-General and Chief of Artillery of Hill's
Corps, was then captain of the battery, and was not
slow to discover what a thorough soldier he possessed in
his young subaltern.   Long afterwards Walker gener-
ously said that Pegram spared him all trouble, and that
commanding a battery, the most troublesome thing in
the world, became a pleasure with such an executive
officer.   In the campaign of '61 the battery was engaged
at Bull Run; Walker received his majority early in
'62, and Pegram became captain on the reorganization.
But it was not until the great struggle in front of Richmond, in July of '62, that the battery came into marked
prominence.   At Mechanicsville it held the post of
honor, and paid the price which the post of honor ever
exacts.   Here first to the Army the young captain gave
proof of that stubborn courage and literal obedience to
orders which all men thereafter looked for in him.   Exposed to a murderous fire of infantry, to the convergent
fire of five six-gun batteries, long after night came
down the thunder of his guns told that he was
tenaciously holding his ground.   But there was surprise mingled with admiration when it became known
to the Army on the next day that of his six guns four
had been disabled before nightfall, that two of his officers had been badly wounded, more than half his
horses killed, and that of the ninety dashing cannoneers
who had on yesterday galloped into action more than
fifty lay killed and wounded on the field.

"The day after 'Mechanicsville' he equipped thoroughly the two guns which had not been disabled, and
again applied to Gen. Hill to have the advance.   Everywhere during the Seven Days that plucky section and
its young captain found their place where the battle
raged hottest.   Richmond, in her joy of triumph, a joy
chastened by the sorrow which victory ever brings, was
not unmindful of her younthful hero.   The town rang
with his praises—praises closest to a soldier's heart—
from the lips of wounded men, who had seen him in the
dust and sweat of battle, and who spoke of him as only

brave men can speak of each other. His name was introduced into the play by one of the actors at the theater, and elicited the most tumultuous applause. The player declared that the boy captain fought at such close quarters because he was too near-sighted to see a dozen yards, and would never open fire until he saw the enemy. At this the bronzed and bearded veterans in the pit rose and cheered lustily. Meanwhile the young captain remained modestly at his camp, riding into the city but rarely to visit his immediate family, and blushing painfully when any one spoke to him of the attention his gallantry had excited. Especially annoying to him were the fulsome praises showered upon him by newspapers. His distress at these paragraphs was a great source of amusement to his comrades. 'Why, this is simply disgusting,' he would say; 'every man at the front will be laughing over it.' But the men at the front were never prone to laugh at good fighters, and gave even more exaggerated accounts of his achievements than did the florid paragraphs of the journals.

"A few days of rest, and his battery, newly equipped and recruited, was on the march to Cedar Mountain with Jackson's flying column. Here again his guns, pushed up within eighty *yards* of the enemy, were served with such rapidity and precision as won a nod of approval even from the great leader, always so chary of praise. About nightfall, when Gen. Jackson had determined to press the retreating enemy, Pegram's guns, supported by Field's Brigade, were advanced within close range of the spot where the enemy was supposed to have halted. In a few moments a heavy column was seen marching on the flank of the guns. Owing to the uncertain light it was impossible to tell whether it was a column of Federals or of our own men. The officers of the support differed in opinion regarding the matter, and time was precious. Pegram at once turned his battery over to his 1st lieutenant, saying: 'McGraw, I shall ride up close to these fellows; keep a sharp look-

out, and if you see me wave my hat, open all the guns.'
In a moment he was galloping towards the column now
within a hundred yards, reined in his horse close to
the silently-moving mass, turned, and waved his hat.
Another moment and he rode at full speed into the
line of guns, where old Stonewall sat on his sorrel
watching the column. Pegram cried out in great glee:
'Pitch in, men; Gen. Jackson is looking at you!' The
enemy were broken in a few minutes by his rapid fire,
but speedily put three batteries into position and returned it. For 2 hours this single battery fought 18
guns of the enemy, and it was not until 10 o'clock that
his heated and disabled Napoleons were silenced. His
loss was proportionally, very nearly as great as at
Mechanicsville; but he was determined to push on with
Walker's Battalion to Manassas, where for the second
time his guns did good service on that glorious field."

CHAPTER XVII

GAINESVILLE AND GROVETON

August 14, McClellan, with the main body of his army began his movement to Fortress Monroe, from which point his troops were to be transferred to the vicinity of Alexandria, for the purpose of moving out to the support of Pope. Burnside's Corps which had reached Fredericksburg began to move up the Rappahannock for the same purpose. Gen. Lee personally took command at Gordonsville on the 15th, to which point Jackson had returned on the 12th. On the 13th, Longstreet's command consisting of 19 brigades was ordered to Gordonsville by rail, and Hood with 2 brigades to Hanover Junction, R. H. Anderson's Division being ordered to proceed from Drewry's Bluff to Louisa Courthouse.* As soon as it was positively learned that Burnside had left Fredericksburg, Hood was ordered to join Longstreet. On the 18th, the Reserve Artillery, which had not taken part in Jackson's operations about Orange, was ordered to proceed by road to Gordonsville.† Leaving his camp about Richmond on the afternoon of the 19th, the same day Pendleton was directed to halt his command upon reaching the North Anna, behind which Ripley had been ordered to mass Smith's Division for the purpose of opposing the reported advance of a Federal column over the Fredericksburg Road. Tarrying here for a time, Pendleton was soon ordered to join Gen. Lee, the Reserve reaching Louisa Courthouse on the 27th. From this point its route was deflected to Rapidan Station. While Pendleton himself, by dint of hard riding, succeeded in joining Gen. Lee on the battlefield of Second Manassas, the Reserve Artillery, as seen, was lumbering along far to the rear at the rate of about 20 miles a day.

---

*Rebellion Records, Series I, Vol. XII, Part III, pp. 928, 929, 931.
†Ibid., p. 965.

On the 19th, Gen. Lee had published his order for the advance of his army from Gordonsville to begin early the following morning. Longstreet's command constituting the right, and Jackson's constituting the left wing, were to cross the Rapidan at Raccoon and Somerville Fords, respectively, moving in the direction of Culpeper Courthouse, the latter followed by R. H. Anderson's Division in reserve, with which Col. S. D. Lee's newly-organized battalion of 6 batteries was to move. This reserve battalion was composed as follows:

Bath Battery,	Capt. J. L. Eubank.
Portsmouth (Grimes') Battery,	Lieut. Thomas J. Oakham.
Bedford Battery,	Capt. T. C. Jordan.
Richmond Battery,	Capt. W. W. Parker.
Rhett's South Carolina Battery,	Lieut. Wm. Elliott.
Ashland Battery,	Capt. Pichegru Woolfolk, Jr.

The mass of Pope's troops was near the Rapidan, opposite Orange Courthouse, where they had been confronting Jackson at Gordonsville. The commanding-general becoming apprised on the 18th of Lee's plans and numbers by means of a captured autograph communication of the latter, at once ordered his army to fall back behind the Rappahannock, where he would be nearer his base and more promptly reënforced by a part, at least, of McClellan's army. By the night of the 19th the Federal Army lay behind the river, its left opposite Kelly's Ford, and its right behind Hazel Run, near Rappahannock Station. The following night the Confederates had crossed the Rapidan, and Longstreet, on the right, had gained contact with the Federal left at Kelly's Ford. On the 21st, Jackson moved forward from his bivouac at Stevensburg to the river, his front extending from the railroad bridge to Beverly Ford. At the latter point, Col. Rosser with two regiments of cavalry crossed the river, dispersing the opposing infantry and disabling one of Banks' batteries which had been posted behind the ford. With a section of Pelham's horse battery, Rosser's force remained on the north side of the river until late in the day, supported from the other bank by Taliaferro's 8 divisional batteries under Maj. L. M. Shumaker. When Stuart withdrew before King's Division and some of Sigel's troops, sent up by McDowell to retake the ford, an active artillery duel ensued during the remainder of the day between the opposing batteries, a cannonade without material results on either side.

The main point to be noticed in connection with the Artillery in this movement is that it was comparatively well organized in divisional masses, only a few batteries being assigned to brigades, and that it was kept well up to the front in the advance, with the exception of the Reserve. It would seem that Pendleton's remonstrance against the inadequate use of the Artillery on the Peninsula had had some effect, though of course the error which had been previously committed with respect to the neglect of the arm had been perceived and appreciated by Gen. Lee. Its organization was now, approximately, as follows:

RIGHT WING OR LONGSTREET'S CORPS

ANDERSON'S DIVISION

Lieut.-Col. Stephen D. Lee, Chief of Artillery

1.	Bath Battery,	Capt. J. L. Eubank.
2.	Portsmouth Battery,	Lieut. Thomas J. Oakham.
3.	Bedford Battery,	Capt. T. C. Jordan.
4.	Richmond Battery,	Capt. W. W. Parker.
5.	Rhett's South Carolina Battery,	Lieut. William Elliott.
6.	Ashland Battery,	Capt. Pichegru Woolfolk, Jr.

WILCOX'S DIVISION

1.	Thomas Battery,	Capt. Edwin J. Anderson.*
2.	Dixie Battery,	Capt. W. H. Chapman.†

HOOD'S DIVISION

Maj. B. W. Frobel, Chief of Artillery

1.	Charleston (S. C.) German Battery,	Capt. W. R. Bachman.
2.	Palmetto (S. C.) Battery,	Capt. Hugh R. Garden.
3.	Rowan (N. C.) Battery,	Capt. James Reilly.

*Wilcox's Brigade.
†Featherston's Brigade.

KEMPER'S DIVISION

1. Macbeth (S. C.) Battery,   Capt. R. Boyce.*

CORPS RESERVE ARTILLERY (RIGHT WING)

Col. John B. Walton, Chief of Artillery

1.	1st Co. Washington Artillery,	Capt. C. W. Squires.
2.	2d Co. Washington Artillery,	Capt. J. B. Richardson.
3.	3d Co. Washington Artillery,	Capt. M. B. Miller.
4.	4th Co. Washington Artillery,	Capt. B. F. Eshleman.
5.	Norfolk Battery,	Capt. Frank Huger.
6.	Goochland (Leake) Battery,	Capt. Wm. H. Turner.
7.	Donaldsonville (La.) Battery,	Capt. Victor Maurin.
8.	Lynchburg Battery,	Capt: M. N. Moorman.
9.	Loudoun Battery,	Capt. A. L. Rogers.
10.	Fauquier Battery,	Capt. R. M. Stribling.

LEFT WING OR JACKSON'S CORPS

Col. Stapleton Crutchfield, Chief of Artillery

TALIAFERRO'S DIVISION

Maj. L. M. Shumaker, Chief of Artillery

1.	2d Baltimore Battery,	Capt. J. B. Brockenbrough.
2.	Alleghany Battery,	Capt. Joseph Carpenter.
3.	Hampden Richmond Battery,	Capt. Wm. H. Caskie.
4.	Winchester Battery,	Capt. W. E. Cutshaw.
5.	1st Rockbridge Battery,	Capt. Wm. T. Poague.
6.	Lee Battery,	Capt. Charles J. Raine.
7.	8th Star Battery,	Capt. W. H. Rice.
8.	Danville Battery,	Capt. George W. Wooding.

A. P. HILL'S DIVISION

Lieut.-Col. R. Lindsay Walker, Chief of Artillery

1.	Fredericksburg Battery,	Capt. Carter M. Braxton.
2.	Richmond Battery,	Capt. W. G. Crenshaw.
3.	Letcher Battery,	Capt. Greenlee Davidson.
4.	Middlesex Battery,	Lieut. W. B. Hardy.
5.	Branch (N. C.) Battery,	Lieut. John R. Potts.
6.	Pee Dee (S. C.) Battery,	Capt. D. G. McIntosh.
7.	Purcell Battery,	Capt. Wm. J. Pegram.

*Evans' Brigade.

EWELL'S DIVISION

Maj. A. R. Courtney, Chief of Artillery

1. Staunton Battery,	Lieut. A. W. Garber.
2. 4th Md. or Chesapeake Battery,	Capt. Wm. D. Brown.
3. Louisiana Guard Battery,	Capt. Louis E. D'Aquin.
4. 1st Maryland Battery,	Capt. Wm. F. Dement.
5. Bedford Battery,	Capt. John R. Johnson.
6. Henrico Courtney Battery,	Capt. James W. Latimer.

Thus with Lee's Army, numbering between 47,000 and 55,000 men, were 43 batteries, with a total of about 175 guns, or something over 3 guns per 1,000 of all arms.* With Longstreet's Corps were 22, and with Jackson's, 21 batteries. The total personnel did not exceed 2,500 men.

In addition to the light batteries of the Army, there were, however, with the cavalry, Pelham's and Chew's horse batteries. About this time the Washington (S. C.) Battery, Capt. James F. Hart, was converted into a horse battery, but it did not rejoin the Army until September 2.

In Longstreet's Corps, a large reserve force of 10 batteries is found collected under the immediate command of Col. Walton, an organization only approximating the corps artillery reserve of the following year, for 6 of these batteries were used at this time in a purely individual capacity.

On the morning of the 22d, Jackson, seeking to gain the enemy's right, left the position he had previously occupied, Longstreet having been ordered over thereto from Kelly's Ford, and moved towards the fords near Warrenton or Fauquier White Sulphur Springs, where he arrived during the afternoon, having crossed the Hazel River at Welford's Mill. Longstreet had, meanwhile, been engaging the enemy in an active artillery combat at Beverly Ford.

Although aware of the movement on his right, Pope held the mass of his army near Rappahannock Station

---

*For strength of Lee's army, see Ropes, p. 198; Allan, p. 199; *Four Years With General Lee*, Taylor, p. 60; *Southern Historical Papers*, Vol. VII, p. 181.

in order to hold the railroad and keep open the route for his reënforcements from Fredericksburg, both of which were threatened by Longstreet. During the various active movements that ensued, resulting after much vacillation, in Pope's occupying with his whole army a position between Sulphur Springs and Warrenton, the Artillery had been actively employed both by Longstreet at Beverly Ford and by Jackson against Sigel, in his flanking movement on the Federal right. On the 24th, Jackson's artillery had also been active along the river from Sulphur Springs to Waterloo, A. P. Hill's Division holding the Confederate side of the river. Practically all of the artillery of the two corps had been engaged.

It now became known that Pope had plans of his own, and that Lee had been foiled in his effort to cross the river. At this juncture it also became evident that Pope's 50,000 men would soon be increased to 130,000 or more, and though Lee's strength would soon exceed 70,000, immediate action on his part was necessary. Without waiting for his reënforcements, since the delay would in effect only contribute to the disparity in numbers between the two armies, Lee now decided to make one more effort to fall upon Pope's rear.

Accordingly, late on the 24th, Jackson, with 22,000 men, was ordered to cross the Rappahannock beyond Pope's right flank, and move by forced marches through Thoroughfare Gap until he struck the Orange and Alexandria Railroad in the Federal rear.

In order to make possible this movement, Lee now gave the most brilliant example of the use of artillery which had yet occurred in the war. The success of Jackson's movement depended absolutely upon its secrecy, and yet it was necessary for him to withdraw his guns from under the very eyes of the enemy. It was accomplished on the following day. Perceiving that the Federals had largely withdrawn from the lower fords along the Rappahannock, Longstreet, leaving but a small force in his old position, was ordered up to re-

lieve Jackson, the latter's guns having maintained their
fire until nightfall, making a brave display of force.
Upon the arrival of Longstreet, his guns were quietly
substituted for those of Jackson under the cover of
night, continuing the fire with great activity at dawn.

Late on the 24th, Jackson's Corps had been assembled about Jeffersonton, where the troops were relieved of all baggage and trains. Nothing in the way
of a train but the ambulance and ammunition wagons
and a few beeves on the hoof was to accompany the
light column and its artillery. Marching northwest to
Amissville, and then north to Salem, with the artillery
in the rear, Jackson covered 26 miles on the 25th. On
the 26th, the column was under way at daybreak, and
now turned eastward. Passing through Thoroughfare
Gap in the Bull Run Mountain, it reached Gainesville
about 3 P. M., from which point Jackson marched to
Bristoe, Ewell's Division arriving there about sunset
after a march of 25 miles. The presence of the Confederates being now discovered, Trimble's Brigade
hastened on another 4 miles to capture Manassas
Junction before reënforcements could arrive from
Alexandria. This he gallantly did, capturing the
Federal works with 2 light batteries complete and fully
mounted. When Jackson arrived at Manassas Junction
early the morning of the 27th, with Taliaferro's and
Hill's divisions, he had with him the entire divisional
artillery. Thus, in little more than 48 hours, Jackson's
21 batteries, with four-horse teams, had covered over 55
miles, no mean performance even with the most superior
full teams of draught animals.

In the meantime, Longstreet by ostentatiously planting fresh batteries and keeping up a heavy fire of artillery in periodical cannonades, had succeded in deceiv-
ing Pope throughout the 25th and the morning of the
26th into believing that a crossing was to be attempted
either at Sulphur Springs or Waterloo Bridge.*
About noon of the latter day, however, leaving Ander-

---

*Rebellion Records, Series I, Vol. XII, Part II, p. 66.

son's Division at Sulphur Springs to observe the enemy, Longstreet with about 25,000 men set out to follow Jackson's route, bivouacking at Orleans that night and reaching White Plains the next day, 24 miles west of Thoroughfare Gap. Meantime, Pope, possessed of a great desire to crush Jackson at Manassas, ordered all his forces to that point on the 28th.

When Pope reached the battlefield on Manassas plains which he had sketched out for himself, his antagonist was not to be found, for Jackson lay hidden in the woods within seven miles of the ruins of Manassas. It was not until 5 P. M. that King's Division of Mc-Dowell's Corps accidentally developed his presence while marching from Gainesville to Centreville to join the main Federal body in pursuance of Pope's orders.

Jackson's position lay about a mile north of the Warrenton pike, near Groveton. As soon as King's brigades began to stream by, utterly unconscious of the former's presence, Jackson ordered Lawton's and Trimble's brigades to the attack, and Wooding's and Garber's batteries to trot forward and open fire upon the center of the column opposite them. Gibbon sent a regiment to drive off the guns, thinking perhaps he had encountered a part of Stuart's Cavalry, with its horse batteries, and also opened upon them with his own two batteries, which, admirably served, soon compelled the Confederate guns to limber up and shift their positions. To the support of Wooding and Garber, Jackson had ordered up from his rear 20 more pieces which failed to arrive, due to the thickness of the woods, though two of Pelham's guns were brought forward. For 2½ hours the conflict raged with heavy loss to both sides, the Federals, who had displayed great courage, finally withdrawing at nightfall. Surprised while marching *en route* by the fire of two batteries that were supported by a large force of infantry, and again when ordered to drive off a supposed small cavalry force, the Federal Infantry as well as their two batteries, neither of which had been in action before, sustained and inflicted serious losses

under circumstances which would have justified confusion among seasoned troops. They could not have
been taken at a greater disadvantage, and while they
lost 1,100 out of 2,800, among the 4,500 Confederates
engaged, the loss was not less than 1,200. The rifled
Federal guns had undoubtedly carried off the artillery
honors.

On the morning of the 29th, Jackson realized, as he
gazed upon the heavy masses forming on the hills opposite him, that the day was a critical one, for whether
Longstreet had broken through Thoroughfare Gap or
not, it would be many hours before he could reënforce
the Second Corps on the battlefield of July 21, 1861.

Jackson's three divisions occupied a long, flat-topped
ridge, standing about a mile north of the Warrenton-
Centerville Road, and commanding the approaches
from the south and east, was an unfinished railroad bed
running some 500 yards below the crest. Before the
right and the right center of the position, about 1¾
miles in length, lay green pastures, almost free of obstacles to the fire of the defenders for a distance of 1,300
yards, and sloping to a brook known as Young's
Branch. The left center, and left, however, were shut
in by a thicket near Groveton, from 400 to 600 yards in
width, which crossed the cut, and reduced the field of
fire at that point. Within the position behind the
copses and folds in the land, there was ample cover for
reserves. Behind the deep cuttings and high embank-
ments of the railroad bed, the advanced line was
strongly placed. The left, slightly refused, rested on a
rocky spur near Bull Run, commanding Sudley
Springs Ford, and the road to Aldie Gap. Between
this eminence and the creek lay an open cornfield.

On the wooded ridge 500 yards to the left rear of the
infantry line, 16 guns were posted and the 24 pieces of
Poague's, Carpenter's, Dement's, Brockenbrough's, and
Latimer's batteries were stationed in rear of the right
center.

The left of the position was occupied by A. P. Hill's Division of 6 brigades in 3 lines; the center by Trimble's and Lawton's brigades of Ewell's Division, and the right by Jackson's old division of 4 brigades, now commanded by Starke, also in 3 lines. Early with 2 brigades and a battery, occupied a wooded knoll where the railroad bed crossed the highroad in the right rear of the main line, and Stuart protected the flanks, meantime endeavoring to gain touch with Longstreet whose approach was from the right rear. Thus Jackson had taken up a most defensible position with his 18,000 men, and placed every gun in position, for which there was room on the ragged crest. Behind the deep ditches and high parapets formed by the railroad bed were roughly 5 muskets per running yard of front, with a clear field of fire, except at one point, up to the limit of their effective range, the same being true with respect to the guns from which a plunging fire would have to be encountered by the attacking infantry.

Jackson's disposition of his artillery was a wise one, from which many advantages were to be expected. If the enemy's long range pieces elected to engage in a duel with the batteries on the ridge above and to the rear of his infantry, then the latter would be relieved of the fire of the opposing batteries, and, should the enemy decide to hammer at his infantry in the railroad cuts and behind the fills with his artillery, the supporting batteries would be free to play either upon the hostile guns or the attacking columns at will. Little effect with common shell could be had, at best, against the natural line of works, which Jackson had availed himself of for his infantry, and before the assaulting columns could gain the position, the fire of the enemy's guns would become masked. From every consideration, then, the Confederates seemed possessed of a position guaranteeing a fire superiority over the enemy. That such proved to be the case in the battle of Groveton is borne out by the repulse of overwhelming numbers. That Jackson and Crutchfield had employed much judgment in the disposition of their artillery is not to be denied, and in this engagement many of the advantages of modern indirect fire accrued to the defense, that is, the attacker, since he did not possess a greatly superior number of guns, was forced to neglect either the artillery or the infantry of his adversary by reason of their entire separation. Again, Jackson gives us the first example of the kind to be found in the operations of Virginia. In the study of his battles too little attention has been paid such considerations, elements of his success, particularly on this occasion, which can not be overlooked. A general who makes good use of his artillery holds in his hand a strong trump card.

CHAPTER XVIII

SHORTLY after 5 A. M. on the 30th, while the Confederates were still taking up their positions, the Federals began to move down the heights near the Henry House about 2 miles distant, in imposing masses, and about 7 o'clock, 4 divisions deployed in several lines at the foot of the hills, their skirmishers engaging the Confederate pickets, and 3 batteries came into action on a rise northeast of Groveton, opposite the Confederate center.

On the right and left of the Groveton wood, Jackson's two large groups of guns had a clean field of fire which they utilized with splendid effect, completely checking the attacking columns in their front, the enemy's infantry entering the wood, however, from which the Confederates, protected in a measure from the fire of Pope's batteries by the thickness of the cover, succeeded in driving them. The batteries of Poague, Carpenter, Dement, Brockenbrough, and Latimer, under Maj. Shumaker, were now thrown forward from the right to shell the retreating columns. These batteries were met by the fire of those of the enemy which had been shelling the woods, and a fierce duel ensued, lasting until perhaps 10:30 A. M., when Shumaker withdrew his batteries. The Federal guns were now moved more to their right to prepare the way for another attack on Hill's right. About noon the second assault was repulsed, although the Federals reached the Confederate position in such strength as to require the third line of Hill's Division to assist in clearing the wood, a section of Pegram's Battery moving out with the infantry to fire upon the retreating foe.

Meanwhile the divisions of Reno, Kearney, and Hooker had reached the field from Centreville, and about 1 P. M. they were ordered to renew the attack.

Kearney on the right was completely foiled by the fire of the left group of guns, but Hooker and Reno entering the woods, portions of their heavy columns actually crossed the railroad line and engaged in the most desperate hand-to-hand encounter with Field's and Thomas' brigades. Again reënforcements were sent forward from Hill's third line and, repelling the assault, pursued the enemy through the wood to the open ground beyond, where Pender's Brigade, encountering a destructive artillery fire, fell back to the thicket somewhat disorganized. Seeing Pender's retirement, Grover's Brigade of Hooker's Division, being in reserve, was ordered to deliver a counterstroke and performed the task with such splendid courage that, unsupported, it carried a considerable part of the Confederate line in the wood.

In the third attack, the Federal infantry column had been well supported by the fire of its guns, 2 of which, rifled pieces, had been moved well forward to the right, causing Braxton's Battery to be ordered to Hill's left to reply to them. Before the fourth assault was undertaken, the batteries of Crenshaw and Latham had also been moved out to the left to drive off the 2 Federal guns and secure oblique fire to their own right. They succeeded in silencing the 2 guns.

While the Federals had forced Hill back about 300 yards, they were themselves thrown into disorder and the arrival of Early's and Lawton's brigades now enabled Hill once more to regain his position and drive the enemy from the wood. He was ably assisted by Crenshaw's and Latham's batteries which delivered a destructive fire upon the enemy at a range of not over 450 yards, and Starke's Brigade captured the two 3-inch Federal rifles which had caused so much trouble.

It was now nearly 6 o'clock. The Federals had never been able to reach close quarters with the Confederates, either on the right or left of the Groveton wood over the approaches dominated by Crutchfield's artillery groups, although, at a cost of 4,000 men, they had four times reached the line in the wood where little artillery fire was encountered. The contrast is significant and clearly illustrates the fact that artillery efficiency is not to be measured by the losses it sustains nor by those which it inflicts. Indeed, it is very often the case that the greater the influence the guns exert upon the course of a battle, as at Groveton, the fewer the losses the detachments sustain, by reason of their ability to hold the enemy at ranges beyond the fire effect of the latter. Had the groups of guns at Groveton proved inadequate to check the attacking columns opposite them, and had those columns been able to advance to close quarters in spite of the fire of the opposing guns, then the artillery, having failed to accomplish the mission assigned it, would undoubtedly have suffered heavy losses. As it was, it suffered little.

Again, the effectiveness of artillery is not to be measured by the losses it inflicts. We often hear the sneering criticism that at such and such a battle but 1 or 2 per cent of the enemy's loss was due to the fire of the artillery. Any such test is entirely erroneous. Not only do the guns exert a tremendous moral effect in support of their infantry, and adverse to the enemy, but they do far more. They often actually preclude heavy damage from the enemy by preventing him from essaying an assault against the position the guns occupy. Then, again, by forcing the enemy to seek cover, they eliminate their antagonists to that extent, and though they are able to inflict little damage upon the enemy while he is under cover, they not only reduce his volume of fire, but render that which is delivered less effective. Let us hear no more of artillery efficiency as measured by the number of its victims.

Had the terrain permitted Jackson to post a large group of guns so as to command the approach to the Groveton wood, the Federal loss would have been much less than it was by reason of the fact that Pope's dense columns would never have come within the zone of effective musketry fire, since they would have been held at arm's length by the artillery. The weakest point of Jackson's line was clearly the one the approach to which was not commanded by his guns, yet at that point the attack being more successful than elsewhere, the heaviest losses were incurred by the enemy, only a small percentage of which were inflicted by the artillery.

Throughout the latter half of the day, the divisions of Longstreet's Corps, which had forced their way through Thoroughfare Gap, were arriving on Jackson's right, to oppose which the troops of Reynolds, McDowell and two of Porter's divisions had taken position. Longstreet, on his arrival, instead of prolonging Jackson's right, had inclined his line forward, thus forming with the former an obtuse angle.

While approaching his position in line, Gen. Hood, about 11 A. M., ordered forward his divisional batteries under Maj. Frobel to assist Jackson's right group of guns in holding Reynolds at bay. Commencing about 1 P. M., a duel with the enemy's batteries near Groveton House continued about 2½ hours in which the hostile guns were silenced and driven from the field. In this duel, Bachman's and Reilly's batteries, Garden's not being engaged because not armed with rifled pieces, expended about 100 rounds. The incident is mentioned because it clearly shows the change which had taken place in the tactical employment of artillery. Here we find a division commander, instead of keeping his battalion in the rear, ordering forward his artillery to cooperate with the guns of another commander, even before the position is reached. To accomplish his movement, it was necessary for Frobel to have the right of way, a thing quite unheard of for the artillery on the Peninsula. So we see that a marked advance is not only to be noted in Jackson's use of his artillery on the defensive, but that indications of better tactical employment while advancing to the attack are to be found in the battle of Groveton, which ended about 9 P. M., after Hood and Evans had overthrown King.

On the morning of the 30th, the Confederate line, about 4 miles long, was occupied by about 47,000 men, exclusive of 2,500 cavalry. Pope with 65,000 men and 28 batteries compactly massed under his own eye, might expect in the course of several hours a reënforcement of 42,000 men from Alexandria.

While the Federal commander was making his dispositions to renew the battle of the day before, a long range and ineffective cannonade was indulged in by the opposing artilleries. Although with the 28 Federal batteries there were not over 125 guns, practically all of them were rifled pieces and many were of heavy caliber. It is quite certain that the 43 Confederate batteries present, with a total of perhaps 175 guns, were outmatched in point of metal, for the best artillery material in Lee's Army was with the reserve which had not yet come up.

The Federal line of battle, when finally formed, was short and strong. From its right on Bull Run opposite Jackson's left, to its left, which rested just across the Warrenton pike, near Groveton, the distance was less than 3 miles. Deployed in the front line were 20,000 infantry, with 40,000 held in great compact masses to be hurled in columns whenever needed, a formation Napoleonic in the grandeur of its density.

Satisfied with his railroad line, Jackson clung to his old position, but a number of changes were effected in the posting of the guns. The left group of 16 guns remained as before, but 18 guns from the right center group were advanced by Col. Crutchfield to a position from which they could enfilade any columns that might attempt to assault the infantry line.* Still farther toward the turnpike and about half a mile west of Groveton, was stationed another group of 18 guns drawn from Longstreet's reserve and in command of Col. S. D. Lee. The ammunition chests of all the batteries had been replenished during the night.

---

*From the batteries of J. R. Johnson, Rice, Wooding, Poague, Carpenter, Brockenbrough, Latimer, and D'Aquin.

Col. Lee's Battalion, composed of the batteries of Eubank, Parker, Rhett, and Jordan, was skillfully posted on the high ground just west of the Douglas House, the guns pointing northeast, or at right angles to Jackson's line, overlooking and commanding the wide tract of undulating meadow stretching away for a mile or more in front of the Stonewall and Lawton's divisions. The entire open space in front of Jackson's line was now, therefore, exposed to a cross-fire from the 3 formidable groups, besides that from the batteries on the infantry line.

To the right of Jackson, Stuart's Hill was strongly occupied by Longstreet, and this wing of the Confederate Army, held always under cover, was gradually swung forward until it occupied a line almost perpendicular to the unfinished railroad.

With slight knowledge of Longstreet's position, it would seem, or at least with an utter failure to grasp the meaning of Porter's reports, Pope, satisfied that Jackson would abandon his position, determined to launch his superb columns once more against it. The weight which he apparently lacked the previous day he thought he had now secured. So, about noon, he sent forward a swarm of skirmishers along his whole front to clear the way for the 3 great lines in their rear.

The advance of the skirmishers did not provoke the fire of the guns, but when the compact lines came within range, the heavens rocked with the roar of the Confederate batteries. Meantime, Jackson's brigades, which had retired to the thickets behind their lines, a move that had misled Pope into believing the position was only weakly held, rushed down the hillside to reoccupy the improvised works of the railroad bed. The whole force of Pope's blow falling on Jackson's thinned line, the pressure was tremendous and reënforcements from Longstreet were called for.

By this time, the left of Pope's assaulting columns had come within the reëntrant angle which Longstreet's line formed with that of Jackson's, and Longstreet grasped the unusual opportunity presented to enfilade with his guns the left of the Federal reserves as they advanced. The rapidity with which the foremost lines of the Federals had reached Jackson's line, masked in large measure the guns on his right which were unable to fire upon the enemy without doing great damage to the Confederates. Crutchfield's and Lee's groups, therefore, turned their attention to the advancing reserves. Though half of their guns were short range pieces, even these proved effective on the nearest part of Porter's column, while the others poured a storm of iron over all parts of the field. Meanwhile, the Federal guns at the Dogan House and elsewhere behind their line devoted themselves principally to Jackson's front in an endeavor to prepare a way for the attacking infantry. But two batteries seem to have engaged Crutchfield and Lee, who had much the better position, and were considerably overshot by the enemy. No serious effort, whatever, was made to neutralize the artillery masses of the Confederates.

It was now that, instead of sending Jackson a reënforcement of infantry as called for, Longstreet ordered Bachman's and Reilly's batteries of Frobel's Battalion over from the hill in front of the Groveton House, where they had been engaged with the Federal guns in the Dogan House orchard, to the right front of S. D. Lee's group, from which advanced point they opened a raking fire with terrific effect into the left rear of Porter's dense column. These two batteries added all that was needed to put an end to the attack. Before the second battery, Reilly's, with its howitzer section gained its position, the enemy began to retire, and in less than 10 minutes after the effect of the guns began to be felt, Porter's troops gave up the contest and retired in confusion to the woods through which they had advanced. In vain now did Pope endeavor to stem the tide of disaster. A great mass of troops from the various commands, which had become mingled, was again gallantly urged forward, but this time their advance not being so rapid as before, Crutchfield's and Lee's guns were able to find the range before the Federals closed with Jackson's line. Thoroughly disorganized by the flanking fire of the artillery, the great Federal column was now driven back by a counter-charge of two of Jackson's brigades, and Pope's battle was lost.

Anticipating Lee's wishes, Longstreet, as soon as he saw Porter's defeat in the center, ordered his whole line forward at the charge, advancing his batteries along the turnpike with the infantry in an endeavor to take the Henry House plateau, on which the Federal regulars and the best troops, including a number of batteries, were making a desperate stand. This force, assisted by a flanking fire from his left upon Longstreet's advancing columns, checked the attack at nightfall, the Federal left crossing Bull Run after dark. The opportunity presented to Longstreet to capture this portion of the Federal Army, had he had a large and well-organized reserve artillery, was an unusual one. But this was not to be. That he used his available guns with exceptional skill is not to be denied.

From the battlefield of Second Manassas, Lee gleaned some 30 pieces of Federal ordnance, while the Confederates lost none.

Some idea of the intensity of the Confederate artillery fire in the battle of Second Manassas may be gained from the expenditures in ammunition of the 1st, 2d, and 3d batteries of Washington Artillery. Capt. Squires reported an expenditure of 400 rounds, Capt. Richardson of 178 rounds, and Capt. Miller of 356 rounds. By one section of the Dixie Battery, 297 rounds were fired; Stribling's Battery expending 354, and a section of Maurin's Battery 119. None of these batteries were engaged as continuously as were those under Crutchfield and Lee. The expenditures of the latter must have been enormous, certainly not less than 600 rounds per battery, or 150 per gun.* Let us compare this expenditure with that in other battles.

---

*The expenditure of Waterman's Rhode Island Battery was 500 rounds, and of Hazlett's regular battery, 6 pieces, 1,000 rounds, *Rebellion Records,* Series I, Vol. XII, Part II, pp. 468, 469.

In the battle of Leipzig, 1813, the expenditure of the Austrian guns was 199 rounds per gun in the 3 days, or 66 per gun per day. The greatest expenditure in one day by a Prussian battery, 1866, was 180 rounds per gun, at Blumenau; by an Austrian battery, 217 per gun at Königgrätz.

In 1870, the Prussian batteries averaged at Vionville, 89 rounds per gun; 35 per cent of the batteries fired over 100 rounds per gun. At Gravellote-Saint Privat, the Prussian guns averaged 55 rounds; 16 per cent of the batteries firing over 100 rounds per gun; the French average being 90 rounds per gun, but no battery exhausted its normal ammunition supply. During the whole war the 15 batteries of the German Guard expended but 270 rounds per gun.

At Gettysburg, the Federals averaged 102 rounds per gun for the 3 days, or 34 rounds per day for each of the 320 guns engaged, the greatest individual battery expenditure reported being 1,380 rounds for the 3 days, or a daily average of 77 rounds per gun per day. The Confederate expenditure on this occasion was probably 100 rounds per gun or an average of 33 per day, the greatest expenditure for 1 battery being 882 rounds, or 73 rounds per gun per day.

At the Sha-ho, in 1904, the Artillery of the 34th Russian Division averaged 278 rounds per gun per day. At Liaoyang, the Artillery of the 1st and 3d Siberian Corps averaged 420 rounds per gun per day. At Tashichiao, Colonel Patchenko's Battery fired 522 rounds per gun, which was the greatest expenditure for a single battery ever reported for one day.

Now, if we confine ourselves to the days of muzzle-loading field pieces, it is seen that the expenditure at Second Manassas compares favorably with that of the greatest artillery conflicts of history, exceeding perhaps that at Gettysburg.

The Confederate Artillery losses in this battle were: killed, about 30; wounded, about 90. In Lee's Battalion there were but 6 wounded, a fact to be borne in mind by those who would rate the service of field artillery by the magnitude of its losses, for probably no one force exerted a greater influence upon the final result of the battle than did this group of 18 guns.

At the battle of Second Manassas, many decided advances in the tactical employment of the Confederate field artillery are to be noticed. It is true, the defensive attitude assumed by Jackson gave him the same advantage in point of time to dispose his guns as was enjoyed by McClellan in the various fights on the Peninsula. Yet, the grouping of his artillery was by no means accidental. It was disposed with a special mission in view and to each piece was assigned a definite sector of fire. Not only were 40 of his guns well massed, but others were posted along the infantry lines in positions from which they were free to move from point to point, as developments might require. The principal features and advantages derived from his artillery position have already been discussed. It has also been noticed that when Longstreet began to arrive, his batteries preceded many of his infantry brigades, instead of being choked off from the field by infantry columns unwilling to give them a right of way. The massing of Lee's Battalion in advance of Jackson's right flank was a masterly move, and showed clearly that the lesson of Malvern Hill had been well digested. And then, as if to demonstrate to the Army the tremendous influence of which even a handful of guns, well served, is capable of exerting, at the very crisis of Pope's powerful infantry attack Longstreet ordered 2 batteries into action with decisive effect, followed by a general rush to the front of the few remaining batteries capable of following up the repulsed attacking columns.

The grave defect in Lee's tactics, from an artillery point of view, was the absence of his reserve. Had Pendleton's battalions with their superior material, a part of which at least was equal to that of the enemy, been on hand to engage in Lee's counter stroke, the fruits of the victory would certainly have been greater.

The comparative ineffectiveness of the Federal Artillery was due to a number of causes. In the first place, the disadvantage of inexperience in the attack now rested upon it. There was no Hunt present to direct the massed fire of the batteries and consequently they frittered away their efforts as individuals. In the second place, Crutchfield and then Lee occupied vastly superior positions from which they invited the fire of the heavier hostile guns, in order to divert it from the infantry line. And, in the third place, the Federal Artillery was definitely assigned the mission of shaking Jackson's Infantry line, which it could not attempt, by reason of his dispositions, without utterly neglecting his artillery. Thus, not only did it fail to neutralize the latter, leaving it sufficient in itself as events proved to hold at bay the attacking columns in all but a single quarter, but roughly handled by the opposing guns more or less free from hostile artillery fire, and quite without the effective zone of musketry, the Federal Artillery was unable to accomplish the undivided task assigned it.

Groveton and Second Manassas were battles in which the rôle of the artillery was a supreme one. In vain do we find their true features disclosed in the numerous accounts of Lee's battles, which have been contributed to history. On the contrary, they have been masked in narratives in which the influence of the infantry position behind the railroad bed is presented as the most potent element of Lee's and Jackson's success. But, far above that accidental field work stood the guns of Stapleton Crutchfield and Stephen D. Lee, in imposing masses with ready thumbs upon the vents and hands upon the rammers. And never in the history of war have more superb or denser columns recoiled before the muzzles of an artillery.

CHAPTER XIX

THE MARYLAND INVASION—HARPER'S FERRY AND SOUTH MOUNTAIN

AFTER the battle of Second Manassas, Gen. Lee decided that the time was a propitious one for the invasion of Maryland and therefore headed his columns towards Leesburg as soon as he was satisfied of the retreat of Pope to Washington, the movement beginning September 3.

On that day the Reserve Artillery arrived at Sudley, Pendleton having reported in person to Gen. Lee during the battle on August 29, after temporarily turning over his command to Lieut.-Col. Cutts on the 17th.

In the meantime, a considerable force of field artillery had been collected about Richmond and Col. T. S. Rhett assigned to the command of the permanent batteries as well as the former. Lieut. James Howard, Artillery Corps, with temporary rank of lieutenant-colonel, and Lieut.-Col. C. E. Lightfoot, Provisional Artillery, were assigned to duty under Col. Rhett to command the permanent works of the inner line and the field guns of the outer line, respectively.

In the defenses about Richmond at this time there was an artillery force of 89 officers and 1,693 men present, with an aggregate present and absent of 2,983, including the companies of heavy artillery. Near Petersburg, Capt. S. T. Wright also had about 120 men and 13 field pieces.*

Between the battle of Malvern Hill and the Maryland invasion, the field artillery passed through a distinct transition. The former affair had, as has been shown, directed the attention of many minds to the artillery problem. The faith of the Army in an arm of such latent ability, vouched for by the high character of

---

*Rebellion Records, Series I, Vol. II, Part II. p. 601.

its officers, was unimpaired. Every one recognized the capabilities of the gunners and felt that a solution would soon be effected. But how to accomplish the results expected of them was a serious task for the gunners. The battle of Second Manassas proved an object lesson of the greatest value. In that battle the Artillery rendered yeoman service, justifying the faith and the expectations of all. The tremendous effect of concentrated artillery fire had left no doubt as to the value of masses of guns. The names of Crutchfield, S. D. Lee, Lindsay Walker, Pegram, and the other gallant artillerymen whose talents had been so ably displayed, were on the lips of every soldier in the Army, and a spirit of intense admiration for the Artillery supplanted the criticisms hitherto so rife. The "long arm" had vindicated itself. Yet, many improvements were possible and steps were immediately taken to raise the standard of efficiency of the Artillery.

It was now generally perceived that more guns should accompany the divisions, and that the old system of isolating batteries by attaching them to brigades simply crippled the power of concentrating them in action. It was also realized that reserve artillery did not mean a great mass of guns rumbling along in rear of the army, but that its true purpose was its active use under the direction of the commanding-general whose wider grasp enabled him to throw the reserve artillery into action with the greatest effect upon the issue.

When Gen. Pendleton's reserve column reached Leesburg, it had with it much of the best material in the service, but many of the batteries with the divisions were much depleted in personnel and horses, and the material of others was of the most defective character. In fact, the Artillery in general showed the effects of the long marches and the severe fighting of the preceding month, the former not less wearing than the latter. It was at once decided, therefore, to weed out those batteries in the poorest condition, using the men and effective animals drawn therefrom for the purpose of strengthening others. The horses were at this time particularly run down.*

The more depleted batteries, including Leake's Goochland, Stribling's Fauquier, Rogers' Loudoun, Fleet's Middlesex, Latham's Branch North Carolina, and Anderson's Thomas batteries, with all the animals of the artillery and train unfit for service, were ordered to be detained at Leesburg in command of Maj. Richardson, who was directed to proceed with them as soon as possible to the neighborhood of Winchester and establish there a remount depot and recruiting station for the Artillery.

In the effort to place the Artillery on a more effective footing, it was designed to attach one battalion to each of Longstreet's 5, and Jackson's 4 divisions, with an additional reserve battalion for each of these corps and a general reserve for the entire army. Each battalion, whether with the divisions or in the reserve, was to have its own field officer. A battalion assigned to a division fell under the command of the Division Chief of Artillery. The foregoing was the general plan of the reorganization, but it was not rigidly adhered to as shown by the assignments of the batteries and battalions in effect during the Maryland campaign.† At one time during the operations in Maryland, D. R. Jones' Division of Longstreet's Corps had with it but one battery and Walker's Division but two batteries. At Sharpsburg, Ewell's Division had with it but two batteries, having left four at Harper's Ferry. On the other hand, D. H. Hill not only had Maj. Pierson's Battalion with his division at Sharpsburg, but Maj. Jones' Battalion of the reserve was also assigned him. With Longstreet's Corps, there were also two reserve battalions, Walton's of four, and Lee's of six batteries, whereas no reserve battalion was assigned as an integral part of Jackson's Corps, Jones' Battalion being first

---

*See G. O. No. 102, A. N. V., September 4, 1862, *Rebellion Records,* Series I, Vol. XIX, Part II, p. 592, and G. O. No. ——, September 5, Ibid., p. 595.
  †*Rebellion Records,* Series I, Vol. XIX, Part I, pp. 803-810. *Battles and Leaders,* Vol. II, pp. 600-603.

detached from the general reserve for the purpose, and later Brown's First Virginia Regiment. Roughly, the batteries and battalions were assigned as follows:

1st CORPS OR RIGHT WING (Longstreet)

Col. Henry Coalter Cabell, Chief of Artillery

McLAWS' DIVISION

Maj. S. P. Hamilton, Chief of Artillery

1. Manly's North Carolina Battery,   Capt. Basil C. Manly.
2. Pulaski (Ga.) Battery,   Capt. John P. W. Read.
3. Richmond Fayette Battery,   Capt. Miles C. Macon.
4. 1st Co. Richmond Howitzers,   Capt. E. S. McCarthy.
5. Troup (Ga.) Battery,   Capt. H. H. Carlton.

R. H. ANDERSON'S DIVISION

Maj. J. S. Saunders, Chief of Artillery

1. Donaldsonville (La.) Battery,   Capt. Victor Maurin.
2. Huger's Norfolk Battery,   Capt. C. R. Phelps.
3. Grimes' Portsmouth Battery,   Lieut. Thompson.
4. Lynchburg Battery,   Capt. Marcellus N. Moorman.

D. R. JONES'S DIVISION

1. Fauquier Battery,   Capt. Stribling.*
2. Loudoun Battery,   Capt. Arthur L. Rogers.*
3. Wise Battery,   Capt. J. S. Brown.
4. Goochland Battery,   Capt. Leake.*

WALKER'S DIVISION

1. Petersburg Battery,   Capt. James R. Branch.
2. Stafford Battery,   Capt. David A. French.

HOOD'S DIVISION

Maj. B. W. Frobel, Chief of Artillery

1. Charleston German Battery,   Capt. W. K. Bachman.
2. Palmetto (S. C.) Battery,   Capt. H. R. Garden.
3. Rowan (N. C.) Battery,   Capt. James Reilly.
4. Macbeth (S. C.) Battery,   Capt. R. Boyce.

---

*Left at Leesburg.

1st Reserve Battalion

Col. John B. Walton

1. 1st Co. Washington Artillery,   Capt. C. W. Squires.
2. 2d Co. Washington Artillery,   Capt. J. B. Richardson.
3. 3d Co. Washington Artillery,   Capt. M. B. Miller.
4. 4th Co. Washington Artillery,   Capt. B. F. Eshleman.

2d Reserve Battalion

Col. Stephen D. Lee

1. Ashland Battery,   Capt. Pichegru Woolfolk, Jr.
2. Bedford Battery,   Capt. T. C. Jordan.
3. Brook's South Carolina Battery,   Lieut. William Elliott.
4. Bath Battery,   Capt. J. L. Eubank.
5. Madison (La.) Battery,   Capt. Geo. V. Moody.
6. Richmond Battery,   Capt. W. W. Parker.

2nd CORPS OR LEFT WING (Jackson)

Col. Stapleton Crutchfield, Chief of Artillery

Ewell's Division

Maj. A. R. Courtney, Chief of Artillery

1. Bedford Virginia Battery,   Capt. Jno. R. Johnson.
2. Louisiana Guard Battery,   Capt. Louis E. D'Aquin.
3. 1st Maryland Battery,   Capt. Wm. F. Dement.†
4. 4th Md. or Chesapeake Battery,   Capt. Wm. D. Brown.†
5. Courtney or Henrico Battery,   Capt. J. W. Latimer.†
6. Staunton Battery,   Lieut. A. W. Garber.†
7. Charlottesville Battery,   Capt. J. McD. Carrington.*

A. P. Hill's Light Division

Lieut.-Col. R. Lindsay Walker, Chief of Artillery

1. Richmond Battery,   Capt. Wm. G. Crenshaw.
2. Fredericksburg Battery,   Capt. Carter M. Braxton.
3. Letcher Richmond Battery,   Capt. Greenlee Davidson.*
4. Purcell Richmond Battery,   Capt. Wm. J. Pegram.
5. Pee Dee (S. C.) Battery,   Capt. D. G. McIntosh.
6. Middlesex Battery,   Capt. Fleet.‡
7. Branch (N. C.) Battery,   Capt. A. C. Latham.‡

*Left in Richmond in August.
†Left at Harper's Ferry, and not at Antietam.
‡Left at Leesburg.

J. R. JONES' DIVISION

Maj. L. M. Shumaker, Chief of Artillery

1. 2d Md. or Baltimore Battery,   Capt. J. B. Brockenbrough.
2. Alleghany Battery,   Capt. Jos. Carpenter.
3. Danville Battery,   Capt. George W. Wooding.
4. Richmond Hampden Battery,   Capt. William H. Caskie.
5. Lee Battery,   Capt. Charles J. Raine.
6. 1st Rockbridge Battery,   Capt. Wm. T. Poague.

D. H. HILL'S DIVISION

Maj. S. F. Pierson, Chief of Artillery

1. Alabama Battery,   Capt. R. A. Hardaway.
2. Jeff Davis Alabama Battery.   Capt. J. W. Bondurant.
3. Peninsula Battery,   Capt. Wm. B. Jones.
4. King William Battery,   Capt. Thomas H. Carter.

GENERAL RESERVE ARTILLERY

W. N. Pendleton, Chief of Artillery

1ST REGIMENT VIRGINIA ARTILLERY

Col. John Thompson Brown

1. Powhatan Battery,   Capt. Willis J. Dance.
2. 2d Co. Richmond Howitzers,   Capt. D. Watson.
3. 3d Co. Richmond Howitzers,   Capt. Benj. H. Smith, Jr.
4. Salem Battery,   Capt. A. Hupp.
5. Williamsburg Battery,   Capt. John A. Coke.

CUTTS' BATTALION

Lieut.-Col. A. S. Cutts

1. "D" Battery, Sumter Battalion, Capt. James A. Blackshear.
2. "C" Battery, Sumter Battalion, Capt. John Lane.
3. "A" Battery, Sumter Battalion, Capt. H. M. Ross.
4. "B" Battery, Sumter Battalion, Capt. G. M. Patterson.
5. Lloyd's North Carolina Battery, Capt. W. P. Lloyd.

JONES' BATTALION

Maj. Hilary P. Jones

1. Morris Louisa Battery,   Capt. R. C. M. Page.
2. Richmond Orange Battery,   Capt. Jefferson Peyton.
3. Goochland Battery,   Capt. W. H. Turner.
4. Long Island Battery,   Capt. A. Wimbish.

NELSON'S BATTALION

Maj. William Nelson

1. Amherst Battery,	Capt. T. J. Kirkpatrick.
2. 2d Fluvanna Battery,	Capt. John J. Ancell.
3. 1st Fluvanna Battery,	Capt. Charles T. Huckstep.
4. Richmond Battery,	Capt. Marmaduke Johnson.
5. Milledge's Georgia Battery,	Capt. John Milledge.

MISCELLANEOUS RESERVE BATTERIES

1. Winchester Battery,	Capt. W. E. Cutshaw.
2. Dixie Battery,	Capt. W. H. Chapman.
3. Magruder Battery,	Capt. T. J. Page, Jr.
4. 8th Star Battery,	Capt. W. H. Rice.
5. Thomas Battery,	Capt. E. J. Anderson.*

CAVALRY CORPS (Stuart's Horse Artillery)

1. Chew's Battery,	Capt. Robert Preston Chew.
2. Pelham's Battery,	Capt. John Pelham.
3. Hart's Battery,	Capt. J. F. Hart.

At the battle of Sharpsburg but two battalions, Cutts' and Nelson's of three batteries each, remained in the general reserve with Pendleton along the river, and many of the batteries with the Army when it left Leesburg soon disappeared, as we shall see.

Though not distributed exactly as contemplated, there appear to have been 29 batteries assigned to the 1st Corps, grouped in 6 battalions, 26 batteries accompanying the Corps in the Maryland operations; and to the 2d Corps 25 batteries, grouped in 4 battalions, 22 batteries crossing the Potomac. In the Reserve we find 4 battalions with a total of 19 batteries and 5 batteries unassigned. There were then on the rolls of the Army some 78 batteries, of which number 71 engaged in the Maryland operations. The total personnel of these 71 batteries approximated but 4,000 men, for numbers of them were so weak as to be either disbanded or consolidated with others at an early date.

In the report of Gen. Pendleton, dated September 24, 1862, it is stated that to each of Longstreet's five battalions was attached a battalion of artillery with a 6th

*Left at Leesburg.

battalion as the corps reserve, with a total of 112 pieces, viz.: 45 rifles, 13 Napoleons, and 54 common smooth-bore guns, and that to each of the 4 divisions of Jackson's Corps was also attached a battalion of artillery with a 5th battalion as the corps reserve, with a total of 123 pieces, viz.: 52 rifles, 18 Napoleons, and 53 common smooth-bore guns. This statement does not include the batteries of E. J. Anderson, Blackshear, J. S. Brown, Chapman, Coke, Fleet, John R. Johnson, Leake, Lloyd, Nelson, T. J. Page, Jr., Rogers, Thompson, and Wimbish, which were disbanded under a general order of October 4, 1862; nor account for those of Cutshaw and Rice, which were consolidated with Carpenter's and Wooding's batteries on September 26; nor for Boyce's, Moorman's, and Woolfolk's batteries. But, as the material, men, and animals of the disbanded batteries were distributed among the remaining ones, it would seem that with Lee's army in Maryland there were 225 guns, in addition to 12 with the three horse batteries and 36 in the Reserve, or a grand total of about 300 guns. McClellan estimated the number at 400, a figure not so absurd as Gen. Early and others have considered it.

In order that the character of the armament of Lee's artillery at this time may be seen, the following table is inserted:

NAME OF BATTERY	20-pounder Parrotts	10-pounder Parrotts	3-inch rifles	24-pounder howitzers	12-pounder howitzers	Napoleons	Whitworths	Blakelys	6-lb. S. B. guns	Total
Lewis		2	2							4
Grandy		2			2				2	6
Maurin		2	1						3	6
Huger		1	1						2	4
Manly			1		2				3	6
Carlton		2			1				2	5
McCarthy		2							2	4
Read		1			1				2	4

NAME OF BATTERY	20-pounder Parrotts	10-pounder Parrotts	3-inch rifles	24-pounder howitzers	12-pounder howitzers	Napoleons	Whitworths	Blakelys	6-lb. S. B. guns	Total
Dearing		1			1				2	4
Macon		2			1				4	6
Stribling				2		4				6
Bachman						4				4
Garden					1	1			2	4
Reilly		2	2	2						6
Branch		1	2		3					6
French		3			3					6
Squires		1	2							3
Miller						2				2
Richardson					2	2				4
Eshleman					2				2	4
Jordan			2		1				1	4
Rhett	2	2								4
Moody			2	2						4
Parker			2		2					4
Eubank			1		1				1	4
Bondurant			2		2					4
R. C. M. Page			2		1				3	6
Peyton (Fry)			1		1				3	5
Hardaway			2				1			3
Carter		1			2				2	5
Braxton			2						4	6
Latham						2			2	4
McIntosh		1	1		1	1				4
Davidson			1			2			1	5
Crenshaw					1	1			2	4
M. Johnson			2		2					4
Pegram		2				2				4
Brockenbrough			1		1			2		4
Raine			3		1					4
Caskie		1							3	4
Lusk		1	1						2	4
Carpenter			2			2				4
Wooding		2	1			1				4
Brown		2	1							3
Balthis									2	2
Dement									4	4
Carrington			2		2				2	6
Latimer			2			2				4
D'Aquin		1	2							3
Poague	2	2								4
Smith		2			2					4
Dance			1		2				1	4
Watson		2			1					*3
Hupp					2				2	4
Brooke					1	1			2	4

*Watson's Battery also had one Hotchkiss rifle.

From the foregoing table it will be seen that absolutely no uniformity of armament obtained in the divisional batteries, either as to the character of the material or the number of pieces. The following table shows the armament of some of the reserve batteries, there being but 12 rifled pieces with Pendleton.

NAME OF BATTERY	20-pounder Parrotts	10-pounder Parrotts	3-inch rifles	Hotchkiss rifle	James rifle	Whitworth rifle	12-pounder howitzers	Napoleons	6-lb. S. B. guns	Total
Lane	2	3				1				6
Ross							2	1		3
Blackshear							3		3	6
Kirkpatrick							2		4	6
Massie									6	6
Milledge		1	3	1	1					6

It is impossible exactly to determine the strength of the Army of Northern Virginia at this time, but the most conservative estimate does not place the maximum strength of the infantry at more than 30,000 men. Taking this figure and 300 as the number of guns with the Army, it will be seen that the proportion had reached 10 guns per 1,000 infantry. Deducting the guns of the Reserve, those of the Horse Artillery, and those left at Harper's Ferry, and the proportion actually with the divisions at Sharpsburg appears to have been about 9 per 1,000, the largest yet found. The assignment of Walton's and Lee's battalions to Longstreet, and Brown's Regiment to Jackson, as corps reserves, foreshadowed the artillery reorganization of 1863, and again we find an analogy in the development of the artillery in the Civil War and in the Prussian campaigns of 1866 and 1870-71.

Hohenlohe, summarizing the revolution in the tactical employment of field artillery which Prussian experience brought about, states that in 1866 great un-

willingness was shown to employ much artillery to prepare the action, but that in 1870, intentionally from the
first, as many guns as possible were brought into play.
He then shows that even at the moment when the fight
was at its height, a strong reserve of all arms was held
out in 1866, a practice which kept at least half of the
great mass of reserve artillery of the 1st Army from firing a shot at Königgrätz, when the fire of every gun
was needed, whereas in 1870 such a practice was so opposed to the tactical ideas of the time that even the
name "Reserve Artillery" was abolished, and replaced
with that of "Corps Artillery." Then again, in 1866,
we find the Prussian reserve marching as near the tail
of the column as possible, and on some occasions days
in rear of the Army, just as in the case of the Confederate reserve in the Cedar Mountain-Second Manassas campaign. Whereas, in 1870, the Prussians even
sent their reserve guns, then called corps artillery,
ahead, as in the case of the Guard and the 3d Corps at
Saint-Privat, and the 5th, 11th, and 12th corps at
Sedan. As a parallel to this we find the reserve battalions of Walton, S. D. Lee, and Brown, moving into
Maryland with the most advanced columns. In
Prussia, two wars were necessary to bring about such
developments, simply because of the brevity of the
first, lasting as it did but seven weeks, whereas in
America the tactics of the artillery had to be developed
in a single period of continuous campaigning. The
Prussians naturally derived a great advantage from the
interim between their activities, which afforded them
a breathing spell during which they found opportunity
for serious reflection upon, and digestion of, their recent
experiences.

By the afternoon of September 7, the mass of Gen.
Lee's army had reached Frederick, Maryland, Gen.
Pendleton reporting with the Reserve Artillery on the
morning of the 8th.

In advancing into Maryland, Gen. Lee, whose army
was greatly depleted by straggling and lack of shoes

for his infantry, took into consideration the character of his old opponent, McClellan. His principal cause of anxiety was not so much the smallness of his army (for in the ranks were those only who had best stood the strain of two campaigns) as it was the difficulty of securing ammunition, especially for the artillery. Without an ordnance officer of Alexander's ability, it is difficult to see how the invasion of Maryland in 1862 would have been possible. The brevity of the campaign, however, coupled with almost superhuman efforts on the part of the ordnance officers, relieved the situation.

When the Army reached Frederick, two developments affected its proposed movements. In the first place, Halleck, instead of following McClellan's advice and ordering the garrison of 12,000 men at Harper's Ferry to fall back, directed it to remain there. In the second place, the people of the North forced McClellan to move out from Washington at once, to drive Lee from Maryland, whether he would or no. It therefore became necessary for the latter to dispose of the force at Harper's Ferry while holding off McClellan, or to return with his whole army to Virginia in the event his new line of communication up the Valley was not cleared of the enemy. Not impressed with the necessity of abandoning Maryland, Gen. Lee on the 9th ordered Jackson to seize Harper's Ferry, and held D. H. Hill with a small force at South Mountain, while Longstreet moved to Boonsboro.

Harper's Ferry was to be invested by three columns, the first under Jackson himself from the south, the second under J. G. Walker from the east, and the third under McLaws from the north. Leaving Frederick on the morning of the 10th, Jackson moved westward and crossed the Potomac at Williamsport on the 11th. After driving in a small portion of the enemy from Martinsburg, he reached Halltown in view of Bolivar Heights, strongly held by the garrison of Harper's Ferry, on the 13th. Meanwhile, Walker reached Loudoun Heights on the east early that day, and find-

ing them unoccupied, succeeded in placing five pieces of
artillery in position before noon the next day. McLaws,
driving a small hostile force into Harper's Ferry, succeeded in occupying Maryland Heights on the north
before the night of the 13th, and the next morning cut
a road to the crest, over which Maj. Hamilton, Divisional Chief of Artillery, dragged two guns from Read's
and 2 from Carlton's batteries, into position before 2
P. M. the 14th.

Bolivar Heights, lying below and to the south and
west of Maryland Heights and Loudoun Heights, respectively, was now commanded by the guns of Mc-
Laws and Walker, so that when a Federal battery
opened upon Walker at 1 P. M. the 14th, the four pieces
on Loudoun Heights silenced it within two hours. The
elevation to the guns of Maryland Heights was so great
that McLaws was free to join in the cannonade without
fear of injury from the Federal guns.

When Jackson on the night of the 13th learned that
McLaws and Walker were both in position, he moved
forward from Halltown. On the morning of the 14th,
he ordered A. P. Hill to advance on the Confederate
right along the west bank of the Shenandoah, directing
him to turn the enemy's flank and get into Harper's
Ferry in his rear, if possible. Lawton, with Ewell's
Division, moved along the Charleston turnpike which
passed over Bolivar Heights about the center of the
Federal position, and J. R. Jones moved against the
enemy's right near the river.

Jones soon seized a position for Poague's and Carpenter's batteries near the river and commanding the
enemy's right, on which the guns of McLaws were
already playing, and during the night Lieut.-Col. R.
Lindsay Walker, Chief of Artillery, A. P. Hill's Division, placed Pegram's, McIntosh's, Davidson's, Braxton's, and Crenshaw's batteries in position on an eminence commanding the Federal left. While Hill and
Jones were thus taking up their positions, Lawton advanced during the night along the pike and formed his

line in front of the Federals on Bolivar Heights. He was supported by batteries posted by Col. Crutchfield on School House Hill. Guns from the batteries of Brown, Dement, Garber, and Latimer, ten pieces in all, were then taken by Crutchfield across the Shenandoah at Kelly's Ford and moved down stream to a position opposite the left of the enemy's line of entrenchments, to which a road for the guns had to be cut. This position, although commanded by Bolivar Heights, yet secured a fire into the rear of a work on the enemy's left, where there was an embrasure battery of four pieces, just opposite A. P. Hill and forming the keystone of the position.

For several hours after dark on the 14th, while Walker and Crutchfield were placing their batteries, the Confederate guns on Maryland and Loudoun Heights engaged in a duel with the Federal Artillery on Bolivar Heights, presenting a scene of surpassing grandeur, but striking terror into the hearts of the besieged.

At dawn on the 15th, the attack was ordered to begin and was opened by the fire of Col. Walker's group of guns, soon joined by those of Crutchfield on the east side of the Shenandoah, the batteries on School House Hill, those near the Potomac, and the guns on Maryland and Loudoun Heights. The gunners were almost immediately driven from the Federal work, commanded by the ten pieces which Crutchfield had so skillfully placed across the river.

After about an hour of concentration upon the enemy's position, his artillery and musketry fire were almost subdued by the great circle of guns, whereupon orders were issued to carry the Federal position by storm. But again the battery in front of Hill's Division was gallantly manned and reopened its fire only to be silenced by Crutchfield's group, after another hour of firing. Meanwhile, Pegram and Crenshaw moved their batteries up to within 400 yards of the Federal works and poured a rapid enfilading fire into them.*

---

*It was not Carpenter's Battery as stated by Allan, but Crenshaw's. See Walker's Report.

As the infantry approached the Federal position, about 8 A. M., a white flag was displayed, and as soon as the artillery could be caused to cease firing the surrender was effected, the Confederates taking 11,500 prisoners, 13,000 stand of arms, 49 field pieces, and 24 mountain howitzers.

The losses in the Confederate Infantry at Harper's Ferry were not over 100, mostly wounded. The Artillery loss probably did not exceed 10 men, yet Harper's Ferry vividly illustrates the power of artillery. An assault on Bolivar Heights by infantry without the support of a large number of guns would have been as costly as it would have been doubtful of success. And this Jackson knew.

From a tactical standpoint, Jackson's movements were splendidly conceived and superbly executed. He employed his artillery, almost every effective piece being brought to bear on the enemy's position, in a way above criticism. True, the opportunity presented for its use was a rare one, yet the fact remains that he grasped it and saved his infantry almost to a man, and those that were lost were not sacrificed in an assault until the hostile guns were practically silenced. Seldom has a general been fortunate enough to secure so thorough an artillery preparation.

The work of Crutchfield, of Lindsay Walker, and of the other artillery officers was brilliant, and again Pegram displayed that dauntless spirit which soon made his name a by-word in the Army.

We look in vain for a parallel to Harper's Ferry in the Civil War, and involuntarily turn to Sedan. The great artillery battle of the Franco-German War was on a grander scale, of course, than that at Harper's Ferry, there being engaged in the terrible "circle of fire" five great artillery groups with a total of 540 guns, whereas Jackson had fewer than 75 in action. Yet, the *mise en scène* of Sedan was not as awe inspiring in its grandeur as that at Harper's Ferry. In fact, no battlefield could be more sublime in its altitudes than the latter.

As soon as possible after the surrender of Harper's Ferry, Jackson prepared to join Gen. Lee, leaving A. P. Hill's Division to take charge of the captured property.

Arriving on the 16th, the Chief of Ordnance at once collected the 73 captured guns, sending them to Winchester along with a large supply of ammunition unsuited to the field pieces. With the exception of canister, there was little field artillery ammunition captured by the Confederates at Harper's Ferry.

While Jackson had been engaged at Harper's Ferry, the 1st and 9th corps of McClellan's army, with 18 batteries, had appeared before D. H. Hill at South Mountain. After a desperate fight, Hill, reënforced by four of Longstreet's brigades, succeeded in checking the advance of the enemy, until the Reserve Artillery and the ordnance trains at Boonsboro could move off to a position of safety.

When the Reserve Artillery under Gen. Pendleton, consisting on the 14th of the battalions of S. D. Lee, Brown, and Nelson—Cutts having been sent to the support of D. H. Hill*—retraced its steps to Boonsboro from Hagerstown, it was first ordered to be placed in position along the Beaver Creek Heights, which was done before nightfall. But when it became apparent that Hill's position had been overlapped and that a retirement was necessary, Gen. Pendleton was ordered to send Lee's Battalion to Centreville to report to Longstreet and take the rest of his command by the shortest route across the Potomac at Williamsport and guard the fords of the river.

Leaving Beaver Creek about midnight, Pendleton's command with Alexander's reserve ordnance train reached the intersection of the Sharpsburg, Boonsboro, Hagerstown and Williamsport roads about daybreak the following morning, at which point information was received that a large cavalry column of the enemy was near at hand. Immediate steps were taken to repel an

*See *Rebellion Records,* Series I, Vol. XIX, Part II, p. 547.

attack and to protect the trains by organizing the stragglers and teamsters at hand. The hostile force consisted of Gregg's Brigade of 3 regiments of cavalry
under Col. Davis, which had escaped from Harper's
Ferry on the 14th. Although narrowly missing Pendleton's column it later met Longstreet's reserve ordnance
train and burned 45 wagons of precious ammunition.

Upon reaching the river the defense of the Williamsport ford and the adjacent lower one was assigned Col.
Brown's Battalion, Gen. Pendleton continuing with
Nelson's Battalion and Alexander's train to Shepherdstown. By 10 A. M. on the 16th, the passage at that point
was also well guarded.

Meanwhile the demands upon the Chief of Artillery
from Sharpsburg, the point upon which Gen. Lee had
determined to concentrate, for long-range field pieces
were becoming most pressing, so that when Jackson's
column arrived, Col. Crutchfield was directed to return
to Harper's Ferry and bring up all the heavy captured
rifles he could find. Upon his return, however, he discovered that Col. Alexander had already directed most
of the captured material to be sent to Winchester. Before leaving Harper's Ferry, Crutchfield had found it
necessary to leave the batteries of Brown, Dement,
Latimer, and Garber, for sheer lack of horses. For the
same reason, Col. Walker was forced to leave Davidson's Battery behind. Impressing a sufficient number
of draught animals for the first three of his batteries
above named, securing two 3-inch captured rifles for Dement, and filling the caissons with a fresh supply of Federal ammunition, Crutchfield now proceeded to Sharpsburg, but arrived too late to take part in the battle of the
17th. Meanwhile, Brown's Battalion had been relieved
from duty at the Williamsport fords and moved forward as the reserve of Jackson's Corps, one battery of
which, Watson's, being the only one engaged in the
battle of Sharpsburg. Nelson's Battalion at this time
consisted of the batteries of Kirkpatrick, Milledge,

Ancell, Marmaduke Johnson, and Huckstep, the armament of which was very light, and therefore they were not called upon.*

The surrender of Harper's Ferry had come in the nick of time. By a rapid night march of 17 miles Jackson arrived at Sharpsburg on the 16th, Walker the same day, and McLaws at sunrise on the 17th, and A. P. Hill, leaving a brigade at Harper's Ferry, arrived during the battle. Thus the Army was concentrated at Sharpsburg before the close of the 17th.

When Longstreet and D. H. Hill had fallen back upon Sharpsburg, the Federal Army passing through the various gaps followed upon their heels. The greater part of the 16th was spent by McClellan in putting his troops in position along the ridge east of the Antietam, a creek flowing along the Confederate front and on the west side of which Longstreet and D. H. Hill were in position.

The Confederate position stretched across the angle formed by the Potomac and the Antietam, the latter a deep stream of more than 60 feet in width, overshadowed by a tangle of trees, that filled the bottom from which the ground on both sides ascends to the ridges. Just beyond the one on the west runs the Hagerstown pike, which is about a mile distant from the stream. On the reverse slope of the western ridge, falling as it does to the Potomac, lay the small village of Sharpsburg, behind the center of the Confederate line, which followed the main crest just east of the Hagerstown pike. A mile north of the village and on the pike Lee's left center rested near the Dunkard church, behind which lay a tract of trees known as the west wood, 500 yards in front of which stood a smaller wood known as the east wood. Extending southward from Sharpsburg the line rested its right on a wooded-spur overlooking the Antietam where it turns westward to the Potomac.

---

*On October 4, 1862, Ancell's and Huckstep's batteries were consolidated and became Massie's Battery.

From the main position just across the Hagerstown pike, open slopes, broken by long ravines, fell eastward to the bottom, affording the Confederates an admirable field of fire to the stream from 1,000 to 2,500 yards distant. Many lanes crossed the Confederate front, the sunken ones, together with the numerous low stone walls near the village, forming natural entrenchments of great strength for the defenders.

In the west wood, not only was there an entire absence of undergrowth, but the ground was intersected with waist-high outcroppings of rock which afforded excellent protection from hostile fire. But this portion of the line was the weak point, for the enemy was able to approach it closely through the east wood, and also threaten the flank under cover of a larger thicket which spread across the pike some distance to the north. Behind and between these screened approaches from the Antietam lay several small farms with orchards and stone fences, among which an attacking force, if checked, might rally, and near the Dunkard church were also a number of cottages and barns which offered cover.

The only ford across the Antietam was commanded by the bluff on the extreme right, yet a number of stone bridges remained intact. That nearest the Potomac, over which the road to Harper's Ferry passed, was defended by rifle pits and enfiladed by batteries. The next, known as the Burnside Bridge, just east of Sharpsburg, was well commanded by the western ridge, and the one opposite the Confederate center could be raked throughout its length. But one more to the north at Pry's Mill was entirely screened from the Confederates' view and fire, and was left unguarded, laying as it did a mile and a half east of the west wood and behind the east and Poffenberger woods.

While the position was an exceptionally strong one with the pike, an excellent lateral communication for the most part under cover, and numerous other intersecting roads, it possessed the grave disadvantage of being paralleled by the ridge east of the Antietam, along which, though slightly commanded by the hostile position, McClellan had ample space to deploy his 275 pieces of artillery. The superiority of his ordnance in weight and range far overbalanced the Confederate advantage in elevation. The range from ridge to ridge in no place exceeded 2,000 yards, but at many points, approached that limit. The Federal guns were therefore able to deliver upon the hostile batteries a damaging fire to which little effective reply could be made. Not only was McClellan able to engage the Confederate 10-pounder rifles and 6-pounder guns with his 20-pounder Parrotts, but a greater discrepancy had to be contended with by the latter, for their projectiles and fuses were of very inferior quality, whereas those of the enemy were of the best. Not alone, then, will a comparison between the guns themselves suffice, for inferior ammunition reduced still further the comparative efficiency of the lighter ordnance. It was his ready grasp of the situation that led Gen. Lee to make such pressing demands upon Pendleton for all the heavy rifled pieces the latter could possibly forward from Harper's Ferry and Shepherdstown on the 16th and 17th.

As his troops arrived, Gen. Lee assigned Jackson to the left of the position with his 5,500 men and the 16 guns he had brought up from Harper's Ferry, and later Hood was placed in his rear. Next, on Jackson's right, came D. H. Hill with 5,000 men and 26 guns. Longstreet with 8,000 men and 50 guns held the center and right, the Washington Artillery commanding the bridge in his front and Eubank's Battery the Burnside Bridge with Richardson's on a hill slightly to its rear. Walker's Division of 3,500 men, and Branch's and French's batteries with 12 guns, was held as a reserve in rear of Toombs' Brigade on the extreme right. Munford's two regiments of cavalry, with Chew's Battery, were stationed on the extreme right to hold the bridge at the Iron Works and keep open the line of communications with Harper's Ferry, while Stuart with Fitzhugh Lee's Brigade of cavalry and Pelham's four guns was

stationed behind the extreme left. Thus on the line from
Nicodemus Run to the Potomac, a distance of three
miles, were about 20,000 infantry, 2,500 cavalry, and
about 2,000 artillerymen with 108 guns, Pendleton holding the fords of the river with 1,000 men, including a
small infantry escort, and 26 guns. Urgent orders had
been dispatched, however, for A. P. Hill to come up
with his 13,000 men and 60 guns.

At 2 p. m. on the 16th, Hooker was ordered to cross
the Antietam at Pry's Mill and attack the Confederate
left. The movement being discovered, Hood was
ordered into the front line, having already placed a
number of his guns on a rise in the open ground east
of the Hagerstown pike. A spirited combat now ensued between Hood and Meade, lasting until dark, resulting in the former regaining the east wood and driving Meade therefrom after he had once taken it. The
artillery on both sides was active, Poague's Battery
rendering valiant support to Garden's, Bachman's, and
Reilly's batteries, of Frobel's Battalion, Hood's Division, all of which were much punished. In this affair,
the howitzer section of Rhett's Battery, Lee's Battalion,
was also engaged. Meanwhile, the rifled sections of
Rhett's and Parker's batteries, and one rifled piece of
Jordan's Battery, of Lee's Battalion, had been engaged
in firing upon the Federal Infantry massing opposite
the center, suffering some loss from the heavier guns of
the enemy. Earlier in the day, Squires' Battery of
rifles, Walton's Battalion, posted near the center, indulged in an artillery duel of about an hour's duration
with the enemy. Before night, however, both Walton
and Lee withdrew their battalions behind the cover of
the ridge forming the infantry position.

On the morning of the 17th, S. D. Lee established a
large group of guns in rear of Longstreet's center, to
support Walton's batteries, all of his guns being
necessarily much exposed to the Federal artillery fire.
Another large group of guns was established by D. H.
Hill not far in rear of his center near the Clipp, Rou-

lette, and Mumma houses. Though Hill's Infantry had been much reduced at South Mountain, he was well supported by artillery, having Jones' reserve battalion of 14 guns, his divisional batteries, or those of Carter, Bondurant, and Hardaway, with their 12 pieces, under Maj. Pierson, Cutts' reserve battalion consisting of Ross's, Patterson's, Blackshear's, and Lane's batteries, with their 24 pieces, and Lloyd's Battery of 4 guns. Of the 16 guns of Jones' and Ewell's divisions of Jackson's Corps present, all except those of Poague's Battery were attached to Stuart, and placed by him under Pelham on the extreme left, Crutchfield not having arrived with Brown's, Dement's, Latimer's, and Garber's batteries from Harper's Ferry.

McClellan, on the morning of the 17th, had available 87,164 men and 275 guns. Upon gaining contact with the Confederates, Gen. Hunt, Chief of Artillery, at once selected an excellent position for 10 batteries of his reserve. In his report he states: "They overlooked the enemy and swept most of the ground between them and our troops. They were well served, especially the guns of Benjamin's Battery. Their field of fire was extensive, and they were usefully employed all day, and so constantly that the supply of ammunition for the 20-pounders ran short." It should here be noted that in Lee's entire army there were but six 20-pounder field pieces.

All during the successive and more or less isolated attacks of Hooker, Mansfield, and Sedgwick on Lee's left, of French and Richardson on his center, and of Burnside on his right, Hunt's great masses of guns played upon the Confederate batteries and their infantry lines, adding the tremendous weight of their metal to that of the corps and division batteries, with the several assaulting columns. As to the effect of Hunt's Reserve Artillery, we may judge from the report of D. H. Hill, who, as we have seen, controlled the largest group of Confederate guns. He wrote: "Positions were selected for as many of these guns as could be used, but all the ground in my front was commanded by the long range artillery of the Yankees, on the other side of the Antietam, which concentrated their fire upon every gun that opened and soon disabled it." And Col. S. D. Lee, the batteries of whose reserve battalion were distributed along the center and left center, afterwards declared that "Sharpsburg was Artillery Hell." The latter statement is no doubt correct, but Hill's is somewhat exaggerated, for the artillery of his portion of the line undoubtedly rendered most effective service, in spite of Hunt's batteries, the fire of which they disregarded when necessary for them to play upon the advancing columns of the enemy.

Jones' Division was all on the left of the pike, drawn up in two lines, facing northward, the first extending from the road to the Nicodemus house, the other in the northern edge of the west wood. Near the turnpike, one of Poague's rifles and two of Raine's howitzers were posted in the front line, while to the left rear Pelham was in position with a number of batteries. On the east of the pike, and in prolongation of Jones' line, was Lawton's Division.

At 3 A. M. on the 17th, Hooker renewed his attack, Doubleday on the right, Ricketts on the left, and Meade in reserve close behind. As this splendid force of 10 brigades and 10 batteries advanced to the attack, Hunt's guns 3,000 yards to the east opened a heavy enfilade fire upon the Confederate left, but disregarding both this and the fire of the batteries in their front, Poague, Raine, and the three batteries of Woolfolk, Parker, and Rhett, which Col. Lee had ordered into position near the Dunkard church, opened a continuous fire upon the infantry of the enemy with splendid effect. But as the Federal Infantry advanced, with Campbell's Battery in the front, Jones' first line was forced back upon the wood and its leader was carried wounded from the field. Poague and Raine after firing a few shots now retired their guns to a position in rear of the west wood, from which they continued to fire.* To the east

*These guns were not abandoned as stated by Henderson. See Poague's Report.

of the road, Lawton's Division, with the three batteries
of Lee's Battalion firing over the infantry from the rear,
first checked Meade and then drove him back upon six
batteries massed on his right, whereupon a section of
Jordan's Battery under Capt. J. S. Taylor was sent
forward by Col. Lee with Lawton's line, but was soon
driven back by the opposing batteries.

About this time the Confederate skirmishers, creeping through the corn in front of the west wood, shot
down the gunners and many horses of Campbell's Battery, all but taking the guns, and Starke, who had succeeded Jones, led his line forward once more. Meanwhile, the fire from Pelham's, Poague's, Raine's, and
Col. Lee's guns near the church, had been most effective,
though the right group suffered severely from Hunt's
fire as well as from that of two of Hooker's batteries.
Col. Grigsby, who in turn succeeded Starke, now held
the original position of his division, but Lawton, having
forced back Meade, was now himself being driven, for
with splendidly-served batteries the Federals were again
pushing forward, only to be checked by the arrival of
Hood's Division, with Frobel's Battalion of divisional
artillery. Capt. Bachman, galloping out into the cornfield with a section of Napoleons, opened fire upon the
enemy at a range of 150 yards. But in a few minutes
Hooker's skirmishers, creeping up to within 50 yards
of the guns, drove them from the field with the loss of
a number of men and many horses. Meanwhile the
rifled section of the battery had gone into action on the
turnpike, Reilly's Battery supporting the infantry from
a position further in rear. Garden's or the third battery
of the battalion had been left in position near Longstreet's center, with Walton's Battalion.

To Hood's support, D. H. Hill now sent over Ripley's, Colquitt's, and Garland's brigades, which in
column in the order named and on Hood's right struck
the left of the Federal attack and assisted in driving the
enemy a second time back upon their guns. Meanwhile, Woolfolk's, Parker's, and Rhett's batteries, much

damaged and with ammunition exhausted, the first leaving a piece on the field, had been ordered to the rear to refit, and Moody's Battery sent into position in their place. But as Hood's line advanced, Moody's guns were masked. Without hesitation the gallant officer with a section of his battery dashed forward 300 yards into a ploughed field and from a position in advance of the infantry for 15 minutes delivered a galling fire upon the enemy. Lieut. Gorey, an officer of another battery, who, seeing Capt. Moody's guns advancing to a post of such danger, had begged to be allowed to accompany them, was shot through the head and killed while sighting for the final shot.

It was now 7:30 A. M. and Mansfield's Corps was rapidly approaching to the support of Hooker's shattered troops which had rallied about their artillery. On Hood's left, J. G. Walker's two brigades and G. T. Anderson's Brigade had arrived from the extreme right, and Early had taken position in the west wood, where the remnants of Jones' Division remained. Pelham, joined by Poague, meanwhile had moved 13 pieces to a position just in rear and to the immediate left of Jones' old line, from which he was able to sweep the open ground from the Nicodemus house to the Dunkard church. Thus with ready perception he had grasped the key-point of Jackson's whole line, and yet placed his guns where they were entirely free from Hunt's fire, which relentlessly continued to play upon the Confederate left. Whatever may be said of McClellan's disjointed attacks in this quarter, Hunt at least did his part in the matter of artillery support. But in Pelham he found an equal in the aggressive handling of artillery, for no one movement on either side bore a greater influence upon the final issue of the battle than did the advancement of Pelham's group during the interim between Hooker's and Mansfield's attacks. This was a move on the chess board, though perhaps by a pawn, which baffled the most powerful pieces of the enemy. It was one of those master strokes by a sub-

ordinate of highly-developed initiative, which has so
often been found to play a major part in the tactical
success of the superior.

It is perhaps incorrect to speak of an interim between
the first two attacks on Jackson, for Mansfield's overlapped Hooker's, his massed divisions pressing forward in time to check Hood's advance, and forcing his
division back with fearful loss through the thirty-acre
cornfield, east of the pike, to the church. Ripley and
Colquitt were also being driven back to the same point
from the east wood, to which they had advanced in
following up Ricketts, by Greene's Division and
Knapp's Battery. At this time Hood and Lawton held
the southern part of the west wood, Ripley's and Colquitt's brigades retiring from the line towards D. H.
Hill's position along the "bloody lane." But, while
the Federals had gained all the ground north of the
church and east of the pike, Jackson's left, by means
of Pelham's guns, had held fast. No troops, however
brave, could cross the space which Pelham's group so
perfectly commanded. The Confederate line, when the
lull succeeding Mansfield's repulse came, ran northward from the Dunkard church, almost parallel to the
pike, while the Federal line near Miller's house faced
south, its center in the east wood, and its left near the
church, facing west. So far, less than 8,000 Confederates with perhaps 35 guns actually engaged, had,
though suffering terribly themselves, foiled both
Hooker's and Mansfield's corps, aggregating not less
than 20,000 men, and 60 or more guns present on the
field.

The lull about 9 A. M. was of short duration, for Sumner's columns were fast approaching from the north,
and Porter was preparing to throw a heavy force, accompanied by his horse batteries, and supported by his
corps artillery as well as Hunt's guns, across the Boonsboro Bridge opposite the Confederate center. Meanwhile Gen. Lee was sending his last reserves then on the
field, McLaws and R. H. Anderson's divisions, to the
front line, the former to Jackson's right at the Dunkard

church, and the latter to the support of D. H. Hill. Before following up Sumner's or the third attack, let us turn to the center.

Soon after Col. Lee withdrew the three batteries of his battalion, and Jordan's section, from their positions near the church, he was ordered by D. H. Hill to mass his battalion along the ridge between the church and Sharpsburg, just west of the pike. From this position he was able to support Hill by firing over his infantry upon the extreme left of the Federal attack, which, overlapping Jackson, fell upon Hill's left. But in this position the batteries were so severely punished by Hunt that upon the arrival of McLaws they were ordered about a mile to the rear to replenish their ammunition and make such repairs as were possible.

After the retirement of the five batteries of Lee's own battalion, viz., Woolfolk's, Moody's, Jordan's, Parker's, and Rhett's, which had been heavily engaged in supporting Jackson, D. H. Hill had in position behind him Cutts' reserve battalion of 5 batteries with 26 pieces in addition to his divisional battalion of 4 batteries with 16 guns under Maj. Pierson. Further to the right, and behind Longstreet's center, was Walton's Battalion with 16 pieces, the 12 guns of Eubank's, Branch's, and French's batteries, the last two having been left by J. G. Walker's Division, being still opposite the Burnside Bridge. Bachman's Battery had also been ordered to the rear to refit. Save for a few companies of skirmishers, not a Federal soldier had yet crossed the Antietam south of the Dunkard church, and they had been driven to cover by Squires' Battery, which then withdrew to cover behind the crest with the other batteries of Walton's Battalion, allowing the enemy to expend many rounds of ammunition in a one-sided duel.

Sumner, who had gained contact with Jackson's line, now threw three divisions, Sedgwick's leading, and all in the closest order, against the west wood and the Roulette house. As the head of the column emerged from the east wood, moving across the cornfield beyond the turnpike, Greene, of Mansfield's Corps, advanced from his position near the church. Early, with a handful of Jones' Division, still holding the west wood, now moved rapidly forward to meet the attack almost solely opposed by Pelham's guns, and striking Greene's left flank drove him back. At this moment McLaws advanced in line through the west wood with the church on his right and struck Sedgwick in flank, and with Early's assistance Sumner's leading division was quickly driven off towards the north, losing nearly 2,000 men in a few minutes.

In vain did Sumner's guns, massed with those of the corps which had preceded him on the slope north of the cornfield, hurl canister at McLaws' and Early's lines. As Col. Cabell brought up McLaws' divisional battalion of artillery, the batteries, plying whip and spur dashed to the front, unlimbering and firing as they advanced. Read's Battery, which went into action in the open on the right of the wood, alone lost 14 officers and men and 16 horses in as many minutes, and Carlton's Battery further to the left and in front of Ransom's Brigade was all but cut to pieces by the opposing guns.

Meanwhile Pelham's group on the extreme left continued its fire with great energy in an effort to beat down the storm of shot, shell, and canister from the Federal Artillery, but while it sought in vain to silence the great group of guns much damage was done them and at least a part of their fire diverted from McLaws and Early. Now again the fleeing mass of Federals rallied upon the artillery position, as Hooker and Mansfield had done before, a position which Stuart had vainly attempted to turn all through the forenoon. During the successive combats it had proved the source of many evils to the Confederates, and never once had the guns of the enemy been driven therefrom, though Pelham, greatly outmatched in the number of pieces as well as the weight of his metal, had with unsurpassed courage and skill done all of which his men and material were capable.

On the right of the west wood, as Early's men forced Greene back upon the east wood, and were about to capture Knapp's Battery, which had so harassed them, "A" Battery, 4th United States Artillery, under Lieut. Thomas, galloped into action beside Knapp, and together they gave a superb exhibition of what light batteries are capable of doing even in the face of point blank musketry fire. In position near the southwest corner of the east wood, on the Smoketown road, almost surrounded by Aiken's North Carolina Regiment, they were saved only by the timely arrival of Smith's Division of Franklin's Corps, the latter now coming upon the field and forming a line between the church and the east wood, sheltered by a rise in the ground. At this juncture, the Confederates having been checked by Franklin's fresh divisions, the fighting was reduced to an active artillery duel, at ranges from 600 to 1,500 yards, and the attention of Cabell's and Pelham's batteries were principally devoted to the most advanced Federal group near the Miller house, composed of Cowan's, Frank's and Cothran's batteries, to the support of which Hancock had been sent. At least 15 Federal batteries were in position to the right front of Pelham. While the infantry of neither side was able to assume the aggressive, the Confederates were well satisfied, since they had repossessed themselves of and continued to hold the west wood, under cover of which their lines had reformed before 10:30 A. M.

At last Jackson's trials were over and opposite him lay three shattered corps and a fourth or Franklin's with all its ardor gone. With less than 19,400 men and 40 guns engaged on his part of the line, he had held at bay at least 30,500 infantry and 25 superb batteries with not less than 100 guns, all of which had been handsomely supported by Hunt's powerful mass of long-range rifles. In their assaults, extending over a period of five hours, the Federals had lost 7,000 officers and men, while the Confederate losses on the left up to 10:30 A. M. were 5,754, or 29 per cent of those engaged.

When Sumner's Corps came upon the field about 9:30 A. M., French's Division overlapped Jackson and fell upon D. H. Hill with great fury, soon joined by two brigades of Franklin's and Richardson's divisions. The main attack fell upon that part of the line from a point just southeast of the church past the Roulette and Piper houses.

At a point about one-third of the way from the church to Sharpsburg, a sunken lane, running from the east side of the turnpike, zigzagged into the Boonsboro road halfway between the village and the Antietam. This erratic route, now know as the "bloody lane" by reason of the slaughter which occurred therein during Hill's defense, at first descending in an easterly direction, soon meets a hollow where the lane to the Clipp house branches to the northeast. From thence the main lane runs southeast, ascending abruptly to the Boonsboro road. North of the sunken lane, and between it and the east wood were the Clipp, Roulette, and Mumma houses in the order named from the south, the last being the "burning building" so constantly referred to in the reports. Within the salient formed by the "bloody lane" is a plateau on which stood the Piper house. In rear of this plateau, or flat-topped hill, the land gently dips to the west, rising again to a ridge of greater elevation just west of the Hagerstown pike, which lies in the depression. It was from this ridge that Lee's Battalion, after firing for some time upon French's left, had been forced to withdraw about 10 A. M. by Hunt's guns, and it was in the depression running along its front to the south as far as the village that Jones, Cutts, and Walton, had held their artillery battalions under cover.

Although French assaulted Hill's position with great vigor, he was able to make little permanent headway, in spite of numerous efforts, but when Richardson came to his assistance the Confederates were forced back out of the "bloody lane" after a desperate defense, through the fields and the orchard in front of the Piper house.

But at the latter point the Federal advance was checked
by a terrific fire from Cutts' guns now with Col. Lee
on the ridge beyond the pike. But on the left of Richardson's line the Federals now gained the rise of ground on
Hill's right and also drove the Confederates defending
it towards the Piper house, exposing the men holding
the sunken lane to a destructive enfilade fire. Cutts'
and Jones' reserve battalions and Hill's divisional batteries under Maj. Pierson, utterly disregarding the tremendous shower of shot and shell which Hunt poured
upon them, now massed across the pike and sought to repel the advancing enemy; but as the foremost batteries
opened fire they were silenced and swept from the field.
Realizing the weakness of Hill's line, Longstreet ordered Miller's Battery of the Washington Artillery to
the support of Hill, which promptly went into action on
the ridge behind the line, but withdrew to cover after
losing a number of men. As the enemy again advanced,
Capt. Miller, dashing forward across the pike with the
remaining section of his battery, two Napoleons, went
into action and for half an hour delivered an effective
fire upon the enemy. Again, he moved forward, almost to the Piper house, ordering a sergeant to bring
up a fresh caisson when his limbers were emptied.
Joined by another piece, Miller's three guns, supported
by a handful of infantry which had rallied about them,
now delivered a rapid fire with canister. But the gunners
falling rapidly, Longstreet, who was watching the battery, ordered his own staff to man the guns, and these
gallant officers, firing with the greatest coolness and
rapidity, succeeded in checking the enemy. Miller with
ammunition exhausted was at this juncture relieved by
Boyce's South Carolina Battery. Exposed to both a
direct and reverse fire from Pleasonton's horse batteries now on the Boonsboro pike, and those in front of
Porter across the Antietam, Boyce's men suffered
heavily. While galloping into action, a caisson exploded, but, unlimbering within a few yards of the Federal line, the gallant battery drove it back with a

furious discharge of canister, firing 70 rounds in a few minutes. This battery lost 19 men and 15 horses. Nothing was ever more gallant than its conduct.

The Federals retiring to the ridge from which they had advanced, now brought up Robertson's horse and Graham's light batteries to drive off Boyce, but Hill had repossessed himself by 1 P. M. of the Piper house and, aided by every battery which could be brought into action, held French beyond the sunken lane and Richardson on the crest beyond the orchard. Thus, with 7,000 men and about 50 guns in action, Hill had repelled a force of not less than 10,000 Federals.

About this time Col. Lee was forced to order all of the batteries in action behind Hill to the rear to refit, but not until relieved by Capt. Moorman in command of Maj. Saunders' Battalion of four batteries of R. H. Anderson's Division.

While this change was being effected four regular batteries of the enemy pushed across the Boonsboro bridge and came into action on either side of the road. Squires' and Garden's batteries on the south side of the road at once uncovered and several times broke the advancing Federal infantry line with their canister, but the enemy renewed his attacks again and again.

In the meantime, about 3 P. M., Squires' Battery was relieved by 12 pieces of Col. Lee's Battalion, all that could be refitted after the wreck of the morning, which, returning to the field, were posted about Sharpsburg. Moody's Battery now moved to the right, two pieces of Parker's and two of Jordan's Battery were placed at the left, and Rhett's two remaining guns went into action on the ridge just north of the village. These batteries as well as those they had relieved were exposed to a heavy fire of infantry and artillery, the skirmishers of the enemy approaching to within 150 yards of them, after having been driven back five or six times by Moody's and Squires' batteries. Finally, Garnett's Brigade, with Moody's Battery firing canister while advancing with the infantry, drove the enemy from the ridge just

northeast of the village which they had taken, and the
other batteries which had been joined by Carter's were
now moved to a more advanced position south of the
Boonsboro pike, which they held until forced to fall
back by Burnside's success on their right.

Though ordered to attack at 9 A. M., it was not until
1 P. M. that Burnside made a vigorous effort to force
the bridge in his front. Upon the crossing, Eubank's
Battery kept up a plunging fire along with Richardson's further to the rear, but the latter, having expended
all its ammunition and having one of its two Napoleons
dismounted by Benjamin's Battery across the stream,
withdrew temporarily. Meanwhile, Eshleman was plying with case and canister the Federals who were attempting to cross the ford below the bridge. But, in
spite of the desperate resistance of the four brigades
guarding the bridge, Burnside with the aid of Tidball's
horse battery drove the Confederate skirmishers from his
front and forced his way over. Pushing rapidly over
the ridge towards Sharpsburg, he was almost unopposed, except by Maj. Frobel's batteries of Hood's Division, which were now returning to the field. Throwing Brown's Battery of D. R. Jones' Division well
forward, Frobel also sent one of Reilly's sections and
Garden's Battery of his own battalion into action at a
range of not over 100 yards from the enemy, and thus
checked the advance, though he lost most of his horses
and many of his men in so doing. In a few minutes, all
but three pieces were disabled, and their ammunition was
exhausted. Running the disabled pieces to cover by
hand, the gallant gunners were now ordered to retire
them as the Federal Infantry rapidly occupied and then
passed the position the batteries had abandoned. As
the swarm of skirmishers almost overtook the guns,
shooting down the cannoneers and horses, Lieut. Ramsay with the 2d section of Reilly's Battery arrived on
the scene from the rear, and boldly going into action
in a field on the right of the road from the bridge, enfiladed the enemy's line with canister, hurling its ex-

treme left back in confusion. To oppose the Federals in this quarter, there being no available infantry, every battery which could be spared from other sections of the field was ordered to the right. First Carter, galloping along the east side of the village, then Poague, came to the support of Ramsay. At this instant occurred one of those incidents which make war grand. As a section of the Rockbridge Battery, which had been detached from Pelham on Jackson's left, with lathered horses and battle-stained men dashed past Gen. Lee on its way to the point of threatened rout, Robert E. Lee, Jr., the youngest son of the great Commander-in-Chief, and a private in the battery, raising himself to an erect posture, saluted with military precision his noble father. Where in all the history of war is such another incident to be found? Where such material for the brush of a Messonier? The kith of Bonaparte bore the baton, but the kin of Lee fought at the muzzle with hands upon the rammer staff.

Truly one might say that Sharpsburg was a day of glory for the Confederate Artillery. Without Pelham's guns, to deny the approach, never could Jackson have withstood the shock of those dense masses still ominously banked against his left. Without the gallant Miller and Boyce to check the onrushing columns of Richardson, and Col. Lee's guns to hold the enemy at bay, D. H. Hill had been swept from the field. And now, when the thin grey lines had been brushed aside like so much chaff by Burnside's dense and ever-increasing force, naught but the shattered remnants of his batteries saved Lee from utter rout. Like bees to honey, the batteries from left and center now swarmed to the post of danger. Miller, Eshleman, Richardson, Squires, Eubank, Garden, Reilly, Bachman, Brown, and Carter, regardless of the hail of iron poured upon them by Von Kleiser's, Taft's, Weed's, Durell's, Clark's, Simmons', Benjamin's, Muhlenberg's, Cook's, McMullen's, and other batteries across the Antietam, and free from molestation, heeded only the task assigned them. Not a one but gladly undertook it, willing to sacrifice men, guns, and self, if only the surging wave of blue could be momentarily checked, for A. P. Hill was now at 3:30 P. M. arriving with his veteran light division from Harper's Ferry, and Lindsay Walker with four batteries was near at hand.

Hill's Division had marched 17 miles in 8 hours. His arrival was in the nick of time, for the Confederate batteries were now either totally disabled, or practically without ammunition, having for some time in the most exposed positions been doing the work of infantry while the superbly served Federal batteries played upon them at will. The village of Sharpsburg was all but taken, with all that that meant to Lee. Toombs alone, with a handful of men in support of the batteries, was formed in the path of the enemy. Dashing through the fields, Braxton's, Pegram's, McIntosh's, and Crenshaw's batteries, the first commanded by Lieut. Marye, heralded the approach of Hill's three brigades under Gregg, Branch, and Archer, and going into action within a few yards of the Federal flank, at once became involved in a desperate struggle for existence. In fact, McIntosh was soon forced to abandon his pieces. On the right of McIntosh and Crenshaw, whose positions were to the right of Toombs' rallied line, Pegram had also been pouring a continuous fire of canister into the enemy's lines, and further still to the right was Braxton.

Gathering their strength, Toombs' and Archer's brigades now swept forward from the road, striking the Federal left in flank, recapturing McIntosh's guns, and driving Rodman back upon the massed guns in front of the bridge. This left Wilcox's Division mainly on the north side of a ravine separating it from the bridge. Quickly perceiving his opportunity Col. Walker ordered Pegram with the only one of his pieces for which ammunition was left, and Braxton's Battery, to an elevation just north of the Snively house from which they poured a terrific enfilade fire down Wilcox's line at a range of about 500 yards.

To the left and in advance of Crenshaw, Carter's and the Donaldsonville Battery under Lieut. Elliott now went into action, Carter, Elliott, Crenshaw, Pegram, and Braxton, almost unaided by the musketry of the infantry, literally driving Wilcox from the field with their fire delivered on his front and both flanks. From their elevated position Pegram and Braxton continued their fire with splendid effect upon the Federals near the bridge until nightfall closed the engagement, the precision of their practice having attracted the attention of friend and foe.

The Confederates made no attempt to follow up the success which had attended the complete overthrow of Burnside, and as darkness enveloped the battlefield, worn out and exhausted by eight days of continuous marching and fighting, dropped to the ground where they stood to seek repose in sleep. But, even more fatigued than their men, the division commanders now sought Gen. Lee to urge, without exception, his withdrawal during the night. Unmoved by the universal opinion, and relying upon his confidence in McClellan's lack of heart for a resumption of the struggle, the great leader, possessing that supreme moral courage which so few possess, even though lions when aroused, merely ordered his generals to collect their remnants, and strengthen the lines for a possible conflict on the morrow.

The morning of the 18th, Lee turned his attention to the offensive plan which Jackson had attempted to execute the preceding day, to turn the extreme Federal right, which Stuart and Pelham had failed to do, reporting the task impossible.

Nothing can so well describe the situation on the morning of the 18th as the account of Col. S. D. Lee, whose gallantry and heroic efforts the day before had more than once saved the Confederate Army from defeat. Sending this officer to make a reconnaissance of the Federal right with Jackson, who had supported the views of Stuart and Pelham, Gen. Lee patiently

awaited their report, continuing to urge Gen. Pendleton to send forward all the rifled pieces and stragglers
he could collect.

Of his reconnaissance, Col. Lee wrote: "During the
morning a courier from headquarters came to my battalion of artillery with a message that the commander-
in-chief wished to see me. I followed the courier, and
on meeting Gen. Lee, he said: 'Col. Lee, I wish you to
go with this courier to Gen. Jackson, and say that I
sent you to report to him.' I replied, 'General, shall I
take my batteries with me?' He said: 'No, just say that
I told you to report to him, and he will tell you what he
wants.' I soon reached Gen. Jackson. He was dismounted with but few persons around him. He said to
me: 'Col. Lee, I wish you to take a ride with me,' and
we rode to the left of our lines with but one courier, I
think. We soon reached a considerable hill and dismounted. Gen. Jackson then said, 'Let us go up this
hill, and be careful not to expose yourself, for the Federal sharpshooters are not far off.' The hill bore evidence of the fierce fight the day before.* A battery of
artillery had been on it, and there were wrecked caissons,
broken wheels, dead bodies, and dead horses around.
Gen. Jackson said: 'Colonel, I wish you to take your
glasses and carefully examine the Federal line of battle.' I did so, and saw a remarkably strong line of
battle, with more troops than I knew Gen. Lee had.
After locating the different batteries, unlimbered and
ready for action, and noting the strong skirmish line
in front of the dense masses of infantry, I said to him:
'General, that is a very strong position, and there is a
large force there.' He said: 'Yes, I wish you to take
50 pieces of artillery and crush that force, which is the
Federal right. Can you do it?' I can scarcely describe
my feelings as I again took my glasses, and made an
even more careful examination. I at once saw such an
attempt must fail. More than 50 guns were unlimbered
and ready for action, strongly supported by dense lines

---

*This hill as suggested by Henderson was probably the one held by Pelham
on the 17th.

of infantry and strong skirmish lines, advantageously posted. The ground was unfavorable for the location of artillery on the Confederate side, for, to be effective, the guns would have to move up close to the Federal lines, and that, too, under fire of both infantry and artillery. I could not bring myself to say all that I felt and knew. I said: 'Yes, General. Where will I get the 50 guns?' He said: 'How many have you?' I replied: 'About 12 out of the 30 I carried into action the day before.' (My losses had been very great in men, horses, and carriages.) He said: 'I can furnish you some, and Gen. Lee says he can furnish some.' I replied: 'Shall I go for the guns?' 'No, not yet,' he replied. 'Col. Lee, can you crush the Federal right with 50 guns?' I said: 'General, I can try. I can do it if any one can.' He said: 'That is not what I asked you, sir. If I give you 50 guns, can you crush the Federal right?' I evaded the question again and again, but he pressed it home. Finally I said: 'General, you seem to be more intent upon my giving you my technical opinion as an artillery officer, than upon my going after the guns and making an attempt.' 'Yes, sir,' he replied, 'and I want your positive opinion, yes, or no.' I felt that a great crisis was upon me, and I could not evade it. I again took my glasses and made another examination. I waited a good while, with Jackson watching me intently. I said: 'General, it can not be done with 50 guns and the troops you have near here.' In an instant he said: 'Let us ride back, Colonel.' I felt that I had positively shown a lack of nerve, and with considerable emotion begged that I might be allowed to make the attempt, saying: 'General, you forced me to say what I did unwillingly. If you give the 50 guns to any other artillery officer I am ruined for life. I promise you I will fight the guns to the last extremity if you will only let me command them. Jackson was quiet, seemed sorry for me and said: 'It is all right, Colonel. Every body knows you are a brave officer, and would fight the guns well,' or words to that effect. We soon reached

the spot from which we started. He said: 'Colonel, go
to Gen. Lee, and tell him what has occurred since you
reported to me. Describe our ride to the hill, your examination of the Federal position, and my conversation
about your crushing the Federal right with 50 guns,
and my forcing you to give your opinion.'

"With feelings such as I never had before, nor ever
expect to have again, I returned to Gen. Lee, and gave
a detailed account of my visit to Gen. Jackson, closing
with the account of my being forced to give my opinion
as to the possibility of success. I saw a shade come
over Gen. Lee's face, and he said: 'Colonel, go and join
your command.' For many years, I never fully understood my mission that day, or why I was sent to Gen.
Jackson. When Jackson's report was published of the
battle, I saw that he stated that on the afternoon of the
17th, Gen. Lee had ordered him to move to the left with
a view of turning the Federal right, but that he found
the enemy's numerous artillery so judiciously posted in
their front, and so near the river, as to render such an
attempt too hazardous to undertake. I afterwards saw
Gen. J. E. B. Stuart's report, in which he says that it
was determined, the enemy not attacking, to turn the
enemy's right on the 18th. It appears Gen. Lee ordered
Gen. Jackson on the evening of the 17th to turn the
enemy's right, and Jackson said that it could not be
done. It also appears from Stuart's report and from
the incident I relate, that Gen. Lee reiterated the
order on the 18th, and told Jackson to take 50 guns
and crush the Federal right. Jackson having reported
against such an attempt on the 17th, no doubt said that
if an artillerist, in whom Gen. Lee had confidence,
would say the Federal right could be crushed with 50
guns, he would make the attempt."

The incident recounted by Col. Lee is a dramatic one.
The temptation offered the brave artilleryman to allow his professional duty to be overborne by the desire to retain the approval of Jackson, the soldier who
had never flinched from even the seemingly impossible,

was a great one. Just as he wrote, Col. Lee could not have known during the battle that Jackson's views coincided with his own. On the contrary, it was most natural for him to believe that Jackson regarded him as unwilling at heart to essay the proposed task.

This whole affair again illustrates those tactical views of Jackson's which we have had occasion to note at White Oak Swamp and Cedar Mountain. He realized the futility of frontal attacks against massed batteries without a proper artillery preparation, and to secure such he knew was quite impossible at Sharpsburg on the 17th and 18th. He knew that even had the Confederate batteries been fresh and full-manned, instead of badly wrecked as they were, another Malvern Hill stared him in the face. Yet, no doubt sensible of the criticism to which he had been subjected for his delay at White Oak Swamp while seeking to subdue the fire of the hostile guns, in order not to sacrifice his infantry, even though confirmed in his view of the situation by Stuart and Pelham, the latter an artilleryman of unquestioned intrepidity, Jackson threw the burden of the decision upon the commander-in-chief himself, through the medium of the latter's technical adviser, Col. Lee. In this his action was well considered, and the delicate manner in which he convinced Gen. Lee of the error in which he was about to fall beautifully illustrates Jackson's loyalty to his chief.

But another feature is to be noted, and that is the submission by Gen. Lee and Gen. Jackson of purely technical questions concerning the guns to skilled artillerymen. In this matter the change for the better is most noticeable. Never once, as far as can be ascertained, had the infantry assaults of the Peninsula been held in abeyance pending an artillery reconnaissance. In every instance until now the columns had been furiously hurled against all but impregnable positions without the slightest deference being paid to the professional opinion of artillerymen; nor were their views even sought. But now we first find Jackson con-sulting Pelham, and though but confirmed by the latter in his views, naïvely suggesting to his commander-in-chief that he, too, avail himself of an expert technical opinion. An artilleryman, and one in whose loyalty, as well as in whose ability and courage, the highest confidence is reposed by him, is sent to make the reconnaissance, and the ultimate decision withheld pending his finding. No longer is the advice of the "old war horse" alone sought on artillery matters, as at Malvern Hill. In vain did Longstreet urge the frontal attack on the 17th as the proper counter-stroke. The certain fate of such a move was painted in lurid colors. The flashes of a hundred guns running together streaked the opposite hillside with a line of red, through which no infantry might hope to pass. Malvern Hill had not been lost in vain, and Gen. Lee turned towards his enemy's flank, waiting, so patiently listening, for some news of Jackson's success. But the Federal move which baffled Pelham was the massing in a single group of 30 heavy rifled pieces on a well-prepared position, about one mile north of the west wood, and 900 yards from the river, at a point where the Hagerstown pike ascends to a commanding ridge. Opposed to this great battery, so skillfully placed, the damaged guns of Pelham would have been almost as useless as old Brown Bess.

When Gen. Lee received from the lips of one of his ablest artillerymen a confirmation of Jackson's report, his troops still lay in line of battle. Not a halo of smoke had hovered above the guns, not a rifle-shot had broken the awful stillness of the morning. With bated breath and tense with anxiety, the two armies lay watching each other so silent it almost seemed the life blood had ebbed from their veins. The stricken hundreds which held the foremost lines were scarce less motionless than those who survived. And what a contrast this the night hour in which Lee set his columns in motion for Virginia bore to that when but recently, with bands playing and mid cheers from 40,000 throats, the sons of the South crossed to the land of their foe. Now, as the dejected, battle-rent regiments, some reduced to mere platoons, waded out into the Potomac, with faces turned southward, even the splashing of feet in the water jarred upon the overwrought nerves of the men. The Army of Northern Virginia was experiencing a new sensation, for though its resolve was never higher, its back was towards the enemy.

We find those who speak of Sharpsburg or Antietam as a drawn battle. So it was in every tactical sense of the word. Strategically, however, the Maryland campaign had ended in defeat and the great battle of September 17 was the culmination. Lee had crossed the Potomac with the intention of carrying the war into the enemy's country. He had scarce crossed before he was fighting for existence, with one foot of his army at all times on the other side of the dividing line. Now he was returning to the southern shore, even thankful that the avenue of retreat lay open. During the night of the 18th, the Army of Northern Virginia, with all its trains and artillery, had recrossed the Potomac at Boteler's Ford. As the rear wagons containing the wounded, and the splintered remains of the last battery to leave its position, approached the ford, Gen. Lee, still at the post of greatest danger near the north shore, with a great sigh and as if to relieve his soul of pain, expressed his thanks to God. No words can so well fix in history the failure of the First Maryland Invasion as that fervent prayer of the Confederate leader with all that it meant. In connection with Gen. Lee's withdrawal from Sharpsburg, one instinctively recalls Moses, the deliverance of the Israelites and of the Confederates both being percarious from a military point of view.

No serious attempt was made by McClellan to press the Confederates until the next day, Fitz Lee's cavalry having held off Pleasanton until the crossing was effected. Meanwhile, Gen. Pendleton, with Nelson's reserve battalion of artillery crowning the heights opposite the ford with its guns, had been collecting other batteries as they crossed and placing them in position to repel the enemy, momentarily expected to appear. Soon 44 guns were thus secured. Capt. Maurin with three rifled pieces was placed to the right, about 250 yards from the river, and Lieut. Maddox with one piece on his left. Upstream then came Milledge with four rifles and a howitzer, and Chapman with one rifle and one Napoleon. On the brow of the cliff overlooking the ford so as to rake it and its approaches, Capt. Marmaduke Johnson, with two 6-pounders and two howitzers, was placed. Above the road leading through the ravine from the ford, Capt. Kirkpatrick with two 6-pounders and two 12-pounder howitzers occupied the brow of the cliff from which position he was able to cross fire with Johnson, and next to him Capt. Huckstep took position with his four 6-pounders. To the left of Huskstep was Braxton's Battery, and further along Capt. Barnwell, of Pendleton's staff, placed a 12-pounder Whitworth and two 10-pounder Parrotts under Capt. Hardaway; two of the Washington Artillery batteries were also posted on the brink of the ravine by Col. Long of Gen. Lee's staff, while eleven pieces were held in reserve for an emergency.

About 8 A. M. on the 19th, Pleasanton appeared at the ford with a large force of cavalry, and Gibson's, Tidball's and Robertson's horse batteries with their eighteen pieces opened on the Confederates. An artillery duel had continued for about two hours when the Federal 5th Corps arrived. The Confederate infantry support of about 600 men left with Gen. Pendleton now replied to the enemy while the guns economized their ammunition as much as possible. About noon the Federal Infantry took cover behind a canal bank on the north side of the river, from which their sharpshooters greatly harassed the Confederate gunners. The situation of the isolated batteries was now critical and though much criticism of Gen. Pendleton has resulted from his failure to hold the ford, it is not suggested by Alexander and others how it should have been done. Pendleton had on the 18th sent Ancell's Battery to Shepherd's Ford, four miles above Boteler's, and on the 19th, he had been forced to dispatch 200 men of his infantry to its support, sending an equal number to the ford below him, opposite which the enemy had appeared with a number of guns and commenced to shell the small cavalry force stationed on the south shore. Lee was not ignorant of the precarious task which had been assigned his Chief of Artillery, for on the 19th he had instructed him by letter to fall back that evening if the pressure of the enemy became too great, adding that a few guns only need be left with the cavalry, which had been ordered to relieve him.* Col. Munford, with his cavalry and Chew's horse battery, had promised to be on hand by night. So any suggestion that Pendleton deserted his post is an improper one.

During the afternoon the battery commanders began to report their ammunition exhausted, but such only as were able to withdraw their guns unseen by the enemy were allowed to retire. Shortly after nightfall, while some of the batteries were moving off, the infantry remaining near the ford broke badly and fled down the road from the river, a large body of skirmishers having rushed across the stream and routed them. Capt. Maurin was now compelled to spike his 10-pounder Parrott, Capt. Milledge and Johnson each a 12-pounder howitzer, and Capt. Huskstep one of his 6-pounders, all of which were abandoned.† In the retirement the Confederate batteries lost 7 men and 26 horses.

While the batteries were moving off from the river as best they could in the night, Gen. Pendleton sought in vain to induce Gen. Pryor, but two miles inland, to return and cover the position he had occupied, but Hood, the division commander, not being found, he continued his search for Gen. Lee, who ordered Jackson to take

---

*Memoirs of W. N. Pendleton, p. 225.

†The piece lost by Milledge was one of the two brass howitzers belonging to the Cadet Battery of the Virginia Military Institute, cast by order of President Taylor, in 1855, and presented to the Corps of Cadets. The mate of the lost piece is now the evening gun of the Institute, and has been used as such since 1866.

the necessary steps to hold the enemy in check. The next morning Jackson sent A. P. Hill's Division towards the river, he and Pendleton accompanying it. As Hill moved up at an early hour in two lines, he found a force of about 3,500 men of Porter's Corps along the Charles Town road. Under cover of a tremendous fire of artillery from the north shore, the Federals maintained a stubborn resistance along the crest of the ravine. But soon Porter ordered Sykes to recross, and, during the attempt to execute the movement, Hill's brigades made a superb charge, driving the remaining regiment into the river, this single command suffering a loss of 282 men out of 800 present.

Hill had not a single gun in action. His divisional battalion under Col. Walker was no doubt blocked on the narrow roads leading south when his orders were received to drive Porter back, and there was no time to wait for them. But his assault on the Federal position in the face of numerous well-served guns cost him a loss of 261 men of his sorely-depleted brigades. The affair indicates that Hill's Infantry, at any rate, had lost none of that fierce *élan* for which the Light Division had ever been famous.

The Federals now desisted from further attempts to overtake Lee's army, McClellan's attention being wholly devoted to Stuart's threat against his rear, the latter having crossed the Potomac near Williamsport.

The actual losses of the Confederate Artillery in material in the campaign had been slight, although the batteries were veritable wrecks, over half of their horses having succumbed either on the road or in battle. Walton's Battalion had abandoned but one caisson before withdrawing from Sharpsburg, and that had been destroyed. At Crampton Gap, Capt. Carlton, of Cabell's Battalion, had lost a 12-pounder howitzer, Read and Lloyd of the same command having lost elsewhere one 3-inch rifle, and one 6-pounder with two caissons, respectively. In Col. Lee's Battalion, the loss was comparatively great, Jordan having lost a howitzer caisson, Rhett a howitzer limber, Parker the rear chests of a howitzer caisson, Moody a forge, Woolfolk a 12-pounder howitzer and limber, and Moorman two 10-pounder Parrotts with part of a caisson. In addition to the foregoing were the losses at the ford by Maurin, Milledge, Johnson, and Huckstep, viz., the four pieces, already enumerated.*

In personnel, Col. Lee's Battalion alone had lost 2 officers and 8 men killed, and 2 officers and 75 men wounded, an aggregate loss of 85, not less than 25 per cent, an enormous percentage for artillery. Col. Walton's Battalion had lost 4 men killed, and 3 officers and 27 men wounded; Jones' Battery of Pierson's Battalion, D. H. Hill's Division, had suffered a loss of 26 men, or fully 50 per cent of its strength. Maj. Frobel's Battalion of Hood's Division sustained a loss of about 23 men. In the division reports of casualties the Artillery losses are in many cases not separately enumerated, but a conservative estimate, based on those reported, fixes the Artillery losses at not less than 300 officers and men.† Among the former were Capt. J. S. Taylor, of Col. Lee's staff, and Lieuts. Dabney and Pringle of Carter's and Garden's batteries, respectively, all of whom fell mortally wounded while performing their duty with great gallantry.

But, as has been remarked before, artillery losses do not spell artillery efficiency and service rendered. In fact, there is little relation between them. Had the Confederate batteries been able to beat down the fire of the powerful Federal guns, especially those of Hunt, they would have saved the infantry hundreds of men. As it was, they were unable to do this, and, in repelling the infantry columns of the enemy, were exposed to more serious losses than if they had for the most part merely engaged in an artillery duel. Surveying the battlefield on the 16th, such men as Cols. Lee and Walton, Majs. Cutts, Jones, Pierson, and Frobel, had all realized at a glance what was before them. They

---

*For above see *Rebellion Records*, Series I, Vol. XIX, Part I, p. 844, and Pendleton's and Barnwell's reports, Ibid., pp. 834, 837.

†See Guild's report, Longstreet's return, Ewell's return, Vol. XIX, Part I, pp. 810, 843, and 974, respectively, also individual reports of Walker, Walton, Lee, Frobel, and others.

saw at once that the work of the gunners was to be
a task of self-sacrifice.   If they were to render the
infantry that service of which they were alone capable,
the artillery of the enemy must be in large measure
ignored by them, for in a duel with the superior ordnance
of McClellan, their guns would be completely outmatched.   With firm resolve, they therefore, determined
to devote their energies to the attacking infantry, heedless of the exposure to the hostile artillery.   Transmitted to the men and officers of their commands, such
was the spirit which animated the Confederate Artillery
in this great battle which Col. Lee afterwards characterized as "Artillery Hell."   How well the gunners carried
out their resolve has been shown.   In every quarter of
the battlefield they saved the day for Gen. Lee.   With
Hill in the center, the Artillery at one critical instant
alone remained in action to check the enemy and save
that portion of the line from rout.   Later Burnside's
advance was stayed by the Artillery unsupported except by Toombs' shattered brigade, utterly incapable of
further effective resistance, and dashing upon the field
the batteries of Walker's Battalion, coming to the relief of those already in action, had hurled Rodman, then
Wilcox, back from Sharpsburg.   Their share in saving
Lee's right is well attested by the insignificant losses
which the infantry of A. P. Hill's Division suffered in
coöperating with them, and again by the Federal reports which repeatedly refer to the Confederate batteries as the cause of the withdrawal of Burnside's divisions.

In the battle of Sharpsburg necessity developed a
mobility among the light batteries which was surprising.   A study of the reports shows that the same battery
was engaged in widely-separated positions, in spite of
enormous losses and deficiencies in horses.   We have
seen how Carter moved from point to point under a
tremendous fire, as occasion required.   And again, how
Poague, after incurring severe losses in the morning on
the extreme left with Jackson and Pelham, reappeared
in action in the afternoon at the threatened point on the

extreme right. These rapid changes of position were
typical of many of the batteries engaged, for the groups
which were originally established were essentially un-
stable by reason of the superiority of the enemy's artillery fire, which forced them to dissolve whenever they
opened. It was necessary, therefore, for batteries to
be constantly shifted about and detached from their
own battalions and groups in order to close with the
attacking infantry. Dispersed, these batteries were
able to assist in repelling the enemy with their canister,
drawing upon themselves only a portion of the hostile
artillery fire when they went into action. Massed, they
were overwhelmed by the concentrated fire of superior
guns. We therefore find the usual order of things reversed, due to the undisputed fire of Hunt's masses. At
Sharpsburg, the Confederate batteries were more effective individually than grouped, because they were
forced to devote their energies to the hostile infantry
wherever it threatened and because by dispersing they
so divided the attention of Hunt that much of the concentrated effect of his guns was lost. Upon whatever
point the great Federal masses of guns shifted their
sheaves of fire, from some other quarter a Confederate
battery sprung into action relieved for a time at least
of the merciless hail of iron soon sure to be directed
upon it. But meanwhile these isolated batteries had
individually inflicted terrific losses upon the attacking
infantry.

Sharpsburg, at which the Federals hurled their
masses upon the Confederate positions, was in no way
similar to Malvern Hill. In the latter battle the artillery superiority rested with the defenders whose guns
completely prevented the artillery preparation for
the infantry attack by sweeping the hostile batteries
from the field. At Sharpsburg, on the contrary, the attack retained its artillery superiority throughout, and
yet, though the effect of the artillery preparation was
tremendous, the infantry was unable to press home.
From a tactical standpoint, this anomaly is solely ex-
plainable (since the courage of the Federal Infantry

was superb) by the unsparing support which the infantry of the defense received from its batteries, the guns of which invariably reopened when the hostile guns were masked by the assaulting columns. This was made possible only by the Confederate batteries moving into the closest proximity with the enemy; and, being willing and able to do that, their ordnance, comparatively inferior in point of range, was almost as effective upon infantry masses with case and canister as the superior material of the enemy would have been in their hands. In fact 6-pounders and light howitzers were even more effective with canister at ranges from 150 to 300 yards, than the heavier rifled pieces with shell would have been. All these matters are worthy of much consideration. It is such factors that enter into the problems presented by many battles.

We have seen that the number of guns borne on Lee's muster rolls at this time aggregated about 300, giving a proportion on paper of between 9 and 10 pieces per 1,000 men of the infantry. But no such proportion was to be found on the battlefield of Sharpsburg. A number of batteries were still on the road from Harper's Ferry with Crutchfield when the battle closed; others remained at Harper's Ferry; some had been left at Richmond, or sent to Winchester. In addition to these, the batteries of Col. Brown's regiment and Maj. Nelson's battalion of the reserve took no part in the action. Yet these two commands were being employed for a purpose closely connected with the maneuvers of the Army, and should not be excluded for that reason. Actively employed, then, whether actually engaged or not, were not less than 200 guns, which, considered in connection with an infantry force of 30,000 men on the field of battle, gave a proportion of between 6 and 7 pieces of artillery per 1,000 men of the other arms, still an unusually large proportion, to which the repulse of McClellan's superior force was in great measure due.

As to the expenditures of the various batteries at Sharpsburg, we have no record. The recordation of

such matters was a refinement little known or appreciated by the gunners of 1862. They were more concerned with a multitude of other matters which demanded their attention than with statistics for future
study, and most of the gallant battery commanders who
fought their guns at Sharpsburg were as unable immediately after the battle as the survivors are to-day to
state with any degree of accuracy whether they expended 200, 300, or 500 rounds on the 17th of September. But every circumstance points to an immense
expenditure on the part of some of the batteries engaged, and it is not extravagant to believe it equaled,
if it did not exceed, the average of Second Manassas.

With the final episode of the first invasion of the
North, the Confederate Artillery already, since Second
Manassas, highly regarded, sprang into a position of
preëminence among its sister arms.* The distinguished
reputation which the artillery branch of the Confederate service had acquired, rested not upon its comparative efficiency with the same branch of the Federal
Army, for all recognized the superiority of the latter, in
organization, drill, discipline, material, and equipment.
It was but the direct result of the personal character of
its officers and men, who, except in courage, were overweighed in all that made for the force of their blows.
In other branches of the Confederate service there were
few names among the subordinate officers as well known
as those of Stephen D. Lee, Stapleton Crutchfield,
John B. Walton, and Lindsay Walker, and those of
gentle Tom Carter, bold Preston Chew, stern Poague,
youthful Willie Pegram, and dashing John Pelham had
become by-words in every Southern household. Few
armies have ever boasted such a brilliant galaxy of
gunners, combining as they did the unflinching resolve
of maturer manhood with the bravery of youth, as was
to be found towards the close of 1862 in Lee's field
artillery.

---

*In a letter from Gen. T. T. Munford, himself a cavalryman, to the author,
he declares the artillery to have been the most distinguished branch of the
Confederate service.

CHAPTER XX

AFTER his retreat from the Potomac Gen. Lee rested his army between Winchester and Bunker Hill, a section still rich in food supplies, while the Cavalry watched the enemy. At last his worn men were given a chance to recuperate their strength, and in the vast rolling meadows of the Valley, with grasses still green and sweet, the weary animals of the Artillery found rest and invigorating food.

The base of supplies of the Army was now Staunton, more than 100 miles distant, but passing back and forth over the metalled highway of the Valley, the wagon trains were kept busy bringing ammunition, food, and clothing, until the Army was again placed on a footing of preparedness for further campaigning. But horses and wagons were particularly scarce, in spite of all that Maj. Richardson and the other artillery officers sent to Winchester from Leesburg had been able to do. As late as October 20, the Chief of Ordnance alone reported a deficit of 55 wagons with their teams for Longstreet's reserve ordnance train, and 41 for that of Jackson's Corps, and in nearly every report and communication of the battalion and battery commanders at this time, the scarcity of horses for their batteries is mentioned. Just after the Maryland campaign the general condition of the field artillery in point of personnel, material, horses, and equipment, was distressing.

On September 22, Col. Crutchfield reported every battery of Maj. Pierson's Battalion, D. H. Hill's Division, as unfit for duty, and ordered them to Martinsburg to refit, and to rest and reshoe the horses. In Jackson's old division the condition of Maj. Shumaker's Battalion, composed of Poague's, Carpenter's, Cutshaw's, Caskie's, Rice's, Wooding's, Brockenbrough's, and

Raine's batteries, was even worse. For the 28 guns of these eight batteries, not less than 128 horses were necessary to make them really serviceable, and 204 were needed to properly mount the batteries. Some of these batteries had actually less than 20 animals available for duty, and their harness was particularly defective, others being equipped with 12-pounder howitzers drawn by 6-pounder limbers.

Of Maj. Courtney's Battalion, Ewell's Division, few of the batteries had been present at Sharpsburg. Crutchfield reported three batteries in excellent order, having been refitted by him at Harper's Ferry, two others in fair condition but needing better guns, and two disabled. The last two were also sent to Martinsburg to refit, and for them alone 30 horses were needed.

In A. P. Hill's Division, such of Maj. Lindsay Walker's batteries as had been refitted at Harper's Ferry were in fair condition, in spite of their service at Sharpsburg.

The condition of the artillery of Longstreet's Corps was undoubtedly worse than in Crutchfield's battalions, for nearly all the batteries of Cols. Lee, Walton, and Cabell, and of Majs. Jones, Cutts, Frobel, and Saunders, had been exposed to a terrific punishment at the hands of Hunt. In fact a number of the batteries were individually reported totally disabled, as was Cabell's entire battalion.

In point of personnel, the extent of the depletion of the batteries in general may be estimated from the return of the strength of Lee's and Walton's battalions on September 22, at which time the ten batteries included in the report mustered 39 officers and 632 men present for duty, an average battery strength of but 64 men. Yet, the minimum strength of a battery was prescribed by law to be 80 men.

Within one week, however, the return of stragglers and absentees brought the strength of Walton's Battalion up to 281 officers and men present for duty, with an aggregate present and absent of 355, or a battery average of nearly 90 men. In Lee's Battalion, 433 officers and men were reported present for duty, with an aggregate present and absent of 561, or a battery average of 93 men. At the same time, the personnel of about 20 reserve batteries was reported as 55 officers and 716 men present, with an aggregate of 1,027 present and absent, which shows an average battery strength of but 50 men.

The 7 batteries of Courtney's Battalion, Ewell's Division, reported an average strength at this time of but 49 men present, but of 72 present and absent.

Such conditions demanded an immediate remedy, and steps were at once taken to place the Artillery on a better footing.

As early as the 26th the batteries of Carpenter and Cutshaw, under command of the former, were consolidated, and Wooding was given command of Rice's Battery consolidated with his own; four guns were allowed each battery, and any that remained were ordered to be turned over to the reserve. Capt. Cutshaw had been badly wounded and Rice had resigned. But further than this Gen. Lee had not cared to go without express authority from the Secretary of War, upon whom he called, September 28, for instructions to reorganize and reconstruct all the unserviceable batteries and to dispose of surplus officers according to their merits.* Gen. Lee's communication to the Secretary of War was at once referred to the President, the latter's attention being called in the endorsement to the fact that Congress had refused to authorize the consolidation of companies, even objecting to the disbanding of them, and that in consolidating batteries it was difficult to select the best officers to remain in the service. But the President wisely declared legislation on this point by Congress unnecessary and sanctioned Gen. Lee's action.

To bring the animals of the Army up to a state of efficiency Gen. Lee now, in a general order, which is a model of its kind, established definite and rigid regu-

---

*See *Rebellion Records*. Series I. Vol. XIX, Part II, pp. 629 and 632, S. O. No. 201, September 26, 1862, and letter of Lee to Randolph, September 28, 1862.

lations for their use and care. Inasmuch as it shows both the importance which the deficiency of horses had assumed, as well as the methods pursued in the Artillery for husbanding the strength of the indispensable companion of the gunner, the order is given in full.*

"HEADQUARTERS, ARMY OF NORTHERN VIRGINIA,

"October 1, 1862.

"ORDERS—No. 115.

"II. The general commanding desires to impress upon all officers in charge of horses of the army the urgent necessity of energetic and unwearied care of their animals, and of preventing their neglect and abuse. Officers in charge of wagon trains will be held to a rigid accountability for permitting their teams to be overdriven, misused, or neglected. Division quartermasters and commissaries will report all instances of the kind in trains under their charge.

"III. Artillery horses especially must be kept in good condition. To this end the Chief of Artillery will personally supervise all the reserve, and see that all instances of neglect are corrected, by penalty when deserved, and by suitable provisions when the evil has resulted from necessity. He will cause every practical arrangement to be made for supplying the horses of his command with sufficient and suitable food, sparing no effort or reasonable expense.

"IV. Division commanders are reminded of their responsibility for the condition of their artillery, and especially of its horses. On the march, they will see that the halting places are selected for their batteries where water and food can be obtained. They will charge their Chiefs of Artillery to secure, by rigid personal attention, adequate supplies of forage from the quartermasters to whom that duty is committed. They will see that, when in the vicinity of the enemy, every possible opportunity is improved for resting, watering, and feeding their horses. When the army is quiet, division artillery will be diligently cared for by division commanders and their Chiefs of Artillery. Their batteries must be kept under control, and not allowed to scatter at will. If scarcity of forage renders impracticable a full supply for the horses retained with divisions, and it becomes necessary to send batteries elsewhere for sufficient food, they must go together with proper officers to supply and supervise them, and report statedly to their division commander, or they must be sent to the reserve camp to be there supplied, and report immediately to the general Chief of Artillery.

*Rebellion Records, Series I, Vol. XIX, Part II, p. 642.

"V.   Horses worn down, past recovery, will be turned in to the chief quartermaster, who will send them off immediately, under proper regulations, to good pasturage, where they must be attended to and cared for under the supervision of responsible agents.

"VI.   Battery horses will in no instance be ridden, except while in use by the usually mounted non-commissioned officers of the company, and by them only on duty.   Their use, except with the battery, and then in battery service, is strictly prohibited, and Chiefs of Artillery will arrest and bring to trial all violating this order.

"By order of Gen. R. E. Lee.

R. H. CHILTON,
Assistant Adjutant-General."

The foregoing order not only gives us an insight into the abuses of the past, but also into the system adopted for the care and preservation of the animals during subsequent campaigns.   In all green armies, the abuse of horses is a constant source of annoyance to the authorities, and one not familiar with the mounted service can scarcely realize how very greatly their neglect cripples the efficiency of the troops.   The Confederate Army was fortunate in this respect, inasmuch as the teamsters and drivers were generally quite accustomed to the handling of horses.   In the South nearly every soldier, whether in the infantry, cavalry, or artillery, had been a horseman from early youth, and they only needed to be directed and controlled in order to get the best results from their teams and mounts.   Then, too, the Southern horse was generally of a better breeding and hardier stock than the heavier animals of the North, and Northwest, in which draft blood preponderated.   Especially was this true in Virginia, where many blooded sires were owned by the gentry.   Hardly a farmer in the State but owned a number of superior horses.   The great sport of the people, since early colonial days had been fox-hunting, and therefore the original supply of horses was drawn from those trained in cross-country runs, and inured to the hardships of field and forest. Such animals were peculiarly fitted for military usage when properly fed and cared for, and largely accounted for the effectiveness of the mounted men of Lee's army before the animals were exhausted by the strain of continuous campaigning.

For the trains a large supply of mules was available, animals especially adapted to the rough work exacted of them, and requiring far less forage and attention than horses. Yet the supply was not unlimited, and became scarcer and scarcer as the war progressed and successes enabled the enemy to take from the Confederacy the great breeding grounds of Louisiana, Mississippi, Alabama, Tennessee, Kentucky, and Missouri.

So far the field artillery had been little troubled with the disease known as "sore tongue and soft hoof," which was ravaging the horses of McClellan's Cavalry, and which early in November had attacked Stuart's mounts to such an extent that the Commander-in-Chief in a letter to the latter took occasion to refer to the matter in a spirit of particular concern.*

As early as November 14 the necessity of purchasing horses in Texas for Stuart's Cavalry had impressed the Secretary of War, and before the 20th, Maj. Hart had been directed to secure 1,000 in that quarter. These small animals were of course unsuited for artillery draught purposes, but their purchase tended to relieve the situation in Virginia by leaving the heavier horses for the light batteries.

On October 2, obedient to the instructions of the Commander-in-Chief, Gen. Pendleton made an extensive report on the condition of the Field Artillery. Declaring the number of light batteries too large, some he stated to be inadequately officered, and some, though well commanded and entitled to the highest respect for the honorable service they had rendered, so reduced in personnel and horses as to preclude the possibility of restoring them to efficiency by reason of the expense and enormous number of horses such a step would entail. He proposed that the fairest possible standard be adopted to determine which batteries should be dis-

*Rebellion Records, Series I, Vol. XIX, Part II, p. 703.

banded, their officers relieved from duty, and their men, horses, and equipment distributed among those batteries retained in service. The proposed test to be applied consisted of: First, services rendered; second, the efficiency of the officers; and third, the existing conditions and prospects of the battery as a whole. In summing up his recommendations in this respect, he wrote:

"1st. Laudable service undoubtedly entitles a company to honorable continuance, provided it be not forbidden under one or both of the other conditions.

"2d. Officers thoroughly efficient have a prior claim. Good service for a season, under special circumstances, may have been rendered where some essential requisites for maintaining a battery through protracted difficulties are lacking. To pass upon such characteristics is delicate, yet, under existing responsibilities, essential.

"3d. Where the two preceding conditions concur, it is probably best to invigorate a battery to the utmost practicable; but if either fails, in case of a company much reduced below the service standard, it would seem right to merge it in some others."*

In pursuance of such views, the Chief of Artillery then recommended that the four companies of the Washington Artillery of Louisiana be consolidated into two 6-gun batteries, for the reason that, in spite of their gallant and meritorious service and the generally high character of the officers, there seemed little prospect of recruiting them up to the minimum strength allowed with volunteers and conscripts from other States. Already, before entering Maryland, it had been necessary to attach to Walton's Battalion while at Leesburg, 32 Virginians, 5 from Leake's Battery, and 27 from Anderson's, and these men were urgently needed for the batteries of their own State. Without these there remained but 212 men present and 227 present and absent for the four Louisiana batteries, or an average strength at best of but 57 men. Under the existing battalion organization of four 4-gun batteries, with a forge and a battery wagon, and three escort wagons for each battery, 310 horses were required, in addition to those

*Rebellion Records, Series I, Vol. XIX, Part II, p. 647.

for battalion headquarters, whereas if consolidated, 210 horses would suffice, and the two resulting batteries with a strong personnel and 12 guns would be more effective than 16 pieces distributed among four weak batteries.

The ten batteries of Col. Brown's reserve command, or the First Virginia Regiment, were recommended to be consolidated into six batteries by disbanding Wyatt's, Young's, Ritter's, and Coke's batteries, the first three of which were on duty in Richmond. It was urged that 1st Lieuts. Thurmond, Pendleton, and Robertson, of Wyatt's, Coke's, and Ritter's batteries, respectively, should be by all means retained in the Artillery, as also 2d Lieut. S. H. Hawes, of Coke's.

In Jones' reserve battalion, it was proposed to consolidate the four batteries into two, by disbanding Wimbish's, and Turner's batteries for inefficiency. In this battalion, Capt. Peyton of the Orange Battery was recommended to be dropped for continued absence and unfitness for command, 1st Lieut. Fry to be promoted to succeed him. Certain other promotions and dismissals among the officers were recommended.

Lieut.-Col. Cutts' Battalion of four batteries was proposed to be consolidated into three, by relieving the officers of Capt. James A. Blackshear's Georgia battery and distributing 22 of his men to Ross's, 29 to Lane's, and 42 to Patterson's batteries, of the Sumter Battalion, thus raising the personnel of each to 150 men present for duty. The Sumter Battalion was one of the strongest in personnel in the Army at this time.

Nelson's reserve battalion, of four batteries, it was also thought, should be reduced to three by disbanding Ancell's Fluvanna Battery, and by dropping Capt. C. T. Huckstep, retaining 1st Lieut. John L. Massie, an admirable officer, and promoting him captain in Huckstep's place, while 1st Lieut. B. F. Ancell was recommended to be assigned to duty with the resulting battery. Many other changes in the officers of the battalion were recommended.

Thompson's Battery, or Grimes' of Portsmouth, was also reported below the standard, and it was proposed to consolidate it with the other two batteries, Moorman's and Huger's, of Saunders' Battalion, R. H. Anderson's Division.

In every case the battalion commanders were to select for the batteries retained the best material, horses, and equipment of the disbanded units, turning in any surplus that might remain.

In the case of other batteries to be disbanded, the recommendations were as follows:

For unfitness for their duties all the officers of Lloyd's Battery, of Cutts' Battalion, were to be relieved and of his 85 men, 55 to be assigned to Manley's Battery of Moore's Battalion, McLaws' Division, and 28 to Reilly's Battery, Frobel's Battalion, Hood's Division, these batteries being all from North Carolina.

Chapman's Dixie Battery, mustering but 32 men present for duty, was to be disbanded and its men and horses assigned to Pegram's Battery of Walker's Battalion, A. P. Hill's Division.

The Wise County Battery, or Brown's, having but 48 men on the rolls, and its gallant captain having been seriously wounded, was to be disbanded and its men and horses transferred to Col. Lee's Battalion. The record of this battery was especially fine. It had served with distinction in every battle from Bull Run to date, and lost two commanders, Capts. Alburtis and Brown.

The Hanover Battery, or G. W. Nelson's, with but 60 men, was also to be disbanded, 20 of the men going to Kirkpatrick's Amherst Battery of Nelson's reserve battalion, and 40 to Woolfolk's Ashland Battery of Lee's Battalion. Capt. George Washington Nelson, though highly regarded as a fighter by his superiors, was thought to be better fitted for duty as a cavalry aide than as a battery commander.

With 52 men and 50 horses on its rolls, J. R. Johnson's Battery, of Bedford County, but recently organized, instead of being given the 48 horses

called for by its captain, was to be disbanded and its
men equally distributed to Dearing's and Stribling's
batteries.

Rogers' Loudoun Battery, though having rendered
good service, was to be disbanded since its captain was
absent, its lieutenants indifferent, and its prospects poor.
Its 45 men were also to be transferred to Stribling's
Fauquier Battery.

The Thomas Artillery, or Anderson's Battery, an
organization with a splendid record, had become so
reduced in efficiency that it had not been allowed to accompany the Army into Maryland. The 29 men still
on duty with this battery, and the 27 to be returned to
it by the Washington Artillery Battalion, with its 22
remaining horses, and two senior lieutenants, were to be
assigned to Caskie's Hampden Battery.

Capt. Leake's Battery, its service having been
principally on the South Carolina coast, bearing but 48
men and 58 horses on its rolls, all in poor condition, was
to be consolidated with Carter's King William Battery.

The Magruder, or T. J. Page's Battery, was to be
disbanded, its 45 men and 25 horses being assigned to
Col. Lee's Battalion. Capt. Page himself was recommended for duty on Col. Lee's staff, and Lieut. Magruder for retention in the service.

Though eulogized by Gen. A. P. Hill and his Chief
of Artillery for the service it had rendered in several
actions, Fleet's Middlesex Battery was to be broken up,
46 of its men having been assigned to Woolfolk's, Ancell's and Marmaduke Johnson's batteries at Leesburg.
For insubordination, and misconduct, its officers were
still under arrest and awaiting trial by court-martial.
The payrolls, descriptive lists, horses and material had
all been greatly neglected, and 50 of its men reported
sick when but four were actually unfit for service. It had
no sergeants and no roll existed when the men were
transferred.

Stribling's and Bondurant's batteries required much
work to place them in serviceable condition.

The changes thus proposed and already effected by the Chief of Artillery involved a reduction of the Artillery by 19 batteries. The entire number borne on the rolls of the Army of Northern Virginia had been 73, so that under the proposed reorganization but 54 batteries were contemplated in addition to the horse artillery.

When the unusually hard service which Lee's artillery had experienced, the general unpreparedness of the Confederate government for the arming and equipping of such a large number of batteries, the peculiar requirements of the arm and the utter lack of training on the part of all its men and many of its officers are taken into consideration, one is not surprised at the recommendations of the Chief of Artillery. On the contrary, the condition of the Artillery at this time in many respects is surprising and argues well for those who had charge of its organization and equipment, and especially for the officers who had led the batteries in battle. The fact that so few officers had proved unsuitable to the artillery service, a service most exacting in its many requirements, is a high tribute to the character of the Southern soldier. But as has been pointed out before, the men of the South were peculiarly adapted to mounted service in the field, and the Army of Northern Virginia was exceptionally favored by circumstances in having a large number of officers available who by no means were mere untrained volunteers. In addition to numbers of efficient artillerymen of the Old Army, such as Magruder, Alexander, Lee, and Pelham, were a great many who had received superior instruction in gunnery at the Virginia Military Institute, under Gilham and Jackson, such as Crutchfield, Walker, Carter, Carpenter, Cutshaw, Chew, Truehart, Latimer, and many others. With a backbone of officers of this character, the efficiency of the Field Artillery was readily to be accounted for. It was perhaps more favored than any other branch of the service in the quality of its officers, with respect to the junior as well as the senior grades. Among the lieutenants of the Field Artillery were to be found many trained and able officers who could not have been induced to transfer even with advanced rank from the service of the guns, which held for them a peculiar fascination. For this reason, men like "Jimmie" Thomson, the Carpenters, Milton Rouse, Huger, and Breathed, were found for years serving as mere subalterns in the Artillery.

The recommendations of Gen. Pendleton were almost immediately adopted, the only departure from them being with respect to the reduction of the Washington Artillery Battalion in deference to Col. Walton's objections, who represented that the circumstances attending the organization of his battalion, and its acceptance into the service of the Confederate States in its original form were peculiar. Unwilling to violate any arrangement or agreement which might have been made in the past, Gen. Lee decided to retain the battalion intact, except that the weakest section of Miller's Battery was directed to turn in its guns to the Ordnance Department. *Special Orders No. 209, A. N. V., October 4, 1862,* in which the proposed changes were made effective, were then forwarded to the Secretary of War and, his attention being called to the fact that the measure was imperatively necessary, his approval was requested. The reduction of Walton's Battalion to three batteries was urged if it could be done without breach of faith, and the meritorious officers relieved from duty recommended to be retained in their present grades, and, if necessary, commissioned in the Provisional Army as ordnance or artillery officers.

To insure the speedy and proper reorganization of the Artillery as ordered the Chief of Artillery was authorized and directed to associate with himself in the work Cols. J. Thompson Brown and Stephen D. Lee.

On October 8, the Secretary of War advised Gen. Lee that his action, though supported by the Adjutant-General, was in his own opinion without authority of law, but that in view of the imperative necessity therefor, he had induced the President to recommend legislation to supply the defect, meanwhile withholding his own decision. The question, a purely political one, fortunately resulted in no embarrassments to Gen. Lee, who was firmly supported by the President and the Adjutant-General. But one may rest assured the reorganization met with serious objections, and produced many heart-burnings, on the part of those most affected, namely, the inefficient officers who were thereby relieved from duty. Upon some of the officers whose commands were disbanded necessary hardships were of course entailed, and such was the case with Capt. John R. Johnson.*

The tri-monthly return of October 10 shows an encouraging increase in the number of men with the batteries. On that date, for Lee's and Walton's battalions, together containing 10 batteries, the personnel is given as 35 officers, 738 men present for duty, with an aggregate present and absent of 1,107 men. The average effective battery strength was, therefore, over 70 men, and on paper about 110.† But Col. Brown's six batteries mustered at this time only 13 officers and 311 men, or an average strength of but 51 men present, the same on paper being nearly 90 men. In the Reserve Artillery, that is in Cutts', Jones', and Nelson's battalions, composed of 8 batteries, a total of 54 officers and 858 men was reported present with an aggregate of 1,027 present and absent. The average effective strength of the reserve batteries was therefore about 107 men. A considerable increase in the number of Brown's effectives, that is 8 officers and about 100 men, appears in the return of November 10.

Before the middle of October and before the consolidation of the batteries and the turning in of the surplus guns, some 40 in number, had been effected, the activity of the enemy became noticeable and in the midst of his work Gen. Pendleton was ordered to pre-

---

*Rebellion Records, Series I, Vol. XIX, Part II, p. 662. See Gen. Lee's letter to Gen. Early on the subject of Capt. Johnson.
†Ibid., p. 660.

pare to move at a moment's notice since it was not designed to give battle about Winchester. But fortunately
a further respite ensued and the work of reorganization
and equipment continued.

The fine ordnance captured at Harper's Ferry proved
a great bone of contention among the battery commanders. Enough requests for McClellan's 73 field
pieces were received to have made the issue of double
the number necessary in order to fill all the demands.
The material of the Artillery was quite deficient, and
was a cause of much anxiety to all concerned. As late
as December 5, Gen. Lee wrote the Secretary of War,
that during the past campaigns he had been much handi-
capped by the superiority of the Federal artillery over
his own, a fact which he attributed in part to the
greater experience of the enemy's gunners but principally to the better quality of their ammunition and
ordnance. Though these advantages were being rapidly
diminished by the increasing efficiency of his artillery
personnel and the substitution of heavier guns for the
light pieces with which his batteries were originally
armed, yet the disparity was still keenly felt. The ammunition, he stated, was being more carefully prepared,
and captured ordnance had been made full use of, but
long-range pieces were urgently needed. If sufficient
metal could not otherwise be secured for their manufacture, he recommended that the Chief of Ordnance
melt up the old bronze 6-pounders, and if necessary a
part of the 12-pounder howitzers for the purpose of
recasting 12-pounder Napoleons. The best material for
field service in his opinion were 12-pounder Napoleons,
10-pounder Parrotts, and the improved 3-inch rifles.
Batteries armed with such pieces would, he declared,
greatly simplify the question of ammunition supply by
reducing the number of calibers in use, and the weight
of metal to be transported. For special service, he requested to be supplied with additional 20- and 30-
pounder Parrotts, closing his communication with an
urgent recommendation that the subject of field ar-

tillery material receive the immediate consideration of the War Department, and the remark that "the contest between our 6-pounder smooth-bores and the 12-pounder Napoleons of the enemy is very unequal, and, in addition, is discouraging to our artillerists."*

This communication was at once referred to Col. Gorgas, Chief of Ordnance, who returned a circular of his department showing that J. R. Anderson & Co., of the Richmond Tredegar Works, had already been given directions to work night and day to turn out material such as Gen. Lee desired, and that Col. Baldwin, Chief of Ordnance, A. N. V., had been requested to turn in all the discarded pieces both at Staunton and with the Army to be recast. This circular, dated November 13, 1862, was as follows:

"Until further order, no artillery will be made except the following caliber:

"Bronze—Light 12-pounder Napoleon guns; caliber, 4.62.

"Iron—For field battery of maneuver, 10-pounder Parrotts, banded; caliber, 2.9. For field battery of reserve, 20-pounder Parrotts on 12-pounder carriages; caliber, 3.67. For siege guns, 30-pounder Parrotts on 18-pounder siege carriages; caliber, 4.2."†

These guns were to be forwarded to the Army as rapidly as completed, and, as we shall see, a few of the heavier ones were received during the first days of December.

Early in October a court of inquiry was appointed to investigate the circumstances connected with the disorderly withdrawal of the two infantry regiments of Lawton's command, which had been left as a support for the Reserve Artillery at Shepherdstown. But in the records no suggestion of misconduct on the part of the artillery officers is to be found, a significant fact for those who insinuate lack of persistence on the part of Gen. Pendleton and his subordinate commanders. If at any time during the months of September and

*Rebellion Records, Series I, Vol. XXI, pp. 1046-7. Letter of Gen. Lee to Secretary of War. Also see Ibid., p. 1048, Lee to Gorgas.
†Ibid.

October the Chief of Artillery appeared to be lacking in energy, despite the results he actually accomplished in the matter of collecting material, horses, and stragglers, in addition to his routine duties during the campaign, and in looking up woolen mills and arranging for the manufacture of clothing and equipment, subsequent thereto, along with the labor of personally directing the reorganization of the Artillery, it is only necessary to state that every communication of Gen. Lee bears the imprint of his undiminished confidence in Gen. Pendleton, whose unfortunate physical condition was nevertheless well known to the Commander-in-Chief. While on the Peninsula, he had contracted a severe case of malaria, which would have justly entitled him to a leave of absence from field duty while recuperating. The anxiety, exposure, and loss of rest during the days and nights, especially from the 14th to the 20th of September had brought on him a return of his debilitating malady. But despite much actual suffering and frequent enforced prostration, the old officer refused to relinquish his labors and kept bravely at his post.

That Gen. Pendleton did not possess the vigor of youth and the initiative which goes with it is undoubtedly true, and there were no doubt those in the service who would have brought to the office he filled superior qualities in many respects. Pendleton certainly did not possess the forceful character of Gen. Hunt, the Federal Chief of Artillery, but he did possess a conservative and mature judgment which Gen. Lee evidently highly valued. Although but 53 years of age at this time, Gen. Pendleton was aged beyond his years, and an old man in the Army of Northern Virginia where the greatest were so young. Jackson, the Hills, Hood, McLaws, and even Longstreet, were many years his juniors, and in his association with his Chief of Artillery, a man of the most intellectual temperament and Christian character, Gen. Lee, himself senior in point of age to most of his officers, must have found much agreeable relief from the cares and harassments of his awful responsibility.

Then there was another factor entering into Pendleton's retention in a position of so great importance and for which, in the opinion of many a man of greater professional aptitude, and more forceful traits of character, mental and physical, might have seemed better suited. Pendleton was the senior in age of all others in his arm of the service, senior even to Walton. Besides, he was a graduate of West Point, which fact added to the priority of his claim. Should he have been relieved from active command, as he might well have been by reason of his physical condition, a serious question as to his successor would at once have arisen and a host of aspirants would have entered into the jealous turmoil incident to the necessity of such a selection. The retention of Pendleton as Chief of Artillery by Gen. Lee is but another evidence of the latter's sagacity, for he realized that he was still free to assign those duties requiring the vigorous qualities of youth to Pendleton's lieutenants whenever circumstances seemed to demand it, and yet retain the many admirable qualities, especially as an administrator, possessed by the senior.

There were covert insinuations made during the war that Gen. Pendleton was lacking in courage, and similar suggestions have recurred since its close. Instead of combating such a belief on the part of those who gave credence to it, Gen. Alexander has strengthened the voice of the scandal-mongers by never failing to take a slap at his own chief. It is not intended here to assert that Gen. Alexander ever declared Pendleton to have lacked courage, but he does expressly charge him in his book with inactivity both in the Peninsula and in the Maryland campaign in such words as to leave a loop-hole for those maliciously inclined. He, of all others, must have known that Gen. Pendleton was not a coward. The Army gossip was well known to him, and it was his duty to express himself in unequivocal terms, if not to defend his former commander. The writer has made it his duty to discuss the matter of Gen. Pendleton's bearing with many of the latter's former subordinates, and no evidence of the truth of the scandalous charges has been found. On the contrary, Capt. William T. Poague, a man of the most dauntless courage and of the highest Christian character, declare that on a number of occasions when exposure was necessary he witnessed the bearing of Gen. Pendleton under fire, and that he was as calm, self-possessed, and apparently as courageous, as any man could well be. Capt. William Gordon McCabe, as intrepid an officer as was to be found in the Army of Northern Virginia, and possessing those qualities which made him the adjutant and fit companion of Pegram, also denies from personal observation that Gen. Pendleton was lacking in courage.

That Pendleton possessed ample courage is a fact exceptionally well established by Lee's regard for him. Gen. Lee did not gather about him, in offices of high trust, men with weak hearts, but that Pendleton was not given to unnecessarily exposing himself and that he was not a man with the reckless bravery of youth is no doubt true. So much by way of defense of an able and courageous officer.

While the Artillery had been resting and recruiting in camp near White Post, its reorganization was completed, the guns captured at Harper's Ferry equitably distributed among the batteries, including the two 20-pounder Parrotts, and in addition two Whitworth rifles, the latter brought up from Richmond. These important pieces were credited with a range of five miles.

The batteries were now formed into organized battalions as fully as possible. The battalions previously formed really possessed little organization as tactical units, but were merely collections or groups of battery units possessing practically no tactical cohesion. The divisional batteries fell under the control of a senior officer simply in his capacity of chief of artillery, and his functions were administrative rather than tactical.

On November 7, the returns of the Army showed the following assignment of the Artillery:

With the First Corps, in command of which Longstreet had been retained with the rank of lieutenant-general, were 30,319 infantry, and about 1,620 artillery, with 112 guns, of which 54 were light smooth-bore pieces.

In the Second, or Lieut.-Gen. Jackson's Corps, were 30,054 infantry and about 1,740 artillery, with 123 guns, of which 53 were also light smooth-bore pieces.

The Reserve Artillery, consisting of Brown's, Cutts', and Nelson's battalions of 12 batteries, 16 rifled, and 20 smooth-bore pieces, mustered at this time an aggregate personnel of 900.

The horse batteries were with the cavalry division of 7,176 men.

The aggregate of Lee's Army November 17 was, therefore, 71,809 men and 291 guns.

Within the next two weeks, however, a considerable change in the Artillery occurred, for the returns of November 20 show a different organization, as follows:

In the First Corps were 5 divisions under McLaws, R. H. Anderson, Pickett, Hood, and Walker, with 2 reserve battalions of artillery of 6 and 4 batteries, respectively, and a personnel of 623 men.

The divisional artillery of the First Corps was assigned as follows: McLaws' Division, Cabell's Battalion, 4 batteries, 18 guns; Anderson's Division, 4 batteries, unorganized, 18 guns; Pickett's Division, 3 batteries, unorganized, 14 guns; Walker's Division, no artillery. Thus in the First Corps with 28,453 infantry, we find 24 batteries with a total personnel of about 1,463 men, and 99 guns, or a proportion of a little over 3 guns per 1,000 men of the infantry.

In the Second Corps were 4 divisions under Ewell, D. H. Hill, A. P. Hill, and Taliaferro, respectively, with Latimer's Battalion of 6 batteries and 26 guns assigned to Ewell; Jones' Battalion of 5 batteries and 22 guns to D. H. Hill, Walker's Battalion of 7 batteries and 28 guns to A. P. Hill; Brockenbrough's Battalion of 5 batteries and 22 guns to Taliaferro.* With the

---

*The battery assignments will be given later.

30,312 infantry of the Corps, there were then 23 batteries with a total personnel of 1,380 and 98 guns, or about the same proportion of guns to infantry as in the First Corps.

The Reserve Artillery consisted of Brown's Battalion with 6 batteries, Cutts' with 3 batteries, and Nelson's with 3 batteries, with a total personnel of 718 men and 36 guns.

With the entire Army of 38 brigades of infantry, aggregating 58,765 men, we therefore find 59 batteries with 233 guns, or a general proportion of about 4 guns per 1,000 infantry.

Two additional batteries of horse artillery had now been raised, to the commands of which Capts. M. W. Henry and M. N. Moorman were assigned.* Pelham had meanwhile been promoted, taking command of the battalion of 5 horse batteries, the old Stuart Horse Artillery falling to his former lieutenant, Capt. James Breathed, than whom no more gallant gunner ever pulled a lanyard. With Pelham's 5 batteries, viz., Chew's, Breathed's, Hart's, Moorman's, and Henry's, were 22 pieces, a number of them imported Blakelys. To the 8,846 men of Stuart's Cavalry, the horse artillery with a personnel of about 300 men, bore a proportion of about $2\frac{1}{2}$ guns per 1,000.

With the Army of Northern Virginia, November 20, 1862, composed of 58,765 infantry, and 8,846 cavalry, there were 63 batteries with a total personnel of 3,861, and 252 guns, in by far the highest state of efficiency, except as to horses and clothing for the men, yet attained by Lee's artillery.

Forage being all but exhausted around Winchester late in October, Gen. Pendleton, who had completed the work of reorganization, was sent by Gen. Lee to explore the routes over the Blue Ridge Mountains and ascertain the capacity of Fauquier and Loudoun counties to the east for maintaining the Army.

---

*Henry's Battery was formed by dividing Pelham's original battery. Henry was soon promoted major and succeeded in command of this battery by McGregor. Moorman's Battery was simply converted from a light to a horse battery.

Now let us go back and follow the operations of the cavalry, in which the horse artillery had of course been engaged.

Only two days of rest were allowed Stuart's command after his return from Chambersburg, for on the 16th of October two Federal columns had advanced, one under Humphreys from Shepherdstown to Smithfield, composed of 6,000 infantry, 500 cavalry and a horse battery, and the other under Hancock from Harper's Ferry to Charles Town, consisting of 1½ divisions of infantry, 4 regiments of cavalry, and 4 pieces of artillery. The purpose of the Federal reconnaissance was to develop, if possible, during Stuart's supposed absence, the whereabouts of Lee's army.

Humphreys' force was skillfully opposed by Stuart in person with Fitz Lee's Brigade, reënforced at Kearneysville near Shepherdstown by Winder's Brigade of infantry, where only a most determined attack on the part of the Federals succeeded in forcing the Confederates back. On the following day Stuart was joined by Hampton's Brigade, and after reaching Leetown, from which point Humphreys reconnoitered towards Smithfield, the Federal column retraced its steps.

Hancock's column had, meanwhile, been opposed by Col. Munford with several regiments of cavalry, one piece of Chew's horse battery, and three pieces of the 3d Company of Richmond Howitzers under Capt. B. H. Smith, Jr. The most stubborn resistance on Munford's part failed to prevent Hancock from occupying Charles Town where he remained until noon on the 17th, when he returned to Harper's Ferry. In the report of his operations, Col. Munford made special mention of the gallantry of Capt. Smith, who lost a foot and was captured in Charles Town as his last piece was retiring from the field. He also commended Lieut. J. W. Carter, of Chew's Battery, who although wounded early in the day returned to his gun as soon as his wound was dressed.

Having ascertained by means of this reconnaissance that the Confederate Army was still in the Valley, McClellan crossed the Potomac at Harper's Ferry with two divisions of the 9th Corps and Pleasonton's Cavalry and pushed back the hostile pickets east of the mountains as far as Snicker's gap. While Gen. Lee was preparing to meet the Federal advance, Stuart with Fitz Lee's Brigade, and Breathed's and Henry's horse batteries with 6 guns under Maj. Pelham, crossed over the mountains into Loudoun County, bivouacking near Bloomfield on the night of the 30th. So depleted was the cavalry by the disease known as "greased heel" among the horses, that the brigade numbered less than 1,000 men. After driving a small force of the enemy's cavalry from Mountville on Goose Creek, Stuart pursued to Aldie, where he met the head of Bayard's Cavalry Brigade coming from Washington, which he defeated in a sharp encounter, driving it to the cover of its artillery well posted on a line of hills east of the village. Pelham's batteries had not been able to keep up with Stuart, but soon arrived and, dashing into position, engaged the Federal guns. Bayard was soon forced out of his position, and during the night, after a vain effort to make a stand, fell back to Chantilly.

While these movements were in progress, D. H. Hill's Division of Jackson's Corps had been dispatched by Gen. Lee to the vicinity of Paris and Upperville, via Ashby's Gap, and on November 1 Stuart disposed his troops to cover its front. Learning that Pleasonton was advancing upon Philemont, he moved through Union to meet him. Pleasonton drove in Stuart's advanced guard, but declined to attack his main column. On the 2d of November, Pleasonton's cavalry brigade with Pendleton's horse battery was reënforced by a brigade of Doubleday's infantry division and a New Hampshire battery, thus giving the Federals the preponderance of artillery in the proportion of 12 to 6 pieces, a circumstance which gave Stuart much concern.

The successful resistance he had been able to oppose to the enemy was in large measure due to the skillful handling of his guns upon which he constantly depended. Maj. McClellan, Stuart's Chief-of-Staff, writes: "Two spirits more congenial than Stuart and Pelham never met on the field of battle. Stuart's fondness for the use of artillery was almost excessive; Pelham's skill in its management amounted to genius. Stuart and Pelham imparted to the horse artillery an independence of action and celerity of movement which characterized it to the end of the war, and which was nowhere equalled or imitated, except in the same arm of the Federal service. The achievements of the batteries attached to both the Federal and Confederate cavalry are worthy of a separate record, and of the careful attention of military men."*

Such were the views of the Confederate cavalrymen regarding their horse batteries and gunners and when expressed by the Chief-of-Staff himself they bear particular weight.

Just what Chew was to Jackson and Ashby, Pelham was to Stuart. "It is doubtful," says Gen. Munford in a letter to the author, "if either could have accomplished what they did without these remarkable artillerymen."

Notwithstanding Pleasonton's superior force, Stuart offered him resistance near Fleetwood on November 2. About 8 A. M. the Federals began to deploy both their infantry and cavalry and some 6 or 8 pieces of artillery in his front, and Stuart, dismounting his troopers, took position behind the stone fences which were very numerous in that section, affording both sides excellent cover. "Having to watch all the avenues leading to my rear, my effective force for fighting was very much diminished, but the Stuart Horse Artillery, under the incomparable Pelham, supported by the cavalry sharpshooters, made a gallant and obstinate resistance, maintaining their ground for the greater part of the day, both suffering heavily, one of our caissons exploding from the enemy's shot."†

---

*The Campaigns of Stuart's Cavalry, McClellan, p. 173.
†Stuart's Report.

It was during this engagement that Pelham performed a feat of arms second only to that which he was soon destined to accomplish at Fredericksburg. Conducting a howitzer some distance in advance of his cavalry supports to a hill, and concealing the piece, he opened fire upon a body of the enemy's cavalry in the valley beneath him, putting it to flight, and then pursuing the panic-stricken men actually captured their standard, a number of their arms, equipments, horses, and some prisoners as well, without the loss of a single gunner or horse of his own battery.

But, in spite of Pelham's prowess, the enemy returned and enveloped the Confederate position which compelled Stuart's withdrawal to Seaton's Hill, about a mile in rear, where the Federals were held at bay until dark. Repeatedly assailing this position, Pleasonton was each time repulsed by the fire of Pelham's guns, the latter sighting the pieces himself. And such was the accuracy of Pelham's aim that on one occasion he struck down a color bearer with a single shot at a range of 800 yards.

During the night Stuart withdrew his command to Upperville, where he proposed to offer further resistance on the 3d. Pleasonton was again reënforced, this time by Averell's Cavalry Brigade and Tidball's Horse Battery, whereas the only reënforcements acquired by Stuart was Hardaway's Battery, with a Whitworth gun from D. H. Hill's Division, which had moved back through the gap toward Front Royal.

About 9 A. M. Pleasonton attacked Stuart, who resisted him as upon the preceding day until late in the afternoon, when the Confederates withdrew. As the Federals approached Paris and Ashby's Gap, Hardaway's Whitworth opened upon them at long range, one of its shells killing Gen. George D. Bayard, of the Federal Cavalry. This same gun, under the same officer, was later stationed on the extreme right near the Yerby house at Fredericksburg, and all through the battle greatly annoyed Burnside's troops on the plain below.

Meanwhile, the fact had been discovered that Mc-Clellan's whole army was advancing southward, and on October 27, Longstreet's Corps had been set in motion to confront it, while Jackson remained about Millwood keeping D. H. Hill opposite Ashby's Gap. The Reserve Artillery was ordered to follow Longstreet at a convenient distance and to encamp upon its arrival at Culpeper. The reserve ammunition train under Col. Alexander accompanied Pendleton. Moving on the 1st of November, and marching *via* Nineveh, Front Royal, Chester Gap, Gaines' Cross-Roads, and Sperryville, the column reached camp at Culpeper on November 4. On the 6th, Col. S. D. Lee, who had acquired a distinguished reputation as an artillerist, and to whose advice at Sharpsburg the Commander-in-Chief had himself deferred, was relieved from the command of his battalion of artillery and ordered to Richmond, receiving there his promotion as a brigadier-general of infantry, and assigned to duty at Vicksburg, Miss. The following day, Lieut.-Col. E. P. Alexander, Chief of Ordnance, A. N. V., was placed in command of Col. Lee's Battalion, but retained immediate charge of the reserve ordnance train, until relieved of ordnance duty and permanently transferred to the Artillery on December 4. On that date, Lieut-Col. Briscoe G. Baldwin, a graduate of the Virginia Military Institute, who had served since the beginning of the war as assistant ordnance officer, was promoted Chief of Ordnance, A. N. V., vice Alexander relieved. Until the surrender at Appomattox, Col. Baldwin fulfilled his responsible office with great success.*

The transfer of Alexander in reality entailed only a slight promotion, but in effect it was more than the mere advancement incident thereto. His abilities as an organizer, and his reputation as a youthful officer with exceptionally mature judgment, as one possessing unusual professional learning, coupled with wide experience in many branches of the service, and as a man

---

Rebellion Records, Series I, Vol. XXI, p. 1046.

of great initiative, and yet not too bold, was well known to the Army. The apparent desire on the part of Gen. Lee was to secure to himself an artilleryman as good as, if not better than, the one whom justice required him to relieve, for the reward given Col. Lee by promoting him was a well-deserved one.

Upon the occupation of Upperville by Pleasonton, Stuart had divided his force, sending Col. Douglas with three of his regiments to Piedmont, as a rear-guard for his trains, and moving his remaining two regiments back to Ashby's Gap, where he joined Hardaway's detachment supported by a small infantry force left with him by D. H. Hill. Pleasonton, though showing little disposition to advance upon the Gap, had sent Averell's Brigade after Stuart's trains, forcing the latter to dispatch Rosser with his two remaining regiments to the support of Douglas, while he repaired to Millwood for instructions from Jackson. Stuart was directed to remain in the Valley, so as to be on McClellan's flank, instead of following Longstreet.

Rosser joined Douglas on the evening of the 3d of November at Markham's, to which point the latter had retired, leaving Averell in possession of Piedmont. The following morning Rosser offered the Federals battle. The engagements which ensued resulted in the Confederates withdrawing after a stiff fight during which reënforcements for Averell were sent up by Pleasonton. As an artillery affair, the action at Markham's is notable on account of the superb gallantry of Henry's horse battery. Averell reported that he actually captured 300 of Rosser's men, and two of Henry's guns, but was forced to relinquish them, which accords with an unwritten tradition among the Confederate Cavalry that on this occasion two of Henry's guns, one of which was the Napoleon with which Pelham distinguished himself at Fredericksburg, were most gallantly handled. These pieces were manned by the famous "French Detachment," which, though surrounded by the Federal cavalry, and attacked at the same time both in front

and rear, kept their guns in action while the gunners
sang the Marseillaise Hymn, being finally relieved by a
charge of one of Rosser's regiments. Though the incident is not officially recorded, the story, resting entirely
upon tradition, but circumstantially corroborated by
Averell's statement, is a pretty one and should be preserved. At any rate we know that Henry's Battery
played an important part in the affair.

Rosser now retired to Barbee's Cross Roads, where
he was joined by Stuart and Hampton's Brigade on
the night of the 4th, and here Stuart determined to
make a stand. Occupying the crest of the hill immediately north of the town with his artillery and
sharpshooters, he held his main body at the Cross Roads.
The enemy attacked at 9 A. M. and a brisk artillery duel
ensued, lasting some hours. But Stuart, having been
informed that the enemy had reached Warrenton, concluded that the attack upon him was but a feint, and at
once withdrew along the Flint Hill and Orleans roads,
the enemy not pursuing.

On November 7, Pleasonton attacked Stuart at
Amissville, where he claimed to have captured two guns.
Gen. Stuart, however, makes no mention of this loss.
Moreover, in his report of the battle near Middleburg,
on June 19, 1863, he distinctly declares that the Blakely
gun, which he was compelled to abandon on that field,
was the first which the horse artillery had lost during the
war.

Pleasonton, following up Stuart on the 8th and 9th
of November, came in contact with Longstreet's Corps
at Corbin's Cross Roads on the 10th. Meanwhile, on
the 7th, Burnside had relieved McClellan and soon the
Federay Army was set in motion towards Fredericksburg, only to find itself again confronted by its vigilant
adversary. W. H. F. Lee's Cavalry Brigade guarded
the lower Rappahannock, while Hampton and Fitz
Lee picketed the river above.

In all Stuart's operations up to this point, and in the
reconnaissances that preceded the battle of Fredericks-

burg, in which the command was almost constantly engaged, either in fighting or marching, the Artillery took
an important part.   Again Stuart pays his tribute to
Pelham.   "The Stuart Horse Artillery comes in for a
full share of this praise, and its gallant commander,
Maj. John Pelham, exhibited a skill and courage which
I have never seen surpassed. On this occasion (Corbin's
Cross Roads, November 10, 1862), I was more than
ever struck with that extraordinary coolness and
mastery of the situation, which more eminently characterized this youthful officer than any other artillerist
who has attracted my attention.   His *coup d'oeil* was
accurate and comprehensive, his choice of ground made
with the eye of military genius, and his dispositions always such in retiring as to render it impossible for the
enemy to press us without being severely punished for
his temerity."   These are words which any soldier might
be proud to have used in connection with his name, and
when we consider that they occur in the report of a
cavalry commander, they should be all the more dear
to the artilleryman.   In the same breath Stuart had to
say of the cavalry the following: "In all these operations, I deem it my duty to bear testimony to the gallant
and patient endurance of the cavalry, fighting every
day most unequal conflicts, and successfully opposing
for an extraordinary period the onward march of Mc-
Clellan."   It should be observed that he does not
mention by name a single officer in his corps for especial
commendation, except the "incomparable Pelham."
This fact gives us some insight into the value he placed
upon the latter's services.

The camp selected for the Reserve Artillery at Culpeper, was an excellent one about a mile from the town,
where clear streams furnished water, and kept the meadows fresh late into the winter, and where woods sheltered
the animals from the bleak north winds. A brief though
welcome rest was here secured for the men and animals.

About this time the field batteries were inspected, and
in order to show the thoroughness of the system of in-

spection, the following abstract from Gen. Lee's comments on the report of Col. Edwin. J. Harvie,
Inspector-General, A. N. V., concerning Frobel's Battalion, of Hood's Division, is quoted: "Capt. Reilly's
Battery is spoken of as being in very fine condition,
showing intelligence and highly-commendable pride in
officers and men, that care having been bestowed upon
horses, guns, etc., which secures true efficiency, and
gives evidence that a due regard for the interests of the
service and a proper attention on the part of officers
will keep artillery horses in good order and guns and
equipment serviceable.

"Captain Bachman's German Artillery is reported,
with exception of 6 horses greatly reduced, as in fair
condition; leather equipment, however hard and stiff,
requiring Capt. Reilly's system to soften and supple
them, the use of Neat's foot-oil, which he obtains from
cattle-feet thrown aside at commissary pens.

"Capt. Garden's Palmetto Light Artillery reported
as inferior to Capt. Bachman's, the horses showing
neglect, axles of pieces and harness requiring grease.
This battery, however, is reported as improving under
your orders."*

Such sidelights as these are very interesting to the
artilleryman. They present a familiar view of great
value as well, and it would seem that the orders on the
subject of the horses were being closely followed up.
But while the equipment of the batteries was being carefully preserved, the necessities of the men were very
pressing. Maj. John J. Garnett, appointed Inspector
of Ordnance and Artillery of Longstreet's Corps,
November 14, 1862, reported on that date 95 of Col.
Alexander's 360, and 64 of Col. Walton's 225 men,
barefooted.† Yet, on the 19th, these battalions and
the Reserve, the men of which were in an equally deplorable condition, were ordered to break camp and
march over muddy, half-frozen roads towards Fredericksburg, special injunctions against straggling be-

---

*Rebellion Records, Series I, Vol. XIX, Part II, p. 719.
†Ibid., Vol. XIX, Part II, p. 721, and Vol. LI, Part II, p. 645.

ing announced, and the gunners were directed to dismount and assist the horses by hand in all difficult places.*

Meanwhile, in the absence of Col. Walton, Col. Alexander had been acting Chief of Artillery, Longstreet's Corps, Col. Walton not returning from sick leave until December 8. Capt. Eshleman commanded the Washington Artillery Battalion in his absence.

After a rough march, extending over five days, the Reserve Artillery arrived in camp near Fredericksburg on November 23. Winter had set in unusually early and with great severity. Provisions were scarce, and often there were short nations even for headquarters. But the men, though barefooted and without heavy clothing, were in excellent spirits and bore their privations with cheerful fortitude, and they made every effort by building shelters to save their horses. It was a noble but pathetic sacrifice on the part of these men, with half-frozen feet, to plod about the hillsides and thickets cutting brush in order that the teams might rest and be protected from the bitter night winds. Similar performances are rarely recorded even in the history of war.

*Ibid., Vol. LI, Part II, pp. 649, 650.

CHAPTER XXI

FREDERICKSBURG

ON November 7, the six Federal corps comprising the Army of the Potomac, which lay between the Bull Run Mountains and the Blue Ridge, contained 125,000 officers and men present for duty, with 320 field pieces.* Accompanying the order of this date superseding McClellan with Burnside, were urgent suggestions that something be done by the latter. Organizing his army into three Grand Divisions under Sumner, Franklin, and Hooker, the new Federal commander promptly issued his orders, and Sumner moved towards Fredericksburg on the 15th, reaching Falmouth just opposite the town two days later. The remainder of Burnside's army took up the march on the 16th, concentrating in rear of Sumner on the 19th.

The batteries of Lee's army were at this time assigned as follows:

1ST CORPS (Longstreet)

Col. J. B. Walton, Chief of Artillery

R. H. ANDERSON'S DIVISION

1. Donaldsonville Battery,	Capt. Victor Maurin.	
2. Norfolk Blues Battery,	Capt. C. R. Grandy.	
3. Norfolk Battery,	Capt. Frank Huger.	
4. Pittsylvania Battery,	Capt. John W. Lewis.	

McLAWS' DIVISION

Col. H. C. Cabell, Chief of Artillery

1. Manly's North Carolina Battery,	Capt. B. C. Manly.
2. Pulaski (Ga.) Battery,	Capt. J. P. W. Read.
3. 1st Co. Richmond Howitzers.	Capt. E. S. McCarthy.
4. Troup (Ga.) Battery,	Capt. H. H. Carlton.

*The strength of Lee's army at this time we have seen was 71,809 men with 275 guns, the latter soon reduced to 255.

PICKETT'S DIVISION

Capt. James Dearing, Chief of Artillery

1. Lynchburg Battery,	Capt. James Dearing.
2. Richmond Fayette Battery,	Capt. Miles C. Macon.
3. Fauquier Battery,	Capt. R. M. Stribling.

HOOD'S DIVISION

Maj. B. W. Frobel, Chief of Artillery

1. Charleston German Battery,	Capt. W. K. Bachman.
2. Palmetto (S. C.) Battery,	Capt. H. R. Garden.
3. Rowan (N. C.) Battery,	Capt. James Reilly.

RANSOM'S DIVISION

1. Petersburg Battery,	Capt. J. R. Branch.
2. Stafford Battery,	Capt. R. L. Cooper.

CORPS RESERVE

1ST RESERVE BATTALION

Col. J. B. Walton

1. 1st Co. Washington Artillery,	Capt. C. W. Squires.
2. 2d Co. Washington Artillery,	Capt. J. B. Richardson.
3. 3d Co. Washington Artillery,	Capt. M. B. Miller.
4. 4th Co. Washington Artillery,	Capt. B. F. Eshleman.

2D RESERVE BATTALION

Lieut.-Col. E. Porter Alexander

1. Bedford Battery,	Capt. Tyler C. Jordan.
2. Bath Battery,	Capt. J. L. Eubank.
3. Madison (La.) Battery,	Capt. George V. Moody.
4. Richmond Battery,	Capt. William W. Parker.
5. Brooks (S. C.) Battery,	Capt. A. B. Rhett.
6. Ashland Battery,	Capt. P. Woolfolk, Jr.

2D CORPS (Jackson)

Col. Stapleton Crutchfield, Chief of Artillery

EWELL'S DIVISION

Maj. A. R. Courtney, Chief of Artillery

1. Charlottesville Battery,   Capt. James McD. Carrington.
2. 4th Md. or Chesapeake Battery,   Capt. Wm. D. Brown.
3. Henrico or Courtney Battery,   Capt. J. W. Latimer.
4. 1st Maryland Battery,   Capt. Wm. F. Dement.
5. Louisiana Guard Battery,   Capt. Louis E. D'Aquin.
6. Staunton Battery,   Capt. W. L. Balthis.

D. H. HILL'S DIVISION

Maj. Hilary P. Jones, Chief of Artillery

1. Hardaway's Alabama Battery,   Capt. R. A. Hardaway.
2. Jeff Davis Alabama Battery,   Capt. J. W. Bondurant.
3. King William Battery,   Capt. Thomas H. Carter.
4. Morris Louisa Battery,   Capt. R. C. M. Page.
5. Richmond Orange Battery,   Capt. C. W. Fry.

A. P. HILL'S DIVISION

Lieut.-Col. R. L. Walker, Chief of Artillery

1. Branch (N. C.) Battery,   Capt. A. C. Latham.
2. Richmond Battery,   Capt. Wm. G. Crenshaw.
3. Fredericksburg Battery,   Capt. Carter M. Braxton.
4. Richmond Battery,   Capt. Marmaduke Johnson.
5. Richmond Letcher Battery,   Capt. Greenlee Davidson.
6. Pee Dee (S. C.) Battery,   Capt. D. G. McIntosh.
7. Richmond Purcell Battery,   Capt. Wm. J. Pegram.

TALIAFERRO'S DIVISION

Capt. J. B. Brockenbrough, Chief of Artillery

1. Alleghany Battery,   Capt. Joseph Carpenter.
2. Danville Battery,   Capt. George W. Wooding.
3. Richmond Hampden Battery,   Capt. W. H. Caskie.
4. Lee Battery,   Capt. Charles J. Raine.
5. 2d Rockbridge Battery,   Capt. J. A. M. Lusk.

2D CORPS RESERVE BATTALION

1ST RESERVE BATTALION

Col. J. Thompson Brown

1. Warrenton Battery,   Capt. James V. Brooke.
2. Powhatan Battery,   Capt. Willis J. Dance.
3. 2d Co. Richmond Howitzers,   Capt. David Watson.
4. 3d Co. Richmond Howitzers,   Capt. Benj. H. Smith.
5. 1st Rockbridge Battery,   Capt. William T. Poague.
6. Salem Battery,   Capt. A. Hupp.

ARMY RESERVE ARTILLERY

Brig.-Gen. William Nelson Pendleton

1ST RESERVE BATTALION

Lieut.-Col. A. S. Cutts

1. "A" Battery, Sumter (Ga.) Batt., Capt. H. M. Ross.
2. "B" Battery, Sumter (Ga.) Batt., Capt. George M. Patterson.
3. "C" Battery, Sumter (Ga.) Batt., Capt. John Lane.

2D RESERVE BATTALION

Maj. William Nelson

1. Amherst Battery,   Capt. Thomas J. Kirkpatrick.
2. Fluvanna Battery,   Capt. John L. Massie.
3. Georgia Regular Battery,   Capt. John Milledge, Jr.

MISCELLANEOUS BATTERIES

1. Ellis' Georgia Battery,   Lieut. W. F. Anderson.
2. Hanover Battery,   Capt. George W. Nelson.

From the foregoing schedule of assignments, it is seen that during the Fredericksburg campaign not less than 63 batteries, exclusive of the five horse batteries, were with Lee's army.

On December 20, the six batteries of Brown's Battalion, which was early taken from the General Reserve and assigned as the corps reserve of Jackson's Corps, mustered 20 officers and 434 men present, and reported an aggregate of 684 present and absent. The average effective battery strength was therefore about 75, and on paper 114. Walton's and Alexander's battalions, with a total of 10 batteries, mustered 41 officers and 629 men present and reported an aggregate present and absent of 966. The effective battery strength was therefore 67, and on paper 96. The eight batteries of the General Reserve reported an effective strength of 42 officers and 683 men, which gives an average effective battery strength of about 90 men, and on paper there appeared an average strength of 120.

Taking the average effective battery strength throughout the Army at 3 officers and 70 men, there must have been in the Army of Northern Virginia an effective artillery personnel of about 200 officers and 4,500 men, while on paper the strength of the Field Artillery was not far from 7,000 officers and men. But for all practical purposes a minimum of 4,500 should be deducted from the figures given for Lee's Infantry, which generally included the Artillery personnel.

Had Burnside upon reaching Falmouth on the 17th immediately crossed the river and taken possession of the hills along the southern bank of the Rappahannock, as he might have done, Gen. Lee would have been compelled to take up a defensive position nearer Richmond. That the possibility of having to fight nearer Richmond was considered by Lee as late as the 23d is shown by the fact that Maj. Moore's Third North Carolina Artillery Battalion which had reported to Pendleton for duty, and which he had ordered on the 22d to rejoin G. W. Smith's command at Richmond, was on the former date directed to occupy a strong position on the south side of the North Anna, and commanding the important railroad bridge between Fredericksburg and Richmond.* Moore reached Richmond before receiving the modification of his orders, but at once retraced his steps, occupying the designated position on the 28th.

Instead of seizing the southern bank, however, Burnside simply occupied the Stafford Heights, or the hills on the north side of the river overlooking the plain of

---

*The horses of this battalion were in poor condition, and Maj. Moore was directed to do all in his power to make them more serviceable.

Fredericksburg, crowning them with his heavy guns under protection of which he began the construction of bridges for his crossing. The narrowness of the Rappahannock, its winding course, and deep bed presented opportunities to accomplish this work practically unopposed by the Confederates, unless they should elect to sacrifice their men and guns to the overwhelming fire of Burnside's batteries.

There were only three Confederate cavalry regiments under Col. Ball guarding the river at Fredericksburg when Burnside commenced his movement in that direction, but on the 15th Gen. Lee ordered a regiment of infantry and Lewis' Battery from near Richmond to reinforce this small force. Reaching Fredericksburg on the 17th, just before Sumner's advance guard arrived at Falmouth, a spirited duel occurred between Lewis' Battery and a rifled battery under Capt. Petitt, the latter having decidedly the best of it as his adversary had but four very inferior guns.

Upon reaching Falmouth, Sumner had favored an immediate crossing, but Burnside would not consent thereto, and for three weeks delayed while the Confederates each day rendered his ultimate move less probable of success. "Opportunity in war is like a woman," Napoleon said. "If you fail to meet her to-day, you need not expect her to meet you to-morrow." Burnside's golden opportunity, offended by his neglect to keep the tryst, had eluded him forever.

On the 20th, his whole army was near Fredericksburg. Longstreet on the day before reached the town, *via* Raccoon and Morton's fords, and rapidly disposed two of his divisions with their artillery on the hills to the west and southwest of the place. On the 21st, Sumner summoned the town to surrender before 5 P. M., under penalty of being bombarded the next day. Of this Gen. Lee wrote: "The weather had been tempestuous for two days, and a storm was raging at the time of the summons. It was impossible to prevent the threat to shell the city, as it was completely exposed to the batteries on the Stafford hills, which were beyond our reach. The city authorities were informed that while our forces would not use the place for military purposes, its occupation by the enemy would be resisted, and directions were given for the removal of the women and children as rapidly as possible. The threatened bombardment did not take place; but in view of the imminence of the collision between the two armies, the inhabitants were advised to leave the city, and almost the entire population, without a murmur, abandoned their homes. History presents no instance of a people exhibiting a purer and more unselfish patriotism, or a higher spirit of fortitude and courage, than was evidenced by the citizens of Fredericksburg. They cheerfully incurred great hardships and privations, and surrendered their homes and property to destruction, rather than yield them into the hands of the enemies of their country."*

Although the weather was most inclement, the thermometer being near zero, almost the whole population removed and found the best shelters they could, cheerfully giving up their homes to the battlefield. The neighboring country homes and churches were filled, some times with dozens of families, to whom rations were issued by the commissaries, and many women and children encamped in the forest in brush and blanket shelters, where the sight of their cheerfully borne sufferings nerved many a heart for the coming struggle. Though the Federals did not shell the town after certain representations were made by the Mayor, it was inferred from the negotiations that the bombardment would simply be postponed, and this understanding was responsible, Gen. Alexander tells us, for the construction of many of the earthworks which contributed to the repulse of Burnside's assaults on Marye's Hill.†

By November 22, Longstreet's other two divisions, with Lane's Battery, had arrived and the First Corps extended its line along the southern heights, overlooking the town, from Banks' Ford on the west to Hamilton's Crossing on the east.

---

*Rebellion Records, Series I, Vol. XXL, p. 551, Lee's Report.
†Gen. E. P. Alexander's Southern Historical Papers, Vol. X, p. 383.

Lee and Jackson had both originally opposed resisting Burnside's advance at this point, by reason of the fact that in case he was defeated the Stafford Heights, which he would undoubtedly hold with a strong rear guard, afforded him too free an escape, whereas if he were overthrown at such a point as the North Anna, with lengthened communications, his retreat would be far more difficult.* But Burnside's procrastination enabled Lee to so strengthen the Rappahannock position that he deemed it wise to avail himself of it for defense in preference to the weaker one on the North Anna, in spite of the foregoing objections and Jackson's reiterated protests. The developments had simply committed the Confederates to the line along which they had gradually by circumstances been led. The Federals had placed themselves behind a broad river, and it is an established fact that rivers influence military operations mainly in that they delay the movements of the attacker, and during the passage afford the defender an opportunity of engaging the attacking troops in detail. Gen. Lee knew this and could not bring himself to relinquish what he perceived to be a real, present advantage for those advantages which might develop later on, provided war with its uncertainties played him no tricks. He also saw that in failing to seize the southern bank of the river, Burnside had placed it in his power to occupy it in force, the time allowed him further enhancing his advantage by enabling the development of communications which only served to increase the mobility of the defense.

Lee's principal fear, and also Jackson's, was that, in view of the difficulty of the attack on a well-defended river line, which is rarely attempted, Burnside would refrain from making an effort to force the Confederate position, and resort to a turning movement. But Lee in dealing with the Federals always minimized the probability of their acting upon the soundest strategical principles. He had learned by experience that they

*Military Memoirs of a Confederate, Alexander, p. 287.

were prone to disregard the rules of war, and was ever willing to take advantage of their neglects. Thus he had divided his army before Pope, and again in the Maryland campaign, where he also fought the battle of Sharpsburg with his back against the Potomac, and with but one avenue of retreat, and that one behind an exposed flank, and later he indulged in a most risky division of force at Chancellorsville. Lee's strategy was based upon his own moral supremacy over his adversaries. In declining to be bound by established principle, he simply availed himself of that supremacy, increasing it by success, instead of neglecting an element which made it possible for him to disregard the dictates of the most approved general principles. With an army possessing great cohesion, in addition to the utmost mobility of its parts, a change in tactics in the face of the enemy is possible, although the whole has been seemingly committed to the original plan of attack. But Lee knew full well from experience that the ever present bungling of his opponents, even when in the execution of a prearranged plan, would render unsuccessful any extemporaneous maneuvers on their part, however brilliantly conceived. At any rate, he felt that tactical surprises, if attempted, would be more apt to present him with opportunities than to take him unawares. We should not attempt to solve Lee's strategy by cut and dried formulæ. The controlling factor in his problems was the character of his adversary, and of that factor he never lost sight. Pitted against a Napoleon and a Moltke, Lee would never have fought the battles of Second Manassas, Sharpsburg, Fredericksburg, and Chancellorsville.

Finding the Confederates determined to contest his crossing at Fredericksburg, the Federal commander endeavored to effect one at Skinker's Neck, about 15 miles below the town, but the premature appearance of a number of gunboats near Port Republic and other movements in that direction disclosed his design, and D. H. Hill's and Early's divisions were ordered up

from Orange Courthouse to oppose the projected crossing. When Burnside endeavored to push across on the
5th, he found it impossible, Hill's and Stuart's artillery
having driven off his gunboats. In this work Pelham's
horse batteries and Milledge's and a section of Poague's
Battery, were most effective, in spite of Gen. D. H.
Hill's sarcasm directed at the gunners. These batteries
were provided with very poor ammunition, and the
flight of the heavy projectiles were, therefore, most
erratic. As they tumbled short, or burst in air, or failed
to burst altogether, the remarks of "Old Raw-Hide"
were extremely biting.*

When Burnside's balloonists reported Jackson's divisions massed behind the guns, he abandoned his project
in this quarter and determined to effect his crossing at
Fredericksburg. His plan was now to cross at the
town, also to push a force around Lee's right at
Hamilton's crossing, thus interposing between the main
Confederate force and that at Skinker's. Something
had to be done, and he could no longer delay in making
his effort.

On December 10, Burnside finally issued his orders
for an attack. In his report he said: "I concluded that
the enemy would be more surprised at a crossing, at or
near Fredericksburg, where we were making no preparations, than by crossing at Skinker's Neck, and I determined to make the attempt at the former place. It
was decided to throw four or five pontoon bridges across
the river, two at a point near the Lacy house, one near
the steamboat landing at the lower part of the town,
one about a mile below, and if there were pontoons sufficient, two at the latter point."†

The pontoon trains were to arrive at their designated
positions by 3 A. M. December 11, and at daylight the
construction of the bridges commenced. It was estimated that these bridges, from 400 to 440 feet long,
with the thermometer at 24 degrees above zero, would

---

*Gen. D. H. Hill, a man of much dry wit and very outspoken, an able officer
whose opportunities were unequal to his abilities, had received the name of
"Raw-Hide" by reason of his having shod numbers of his men with moccasins.
†*Rebellion Records*, Series I, Vol. XXL, p. 87.

be completed in between two and three hours, the working parties being screened from the Confederate fire by the town. On the Stafford hills above the plain 179 Federal guns were placed in position during the night to cover the proposed crossing, and to keep down any hostile musketry fire from the opposite bank. Where two bridges were thrown, one was to be reserved for the batteries.

Among the Federal guns which crowned the Stafford Heights, from Falmouth to Pollock's Mill, a distance of some 3½ miles, were six 20-pounder Parrotts, and seven 4.5-inch siege guns so placed as to be able to sweep the town of Fredericksburg and the plain, and to bring to bear a formidable fire upon the most distant heights occupied by the Confederates.

The Federal commander had not reckoned upon the all but impregnable character of Lee's position. It might have been turned, as pointed out by Jackson, by way of the upper fords, but a frontal attack was destined to fail. The Rappahannock, navigable to Fredericksburg, is there about 140 yards wide. The Stafford Heights along the north side have an elevation of about 150 feet, and completely command the plain below and across the river. On the southern side is Taylor's Hill close to the river and 1½ miles upstream and across from Falmouth. From Taylor's Hill an irregular ridge extends southeastward, which leaves between it and the river a plain gradually spreading out to a width of a mile at Fredericksburg, and increasing below the town. This plain, with an elevation of about 30 feet above the river, is intersected by Hazel Run just below, Deep Run about half a mile, and the Massaponax River some four miles beyond the town, all flowing through deep, ravine-like banks from the highland across the plain to the river. Lengthwise, and near the middle from end to end, the flats were intersected by a broad, unpaved, worn-out stage road, which descending into the plain from Taylor's Hill passed through the town, and bifurcated just short of the Massaponax, its branches leading to Port Republic and Richmond respectively. This hollowed-out roadway was bordered by ditches and low cedar hedges which afforded excellent cover for infantry. Not far from the base of the foothills southeast of the town, and almost parallel to the stage road, ran the Richmond and Fredericksburg Railroad, with an embankment about 3 feet high, almost parallel to the stage road until it reached Hamilton's Crossing, at which point it turned southward towards Richmond.

The northern end of the ridge or that portion consisting of Taylor's, Stanbury's, and Marye's Hills, was for the most part open, though much cut up by the headwaters of Hazel Run. The center and southern portions, consisting of Lee's Hill, the Howison house ridge, and Prospect Hill, were covered with a dense wood, which nowhere extended into the plain, except between Deep Run and Hamilton's crossing where the swampy sources of a small stream were covered with brush and timber to a point midway between the railroad and the stage route. Low in front, with an elevation above the plain of between 40 and 50 feet, with many indentures sloping towards the river, the ridge gradually rises to a crest, lower in elevation than that of the Stafford Heights, and then falls towards the south and the Massaponax. About one mile from the northern limit of the plain, and directly east of Stansbury's and Marye's hills, was the main part of Fredericksburg, a town of about 4,500 inhabitants, extending halfway back to the base of the ridge from the southern bank of the river. On the north edge of the town was a mill, to which two branches of a canal flowed, one from the river at the base of Taylor's Hill, and one from the river immediately opposite Falmouth. Leaving the western branch of the canal at a point just in front of Stansbury's Hill, a race or ditch ran almost parallel to the river and behind the town into Hazel Run. This ditch lay in a depression, the south bank of which also afforded cover for troops. Leaving the center of the town in a direction perpendicular to the river, the Plank Road to Orange Courthouse, crossing the mill race, passed over Marye's Hill. The Telegraph road, leaving the town just below the former, continued parallel with it until it reached the foot of Marye's Hill, when it followed the base around to its right for half a mile to Hazel Run, which it crossed, then ascended Lee's Hill, whence it took a southeasterly course toward Richmond. At the circular base of Marye's Hill, this road, hollowed out by long use, was bounded by stone fenses.

The Confederate position was well taken along the ridge to the south and west of Fredericksburg, that is from Taylor's Hill to the Massaponax. Realizing the inequality of the contest which he would be called upon to wage when activities were resumed, Lewis on the extreme left had, on the night of the 23d, taken up a position on the plateau to the right of and below the summit of Taylor's Hill and had begun to construct gun-pits and epaulments for his guns. Meantime, Grandy's Battery of Anderson's Division had also arrived, coming up from Richmond, and prepared a position in like manner on Lewis' right. On the 17th, Gen. Lee, learning of Sumner's movement, had ordered Longstreet with McLaws' and Ranson's divisions, with Cabell's Battalion of the former, and Branch's and Cooper's batteries of the latter, to Fredericksburg, and Lane's Battery of the General Reserve with its two 20-pounder Parrotts, was sent forward with them. Lane at once intrenched on the heights overlooking the bend of the river above Falmouth, retaining his position on the extreme Confederate left. Overruling Col. Cabell's advice to occupy Taylor's Hill with his artillery, McLaws placed his batteries on the crest of the hill between the Telegraph road and Howison's barn. In this position Read, with one 10-pounder Parrott, one 12-pounder howitzer, and one 3-inch rifle; Manly with three 6-pounders, one 3-inch rifle and two 12-pounder howitzers; Carlton with two 10-pounder Parrotts; and

McCarthy with two 3-inch rifles, at once intrenched, while the less effective pieces of their batteries were held under cover only to be used against attacking infantry. Cooper's and Branch's batteries of Ransom's Division joined Cabell's batteries, the former with three 10-pounder Parrotts also intrenching.

On the 19th, the remaining divisions of Longstreet's Corps were ordered up, the Reserve Artillery and the ordnance train following. At the same time Jackson was directed to proceed to Orange Courthouse with all dispatch. Leaving his old camp on the 19th, he set out from Winchester on the 22d. He passed through Strasburg on the 25th, and Madison Courthouse on the 26th, and reached his appointed rendezvous, without a straggler, the following day, having marched 120 miles over execrable roads in eight days, two of which were devoted to rest.

On the 29th, Lieut. W. F. Anderson in command of Ellis' Georgia Battery arrived from Richmond with two "Long Toms,"* or 30-pounder Parrotts, sent forward by Col. Gorgas, and pits were constructed for them near the Howison house group under Col. Cabell, and his assistant, Maj. S. P. Hamilton.

In the meantime the two remaining batteries of Anderson's Division, Maurin's and Huger's, came up and intrenched immediately north of the Plank Road, and Moorman's, Macon's, and Stribling's batteries of Pickett's Division, joined Cabell's group on the ridge behind McLaws' Division, all except one 10-pounder Parrott of Macon's and a similar piece of Moorman's being well retired. Frobel's Battalion of Hood's Division, consisting of Reilly's, Bachman's, and Garden's batteries, intrenched along the northern part of the ridge, running from Deep Run to Hamilton's Crossing, the guns commanding the valley of the stream.

Of Walton's reserve battalion which occupied Marye's Hill from the Telegraph to the Plank Road, two 3-inch

---

*"Long Tom" was the name given the big 30-pounder Parrott captured at First Manassas. The name was also used by the Boers in 1899 to designate their big guns.

rifles and one 10-pounder Parrott of Squire's 1st Company, two 12-pounder Napoleons of Miller's 3d Company, and two 12-pounder howitzers and two 12-pounder Napoleons of Eshleman's 4th Company, or nine pieces in all, were placed in individual pits and epaulments on the military crest. Richardson's 2d Company was on detached duty with Pickett's Division. Further to the left and beyond Maurin and Huger, Alexander's reserve battalion occupied the Stansbury Hill, Rhett's Battery, however, being established south of the Plank Road; two rifles of Parker's Battery occupied pits in front of the Stansbury house, while his two howitzers were concealed behind the buildings for use against the infantry columns of the enemy. The batteries of Jordan, Woolfolk, and Moody were also held behind the rear crest of the plateau, from which position they could move into pits on the forward crest, or be sent to the most threatened points as needed. The sixth battery of the battalion, or Eubank's, joined Cabell's group behind McLaws, as did the General Reserve. The batteries under Alexander and Walton and those of R. H. Anderson's Division thus commanded the entire plain from Hazel Run northward to the westward bend of the river, as well as the opposite bank, at a range of 1½ miles, while Cabell's group of nearly 50 pieces could sweep the flats from Fredericksburg southward, crossing fire with Frobel's guns beyond Deep Run. The distribution of the artillery was excellent in every respect, and illustrates the correct method of guarding a line of river by a series of strong artillery groups so placed as to be able to concentrate their fire on the various approaches to the position to be held. Furthermore, the tactics employed were far superior to those at Antietam, for at Fredericksburg the inferior artillery was not ruthlessly exposed, but held entirely under cover until it could be effectively brought into action, thus concealing as well as protecting the lighter pieces from the superior fire of the enemy while the heavier guns, necessarily placed in position, were intrenched. The whole plan was most skillfully conceived.

Its main features were as follows: the long range pieces, protected by intrenchments, would engage in the preliminary action, conserving their ammunition and refraining from any waste in a useless duel with the superior artillery of the enemy. These guns were to inflict as much damage as possible, however, on the enemy while crossing the river and forming for attack, and to take advantage of all exposures on his part in whatever quarter of the field. In so doing they would necessarily disclose their positions. It was not expected that they could subdue to any great extent the hostile artillery fire. When the infantry columns of the enemy with their light batteries advanced to the assault and came within range of the lighter pieces, they would move into hitherto undisclosed positions, and open with the maximum effect, assisting in the overthrow of the attacking columns, before they were silenced by the guns of the enemy. So soon as the fire of the enemy's batteries of position were shifted to the fresh batteries, the heavier Confederate guns would be free again to play upon the hostile groups, shaking their fire, or to assist in the repulse of the infantry, as circumstances dictated to be best.

By reason of the character of the terrain, Gen. Lee had wisely determined only to resist the enemy after he had effected his crossing, and as the southern hills were commanded by the opposite heights, it became necessary to construct earthworks for his artillery. The work of locating the Confederate batteries had been assigned to Gen. Pendleton, who with the skillful aid of Cols. Cabell and Alexander and Capt. S. R. Johnson, of the Engineers, after making a most comprehensive reconnaissance, prepared the general plan of defense. In this work the services of Col. Alexander were of course invaluable. Both an engineer and an artilleryman of experience, he had constantly before him the necessities of communication, necessarily fore-most in the mind of one so familiar with the duty of am-munition supply. The Confederate dispositions were hence most judicious.

Until Lee's army was concentrated at Fredericks-burg, the burden of the defense had fallen upon the Artillery. While Burnside's men were working like beavers planting their heavy batteries, Pendleton and his artillery officers had also been busily at work. The Confederate batteries, such as they were, were carefully classified and marked so that every staff officer might readily find them. So placed that the maximum field of fire might be secured to the guns, the best possible lateral communications were prepared by the engineers. In the preparation of the position, the services of the infantry as well as of the gunners were utilized to the utmost, and gangs of negroes were brought up to assist in the work of intrenching.

The weather was extremely severe during all this work. Lack of tools and frozen ground made the work slow, and when Burnside finally attacked, individual pits for about 40 guns had been dug, but these were without shelter for ammunition or infantry supports. Along the Telegraph road at the base of Marye's Hill a ditch had been dug on the lower side of the road and the dirt thrown forward and banked against the stone fence which bounded it. A work was constructed near the mouth of the Massaponax, in which Capt. Ross's Battery of the Reserve was placed to stop any gunboat which might pass Pelham's guns further down the river. Little artificial cover could be provided for the infantry, in view of the labor that intrenching entailed under the existing conditions. In this execrable weather the only shelter for the men, a few still without shoes, and most of them totally unprovided with adequate clothing, consisted of "lean-to's" constructed by throw-ing tarpaulins and blankets over poles, or fashioned with brushwood, leaves, and mud. But fire-wood was plentiful and in some way the men managed to keep the blood coursing through their veins. Provisions were none too bountiful. Beef on the hoof, cornmeal, and black-eyed peas comprised the great bulk of the commissary issues, coffee and hog meat being rare treats even for the general officers and their staffs.

On the morning of the 11th, Longstreet's Corps held the ridge in rear of Fredericksburg, with Anderson's, McLaws', Ransom's, Hood's, and Pickett's divisions, aggregating 33,400 infantry, and about 1,500 artillery-men, with about 100 guns.* Of Jackson's Corps, A. P. Hill's Division of 11,533 infantry, and about 450 ar-tillerymen, with 7 batteries, was near Yearly's house, five miles south of Fredericksburg; Taliaferro's Divi-sion of 4,690 infantry, and about 325 artillerymen with 22 guns, was at Guiney Station, nine miles south of Fredericksburg; Early's Division of 7,340 infantry, and 380 artillerymen, with 26 guns, was at Skinker's Neck, 12 miles down the river; and D. H. Hill's Divi-sion of 8,627 infantry and 325 artillerymen, with 22 guns, was at Port Royal, 18 miles below the town.

Pendleton with the Reserve Artillery, less Brown's Battalion, now assigned as reserve of the Second Corps, with 752 officers and men, and about 20 guns, was in rear of Longstreet's line.

Of the cavalry division under Stuart, aggregating 9,146 present for duty, Hampton's Brigade was im-mediately on the left of Longstreet along the river and watching Banks' and United States fords; Fitz Lee's Brigade was with Longstreet; W. H. F. Lee's Brigade was along the river near Port Royal, and Rosser's Bri-gade was in rear near the Wilderness Tavern, watching the left flank and upper fords.

Including the staffs and the five horse batteries the grand total, present for duty, December 10, was 78,513 and about 250 guns, the largest concentrated army Gen. Lee had yet handled.

---

*The return of the 1st Corps for December 10 shows a total of 34,944 officers and men present for duty. See *Rebellion Records,* Series I, Vol. XXI. p. 1057. Of this number there were 37 officers and 586 men in Walton's and Alexander's reserve batteries, and there were 14 divisional batteries besides, with a total of not less than 50 officers and 840 men present for duty. Deduct-ing the artillery personnel of about 1,500 officers and men from the total present for duty we have about 33,400 as the strength of Longstreet's Infantry.

Opposed to him was an army of 118,952 men and 324 guns, with reënforcements aggregating 27,724 men near at hand and actually *en route,* and in addition a force about Washington of 51,970 with 284 guns of position and 120 field pieces. For the advance upon Richmond and the defense of Washington, the Federals had, therefore, 198,546 men present for duty and about 900 guns. If Burnside should defeat Lee, Richmond would be lost. But if Lee defeated Burnside and captured his entire army, the most serious part of his work would not have begun.

Burnside's attempt to cross the river in his front had been expected for some days, notice of which was to be given the Confederates by the firing of two guns of Cabell's group. At 2 A. M. on the 11th, the pickets reported that pontoon trains could be heard in motion, and at 4:30 A. M. the Federal working parties had commenced to throw their bridges. About 5 A. M. the signal guns were fired and the Confederate brigades and batteries at once moved into their appointed positions, the latter having been held behind the crest of the ridge, so as not to disclose their whereabouts until they actually opened fire.

Gen. Lee had committed the task of resisting the crossing to Barksdale's Mississippi Brigade supported by a regiment or two from Anderson's Division. At Deep Run, the Confederate skirmishers having little or no shelter from the hostile guns, were capable of but little resistance, and before noon the Federals had completed two bridges at that point. At the town Barksdale's men, under cover of the houses, were more successful, repeatedly driving off the working parties until at last, about 11 A. M., the engineers abandoned the task. Burnside now ordered every gun in range to fire 50 rounds into the town. About 100 pieces responded with terrific effect upon the buildings, many of which were either completely demolished, or set on fire, but none of the Confederates were injured. The bombardment was simply one of those useless expenditures of ammunition resorted to for lack of more effective measures. The heavy fog of the morning had now almost disappeared, and the panoramic view from the Confederate position was superb. Gen. Alexander thus describes it: "The city, except its steeples, was still veiled in mist, which had settled in the Valley. Above it and in it incessantly showed the round white clouds of bursting shells, and out of its midst there soon rose three or four columns of dense black smoke from houses set on fire by the explosives. The atmosphere was so perfectly calm and still that the smoke rose vertically in great pillars for several hundred feet before spreading outward in black sheets. The opposite bank of the river, for two miles to the right and left, was crowned at frequent intervals with blazing batteries, canopied in clouds of white smoke.

"Beyond these, the dark blue masses of over 100,000 infantry, in compact columns, and numberless parks of white-topped wagons and ambulances massed in orderly ranks, all awaited the completion of the bridges. The earth shook with the thunder of the guns, and high above all, a thousand feet in air, hung two immense balloons. The scene gave impressive ideas of the disciplined power of a great army, and of the vast resources of the nation which had sent it forth."

But the grand cannonade failed to drive Barksdale's men from their posts of vantage, and again they opened fire upon the returning bridge builders. At last, at the suggestion of Gen. Hunt, still Chief of Artillery, Army of the Potomac, volunteers crossed the completed bridges under cover of the artillery fire, and approaching the town occupied the Confederate sharpshooters sufficiently to enable the bridges opposite the town to be completed, the attempt being resumed about 4:30 p. m. During the continuance of Barksdale's street fighting, which lasted until after dark, the Confederate batteries had for the most part remained silent by reason of the fog, which hid the crossings from view during the morning, making good practice impossible. The

orders against wasting ammunition in useless cannonades were most stringent. This was left to the enemy
who fired intermittently throughout the day upon the
Confederate position, inflicting only slight damage
upon the men and guns by reason of the works which
sheltered them.

Late in the day, observing a small column of hostile
infantry approach the upper pontoon bridge, Lewis'
Battery opened fire and drove the enemy behind the
Lacy house, and shortly afterwards it again fired upon
some cavalry and artillery which made its appearance
across the river, but the action of this battery was not
unnecessarily prolonged. Maurin's Battery near the
Plank Road also fired a few shots towards evening.

About 7 P. M., the Federals having occupied Fredericksburg, Col. Walton was directed to make his preparations to rake the streets of the town at the first signal
of their advance, and Ransom, who had posted his two
batteries, Branch's and Cooper's, on the Telegraph
Road, was ordered to do the same, also being directed
to secure tools from Gen. McLaws and connect the
small gun pits in his front with rifle-trenches.* Not a
gun was fired by Alexander's, Walton's, Cabell's, and
Frobel's groups during the day, though they had all
received orders during the early morning to do what
they could to impede the construction of the bridges.

Thus passed away Thursday, the 11th, on which day
Burnside only succeeded in throwing his six bridges, his
artillery utterly failing to uncover the Confederate batteries. Lee now ordered A. P. Hill and Taliaferro to
come up from the rear and relieve Hood and Pickett,
who were to close on the center and hold the ground
between Deep and Hazel runs. During the night, with
the thermometer 26 degrees above zero, Hill and Taliaferro completed their preparations, and, breaking camp
before daybreak, arrived at their designated positions
about noon on the 12th. Col. Crutchfield, who had preceded the movement of these divisions and reconnoitered

*Rebellion Records, Series I, Vol. LI, Part II, pp. 661, 662.

the position assigned them, directed Col. Walker to select positions for his guns along the ridge from Hamilton's Crossing to Deep Run. As soon as they arrived, Col. Walker placed McIntosh's and Pegram's batteries with sections from Crenshaw's, Latham's, and M. Johnson's batteries, the latter commanded by Lieuts. Clutter, Potts, and Ellett, respectively, or a total of 14 guns, on the height immediately above the railroad on the extreme right of the ridge known as Prospect Hill.

Braxton's Battery in command of Lieut. Marye with 5, and Davidson's with 4 guns were sent to the left of the line, where they were mingled with those of Taliaferro's Division. The 21 guns assigned to the left were placed in position as follows: just at Bernard's cabins and to their left 9 guns, consisting of 6 rifles, 2 Napoleons, and one 6-pounder of the batteries of Raine, Caskie, and Braxton, all under the immediate charge of Capt. Davidson, and about 200 yards in front of these, to their right and across the railroad, 6 rifles, 3 Napoleons, and three 6-pounders from the batteries of Carpenter, Wooding, and Braxton, all under the immediate command of Capt. J. B. Brockenbrough. Hood's three batteries meanwhile moved from their position on the northern salient ridge south of Deep Run to one at the base of the hills north of the run and immediately across from Franklin's bridge.*

During the 12th, Sumner at the town and Franklin at the Deep Run bridges took over their grand divisions, which, when in line, extended from the center of the town towards Deep Run about parallel to the river and between it and the Richmond road. No attempt was made by the Federals on the Confederate position, nor did Gen. Lee make any serious opposition to the crossing, though the long-range guns were again ordered to inflict as much damage as they could upon the enemy.† Rhett's and Parker's batteries from their

*Henderson is mistaken as to the number of guns with the Light and Taliaferro's divisions. He shows a disposition of 47 guns; there were but 35. He counted Brockenbrough's group twice. See Crutchfield's Report, *Rebellion Records*, Series I, Vol. XXI, p. 636. Henderson merely copied the error of Allan. Alexander also copied the error.

†*Rebellion Records*, Series I, Vol. LI, Part II, p. 661.

positions near the Plank Road and the Stansbury house,
respectively, fired upon the town, enfilading the main
streets, but always drawing upon themselves a storm
from the opposite bank. During the day one of Col.
Cabell's batteries, discovering a light battery in position
along the enemy's line, drove it beyond Deep Run,
where it joined a number of others, all too far removed
from the Confederate position to be harmful. Lewis'
Battery on the extreme left of Longstreet's line was also
engaged about 3 P. M., firing upon an infantry brigade,
and later upon a cavalry column, which made their appearance at the ford opposite his position, and Maurin's
Battery dropped a few 10-pounder shells among some
skirmishers near the town, and occasionally fired upon
the masses across the river.

About 2 P. M., the fog having lifted sufficiently to enable Col. Walton's gunners to see as far as the river,
his batteries fired upon a column of the enemy below the
town for a few minutes until it dispersed and sought
cover behind the inequalities of the ground. Hundreds
of rounds of ammunition were wasted by the enemy in
a one-sided cannonade during the 12th. That night the
various artillery commanders were informed that the
enemy was expected to attack Longstreet's right and
Jackson's front in the morning. Jackson was now
ordered to Fredericksburg with Early's and D. H.
Hill's divisions, both of which with their artillery arrived at Hamilton's Crossing about dawn on the 13th,
Hill having marched 18 and Early 12 miles during the
night. Upon arriving, Capt. Latimer, Acting Chief of
Artillery, Early's Division, reported to Col. Crutchfield
and was ordered to hold his six batteries under cover in
rear. Behind D. H. Hill's Division on the extreme
right, Capt. Carter, Acting Chief of Artillery, also
held his five divisional batteries in readiness to relieve
those under Col. Walker on Prospect Hill, and Col.
Brown's Corps Reserve was kept under cover in the rear.
Across the railroad from Prospect Hill were two of
Stuart's cavalry brigades, and Maj. Pelham with sev-

eral horse batteries, and Milledge's and Lane's batteries of the General Reserve, the latter with two 20-
pounder Parrotts. In all, Pelham had 18 guns. An
imported Whitworth rifle of large caliber and great
range was posted on the wooded heights northeast of the
Yerby house in charge of Capt. Hardaway.

During the night Ross's Battery returned from its
position below the Massaponax, and was assigned to
Maj. S. P. Hamilton's group of Cabell's guns on the
hill behind McLaws. A section of 6-pounders from this
battery with Patterson's Battery of Cutts' Battalion
was dispatched to Hood's front in charge of Maj. T. J.
Page, Jr. Capts. Barnwell and G. W. Nelson were
now placed in charge of the two 30-pounder Parrotts
of Ellis' Battery on Lee's Hill. With Kirkpatrick's
and Massie's batteries, Maj. Nelson was then directed
by Gen. Pendleton to take up a position near the Telegraph Road, in rear of and commanding the plateau of
Marye's Hill, so that it could be swept if carried by the
enemy. Rhett's Battery was similarly stationed near
the Plank Road.

Burnside's belated plan was now to seize Prospect
Hill with Franklin's Corps, and Marye's Hill as well
as the heights occupied by Cabell's and Hamilton's batteries with Sumner's Corps. Franklin was to move
around to the right of Hamilton's Crossing and sweep
along the avenues of communication, which the Confederates had prepared in rear of their position, from
Prospect Hill to the Telegraph Road, thus connecting
with Sumner. The plan, if successful, would not only
cause the Confederates to evacuate their strong lines in
the woods along the base of the hills and behind the railroad embankment, but would prevent the withdrawal of
the artillery groups under Walker, Carter, Latimer,
Davidson, and Brockenbrough, in position along the
forward crest of the ridge. Hooker was to hold four divisions in support of Sumner and to send two to Franklin.

Burnside had detected the weakest point in the Confederate line, which was in A. P. Hill's front about op-

posite the middle of the ridge from Hamilton's Crossing to Deep Run. Although Jackson held a line of but
2,600 yards with 30,000 men or about 11 men to the
yard, his formation was very deep and not dense in the
front line held by A. P. Hill. Just to the left of Walker's
batteries, posted in a trench within the edge of the
woods, was Archer's Brigade of Hill's Division with its
left resting on a coppice extending well forward into
the flats. Beyond the coppice, but nearer the railroad
embankment, lay Lane's Brigade of the same division
with its right about 600 yards from Archer's left. In
the gap behind the coppice was an open field 200 yards
in breadth. About 500 yards in rear of the gap, along
the military road constructed by the Artillery as a
lateral communication, lay Gregg's Brigade. On
Lane's left rear was Pender's Brigade, in front of which
was Capt. Davidson's group of 9 guns, the 12 pieces
under Brockenbrough being in front of and across the
embankment from Lane. Field's Brigade supported
Walker's group on the extreme right and Thomas' Brigade was held in rear of Pender's right and Lane's left.
Across Deep Run was Hood's Division, with Frobel's
artillery group. Jackson's disposition had been made
before Early and D. H. Hill came up and they with
Taliaferro were left in the third line farther back even
than Gregg, a change under fire being deemed hazardous. His position was very similar to that occupied by
him at Second Manassas. In his front was the railroad embankment, in his rear were the wooded heights,
upon his flanks were the massed batteries under the general supervision of Crutchfield, and opposite his center
was the wood projecting beyond the embankment, forming the same defect from which he was again to suffer.
Maj. Von Borcke, a Prussian officer of Stuart's staff,
had on the 12th seen the danger lurking in the gap and
had suggested that the thicket should be levelled, but it
was considered too miry to be passable and no steps were
taken to correct the evil. Col. Crutchfield, who saw
that a space of 800 to 1,000 yards of Jackson's front

was undefended by direct artillery fire, examined the wood most carefully with a view to establishing howitzer batteries behind it, which by canister fire might keep it clear, but found it impracticable to do so in the time left him before the action, but he instructed Capts. Brockenbrough and Davidson to reserve their fire until the enemy's infantry had approached to within close range. By the fire of their advanced pieces he hoped that the approach to the wood would be commanded. Col. Walker's group could only cross-fire with them by firing very obliquely to the left.

Early in the morning, Meade's Division moved down stream about 700 yards beyond the ravine near the Smithfield house, and turning sharply to the right crossed the Richmond road. While Meade was forming his division in column of brigades opposite the coppice which projected from the dip in the ridge held by A. P. Hill, under cover of a rise in the ground between the road and the embankment, his supporting batteries opened a desultory fire upon the Confederate position as if feeling its strength, but no reply was elicited.

Maj. Pelham commanding Stuart's horse batteries, and the light batteries assigned to Jackson's extreme right, had moved his guns forward with the dismounted cavalry, which occupied a line extending from the southern base of Prospect Hill towards the river on the north side of the Massaponax. With the unerring eye of genius, he now seized the opportunity which the exposed flank of Meade's column presented him. Galloping forward with two 12-pounder Napoleons of Henry's Battery, along the road leading from Hamilton's Crossing to the Richmond Road, and concealing his movements by using the cover of the ditches and hedges, he gained a tangled ravine just beyond a marshy stream less than 400 yards from Meade's flank, from which point he opened a rapid fire upon the astonished Federals. Meade's leading brigade at once began to waver and seek cover, threatening to throw the whole division

in confusion, while four Pennsylvania batteries, called to
the left by Meade, and soon joined by two others, together sought to overthrow Pelham. One of his pieces
was soon disabled, but rapid changes of position enabled
him to defy the opposing batteries for nearly an hour,
though well in advance of Jackson's line and unsupported except by several small troops of dismounted
cavalry. Pelham finally retired in obedience to Stuart's
peremptory order, but not until his limbers had been
emptied, nor until he had delayed the advance of 4,500
Federals and caused Franklin to dispatch Doubleday's
entire division to guard Meade's flank, a task which absorbed its efforts during the remainder of the day. He
had also caused the explosion of one of the enemy's
caissons.

Upon his withdrawal, Pelham took up a position with
all the batteries under his command across the railroad
from Hamilton's Crossing, from which he was able to
cross-fire to some extent in front of Hill's center with
the guns of Brockenbrough's group advanced beyond
the railroad.

Gens. Lee and Jackson were present together on the
extreme Confederate right, and were eye-witnesses of
the contest between Pelham's Napoleon and the Federal batteries.

Franklin had now advanced several batteries to the
Richmond Road, which, together with the batteries on
Stafford Heights, for half an hour subjected the wooded
ridge occupied by Hill to a heavy cannonade, the effect
of which was generally slight, except upon Walker's
batteries. The position of these batteries, though obscured from the view of the enemy, were more in the
open than the infantry, but Walker's guns remained
silent, as did the infantry, reserving their fire for
Meade's column at closer range. About 11 A. M., the
Federal advance was resumed under cover of a great
number of guns, and when the first line came within
800 yards of Jackson's center the silent woods awoke.
First Walker, then Davidson, then Brockenbrough,

pushed their guns from the covert, and as Jackson's 35 guns, aided by those of Pelham to the right, which were promptly advanced, opened fire, the Federal leader realized the insufficiency of his artillery preparation. "From front and flank came the scathing fire; the skirmishers were quickly driven in and on the closed ranks behind burst the full fury of the storm. Dismayed and decimated by this fierce and unexpected onslaught, Meade's brigades broke in disorder and fell back to the Richmond Road."*

Upon Meade's troops the effect of Pegram's and McIntosh's fire from Walker's group was especially destructive, but the troops on their left were not so promptly checked. Gibbon's Division had come under the fire of Brockenbrough's and Davidson's guns, which succeeded in at once driving off the skirmishers with canister, but in doing so they disclosed their positions and drew upon themselves the concentrated fire of a number of field batteries which caused them much loss. Again and again the skirmishers advanced into the woods, and finally working around to the right, began firing upon the batteries. While serving as gunners, Capts. Brockenbrough and Wooding were both shot. The axles of two rifled field pieces in Wooding's and Caskie's batteries breaking from the recoil, and the ammunition of Raine's Battery proving so defective that none of the shells burst, it became necessary about 10:30 A. M. for Brockenbrough to retire from his advanced position, and for Col. Crutchfield to order Capt. Latimer, Early's Acting Chief of Artillery, who was holding his divisional batteries in reserve, to take the rifled section of his own, and the three rifles of Brown's Chesapeake Battery, under Lieut. Plater, to the left to replace the five pieces disabled or withdrawn.

For the next hour and a half an artillery duel, in which over 400 guns took part, raged over the whole field, and in some way the Confederate batteries managed to hold their own with the powerful ordnance of

*Henderson, p. 388.

the Federals. The fire of Crutchfield's three groups and Pelham's guns had almost alone hurled Meade and Gibbon back, so completely sweeping the open ground in Walker's front that the attack in that quarter was not renewed. Meantime Col. Crutchfield had also directed D'Aquin's Battery, and the Staunton Battery under Lieut. Garber, both of Latimer's Battalion, to join Maj. Pelham, to whom, about noon during the lull succeeding Meade's repulse, he also sent Graham's 10-pounder Parrott section of Poague's Battery, the rifled section of the 3d Howitzer's under Lieut. Utz, and a short while later, Watson's 2d Howitzers with two 10-pounder Parrotts and a brass rifle, and one 3-inch rifle of Dance's Battery, all of Col. Brown's Corps Reserve then being held in readiness behind Hamilton's Crossing. When these pieces reached Pelham, Gen. Stuart ordered Col. Rosser to take one of Watson's rifles under Lieut. Pleasants, and Dance's piece, and move out to the point from which Pelham had fired upon the enemy during the morning, but little good was now accomplished since the enemy's flank was well protected, and the horses and gunners suffered greatly before the pieces were retired.

Nothing had been accomplished by Reynolds' attack, except that Gibbon on Meade's right had succeeded, with great loss, in driving Brockenbrough's twelve pieces back across the railroad, the artillery on Jackson's left meanwhile having been reënforced by Latimer's fresh guns. The Confederate line, as a whole, remained unshaken, and its artillery, which had borne the brunt of the contest, with a few exceptions, had suffered slight loss, that having been more than made good by ordering into position a number of the batteries which had been held in reserve. Truly Second Manassas was being repeated.

Before Reynolds' attack on Jackson's line had come to a standstill, Burnside about 11 A. M. had ordered Sumner to make a diversion against Lee's left in favor of Franklin. Unfortunately for Sumner the strongest

point of the Confederate position, Marye's Hill, was
designated as his point of attack, and added to the impregnable character of the position was the necessity
of his crossing the mill race between the heights and
the town before the assaulting columns could deploy.
Having crossed the obstacle, however, a rise in the
ground enabled the Federals to deploy under cover.
From this inequality of the ground the land, open and
somewhat broken, gently rose to the Telegraph Road,
at the base of Marye's Hill.   Towards the left of the
attacking column, the Hazel Run ravine, which separated Marye's Hill from Lee's Hill, or Cabell's
position, ran out into the plain.   Along the depression
ran the unfinished roadbed of the Fredericksburg and
Orange Railroad, which branched off from the main
line, passing southward through the flats, just below
the town.   Between the old railroad bed, and the Plank
Road lay the ground over which Burnside directed
Sumner to advance.

At the base of the hill and in the wide roadbed of the
Telegraph Road, sunken about four feet and artificially
prepared by throwing dirt forward over the stone wall
which bounded it, Gen. Cobb of McLaws' Division,
with three regiments of infantry, was in position.   From
the point where the Telegraph Road struck the base of
Marye's Hill and turned southward, the Confederate
line was prolonged northward to the Plank Road by a
shallow trench, in which the 24th North Carolina lay.
All along the line the infantry could move under cover.
To the rear and well above them, occupying a front of
about 400 yards, were the nine gun-pits of Walton's Battalion, supported by Cooke's Brigade of Ransom's Division 200 yards in rear, and the remaining regiments of
the same division 400 yards further back with Moseley's
Battery of 6 guns.   Walton's guns, 2 rifles of Maurin's
and 3 pieces of Moody's Battery now north of the Plank
Road, bore directly upon the approaches to Marye's
Hill, and Cabell's and Hamilton's groups on Lee's Hill

were able to cross fire in its front with Alexander's and R. H. Anderson's batteries on the Stansbury Hill, but only at a point well forward.

Sumner's troops had been formed in the town early in the morning, French's Division of the 2d Corps in the lead. When Longstreet detected signs of their advance, he directed Alexander "to throw a hundred shells down the streets of the city, and towards the (pontoon) bridges," and this fire had hardly begun when French moved forward about noon, Parker's, Rhett's, Moody's, and Maurin's batteries continuing their fire all the while. The instant French cleared the town, Walton's guns opened with great precision, the effect of their fire being so destructive that Longstreet himself sent him a note in which his congratulations were included, urging him by all means to keep his batteries well supplied with ammunition.* Cabell's heavier guns, including the two 30-pounder Parrotts under Capts. Barnwell and Nelson, also opened with effect until French succeeded in crossing the mill race about 300 yards from the town and so sought shelter behind the rise 400 yards from the base of Marye's Hill. Sturgis' Division, meanwhile, had been directed to support French's on the left. Thrown forward, Ferrero's Brigade and Dickenson's Battery were immediately brought under the fire of Cabell's guns on Lee's Hill, which completely commanded the ravine and the unfinished railroad bed by means of which the enemy was seeking to reach the right rear of Marye's Hill. The conformation of the ground was such that Walton's guns were unable to sweep down this ravine. Dickenson was almost immediately killed, and his battery disabled and withdrawn. Ferrero was checked by Cabell's fire and held under cover of a depression in the ravine from which his men engaged in a heavy musketry fire, principally upon the batteries on Lee's Hill. The various brigades and divisions which during the day endeavored to advance by way of the ravine all met the same fate. It was simply impassable for infantry.

---

*Rebellion Records, Series I, Vol. LI, p. 662.

During French's deployment, Arnold's regular battery went into action on the edge of the town and opened upon Marye's Hill, and the great mass of guns on Stafford Heights, which had been shelling the Confederate position generally, now concentrated their fire on Walton's batteries, the gunners of which behind their earthworks devoted their energies solely to the infantry columns of French, who had, after deploying, sent forward three regiments of skirmishers. As the line cleared the cover behind which the Federals had deployed, Cobb's Infantry from behind the stone wall rose and opened a rapid musketry fire upon it at a range of less than 500 yards, and Walton now began to hurl canister at the enemy until the skirmish line disappeared behind a low terrace about 250 yards from the Confederate Infantry, seizing some of the small houses on the Telegraph Road to the right. The remainder of Kimball's Brigade now reached Col. Mason's three regiments, but as Andrews' and Palmer's brigades left their cover they were swept from the field in great confusion by the fire of Walton's and Alexander's guns, a few only reaching Kimball's line, the great majority returning to their former position. After eleven separate efforts on the part of the Federals to reach the hill, a lull of about 20 minutes occurred while Hancock was preparing to attack. French, Sturgis, and Griffin had all been repulsed with great loss, and the Confederates were little shaken by the tremendous cannonade of the Federal batteries, although they had lost both their 30-pounder Parrotts by explosion, one bursting at the 39th and the other at the 54th round, after most effective use. Near the left one of these big guns under Capt. Nelson, Gens. Lee, Longstreet, and Pendleton had watched the awe-inspiring conflict, the Chief of Artillery himself frequently directing the fire of the big piece. Longstreet and Pendleton were both standing within 10 feet of it when it burst. A smaller Parrott was immediately substituted, and orders sent to Capt. Lane to bring the big

Whitworth to Lee's Hill from its position below the Massaponax in front of the Yerby house, but it did not arrive until after dark.

Before Hancock commenced his attack, Longstreet, desiring to drive Kimball's men from behind their cover, directed Capt. O. Latrobe of his staff to take a 10-pounder Parrott of Maurin's Donaldsonville Battery from out its pit, and, moving it forward to the left, enfilade the enemy's line. The attempt meant almost certain destruction, as two Federal batteries had been concentrating their fire throughout the morning on Maurin's gun-pits, having almost silenced his pieces after he had fired about 200 rounds. The suggestion was no sooner made than acted upon, however, but a staff officer alone was not to do the work, for Lieut. Landry directed his gunners to move the pieces forward by hand to the designated position. Before the first three shots were fired, five gunners were down, including the corporal, and as the piece was loaded for the fourth time, it was struck by a shell which destroyed a wheel. But the three shots directed by Landry and Latrobe were not wasted, for not only did the shells burst in the very midst of the crouching Federals, but the daring deed, seen by hundreds of the Confederate soldiers, inspired them in a way that nothing but such heroic actions on the field of battle can do. The names of Lieut. Landry, of Corporal Morel, of Cannoneers Dernon Leblanc, Francis Perez, Claudius Linossier, Adolph Grilke, and Francis Babin, are worthy of the best traditions of their ancestors who fought with the great Napoleon.

Just as Hancock's advance commenced, Ransom sent Cooke's Brigade to the crest of Marye's Hill, one regiment going down to the sunken road to reënforce the Georgia regiments, Cobb having been killed by a sharpshooter.

Hancock's superb division now pressed forward in column of brigades with intervals of 200 paces, Cook leading, then Meagher, with Caldwell in rear. Issuing from the town under a terrific artillery fire, they formed along the canal, and then charged up the slope towards the sunken road. On past French's isolated skirmishers dashed Hancock's men. As they advanced up the slopes towards the Confederate position, the supporting batteries from the Stafford Heights were caused to cease firing upon Marye's Hill for fear of throwing shells among their own infantry. It was now about 1 P. M., and as the Federal batteries became masked the smooth-bore or lighter Confederate pieces uncovered and went into action, adding their fire to that of the heavier guns, without fear of the hostile artillery. The Confederate canister swept great gaps from end to end through the Federal column, while the shells bursting among the charging lines hurled small groups of men into the air. As they swept on to within 100 paces of the hill, Walton's guns also poured canister among them, and the musketry fire both from the sunken road and the crest of Marye's Hill redoubled in intensity. Under this murderous maelstrom of iron and lead, the Federal Infantry was at last checked, and, falling like leaves, retired to the cover which marked French's farthest advance, but not until a number of the bravest men had actually approached to within 25 yards of the sunken road, only to be shot down or taken prisoners. Meagher's Brigade kept on to the town. Of the 5,006 men led forward by Hancock, 2,013 remained dead or wounded upon the field. In the sunken road and on the crest were less than 2,000 infantry. In the charge of 400 yards they could not have averaged more than two shots apiece. From this fact, we are able to appreciate what must have been the deadly effect of the Confederate guns. In several of the Federal accounts of the battle, it is stated that one-fifth of the casualties suffered by Burnside were from the fire of artillery. This estimate covers the losses on the whole field, so that in the charge of Hancock's Division on Marye's Hill, it is fair to assume that not less than half of the losses were due to the artillery, a remarkable record. This belief is borne out by the fact that the killed were found in great numbers behind cover impenetrable to the musket balls.

So soon as the Federal batteries were unmasked by the withdrawal of Hancock's troops, the short-range Confederate guns again sought cover from their fire. A lull now ensued, and only the field batteries near the town continued to fire upon Marye's Hill, Cabell and Hamilton concentrating their guns upon these.

Hancock, also, had been severely repulsed, but Howard was moving out of the town with his division to renew the assault. Meantime the four Confederate regiments in the sunken road were reënforced by four more while the infantry force on the forward crest was also increased by Ransom, and additional reserves brought up under cover of the ridge. Behind the stone wall the Confederates now stood in four ranks.

Howard's Division charged forward as gallantly as had Hancock's, and with the same result. Again the assaulting columns masked the supporting batteries, and again did the lighter pieces of the Confederates, more effective even than the rifled guns at short range, uncover, and pour canister and shell into the dense blue masses. Here and there the Federals sought the available shelter, but most of those who escaped unwounded retired upon the town. Fearing a counter attack, Gen. Couch ordered Hazard's regular battery into action near the edge of the town at a point about which the defeated infantry might rally.

It was now 3 P. M. and four of the five divisions under Sumner's command had been dashed to pieces against Marye's Hill, and two under Franklin against Prospect Hill. In neither quarter were the Confederates shaken, but Burnside ordered the attack to be renewed all along the line.

Meanwhile, Poague had alone been engaging Reynolds' batteries with his 20-pounder section, which Col. Crutchfield had ordered Col. Brown to send up to Walker. The exact range of the Confederate batteries having been obtained by the enemy, the lighter pieces were withdrawn again to cover. While bringing up the howitzer section of Dance's Battery, Lieut.-Col. Coleman of the Corps Reserve Battalion was severely wounded, and Lieut. J. B. McCorkle of Poague's Battery was killed. Severe losses were being sustained from the accurate fire of the Federal batteries. It should be mentioned here that Poague's Battery had, upon receiving orders late the night before to rejoin its corps, marched 16 miles in the night over the most difficult half-frozen roads, in four hours, a fact which seems all but incredible.

About the time French was assaulting Marye's Hill, on the Confederate left, Reynolds was reforming under the cover of his batteries to make another assault on Jackson's position. Meade's Pennsylvanians were rallying, Gibbon was constantly strengthening his line, and the flank was well protected by Doubleday, who was still, however, fully occupied by Stuart's dismounted men and Pelham's guns. When Meade and Gibbon were at last ready to renew their efforts, Hancock had just about begun his assault on Marye's Hill.

Reynolds had posted 21 guns on the right of Gibbon, and 30 on the left of Meade, both groups near the Richmond Road, those on the Stafford Heights forming a second tier. Preceded by clouds of skirmishers, and under cover of a tremendous artillery fire, Meade and Gibbon advanced in columns of brigades, the whole covering a front of about a thousand yards. As they rushed forward, Crutchfield's guns opened as before, but with less effect than formerly, by reason of the overwhelming and accurate fire of the batteries of the enemy concentrated on his positions, hitherto disclosed. Even Pelham's group of guns was receiving full attention from the enemy. Those portions of the Federal line opposite Lane and Archer, which came under the direct fire of Crutchfield's guns, were soon checked, however, but the center reached and entered the tongue of woods extending into the plain, thus at once threatening Archer's left and Lane's right flank. As the Federals swept onward through the wood they brushed aside the regiment which Archer had sent into the thicket, and, forcing back Lane's and Archer's exposed flanks, took a number of prisoners. So rapid was their advance that Gregg's line 500 yards in rear was reached almost before he was aware of the enemy's approach, and mistaking the charging columns for a Confederate command retreating, he was struck down in front of his brigade, while endeavoring to stay its fire. A desperate struggle now ensued between Gregg's men and the Federals, a part of the former having been thrown into confusion by the suddenness of the attack. But Jackson, having detected the victorious advance of the enemy, had sent for Early's and Taliaferro's divisions, which soon hastened up and, threatening to surround Sinclair's Brigade in the lead, drove it back in confusion through the gap into which it had penetrated, involving Magenton's supporting brigade in the disorderly withdrawal. Hoke's Brigade of Early's Division meantime drove off the Federals who had carried the trenches on Archer's left, and the whole of Meade's Division was again in retreat. Early pursued the routed enemy beyond the railroad, but as Birney's troops of Hooker's Corps advanced to Meade's assistance, he fell back and took position behind the embankment.

While Meade was forcing his way through the center, Gibbon was engaged in an assault upon A. P. Hill's left center, held by Lane. Bringing Hill's, Thompson's, and other batteries into action against Davidson's and Latimer's guns in front of the Bernard cabins, Gibbon's Division advanced in three lines, the first two being hurled back by Lane's musketry and the left group of guns. The third line under Root, however, was not to be checked, and sweeping over Lane's trenches drove his men back into the woods at the point of the bayonet. But, just as Early and Taliaferro arrived and drove back Sinclair's leading brigade of Meade's Division, thus uncovering Root's left flank, Thomas' Brigade of A. P. Hill's Division, which had been held in reserve behind Pender on the left of Hill's line, came up and struck Root's exposed right. After a stubborn struggle, Root's Brigade retired in confusion to the stage road, from which it had advanced.

On the right of Reynolds the batteries of Smith's Corps had kept up a heavy cannonade upon the guns of Latimer and Davidson, and Frobel's group with Hood north of Deep Run, but it was not until about 3 P. M., after Gibbon and Meade had both been repulsed, that a serious effort was made by Brooks' Division of Smith's Corps to seize the line of the railroad in its front. On the south side of the run was Pender's Brigade, of A. P. Hill's Division, with skirmishers behind the embankment, and on the north side was Law's Brigade of Hood's Division. Moving under cover of the Deep Run ravine, the Federals came upon the flank of Pender's advanced line and drove it from the railroad, but while waiting for reënforcements, two regiments of Law's Brigade and one of Pender's charged, driving them back with severe loss to the Richmond Road and reoccupying the line of embankment.

Such was the situation of the Confederate right when Sickles' Division of the 3d Corps came up to the support of Reynolds and made a counter-attack impracticable on the part of Jackson. Doubleday's Division, on Reynolds' left, had been completely neutralized by Stuart's constant threat, and the fire of Pelham's guns. Franklin's efforts had thus come to a standstill by 2:30 P. M. Indeed, he was not only defeated, but had probably been saved the loss of his field batteries by the timely arrival of Sickles.

When about 3 P. M. Burnside's order came to Franklin to renew his attack, the latter took upon himself the responsibility of remaining quiet, his failure to obey the orders he received leading to his subsequent removal from command. The sole activity on his part for the rest of the day was a heavy artillery fire from his batteries, causing considerable loss to Crutchfield's men.

About 3:30 P. M., it became necessary to relieve Pegram's and McIntosh's batteries, both having exhausted their ammunition and suffered severe losses. The fresh batteries of the corps reserve were then brought forward to take the place of the batteries withdrawn, and Hupp's Battery was sent beyond the railroad later in the day, to drive off the sharpshooters of the enemy, which had for some time annoyed the gunners. Col. Brown's six batteries lost during the remainder of the day no less than 10 killed and 26 wounded.

At 1:30 P. M., Hooker had been ordered to cross the river and attack Marye's Hill, but with a knowledge of what had befallen French, Hancock, and Howard, and that Franklin's efforts on the left had again been unsuccessful, he urged that the attempt to drive Lee from his strong position be abandoned, at least for the day. But Burnside was relentless.

The Confederates employed the lull during Hooker's preparations to reënforce the force in the sunken road by still another regiment, and to bring up some of the reserves to the infantry position along the crest. Meanwhile the caissons were rapidly being refilled from the reserve ammunition train, and the Artillery was generally taking a long breath except the batteries on Lee's Hill, which continued to fire on the Federal masses near the town and in the Hazel Run ravine.

With eleven regiments in the sunken road, and six on the forward crest, all fully resupplied with ammunition, Marye's Hill was now even more securely held than during the previous attacks upon it. The fresh assault was preceded by the heaviest artillery preparation the Federals had yet attempted. Among the field batteries Randall's and Hazard's were especially active and effective.

When the artillery fire was at its height, Hooker launched Humphreys' Division along the Telegraph Road, with Sykes' to the right *en échelon*. As these troops advanced, Griffin's Division moved forward

from near the railroad depot and joined Humphreys'
left. Their advance to the line occupied by the men of
the commands which had preceded them was quite successful and rapid, for they were all but free from the
fire of artillery. Just after the attack commenced Col.
Walton's Battalion had exhausted its ammunition and
the refilled caissons had as yet failed to return from the
ammunition train in rear, necessitating the substitution
in the pits of other pieces. Col. Alexander had held
Woolfolk's and Jordan's batteries under cover of the
ridge during the day and now, quickly ordering forward the four pieces of the former and two guns of the
latter, he undertook to relieve Col. Walton's batteries
in the face of a heavy fire, losing many horses and men
in so doing. Moody was also directed to transfer three of
his pieces from his own pits to the left to those formerly
occupied by Capt. Miller's guns. In making the change
a piece was capsized which added to the delay in opening fire with the guns which did not begin their work
until the enemy was within 300 yards of the position.
When Alexander's nine guns opened upon the advancing infantry which had reached the cover behind
which the men of the preceding commands were lying,
Humphreys' leading brigade dropped to the ground
and commenced to fire wildly. Walton's guns were
now seen galloping to the rear and the rumor sped down
the Federal line that the hill was being evacuated, which
enabled Humphreys to get his men to their feet. Placing himself, mounted, with great gallantry at their
head, he induced them to make a final effort to cross
the 200 yards of intervening ground, being received by
a whirlwind of musketry fire from behind the stone
wall, and canister from Alexander's guns, which now
opened from above. But when the brigade came within
80 yards of the Confederate Infantry, it broke and fled
to the rear. Tyler's, or his second brigade was now
coming up, and Humphreys, after having the Federal
batteries directed to cease firing, again essayed to lead
his men to the Confederate position, with a view of

carrying it with the bayonet. After they had mingled for a time with those seeking cover in their path, as in the case of Allabach's Brigade, Humphreys was also able to lead Tyler's men forward, but all in vain. The shriveling fire of the Confederates simply swept them from the field. Over 1,000 men of the division commanded by the noble Humphreys lay killed and wounded upon the ground.

Added to the fire of the guns on Marye's Hill, was that of Parker's Battery, which Alexander had posted near the Stansbury house. The fire of this battery was so oblique that many of the Federal officers mistook it for the fire of their own guns from the rear.

Griffin's Division, exposed to the fire of Cabell's and Hamilton's guns, had been checked on the left of Humphreys, and Hooker, seeing their failure, had recalled Sykes. Although several fresh brigades pressed forward to Griffin's most advanced line before dark, when night fell the Federals had been hopelessly defeated, and the shattered troops under cover of Sykes' Division, which was sent forward about 11 P. M. to relieve them, withdrew to the town or were reformed along the canal bank and from thence retired from the field.

The Confederate fire ceased only when the flashes of the Federal guns no longer gave targets, but no one in Lee's army conceived that the battle was over, for only four of the nine Confederate divisions had been engaged. Nor had Burnside himself abandoned the idea of driving the Confederates from their positions, proposing during the night to form the Ninth Corps in column of regiments and lead it in person against Marye's Hill at dawn. During the night he issued the necessary orders for the renewal of the attack, but subsequent to the issuance of these orders, he was dissuaded by certain of his officers from making another effort. This was very fortunate for the Ninth Corps, for a copy of the order directing it to assault at dawn had come into the possession of the Confederates. With full knowledge of the plan of attack, and the point to be assaulted, Longstreet had strengthened his intrenchments and the force holding them, and had caused most careful arrangements to be made during the night for reënforcing the front line, and supplying the men engaged with water and ammunition. Every gun which could be spared from other parts of the line was brought up by the Chief of Artillery, and placed in a covered position, from which it would bear directly upon the ground over which the dense Federal column was to attack, and a long line of reserve caissons was placed immediately behind the ridge from the filled chests of which a plentiful supply of ammunition could be quickly drawn for the already well provided batteries. Not a serviceable piece was left in reserve, except those the gun detachments of which were so depleted and exhausted as to render them unfit for further exertions, such being the case with Maurin's Battery, which was relieved by Moody's 24-pounder howitzer section, and a rifled piece of Jordan's Battery. The 12-pounder howitzer section of Moody's and the 6-pounder section of Woolfolk's batteries had also to be relieved.

Maj. Nelson's battalion of 6-pounder batteries was so disposed as to be able completely to sweep the ascent to Lee's Hill, and Walton's Battalion, much damaged, was held immediately in rear of Marye's Hill.

During the night, Capt. Parker discovered a position from which the canal bank in his front could be enfiladed, and the Federals thus prevented from forming under cover as before. Col. Alexander immediately ordered Moody to take his 12-pounder section which had been relieved, filling up his detachments from Woolfolk's Battery, and construct pits for his guns in this position.

Fearing lest Burnside might renew the attack under cover of darkness, Gen. Pendleton with the assistance of his staff prepared a number of incendiary shells, with which the buildings along the Telegraph Road in front of the Confederate position might be set on fire, thus illuminating the field, but as events turned out these shells were not used.

On the right, Jackson had brought up to his front line every battery in his corps capable of going into action. Capts. Carter and Latimer, Acting Chiefs of Artillery, of D. M. Hill's and Early's (Ewell's) divisions, respectively, had the day before fully engaged all their batteries towards the close of the day, and the corps reserve had also been entirely engaged in order to relieve Walker's batteries. The latter, meantime, had found time to rest and refit.

In the Confederate ranks the utmost confidence of administering a more crushing repulse than had been previously administered to the Federals was entertained, and the men, especially the gunners, the effect of whose fire was more noticeable than that of the infantry, awaited the enemy's attack with keen impatience. Never in the history of war, perhaps, was an army on the defense more willing to be attacked by overwhelming numbers. The Confederates were even anxious less Burnside might fail to hurl his masses upon them, the plan of the latter having been fully disclosed to the troops in order to expedite the necessary preparations which had to be made during the night. Not only were those upon whom the assault was expected to be made pleased to occupy the post of greatest danger, but the men in less threatened quarters were disappointed that the brunt of the fighting was not to fall upon them. In their zest for the fray, there was even something savage, though not inhuman. It was simply the desire of strong men to strike hard when the time came. So when the day at last broke, the Confederates eagerly looked and listened for signs of Burnside's advance. The long hours passed away in silence until about 10 o'clock, when the fog lifted and a vicious sharpshooting broke out from Sykes' regulars in front of Marye's Hill. A desultory cannonade from Stafford Heights also commenced.

Seeing Sykes' men lying down in the swale, and, in the language of Burnside, "holding the first ridge," Capt. Moody, from the advantageous position in which he had placed his 12-pounders, opened upon them from their right. The Federals were amazed, and, after a few shots from Moody's guns, those who were unable to find fresh shelter broke and fled to the town, pursued by the fire of the guns on Marye's Hill. This ended for the day the annoying sharpshooting from the "first ridge."

The day wore on without any serious effort being made by the Federals, whose batteries across the river all but ceased firing on Marye's Hill, by reason of a number of premature explosions of their shells having caused losses among their infantry in advance of the town. Relieved of the fire of these batteries as well as of that of the sharpshooters, the Confederate gunners were free to work in their pits and continued to fire throughout the day upon any masses which appeared in or about the town.

During the night of the 14th, the earthworks and lines were still further strengthened by the Confederates, abattis being prepared and arrangements of all kinds for defense being more fully completed. A large supply of ammunition arriving from Richmond, the ordnance trains moved up closer to the Confederate position, and even more batteries were now ready to resume activities. But again, on the 15th, the Federals remained inactive, while the Confederates worked openly at their defenses, and that night in the midst of a heavy storm, the noise of the wind preventing his movements from being heard by his enemy, Gen. Burnside withdrew his tremendous army from the plain, crossing the Rappahannock with all the troops and guns between 7 P. M. the 15th and 7 A. M. the 16th. The feat was a superb one, and, as Gen. Alexander states, its successful accomplishment reflected upon the vigilance of the Confederates. The real opportunity for the use of Pendleton's incendiary shells was lost.

Had Burnside's movement been detected, the river
crossing lit up by the flames of nearby buildings would
have presented a rare spectacle to the Confederates.
A few shells from the longer range pieces, the Whitworth and Poague's 20-pounder Parrotts, for instance,
would most certainly have thrown the Federal columns
into confusion, or forced them to forego the crossing
and remain in the plain. Had they persisted in the attempt to cross the river a second Borodino would have
ensued, for sending only a part of his infantry forward
to the town, with perhaps a dozen short-range batteries,
Gen. Lee would have been able to throw Burnside's
army into a veritable panic. Meanwhile, the bulk of
his army with the longer range batteries could have
held the position against a possible reverse, the guns
neutralizing to some extent the batteries on Stafford
Heights. But those batteries would in all probability
have been unable to fire upon Lee's pursuing columns,
all but mingled with the enemy, and it is quite im-
probable that in the circumstances Burnside's troops
would have remained sufficiently in hand to deliver an
effective counter-stroke. Night, the noise and confusion incident to the storm, the turbulence of the river,
the uncertainty of the number of the enemy upon their
heels, and the inevitable losses which even the few Confederates would have been able to inflict upon the struggling masses at the bridges and the crowded approaches
thereto, are all elements which would have contributed
to a direful disaster to the Federal Army. It is indeed a grave question whether, when once the withdrawal had begun, Burnside could have held a rear
guard in position. But assuming that he could have
held off the Confederates, he would have at least
suffered tremendous losses at the bridges and the almost certain loss of his rear guard, or been forced to
forego the withdrawal. There would have then remained for him the alternative of renewing the effort
to cross the river a succeeding night, or the task of
cutting his way out of the plain through Lee's position.

A subsequent attempt to recross the river would have been anticipated by Lee, whose preparations to prevent the withdrawal would have been complete, and there is every reason to believe that other assaults on the Confederate position would have been more disastrous than those already made. Indeed, Burnside's Army, conscious of the *cul-de-sac* in which it had been placed, would have been in much the same plight as that of the French Army at Sedan. Desperation, unattended by discipline and confidence, would have taken the place of the fine *morale* which inspired the Federals in their first attacks, and while, no doubt, they would have defended themselves with the stubbornness of the wild animal driven to bay, the army would have been utterly lacking in cohesion and that collective will-power which makes successful effort possible. Surely it cannot be argued that in such circumstances Burnside could have secured that coöperation which under the most favorable conditions he had failed to attain.

The inertia of the Confederates is difficult to explain. The escape, for escape it was in every sense of the word, of Burnside was but the realization of the fear which had led both Lee and Jackson originally to oppose the defensive position of Fredericksburg. True, Jackson had urged a counter-stroke in the form of a night attack on the 13th, his proposition being overruled as too hazardous. Gen. Lee's views on this point were no doubt well considered and correct, for the conditions on that night were by no means similar to those obtaining two nights later. The very essentials of the Confederate ability to destroy Burnside's army lay in the latter's attempt at recrossing the river, no thought of which was entertained by the Federals when Jackson proposed to attack them. But Gen. Lee had every reason to believe that Burnside would make another great effort to drive him from his position, the very order for the attack being in his hands. There was every indication that the Federal effort was but postponed, and he believed that his task of destroying the enemy would be all the more simple after the latter had received another crushing repulse.

Yet, while Gen. Lee's tactical attitude may be reasonably explained, the question arises, why was he not informed of the move in the game which would, if known to him, have required aggressive action? The same answer has to be made to this question that has been made to many others—imperfect provision for securing information. In this instance no one in particular was at fault. The men were exhausted by cold, hunger, and long sustained effort. For hours they had remained under the greatest tension of expectancy, and at last when it became apparent to all that the enemy would not assault in the blinding storm, the nervous relaxation was overpowering. Not only did the outposts, videttes, and contact patrols naturally seek shelter from the elements, thereby blinding the army as a whole, but Burnside took every precaution to see that they should remain in their blind security and assurance that no offensive move would be made by him. Thus coupled with the negative efforts of Lee's outposts, were the positive efforts of the enemy to keep them in darkness.

To the cavalry especially no blame whatever should attach in connection with Burnside's withdrawal. The peculiar situation of the two armies was such as to preclude its presence except on the flanks, and in its proper sphere of action Stuart's brigades had more than done their duty. Particularly was this true as regards Lee's right flank, where Stuart and Pelham both rendered splendid service. Recognizing that a large cavalry force assigned to the duty of guarding a flank should not remain passive and merely wait until it suited the enemy's turning columns to move against it and drive it back, Stuart had adopted the adage that "prevention is better than cure" and had hung on the enemy's flank, thereby meeting him more than half way. He clearly saw that by pushing forward into contact with the enemy's flank, any enveloping movement on the latter's part would be abandoned, unless in force, or in any circumstances the enemy's infantry masses could be delayed sufficiently long to enable Gen. Lee to make the necessary dispositions to meet them. Stuart's tactics at Fredericksburg might well have contained a lesson for Kuropatkin's cavalry at Mukden, where great masses of troopers remained inert on a line with, or in rear of, the flank they were supposed to protect, waiting for the Japanese to arrive before even the mere intelligence of their coming was transmitted.*

Pelham has for all time illustrated the power of guns in the hands of a dashing and energetic horse artillery-man, associated with a bold cavalry leader. Almost unaided and with a single piece he entirely neutralized Doubleday's whole infantry division throughout the critical hours of the battle after first breaking the shock of Meade's column already moving to the assault. Hanging upon the exposed flank of the enemy, appearing and reappearing when and where least expected, like a gnat in the eye of a great beast, he was never driven from the field, but, retiring to a more secure position from which at any time he was free to return to the immediate flank of his opponent, he brought more and heavier guns into action. Thus when his original liberty of action was denied him, he did not remain idle, but constantly maintained his threat as a cavalryman, while rendering yeoman service as a light artilleryman.†
And so, it may be remarked, the study of Fredericksburg is fruitful of many positive lessons in the tactics of the mounted arm, both for its troopers and its gunners.

As to the tactical employment of the artillery in general, little need be said, for the narrative of events has already disclosed lessons which the most casual reader could not fail to detect. As an example of the manner in which an inferior artillery should be employed,

---

*Cavalry in the Russo-Japanese War, Count Gustav Wrangel.
†Horse artillery is cavalry in one sense of the word.

Fredericksburg has few superiors. The expectations which prompted the disposition of the Confederate guns were more than realized. Refusing to sacrifice his artillery in a duel against great odds, Lee simply held the bulk of it under cover until the superior guns of the enemy were masked, whereupon it went into action with the utmost liberty and effect. Generally speaking, only his heavier ordnance was pitted against the artillery of the enemy, and that was protected by intrenchments which Sharpsburg had taught to be necessary. Thus the numerical superiority of the enemy's guns was in a measure offset by art.

Fredericksburg was in a much higher degree than either Second Manassas or Sharpsburg an artillery affair. The Federal Army was overthrown by the guns of Lee's army. The fact that Burnside was vastly superior to Lee in point of artillery is the best evidence of the service the Confederate gunners rendered. One-half of Lee's infantry, or five out of nine infantry divisions were engaged, while the batteries which crowned the heights above them were in almost continuous action. When Pendleton, Alexander, Brown, Cabell, Walker, Pelham, Hamilton, Nelson, Jones, Carter, and Latimer contemplated the extent to which they had warded off the blow directed at the gallant infantry, they must have experienced a feeling of supreme satisfaction in the knowledge that they had done their duty. No higher ambition can come to the gunner than to merit the full confidence of his sister arm. It should be his one desire, as it is his duty, to relieve the infantry of so much of the shock of battle, as he can divert to himself, even if he succumb under the blow. By such unselfish conduct alone can he win the esteem and the confidence of the whole army and instill in the breasts of his comrades in arms that affectionate regard for the artillery which Lee's gunners had won for their arm before the close of 1862. No spirit of caste jealousy now existed between the gunners and the infantry of the Army of Northern Virginia. No feeling on the part of either that they had left aught undone which they well might have done made them resentful of the other's prowess and attainments. Only a feeling of mutual respect existed between them, and willingly the infantry pressed to the roadside to help forward their batteries. For each there was an allotted task and confidence in the other's ability to perform the work assigned it was mutual. The *esprit de corps* of many of the batteries was superb. They were but clans with tartans distinct, their chieftains known to all, and as some gallant gunner at the head of his battery galloped to the front, the infantrymen by the wayside, or in the trenches, vied with each other in springing to their feet to wave a generous salute of recognition. In the advancing rush and rumble of the guns, there was an inspiring note for the foot soldier, and in the knowledge that no sacrifice in their support would be too great for the infantry, there was encouragement to the gunners to make that sacrifice unnecessary. The *entente cordiale* existing between the sister arms was the natural consequence of services rendered. It could never have arisen from mere theoretical potency. What soldier of Jackson's army could suppress his admiration for Pelham and his men, who under the very eyes of the whole corps had with dauntless courage assailed, unaided, a Federal division? What soldier of Longstreet's Corps whose heart failed to respond to the emotions which such deeds as those of Landry and of Parker are wont to generate?

Verily the plain of Fredericksburg was an amphitheatre upon which the Confederate Artillery won the proud acclaims of a martial race, the leaders of which, whether friend or foe, have echoed their applause through the pages of history. Gens. Lee, Longstreet, Jackson, A. P. Hill, McLaws, in fact all the Confederate commanders, in their reports of the battle of Fredericksburg, speak again and again of the "rapid," "destructive," "well-directed," "demoralizing," "murderous," "accurate," "efficacious" fire and "extraordinary" effect of their guns at all points, and of the "unflinching" courage, "unshaken steadiness," "animation and spirit" with which they were "admirably served," and repeatedly mention with high commendation individual commanders and batteries.

The tribute paid the Confederate Artillery by the Federal commanders is even more emphatic as to the important and preëminent part it played in the repulse of Burnside's Army. Their reports—from those of Gens. Burnside, Franklin, Sumner, Hooker, French, Hancock, Howard, Couch, Meade, Reynolds, Birney, and Doubleday, to those of officers commanding brigades, regiments, companies, and especially batteries,— characterize the fire of the opposing artillery as murderous, deadly, terrific, destructive, continuous, severe, galling, vigorous, furious, heavy, enfilading, cross, and concentrated. In some instances special reference is made to the effect of individual batteries or guns, which unless exceptionally well served would have made no particular individual impression.

But of all the encomiums bestowed by the commanders of high or low degree, the most prized by the soldiery of the Army was that epithet, dearer than life itself to a soldier, which Lee himself applied to a gunner when he wrote in his report of the heroic exploit of "the gallant Pelham." Was it mere opportunity, was it fate, or was it genius which enabled this youth to act such an heroic part upon the stage of immortality? Glorious indeed was that feat which wrested from a great commander such mention of a subaltern's name in a brief account of so great a battle.*

Of the battery expenditures in the battle of Fredericksburg there is, as in the case of Sharpsburg, no record.

The losses of the Artillery as itemized, and only in part separated from those of the infantry, aggregate about 50 killed and 250 wounded. The entire loss probably exceeded 400, or about 10 per cent of the personnel engaged. This figure is relatively enormous, as

*Gen. Lee's report of the whole battle of Fredericksburg covers less than two pages in the Official Records.

compared with the losses of the Confederate Army, which were 608 killed and 4,116 wounded. Col. Walker's Battalion alone lost 11 killed and 88 wounded, including a disproportionate number of officers, while Brown's Battalion lost 10 killed and 26 wounded. The batteries of Taliaferro's Division, under Brocken-brough, lost 2 killed and 28 wounded, while Pelham's casualties were 3 killed and 22 wounded, and Latimer's 4 killed and 21 wounded.

On the left the artillery was less exposed to the musketry fire of the infantry and the losses of Alexander's, Cabell's, and Hamilton's batteries, principally by reason of the pits which protected the detachments, were less than those sustained by Jackson's gunners, although they were more constantly engaged.

The heaviest individual losses were those of Poague's Battery, in which the casualties were 6 killed and 10 wounded of a personnel of 60 men; and Carpenter's, in which the losses were 1 killed and 25 wounded out of 65 men.

While the Confederates lost no guns and captured none, the loss of the batteries in horses was especially heavy. Long exposure to the elements in the severe weather which had prevailed added a heavy toll to the number killed in action.

CHAPTER XXII

THE battle of Fredericksburg was over, but Burnside's army rested securely under the protection of its batteries beyond the river, the Confederates still holding with their pickets the line formerly occupied by them. The troops, meanwhile, were withdrawn and immediately commenced the construction of cabins, huts, and every form of shelter both for the men and horses, but all remained near at hand in rear of their positions in line. Walton's three batteries and a number of others were at first left in position on outpost duty, but most of these were withdrawn to the rear on the 18th. The signal for the various batteries, brigades, and divisions to hasten back to the lines was to be given by Anderson's batteries on the left, if danger threatened in that quarter, and by one of Hood's or Pickett's batteries if on the right, in either case repeated by Cabell. On the morning of the 19th undue activity on the part of the enemy, his bridges still being intact, caused the alarm to be given, and immediately the troops moved forward to repel an attack, but the alarm proved to be a false one and the Confederates returned to their unfinished camps.

As soon as actual hostilities ceased, many citizens of Fredericksburg returned to their homes and all orders to destroy the enemy's bridges were countermanded, for fear of drawing the fire of the hostile batteries upon the town. The suffering of the people had been great enough, many returning to find their dwellings in ashes and their effects destroyed or removed. So great were the hardships imposed upon the residents of Fredericksburg that Gen. Longstreet invited his troops in a general order of the 18th to contribute to a fund for their relief. The response from the soldiery was immediate. The officers and men of the Washington Artillery Battalion had previously collected a purse of $1,391 for the relief of the Charlestonians, whose more-pressing wants, however, having been adequately supplied, they now unanimously voted to divert the fund to the aid of the destitute people of Fredericksburg. Thus we see that these generous Louisianians not only contributed their blood and valour to the defense of Virginia, but gave of their wealth for the alleviation of her people's suffering as well.

On the 24th, by reason of the scarcity of forage, it became necessary to disperse the batteries of the Army. Lane's Battery of the General Reserve, Rhett's of Alexander's Corps Reserve, Lewis' of Anderson's, Read's of McLaws', Stribling's of Pickett's, Reilly's of Hood's, and French's of Ransom's divisions, were retained near the positions they had occupied along the front of Longstreet's Corps. In Jackson's Corps, Poague's Battery of the Corps Reserve, Hardaway's of D. H. Hill's, Carpenter's of Taliaferro's, and Brown's of Early's divisions, were also retained. The remaining batteries of the 1st Corps were sent under the command of Col. Walton, Chief of Artillery, to the vicinity of Childsburg, about midway between the Mattapony and the North Anna rivers, Col. Crutchfield conducting those batteries of the 2d Corps which had been relieved to a point about five miles from Bowling Green. The General Reserve Artillery and Alexander's Battalion were ordered to be placed in cantonments by the Chief of Artillery along the North Anna, as he might see fit, and Gen. Pendleton was charged with the supervision and administration of the entire arm, and with the rigid enforcement of the regulations for the care of the animals, lest many of the batteries should have to be disbanded in the spring for lack of horses.* The sections to which the Artillery was thus assigned for winter quarters possessed particularly good

*Rebellion Records, Series I, Vol. XXI, p. 1109.

grass lands and it was hoped that a sufficient supply of forage would be found to carry the horses through the winter.

Longstreet with the divisions of Hood and Pickett and their respective divisional artillery battalions under Majs. Henry and Dearing, after the inactivity of Burnside was assured, was ordered February 18 to the district south of Petersburg, where the ravages of war had not yet been seriously felt. Jackson's Corps, with McLaws' and Anderson's divisions of the 1st Corps, remained along the Rappahannock guarding the line from United States Ford above Fredericksburg to Port Royal, 25 miles below.

Late in January, the Federals, by extending along the north of the river, seemed to threaten renewed activities, and Jackson's men were kept busy preparing to meet the enemy wherever he might attempt a crossing. Meanwhile, Gen. Lee was urging forward the work on the Napoleons and the Whitworth gun carriages, which he had called upon the Ordnance Bureau to make for use along his front.*

The strength of the Field Artillery of the Army on the last day of 1862 shows an increase in spite of the inroads of the Fredericksburg campaign. The General Reserve consisted of 5 batteries, 30 pieces, and 437 horses, with a personnel of 30 officers and 549 men present for duty, and an aggregate present and absent of 778. In the 1st Corps were 19 batteries, 83 pieces, and 405 horses, 70 officers and 1,576 men present for duty, with an aggregate present and absent of 2,311, and in the 2d Corps there were 31 batteries, with 125 guns, and about 700 horses, 99 officers and 2,365 men present for duty, and a paper strength of 3,966.

The Field Artillery then consisted of some 65 batteries, 240 guns, 1,550 horses, 199 officers, and 4,490 men present for duty. The average battery in the field, therefore, was composed about as follows: 3 officers, 81 men, 4 guns, and 30 horses, with a paper strength of about 130 officers and men.†

* *Rebellion Records*, Series I. Vol. XXI, p. 1109.
† *Rebellion Records*, Series I, Vol. XXI, p. 1082.

Considering the vast improvement which had already been made in its material and the measures in process of completion for its better armament, the increase both in the experience and the numbers of its personnel, the condition of the Artillery was relatively good in all respects, except as to the horses and the horse equipment, the deficiency in these two items being a serious menace to the general efficiency of the arm at all times.

The returns for January 1863 show no depletion in artillery personnel, so there could have been few deserters.

Early in January, Gen. Pendleton assigned Capt. G. W. Nelson, and 1st Lieut. E. P. Dandridge, both unattached, to batteries, the first to duty as Inspector of the Artillery of the First Corps and the General Reserve, and the latter to the same duty in the Second Corps. They were ordered to enter immediately upon the work of inspection, and were particularly directed to report upon the following points:

"1st. Condition of horses, guns, harness, ammunition, and wagons.

"2d. The strength of each battery in officers, enlisted men, horses, and equipments.

"3d. The supply of forage, its source, and prospect in future.

"4th. The position of camp, its advantages or evils.

"5th. The attention to, or violation of, rights of citizens, etc.

"6th. They will also report absences and their occasion; they will attend to all matters of importance to the service in each case, as, for instance, what hospital arrangements are made; they will regularly record the result of their observations and inquiries, and make punctual and exact reports of the same. When horses are presented for condemnation, they will carefully examine them and pass upon their condition, reporting at the same time the apparent causes thereof. It is very desirable that these inspections should be made promptly, and to this end great diligence will be needed."*

The foregoing plan of inspection gives one an excellent idea of the measures adopted to bring up the batteries to a more efficient footing. The inspections were industriously carried out as ordered, and Pendle-

---

*Rebellion Records, Series I, Vol. XXV, Part II, p. 613.

ton exerted himself to the utmost to see that every effort was made to correct or to counteract defects as they developed. In addition to this work he had, after collaborating with Cols. Crutchfield and Alexander, whose judgments he most respected of all his officers, prepared a comprehensive plan for the reorganization of the Artillery, and on February 11, submitted it in writing to the Commander-in-Chief.* In this plan it was contemplated that the Artillery should be completely organized into battalions, a thing which had only partially been effected. We have frequently spoken of a group of batteries assigned to a division as a divisional battalion when in fact it was not. The plan also included the promotion of many officers in order to furnish the requisite field officers for the proposed battalions. Promotion on a large scale at once involved a serious question. The more southern states were acutely jealous of Virginia in the matter of commissions, and, cognizant of this spirit on their part, Gen. Lee had ever sought to minimize the evil effects resulting therefrom by limiting Virginia to a number of field officers in proportion to the number of troops she furnished. Even then, the Old Dominion possessed a preponderance of the higher officers. But no man could say that Virginians unduly profited from favoritism. In fact, good men were frequently kept from well-deserved promotion in deference to this rule of policy.

Pendleton's recommendations comprise a brief history of the artillery arm up to the time they were made. Between the lines one familiar with the politics of the Army may read much. From a perusal of these lines of the Chief of Artillery, replete with suggestions, one gains a most comprehensive idea of conditions as they were, and, in order that nothing may be lost from the meaning of Pendleton's words, they are here given as he wrote them:

"The objections to the brigade batteries and division groups now existing are obvious. Burdened as are brigade and division commanders, they can scarcely extend to batteries thus assigned

---

*Rebellion Records, Series I, Vol. XXV, Part II, p. 614.

that minute supervision which they require, and the supply officers, whose chief care lies with considerable bodies of infantry, cannot devote to one or more batteries the time and attention they imperatively need. This is injuriously experienced in time of pressure. The existing arrangement moreover affords insufficient scope for field officers of artillery. Batteries, besides, permanently attached in this way, can scarcely be assigned elsewhere, whatever the emergency, without producing some difficulty, almost as if a vested right were violated. But, most injuriously of all, this system hinders unity and concentration in battle.

"Toward remedying these evils, it is respectfully proposed that in each corps the artillery be arranged into battalions, to consist for the most part of four batteries each, a particular battalion ordinarily to attend to a certain division, and to report to, and receive orders from, its commander, though liable to be divided, detached, etc., as to the commanding general or corps commanders may seem best; past associations to be so consulted in the constitution of these batteries as that each shall, as far as practicable, contain batteries that have served together, and with the division which the battalion is still ordinarily to attend. These battalions ought to have, it is believed, two field officers each, a surgeon, an ordnance officer, and a bonded officer for supplies, if not both quartermaster and commissary. Such battalions, with the officers proposed to command them, are presented to view in the accompanying schedule.

"It will be noticed that two batteries are proposed to be transferred from the Second Corps to the First, in order to equalize them as nearly as may be. One of these, Thompson's, the Louisiana Guard Artillery, heretofore attached to Gen. Early's Division, is in the schedule put into the Battalion P, to operate with Gen. Pickett's Division. The other, Latham's, a North Carolina Battery, heretofore attached to Gen. A. P. Hill's Division, is placed in the Battalion H to operate with Gen. Hood's Division.

"In the Second Corps, Dement's Battery, now attached to Gen. Early's Division, is proposed to be placed in the Battalion T to operate with Gen. Trimble's Division, because Lieut.-Col. R. S. Andrews, proposed to command that battalion, expressly requests it, that being his original battery. In this corps, also, five batteries are proposed to constitute the battalion to operate with Gen. A. P. Hill's Division, because that is a large division, and because it has hitherto been attended by a strong artillery force.

"Four batteries remaining in the Second Corps, after thus constituting battalions to attend the several divisions, are combined in a new reserve battalion, corresponding in that corps with the Washington Artillery, First Corps.

"It will be seen that this plan involves the least possible disturbance to existing relations, while it equalizes force and provides a more effective organization. Existing reserve battalions are proposed to remain as they are.

"Batteries, it is recommended, should be rendered homogeneous in armament as soon as practicable by interchange of guns with other batteries. All the batteries of each corps to be supervised by and report to the Chief of Artillery for the corps, as representing the Lieutenant-General commanding, and the whole in both corps to be superintended by and report to the general Chief of Artillery, as representing for this arm the General commanding.

"For convenience, a certain alphabetical designation is suggested for the battalions, the initials of the division commanders at the present time being adopted, rather than the usual letters in order, because the latter might seem like a numerical designation to assign some precedence of one battalion over another.

"Attention is asked to a few words respecting the officers proposed.

"*First Corps: Battalion A:* Maj. J. J. Garnett, who is well known to Gen. Longstreet, and highly appreciated by him as an efficient officer. His merit and services no doubt entitle him to the command and grade of Lieutenant-Colonel proposed for him.*

"Maj. Charles Richardson, with Gen. Anderson, may well be retained as the Second Field Officer of that battalion. These officers are both from Virginia.

"*Battalion M:* Col. Cabell, of Virginia, and Maj. Hamilton, of Georgia, who have long directed the artillery attached to Gen. McLaws' Division, should probably have command of this battalion.

"*Battalion P:* Maj. Dearing, well known to and approved by Gens. Longstreet and Pickett, and recently promoted to command the artillery attached to Pickett's Division, can well command this battalion. He is from Virginia.

"Capt. Read, of Georgia, now commanding a battery in Gen. McLaws' Division, has been heretofore recommended several times, I believe, for promotion as a gallant, intelligent, and meritorious officer, and may be usefully and justly made Major, to coöperate with Maj. Dearing in his battalion.

"*Battalion H:* Maj. Kemper, so justly appreciated for his gallantry and for long and efficient service, may well be given command of this battalion, with the rank of Lieutenant-Colonel. He is from Virginia.

"Maj. Thomas Jefferson Page, Jr., heretofore associated for a season with Maj. Kemper, and at another time with Gen. Hood, might serve well as the Second Field Officer in this battalion.

"*Washington Artillery Battalion:* Col. Walton, of course, remains as long as he wishes in command of this. He is known to be from Louisiana.

---

*Maj. Garnett had previously served on Longstreet's staff, having rendered valuable services in the Artillery on the Peninsula.

"Alexander's Battalion: Lieut.-Col. Alexander, of Georgia, is really entitled to the full rank of Colonel at the head of this battalion. We have no more accomplished officer. His commission should date from his original assignment to the command.

"Maj. J. R. C. Lewis, for some time attached to the battalion as its Second Field Officer, should probably retain the position. He is from Virginia.

"It is respectfully suggested that the officer to act as Chief of Artillery to the Corps might be most efficient in that capacity if relieved from the burden of a special command.

"Second Corps: Battalion R: Maj. T. H. Carter, some time since promoted to command the artillery of Gen. D. H. Hill's Division, was even then recommended for the rank of Lieutenant-Colonel, as fully earned by his distinguished services, and eminent merit, and may well be made Lieutenant-Colonel and given command of this battalion. He is from Virginia.

"Capt. C. M. Braxton, now commanding a battery in Gen. A. P. Hill's Division, has been recommended for promotion. He also has fully earned it by efficient service and would, no doubt, be highly approved by Lieut.-Col. Walker and by Gen. Hill as the Second Field Officer in this battalion. He is from Virginia.

"Battalion L: Lieut.-Col. R. L. Walker, of Virginia, so justly distinguished for long and gallant service, has been recommended for the full rank of Colonel. He might justly receive it and have command of this battalion.

"Capt. W. J. Pegram, now commanding a battery in Gen. A. P. Hill's Division, has been recommended for promotion. He has also fully earned it by efficient service, and would no doubt be highly approved by Lieut.-Col. Walker and by Gen. Hill as the Second Field Officer in this battalion. He is from Virginia.

"Battalion T: Maj. R. S. Andrews, so severely wounded at Cedar Mountain, but now nearly recovered and on duty in Richmond, desires and richly deserves the rank of Lieutenant-Colonel and the command of this battalion. We have no more brilliant and thoroughly meritorious artillery officer. His recommendations are ample, nor can a doubt remain as to the propriety of his having this promotion and command. He is from Maryland.

"Capt. J. W. Latimer, now commanding a battery in Gen. Early's Division, is highly recommended by Col. Crutchfield, and earnestly desired by Maj. Andrews to be promoted and associated with him as the Second Field Officer in this battalion. He is from Virginia.

"Battalion E: Maj. H. P. Jones, now in command of the artillery of Gen. Trimble's Division, under special request from Gen. W. B. Taliaferro, when in command of that division, has been recommended for promotion, and might worthily be made

Lieutenant-Colonel and have command of this battalion. In addition to much gallant service he is a very judicious and faithful officer. He is from Virginia.

"Capt. J. Gibbs Barnwell, of South Carolina, is well entitled to promotion, and would make an excellent field officer in this battalion. He has mainly served as an ordnance officer with the General Reserve Artillery, but in repeated instances has taken command in action and admirably performed his part. He is a capital artillerist, and in general merit has perhaps no superior.

"*Battalion N, Reserve:* Capt. Hardaway, now commanding a battery in the division lately under Gen. D. H. Hill, at present under Gen. Rodes, is a fine officer entitled to promotion, and some time since recommended for it; indeed, his initials were, to the end he might be commissioned as Major, asked of the undersigned by the War Department. His merit and his services entitled him to this rank, and it is believed he would well command this battalion. He is from Alabama.

"Capt. Brockenbrough, of Virginia, now suffering from a painful wound received at Fredericksburg, has been recommended for promotion. He has well served since the beginning of the war, and would do well as the Second Field Officer in this battalion.

"*Brown's Battalion:* Col. J. T. Brown, of Virginia, for months past in command of this battalion, should of course retain it.

"Capt. Poague, of Virginia, now commanding a battery in this battalion, is a superior officer, whose services have been scarcely surpassed. He has been recommended for promotion, and should justly receive it. He might well be made a Major in this battalion.

"*General Reserve: Cutts' Battalion:* Lieut.-Col. Cutts, an efficient officer, should retain command.

"Capt. Lane, commanding a battery in this battalion, a trained officer, gallant, and efficient, has been recommended for, and deserves promotion. During a long furlough of Lieut.-Col. Cutts, he has commanded the battalion, and would make for it a good Major. The companies are large, the batteries have each six guns, and a second field officer would secure its greater efficiency. Capt. Lane is from Oregon, though accredited to Georgia.

"*Nelson's Battalion:* Maj. William Nelson, long in command of this battalion, is as gallant and efficient an officer as we have in his grade. He has served from the beginning of the war as Captain and Major, has exhibited courage of the highest order and fidelity undeviating, and well deserves the rank of Lieutenant-Colonel. He is from Virginia.

"Maj. A. L. Rogers, also of Virginia, might usefully serve as the Second Field Officer in this battalion. Its batteries are all of six guns.

"The recommendations for promotion are believed to be in strict accordance with the merits of the officers and the wishes of Gens. Longstreet and Jackson, and of other commanders best qualified to judge.

"The proportion between the number of field officers of artillery thus proposed belonging to Virginia and those from other States is very nearly coincident with that between the number of batteries from Virginia and those from other States. Of the whole number of batteries, 35 are from Virginia and 24 from other States. This would give of the 28 field officers proposed, about 17 from Virginia and 11 from other States. Of those actually recommended 18 are from Virginia and 10 from other States.

"Should this organization be mainly approved and ordered, ordnance officers, surgeons, and supply officers can be applied for by the several battalion commanders.

"Toward accomplishing an efficient adjustment of the whole in time for the probable opening of the spring campaign, it is important that an adequate supply of suitable guns be furnished as soon as possible by the Ordnance Department. Nearly all the bronze short-range guns of the Second Corps were several weeks ago sent to Richmond to be recast into Napoleons. None have been sent from the First Corps, nor from the General Reserve, because Col. Gorgas advised against it, on the ground that the Department had as much metal as it could cast for a number of weeks.

"Four battery battalions might be armed with good rifles and Napoleons in nearly equal proportions, two batteries to have rifles altogether, and two to have Napoleons altogether. Larger battalions to have perhaps a corresponding proportion, or more Napoleons. Batteries in reserve to have heaviest metal. It is hoped that, much as a number of battery horses will probably be reduced in strength by the occasional scarcity of food incident to the difficulty of transporting it, in spite of all efforts, a sufficiency will be at hand for the batteries proposed when the campaign opens. Some 400, sent for to Georgia in the fall by the undersigned, have, under advisement with the Quartermaster's Department in Richmond, been stopped on the border of North Carolina, for the sake of being easily foraged. Other droves the Quartermaster's Department will, it is hoped, have collected, so that such animals as are unserviceable with the batteries may be replaced by others comparatively fresh and strong."

The proposals of Pendleton contemplated that in the First Corps there should be 4 divisional battalions and 2 corps reserve battalions, with a total of 26 batteries and 112 guns; and in the Second Corps 27 batteries with

116 guns, organized into 6 battalions as in the First Corps. The General Reserve was to consist of 2 battalions, of 3 batteries each, with a total of 36 pieces. Thus in the entire Army there were to be 14 artillery battalions, each with 2 field officers and a staff, and a total of 264 guns, exclusive of those of the Horse Artillery.

Four days after the receipt of Gen. Pendleton's recommendations, the Commander-in-Chief promulgated the proposed organization of the Artillery, withholding, however, the appointment of the additional field officers pending an investigation of their individual merits. On March 2, Gen. Lee forwarded his recommendations to the President with such revisions in Pendleton's as seemed proper to him for one reason or another, the appointments being soon made, and finally announced in *Special Orders No. 106, A. N. V., April 16, 1863.*[*] The Field Artillery organization was now as follows:

1st CORPS

Col. John B. Walton, Chief of Artillery

CABELL'S BATTALION

Col. Henry Coalter Cabell
Maj. S. P. Hamilton

1. Troup (Ga.) Battery,	Capt. Henry H. Carlton.
2. Pulaski (Ga.) Battery,	Capt. John C. Fraser.
3. 1st Co. Richmond Howitzers,	Capt. E. S. McCarthy.
4. "A" Battery, 1st N. C. Reg't,	Capt. B. C. Manly.

GARNETT'S BATTALION

Lieut.-Col. John J. Garnett
Maj. Charles Richardson

1. Norfolk Light Artillery Blues,	Capt. Chas. R. Grandy.
2. Pittsylvania Battery,	Capt. John W. Lewis.
3. Donaldsonville (La.) Battery,	Capt. Victor Maurin.
4. Norfolk (Huger's) Battery,	Capt. Jos. D. Moore.

Rebellion Records, Series I, Vol. XXV, Part II, pp. 651, 728.

DEARING'S BATTALION

Maj. James Dearing
Maj. J. P. W. Read

1. Fauquier Battery,	Capt. R. M. Stribling.
2. Richmond Hampden Battery,	Capt. Wm. H. Caskie.
3. Richmond Fayette Battery,	Capt. Miles C. Macon.
4. Lynchburg Battery,	Capt. Joseph G. Blount.

HENRY'S BATTALION

Maj. M. W. Henry

1. Charleston German Battery,	Capt. W. K. Bachman.
2. Palmetto (S. C.) Battery,	Capt. Hugh R. Garden.
3. Rowan (N. C.) Battery,	Capt. James Reilly.
4. Branch (N. C.) Battery,	Capt. Alexander C. Latham.

CORPS RESERVE

ALEXANDER'S BATTALION

Col. E. Porter Alexander
Maj. Frank Huger

1. Bath Battery,	Capt. J. L. Eubank.
2. Bedford Battery,	Capt. Tyler C. Jordan.
3. Madison (La.) Battery,	Capt. Geo. V. Moody.
4. Richmond Battery,	Capt. Wm. W. Parker.
5. Brooks (S. C.) Battery,	Capt. A. B. Rhett.
6. Ashland Battery,	Capt. Pichegru Woolfolk, Jr.

WASHINGTON ARTILLERY BATTALION

Col. John B. Walton

1. 1st Co. Washington Artillery,	Capt. C. W. Squires.
2. 2d Co. Washington Artillery,	Capt. John B. Richardson.
3. 3d Co. Washington Artillery,	Capt. M. B. Miller.
4. 4th Co. Washington Artillery,	Capt. Benj. F. Eshleman.

2D CORPS

Col. Stapleton Crutchfield, Chief of Artillery

WALKER'S BATTALION

Col. Reuben Lindsay Walker
Maj. William J. Pegram

1. Pee Dee (S. C.) Battery,	Capt. E. B. Brunson.
2. Richmond Battery,	Capt. Wm. G. Crenshaw.
3. Richmond Letcher Battery,	Capt. Greenlee Davidson.
4. Richmond Purcell Battery,	Capt. Jos. McGraw.
5. Fredericksburg Battery,	Capt. E. A. Marye.

CARTER'S BATTALION

Lieut.-Col. Thomas H. Carter
Maj. Carter M. Braxton

1. Jeff Davis Alabama Battery,   Capt. Wm. J. Reese.
2. King William Battery,   Capt. W. P. Carter.
3. Richmond Orange Battery,   Capt. C. W. Fry.
4. Morris Louisa Battery,   Capt. R. C. M. Page.

ANDREWS' BATTALION*

Lieut.-Col. R. Snowden Andrews
Maj. Joseph W. Latimer

1. 4th Md. or Chesapeake Battery, Capt. Wm. D. Brown.
2. Alleghany Battery,   Capt. Jos. Carpenter.
3. 1st Maryland Battery,   Capt. Wm. F. Dement.
4. Lee Battery,   Capt. Chas. J. Raine.

JONES' BATTALION

Lieut.-Col. Hilary P. Jones
Maj. J. B. Brockenbrough

1. Charlottesville Battery,   Capt. James McD. Carrington.
2. Staunton Battery,   Lieut. Alexander H. Fultz.
3. Richmond Courtney Battery,   Capt. W. A. Tanner.
4. Louisiana Guard Battery,   Capt. C. Thompson.

CORPS RESERVE

BROWN'S BATTALION

Col. John Thompson Brown
Maj. R. A. Hardaway

1. Warrenton Battery,   Capt. James V. Brooke.
2. Powhatan Battery,   Capt. Willis J. Dance.
3. 1st Rockbridge Battery,   Capt. Archibald Graham.
4. Salem Battery,   Capt. A. Hupp.
5. 3d Co. Richmond Howitzers,   Capt. Benj. H. Smith, Jr.
6. 2d Co. Richmond Howitzers,   Capt. David Watson.

McINTOSH'S BATTALION

Maj. D. G. McIntosh
Maj. Wm. T. Poague

1. Alabama Hardaway Battery,   Capt. William P. Hurt.
2. Richmond Battery,   Capt. Marmaduke Johnson.
3. 2d Rockbridge Battery,   Capt. John A. M. Lusk.
4. Danville Battery,   Capt. Geo. W. Wooding.

*For final assignment of Thompson's, Brown's, and Caskie's batteries, see *Rebellion Records,* Series I, Vol. XXV, Part II, p. 667, Special Order No. ——, March 14, 1863.

GENERAL RESERVE

Brig.-Gen. William Nelson Pendleton

CUTTS' BATTALION

Lieut.-Col. Allen S. Cutts
Maj. John Lane

1. Battery "A", Sumter (Ga.) Batt., Capt. H. M. Ross.
2. Battery "B", Sumter (Ga.) Batt., Capt. Geo. M. Patterson.
3. Battery "C", Sumter (Ga.) Batt., Capt. John T. Wingfield.

NELSON'S BATTALION

Lieut.-Col. William Nelson
Maj. Thomas Jefferson Page, Jr.

1. Amherst Battery,   Capt. Thomas J. Kirkpatrick.
2. Fluvanna Battery,   Capt. John L. Massie.
3. Georgia Battery,   Capt. John Milledge, Jr.

HORSE ARTILLERY

Maj. R. F. Beckham

1. Chew's Battery,   Capt. R. Preston Chew.
2. Stuart Horse Artillery,   Capt. James Breathed.
3. Lynchburg Beauregards,   Capt. Marcellus N. Moorman.
4. 2d Stuart Horse Artillery, Capt. Wm. N. McGregor.
5. Washington (S. C.) Battery, Capt. James F. Hart.

Thus we see that the only changes in Pendleton's plan were the substitution of Maj. M. W. Henry as a battalion commander for Maj. Del. Kemper, and Maj. D. G. McIntosh for Maj. R. A. Hardaway, the latter, however, being given his majority, while neither Capt. Squires nor Capt. Barnwell was promoted. Longstreet desired to wait until Col. Walton's return in the case of the former, Walton being on recruiting duty in Louisiana. Majs. J. R. C. Lewis and A. L. Rogers were also omitted in the new organization. The former transferred to another arm of the service, and was succeeded by Capt. Frank Huger, the only West Pointer still commanding a battery.*

_____

*See letter of Pendleton to Lee, *Rebellion Records*, Series I, Vol. XXV, Part II, pp. 628-9.

The law approved January 22, 1862, authorized field officers for the Artillery in the proportion of a colonel for every 40, a lieutenant-colonel for every 24, and a major for every 16 guns. Based upon 264 guns, the Army was entitled to 6 colonels, 11 lieutenant-colonels, and 16 majors. The organization as completed included 6 colonels, 7 lieutenant-colonels, and 16 majors.* But three vacancies existed, therefore, among the field officers.

The departure from Pendleton's recommendations for promotion in the Second Corps were due almost entirely to Col. Crutchfield, who warmly advocated the promotion of either Brockenbrough or Chew in preference to Maj. Jones and Capt. Barnwell, and in his opposition to the advancement of the latter officers he was supported by Jackson.†

Col. Crutchfield particularly urged the promotion of McIntosh, which he finally secured, yet Jones was also promoted. The placing of Hardaway in command of a battalion was also opposed by Crutchfield. "He is an excellent artillerist, a good shot, and very fond of the scientific parts of the service," said Crutchfield, "but not good at managing men, hard on his own horses, and not at all apt to require the captains of batteries under him to take good care of their horses. He is rather indifferent to what he regards as the drudgery of the service, and while the qualifications he does possess will render him a very valuable field officer of artillery, it will not be in the sphere of the constant commandant of a battalion."

The foregoing remarks are quoted because they give us some idea of the qualities which were considered requisite on the part of a battalion commander. More than mere brilliancy seems to have been required.

The correspondence between Lee and Jackson respecting the appointment of artillery officers in the Second Corps is quite interesting, the latter's attitude

---

*Including Lieut.-Col. L. M. Coleman, of Brown's Battalion, invalided from wounds received at Fredericksburg.
†*Rebellion Records,* Series I, Vol. XXV, Part II, p. 633-4.

being characteristic. He insisted upon the privilege of exercising control over promotions in his corps. "I have had much trouble resulting from incompetent officers having been assigned to duty with me, regardless of my wishes," he wrote. "Those who assigned them have never taken the responsibility of incurring the odium which results from such incompetency."* This was strong language to address to the Commander-in-Chief.

When Gen. Lee forwarded his recommendations for promotion in the Artillery to the President, he took occason to state that "No class of officers in the Army has learned faster or served better than the Artillery."†

Before the end of February, Longstreet, having been informed by Col. Crutchfield that Jackson had asked for Col. Alexander to be made brigadier-general of infantry, vice Lawton, wrote Gen. Lee inquiring if Maj. Pelham could be spared by Stuart to fill Alexander's place, suggesting Pelham's promotion, and Maj. Terrell's appointment to succeed him in command of the Horse Artillery. But nothing came of the matter, probably by reason of Alexander's unwillingness to relinquish his commission as colonel in the Artillery for one as a brigadier-general of infantry. His present duties were far more important and attractive to one of his tastes than those incident to the office of a brigadier. At any rate he was not transferred, though his promotion was requested by Gen. Lee.‡

On February 20, Lieut. Dandridge returned his report covering the inspection of 29 batteries of the Second Corps.§ The items of the report comprise an accurate and complete record of the condition of Jackson's artillery, which may be regarded as typical of the arm. The harness and ammunition was generally reported as good and most of the horses, of which there was an average number of about 55 to a battery, were

---

* *Rebellion Records,* Series I, Vol. XXV, Part II, pp. 644-5-6.
† Ibid., p. 651.
‡ *Rebellion Records,* Series I, Vol. XXV, Part II, p. 645.
§ Ibid., pp. 634, 638.

found in a serviceable condition, very few instances of neglect having been detected. Most of the batteries possessed several two- or four-horse wagons for purposes of foraging, having to haul their hay and grain varying distances, some as far as 60 miles over execrable roads, until provision was made to transport forage by rail to the artillery camps. Until these arrangements were completed, corn was principally secured in Essex County, and from Hanover Courthouse. Some forage was found about Guiney Depot, Hamilton's Crossing, Milford, and in King William County.

Most of the batteries mustered a personnel of about 100 officers and men, and some as high as 140, but few less than 90. The number of absentees exclusive of the sick was not excessive, though there were exceptions. Carter's Battery reported 2 officers and 133 men present for duty, 1 officer and 6 men detached, 4 absent with leave and 71 deserters. The last figure must have been for the whole period of the war. Sickness was prevalent, many of the batteries having as many as 20 men on the sick list, and few less than 8. Latham's Battery with 4 officers and 114 men present, 1 man on furlough, 1 absent without leave, and 9 on detached duty, reported 39 sick, while Pegram's Battery with 3 officers and 108 men present, 1 officer on leave, 1 man on detached duty, and 3 absent without leave, reported 55 men absent sick. But it must be remembered that frequently men not sufficiently well clad, or who did not possess shoes good enough to permit of their exposure to the cold and mud of winter, were carried on the rolls as sick. At any rate, the poor clothing with which the men were provided would account for many minor cases of sickness during this exceptionally severe winter.

The condition of the men with respect to clothing was perhaps no better or no worse than in the Army in general. Nothing gives a better understanding of the wants in this respect than the following anecdote concerning the Chief of Artillery himself. Late in Decem-

ber, Gen. Pendleton was found one afternoon by Maj.
Page of his staff busily engaged with needle and thread.

"What are you doing, General?" he asked.

"Mending my trousers. The only thing I could find
for a patch was this old piece of collar," replied the
Chief.

"Well, it's a great waste of time, for nobody will
ever be able to tell one end of your shirt from the other,"
rejoined the Major.

Knowing that the Chief of Artillery was forced to
rob his shirt for the benefit of his breeches, we are led
to wonder how the private gunner managed to hide his
nakedness!

Fortunately for the poor soldiers, timber was plentiful with which to erect crude but comfortable cabins.
For an insight into the life they led during the cold
winter of 1862-63, surrounded on all sides by poverty
and distress, the reader would do well to peruse those
vivid pages which so well and so touchly record the
minutiæ of a private soldier's life in the Army of Northern Virginia.* The story is a pathetic one, told in a
vein of ineffable sweetness in spite of the ghastly features which the recollections must have conjured up before the writer. It is a classic of its kind, and serves to
show that the lowering clouds of war could not keep at
least a few beams of sunlit happiness from sifting
through the chinks in the huts and hearts of the Confederate gunners during that long and trying winter.

January, February, and March, 1863, were months
of ceaseless activity on the part of the artillery officers,
of whom great diligence was required to provide the
necessary forage which had to be located, collected and
brought in from the back country. Then, too, the work
of overhauling harness and equipments, refitting the material, and culling out and turning in the inferior
ordnance to be replaced by the new Napoleons, kept
them busy. Some were dispatched to other parts of the

---

*Soldier Life, A. N. V., written by Carlton McCarthy, a private soldier in the
2nd Co. Richmond Howitzers.

South to look for horses, others to collect stores and supplies of all kinds. Col. Cutts even visited Georgia and Florida where he reported a large supply of provisions and thousands of beef cattle to be available for the Army.* Cutts had been absent on furlough since the return of the Army from Maryland.

Maj. John Page, Chief Quartermaster, Artillery Corps, was forced before the 1st of February to scour the country between Richmond and Gordonsville along the Virginia Central Railroad, and the rich James River Valley, for the necessary hay and grain for the batteries, the supply in Caroline County having all but been exhausted.†

Constant efforts were now being made not only to expedite the delivery of the new guns being manufactured by the Bureau of Ordnance, but to complete the quota of horses for every battery in the Army. Late in March statements of the various battalion commanders showed that in addition to those already furnished, at least 1,200 horses were needed for the battalions, exclusive of 170 for the General Reserve.‡ The Chief of Artillery, in his report to the Inspector of Transportation, stated three causes for the unusual deficiency in spite of the extraordinary efforts which had been made to maintain the draught animals in a state of efficiency. First, there were the losses in action, incident to the battles of the late fall and early winter; second, the breaking down and sickness of many animals due to the labor of hauling forage, the insufficiency of feed, and the rigours of the winter season; and third, the additional demand by reason of the substitution of heavier ordnance for the discarded 6-pounders, the former requiring 6-horse teams.

By April 1 the weather had so moderated that the deficiency of forage was partly counteracted by turning the horses into the meadows where the droves might browse and rest, the shoes of the horses being removed.

*A sufficient supply for two years, Ibid., p. 738.
†*Rebellion Records,* Series I, Vol. XXV, Part II, p. 599.
‡Ibid., p. 695.

The condition of the horses of the Army, and the deficiency in their number, was a source of grave concern to Gen. Lee. On April 16, in a letter to the President, in which he expressed the opinion that the aggressive should be resumed by May 1, he declared that his only anxiety arose from the immobility of the Army, owing to the condition of the horses and the scarcity of forage and provisions.* And again, on April 25, he wrote Gen. Pendleton that the destruction of horses in the Army had been so great he feared it would be impossible to supply all wants.

In an effort to economize horses the Chief of Artillery had ordered the field transportation in each battalion for staff purposes to be reduced to one 4-horse and one 2-horse wagon. The former was to suffice for the mess outfit, desks, papers, and tents of the field and staff, while the other was set apart for the surgeon and his medical supplies. The batteries were limited to one wagon per section for men and foraging purposes. The allowance for the batteries was considered inadequate by Col. Crutchfield, who asserted that three wagons to a battery were absolutely necessary, that being a reduction of one-fourth the number previously allowed. It was necessary, he claimed, to have an ordnance wagon in which spare harness, stores, and mess equipment could be transported, in addition to two forage wagons, one carrying the horse feed, while the other remained free to forage. The escort wagon in use in the Artillery had a capacity of 6 barrels of corn, that was 168 rations of 10 pounds each, or only two days' rations of corn for the battery complete. With but one forage wagon, the battery could not secure its provender until after it had reached camp and unloaded the wagon, the team having been on the march all day, whereas with an extra wagon, forage could be collected on the march, the teams saved extra work, and the battery horses regularly fed. Col. Crutchfield's views were adopted and the field transportation allowance of the Artillery fixed at three per

---

*Ibid., p. 725.

battery. Thus for a battalion of 4 batteries, the train consisted of fourteen 4-horse wagons. The Artillery train of the entire army, exclusive of ammunition columns, consisted of not less than 250 wagons and 1,000 horses, a saving of at least half of that number having been effected by Pendleton's rigid measures. Orders were also promulgated providing that no part of a battery or train should remain on a road when disabled, the officer in charge being required promptly to remove the carriages from the roadway. Batteries and trains were also prohibited from stopping in the line of march to water, or from attempting to regain their place in column when once having lost it for any reason.* The packs of dismounted gunners were to be carried by the men, and the baggage of field officers was limited to 65, and that of battery officers to 50 pounds. But one wall tent was allowed battalion headquarters, and one tent fly to the officers of each battery.†

The officers and men of the batteries with Jackson, were the most actively engaged of all during the winter. Of the work in which they were ceaselessly engaged, Maj. A. S. Pendleton of Jackson's staff, son of the Chief of Artillery, wrote on April 26:

"The greatest destruction and change in the appearance of the country is from the long lines of trenches and the redoubts which crown every hillside from ten miles above Fredericksburg to twenty miles below. The world has never seen such a fortified position. The famous lines of Torres Vedras could not compare with them. As I go to Moss Neck (Jackson's headquarters) I follow the lines, and 'have a ride in the trenches.' These are 5 feet wide and 2½ deep, having the earth thrown forward towards the enemy, making a bank still higher. They follow the contour of the ground and hug the bases of the hills as they wind to and from the river, thus giving natural flanking arrangements; and from the tops of the hills frown the redoubts for sunken batteries and barbette batteries, *ad libitum,* far exceeding the number of our guns; while occasionally, where the trenches take straight across the flats, a redoubt stands out defiantly in the open plain to receive our howitzers. . . . "

*G. O. No. 26, Second Corps, April 13, 1863, Ibid., p. 719.
†G. O. No. 58, A. N. V., April 20, 1863, Ibid., p. 739.

Before spring arrived much had been done under Pendleton's administration to place the batteries on a more effective footing. The losses among the officers had been especially large, and the comparatively few unsuited to command who remained were ruthlessly culled out, making way for the more efficient. In this respect the Field Artillery was especially favored. The peculiar character of the service of the guns is such that no officer may hide his inefficiency beneath the cloak of collectivism. At every turn even the junior officer of a battery is called upon to exercise positive command and to lead, not follow. Thus in the Field Artillery the laggard, the incompetent, is soon discovered.

One great incident of the winter should not be ignored inasmuch as Gen. Pendleton, Chief of Artillery, was not only constantly engaged in it, but actually led the movement. Religious interest and services had been kept up among the artillery commands from the beginning of the war under Gen. Pendleton's direction and guidance. Under the influence of Lee, Jackson, and Pendleton, the spirit of religion spread broadcast through the Army during the period of winter quarters from the battle of Fredericksburg to the spring campaign of 1863. Log chapels everywhere sprang up along Jackson's lines, and in them the men of all arms gathered together during the long winter evenings to hear the word of God. To systematize the religious work providing every portion of the field army with devout, faithful chaplains, was a task to which Jackson and Pendleton both addressed themselves with fervor, But the number of chaplains proving inadequate to meet all demands, the men themselves not infrequently preached to their fellows. The spirit of revival swept on and on through the ranks until few, however callous, held aloof from the meetings where so much of peaceful promise was to be found, and over all there seemed to spread a spirit of sanctity which did much to lighten the burdens of the soldiery, and inspire them to a faithful discharge of their duties. Christ walked abroad in the camps, and whispered many a word of consolation, of cheer, of forgiveness for their sins, to those lonely desolate men, who, in spite of cold, of hunger, of doubt, of loss of loved ones, and separation from everything dear to their lives, clung to their posts through that awful winter. "Courage, despair not," the sweet and hopeful voice whispered in their ears, and each dawn found the Confederate sentinel watching upon the post of consecrated duty.

He who fails to accord great weight to the religious influence projected into the Confederate cantonments along the Rappahannock while Jackson confronted the Federal host, fails utterly to understand why, when the men of the Northern Army, bountifully supplied with all that a wealthy nation could furnish, were deserting at a rate of 200 a day, the half-starved, half-naked, unpaid Confederates stuck to their tattered colors.* He fails to understand that it was that divine faith in themselves and in their cause, instilled by their leaders into their hearts along with a trust in God, and the promise of that "peace which passeth all understanding" which kept the soldiers of the Confederacy in the ranks, and made it possible for the frosted colors to be once more unfurled to lead them on to fresh victories. To such factors in war, the ordinary strategist, tactician, military historian, accords little consideration. He is too prone to deal merely with words of command and numbers. In disregarding the tears of repentance which wet the cheek of the Army of Northern Virginia in the winter of 1863, he but neglects the very cause of the steeling of its heart to all the sacrifices, all the sufferings, all the privations it was called upon to endure. "In war men are nothing; it is the man who is everything. The general is the head, the whole of an army. It was not the Roman Army that conquered Gaul, but Cæsar; it was not the Carthaginian Army that made Rome tremble in

---

*Hooker stated before the Committee on the Conduct of the War that when he relieved Burnside desertions were at the rate of 200 a day in the Army of the Potomac, and that the returns showed 2,922 commissioned officers and 81,964 enlisted men absent, the majority from causes unknown.

her gates, but Hannibal; it was not the French Army that carried the war to the Weser and the Inn, but Turenne; and it was not the Prussian Army which, for seven years defended Prussia against the three greatest powers of Europe, but Frederick the Great." So spoke Napoleon, and many military writers tell us that an army is but the reflex of its commander. The leader of the Army of Northern Virginia in the winter of 1863 was Christ. Its moral stamina was, in the highest sense of the word, God-given.*

As spring began to approach there were signs of renewed activity in both armies. As early as the 9th of February, Fitz Lee's Cavalry Brigade had broken camp in Caroline County, and leaving its winter quarters moved to Culpeper Courthouse, where, on the 12th, it relieved Hampton's Brigade from the duty of picketing the upper Rappahannock. Crossing the river on the 24th, at Kelly's Ford, Fitz Lee reconnoitered towards Falmouth, encountering the enemy's cavalry at Hartwood church and actually driving it back into the camps of the 5th Federal Corps. On the 26th, he returned to his new camp after taking 150 prisoners and providing his men with a number of horses, much equipment, forage, etc. This exploit provoked the Federals and Brig.-Gen. Averell, with his cavalry brigade, was ordered on the 18th of March to cross the river at one of the upper fords and to "attack and rout or destroy" Fitz Lee's Brigade reported to be in the vicinity of Culpeper Courthouse. After detaching a force of 900 men to look after the Confederate patrols north of the river, Averell with 2,100 men and a horse battery reached Kelly's Ford on the morning of the 17th. Lee's pickets guarding the ford were driven off, and then Averell set about crossing his command. The river was high and swift, and the caissons and guns were entirely sub-

---

*The reader is invited to consult *Soldier Life, A. N. V.,* McCarthy; *Four Years Under Marse Robert,* Stiles; *A Cannoneer Under Stonewall Jackson,* Moore; *Three Years in the Confederate Horse Artillery,* Neese; *A Soldier's Recollections,* McKim; and in marked contrast with these is *Recollections of a Private Soldier of the Army of the Potomac,* Wilkeson.

merged, the artillery ammunition being carried across
in the nose-bags of the troopers. By 10 A. M. he was
ready to advance.

In the meantime, Fitz Lee at his camp near Culpeper
Courthouse had learned that the ford had been forced,
and immediately set his command in motion, meeting
Averell's column within half a mile of the ford. The
Federal line extended from the river near Wheatley's
Ford to the Brooks house, with sharpshooters posted
behind a stone fence running along the front and the
mounted reserves drawn up in the fields and woods in
rear on both sides of the road branching off from
Wheatley's to Kelly's Ford. Along his front, Averell
had deployed two regiments armed with carbines, and
supported by two sections of his horse battery. Fitz
Lee's leading regiment charged down the stone fence in
columns of fours, the men emptying their pistols as they
galloped along and driving off the defenders.

Gen. Stuart and Maj. Pelham had been attending the
session of a court-martial in Culpeper Courthouse as
witnesses and, expecting to return to Fredericksburg
on the 17th, borrowed horses and joined Lee's Brigade
when they learned of the impending cavalry fight. Being present by mere accident, Stuart declined to exercise command, but Pelham could not remain inactive on
the battlefield, and, seeing Lee's 3d Virginia Regiment
preparing for the charge described, rushed to its head
to assist Col. Owen in leading it. With the shout of
victory upon his lips, and while waving his hat aloft, he
was struck in the head by a piece of shell just as the
column passed by the Wheatley house. A single Confederate trooper reined up to carry the all but lifeless
body from the field across his pommel. Thus was the
body of the "gallant and incomparable" Pelham saved
from the enemy.

The leading Confederate regiments were met near the
Wheatley house by a part of the Federal reserves and
checked after a sanguinary mounted combat, the result
of which in view of Averell's superior force was to com-

pel Lee, for reasons of prudence, to retire to a strong position where he could employ his artillery with effect. Withdrawing to the road from Brandy Station to Kelly's Ford, he now formed a line across it near Carter's Run with an open field about 600 yards wide in his front. On a hill north of the road, Capt. James Breathed's Battery of four guns, formerly commanded by Pelham, took up its position. Soon the enemy made his appearance and opened fire with three pieces of Lieut. Brown's section at long range. After awaiting Averell's attack for some time, Fitz Lee, growing impatient, ordered a charge, and, routing the enemy, all but captured his guns, the troopers driving the gunners from their pieces in spite of their double-shotted canister and spherical case.

Maj. McClellan states that Pelham was dead when his body was removed by the trooper. John Esten Cooke states that he lingered until after midnight, at which time Stuart, grieved beyond all measure, telegraphed the family of Pelham in Alabama:

"The noble, the chivalric, the gallant Pelham is no more. He was killed in action yesterday. His remains will be sent to you to-day. How much he was beloved, appreciated and admired, let the tears of agony we have shed, and the gloom of mourning throughout my command, bear witness. His loss is irreparable."[*]

The young artilleryman's body was sent to Richmond and there laid in state in the Capitol of Virginia at the feet of Houdon's statue of the Arch Rebel, Washington.[†] Cooke tells us that "some tender hand deposited an evergreen wreath, entwined with white flowers, upon the case that contained all that was mortal of the fallen hero." Soon his family conveyed the youthful soldier's remains to his home in the far South, Virginia, the field of his undying fame, surrendering them to Alabama, the land of his birth.

"The Major-General commanding," wrote Stuart in a general order, "approaches with reluctance the painful

---

[*]Pelham, "the Gallant," in *Wearing of the Gray*, by John Esten Cooke, p. 127; *The Campaigns of Stuart's Cavalry*, McClellan, p. 211.
[†]See Col. William F. Gordon's famous poem, *Secessia*.

duty of announcing to the division its irreparable loss in
the death of Maj. John Pelham, commanding the Horse
Artillery. He fell mortally wounded in the battle of
Kellysville, March 17, with the battle cry on his lips,
and the light of victory beaming from his eye.

"To you, his comrades, it is needless to dwell upon
what you have so often witnessed—his prowess in action,
already proverbial. You well know how, though young
in years, a mere stripling in appearance, remarkable for
his genuine modesty of deportment, he yet disclosed on
the battlefield the conduct of a veteran, and displayed in
his handsome person the most imperturbable coolness
in danger.

"His eye had glanced over every battlefield of this
army, from the First Manassas to the moment of his
death, and he was, with a single exception, a brilliant
actor in all.

"The memory of the gallant Pelham, his many
virtues, his noble nature and purity of character, is
enshrined as a sacred legacy in the hearts of all who
knew him.

"His record has been bright and spotless, his career
brilliant and successful.

"He fell—the noblest of sacrifices—on the altar of
his country, to whose glorious service he had dedicated
his life from the beginning of the war."

The written records of the American conflict fail to
disclose another such tribute from so great a commander
as Stuart. The evergreen wreath placed upon his bier
has long since shriveled and died—these words can never
fade from the pages of history. Pelham is now a tradition of the Southland, nay more, of the American
people. His fame is the heritage of a united country
and an inspiration for all time to the soldier of whatever race. Of his death, the poetic Cooke wrote:

"Thus passed away a noble, lofty soul; thus ended a career
brief it is true, but among the most arduous, glorious, and splendid
of war. Young, but immortal—a boy in years, but heir to undying
fame—he was called away from the scene of his triumphs and

glory to a brighter world, where neither wars nor rumours of wars can come, and wounds and pain and suffering are unknown; where

> "Malice domestic, foreign levy, nothing
> Can touch him further!"

It would be vain indeed for the author to attempt to trace the record of Pelham's 24 years of life when already it has been done in the beautiful words of one of his comrades. In order that not even language may detract from his due, the following extract from John Esten Cooke's sketch is inserted:

"A son of the great State of Alabama, and descended from an old and honorable family there, he had the courage of his race and clime. He chose arms as his profession, and entered West Point, where he graduated just as the war commenced; lost no time in offering his services to the South, and received the appointment of First Lieutenant in the Confederate States Army. Proceeding to Harper's Ferry, when Gen. Johnston was in command there, he was assigned to duty as drill officer of Artillery, and in the battle of Manassas commanded a battery, which he fought with that daring courage which afterwards rendered him so famous. He speedily attracted the attention of the higher generals of the Army, and Gen. J. E. B. Stuart entrusted him with the organization of the battalion of Horse Artillery, which he subsequently commanded in nearly every battle of the war upon Virginia's soil. Here I knew him first.

"From the moment when he took command of that famous corps, a new system of artillery fighting seemed to be inaugurated. The rapidity, the rush, the impetus of the cavalry were grafted upon its more deliberate brother. Not once, but repeatedly, has the Horse Artillery of Pelham given chase at full speed to a flying enemy; and far in advance of all infantry support, unlimbered and hurled its thunders on the foe. It was ever at the point where the line was weakest; and however headlong the charge of the cavalry, the whirling guns were beside it, all ready for their part. 'Trot, march!' had yielded to 'gallop!' with the battalion; it was rushed into position, and put into action with a rush; and in and out among the guns where the bolts fell thickest was the brave young artillerist, cool and self-possessed, but, as one of his officers said the other day, 'as gay as a schoolboy at a frolic.' He loved his profession for its own sake; and often spoke to the officers above alluded to of the 'jolly good fights' he would have in the present campaign; but I anticipate my subject.

"Once associated with the command of Stuart, he secured the warm regard and unlimited confidence of that general, who employed his services upon every occasion. Thenceforth their fortunes seemed united, like their hearts, and the young man became known as one of the most desperate fighters of the whole army. He was rightly regarded by Jackson, and others, as possessed of a very extraordinary genius for artillery; and when any movement of unusual importance was designed, Pelham was assigned to the Artillery to be employed.

"His career was a brief one, but 'how glorious'! Let us glance at it.

"When the Southern forces fell back from Manassas in 1861, his batteries had their part in covering the movement and guarding the forks of the Rappahannock. During the campaign of the Peninsula, his Blakely was as a sentinel on post near the enemy; and at the battle of Williamsburg his courage and skill transformed raw militia into veterans. In the Seven Days' battles around Richmond, he won fadeless laurels. With one Napoleon, he engaged three heavy batteries, and fought them with a pertinacity which made the calm face of Jackson glow; and the pressure of that heroic hand, warm and eloquent of unspoken admiration. Soon afterwards, at the White House, he engaged a gunboat, and driving it away, after a brief but hot encounter, proved how fanciful were the terrors of these 'monsters'.*

"His greatest achievements were to come, however, and he hastened to record them on the enduring tablets of history. From the moment when his artillery advanced from the Rappahannock, to the time when it returned thither, to the day of Fredericksburg, the path of the young leader was deluged with the blood of battle. At Manassas he rushed his guns into the very columns of the enemy almost; fighting their sharpshooters with canister, amid a hurricane of balls. At Sharpsburg he had command of nearly all the artillery on our left, and directed it with the hand of a master. When the Army crossed back into Virginia, he was posted at Shepherdstown and guarded the ford with an obstinate valour, which was spoken in the regular and increasing reverberation of his deep-mouthed Napoleons, as they roared on, hour after hour, driving back the enemy.

"Of the day which succeeded that exciting period, many persons will long hold the memory. It was in an honest old country-house, whither the tide of war bore him for a time, that the noble nature of the young soldier shone forth in all its charms. There, in the old hall on the banks of the Opequon, surrounded by warm hearts who reminded him perhaps of his own beloved ones in Alabama; there in the tranquil days of autumn, in that beautiful country, he seemed to pass some of his happiest hours. All were charmed with his kind temper and his sunny disposition; with his refine-

---

*This was later done by Confederate batteries along the Rappahannock, and by Forrest's batteries in Tennessee.

ment, his courtesy, his high breeding, and simplicity. Modest to a fault, almost blushing like a girl at times, and wholly unassuming in his entire deportment, he became a favorite with all around him, and secured that regard of good men and women which is the proof of high traits and fine instincts in its possessor. In the beautiful autumn forests, by the stream with its great sycamores, and under the tall oaks of the lawn, he thus wandered for a time,— an exile from his own land of Alabama, but loved, admired, and cherished by warm hearts in this. When he left the haunts of 'the Bower' I think he regretted it, but work called him.

"The fiat had gone forth from Washington that another 'On to Richmond' should be attempted; and where the vultures of war hovered, there was the post of duty for the Horse Artillery. The Cavalry crossed the Blue Ridge, and met the advancing column at Aldie, and Pelham was again in his element. Thenceforward, until the banks of the Rappahannock were reached by the Cavalry, the batteries of the Horse Artillery disputed every step of ground. The direction of the Artillery was left, with unhesitating confidence, by Stuart to the young officer; and those who witnessed, during that arduous movement, the masterly handling of his guns, can tell how his confidence was justified. It was the eye of the great soldier, the hand of the born artillerist, which was evident in his work, during those days of struggle. He fell back neither too soon nor too late, and only limbered up his guns to unlimber again in the first position which he reached. Thus fighting every inch of the way from Aldie, round by Paris, and Markham's, he reached the Rappahannock and posted his artillery at the fords, where he stood and bade the enemy defiance. That page in the history of the war is scarcely known; but those who were present know the obstinacy of the contest, and the nerve and skill which were displayed by the young officer.

"That may be unknown, but the work done by Pelham on the great day of Fredericksburg is a part of history now. All know how stubbornly he stood on that day—what laurels encircled his young brow when night at last came. This was the climax of his fame—the event with which his name will be inseparably connected. With one Napoleon gun, he opened the battle on the right, and instantly drew upon himself the fire, at close range, of three or four batteries in front, and a heavy enfilading fire from thirty-pound Parrotts across the river. But this moved him little. That Napoleon gun was the same which he had used at the battle of Cold Harbor—it was taken from the enemy at Seven Pines,—and, in the hands of the young officer, it had won a fame which must not be tarnished by defeat! Its grim voice must roar, however great the odds; its reverberating defiance must roll over the plain, until the bronze war-dog was silenced. So it roared on steadily with Pelham beside it, blowing up the caissons, and continuing to tear up the enemy's ranks. Gen. Lee was watching it from the hill above, and exclaimed, with eyes filled with admiration, 'It is glorious to see such courage in one so young!' It was glorious indeed to see that one gun, placed in an important position, hold its ground with a firmness so unflinching. Nor, until his last round of ammunition was shot away, did Pelham retire; and then only after a peremptory order sent to him. He afterwards took command of the entire artillery on the right, and fought it until night with a skill and courage which were admirable. He advanced his guns steadily, and at nightfall was thundering on the flank of the retreating enemy, who no longer replied. No answering roar came back from those batteries he had fought with his Napoleon so long; he had triumphed. That triumph was complete, and placed forever upon record when the great commander-in-chief, whom he loved and admired so ardently, gave him the name in his report, of 'the gallant Pelham.'

"Supreme tribute to his courage—immortalizing him in history! To be the sole name mentioned beneath the rank of Major-General in all that host of heroes—and mentioned as 'the gallant Pelham'!"

"Thenceforward there was little for him to desire. He had never cared for rank, only longed for glory, and now his name was deathless. It is true that he sometimes said, with modest and noble pride, that he thought it somewhat hard to be considered too young for promotion, when they gave him great commands at Sharpsburg and Fredericksburg,—and called on him when the hardest work was to be done. But, he never desired a mere title he had not won, and did his soldier's duty thoroughly, trusting to time. So noble and important, however, had been his recent services that promotion was a matter of course. The President said, 'I do not need to see any papers about Maj. Pelham,' and had appointed him a Lieutenant-Colonel; and it only awaited the formal confirmation of the Senate, when he fell on the Rappahannock. His fall was a public calamity to the nation, but none to him. It was fit that such a spirit should lay down its great work before the hard life of the world had dimmed the polish of the good knight's spotless shield. He wanted no promotion at the hands of men. He had won, if not worn, the highest honors of the great soldier; and having finished his task, the gentle spirit took its flight, promoted by the tender hand of death to other honors in a brighter world."*

Such was the character, such were the military services of Maj. John Pelham, who in two years had thrice won the personal thanks of Jackson, and individual mention by the Commander-in-Chief, these two

---

*Pelham, "the Gallant," in *Wearing of the Gray*, Cooke.
Every child should read Cooke's Surry of Eagle's Nest, Mohun, Fairfax, etc.

being among the best and the bravest men, and certainly the greatest soldiers, in the Army of Northern Virginia. Well might Jackson have said to Stuart on the bloody field of Fredericksburg, "Have you another Pelham, General? If so, I wish you would give him to me!"

Pelham has been likened to both Murat and Marceau. Had he merely embodied the characteristics of such soldiers so extensive a mention of his name had not been made. He was far more than a skilled and dashing soldier. He was not only the pattern of his arm, injecting into the service of the guns an *élan* and spirit of self-sacrifice remarked by all, but he is to-day the Galahad, *sans peur et sans reproche,* of all artillerymen. Modern formulæ have by no means rendered impossible the deeds of another Pelham, nor is the effectiveness of field artillery yet determined by the rank of the gunner who lays the piece.

Pelham's brilliant career was but a phase of the Confederate artillery service. In the final analysis of his deeds, it was not so much what he actually did as what his name stood for among his comrades and his associates. The influence of such a spirit as his is far reaching. It is easy to place limits upon his actual accomplishments in a tactical sense—it is impossible to define the extent of his moral ascendency.

Yet, it must not be thought that the Field Artillery of Lee's army boasted no other figures of exceptional individualism. Indeed, there were many in whom may be noted those strong traits of character which typified the arm. Crutchfield, Walker, Alexander, Carter, Pegram, Chew, Caskie, McIntosh, Haskell, Breathed, McGraw, McCabe, Cutshaw, Thomson, Latimer, Carpenter, Poague, and many others were the very embodiment of all that was skillful, courageous, gallant, each possessing a peculiar individualism developed to the highest degree. From the sentiments and character of these men were developed the *élan* and the *morale* which gave to their arm that distinctive mien so characteristic of the

Field Artillery.   In their make-up there was decidedly something of the Cavalier; their features were unhidden by the helmet of uniformity.   No cuirass concealed their familiar figures; their hearts were encased only by that heroic resolve which, though powerless to shield from the dangers of mortal conflict, kept their souls unsullied, enabling them to breach the works of fame and transcend the ordinary limits of military glory.

CHAPTER XXIII

THE BATTLE OF CHANCELLORSVILLE—PRELIMINARY DISPOSITIONS

THE Army of the Potomac, now under Hooker, numbered May 1 not less than 111,000 infantry, 11,000 cavalry, and 8,000 artillery with 404 guns, organized in seven corps.* To this impressive force, Lee was prepared to oppose less than 60,000 men of all arms and about 228 guns.†

The Confederate Artillery was distributed as follows:

1st Corps

McLaws' Division, Cabell's Battalion, 4 batteries, 18 guns.

R. H. Anderson's Division, Garnett's Battalion, 4 batteries, 18 guns.

1st Corps Reserve Artillery, Alexander's Battalion, 6 batteries, 23 guns, and Walton's Battalion, 4 batteries, 13 guns, the effective personnel of the two battalions numbering about 850, or 85 officers and men per battery.

2d Corps

A. P. Hill's Division, Walker's Battalion, 6 batteries, 24 guns.

Rodes' Division, Carter's Battalion, 4 batteries, 18 guns.

Early's Division, Andrews' Battalion, 4 batteries, 18 guns.

Colston's Division, Jones' Battalion, 4 batteries, 18 guns.

2d Corps Reserve Artillery, Brown's Battalion, 6 batteries, 24 guns, and McIntosh's Battalion, 4 batteries, 16 guns, with a total effective personnel for the two battalions of about 900, or 90 officers and men per battery.

General Reserve Artillery

Cutts' Battalion, 3 batteries, 14 guns, and Nelson's Battalion, 3 batteries, 12 guns, with a total effective personnel for the two battalions of about 600, or 60 officers and men per battery.

Horse Artillery

Beckham's Battalion, 4 batteries, 18 guns.‡

Rebellion Records, Series I, Vol. XXV, Part II, p. 320.
†Hood and Pickett with Dearing's and Henry's battalions, or 8 batteries, with a total of about 35 guns, were still detached from the 1st Corps.
†Chew's Battery was detached with Jones' Brigade, and on duty in Western Virginia.

Thus, there were 54 batteries present with 232 guns and a total artillery personnel of about 5,000 officers and men. In this campaign we should figure on the Confederate divisional battalions as possessing about 95 officers and men per battery, whereas the average strength of Hooker's 74 batteries was not less than 135.

When Lee should have had every man and gun available to ward off the blow which Hooker proposed to deliver to him, he found himself deprived of three of Longstreet's divisions, numbering about 20,000 effective infantry, and two battalions of artillery with a total personnel of about 30 officers, and 800 men, with over 30 guns.*

Soon after the battle of Fredericksburg, Gen. D. H. Hill had been placed in command of the force defending the seaboard of the Carolinas, and at the beginning of the New Year, Ransom's Division of the 1st Corps had been detached from the Army of Northern Virginia and assigned to this command. The strength of this division was not far short of 4,000 men. About the middle of February Gen. Lee had also been induced by Mr. Seddon to send Longstreet with the divisions of Hood and Pickett to cover Richmond, which the administration believed to be menaced from the directions of Fortress Monroe and Suffolk. While Lee deemed a single division sufficient to ward off the danger, he submitted to the detachment of the two divisions, which numbered about 15,000 officers and men, but cautioned Longstreet to so dispose his troops that they could return to the Rappahannock at the first alarm. The warning, however, was totally disregarded, nor was Gen. Lee able in spite of persistent representations to Mr. Davis and the Secretary of War, Mr. Seddon, to overcome their fears and have these troops ordered to rejoin him. In their counsels, the President and the Secretary held Longstreet's views superior to those of Gen. Lee, whose lieutenant had become wedded to the idea of operations independent of the main army. And so, when Hooker was becoming active on the Rappahannock, thoroughly informed by Gen. Peck at Norfolk of Lee's weakened condition, Longstreet was puttering about east of Richmond 120 miles away from his proper post, either ignorant of the value of concentration, or careless of the necessity therefor, in order that his own pet project might be carried out.

While many of the accusations brought against Longstreet since the war are to a great extent the outgrowth of political prejudice, this willful desertion of his commander-in-Chief is the most unpardonable error of which he was guilty. He left Gen. Lee with a thorough understanding between them that he would return in the spring. So soon, however, as he tasted the sweets of independence, he found himself unable to accede to the wishes and the views of his commander-in-chief, and actually played upon the fears of the President and Mr. Seddon to the end that his own wishes prevailed. It seems certain that Mr. Davis would never have taken the responsibility of going counter to Gen. Lee's advice had Longstreet properly supported his commander-in-chief. Longstreet's conduct is in marked contrast to that of Jackson, who, without delay, hastened from the Valley to the Peninsula in June, 1861, when summoned by Lee. The true value of a lieutenant lies in his ability and willingness to subordinate his own desires to those of his captain. This Jackson did, and this Longstreet failed to do.

Of Longstreet's detachment from the Army, Gen. Alexander has this only to say: "The great need of rations for the coming summer led the War Department to send Longstreet with two divisions for a campaign in the vicinity of Suffolk. Its object was to collect forage and provisions from counties near the Federal lines. The campaign was not initiated by Lee, and he thought but one division would have been sufficient, as the result showed. For the little fighting done was unnecessary, being initiated by the Confederates.

And, although Lee at Chancellorsville repulsed Hooker's attack, it was poor policy to take the risk of battle against enormous odds, with one-fourth of his infantry absent."*

Truly this is a remarkable criticism! Poor policy on the part of whom? The insinuation is at least an involved one. It is clearly directed at Lee, who in the very words of the writer was not to blame for the poor policy pursued. After spending the whole winter fortifying and strengthening his lines, was Gen. Lee to desert them without striking a blow and take up a less favorable position to resist Hooker? The suggestion is absurd. Or perhaps Gen. Alexander meant that the Army of Northern Virginia should have conformed to Longstreet's movements! We agree with him that an error was committed which prevented the Confederates from reaping the fruits of the victorious battle which necessity forced upon Lee, but Longstreet and others, and not Lee, were guilty of the poor policy of which he complains. It is strange how one, generally so scathingly critical of others as Gen. Alexander was, can dismiss so important a question involving Longstreet, his commander, in so few words. The way in which he has almost ignored the point is indicative of a total lack of real defense. Longstreet attempted none for himself except to state that his trains were busy collecting forage and that he could not rejoin Lee without abandoning them. Why, we may ask, did he set about collecting forage at so important a crisis?†

The absence of Dearing's and Henry's battalions, and the batteries of Blount, Macon, Stribling, Thompson, Bachman, Garden, Latham, and Reilly, from the field of Chancellorsville, was, as we shall see later, keenly felt by Gen. Lee.

With the exception of Burnside's famous "Mud March" shortly after the battle of Fredericksburg, and the cavalry fight on March 17, at Kelly's Ford, nothing

*Military Memoirs of a Confederate, Alexander, p. 319.
†From Manassas to Appomattox, Longstreet, p. 326.

of interest in the main theater of war had transpired since the great battle of December. On the former occasion, some of the Artillery had been ordered up from the camps along the North Anna, but had returned after traversing about half the distance to the front. But the Artillery had not been inactive elsewhere.

When Jackson was ordered across the Blue Ridge in November, Chew's Ashby Battery was attached to Gen. W. E. Jones' Cavalry Brigade, which had been left in the Valley with headquarters at New Market, to coöperate with Gen. George H. Steuart's mixed command known as the Maryland Line. The Artillery of Steuart's force consisted of the 2d Baltimore Battery, or the Baltimore Light Artillery, formerly commanded by Capt. Brockenbrough and now by Capt. William H. Griffin. The operations in which Steuart and Jones engaged during the severe winter of 1862-63 were very trying, for they were kept constantly on the alert guarding Lee's flank against hostile movements up the Valley. April 21 Chew's and Griffin's batteries accompanied Jones on his raid into West Virginia, where, coöperating with Gen. J. D. Imboden, much damage was done to the Northwestern Railroad. It was for the purpose of this expedition that Griffin's Battery was fully mounted and thus converted into a horse battery.

All through the winter Chew's and Griffin's batteries had rendered splendid service, in repelling the raiding parties of the enemy, and although they had not been present at Fredericksburg and only returned to Harrisonburg from West Virginia on May 1, too late to participate in the Chancellorsville campaign, it is safe to say that no other batteries of the Army had seen as much arduous service as they had since the return of the Army from Maryland in the fall.

As early as April 13 Hooker had dispatched Stoneman at the head of 10,000 finely-equipped cavalry to ascend the Rappahannock and, swinging around, to attack Stuart's troops wherever they might be found, and "Fight! Fight! Fight!" Receiving intelligence on the 14th of the concentration of the Federal Cavalry on the upper Rappahannock, Stuart in person had moved with Fitz Lee and two regiments of W. H. F. Lee's Brigade, accompanied by Hart's and Moorman's Horse batteries, to oppose the movement. This opposition, together with the swollen condition of the river, checked Stoneman's passage to the south side and so deranged Hooker's plans that he was constrained to suspend his advance until the 27th. He had hoped that his splendid cavalry column would at once gain the railroad between Fredericksburg and Richmond, by which Lee received his supplies, and by cutting the main line of their communications compel the Confederates to evacuate their fortified line and fall back upon Richmond. The Federal commander also anticipated that in drawing off Stuart, Stoneman would make it possible for the bulk of his army to be transferred to the south side of the river with little or no resistance, and having effected the crossing he expected to find space to maneuver his immense force.

Hooker's grand movement was preceded by several demonstrations intended to deceive Lee. On the 21st small bodies of his infantry had appeared at Kelly's Ford and the Rappahannock Bridge, and on the 23d, a small force had been thrown across the river at Port Royal. From such activity on the part of the enemy Lee at once concluded active operations were soon to be resumed in earnest by Hooker.

At this time, the Confederates occupied the powerful line of works they had constructed during the winter, reaching from near United States, or Bark Mill Ford on the west, to Port Royal on the east, a distance of about 30 miles. The brigades of Mahone and Posey, of Anderson's Division, with Grandy's and Lewis' batteries, observed United States Ford; that of Wilcox, with Maurin's and Huger's batteries, Banks' Ford; while the remaining troops of the division held the heights about Fredericksburg, including Marye's Hill. McLaws' Division held the works on Lee's Hill and the line running to Hamilton's Crossing, and Jackson's Corps lay in position between that point and the extreme right at Port Royal. Stuart, with the main body of the cavalry, some 2,400 strong, at Culpeper, was now observing the Federal horsemen at Warrenton Junction, while picketing the Rappahannock with the rest of his command.

Early on the 27th Hooker set his 11th and 12th corps in motion for Kelly's Ford, 25 miles up the river, where they concentrated on the evening of the 28th. The 5th Corps left the Federal camp on that day. The object of the expedition was unknown even to the corps commanders until after their arrival at the ford. The 11th Corps crossed the Rappahannock at once, followed in the morning by the 12th and 5th corps, the first two striking for Germanna Ford on the Rapidan, and the last for Ely's Ford lower down that stream.

After having been forced to deploy the advance guard several times, and much annoyed by one of Fitz Lee's regiments with Lieut. Phelps' section of Moorman's Battery at Wilderness Run, and again being checked at Wilderness Tavern by Stuart himself, who had arrived from Culpeper with the rest of the brigade, and Breathed's and McGregor's batteries, the heavier or more southern column of the enemy under Slocum arrived at Chancellorsville the evening of the 30th. In the meantime, Meade with the 5th Corps had also arrived at the designated point of concentration. But, while Stuart had been powerless to stay the advance of the enemy, he had secured the information which enabled Lee to fathom Hooker's design, until now skillfully concealed.

In order to confound the enemy, Hooker had assembled his 1st, 3d, and 6th corps under Sedgwick, at Franklin's Crossing, and Pollock's Mill, about 3 miles below Fredericksburg, before dawn on the 29th, and thrown two pontoon bridges across the river, and on the 28th, holding a single division in camp at Falmouth in view of the Confederates, he had withdrawn the other two divisions of the 2d Corps and dispatched them with all haste to Banks' Ford four miles upstream. Finding this crossing held by Wilcox, the column continued to United States Ford, from which Mahone and Posey had been forced to retire by Meade's advance on the 29th. Throwing a pontoon bridge at this point they reached Chancellorsville the same night as the 5th, 11th, and 12th corps. The same day, the 30th, Sedgwick was instructed to place a corps across the river and make a demonstration against the Confederate line below Fredericksburg in his front, and the 3d Corps was ordered to proceed with haste to Chancellorsville where Hooker arrived and established his headquarters during the evening.

Immediately upon discovering the movement of the enemy across the Rappahannock on the 28th, Stuart had reported the fact, and been instructed by Gen. Lee to take the necessary precautions to protect the property along the railroads. For this purpose, W. H. F. Lee with two regiments of his brigade, Hart's Battery and Shoemaker's section of Moorman's Battery, was ordered to proceed by way of Culpeper Courthouse to the Rapidan, and endeavor to cover Gordonsville and the Virginia Central Railroad. The manner in which W. H. F. Lee with the 9th and 13th Virginia Cavalry, Hart's Battery, and Shoemaker's two guns, clung to Stoneman's overwhelming force for the next week, impeding its movements by reappearing in his front at every defensible position, threatening his flank by day and night, and dropping shells into his columns whenever opportunity presented, is a story in itself, a part of the glory of which is due the Horse Artillery. Hart and Shoemaker returned with exhausted horses and men, but the Federal Battery of six pieces, with which they had been frequently engaged during the seven days of constant marching, had never once silenced the Confederate guns.

While Stuart was attempting to delay the Federal advance and secure all the information he could, Gen.

Lee was actively engaged in moving the larger part of his army to the left to meet the Federal advance. At 9 P. M. on the 29th Anderson was directed to proceed with his division to Chancellorsville and cover the roads leading therefrom to Fredericksburg with Mahone's, Posey's and Wright's brigades, the first two of which had retired to that point from United States Ford. The following morning Anderson withdrew to the intersection of the Mine and Plank Roads, near Tabernacle Church, and began to intrench. Mahone was placed astride the old turnpike, and Wright and Posey on the Plank Road. That afternoon, leaving a portion of his force to observe the Federals, Stuart marched by way of Spotsylvania Courthouse to Todd's Tavern, from which point he proceeded in person with his staff to join Lee.

On the forenoon of the 29th, Gen. Pendleton at Artillery Headquarters, near Chesterfield Depot on the Richmond and Fredericksburg Railroad, received telegraphic orders to bring up all the Artillery. Col. Crutchfield with most of the artillery of the 2d Corps, in camp near Bowling Green, and Alexander's Battalion, two batteries of Cabell's, and one of Garnett's Battalion of the 1st Corps, in camp at Mt. Carmel Church, about five miles north of Hanover Junction, took up the march to Fredericksburg at 1 o'clock that afternoon. The following morning Walton's Battalion and Nelson's and Cutts' battalions, of the General Reserve, broke their camps about Chesterfield.* In spite of the extremely bad condition of the roads and the heavy rain which fell during the night of the 29th, Alexander's Battalion reached Tabernacle Church at 10 A. M. on the 30th, Jordan's Battery at once went into position on Anderson's line, an attack being expected, while the other batteries were held in reserve. Manly's and Carlton's batteries of Cabell's Battalion under Maj. Hamilton reported to McLaws during the afternoon. McCarthy's and Fraser's, the other two batteries of

---

*Lane's Battery of Cutts' Battalion was on detached duty with Longstreet.

Cabell's Battalion, had remained at the front with the infantry during the winter and were already in position on Lee's Hill.

During the movement of the Artillery to the front, Gen. Pendleton himself remained on the road near Massaponax Church, where he arrived about noon on the 30th. All the batteries in the rear had reached this point from their camps by nightfall, and were parked awaiting orders from the commander-in-chief, except those of Walton's Battalion which lost the road.

Meantime, the enemy below Fredericksburg had continued inactive, and it became apparent from Stuart's reports that the main attack would be made in the direction of Chancellorsville or on the Confederate left rear. Gen. Lee, therefore, determined to leave a sufficient force to hold the intrenched line, and with the main body of the Army to oppose Hooker's turning column. Early's Division of the 2d Corps and Barksdale's Brigade of McLaws' Division of the 1st Corps were held in position opposite Sedgwick, and at midnight on the 30th McLaws marched with the rest of his command toward Chancellorsville, Jackson following at dawn with the divisions of Rodes, Colston, and A. P. Hill, and all of his artillery except Maj. Andrews' Battalion, which remained with Early.

The brigades of Kershaw, Semmes, and Wofford, left their works at 12:30 A. M. May 1 and marched along the Plank Road. By 6 A. M. they were in position behind the rifle pits about Smith's Hill, McLaws' left joining Anderson's right, thus protecting the approaches from the United States Ford, and that from Chancellorsville on the right. Maj. Hamilton, leaving Fraser's and Carlton's batteries of Cabell's Battalion in the works on Lee's Hill, followed the division with Manly's and McCarthy's batteries at 2 A. M. Upon the departure of part of the battalion Carlton at once placed two of his Parrotts in the works opposite Deep Run, a third in a pit in rear of the Howison house, holding the fourth piece, a 12-pounder howitzer, in reserve.

While Mahone's, Posey's, and Wright's brigades of Anderson's Division, and Kershaw's, Semmes', and Wofford's brigades of McLaws' Division, Manly's and McCarthy's batteries of Cabell's Battalion, Granby's and Lewis' batteries of Garnett's Battalion, and Jordan's, Moody's, Woolfolk's, Eubank's, and one section of Parker's Battery of Alexander's Battalion, were opposing Hooker's four corps at Chancellorsville, and Jackson's divisions were rapidly moving from Hamilton's Crossing to unite with them, it will be well to see what had been done to hold Sedgwick in check.

When the regiment on picket at the mouth of Deep Run reported to Early at dawn on the morning of the 29th that the enemy had thrown a brigade across the river in boats under cover of the fog, he at once notified Jackson and without orders moved his division to the front, deploying three regiments as skirmishers along the River Road. Meantime, however, the Federals had thrown a bridge and crossed over an entire division of infantry with its batteries. About a mile lower down the river, Sedgwick also succeeded in throwing a bridge but, due to the opposition of the Confederate pickets, was delayed in effecting a crossing until after 10 A. M., when another division was sent over. The Federal troops, protected by the steep river banks, at once commenced to intrench and construct epaulments for their guns, and on the opposite bank great masses of infantry appeared. To resist the threatened attack, Early placed some of Andrews' guns behind his right on Prospect Hill, and others in rear of his left. Jackson soon sent forward Rodes' Division which extended Early's line to the right across Massaponax Creek, and a Whitworth gun of large caliber under Lieut. Tunis was placed in position near the Yerby house hill, from whence, safe from hostile fire, it could enfilade the ground in Early's front. Colston's and A. P. Hill's divisions were brought up during the day and the latter was placed in position in rear of Early. McLaws' Division manned the lines on Early's left, and, beyond, three brigades of Anderson's Division were intrenched, Barksdale's Brigade occupying the town. During the day, the Federals made no attempt to advance and the Whitworth effectually kept down the fire of the enemy's batteries whenever they showed a disposition to open. On the 30th there was no increase in the activity of the enemy, but the diminution of his force on the opposite bank by the movement of the 3d Corps to Chancellorsville was apparent. Such was the condition of affairs when Anderson's, McLaws', and Jackson's divisions were withdrawn and Early was left to hold the line he had established with his own division, and Andrews' Battalion, now reduced to 12 pieces, viz., six Napoleons, three 3-inch rifles, and two 10-pounder Parrotts. Barksdale's Brigade of McLaws' Division was left to occupy Fredericksburg, and Tunis with the Whitworth was placed under Early's command. At daybreak on the 1st, however, the Chief of Artillery was assigned the artillery defense of the lines, and directed to report to Gen. Early. No more batteries were to be sent to the left from his reserve column, then parked at Massaponax Church.

When Pendleton arrived on the scene he at once in company with Early made a reconnaissance. The weakness of the line was apparent to them both. With six miles of front to defend, there were but 9,000 muskets available, including Barksdale's men. Since it was impossible to occupy the whole line, the interval between Deep Run and the base of Lee's Hill had to be left vacant. The principal threat was on the right, for the enemy was below Deep Run.

Turning over the artillery defense of the right to Maj. Andrews, Pendleton directed his attention to the left. Andrews had placed four Napoleons and two 3-inch rifles under Maj. Latimer in gun-pits behind Early's left, and two Parrotts on Prospect Hill. Graham's 1st Rockbridge Battery of four rifles, which had been sent him by Pendleton, was also posted at this point. Below Hamilton's Crossing, two Napoleons and two rifles were posted in a grove of pines, while the Whitworth, entirely unsupported, still occupied the Yerby height across the Massaponax. There were thus 17 pieces under Andrews disposed in three groups, so as to give a cross fire on Early's front.

By 10 A. M. Pendleton had occupied the gap north of Deep Run with Nelson's Battalion of the General Reserve, Massie, Milledge, and Kirkpatrick placing their 12 pieces on the slope to the left of the broad flat extending past the infantry line behind the railroad.

On the extreme right of Lee's Hill, Carlton's Battery of Cabell's Battalion had already taken position, with Fraser's on the left. Rhett's Battery of Alexander's Battalion had also been left behind to occupy the center, with three 20-pounder Parrotts. Alexander had sent back a section of Parker's Battery under Lieut. J. Thompson Brown, Jr., to man two of the 10-pounder Parrotts of Rhett's Battery, which at this time were the only guns in position on Marye's Hill. Pendleton therefore ordered Ross's Battery of Cutts' Battalion to occupy this important position, having been forced to dispatch Patterson's to Port Royal, where two Federal gunboats were reported to be shelling the place.* The Washington Artillery was momentarily expected to arrive, but did not make its appearance until the afternoon. Fortunately the enemy had not been active. During the evening, in response to a call from Early for a battery of rifled pieces, Richardson's Battery of this battalion was directed to report to Maj. Andrews. The following morning Walton was directed to assume charge of the artillery defense of the left and place two guns to the right of the Marye house near the old graveyard, to command the plain in front; two in the epaulments to the left to sweep the Telegraph Road and the Plank Road; and several in the works on the Stansbury Hill, to command the bridges over the canal in front.

---

*The third battery, Lane's, of this battalion was on detached duty with Longstreet.

Upon examining the foregoing dispositions one is much impressed by Lee's lack of artillery on his right. At no place could guns have been used to better advantage or have so well contributed to overcome the deficiency in the infantry available for the defense of the heights, which Early was expected to hold. The setting, as we have before noted, was ideal for the employment of artillery to the fullest extent. But in the absence of Henry's and Dearing's battalions, even Pendleton's batteries had to be absorbed in the first line of defense, thus leaving Lee without an artillery reserve.

Turning to Chancellorsville, it is to be noted that Hooker's movements up to the night of the 30th had been attended with the greatest success. Full of confidence, his troops had marched with a celerity hitherto unknown to the Army of the Potomac. In three days, Hooker's turning column of 70,000 men had marched 46 miles over bad roads, had forded two difficult rivers, thrown several bridges, brushed aside Stuart, and concentrated in a position which not only took Lee's entire system of river defense in reverse, but lay upon the principal roads leading to his line of communication.

In order, however, to gain the advantages of the position Hooker held by concentrating three corps at Chancellorsville, it had been necessary to divide his army, and the line of communication between the wings by way of United States Ford was not less than 20 miles long. It was imperative that this line be at once shortened since a bold enemy lay between the two wings and the seizure of Banks' Ford became more important to Hooker with every hour of his occupancy of Chancellorsville. Yet, nothing was done on the night of the 30th but to send out a cavalry regiment towards Spotsylvania Courthouse to feel for the enemy.

Colliding with Stuart by chance this small Federal column was driven back without securing the slightest information of importance.* No effort whatever was

*See Pleasonton's extravagant account, *Battles and Leaders of Civil War,* Vol. III, p. 172.

made to sweep down on Wilcox and secure Banks' Ford, which might have been done with ease had the proper amount of energy been expended.

There were three roads over which Hooker's right wing could move upon Fredericksburg and Lee's rear: the Orange Turnpike from the west passed through Chancellorsville and was the most direct; the United States Ford Road, which, crossing the former at Chancellorsville, became the Plank Road, bent to the left and united with the turnpike five miles or so from Chancellorsville toward the Rappahannock, passed along by Banks' Ford, six miles distant, and continued to Fredericksburg. The two important points were Chancellorsville, which consisted of a large dwelling, and Tabernacle Church, some four miles nearer Fredericksburg, both owing their importance to the junction of the various roads at those places. The satisfaction Hooker displayed over his successful concentration at Chancellorsville was marked. He had evidently studied his map, and on paper his move was a masterstroke, but one which splendidly illustrates the impractical character of "Kriegspiel." It is not merely location in war, but position with regard to terrain, that is of practical value. It is not so much the number of miles as the topographical features which separate the hostile forces that are of practical importance, and of these facts Hooker displayed striking ignorance. His expressed intention was to gain elbow room in which to maneuver. He should never have halted his magnificent corps until that was gained, especially since no opposition was to be encountered in gaining it. Meade, whom he had halted at Chancellorsville late on the 30th, might just as well have pushed on towards the line occupied by Anderson and McLaws, and, with Slocum's two divisions following hard behind, the open country would have enabled the Federal masses to deploy. As it was, only the cavalry followed up Anderson and McLaws as they retired. Instead of elbow room Hooker found his turning column choked in the dense woods surrounding Chancellorsville, from which point only a few narrow and difficult roads issued to the open country. The shock he was able to deliver to his enemy was not the dynamic power of the mass, but merely that of the small currents which he could bring into contact with the resisting force. His map had deceived him. It would have been better had Stoneman's command been sent to clear Hooker's way and seize the true point of vantage from which the latter might maneuver than it was to eliminate the services of so valuable a body of horsemen.

CHAPTER XXIV

CHANCELLORSVILLE—MAY 1ST

On the morning of May 1 Hooker reconnoitered the Confederate position and issued orders for a general advance. Delays now supplanted the celerity which had hitherto characterized the Federal movements, for it was hours after daylight before the start was made. Meade was finally pushed out on the left over the River and Turnpike roads, Slocum and Howard on the right along the Plank Road. Meade was directed to arrive near Banks' Ford by 2 P. M. and the right column at Tabernacle Church by noon. But the movement was undertaken just 12 hours too late, as we shall see.

Jackson's three divisions with all the artillery of the 2d Corps, except Andrews' Battalion, moved at 3 A. M., May 1, along the Military Road, and then following the Plank Road arrived at the line held by Anderson and McLaws about 8 A. M., Jackson taking command of the left. By his orders work was at once discontinued on the intrenchments and preparations for an advance were made. About 11 A. M. Anderson was directed to advance along the turnpike with Mahone's Brigade leading. Wilcox supported McLaws' right. Soon the enemy was encountered in force and Mahone deployed across the turnpike with Jordan's Battery in the front line while Semmes formed line on his left with Wofford and Perry on his right covering the Mine Road. Wright and Posey with Moody's, Woolfolk's and Eubank's and a section of Parker's Battery advanced along the Plank Road.* Lieut. James Woolfolk, of the Ashland Battery accompanied the skirmishers with a howitzer and rendered conspicuously gallant service. Jackson's divisions in column followed Anderson along the Plank Road.

---

*Eubank's Battery was commanded by Lieut. O. B. Taylor at this time, and is frequently referred to in the records as Taylor's Battery.

The enemy was soon encountered on both the Plank Road and the turnpike and heavy skirmishing with infantry and artillery ensued. A strong attack upon McLaws was repulsed by Semmes' Brigade, and one gun of Jordan's and one of Grandy's batteries repulsed a body of cavalry, which bravely sought to take the leading guns. Grandy's Battery had been brought up from the intrenchments held by Mahone and Semmes, to the support of Jordan's single rifle. But, only one piece under Lieut. Wm. T. Peet could be brought into action which, together with Jordan's, engaged Weed's regular battery for over an hour, alternating their fire by pouring canister at a range of 300 yards upon Sykes' Infantry on the turnpike. In this affair, Grandy's Battery lost 1 killed, and 6 wounded, including Lieut. Peet, whose platoon was not withdrawn until but two men remained to work the gun. After going into position again the next day on the Plank Road, Gen. Lee in person at 6 P. M. ordered Grandy to withdraw his guns, most of which were light pieces, and to proceed to Chesterfield Depot to remount his command, the horses of which were so much worn and depleted in number as to render the battery unfit for further service.*

When Hooker heard heavy firing in his front and learned that strong opposition had been encountered, he ordered Couch to take Hancock's Division and proceed to the front. Moving out along the turnpike about 1½ miles Couch encountered Sykes' Division of regulars, which was heavily engaged with Mahone and Semmes. Soon after he deployed Hancock's men both he and Sykes were ordered by Hooker to withdraw their divisions to Chancellorsville. The move, in view of the importance of gaining the open country in their front, appeared so undesirable to all those on the spot, that Couch requested a change of orders, but instead of being allowed to proceed, he was peremptorily directed to re-

---

*From Chesterfield Depot Grandy was ordered by Gen. Pettigrew to Hanover Junction to guard the bridges at that point.

turn. While Couch was withdrawing, Hooker again changed his mind and ordered him about 2 P. M. to "hold on till 5 o'clock."

The resistance of the enemy proving stubborn, Anderson had directed Wright about noon to proceed to the left along the unfinished railroad and endeavor to turn the Federal right. About 6 P. M. Wright reached the Welford Iron Furnace, 1½ miles southwest of Chancellorsville, where he was informed by Stuart that the enemy occupied a strong position in the woods north of the furnace. At this juncture Maj. Beckham arrived at the furnace from Spotsylvania Courthouse where the Horse Artillery had bivouacked the night before, and joined Wright with six guns, three of Mc-Gregor's, one of Breathed's, and Phelps' section of Moorman's Battery.

It was supposed that the force of the enemy some 1,200 yards north of Wright possessed no guns. As there was little room for the movement of artillery, Beckham was able to bring but four pieces into action in support of Wright's attack. The infantry assailed the enemy with great fury, and together with the fire of Mc-Gregor's and Moorman's four guns scattered the more advanced Federals and drove them back upon their works from which two well-masked batteries at once opened a destructive fire. Beckham now shifted the fire of his guns upon the hostile artillery and engaged it in a duel for nearly an hour in which the Federal guns had the advantage of position. But as Wright's advance ceased, the fire of the enemy's guns slackened and Beckham was ordered to withdraw his guns.

The officers and men of the Horse Artillery engaged in the duel with the two Federal batteries subsequently declared this affair to be one of the hottest they had ever participated in. It is certain that Beckham's gunners were severely punished. One piece of McGregor's Battery under Lieut. Burwell had every cannoneer wounded but one, and another piece of the same battery was struck by a shell. Beckham's loss was 1 officer, Lieut.

Burwell, and 2 men killed, 5 men wounded, 3 horses and 1 piece disabled. Lieuts. Burwell, Ford, and Wigfall were especially gallant in their conduct.

While Beckham was engaged at the furnace, Breathed, who had accompanied Fitz Lee's Brigade on a reconnaissance of the enemy's right, had been engaged with the enemy occupying Talley's farm. Unopposed by artillery he had moved up with two rifled pieces to within a few hundred yards of a heavy mass of infantry and without loss to his own battery killed and wounded probably 100 of the enemy, driving them to the cover of their works.

Meantime, McLaws had been checked on the right and it was reported that the enemy was advancing in strength along the Mine Road. Kershaw was now extended beyond Semmes' left and Wilcox with Lewis' and Huger's batteries came up on McLaws' right and occupied the rifle pits running from Banks' Ford to the Mine Road. Lewis' Battery from a position near the turnpike at once engaged the enemy's batteries, which soon ceased firing.

McLaws and Anderson had been ordered to advance about 4 p. m. and pressed forward with energy, assisted by the fire of their own guns and Walker's Battalion under Pegram, which arrived later in the day. As the Federal troops moved back the whole Confederate line followed them closely to the new position in which they established themselves about a mile from Chancellorsville. "Here the enemy had assumed a position of great natural strength, surrounded on all sides by a dense forest, filled with tangled undergrowth, in the midst of which breastworks of logs had been constructed, with trees felled in front, so as to form an almost impenetrable abattis. His artillery swept the few narrow roads by which the position could be approached from the front, and commanded the adjacent woods."*

During the night the Confederates held a line from the Mine Road on the right to Welford's or Catherine

*Lee's Report.

Furnace on the left. Wilcox had been ordered to
Banks' Ford. Two regiments of cavalry held the River
Road while Stuart with the rest of Fitz Lee's Brigade
was on the extreme left near the furnace. McLaws'
Division bivouacked along the crest just east of Big
Meadow Swamp where the Mine Road and Turnpike
intersect, and Anderson continued the line to the left.
At 11 P. M. Wright returned to the Plank Road along
which Posey had pressed to within a short distance of
the enemy's works.

The Federal line extended from the Rappahannock
on the left to the vicinity of Wilderness Church, a point
two miles west of Chancellorsville, on the right. For
nearly the whole of that distance it ran through an almost impenetrable forest of scrubby oak and pine,
which had given to the region the name of the Wilderness. Beginning near Tabernacle Church on the east,
the forest extended over 10 miles westward and perhaps an equal distance southward from the Rappahannock. Once within the confines of this densely-wooded
region, in which there are few commanding eminences,
it was difficult to determine what was transpiring a few
yards away. The thoroughfares, if the crude roadways
penetrating the forest and connecting the various
portions of the Federal position could be so called, were
few in number, and the bordering woods which stood in
a sea of dense underbrush would hardly permit the
movement of foot troops through them. The movement of artillery was therefore restricted to the roads,
except when by great labor communications were cut
through the forest. While the abundant supply of
timber made the construction of breastworks for a defense a simple undertaking, every *débouché* from the
forest towards Fredericksburg, or the pike, the Plank
Road, the unfinished line of railway a mile south of
their junction, and the River Road, about two miles
north, was commanded from the Confederate position.
The position which Hooker had abandoned was one on
high ground, more or less open in front, over which an

army might move freely, maneuver and employ artillery to the best advantage.   In directing the retrograde movement, not only did Hooker shut his army up in the forest, thereby sacrificing all freedom of movement, but he at once destroyed confidence in him on the part of that army which he declared to be the finest on the planet.   Having advanced with high expectation of victory, his officers and men now found themselves preparing to fight a defensive battle behind breastworks, with no telling what odds against them.   The very nature of the country seemed to harmonize with the gloom of their suddenly downcast spirits.   Thus does the single act of a leader depress the *morale* of an entire army and change enthusiasm to despondency.

Within the Federal position were a number of clearings which Hooker's masses occupied, and in which his reserve artillery and trains were parked.   On the extreme right of his line and north of Chancellorsville a narrow expanse of open land extended from the neighborhood of Quisenberry's Mill near Ely's Ford on the Rapidan, along the road from that ford in a southwesterly direction, past the White House and the Bullock Road, terminating several hundred yards north of the Chancellorsville house.   The main clearing about the Chancellorsville house began at Mott's Run, followed the road in a narrow strip until within a few hundred yards of the house, and then opened out northward to the strip of woods separating it from the White House clearing, and southward for perhaps a half-mile, where it turned sharply to the west.   Narrowing towards the southwest corner half a mile below the Plank Road, the Chancellorsville clearing joined a smaller one about a mile from the Chancellorsville house, the latter embracing an eminence known as Hazel Grove, which lay on the north of Scott's Run.   Hazel Grove at this point was about three-fourths of a mile north of Catherine Furnace.   From the Chancellorsville house, the Plank Road ran almost due west past the Wilderness Church, at a distance of about two miles.   About the church spread out an irregular clearing for half a mile in all directions with its eastern edge not over a mile from the western limit of the Chancellorsville clearing on the Plank Road, and its southern boundary along Scott's Run less than half a mile from the Hazel Grove clearing. Near the church and on the road stood Dowdall's Tavern, occupied as a residence by Dr. Melzi Chancellor.

During the night of the 1st, Hooker's troops were disposed solely for purposes of defense. Meade with the 5th Corps held the left, covering the River and Mine roads and extending to the Rappahannock. On his right was Couch's, or the 2d Corps blocking the pike. Slocum with the 12th Corps occupied the lines east and south of the Chancellorsville clearing, while Sickles with the 3d Corps held those about Hazel Grove. On the extreme right, the 11th Corps under Howard occupied a line of hasty intrenchments running south of the road through the church or Dowdall clearing, westward as far as a small clearing known as Talley's farm. Strong outposts of infantry were thrown out into the woods, and the men worked steadily during the night throwing up intrenchments. Batteries were disposed so as to sweep every approach from the south, southeast, and southwest, and the line was held by no less than five muskets to every yard of parapet. The whole line, however, was six miles long from flank to flank, and in order to strengthen the defense, about 2 A. M., May 2, Hooker ordered Sedgwick to send the 1st Corps to Chancellorsville, although his corps commanders had declared their ability to hold their respective positions. Earlier in the night, a brigade of infantry and 34 guns, principally of the Horse Artillery, had been dispatched from Falmouth to Banks' Ford, this being the move of the enemy which had necessitated the return of Wilcox to that point.

Among the Federal leaders differences of opinion developed at a council of war held during the night. Some advised an immediate advance in accordance with the

original plan, and others a strictly defensive attitude.
Hooker, lacking the divine genius for war possessed by
Lee, decided upon the latter course, much to the disgust of his bolder lieutenants.   But in the conference
between Lee and Jackson as they sat upon the Federal
cracker boxes in the woods three miles down the Plank
Road, there was no conflict of views.   Jackson's reconnaissance of the Federal left had discovered it to be
all but impregnable, but Fitz Lee had found a weak
spot and reported through Stuart that Howard's right
on the Plank Road beyond the Wilderness Church was
completely in the air, protected by no natural obstacle.
Such breastsworks as there were in this quarter faced
south, and thus again had Hooker paid too much regard
to his map and too little to the topography of his position.

Jackson proposed to turn Hooker's right with the
2d Corps while Lee held his left in check with the divisions of Anderson and McLaws.   The plan was a bold
one, and violated the first principle of war.   With less
than 42,000 muskets, Lee was in the presence of 70,000.
To divide his army in such circumstances was indeed
hazardous, but the very audacity of the maneuver, if it
could be executed with secrecy and dispatch, was a
guarantee of success, and Jackson was directed to carry
it out.

CHAPTER XXV

ORDERS for the movement of the 2d Corps, which had bivouacked along the Plank Road, were at once given. Rodes' Division was to lead, followed in order by Colston's and A. P. Hill's divisions. Alexander's Battalion was directed to accompany Jackson's column. About 6 A. M., or one hour after sunrise, the column took up the march. Manly's and McCarthy's batteries of Cabell's Battalion, under Maj. Hamilton, soon relieved the batteries of Walker's Battalion, which Maj. Pegram had taken into action about 6:30 A. M. on Anderson's right. Pegram had been ordered to advance as many rifled pieces as possible along the turnpike and shell the enemy's infantry behind their works in the woods. While placing his batteries in position two Federal batteries opened a brisk fire upon them. In the long-range duel which ensued for 20 minutes or more, McGraw's Purcell, and Brunson's batteries, and a section of the Letcher Battery, only were engaged, while some of the guns of these batteries were directed by Pegram to fire only upon the woods. Soon reporting the cannonade to be but a waste of ammunition, Pegram was ordered by Gen. Heth, who commanded at this point, to withdraw, whereupon the battalion followed Jackson's column already under way. McGraw's Battery had suffered heavily from the explosion of a number of caissons.

Maj. Hardaway was placed in command of the artillery from the Plank Road to Mine Creek near the furnace. Including Jordan's Battery of Alexander's Battalion, he had but eight pieces at his disposal. Ordering Jordan's Battery over from its position left of the turnpike, he placed one rifle and one Napoleon so as to sweep the Plank Road, two howitzers 120 yards to their

left, commanding a woods road leading from Chancellorsville, and the others at intervals of about 400 yards
along the Mine Road commanding the ravines leading
into Mine Creek.*

Maj. Hamilton commanded the artillery along the
turnpike, consisting of only two batteries, while Maj.
Garnett exercised general supervision over the battalion
distributed between Wilcox at Banks' Ford and Mc-
Laws.

Cols. Alexander and Brown joined the extreme rear
of Jackson's column at the intersection of the Plank
and Mine roads near the furnace about 10 A. M. With
the exception of Breathed's and Moorman's horse batteries, the artillery battalions followed their respective
divisions, while the reserve battalions and trains brought
up the rear.

One again pauses to note how valuable to Lee would
have been a strong reserve force of artillery at this time.
With McLaws and Anderson, and spread over a front
of seven or eight miles, were not over 32 guns. Had Lee
had the equivalent of Longstreet's two battalions of 32
guns, he could have retained both Alexander's and
Brown's corps reserve battalions to strengthen the attenuated line which McLaws and Anderson held, thus
overcoming in a measure the deficiency in the number of
muskets. It was for just such purposes that the reserve
battalions of his army were created, but Lee was robbed
of the benefits which he had a right to expect from them
by the absence of part of his artillery from the main field
of operations.

Jackson's column consisted of three divisions of
infantry, or 70 regiments, 4 regiments of cavalry of
Fitz Lee's Brigade under Stuart himself, the artillery
battalions of Brown, 4 batteries present,† Walker's Battalion of 5 batteries, Jones' of 4, McIntosh's of 4, or

---

*The Mine Creek and Mine Road here referred to are in the neighborhood of
the furnace and northeast thereof, and not generally shown on the maps. The
Mine Road connected the furnace with the Plank Road. Mine Creek runs north
from Lewis' Creek almost to Chancellorsville.

†Graham's or the 1st Rockbridge Battery was left with Early and Brooke's
with Hardaway.

17 batteries of the 2d Corps, 3½ batteries of Alexander's Battalion of the 1st Corps, and Beckham's 2½ horse batteries.* Thus exclusive of the Horse Artillery there were under Crutchfield's command as Chief of Artillery 20½ batteries with about 80 guns.

Turning to the left from the Plank Road about half a mile in rear of Anderson's line, Jackson led his column by the Mine Road to Catherine Furnace through the dense forest south of Chancellorsville. While his column was moving off to the west, the 10,000 Confederates which Lee held opposite the Federal left kept up a brisk demonstration, Hardaway's and Hamilton's guns maintaining an active fire in order to divert the enemy's attention. But as early as 8 A. M. Birney, from his commanding position at Hazel Grove, looking down the valley of Lewis Creek, had detected Jackson's column and reported it to Sickles, and the latter in turn to Hooker. At the furnace the road turned due south from the direction of Jackson's march, and from the fact that trains were visible in rear of the column Hooker at once concluded that Lee's army was retreating towards Gordonsville. Moving on a mile or more to the south the Confederate column turned westward, crossed the Brock Road after following it a short way southward and then moved north by way of a woods road over which a resident of the section led the way to the Orange Plank Road, about four miles west of Chancellorsville. Meanwhile, Stuart guarded the flank of the column, the head of which advanced at the rate of only about 2½ miles and the rear about 1½, in spite of all efforts to press on more rapidly. The whole column was perhaps ten miles in length, of which the infantry occupied only six miles, the artillery and ammunition trains the rest.

As the long column continued to file by the furnace, Birney secured permission to open with Clark's rifled battery at Hazel Grove, the range being about 1,600 yards. A few shots dispersed the troops in sight, and

*Hart's Battery was with Hampton's Brigade and not present during the campaign.

caused the column to seek another route further to the south, out of reach of the Federal guns and out of sight of Hazel Grove. About noon, Berdan's sharpshooters were thrown forward by Sickles and advanced towards the furnace, and soon Birney's Division followed by Whipple's moved out from Hazel Grove. While Anderson from his position astride the Plank Road engaged the left of this force, a part of Birney's Division pressed on down the Furnace Road, actually reaching the unfinished railroad, thus threatening to cut Lee's army in two. Sickles' men had actually captured the greater part of the 3d Georgia Regiment, acting as rear guard for Jackson's train, and were pressing rapidly down the Furnace Road when Col. Brown, whose battalion was passing nearby, threw one of his batteries into action near the Welford house and drove the more advanced skirmishers and a Federal battery back. Entirely unsupported in this position except by a few of the Georgia infantrymen, who had escaped capture, Brown with a single battery had rendered a most valuable service. Had Sickles' men reached the trains, the success of the whole movement might have been endangered. But, while single-handed Brown held the enemy at bay, Archer's and Thomas' brigades rapidly retraced their steps from the rear of the column and saved the situation. Meanwhile Hardaway had brought up a howitzer to the support of Anderson's extreme left, and together with the infantry succeeded in checking the left of Sickles' column. He then brought Jordan's Battery over to Anderson's left and soon the enemy gave up the attack. Archer's and Thomas' brigades and Brown's Battalion after remaining in observation for an hour or more continued their march, but failed to overtake the column until after nightfall.

Henderson, Alexander, and others state that Jackson was responsible for the timely action which Col. Brown took with his guns near the furnace, but no authority is to be found for such a belief. Brown's Battalion happened to be a part of Jackson's force and this fact alone probably gave rise to the assertion that its commander was acting under the direct orders of the corps commander. That such was the case seems obviously incorrect, for Jackson was at least ten miles from the Welford house when Sickles commenced his attack, and in the short interval of time between the advance of Berdan's men which commenced about 11 A. M., and the moment when Brown threw his battery into action at noon, it would have been quite impossible to communicate by courier with Jackson. There were no field wires connecting the head and rear of the column. To Col. Brown alone seems to belong the credit. Yet, after all, he simply performed the duty which was his, for he had been ordered to join the rear of the column as it filed past a stated point. Upon him, therefore, fell the responsibility of the artillery commander of the rear guard. Alexander states that Archer and Thomas retraced their steps without orders. If Jackson did not send them back, he certainly did not direct Brown, unsupported, to oppose the enemy.

Between 1 and 2 P. M., Jackson arrived at a point on the Orange Plank Road, about two miles south of the Talley farm, where he met Gen. Fitz Lee, who took him to the top of the elevation at Burton farm. From this point he secured a perfect view of the position of the enemy's 11th Corps at the Dowdall clearing, some two miles along the road to the east. Most of Howard's troops were in sight at the Dowdall and Talley farms, and some of those at the Hawkins farm half a mile north of the Wilderness Church, but a part of Devens' Division was concealed in the woods, and the whole of Von Gilsa's Brigade which formed the extreme Federal right was in the woods north of the pike and half a mile west of the Talley house. But two guns commanded the road. The position of Von Gilsa was not discovered until the middle of the afternoon when a party of cavalry drew his fire.

Until now, it had been Jackson's intention to attack that part of the enemy's line between the Dowdall and the Talley farms, by way of the Plank Road, but his personal reconnaissance led to a change of plans. Ordering the Stonewall Brigade under Paxton to advance along the Orange Plank Road to within 1½ miles of the Wilderness Church, and the four regiments of cavalry under Fitz Lee to occupy the Burton farm on the same road, he led his column northward to the Luckett farm on the turnpike, two miles west of Dowdall Tavern, where Howard's headquarters were located.

It was about 4 P. M. when Rodes' Division at the head of Jackson's column began its deployment on both sides of the turnpike, and it was after 5 P. M. when eight of the twelve Confederate brigades had formed in two lines, Rodes' four in front, Colston's four a hundred yards behind. A. P. Hill's Division was designated for the third line. Only a part of this division was deployed, the rest in column following the road. The attacking column now presented a front of two miles, extending a mile or more north of the pike and to the rear of the 11th Corps, which still faced south. A heavy skirmish line led by Cols. Willis and Blackford was thrown out 400 yards to the front by Rodes, and Breathed with two Napoleons on the road accompanied the first line, closely followed by his other section. Behind Breathed, McGregor's Battery and Phelps' section of Moorman's Battery occupied the road, there being space only for the deployment of two pieces at a time. The Horse Artillery under Beckham, consisting of 2½ batteries, had joined the head of Jackson's column when it reached the Orange Plank Road about noon.

In about 1½ hours, notwithstanding the dense woods, the Confederate divisions were deployed. Jackson was determined that the lines should move forward in good order and minute instructions had been given every brigade commander, while staff officers were detailed to maintain the general direction and alignment. The three lines were to move forward simultaneously through the woods without pausing until the open hill in the Talley clearing about 1,000 yards eastward was carried. If, after the seizure of this hill which commanded the ridge running north from the road at Dowdall's Tavern, the Federals showed a determined front in their secondary position, Rodes was to halt under cover until Beckham's batteries could dislodge them. But under no other circumstances was a halt to be called. A regiment of the first line was detailed to guard the left flank and Ransom's Brigade to guard the right. The field hospital was established at the Wilderness Tavern in the rear and Crutchfield was already assembling some of his artillery in the open spaces thereabout preparatory to moving forward when needed.

It has frequently been stated that the avalanche which fell upon Hooker's right flank May 2 was entirely unsuspected, and even Henderson fell into this error.* But nothing is further from the truth, nor was the much maligned 11th Corps at fault for the disaster which befell Hooker's right. No troops in the same circumstances could have opposed a firmer resistance to Jackson's immense column. The fault was with those higher up and not with the gallant German troops which received the shock of the blow. One would suppose from the ordinary account of the battle of Chancellorsville that these men alone failed Hooker. But as a matter of fact, their conduct in the main was superb, and it was Hooker who failed them. He and others cast the obloquy of defeat upon innocent shoulders in order to excuse their own defaults. Hooker had made up his mind that Lee was retreating in spite of many warnings of the impending attack on the right. Sickles was positive that such was the case, and repeatedly represented that he was actually among the fleeing foe. So firmly had the belief taken root that Howard's supports were withdrawn to assist Sickles on his wild-goose chase to the south, at the very instant Jackson was massing his column of attack three miles to the north and west. Hooker's conduct on May 2 is a military anomaly. It would almost seem that his powers of reason left him the

*See p. 539, Henderson's *Life of Jackson*.

minute he established his headquarters in the Chancellorsville house. With Anderson and McLaws thundering away on his left, with Early firmly planted before
Sedgwick at Fredericksburg, and with Wilcox still holding the crossing at Banks' Ford, yet, he was convinced
that the Army of Northern Virginia was retreating to
Gordonsville or some other point.

If Lee had undertaken to withdraw his army, surely
he would not have retreated squarely across the Federal
front. In the nature of things, his trains would have
moved more to the rear and the troops farthest from
the point upon which his army was to fall back would
have moved off first. With Gordonsville as the point of
concentration, Early, then Wilcox, would have receded
before the enemy, then McLaws and Anderson in turn.
Nor would every available Confederate gun on
Hooker's left have been kept continuously in action to
tempt Hooker to move out and interfere with the withdrawal. No. Hooker's wish on this occasion was father
to the thought, and Sickles by his absurd reports did
much to create the delusion. In the morning the Federal commander had ridden his lines from left to right
and upon his return to headquarters had, at 9:30 A. M.,
cautioned both Howard and Slocum to beware of a
movement of the enemy to their right, a movement which
he had good reason to suspect. This warning on the
part of Hooker does not excuse him, but all the more is
he guilty of a gross neglect in allowing Barlow's Division, or Howard's reserve, to be withdrawn in favor
of Sickles later in the day. The minute a more-
favorable interpretation of the enemy's movement was
advanced, Hooker seemingly forgot all about the danger
of his right, and supinely waited for the outcome of
Sickles' movement. Instead of cautioning Howard
and Slocum he should have himself directed the necessary dispositions to counteract the threatened danger.

But in the 11th Corps the danger was not overlooked.
Hooker's order of the morning had been received and
opened by Gen. Carl Schurz, who had temporarily as-

sumed command, while Howard was resting. Schurz, convinced that an attack would be made from the west, urged Howard to allow him to withdraw Devens' Division and part of his own from the Talley and Hawkins farms and the woods beyond, and place them in a strong position behind Hunting Run, east of the junction of the Orange Plank Road from the southwest and the turnpike from the west, the new line facing directly to the west. From the proposed position, which was one of great strength, the artillery would have a clear field of fire across the Hawkins and Talley clearings, and command both roads over which the enemy could attack. But Howard saw no need of any change, and the only one that was made by Schurz was of his own volition when he changed the front of some of his regiments at the Hawkins farm to the west. These troops about 11 A. M. threw up a line of shallow rifle pits, but Devens did nothing. And in spite of Hooker's order, Warren, his Chief Engineer, although apprised of the movement of a heavy column past the furnace, did not visit the right, a fact which testifies to the views at headquarters.

Although nothing of moment was done by Howard, the new commander of the 11th Corps, to ward off the threatened danger, the feeling was more or less general among his subordinate officers that something momentous was impending. These men had had experience in the Valley with Jackson, and agreed among themselves that "it was never too late for him to turn." Until they learned that he was positively placed it was their habit to look for him in the most unlikely quarter. They seemed to feel the spell of the forest, the mystery of its forbidding silence, and as the day wore on even the men of the Corps began to believe that danger was lurking in the impenetrable fastness which closed in upon them from all sides. Early in the morning a field-officer in charge of a portion of the picket line had heard the rumble of a large number of wheels past his front to the west and upon reporting the fact was told that his

fears were unduly aroused. At 10 A. M. other officers
actually observed troops moving towards the right, and
later on, Col. Friend, the officer of the day of Devens'
Division, reported a movement of the enemy to the
right rear, but each report was discredited and made
light of by Howard, and Friend was actually rebuked
and warned not to bring on a panic by circulating such
a tale. More than ever confirmed in his views by the
occurrences of the morning, Gen. Schurz, who had,
meanwhile, himself observed the enemy marching in a
southwesterly direction, ordered Capt. Hubert Dilger
to examine the rear of the line, with a view to meeting
an attack from that direction. Dilger, who commanded
an Ohio Battery attached to Schurz's Division, had been
an officer in the German Horse Artillery, resigning to
take part in the American Civil War. He was not only
a trained soldier and regarded as one of the best artillery
officers in the Army, but his veteran battery was considered to be the best in the 11th Corps.

Early in the afternoon, accompanied by a single
orderly, the young artilleryman set out to reconnoiter
the terrain in his rear and determine for himself the condition of affairs. Passing westward along the pike, he
was met and urged by Gen. Von Gilsa not to proceed
further lest he should be captured. Von Gilsa was absolutely satisfied that the enemy was massing a large
force down the road beyond his brigade and had sent
numerous reports to that effect to Devens. But Dilger
kept on for about a mile when he ran into Rodes' men
deploying north of the Luckett farm. Cut off from the
road by a body of cavalry and pursued northward for
some distance, he finally succeeded in eluding his
enemies in the woods, and reached the United States
Ford Road, which he followed direct to Hooker's headquarters at Chancellorsville. It was perhaps 4 P. M.
when Dilger informed a member of the commanding
general's staff of what he had seen only to be insulted
for bothering superiors with "such a yarn." Immediately he galloped back to the headquarters of the

11th Corps, where he was in effect reprimanded for his trouble and assured in no uncertain terms that Lee was in full retreat towards the south with Sickles on his heels! But Dilger, confident that the storm would soon burst, returned with haste to his battery near the church, placed his guns in the best possible position, and even refused to allow his teams to be taken to water. Hardly had his dispositions been made when the distant popping of Rodes' skirmishers announced the advance of the enemy.

The foregoing are but a few instances of personal knowledge on the part of Howard's officers of the presence of the enemy on their right and rear. Gen. Devens, who commanded the extreme right, and who, like Howard, was also a newcomer in the Corps, was repeatedly informed by field officers of the fact, but even after the pickets were attacked, when there was time to change front, Devens refused to do so.*

While the eager but silent Confederates were being deployed, their quick intelligence having already grasped the situation, Jackson sat astride "Little Sorrel" on the road. With his old slouch hat pulled well forward and his lips tightly compressed, he calmly but impatiently awaited the completion of the dispositions for advance. Who shall know what were his feelings during this, the supreme hour of his life? Certainly few soldiers since the world began have been so situated. Less than half a mile before him lay the vulnerable flank of his enemy entirely unprepared to meet the rush of his battalions. It almost seemed that Fame, even had she never favored him before, had already spread over his shoulders the cloak of immortality! With that supreme confidence in himself and a confidence in his men which few leaders have ever experienced in so high a degree, the hawk of the Valley was deliberately spreading his pinions for the sudden swoop. On the familiar faces of his leaders, Jackson

*See Chapter VI entitled "Warnings of Danger Unheeded," in a remarkably accurate and able work on the battle of Chancellorsville, by Lieut.-Col. A. C. Hamlin.

discovered only the expression which gladdened his heart and forbade thought of failure. There were Rodes and Colston in front, whom he had tutored in the game of war, and led to manhood's estate, and in their divisions were not less than 200 brigade, regimental, battalion and company leaders whom he had drilled upon the parade ground at Lexington for this, the greatest maneuver of his life. On his right at the head of the leading regiment of cavalry was the dashing Munford, and in his rear the brilliant Crutch-field in command of the Artillery, both of whom had been his pupils, then associates, in the Faculty of Virginia's great School of Arms. Small wonder was it that the inspiration which animated the soul of the chieftain penetrated to the very core of his army. With these facts in mind, one may readily understand Jackson's remark as he set his column in motion in the morning: "The Virginia Military Institute will be heard from to-day."*

At 5 o'clock Jackson said to Rodes, "Are you ready?" "Yes," replied Rodes, who then nodded to the commander of the skirmish line. At 5:15 P. M. the signal for the general advance was given and almost immediately Willis' skirmishers struck the Federal pickets along the pike, who fell back, giving the alarm. The Confederate bugles rang out all along the advancing line like the cry of wild fowl in the teeth of a gale. On past the foremost skirmishers dashed Breathed with the leading section of his battery, and, unlimbering on the pike, from each of his two guns was fired a round of solid shot, which raked the roadway and, bounding on, fell in the front yard of the Talley house, a mile distant,

---

*In addition to the officers named many other prominent actors in the battle of Chancellorsville had been cadets under Jackson. Gen. James H. Lane; Maj. T. S. Tosh, Colston's Adjutant-General; Col. Thomas H. Carter, Chief of Artillery of Rodes' Division; Capt. H. E. Whiting, A. A. G., Rodes' Division; Col. John M. Brockenbrough, commanding Heth's Brigade; Col. R. M. Mayo, 47th Virginia; Col. Frank Mallory, 55th Virginia; and Lieut.-Col. T. W. Cox, Lieut.-Col. E. P. Taylor, 22d Virginia Battalion; Gen. R. Lindsay Walker, Chief of Artillery, A. P. Hill's Division; Col. Briscoe G. Baldwin, Chief of Ordnance, A. N. V.; Col. R. W. Carter, 1st Virginia Cavalry; Col. Thomas H. Owen, 3d Virginia Cavalry; and Col. W. H. Payne, 4th Virginia Cavalry, were among the graduates of the Institute. Thus it is seen that all four of Jackson's cavalry regiments, two of his divisions, and two battalions of his artillery were commanded by former pupils, besides many batteries and regiments.

where Devens was resting. But still Devens refused to allow his division to change front. In the meantime, Rodes' line, rushing forward like a tornado, had swept all before it and captured the two guns of Dieckmann's Battery, which were in position on the pike, after they had fired but a few rounds. Von Gilsa's Brigade in the woods to the north was almost immediately overlapped, and Devens' men facing south along the pike were subjected to a whirlwind of musketry fire from flank and rear as they finally endeavored to change front. A few of the latter crossed the road and joined Von Gilsa's men, and together, though not over 1,000 in number, they checked Rodes' advance until Colston's line pressed forward and overbore them. Retreating after firing three volleys, the wreck of Von Gilsa's Brigade fell back upon a Federal regiment forming line some 400 yards to the rear. Upon the new line, Breathed poured a deliberate fire of canister at close range, while two Confederate brigades assailed it, the men firing as they trotted forward. In ten minutes the survivors, after losing a great number of officers and men, were swept back 500 yards to the line forming in front of the Talley house, consisting of portions of Von Gilsa's and Devens' men. All about them the Confederate Infantry were now swarming, while Breathed on the pike plied his guns with renewed vigor. It was no longer a fight but a massacre. Musketry fire and canister literally swept the brave Federals from their feet, and soon bore them back towards the church where Schurz had formed his division in a secondary line of defense. A large number of Devens' men rushed through Schurz's line, intermingled with two of his veteran regiments in the act of changing front, and carried them on down the pike to the Dowdall Tavern, where the panic-stricken mob was met by Howard. Seizing the colors of one of the broken regiments, the Corps Commander sought to check the fleeing men. Many kept on while others rallied on Schurz's and Buschbeck's lines and continued in the fight.

In 30 minutes Jackson had swept Devens' Division
of 4,000 men from his path, and all but destroyed it, and
before 6 P. M. he had seized the Talley plateau. But his
attack had in part miscarried, for Colquitt, who commanded Rodes' right brigade, in spite of the most
positive orders to press forward had delayed to investigate a supposed threat to his flank and was not in sight
when Jackson reached the Talley house. Instead of
having reached Dowdall's Tavern as he had been expected to do, he had changed front to the south just before reaching the Burton farm. Not only had he failed
to move forward himself, but having the right of way
he had blocked the Stonewall Brigade and Fitz Lee's
Cavalry on the Plank Road and brought Ramseur's Brigade in his rear to a standstill. And so, by an act of
singular stupidity, Colquitt held 17 regiments, including
all the cavalry, out of action for 45 minutes. Had
Colquitt pressed on and allowed Fitz Lee and Paxton
to do the same, it is doubtful if Schurz could have
formed to retard Jackson's advance, for the Stonewall
Brigade and the cavalry would have debouched from
the woods on the immediate flank of the position in
which he subsequently resisted Jackson's advance long
enough to allow Buschbeck to form in his rear.

The Confederates in their advance, after taking
Dieckmann's two guns, had, fortunately for them, encountered very little artillery. When the attack commenced Dilger's Battery and a part of Weidrick's
occupied a position on a slight rise abreast of the church,
and facing northwest had done what they could to support Von Gilsa's men as the enemy crossed the Hawkins
farm. Wheeler's Reserve Battery in their rear also
came into action and fired over the heads of the infantry
upon the enemy half a mile distant. Dilger's conduct
throughout was heroic and though scarcely mentioned
in the accounts of the battle, his services would have won
for him from a Napoleon instant promotion on the field.
But Dilger was a German of the despised 11th Corps,
and remained a captain to the end of the war, though
recommended many times for promotion.

Shortly after the attack commenced he moved his battery to the western edge of the Dowdall clearing near the road and, leaving the way open, as soon as Devens' men rushed by, opened fire with his six pieces upon the enemy as they cleared the woods 1,000 yards away. In a few minutes Hill's Battery of 3-inch Rodman rifles swung into action on Dilger's left and opened on the Confederate line advancing across the Talley fields south of the pike. Weidrick's and Wheeler's batteries from their positions were unable to fire down the pike, so for more than 30 minutes Dilger, single-handed, maintained his position, changing from shell to charges and double charges of canister, as the enemy crept forward through the little thickets in his front. Hill's Battery, entirely without canister, had been sent to the rear. Finally, after staying the advance along the road for some time, Dilger, not wishing to sacrifice his guns, reluctantly gave the order to retire, but too late to save the entire battery, for one piece, which had lost nearly all its horses, had to be abandoned after a vain attempt to drag it to the rear by hand. Some time before Dilger withdrew, Weidrick's Battery had also been driven from its second position south of the Dowdall house and in front of Buschbeck, by the Confederate skirmishers passing around his flank below the road, and two of its pieces had been captured, all of the horses of one and the cannoneers of the other having been wounded. All of the Reserve Artillery had been ordered to retire sometime previously, as there was no opportunity to use it in the narrow space in rear of the line of rifle pits in the woods. Up to this time the Confederates had taken eight pieces of ordnance and lost none. Breathed's and McGregor's batteries had kept up with the infantry, seizing every available position from which to fire upon the Federals, paying particular attention to their batteries. Beckham had reaped a rich reward for his services. From the first salvo of his guns the daring of the horse batteries had attracted the attention of Jackson. As Breathed would dash forward, often in advance of the infantry, Lieut. Johnston with his rear section continued the fire soon in turn to limber up and gallop to the first position beyond Breathed, while Beckham, always in the lead, encouraged the gunners by his example. The strain upon the men and horses was tremendous, but Moorman relieved them from time to time by sending up his own cannoneers for the use of whose guns no space was available, to take the place of the exhausted men of the more advanced batteries. Meeting the young major in the road at the first pause in the advance of the infantry, the great leader leaned forward on his horse and extended his hand to Beckham saying, as he passed, "Young man, I congratulate you." Thus did the successor of the heroic and lamented Pelham lead the Horse Artillery in the first great battle in which he commanded it. Beckham was no doubt the last one to grasp the hand of Jackson before it hung limp and all but lifeless by his side.

While Dilger remained in his isolated and exposed position near the road, maintaining the fire of his single piece against Breathed's four guns and the musketry of the approaching infantry, he was all but captured by the latter. Thrown heavily to the ground by the fall of his wounded horse, a number of the enemy were almost upon him when he succeeded in extricating himself and took to his heels. Running about 100 yards down the pike before his pursuers, he was unexpectedly succoured by a little boy friend named Ackley, who, missing his devoted companion from the battery as it retired, had ridden to the front under fire in search of him. Springing from his horse and assisting Dilger to the saddle, together they escaped on the single mount. Dilger overtook the remains of his battery in rear of Bartow's incomplete line of rifle pits, and ordering his lieutenant to retire with four pieces he kept the other on the road in the gap in the line of intrenchments, and again opened rapid fire to the front. Meanwhile, Buschbeck had occupied the line of pits constructed in the morning by Barlow, and upon which Schurz now fell back partly under cover of Dilger's single piece.

The exploits of Capt. Dilger have been gone into in some detail for a dual reason. First to illustrate the power which a bold battery commander holds in his hand, and the influence which even a single piece well handled may exert in battle, and in the second place to show that the Federal gunner wore the same stripe as his Southern brethren whose deeds are recounted in these pages. We read much of Hunt, of Ricketts, of Griffin, of Hazlett, of Greble, and of other gallant Federal artillerymen, but seldom do we find mention of "Leather-breeches" Dilger, the soldier of fortune from Baden, who was the peer of the best of them. And as for his little friend Ackley, there are no words in which to commend adequately his act of heroism. It is such incidents as that of Dilger and the boy that make war live in story and in song when the more formal record of history is forgotten.

Here it should be stated that modern developments have by no means precluded the element of individualism among field gunners. Indeed, with the increased power and efficiency of the modern weapon, greater opportunities for the individual prowess of a subordinate will present themselves. If with a muzzle-loading piece capable of firing under extraordinary circumstances from three to four rounds a minute, a battery or platoon commander was able to stay the advance, check the attack, and even turn the assault of an entire army into a rout, surely with the modern field gun the effect of which is equivalent to that of many of the earlier ones, the results which one may expect from artillery officers of ready perception, consummate skill, and high courage, cannot be limited. Nor is this expectation a problematical one. In the battle of Motienling, a brave Japanese officer with a battery of mountain guns, secured a victory when the issue was at least doubtful. And there were numerous other instances in Manchuria where artillery subalterns, acting solely upon their own initiative, altered the complexion of a battle.

The shallow line of intrenchments held by Buschbeck
ran just west of the woods bordering the Dowdall clearing on the east, and extended some 1,000 yards north
well into the forest, and less than half that distance south
of the road.   In the latter quarter the line was held by
three regiments of Steinwehr's Division and a few of Devens' and Schurz's men, while that part of the line north
of the road from left to right was defended by three regiments of Steinwehr's Division, a mingled mass of
Devens' and Schurz's men, two more regiments of Steinwehr's Division at the edge of the woods, and two unbroken regiments of Schurz's Division within the woods.
Behind the extreme right another regiment was held in
reserve.   Dilger's single gun on the road was the only
piece of artillery present.   Of Howard's entire corps of
11,000 men, less than 5,000 remained on the Buschbeck
line.   Barlow's Brigade was three miles away at the
furnace, 1,500 men killed and wounded lay upon the
field, about 1,000 had been captured, and perhaps 2,000
had fled towards Chancellorsville.   Yet from three successive positions Jackson had been resisted by these
troops for over an hour without the slightest aid from
without the Corps.   In fact, Hooker had just learned
of the disaster which had befallen Howard.

The line of intrenchments commenced by Barlow in
the morning before he was called away was so shallow
that it afforded only slight shelter for the defenders
when kneeling.   In front from the ravine south of
Dowdall's house well into the woods north of the Hawkins farm and beyond their right, the dense Confederate line, from four to eight men deep, surged like a
tidal wave of bayonets.   Along the road and about the
Talley house Breathed's and McGregor's batteries were
in action and behind them glistened the forest of
bayonets of A. P. Hill's Division in the third line.   Fitz
Lee, Paxton, Colquitt and Ramseur were now pouring
out of the woods into the Plank Road half a mile away
and hurrying forward to the battlefield.

Buschbeck's men resisted Jackson's third assault for perhaps 20 minutes and not until the flanks were turned by Iverson's and Nichols' brigades on the right and Colquitt's and Ramseur's on the left and the enfilading fire from both directions reached their center did they retire. It was about 7:15 P. M. when the Federal regiments in perfect order moved slowly back within the edge of the woods where well under control they were again halted to check pursuit. Dilger deliberately moved his piece down the road, firing both canister and solid shot as he retired, Gen. Howard and Schurz mingling with and encouraging the gunners.

The effort to force the Buschbeck line broke the impetus of Jackson's attack. So commingled had the Confederate divisions, brigades, regiments and even companies become, that a halt was declared by Gen. Colston to be a necessary evil, for the men had become much disorganized during the rapid advance through the dense thickets and it would have been impossible to lead them farther in the gathering dusk. But whether necessary or not, the delay which Jackson reluctantly consented to seems now to have been a fatal one, for the White House was but 2,000 yards along the Bullock Road in his front, and the only force to oppose his advance in that direction was some 1,200 men of Schurz's Division, which had fallen back through the woods from the Hawkins farm and were halted on the dirt road, Buschbeck's regiment and Dilger having passed along the Plank Road to Fairview on the Chancellorsville plateau.

Confusion and dismay suddenly succeeded the utter peace which had reigned at Army Headquarters during the day. Hooker had been resting quietly on the veranda of the Chancellor house. Sickles and Pleasonton had long since disappeared in the forest and the 12th Corps was engaging Anderson and McLaws. There were hardly any troops in sight, for only a few reserve batteries, wagons, and ambulances remained on the Chancellorsville plateau. A desultory fire was to be heard to the eastward and in the south the sound from

Sickles' guns grew fainter and fainter. There was nothing, in fact, to indicate unusual activity in any quarter. Even Dilger had been driven off with his absurd yarn about the enemy before he could disturb the commanding general's peace of mind. Suddenly about 6:30 P. M., however, the heavy roar of a cannonade was heard in the west, and while Hooker and his military family were speculating on what this might mean, one of the officers detected Howard's fugitives rushing up the Plank Road. "My God, here they come!" he cried. Springing upon his horse and riding rapidly along the road, Hooker met the panic-stricken fugitives inextricably mingled with wagons, ambulances, pack-mules, caissons, and the other impedimenta of an army. "The whole of the right wing has been overwhelmed by Stonewall Jackson and is falling back in disorder upon Chancellorsville," the stragglers cried as they fled by.

Hooker's situation was a deplorable one, but he had no one to blame but himself. For years an effort was made to saddle the blame on the 11th Corps, the men of which in the face of an overwhelming force on their flank and rear had, by their stubborn resistance alone, disorganized the attacking column and checked it long enough for night to fall and prevent Jackson from reaping the fruits of victory.

The Federal center was held by only two brigades of the 12th Corps at the Fairview Cemetery, while the works at Hazel Grove, the key-point of Hooker's whole line, were occupied by a small force of artillery and some trains. Couch and Meade were fully occupied by McLaws and Anderson, who increased the activity of their demonstrations upon hearing Jackson's guns. Sickles with the 3d Corps had wandered off in the forest and was all but cut off from the Army, while the line of retreat to United States Ford and the Bullock Road to the White House were entirely unprotected. But, while Jackson was urging A. P. Hill's Division forward to resume the advance along the Bullock Road,

and chafing at the necessary delay caused by the disorganization of Rodes' and Colston's divisions which
had become mingled and were in great confusion in the
woods, Hooker found time to throw a small force across
the path of the Confederates. The only troops immediately at hand were those at Fairview, and those he
ordered to move forward rapidly and occupy the ground
Howard's men had abandoned, also sending word to
Sickles to retrace his steps in hot haste. Of course,
Berry and Hayes could not retake the lost ground, but
they did occupy a line in the woods in front of and below the Fairview position, and thus presented a front to
the Confederates behind which other troops soon formed
while the Federal artillery began to mass on the edge
of the plateau. Meanwhile, the general confusion
within the Federal position was increased by Hardaway's activity, whose guns from Anderson's left front
were hurling shell and solid shot into the trains on the
high ground at a range, however, which rendered accurate practice impossible.

When Jackson consented to the fatal halt, he had five
brigades of Rodes' and Colston's divisions intact near
the Wilderness Church. Rodes' Brigade, the foremost
of Rodes' Division, halted in the woods on the eastern
edge of the Dowdall farm, south of the road, while Colquitt's and Ramseur's brigades rested in the rear of the
Dowdall farm house. Paxton's Brigade was drawn up
in line north of the house, across the field in front of the
rifle pits. Iverson and Nichols had come to a standstill
in the woods on the north side of the road, and near the
log hut, where Colston was endeavoring to reform his
men. Stuart with the cavalry was near the church preparing to move with a small infantry support around
the Federal right. The command to halt was not heard
by the extreme right of Rodes' line, and several groups,
leaving the road to avoid the fire of Dilger's gun, pushed
slowly on through the woods to the south and soon ran
up against the log works in the woods of Williams' Division of the 12th Corps some distance in front of Fairview

Heights and held by three or four companies of a New York regiment. While the Confederates were demanding the surrender of Williams' men, a great battle, entirely mythical however, was occurring at Hazel Grove. It is mentioned with the sole purpose of contributing something to dispose of a fictitious artillery affair which has been accepted in good faith, even by such an eminent and usually accurate historian of the war as Col. Willam Allan, Jackson's Chief of Ordnance.*

Before moving out into the woods towards the furnace about noon, Sickles had left the three batteries of Whipple's Division in park under Capt. Huntington, the divisional chief of artillery, at Hazel Grove, and finding the country unsuitable for the use of cavalry, Gen. Pleasonton had also returned to that point with his regiments and Martin's Horse Battery about 6 P. M. Pleasonton, sublimely ignorant of all that was occurring within two miles of Hazel Grove, received orders from Sickles to dispatch a cavalry regiment to Howard at Dowdall's Tavern, and directed the 8th Pennsylvania Regiment to proceed to that point. As the regiment moved off to the northeast along a dirt road which connected Hazel Grove with the Plank Road a mile away, it was followed by the immense ammunition pack train of the 3d Corps under Col. Hall, who desired to return to Chancellorsville with the mules and ambulances of his column. Soon the cavalry regiment unexpectedly collided with some of the Confederates in the woods and was forced to cut its way through them to escape by the Plank Road, but the pack train stampeded to the rear and dashed pellmell through the batteries and cavalry which had remained at Hazel Grove. This was the first indication Pleasonton had of any trouble. Not a sound had disturbed his repose. The batteries were at once prepared for action and the troopers sprang to their horses. In a short while about 200 Confederates under Cols. Mercer and Winn wandered through the woods

*Chancellorsville, Hotchkiss-Allan, p. 52. Also see *The Campaigns of Stuart's Cavalry*, McClellan, p. 238.

to the western edge of the Hazel Grove clearing and began to fire upon the Federals. Whereupon Huntington's batteries opened upon them, as did Martin's under Pleasonton's direction, and soon drove the small force of surprised Confederates off. Pleasonton afterwards greatly exaggerated this accidental brush, claiming in effect that by his remarkable presence of mind and by assuming charge of the 30 or more guns at Hazel Grove, he had repulsed not less than 5,000 Confederate infantry! Huntington, who was not the least disturbed, and was really cool, handled his own batteries, however, and made no such extravagant claims, characterizing Pleasonton's account as an impertinent falsehood, which it was. In his excitement, Pleasonton also mistook Sickles' pack train as it dashed past for the routed 11th Corps, which at the time he did not know was routed! Pleasonton's brilliant and graphic report to Hooker and his subsequent account of the affair at Hazel Grove in which he claimed that he sent the Pennsylvania Regiment on a death charge to retard the masses of the enemy, while he personally directed the fire of his great battery of 22 pieces, are among the greatest pieces of fiction concerning the Civil War.* He even went so far as to explain the manner in which he employed the principal of ricochet of solid shot in sweeping the dense lines of the enemy from the field, thus catching the poor Confederates both "coming and going," as it were, on the rebound! Thus did he adopt that general principle of the equality of the angles of incidence and reflection to the fire of his guns! It was no doubt the intense concentration of his mental faculties upon this physical phenomenon that kept him in ignorance of what was really transpiring about him.

In the gathering gloom Berry and Hayes had formed in the woods at right angles to and north of the road, while Buschbeck's and Williams' brigades prolonged his line to the left and immediately in front of the Fair-

*See *Battles and Leaders*, Vol. III, p. 172, but also pp. 186-188; and the *Battle of Chancellorsville*, Hamlin, pp. 82-96.

view Cemetery. Not less than 3,000 men of the broken 11th Corps, including those of Buschbeck's intact brigade, rallied on the new line nearly two miles east of Dowdall's Tavern, and one and a half miles from the point where the Confederate advance was halted. Immediately upon learning of the rout of Howard's Corps, Capt. Best, Chief of Artillery of the 12th Corps, had occupied Fairview Cemetery with his own and some of the batteries of the 11th Corps, and was later joined by the indefatigable Dilger. In all Best massed 34 pieces in this position which completely dominated the Plank Road approach and the woods on both sides. Including the 22 pieces under Huntington and Pleasonton at Hazel Grove, a mile southeast of Fairview, to the support of which two of Sickles' infantry regiments had come up from the south, Jackson was now confronted by 56 guns in strong positions.

It was some time before A. P. Hill was ready to advance in spite of Jackson's exhortations to push on, and at last about 8 P. M., when Lane's Brigade was ready to resume the movement, an unfortunate incident occurred. About 6:30 P. M. Col. Crutchfield at the Wilderness Tavern had directed Maj. Pegram of Walker's Battalion to send two guns to Gen. Pender on the Plank Road and two to Gen. McGowan in the woods to the south, and about the same time Carter was ordered to lead the artillery column forward. Crutchfield, himself, taking a section of Napoleons and a Parrott from the King William Battery of Carter's Battalion, moved on to join the infantry behind which Carter was ordered to follow at a distance of half a mile. When Crutchfield reached a point about 1,200 yards from Fairview, for some unknown reason the three guns with him were opened upon the Federal artillery position, on which by this time 43 guns had been massed, whereupon six of Capt. Osborne's pieces replied. Lane, urged on by Jackson himself, had moved up to the rear of Crutchfield's guns when the rapid return fire of Osborne's artillery raked his column in the road and forced him to

seek cover in the woods to the left, where he remained
until Hill directed Crutchfield to cease firing. In the
meantime, under the hail of shell and canister from the
Federal guns the artillery horses of Carter's Battalion
in the road had become unmanageable, and were with
difficulty prevented from stampeding to the rear by the
personal efforts of Jackson, Colston and their staff
officers. The Federal fire ceased with that of Crutchfield's guns.

To fire upon the enemy, especially upon so formidable an array of hostile guns, in such circumstances was
a mistake which nothing can excuse. It was indeed
stirring up a hornets' nest. There is no question about
a mistake having been committed. The sole inquiry is,
who was to blame? Alexander, who was miles away in
the rear at the time, states that the error was due to
Crutchfield's partaking of Jackson's impetuosity. Perhaps so, but this statement in itself is not an illuminating
one. There is something so inconsistent in this affair
with our knowledge of Crutchfield's character, and especially his ability as an artillerist, that it is difficult to
believe he was entirely to blame for committing so
grievous an error. The reports throw very little light
upon the subject. Lane, who was actually among
Crutchfield's guns and suffered most from the enemy's
fire, stated in his reports that just as he was deploying
in the road, the enemy "opened a terrific artillery fire,
which was responded to by our batteries." Had Crutchfield been responsible for provoking the enemy's fire, it
seems certain Lane would have known who fired first and
attributed the blame to Crutchfield. On the contrary he
expressly declares that the Federals opened first.
Captain Osborne, however, states that the Confederate
battery fired first, and that its challenge was accepted
by two of his lieutenants. But Osborne was not himself responsible for the duel and was obviously only repeating what had been reported to him. When the men
of Rodes' and Colston's lines became mingled and disorganized, Rodes, after calling a halt in the woods, rode

forward to reconnoiter the front and satisfied himself
that there was no enemy between him and the Fairview
Heights. On his return he informed Col. Crutchfield,
then on the road with his three guns, of the result of his
reconnaissance "and he opened his batteries on that
point," wrote Rodes in his report. He also wrote that
"the enemy instantly responded by a most terrific fire,
which silenced our guns. It did but little execution on
the infantry, as it was mainly directed down the Plank
Road, which was unoccupied, except by our artillery."

The evidence of Lane, Osborne, and Rodes, suggests
that even if Crutchfield provoked the unfortunate duel
the information and advice of Rodes, the commander
of the advance line, had something to do with it. Unless Rodes desired some action on the part of his artillery
support, it is hardly probable that he would have so
promptly communicated the result of his personal reconnaissance to Crutchfield. It is unfortunate that the
latter, who was wounded within a short time, left no report. Had he done so, his almost inexplicable conduct
would no doubt have been accounted for. The writer
it loath to believe to the contrary.

In this connection we are bound to note with some degree of satisfaction the manner in which Crutchfield had
pressed forward with his available artillery to the very
foremost line. The Wilderness was no less unsuited to
the maneuver of artillery masses than the Peninsula,
yet, instead of lurking far in the rear we find all the batteries which had come up well to the front, and therefore
available for use in any emergency. Crutchfield was
at least prepared to secure the ground that Jackson had
taken against recovery by the enemy.

After the delay of some 15 minutes occasioned by the
artillery duel, A. P. Hill's Division advanced. Lane
in the lead soon came upon Williams' deserted log
works in the woods south of the road, while two brigades
of the rear lines were ordered into position to guard the
road from Hazel Grove. Meanwhile Jackson was urging Hill to press on and cut the enemy off from the

United States Ford road, offering him the services of Capt. Boswell, the chief engineer officer of his staff, and one familiar with the terrain, to act as guide to the White House. Passing rapidly to the front along a woods road just above the Plank Road with his staff, Jackson then undertook to make a personal reconnaissance of the ground in his front. The Federals could be plainly heard chopping trees and at work on their intrenchments. The fire of musketry had broken out south of the Plank Road, occasioned by a collision between some of Sickles' men, who were returning to occupy the line of deserted works, with Lane's skirmishers. Turning his horse to the rear, Jackson met A. P. Hill and his adjutant. The firing of the pickets of both armies had now become active, and rolled along the Federal front to the north of the road, causing Lane's men in the wood in rear of Jackson to become very alert. Hearing the rush of a small party of Confederate horsemen on the pike, but seeing only those in the woods 80 yards to his front, Maj. Barry, in command of the left wing of the 18th North Carolina Infantry, whose men were already aroused by the musketry fire of the enemy in their front, and had not seen Jackson's party pass in that direction, gave the order to fire and repeat the firing. The first volley was a fatal one, for inflicting three wounds upon Jackson, it also destroyed the right arm of Lee. With a bullet in the palm of his right hand and two in his left arm, one of which crushed the bone just below the shoulder and severed the main artery, Jackson was unable to control his horse, which plunged forward towards the enemy's line to escape the fire of Lane's men. As "Little Sorrel" dashed across the path, a heavy oak branch struck his wounded rider a heavy blow in the face and all but unseated him, but seizing the bridle with his bleeding hand, Jackson managed to stop the horse as he fell from the saddle into the arms of Capt. Wilbourne of his staff. Soon A. P. Hill arrived and assumed command, while the stricken chieftain was tenderly borne to the rear along the Plank Road.

It was now bright moonlight and objects could be plainly discerned in the roadway. Capt. Osborne, who happened to be with two Federal guns some 800 yards down the Plank Road at the base of the hill, saw the party bearing Jackson from the front and opened fire with canister. The discharge of the picket guns was taken as the signal of alarm by the enemy, and at 9:30 p. m. the 43 guns at Fairview directed a terrific fire down the Plank Road in which Carter's artillery, still in column of pieces, and probably 20,000 infantry were massed. The effect was fearful. Jackson's litter bearers were struck down twice, causing him to fall heavily to the ground upon his side and the injured arm. As he continued on his way to the rear he heard Gen. Pender, whose brigade in column in the road was being torn to pieces, declare his inability to hold his men in position, and it was to Pender that Jackson gave his last order on the field of battle. Raising himself upon his elbow as best he could, the wounded leader emphatically exclaimed: "Pender, you must hold your ground!" Repeated along the column these last words of their leader had a magical effect upon the sorely-tried men, and the wild confusion into which the Federal artillery fire had thrown them, threatening to break up two whole divisions, soon gave way to order. Meanwhile, however, A. P. Hill, Col. Crutchfield and many other valuable officers had been wounded.

Although the Federal Artillery continued to fire until after 10 o'clock, the sole part taken in this affair by the Confederate guns was the firing of a few rounds of shell over the heads of the infantry by the two pieces which had been sent to Pender, and by the section of Napoleons under Lieut. Chamberlayne, with McGowan on the road to Hazel Grove. Of course the fire was random and accomplished nothing, as no Federals were advancing to the attack. Yet, even so accurate an officer as Pegram, under whose direction the fire was conducted, reported that heavy loss was inflicted upon the enemy. And here it should be remarked that the statements of artillery officers as to the effect of their fire, the number of losses it inflicts, the batteries it silences, etc., etc., are ordinarily valueless. It was even more impossible for Pegram to observe the effect of his fire in the circumstances in which he found himself, than it was for Osborne and Best to see the damage they had done, and Osborne had no knowledge whatever of the destruction he had caused, except that subsequently acquired from captured Confederates. Had the officers engaged in the Civil War confined their reports to detailed accounts of their movements, positions, matters of ammunition expenditure, and their own losses in men, horses, and equipment, and not filled them with useless speculations as to the loss of the enemy and congratulations for their men, the official records would be more illuminating and far less confusing.

While Stuart, who had moved towards Ely's Ford with his cavalry and some of Beckham's batteries to attack the enemy's camps and trains, was being sent for to take command after Hill was wounded, Rodes assumed general control and immediately commenced to prepare for an attack in the morning, cheerfully relinquishing command when Stuart arrived at midnight. Throughout, his whole conduct was marked by the greatest magnanimity of spirit. Poor Crutchfield, with a leg shattered, had been borne to the rear in the same ambulance with Jackson. For a second time during the war this gallant soldier had received a desperate wound. Meanwhile Col. Alexander had arrived on the scene, and upon him devolved the duties of Chief of Artillery, while Col. Brown assumed command as Chief of Artillery of the 2d Corps. Carter's Battalion was now ordered to retire to the Dowdall house, and refit for the work of the morning, and went into bivouac in the surrounding fields, where Alexander's, Brown's, Walker's, Jones', and McIntosh's battalions were also parked for the night, most of the batteries of which had arrived about 8 P. M. Beckham's batteries bivouacked for the night nearby.

A. P. Hill's Division now held the advance line of the Confederates, while Rodes and Colston were withdrawn and bivouacked in line near the Dowdall Tavern, after reforming in the open fields. Jones' Brigade of Colston's Division was detached to guard the road from the furnace, and Colquitt's Brigade of Rodes' Division assigned to a similar duty on a road also from the south, but farther to the west. Paxton's Brigade occupied the Buschbeck intrenchments.

Learning that the Confederate attack had come to a standstill before the Fairview line, and that the Confederate right extended toward Hazel Grove, Hooker ordered Sickles, who had reached the latter position, to attack by moonlight. Forming Birney's Division in two lines, with supporting columns, Sickles set his corps in motion through the forest south of the Plank Road about midnight. The left wing of his column grazed the skirmishers of McGowan's Brigade, and later struck the right flank of Lane's line, of which several regiments became engaged. But Sickles' whole column glanced off towards Fairview, a part of his men reoccupying the deserted works which Williams had constructed and from which Lane had withdrawn. Meantime his troops, advancing almost northeast, were engaged in a desperate conflict with the Federal Infantry in front of Fairview, while the Federal guns about the cemetery shelled the underlying woods with vigor. During this assault which Sickles made upon his friends, and in which the participants on both sides suffered heavily, the puzzled Confederates listened to the roar of artillery and musketry and the cheering of the enemy with profound amazement. Not until Sickles' report was published were many of them able to learn what had befallen them. Sickles says that his men, in spite of a terrific fire of musketry and of 20 guns at Dowdall's Tavern, regained the Plank Road; that Howard's rifle pits were reoccupied; that all.the guns, caissons, etc., of the 11th Corps were recovered; that two guns and three caissons of the enemy were captured, and that Jackson was wounded; and that, thrown into confusion on their right, the enemy, after being also repulsed by Berry on the left, were so completely taken by surprise that they fell back, etc., etc.! Of course, the Confederate Artillery in bivouac over a mile away did not fire upon Sickles. Lane's loss was trifling; the Confederates, while surprised at the roar of the battle in their front, did not fall back; Howard's guns were not recovered, and the Confederates were not repulsed by Berry. The guns taken by Sickles were those of the Federal 3d Corps, which Winn had captured and left in the dirt road when driven off by Huntington and Pleasonton from Hazel Grove, and the works Sickles occupied were those which Lane had withdrawn from and were over 1½ miles from Buschbeck's works in the Dowdall clearing, or the nearest intrenchments of Howard's Corps. So we see that Sickles was imaginative if not accurate and must be relegated to the same category to which Pleasonton has been assigned. What a combination Sickles as commanding-general and Pleasonton as his cavalry leader would have made! Together their reported deeds furnish material for a wonderful work of fiction. But while the midnight fiasco of Sickles' desperate attack by moonlight is in many ways one of the comical incidents of the war, yet there is an element of sadness about it, for many brave men were sacrificed during the hour or two of its duration.

CHAPTER XXVI

WHEN Stuart arrived and took command, he was entirely ignorant of the situation except as to its general features. Rodes' plan to wait for the morning was approved by him and all activity was postponed until dawn. Stuart then set about making a personal and general reconnaissance and directed Col. Alexander, in his capacity as Chief of Artillery, to examine the ground for artillery positions.

A careful reconnaissance extending throughout the night convinced Alexander that a frontal attack through the dense woods against the enemy's works and artillery position would prove most costly to the Confederates, even if successful. The Federal infantry in the far edge of the forest not only lay behind exceptionally strong breastworks, with the approaches well protected by abattis, but a powerful artillery was massed behind individual epaulments on the crest of the hill behind and within easy canister range of the woods, through which an attack would have to be made. He soon found that there were but two possible outlets by means of which the Confederate artillery could be brought to the front. The first was the direct route of the Plank Road debouching from the forest beyond the schoolhouse and the junction of that road with the Bullock Road at a point not over 400 yards from the position of the hostile guns, part of which enfiladed the roadway for a long distance towards the woods. In advance of their main artillery position, the enemy had placed three pieces of Dimick's Battery behind an earthwork across the road and abreast of the infantry line. Even a casual examination of this route was sufficient to convince Alexander of its impracticability for the advance of artillery, which could only move up the narrow road in column of pieces and would, therefore, be destroyed piecemeal before it could be thrown into action. The utmost dash and gallantry of the gunners would simply be sacrificed in such circumstances.

The second outlet was a vista, some 200 yards long, a lane cleared on both sides to a width of 25 yards, which ran parallel to the Plank Road about 400 yards to the south. This vista terminated at its eastern end in the narrow dirt road leading from Hazel Grove to the Plank Road and it was in this clearing that Col. Winn's men had abandoned the two guns and three caissons, which they had captured from the train of the 3d Corps about 6 p. m., subsequently recovered by Sickles. It was reached from the Plank Road not only by the dirt road running to Hazel Grove 1,000 yards to the south, over which route Pleasonton had dispatched the regiment of cavalry to Howard's assistance, but by a second road half a mile to the rear of the Confederate infantry line. Pegram had from the first appreciated the value of the opening, and, as we have seen, had posted Chamberlayne with a section in it the evening of the 2d in support of McGowan's right, from which position Chamberlayne had been able to deliver a more or less random fire through the woods when Sickles' left collided with McGowan's right, about midnight.

At dawn, Alexander posted 17 guns as follows: Capt. E. A. Marye, of Walker's Battalion, with two Napoleons and two rifles in the clearing about the schoolhouse, at which point Pender's line crossed the Plank Road, and a short distance in rear, and also on the road, Capt. Brunson with his battery of four rifles, of the same battalion. It was necessary for the latter to fire over Marye's head, for in no other way could the guns be placed. Capt. R. C. M. Page, of Carter's Battalion, was placed with three Napoleons in the thin woods some 300 yards south of the Plank Road and on the dirt road leading to Hazel Grove, to fire upon the enemy's infantry lines until ordered elsewhere. Lieut. Chamberlayne of Walker's Battalion, with two Napoleons, was masked in the pines at the eastern end of the vista to assist the infantry in its advance and then accompany it, while Maj. Pegram, with Davidson's and McGraw's batteries of Walker's Battalion, took position at the western end of the vista. Placing four Napoleons on a small cleared knoll 400 yards to his rear to fire over the trees at the enemy's smoke, he held his entire command well in hand to advance down the vista and the dirt road towards Hazel Grove, when circumstances should permit the occupation of that position. Alexander's, Brown's, Carter's, Jones', and McIntosh's battalions were held in the rear in column along the Plank Road.

Col. Alexander convinced Stuart that the Hazel Grove position, which commanded Fairview Heights, was the key to the Federal line, and Archer's Brigade which had come up during the night and formed on McGowan's right, thus occupying the extreme right of the Confederate line, was ordered at daylight to seize the hill, which Sickles had all but abandoned. Archer at once advanced through the woods, driving the handful of Federal skirmishers before him, and charged about 400 yards across the open fields in front of the Hazel Grove position. Pressing up the slope, his men seized the hill and captured the four pieces of artillery. Within 90 minutes after the attack commenced, Hazel Grove was in possession of the Confederates, its wanton desertion by Sickles having destroyed all chance of a successful resistance by Hooker, in the lines then occupied by his troops.

Stuart was now to reap the benefit of Alexander's judicious disposition of the artillery, for at 5 A. M. the latter ordered Maj. Pegram to move forward and occupy Hazel Grove, and Col. Carter to move as many of his pieces as possible up to the schoolhouse. Pegram, all in readiness, responded, and before 6 A. M. had placed Chamberlayne's Battery of his own battalion and Page's of Carter's Battalion in position on the forward crest of Hazel Grove. The sight that met his eyes was one to fill the soul of an artilleryman with joy. Less than 1,500 yards to the northeast the enemy's position

lay before him, and his own guns almost completely enfiladed those of the enemy in the road and were able to
deliver an oblique fire upon the others on Fairview
ridge. Meantime, Col. Carter had moved up to Marye's
position at the schoolhouse, with six pieces of his own
battalion. Without hesitating a moment, Pegram
opened with his eight pieces upon the enemy, joined by
Carter's group of ten on the road, thus at the outset
subjecting the enemy's guns to a cross fire.

But until the Artillery opened fire, Stuart had not
recognized the vast importance of Archer's capture, and
while Pegram and Carter were getting into position, a
useless sacrifice of Lane's and Ramseur's men had been
made by furiously hurling them against Berry's and
Williams' intrenchments in the woods, from which the
Federals were, however, driven back upon their main
line just in front of Fairview. After an hour of
desperate fighting, Stuart's whole line was in turn
driven out of the works, and Archer himself was forced
to fall back to Hazel Grove, where he took up a position
in support of Pegram's guns. It was clear now that
extreme efforts would be required to drive the Federals
from their strong position, for Hooker had established
the 1st, 2d, and 5th corps on his line, threatening to turn
the Confederate left where a desperate conflict was
raging.

Meanwhile Stuart had seen the value of Pegram's
position, to which Alexander had, meantime, ordered
Moody's and Woolfolk's batteries and Parker's section
of his own battalion, with ten guns under Maj. Huger,
and Brooke's, Smith's, and Watson's batteries of
Brown's Battalion under Capt. Watson, Lusk's, and
Wooding's batteries of McIntosh's Battalion under
Maj. Poague, and Tanner's and Carrington's batteries
of Jones' Battalion, all of which immediately went into
action. McIntosh with a rifled section of Thompson's
Louisiana Battery of Jones' Battalion moved down the
road to Brunson's position, while Maj. Jones with
portions of W. P. Carter's, Reese's, and Fry's batteries

of Carter's Battalion, Tanner's Battery of his own, and a section of Taylor's Battery of Alexander's Battalion, twelve pieces in all, moved further to the front and to the left of the schoolhouse group of ten pieces, now under Maj. Braxton. Col. Carter about this time assumed control of his own, Huger's, and Poague's batteries at Hazel Grove and Col. Walker of Brown's, Pegram's, and Jones' batteries at that same point.

Alexander states that perhaps 50 guns were engaged at Hazel Grove, though not over 40 at any one time, as the batteries had to be relieved from time to time to replenish their ammunition. The fire which Pegram, then Walker and Carter, conducted from this point was perhaps for an hour the most continuous and rapid ever delivered by the Confederate Artillery. Every caisson had to be well filled during the night, yet many of them were emptied within the hour, some of the better-served pieces, those under Pegram, firing as rapidly as three rounds a minute, which was an exceptionally rapid rate for the time.

As an artillery position, Hazel Grove was ideal and Alexander's battalion commanders made the best of it. Somewhat greater in elevation than Fairview, its bushy crest all but obscured the Confederate guns, well drawn back from the view of the enemy, whose shells bursting beyond the narrow ridge, or in the depression in front, were quite harmless. Few reached their difficult target, while the Federal position presented an extensive and easy target to the Confederate guns. It is remarkable how the Federal cannoneers managed to maintain their fire against such odds, yet they did so and although severely punished by Alexander's artillery, their guns formed the rallying point for Hooker's troops below them in the woods, and they inflicted terrible losses upon Hill's attacking infantry. Had the Confederates been provided with good ammunition for their guns, it is doubtful if the Federal Artillery could have made the stand it did. An extraordinarily large percentage of the Confederate shells failed to burst, and many were even more ineffective by reason of premature explosions. With the very best ammunition the error of the fuse, and consequently the area of dispersion, is large, but the mean burst is easily ascertained and ranging becomes fairly simple and accurate. On the other hand, ranging with the Confederate ammunition was extremely difficult. The writer has heard this point discussed by numerous Confederate artillery officers, who declared that ranging with them was ordinarily mere guess work, and that frequently a dozen bursts gave them no knowledge whatever of the true range. Indeed it was most discouraging to the Confederate gunners to fire and fire upon a perfectly visible target under the easiest conditions, and see not a sign of effect from their shells, and this is a fact which must be considered by the artillery student of the war.

Soon Anderson united with Stuart's right, the former moving his left up to Mine Creek from the furnace, while Hardaway followed with three rifles of Jordan's Battery. Before moving off, Hardaway left Capt. Dance with one rifle of Jordan's Battery, one Napoleon, and one howitzer of Hupp's and two howitzers of Hurt's, with instructions to follow Mahone's advance along the Plank Road to the east. Dance at once occupied a fine position on a knoll to the right of the road, and about 900 yards from the enemy's breastworks.

Proceeding along the ravine, Hardaway encountered Gen. Lee, who had selected a position on a wooded hill, which the Major was directed to prepare for his three guns, and from which he opened an active fire upon the Fairview guns, after the axmen with great labor had cut a roadway thereto.

By 9 A. M. the Federal artillery fire had appreciably slackened, many of the guns having exhausted their ammunition since no provision was made to resupply them in spite of the urgent requests of the officers. Besides, the Federal Artillery had suffered severely from the terrible cross fire, which Carter, Pegram, and McIntosh, now reënforced by Hardaway's guns, had been directing for nearly two hours upon Fairview.

It was at this juncture that the veteran commander of the Richmond Letcher Battery, Capt. Greenlee Davidson, received his mortal wound at the very moment of victory. In the words of Maj. Pegram, he was "one of the most gallant, meritorious, and efficient officers in the service."

About this time Col. Walker assumed the active direction of his battalion, of which Pegram had sent Davidson's and Chamberlayne's, together with Page's of Carter's Battalion, to the rear to replenish their ammunition. Col. Brown also assumed active control of the artillery of the 2d Corps.

Concerning the Federal artillery position and the effect of the Confederate fire, Capt. Clermont L. Best, 4th United States Artillery, Chief of Artillery, 12th Corps, after explaining how his guns had been intrenched during the night of May 3d, had the following to say: "Our position would not have been forced had the flanks of our line of guns been successfully maintained. An important point, an open field about a mile to our left and front, guarded by a brigade of our troops (not of the 12th Corps) and a battery—was seemingly taken by a small force of the enemy and the battery captured and turned on us with fearful effect, blowing up one of our caissons, killing Capt. Hampton, and enfilading Gen. Geary's line. It was most unfortunate. My line of guns, however, kept to its work manfully until 9 A. M., when, finding our infantry in front withdrawn, our right and left turned, and the enemy's musketry so advanced as to pick off our men and horses, I was compelled to withdraw my guns to save them. We were also nearly exhausted of ammunition."

The remarks of Capt. Best are much more conclusive of the service rendered by Alexander and his batteries than anything the Confederate gunners themselves might have said. The effect of Alexander's fire Gen. Hunt also characterized as fearful.

The Federal line of battle was now along the heights below and a short distance west of Fairview. Sickles' Corps connecting with Slocum's on the left, occupied this line to the Plank Road and across it. On his right was a portion of the 2d Corps and beyond behind breastworks thrown up during the night along the Ely's Ford Road, and separated by a small interval from Couch, lay the 1st Corps under Reynolds. On Slocum's left and facing towards Fredericksburg the 5th Corps opposed McLaws, while the remnants of Howard's Corps was massing beyond Meade. Thus Hooker still had 60,-000 infantry in line while the combined strength of Stuart, Anderson, and McLaws, after the losses of the 1st and 2d, was not over 40,000. But the *élan* of Stuart's men had not waned in spite of the unsuccessful attempts of the morning to drive the enemy from their strengthened line, and each minute the efforts of the Confederate Artillery became more telling. There was nothing for Stuart to do but to organize a fresh attack. The spirit of the brave leader as he rode the lines encouraging his men was contagious. Entirely relieved of anxiety for his right flank by the union with Anderson's line in that quarter, he now massed his infantry on the left to drive the enemy out of the position from which they were threatening his flank, to the support of which Ramseur's Brigade had been sent. Finally, about 9:30 A. M., a third assault was made and the Federal line was broken by the sheer valour of Jackson's infantry. The Artillery had meantime crushed the Fairview batteries, the very keystone of the whole structure of resistance.

As the Confederate infantry surged forward through the woods, Carter, Jones, and McIntosh dashed down the road and up the slopes of Fairview to the crest, while the batteries at Hazel Grove crossed the valley in their front, and, joining with the others in action, poured a whirlwind of fire upon the retiring Federals and their batteries, the latter withdrawing to their ammunition trains.

The Federals now endeavored to make a stand near the Chancellorsville house, but without success. Enfiladed from the west by Carter's group, fired upon from their right front by Pegram's batteries and from their front by Jordan's guns, which Hardaway had meantime brought upon the southern edge of the plateau, and entirely without breastworks, their resistance was gallant but brief. At this juncture, Hooker, while standing on the porch of the Chancellor house, was put *hors de combat* by a fragment of brick torn from a pillar by one of Jordan's shells, and did not recover for several hours. For a time his defeated army was without a leader.

About 1 A. M., Lee joined Stuart near the Chancellor house and directed that both infantry and artillery replenish ammunition and renew the assault. The enemy having stubbornly fallen back to a line of works prepared by Warren, running along the Ely's Ford and United States Ford roads, with its apex at the White House, thus covered their avenues of retreat.

When the Federals fell back to their works after being shelled for about an hour, the Confederate batteries at once advanced to the turnpike and threw up hasty intrenchments from which a desultory fire was maintained upon that portion of the line near the White House. About 3 P. M. Colston's Division, which had been temporarily withdrawn, reformed, and, resupplied with ammunition, was ordered by Gen. Lee to move forward towards the United States Ford for the purpose of developing the enemy's position. Page's Morris Battery of Napoleons accompanied Colston. Hardly had Colston's men been set in motion when the enemy opened upon them with twelve pieces of artillery from a barbette battery on an eminence, and although Page replied to this fire for half an hour or more, nothing serious was attempted and Colston was directed to draw off and intrench. Meanwhile Maj. Hardaway with thirteen rifled pieces, including two of Fry's, two of Marye's, and two of W. P. Carter's, Jordan's four rifles

and three of Hurt's, was ordered to accompany Gen.
Anderson to the river for the purpose of shelling the
enemy's wagon trains on the north bank near Scott's
Dam, about 1½ miles below the United States Ford.

The Confederates had before noon practically come
to a standstill on the Chancellor plateau, for disquieting
news had reached Gen. Lee from the rear. Sedgwick
had finally forced Early's flimsy line and compelled the
Confederates opposite Fredericksburg to fall back.
Operations about Chancellorsville were perforce suspended while Gen. Lee's attention was directed to the
new danger.

CHAPTER XXVII

WE left Early and Pendleton on the morning of the 2d disposing their men and guns to oppose as best they could Sedgwick's advance, the Federals pretty much in the same position and attitude they had assumed the evening before. Before 10 A. M. Gen. Early, however, directed Maj. Andrews to feel the enemy with his guns, and accordingly Maj. Latimer opened with two rifles on that portion of the hostile line near Deep Run, while Graham's and Brown's Parrotts on Lee's Hill directed their fire upon the infantry and batteries massed near the Pratt house, driving them to cover. Latimer drew no fire, but two batteries on the north bank and several on the south side of the river responded with energy to that of Graham's and Brown's guns. Soon after this affair, Early rode to the left to confer with Pendleton, who was directing the disposition of Walton's guns along the Stansbury Hill, with a view to firing upon the enemy's masses about Falmouth. While he was with Pendleton, Col. Chilton, Gen. Lee's Adjutant-General, arrived with verbal orders for him, directing that he move at once to Chancellorsville with all his infantry but one brigade, and that Gen. Pendleton should withdraw all the artillery along the Telegraph Road, especially all the heavier pieces, to Chesterfield, except eight or ten guns which were to follow the rest when forced by the enemy to do so. Early and Pendleton both advanced many objections to the withdrawal of their forces at such a time, which in their opinion would only invite the advance of the enemy, but were informed that the commanding general was convinced of the wisdom of crushing Hooker's force and that, having done so, he could then return to Fredericksburg and drive Sedgwick off if necessary. To do this, all his infantry was needed, but more artillery about Chancellorsville would be superfluous, and the small detaining force was only expected to delay Sedgwick long enough for the Artillery and trains to withdraw. Such was the substance of Chilton's remarks. The orders as delivered to Gen. Early left him no discretion and, much against their will, he and Pendleton, about noon, set about executing them. Hays' Brigade was directed to relieve Barksdale's Regiment in the town and to remain with Pendleton's artillery force. It was late in the afternoon, however, before the infantry column moved off from Early's line along the military road from Hamilton's Crossing to the Telegraph Road, and then along a cross road leading into the Plank Road, followed by Maj. Andrews with his own battalion and Graham's Battery.

Pendleton had, before noon, ordered Nelson's Battalion to withdraw first since it was least exposed to the view of the enemy. The three 20-pounder Parrotts of Rhett's Battery were replaced by the lighter and less valued pieces of Patterson's and Fraser's batteries. Lieut. Tunis with the Whitworth moved over from the extreme right and with Rhett's Battery and Nelson's Battalion retired along the Telegraph Road while Richardson's Battery which Walton had detached to Early's line rejoined its battalion. Col. Cabell also withdrew Carlton's Battery from Lee's Hill and moved to the rear in command of the entire column of 22 pieces. Pendleton, therefore, retained in position after noon but 15 guns. Of these six guns of the Washington Artillery and Parker's two 10-pounder Parrotts were held in position on Marye's Hill and the ridge to the left, Fraser's three and one of Patterson's guns on Lee's Hill, and three of Patterson's on the ridge back of the Howison house. During the withdrawal of his batteries, Pendleton resorted to every subterfuge to make it appear to the enemy as if additional guns were being brought into position. After remaining idle the greater part of the afternoon, the Federals at last began to send forward their skirmishers and to mass on the north bank as if to cross. Pendleton now ordered Col. Cabell to return with Carlton's Battery.

Upon arriving with the head of his column at the Plank Road leading to Chancellorsville just before dark, Early received a note from Gen. Lee saying that he was not expected to withdraw his division from Fredericksburg, if by remaining Sedgwick could be checked, as by neutralizing the 30,000 Federals with his 10,000 men Early could render far greater service than he could at Chancellorsville. Thus had Chilton misunderstood the commanding general's directions, and led to an all but disastrous movement in Lee's rear by denying Early and Pendleton all discretion in the execution of the orders he transmitted to them. The incident well illustrates the danger of verbal orders and from orders in any form emanating from one not actually conversant with the conditions in remote quarters of the field of operations. What Gen. Lee had intended for instructions were transmitted as positive orders.

Early had hardly received the message from Gen. Lee when he was informed by Gen. Barksdale through a courier, at the rear of his column, that the enemy had advanced in force against Hays' weak line, and that both Hays and Pendleton had sent word that all the artillery would be captured, unless they received immediate relief. Meantime Barksdale, with rare good judgment, and in the exercise of that initiative on the part of a subordinate so valuable on such occasions, had retraced his steps with his own regiments, followed by Gordon's Brigade. Early at once gave the order for his main column to do the same.

Sedgwick, upon discovering the Confederate withdrawal, had crossed the remainder of his corps about dark, and moved towards the River Road, or Bowling Green Road, below the town, driving Col. Penn's Regiment of Hays' Brigade back to the line of the railroad, and then formed line with his main body along the river. Fortunately, he had not seriously attempted to take the town. The heavy masses of the enemy seen at Falmouth, earlier in the day, were the troops of the 1st Corps under Reynolds moving to the left to reënforce Hooker.

Between 10 and 11 P. M. Early's Division reoccupied its old line and skirmishers were thrown out towards the River Road, Barksdale again occupying the town and Hays moving to Early's right. Before notice of Early's decision to return reached Pendleton he had, after deliberate consultation with Hays, withdrawn the Artillery, Walton's batteries moving off first, followed by those on Lee's Hill. But Pendleton had scarcely reached the Telegraph Road with the rear batteries, when he met Barksdale returning to the field and was told by him that the orders were to hold Fredericksburg at all hazards. Pendleton, as well as Hays, who was at Marye's Hill supervising the final preparation for the retirement of his brigade, was naturally much puzzled by the incomprehensible conflict of orders they had received during the day, but was finally assured by Early himself that the confusion had resulted from Chilton's mistake, and that since Barksdale and Gordon had both returned of their own accord he had thought best to reoccupy his lines so long as it was possible to do so. Pendleton, in complete coöperation with Early, though much perplexed, and weakened by having sent so many of his guns to the rear, promptly directed Walton and Cabell to reoccupy their positions, the former being assigned to the command of the artillery on Marye's Hill and the latter to that on Lee's and the Howison Hill. It was 1 P. M. when the 19 guns, including those of Carlton's Battery, remaining for the defense of so important a position, were reëstablished in position.

At 11 P. M. Sedgwick received a much belated order from Hooker to march upon Chancellorsville with all haste. Leaving one division to cover his rear and skirmish with the Confederates in its front, he moved his other two divisions up the river towards Fredericksburg. Had Hooker's orders been duly received, his advance would have been all but unopposed. Even now delays occurred, and although Gen. Warren arrived at 2 A. M. to hasten forward his movement, the head of Sedgwick's column did not enter the town, but 3 miles from the bridge at Franklin's Crossing, until daylight. Having detected the movement of the enemy, and believing that Sedgwick's main effort would be made on the left, Pendleton at once advised Early, who dispatched Hays' Brigade from his right, to reënforce Barksdale near the town.

Meanwhile, Gibbon had thrown a bridge at the town and crossed over with his division of the 2d Corps. With the Federal advance were several batteries, to engage which Pendleton directed Walton to send a section of artillery to the most advanced works on the left. Meantime Barksdale had directed Maj. Eshleman to move a piece of Miller's Battery, which commanded the Plank Road leading from the town, to the left front, thus unknown to Pendleton uncovering the most important approach to Marye's Hill.

To meet the enemy, Early now had 7 companies of Barksdale's Brigade between the Marye house and the Plank Road, 3 companies on the Telegraph Road at the foot of Marye's Hill, and 2 regiments on the ridges of Lee's and Howison's hills, while one of Hays' regiments covered Barksdale's right and 2 occupied the Stansbury ridge. The extreme right was held by Hoke's and Smith's brigades with Andrews' Battalion of artillery and Richardson's and Graham's batteries in their old works.

Very shortly after daylight Sedgwick commenced demonstrations at Deep Run as if to turn Hoke's line, throwing forward his skirmishers up the ravine formed by the stream. In spite of Latimer's fire, a large body succeeded in reaching the railroad behind which it remained while several Federal batteries played upon Latimer's guns. Andrews now brought Graham's and Brown's batteries from the right to the support of Latimer's two Napoleons, and also Carpenter's rifled section, which engaged in a duel with the enemy's artillery as well as firing upon their infantry. Finally Hoke moved out and drove the enemy from behind the railroad embankment, while Andrews' batteries played upon the retiring troops.

As soon as the advance division (Newton's) of Sedgwick's Corps had entered the town, four regiments were sent forward to attack the Confederate line in rear of it, advancing over the ground made famous in December by the desperate charges of Burnside's divisions. Once more the brave Federal infantry pressed up to within a few paces of the stone wall and rifle pits at the base of the hills, while Pendleton's batteries poured shell and canister into their ranks with dreadful effect, and Barksdale's men, reserving their fire until the last moment, hurled the attacking columns back in a blizzard of musketry fire. Once more the enemy withdrew to cover behind the accidents of the ground, while their batteries in the town poured their fire with unrelenting vigor upon Marye's Hill. At all points Sedgwick's men were repulsed, but it was apparent to the defenders that the ever-increasing force in the town was only temporarily balked. The glorious news of Jackson's victory at Chancellorsville, which had just been received, inspired the gray line to redouble its efforts.

Sedgwick now determined to turn the Confederate position and directed Howe with his rear division, on the left of Hazel Run, against the opposing line, while Gibbon was ordered to move up the river from the town and turn the Confederate left. But Howe found the works in his front and those which extended beyond his left occupied, while the stream on his right deterred him from assaulting Marye's Hill in flank, and Gibbon's advance was barred by the canal behind which on the Stansbury Hill were the men of Hays' Brigade, and the pickets of Wilcox's Brigade on Taylor House Hill. Information of Gibbon's movement was at once sent Wilcox, who, leaving one section of Lewis' Battery and

50 men at Banks' Ford, had hastened down in person
with the other section of the battery under Lieut.
Nathan Penick, and threw his guns in action first on the
Taylor House Hill, then on the Stansbury ridge. Soon
he also brought up Moore's (Huger's) Battery, two
rifles of which on the Taylor House Hill engaged the
enemy's guns in Falmouth and on the plain below, for
about two hours, while the latter sought to prepare for
Sedgwick's final efforts.

When Gibbon and Howe, whose men unable to advance also sought the cover of the ground, reported the
impracticability of turning the Confederate position, the
resolute Sedgwick determined to storm the opposing
works. For this purpose, Newton's Division in front
of the town was to be organized into two columns for the
assault of Marye's Hill, while Howe was to move up
Hazel Run and attack Lee's Hill. Newton's two columns, of two regiments each, with two regiments in support, moved forward on the right of the Plank Road
while Col. Burnham with four regiments in line of battle, to the left of the road, charged directly upon the
rifle pits at the base of Marye's Hill. The works against
which these troops charged were now held by but two
regiments supported by six guns on the hill above under
Walton, who directed a withering fire of canister upon
the enemy. As before, the Federals reeled and broke,
only to be rallied and led back with the same result. But
under a flag of truce for the purpose of allowing the
enemy to recover their dead, the fire in this quarter was
now suspended. This action by the Confederates was entirely unauthorized by proper authority and was due to
the strange good nature of a gallant officer, Col. Griffin
of the 18th Mississippi, who received the flag and honored the request in spite of the fact that Howe was
actively engaged in attacking Hays' line only a few hundred yards to his right. Not only did Griffin suspend
the fire on his portion of the line, but he allowed his men
to show themselves, and when Newton was apprised by
his returning officers how weak the line was which had

repulsed him, the three columns were ordered forward again upon the termination of the local truce. It was now that the full effect of Chilton's dreadful blunder, as well as Barksdale's unwarranted interference with Pendleton's dispositions, were to be felt. Instead of 37 guns in position to repel the enemy, there remained less than half that number, and the direct approach up the Plank Road instead of being completely dominated by Miller's guns was exposed only to the fire of the six pieces on the hill, above and behind the stone wall, the few defenders of which finding themselves assailed from every side by superior numbers were unable to check the onset. The Federals dashed on up to and over the works, completely overpowering the Mississippians, most of whom were either killed, wounded or captured in the desperate hand-to-hand conflict which ensued. Thus did Griffin reap the whirlwind which he had sown. It was now 11 A. M., and so rapid had been Newton's final assault that Hays and Wilcox, the latter having by this time assembled a portion of his brigade on Taylor's Hill, had not had time to come to Barksdale's aid. The enemy, after securing the works at its base, swarmed up Marye's Hill and seized five of Walton's guns and Parker's two to their left, before they could be withdrawn, but the gunners kept to their work to the last. Seeing Newton's success, Pendleton at once caused the guns on Lee's Hill to be directed on the enemy on Marye's Hill, and brought up two pieces of Patterson's Battery from near the Howison house, which opened fire from the brow near the Telegraph Road. Just at this moment Richardson's Battery arrived at the Howison Hill from the right, from whence it had been dispatched by Early, and was sent by Pendleton to join Walton, who assumed direction of the guns firing upon Marye's Hill, while Barksdale formed a regiment in line to the left of the Telegraph Road in their support.

The enemy now advanced his batteries on the plain in support of Howe's column, which vigorously assailed Lee's Hill. Upon these Carlton's and Fraser's batteries under direction of Col. Cabell poured a rapid fire of canister, but they, too, were forced to withdraw as the infantry supports in their front fell back along the Telegraph Road, contesting every foot of ground. In withdrawing, Richardson was compelled to abandon a piece, the horses of which were all shot down. Fraser, in the meantime, had been directing the fire of his left piece upon Marye's Hill, while his other piece and Carlton's Battery continued to hurl canister upon Howe's men. Not until the enemy all but reached their guns did Fraser and Carlton withdraw them, the former saving both his guns by substituting a caisson limber for a gun limber which had been blown up. While directing this difficult task under a galling fire, Lieut. F. A. Habersham, of Fraser's Battery, was struck in the head and killed by a large fragment of shell, but his body was borne from the field on the shoulders of his cannoneers. Cabell now led his two batteries to the rear along the Telegraph Road and formed Carlton's for action near the pump at the Leach house, while Early hurried up with his troops from near Hamilton's Crossing and formed them on the line which the remnants of Barksdale's Brigade was holding in front of the Cox house, about two miles in rear of Lee's Hill. Walton had been ordered to the rear along the Telegraph Road, and directed to occupy the first favorable position with his remaining guns. Soon the enemy brought a battery into action near the brick house in rear of the Howison house and engaged Carlton, who replied until his ammunition was expended, when Walton was ordered to bring up his ten pieces and relieve Carlton and Fraser, the former having lost one man killed and eight wounded in the duel.

One incident in connection with Carlton's Battery should here be mentioned, as it illustrates the coolness and heroism of the Confederate gunner. An unexploded shell fell among Carlton's guns with the fuse still burning. Its explosion would have certainly caused the death of several men. Without pausing an instant in his work, Lieut. Thomas A. Murray, who was busily engaged in sighting his piece, called private Richard W. Saye's attention to the dangerous projectile which lay at their feet and Saye, picking it up, hurled it over the parapet of the work. The shell burst as it fell to the ground in the ditch beyond.

Pendleton in his report mentions the mortification he experienced in seeing Walton's and Patterson's guns captured by the enemy. Fortunately the day has come when it is considered an honor and not a disgrace for the artillerymen to lose guns in such circumstances. In this affair it does not appear that any criticism can be made to the discredit of the gunners, for they remained at their posts until the last, and by the nature of the ground were cut off from saving their guns. The artilleryman who feels that he must save his pieces, or be disgraced before his comrades in arms, finds a strong incentive to "pull out" before actually necessary, and where such a spirit prevails the subaltern who cannot view the whole field in its general aspect is too apt to anticipate the crisis and retire his guns when by remaining in action a few minutes longer he might materially influence the issue. Then, too, the guns give the bravest infantry additional assurance. Nothing is more inspiring to a sorely pressed infantry than the nearby crash of supporting guns and nothing more disheartening to the foot soldiers than the sight of their artillery supports drawing off from the post of danger. Upon such facts the more modern and sounder rule has been based that artillery when practicable must seek positions in close proximity to the advanced infantry, and remain with it until to do so longer becomes but a useless sacrifice of men and guns. The mere personal knowledge that their batteries are still in the fight is of great moral support to the infantrymen who must after all bear the ultimate shock of an assault driven home. If by losing a single piece or many, the force of the enemy's blow can be reduced by the artillery to within the limits of the defending infantry's power of resistance, then by all means the guns should be gladly lost and much honor accorded the gunners who are resolute enough to lose them, for it must be remembered that if the infantry is overborne and swept from the field, the artillery as a rule must fall with it. Let us all be thankful that the old idea that under no circumstances must a gun be lost, a rule which continued to be accepted from the time of the War of Liberation to the Franco-German War, has at last been abandoned, and that Bernadotte's proud boast that in all his battles he had never lost a piece no longer does him any credit in the eyes of the world.

This point is well covered by Hohenlohe, who discusses at length the evils which flowed in 1866 from the Prussian batteries withdrawing from the front line to refit, or when their ammunition ran short. Of course, there were exceptions even then, such as in the case of Von der Goltz's Battery at Königgrätz. Ordinarily, however, they were too prone to fall back when custom and the regulations warranted it. But before 1870, the German artillerymen had learned that to lose guns was not dishonorable and at Chateaudun instead of a battery withdrawing when its ammunition had been exhausted and its material greatly injured, the battery commander made his cannoneers mount the limbers and sing the "Wacht am Rhine" until the commanding general should see fit to order them to retire or until a fresh supply of ammunition might arrive.

That Pendleton's batteries remained long enough at their posts at Fredericksburg is amply attested by their losses. In Walton's Battalion of Washington Artillery, there were four men killed, and four wounded, including Lieut. De Russy, besides the losses in material etc., which was two 3-inch rifles of Squire's, one 12-pounder howitzer of Richardson's, one 12-pounder Napoleon of Miller's, and a 12-pounder howitzer and a 12-pounder Napoleon of Eshleman's Battery, four limbers, one caisson, and 29 horses. In Lieut. Brown's section of Parker's Battery, the loss including the section commander was 23 officers and men captured, two 10-

pounder Parrotts, 2 limbers, 2 caissons, and 28 horses.
Patterson of Cutt's Battalion lost 3 men wounded, one
Napoleon, one 13-pounder howitzer, 2 limbers disabled,
and 4 horses killed, while Fraser lost one officer killed
and one caisson and limber by explosion. Carlton's loss
was one man killed, 10 wounded and 3 horses. Later
Patterson's two pieces were recaptured, so the total
loss of the artillery under Pendleton was 6 officers, 64
men, total 70; 8 guns and limbers, 4 caissons and 64
horses.

Sedgwick, as we have seen, did not press along the
Telegraph Road, but followed the direct route to Chancellorsville along the Plank Road. Wilcox, cut off by
the Federal advance from Early, instead of trying to
establish connection with him, determined to delay
Sedgwick's progress as much as possible. He, therefore, and with a keen perception of the best part he was
able to play, drew up his brigade in line on a ridge
running from Stansbury Hill to a point on the Plank
Road some 500 yards in front of the Guest house, and
placing two rifled pieces of Moore's and Lieut. Barksdale's section of Penick's (Lewis') batteries in his
front, shelled the Federal troops on Marye's Hill and
the adjacent height at a range of about 800 yards. For
a time this checked the enemy, but soon their skirmishers
advanced to within 400 yards of the guns with dense
lines following. A force that was sent below the Plank
Road threatened to turn Wilcox's right, whereupon he
ordered Moore and Penick to retire and withdrew his
men along the River Road to a point half a mile in rear
of Dr. Taylor's house. In this affair, Lieut. Barksdale,
of Lewis' Battery, was severely wounded. So active
were Moore and Penick that Sedgwick mistook them
for a horse battery.

The slowness and caution with which the Federals
advanced encouraged Wilcox to move back to the Plank
Road and again seek to delay their progress towards Chancellorsville. Deploying a troop of cavalry
which he happened to have with him, in some pines in
rear of Downman's house, he moved his brigade and five

batteries to Salem Church, about five miles from Fredericksburg, where Cobb's rifled section of Penick's Battery went into position near the toll gate, while Moore's Battery sought a position 1,000 yards to the rear near the church itself. In the meantime one of Early's aides had informed Gen. Lee of the loss of the position in his rear, whereupon, as we have seen, he postponed his assault on Hooker's new lines, and dispatched McLaws with Mahone's, Wofford's, Semmes', and Kershaw's brigades to the support of Wilcox.

Upon forming line in front of Salem Church, Wilcox calmly awaited the arrival of the head of Sedgwick's column, which soon came up pushing Maj. Collins' small cavalry detachment down the road. Lieut. Cobb now opened fire with his two pieces, but was almost immediately driven from his position by a battery with the Federal advance guard, and fell back upon Moore's position, soon followed by Wilcox's Brigade, which reformed on the line already occupied by McLaws' troops at Salem Church.

Leaving Wofford at the junction of the turnpike and Plank Road, McLaws formed his line of battle perpendicular to the latter in front of the church, with Mahone on the left, Semmes next, then Wilcox across the road, and Kershaw on the right. Wofford took position on Kershaw's right when ordered up, while the two batteries remained in the road. Wilcox placed a number of his men in the church and also some in a schoolhouse about 60 yards in advance of his line. These dispositions had hardly been made when Brooks' Division moving forward rapidly in line of battle, and athwart the road, with Newton's Division in close support, rushed into the open space between the toll gate and the church, while Sedgwick's batteries drove Moore and Penick from the road after the latter had fired a single shot. Thus McLaws was left entirely without artillery in the engagement which followed. The Confederate line, however, lay well retired, in a thick growth of woods which afforded much shelter from the hostile guns.

After shelling the woods for about 20 minutes, the Federals advanced, Bartlett's Brigade, which boasted it had never been repulsed, on the left of the first line. On came the charging troops, cheering as they entered the woods, but when they had pressed to within 80 yards of the Confederate line they were received by a tremendous volley of musketry which momentarily checked the advance. In spite of the Confederate fire, Bartlett's brave men soon recovered their formation and swept on, taking the schoolhouse and its small garrison as it passed. But Wilcox, having held a regiment in reserve, now hurled it upon Bartlett's disordered line, and after a desperate encounter at close quarters, the Federals were broken and pressed back past the schoolhouse. Brooks' right had also been checked and broken. Sedgwick hurried forward his second line to save the day, but all in vain, for Semmes and Wilcox advanced their entire brigades and drove the enemy from the field clear back to the toll gate in a dangerously prolonged pursuit. At that point Sedgwick's massed reserves, together with the closing in of night, forbade further progress on the part of the Confederates. Meanwhile, Col. Alexander with his battalion and Maj. Hamilton with Manly's and McCarthy's batteries of Cabell's Battalion, had been ordered from the Chancellorsville plateau down the Plank Road to the support of McLaws, but arrived too late to take part in the engagement. The necessity of withdrawing these guns from so critical a point was due simply to the fact that Gen. Lee was entirely without an artillery reserve. Every piece, except those of Nelson's Battalion, which had been ordered to the rear as a result of the disastrous verbal order erroneously transmitted by Chilton, was engaged. Salem Church was in effect a rear guard action, and for use in such a contingency reserve artillery was created. One cannot fail to see how crippled the commander-in-chief had been by the loss of two of his battalions. Had they been present, Pendleton's two battalions would no doubt have been available as a reserve, instead of being committed at the outset. As a reserve, these battalions would have been held at Gen. Lee's immediate disposal, and would have, therefore, been among the first troops to arrive at Salem Church in support of Wilcox. McLaws would then have had Nelson's and Cutts' six fresh batteries, with which to repulse Sedgwick instead of parts of two much-damaged ones, without ammunition enough to remain in action at the critical moment. Since Gen. Lee was able to withdraw Alexander's four and Hamilton's two batteries from Chancellorsville, it is apparent that he would have been free to dispense with Pendleton's six batteries had they been present, and without weakening his front by taking so many guns from his advanced lines.

The sturdy Wilcox had, however, almost without artillery fought a superb rear guard action. Few better examples of the kind are to be found. In the nick of time, he had interposed his small force between the enemy and Lee's rear, after Early and Pendleton had been forced from the path. But much credit is also due Early and Pendleton, for they with 10,000 men and a few guns had for the better part of two days neutralized Sedgwick's whole corps of 30,000 men. Wilcox's Brigade had lost 500 officers and men, but Bartlett's Brigade alone of some 1,500 men had experienced casualties aggregating 580.

Sedgwick's line now extended from the river above Banks' Ford to Fredericksburg, and during the night a bridge was thrown at the ford.

CHAPTER XXVIII

An hour before sunset on the 3d, Early was informed that McLaws was moving down the Plank Road to meet Sedgwick, and that he, Early, was expected, if possible, to coöperate with McLaws in overwhelming the enemy's column. Early was then three miles from Salem Church and, satisfied that he could render no assistance to McLaws at so late an hour, advised him that he would concentrate his force during the night, and endeavor to drive the enemy from Lee's and Marye's hills at dawn, throwing forward his left to connect with Wofford on the right of Salem Church. Both Lee and McLaws approved this plan.

It was late in the evening when Early succeeded in concentrating his division, one battery only with a regiment of infantry in support being left on the right of the Cox house ridge, so as to guard the flank beyond the Telegraph Road against any movement of the enemy up the Deep Creek Valley. Early's plan was to advance along the Telegraph Road with Gordon's Brigade in the front line, followed by Andrews' Battalion of artillery and Graham's Battery, with Smith's and Barksdale's brigades in rear forming a second line, and to throw Hays' and Hoke's brigades across Hazel Run opposite his position so as to move down the left bank while he attacked the heights held by the enemy along the road. Upon recovering Marye's and Lee's hills, he proposed to occupy them with Pendleton's batteries and Barksdale's men while Hays and Hoke, crossing Hazel Hun at the ford on his left, connected with McLaws, and Gordon and Smith moved along the Plank Road up river.

At dawn, Gordon moved off along the Telegraph Road and found Lee's Hill unoccupied, but a body of hostile infantry moving westward along the Plank

Road halted and took position behind an embankment of the road between Marye's Hill and the ridge above. In the valley between Guest's and Downman's houses, there was also a large body of the enemy's infantry and a battery at the latter house. Andrews, who had accompanied Gordon, now placed Graham's Battery in position on the Telegraph Road along the western face of Lee's Hill, and opened on the enemy's troops in the valley, while Gordon's skirmishers descended the hill and advanced upon them. At this juncture, two large bodies of hostile infantry, probably brigades, crossed the ridge just beyond the Alum Spring Mill and threatened Gordon's left, as his line advanced, but Graham shifted his fire upon them and drove them to cover. Gordon then made a dash across the run and after a sharp encounter drove off the enemy behind the road embankment, captured some prisoners, several commissary wagons, and a battery wagon and a forge with their teams. This gave Early possession of Marye's and Cemetery hills again, and while Smith moved up to the support of Gordon, Barksdale reoccupied the sunken road behind the wall at the base of Marye's Hill, under a heavy fire from the batteries on Stafford Heights, and was ordered to seize the town itself, the bridge head, and a large wagon camp seen there. But Barksdale was unable to occupy the town, which was still held by Gibbon's Division of the 2d Corps, and the wagon train decamped.

Having disposed of the enemy's infantry, Graham turned his two 20-pounder Parrotts upon the battery at Downman's which had been free to fire upon him, and drove it off to the Guest house out of reach.

The enemy now held a line of shallow trenches extending from Taylor's Hill to the brow of the hill beyond Alum Spring Mill, while Gordon and Smith had occupied the trenches along the crests from the Plank Road towards Taylor's Hill, with their backs towards Fredericksburg. Smith was now ordered to advance towards Taylor's Hill, and in pressing forward up the slope was opened upon by the Federal batteries at the Taylor house with such effect that his movement was checked. The enemy appeared in such strength and inflicted such losses upon him that his brigade was withdrawn to its former position.

Hays' and Hoke's brigades had, meanwhile, moved down the left bank of Hazel Run, and had taken up a position from which they could connect with McLaws' right, by moving across the ridge on which Downman's house stood, and of this fact Early now notified McLaws. McLaws did not attack, however, but informed Early that Anderson was coming up to his support. When these troops began to arrive at Salem Church, Early drew Hays and Hoke further back to his right, placing the former in line at the base of the Alum Springs Hill, from which concealed position the brigade might move up the wooded slope on to the plain above, which was occupied by the enemy. Hoke was concealed in the woods on the lower end of the Downman house ridge. Gen. Lee now arrived and, personally examining Early's dispositions, approved his plan of attack, which was for Hays and Hoke to press forward to the Plank Road, while Gordon supported by Smith endeavored to sweep the crests in front of him, and to turn the Federal left resting on the river.

Sedgwick's main line covered the Plank Road for some distance on the south side, its center on the ridge along which the road runs and both flanks retired and resting on the river above and below. His main artillery position was within his line and at the Guest house, while other guns were on his left front facing Early. Skirmishers were thrown out upon the ridges in his front.

When dawn broke, no communication had yet been received from Hooker by Sedgwick, and he was still under orders to move to Chancellorsville. At an early hour, Early's movements in the latter's rear had caused him to deploy Howe's Division facing to the rear and perpendicular to the Plank Road. His scouts had reported that a column of the enemy, 15,000 strong, had arrived from Richmond and occupied the heights at Fredericksburg. At once abandoning all idea of taking the aggressive, Sedgwick was bent only upon crossing the river, but this in spite of the bridge at Banks' Ford, now within his line, he did not dare attempt by daylight. And so, with a line much attenuated and facing in three directions, east, south, and west, he awaited events. At last a welcome dispatch from Hooker, which authorized him to cross at Banks' Ford, or fall back upon Fredericksburg, and directing him not to attack, was received; but a little later another message arrived urging Sedgwick to hold a position on the south bank, to which he replied that he was threatened on two fronts, that his line was a poor one for defense, and that his bridge was endangered, closing with a request for assistance. Receiving no reply to this message he decided to remain in position until nightfall. Howe's Division still extended from the river to a point a short distance south of the Plank Road. Brooks' Division was on the right of Howe, forming line at right angles with him, and parallel to the road, while Newton's Division formed the west front occupying its position of the evening before and extending to the river above the bridge.

Anderson had arrived at Salem Church by midday, and after some delay his three brigades were moved into line on Early's left. Between Anderson's left and McLaws' right, the latter confronting Newton's Division, a large gap existed which was to be closed as the whole line advanced upon the enemy. The Confederate line from Lee's Hill to McLaws' left was six miles or more in extent.

Pendleton after reëstablishing Walton's guns on Marye's Hill and Fraser's Battery with a number of others on Lee's Hill, moved Carlton's Battery and Ross's which had rejoined him from Port Royal during the night, as far forward from the Telegraph Road towards the Guest house as possible, and also attempted to find a good position for the Whitworth with which Lieut. Tunis had returned. Andrews with his battalion occupied positions along the Telegraph Road, while Alexander had sent Taylor's (Eubank's), Woolfolk's, and Moody's batteries of his own battalion under Maj. Huger to coöperate with Anderson's brigades. Moody's Battery moved far off to Anderson's right towards the Telegraph Road. Manly's Battery remained with Wilcox near the church.

It was not until 6 p. m. that McLaws gave the signal for attack, when Hoke moved at once across the plateau between Downman's house and Hazel Run, under cover of Ross's and Carlton's fire, then down the slope, across the valley, and up the steep ascent of the Plank Road ridge, driving the enemy's skirmishers before him, while the hostile guns at the Guest house played upon, but failed to break, his line. Hays also swept the enemy's advance line from his front. These two brigades with unsurpassed ardor pressed on without halting for a moment, and were lustily cheered by the gunners in their rear whose fire was masked by the advance. From the artillery positions along the Telegraph Road, the sight was indeed an inspiring one, and filled the hearts of the artillerymen with enthusiasm and admiration for the gallant infantry which they were powerless to assist.

Gordon had advanced along the Plank Road ravine, formed in line, and with the utmost *élan* swept on towards the Taylor house. Brushing the enemy's skirmishers from the forward crests, he forced the artillery on that flank to retire rapidly, only halting when the Federals had been driven pellmell from Taylor's Hill towards Banks' Ford. Even the guns at the Guest house had been compelled to fly in order to escape capture. Thus had the enemy been thrown into confusion on all sides when Hoke was wounded, and his brigade, colliding with Hays' men in the woods, lost its direction and was thrown into confusion beyond the Plank Road. Hays' Brigade pressed on with such men of Hoke's as had mingled with it, but having also be-

come disordered in the woods, was checked by a retiring force of the enemy, which had been rallied to meet
the advance and which drove the Confederates back to
the Plank Road. Here Hays succeeded in rallying the
regiments of the two brigades to the support of which
Early brought up a part of Smith's Brigade. But before the Confederates could be reformed, night had
fallen, and with Smith's two regiments in front, Hays'
and Hoke's brigades rested in position along the Plank
Road. Gordon had also come to a standstill by reason
of the approach of darkness, on the Taylor House Hill
confronting the enemy's left. McLaws' Division had
not advanced at all. Anderson's Division had pressed
forward on Hoke's left, driving the enemy's skirmishers,
which confronted his center, from the Downman house
and the upper part of the ridge, but it did not cross the
Plank Road until dark, and none of its batteries were
engaged. When the attack came to an end, Posey extended Early's left, with Wright further down the road,
towards Salem Church. Beyond Anderson was Mc-
Laws with two of Alexander's batteries and Hardaway's group on the river road on his left.

During the early morning Alexander had been
directed to post some of his guns so as to prevent Sedgwick from advancing along the River Road to unite with
Hooker at Chancellorsville, and for this purpose he had
placed Jordan's Battery on a bluff commanding the
road, where the guns were intrenched. These guns were
now able to fire upon Banks' Ford, as were those of
Andrews' Battalion, which had been moved up to
the Taylor House Hill when the battle ended. Manly's
Battery was also most effective in firing upon the retreating enemy, while Hardaway with a number of batteries was nearby.

We have seen that after the seizure of the Chancellorsville plateau on the 3d, Hardaway had been dispatched
to Scott's Dam with 13 rifled pieces. Some time
was required for the assembling of his force, the organization of his column, and the refilling of his caissons.

The roads were also very heavy and difficult and it was well after dark before Hardaway, moving northward along the River Road, came up to the position of the 3d Virginia Cavalry near the Hayden house, with 10 of his guns. Gen. Anderson had meantime halted Hurt's three pieces on the road some distance in rear, as the weight of the carriages was such that it was doubtful whether the teams could draw them through the mud.

Hooker's wagon trains, in park and with camp-fires burning, were plainly visible at the base of a hill about a mile from the bluffs on the south bank of the river, when Hardaway in company with an engineer officer reconnoitered the ground. About 3 A. M. he brought up his 10 guns to the bluff in front of the Hayden house, and after firing 15 rounds per gun, the pieces were limbered up and started back through the mud to Chancellorsville, while Hardaway remained to discover by daylight the effect of his fire. The horses of the train when fired upon had been picketed in a field on the slope of the hill on the river side of the wagon park. Many of them had been killed or injured, as well as some of the teamsters, and a number of wagons had been destroyed by shelling. But the results of such an enterprise are never very serious, and have practically no effect upon the main operations of the enemy. It is exceedingly doubtful if in this case the injury inflicted by Hardaway was worth the ammunition expended.

While the column was returning the enemy made a demonstration on the south side of the river below United States Ford as if to cut off Hardaway's command, whereupon the batteries were hurried to the rear, leaving Anderson's skirmishers to check the attack, which proved not to be serious.

Anderson was now ordered to proceed to Salem Church, and Hardaway's artillery detachment was directed to follow. Upon approaching the church, Alexander halted Hardaway's command, directing Parker with his remaining section to join it. Sending Jordan's Battery to the position on the River

Road before referred to he set out to determine what position was best for Hardaway to occupy. In a short while the latter was directed to move his guns from the Plank Road to Smith's Hill to the north and drive off a Federal battery on the north bank of the river, which had enfiladed McLaws' line whenever it attempted to advance towards Fredericksburg. It was now about 10 A. M., and meanwhile Anderson had commenced to move forward, directing Hardaway to follow him to the right of the church. Under this conflict of orders, Hardaway galloped forward to consult Anderson, who referred him to Gen. Lee. Since Alexander had sent Maj. Huger with the 10 guns of his own battalion to the right in support of Anderson, Hardaway was ordered to comply with the orders of the Chief of Artillery, which he proceeded to do.

Hardaway had been informed that he would find pits for his guns at Smith's Hill, but upon arriving at the designated position, found intrenchments for but four pieces. Many of his men and horses had been without rations for 24 hours, while they had been continually on the move since leaving Chancellorsville the evening before. So sultry and oppressive was the day that a number of his gunners fainted while engaged in the work of clearing away the timber and digging gun pits. But at last the axe details from the gun detachments completed their work, and most of the pieces were in position and fairly well protected before the attack was ready to be made.

To the left of Jordan's four pieces, which occupied a position across a ravine, and some 900 yards down the road, W. P. Carter's four guns were posted on the bluff, with Fry's two guns to the left of him. Parker's section and three pieces of Penick's (Lewis') Battery occupied pits on a knob to the left rear and some 40 feet higher than the bluff on which Carter and Fry were posted. Hurt with a Whitworth occupied a pit at the bend of the ridge 80 yards or more to the left of the knob, while 200 yards to the rear and 100 to the left McCarthy's two guns and Marye's two held the ridge. Lieut. Ferrell's section of Hurt's Battery was kept in reserve.

The part played in the action of the day by Hardaway's command, while a secondary, was quite an important one. As soon as Early, Anderson, and McLaws became engaged, his guns opened upon the Federal Battery of eight pieces in earthworks about a house on the bluff of the north bank, and immediately opposite Smith's Hill. Other Federal guns soon came into action, two from a point 400 yards below, and two in a thicket 200 yards above the main battery. The fire of these 12 guns was principally directed at the four guns of McCarthy's and Marye's batteries and the Whitworth, all of which stood in the open. At one time the fire of Hardaway's right guns was all but silenced, which enabled the enemy to concentrate more successfully on those to the left. But going to the right of his position, Hardaway in person encouraged his gunners to redouble their efforts.

Never in the war was a duel with the Federal artillery conducted under more disadvantageous circumstances. Although the shells were provided with the fuse-igniter attachment, but one Confederate shell in fifteen burst while the Federal ammunition was most effective. Hardaway, an officer of much scientific knowledge, afterwards declared that the meal powder was knocked off the fuses while they were being driven home with the mallet, but in spite of the fact that he was in effect using solid shot almost entirely, six of the enemy's guns in the central work were disabled, and the other two were driven from their position, while the remaining four pieces were practically silenced, though they maintained a desultory fire until after dark. Meantime, McCarthy's section, which had expended its ammunition, had been relieved by Ferrell's section of Hurt's Battery, and sent to the rear. Hardaway's task had been well executed, for by the continuous action of his guns, the fire of the Federal artillery on McLaws' left, hitherto so destructive to the infantry, had been completely diverted.

As night closed in a thick fog had settled over the field which added greatly to the difficulties of the Confederates, who were thus again balked of the fruits of victory by darkness, and the delay in attacking. Under cover of the fog, Brooks' and Newton's divisions reformed about the ford, and upon them Howe's broken division fell back and also reformed under cover of 34 guns on the north bank, protecting the bridge at Banks' and the one at Scott's Ford, a short distance below.

Sedgwick had suffered too severely to think of another day's battle with his troops in their present position. In two days he had lost over 5,000 of his men. He, therefore, advised Hooker that his position was commanded by the enemy's guns on the Taylor House Hill, and asked if he should risk remaining on the south bank. At 1 A. M. he received orders from Hooker's Chief of Staff to "withdraw under cover," and by 5 A. M. the entire corps had crossed the river and taken up its bridges. But the crossing had not been accomplished without some loss, for Alexander had during the afternoon busied himself establishing points of direction for night firing upon the position about the ford in anticipation of Sedgwick's retreat, and during the night Jordan was able to fire upon the masses huddled about the crossing, causing the enemy much annoyance.

This was perhaps the first instance of the employment of indirect fire by the Confederate Artillery. Jordan's position along the bluff to the left of the River Road, facing towards Banks' Ford, was obscured from the latter point by intervening ridges and thickets over which by means of Alexander's deflection marks the fire could be directed upon the enemy. About 1 A. M. Hardaway had also withdrawn Carter's and Fraser's four pieces on his right and shifting his line so as to face the ford, opened fire down the ravine leading thereto, but was soon directed by Alexander to cease firing as McLaws was sending two brigades in that direction. Riding forward to the picket line of the infantry to secure the exact direction of the pontoon bridges, and hearing the artillery of the enemy crossing, Hardaway returned and again shifted his guns so as to deliver an indirect fire upon the approaches to the ford on the north side of the river, and caused his guns to fire from right to left, at the rate of about one shot a minute. About 2 A. M. Hurt's Whitworth was directed upon a deep hollow leading towards Falmouth, in which many stragglers, wagons, etc., could be seen by the light of the numerous fires along the line of retreat. Later it was turned upon a large wagon train concentrated at the junction of the Aquia Creek and United States Ford roads. Although the range was about 3 miles, the fire of the Whitworth was soon adjusted and created consternation in the wagon park, causing the train to disperse in the utmost disorder. The ammunition for the large rifle being very scarce and expensive the fire soon ceased.

All day on the 4th, Brown's, Walker's, McIntosh's, and Jones' battalions had been held in position along the Chancellorsville plateau, the cannoneers requiring no encouragement to throw up hasty works for the guns. With the exception of Walker's batteries, which had been turned over the night before to Maj. Pegram, none of the Artillery was seriously engaged, though most of the batteries fired upon the enemy's works from time to time. Early in the morning, 18 or 20 Federal guns opened fire upon Pegram's position on the Plank Road, and, after a somewhat protracted duel, ceased to fire. In this affair, Pegram seems to have had the better of it, for his guns all remained in position until the morning of the 6th, when the enemy's withdrawal was discovered.

While Sedgwick's last brigade was crossing, he received an order from Hooker countermanding the authority previously given for the withdrawal to which, at 5 A. M. Sedgwick replied that it was too late, and that the bridges were already being taken up while his men were much exhausted.

In spite of the fact that the enemy had escaped, it was with great elation on the morning of the 5th that Huger's and Andrews' guns fired the last shots across the river at Sedgwick's retreating columns, and that the Confederates at sunrise found themselves in complete possession of the southern bank of the river from Fredericksburg to Hooker's contracted position above Chancellorsville. The movement against Sedgwick had been a complete success, and even Gibbon had been withdrawn across the river from the town during the night, while Hooker had not ventured from his works to assist the inferior force which he had ordered up to his own relief. The whole situation presents a tactical anomaly. Hemming a vastly superior enemy up in his works in front of United States Ford, Lee had withdrawn much of his artillery and the larger part of two divisions of infantry from his front to hurl upon an equal force, which had already pushed his rear guard aside, and, uniting them with that broken rear guard, had assailed an entire Federal corps of 30,000 men, rated among the best of his adversaries, overthrowing it and driving it across the river at Banks' Ford, in some disorder at least, in the very face of the main army of the enemy. But still the bold commander-in-chief was not satisfied with what he had done. He knew that Sedgwick's Corps had suffered so severely in men and *morale* that it was not available for immediate service, even had it been transferred to Chancellorsville, instead of being headed for Falmouth. During the afternoon of the 5th, therefore, leaving Early's Division, Barksdale's Brigade and Pendleton's artillery to guard the river from Banks' Ford to the crossings below Fredericksburg, he ordered Anderson and McLaws to return to Chancellorsville with a view to assailing Hooker's position. What was known of that position satisfied every man in the Confederate Army that the worst was yet to come. Ninety thousand men behind works covering a front of five miles, which they had had 48 hours to prepare, with all the advantages which un-

limited quantities of timber, broken ground, and difficult approaches through a dense forest gave them for
defense, with three-fourths of their front covered by
streams on their southwest and northwest, and both
flanks resting on a wide river,—this was the proposition now before some 35,000 Confederates. Not only
would the attack have to be directed squarely on the
Federal front, but little assistance could be expected
from the Artillery. Impenetrable abattis covered the
entire line, and the crest of the works was everywhere
surmounted by head logs with loopholes, while in rear
separate structures were provided for officers and supports from which the former could see and exercise control over the defenders, and from which the latter could
be moved up to the advanced works under cover.

It is doubtful if in the whole military career of Gen.
Lee, a bolder resolve on his part can be discovered
than this one to hurl his troops upon Hooker's final
position at Chancellorsville. But again, it must be
conceded that in arriving at a decision, seemingly so
rash, if not desperate, he had considered the moral attitude of his adversary. Again he did not count the
number of noses and muskets as the supreme factor of
his problem. The moral power of the enemy he regarded inversely as the strength of his breastworks and
preparations for defense. It was the same unflinching
determination which led him to order Longstreet and
Jackson back to their lines at Sharpsburg the preceding
September, that now enabled the great commander to
approach the task before him in so resolute a manner.
He saw too well in both cases the results which would
flow from a more timid course, and he knew that
Hooker, like McClellan, would fall a victim to im-
position. Lee has been harshly criticised for even con-
templating an assault on Hooker's lines, but the question
may be asked his critics, what his position would have
been had he lain supine upon the fields he had won?
In a frank answer to this query is the vindication of his
action, if any justification is needed. It was certainly

not for him to admit to the enemy by inactivity that his last bolt was spent, and invite the Federals to move out upon his army, weakened as it was by four days of tremendous effort and constant strain. Why, may we also ask, should Lee at this juncture, after once having assumed the aggressive, and with unparalleled audacity having divided his army in the face of a superior enemy, now resort to the defensive? Was the resolve to attack Hooker on the 5th more reckless than the actual attack which had been made on the 2d? Of the two decisions, the writer is inclined to consider Jackson's turning movement by far the more daring. But, whether so or not, Lee's willingness to take upon him the consequent risk of the maneuver, retaining under his immediate control but two small divisions, with a powerful enemy both in his front and rear, displayed a higher courage than was ever evinced by any other mortal man upon the field of battle. The maneuver of Jackson, the lieutenant, the lustre of which has all but obscured the other incidents of the campaign, was indeed brilliant, but the courage of Lee, the captain, who permitted it, was far more superb, for victory alone was not the stake—a nation hung in the balance.

No. On May 5, Lee did just what a general with exceptional power to divine the enemy's thoughts, and the boldness to act upon the latter's fears, should have done. He drew his sword once more to strike, knowing that the flash of the blade would itself strike terror to a heart already taking counsel of a timorous mind. And so, when his forces were again marshalled for attack, the blow became unnecessary; there was no adversary to meet him. Critics deal too much in numbers. They forget that moral force, in the words of Napoleon, is everything in war. Who shall say that the violent storm which caused Lee to postpone his attack on the afternoon of the 5th was not as welcome to Lee as to Hooker? We may surmise this with respect to the former. We have evidence from his hasty withdrawal across the river under its protection that it was welcome to the latter.

During the afternoon and before Anderson's troops had come up from Salem Church, the rain fell in torrents, converting the spongy soil into a vast quagmire. In spite of the almost impassable condition of the roads, Alexander who had reconnoitered the extreme Federal left during the morning, and had directed the scattered batteries to report to their respective corps, moved his own battalion by the River Road and set his men to work digging pits and preparing a position near the Childs house, from which to open upon the enemy behind Mine Run. The rain continued to fall, but all night the cannoneers kept at their work. Alexander's position, partly around the bend of the river and near the bank, was such as to enable his guns to deliver an oblique fire upon a hostile group of artillery on the enemy's extreme left.

As soon as Hooker learned from Sedgwick that the 6th Corps had abandoned the southern bank of the river, he too determined to withdraw to the north bank, but went through the idle form of calling his corps commanders together to hear their views. As it happened, the majority were of his own opinion, but judging from the frame of mind of the commander-in-chief, it is doubtful if he would have waived his own views had they all been opposed to them. During the 5th preparations were made for recrossing the Rappahannock and an interior line of works, running from Scott's Dam to the mouth of Hunting Run, was constructed to cover the withdrawal. At nightfall the retreat, greatly favored by the storm, began. First the Artillery crossed over the bridges, the ends of which were all but submerged by the rising current which threatened their destruction. By daylight the great mass of the Federal Army was on the north side, and by 8 A. M. the rear corps under Meade had crossed, leaving behind nothing but several field hospitals full of wounded soldiers. Meanwhile, at early dawn on the 6th, the storm unabated, while Lieut. Taylor of Eubank's Battery was placing his four Napoleons and

Lieut. J. D. Smith, of Jordan's battery, his section in the six epaulments, which Alexander had constructed near the river during the night, they were suddenly fired upon by a group of guns across the river and squarely on their own flank. A number of men and horses were wounded and several dismounted limber chests exploded before the detachments succeeded in getting their pieces under cover. To this fire, Capt. Jordan, in command of the guns, was quite unable to reply. During the night the enemy had constructed works on the hill some 800 yards distant in which two batteries had been placed to prevent the occupation of Jordan's position, which commanded the lower bridge at Scott's Dam, and it was only now that it was discovered by the Confederate pickets that Hooker had abandoned his advanced lines, and that few Federal troops remained on the south side of the river.

The batteries on the north bank continued to hammer at Jordan until 9 A. M. when Alexander brought up Moody's Battery, a section of Parker's, and a 24-pounder howitzer of Woolfolk's Battery, seven pieces in all, which, aided by Jordan's guns, engaged the enemy. During the duel which ensued two fresh hostile batteries to the right of the others uncovered, and all being well protected Alexander commanded his guns to cease firing. Jordan's six pieces remained under cover in their pits, while the enemy continued to fire upon him until the other guns were withdrawn. This incident closed the operations of the Confederate Artillery in the battle of Chancellorsville, in which Alexander's Battalion alone had lost Brown's entire section of Parker's Battery by capture, 6 men killed, 25 wounded, 21 missing, and 46 horses killed, disabled, or captured, or a total loss in officers and men of 62, which was about twenty per cent of those engaged. The losses of Walton's and Cabell's battalions of the 1st Corps were 28 and 45, respectively, while Garnett's loss was probably not less than 25. In the 2d Corps, Brown, Walker, Carter, Jones, McIntosh, and Andrews together lost 150 men, while the total loss in Cutts' and Nelson's reserve battalions and Beckham's horse batteries was about 30. The aggregate Artillery loss in personnel at Chancellorsville was, therefore, not less than 275, or in the neighborhood of seven per cent of the number actually engaged. For field artillery at this period the loss was enormous. But the loss inflicted upon the enemy's artillery had been still greater. In a report of casualties, which Gen. Hunt characterized as "imperfect," he states his losses as 5 officers and 50 men killed, 13 officers and 268 men wounded, 53 captured or missing, or an aggregate loss in personnel of 389, not including the horse batteries. In horses the loss was 389, and 14 pieces of superior ordnance were taken by the Confederates who themselves lost but 8. Although Hooker's entire loss aggregated 16,844 of all arms, that of his artillery was disproportionately large for the circumstances under which it was engaged.

Nor had the Federal Artillery by any means measured up to its former standard of efficiency. The reason is not difficult to discover. The command of the Artillery which had been committed to Hunt by both McClellan and Burnside was withdrawn from him by Hooker, and the splendid soldier whose services at Malvern Hill, Sharpsburg, and Fredericksburg had won great fame for him as an artillerist, was relegated to a purely administrative duty. Not only was the superb organization which he had perfected much broken up by scattering the Artillery here and there, and giving the various corps and division commanders too high a degree of control over it, but many of the batteries, unknown to Hunt, were ordered to be left in camp on the north side of the river when Hooker's main force moved to Chancellorsville. The promotion and transfer of numbers of the old regular artillery officers to other branches of the service also deprived many of the divisional battalions of experienced commanders, and throughout the arm a great deficiency in the quality and number of field officers existed. For the command and administration of an arm with 412 guns, 980 carriages, 9,543 officers and men, and 8,544 horses, besides the immense ammunition trains requisite for such a force of artillery, there were during the Chancellorsville campaign but five field officers of artillery present with the Army, and they were provided with miserably-inefficient staffs! Add to this the fact that there was no active head to the Federal Artillery until Col. Wainwright took command at Fairview on the morning of the 3d, and that Gen. Hunt was not given entire control until 10 P. M. that night, and the wonder is that Hooker's scattered batteries maintained themselves as well as they did. If Hooker were open to criticism as a general in no other respect the gross mismanagement of his artillery, the Federal arm *par excellence,* already famous the world over for the superiority of its organization and material and the high efficiency of its officers and men, would appear to be inexcusable.

Many writers speak of Hooker's movements up to the time his three corps reached Chancellorsville on the 30th, as exceptionally fine. If to dispatch one's entire cavalry force, with the exception of a small brigade, to another quarter of the universe on a wild-goose chase; if to leave a great part of one's artillery at the base and provide no chief for the rest, but commit it entirely to the control of corps and division commanders; if to pen one's infantry up in the heart of a forest without having even attempted a reconnaissance of the surrounding country, and leave every approach, except a single line of communication, open to be blocked by a nearby enemy known to be exceptionally bold and active; if such movements are correct, then Hooker's conduct of the campaign was indeed fine. But it seems to the writer that Hooker in disposing of his cavalry and demolishing his artillery in the way he did, committed acts which alone are enough to condemn any general guilty of such acts as inefficient and lacking in the fundamental conceptions of the tactics of the three arms combined. And such a view, it is believed, will universally obtain as time progresses and knowledge of events at Chancellorsville becomes more general.

But now as to the tactical employment and services of the Confederate Artillery, the actual operations of which have been so closely followed. From the standpoint of the effectiveness of its fire, we have but to consider the results it undoubtedly accomplished in the conflict with an artillery superior in numbers and material. Again the Federal reports teem with references to the severity and accuracy of the Confederate artillery fire; not one but mentions the Confederate guns in a way showing that the writer had in mind their fire as bearing a direct influence upon the issue of events at every point, and this in spite of the inferior grade of ammunition with which Lee's gunners were provided. We must at least concede, that with such a serious defect to overcome, an exceptional degree of energy and efficiency was required on the part of the personnel to accomplish even what might have been expected of ordinary artillery.

The mobility which the Confederate batteries displayed in this campaign is astounding when the deficiency in the number and quality of their draught animals is considered. In no battle of the war was artillery called upon for greater activity on the march after contact with the enemy had been gained. Beginning with April 29th, when Lee directed his Chief of Artillery to set the reserve battalions in motion, there was not a day when a great part of his artillery was not on the march. The transfer of the Artillery of the 2d Corps from below Hamilton's Crossing to the vicinity of Chancellorsville on the night of the 30th, was rapid and conducted in such a successful manner over a single road that there is an entire absence of complaint on the part of division and brigade commanders about blocked roads, etc., to which infantry commanders are so prone to attribute the causes of their own delays. With little rest, again the great column was set in motion and whirled over 15 miles or more of despicable roads, both narrow and difficult, and not only did it arrive at the designated point of rendezvous in good order and in good time, but some of the battalions were forced impatiently to remain in the clearings near the head of Jackson's column, when the signal for the infantry attack was given. Indeed, the Artillery seems rather to have been too forward, as in Crutchfield's case and that of Carter on the night of the 2d, instead of being tardy in its arrival. In spite of darkness and the forbidding character of the terrain, when dawn of the 3d broke every gun of both corps was in the best position which those responsible for the posting of the Artillery could select, a fact which enabled Alexander, who accompanied Archer in his attack on Hazel Grove, to secure the position with Pegram's batteries the instant the Federals abandoned it, and instead of his lacking guns at the critical point, there was actually a surplus of them at hand in the foremost line. The coöperation of Alexander, with Stuart, was extraordinary and elicited from Stuart himself the statement that the action of the Artillery was superb, attributing the rapid movements of the batteries as he did to the improved battalion organization. But, if Alexander's coöperation with his corps commander was active and complete, no less so was that of Brown, Walker, Jones, McIntosh, Poague, and Huger with their respective chiefs. Everywhere we found them striving to be at the right point at the right time. The activity displayed by Hardaway was also noticeable. Stumbling through trackless thickets, cutting his way with pick and axe to the front, we find him moving a part of his guns, at least, forward with the infantry as it advanced from the south to the Chancellorsville plateau, soon to move to a distant point of the theater of operations, only to push on over bottomless roads to a more active conflict, after a distressing night of toil and hunger. On the 4th we find Alexander's Battalion whisked from Chancellorsville after five days of constant marching or fighting, many miles to the rear and then back again to the river, where the morning of the 6th it was as active as when "boots and saddles" was blown at Hanover Junction a week before. In this week a number of the batteries of this battalion marched over 100 miles, in addition to being actually engaged three days and three nights. We have seen that the Horse Artillery under Beckham had lost nothing of its old dash so well known to the enemy. Yet, at least two of the light batteries, Moore's and Penick's, maneuvered with such rapidity in action as they dashed from hill to hill before Sedgwick's column on the 4th, always in the front and retarding the enemy, that they were mistaken by the Federal commander himself for horse artillery.

Another fact to be discerned from the records is the entire absence of friction in the Confederate Artillery, and between it and the Army as a whole at Chancellorsville, while so much discord and lack of cohesion existed in the same arm of the Federal Army in this campaign. In Hooker's army, after the battle, there was a widespread feeling that the Federal Artillery had failed, a sentiment so prevalent that Gen. Hunt himself saw fit to offer explanations of the cause in his report. While one is forced to absolve the Federal Artillery itself of all blame, yet the fact remains that, though not of its own doing, it was rendered collectively inefficient throughout the campaign in spite of the individual gallantry and prowess of Dilger, Weed, Best, Osborn and others. Its very losses, which included about 20 officers, are sufficient evidence of the courage and fighting capacity of the Federal gunners, and it seems a pity that so superb a fighting machine as that which under Hunt was inherited by Hooker, should have been wantonly sacrificed to the ignorance and stupidity of one whom the world at large has seen fit to credit with unusual skill as an organizer, palliating in a measure thereby his miserable failure as an army commander.

It has already been remarked that the Confederate Reserve Artillery was by necessity perverted from its true function in the campaign. Unless battalions which must be committed to the first line before a shot is fired can be classed as an artillery reserve, Lee had none at

Chancellorsville, and in this respect was sadly crippled. In the narrative of events we have noted numerous occasions when such a force might have been, and had it been available would have been, employed with controlling influence upon the issue. All that can be said of the nominal reserve artillery is that in the sphere of duty assigned it, the services it rendered fully measured up to the expectations of the commander-in-chief, who in the conclusion of his report paid high tribute to the Artillery of his army in the following words:

"Cols. Crutchfield, Alexander, Walker, and Lieut.-Cols. Brown, Carter, and Andrews, with the officers and men of their commands, are mentioned as deserving especial commendation. The batteries under Gen. Pendleton also acted with great gallantry." And later: "The Horse Artillery accompanied the infantry, and participated with credit to itself in the engagement."

In concluding this account of the great campaign of May, 1863, the direct influence of the Confederate Artillery upon the issue demands notice by reason of the fact that history has almost completely ignored the matter. Without calling further attention to the service rendered by Pendleton at Fredericksburg, which was jointly rendered with that of Early's infantry, at least two instances may be cited when the Artillery exercised a direct and determining influence upon the ultimate result attained by Lee. Had Sickles not been checked by Col. Brown at the furnace on May 2, he would most certainly have developed the line of least resistance in that direction, and thrown the main column of his corps towards the southwest instead of, by a more easterly movement, becoming involved with the left of Anderson's Division. Had he, while engaging Anderson with his own left, been free to follow up Jackson's column with the force which Brown's prompt action balked in its advance, the trend of that column would have been more accurately determined, and at an early hour in the day, that is before 1 P. M., Hooker would most certainly have been advised of its true direction, for already the head of the column had turned northward at a point less than two miles from Brown's position, and nothing seems more probable than that this fact would have been discovered through flanking parties of Sickles' Corps drifting up against it during the advance of their main body. Already Berdan, with a division close behind, had almost reached the unfinished railroad; had he reached and freely possessed himself of it, this road would have formed the natural line of extension for the troops behind in their effort to turn the flank of any force which might seek to block their advance. Possessed of this railroad Sickles' men would have had a short route to the Brock Road, from which Jackson's movement to the north would have been plainly visible, and the very denseness of the country intervening between the furnace and the Brock Road would have led small parties of the Federals to search for points of vantage from which to observe the movements of the enemy. From the point where Berdan was actually checked by Brown to the point along the railroad from which a clear view of Jackson's column moving to the north across Poplar Run and the railroad itself, and ascending the Trigg House Hill might have been had, the distance was not over $1\frac{1}{2}$ miles. The information which Sickles would thus have secured would at once have corrected the false impression under which he labored, and which he created in Hooker's mind about the enemy's movement to the south, and, added to the reports coming in from Howard's front, would have altered the whole estimate of the situation at headquarters, giving Hooker and Howard some five hours to prepare to meet the attack. In half that time, the 11th Corps alone, with such reserve artillery as was available for use on the Federal right, could have been so disposed behind Hunting Run as to present an impregnable front. With Barlow and every available reserve hurrying to Howard's left, and Sickles already wedged into the immense gap below the furnace, it would not have required a tactician of the first order to cut Lee's Army in twain. In fact, Brown's single battery at one time stood between Hooker and the accomplishment of this task. But let us pass from what may appear too speculative, to that which is beyond the realm of conjecture, and which savors of reality.

When Stuart arrived at the scene of action along the Plank Road at midnight, May 2, he was totally ignorant of the situation, and none of Jackson's staff except Col. A. S. Pendleton reported to him. Fortunately, however, he found Col. Alexander, who had the situation in its broad aspects in hand. Rodes and Colston were of course willing and anxious to give Stuart the benefit of all the information in their possession, but their observations had been necessarily hasty and local in character. It seems certain that no one at the moment was so familiar with the situation as the Chief of Artillery, whose very duties had led him to make a thorough reconnaissance of the paths and roads leading to the front. That Stuart appreciated this fact, is evidenced by his immediately associating Alexander with him for the purpose of making a general examination of the ground. It is now important to note from the tenor of Stuart's report that Alexander, and not he, discovered the Hazel Grove position and at once grasped its importance. This fact is proved by the useless and costly effort which Stuart made with Lane's and Ramseur's brigades in the morning along the road, while Alexander was massing his batteries in readiness in the vista to seize Hazel Grove, at the first opportunity. From the moment he had first laid eyes on Hazel Grove, Alexander never lost its importance from view, and in the light of what transpired, it seems fortunate for the Confederates that its seizure was not seriously attempted on the night of the 2d, before Sickles and Pleasanton abandoned the position. Had this been done, the attention of the Federals might have been called to the point, and the head instead of the tail of Sickles' column of attack would have been directed towards the Confederates, thereby saving the key-point of Hooker's line of defense, and many men who met their fate in the midnight fiasco.

Conceding then, that the occupation of Hazel Grove was primarily due to the ready perception of Stuart's Chief of Artillery, we must now go further and consider the controlling influence its occupation by the Artillery exerted upon the issue. In the first place, there is no reason to suppose that having twice failed on the morning of the 3d to carry the Federal works in front of Fairview, although aided by Pegram's artillery, Stuart's infantry could have succeeded in a third attempt without artillery. In fact, the Federals themselves unanimously ascribed the loss of their line of defense to the Confederate batteries at Hazel Grove, the oblique fire of which Best's and Osborn's guns were unable to withstand. The great mass of guns at Fairview Cemetery comprised the very bulwark of the Federal defense, and it was those guns in large measure which had swept back Stuart's gallant infantry from the works they had taken, while the Confederate left was subjected to an increasing pressure. To the threatened point, Stuart's attention was more and more directed, but meantime Alexander was moving the bulk of his artillery to the extreme right, and when finally his artillery preparations were well under way it must be observed that it was not the Federal right, but that portion of the line upon which the Confederate Artillery exerted its influence, that yielded, which of course relieved the intense pressure on Stuart's left. It is thus seen that the superiority of fire attained by Alexander over the Federal Artillery, alone made possible the success of Stuart's third infantry assault, for it was the withdrawal of their artillery that broke the backbone of the enemy's resistance.

There are few better examples to be found than this one of the power of artillery when once it has attained a superiority of fire. Then it is that the crisis of the battle has arrived, and whatever may be the timber of the defending infantry, unless there are close at hand fresh guns, as in the case of the Confederate short-range batteries at Sharpsburg and Fredericksburg, to uncover when the hostile artillery becomes masked, the day is usually lost if the assaulting infantry is in earnest and numerically adequate to its task.   Stuart was fortunate in possessing such an infantry, and it drove home with all the ardor of its old recklessness favored by the fact that almost until "cold steel" was the word, the supporting batteries were able to maintain over its head a heavy fire upon the somewhat elevated line of works held by the enemy.

The loss of Fairview was but the precursor of Hooker's withdrawal from the south side of the river, for by its fall the Federal left was compelled to retire before Anderson and McLaws. Even before it fell, Hooker's heart had become set upon a general retrograde movement. Otherwise, he would surely have allowed his batteries to be supplied with ammunition, however hopeless their struggle might have appeared.

CHAPTER XXIX

WHEN it became certain that Hooker had withdrawn his immense army from the upper fords and had reestablished his old camps about Fredericksburg and Falmouth, Gen. Lee ordered his troops back to the lines held by them during the winter.

Col. Walton immediately placed the bulk of the artillery of the 1st Corps in camp at Stanard's farm, a few miles below Massaponax Church, while Col. Brown moved his batteries to the old artillery camping grounds in rear of Hamilton's Crossing and about Guiney's Station. Alexander, however, moved his battalion to the immediate neighborhood of Bowling Green, a point which was thought by both Gens. Lee and Pendleton to be too far to the rear in case of emergency. Meanwhile, the horses of the various artillery commands, which were greatly worn down and depleted by the strain of the recent campaign, were turned out to pasture, although the orders were general that the Artillery should be kept well in hand and prepared to move at a moment's notice. Reports of the condition of the batteries, detailing the number of serviceable guns, horses, and the strength in personnel of each were directed to be made, in order that all deficiencies might be made up as far as possible.

The old idea that artillery battalions were an integral part of infantry divisions had by this time almost disappeared, an advance in the right direction which had taken long to accomplish. But still the old view continued to crop out on occasions, as in the case of Col. Cabell, who, instead of moving his battalion along the Telegraph Road, as directed, to join Walton and rest his horses, maintained his position on Lee's Hill in accordance with Longstreet's views until he was peremp-

torily ordered by Pendleton to repair to the rear.   Cabell, it seems, had preferred to consider his command as
permanently attached to one of Longstreet's divisions,
and had been most remiss in rendering his reports
through Col. Walton, Chief of Artillery 1st Corps.

Gen. Longstreet had arrived at Fredericksburg on
the 6th of May and soon after Pickett's and Hood's
divisions began to arrive with Dearing's and Henry's
battalions of artillery.   On the day Longstreet arrived
A. P. Hill resumed command of the 2d Corps, Stuart
returning to his own division.   Gen. Lee had also urged
the return of Ransom's Division, which the Secretary
of War, on the 6th, directed D. H. Hill in North Carolina to set in motion for Fredericksburg, if it could be
done with safety.

The great shock of the campaign now occurred, for
on May 10, Gen. Jackson succumbed.   The story of his
last hours on this earth is one full of pathos, as well as
of the most inspiring lessons for the soldier.   In the
hour of his death he was as great as when upon the
various battlefields of his career, with exalted mien and
superb composure, he led his men to victory.   Concerning his wounding and death, Longstreet wrote: "The
shock was a very severe one to men and officers, but the
full extent of our loss was not felt until the remains
of the beloved general had been sent home.   The dark
clouds of the future then began to lower above the
Confederates."   Gen. Lee in a note to the wounded
general on the 3d, in the midst of battle had already declared that, could he have directed events, he should
have chosen, for the good of the country, to have been
disabled in Jackson's stead.   In closing his message, he
congratulated Jackson upon the victory his "skill and
energy" had won, but the latter, expressing appreciation
of his superior's remarks, declared that Gen. Lee should
give the praise to God and not to him.

Soon after his wounding, he had been removed by
order of Gen. Lee to the Chandler house near Guiney's
Station, where Dr. McGuire did all in his power to save

him, but on Thursday the 7th he developed pneumonia of the right lung, doubtless attributable to the fall from the litter the night he was wounded. Fortunately for the peace of his mind, Mrs. Jackson arrived this day with their infant child, and took the place of his chaplain who had remained almost constantly with him. By Saturday, Drs. Hoge, Breckenridge, and Tucker had joined McGuire in an effort to save him, and noting their presence he said to Dr. McGuire: "I see from the number of physicians that you think my condition dangerous, but I thank God, if it is His will, that I am ready to go." When informed by Mrs. Jackson at daylight the next morning that he should prepare for the worst, he was silent for a moment and then said, "It will be infinite gain to be translated to heaven." And so we see that although this wonderful man still clung to a hope of recovery, his confidence in the future was as supreme as his self-confidence had been on earth. Never once did he express a doubt of his ability to rise paramount to present difficulties or to meet the future. His sole request was to be buried in Lexington, in the Valley of Virginia, where as a simple and unassuming professor of the Science of War he had kept the smothered fire of his genius aglow while preparing himself and a host of his pupils for the inevitable struggle which he had foreseen. When told by his wife that before sundown he would be in Heaven, he called for Dr. McGuire and asked him if he must die. To the affirmative answer he received, his reply was, "Very good, very good, it is all right." His efforts then were to comfort his heart-broken wife, and when Col. Pendleton, whom he had trained as a soldier and loved very dearly, entered his room about 1 P. M., he asked who was preaching at headquarters on this his last Sabbath. Being informed that the whole Army was praying for him, he said, "Thank God, they are very kind. It is the Lord's day; my wish is fulfilled. I have always desired to die on Sunday."

His mind now began to weaken while his lips frequently muttered commands as if he were on the field

of battle, then words of comfort for his wife. When
tendered a drink of brandy and water, he declined it,
saying, "It will only delay my departure and do no
good. I want to preserve my mind, if possible, to the
last." Again he was told that but few hours remained
for him, and again he replied, feebly but firmly, "Very
good, it is all right." In the delirium which preceded
his death he cried out, "Order A. P. Hill to prepare for
action, pass the infantry to the front rapidly,—tell Maj.
Hawks—" and then, pausing, a smile of ineffable sweetness spread over his pallid face and with an expression
as if of relief, he said, "No, no. Let us cross over the
river and rest under the shade of the trees."* Then
without sign of pain, or the least struggle, his spirit
passed onward and upward to God.

Such were the final moments of the great soldier.
With body all but cold in death, so long as his pulse
continued the dictates of his heart were pure. Almost
to the instant that heart ceased to beat, his mind gave
evidence of the quality of the man in the flash of the
will, though now subconscious, which possessed his
spirit. Still his mind dwelt upon rapid action and the
rush of infantry, which ever filled his soul with joy, but
then, even in the last flicker of his intellect, he realized
that the flag of truce had been raised by his enemies and
interposing the stay of his final words "No, no—," he
died in the happiness of the earthly victory he had won.
Let us be thankful that he saw his men preparing to
rest upon their arms—not engaged in the heated
turmoil of the charge when he bade them farewell. Let
us be thankful that this dispensation was granted him
by the Maker who gently led him to the shade of the
river side where rested all those gallant associates who
had preceded him. No longer were they his pupils and
his subordinates in war, but his equals in the eternity of
peace. But yet an earthly rite remained to those whom
he had left behind, for far off from the scene of conflict,
that youthful band, bound together then as it is now,

*This remark was as given above, according to Capt. James Power Smith
of Jackson's staff, and not merely as usually quoted without the two first words.

by the traditions of his fame, bore his body to the grave. How fitting that a caisson of the cadet battery with which he had for so many years drilled his pupils and the Confederate Artillery should form his hearse, and that his body should lie in state in the old tower class-room, wherein he had set so noble an example to youth. It was in that very room that he had declared, "If war must come, then I will welcome war," and that the South in such event should "throw away the scabbard."

In the shadow of the majestic Blue Ridge, with the great North Mountain as his head stone, which like a huge sentinel stands guard beside the parade ground of his life, tenderly was his body laid to rest by the youthful soldiers he loved so well, but still, wielding the uncovered blade of immortality,

> "His spirit wraps yon dusky mountain;
> His memory sparkles o'er each fountain;
> The meanest rill, the mightiest river,
> Rolls, mingling with his fame forever."

For one part of the Army, at least, it was Jackson, the artilleryman, that had gone, for he in a higher degree than any of Lee's lieutenants had endeared himself to the gunners to whose welfare he was ever attentive and of whose success he was ever proud. The old love of the arm which he could not overcome in spite of the more general command he had been clothed with, coupled with the knowledge of the gunners that their leader had once commanded a battery, created and maintained a bond of sympathy between Jackson and his artillery evidenced by innumerable little incidents in his career as a general. One thing is certain, he was the first of Lee's lieutenants to grasp the idea of artillery as an entity and to employ it accordingly, and in this he was ably assisted by Col. Crutchfield, between whom and his chief the most thorough confidence existed. No such relations as theirs existed between Longstreet and Walton, neither of whom proceeded upon the principle that the Chief of Artillery should be able to read the

very soul of his commander, and by that constant and
close association which alone can breed the highest confidence between men, especially between soldiers, be able
to frame his every action in conformity with his superi-
or's views. Mutual confidence between a commanding
general and his chief of artillery is certainly essential
to the success of the artillery, if not to the army as a
whole, for occasions will arise when the supreme commander must needs direct the movements of his batteries and there is always danger that the limitations and
necessities of the special arm may be lost sight of by one
who views the situation in its general aspect. Now, if
the chief of artillery has by his obedience, by his
readiness to act, and by his sympathy with the wider
problems of the general, won a personal place in addition to his official position on the staff of his commander, he is prepared to suggest, without danger of
giving offense to his superior, a change here and there
which will at once inure to the benefit of his arm, and
enable it to accomplish the best results. If, however,
there is a want of sympathy between the two, or if the
subordinate holds himself aloof, or stands upon his
dignity and receives his orders in a perfunctory way,
rather suggesting by his conduct a superior specialized
knowledge, lack of harmony is sure to result with its
many evil consequences. We must concede, in view of
these facts, that Jackson was most fortunate in possessing Crutchfield, from whose relations with the commanding general the artillery of his corps in turn
directly benefited.

The loss of Jackson was accepted by Lee in the same
spirit of Christian fortitude for which he was ever conspicuous, and the day following his death the highest
tribute ever paid a soldier was published in the following
words:

"With deep grief, the commanding general announces to the
Army the death of Lieut.-Col. T. J. Jackson, who expired on the
10th inst., at 3:15 P. M. The daring, skill, and energy of this great
and good soldier, by the decree of an all-wise Providence, are now
lost to us. But while we mourn his death, we feel that his spirit

still lives and will inspire the whole army with his indomitable courage and unshaken confidence in God as our hope and strength. Let his name be a watchword to his corps, who have followed him to victory on so many fields. Let his officers and soldiers emulate his invincible determination to do everything in the defense of our beloved country.

> "R. E. LEE,
> *"General."*

And to Stuart, the bereft Commander-in-Chief wrote, "May his spirit pervade our whole army; our country will then be secure."*

These words of Lee are referred to as the greatest tribute ever paid a soldier, for never before or since has so great a commander-in-chief as Lee appealed to the love and memory of a lieutenant as the spirit which diffused should prove the motive power of his army.

On May 11th, the Chief of Artillery, 2d Corps, reported that immediate steps had been undertaken to reorganize and refit his batteries. As it shows the condition of the Artillery in general, the substance of his report is given.

Many guns were rendered unserviceable through lack of horses. The available ones were as follows.

Walker's Battalion of 5 batteries, 14 guns in camp and 4 on picket near Hamilton's Crossing.

Jones' Battalion of 4 batteries, 8 guns in camp and 4 on picket on the left.

Carter's Battalion of 4 batteries, 13 guns in camp and 3 at the repair train in rear.

Andrews' Battalion of 4 batteries, 14 guns in camp.

Hardaway's (Brown's) Battalion of 6 batteries, 12 guns in camp, and 4 on picket in the center.

McIntosh's Battalion of 4 batteries, 14 guns in camp.

Thus it is seen that but three batteries had been left along the front while there were 87 guns available for service in the 2d Corps.

Meantime, Col. Brown had sent out two officers from each of his battalions amply provided with money to

---

Rebellion Records, Series I, Vol. XXV, Part II, pp. 792-3.

buy fresh horses and authorized to sell the condemned battery horses to farmers who might be willing to purchase them for future use.

The condition of Cabell's Battalion on the 15th is indicative of that of the others of the 1st Corps. McCarthy's Battery with two 3-inch rifles, two 6-pounders, one 4-horse battery wagon and two quartermaster wagons, had 54 horses of which 12 were unserviceable. Manly's Battery had one 3-inch rifle, two 20-pounder howitzers, two 4-horse battery wagons, two quartermaster wagons, and 90 horses, of which 20 were unserviceable. With Carlton's Battery, there were two 10-pounder Parrotts, one 12-pounder howitzer, three battery wagons with 12 mules and 73 horses, seven mules and twelve horses being unserviceable, while Fraser's Battery had one 10-pounder Parrot, one 3-inch rifle, one 12-pounder howitzer, one forge, three wagons, and 62 horses, of which six were unserviceable. Including mounts for the battalion sergeant-major, forge master, wagon master, quartermaster-sergeant, and mounted courier, 88 horses were required to complete the complement of this battalion alone, while two Napoleons for McCarthy, three for Manly, two for Carlton, and a 12-pounder Blakely for Fraser were soon expected to arrive from Richmond.

Gen. Pendleton made every effort to secure the horses needed for the Artillery, but before the end of the month was able to secure but 396. The condition with respect to horses of the various battalions after the preceding campaign is shown by the distribution of this supply, which was as follows:

Hardaway's Battalion _____ 112
Jones' Battalion _____ 17
Walker's Battalion _____ 56
Carter's Battalion _____ 14
McIntosh's Battalion _____ 34
Andrews' Battalion _____ 40
Eshleman's Battalion _____ 32
Garnett's Battalion _____ 26
Cabell's Battalion _____ 10
Alexander's Battalion _____ 55

This issue by no means supplied all the wants, which fact gives a pretty good idea of the suffering and service which the field artillery horses had undergone during the short space of a single week, for it will be recalled that the batteries were fairly well mounted when they left their winter quarters the 29th of April.

Extraordinary efforts were now being made by the Bureau of Ordnance to provide the necessary material, and Col. Gorgas himself was present to examine into the exact needs of all, and found that in general a marked improvement in the ammunition was reported. The shells for the 20-pounder Parrotts, due to defects in the castings, were still unsatisfactory, for many of them were reported to have burst near the muzzle. The new projectile for the Whitworths, which had been fabricated in Richmond, however, proved a great success. In the main, the field ordnance operations had been well conducted during the campaign and satisfaction in that respect was general. Capt. William Allan, Chief of Ordnance, 2d Corps, had displayed unusual ability, and his promotion was again urged by Col. Gorgas.

Nothing is so indicative of the growing appreciation of the importance of the Artillery as the increased interest now displayed in the theoretical features of gunnery. By a special order of June 8, a board to consist of not less than three nor more than six artillery officers, to be designated by the Chief of Artillery, was created and directed to meet the first day of each month, or as soon thereafter as practicable, to report such facts in regard to material, ammunition, and any other matters concerning the Artillery, and to make recommendations for its improvement. The board was also directed to compile range tables for the various types of guns in use. On the 15th, Gen. Pendleton appointed Col. Alexander, Majs. Dearing and Henry, Capts. Reilly, Blount, and Fraser to the board, and immediately they set to work, extending their investigations over a wide field and contributing in innumerable ways to the betterment of the arm.*

It was at once found that a number of vacancies existed among the superior officers of the Field Artillery, which hampered the effective administration and leadership of the battalions. The number of guns with the Army entitled the arm, under the law, to 3 brigadier-generals, 7 colonels, 11 lieutenant-colonels, and 17 majors, whereas there were actually commissioned but 1 brigadier-general, 6 colonels, 6 lieutenant-colonels, there being, however, 19 majors, or two more than for which authority of law existed. Already several promotions of importance had been made, among which was that of Capt. Benj. T. Eshleman, of the Washington Artillery Battalion, as its major with rank as of March 26, 1863. This battalion had not only furnished the Chief of Artillery of the 1st Corps, but three majors besides, namely, Garnett, Dearing, and Eshleman, while one of its original captains, Thomas L. Rosser, had already become a colonel of cavalry. Both he and Dearing later became major-generals of cavalry.†

It was but a few days before the artillery board of which Col. Alexander was president, and in the deliberations of which he played a leading rôle, drafted a plan for the reorganization of the Artillery and submitted it to the commander-in-chief, with what result we shall see.

By special order dated May 30, the Army of Northern Virginia was reorganized into three corps with Longstreet, Ewell, and A. P. Hill as corps commanders. The 1st Corps now consisted of McLaws', Hood's, and Pickett's divisions, the 2d Corps of Early's, Edward Johnson's, and Rodes' divisions, and the 3d Corps of R. H. Anderson's, Heth's, and Pender's divisions. Rodes' and Anderson's divisions each contained five,

---

*Rebellion Records, Series I, Vol. XXVII, pp. 873, 895.

†Rosser, Garnett, and Dearing were members of the graduating class at West Point when they resigned in April, 1861. When the Washington Artillery Battalion reported in Richmond in May they were assigned to duty with it, the first as a captain and the others as lieutenants.

Pickett's three, and all the others four brigades. The Chief of Artillery was directed to designate the artillery for the various corps and the General Reserve Artillery was abolished.* This order marks a great crisis in the development, not only of the Confederate, but of the artillery organization of the world. For the first time practical effect was to be given the growing recognition of the fact that a general reserve artillery was no longer necessary, and that the better tactical employment of the arm required the distribution of all the guns among the corps, if the danger of part of them being left inactive in the rear was to be overcome. The advantages of corps artillery have been previously discussed at length. Suffice it to repeat that together with the change of name came also a change of position in the order of march, and that every leader of troops and every staff officer were at once compelled to recognize that no part of the artillery was to remain in idleness, but that all was to take a place in the line of battle since improved material with its increased range enabled the withdrawal of battalions for special missions, even after they had once become engaged. It should here be noted that Lee in the employment of his artillery had anticipated the actual change in organization, which was, therefore, in large measure, but the logical result of a gradual process of development in his tactics. Whatever may be claimed as to the theoretical development of artillery organization and tactics, the Confederates certainly gave practical form to the conception of corps artillery in its highest sense, and the innovation was soon accepted and adopted by the armies of the continent.

On June 2 and 4, Pendleton gave form to the new artillery organization by first designating three divisional and two reserve battalions for each of the three corps of the Army, and then assigning a chief of artillery to each. The completed organization was as follows:

*Rebellion Records, Series I, Vol. XXV, Part II, p. 850, Special Order No. 146.

1ST CORPS (Longstreet)

Col. James B. Walton, Chief of Artillery

DIVISIONAL BATTALIONS

CABELL'S BATTALION
Col. Henry Coalter Cabell

1. "A" Battery, 1st N. C. Reg.,	Capt. Basil C. Manly.
2. Pulaski (Ga.) Battery,	Capt. John C. Fraser.
3. 1st Co. Richmond Howitzers,	Capt. Edward S. McCarthy.
4. Troup (Ga.) Battery,	Capt. Henry H. Carlton.

DEARING'S BATTALION

Maj. James Dearing

1. Fauquier Battery,	Capt. Robert M. Stribling.
2. Richmond Hampden Battery,	Capt. William H. Caskie.
3. Richmond Fayette Battery,	Capt. Miles C. Macon.
4. Lynchburg Battery,	Capt. Jos. G. Blount.

HENRY'S BATTALION

Maj. M. W. Henry

1. Branch (N. C.) Battery,	Capt. Alexander C. Latham.
2. Charleston German Battery,	Capt. Wm. K. Bachman.
3. Palmetto (S. C.) Battery,	Capt. Hugh R. Garden.
4. Rowan (N. C.) Battery,	Capt. James Reilly.

ALEXANDER'S BATTALION

Col. E. Porter Alexander

1. Ashland Battery,	Capt. Pichegru Woolfolk, Jr.
2. Bedford Battery,	Capt. Tyler C. Jordan.
3. Brooks (S. C.) Battery,	Lieut. S. C. Gilbert.
4. Madison (La.) Battery,	Capt. Geo. V. Moody.
5. Richmond Battery,	Capt. William W. Parker.
6. Bath Battery,	Capt. Esmond B. Taylor.

ESHLEMAN'S BATTALION

Maj. Benj. F. Eshleman

1. 1st Co. Washington Artillery,	Capt. C. W. Squires.
2. 2d Co. Washington Artillery,	Capt. J. B. Richardson.
3. 3d Co. Washington Artillery,	Capt. M. B. Miller.
4. 4th Co. Washington Artillery,	Capt. Joe Norcom.

2D CORPS (Ewell)

Col. John Thompson Brown, Chief of Artillery

DIVISIONAL BATTALIONS

CARTER'S BATTALION

Lieut.-Col. Thos. H. Carter

1. Jeff Davis Alabama Battery,   Capt. William J. Reese.
2. King William Battery,   Capt. William P. Carter.
3. Louisa Morris Battery,   Capt. R. C. M. Page.
4. Richmond Orange Battery,   Capt. Chas. W. Fry.

JONES' BATTALION

Lieut.-Col. Hilary P. Jones

1. Charlottesville Battery,   Capt. Jas. McD. Carrington.
2. Richmond Courtney Battery,   Capt. W. A. Tanner.
3. Louisiana Guard Battery,   Capt. C. A. Green.
4. Staunton Battery,   Capt. Asher W. Garber.

ANDREWS' BATTALION

Maj. James W. Latimer

1. 1st Maryland Battery,   Capt. Wm. F. Dement.
2. Alleghany Battery,   Capt. John C. Carpenter.
3. 4th Md. or Chesapeake Battery,   Capt. William D. Brown.
4. Lee Battery,   Capt. Charles J. Raine.

CORPS RESERVE BATTALION

FIRST VIRGINIA ARTILLERY

Capt. Willis J. Dance

1. 2d Co. Richmond Howitzers,   Capt. David Watson.
2. 3d Co. Richmond Howitzers,   Capt. Benj. H. Smith, Jr.
3. Powhatan Battery,   Lieut. John M. Cunnigham.
4. 1st Rockbridge Battery,   Capt. Archibald Graham.
5. Salem Battery,   Lieut. C. B. Griffin.

NELSON'S BATTALION

Lieut.-Col. William Nelson

1. Amherst Battery,   Capt. Thomas J. Kirkpatrick.
2. Fluvanna Battery,   Capt. John L. Massie.
3. Georgia Regular Battery,   Capt. John Milledge.

3D CORPS (A. P. Hill)

Col. Reuben Lindsay Walker, Chief of Artillery

McINTOSH'S BATTALION

Maj. David G. McIntosh

1. Danville Battery,   Capt. R. S. Price.
2. Alabama Battery,   Capt. W. B. Hurt.
3. 2d Rockbridge Battery,   Lieut. Samuel Wallace.
4. Richmond Battery,   Capt. Marmaduke Johnson.

GARNETT'S BATTALION

Lieut.-Col. John J. Garnett

1. Donaldsonville (La.) Battery,   Capt. Victor Maurin.
2. Norfolk Battery,   Capt. Jos. D. Moore.
3. Pittsylvania Battery,   Capt. John W. Lewis.
4. Norfolk Blues Battery,   Capt. Chas. R. Grandy.

POAGUE'S BATTALION

Maj. William T. Poague

1. Albemarle Battery,   Capt. James W. Wyatt.
2. Charlotte (N. C.) Battery, Capt. Joseph Graham.
3. Madison (Miss.) Battery,   Capt. George Ward.
4. Warrenton Battery,   Capt. J. V. Brooke.

CORPS RESERVE BATTALIONS

PEGRAM'S BATTALION

Maj. William J. Pegram

1. Richmond Battery,   Capt. Wm. G. Crenshaw.
2. Fredericksburg Battery,   Capt. Edward A. Marye.
3. Richmond Letcher Battery,   Capt. Thomas A. Brander.
4. Pee Dee (S. C.) Battery,   Lieut. Wm. E. Zimmerman.
5. Richmond Purcell Battery,   Capt. Jos. McGraw.

CUTTS' BATTALION

1. "A" Battery, Sumter (Ga.) Batt.,   Capt. Hugh M. Ross.
2. "B" Battery, Sumter (Ga.) Batt.,   Capt. Geo. M. Patterson.
3. "C" Battery, Sumter (Ga.) Batt.,   Capt. John T. Wingfield.

From the foregoing we see that there were now with
the Army 15 battalions with a total of 62 light bat-

teries.   Each battalion had a field-officer in addition to
its commander, and a complete commissioned staff.   The
five battalions comprising the artillery of each corps constituted a division of artillery under the corps chief of
artillery, who reported to and received orders direct
from the corps commander, while the chief of artillery of the Army reported to and represented the
commander-in-chief in his dealings with the corps artillery.   In the whole scheme of reorganization, one
cannot but see the features of the brilliant Alexander
cropping out, and the final success of his efforts to di-
vorce the artillery from the tactical control of Gen.
Pendleton, except in so far as he represented the commander-in-chief in his capacity as administrative chief
of artillery.

By the time the reorganization was completed, Col.
Baldwin, the Chief of Ordnance, had received a fresh
consignment of 14 Napoleons from Gorgas, who was
energetically pushing forward the manufacture of the
improved gun in Richmond.   These, in addition to the
14 captured pieces, were at once issued to the battalions
in the field in as equitable a manner as possible, only
two 3-inch rifles going to the Horse Artillery.   The
distribution of guns was now as follows:

Cabell's Battalion, 8 rifles, 8 Napoleons.
Garnett's Battalion, 11 rifles, 4 Napoleons, 2 howitzers, and
one 6-inch Whitworth.
Dearing's Battalion, 5 rifles, 12 Napoleons, 1 howitzer, and one
6-inch Whitworth.
Henry's Battalion, 4 rifles, 12 Napoleons, 1 howitzer, and one
6-inch Whitworth.
Eshleman's Battalion, 10 Napoleons, 1 howitzer, and one 6-inch
Whitworth.
Alexander's Battalion, 11 rifles, 9 Napoleons, 3 howitzers.
Carter's Battalion, 8 rifles, 6 Napoleons, 2 howitzers.
Jones' Battalion, 4 rifles, 10 Napoleons.
McIntosh's Battalion, 10 rifles, 6 Napoleons.
Andrews' Battalion, 10 rifles, 6 Napoleons.
Pegram's Battalion, 8 rifles, 9 Napoleons, 2 howitzers.
Dance's Battalion, 10 rifles, 8 Napoleons, 4 howitzers.
Cutts' Battalion, 10 rifles, 3 Napoleons, 5 howitzers.
Nelson's Battalion, 6 rifles, 8 Napoleons, 4 howitzers.

Thus, it is seen that about equally distributed among the three corps were one hundred and three 3-inch rifles, one hundred and seven 12-pounder Napoleons, thirty 12-pounder howitzers, and four 6-inch Whitworths, or a total of 244 guns of comparatively superior type to those which had been in use within the past few months. But, while the material was much improved by substituting the captured rifles and the Napoleons of home manufacture for the old 6-pounders, and while the batteries were equally equipped in the number of pieces, that is four to a battery, a distressing lack of uniformity in material existed. This was of course a glaring defect, greatly increasing the difficulty of ammunition supply and impairing the general efficiency. Theoretically it was capable of correction, but practically there were many difficulties in the way. Some batteries wanted rifles, others Napoleons, and few were willing to be armed with howitzers alone. The gunners in the various batteries had become familiar with their material of whatever character, and the mere suggestion that uniformity of battery armament should be enforced at once raised a hue and cry on the part of all for the material of their individual preference. For the sake of general uniformity none were willing to waive those preferences. After all, this attitude was natural, and it would have required a bold chief indeed to ignore the human phase of the situation. Believing that the good to be accomplished by unifying the battery armaments was not commensurate with the general dissatisfaction such a step would surely arouse, Gen. Pendleton declined to raise the issue and so a great evil was allowed to exist to the very end.

In the selection of a chief of artillery for the new corps, the services of one who had been actively engaged in every battle from Bull Run to date were recognized. In the whole army, there was not one who deserved promotion more than Reuben Lindsay Walker, and his elevation was welcomed by all and accepted in a spirit of profound satisfaction by the Artillery. Less brilliant

than Alexander, he yet possessed the highest virtues
both as a man and as a soldier, and throughout his long
career gave many evidences of his peculiar ability as an
artillerist, especially as an organizer.

Here it should be remarked that in no arm of the
service was promotion so slow as in the Field Artillery.
In the list of battery commanders in May, 1863, we find
a number who had served in that capacity since the outbreak of the war, and less than 30 of the original artillery officers had attained the rank of field-officers
after two years of honorable and arduous service.
Many of these were among the most efficient officers in
the Army from every standpoint.   Col. Long, Lee's
military secretary, said that the personnel of the Artillery was unsurpassed by any troops in the Army,
and many officers in other arms have declared that the
Artillery was the most distinguished arm of the service.
It was the *esprit de corps* of the Artillery alone which
kept its officers true to their stripe, notwithstanding
the unfavorable opportunity for their advancement, and
few sought promotion by transferring to other arms,
Rosser, Dearing, and J. R. C. Lewis being among the
exceptions, while Col. Stephen D. Lee was promoted
out of the Artillery.

It has become the habit of historians to declare that
the Federal at all times excelled the Confederate artillery in material and personnel.   Even Col. Henderson in his Aldershot lecture on the American Civil War
fell into the error of making so general and unqualified
an assertion.*   Certainly, as far as the Army of Northern Virginia is concerned, the quality of the personnel
of the Field Artillery was not surpassed if equalled by
any similar arm then in existence, a fact which seems to
be indisputable when the inferiority of its material, ammunition, equipment, stores, horses, training and all the
other disadvantages under which it labored are considered.

---

*Science of War, G. F. R., Henderson, p. 245.   But see Evolution of Modern
Strategy, by Lieut.-Col. F. N. Maude, in which it is said that the three arms of the
Confederate Army were intrinsically superior at the beginning of the war.

At the outbreak of the war the regular batteries served as models to the Northern volunteers. One of these was grouped with three manned by volunteers, and the latter very naturally profited by the example set them. Again, the supply of horses in the North and West was practically inexhaustible, while in the South there were few left at the close of the second year of the war. Not only did the North possess the national school of arms, which it was able to maintain in uninterrupted activity for the technical education of its more scientific officers, but it also conducted several schools of gunnery while its armies operated in the field. In a measure, West Point was offset by the Virginia Military Institute, but had the South been free to conduct schools of gunnery for its artillery officers, it would have been unable to provide them with ammunition. After the war commenced its only school of instruction was that of actual experience, and a large majority of its junior artillery officers fired a gun for the first time on the field of battle. Surely the personnel must have possessed equal if not superior qualities to those of their antagonists, to accomplish the results they did. One need only follow the rapid development which they brought about to be satisfied that they were not ordinary or inefficient men. We have seen what the stage of this development was in May, 1863. Now let us examine conditions in the Federal Artillery at the time.

If we accept the evidence of Gen. Henry T. Hunt, Chief of Artillery Army of the Potomac, an officer of great ability and unsurpassed special knowledge as an artillerist when he wrote, the Federal Artillery in May, 1863, was in a most unsatisfactory condition.* In spite of the splendid organization which McClellan had given it and its initial services in the war under Hunt, a general decline in the efficiency of the arm had set in before the end of 1862. Field-officers of artillery had become to be regarded as an unnecessary expense, and their muster into the service was forbidden; so just at the time

---

*Battles and Leaders, Vol. III, p. 259.

the Confederates were doing all in their power to improve the organization of their artillery by creating battalions with an adequate number of competent field and staff officers, the Federals were destroying the tactical cohesion of their artillery by denying it the necessary officers, and instead of remaining in the artillery irrespective of promotion, many of the best artillery officers in the Army of the Potomac at once transferred to other arms in which better opportunities for advancement were to be found. Thus, such experienced artillerists as Hays, De Russy, Getty, Gibbon, Griffin, and Ayres sought promotion in the cavalry and infantry. While every effort was made to maintain the Confederate batteries at full strength, however depleted the units of the other arms, in the North no adequate measures were taken to supply recruits for the artillery, and the batteries were frequently dependent on the troops to which they were attached for men enough to work the guns in action. While Pendleton was maintaining a remount depot for his command at Winchester under Maj. Richardson, inadequate as it was, and scouring the country, even as far as Georgia and Florida, for draught animals, always being favored by the Quartermaster-General in the matter of horses, the Federal batteries were often forced to wait for remounts until the cavalry, and even the medical and quartermaster trains had been supplied, a fact which illustrated the general feeling in the army towards the field artillery. While the Confederate organization was being solidified and molded along the lines dictated by experience, in the North all experience was ignored and the Chief of Artillery was in effect relieved by Hooker from all but administrative work. In lieu of the perfect mechanism of the arm under Hunt on the Peninsula, Hooker substituted chaos. With the command of the Artillery at his own headquarters to be exercised by his chief only upon specific orders, there resulted such confusion and disorder that the artillery had to be practically reorganized after a splendid organization had already been attained and sacrificed. Thus while the Confederates were building up, the Federals had been tearing down. During the period in which the former were organizing their artillery into corps divisions, all under a strongly-centralized command, and appointing more and more field officers, the Army of the Potomac had no artillery commander-in-chief, and of the 14 artillery brigades it possessed, nine were commanded by captains and one by a lieutenant, in addition to their battery duties, while but four were commanded by field officers!

Such was the condition of the Federal Field Artillery, when it entered upon the Gettysburg campaign, with its 65 batteries and 370 splendid guns, It will, therefore, as stated by Gen. Hunt himself, be perceived by comparison that the organization of the Federal Artillery was at this period in every way inferior to that of the Confederates. Nothing but the same individual courage and intelligence among the Northern artillerymen, as was to be found in the corresponding arm in Lee's Army, saved the former from a complete breakdown at Gettysburg. All the more honor is due them for the account they there gave of themselves, but let us hear nothing more of the superiority of the Federal Artillery personnel, except in point of numbers. In that respect the Confederates were greatly outclassed.

The return of May 20 gives the artillery personnel of Lee's Army as 253 officers and 4,708 men present for duty, and a paper aggregate of 7,279. These figures do not include Dearing's Battalion and two batteries on picket, nor two others with Ransom. The return of May 31, the last before the battle of Gettysburg, gives the Artillery, less Alexander's and Garnett's battalions, a total effective strength of 4,460. The 52 batteries reported therefore averaged 86 officers and men present, and adding 860 for the 10 batteries not included in the return, an effective aggregate of 5,320 is obtained. This is not far from correct, since the aggregate present on May 10 was 5,010. From these figures it is seen that the average battery strength was about 3 officers and

80 enlisted men, a fact which well illustrates the importance Lee attached to the efficiency of his artillery, and
the tremendous effort which had been made by the Chief
of Artillery and his subordinates to maintain the batteries at a serviceable strength. In the infantry and
cavalry there were battalions and squadrons at this time
with less than 100 men.

The aggregate strength of the Federal Artillery engaged in the Gettysburg campaign was 7,183, the number of batteries 65, and the number of guns 370, or
about 110 officers and men and 6 pieces to the battery.

Having examined the organization of the Field Artillery, let us look into that of the Confederate Horse
Artillery.

Immediately after the battle of Chancellorsville,
Stuart was directed to concentrate his division at Culpeper, meanwhile guarding his front and the Confederate left along the Rapidan, and before May 9, Jones'
Brigade with Chew's Battery was ordered from the
Valley to join him. By May 20, the strength of his
division, including the Horse Artillery, was 8,193
present and 11,905 present and absent.

Early in April the horse batteries had been organized
into a separate corps under Maj. R. F. Beckham, but
were temporarily left with the brigades with which they
had served, subject to the orders of the brigade commanders.* The first step in the organization of the
Horse Artillery into a tactical unit had therefore been
taken when the Army was reorganized on May 30.

The growth of the battalion had been slow but sure.
Stuart from the first had proved an ardent advocate of
the increase in the number of horse batteries, placing
great reliance upon their services, and displaying unusual interest in their proper development. Indeed,
though his historians do not include the horse batteries
in the organization of the cavalry, Stuart considered
them as much a part of his command as the cavalry regiments themselves. After Ashby raised Chew's Battery

*Rebellion Records, Series I, Vol. XXV, Part II, p. 858.

and employed it so successfully, Stuart, it will be recalled, had organized the Stuart Horse Artillery. Its
original commander, as we have seen, was John Pelham,
who, just graduated from West Point, had been commissioned by the Confederate Government at Montgomery as a lieutenant of artillery, and sent to Lynchburg in charge of the ordnance office there. From that
point he was ordered to Winchester, where he organized
and drilled Alburtis' Wise Battery, which he commanded at Bull Run with conspicuous efficiency. When
assigned in the fall of 1861 to the duty of organizing
Stuart's Horse Battery, he gathered about him a most
remarkable and superior set of men, mostly from the
cavalry, some from Virginia, and some from Maryland,
under Dr. James Breathed. To these were added about
40 from Talladega County, Alabama, under Lieut.
William M. McGregor. It was not long before Hart's
light battery of Washington, South Carolina, was converted into a horse battery.

The experiences of the first Maryland invasion in
which the cavalry was so active and opposed to an enemy
well provided with horse batteries, convinced Stuart of
the urgent need of more artillery for his own command.
The day after the battle, Pelham's Battery, which had
received a large accession of recruits from Maryland,
was drawn upon for the men with which to create a new
horse battery, to the command of which Capt. M. W.
Henry was assigned, and on November 18 the light
battery of Capt. Marcellus N. Moorman, from Lynchburg, was converted. The men of Moorman's Battery
had been mustered into the service April 25, 1861, as a
company of infantry, under the name of the "Beauregard Rifles," and sent to Norfolk, where for lack of
muskets it had been temporarily armed with Parrott
guns. When the Army was reorganized a year later
it was still serving as artillery at Sewell's Point and elsewhere about Hampton Roads, and was then definitely
mustered into the Confederate service as a battery of
artillery, and placed in a battalion with Grimes',

Huger's, and Nichols' light batteries, under Maj. John S. Saunders. Before its conversion it had, therefore, served, and with great credit, throughout the Peninsula, Second Manassas, and Maryland campaigns.

When Pelham was promoted major of horse artillery, Breathed succeeded to the command of his battery, while McGregor succeeded Henry upon the latter's promotion. During the winter of 1862, Brockenbrough was promoted major, and his battery, the 2d Baltimore Artillery, which had been detached for duty in the Valley with Jones' and Steuart's brigades, was also converted and placed under the command of Capt. William H. Griffin. Another horse battery, McClannahan's, had been formed by converting Imboden's Staunton battery, but this battery was not regularly brigaded with Stuart's Battalion until 1864, and Griffin's battery did not join Beckham's Battalion until Jenkins arrived at Gettysburg.

When Stuart finally concentrated his division at Culpeper towards the end of May, the Stuart Horse Artillery Battalion was composed as follows:

Maj. R. F. Beckham

1.	Ashby Battery,	Capt. Robert Preston Chew.
2.	1st Stuart Horse Artillery,	Capt. James Breathed.
3.	Washington (S. C.) Battery,	Capt. James F. Hart.
4.	2d Stuart Horse Artillery,	Capt. William M. McGregor.
5.	Lynchburg Battery,	Capt. Marcellus N. Moorman.
6.	2d Baltimore Battery,	Capt. William H. Griffin.

There was, therefore, a battery of horse artillery for each of the six cavalry brigades under Hampton, Fitz Lee, W. H. F. Lee, Jones, Robertson, and Jenkins, respectively, as well as one for Imboden's independent cavalry command.

At the end of May, the strength of the five batteries of horse artillery present with Stuart at Culpeper was 18 officers and 519 men present for duty, with a paper aggregate of 701, or an average effective battery strength of about 107. These five batteries together possessed 24 pieces of artillery, three being armed with four and two with six pieces.

Stuart, who was making every effort to increase the strength of the Horse Artillery in material, as well as in personnel, sought to retain all the captured pieces in his possession for his own batteries, and this led to an altercation between him and the Chief of Ordnance, who was unable to recover the guns for distribution. In the correspondence which ensued, Stuart resented the use of the expression that these guns had been "appropriated by the Stuart Horse Artillery," which he erroneously, and no doubt because of a guilty conscience, attributed to Col. Baldwin. The difficulty was finally adjusted, however, by Gen. Lee assuming the burden of the remark, which he denied was used by him in any objectionable sense, and Stuart was allowed to retain two 3-inch rifles and directed to turn in the three other captured guns in his possession.

Beckham was endeavoring to provide all his batteries with six pieces, a step which met with the disapproval of the Commander-in-Chief, and the Chief of Artillery, for the sole reason that the additional horses for this increase in armament were not available. Even the dismounting of some of the light batteries had become almost a necessity for lack of horses, but in some way Beckham soon managed to supply the necessary number to complete the quota of his battalion in spite of the fact that the ambulance and ammunition trains were so poorly provided with animals as to be almost unserviceable. Concerning Beckham's work in refitting his battalion and establishing it upon a sounder basis, Stuart in his letter to headquarters was most complimentary.

Meantime, Hampton, Fitz Lee, and W. H. F. Lee, and the horse batteries of Breathed, McGregor, Hart and Moorman, lay about Culpeper. The Artillery was encamped on the farm of John Minor Botts, who was a strong anti-secessionist and bitterly complained that "Ten thousand men should burn his rails without splitting any." Jenkins' Brigade with Griffin's Battery had been assigned to duty in the Valley. On the 22d of May, Gen. Stuart reviewed that portion of his division present, many distinguished personages appearing, among them Gens. Hood and Randolph. Great numbers of ladies also attended, which of course pleased the gallant cavalry commander. Shortly afterwards, Robertson's Brigade arrived from North Carolina, and on June 4, Jones' Brigade with Chew's Battery from the Valley, so that the following day another review of the entire division was held, at which Gen. Lee was expected to be present. In this Stuart was much disappointed, but the "pageantry of war proceeded." Eight thousand cavalry, with the battalion of artillery in the lead, passed under the eye of the division commander in column of squadrons.

So unique is this incident in the career of that grim fighting machine, the Army of Northern Virginia, that especial interest attaches to it. One is involuntarily impelled to pause and reflect upon the exuberance of the spirit of that youthful soldier, who, in spite of war's dreadful tragedy all about him, and in which he himself was a leading actor, could so indulge his fancy in the very presence of the enemy. The following interesting account of the review is taken from the war-time diary of one of Stuart's gunners:

"Early this morning we started to the field, where the troops were to be reviewed by passing by the eagle eye of their great commander. The place where the review was held is a beautiful and nearly level plain about four miles northeast of Culpeper Courthouse, and little over a mile southwest of Brandy Station, and on the west side of the Orange and Alexandria Railroad.*

"When we, Chew's Battery, arrived on the field some of the Cavalry regiments were already forming in dress parade order for the review procession. At about 10 o'clock the whole column, which was about two miles long, was ready and in splendid trim to pass in review before its illustrious and gallant chief, and his brilliant staff.

"As soon as the whole line was formed, Gen. Stuart and his staff dashed on the field. He was superbly mounted. The trappings on his proud, prancing horse all looked bright and new, and

---

*Now Chesapeake & Ohio R. R.

his side arms gleamed in the morning sun like burnished silver. A long black ostrich plume waved gracefully from a black slouch hat, cocked upon one side, and was held with a golden clasp which also stayed the plume. Before the procession started, Gen. Stuart and staff rode along the front of the line from one end to the other. He is the prettiest and most graceful rider I ever saw. When he dashed past us, I could not help but notice with what natural ease and comely elegance he sat his steed, as it bounded over the field, and his every motion in the saddle was in such strict accordance with the movements of his horse that the rider and his horse appeared to be but one and the same machine. Immediately after Gen. Stuart and staff had passed along the front of the whole line, he galloped to a little knoll in the southwest edge of the field near the railroad, wheeled his horse to front face to the field, and sat there like a gallant knight errant, under his waving plume, presenting in veritable truth every characteristic of a chivalric cavalier of the first order. He was then ready for the review, and the whole cavalcade began to move and pass in review before the steady, martial, and scrutinizing gaze of the greatest cavalry chieftain of America.

.   .   .   .

"Three bands of music were playing nearly all the time while the procession was moving, a flag was fluttering in the breeze from every regiment, and the whole army was one grand, magnificent pageant, inspiring enough to make even an old woman feel fightish.

"After the whole cavalcade passed the review station, at a quick walk, the column divided up into divisions, brigades, and regiments, which maneuvered all over the field. The last and most inspiring and impressive act in the scene was a sham battle, the cavalry charging several times with drawn sabers and the horse artillery firing from four or five different positions on the field. I fired ten rounds from my gun.

"Hundreds of ladies from Culpeper Courthouse and surrounding country stood in bunches on the hills and knolls around the field looking at the grand military display.

"A special train from Richmond stood on the track just in rear of the review stand, crowded with people, and, judging from the fluttering ribbons at the car windows, the most of the occupants were ladies. Gen. Hood's Division of infantry was drawn up upon the north side of the field, viewing the cavalry display, and also for support in case the Yanks would have attempted to take a hand in the show. There is a heavy force of Yankees camped on the north bank of the Rappahannock, only about five miles from the review stand.

"By about four o'clock this evening the whole affair was over, and the troops withdrew from the field and repaired to their respective camps."*

*Three Years in the Confederate Horse Artillery, Neese, p. 168.

One would have thought that this affair was sufficient to satisfy Stuart's love of the "pomp and circumstance" of war. But no. When he found that Gens. Lee, Longstreet, Ewell, and Pendleton would arrive at his camp on the 8th, another pageant was ordered to be held. But much less of that display for which Stuart had so great a weakness was attempted on the occasion of the third review, for Gen. Lee, always careful not to tax his men unnecessarily, would not allow the cavalry to take the gallop, nor the artillerymen to fire their guns.

On this occasion an incident occurred which, aside from its amusing features, is of valuable interest to the student because of its bearing on Stuart's character. Capt. Chew had not come to Culpeper with any exalted ideas as to the pomp of war. In fact, his battery was reduced in point of appearance to the lowest plane to which constant hardship and service could bring it. He had only arrived from the Valley the night before and with horses and men equally worn, found himself suddenly on parade before the Commander-in-Chief. What wonder then if, conscious of the ungainly appearance of his half-starved horses, and in a spirit of pride, the battery first sergeant should seek to improve the outward appearance of the battery by bestriding a fine, sleek mule! Just as the far-famed Ashby Battery, the senior in rank in its battalion, and certainly the equal of any other in point of service, approached the reviewing stand in the very lead, Stuart's proud eye detected the active ears of the mule at the head of the battery, and with extreme impatience and disgust quickly dispatched one of his aides to direct Capt. Chew to have both his first sergeant and the mule leave the field! Says the sergeant in his diary, "I cared very little about the matter, but the mule looked a little bit surprised, and, I think, felt ashamed of himself and his waving ears, which cost him his prominent position in the grand cavalcade.

"No doubt Gen. Stuart is proud of his splendid cavalry, and well he may be, for it certainly is a fine body of well mounted and tried horsemen. . . . True a mule was not built for the purpose of ornamenting a grand review or embellishing an imposing pageant, but as mine so willingly bears the hardships and dangers of the camp and field, I thought it not indiscreet to let it play a little act in some of the holiday scenes of war."

One can picture the amusement this whole incident afforded the youngsters of Stuart's staff, at their chief's expense, not to mention Gens. Lee, Pendleton, and the distinguished foreigners, who composed the reviewing party. Perhaps no other general in the Confederate Army would have paid the slightest attention to that worthy mule. Of one thing we are certain,—there could not have been many mules in use as mounts in Stuart's Cavalry and Horse Artillery at this time, this one having slipped in, so to speak, over night!

But few other instances of such military frivolity on the part of the Confederates are recorded. When in March, 1864, Gen. Pendleton was sent to Dalton, Ga., to inspect the artillery of Johnston's Army, after reviewing Hood's and Hardee's artillery and seeing it drill on a number of occasions, he was tendered a grand sham battle by Hood's entire corps, in which blank ammunition was used. The precedent for this display was no doubt that which Hood and Pendleton had both witnessed a year before at Culpeper.

Before Stuart's participation in his "horse play" at Culpeper, the movement of Lee's army which resulted in the Gettysburg campaign had commenced. Longstreet's and Ewell's corps had already reached Culpeper Courthouse, while Hill's Corps was left in front of Hooker at Fredericksburg. After the review the cavalry brigades were immediately assigned to posts along the river, and Beckham proceeded towards Beverly Ford that night, and placed four of his batteries in camp near Saint James Church. Fitz Lee's Brigade under Munford was assigned to the duty of picketing the upper Rappahannock. Munford established his camp across the Hazel River in the vicinity of Oak

Shade. W. H. F. Lee established his brigade and Breathed's Battery near Welford's house on the Welford Ford Road; Jones' Brigade held the Beverly Ford Road, and Robertson's remained at the Botts and Barbour farms picketing the lower fords. Saint James Church stood about 200 yards to the west of the main road to the ford and opposite it, and on the east of that road in a large grove of trees stood an old brick house known as the Thompson or Gee house, on an elevation from which the fields on both sides of the road for a distance of 500 yards to the north were commanded. The grove was occupied by one regiment of Jones' Brigade, the others bivouacking in the edge of the woods, which skirted the fields to the north of the church. Beckham, with Chew's, Moorman's, McGregor's, and Hart's batteries, bivouacked in the edge of the woods beyond, in sight of though in advance of the cavalry. Beyond the camp of the battalion, unbroken woods extended on both sides of the road for more than a mile, and as far as the highland overlooking the river lowgrounds and Beverly Ford. From the latter point, Beckham's and Jones' camps were about 1½ to 2 miles.

Stuart, with his train in readiness for an early start, had established his headquarters at a residence on Fleetwood Hill, about a half mile east of Brandy Station, two miles down the road in rear of Saint James Church. Fleetwood Hill completely commanded the large open plain which surrounded it, with the exception of the Barbour House Hill, of slightly greater elevation. Such was the situation on the night of the 8th when Stuart, entirely ignorant of any concentration of the enemy's cavalry on the north side of the river, issued his orders to march at an early hour.

Meantime, Pleasonton was approaching from the north, with orders to make a reconnaissance in force as far as Culpeper Courthouse if possible, to verify the reports that the Confederates were moving westward from Fredericksburg. Pleasonton's force consisted of two small brigades of infantry, some 3,000 men in all, and about 8,000 cavalry, including Robertson's Brigade of horse artillery of four batteries. Dividing this force into two columns of equal strength, he ordered the first under Gregg to cross at Kelly's Ford at dawn, and the second under Buford, which included all of Ames' infantry, to move by way of Beverly Ford, about 1½ miles above the railroad bridge, and 5½ miles above Kelly's Ford. Great care was exercised by the Federals during the night to conceal their presence from Stuart's pickets, and in this they succeeded.

At 4:30 A. M. on the 9th Buford's two leading regiments dashed across Beverly Ford and rapidly drove the troops on picket there back towards the woods north of Saint James Church. Upon learning that the enemy was advancing from the ford, Beckham directed Capt. Hart, whose battery was on the right of the battalion, to place a gun in the road by hand, while the batteries were ordered to hitch up and gallop back to the Gee House Hill, some 600 yards in rear, and to go into position there. Before the teams could be harnessed, however, the enemy was almost upon the artillery camp, and had begun to fire upon the horses at the picket lines. But at this juncture Maj. Flournoy, with about 100 men of the regiment which had bivouacked in the grove, dashed forward and temporarily checked the enemy, which not only saved Beckham's guns, but gave time for Jones to bring up the 7th Virginia Cavalry from the main camp. Meantime, Hart had thrown two pieces into action by the road, and Beckham in less than 20 minutes after the first alarm was establishing his guns at the grove. The 7th Regiment, upon coming up, immediately charged, but was repulsed and driven back along the road past Hart's two guns, leaving them entirely isolated. Says Maj. McClellan, of Stuart's staff, "These gallant cannoneers on two occasions during this memorable day proved that they were able to care for themselves. Although now exposed to the enemy, they covered their own retreat with canister, and safely retired to the line at Saint James Church, where they found efficient support."*

During the charge of the 7th Regiment, the gunners, standing in silent awe by their pieces perfectly aligned along the wave-like swell north of the brick house, watched the savage conflict between the horsemen in their front, fascinated by the scene, and as Hart fell back, alternately retiring his two guns from point to point along the road, a wild cheer from Beckham's line preceded the simultaneous flash of his 16 guns. Just as the sun rose, the crash of the guns burst upon the ears of the enemy's troopers, and soon the woods which they had entered were rent with shrieking shells. Beckham's steady fire forced the enemy to cover, while they sought positions in which to place their artillery, none of which had yet arrived from the ford. Thus did the Horse Artillery hold Buford at bay, having lost nothing but the field desk of the major, which jostled from the headquarter's wagon as it galloped off to safety.

The other regiment of Jones' Brigade now took position on the left of the church, and Hampton with four of his regiments occupied the rise between it and Beckham's guns at the grove. About 8 A. M., W. H. F. Lee moved down from Welford Ford towards the sound of the firing and placed his dismounted troopers behind a stone fence on the Cunningham farm, while Johnston's section of Breathed's Battery moved down stream from Freeman's Ford where the battery had been on picket, crossed the Hazel River, and took up a position near the Green House on a hill behind W. H. F. Lee's line, from which it had a clear field of fire in every direction. This position soon proved to be the key-point of the Confederate line of defense. The other section of Breathed's Battery moved back from Freeman's to Starke's Ford.

A determined attack was made by the enemy's dismounted men, supported by a battery of four pieces,

*The Campaigns of Stuart's Cavalry, McClellan, p. 266. Also see article in Philadelphia Weekly Times, June 26, 1880, by Maj. J. F. Hart.

upon W. H. F. Lee's line, but it was repelled by the
Confederate sharpshooters, and Johnston's guns, but
not until several mounted charges made by the 10th Virginia and 2d North Carolina Cavalry cleared the field,
driving the Federals back to the cover of the woods
along the Beverly Ford Road, and seriously threatening their flank. Hampton had, meantime, extended his
right beyond the church, so as to partially envelop the
enemy's left, and together with Jones now advanced.
From this time until 10 A. M. the lines swayed back and
forth. During the early morning, the 6th Pennsylvania Cavalry, supported by the 6th United States
Regiment, made a superb mounted charge upon the
Confederate artillery position, over a plateau some 800
yards wide. The regulars, heedless of Beckham's shrapnel, shell, and canister, actually reached his guns, and,
dashing between them, passed on only to be attacked
simultaneously on both flanks by the Confederate
troopers, who drove the survivors back. There are few
instances recorded of a simlar charge upon so strong
a line of artillery. Scarlett's charge at Balaclava was
no more daring than the one which Smith led at Saint
James Church, the latter possessing the additional feature that it was premeditated and not the result of accident.

Beckham's pieces now redoubled their fire, having
suffered none from the charge, and furiously shelled the
woods in their front, where the enemy was gathering in
increasing numbers. The artillery position was a commanding one, and no doubt, had its flanks been guarded,
could have been held indefinitely. But the situation was
becoming serious in another quarter, for the head of
Gregg's column was approaching Stevensburg from
Kelly's Ford. Stuart had dispatched two regiments
under Wickham and Butler and one of Moorman's guns
to the support of Robertson's Brigade, which had moved
forward to Kelly's Ford early in the morning, and believing the force of 1,500 men between Brandy Station
and the ford sufficient to guard the road to Culpeper

Courthouse, proceeded to the church. His camp of the night before had been broken and nothing remained at Fleetwood Hill but a section of Chew's Battery under Lieut. John W. Carter, which had been retired from the fight after its ammunition was all but exhausted.

When Pleasonton found that Buford's column could not overcome the resistance of the three Confederate brigades opposed to it in front of Beverly's Ford, he decided to wait until Gregg could move up to his assistance. The latter had readily effected a crossing at Kelly's Ford about 6 A. M., Col. Duffie with four regiments of cavalry and a section of Pennington's Battery in the lead. Duffie's orders were to move on Stevensburg, whilst Gregg with the rest of the column proceeded towards Brandy Station in order to effect a junction with Buford. Robertson had fallen back along the direct road from Brandy Station to Kelly's Ford, and the two regiments dispatched by Stuart to his support were unable in spite of the most gallant efforts to prevent Duffie's advance upon Stevensburg. But orders now came for Duffie to join Gregg's main body and he at once commenced to retrace his steps towards Madden's, covering the movement with his guns while Wickham's regiment retarded his progress in every way possible. Meantime, unknown to Robertson, Gregg had advanced directly upon Brandy Station, and actually came within sight of Fleetwood Hill directly in the Confederate rear before his approach, which had been concealed by numerous groves, was discovered by Stuart's Adjutant-General, who had been left behind to maintain communications. The leading regiment of Wyndham's Brigade was already emerging into the open about Brandy Station, within cannon shot of Carter's guns. Without hesitating an instant, the young lieutenant brought one of his pieces from the road to the top of the hill and boldly pushed it to the forward crest. A few imperfect shell and some round shot was all the ammunition in the limbers, but with these a slow fire was at once opened upon the enemy's moving column, while

first one and then another of the mounted cannoneers
was sent to inform Stuart of the peril.

The bold front which Carter put up led Gregg and
Wyndham to conclude that the hill was more formidable
than it was.   At any rate, there was some hesitation on
their part and considerable delay while Clarke's section
of Pennington's Battery sought to prepare the road for
a charge.   Every moment of this delay was precious to
the Confederates, for had Gregg succeeded in planting
his guns on Fleetwood Hill, Stuart's position would
have been most precarious.   The first courier found
Stuart among Hart's guns near the church, and not until the second message arrived, and he heard the sound
of Carter's and Clarke's guns in his rear, did he counter-
mand his order to Capt. Hart to ride back and verify
the report.

The 12th Virginia and the 35th Battalion were immediately withdrawn from Jones' line, 1½ miles from
Fleetwood Hill, and ordered by Stuart to gallop back
to Carter's assistance.   Minutes seemed like hours to
Carter.   Not a man but the cannoneers of his section
and Maj. McClellan of Stuart's staff occupied the hill.
The enemy had been imposed upon for a time, but at
last Wyndham's regiment in column of squadrons, with
standards and guidons fluttering, galloped forward and
commenced the ascent of the hill.   Just as Carter was
retiring his guns, the enemy not 50 yards away, and the
last round having been fired, Col. Harman with the
leading files of the 12th Virginia galloped up to the
crest from behind, and without hesitating dashed at the
enemy.   The rest of the regiment had strung out along
the road in great disorder due to the rapidity of his
movement, and as the men arrived in small groups, they
were no match for Wyndham's more collected force.
Stuart arived in a few moments, having ordered Hampton and Jones to retire from the church and concentrate
at Fleetwood, while Robertson on the Kelly's Ford
Road was advised of the situation.

Reforming his regiment Harman desperately engaged the enemy, while charge and counter-charge swept across the face of the hill. Lieut.-Col. White, with the 35th Battalion, had arrived shortly after Col. Harman, and with two squadrons dashed around the west side of the hill, and charged three guns of Martin's Battery, which Gregg had already brought up, driving off the cavalry support. But the gunners stood firm and a hand-to-hand struggle ensued, in which neither side asked quarter. This battery was the horse battery which Pleasonton had with him at Hazel Grove on May 2, when together with Huntington's batteries it repulsed Winn's attack. In his report, Martin says: "Once in the battery, it became a hand-to-hand fight with pistol and sabre between the enemy and my cannoneers and drivers, and never did men act with more coolness and bravery, and show more of a stern purpose to do their duty unflinchingly, and above all to save their guns; and while the loss of them is a matter of great regret to me, it is a consolation and a great satisfaction to know that I can point with pride to the fact that, of that little band who defended the battery, not one of them flinched for a moment from his duty. Of the 36 men that I took into the engagement, but 6 came out safely; and of these 30, 21 are either killed, wounded, or missing, and scarcely one of them is there but will carry the honorable mark of the sabre or bullet to his grave."

White's men did not long retain possession of Martin's guns, for the few troopers he had with him were soon surrounded by superior numbers and were compelled to cut their way out.

When the retirement of the Confederate line commenced, one of Beckham's guns, as we have seen, was with Butler's regiments, then engaged with Duffie; one of Hart's and two of McGregor's pieces had become disabled from the shock of recoil, a section of Chew's Battery had been sent to the right to join Robertson, and Carter's section of this battery was at Fleetwood Hill. Thus there were but eight guns still in action at the church at the time. Leaving Moorman's remaining three pieces with Jones' 11th Virginia Regiment in position at the church, Beckham with the rest of the artillery, including Hart's and McGregor's batteries, accompanied Hampton's brigades to the rear, which came into action just after Flournoy's Regiment of Jones' Brigade had charged the 6th New York Battery, a section of which it captured, but soon relinquished. Hampton's Brigade advanced at a gallop in magnificent order, in column of squadrons, with Hart's and McGregor's batteries abreast of the leading line. As the column approached the hill, its summit and the plateau east of the hill and beyond the railroad was covered with Federal cavalry. Diverging to his left, Hampton crossed the railroad east of the hill, striking the enemy's flank with the head of his column, while Hart galloped his battery to the crest of the hill and opened fire on the enemy who had been driven from the summit. But he only succeeded in firing several shots with a single gun before the carriage which had been partly repaired was permanently disabled. McGregor now succeeded in placing two pieces in position on the crest, and hardly had they gone into action when the guns were charged by a party of the enemy's cavalry, which from the extreme Federal left came thundering down the narrow ridge, striking the unsupported batteries in flank, and trying to ride down the cannoneers. The charge was met by the gunners alone, who, with pistols, sabers and rammer staffs drove the hostile troopers from among the guns and caissons. Lieuts. Ford and Hoxton with their pistols killed both the brave leader of the charge, Lieut.-Col. Broderick, and Maj. Shelmire, while private Sudley of McGregor's Battery knocked one of the enemy from his saddle with a sponge staff.

About the time the desperate attempt of the 1st New Jersey Regiment to take the guns was repulsed by Beckham, Jones' last Regiment with Moorman's three guns arrived from the church, as did Capt. Chew with the section which had been with Robertson. Beckham quickly placed every available gun in position along the crest and opened fire upon the enemy about Brandy Station.

Hampton was more than holding his own on the plain to the east, but the enemy was still contending for Brandy Station, and a few were desperately defending Martin's silent guns near the eastern base of the hill. Lomax's 11th Virginia spreading out on both sides of the road to the station finally charged the latter, rode completely over Martin's guns and pursued the defenders for some distance down the Stevensburg Road. In the meantime, Hampton had, after a desperate hand-to-hand fight with pistol and saber, overborne the enemy in his front and followed upon their heels until compelled by the well-directed fire of Beckham's guns to forego the pursuit. It was impossible even at close quarters by reason of the dust and smoke to tell friend from foe, and Beckham, rather than lose the effect of his fire, continued to direct it upon the immense mass of horsemen flying down the road in his front. The artillery fire from Fleetwood Hill was most accurate and effective and had, before the withdrawal of the enemy commenced, several times broken the formations of his cavalry.

Meantime W. H. F. Lee's Brigade with one regiment of Jones' Brigade and Johnston's section of Breathed's Battery had, by threatening Buford's rear, kept the latter's force from advancing to the aid of Gregg, in spite of the fact that the direct route lay practically open, and before dispositions could be made for the advance Gregg had been repulsed. As soon as Gregg withdrew, Stuart promptly formed a new line along the eastern slope of the range of hills which, commencing at Fleetwood, extended irregularly to the river at Welford's Ford. Soon after Jones withdrew from the church, exposing W. H. F. Lee's right flank, the latter retired and occupied the hills overlooking the Thompson house, his line connecting with and prolonging that which Stuart had established. Munford, with Fitz

Lee's Brigade, was momentarily expected to arrive and occupy the commanding ground about the Welford house.

To the South, Duffie had arrived near Brandy Station in time to cover Gregg's withdrawal by Rappahannock Ford, and the activity of the Federals was now shifted to Buford, who, extending further and further to his right, until W. H. F. Lee's left was enveloped, launched an attack from the high ground just south and west of the Green House. The movement of the enemy had forced Johnston to withdraw his guns about 2 P. M., and in doing so he was joined by Breathed with the other section of his battery, the whole retiring from point to point and firing upon the advancing Federals. Buford now sent forward a part of his infantry, and followed up its advance with a mounted charge of two regiments, which was quickly repelled. In the struggle W. H. F. Lee was wounded about 4:30 P. M. Before the attack had been repulsed Munford arrived on W. H. F. Lee's left with three regiments of Fitz Lee's Brigade from Oak Shade and at once threw forward a heavy line of skirmishers with which Breathed's Battery advanced. But Buford was already falling back upon Beverly Ford. Munford followed the Federals up closely while Breathed doggedly hung upon their heels with three guns and plied the retreating column from every available position until the pursuers were checked by the enemy's infantry and several batteries in position near the ford.

Pleasonton afterwards attributed his retirement to the fact that the purpose of his reconnaissance had been accomplished since the presence of the Confederate Infantry at Brandy Station was developed by his column. But he must have kept his information from Hooker, who on the 12th of June was, according to his own words, entirely in the dark as to the Confederate movements on his right, and Gen. Lee's intentions.* Pleasonton's statement that the Confederate Infantry

*Conduct of War, Vol. I, p. 158.

was seen disentraining at Brandy Station is wholly false, for the first division of Ewell's Corps marched to Stuart's assistance from Rixeyville, four miles north of Culpeper Courthouse, by way of Botts' farm to Brandy Station, and did not begin to arrive at the latter point until Pleasonton had made his dispositions to withdraw. So again it is seen how prone to error this "Knight of Romance" was.

The battle of Brandy Station has been gone into in some detail, because it was the first engagement in which mounted troops were almost exclusively engaged on both sides, and because it was one in which the Confederate Horse Artillery displayed a most surprising degree of mobility. Its successful employment was in marked contrast to the comparatively ineffective use of the Federal batteries. At every important point of the field, we have found Beckham's guns playing a leading rôle, but we search in vain for any material influence which the guns of Pleasonton's column bore upon the issue. The few which were brought into prominent action were handled with great courage by the gunners, but they apparently had little or no effect, whereas the position taken by Beckham at the church had proved the nucleus about which the whole defense formed. Furthermore, the fire of Beckham's massed batteries at that point had practically brought Buford's column to a standstill, enabling W. H. F. Lee to move upon the Federal flank and check all hope of successful attack until the Federal front could be partially changed to meet his threat, and in the defense of Lee's line, almost at right angles to that of Jones' and Hampton's, Johnston's two guns had played an important part.

Again, when Gregg had all but occupied Fleetwood Hill with his batteries, it was Carter's section of Chew's Battery which snatched the opportunity from the enemy and by the unaided efforts of a handful of bold gunners saved Stuart, certainly from defeat, if not from a rout. Beckham's rapid movement with Hampton to the rear and the prompt massing of his batteries at Fleetwood

not only secured the position which Carter had prevented Gregg from taking, but contributed materially
to the breaking of the Federal column on the plain below with which Hampton was desperately engaged,
and the fire of the batteries was most effective upon the
retreating enemy. One of Moorman's guns had rendered splendid service with Butler's regiment in opposing Duffie, while Chew with a section of his battery
in moving to the support of Robertson's Brigade on the
Kellysville Road, and then rapidly back to Fleetwood
at Beckham's summons, had traversed the field from
end to end in time to arrive at the decisive point at the
critical moment. The movements of the various batteries of Beckham's command exhibited not only remarkable mobility, and a rare ability on the battalion
commander's part to obtain concert of action between
his battery units, but also a most exceptional amount
of initiative on the part of his battery commanders who,
when assigned a special mission by direct order or by
chance, solved the problem which fell to them with skill
and determination.

In no battle of the war did the Artillery display a
higher degree of independence. This was as it should
have been, for if one objection to horse artillery exists,
it is as to its vulnerability on account of the large target it presents while in motion due to the great number
of animals it requires. Then, too, it is sometimes
argued that much time is lost in the care and disposition
of the cannoneers' mounts. But such objections are
specious, and, even were they material, would be more
than counterbalanced by the celerity of movement and
the consequent diminishment in the time of exposure.
However this may be, Beckham's batteries certainly
proved the ability of the Confederate Horse Artillery
to take care of itself, for twice in one day the same
batteries were ridden over by the enemy's cavalry, and
yet the gunners managed to save themselves and their
material from harm by their own defensive power. Not
so much as a trace was cut, nor a team stampeded by
the enemy. It is true this immunity from serious injury

was due, in a measure, to the fact that the troopers who got in among the guns on both occasions were mounted, and therefore unable to secure the guns, etc., which they might have captured had the attacking force been dismounted. But, then it must be remembered that the speed of the mounted men alone enabled the enemy to reach the guns which would have been quite impossible under the circumstances of each case for foot troops. It was that same mobility which made it possible for Hart and McGregor to move at the head of Hampton's Brigade from the church to Fleetwood Hill, that made it possible for Smith to dash across the open in the face of the artillery, and for Broderick to rush down upon the flank of the guns before they could change front.

But even when cavalry possesses the requisite boldness and dash to accomplish such feats as those of Smith's and Broderick's men, the gunners will always possess a great advantage in the brief hand-to-hand conflict which will ensue, for the majority of the mounted men will as a rule pass on through the guns, unable to draw rein. This was certainly the case in both instances when Beckham's batteries were reached by the Federal cavalry, and also when Flournoy charged Clarke's and Martin's batteries. In the last instance, the Federal gunners remanned their guns after Flournoy swept by, and continued in action until finally overpowered by Lomax, by whom the three guns were turned over to Hart's Battery, the gunners of which opened fire with two of the captured pieces.

In the battle of Brandy Station, the Confederate Artillery loss was 1 killed, 10 wounded, and 1 missing, the heaviest individual battery loss being in Moorman's Battery, in which there were 1 man killed, 3 wounded, and 1 captured.*

---

*Maj. McClellan, in his history of Stuart's campaigns, does not mention Moorman's Battery in connection with this battle, and in the excellent account of the battle by Lieut. G. W. Beale, 9th Va. Cavalry, which appeared in the *Richmond Times-Dispatch*, of August 11, 1912, no mention whatever of Moorman's Battery is made. But see Beckham's report and the history of the battery by Capt. J. J. Shoemaker, p. 39. The author also has a letter from Capt. Shoemaker, who was 1st Lieutenant of the battery at the time, graphically describing the part of the battery in the battle.

Some idea of the ammunition expenditure of the
Horse Artillery may be gathered from the fact that a
single piece of Chew's Battery is reported by its gunner to have fired during the engagement 160 rounds.
But that such an enormous expenditure for a single
piece was by no means general is proved by the fact that
this gun burnt out at the breech before the day was over,
and was turned in as disabled.*

Of the part of the Artillery in the fight, Stuart in his
report has to say: "The conduct of the Horse Artillery, under that daring and efficient officer, Maj. R. F.
Beckham, deserves the highest praise. Not one piece
was ever in the hands of the enemy, though at times the
cannoneers had to fight, pistol and sword in hand, in its
defense. The officers and men behaved with the greatest gallantry and the mangled bodies of the enemy
show the effectiveness of their fire."

We must now leave Stuart and the Horse Artillery
in order to follow the movements of the main army.
But, before doing so, it should be said that in all the
operations of the cavalry leading up to Gettysburg,
Beckham's guns took an active part. It should also
be said that in crossing the Potomac at Rowser's Ford
on the 27th of June, the practice of submerging the
guns and caissons and towing them across stream on
the river bottom while the ammunition was carried over
in feed bags, was resorted to by Beckham and was,
therefore, not one exclusively employed by Forrest in
the west, as some writers seem to think.

---

*Three Years in the Confederate Horse Artillery, Neese, p. 179.

CHAPTER XXX

FROM FREDERICKSBURG TO GETTYSBURG

DURING the winter of 1862-63, Jackson had caused his Topographical Engineer to prepare a detailed map of the districts through which it would be necessary to pass in going from the lower Valley through Maryland to Pennsylvania.* This map was the most accurate and remarkable one of its kind made during the war. It showed every defensive position from Winchester to Carlisle, and upon a study of this map Lee matured his plans for the next campaign, which he desired to make a decisive one. Longstreet proposed to send a force into Tennessee to unite with Bragg and Johnston, the latter then being at Vicksburg, which place it was impossible for him to save. By concentrating such a large force in Tennessee, Longstreet believed Rosecrans could be crushed, Cincinnati threatened, and Grant drawn off from Vicksburg.† But Lee preferred to invade the North, agreeing with Longstreet that in taking this step the campaign should be offensive in strategy, but defensive in tactics. Lee's idea was to force Hooker to attack him in a strong position of his own selection and he no doubt felt as Jackson did when he said "we sometimes fail to drive the enemy out of his position, but they always fail to drive us out of ours."

Gen. Lee's decision was reached near the close of May and by the 1st of June he had completed his arrangements for the ensuing campaign. Before the movement began, his plans were so fully matured and made with such precision that the exact locality at which a conflict with the enemy was expected to take place was indicated on his map. This locality was the town of Gettysburg.‡ He was satisfied that if he could defeat

---

*Prepared by Capt. Jed Hotchkiss of his staff.

†*Lee's Invasion of Pennsylvania*, Longstreet; *Battles and Leaders*, p 245; also see *From Manassas to Appomattox*, Longstreet, p. 336.

‡*Memoirs of Robert E. Lee*, Long, pp. 267, 268.

the Federal Army he could also drive it across the Susquehanna and possess himself of Maryland, Western Pennsylvania, probably West Virginia and Washington, as well as relieve the pressure in the west and southwest. The plan being fully approved by Mr. Davis in a personal interview, Lee commenced the movement on June 2 by sending Ewell's Corps to Culpeper Courthouse, soon followed by Longstreet, while A. P. Hill was left in observation of the enemy at Fredericksburg, charged with the duty of screening the movement to the west. By the 8th of June, the main body of the Army was concentrated in the neighborhood of Culpeper Courthouse, from which point Lee on the 9th was able to send forward some of his infantry and Carter's and Alexander's battalions of artillery to the relief of Stuart at Brandy Station when, as we have seen, he was assailed by Pleasonton.

On the 5th, when preparations were in progress for the removal of army headquarters from Fredericksburg, two corps having already left, the enemy appeared in force on the opposite bank, and in the afternoon opened a heavy artillery fire near the mouth of Deep Run, under cover of which they established a pontoon bridge, over which a small body of infantry was crossed. The evening and night was spent by Pendleton in establishing the artillery defense with the batteries of the 3d Corps, but the enemy's movement proved to be a feint, and soon after midday of the 6th, in company with the Commander-in-Chief, the Chief of Artillery proceeded to Culpeper, arriving there the morning of the 7th. The Artillery of the 1st and 2d Corps had accompanied their respective corps to the point of concentration.

June 10, Ewell's Corps left Culpeper for the Valley. Milroy's Federal Division, about 9,000 strong, occupied Winchester, while McReynolds' Brigade held Berryville. Kelly's Division of about 10,000 men was at Harper's Ferry with a detachment of 1,200 infantry and a battery, under Col. Smith, at Martinsburg. Ewell reached Cedarville, *via* Chester Gap on the evening of the 12th, whence he detached Jenkins' Cavalry Brigade with Griffin's Battery, and Rodes' Division with Carter's Battalion to capture McReynolds who, discovering the approach of the Confederates, withdrew to Winchester. Rodes then pushed on to Martinsburg, and by the fire of Carter's Battalion, almost unaided, drove the garrison out of its works and across the Potomac at Shepherdstown. Smith's Federal battery in retreating by the Williamsport Road was pursued by Jenkins, and lost five guns with all their caissons, teams, and 400 rounds of ammunition. In the meantime, Ewell with Early's and Johnson's divisions and the corps artillery had arrived near Winchester on the evening of the 12th. The next morning Early's Division, with Jones' and Dance's battalions of artillery, was ordered to Newtown, where they were joined by a battalion of Maryland infantry and Griffin's Battery. Johnson moved along the direct road from Front Royal to Winchester driving in the enemy's pickets, while Early advanced along the pike to Kernstown and then to the left so as to gain a position northwest of the town, from which the defensive works could be attacked with advantage. While Early was maneuvering for a position, Johnson formed line of battle two miles from the town preparatory to making an attack and was opened upon by a battery of artillery near the Millwood Road. Col. Andrews at once brought up Carpenter's Battery in command of Lieut. W. T. Lambie, which from a position to the left of the Front Royal Road blew up one of the enemy's caissons and drove off his guns. But almost immediately 12 or 15 long-range pieces in and near the town uncovered and opened upon Lambie's guns, forcing them to retire. Dement's Battery in reserve also suffered some loss and was driven from the field.

It was late in the day before Early was ready to attack. His progress had been opposed by a battery on Pritchard's Hill, which compelled him to make a longer detour than he had anticipated. But finally Hays' Brigade was moved around through the woods to the Cedar Creek Pike, and along the road to a suitable position, from which to assail Pritchard's Hill. This hill was found by Hays to be occupied by a considerable force of infantry, as well as by the battery, and Gordon was sent by the same route pursued by Hays, to join the latter in the attack. Together Hays and Gordon drove the enemy across the Cedar Creek Pike, and Abraham's Creek as far as Milltown Mills, and into their fortifications on Bower's Hill, the latter being an exceptionally strong position, well defended by artillery, and most difficult of access by reason of the boggy creek bed in its front. During the retirement of the enemy from Bower's Hill, Maj. Latimer directed Carpenter from the position to which he had retired to open with a section of rifled pieces upon them, which was done with excellent effect, but again the enemy's massed artillery actively replied, whereupon about dark Latimer withdrew the battery and placed it in park with the rest of Andrews' Battalion, which was not engaged again that night or the following day. Early reformed his division, three brigades in the front line and one in reserve, while the enemy vigorously shelled his troops and Lambie's guns further to the right. Night fell before the attack could be organized and the men slept in position on their arms, while a terrific storm raged and torrents of rain fell upon them.

During the night, the Federal artillery was withdrawn from Bower's Hill and the south and west side of the town, only a thin line of skirmishers being left to confront Early and Johnson. Before 9 A. M. on the 14th, Early gained Bower's Hill, from which Ewell was able to see the enemy's main work to the northwest of the town. Early was accordingly directed to move to the west of the town and seize a small open work near the Pughtown Road, which commanded the main work, while about 11 A. M. Johnson moved east of the town to divert attention from Early and interfere as much as possible with the work of fortification which the Federals were busily engaged in. He accordingly advanced to a point between the Millwood and Berryville roads and threw forward a regiment in skirmish order which successfully engrossed the enemy's attention.

Leaving Gordon's Brigade and the Maryland Battalion with Griffin's and Hupp's batteries at Bower's Hill, Early with the rest of his division, Jones' Battalion of artillery under Capt. Carrington, and Brown's Battalion, less Hupp's Battery, under Capt. Dance, moved by a long circuit of some ten miles under cover of the intervening ridges and woods, and about 4 P. M. gained a wooded hill (one of the ranges known as Little North Mountain), opposite the enemy's position and within easy artillery range of it. While Col. Jones was engaged in placing the guns the men were allowed to rest. At the north extremity of the ridge, just south of the Pughtown Road, a cornfield, and at the south end an orchard, afforded excellent positions for artillery to fire upon the opposing works. The enemy had no pickets thrown out towards the north and west, although their main advanced work consisted of a bastion front facing Early's position. From this work a line of parapets ran northward about 150 yards across the Pughtown Road to a small redoubt, occupied by two guns and an infantry support. So completely were the Federals unaware of Early's presence, that two miles to the right of the position he had gained, the rear of their line confronting Gordon at Bower's Hill could be seen.

Jones immediately upon arriving at the ridge carefully reconnoitered the position with his battery commanders and directed a battery of his own and two batteries of Dance's Battalion, 12 guns in all, to be brought up by Dance to the position on the right of the ridge, which position was about three-fourths of a mile to the left front of the bastion. Carrington with two of Jones' batteries was then directed to occupy the cornfield on the left of the ridge, a position somewhat nearer the enemy's work, well to its right front, and from which it could be partially enfiladed. All of the guns were held under cover on the rear crest immediately in rear of the positions assigned them, extra ammunition brought up, and each battery commander and gunner pointed out his special portion of the target. The remaining batteries were held in reserve at the rear base of the ridge, ready to relieve those in position.

Hays' Brigade, with Smith in support, was brought up by Early and prepared to advance under cover of Jones' fire. When the infantry had been refreshed after a rest of about two hours, Jones gave the signal for Dance and Carrington to open. Instantly the twenty guns were pushed forward to the military crest by hand and opened simultaneously, crossing their fire on the opposing works. The Federal guns immediately opposite Early's position were helpless from the first, although an effort was made to keep them in action. As soon as the Confederate fire commenced, the line opposite Gordon began to fall back towards the main work, and it was upon these troops that Latimer, east of the Pike, caused Lambie to fire.

If the guns in the bastion and the small work on its right replied to Carrington's group Dance was free to fire upon them with the greatest deliberation, and if they shifted to the Confederate right group, Carrington's nearer group had necessarily to be neglected by them. Nor were they able under the most accurate cross-fire of the two groups to concentrate with effect upon Hays' line as it advanced leisurely across the intervening space. The works constructed for their cover were well defined targets for the Confederate gunners, who had no doubt whatever as to their true objective, and under such circumstances it was but a question of a few minutes before a superiority of fire was attained by the Confederate guns in their unexpected and suddenly disclosed positions.

As soon as Early had seen that the Federal defense was overwhelmed by the fire of his artillery, he had sent Hays' Brigade forward, the men of which ad-

vanced without molestation across the open to within
200 yards of the enemy's works. Within thirty minutes
the hostile fire was completely subdued, and the defenders began to leave their intrenchments and fall back
upon the supports forming in the rear, whereupon the
signal for Jones to cease firing was given and the Confederate assaulting column rushed up the slope, through
the brushwood abattis, and into the larger work,
bayoneting the cannoneers who remained at their
posts. Of the six rifled guns in this work, two were
immediately turned upon the fleeing enemy and the
troops forming to advance to the support of the
captured line. The Federals now abandoned the small
works to the north of the bastion, which were promptly
occupied by Smith's men, whereupon Dance shifted
his fire to the main Federal fort, holding his original
position in order that he might sweep the opposite ridge,
should it be recovered by the enemy.

The occupancy of the whole line of detached works
gave the Confederates complete command over the main
Federal position. Thus had the artillery, much as at
Harper's Ferry the year before, but with even smaller
loss, enabled the infantry to seize an exceptionally
strong defensive line. No wonder the latter was filled
with enthusiasm for the gunners.

In the operations leading up to so successful a result Jones and his battery commanders displayed
marked ability and most excellent judgment. In the
first place, though always well up to the front in the
turning movement, they exhibited no undue haste, and
before rushing into position saved time and guarded
against mistakes by thoroughly reconnoitering the
position to be occupied by the guns. This having been
done, the batteries were brought up quietly, and without
the slightest confusion assigned their tasks. Nor were
the pieces exposed until the instant all were ready to
open fire. The method of bringing them into action on
this occasion is known as "creeping." Although a most
ordinary proceedure, and one which common sense

would always seem to dictate in circumstances like those in which Jones found himself placed, a perfect storm of discussion concerning "creeping" at one time broke out among the artillerymen of the Continent, the *pros* and *cons* appearing in numerous pamphlets.* It is such artificial issues that overcome the patience of practical soldiers to whom it seems that they have no place whatever in serious treatises on the technique and tactics of artillery.

As soon as Hays and Smith had secured the hill, Carrington moved his eight guns to its crest. In the meantime, Hays had been reënforced by Smith, and had with the captured guns dispersed the column which endeavored to recapture the position. An attack upon Gordon's position at Bower's Hill had also been repulsed, so that the Federals contented themselves by turning all the guns in the main fort and those in the redoubt on the ridge to its north upon Early, to which Jones replied as soon as he had brought up his batteries. From the captured position the Confederate guns were able to fire into both of these works, as well as upon the infantry masses near them, and continued in action until nightfall. Although Hays' and Smith's brigades had been formed along the rear crest of the ridge for an attack upon the main work of the enemy, the number of the latter, the difficulty of the intervening ground, and the growing darkness, all combined, rendered a further advance unadvisable. But it was apparent to all that the enemy had suffered severely from Jones' fire and that his position was untenable. Furthermore, Jones had early in the night brought all of his guns up and placed them behind the abandoned works.

Anticipating that Milroy would endeavor to escape during the night, Ewell, just after dark, ordered Johnson with a part of his division, and Lieut.-Col. Andrews with Dement's Battery of Napoleons, and Raine's

---

*See *Field Artillery With the Other Arms,* May, p. 126; also see Von. Schell, p. 43.

and Carpenter's rifled sections, eight guns in all, to move to a point about 2½ miles north of Winchester on the Martinsburg Pike to intercept the enemy's retreat, or to attack from the north at daylight, in concert with Early and Gordon, should he hold his ground. The remainder of Andrews' Battalion was left with Latimer in front of Winchester, somewhat to the southeast of the town.

Finding the direct road to the designated point almost impassable in the night, Johnson moved across country until he struck the road leading from the Winchester and Martinsburg Pike to Charles Town, and marched *via* Jordan Springs towards Stephenson's Depot, five miles from Winchester. By 3 A. M. he was within four miles of the Martinsburg Pike, marching rapidly towards it, Andrews' guns well closed up upon the infantry. As the head of the column reached the railroad some 200 yards from the pike, it was discovered that the enemy, who had abandoned all his guns, was moving north in full retreat, and almost instantly the fire of musketry broke out between the heads of the two columns. Johnson promptly formed his infantry in line across the Winchester-Harper's Ferry Road, over which he had approached the pike, a stone wall providing excellent cover for the men. In the meantime, the batteries had been halted about 200 yards from the railroad, and the leading gun of Dement's Battery ordered forward to the depot, whence it was directed to be placed in the road near the railroad bridge. Soon the other piece of the same section of Dement's Battery was ordered to occupy a position on the left of the road, and well to the front. Neither of these pieces was able to fire upon the pike at this time, however, on account of the skirmishers in their front. But soon the skirmishers fell back, followed by the enemy, and Dement's guns opened with canister at a range of less than 150 yards, and became desperately engaged in defending themselves against the Federal infantry. Andrews now posted Dement's second section and Raine's section

along the edge of the woods to the left of the road, and
somewhat further from the pike than Dement's two
guns, and Lambie's section of Carpenter's Battery at
a point about 200 yards to the right of the road to guard
the flank of Johnson's line.   Hardly had these dispositions been made when Milroy came on with his infantry and cavalry, and attacked, making repeated and
desperate efforts to cut his way through to Martinsburg.
The 1,200 men which Johnson had in his first line were
now reënforced by Walker's belated brigade, and after
failing in several frontal attacks, and then in an effort
to turn the Confederate flanks, a part of the Federal
column, some 2,300 men, surrendered.   The rest
scattered through the woods and fields, Milroy himself,
with about 250 cavalry escaping to Harper's Ferry, but
before morning, the Confederate cavalry had rounded
up many of the Federal stragglers.

In the fighting at Stephenson's Depot, Andrews
handled his guns with remarkable ability, all of them
being heavily engaged with the enemy's infantry at
close range for nearly two hours.   The guns were shifted
from point to point with unusual celerity, and met each
attempt to turn Johnson's flanks with a well directed
and rapid fire of canister, following up the enemy's
dispersed groups after his column was broken.   One of
Raine's guns, with an infantry support of but seven men,
compelled several hundred Federals retreating in disorder along the Jordan Springs Road to surrender.
This instance illustrates the tremendous moral influence
of pursuing guns upon disorganized troops.   Especially
effective was one of Dement's guns which during the
action occupied the railroad bridge and held it against
a large body of the enemy that endeavored to cut its
way over.   In this section commanded by Lieut. Contee,
the loss was 1 killed and 13 wounded, the latter including the section commander.   In the same section, 15
horses were killed or disabled.

In his account of the affair, Gen. Edward Johnson
says: "Before closing the report, I beg leave to state

that I have never seen superior artillery practice to that of Andrews' Battalion in this engagement, and especially the section under Lieut. Contee (Dement's Battery), one gun of which was placed on the bridge above referred to, and the other a little to the left and rear. Both pieces were very much exposed during the whole action. Four successive attempts were made to carry the bridge. Two sets of cannoneers (13 out of 16) were killed and disabled. Lieut.-Col. Andrews and Lieut. Contee, whose gallantry calls for special mention, fell wounded at this point. Lieut. John A. Morgan, First North Carolina Regiment, and Lieut. Randolph H. McKim, took the place of the disabled cannoneers, rendering valuable assistance, and deserving special mention."*

Johnson's total loss in the operations of the 13th, 14th, and 15th was but 14 killed, and 74 wounded. Some idea of the desperate work done by Andrews' gunners at Stephenson's Depot may be got from the fact that on that occasion he lost 2 men killed, 2 officers and 12 men wounded, more than 10 per cent of those engaged, whereas the infantry loss was less than 2 per cent of the force engaged. The total number of captured Federals was about 4,000, including 108 officers. The enemy abandoned 300 loaded wagons, 300 horses, a large quantity of commissary and quartermaster stores, and all their guns. Including those captured by Early, 23 pieces of ordnance were secured. Ewell's total loss was 47 killed, 219 wounded, and 3 missing, aggregate 269.

Ewell at once informed Rodes at Martinsburg of Milroy's flight, but as Jenkins was on the Potomac near Williamsport on the morning of the 15th, there was no cavalry with which Rodes could intercept the escaping Federals. That evening, Rodes crossed the river at Williamsport with three brigades, sending Jenkins forward to Chambersburg, and on the 19th moved his entire

---

*See account of this affair in *Recollections of a Soldier*, by the Rev. Randolph H. McKim.

division to Hagerstown, where he encamped on the road to Boonsborough, while Johnson crossed to Sharpsburg, and Early moved to Shepherdstown to threaten Harper's Ferry. In these positions, Ewell's divisions rested until June 21, while Longstreet and Hill closed up. The 2d Corps in a brief series of operations had not only swept the route clear for the advance, with the exception of 11,000 Federals at Harper's Ferry, but had secured 28 pieces of superior ordnance with which to complete the armament of its batteries besides turning over the surplus guns and a large amount of supplies to the Army.

On June 13, as Ewell's Corps approached Winchester, Hooker put his army in motion from Falmouth for Manassas. His plan to interpose between Lee's flanks was opposed by Lincoln, Halleck and Stanton, in spite of the fact that the Army of Northern Virginia was spread over a distance of more than 100 miles, and as Lincoln surmised, "was very slim somewhere." When Hooker abandoned his position along Stafford Heights, Hill started on the 14th for the Valley *via* Culpeper Courthouse and Front Royal, Garnett's, Poague's, and Cutts' battalions accompanying Heth's, Pender's, and Anderson's divisions, respectively, with the battalions of McIntosh and Pegram organized as a corps reserve.

Longstreet's Corps, with Henry's, Cabell's, and Dearing's battalions accompanying Hood's, McLaws', and Pickett's divisions, respectively, and Alexander's and Eshleman's battalions organized as the corps reserve, left Culpeper on the 15th and moved along the eastern slope of the Blue Ridge to cover the gaps. Hill passed in rear of Longstreet, and when he was safely in the Valley, the latter moved westward through Snicker's and Ashby's gaps, the two corps uniting near Winchester about the 20th. The march along the eastern slope of the Blue Ridge had been an arduous one for Walton's battalions, for not only were the roads followed extremely rough and difficult, and the heat oppressive, but the artillery was frequently called upon to make long digressions from the route to support the cavalry and detachments of infantry in meeting the threats of the enemy on the flank of the column. The Cavalry with the Horse Artillery had, while endeavoring to screen the movement, been almost constantly engaged, encountering the enemy at Aldie, Middleburg, and Upperville, and losing over 500 men in these operations.

On the 16th the Chief of Artillery, after a week of strenuous labor at Culpeper supervising the organization of the artillery trains, and assisting in arranging for the reserve supply of ammunition, left for the Valley and soon joined army headquarters which was with the 1st Corps. Between the 23d and 25th, after resting in camp near Millwood and Berryville for four or five days, the 1st Corps crossed the Potomac at Williamsport, and the 3d Corps at Shepherdstown. Robertson's and Jones' brigades of cavalry with Moorman's and Breathed's batteries remained at Ashby's Gap, while Chew's, McGregor's, and Hart's batteries, as we have seen, accompanied Stuart in his movement around the enemy's rear with Hampton's, Fitz Lee's, and W. H. F. Lee's brigades.

On the 21st, Gen. Lee ordered Ewell to move forward and take possession of Harrisburg, and the following day Rodes and Johnson with Carter's and Andrews' battalions, the latter under Latimer, and Early with Jones' Battalion, took up the march. Rodes and Johnson proceeded *via* Chambersburg to Carlisle, and Early's Division moved *via* Greenwood and Gettysburg to York, with orders to join the main body at Carlisle after destroying the Northern Central Roalroad, and the bridge across the Susquehanna at Wrightsville. Brown's and Nelson's battalions organized as the corps reserve accompanied Johnson's Division.

On the 25th and 26th, Hooker also crossed his army over the Potomac at Edward's Ferry, and moved to the vicinity of Frederick. Here he threatened the Confederate rear through the South Mountain passes, should Lee move north, and also covered Washington, but he soon found that his hands were tied by Stanton and Halleck, who did everything possible to compel his resignation, which was tendered and accepted on the 27th. At midnight, Meade was placed in command of the Army of the Potomac. Meanwhile, Lee with the 1st and 3d corps had reached Chambersburg and ordered Longstreet and Hill to join Ewell at Harrisburg. Ewell with Johnson's and Rodes' divisions had reached Carlisle. The following day, the 28th, Early reached York and sent Gordon forward to destroy the bridge, which was done, however, by a small party of Federal militia, falling back before the Confederate advance. Gen Lee did not learn until this day of Hooker's crossing, for Stuart with the larger part of the cavalry was entirely out of touch with the Army, and Robertson with his own and Jones' Brigade had not moved into Pennsylvania with the Army. Therefore, Lee was in utter ignorance of the movements of the enemy (just as Hooker had been at Chancellorsville), until one of Longstreet's spies arrived about midnight on the 28th, with accurate information as to the position of five of Meade's corps, and Lee now learned that Meade was at Frederick. That the absence of Stuart from the immediate front and flank of the Army during its advance into Pennsylvania was a grievous error on somebody's part seems certain, but the point cannot be gone into at length here. It is by no means clear, however, that the mistake is justly attributable to Stuart. Before he separated from the Army with the larger part of his division, he placed one brigade and part of another in immediate touch with army headquarters, and this force was at all times subject to the directions of Stuart's superiors. The force was not used, but that was not Stuart's fault. Stuart certainly had the sanction of Gen. Lee for the movement he undertook, and if the troops he left with the Army had been properly employed, irrespective of what orders Stuart may have left with Robertson, the absence of the cavalry would never have been assigned as one of the causes of the Confederate reverses in Pennsylvania. There is much ground for the belief that Lee counted on Stuart doing that which he had authorized Stuart to leave for Robertson to do, whereas Robertson, without direct orders from Lee failed to do without any fault on his part what Stuart would have done in similar circumstances. It would, therefore, seem that Lee suffered more from the absence of Stuart than from that of the cavalry, some of which he had but did not use; and again, it may be said, that since Stuart was authorized to separate from the Army of Lee, the latter as commander-in-chief must bear the blame for all consequent mishaps.*

As soon as Lee learned of Hooker's move across the Potomac and that the Federal army was marching towards South Mountain, he at once arrested the movements of his corps which had been hitherto ordered and determined to concentrate his army at Cashtown. Hill's Corps was accordingly ordered to move toward that point on the 29th, and Longstreet to follow the next day, leaving Pickett's Division at Chambersburg to guard the rear until relieved by Imboden's command from the Valley. Ewell was also recalled from Carlisle to the point of concentration, and on the evening of the 30th his reserve artillery and trains with Johnson's Division as an escort arrived near Chambersburg, and Ewell himself with Early and Rodes reached Heidlersburg. Since Jenkins' Brigade with Griffin's Battery, which had covered Ewell's advance towards Harrisburg, were the only mounted troops present, the advance of the Federals upon Gettysburg was unknown. Heth's Division of Hill's Corps had reached Cashtown on the 29th, and the following morning Pettigrew's Brigade of that division, which had been sent forward to procure a supply of shoes, found Gettysburg occupied by the enemy, and returned nine miles to Cashtown, its commander being unwilling to hazard an attack with his

*See *Stuart's Cavalry in the Gettysburg Campaign*, Mosby; also Col. Mosby's and Col. Robertson's articles in *Battles and Leaders; Campaigns of Stuart's Cavalry*, McClellan; *The Battle of Gettysburg*, Henderson; and numerous other authorities pro and con.

single brigade. Buford had early on the morning of the 29th crossed into and moved up the Cumberland Valley, *via* Boonesborough and Fairfield, with Gamble's and Devens' cavalry brigades, after sending Merritt's to Mechanicstown as a guard for his trains, and on Tuesday afternoon, June 30, under instructions from Pleasonton had entered Gettysburg.

Meade, who, like Lee, desired to fight a defensive battle, very soon after taking command on the 28th selected a strong position for his line along Parr's Ridge, behind Pipe Creek. This ridge formed the divide between the waters of the Potomac and Chesapeake Bay. From Gettysburg, near the eastern base of the Green Ridge and covering all the upper passes into Cumberland Valley, good roads led to all important points between the Susquehanna and the Potomac, as a result of which the town was of great strategic importance. On the west of the town, distant nearly half a mile, there is a somewhat elevated ridge running north and south with the Lutheran Seminary on the crest. This ridge, known as Seminary Ridge, was covered throughout its whole length with open woods. From the crest the ground slopes gradually to the west, and again rising forms another ridge about 500 yards from the first, upon which, nearly opposite the Seminary, stood the McPherson farm buildings. The western ridge, wider, smoother, and lower than the first, intersects the latter at Oak Hill, a commanding knoll at its northern extremity, and about one and a half miles north of the Seminary. From Oak Hill, the southern face of which was bare, there is a clear view of the slopes of both ridges and the valley between them. West of McPherson's ridge, Willoughby Run flows south into Marsh Creek, and south of the farm buildings and directly opposite the Seminary, a wood bordered the run for about 300 yards, and stretched back to the crest behind. The Seminary stands midway between two roads and about 300 yards from each, the first running from Gettysburg southwesterly to Hagerstown, *via* Fairfield; the second northwesterly to Chambersburg, *via* Cashtown. Parallel to and 150 yards north of the Chambersburg Pike is the bed of an unfinished railroad, with deep cuttings through the two ridges. North of the town the country is comparatively flat and open; on the east of it Rock Creek flows south. South of the town, and overlooking it, is a ridge of bold high ground, terminated on the west by Cemetery Hill, and on the east by Culp's Hill, which bending around to the south extends half a mile or more and terminates in low grounds near Spangler's Spring. Culp's Hill is steep and well wooded on its eastern face, which slopes downward to Rock Creek. From Cemetery Hill, a ridge known as Cemetery Ridge extends southward for a mile or more nearly parallel to Seminary Ridge, 1,000 yards to the west. On a line in prolongation of Cemetery Ridge rise two bold knolls, known as Little Round Top and Big Round Top, respectively. The configuration of the ground comprising Cemetery Ridge is such that its crest forms a line similar to the shank of a fish hook, with the crest line of Culp's Hill as the barb. The intervening ground between Cemetery and Seminary ridges consisted of rolling fields, intersected by numerous fences. Between the two ridges runs the Emmittsburg Road, which leaving the southern extremity of Seminary Ridge crosses the depression in a northeasterly direction, and passing over Cemetery Hill descends to the town. Such are the general features of the battlefield of Gettysburg.

So impressed was Buford with the strength of the various positions about Gettysburg, that no sooner had Pettigrew withdrawn before his advance, than he decided to secure them to Meade. Expecting the early appearance of the Confederates in force, he assigned Devens' Brigade to the quarter of the field north, and Gamble's to that west of the town, sent out scouting parties along all the roads to collect imformation, and informed Reynolds of the situation. His pickets extended from below the Fairfield Road along the eastern bank of Willoughby Run to the railroad cut, then easterly some 1,500 yards north of the town to a wooded hillock near Rock Creek. Meade arrived on the night of the 30th, with his headquarters and the Reserve Artillery under Hunt at Taneytown, about 12 miles south of Gettysburg. The 1st Corps was at Marsh Run, the 11th at Emmittsburg, the 3d at Bridgeport, the 12th at Littletown, the 2d at Uniontown, the 5th at Union Mills, the 6th and Gregg's cavalry at Manchester, and Kilpatrick's cavalry was at Hanover. Thus, while the Confederates were concentrating near Gettysburg, the Federal Army was widely scattered over the region to the south and east of it. But Meade was soon convinced that the movement of the enemy towards the Susquehanna had been abandoned, and while he issued carefully drawn orders to prepare the Pipe Creek line for defense, he also provided for an offensive movement in case developments should justify it.

At this time the three Confederate corps were converging by easy marches on Cashtown, where Lee, now more or less conversant with the positions of the Federal corps, proposed to await an attack. Stuart was still out of touch with the Army, and Robertson and Imboden had not had time to come up. Pickett's Division had been left at Chambersburg to await Imboden's arrival, and Law's Brigade had been detached from Hood's Division and sent to New Guilford Courthouse, a few miles south of Fayettesville, with orders to remain there until Robertson's command arrived.

As soon as Hill on the 30th learned from Pettigrew that the enemy was in Gettysburg, he informed Lee of the fact and also Ewell that he intended to advance the next morning and discover what was in his front. His orders were specific not to bring on an action, but his thirst for battle was unquenchable, and like the German lieutenants in 1870 he rushed on, and, as we shall see, took the control of the situation out of the hands of the commander-in-chief. It was Hill, therefore, who committed the second great mistake of the Confederate campaign, the practical elimination of the cavalry being the first.

CHAPTER XXXI

GETTYSBURG—JULY 1

THE Confederate situation on the morning of July 1 was briefly as follows: Of the nine divisions, eight with the exception of Law's Brigade were in motion towards Gettysburg, Ewell, in conformity with Hill's plan, having at an early hour ordered Rodes and Early to move on that point from the roads they were pursuing toward Cashtown. Six of the divisions with the reserve artillery of the three corps and the trains were concentrated upon the turnpike from Fayettesville to Gettysburg.

At 5 A. M., Hill with Heth's and Pender's divisions and Pegram's and McIntosh's battalions of artillery had left Cashtown, and at 8 A. M. Buford's scouts, about three miles west of Gettysburg, on the Cashtown Road, reported Heth's advance. Heth pressed on and found Gamble's cavalry brigade in position on the McPherson Ridge from the Fairfield Road to the railroad cut, supported by Calef's regular battery, one section of which was stationed near the left of the line and the other two across the Chambersburg or Cashtown Pike.* Devens' squadrons prolonged Gamble's line to Oak Hill.

As Heth advanced, he threw Archer's Brigade to the right and Davis' to the left of the Cashtown Pike with Pettigrew's and Brockenbrough's brigades in support. Pegram's and McIntosh's battalions, though well up, were unable to gain positions from which to prepare the attack before Heth launched his brigades, and the batteries were left to act as best they could, without any definite plan or objective. Hence, Heth's first attack was well resisted by Buford's dismounted troopers, who would have been unable to hold their lines had they been first subjected to a heavy artillery fire. Heth

*This battery was distinguished as Duncan's Battery in the Mexican War.

would almost certainly have been able by a proper concert with Pegram and McIntosh to seize Buford's position before the latter was reinforced.

Upon receiving Buford's report, Reynolds started for Gettysburg with Wadsworth's small division of two brigades, and Hall's 2d Maine Battery, ordering Doubleday and Howard to follow with their corps. Hearing the sound of battle as he approached the town, Reynolds directed his troops to cross the fields towards the firing, and himself joined Buford at the Seminary. It was now past 10 o'clock, and Heth had formed for attack. Reynolds placed three of the regiments which he had brought up north of the railroad cut, and two south of the pike, substituting Hall's Battery for Calef's, thus relieving the dismounted troopers, who had alone opposed Hill for the past two hours. Cutler's regiments were hardly in position when they were furiously charged by Davis' Brigade and swept back to Seminary Ridge under the fire of Pegram's guns, which also forced Hall to retire his battery by sections. Reynolds had meantime sent to the rear to hurry Doubleday forward and one of the latter's regiments, together with the two which had been posted south of the pike under Col. Fowler, charged Davis' Brigade and drove it from the cut with terrible loss to both sides. The Confederate brigade, losing all its field-officers but two, and many of its men, was disabled for the rest of the day. Just as Davis' Brigade overlapped Cutler's on the right, so Meredith's, the other brigade which Reynolds had brought up, overlapped Archer's on the latter's right. As Meredith's Brigade entered the wood west of the Seminary, it was ordered forward by Reynolds in a furious charge upon Archer's Brigade, turning the Confederate flank, capturing Archer and most of his men, and pursuing the others beyond Willoughby Run. Almost at the moment of victory, the superb Reynolds, who with that magnanimity which characterized his soul, had disregarded the affront of Meade's appointment over him, and had only sought to aid his new commander and serve his country to the utmost of his ability, was killed in the wood by a sharpshooter. But with Wadsworth's Division he had, with rare promptitude and gallantry, "determined the decisive field of the war." In the words of Gen. Hunt, it may be said that " to him may be applied in a wider sense than in its original one Napier's happy eulogium on Ridge: 'No man died on that field with more glory than he, yet many died, and there was much glory.' "

Soon after the repulse of Davis and Archer, Rowley's and Robinson's divisions of two brigades each with the four remaining batteries of the Corps arrived. Of Rowley's Division, Stone's Brigade occupied the interval between Meredith and Cutler, and Biddle's Brigade with Cooper's Battery took position on the ridge between the Fairfield Road and the wood. Reynolds' Battery replaced Hall's, and Calef's rejoined Gamble's Brigade, which with Devens' had been withdrawn from the field about 11 A. M. and stationed as a reserve in rear of the Federal left. Robinson's Division was also held as a reserve near the base of Seminary Ridge. Gen. Howard arrived about noon and, assuming command, directed Gen. Schurz commanding the 11th Corps to prolong Doubleday's line towards Oak Hill with two of his divisions and three batteries, and to post his third division and two batteries on Cemetery Hill as a rallying point.

Heth had, meantime, been preparing to renew the attack, and, as soon as Pender arrived to support him, was ordered to advance by Hill. The greater portion of Heth's line now moved to the attack south of the Cashtown Pike, with Pender's Division formed in a second line. The nine batteries of Pegram's and McIntosh's battalions occupied positions west of Willoughby Run, with Lane's, Poague's, Cutts', and Garnett's battalions held in reserve along the pike some distance to the rear. Pegram's entire battalion went into action on a low crest just to the right of the turnpike, while Rice's Battery and Hurt's section of Whitworths joined it. Johnson's Battery and Hurt's other section occupied a commanding hill further to the right near the Fairfield Road, while the 2d Rockbridge Battery, under Lieut. Wallace, was stationed just to the left of the pike. The two battalions at once opened with a slow fire which gradually grew in intensity as the Federal guns uncovered. Hurt's Whitworths were energetically employed in shelling the woods and soon Maurin's Battery of Garnett's Battalion moved up to the relief of one of Pegram's batteries, which had exhausted its ammunition.

At this juncture there were nine batteries engaged on either side. But Hill was not to deliver the attack unaided, for, approaching Gettysburg and guided by the sound of battle, Rodes had directed his march along the prolongation of Seminary Ridge, with three brigades on the western and two on the eastern slope, while Ewell ordered Carter to seize Oak Hill for his battalion of artillery. By 1 o'clock the approach of Ewell had been detected, and by 2 o'clock the column had begun to arrive over the Middletown Road and Carter was establishing his guns in position. Whereupon Howard called on Sickles at Emmittsburg, and Slocum at Two Taverns, for aid.

Col. Carter moved out ahead of Rodes' line, and placing W. P. Carter's and Fry's batteries in position on Oak Hill opened a destructive fire upon the enemy's line running along the ridge west of the town to the railroad cut. The effect of these two batteries, though in a position much exposed to the artillery and musketry fire of the enemy, was such as to cause Schurz, who had prolonged Doubleday's line to the right, to change front with his two divisions and occupy a low ridge half a mile north of the town. This change of front left a gap between his left and Doubleday's right covered only by the fire of Dilger's and Wheeler's batteries posted behind it. To meet the movement effected by Schurz, whose line was now at right angles to that of Doubleday and confronting Rodes, Carter moved Page's and Reese's batteries to the

Confederate left. Page's Battery went into action at the foot of the ridge occupied by O'Neal's Brigade, and opened with canister upon the enemy's infantry, which advanced to the attack. Disregarding at first the fire of the Federal batteries, a number of which had taken position in the valley north of the town and had concentrated upon him, Page was finally driven back to a more retired position. How persistently W. P. Carter at Oak Hill and Page maintained their fire is shown by the fact that within a short space of time the former lost 4 men killed and 7 wounded, while the latter lost 4 men killed and 26 wounded, and 17 horses.

McIntosh and Pegram had from the first crossed fire with Carter, and from their positions had not only assisted in forcing Schurz to abandon his original line, but had been able, by advancing two of McIntosh's batteries to the hollow east of Willoughby Run, to enfilade a large mass of infantry in the railroad cut, completely clearing it of the enemy.

The Federal attack on Rodes' left had become serious. Not only was Page's Battery compelled to retire, but Iverson had lost three of his regiments, or about 1,000 of his men, and the flank was being gradually turned. Leaving Fry's Battery in its original position on the ridge, Col. Carter rapidly moved Carter's, Page's, and Reese's batteries to its eastern base behind Doles' Brigade, which now held the extreme Confederate left. These batteries, by a tremendous effort, succeeded almost single-handed in checking the Federal advance and driving back both the infantry and artillery of the enemy from the threatened point. Carter's Battery, though much depleted and damaged, delivered a most effective fire with reckless daring.

At this juncture, about 3:30 P. M., Early's Division began to arrive on Rodes' left, and Devens' dismounted troopers who had been holding a hillock on Rock Creek were driven off by Doles' skirmishers. Barlow, however, advanced his division supported by Wilkerson's Battery, and recovered the position, but in order to connect with Barlow's left, it was necessary for Schurz to push forward his center, and still further attenuate his line.

As Early arrived, he took in the situation at a glance, and directed Jones to throw his battalion into action east of Rock Creek, and somewhat north of Barlow's position. With twelve pieces Jones soon opened at easy range upon the flank of Barlow's massed division, taking part of it in reverse. No troops could withstand such a fire long. No sooner had Jones opened than Gordon's, Hays', and Avery's brigades in line, with Smith's in support, moved out and attacked Barlow, Gordon on the right connecting with Doles on Rodes' left. The Confederate line was now, about 4 P. M., thoroughly reëstablished, and from right to left consisted of Heth's, Rodes', and Early's divisions, supported by four battalions of artillery, or seventeen batteries, all in action.

A bloody contest now ensued between Barlow and Early in which the former was desperately wounded, and Wilkerson's Battery severely punished after losing its commander. The whole 11th Corps or right wing of the Federal line was soon driven back almost to the town, where Schurz sought to establish a new line upon a brigade and Heckman's Battery which he drew from Cemetery Hill for the purpose. Jones had suffered the loss of several men and one gun, which was struck and bent by a solid shot. Three of his pieces had also been rendered temporarily unserviceable by projectiles wedging in the bore. But as soon as Early's advance had masked his fire upon Barlow's retreating masses, he sent Carrington's Battery across the creek in order that it might secure a better position in front of the town.

Doubleday had been vigorously attacked by Rodes on his right, and both Heth and Pender of Hill's Division on his left. Early's success completely uncovered his right, which was overlapped a quarter of a mile or more by Rodes. But still retiring slowly to the base

of Seminary Ridge, where Col. Wainwright commanding the artillery of the 1st Corps had massed 12 guns
south of the Cashtown pike, and Stewart's Battery
slightly north of it, the Federals offered a desperate resistance. Buford had thrown about half of Gamble's
dismounted troopers forward on the left, south of the
Fairfield Road. Heth's Division had suffered severely
and Pender had moved into the front line. On the Confederate side, Gen. Pendleton was seeking to move
Johnson's Battery to a position well to Heth's right,
from which to enfilade Doubleday's left, and had
ordered Garnett's Battalion forward along the pike and
Poague's Battalion to move up under cover to the right
between Johnson and Pegram. The artillery cordon
was thus almost completed from the Fairfield Road to
Rock Creek, when about 4 P. M. the whole Confederate
line advanced to the final attack. Schurz, then Doubleday, gave the order to fall back upon Cemetery Hill, but
not until Davison's section of Stewart's Battery had
raked Scale's Brigade in column on the pike, and
Wainwright's guns had inflicted great punishment upon
Perrin in spite of Pegram's and McIntosh's fire. Wainwright, mistaking the order, had clung to Seminary
Hill, until, seeing the infantry retreating to the town,
he moved his batteries down the Cashtown Pike, where
they were overlapped on both sides by the Confederate
skirmishers at close range. There, he was compelled to
abandon a gun all the horses of which were killed.
Schurz was also compelled to leave a gun on the field.

The Confederate batteries now advanced rapidly
from their several positions, and at once went into
action along Seminary Ridge, while the infantry pursued the retreating Federals through the town, which
was taken about 4:30 P. M. along with some 5,000
prisoners, principally men of the 11th Corps, who had
lost their way in the streets on the way to the rear.

Doubleday's and Schurz's men rallied upon Steinwehr's Division of the 11th Corps. Steinwehr's men
had been well posted behind the stone walls along the

slopes of the hill, and in the houses thereon. As they
arrived, the troops of Doubleday's Corps were formed
on Steinwehr's left and Schurz's on his right. Buford
assembled his squadrons on the plain west of Cemetery
Hill, covering the Federal left flank and checking the
pursuit, while Wainwright and Osborn posted the ten
batteries of the two corps in strong positions on the hill
covering every approach to its summit. A regiment
comprising the train guard was promptly placed by
Wadsworth on Culp's Hill. Hancock, much beloved
and admired by the Federal troops, now arrived and
assumed command, and soon under the energetic
direction of Hancock, Howard and Warren, strong entrenchments of stone, earth and timber began to appear
all along the crests of Cemetery and Culp's hills. The
sorely-tried Federals, much inspired by Hancock's
presence and the knowledge that his corps would soon
arrive, had no thought of abandoning their small Gibral-
tar upon which the tide of defeat had washed them,
without the most desperate resistance.

While the Federals were busily occupied in preparing their position for defense, Gen. Pendleton with his
staff was engaged in reconnoitering Seminary Ridge
as far south as the road leading eastward from the ridge,
through the Peach Orchard and Devil's Den. Garnett's Battalion had already been ordered up along the
Fairfield Road to the ridge, where Pendleton had intended to mass a large number of guns, within easy
range of Cemetery Hill, but Gen. Ramseur, whose brigade had just occupied the town, met Pendleton while
selecting positions for his guns and urged him not to go
into action at the point decided upon, lest the enemy's
batteries should be provoked into firing upon his men,
who were much exposed. Leaving Capt. Maurin with
the batteries of Garnett's Battalion in park just behind
the crest opposite the town, Pendleton again set about
the exploration of the ridge, soon sending Col. Walker
an order to move up his battalions, and the Commander-
in-Chief detailed information about the road leading
past the enemy's left flank.

From his station on Seminary Hill, Gens. Lee and Longstreet had witnessed the enemy retreating to Cemetery Hill. Lee's desire was to have Ewell secure possession of the heights in his front. An order to do this was sent Ewell by Lee, but with the caution not to bring on a general engagement until the Army was all up. The position was a formidable one, and its strength was being rapidly increased. The 2d Corps had been much cut up. Rodes had lost 3,000 men or more, and besides a loss of about 500 of his men, Early had sent two of his brigades well out to his left to watch the York Road, over which the approach of part of the 12th Corps was reported. Hill's two divisions had been very roughly handled and had lost heavily. They had been withdrawn to Seminary Hill, as soon as Early's troops entered the town, leaving Ewell with only about 8,000 men to hold it and secure the prisoners. Ewell, by acquiescing in the order he received, led Lee to believe that the attempt to take the hill would be made and offered no objection to its execution. But Johnson's Division with Latimer's, Dance's, and Nelson's battalions of artillery under Col. Brown, were momentarily expected by Ewell, and he delayed pending their arrival. These troops, however, did not arrive until near sunset, and meantime the firing had all but died out. During the fatal delay, portions of the Federal 12th and 3d Corps arrived. Before Johnson's Division came up, the enemy was reported to Ewell to be moving to his left flank, and upon its arrival he ordered it to move around to meet the threat and occupy Culp's Hill, half a mile to the east of Cemetery Hill, and Col. Brown at once set about a search for a route by which to move his artillery into position on Culp's Hill, which he expected would soon be in Johnson's possession. At this juncture, orders arrived from Gen. Lee for Ewell to draw his corps to the right, but Ewell in person persuaded the Commander-in-Chief to permit him to carry out his original design. Unknown to Ewell, Culp's Hill had been occupied early in the evening by Wadsworth's Division, and so when at midnight Johnson's Division was moved around to its base, a reconnoitering party found the enemy in possession, and no attempt was made to seize it. Latimer had meantime moved his battalion to the extreme left by a wide detour, and gone into position on Benner's Hill, between the York and Baltimore roads in front of Culp's Hill, where the batteries were parked for the night.

General Hunt states that a Confederate attack on Cemetery Hill was impracticable before 5:30 P. M., and that after that the position was perfectly secure. But this statement is too general, and therefore not at all satisfactory. That Ewell was guilty of unnecessarily delaying seems quite clear. The truth seems to be that he did not grasp the rare opportunity presented him and that it slipped by while he intentionally awaited the arrival of Johnson's Division and Brown's Artillery. It is not contended that Ewell should have assaulted after 5:30 P. M. After that time, the Federal position on Cemetery Hill was, as Gen. Hunt declares, no doubt perfectly secure against the force Ewell could hurl against it, and Johnson was undoubtedly too weak to carry Culp's Hill later in the night. The time at which Ewell should have taken the position was when Schurz fell back in more or less disorder before him. At that time, Culp's Hill was entirely unoccupied, and Steinwehr was alone in position on Cemetery Hill. It would seem that Ewell's troops could have followed Schurz up the slopes practically protected against the fire of Steinwehr's men by the enemy retreating in his front. Gordon had practically routed Barlow's Division and was actually among the latter's men when Ewell himself ordered the pursuit to cease. Hear what Gordon has to say: "The whole of that portion of the Union Army in my front was in inextricable confusion and in flight. They were necessarily in flight, for my troops were upon the flank and rapidly sweeping down the lines. The firing upon my men had almost ceased. Large bodies of Union troops were throwing down their arms and sur-

rendering because in disorganized and confused masses
they were wholly powerless either to check the movement or return the fire. As far down the lines as my
eye could reach, the Union troops were in retreat.*
Those at a distance were still resisting, but giving
ground, and it was only necessary for me to press forward in order to insure the same results which invariably follow such flank movements. In less than half
an hour, my troops would have swept up and over those
hills, the possession of which was of such momentous
consequence. It is not surprising, with a full realization
of the consequences of a halt, that I should have refused
at first to obey the order. Not until the third or fourth
order of the most peremptory character reached me, did
I obey."† Now, here it is to be observed that if Doubleday was still resisting well out to Gordon's right, as he
certainly was at the time Gordon pressed forward to
the town, he could not have been securely intrenched
on Cemetery Hill. As a matter of fact, Steinwehr
alone, as we have seen, was there. Gen. Hunt himself
states that Doubleday reached the hill after Howard's
two divisions fell back on Steinwehr, and also that the 1st
Corps was reformed before the 11th Corps. He also
states that the 11th Corps was reformed with some difficulty and that not until Doubleday and Howard had
established their line did Wadsworth occupy Culp's
Hill with the 500 men of the train guard. It appears
then, from his own words, that during the interim between Gordon's enforced halt north of the hill and near
its base and the time Doubleday reformed, a period of
at least half an hour, there were no troops whatever on
Culp's Hill and only Steinwehr and the two other divisions of the 11th Corps, the latter in a state of disorganization, on Cemetery Hill. Little should have been expected by Ewell in the way of an artillery preparation
for his attack. In fact, the terrain offered few good
positions for his artillery, and even had it been capable

---

*No doubt Gordon could see the retrograde movement of Doubleday's line
before Rodes and Pender.

†*Reminiscences of the Civil War,* John B. Gordon.

of rendering him valuable aid, that fact does not extenuate the grievous error of his allowing the enemy to intrench and reinforce himself. When he did move, it was in a manner contrary to the wishes of the Commander-in-Chief, though the latter's consent was finally secured and Johnson's entire division, too weak to carry Culp's Hill, was placed in a position from which communication with the rest of the Army was most difficult. In fact, it was practically eliminated from the field of utility for the remainder of the battle.

As to the point of Ewell's ability to take Culp's Hill and Cemetery Hill on the evening of the 1st, there is, however, the greatest diversity of authority. One of his own staff officers declares as the result of a personal reconnaissance that it was perfectly practicable.* At any rate, Lee's original orders should have been obeyed and the attempt made. In failing to do this, Ewell committed the third great mistake of the campaign. The fact that Lee's consent to the movement of Johnson's Division around to the left had been secured does not in any way signify that his original views were altered by Ewell's representations. When that division arrived, Lee had learned through the personal reconnaissance of Col. Long of his staff that it was no longer practicable to assault Cemetery Hill. He knew that Ewell had by his procrastination allowed the golden opportunity to slip through his fingers, and that some other move was necessary.

But now let us view the situation from another standpoint. Let us regard Ewell's action in the most favorable light possible, assuming, contrary to the fact, that he received no order from Lee to follow up Schurz. Even then it would seem he was guilty of a most inexcusable tactical blunder, for certain it is no general should halt his troops in pursuit, with a hill immediately in front obviously offering a rallying point for the enemy. The mere fact that a routed or even a defeated

*Capt. James Power Smith. See his valuable paper, "General Lee at Gettysburg," read before the Military Historical Society of Massachusetts, April 4, 1905.

enemy makes for a particular point is sufficient to
prompt an energetic commander to seek in every way
possible to deny his adversary access thereto. Cemetery
and Culp's hills by their very nature should have filled
Ewell with a consuming desire to reach their crests and
discover what lay beyond them. He should have longed
to secure their summits if for no other reason than to
keep the enemy from doing so. So long as a single regiment of his corps was capable of pushing on in fairly
good order, it should never have been allowed to halt until stopped by exhaustion or by the enemy. Troops, however weary, do not rest on ordinary hillsides with the
great unknown on the rear crest, and had whatever force
Ewell may have sent forward in this case been checked
in its ascent by Steinwehr, the strength and exact location of the latter would have been discovered. The information thus secured would have at once enabled
Ewell to seize Culp's Hill, if not Cemetery Hill,
and with the former in his possession the latter would
have soon become untenable along with the whole position subsequently occupied by Meade's troops.

The Confederates had now become hopelessly committed to the offensive, and just as Lee was compelled to
abandon the position near Cashtown as his line of defense, so Meade was being gradually drawn away by
circumstances from the defensive position he had selected behind Pipe Creek. Gettysburg, like a great
magnet, had drawn both armies forward from their
chosen fields of action, for neither Lee nor Meade was
able to overcome its attraction. Meade was compelled
to reinforce Buford, then Reynolds, then Howard, then
Hancock, to save them, while Lee was unable to relinquish the contact which Hill, contrary to the general
plan of campaign and specific orders, had brought
about.

When Meade was thoroughly informed of the situation at Cemetery Hill by Hancock and others, he immediately set his remaining troops in motion for
Gettysburg by forced marches, wisely recognizing Gen.

Hunt as his tactical Chief of Artillery and directing him to make all necessary dispositions concerning the arm. Leaving Taneytown about 11 P. M. Meade and Hunt reached the battlefield shortly after midnight and soon reconnoitered the position. The general features of the field have been explained. The Federal line, though hurriedly established upon the natural ridges, overlooked the open country to the north and the depression to the west. From Big Round Top on the south to Culp's Hill at the point of the fish hook on the east, the distance was about three miles. The line possessed a great advantage in that troops could be quickly transferred from point to point of the crest line by moving them across the interior area. Meade saw at once that the position and his force would permit him to establish about 25,000 infantry and 100 guns along each mile of his front, and that his flanks were at once unassailable and unturnable if properly defended. Not only did the natural flanks of the position rest upon precipitous and rocky slopes, but they were screened from artillery fire by thick growths of trees. As he viewed the favor which fortune had bestowed upon him, Meade's regrets concerning the necessary abandonment of Pipe Creek were dispelled.

Running roughly parallel to the shank of the Federal hook, which was some two miles long from Little Round Top to the bend at Cemetery Hill, nature with a bold hand had marked out the main Confederate position along Seminary Ridge. At the close of the 1st of July, Ewell's Corps covered the front from Benner's Hill around Culp's and Cemetery Hill, to Seminary Hill and the Fairfield Road, his line passing through the town. Johnson was on the left, Early in the center, and Rodes on the right. Hill's line occupied Seminary Ridge, his left connecting with Ewell. Trimble, vice Pender, was on the left, Anderson on the right, and Pettigrew, vice Heth, in reserve on the rear slope of the ridge. The Artillery of the 2d and 3d Corps bivouacked that night along the line, generally in rear of the infan-

try. Latimer occupied Benner's Hill, while Brown held
Jones' and Dance's battalions for the night somewhat
in Johnson's rear in readiness to be moved to Culp's
Hill should it be taken. Carter's batteries remained in
position along the ridge north of the town, together with
Nelson's Battalion. Col. Walker held Pegram's, Mc-
Intosh's, Lane's, Poague's, and that part of Garnett's
Battalion which had not been placed in position by
Pendleton, along the rear crest of Seminary Ridge,
ready to take up positions on the forward crest at dawn.

The exterior line of the Confederates is thus seen to
have been not less than 5 miles in extent with communication from point to point rendered most roundabout
and difficult by reason of its concavity towards the
enemy. Furthermore, Lee's force enabled him to occupy this line with not over 13,000 infantry, and 50 guns
per mile, or about half the number of guns and muskets
per mile of the enemy's position. The Federal formation was deep and narrow, while that of the Confederates was extensive in width and shallow. The relative
disposition of the two armies was, therefore, such that
the utmost coöperation between the various parts of the
exterior line, together with the concentration of its fire
effect, was essential to compensate, in an attack upon the
interior line, for the lack of the momentum of a superior
mass at any given point of assault. Without these two
elements, it now seems evident that any attack, however gallantly delivered, was predestined to fail through
sheer lack of momentum. No problem could be presented which involves to a higher degree than did
Gettysburg the absolute necessity of fire superiority to
the success of the offensive.

Such was the condition of affairs at the close of the
1st of July. While Lee's original desire to seize Cemetery Hill during the early part of the evening had been
thwarted, he still believed the important position could
be successfully assailed at daybreak in spite of Longstreet's advice to turn his attention to the enemy's
left in the vulnerable quarter to which Pendleton had

called attention. But while the views of Lee and Long-street differed at this time, the fact remains that the latter had already been urged to hasten forward his troops in order to be ready to discharge and carry out the part which circumstances might dictate. But Long-street at heart never accepted the necessity for the abandonment of the original plan to fight a defensive battle. While with Lee on Seminary Hill on the afternoon of the 1st, he openly expressed his disapproval of the former's intention to attack Cemetery Hill in the morning, saying, "If the enemy is there in the morning, it is because he wants to be attacked." He left his commander-in-chief, according to his own statement, with these parting words upon his lips, and such an expression on his part gives a fair insight into the spirit in which he set about the task of conforming to the general plan. To say the least, he was not enthusiastic, and lacking enthusiasm, that great lubricant of the military machine, it is small wonder that his subsequent movements were characterized by delays. When one's heart is not in his work, difficulties which otherwise might be easily disregarded, and in a large measure overcome, at once become all but insurmountable. To understand Longstreet's movements from now on, one must recognize the fact that he was at least an unwilling actor of a most important rôle, a rôle in which every particle of his old energy and enthusiasm was necessary to bring about success.

Whatever orders were given Longstreet and the other corps commanders, it seems certain that on the night of July 1 every available man was expected to be at the front early the following morning, and so when late in the evening, after conferring with some of his corps and division commanders, Lee finally accepted their view and decided to attack as advised by Long-street, he had every reason to expect that the 1st Corps would be on hand and ready to undertake its mission. After the engagement of the first day, Gen. Pendleton had again examined the ground southwest of the town,

and finding the ground in front of the southern part of
Cemetery Ridge much less difficult than that opposite
Hill's troops which were already in position opposite
Cemetery Hill, its practicable character was again reported to Gen. Lee. By that time, Col. Long had reconnoitered the Federal right and reported adversely
against the chances of a successful attack in the morning
in that quarter, and the Commander-in-Chief had conferred with Ewell and his division commanders whose
views coincided with Pendleton's about the proper
quarter in which to make an assault. Gen. Pendleton
declared that Lee told him when he reported the result
of his second reconnaissance that he had already
ordered Longstreet to attack by way of the Peach
Orchard at sunrise the next morning, and requested
him to reëxamine the ground in that direction at dawn.*

Whether Longstreet was directly ordered by Lee to
attack the Federal left at daybreak on the 2d or not, is
immaterial to this record. Suffice it to say, a great
blunder, the fourth of the campaign, was committed
either by Gen. Lee or by Gen. Longstreet. Much
authority both adverse to, and in support of, the latter
exists. If he was not ordered to attack at an early hour,
he should have been, and if he was directed to do so, he
failed to execute his orders.†

---

*Longstreet, in a vicious article in *Battles and Leaders* and later in his
book, endeavored to discredit the statements of Gen. Pendleton relative to this
reconnaissance. Not only has he been the only one to question the word of the
Rev. Wm. Nelson Pendleton, whose whole life was devoted to truth and the
service of God, but he has, also, been the only soldier of the Confederacy to
impugn the character of Gen. Lee. In expressing sentiments in his writings
entirely at variance with those of Longstreet, the general, Longstreet, the em-
bittered politician, simply weakened the force of his arguments. Into this he
was undoubtedly provoked by the animosities and criticisms of *post-bellum*
politics. One is almost glad to believe, as claimed by many, that he never
really wrote *From Manassas to Appomattox*, but, after all, whether he did or
not, he is responsible for the sentiments expressed by his literary agent, and it
is doubtful if so much jealousy of Virginia and Virginians as that which is
evidenced in this book could have been engendered in his soul subsequent to the
war, unless the germ had lain there from the first. The writer, though but a
child of six years at the time, vividly recalls a conversation between his father
and Gen. William Mahone, while he was perched upon the latter's knee, in
which the General said, "It is too bad Longstreet has let them goad him into
mixing up his military record with politics," or words to that effect. Both
Mahone and the writer's father were victims of much the same political odium
attaching to Longstreet, at the time, but Mahone was wiser than Longstreet,
and though the superb little soldier was actually charged by his more un-
scrupulous enemies with cowardice, he was never provoked into defending himself against the absurd accusation. His remark made a lasting impression upon
the writer's mind, though its meaning was not fully comprehended for many
years.

†See *Military Memoirs of a Confederate,* Alexander, and *Advance and Retreat,*
Hood, both in support of Longstreet.

Longstreet's supporters make entirely too much of the technicality of whether or not a specific order was received by him to attack at an early hour. He was culpable in not having his corps on the field ready to attack, should the developments of the night require it. He was with Lee the afternoon of the 1st, and has frequently declared that he was conscious of a state of mental distress and uncertainty on the part of his commander-in-chief. Since he did not know himself and did not believe that Lee knew what to expect on the morrow, all the more incumbent was it upon him to have his troops present and prepared for any contingency. Longstreet knew that Ewell and Hill had both been heavily engaged and that they had run up against a snag. From this he must have known that the exigency of the occasion required the immediate presence of the 1st Corps. His troops had been set in motion for Gettysburg. The question whether or not he was to attack the next day was immaterial. His duty, irrespective of an order for attack, or further orders of any kind, was to bring his command up at the first practicable hour. That a large part of the 1st Corps could have arrived much earlier than it did is not denied, for the main body of that corps went into bivouac within four miles of the field at midnight. In not appearing as soon as possible, Longstreet was guilty of the same lack of the spirit of coöperation which kept him away from Chancellorsville. Had he done at Gettysburg what the situation as known to him should have disclosed to the commander of one-third of the entire army to be necessary, he would have been present when needed and no delay would ever have occurred, even had no orders for attack been issued on the 1st. But here it should be said that Longstreet's delay was not the sole mistake made at Gettysburg, though many people entirely lose sight of those which had preceded it. Had Stuart been present, no battle would have been fought on the 1st. Had Hill obeyed orders, no battle would have been fought on the 1st. Had Ewell risen to the occasion on the 1st, Longstreet's attack on the 2d would not have been necessary. How can it be justly said that Longstreet lost the battle of Gettysburg? Longstreet, Ewell, and Hill together and in an equal degree contributed to the failure of the campaign. As to the battle itself, it is inconceivable how one can distinguish between the wanton sacrifice of opportunity on the part of Ewell, and the delay of Longstreet, in favor of the former.

CHAPTER XXXII

THE Artillery of the 2d and 3d corps, as well as all the divisions thereof, were upon the field and in position on the morning of the 2d. The Reserve Artillery of the 1st Corps had been held in camp near Greenwood the preceding day, and Cabell's, Henry's, and Dearing's battalions were attached to McLaws, Hoods, and Pickett's divisions, respectively, as usual. Little information had sifted back to the rear during the day of the events transpiring at the front. Early in the evening, however, the news reached the various portions of the 1st Corps that Hill and Ewell had been heavily engaged and were driving the enemy. At 4 P. M., McLaws and Hood with Cabell's and Henry's battalions left Greenwood, and marching 13 miles went into bivouac at Marsh Creek, four miles west of Gettysburg. Marching again at dawn they arrived near the field between 6 and 8 A. M.

Late in the evening of the 1st, information was received in the rear that Hill and Ewell had come to a standstill before the enemy in a strong defensive position, and soon orders arrived for the Reserve Artillery of the 1st Corps consisting of Eshleman's Battalion, 9 guns, and Alexander's, 26 guns, to move forward at 1 A. M. Marching steadily over good roads with a bright moon, the two battalions halted in a grassy, open grove about a mile west of Seminary Ridge at 7 A. M., where the animals were watered and fed. At this juncture, Col. Alexander was sent for by Longstreet, and riding forward found him with Lee on Seminary Ridge. It was explained to Alexander that the 1st Corps would assault the enemy's left flank and he was directed to take command of the corps artillery and reconnoiter the sector assigned him. He was particularly cautioned to keep his batteries out of sight of the signal station on

Big Round Top, in moving them into position. Placing Maj. Huger in command of his own battalion, Alexander at once set about making his reconnaissance, which was most thorough, extending over about three hours. By noon Alexander had led his own, Cabell's, and Henry's battalions by a meadow screened from the Federal signal station to a point in the valley of Willoughby Run, where they remained behind that portion of Seminary Ridge to be occupied by Longstreet's infantry. After disposing his batteries he rode back to learn the cause of the non-arrival of Hood and McLaws. Dearing's Battalion was with Pickett, and Eshleman's was held in reserve by Alexander in rear of the ridge, with the ordnance train.

Col. Walker had early in the morning posted the artillery of the 3d Corps along Seminary Ridge with the exception of Poague's and part of Garnett's battalions, the latter under Maj. Richardson, both of which he held in reserve on the rear crest. Thus Alexander's line of guns was extended to the left by Walker's as far as the Seminary. In the 2d Corps Col. Brown still held the extreme left with Latimer's Battalion. About 4 A. M. Latimer had after a most careful reconnaissance selected the only eligible position which was on the face of Benner's Hill, where he experienced much difficulty in securing proper cover for his caissons and limbers. His position was directly in front of Culp's Hill, and just across Rock Creek therefrom. Brown's Battery occupied the right of the line, Carpenter's the center, and Dement's and one section of Raine's the left. The guns were much crowded, and no room existed for the 20-pounder Parrott section of Raine's Battery, which under Lieut. Hardwicke, with Graham's Battery of Dance's Battalion, was posted further to the rear and right near the toll gate on the Hanover Road. Carter's Battalion still occupied the ridge held by Rodes' Division northwest of the town. Dance's Battalion was placed under Col. Carter's command early in the morning, and, after sending Graham's Battery to the left,

Carter posted Watson's Battery on the ridge just to the left of the railroad cut, Smith's on its right near the Seminary, and Dance's own battery under Lieut. Cunningham on the right of Seminary Hill and to the left of the Fairfield Road. Hupp's Salem Battery under Lieut. Griffin was held in reserve. Jones' Battalion was held well in rear of Ewell's left to guard against any attempt to turn that flank and was therefore eliminated from the action of the day. Just before sunset, he sent the Parrott section of Green's Battery at the request of Stuart to join Hampton at Hunterstown, three miles distant, and at 3 P. M. Tanner's Battery, which had exhausted its ammunition on the 1st, was ordered to the rear with the trains. Nelson's Battalion was held in reserve in rear of the ridge and about 500 yards to the left of the Cashtown Pike until 11 A. M., when it was moved into park immediately in rear of the Seminary, where it remained until dark in readiness to occupy a selected position in the front line. Thus it is seen that Ewell and Brown had not more than 48 of their 80-odd guns actually in position, and bearing on the Federal lines on the 2d of July, for Jones' and Nelson's battalions and Hupp's Battery were not engaged during the day. Yet, Gen. Lee had directed Ewell to create a diversion in Longstreet's favor, as soon as the guns of the 1st Corps were heard, converting it into a real attack if a favorable opportunity offered.

Early in the morning when nearly all the Confederate Army had reached Gettysburg, or its immediate vicinity, a great number of Meade's troops were still on the road. The 2d Corps and two divisions of the 5th under Sykes arrived about 7 A. M., and Crawford's Division joined about noon. Lockwood's Brigade arrived from Baltimore at 8; De Trobriand's and Burling's brigades of the 3d Corps at 9, and the Artillery Reserve, with an ammunition train close in its rear, containing besides the usual supply, 20 additional rounds of ammunition for every gun in the Army, from Emmittsburg at 10:30 A. M.

The lack of energy on the part of the Confederates in completing their dispositions for attack was in marked contrast to Meade's activity. At every point of his line of defense, the Federal commander and his staff officers were to be seen. As the Federal troops came up, all but exhausted by their long forced marches, which extended throughout the night and morning in spite of the oppressive heat, they were not allowed to rest until placed in position. The 12th Corps (Slocum's under Williams) occupied Culp's Hill on Wadsworth's right, the 2d Corps Cemetery Ridge from which the 3d Corps was drawn to prolong the line to Round Top; the 5th Corps was placed in reserve along the Baltimore Road near Rock Creek; and the Reserve Artillery, under the immediate command of Gen. Tyler, in a central position on a cross road from the Baltimore Pike to the Taneytown Road. A part of Buford's cavalry occupied the left, while Kilpatrick's and Gregg's cavalry divisions were posted well out on the right flank. The 1st and 11th Corps still held Cemetery Hill. The batteries of the various corps were strongly posted in rear of the infantry lines, and the more advanced guns on Cemetery and Culp's hills were protected by epaulments and gun pits.

Some slight demonstrating on the part of Ewell at daybreak had led Meade to order Slocum to attack the Confederate left with the 5th and 12th Corps, so soon as the 6th Corps should arrive to support him, but as the ground in his front was found unfavorable by Slocum, and the 6th Corps did not arrive before Ewell's activity ceased, the offensive was not assumed in this quarter by the Federals. Furthermore, Meade was apprehensive about his left, and was well satisfied to remain passive as long as each hour enabled him to strengthen his line in that quarter with the constantly arriving troops. In the meantime, Gen. Hunt, by his foresight in providing extra reserve ammunition, was able to replenish the caissons of the 1st and 11th Corps, which had been practically emptied the preceding day.*

At the first blush of dawn, Gen. Pendleton made his reconnaissance as directed, examining the ground almost up to the Federal position. Finding no difficulties which appeared to him insuperable, but detecting the movements of large masses of the enemy's infantry in the rear of the hostile line, he communicated with both Lee and Longstreet, urging upon them both that an immediate attack be made. Again and again he sent messages to the Commander-in-Chief by his staff officers, to impress him with the necessity of prompt action, and was informed that they were invariably transmitted to Longstreet by Gen. Lee, who was much annoyed by the latter's procrastination. But Longstreet did not arrive with Lee to examine the ground until noon. As they finally viewed the enemy's position from Seminary Ridge, near the Warfield house, the main features of the enemy's position appeared as follows: near the base of Cemetery Hill was Zeigler's Grove a mile and a half due north of the base of Little Round Top. From Zeigler's Grove Cemetery Ridge, with a well defined crest, ran 900 yards or more south to a smaller but prominent clump of trees, where it turned sharply back for 200 yards, then south again for 700 yards to Weikert's house. So far the ridge was smooth and open, in full view of and from 1,400 to 1,600 yards distant from Seminary Ridge. At Weikert's, it was lost in a large body of rocks, hills, and woods, lying athwart the direct line to Big Round Top, the Taneytown Road bending around to the east of the broken ground. This rough space extended some 400 yards west of the line of the ridge prolonged toward Plum Run. Along its southern edge, it was bounded by low marshy ground, stretching back to the base of Little Round Top, half a mile or more from Weikert's house, and its western boundary was wooded from north

---

*Hunt had formed the special ammunition train previously referred to upon his own responsibility and unknown to Hooker, who had never accorded his Chief of Artillery much consideration in the way of assigning him to the tactical direction of the arm.

to south. In front of these woods and Plum Run, stretched an open space 300 yards wide, a continuation of the rolling fields in front of Cemetery Ridge. Plum Run flows in a southeasterly direction towards Little Round Top, and then bends to the southwest at a point where it receives a small branch from Seminary Ridge. In the angles formed by these streams is a bold, rocky height, 100 feet lower than and 500 yards due west of Little Round Top. With a steep eastern face the hill is prolonged as a ridge generally in a northwesterly direction between Plum Run on the north and Plum Run Branch on the south to Seminary Ridge from which it springs towards the east as a spur. The surface of the northern face of Devil's Den Hill proper is intersected by innumerable ledges and outcroppings of rocks, among which are many holes and bowlders. From these peculiar formations the hill takes its name. The marshy bottom forming the valley of Plum Run, and the slopes of the two conical hills known as the Round Tops, are also strewn with massive bowlders. A cross road running along the north of Devil's Den and the Taneytown Road intersected the Emmittsburg Road at a peach orchard on the Devil's Den Ridge, 1,100 yards west of Plum Run. For a distance of 400 yards from the stream, the road was bounded on the north by trees and on the south by a wheat field. From the Peach Orchard, the Emmittsburg Road ran diagonally across the rolling fields between the Seminary and Cemetery ridges, a mile and a half to Zeigler's Grove. For half a mile from the orchard the road ran along a ridge perpendicular to the Devil's Den Ridge, and nearly parallel to and 600 yards distant from Seminary Ridge. From Devil's Den to the wooded crest of Seminary Ridge the distance was therefore about 1,700 yards. The junction of the two bold ridges at the orchard formed the salient of the Federal lines, and it was upon this point that Longstreet's Corps was to be hurled. If the enemy could be driven from the orchard by Longstreet, Gen. Lee believed the latter's artillery massed at that commanding position would be able to assist the infantry in reaching Cemetery Ridge. From the Peach Orchard Longstreet's attack would be in oblique order, and if driven home would roll up the Federal left. Had the attack been rendered before 9 A. M., before the Federal 3d and 6th Corps and the Reserve Artillery were in position, and before the enemy's lines were strengthened by nearly a whole day of energetic labor on the defensive works, the Confederates would undoubtedly have accomplished their design. The first indication the Federals had of Longstreet's presence was when Sickles at Hunt's suggestion sent forward a party to reconnoiter the woods 600 yards in his front. The presence of the enemy, however, when detected gave Sickles little concern, for already news of Sedgwick's near approach with the 6th Corps, the largest in the Federal Army, had been received, and Hunt, who from Devil's Den Ridge had been attracted by the superior command of Big Round Top, had set off to examine the extreme left and see that proper precautions were taken in that quarter to save the conical height from falling into the hands of the Confederates. When Hunt returned to the Peach Orchard after visiting Round Top and reporting all safe to Meade, Birney's Division was posted along the Emmittsburg Road on the Devil's Den Ridge, Graham's on Birney's right in two lines in front of the Smith house, and Burling had been ordered up to reinforce Birney at the salient. Hunt had already sent to the Reserve Artillery for some of his batteries, and as Turnbull's arrived, he replaced with it Seeley's Battery of the 3d Corps, which Capt. Randolph had placed on Graham's right, the latter shifting its position to the left of the Smith house. Randolph had also posted Smith's Battery on the rocky hill at Devil's Den, Winslow's in the wheatfield, Clark's on the left face of the salient or southern slope of the ridge, and his own at the angle looking west.

Sickles' Corps was obviously too weak to hold the advanced line or salient formed by the junction of the two ridges at the orchard, and Sykes' 5th Corps which had been ordered to reinforce him was momentarily expected. No sooner did the Confederate fire open than Meade also sent for Caldwell's Division on Cemetery Ridge, a division of the 12th Corps on Culp's Hill, and soon after for part of the recently arrived 6th Corps. McGilvery's Artillery Brigade also soon arrived from the Reserve, and Bigelow's, Phillips', Hart's, Ames', and Thompson's batteries were ordered into position along the crests.

Pickett's Division had left Chambersburg at 2 A. M., but after a march of 22 miles went into camp, three miles from the field at 4 P. M. Yet McLaws' entire division and Hood's, with the exception of Law's Brigade, had arrived within striking distance of the field early in the morning. Longstreet deliberately waited for the arrival of Law's Brigade before he made the slightest effort to place his infantry in position. This alone was not the only cause of delay, for leaving New Guilford Courthouse with Bachman's Battery at 3 A. M. Law had rejoined Hood before noon. At this time Hood and McLaws were on the Chambersburg Road about a mile west of the town. We have seen that Alexander had easily avoided the exposed point with his artillery column, and had ridden back to discover the cause of Longstreet's delay. Yet, he has subsequently sought to defend that delay when it is proved by his own action that there was no reason for it. Longstreet had caused his infantry to countermarch and take a devious route *via* Black Horse Tavern, in order to avoid detection from the Federal signal station. At length, after many vexatious and useless halts, his column arrived, Hood in front, at the Emmittsburg Road along Seminary Ridge opposite Little Round Top, and on the right of Anderson's Division of the 3d Corps which had been extended towards the south during the morning. In spite of Longstreet's devious route to screen his flank movement, it had been discovered by the Federal signal party.

Both Pendleton and Col. Long of Lee's staff had examined the positions which Walker's batteries had taken along Seminary Ridge from which to support the advance of the 1st Corps, and all was at last ready. Gen. Lee had been sorely tried throughout the day by what appeared to him, at least, to be an inexplicable delay on Longstreet's part. Ewell's and Hill's artillery had already opened upon Cemetery Hill by way of diversion in favor of the 1st Corps.

Upon arriving Longstreet deployed his divisions each in two lines with Hood on the right and extending east of the road to a point about 1,000 yards south of the orchard, his left prolonged by McLaws, whose line crossed the road to the rear. Reilly's, Latham's, Garden's, and Bachman's batteries of Henry's Battalion of 20 guns, were posted among the trees on the ridge in rear of Hood. Although there was no sign of any enemy on the right, as a precaution a regiment was detached and stationed at Kern's house, half a mile down the Emmittsburg Road. While forming his line, Law had been greatly attracted by Big Round Top, and learning from some prisoners, which the mounted scouts he had sent to reconnoiter its southern base had captured, that it was weakly held and that the Federal medical and ordnance trains were unguarded in its rear, and could be reached by a good farm road, he protested to Hood against a frontal attack and begged to be allowed to make a detour around the Federal flank. Hood's orders were positive, but he was induced by Law's persistent representations to communicate the information the latter had secured to Longstreet. Soon Capt. Hamilton of his staff, by whom the message was sent to the corps commander, returned and directed Hood by Longstreet's order to begin the attack at once as previously planned. If Hood's message reached Longstreet, he, Longstreet, had no just ground for his subsequent contention, that he had urged in vain to be allowed to turn the Federal left, instead of making a frontal attack. Whether Lee had previously insisted upon such an attack or not, it seems certain that his views would have been materially altered by such information as that in Law's possession. And, again, while the ground in his front was such that Longstreet's attack necessarily became a frontal one, the movement of his corps with respect to the whole army was designed to be tactically a flank attack. Upon discovering that his blow would fall short of the flank, a fact unknown except to him, it was Longstreet's duty to inform the Commander-in-Chief. Yet, he subsequently had the effrontery to declare that "he would and could have saved every man lost at Gettysburg, had he been permitted to do so." No. Longstreet was stubborn. He had been ordered to do that which he did not want to do, which was to participate in an offensive engagement, and he did not propose to contribute anything on his own initiative to the success of a battle, the fighting of which he had all along opposed. The severest arraignment of Longstreet ever penned is the account of the battle of Gettysburg by Gen. Law, in which, in an attempt to shoulder the blame on Lee for its loss, he unwittingly fixes the responsibility for Longstreet's failure to turn the left flank, beyond peradventure of a doubt, upon Longstreet himself.*

The order of attack issued by Longstreet as soon as his divisions were in line of battle was for the movement to begin on the right, Law's Brigade leading, the others taking it up successively toward the left. It was near 5 P. M. when the infantry advanced. The artillery on both sides had already been warmly engaged the better part of an hour. Alexander's Battalion with 18, Cabell's with 18, and Henry's with 10 guns had been in action since about 3:45 P. M. Henry's Battalion had moved out with Hood, and as the Federal Artillery was well posted and prepared for the attack, his batteries were soon after coming into view heavily engaged. Cabell's Battalion had

---

*See "The Struggle for Round Top," E. M. Law, *Battles and Leaders*, Vol. III, p. 322.

at once gone into action behind a stone fence near
Snyder's house, about 700 yards from the Federal batteries, to support Henry. His position afforded little
cover for the guns, and the well-directed fire of the opposing artillery at once caused him serious loss in men
and horses. To help him, Alexander had Huger move
Moody's, Ficklin's, Parker's, and Taylor's batteries with
their 18 guns to the Warfield house and open at a range
of 500 yards from the orchard. Alexander now had 54
guns of the 1st Corps in action, which he and Longstreet
both believed would in a short while be able to crush in
Sickles' line and silence his batteries. But so accurate
was the practice of the Federal guns, that two of
Fickling's pieces were soon dismounted. The labor of
running the guns up after each recoil to the crest of the
rocky slope was so exhausting to his cannoneers that
Moody was compelled to call for volunteers from
Barksdale's Brigade nearby to handle his four 24-
pounder Parrotts and two 12-pounder Napoleons.
Eight infantrymen promptly responded, two of whom
were killed and three wounded before night.

When Hood finally launched his infantry, it advanced rapidly across the valley in front of the left
leg of the salient angle held by the Federals, all the
time under a heavy fire from the enemy's batteries, and
brushing his skirmishers out of the way, soon struck
Sickles' main line. The advance continued steadily,
driving the enemy to the confines of Devil's Den, where
the troops of both sides on this portion of the field
seemed to dissolve in the rugged area. In less than an
hour Hood's troops had carried Devil's Den opposite
his center and captured three pieces of Smith's Battery,
which from the rocky height had severely punished the
attacking infantry. In the meantime, Law, supported
by a part of Robertson's Brigade, had in spite of Hood's
orders, swept over the northern slope of Big Round
Top, cleared it of the enemy, and, turning somewhat to
the left, advanced upon Little Round Top in rear of
the hill which Hood's center had carried. Henry's Bat-

talion had done all in its power to support Hood's
infantry, devoting much attention to Smith's Battery
on Devil's Den Road, which had enfiladed and inflicted
much loss upon the attacking troops. Cabell had also
turned two of his guns upon this battery with fine effect.
In the meantime, however, Hood's left brigade had
been subjected to great annoyance and loss by the fire
of the enemy along the ridge on its left and had been
frequently compelled in its advance to change front to
repel the movements against its flank. McLaws had
held his men well under cover during the artillery preparation. In spite of the superior number and metal of
the enemy's guns, Alexander's own batteries stood manfully to their task, determined to shake the Federal line
at the angle, and save McLaws' infantry as much as
possible in their advance. The ammunition expenditure
was enormous, but fortunately the reserve supply was
close at hand behind the ridge. At such close range, the
Confederate fire was more accurate than usual, while
many of the Federal projectiles passed over the crest
behind the Confederate batteries, and were lost in the
valley beyond. The thick growth of trees on the ridge
also served to reduce the effect of the shells that burst
short of the crest. But the Federal batteries were still
holding their own when Alexander, about 6 P. M.,
ordered Maj. Dearing, who had arrived in advance of
his battalion, and reported to him, to move up Woolfolk's and Jordan's batteries with their ten pieces, which
had been held in reserve behind the ridge, to the support
of the other four batteries of the battalion under Huger.
But before these batteries joined Huger, at the Warfield house, Cabell had ceased firing and given the signal
with three guns for McLaws' Division to charge.
Leaping the wall behind which they had lain, McLaws'
men rushed past the guns in Kershaw's front, crushed
in the angle of Sickles' line by seizing the Peach
Orchard, and drove the enemy back in confusion from
their salient position, thereby relieving the pressure on
Hood's left.

The breaking in of the Peach Orchard angle exposed the flanks of the batteries on the advanced crests, which fell back firing in order to cover the retirement of the infantry behind Plum Run. Many guns of different batteries had to be abandoned by the Federals because of the destruction of their teams and cannoneers. Some were hauled off by hand, but the loss was heavy. Bigelow's 9th Massachusetts Battery made a stand close by the Trostle house in a corner of a field to which the guns were hauled by prolonges, where it was ordered by McGilvery to remain in action at all hazards until a line of artillery could be formed in front of the wood beyond Plum Run. This line was soon formed by collecting all the serviceable batteries and fragments of batteries which had been withdrawn, and, together with Dow's Maine Battery fresh from the reserve, Bigelow succeeded in checking the pursuit and enabling all but one of the abandoned guns to be recovered.

As McLaws' Division rushed past the guns at the Warfield house, masking their fire, Alexander ordered all six of his batteries to limber to the front, and charged with them in line across the plain, going into action again at the orchard. Perhaps no more superb feat of artillery drill on the battlefield was ever witnessed than this rapid change of position of Alexander's Battalion. For 500 yards the foaming horses dashed forward, under whip and spur, the guns in perfect alignment, and the carriages fairly bounding over the fields. Every officer and non-commissioned officer rode at his post, and not a team swerved from the line, except those which were struck down by the blizzard of Federal shell. Fortunately most of the enemy's projectiles overshot their mark, and as the great line of six batteries with over 400 horses reached the position abandoned by the enemy, "action front" was executed as if by a single piece. Hardly had the teams wheeled, and the trails of the pieces cleared the pintle-hooks when again a sheet of flame burst from the 24 guns of Alexander's magnificent battalion. Few artillerymen have experienced the sensation which must have come to Alexander at this moment, for seldom has such a maneuver been executed on the battlefield.

The ground over which the battalion had advanced was generally good, but obstructed in one place by a rail fence. Seeing a body of Federal prisoners being moved to the rear, Dearing had shouted to them to remove the rails in the path of the artillery. "Never was an order executed with more alacrity. Every prisoner seemed to seize a rail, and the fence disappeared as if by magic." But the joy of the charge was not all. It was the artillerist's heaven to follow the routed enemy after a prolonged duel with his guns, and to hurl shell and canister into his disorganized and fleeing masses. To Alexander's ears, the reports of his guns sounded louder and more powerful than ever before, and the shouts of his gunners directing the fire in rapid succession thrilled his own and the soul of every witness of the fight with exultant pride.

There is no excitement on earth like that of galloping at the head of a rapidly advancing line of artillery, with the awe-inspiring rumble of the wheels, mingling with the clatter of innumerable feet close behind. The momentum of the great mass of men, animals, and carriages almost seems to forbid the thought of attempting to check the force which has been set in motion. With his mount bounding along almost as if borne on the breeze of the pursuing storm, the eye of the commander instinctively searches the terrain for his position, while a hundred, perhaps five hundred, human beings, and as many dumb warriors, joyfully laboring in the traces, watch his every movement. At last the leader's right arm shoots upward, then outward. No words are necessary, and if spoken would be superfluous. In that dull roar of the onrushing mass no voice but that of Jove could be heard. The swoop of the fleetest hawk is not more graceful nor more sudden than that which follows. Every man and horse knows his part and must perform it, for mistakes at such a moment are fatal. But, first

of all, out of the orderly chaos which ensues, the dark
warriors come to rest as if in the ominous silence gathering breath with which to shout their defiance, while the
attending men and beasts are springing to their posts.
The joy of the charge is forgotten. Though every hand
and limb is still trembling with the old thrill, a greater
joy is now in store for all, for flash! bang! scre-e-ch—bo-
om—a shell has burst among the flying foe. Small
wonder then that Alexander cherished no regret over
having declined the command of a brigade of infantry.
Surely there was glory enough for any soldier to be
found at the head of such a command as he led across
the fields and into action in front of Little Round Top!

After the enemy fell back upon the ridge in their
rear, Longstreet's batteries fired upon every part of the
hostile line in range, especially devoting their attention
to McGilvery's group of 28 guns behind Plum Run.
Three of Anderson's brigades, Wilcox's, Perry's, and
Wright's, pressed forward against Humphreys' line
and forced it back to Cemetery Ridge, under cover of
two of Gibbon's regiments and Brown's Rhode Island
Battery. Later they succeeded in breaking the Federal
line and seized many guns, but were driven out and fell
back about dusk under a heavy artillery fire from Mc-
Gilvery's massed batteries.

Further to the right one Confederate regiment alone
succeeded in crossing Plum Run and actually got in
among Bigelow's Battery fighting hand to hand with
the cannoneers. Although, of the 104 men and 88 horses
of this battery, 28 men and 65 horses were killed or
wounded, still it maintained itself without losing a gun,
and the gallant captain, who himself was wounded, faithfully discharged the important trust committed to him.
In doing so, he gave evidence, as in the case of Beckham's gunners at Brandy Station, of the great resisting
power of artillery, even when unsupported.

Hood's center, as we have seen, had seized and still
held Devil's Den, but Law, who had reached the slope of
Little Round Top, had been driven back to its base by

Weed's and Vincent's brigades and Hazlett's Battery, which Warren on his own initiative had stationed at the summit, just as Longstreet's attack commenced. The placing of Hazlett's six guns in this position was a marvelous feat, and one which, in view of the precipitous and rugged slope of the mountain would have seemed impossible under ordinary circumstances. But, together the infantry and the cannoneers dragged them to the top just in time to repel Law's troops, who were already clambering up the slopes. The fighting for the possession of Little Round Top was desperate. Weed and Hazlett were both killed and Vincent wounded. The first had himself won great distinction in the Peninsula campaign, as an artillerist, and again at Chancellorsville, where he served as chief of his corps artillery. Shortly before his death he had been promoted from a captain of artillery to a brigadier-general of infantry. Brave Hazlett, whom we have met on other fields, fell while bending over his former chief to receive his last message. Hood's men, however, clung to the base of the mountain, Devil's Den and its woods, and captured three of Smith's guns.

It was now after 7 P. M. and Longstreet's troops, who had become disjointed in their attack, were engaged in more or less isolated combats. His artillery took part wherever it could. "The fuses of the flying shells streaked the darkening sky like little meteors."

As the Federal reinforcements had arrived piecemeal, they had been beaten in detail until by successive accretions they greatly outnumbered Hood and Mc-Laws. The fighting had been confined largely to the Peach Orchard, Little Round Top, and the rugged area of Devil's Den, behind the ledges and bowlders of which the sharpshooters of both sides had been thickly posted. At the close of the day, the Confederates held the base of both the Round Tops, Devil's Den, and the Emmittsburg Road, with skirmishers thrown out as far as the Trostle house. The Federals held the summits of the Round Tops, the Plum Run line, and Cemetery Ridge.

Before 8 P. M. the fire on both sides began to slacken, and by 9 the field was silent and Longstreet's men rested on their arms conscious of the fact that their work had only begun.

Now let us see what had been done on other parts of the field to support Longstreet's attack. We have seen that Anderson's three brigades assaulted Humphreys on the left of the 1st Corps. In this movement Wilcox was ably supported by Patterson's Battery of six pieces, and one gun of Ross's Battery, all of Lane's Battalion. That Anderson's troops were desperately engaged is shown by the fact that at one time Wilcox took 8 and Wright about 20 pieces of the enemy's artillery.

Of Hill's artillery, Poague's Battalion took position along Anderson's line in two groups. The left group consisting of five pieces of Graham's and Wyatt's batteries under Capt. Wyatt occupied the ridge behind Anderson's left, while Capt. Ward with five guns of his own and Brooke's Warrenton Battery moved out to the crest some 500 yards in advance of the ridge, when Anderson's brigades advanced. On Poague's left, Pegram's Battalion under Brunson occupied a position behind a stone wall on the ridge opposite Cemetery Ridge, losing during the day 9 men and 25 horses. Further to the left and behind the same wall, McIntosh was posted. Poague and Brunson both succeeded in partially enfilading the Federal batteries along the Emmittsburg Road and greatly aided Alexander in subduing their fire and driving them from their advanced positions. In this McIntosh also assisted, but was principally engaged in diverting the fire of the batteries on Cemetery Ridge from Longstreet's and Anderson's troops. On McIntosh's left, Lane with the two 20-pounder Parrotts and three 3-inch navy rifles of Wingfield's Battery, and the five remaining pieces of Ross's Battery, engaged the Federal Artillery on Cemetery Hill. Beyond Lane, and just to the right of the Fairfield Road, Maj. Richardson with nine pieces of Garnett's Battalion also fired actively upon the same guns, and was late in the day able to divert the fire of some of them from Ewell's troops. So much for the part of the 3d Corps. In the main, Walker's batteries were active and effective, and no complaint whatever is to be made of the support rendered by the artillery of the 2d Corps, 55 guns of which were engaged though mostly at extreme range.

Ewell like Hill had been ordered to support Longstreet's attack by active demonstrations. The successful performance of his rôle was essential to the success of the main attack in order that Meade might not draw troops from the point of the hook to support those at the end of the shank. We have seen that but 48 pieces of his artillery had been placed in position in the morning, a fact which almost presaged a lack of energy on his part. But 32 of these were actively engaged. About 4 P. M. Latimer was ordered to open from his position at Benner's Hill. As soon as his guns were unmasked, the enemy replied with a superior number of guns from Cemetery Hill and Culp's Hill, causing many casualties in the battalion. Soon the Federals planted some guns well out to Latimer's left front, enfilading Carpenter's Battery and practically silencing it. By this time one section of Dement's Battery had entirely exhausted its ammunition, and one of Brown's pieces had been disabled. Brown himself was wounded and his men so cut up that but two pieces could be maintained in action. Latimer was now compelled to retire his battalion with the exception of four pieces which he left under cover to repel any advance which the enemy might attempt.

It was now sunset. Jones' Battalion was absent from the field altogether, and neither Carter's nor Nelson's had fired a shot. The three batteries of Dance's battalion in position behind Ewell's right had alone, of all the artillery of the 2d Corps, supported Latimer by firing upon Cemetery Hill and the batteries posted there. Latimer's contest had been most unequal. Ewell's demonstration which should of course have been made soon after Latimer opened fire was delayed, and the infantry only got fairly to work after he had been terribly cut up and compelled to withdraw his guns. Finally Johnson's Division advanced and Latimer boldly opened with the four pieces which he had left in position, drawing the overwhelming fire of the massed batteries of the enemy upon him. Perceiving that the Federals were shifting the position of many of their guns so as to play upon Latimer and Johnson, Richardson on Hill's left redoubled his efforts to divert their fire and partially succeeded. It was at this juncture that the overbold and youthful Latimer was struck down, while heroically cheering on the few cannoneers that remained at their posts. The wound which the "boy major," as he was called, received in his arm, resulted in his death from gangrene on August 1st. Col. John Thompson Brown, the Chief of Artillery of the 2d Corps, characterized Latimer as a gallant and accomplished officer, and a noble young man. "No heavier loss," said he, "could have befallen the Artillery of this corps." And Ewell, who was not given to flattery as his reports will show, wrote of him, "The gallant young officer served with me from March, 1862, to the second battle of Manassas. I was particularly struck at Winchester, May 25, 1862, his first warm engagement, by his coolness, self-possession, and bravery under a very heavy artillery fire, showing when most needed the full possession of all his faculties. Though not twenty-one when he fell, his soldierly qualities had impressed me as deeply as those of any officer in my command." And writing of the battle Gen. Pendleton said, "Here the gallant Maj. Latimer, so young and yet so exemplary, received the wound which eventuated in his death." While Gen. Lee did not mention Latimer in his report of the battle his admiration of the youthful artillerist was unbounded and frequently expressed.

Entering the Virginia Military Institute in 1859, Latimer promptly volunteered when the Corps of Cadets was sent to Richmond in April, was at once assigned to duty with the artillery being organized in the camp of instruction, and was soon commissioned a lieutenant in the battery raised by Capt. A. R. Courtney. During his military career, he occupied many posts of honor and responsibility and enjoyed the perfect confidence of his men and officers. When a lieutenant and under the command of Jackson, his old tutor, the latter wrote of him in his report of the Valley campaign: "This young officer was conspicuous for his coolness, judgment, and skill with which he managed his battery, fully supporting the opinion I had formed of his high merit." Ewell constantly referred to him as his "Little Napoleon." After receiving his wound at Gettysburg, and being removed from beneath his horse, which had fallen upon him, he continued, though half dazed by his fall, to supervise and direct the movements of his battalion. That night he was sent to the rear, and later removed to Harrisonburg from Winchester, where he died. As his final hour approached, the attending physician, seeking to secure his last message, asked him if he feared to die. "No," was his reply, "for my trust is in God." The day before a friendly chaplain who sought to console him asked him upon what he based his hopes for the future. "Not on good works," he replied, "but on the merits of Jesus Christ alone." Such was the spirit which inspired his indomitable soul. That he rests with Jackson who can doubt? And what higher tribute may be paid the memory of the "Boy Major" whose portrait now hangs with those of Crutchfield, and Cutshaw, and Rodes, and Colston, and Allan, and Paxton, and a host of others, among his comrades at the Virginia Military Institute, garlanded with laurels of immortal fame, than to say that he was the peer of any of them, and that in his own arm of the service, he was the fit companion of Pelham, of Breathed, of Chew, and the others whose deathless names fill these pages.*

When Johnson advanced against Culp's Hill, he found only one brigade—Greene's of the 12th Corps—in position, the others having been dispatched to the aid

---

*For a full account of Joseph White Latimer's military career, see *Memorial Virginia Military Institute*, Walker, p. 328.

of Sickles at the Peach Orchard.   This, of course, was the very contingency against which Lee by directing Ewell's demonstration had sought to guard.   Greene, supported by a large number of guns, fought with desperation, and soon, reinforced by about 1,000 men of the 1st and 11th Corps, succeeded in holding his own intrenchments.   Johnson, however, seized those abandoned by Geary and Ruger near the Baltimore Pike, but darkness prevented him from profiting by the advantage within his reach.   Early, with great spirit, assaulted and carried a part of Cemetery Hill, ascending by way of the ravine between it and Culp's Hill.   Breaking the line of the 11th Corps and overrunning Ricketts' reserve batteries, the two assaulting brigades were soon face to face with the excellent position occupied by Stevens' Battery of 12-pounders, which swept the head of the ravine.   Without support from Rodes, who had also been ordered to attack, Early's troops were driven from the hill.   As they fell back the cannoneers of Ricketts' two batteries heroically recovered their guns by a vigorous attack upon the disorganized Confederates, driving off with hand spikes, rammers, stones, and even fence rails, those attempting to secure the pieces.   Thus did Ewell's effort miscarry, which enabled Longstreet to be checked by Meade, who was free to transfer troops almost at will from his right to his left.   In the words of Col. Taylor, "The whole affair was disjointed.   There was an utter absence of accord in the movements of the several commands, and no decisive results attended the operations of the second day."   Longstreet had failed to attack at the time he was expected to do so, which, as has been said, was the fourth great mistake of the campaign. The fifth was committed by Ewell in failing to cooperate with him.

While all had by no means worked smoothly on the Federal side, due to the frequent disregard of orders by Meade's corps commanders, yet, in the main, the tactical conduct of the defense was as fine as that of the offense was faulty.   This fact was largely due, of course, to the peculiar character of the Federal position, which was so compact, as well as covered by the accidents of the ground, that troops could easily be shifted from point to point. Nevertheless, full advantage was taken of this fortunate circumstance by Meade. Again Hunt proved to be the Nemesis of the Confederates, and time and again his artillery was found massed just at the right point to deny them success, for it was McGilvery at Plum Run, who checked Longstreet, and it was Stevens on the right who hurled Early from the ridge he had all but won. During Longstreet's attack, Hunt had supported Sickles with 11 batteries with 60 guns of his general reserve alone. In addition to these guns, the 2d, 3d, and 5th Corps had 80 guns in action. Against these 140 pieces, Longstreet had but 62 guns on the field, and Anderson's Division but 5 in advance of Seminary Ridge.

While the artillery on both sides suffered severely in men and horses, the total loss of ordnance was three Federal guns, two of which only could be removed by the Confederates from the field.

The fire of the Confederate Artillery was most effective, but it was hopelessly outmatched in numbers. Longstreet's batteries were assigned an almost impossible task, for after driving battery after battery from the field, fresh ones continued to appear. Hunt's report says: "The batteries were exposed to heavy front and enfilading fires and suffered terribly, but as rapidly as any were disabled they were retired and replaced by others." And so, after the most persistent and heroic efforts on the part of Alexander's artillerymen to silence the enemy's batteries, at the close of the day they were rewarded by seeing not less than 75 Federal guns in position with ever-increasing infantry supports near-by. Yet there was no sign of discouragement in the Artillery.

When night fell, the Confederate Infantry, with the exception of Hood's and McLaws' Division on the right, and Johnson's on the extreme left, bivouacked approximately in the positions it had occupied in the morning. But while the Infantry rested, it was necessary for the Artillery to be refitted for the morrow. A splendid moon lit up the field and greatly assisted the work. The sound horses were watered and fed, while those killed and disabled were replaced by drafts from the wagon trains in rear. Extra caissons were brought up, ammunition issued, the lines rectified and such cover as was possible provided for the guns and their detachments.

The losses in Alexander's own battalion had been very heavy, probably not less than 75 men and twice that number of horses. Taylor's Battery alone lost 9 men. But the heaviest loss was in Fickling's (Rhett's or Brook's) South Carolina Battery, which had two 12-pounder howitzers dismounted and 40 cannoneers killed or wounded.

An incident in connection with Taylor's or Eubank's Battery is especially worthy of being preserved. While it was dashing forward to the orchard corporal Joseph T. V. Lantz, a veteran gunner, was struck down by a shell, which broke both his legs above the knees, and soon died. When some of his companions attempted to remove him from the field, he said, "You can do me no good; I am killed; follow your piece." Nearby lay the body of a young cadet, Hill Carter Eubank, who only a few days before had left the Virginia Military Institute to enlist in the battery originally commanded by his father. The facts are stated simply to show the character of the men who manned the Confederate guns. No artillery ever possessed a more superb personnel, and equally heroic incidents concerning them might be recounted indefinitely.

In Cabell's Battalion, the losses were unusually severe. McCarthy's Battery lost 9 men and 13 horses. Lieuts. R. M. Anderson and John Nimmo, with the rifled section of this battery alone, expended 200 rounds of ammunition in less than 2 hours, in a duel with Smith's Battery on Devil's Den Hill. Manly's Battery had moved forward to the orchard with Alexander's

Battalion and suffered accordingly. Fraser's Battery not only lost its veteran commander, but one of its lieutenants and 11 men. When Lieut. Furlong succeeded to the command of the battery, he was able to man but two pieces. Capt. Carlton was also wounded, Lieut. Motes succeeding to the command of the Troup Battery. During the night it was withdrawn to be refitted. In Henry's Battalion, which had been actively engaged from the first in support of Hood, the losses were also severe. One of Reilly's 3-inch rifles had burst, but two 10-pounder Parrotts captured by Hood's men from Smith's Battery were turned over to and secured by the battalion. Although Dearing had reported in person to Alexander before the capture of the Peach Orchard and had taken part in the fight, his battalion did not arrive upon the field until after dark, when it went into bivouac behind the ridge.

During the night it became known that the artillery along the whole line would be called upon to open at an early hour, and before morning Eshleman's and Dearing's battalions were moved up to Alexander's left, with Cabell and Henry on his right. Gen. Pendleton and Col. Long visited every portion of the line before morning, verified the positions of the guns, and gave specific directions to the Artillery of all three corps as to its part on the morrow. With the exception of the massing of all the batteries of the 1st Corps along the ridge at the Peach Orchard, the positions of the Artillery remained generally unchanged. Brown and Walker, like Alexander, made every effort to prepare their batteries for the renewal of the battle, and everywhere the fullest confidence reigned in the Artillery. Apparently there was no uneasiness over the small supply of reserve ammunition at hand, a matter with which the gunners, as a whole, were unfamiliar, perhaps fortunately so. But it seems certain that some account should have been taken of the condition of the ammunition supply, as a matter of extreme importance to the success of subsequent operations. The expenditure of the past two days had been enormous, and it was apparent to all that an unusual amount would be required the day following. It would be interesting indeed to be able to follow the movements of the ammunition trains and their methods of supply, but one searches in vain for a record of these things. Fortunately, nowadays, the trains, especially the ordnance trains, are both regarded and treated as an integral part of an army.

CHAPTER XXXIII

THE dawn of July 3d found the two armies approximately in the positions occupied by them at the close of the fighting the evening before. Though Cemetery Ridge remained intact in the hands of the Federals, yet the operations had resulted at every point in an advantage to the Confederates in spite of the fact that they had failed to accomplish all they had attempted to do. Longstreet had seized and occupied the advanced Federal position on the left, Ewell's left held the breast-works on Culp's Hill on the extreme Federal right, and tremendous loss had been inflicted on Meade's army. The advantage gained by Ewell would, it was believed, enable him to take the Federal line in reverse. Gen. Lee, therefore, determined to renew the assault. Longstreet, in accordance with this decision, was reinforced by Pickett's three brigades and Dearing's Battalion of artillery, which arrived after dark, and ordered to assail the heights in his front at dawn, while Ewell was directed to make a simultaneous assault on the enemy's right. But Meade did not supinely await the development of the Confederate attack as planned. A great group of guns was placed in position during the night, to bear on Johnson's Division, which had been strongly reinforced, and at 4 A. M. Geary and Ruger advanced under cover of the artillery to wrest their intrenchments from the Confederates. By 8 A. M. Ewell, in spite of the most desperate efforts on the part of Johnson's men, was forced to relinquish the captured works. Longstreet's dispositions had again been delayed and the fighting on the left had commenced long before the 1st Corps was ready to coöperate. It rendered Ewell no effectual support whatever. The sixth great mistake had been committed in this failure on the part of the

2d and 3d Corps to attack simultaneously, and again Meade had been free to reinforce one of his flanks at the expense of the other.

The change in the condition of affairs compelled Gen. Lee to alter his plan of attack. A reconnaissance disclosed to him that the Federal position from Round Top to Culp's Hill was occupied at every point by infantry and artillery. There was, however, one point upon which an assault could be directed with a reasonable prospect of success. The word reasonable is used because subsequent events showed that success would have been attained had Lee's orders been executed. This point was where Cemetery Ridge sloped westward to form the saddle over which the Emmittsburg Road passed. Lee believed that by forcing the hostile line at that point and directing his attack toward Cemetery Hill, he could take the Federal right in flank. He also perceived that once having gained the saddle in the ridge, the fire of the enemy's left would be neutralized, since it would be as destructive to friend as to foe. The task was accordingly assigned to Longstreet, while as before Hill and Ewell were to support him, and about 150 guns were to be massed to prepare for the assault. These conclusions were reached at a conference held during the morning on the field in front and within cannon range of Round Top, there being present Gens. Lee, Longstreet, A. P. Hill, and various staff officers. The plan of attack was fully discussed and it was decided that Pickett, whose men were fresh and thirsting for battle, should lead the assaulting column supported by McLaws and Hood. A. P. Hill was also to support the attack with such force as he could spare. It was never in any way contemplated that Pickett should alone make the assault. He was to be given the lead for the sole reason that since his troops were unweakened by previous fighting it was naturally assumed they would be more effective than Hood's and McLaws', which had been terribly punished. Any one familiar with war knows that soldiers are not like wolves which become more fierce at the sight of blood. The best troops are the most human men, and while the best troops are able temporarily to set aside, they are never able entirely to dispel, their fears of death. The more losses they sustain, the more difficult it is for them to set aside those fears. Pickett's men were not only fresh, but were inspired by a desire to reap their share of the glory of the battle, which had been denied them by their absence from the field the day before. While it had remained in the rear, its veteran soldiers, though individually glad to escape the horrors of battle, were none the less collectively fearful less they might arrive too late to satisfy the pride of their command.

The sole objection offered by Longstreet to the plan proposed at the conference was that the guns on Little Round Top might be brought to bear on the right flank of his column, but this point was disposed of apparently to his entire satisfaction by Col. Long of Lee's staff, who suggested that they could be neutralized, if not silenced, by a group of Confederate guns massed for the purpose. None of the awful forebodings which Longstreet has subsequently declared he entertained were expressed by him. He made no attempt to point out the inevitable failure of the attack, and gave no evidence of a feeling that the post of honor assigned his corps was virtually a forlorn hope, in which it was to be ruthlessly sacrificed by the "blood-thirsty Lee."* Yet he has declared that he used the following words to the Commander-in-Chief at the conference: "That will give me 15,000 men. I have been a soldier, I may say, from the ranks up to the position I now hold. I have been in pretty much all kinds of skirmishes, from those of two or three soldiers up to those of an army corps, and I think I can safely say there never was a body of 15,000 men who could make that attack successfully." These remarks, which Longstreet in fact would hardly have dared make, are important if they were actually made, for they show that his heart was still not in his work, and

*See Longstreet's absurd article in *Battles and Leaders,* Vol. III, p. 339, and also his book.

prove as previously stated that his spirit throughout the battle was not one of coöperation, and also, that he positively did not gather from the discussion at the conference that Pickett's Division was alone to assault. Yet he also argues that Pickett was wantonly sacrificed by Lee in spite of the fact that he, Longstreet, made not the slightest effort to support the division which, actually by his own words, accomplished all the entire corps was expected to do. The narrative will show that it was Longstreet himself who sacrificed Pickett's Division, and also that its much misunderstood charge, so commonly and erroneously attributed as a grievous error to Lee, was in fact a feat which vindicates the Commander-in-Chief of any possible blame for having attempted the impossible. To believe Longstreet is to recognize that he had in a sense staked his professional opinion against the possibility of the successful issue of the battle. It was then with his moral force, the greatest power of any general, set against the successful performance of his part, that Longstreet undertook the execution of his orders. He says, "With my knowledge of the situation, I could see the desperate and hopeless nature of the charge, and the cruel slaughter it would cause. My heart was heavy when I left Pickett." Picture Longstreet, the "old war-horse," the "Sledge Hammer" of the Army of Northern Virginia, beset with anticipations of loss in battle! Can anything be more absurd, for among all his other virtues as a general that of ability to steel his heart against inevitable losses and not count the cost when occasion demanded was by far the finest. Well might his heart have been heavy when he left Pickett, for he must have known that no steps had been taken, and that he did not intend to take any, to support him.

Upon the representation that he could not uncover his right by withdrawing Hood and McLaws, Longstreet was assigned seven brigades of Hill's Corps. These with Pickett's made ten brigades for the column of attack.

Alexander was early apprised of the alteration of the plan, and in order to bring his guns to bear on Cemetery Hill a good many changes in the positions of the 1st Corps batteries were necessary. The batteries had been posted before daylight on the rolling ground about the Peach Orchard, and by reason of the open character of the position were necessarily exposed. The enemy's guns were generally in pits or behind epaulments along the ridge opposite, and though they fired occasional shots during the morning, Alexander reserved his fire in order to save ammunition. The shifting of his batteries to meet the change of orders was conducted as quietly as possible by Alexander, but with his usual energy and skill, and although the enemy's artillery became somewhat more active, the new line was established by 10 A. M. Alexander now had in position 75 guns, all well advanced, in an irregular curved line about 1,300 yards long, beginning in the Peach Orchard and ending near the northeast corner of the Spangler wood. Along this line Cabell's, Dearing's, Eshleman's, Alexander's under Huger, and Henry's battalions were posted in the order named from left to right. Maj. Richardson, with the nine 12-pounder howitzers of Garnett's Battalion, also reported to Alexander by Pendleton's orders, and his pieces which were of too short range to be effective along Hill's front were directed to be held under cover close in rear of the forming columns of infantry, with which it was intended they should advance. Pickett's Division had already arrived at the orchard and the men were eating and resting, ignorant of the fate which awaited them, but all conscious of serious work ahead.

A few hundred yards to the left and rear of Alexander's line began Walker's line of 60 guns, the batteries of which were generally posted as on the previous day, extending along the ridge as far as the Hagerstown Road. Nearly a mile to the north of Walker's left, two Whitworth rifles of Hurt's Battery were posted on the same ridge. In the interval 10 guns of Carter's Battalion occupied positions on the right and left of the railroad cut, and to their right connecting with Walker's left, Watson's and Smith's batteries and a section of Hupp's of Dance's Battalion, with 10 guns, took position. Latimer's Battalion, now under Capt. Raine, remained in rear of Johnson's left, as did Jones' Battalion, while Nelson's Battalion had also been ordered to that point with directions to engage the enemy's guns on Culp's Hill, if practicable. Capt. Graham, with four guns, occupied a hill about 2,500 yards northeast of Cemetery Hill, and was alone of the three battalions on Ewell's left engaged during the day. Thus in the 2d Corps, Brown placed in position but 25 pieces on the morning of the 3d, and these were restricted to the use of solid shot because of the utter unreliability of the fuses provided for their shell.

The sole activity on the part of the Confederate Artillery during the morning had been that of Wyatt's five guns, or the left group of Poague's Battalion, which opened fire upon the enemy's position about 7 A. M. A number of Federal batteries soon concentrated their fire on Wyatt, and Poague promptly ordered him to desist from a further waste of ammunition in so unequal a contest, in which nothing was accomplished but the explosion of a Federal caisson, and the loss of 8 Confederate horses. Col. Poague afterwards learned that Wyatt had been ordered by A. P. Hill to engage the enemy.

On the Federal side, Hunt had placed 166 guns in position before the attack commenced, and during the engagement 10 more batteries from the reserve were brought in action, raising the number of his guns to 220, as against 172 employed by the Confederates. If there was ever an occasion when every available piece was needed in the front line, it was that of the artillery preparation preceding Longstreet's assault, yet there remained unemployed in the 2d Corps 25 rifles and 16 Napoleons, and in the 3d Corps fifteen 12-pounder howitzers. As the Chief of Artillery had since daybreak on the 3d been busily engaged visiting every portion of the Confederate position from left to right he must have known of the absence of many of these guns from the line. Specific orders were personally given by him to the various group and even battery commanders. His aim was to secure a concentrated and destructive fire, under cover of which the infantry might advance. The problem now seems to have been a simple one so far as the posting of the batteries was concerned, for even had it been impracticable to place them all actually in position, they might have all been held in readiness under cover. Most careful instructions were given by Pendleton on this point, and while he did actually supervise the convenient placing of the ordnance trains, he seems to have failed for some reason to verify personally the posting of the batteries. Subordinate artillery commanders are of course responsible for such neglects as the actual failure to bring their own guns into action, and in this respect, Col. Brown, of the 2d Corps, was undoubtedly remiss, subject, however, to the limitations imposed upon him by the orders of his corps commander, and those orders, it would seem, were responsible for the elimination of Nelson's, Jones', and Raine's battalions. Walker's failure to engage his 15 howitzers was due solely to the ineffectiveness of their range, so no fault is to be found with the artillery dispositions of the 3d Corps, and Alexander brought every piece of the 1st Corps into action.

Viewing the disposition of the Confederate Artillery before the attack, a grave error should have been detected, and for this error the Chief of Artillery, subject also to the orders from the Commander-in-Chief, was responsible. Since Lee assumed no direct control over his artillery, only informing himself of its general situation through Col. Long of his staff, Pendleton must receive the blame. Not only did he permit 56 of his guns to remain idle as pointed out before, but he allowed 80 of the 84 guns of the 2d and 3d Corps, which were engaged, to be brought into action on a mathematically straight line, parallel to the position of the enemy and constantly increasing in range therefrom to the left or north! It was indeed a phenomenal oversight on his part, as declared by Col. Alexander, not to place a part of the Artillery, at least, north of the town and east of the prolongation of his line of guns at the center to enfilade the shank of the fish-hook, and cross fire with the guns on Seminary Ridge. Even had Nelson's and Jones' battalions, or either of them, both of which remained idle with the exception of Milledge's Battery of the former, been massed in such a position, far greater effect would have been obtained by the Artillery, and the actual disposition of the rest of the battalions, which for some reason unknown to us might have been necessary, need not have been altered. Concentrated fire does not necessarily mean massed batteries. And especially is this true when the artillery of the offense may be disposed about the arc of an enveloping line. With batteries widely dispersed about such an arc, the enemy at the more interior or more restricted position is at a great disadvantage, for just as the sheafs of the surrounding groups converge upon a comparatively small area, so the artillery fire of the defense becomes divergent and hence less concentrated. No more beautiful illustration could exist of the possible relative effectiveness of artillery fire under such circumstances than the terrain of Gettysburg. There, artillery disposed about the outer arc would necessarily inflict overwhelming and simultaneous losses upon the thickly-massed batteries and infantry supports on Cemetery Ridge and its adjoining spurs, whereas the fire of the defending batteries would, by virtue of the depression in their front, either be compelled to ignore the attacking infantry, or the opposing batteries beyond and above it. And even if part of the artillery of the defense was assigned to each of these missions, concentration would be greatly reduced. Furthermore, artillery fire directed at Seminary Ridge was either effective to the highest degree, or totally noneffective, for "overs" and "shorts" were lost. There was no infantry between

and beyond to suffer from wild shots as there was on
the heights occupied by the Federals. Again, whatever
the target selected by the inner batteries, their fire would
have been frontal with respect to the guns on the outer
arc, whereas every group on the latter line would have
crossed its fire with that of some other group. Hunt
occupied a position similar to that at the hub of a
wheel; Pendleton could have and should have grouped
his batteries about a part of the rim. The lines of the
spokes clearly illustrate what the comparative result
of the fire of the two artilleries would have been, and it
is not unreasonable to assume that the superiority of the
Federal guns in number and weight of metal would
have been more than compensated for by the natural
advantages of the Confederate position in so far as the
artillery was concerned. Certainly Hunt would have
been put to it to shift his batteries from point to point.
In fact, it would have been impossible for him to do
so, for they were terribly cut up even by the frontal
fire which was actually encountered.

These conclusions are not speculative, but are fully
borne out by an incident of the battle, which shows
what the possibilities really were. Quite by accident,
during the cannonade preceding Pickett's charge,
Milledge's Battery of Nelson's Battalion fired 48
rounds upon Cemetery Hill—the most vulnerable point
to artillery fire, by reason of the practicability of enfilading it, along the whole Federal line. The effect of
Milledge's fire is described by Col. Osborn, Chief of
Artillery, 11th Corps, as follows:

"The fire from our west front had progressed 15 to
20 minutes when several guns opened on us from the
ridge beyond and east of Cemetery Hill. The line of
fire from the last batteries, and the line of fire from the
batteries on our west front, were such as to leave the
town between the two lines of fire. These last guns
opened directly on the right flank of my line of batteries.
The gunners got our range at almost the first shot.
Passing low over Wainwright's guns, they caught us

square in flank and with the elevation perfect. It was admirable shooting. They raked the whole line of batteries, killed and wounded the men and horses, and blew up the caissons rapidly. I saw one shell go through 6 horses standing broadside.

"To meet this new fire I drew from the batteries facing west the 20-pounder Parrott Battery of Capt. Taft, and wheeling it half round to the right brought it to bear on them. I also drew from the reserve one battery and placed it in position on Taft's right.

"Fortunately for us, these batteries, placed in the new line, at once secured the exact range of their immediate adversaries. In a few minutes the enemy's fire almost ceased, and when it again opened, and while the fire was progressing, it was irregular and wild. They did not again get our range as they had it before we replied."*

Col. Osborn had in position over 60 guns along the line of the 11th Corps. If less than 50 rounds of Confederate ammunition caused so much damage to that enormous group of artillery, what, may we ask, would several thousand have done?

The formation of the column of attack consumed more time than had been contemplated, and about 11 A. M. before it had been completed some of Hill's skirmishers provoked the enemy into premature activity by attempting to seize a barn between the lines. Gradually the Federal Artillery opened up, which tempted Walker's guns to reply, and before long Hill's line was subjected to the cannonade of over 100 guns. But soon the roar of artillery died out and the field was again as silent as a churchyard.

On the Federal side, Hancock's Corps held Cemetery Ridge with Robinson's Division of the 1st Corps on Hays' right in support, and Doubleday's at the angle between Gibbon and Caldwell. Newton, who had succeeded to the command of the 1st Corps, vice Reynolds, was in charge of the ridge held by Caldwell. Com-

*Philadelphia Weekly Times, May 31, 1877.

pactly arrayed on its crest was McGilvery's artillery consisting of his own batteries and a number from the Artillery Reserve. This group consisted of 41 pieces. Well to the right of McGilvery, Capt. Hazard had massed the 26 guns of the 2d Corps in front of Hays and Gibbon. Woodruff's Battery was posted in front of Zeigler's Grove, and on his left in succession were posted Arnold's Rhode Island, Cushing's United States, Brown's Rhode Island, and Roity's New York batteries. The two last named batteries had been heavily engaged the day before, and so much cut up that they now brought into action but four guns each. Besides these, Daniel's Horse Battery was posted at the angle, and soon after the action commenced Cowan's First New York Battery with 6 rifles was placed on Roity's left. A number of the guns on Cemetery Hill, as well as those of Rittenhouse on Little Round Top, could also be brought to bear on the point selected for Longstreet's assault. Leaving out the latter, which were partially neutralized by hostile groups, there were, therefore, 77 guns in two groups along the front of the 2d Corps, occupying the actual crest and plainly visible to the Confederates, who had brought to bear upon them approximately 150 pieces.

Aware of the great strength of their position, the Federals, after the early cannonade died out, simply sat still and waited for developments. On the Confederate side, it had been arranged that when the infantry column was ready, Longstreet should announce the fact by the fire of two guns of the Washington Artillery. At this signal all the Confederate guns were to open simultaneously on the batteries on Cemetery Hill, and the ridge extending towards Little Round Top. Alexander was to observe the fire and give Pickett the order to charge. Accordingly he established his observing station about noon at a favorable point near the left of his line of guns. Soon after establishing his station, Alexander received the following note from Longstreet:

"COLONEL—If the artillery fire does not have the effect to drive the enemy or greatly demoralize him, so as to make our efforts pretty certain, I would prefer that you should not advise Gen. Pickett to make the charge. I shall rely a great deal on your good judgment to determine the matter, and shall expect you to let Gen. Pickett know when the moment offers."

This note naturally startled Longstreet's Chief of Artillery, who did not wish to substitute his judgment for that of the Commander-in-Chief who had ordered the attack to be made. No matter what Alexander may have thought at the time, he must have felt that too much responsibility was being shifted upon his shoulders by his corps commander. He therefore sent Longstreet the following message:

"GENERAL—I will only be able to judge of the effect of our fire on the enemy by his return fire, for his infantry is but little exposed to view and the smoke will obscure the whole field. If, as I infer from your note, there is any alternative to this attack, it should be carefully considered before opening fire, for it will take all the artillery ammunition we have left to test this one thoroughly, and if the result is unfavorable we will have none left for another effort. And, even if this is entirely successful, it can only be so at a very bloody cost."

Oh, the wisdom of that message, the able cunning, may we say, of the subaltern who sent it! Nothing that has ever been written or said can half so well give us an insight into Alexander's character. It shows us that not only was this able artilleryman prepared to execute his orders irrespective of personal views concerning the advisability of the general plan, that not only did he have a most thorough grasp of the situation in its present, as well as it future aspects, but that he also had an eye to the propriety of the shifting of authority upon subordinates. He at least did not propose to subject himself nor the Artillery to the possibility of becoming a scape-goat in event of a disaster, and promptly put the matter up to the subtle Longstreet in that light. *"If, as I infer from your note, there is any alternative to this attack, it should be carefully considered before opening our fire, etc."* Well did Alexander use these words, and it may be said here that when the Chief of Artillery himself, whose duty it was to prepare the assault, inferred from the tone of the orders of the Corps Commander that there was an alternative plan, no other fact is necessary to prove that Longstreet entertained such an alternative. Where, may we require, did he find authority for it? Certainly his orders had been specific to make the attack, and those orders have been repeatedly held up to the world by him as not only faulty in the extreme, but as allowing him no alternative. He has even declared that he did not "dispute them further, because he saw that Lee's mind was made up," or words to that effect.* It is such fallacies as those which Longstreet has recorded that makes the world cry out, "Would that mine enemy would write a book!" And when one's enemy writes several books, it is even more delightful to read them.

To Alexander's astute dispatch, the following reply soon came from Longstreet:

"COLONEL—The intention is to advance the infantry, if the artillery has the desired effect of driving the enemy off, or having other effect such as to warrant us in making the attack. When the moment arrives, advise Gen. Pickett, and of course advance such artillery as you can use in aiding the attack."

Let us underscore the "if" in this message, and again ask whence came the pernicious word. There was no "if" in Lee's orders. It was clearly of Longstreet's adoption. In other words he had set about his task prepared to complete it "if" he chose to do so, and this is not the spirit of a lieutenant who is committed heart and soul to the success of his superior. Jackson used no "ifs" in his orders for the execution of Lee's plans. He made his orders mandatory, and said to his subordinates, "You will do so and so," nor did he ever seek to shift responsibility upon his Chief of Artillery. He loved responsibility and never parted with it. This is what Lee subsequently meant when he said he would have won the battle of Gettysburg, had Jackson been present. Lee must have been keenly conscious of Longstreet's

---

*See *Battles and Leaders*, Vol. III. p. 343.

unsympathetic support from the very beginning of the campaign, and cognizant of that dragging influence imposed upon his operations by the latter from the start, he would most certainly have assigned the 1st Corps to the less active part assigned to Hill after the first day, and placed the more enthusiastic Jackson on his right, where energy and promptitude were most required. Who can doubt that Jackson and not Alexander, Brown, or Walker, would have occupied the important station actually turned over by Longstreet to Alexander? Can we doubt that Jackson and not a subordinate, however able, would have himself selected the moment for the advance of his infantry? He did it at Chancellorsville, and why would he not have done it at Gettysburg?

Upon the receipt of Longstreet's reply, which on the whole, however, was couched in quite a different tone from his first message, Alexander was still unable to determine the extent of his discretion, nor was Gen. Wright, who happened to be present, able to help him out. Wright did say, however, that the Federal position was not as difficult to reach as it appeared to be, for he had almost carried a part of it the day before. Influenced by Wright's minimizing the difficulties to be encountered, and somewhat as he tells us "by a sort of camp rumor which I had heard that morning that Gen. Lee had said that he was going to send every man he had upon that hill," Alexander was reassured that no discretion as to the attack was intended and resolved to carry out his part in the way he believed to be in conformity with the decision of the Commander-in-Chief. His position was not an enviable one, and it is not surprising if his confidence was somewhat shaken by that intangible evidence of irresolution on the part of his immediate superior, which in some indefinable way makes itself so quickly felt to all. In this spirit it was that he rode back to see Pickett, whose division was but a short distance in his rear. Alexander did not express his feelings to Pickett, nor did he question him as to his views.

But by those means which human natures possess, he adroitly discovered Pickett's sentiments. Pickett he found to be unusually sanguine of success and highly gratified that his luck had favored him by giving him the chance to make the charge. This was the soldier over whose fate Longstreet's heart was so heavy. What a pity it seems that some of Pickett's spirit was not transmitted to Longstreet, and that the "camp rumor" concerning Lee's resolution, which in itself bespoke the high moral of the troops, did not engender more confidence in his lieutenant. But, while his troops were burning with ardor for the fight, their great, soft-hearted leader was sorely oppressed—his heart was already bleeding for them!

A few minutes with the fiery Pickett sufficed to dispel Alexander's uncertainty of mind, and he returned to his post stimulated by the contagious spirit of the gallant infantry leader. No delay could now be made, and no indecision on his part should contribute to the miscarriage of the attack, so he wrote Longstreet: "General: When our artillery fire is at its best, I shall order Pickett to charge." Note the word "shall" in this message. That word spelt a resolution born of Pickett which had supplanted the previous irresolution born of Longstreet.

All these things are moral factors it is true, and are no part of the tactics employed in the battle, but nevertheless it is such things that induce victories and defeats, and in them is often to be found the reasons for what would otherwise remain inexplicable. Not only the *esprit* of the officers and men at the moment of attack and the physical condition of the troops, but the general state of their military digestion, so to speak, is important when one undertakes to reason from effect to cause. It is not the mere tactical conception as included in orders that wins battles, and yet with absolutely no other knowledge we frequently arrive at conclusions concerning the reasons for the military failures and successes of the past. The most faultless tactics are frequently set at nought by adverse psychological conditions, whereas the sheer *élan* of the troops will often counteract the most egregious tactical blunders. In the final analysis the whole theory of attack may be resolved into the truth that poor tactics, executed with spirit and confidence in the leaders, will more often guarantee success than those of the most approved form when the driving force of enthusiasm is lacking. This fact is more readily grasped if one but realizes that the culmination of attack is close contact, and that there will be no close contact gained by the offense unless the tactical plan, however perfect, is developed with a certain amount of rapidity, in order that changes may not be enforced by the enemy's movements. Enthusiasm alone will produce rapidity of execution. All this well illustrates the causes of Longstreet's lapses at Gettysburg. He himself has admitted that he was woefully lacking in enthusiasm for the part assigned him. Lacking this fundamental element of success, his movements were consequently not only tardy as a rule, but, when finally undertaken were not characterized by that vigorous push for which he was noted.

We have examined the situation on the Confederate side. Now let us view it from Cemetery Ridge as it appeared to Gen. Hunt about 11 A. M., using his own graphic description: "Here a magnificent display greeted my eyes. Our whole front for two miles was covered by batteries already in line, or going into position. They stretched—apparently in one unbroken mass—from opposite the town to the Peach Orchard, which bounded the view to the left, the ridges of which were planted thick with cannon. Never before had such a sight been witnessed on this continent, and rarely, if ever, abroad.* What did it mean? It might possibly be to hold that line while its infantry was sent to aid Ewell, or to guard against a counter-stroke from us, but it most probably meant an assault on our center, to be preceded by a cannonade in order to crush our batteries

*Königgrätz and Sedan had not then been fought.

and shake our infantry; at least to cause us to exhaust our ammunition in reply, so that the assaulting troops might pass in good condition over the half-mile of open ground, which was beyond our effective musketry fire." Here let it be interpolated that Hunt, with the skill of the fine soldier that he was, accurately divined the intentions of the Confederates, expressing his conclusions as follows: "With such an object, the cannonade would be long, and followed immediately by the assault, their whole army being held in readiness to follow up a success. From the great extent of ground occupied by the enemy's batteries, it was evident that all the Artillery on our west front, whether of the Army Corps or of the reserve, must concur as a unit under the Chief of Artillery in the defense. This is provided for in all well-organized armies by special rules, which formerly were contained in our own army regulations, but they had been condensed in successive editions into a few short lines, so obscure as to be virtually worthless, because like the rudimentary toe of the dog's paw, they had become, from lack of use, mere survivals,—unintelligible except to the specialist. It was of the first importance to subject the enemy's infantry, from the first moment of their advance, to such a cross fire of our artillery as would break their formation, check their impulse, and drive them back, or at least bring them to our lines in such condition as to make them an easy prey. There was neither time nor necessity for reporting this to Gen. Meade, and beginning on the right, I instructed the chiefs of artillery and battery commanders to withhold their fire for 15 or 20 minutes after the cannonade commenced, then to concentrate their fire with all possible accuracy on those batteries which were most destructive to us,—but slowly, so that when the enemy's ammunition was exhausted, we should have sufficient left to meet the assault."

Before the Confederate Artillery was ordered to open, Alexander sent a courier to the rear with directions to Maj. Richardson to move up with Garnett's nine howitzers, which he had decided to lead forward nearly to musket range at the head of Pickett's Infantry, where they would be of more service than in its rear. But unfortunately for Pickett, though fortunately perhaps for Pickett's batteries, Gen. Pendleton had sent them to cover behind Hill's line, where they were not found in time to be used by Alexander. Inasmuch as the Chief of Artillery had placed these batteries at Alexander's disposal he was guilty of a grave mistake in detaching them without advising his subordinate. True, he moved them in order to shelter them more thoroughly, but the act was one of unwarranted interference, in the circumstances in which it was done.

Just before 1 P. M. a courier dashed up to the Washington Artillery and handed its commander an order written on the fly leaf of a memorandum book. Addressed to Col. Walton, its contents were as follows: "Headquarters, July 3, 1863. Colonel: Let the batteries open. Order great care and precision in firing. If the batteries at the Peach Orchard cannot be used against the point we intend attacking, let them open on the enemy on the rocky hill. Most respectfully, J. Longstreet, Lieutenant-General commanding." The order to fire the signal guns was immediately communicated to Maj. Eshleman, and the report of the first gun of Miller's Battery soon rang out upon the still summer air. There was a moment's delay with the second gun, a friction primer having failed to explode. The interval was but a short one, but during it the heart of two great armies could almost be heard to throb. Instantly a canopy of smoke spread over the Peach Orchard, and exactly at 1 o'clock, the roar and flash of 138 Confederate guns announced the opening of the conflict. In a few seconds, the artillery of both armies rent the air with the deep notes of the guns, and the crescendo of bursting shell, while the earth trembled as if Jove had placed his feet upon the pedals of a great organ. Truly might Mars have applauded the tremendous throb and looked down with delight from his Olympic seat upon the fire-wreathed arena of Gettysburg, for never in this world had such a warlike scene been set before. The Federal position seemed to have broken out with flashing guns at every point, and from Little Round Top to Cemetery Hill the ridge blazed like a volcano. Hunt had just completed his dispositions at Little Round Top when the Confederate signal guns were heard. Describing the field as he viewed it from that point, he says: "The scene was indescribably grand. All the Confederate batteries were soon covered with smoke, through which the flashes were incessant, whilst the air seemed filled with shells, whose sharp explosions, with the hurtling of their fragments, formed a running accompaniment to the deep roar of the guns. Thence I rode to the Artillery Reserve to order fresh batteries and ammunition to be sent up to the ridge as soon as the cannonade ceased; but both the reserve and the train had gone to a safer place. Messengers, however, had been left to receive and convey orders, which I sent by them; then I returned to the ridge. Turning into the Taneytown Pike, I saw evidence of the necessity under which the reserve had "decamped," in the remains of a dozen exploded caissons, which had been placed under cover of a hill, but which the shells had managed to search out. In fact, the fire was more dangerous behind the ridge than on its crest, which I soon reached at the position occupied by Gen. Newton, behind McGilvery's batteries, from which we had a fine view, as our guns were now in action." Describing the Artillery fire of both sides, Hunt further says: "Most of the enemy's projectiles passed overhead, the effect being to sweep all the open ground in our rear, which was of little benefit to the Confederates,—a mere waste of ammunition, for everything there could seek shelter. . . . I now rode along the ridge to inspect the batteries. The infantry were lying down on its reverse slope, near the crest, in open ranks, waiting events. . . . Our fire was deliberate, but on inspecting the chests, I found that the ammunition was running low, and hastened to

Gen. Meade to advise its immediate cessation, and preparation for the assault, which would certainly follow.
The headquarters building, immediately behind the
ridge, had been abandoned, and many of the horses of
the staff lay dead. Being told that the General had gone
to the Cemetery, I proceeded thither. He was not
there, and on telling Gen. Howard my object, he concurred in its propriety, and I rode back along the ridge,
ordering the fire to cease. This was followed by a cessation of that of the enemy, under the mistaken impression that he had silenced our guns, and almost immediately his infantry came out of the woods and
formed for the assault. On my way to the Taneytown
Road to meet the fresh batteries, which I had ordered
up, I met Maj. Bingham, of Hancock's staff, who informed me that Gen. Meade's aides were seeking me
with orders to 'cease firing.' So I had only anticipated
his wishes." So much for the Federal side.

Before the cannonade opened Alexander had made
up his mind to give Pickett the order to advance within
15 or 20 minutes after it began, but when he observed
the full development of the Federal batteries, knowing
that the enemy's infantry was suffering little behind the
accidents of the ground and the sheltering walls along
the ridge, he could not bring himself to give the word.
He afterwards said that it seemed madness to launch
the infantry into that fire with an open area about 1,300
yards wide to traverse. So he let 15 minutes pass into
25, hoping vainly that the effect of the Confederate artillery fire might soon produce more serious effects. At
the end of this time he wrote Pickett: "If you are coming at all, you must come at once, or I cannot give you
proper support; but the enemy's fire has not slackened
at all; at least 18 guns are still firing from the cemetery
itself." Five minutes after the sending of the message,
Hunt ordered his batteries to cease firing, and those at
the Cemetery were seen to limber up and retire to the
rear. It had not been the custom in the Federal Artillery to withdraw temporarily in anticipation of an

infantry assault, in order to save ammunition, though such a practice had all along been followed by the Confederates. So Alexander believed that if fresh batteries were not shortly brought up by the enemy, the position could be carried. Observing with his glass for five minutes or more the crest which was still swept by the fire of the Confederate guns, he was unable to detect a sign of life on the deserted position. The dead and wounded men and horses, together with numerous disabled carriages, alone occupied the ground. He then wrote Pickett: "For God's sake, come quick. The 18 guns are gone; come quick, or my ammunition won't let me support you properly."

Pickett had taken Alexander's first note to Longstreet, who read it and said nothing. Pickett then said, "General, shall I advance?" Longstreet, unwilling to take upon himself the responsibility of ordering him not to do so, but equally unwilling to give the word for the charge in pursuance of Lee's orders, simply turned his head away, with the result that Pickett, whose heart was in the right place, saluted and said, "I am going to move forward, sir," and then galloped off to his division, and immediately put it in motion.

Longstreet claims that he nodded his head in answer to Pickett's question. But even if he did, that was a remarkable way for a corps commander to set his assaulting column in motion. His whole attitude and conduct was not well calculated to impart to the leader of his column that fiery ardor which alone could win success. Fortunately, Pickett's nerve was unimpaired by Longstreet's conduct. Had a less bold spirit been in the lead, the 1st Corps would never have made the attempt. The whole incident is chilling to the spirits of one who follows it, though it had no such effect on Pickett. In the light of after events, it seems almost too bad he had the resolution to make the attempt, for we are now able to see that with the exception of his individual enthusiasm and that of his men, not one element of success was present.

Most of the Confederate reports declare that at this juncture the Federal batteries were silenced, in the sense than they were subdued. Again we see how dangerous it is to reach the conclusion that silent guns are harmless guns, for in this instance their retirement was but the calm before the storm which was to break out with renewed fury. The moment was in fact far more ominous of what was to follow, than propitious for the assault.

Leaving his staff, Longstreet rode to Alexander's observing station. It was then about 1:40 P. M. Alexander explained the artillery situation to him, feeling then more hopeful of success, but expressing a fear less his ammunition might be exhausted before the crisis of the attack. "Stop Pickett immediately and replenish your ammunition," said Longstreet. But Alexander demurred on the ground that the effect of the artillery preparation would be lost, and also because there was but a little reserve ammunition left. Longstreet then said to him: "I don't want to make this attack. I would stop it now, but that Gen. Lee ordered it and expects it to go on. I don't see how it can succeed."

Let us pause again and ask ourselves if this was not a pitiful situation in which the superb 1st Corps found itself. Think of it! How could aught but disaster ensue with such a one at its head? Its bold leader had utterly succumbed and instead of being his old self, the man of iron nerve and will, he was now at the crucial instant of the war, suffering from all the frailties of a weak mortal. We know that Longstreet possessed great personal courage, but as a leader, on this occasion, he was most certainly, as proved by his own words, the victim of "cold feet." It was his duty to order that charge. If, in his opinion, it was so grievous a mistake as he later declared it to have been, his course was clear. He should have, in the presence of Lee and his staff, made his protest, in writing, if necessary, and upon being overruled, he should have gone back to his command with teeth set and sought to impress his division and brigade commanders not only with the necessity of success, but with the practicability of the assault. Had he done this, the attack would probably have succeeded, but even had it failed, Longstreet would have been scot-free of all blame and Lee would have been the first to publish his protest, in order that his lieutenant might be promptly and absolutely absolved before the world. As it was, the magnanimous Lee assumed all the blame in order that his lieutenant might not be rendered less efficient as a leader, by the destruction of the confidence of his men. Lee knew that his own character, record, and motives alone could stand the strain which the blame for the loss of Gettysburg would impose upon the one who assumed it, and it was his willingness to shoulder the responsibility of the many risks that he took during the war, which made him the moral equal, if not superior of, any captain of history. It is interesting to speculate what the career of a soldier with such moral force might have been had he possessed the means at the disposal of, and the ambitious lust for power which inspired Alexander, Cæsar, and Napoleon. Though not generally classed with these as a great captain, history will in the course of time liken him with respect to the higher virtues of the soul to Hannibal, who from the dispassionate record now appears to have been the strongest man that ever bore arms. Eventual success in war is the most potent irrigant of that fame which grows greener and greener with time. Defeat is the blighting sun which scorches and shrivels military reputations until nothing remains but the gullies and waste places of failure, from which no garlands are plucked. These are facts which the names of Hannibal and Lee alone have set at naught. But to return again to our narrative.

What Col. Alexander's feelings were upon hearing Longstreet's words is difficult to imagine. We can hardly assume that he was surprised, but we can be sure of one thing,—he was not shaken in his resolve to do his best. The heart of Pickett himself was no bolder than that which beat in Alexander's breast. He listened, but dared not offer a word. He realized that the battle was lost if he ordered his guns to cease firing, for he knew that the ammunition supply was too low to permit of another artillery preparation; the guns had hardly cooled during the past three days. There was still a chance of success, and it was not his part by word or deed to sacrifice it, and though he failed to see it, the recordation of these sentiments on his part remains one of the greatest indictments of the superior whom he has so ardently sought to defend.

While Longstreet was still speaking to his Chief of Artillery, the die cast itself, for Pickett's immortal division swept out of the woods in rear of the guns and presented its gray breast to the enemy. The line swept on with bayonets flashing in the sun like the spray on the crest of a great wave. At the head of his brigade rode Gen. Dick Garnett, of the old 9th Infantry, just out of the ambulance, but stimulated with hope of fresh glory. As he passed Longstreet, he threw back the cape of his frazzled blue overcoat and, raising himself erect in the saddle, waved a grand salute to his corps commander.

After riding forward with Garnett a short distance, Alexander returned to his line, with a view to select such of his guns as had enough ammunition to follow Pickett.

While the great artillery duel had been in progress, and before the infantry advanced, a serious danger threatened Longstreet's right. This was the appearance of Kilpatrick's division of cavalry, which moved upon that flank and commenced massing in the body of timber extending from the base of Big Round Top westward to Kern's house on the Emmittsburg Road. Reilly's and Bachman's batteries of Henry's Battalion had been promptly ordered to change front to the right and had opened fire upon the enemy's cavalry with such effect as at once to drive it beyond the wood and out of sight. In the meantime, part of Stuart's Cavalry was arriving on the right and soon formed line at right-angles to that of Hood's Division, while Hart's Horse Battery was stationed on the Emmittsburg Road at the angle, and later succeeded in driving off Merritt's Federal Cavalry Brigade which deployed for the attack.

The infantry column led by Pickett had been poorly formed. Six brigades, or those of Brockenbrough, Davis, McGowan, Archer, Garnett, and Kemper, with about 10,000 men, were in the first line, with a second line composed of Lane's, Scale's, and Armistead's brigades, very much shorter than the first on its left, following 200 yards in rear. The remaining brigade, Wilcox's, was posted in rear of the right of the column, both flanks of which rested in the air with no support in its rear. As the infantry rushed through the line of guns and debouched upon the plain in front of the ridge, the Federal Artillery, which had become almost silent, broke out again with all its batteries, the 18 guns at the cemetery promptly reappearing in action. The Confederate batteries, which had been compelled to reserve their fire while the infantry was moving past them, reopened over its head, as soon as the attacking troops advanced about 200 yards. But the Federal guns which had been so skillfully concealed for the time being and shoved to the forward crest to repel the assault, utterly ignored the Confederate batteries, and concentrated with the utmost precision upon the infantry. Meantime, Alexander had formed about 18 guns, including five from Garden's and Flanner's batteries, of Henry's Battalion, on the right under Maj. John C. Haskell, and four from the Washington Artillery on the left, three under Capt. Miller, and one of Norcom's or Eshleman's old battery under Lieut. Battles. In the center only about one gun in every four could be ordered forward. The ammunition had all but run out along the line, and the caissons which had been sent to the ordnance train had not returned. The train had also been moved by Pendleton to a more distant point than the one it first occupied, to escape the fire, which had been directed at the batteries on the right of Walker's line on the ridge. Alexander soon advanced with Eshleman's, Haskell's, Lieut. Motes' Troup Artillery (Capt. Carlton having been wounded), and several other guns, to a swell of the ground just west of the Emmittsburg Road, where he sought to protect Pickett's column by firing upon the enemy's troops, advancing to attack its right flank. The four guns which Haskell advanced from the Peach Orchard and the four on his left under Capt. Miller and Lieut. Battles of the Washington Artillery, were so far to the front of Pickett's route that they were able to enfilade the Federal Infantry massing to meet the assault. The effect of their fire was for a time terrific, but soon attracted that of not less than 20 guns which practically silenced them after disabling a number of pieces and many men and horses.

The troops of Heth's Division, decimated by the storm of deadly hail which tore through the ranks, had faltered and fallen back before the combined artillery and musketry fire of the enemy. This had impelled Pender's Division to fall back also while Wilcox's Brigade, perceiving that the rest of Hill's troops were unable to reach the Federal position, had failed so far to move forward to Pickett's support. The disintegration of the infantry column had set in when the column had traversed about half the intervening space. The Federal line overlapped it on the left 800 yards or more, and was crowded with guns. The fire upon the unsupported left, the advance of which was retarded by numerous fences, could be endured but a short time. Already the artillery support which had been expected from the 3d Corps was failing, by reason of the batteries having indulged in the earlier duel of the morning. That useless waste of ammunition was now to be sorely felt. Garnett and Armistead had been killed, Kemper wounded, and over 2,000 of Pickett's men had fallen within 30 minutes, before the end of which time the shattered remnants were driven from the position they had carried.

Just as the Confederate column began to advance, the reserve batteries which Hunt had ordered up had arrived, and Fitzhugh's, Weir's, and Parsons' were put in near the clump of trees, while Brown's and Arnold's batteries, much crippled, were withdrawn, Cowan's being substituted for the former. McGilvery's group had promptly reappeared and opened a destructive oblique fire upon the right of the assaulting column, greatly aided by Rittenhouse's six rifles on Little Round Top, which were served with remarkable accuracy in enfilading the Confederate lines. The steady fire from McGilvery's and Rittenhouse's groups caused the column of attack to drift to the left out of its true course, so that the weight of the assault fell directly upon the position occupied by Hazard's group of batteries. Hunt had counted on the cross fire of his artillery groups halting the Confederate column before it reached the Federal position, but in this he was disappointed, for Hazard, who had exhausted his shell, was compelled to remain silent until the Confederate Infantry arrived within the zone of canister effect. The orders of the corps commander, which, contrary to Hunt's directions, had resulted in Hazard's expenditure of all his shell in the artillery duel preceding the assault, deprived the defense of nearly one-third of its guns in the early stage of the attack, and entirely of the effect of the cross fire which had been planned. Hunt subsequently declared that Pickett's troops could never have reached Hazard's batteries had his orders not been superseded. But this is neither here nor there. They did reach the ridge in spite of the tornado of canister fire which Hazard opened upon them when within about 200 yards of his batteries.

As the Confederate brigades closed upon the Federal position, the fire fight of the infantry commenced in earnest. It lasted but a short time and soon Pickett's men, who with the exception of the more-advanced ones had never halted, surged on. As the rear line merged with the first the troops swarmed over the fences and disappeared in the smoke and dust which concealed the enemy's guns. Already the Confederate guns, except those with which Alexander was engaging the enemy on

the right, had been compelled to suspend their fire. The
stars and bars were now discerned fluttering among the
Federal guns, but the enemy was closing in upon
Pickett's men from all sides in spite of every effort
which Walker's and Alexander's batteries made to prevent it. Ewell's Infantry and Artillery were all silent,
leaving Meade free to draw troops from his right to assist in the repulse of Pickett.

From the Confederate position, the awesome tragedy
was grand and thrilling, and the onlookers watched it
as if life and death hung upon the issue. "If it should
be favorable to us," wrote one of the Confederate officers, "the war was nearly over; if against us, we each
had the risks of many battles yet to go through. And
the event culminated with fearful rapidity. Listening
to the rolling crashes of musketry, it was hard to realize
that they were made up of single reports, and that each
musket shot represented nearly a minute of a man's
life in that storm of lead and iron. It seemed as if 100,-
000 men were engaged, and that human lives were being
poured out like water."

Just as Pickett's troops had reached the Federal position, Col. Freemantle, of Her Majesty's Army, who
until then had occupied a post of vantage behind Hill's
Corps on the ridge, came upon the field, and in the belief that the attack had fully succeeded declared to
Longstreet that he would not have missed the scene for
anything in the world.

When Pickett, who was riding with his staff in rear
of his division, saw that Hill's brigades on his left were
breaking up, after sending two aides to rally them, a
third was sent to Longstreet to say that the position in
front would be taken, but that reinforcements would be
required to hold it. Longstreet, in reply, directed
Pickett to order up Wilcox, and Pickett sent three messengers in succession to be sure that the order was
promptly acted upon. As the fugitives from Pettigrew's Division came back, Wright's Brigade of Anderson's Division was moved forward a few hundred yards

to cover their retreat. Already a stream of fugitive and wounded soldiers had begun to flow from the ridge to the rear, pursued by the enemy's fire from the right and left, and it was apparent to all that Pickett's men, unless strongly reinforced—could not hold on. After about 20 minutes, when the fire had all but ceased, and during which time ever-increasing masses of Federal infantry were seen to be moving from all directions upon his men, Wilcox's Brigade of about 1,200 men, with some 250 of Perry's Florida Brigade on its left, charged past the more-advanced Confederate batteries. Not another man was ordered forward, and nothing remained for them to support, for Pickett's Division had by this time simply crumbled away under the terrific infantry and artillery fire, which had been concentrated from all sides upon it.

The victory which for a moment had seemed within their grasp had eluded the Confederates, 4,000 of whom had fallen or been captured in the assault. No troops could have behaved more gallantly than those who participated in the attack, and none could have displayed higher qualities of courage and discipline than those of the whole army when it became apparent that Pickett had been repulsed. While Wilcox's Brigade was making its charge, Gen. Lee, entirely alone, had joined Col. Alexander. The Artillery of the 1st Corp had ceased firing in order to save ammunition in case the enemy should attempt a counter-stroke. Wilcox's charge was as useless as it was tragic. The brigade advanced but a short distance before it was overcome by the fire of the enemy, and compelled to halt, whereupon Lee ordered it to be withdrawn and placed in position behind the batteries with Wright's Brigade to oppose the enemy, should they advance. The Commander-in-Chief was no doubt apprehensive of such action on Meade's part and personally did everything he could to encourage his troops, especially the disorganized stream of fugitives moving to the rear. "Don't be discouraged," said he to them, "It was my fault this time. Form your ranks again when you get under cover. All good men must hold together now." Only when they had all passed, and it was seen that no attack by the enemy was intended, did Gen. Lee leave the threatened point. The officers of every grade on that part of the field seconded his efforts to preserve order and reform the broken troops, and the men so promptly obeyed the call to rally that their thinned ranks were soon restored and the line reëstablished. There was no sign, whatever, of panic or even discouragement. The troops, though mortified over their repulse, longed for the enemy to attack in order that they might efface the blot of their first serious defeat.

While the broken infantry was streaming to the rear and being reformed, Alexander's guns alone and entirely unsupported opposed the enemy at the Peach Orchard. His ammunition was now almost entirely exhausted, so no notice was taken of the desultory fire of the hostile batteries. Occasionally Alexander's batteries were compelled to fire with canister upon the Federal skirmishers, which were thrown forward, but the enemy's guns refrained from molesting the Confederate batteries. Already some of Alexander's batteries had withdrawn entirely from the field to refit, and those in the best condition now returned after having partially refilled their chests with ammunition and boldly remained in advanced positions until late in the day without a single infantryman in their fronts along certain portions of the line. But Meade's Army was so much shattered and discouraged by the losses it had incurred that he did not feel able to attempt to follow up his success. He saw that Lee had merely been repulsed and not routed, and that two whole divisions, those of McLaws and Hood, lay across his path. Swinton also declares that besides the heavy losses they had sustained in repulsing the attack, the Federal troops were thrown in much confusion by the intermingling of the various commands. The aggregate Federal loss of the three days had reached the enormous figure of 23,000 men, including Reynolds, Gibbon, and many other of the most valuable officers; Hancock was wounded. While the Confederates had been defeated, it is very easy to see why Meade was unable to reap the fruits of his victory. The idea that there was a gap in the Confederate right is absurd, and had Meade attacked Lee, it seems certain he would have received as bloody a repulse as had been inflicted upon Pickett. In this respect we must agree with Longstreet, Hunt, and Swinton, in preference to the views of Alexander. The largest bodies of organized Federal troops available at the close of the attack were on Meade's left. An advance to the Plum Run line of the troops behind it, as Hunt points out, would have brought them directly in front of Alexander's batteries, which still crowned the ridges along the Emmittsburg Road; a farther advance would have brought them under a flank fire from McLaws and Hood. It is true that Alexander possessed little ammunition for his guns, but most of what was left was canister and the field of fire which the Federal Infantry would have had to traverse would have presented the opposing artillery with an opportunity not less favorable than that at Second Manassas. Only a few rounds per gun would have been necessary.

Finding that Meade was not going to follow up his success, Longstreet prepared to withdraw his advanced line to a better defensive position. Hood and McLaws were ordered to fall back slowly before Meade's skirmishers, and during the afternoon Alexander withdrew his guns from the Peach Orchard one by one. By 10 p. m. the batteries of the 1st Corps had been retired to the positions occupied by them along Seminary Ridge on the 2d of July, and the infantry was firmly established with the Peach Orchard still in its possession. Stuart had rejoined the Army on the night of the 2d, and had promptly assumed the duty of protecting the flanks, which he still guarded.

Merritt's attack on the Confederate right had been followed up by a bold charge of the Federal Cavalry led by the gallant Farnworth, who had lost his life in the fight. On the Confederate left, four of Stuart's brigades had successfully opposed three of Gregg's near Cress's Ridge, $2\frac{1}{2}$ miles east of Gettysburg. Stuart's position offered excellent opportunities for the use of his horse artillery, reinforced by a section of Green's Battery of the 2d Corps, Griffin's Horse Battery of Jenkins' Cavalry Brigade, and Jackson's new horse battery. In this affair Breathed and McGregor had taken no part at first by reason of lack of ammunition, but later in the day had appeared on the field and rendered valiant service, holding Gregg in check until nightfall. In this quarter, both Stuart and Gregg held approximately their original positions, but the Federal Cavalry had succeeded in foiling Stuart's design to fall upon Meade's rear. Chew's and Moorman's batteries were not engaged at Gettysburg with the Cavalry, having been left in the rear between Hagerstown and the river, and Imboden's independent Cavalry Brigade with McClannahan's Horse Battery of six pieces only reached the field late on the 3d. It had been engaged throughout the campaign in raids on the left of the advancing army.

During the afternoon of the 3d, Lee abandoned his plan to dislodge Meade and determined upon immediate retreat to Virginia, and under cover of darkness withdrew Ewell's Corps to the ridge, and drew back Longstreet's right to Willoughby Run. Imboden, with his 2,100 men, was assigned the duty of organizing all the transportation of the Army into one vast train 14 miles long, and conducting it without a halt to Williamsport, and from thence to Winchester. Eshleman's Battalion with eight pieces, Tanner's 4-gun battery of the 2d Corps, Lieut. Pegram of Hurt's Battery with a Whitworth, and Hampton's Cavalry Brigade with Hart's Battery were ordered to report to him, so that the escort included 23 guns in all.

The great battle was over with the close of the third day. Nothing will so impress the student with its magnitude as the statistics of the Artillery arm.

Allowing the Confederates a maximum of 55,000 infantry present on the field during the three days and 272 guns, we find that in the battle the proportion of artillery to infantry was about five pieces per thousand men. Meade had engaged about 78,000 infantry with 310 guns, exclusive of the Horse Artillery. The Federal proportion of artillery to infantry was therefore smaller than that of the Confederates, being about four guns per thousand men. As a matter of fact, however, the proportion actually engaged was larger, for practically all of Meade's artillery was utilized at one time or another, while much of Ewell's artillery was idle. The supply of ammunition carried into the field for the Federal artillery consisted of 270 rounds per gun, whereas that for the Confederate artillery was but 150 rounds per gun. This fact still further increased the relative superiority of the Federal artillery.

Gen. Hunt reported an expenditure in action for the Federal artillery of 32,781 rounds, an average of 106 per gun. Ewell's Corps reported 5,851 rounds expended, and Hill's Corps 7,112 rounds. Ewell, therefore, averaged 90 rounds per gun, and Hill about 110 for the 65 guns which they each brought into action.

The greatest reported individual expenditure of a Confederate battery was that of Manly's which expended 1,146 rounds during the campaign, or an average of about 287 rounds per gun. This battery was principally engaged on July 3. McCarthy's rifled section, however, expended 600 rounds, or 300 per gun, and one piece of his battery under Lieut. Williams alone expended 300 rounds of shell and canister on the 3d.

The intensity of the fire of the two artilleries was, as may be seen from the foregoing figures, greatly in favor of the Federals whose relative strength in artillery, based upon the Confederate average expenditure per gun, was as 318 to 213, instead of 310 to 272, for it is not merely the number of guns present during the battle that determines the volume of fire. No report was

made of the expenditure in the 1st Corps, but all 83 of
its guns were engaged and undoubtedly averaged as
many rounds as those of Hill's Corps, or 110 each.
Their expenditure was, therefore, fully 9,000 rounds,
which brings up the aggregate for the Army during the
battle to 90,000 rounds. Thus for the 213 guns engaged, excluding the Horse Artillery, the Confederate
expenditure averaged 103 rounds per gun as compared
to 106 for the Federal guns. Again, losses alone do not
determine density of fire. In the solution of this problem we must also consider the relative positions of the
adversaries. It is apparent that a less intensive fire
upon the compact Federal position, upon which nearly
all the defenders were massed, would cause greater loss
per gun than a much heavier fire upon the more extended outer line. This is proved by the fact that the
killed and wounded, exclusive of the missing, in the Federal reserve, with 108 guns engaged, numbered 230 or
an average of 2.1 per gun, whereas in Longstreet's Artillery with 83 guns, the total loss was 271 or an average
of 2.6 per gun. It must also be borne in mind that
normally the loss incurred by offensive artillery in the
open and within the zone of musketry effect is greater
than that inflicted upon the defensive artillery more or
less under cover. In Ewell's Corps, the total artillery
loss was 132, and in Hill's Corps 128, or an average for
each of 2 per gun.

The destruction of artillery horses on both sides was
very great. In the 3d Corps alone, with a total of 77
guns, 190 horses were killed in action, 80 captured, 187
abandoned on the road, and 200 subsequently condemned as unserviceable, or a total of 627 lost in the
campaign! The average loss per battery must, therefore, have been about 50 animals or two-thirds of the
original number.

The heaviest loss in personnel sustained by any battalion was of course that of Huger's, or Alexander's own
command. In that battalion with 6 batteries and 26 guns,
138 men and 116 horses, or over 5 men and 4 horses per

gun, were killed or wounded. As the personnel of the battalion did not exceed at the outset a total of 480, its loss in the battle itself, not counting the missing, was not less than 28 per cent of the whole, principally due to artillery fire. But if these figures, applicable to a special case, seem astounding, what of those concerning the whole Artillery Corps for the campaign? We have seen that the Artillery personnel on May 31 did not exceed 5,300 officers and men in number. Certainly not over 4,500 of these came upon the battlefields of the campaign. Of that number 94 were killed, 437 wounded, and in marked contrast but 77 were reported missing! The aggregate loss sustained by Lee's Artillery between July 1 and his return to Virginia two weeks later, was, therefore, 608, or a loss of 13.5 per cent of the entire effective personnel! When we consider that but a handful of men were captured no further evidence is necessary as to the character of the service rendered by his artillerymen. It is such figures that make one realize that Gettysburg was more than a defeat. It was a disaster from which no army, in fact no belligerent state, could soon recover. The destruction of artillery material, in spite of the fact that but five guns were lost, was enormous. Two of these guns were abandoned near the Potomac by reason of the failure of their teams, two disabled pieces were left on the field, and a third disabled piece which had been withdrawn was later captured by the enemy's cavalry. The guns were more than replaced by the seven captured pieces, but not the harness, fittings, equipment, and horses, and hundreds of its staunchest veterans were lost to the Artillery forever. Latimer, Fraser, and Morris, were but three of the six artillery officers who sealed their devotion to the cause with their life, but among the 26 wounded were such valuable men as Majs. Read and Andrews, and Capts. Brown, Woolfolk, Page, Carlton, Thompson, and Norcom.

CHAPTER XXXIV

July 4 found the Artillery generally posted along Seminary Ridge, with some of Alexander's batteries on the right drawn back towards Willoughby Run. An anxious inventory of the ammunition on hand had been taken late the day before, and much to the relief of all it was found that enough remained for one day's fight. Fortunately Meade was not in an aggressive mood and nothing was attempted by him, so the Artillery was not engaged during the day.

Shortly after noon, a rainstorm of almost unsurpassed fury broke upon the field and soon bemired the roads, causing great difficulty in assembling the train about Cashtown, and much suffering to the teams. Wagons, ambulances, and artillery carriages by hundreds were mingled in the roads and adjacent fields in one great and apparently inextricable mass, while the wounded found no shelter from exposure to the storm. Every vehicle was loaded with wounded men, whose sufferings could not be alleviated. The situation was awful. But about 4 p. m. the head of the train was put in motion from Cashtown and the ascent of the mountain in the direction of Chambersburg began. For the terrors of the retreat, which ensued, one must consult Gen. Imboden's graphic account.* Suffice it here to say that by daylight on the 5th the head of the column had reached Greencastle, 15 miles from Williamsport, having traversed two-thirds of the distance to the Potomac.

About dark on the 4th, the withdrawal of the Army began. Hill's Corps followed immediately after the train, taking the Fairfield Road, while Longstreet followed Hill. But the storm and the consequent condition of the roads impeded the movement so that Ewell was unable to leave his position until daylight on the morning of the 5th.

*Battles and Leaders, Vol. III, p. 420.

The retreat was a terrible march for the Artillery, crippled as it was by the loss of so many horses in battle, and the exhaustion of others. So many, lacking shoes, became totally lame on the stony roads, that squads of cannoneers had to scour the country along the route for horses which were requisitioned when the farmers would not sell them.

Walker's battalions were withdrawn from Hill's old line about dusk and ordered to follow the 3d Corps, while Alexander's moved to Black Horse Tavern about 5 P. M. where they were held in a great meadow adjoining the Fairfield Pike with orders·to watch the passing column, and take their place immediately behind Walker's command. Here the horses, still in harness, were allowed to graze during the night as Walker's batteries did not pass by until 6 o'clock the following morning. The refreshment thus gained for the worn animals was most welcome and enabled them to march for 19 hours to Monterey Springs with hardly a halt, and after resting from 1 to 4 A. M. to resume the march for 14 hours more, not going into bivouac until they reached Hagerstown at 6 P. M. the 7th. It was on the march of the 5th that Maj Henry was compelled to abandon two howitzers for lack of teams. Upon reaching camp about one mile from Hagerstown, the Artillery of the 1st and 3d corps was given a rest of several days.

Ewell's Corps did not withdraw from before Gettysburg until the morning of the 5th. Green's Battery, which had served on the left with Hampton, had joined its battalion the preceding night while Tanner's had accompanied Imboden. Capt. Raine, who succeeded Latimer in command of Andrews' Battalion, had fallen back on the 4th to a position astride the Cashtown Road with Nelson's Battalion on its left. Dance's and Carter's battalions followed Johnson's and Rodes' divisions to the rear during the night while Jones' Battalion remained in position with Early's Division as the rear guard. Brown, therefore, held three of his battalions across the enemy's path until the last infantrymen moved off. Practically all of his field transportation, together with that of the other artillery commands, was taken to convey the wounded to the rear. Carter, Jones, and Dance, never saw their wagons again, as they were captured or destroyed by the enemy's cavalry on the retreat. Brown's entire command reached the artillery rendezvous at Hagerstown on the morning of the 7th after an arduous but undisturbed march with the rear guard of the Army.

In spite of the awful disaster which had befallen it, the magnitude of which was not at first realized by the Army, the spirits of the men were buoyant and the Army as a whole was by no means discouraged. They simply viewed the unsuccessful issue of the campaign as unfortunate because more fighting would be necessary, but never once did the idea of ultimate defeat take hold of them. The storm of the 4th and 5th was far more responsible for the gloominess of the situation than the defeat of Gettysburg, and with the reappearance of sunshine, the irrespressible spirits of the men quickly rose. Thus it was that they plodded back to old Virginia rollicking and making the best of the hardships of the retreat. To their good humor and enjoyment the queer German inhabitants of the region through which they passed contributed much.

The practice of forcible requisition was one in which the gunners especially had had long experience at home, as well as abroad, and was known to the service as "pressing for shorts." By this process alone were the batteries able to save their guns and it was certainly, in the circumstances, justifiable. An incident recounted by Col. Alexander is so amusing and full of interest that it is here given in his own words to illustrate the method of securing draught animals on the retreat:

"Near Hagerstown I had an experience with an old Dunkard which gave me a high and lasting respect for the people of that faith. My scouts had had a horse transaction with this old gentleman, and he came to see me about it. He made no complaint, but said it was his only horse, and as the scouts had told him we had some hoof-sore horses we should have to leave behind, he came to ask if I would trade him one for his horse, as without one his crop would be lost.

"I recognized the old man at once as a born gentleman in his delicate characterization of the transaction as a trade. I was anxious to make the trade as square as circumstances would permit. So I assented to his taking a foot-sore horse, and offered him besides payment in Confederate money. This he respectfully but firmly declined. Considering how the recent battle had gone, I waived argument on the point of its value, but tried another suggestion. I told him that we were in Maryland as the guests of the United States. That after our departure the government would pay all bills we left behind, and that I would give him an order on the United States for the value of his horse, and have it approved by Gen. Longstreet. To my surprise he declined this also. I supposed then he was simply ignorant of the bonanza in a claim against the Government and I explained that; and telling him that money was no object to us under the circumstances, I offered to include the value of his whole farm. He again said he wanted nothing but the foot-sore horse. Still anxious that the war should not grind this poor old fellow in his poverty, I suggested that he take two or three foot-sore horses, which we would have to leave anyhow, when we marched. Then he said, 'Well, sir, I am a Dunkard, and the rule of our church is an eye for an eye, and a tooth for a tooth, and a horse for a horse, and I can't break the rule.'

"I replied that the Lord, who made all horses, knew that a good horse was worth a dozen old battery scrubs; and after some time prevailed on him to take two, by calling one of them a gift. But that night, about midnight, we were awakened by approaching hoofs, and turned out expecting to receive some order. It was my old Dunkard on one of his foot-sores. "Well, sir,' he said, 'you made it look all right to me to-day when you were talking; but after I went to bed to-night I got to thinking it all over, and I don't think I can explain it to the Church, and I would rather not try.' With that he tied old foot-sore to a fence, and rode off abruptly. Even at this late day it is a relief to my conscience to tender his sect this recognition of their integrity and honesty, in lieu of the extra horse which I vainly endeavored to throw into the trade. Their virtues should commend them to all financial institutions in search of incorruptible employees."

Upon reaching Greencastle on the 5th with his convoy, Imboden's trouble began. Not only did the citizens assail his train, but the Federal Cavalry in small foraging parties began to molest his progress. He was almost captured himself, but succeeded in throwing a section of McClannahan's Horse Battery in action with canister, which drove off the largest band. After a great deal of desultory fighting during the day, he succeeded in reaching Williamsport that afternoon with the head of his column, the rear arriving next day with Hart's Battery, the cavalry meanwhile guarding the route on the west. Thus did this energetic officer reach the Potomac with all the wagons of the Army, not less than 10,000 draught animals, and practically all the wounded which were able to be removed from Gettysburg—several thousand in number. Only a small number of wagons had been lost and few horses, this in spite of the fact that during that awful march of fifty-odd miles, there were neither rations for the men, nor forage for the animals. But Imboden soon set the inhabitants to work cooking for the wounded Confederates and his train guard, and at last for the first time since leaving Gettysburg the horses were unharnessed and turned out to graze. This welcome halt was an enforced one, for the enemy's cavalry had destroyed the bridge across the river, which was unfordable by reason of the freshet. At Williamsport the train guard was fortunately strengthened by the arrival of two regiments of Johnson's Division, returning from Staunton whither they had escorted the prisoners taken at Winchester on the advance. They brought a supply of ammunition both for the infantry and artillery.

The morning of the 6th it was reported that 7,000 Federal cavalry with 18 guns were approaching Williamsport. Imboden promptly placed his guns under Capt. Hart in position on the hills which concealed the town, and set about organizing and arming his teamsters as a support for his infantry and dismounted troopers. By noon, about 700 of the wagoners, led by convalescent officers, were available for the defense. A heavy fight ensued in which Eshleman's Battalion, Richardson's two batteries of Garnett's Battalion, Hart's and McClannahan's batteries, all took part.

By making a bold display of his artillery and marching his wagoners hither and thither, causing them to appear at widely separated points, Imboden greatly imposed upon Buford, and Kilpatrick, and succeeded in holding them in check until Fitz Lee arrived in their rear, and caused them to withdraw along the Boonsborough Road. In this affair, which was opened by the artillery on both sides, Eshleman, by the bold advance of his four batteries, secured an enfilade fire upon the enemy, and aided by McClannahan's guns inflicted great loss upon them while the infantry, a part of which was led by Capt. Hart, together with the dismounted troopers, charged the Federals and forced them back, capturing 125 before they reached their horses. The teamsters fought so well that this affair has been called the "Wagoners' Fight." Very fortunately for the Army, Imboden had been able to ferry two wagon loads of shell across the river from the ordnance train during the action in the nick of time, Moore's Battery having already exhausted its ammunition when the fresh supply arrived. It may here be added that this ordnance train had been ordered by Gen. Lee to Gettysburg from Winchester and would have reached the Army certainly by the 8th had it not retreated.

By extraordinary energy and good management, Gen. Imboden had been able to save the transportation of the entire Army, which could not have been replaced.

The next morning the Army began to arrive at Williamsport and the work of constructing bridges commenced. Over 4,000 Federal prisoners, who had been escorted to the rear by the remnants of Pickett's Division, with Stribling's and Macon's batteries, were ferried across the river before the 9th, and sent on to Richmond, *via* Staunton, in the charge of Imboden, with a single regiment. In the meantime, Maj. John A. Harman, noted for his energy and ability, was tearing down warehouses along the canal and building pontoons with the timbers thus secured to repair the bridge at Falling Waters, which, however, was not completed until the night of the 13th. During the time which intervened the Army was in a precarious position. A line of battle had been selected and prepared by the engineers with its right flank on the Potomac near Downsville, passing by St. James' College and resting its left on the Conococheague. The 1st Corps held the right, the 3d the center, and the 2d the left as at Gettysburg. The Artillery marched from Hagerstown on the 9th and 10th and occupied the line, and for the next three days was engaged with the infantry in continuous labor fortifying the position. The Commander-in-Chief had called upon the whole Army for a supreme effort and in furthering his plan of defense, Gen. Pendleton and his subordinates were most energetic in their coöperation. Alexander with his own and Dearing's and Henry's battalions occupied a position on the extreme right near Downsville. Three batteries of Cabell's Battalion were posted astride the Williamsport and Sharpsburg Pike, Lieut. Motes with Carlton's Battery being attached to Wofford's Brigade near St. James' further to the left. Walker's battalions occupied the center north of St. James' between Hagerstown and the Potomac. McIntosh's and Brunson's battalions, or the Corps Reserve, generally occupied those portions of the line held by Anderson and Heth, respectively, while Lane, Garnett, and Poague supported the divisions to which they were usually assigned. Brown's battalions occupied the left of the line, Nelson's batteries covering the Williamsport and Funkstown roads. Carter's Battalion was posted in a strong position to the rear in front of the bridge at Falling Waters.

From the 8th to the 12th of July, Stuart with Chew's, Breathed's, McGregor's, Moorman's, and Griffin's horse batteries covered the Confederate front. These days were occupied by severe fighting between the Confederate Cavalry and the divisions of Buford and Kilpatrick at Boonsborough, Beaver Creek, Funkstown, and on the Sharpsburg front. While both sides claimed the advantage, Stuart succeeded in delaying the advance of Meade's army until the Confederate Infantry and Artillery were thoroughly intrenched, so that when he uncovered the front the Federals found it too strong to be assailed without carefully maturing their plans. The 6th Corps had alone followed Ewell on the 5th as far as Fairfield, the rest of the Federal Army remaining on the battlefield for two days burying the dead, caring for the wounded, and bringing order out of the chaos into which the troops had been thrown by their prolonged defense. A third day was lost to the pursuit at Middle-town to procure supplies and bring up the trains, and had it not been for the storm of the 4th and 5th and further rains on the 7th and 8th the Con-federates would have safely crossed the Potomac before they were overtaken. As it was, Meade might have attacked on the 12th, but simply contented him-self with a reconnaissance resulting in his determination to feel Lee's line on the 13th. A general attack was to follow if a favorable opening was discovered. But, by the 13th, the ford at Williamsport was passable, the bridge lower down stream had been completed, and Lee issued orders for the crossing of his army during the night. Ewell was to cross at the ford, and Long-street followed by Hill with the Artillery of the three corps at the pontoon bridge. Caissons were ordered to start from the lines at 5 P. M., and the infantry and guns at dark. The withdrawal was effected with great skill and celerity, in spite of almost insurmountable obstacles, so that when the Federals, after making various demon-strations the day before, advanced to the attack on the 14th they found but a few hundred stragglers in their path.

The night movement on the part of the Confederates entailed the utmost hardship upon the Army, especially upon the Artillery. A heavy rainstorm had set in before dusk, and continued almost until morning. The routes to the crossings generally lay over narrow farm roads, rough and hilly, which were soon churned into all but impassable mires by the leading artillery carriages. No moon lit the way and the night was unusually dark, but large bonfires along the shore illuminated the crossings. From sunset to sunrise the artillery battalions, in spite of the most tremendous exertions on the part of the men, were able to cover but three or four miles, and many horses perished from exhaustion. Nevertheless all the Artillery was saved except two unserviceable howitzers of Henry's Battalion, which became stalled and were abandoned. After daylight, the weather cleared so that by 1 P. M. Hill's rear guard crossed the river under cover of Carter's guns at the bridge head. The Artillery then retired before the enemy's skirmishers which had been pressing the pursuit during the morning and took up a strong position on the south bank, while six of Garnett's, Lane's 20-pounder Parrotts, and Hart's two Whitworths were posted on his right and left by Gen. Pendleton, who personally conducted the defense of the crossing. For ten hours the old officer remained at this important post, unaided by a single member of his staff, all of whom were without horses and some of whom themselves were broken down by their exertions of the past two weeks. For 28 hours the Chief of Artillery was without a morsel of food, and for 40 was unable to gain a moment's rest.

Lee had intended to cross the Blue Ridge into Loudoun County, and there oppose Meade's advance, but while waiting for the Shenandoah River to subside, the Federals crossed below and seized the passes he had expected to use. Pushing his army southward along the eastern slope of the mountains, Meade threatened to cut Lee off from Gordonsville and the railroad. The danger was averted, however, by Longstreet's timely arrival at Culpeper on the 24th, followed by Hill, while Ewell moved up the Valley and crossed the Blue Ridge at Thornton Gap. By August 4, the entire Army was united behind the Rapidan with Stuart in its front at Culpeper, and the enemy behind the Rappahannock. Thus did the second invasion of the North terminate.

Livermore's estimate, which is believed to be more accurate than the Confederate returns, places the aggregate Confederate loss in the battle of Gettysburg at 28,063, of which number 3,903 were killed, 18,735 wounded, and 5,425 missing, as opposed to a Federal loss of 3,155 killed, 14,529 wounded and 5,365 missing, aggregate 23,049. The losses of the Confederate Artillery itemized by battalions were:

	Killed	Wounded	Missing	Total
Cabell's Battalion _____	8	29	0	37
Dearing's Battalion _____	8	17	0	25
Henry's Battalion _____	4	23	0	27
Alexander's Battalion _____	19	114	6	139
Eshleman's Artillery _____	3	26	16	45
Jones' Battalion _____	2	6	0	8
Andrews' Battalion _____	10	40	0	50
Carter's Battalion _____	6	35	24	65
Dance's Battalion _____	3	19	0	22
Nelson's Battalion _____	0	0	0	0
Lane's Battalion _____	3	21	6	30
Garnett's Battalion _____	0	5	17	22
Poague's Battalion _____	2	24	6	32
McIntosh's Battalion _____	7	25	0	32
Pegram's Battalion _____	10	37	1	48

The aggregate loss of the Confederate Artillery was therefore 582 as opposed to a loss of 736 in the Federal Artillery, exclusive of the Horse Artillery on both sides.

In the battle we have had occasion to note the absence of a number of prominent Confederate Artillery officers, but, Pegram, Andrews, Cutts, Hardaway, and Garnett joined their commands either near the end or soon after the close of the campaign. In Maj. John C. Haskell, of Henry's Battalion, a new character in the drama, and one destined to play a leading rôle henceforth, has appeared. We heard little of Col. Walton at Gettysburg, though he was present. As stated by Longstreet, he was getting too old for active command and his health had stood the rigours of the Virginia winters very poorly. He had already expressed a desire to be transferred to the southern department, but was retained as Chief of Artillery of the 1st Corps for some time.*

*Rebellion Records, Vol. XXIX, Part II, p. 699.

From the magnitude of Gettysburg as an artillery battle it may seem at first glance to require extended criticism, but upon closer examination such is not the case as far as the Confederate Artillery is concerned. Other than the criticisms already offered, few others need be made. The battle of the 3d of July was not lost through lack of artillery support, as asserted by many critics. True, the artillery fire was not maintained as vigorously to the end as it might have been had there been an abundance of ammunition. But it has been clearly shown that the artillery preparation was as thorough in Longstreet's front as the position of the guns would allow up to the very crisis of the attack which was when Pickett's column engaged in the infantry fire fight. Had Alexander and Walker possessed all the guns that could have been brought into action, they could not have maintained Pickett in his advanced position without the timely coöperation of a large infantry support. In fact the assaulting infantry itself masked the guns actually in action. Men, not shell, were needed at the high tide mark. Artillery can help infantry forward, but it cannot prevent overwhelming numbers converging under cover of the terrain upon it from many directions. That there were grave errors committed in the disposition of the artillery is not disputed, but this point is not usually made. The general criticism is that the artillery preparation for Longstreet's attack failed. That this is not true is proven by the very fact that Longstreet's Infantry did reach the enemy's guns and advanced much of the distance free from serious opposition on the part of the hostile artillery. His failure, then, was due to the lack of weight at the decisive point, both because he attacked with lack of concert among his troops, and because with whatever force he assaulted, the enemy remained free to outnumber him by transferring troops from other quarters of the field. The lack of coöperation of the 2d Corps Artillery was not due to Pendleton, nor to Brown, but to Ewell, the corps commander.

CHAPTER XXXV

THE period of several weeks of inactivity following upon the arrival of the Army behind the Rapidan was one of welcome and necessary rest. During this time so many convalescents and absentees returned to the Army that soon it was raised to a strength of nearly 60,000 men. The organization of the Artillery remained for a time unchanged with the exception of the temporary addition of Capt. Thomas E. Jackson's Charlottesville Battery to Beckham's Horse Artillery Battalion. McClannahan's Horse Battery, meantime, continued under Imboden's detached command, so that with Stuart's Division there were now seven horse batteries.

The distribution of the Artillery on July 31 was as follows:

1st Corps, 5 battalions, 22 batteries, 83 guns, 96 officers, and 1,724 enlisted men present for duty, aggregate present and absent 2,873.*

2d Corps, 5 battalions, 20 batteries, 84 guns, 95 officers, and 1,448 enlisted men present for duty, aggregate present and absent 2,392.

3d Corps, 5 battalions, 20 batteries, 62 guns, 86 officers, and 1,564 enlisted men present for duty, aggregate present and absent 2,727.

The effective strength of the Artillery with the Army was therefore over 5,000, and the paper strength nearly 8,000, with 229 guns. Before August 10 the present for duty increased to 5,747, and the aggregate paper strength to 8,325. With the 1st Corps there were then 83, with the 2d Corps 81, and with the 3d Corps 77 pieces of artillery, or a total of 241 guns. Of this num-

---

*For guns of 1st Corps at this time see *Rebellion Records,* Vol. LI, Part II, p. 740, Walton's letter.

ber there were twelve 20-pounder Parrotts, thirty-nine 10-pounder Parrotts, sixty-four 3-inch rifles, two Whitworths, ninety-eight Napoleons, five 24-pounder howitzers, and twenty-one 12-pounder howitzers. In the entire Corps there were but 8 battery wagons, and 32 forges, while there were 228 caissons or nearly one per gun.*

In the Gettysburg campaign, Lee had engaged, according to Col. Taylor, 50,000 infantry, 5,000 cavalry, and 4,000 artillery, but this estimate of the Artillery is, we believe, too small by 500 men. By August 10, however, it is certain that there was one man in the Artillery for every ten present in the Infantry. Thus it is seen that Lee, like Frederick and Napoleon, compensated for the decrease in his infantry by maintaining his artillery in the face of all difficulties.

Besides the Field Artillery actually with the field Army, there was a large force under Gen. Arnold Elzey, in and about the defenses of Richmond. Lieut.-Col. C. E. Lightfoot commanded a battalion consisting of Smoot's Alexandria, Thornton's Caroline, Rives' Nelson, and Hankins' Surry batteries. This battalion occupied the works together with Col. T. S. Rhett's four heavy artillery battalions. Serving with Ransom's Division in the Department of Richmond were four battalions as follows:

MOSELEY'S BATTALION

Maj. E. F. Moseley

Richmond Battery,	Capt. W. J. Dabney.
James City Battery,	Capt. L. W. Richardson.
Goochland Battery,	Capt. Jonathan Talley.
Yorktown Battery,	Capt. E. R. Young.

BOGGS' BATTALION

Maj. F. J. Boggs

Richmond Battery,	Capt. S. Taylor Martin.
Albemarle Battery,	Capt. N. A. Sturdivant.
North Carolina Battery,	Capt. L. H. Webb.

*See *Rebellion Records,* Series I, Vol. XXIX, Part II, p. 636, for complete summary of material, August 10, 1863.

BRANCH'S BATTALION

Maj. James R. Branch

Mississippi Battery,	Capt. W. D. Bradford.
South Carolina Battery,	Capt. J. C. Coit.
Petersburg Battery,	Capt. R. G. Pegram.
Halifax Battery,	Capt. S. T. Wright.

UNATTACHED

Battery "E", 1st N. C. Reg't,	Capt. Alexander D. Moore.
Macon (Ga.) Battery,	Capt. C. W. Staten.

STARK'S BATTALION

Maj. A. W. Stark*

Mathews' Battery,	Capt. A. D. Armistead.
Giles Battery,	Capt. D. A. French.

These 15 light batteries must have possessed a total personnel of not less than 1,000 men and 60 guns. There was, therefore, a large reserve force of artillery in his immediate rear, which Lee could call upon in an emergency, though of course the service of the officers and men who had been held at the base had not been such as to make them as efficient as those with the main army.

Since the reorganization of the Artillery in May, it had greatly increased in efficiency, but the Pennsylvania campaign had practically destroyed its field transportation, and the batteries were themselves almost dismounted. During the retreat it had, therefore, been necessary to still further reduce the baggage allowances in order to supply the batteries and ordnance trains with teams. At this time, the artillery transportation was fixed at two 4-horse wagons for the Chief of Artillery and his entire staff, including the medical officers, one 4-horse wagon for each corps chief and his staff, one 4-horse wagon for each battalion headquarters, one 4-horse wagon for all the battery officers of each battalion, and two 4-horse wagons for the forage and

---

*Attached to Wise's Brigade.

supplies of each battery.   Surplus baggage was directed to be turned over to the Chief Quartermaster at once.*

The following April a slight additional reduction was made in the allowance of transportation, and but one 4-horse wagon was authorized for the Chiefs of Artillery and their entire staffs, while one 2-horse wagon for the medical supplies of each battalion and one 4-horse wagon for the mess equipment of every 500 men actually present were added.   Thus it is seen that the baggage train of the Artillery of the Army when complete consisted of not more than 160 wagons, requiring only about 650 horses.   It is doubtful if any other equal force of artillery ever took the field with such a limited train.   But we must remember that but two wagons were allowed army, corps, and division headquarters, and but one for brigade headquarters, at this time.   By a rigid enforcement of the orders relative to the baggage allowance, the field batteries were provided with an average of about 50 horses before August 10, though some of them were still sadly deficient in the number of their animals.

While the Artillery of the 1st and 3d corps lay in camp near Orange Courthouse and that of the 2d Corps at Liberty Mills, the most strenuous efforts were made by Gen. Pendleton to fully rehorse his command.   His investigations of the horse problem were wide and thorough.   Learning that horses temporarily disabled were not adequately cared for by the agents of the Quartermaster Department, and that numbers of them which under a proper system might be restored to a serviceable condition were allowed to perish from neglect, he reported the condition of affairs to the Commander-in-Chief.†   He suggested that animals unfit for service should be turned over to individual farmers who should be encouraged to save them for their own needs, and not allowed to be herded in great droves.   Under

*G. O. No. 77, A. N. V., July 16, 1863.
†*Rebellion Records,* Vol. XXXIII, p. 1262.
    See his interesting letter, *Rebellion Records,* Vol. XXIX, Part II, p. 643, August 13, 1863.

the prevailing system, diseased animals merely spread contagion and none could receive individual attention. A farmer would ordinarily be only too glad to secure one or two horses for light work, and he would in many cases improve rather than impair their unfortunate condition, which was principally due to exposure and lack of nourishment. Gen. Pendleton also declared that not less than 300 good artillery horses could be secured in Albemarle County alone, if the proper methods were pursued. Quartermasters and their agents, unknown to the people, could not secure these animals, he said, but artillery officers, whose interest in the service was necessarily greater than that of mere purchasing agents, would by tact and good judgment be able to purchase them for about $600.00 apiece, or even perhaps trade worn and feeble battery horses for the fresh ones. At any rate, many could be secured by impressment as a last resort. But very little seems to have been done at this time, however, to remedy conditions, and again, on September 3, the Chief of Artillery called the Commander-in-Chief's attention to this very vital matter, which threatened the efficiency of the whole artillery arm. His recommendations to the Superintendent of Transportation at Richmond were now as follows:

"*First.* The establishment of a sort of general horse district in the counties of Halifax, Pittsylvania, Henry, Patrick, Franklin, Campbell, and Bedford, with depots, stables, etc., under the care of a responsible superintendent, who should select his own agents, and have the care of all the horses of this army to be resuscitated, etc.

"*Second.* The procurement from time to time, by this same officer or others in connection with his charge, of a number of fresh horses, to be taken to the depots in said district and kept with those renovated, for transfer when needed to the field.

"*Third.* The establishment of suitable places of accommodation for horses removed to and from this district and the army, so as to insure their being suitably provided for in transit."*

As far as we know this plan, which in its general aspect was adopted, was one of the first attempts to

---

Rebellion Records, Vol. XXIX, Part II, p. 697. Ibid., p. 715.

organize a remount depot in this country, certainly in the Confederacy. It was to be established in a region still fat with forage, where slave labor was cheap and plentiful and one well removed from the theater of military operations.

So well received were Pendleton's suggestions that Maj. Paxton, whom he recommended to be placed in charge of the establishment, was soon appointed and directed to organize the remount department, with headquarters at Lynchburg. Before spring he had accomplished much in seggregating diseased animals and restoring them to health by means of infirmaries, as well as in collecting animals for future use. Yet, disease was so widespread, extending throughout the section and as far as the North Carolina line, that of the 3,000 animals in Paxton's charge over 600 died before February. The system adopted by the Department for parceling out the animals in small herds, foraging, exercising, and caring for them, was nevertheless such an apparent improvement over old methods that the Chief of Artillery recommended that the 1,500 animals which would be required to rehorse his command be left in charge of Maj. Paxton, until actually needed in the spring. More apprehension was entertained at this time concerning the lack of transport animals than remounts, and Gen. Pendleton urged that his agents be allowed to draw upon the supply of mules in Mississippi, Georgia, and Alabama, and this suggestion was approved by the Commander-in-Chief.*

Early in September Longstreet's suggestion to transfer troops from Virginia to Tennessee for the purpose of reinforcing Gen. Bragg was adopted. There remained several months of open weather and it was hoped that some success could yet be won in the West. But before the movement commenced the short route to Chattanooga, *via* Bristol and Knoxville, was no longer available, and Longstreet was compelled to take the roundabout route from Petersburg *via* Weldon,

---

Rebellion Records, Vol. XXXIII, pp. 1182, 1188.

Wilmington, and Augusta. Leaving Orange on the 9th, the infantry of the 1st Corps was moved to Petersburg by rail, while Alexander's, Walton's, and Dearing's battalions marched. Hood's and McLaws' divisions and Alexander's six batteries with 26 guns entrained on the 17th and reached their destination after a tedious journey, in which it took nearly eight days to cover less than 850 miles. Meanwhile, Pickett's Division with Dearing's Battalion of Artillery was assigned to duty along the James River, relieving Jenkins' and Wise's brigades, the former having accompanied Hood and the latter going to Charleston, S. C. Walton's Battalion remained at Petersburg. On the 23d, Pickett was assigned to the command of the Department of North Carolina, with headquarters at Petersburg, Va. Henry's and Cabell's battalions moved to Hanover Junction with Pickett's Division, but on the 13th were ordered by easy marches into camp in the neighborhood of Gordonsville *via* Louisa Courthouse. On October 5, Lamkin's Nelson Battery was attached to Henry's Battalion, to the permanent command of which Maj. John C. Haskell had succeeded. But on the 9th this battery, which was unarmed, was transferred to Cabell's Battalion. Maj. Henry had been promoted and transferred to the West.

An important promotion had meanwhile been made in the Artillery Corps. It was apparent that Col. Crutchfield would be *hors de combat* for many months, and a permanent Chief of Artillery for the 2d Corps was much needed. Accordingly one of the two existing vacancies in the grade of brigadier-general of artillery was filled by the promotion of Col. Armistead Lindsay Long, formerly Military Secretary of the Commander-in-Chief, and he was assigned to duty as Chief of Artillery of the 2d Corps. The circumstances connected with the selection of Long for this position will be discussed later. Suffice it to say here that while he was in every way competent to fulfill the position to which he was appointed, yet his assignment to this high tactical

command was thought by some to overslaugh the claims
of Col. Brown to seniority in the Artillery of Ewell's
Corps during the absence of Crutchfield. While there
was no open resentment of his appointment, nevertheless it would seem that Col. Brown's claim to seniority
in the 2d Corps was disregarded nothwithstanding the
fact that he was a highly efficient officer and had exercised command in every campaign since April, 1861.
It will be recalled that he was the original battery commander of the 1st Company of Richmond Howitzers
when it left Richmond for Yorktown. From that time
to the day of his death he never missed an hour of duty.
Although an officer with no military training prior to
the war, he was a natural soldier and had no superiors
in point of courage. He was a man of too high a sense
of duty to allow any disappointment which he may
have felt to affect him. He never complained to his associates, and showed no signs of bitterness to his superiors. His personal and family correspondence shows
that he himself accepted conditions in a most magnanimous spirit, but his friends were less philosophical in
the matter. They felt that again the West Point influence had overreached a gallant, meritorious officer
who, irrespective of the fact that he was a civilian before
the war, had proved himself to be eminently qualified to
command and, therefore, entitled to consideration upon
his military record in the service of the Confederacy,
without regard to circumstances before the war. This
belief was heightened by the fact that Col. Brown had
served as Acting Chief of Artillery of the 2d Corps
since the day of Crutchfield's elimination, and that although he had not shown any particular brilliance at
Gettysburg, the minor part played by his command
there was known to have been due to Ewell's and not
his fault.

During the period of inactivity, in which the Confederate Army was gradually recuperating its strength,
two corps were detached from the Army of the Potomac
and sent to reinforce Sherman's Army, and in spite of

Longstreet's absence the two armies were numerically more nearly equal than in the past campaign. This condition induced Lee to attempt to force Meade to an engagement while his army was reduced. Crossing the Rapidan on the 9th of October, Lee moved to Madison Courthouse and thence eastward, screening his movements by the cavalry and the mountain spurs and forests between himself and his enemy. But before Lee arrived near Culpeper Courthouse on the 11th, Meade had learned through his cavalry of the danger to his right, and withdrew along the railroad to the line of the Rappahannock, Stuart driving Pleasonton from the old field of Brandy Station back upon the Federal Army. Cabell's Battalion had been left in front of Gordonsville, and Haskell's had been moved forward to Liberty Mills. The rest of the Artillery accompanied the Army on its circuitous march and throughout the subsequent campaign in which there was much skillful maneuvering on both sides and very little fighting. By the 18th, Lee was back again on the Rappahannock. The main Army lay in camp about Culpeper, while Stuart occupied the country on the north side of the river. By November 7, Meade reached the Rappahannock immediately behind which and in his front lay Ewell's Corps, with Early's Division behind Brandy Station, Rodes' covering Kelly's Ford on the right, and Johnson's between them. Hill's Corps held the line of the river on Ewell's left. A pontoon bridge had been thrown at the site of the old Rappahannock Bridge and the *tete de pont* on the north bank was alternately picketed by a single brigade of Early's and Johnson's divisions and a battery of artillery. When the Federals reached the river Hays' Brigade and Green's Louisiana Guard Battery held the work on the north bank, while Dance's and Graham's batteries occupied a redoubt on the south side of the stream where they were placed merely to prevent a crossing should the bridge-head be taken, but they had no command whatever of the terrain on the north shore.

The Federal advance consisted of the 5th and 6th Corps, which promptly occupied the hills in front of Hays, and opened fire upon the work on the north bank with a battery. To this, Lieut. Moore in command of Green's Battery boldly replied, but was soon overwhelmed by two other batteries while Graham and Dance vainly sought to assist him. At dusk a heavy mass of the enemy's infantry rushed Hays and captured most of his men, and the Louisiana Battery. Of the two officers and 76 enlisted men of the battery, but 28 of the latter escaped, with 9 of their 54 horses. The two 10-pounder Parrotts and the two 3-inch Dahlgren rifled pieces of the battery were taken by the enemy along with all the carriages and about 400 rounds of ammunition.

In the meantime, Early had ordered up his infantry and Jones' Battalion, while Massie's Fluvanna Battery of Nelson's Battalion also arrived and engaged the Federals. But at daybreak on the 8th, Lee withdrew to his former position on the Rapidan. Although the season was late, and Meade had first eluded Lee and then recovered his original position, he was not willing to go into winter quarters until he had himself undertaken offensive maneuvers in order, by some success, to satisfy the expectations of the administration in Washington.

Ewell's Corps now occupied a line from the base of Clark's Mountain to Mine Run, a small tributary of the Rappahannock, and covered Mitchell's, Morton's, Raccoon, and Summerville's fords; Hill's Corps that from Orange Courthouse to Liberty Mills; while Stuart, as usual, covered the front and flanks of the Army. Both corps had been much reduced by winter furloughs, no further operations before winter being expected. Already the Confederates had begun to prepare for a long rest, when at dawn, on November 26, Meade set his entire army in motion towards Germanna Ford, hoping to cross the Rapidan at that point and surprise Lee. But his movement, though shrouded with the utmost secrecy, was instantly discovered by Stuart. Lee at

once ordered Hill to form a junction with Ewell at
Verdierville, and the latter to occupy a strong position
behind Mine Run. In spite of every precaution, many
delays impeded the Federal advance, and Meade's
troops did not cross the Rapidan until the morning of
the 27th. Meanwhile the Confederates had completed
their concentration and thrown up strong log and earth
breastworks. When Meade finally arrived in front of
Lee on the morning of the 28th, he found himself confronted by 30,000 infantry and 150 pieces of artillery
behind works even stronger than those his own men had
thrown up at Chancellorsville. This was a bitter disappointment to the Federal commander, but he diligently set to work to find an opening and next day
Warren reported favorable conditions for assault on the
Confederate right, while Sedgwick seemed to have discovered equally good ones on the other flank. Orders
for the simultaneous attack on both flanks were issued,
but when the Federal artillery of the center and right
opened not a sound came from Warren. His men had
sized up the strength of Lee's works more accurately
than their leader, for each had pinned a slip of paper
on his breast with his name on it in order that the wearer
might be identified. Reconnaissances both by Warren
and Meade satisfied them of the futility of an assault,
which if successful would be at the cost of not less than
30,000 men. Lee, too, was much disappointed by the
retreat of the Federals across Ely's Ford to Culpeper
Courthouse on the night of December 1, and so suddenly
and rapidly was it accomplished that he was unable to
overtake them on the 2d. Thus ended the Mine Run
campaign and the operations of 1863.

The Army was now promptly prepared to go into
winter quarters. The Infantry was generally held along
the Rapidan, while the Artillery with the exception of
two or three battalions was scattered along the line of
the Virginia Central Railroad for the greater convenience of foraging the horses. Gen. Long's 2d Corps
Artillery with the exception of Nelson's Battalion,

which was kept on picket duty along the Rapidan, was located in and about Frederick Hall, and four of Col. Walker's 3d Corps battalions, after camping for a month on the farm of Maj. Lee near Madison Run in Madison County, erected their huts in the neighborhood of Cobham and Lindsay stations, about 10 miles west of Gordonsville, with headquarters at Meeksville, while Cutts' Battalion like Nelson's remained on picket near Rapidan Station. It was at this time that Lieut. Richard Walke, ordnance officer on Mahone's staff, was promoted captain of artillery and assigned to duty as Inspector-General of the 3d Corps Artillery, while Maj. Herbert M. Nash was appointed Surgeon. Captain William W. Chamberlaine had served on Col. Walker's staff for some time as Corps Adjutant.

The Horse Artillery, which was continuously engaged in the cavalry operations during the months of September, October, November, and December, was ordered into winter quarters at Charlottesville on December 21st. Gen. Lee and Governor Letcher had reviewed the infantry and Stuart's command at Culpeper Courthouse on November 5, when again Beckham's Battalion passed before the great soldier at the head of the cavalry, to the tune of Hampton's mounted band.

Leaving the Rapidan country the horse batteries, worn and depleted by months of continuous fighting and marching, toiled over the bottomless roads to the Rivanna, which they reached on the 22d. The camp site selected for the battalion was located on the Earlyville Road, about five miles from Charlottesville. For the next two weeks, the men were busily engaged erecting log huts and stables. It was in this very locality that Burgoyne's Hessians had been cantoned by Washington after their capture at Saratoga during the Revolutionary War.

Officers of the Horse Artillery declare that the winter of 1863-64, part of which they spent at Charlottesville, was the severest ordeal through which they passed while in the service. The cold winds which swept over the mountainous district, and the heavy falls of snow caused the greatest suffering to men and beasts. Alternately bemired and frozen, the roads were impassable and the fields offered no opportunity for exercise. The period of winter quarters was simply a struggle by horses and men for existence, with scant provender for the former, and an unusual deficiency in rations and clothing for the latter. But these conditions were quite general in the artillery camps.

Soon after placing his corps in winter quarters, Gen. Pendleton, with headquarters at Louisa Courthouse, assigned Majs. Page and Wolffe, and Lieuts. Peterkin and Dandridge of his staff to the duty of examining the forage conditions in the region between the railroad and the James River, from a point slightly west of Charlottesville, to one just east of Beaver Dam Depot. These officers were required to locate, and report by December 10 upon, the available supply of corn, oats, hay, straw, and fodder, as well as the grist mills in the respective districts designated for their inspection. Thus it is seen that the rich farming lands of the James River Valley, hitherto free from the presence of the armies, was expected to support the Artillery during the winter. The river counties with their Nile-like low grounds had before the war comprised the finest agricultural section of the state, and although the James River Nabobs were no longer personally superintending the cultivation of their estates, being off with the Army, their wives remained at home and managed to keep most of their slaves at work, thus supporting their own as well as a great number of refugee families from the more exposed parts of Virginia. The Valley of Egypt was hardly more fertile than the bottom lands between Lynchburg and Richmond along the James, and those along the Rivanna from Charlottesville to Columbia.

Many vacancies in the Artillery now existed, so that numerous officers, who had previously been confined to the lower grades, at last had before them prospects of advancement. Early in November, Gen. Pendleton had been called upon for his recommendations for promotion, and after conferring with Gen. Long, Col. Walker and Gen. Stuart, submitted them on November 20.* The authorized commissioned personnel at this time was based, of course, upon the number of guns with the Army. Including those of the 1st Corps with Longstreet in Tennessee, and those of the Horse Artillery, the number actually in service was 244, while the full legitimate armament entitled the Artillery to 276. Arrangements were already nearly completed to supply the deficiency by substituting more Napoleons for the howitzers that had been lost and become unserviceable through ordinary wear and tear. The authorized complement of officers included, therefore, 3 brigadier-generals, 7 colonels, 11 lieutenant-colonels, and 17 majors, whereas there were actually commissioned but 2 brigadier-generals, 6 colonels, 6 lieutenant-colonels, and 17 majors. The existing general and field-officers were as follows:

Brigadier-Generals—W. N. Pendleton and A. L. Long.

Colonels—S. Crutchfield, J. B. Walton, J. T. Brown, H. C. Cabell, R. L. Walker, and E. P. Alexander.

Lieutenant-Colonels—A. S. Cutts, R. S. Andrews, T. H. Carter, H. P. Jones, W. Nelson, and J. J. Garnett.

Majors—B. F. Eshleman, S. P. Hamilton, F. Huger, R. F. Beckham, James Dearing, T. J. Page, W. J. Pegram, D. G. McIntosh, W. T. Poague, J. B. Brockenbrough, C. M. Braxton, J. Lane, R. A. Hardaway, J. C. Haskell, J. P. W. Read, C. Richardson, and Jas. Reilly.

Of these many were unfit for active service. Col. Crutchfield, whom Jackson had earnestly sought to have made a brigadier-general, and whose service had been distinguished from the first, was practically disabled by the wound he had received at Chancellorsville. For him, the Chief of Artillery recommended service about the defenses of Richmond. Col. Walton was no longer capable of performing active service, and his re-

---

*Rebellion Records, Vol. XXIX, Part II, p. 839, and Memoirs of W. N. Pendleton, p. 309.

quest to be assigned to duty at Mobile was endorsed by Pendleton, while Alexander was recommended to be made permanent Chief of Artillery of the 1st Corps. Col. Cabell, an officer of great integrity and personal courage, but lacking in energy and ability as a field soldier, was recommended to be transferred to the command of the battalion of field artillery at Richmond, and Lieut.-Col. Lightfoot transferred to the field army and placed in command of Cabell's Battalion. Lieut.-Col. Andrews, an officer of tried ability, was still an invalid from the wounds he had received at Cedar Run, in 1861, and Stephenson's Depot, in June, 1863. In justice to him, it was declared that he should be assigned to a less active field, preferably to ordnance duty, for which he was well qualified. Lieut.-Col. Garnett, in the opinion of the Chief of Artillery, in spite of his training and the high expectations of all, had proved unsuited to the artillery service. It was believed he could be more useful on conscript service than in his present position, and such a change was recommended. Maj. Brockenbrough, though a most efficient officer, was still disabled from the wound he had received at Fredericksburg, and was incapable of performing active duty. Accordingly Gen. Pendleton recommended Col. Alexander to be brigadier-general; Lieut.-Cols. Carter, Jones, and Cutts to be colonels; Majs. Dearing, Eshleman, Huger, Braxton, Pegram, McIntosh, Poague, Beckham, Hardaway, and Richardson, to be lieutenant-colonels; and Capts. Cutshaw, Jordan, Miller, Stribling, Raine, R. C. M. Page, Watson, McGraw, M. Johnson, Ward, Maurin, Moorman, Chew, and Breathed, to be majors with the following general assignments:

Brig.-Gen. W. N. Pendleton, Chief of Artillery

1st CORPS

Brig.-Gen. E. P. Alexander, Chief of Artillery

Huger's Battalion,	Lieut.-Col. F. Huger, South Carolina.
	Maj. T. S. Jordan, Virginia.
Beckham's Battalion,	Lieut.-Col. R. F. Beckham, Virginia.
	Maj. J. P. W. Read, Georgia.

Eshleman's Battalion, { Lieut.-Col. B. F. Eshleman, Louisiana.
                      { Maj. M. B. Miller, Louisiana.

RESERVE

Col. H. P. Jones, Virginia

Lightfoot's Battalion, { Lieut.-Col. C. E. Lightfoot, North Carolina.
                       { Maj. S. P. Hamilton, Georgia.

2D CORPS

Brig.-Gen. A. L. Long, Chief of Artillery
Col. T. H. Carter, Assistant Chief of Artillery

Page's Battalion, { Maj. R. C. M. Page, Virginia.
                  { Maj. M. N. Moorman, Virginia.

RESERVE

Col. J. T. Brown, Virginia

Cutshaw's Battalion, { Maj. W. E. Cutshaw, Virginia.
                     { Maj. R. M. Stribling, Virginia.
Hardaway's Battalion, { Lieut.-Col. R. A. Hardaway, Alabama.
                      { Maj. T. J. Page, Virginia.

3D CORPS

Col. R. L. Walker, Chief of Artillery

Pegram's Battalion, { Lieut.-Col. W. J. Pegram, Virginia.
                    { Maj. Joseph McGraw, Virginia.
McIntosh's Battalion, { Lieut.-Col. D. G. McIntosh, South Carolina.
                      { Maj. Marmaduke Johnson, Virginia.
Poague's Battalion, { Lieut.-Col. W. T. Poague, Virginia.
                    { Maj. George Ward, Mississippi.

RESERVE

Col. A. S. Cutts, Georgia

Richardson's Battalion, { Lieut.-Col. Charles Richardson, Virginia.
                        { Maj. Victor Maurin, Louisiana.
Cutts' Battalion, { Lieut.-Col. A. S. Cutts, Georgia.
                  { Maj. John Lane, Georgia.

HORSE ARTILLERY

Lieut.-Col. James Dearing, Chief of Artillery
Chew's Battalion,   Maj. R. P. Chew, Virginia.
Breathed's Battalion,   Maj. James Breathed.

The foregoing schedule includes 2 colonels less and 1 lieutenant-colonel and 3 majors more than the law allowed, and provided for 7 promotions from the 1st, 8 from the 2d, and 9 from the 3d Corps, and 4 from the Horse Artillery, which was about as fair a distribution as could be made. It will also be observed that the two reserve battalions of each corps were grouped under a single field officer, which was done at the suggestion of Gen. Long. It is also to be noticed that Maj. M. W. Henry, to the command of whose battalion Haskell succeeded, had dropped out by transfer to the Western Army. It seems strange that Dearing should have been recommended to succeed Beckham as senior officer in the Horse Artillery. This must have been at the instance of Stuart with whom Pendleton had conferred, for no such transfer would have been proposed except at his request. Dearing had a natural love for the cavalry and later transferred to that arm as a brigadier-general.

The foregoing recommendations of the Chief of Artillery with the reasons upon which they were based, give one a valuable insight into the affairs of the Artillery at the time, but the welfare of the arm seems not to have been the only consideration before the appointing power. Influence, prejudice, politics, the bane of armies, were not foreign to the Confederacy, and it was many months before the needs of the service overcame the obstacles thrown in the way of final action. Garnett, meanwhile, retained his command, while Col. Walton remained in Virginia until spring in command of the Artillery with Pickett, consisting of Eshleman's and Dearing's battalions. Cabell was also retained and his battalion was held throughout the winter at the front as an army reserve with Fraser's, Manly's, and McCarthy's batteries at Somerville, Raccoon, and Morton's Fords, and Carlton's Battery in support in rear of the last two. Haskell's Battalion was temporarily attached to the 3d Corps, in the absence of Longstreet. Col. Cabell seems to have been well aware of the fact that he was not in favor, but was determined that he should not be ousted and resolutely held on to the last, giving up his guns only at Appomattox.

As time wore on and it became apparent to Pendleton that the needs of the Artillery were simply being disregarded, he again addressed Gen. Lee on the subject of the necessary promotions as follows:

"Although I know you are anxious to secure the promotion of our many meritorious officers, and regret, as I do, the obstacles that have hitherto hindered favorable action upon the recommendations in their behalf, I deem it my duty to submit for your consideration some additional facts recently brought to my notice.

"*First.* Some of the best officers in the corps, finding how extremely difficult it is to rise in it at all, in proportion to service and merit, are making arrangements for more promising positions in other arms; nor can this be wondered at or even objected to as unpatriotic. Men the most devoted must be expected to value rank alike, as an evidence that their services are appreciated, and as an important condition toward more extended service. No man of merit ever disregards the question of promotion, and much as officers may be willing to sacrifice at times like these, they cannot ignore so universal and powerful a sentiment as that associated with martial honor.

"Even those officers who have no idea of seeking other service, and whose simple sense of duty will keep them steadfast until the end, in spite of disproportionate reward, are compelled to consider themselves and their commands regarded with less than justice, and after all that can be allowed for high principle, we must conclude that it is not in human nature not to be more or less disturbed by such a reflection, nor can such disturbance be without its injurious effects upon the public service.

"In addition to these considerations, the fact is worthy of particular attention that a number of the battalions have with them only one field officer, so that in contingencies frequently occurring, the senior captain, not always well qualified for the charge, has to command a battalion, serious as are the responsibilities belonging to the position. It is certainly important that this difficulty be corrected before the next active campaign.

"You will, I know, appreciate the case, and again ask for such action on the part of the President and the Secretary as may be practicable toward remedying the evil indicated."*

These were strong arguments, and were too true to be further neglected. At this time, there were in the

Rebellion Records, Vol. XXXIII, p. 1193, letter dated February 22, 1864.

three corps and the Horse Artillery 214 artillery officers present for duty, with an effective strength for their arm of 4,893, and a paper strength of 7,137.* The grand total of the Army of Northern Virginia, exclusive of Longstreet's command, was but 85,000 officers and men on paper, yet there were 2,418 officers of infantry and 331 of cavalry. These figures give some idea of how little opportunity the artillery arm afforded for promotion as compared to the others, notwithstanding the fact that the proportion of the artillery personnel to that of the infantry and cavalry, combined, was as 1 to 10. We must also consider that casualties in the Infantry and Cavalry were by virtue of the nature of those arms much greater among the commissioned personnel than in the Artillery.

That the matter of promotions in the Artillery was vigorously pressed by Gen. Lee is certain, for by S. O. No. 77, A. N. V., March 19, 1864, the following assignments were made:

Brig.-Gen. William Nelson Pendleton, Chief of Artillery

1st CORPS

Brig.-Gen. Edward Porter Alexander, Chief of Artillery

Cabell's Battalion,	Col. Henry Coalter Cabell.
	Maj. S. P. Hamilton.
Haskell's Battalion,	Maj. John Cheves Haskell.
	Maj. James Reilly.
Huger's Battalion,	Lieut.-Col. Frank Huger.
	Maj. Tyler C. Jordan.
Jones' Battalion,	Col. Hilary P. Jones.
	Maj. John P. W. Read.
Washington Artillery,	Col. Jas. Birge Walton.
	Maj. Benj. F. Eshleman.

2d CORPS

Brig.-Gen. Armistead Lindsay Long, Chief of Artillery

Braxton's Battalion,	Lieut.-Col. Carter M. Braxton.
	Maj. Marcellus N. Moorman.
Brown's Battalion,	Col. John Thompson Brown.
	Lieut.-Col. Robert A. Hardaway.

*Ibid., p. 1191.

Carter's Battalion,	Col. Thomas H. Carter.
	Maj. Richard C. M. Page.
Cutshaw's Battalion,	Maj. Wilfred E. Cutshaw.
	Maj. Robert M. Stribling.
Nelson's Battalion,	Lieut.-Col. William Nelson.
	Maj. David Watson.

3D CORPS

Col. Reuben Lindsay Walker, Chief of Artillery

Cutts' Battalion,	Lieut.-Col. Allan S. Cutts.
	Maj. John Lane.
Pegram's Battalion,	Lieut.-Col. William Johnson Pegram.
	Maj. Joseph McGraw.
McIntosh's Battalion,	Lieut.-Col. David Gregg McIntosh.
	Maj. Marmaduke Johnson.
Poague's Battalion,	Lieut.-Col. William T. Poague.
	Maj. George Ward.
Richardson's Battalion,	Maj. Charles Richardson.
	Maj. M. B. Miller.

In this assignment, Jones was given Dearing's Battalion, Cutshaw succeeding to the command of Jones' old battalion, while Richardson succeeded Garnett, and Braxton succeeded Andrews.

Soon Gen. Long divided his artillery into two divisions, the first under Brown, consisting of Nelson's, Hardaway's, and Braxton's battalions, and the second under Carter, consisting of Cutshaw's and Page's battalions.* Hardaway and Page then commanded Brown's and Carter's old battalions, respectively.

Early in March Beckham was promoted and transferred to the western army, whereupon Dearing was promoted and succeeded to the command of the Horse Artillery, the organization of which was now as follows:†

HORSE ARTILLERY‡

Lieut.-Col. James Dearing
Maj. Robert Preston Chew

Ashby Battery,	Capt. James W. Thomson.
1st Stuart Horse Artillery,	Capt. James Breathed.

*Rebellion Records, Vol. XXXIII, p. 1267.
†For Dearing's assignment to H. A., see ibid., p. 1264.
‡Griffin's Battery attached to Maryland line under Gen. Bradley T. Johnston. Jackson's Battery with Jones in Department of Western Virginia.

2d Stuart Horse Artillery,	Capt. Wm. M. McGregor.
Lynchburg Beauregards,	Capt. J. J. Shoemaker.
Washington (S. C.) Battery,	Capt. J. F. Hart.

Before the opening of the next campaign, Eshleman was also promoted and given command of a newly-organized battalion from among the batteries around Richmond, and Capt. William Miller Owen, formerly adjutant of the Washington Artillery, became its major and battalion commander. Thus, with the exception of the retention of Cabell in active command, we see that the original recommendations of the Chief of Artillery were finally very closely followed, and general satisfaction prevailed. It was about this time that Lieut.-Gen. J. C. Pemberton, the unfortunate defender of Vicksburg, tendered his resignation and requested to be assigned to the Artillery with the rank of lieutenant-colonel.* On May 12 he was assigned to Ransom's Division in the Richmond defenses as Chief of Artillery.†

Favorable weather in February tempted Meade to undertake a renewal of operations, but the prompt appearance of Lee induced the Federal commander to forego his activity, not, however, until he had attacked Ewell's line. Nearly all the Confederate pickets were taken. The preparedness of Brown's Artillery alone saved the breaking of the Confederate line. The batteries of the 2d Corps, unaided, hurled the Federals back and administered a bloody repulse to them with slight loss to themselves. But for their prompt and energetic action, instead of being a small affair, a disaster would have befallen the Army.

On the 29th of February, Gen. Custer with about 2,500 picked troopers and a section of horse artillery, moving along the Earlyville Road, approached within one mile of the Horse Artillery camp before he was discovered by the merest accident. It so happened that Capt. Moorman with two of his men while going fishing

saw the raiders approaching, and galloped back to camp
to give the alarm. The enemy appeared so suddenly
that the parked guns were all but captured. By the
time Maj. Chew was able to get his batteries hooked up,
the raiders were actually among the huts looting the
camp and shooting down the stray horses which it had
been impossible to drive in from the fields in which the
animals had been turned out. A few shots from Moorman's guns while the teams were being brought up
served to check the enemy sufficiently to enable Chew
to place his batteries in position and open upon the
raiders, who were seemingly more intent upon the destruction of the camp than the capture of the guns. The
artillery fire soon drove Custer off, and thus did Chew
entirely unsupported by infantry or cavalry save Charlottesville, with about 200 cannoneers, including the
sick and the dismounted men who were always called
in the Artillery Company "Q". In accomplishing this
result, an interesting stratagem was utilized. The 16
guns present were formed in line, and manned by the
dismounted cannoneers, while the rest of the men, bearing an old standard, were formed by Chew and Breathed
into a squadron behind the guns. There was not a
musket or carbine in the outfit, few pistols, and fewer
sabers. Most of the men, however, bore sticks and
clubs to represent arms. The few small arms were, of
course, ostentatiously employed, with such effect that
the enemy mistook the line of mounted cannoneers for
a cavalry support. In the meantime, the guns were
actively plied, while Custer held most of his men beyond the river, uncertain as to the number of his enemy.
He had captured Capt. Moorman's two companions before they reached camp. From them little information
could be secured. In fact they intentionally assumed
a most puzzling manner. Custer, himself, then ques-
tioned a negro inhabitant of the neighborhood, who
stated with every appearance of candor that the artillerymen had lied, and that Confederate troops were

encamped all the way from the river to Charlottesville, and had with them not less than 60 guns. This interview was on the south side of the river on a hill above the bridge at Burnley's Mill, about a mile from the Artillery camp, and while it was transpiring several shells burst near the group. About the same time, Chew moved his pseudo cavalry to the flank of the guns and cried out in a loud voice, "Tell Col. Dulaney to bring up the Seventh Regiment." The Federals heard the command, and naturally assumed the superb cavalry regiment had been moved from the Valley, where it was actually in camp, to the defense of Charlottesville. That night Custer retired towards the Rappahannock, having accomplished nothing but the burning of the Horse Artillery cantonments and Burnley's Mill, while Chew moved his battalion four miles down the Scottsville Road, unwilling to rely on Dulaney's support. But the next day, when Custer was found to have decamped, he returned to his old quarters, and rebuilt his huts. The men had lost nearly everything they possessed in the way of surplus clothing. The bountiful supply must have greatly improved the outfit of the Federal raiders. For the next few days rumors of Custer's return were rife and a bold lookout was maintained. On the 20th of March, the battalion was ordered to Gordonsville for security, where it remained until the opening of the next campaign, in camp on the farm of Bolling Haxall. While there a large supply of fresh horses was expected by the batteries, but the total number received was 38.

Meanwhile the following resolutions were received by the Horse Artillery Battalion from the Town Council of Charlottesville, as a testimonial of the appreciation of its people:

"*Whereas,* The recently attempted raid of the Yankees on this place was undoubtedly checked and finally repulsed by unequaled coolness and courage of the gallant officers and men of the artillery battalion, encamped a few miles north of Charlottesville, wholly unsupported as they were by either infantry or cavalry; and,

"*Whereas,* Our town was thus unquestionably saved from pillage, and the public stores and the railroad bridges from destruction; therefore, be it

"*Resolved,* That on behalf of the citizens of Charlottesville we, the council of the town, do hereby return our thanks to the officers and men of the said artillery battalion for their gallant and heroic conduct on the occasion above mentioned, with the assurance of our lasting and grateful appreciation of the service thus rendered us.

"*Resolved,* That the above preamble and resolutions be handed to the commander of the battalion, in order that he may communicate the same to the officers and men of his command in the manner he may deem most appropriate.

"By order of the Council, March 7, 1864.

"A. ROBERT MCKEE, *Clerk.*

"To Maj. M. N. Moorman,
    "Commanding Battalion,
        "Stuart Horse Artillery."

It was after the arrival of the battalion at Gordonsville that Capt. Moorman was promoted major and transferred to Braxton's Light Artillery Battalion, then at Frederick's Hall, Lieut. J. J. Shoemaker succeeding him as Captain of the Beauregard Rifles Battery of Lynchburg, while Maj. Chew became the battalion commander with the rank of lieutenant-colonel.

The next hostile move after Custer's raid was in March when two columns of Federal cavalry under Gen. Kilpatrick and Col. Dahlgren, respectively, moved out from Culpeper Courthouse, the first towards Richmond, and the second with orders to destroy the artillery at Frederick Hall, and then proceed down the James River, form a junction with Kilpatrick's column, capture Richmond, destroy the city, and liberate the prisoners on Belle Isle. This was a big order for Dahlgren. Nearly succeeding with respect to reaching Richmond, he would certainly have succeeded in destroying the 2d Corps artillery, had it not been for the foresight of Gen. Long. Anticipating a cavalry raid upon his camp, he had early applied for two regiments of infantry as a guard. When refused this support, he secured 125 muskets, which he distributed among his cannoneers and organized them by battalions into companies of riflemen.

Dahlgren captured the pickets at Germanna Ford, crossed the Rapidan, and arrived within a few miles of the Artillery camp before his approach was reported. Gen. Long, immediately upon learning of the danger, ordered Lieut.-Col. Braxton to place a battery in position to command the road over which the enemy was approaching, to deploy his company of sharpshooters as skirmishers, and to withdraw his other batteries to a position near the railway station. At the same time, Col. Brown was directed to place his battalion in position to guard the approaches below the depot, while Cutshaw's and Carter's battalions were held in rear of Brown's and Braxton's, and sharpshooters from the supporting batteries were also sent forward and deployed. These dispositions were barely completed when the Federal raiders came in view of Marye's Battery on the road. Seeing the battle flag flying above the guns, and catching a glimpse of the bayonets of the sharpshooters, Dahlgren halted in some surprise, having been led to believe that the artillery at Frederick Hall was without an infantry support. He now inquired of a local contraband whether or not there was infantry with the artillery, to which the negro replied, "Yes, Massa, plenty of it." Being doubtful whether the negro knew what was meant by infantry, Dahlgren asked how he knew it. "Because," was the answer, "the infantry had stickers on the ends of their guns." Convinced by the evidence of the negro that the artillery was not unprotected, Dahlgren made a detour to the left, keeping beyond the range of the guns. The only loss sustained by the Artillery was that of the members of a court-martial, which was in session in a house on the enemy's line of march; whereupon a wag remarked that as the court, prisoners and witnesses were all present the trial might go on and the proceedings be sent to Gen.

Long, from Point Lookout, or Fort Delaware. The prisoners escaped, however, with one exception, during the following night. The two raiding columns failed to coöperate, due to Dahlgren being led astray by a faithful negro slave. Kilpatrick reached the inner line of defenses of Richmond, and, attacking alone, was repulsed. Dahlgren moving down the James River Valley, some of the distance on the tow path of the canal, burned many barns, seized all the horses for his men he could lay his hands on, and almost captured Mr. Sedden, the Confederate Secretary of War, and Gen. Wise, who were visiting their families at "Sabot Hill" and "Eastwood." But these worthies escaped on fleet horses, and took the news of the Federal approach to Richmond, where the Richmond School Cadets, and a nondescript band of departmental clerks and Home Guards, the latter consisting of old men and boys, were hastily thrown across Dahlgren's path, while the Tredegar Iron Works Battalion turned out to guard Belle Isle. The raiders galloped into an ambush which had been skillfully laid for them and were signally defeated. Dahlgren himself, and many of his men, were killed, and only a remnant of his band escaped.* Thus did the Federal plans come to naught, and thus did Gen. Long by the most admirable foresight save the Artillery of the 2d Corps. On three separate occasions a negro had materially befriended the Artillery.

Gen. Pendleton had spent the month of January on leave of absence in Lexington with his family, but returned to Artillery Headquarters at Louisa Courthouse on February 3. He was soon summoned to Richmond, and ordered to Dalton, Ga. Gen. Joseph E. Johnston, commanding the Army of Tennessee, had, upon taking command, found the Artillery of that Army in a highly-disorganized state and at once applied to the War Department for Col. Alexander to be sent to straighten things out. Writing on December 27 about the con-

---

*See *Memoirs of Robert E. Lee*, Long, p. 320, and *Battles and Leaders*, Vol. IV, p. 95. Also an interesting personal narrative in the *Century Magazine*, April, 1894, by Mrs. Ellen Wise Mayo.

ditions of his army, to Gen. Bragg, who was virtually
Mr. Davis' Chief of Staff, Gen. Johnston said:

"The artillery also wants organization, and especially a competent commander. I, therefore, respectfully urge that such a one
be sent me. I have applied for Col. Alexander, but Gen. Lee
objects that he is too valuable in his present position to be taken
from it. His value to the country would be more than doubled, I
think, by the promotion and assignment I recommend."* To this
communication, Gen. Bragg replied in March, in part, as follows:

"Col. Alexander, applied for by you, as Chief of Artillery, is
deemed necessary by Gen. Lee in his present position. Brig.-Gen.
W. N. Pendleton, an experienced Officer of Artillery, has been
ordered to your headquarters to inspect that part of your command,
and report on its condition.

"Should his services be acceptable to you, I am authorized to
say you can retain him.

"I am exceedingly anxious to gratify you on that point, for I
know the deficiency existing.

"It is more than probable that such a junction may soon be made
as to place Col. Alexander under your command."†

The foregoing correspondence gives one an idea of
the estimation in which Alexander was held throughout
the service. Since Gen. Pendleton exercised only an
administrative command of the Artillery, he was
naturally more available than Alexander for such duty
as required by Gen. Johnston. Leaving Louisa Courthouse, March 4, he arrived at Dalton, *via* Atlanta, a
week later, with Lieuts. Peterkin and Hatcher, of his
staff, and immediately set to work. There is no reason
to believe that his assignment was not satisfactory to his
new commander, notwithstanding the fact that a
younger officer had been applied for. Gen. Johnston's
greeting was most cordial, and the artillery situation in
its general aspects was at once laid before Gen.
Pendleton.

The personnel of Johnston's Artillery at this time
numbered approximately 4,500, exclusive of Alexander's command. Energetic measures had already
been taken to supply the western batteries with a full

---

*Johnston's Narrative, p. 288.
†Johnston's Narrative, p. 289.

complement of horses. Maj. Beckham had recently been promoted colonel, and transferred from Stuart's Horse Artillery to Johnston's Army, having been succeeded by Dearing, who had also been promoted. Maj. Bondurant had also been promoted at the instance of Gen. D. H. Hill, and transferred, as a lieutenant-colonel, and Chief of Artillery of D. H. Hill's Division. Pendleton at once took occasion to recommend for the position of Chief of Artillery, Col. Thomas H. Carter, of Virginia.

Some idea of the old general's energy and his peculiar fitness for work of the character to which he had been assigned may be had from the fact that although he only arrived in Johnston's camp at daybreak on the 11th, he commenced his inspection of the three reserve battalions commanded by Lieut.-Col. Hollinguist at noon the same day. This command constituted about one-third of all the artillery with the Army. Accompanied by Maj. Preston, Inspector-General of Artillery, and one of his aides, and provided with one of Gen. Johnston's own mounts, he made a minute inspection of the battalions assembled on the usual drill grounds, including the material, harness, field transportation, horses and stables. He was surprised to find the animals in fair condition, the guns, carriages and harness in very good order, and much evidence of intelligent care and energy. Conditions were so much better than he had expected to find them that at once he recognized the fact that the trouble lay elsewhere.

A grand review of the Artillery of Hood's and Hardee's corps was appointed for the 12th, to be followed by minute daily inspections of their various battalions. By the 16th, the actual work of inspection had been completed, and written inquiries submitted to the battalion commanders, in which various interrogations relative to the service were propounded. On the 16th, Gen. Hood conducted an imposing drill of his corps for the benefit of Gen. Pendleton, followed by combat exercises in which about 20,000 men, including infantry, artillery, and cavalry, engaged with blank ammunition.

Much to the disappointment of the Chief of Artillery notice was received the 19th that Brig.-Gen. Shoup had been ordered from Mobile to join Johnston as his Chief of Artillery. Shoup was a graduate of the United States Military Academy, had served at Vicksburg with great credit, and was reputed to be an able officer, but his preferment over Carter appears to have been only another evidence of the advantage held by West Pointers. Certain it is that his service had not been as illustrious as that of "Tom" Carter, of Pampatyke, a distinguished graduate of the Virginia Military Institute, a kinsman of Gen. Lee, a man of unblemished personal character, and with a record as a soldier second to none in the Confederacy.

Another great artillery drill and sham battle was tendered Pendleton by Gen. Hardee. But the event, while equally inspiring, was less eventful than the former one, on which occasion one of Hood's major-generals and part of his staff had been unceremoniously unhorsed by their affrighted mounts. This incident no doubt established the precedent for the grand review in Paris in 1910, when the Commander-in-Chief of the French Army was thrown at the feet of the President of the Republic. Gen. Hardee's bride was evidently more at home in the saddle than some of the western knights, for she attended the review mounted, and accompanied by a number of brilliant staff officers, without accident.

While in the West, Gen. Pendleton preached to the troops on many occasions. His military views and suggestions were in the main approved by Gen. Johnston, and reorganization had so far progressed during his presence that the task remaining for Gen. Shoup was much simplified. The main trouble had been found to be with the senior officers. Returning to Richmond, on March 29, *via* Charleston, where he and his staff officers inspected the harbor defenses, Pendleton promptly laid his report on the Artillery of the Army of Tennessee, and his recommendations regarding it, before the President. A conference with Mr. Davis, Mr. Sedden, and Gens. Bragg and Cooper, resulted in his being ordered back to Dalton to urge Gen. Johnston to make an aggressive move as speedily as possible, in order to distract the Federals and prevent the massing of more troops under Grant in Virginia. But before returning to the West, he visited Gen. Lee at the front, who concurred in the importance of his mission. Remaining with Johnston but two days, during which time he pressed upon him the desires of the administration, Gen. Pendleton was back in Richmond again by April 21, and soon joined the Army.

We have seen that in personal appearance he much resembled Gen. Lee. An amusing incident which occurred during his presence in Richmond should here be recounted. One afternoon he was stopped by a tipsy Irishman on Broad Street, who began haranguing and gesticulating violently as he detailed some fancied grievance. The ladies of the party wished to go on, but the General insisted on listening patiently for a few moments, then said, "My friend, you are talking to the wrong person." "My," said Paddy, "ain't you Mass' Bob?" "No," replied Gen. Pendleton. "Look and see if you don't know me." This answer seemed to steady the excited soldier. He came a little closer, peered into the General's face a moment, then giving himself a violent slap on the leg, exclaimed, "I'll swear if it ain't old Artillery." And with many apologies the embarrassed soldier allowed the general to pass on.

When Gen. Pendleton returned to the Army he found not only that Longstreet had returned to Virginia, and that many changes had occurred, but that all was not running smoothly in the administration of the Artillery. Gen. Long, it seems, desired that all connection between the Artillery and the Infantry in so far as the authority of division commanders was concerned, should be officially severed by order, and that the corps chiefs should be free to administer their commands as integral units. While this view was clearly expressed in *Orders No. 69, June 4, 1863,* reorganizing the Artillery, and while the Commander-in-Chief deprecated a clash of authority by reason of its misinterpretation, yet he was unwilling to destroy the old associations between the artillery battalions and the divisions with which they had so long served. These associations he regarded as a distinct asset. In this respect Gen. Long was overruled, and soon a better understanding ensued.

A further effort was also now made to equalize the armament of batteries and the strength of the battalions, and as more horse batteries were needed, Alexander and Long were each called upon to recommend a battery for conversion, the first from Huger's, and the second from Hardaway's Battalion. Alexander was also called upon to use his influence to secure the assignment of King's Battalion, to the 1st Corps of the Army of Northern Virginia.* Longstreet had returned to Virginia with his two divisions and Alexander's own battalion some time before this and had gone into camp near Mechanicsburg, about six miles south of Gordonsville. The return of Longstreet's men, who had served with marked distinction in the West, was honored by their being reviewed by Gen. Lee, the first ceremony of the kind he had conducted since October, 1862, when he reviewed his army in the Shenandoah Valley. Describing the scene, Gen. Alexander wrote: "It took place in a cleared valley with broad pastures, in which our two divisions of infantry, with my old battalion of artillery, could be deployed. . . . It is now over 40 years, but in imagination I can see to-day the large square gate posts, without gate or fence, for troops had been everywhere in that vicinity, marking where a country road led out of a tall oak wood upon an open knoll in front of the centre of our long double lines. And as the well-remembered figure of Lee upon Traveller, at the head of his staff, rides between the posts and comes out upon the ground, the bugle sounds

---

Rebellion Records, Vol. XXXVI, Part II, pp. 944, 945. This battalion had been serving in Southwest Virginia in a different department.

a signal, the guns thunder out a salute, Lee reins up Traveller and bares his good gray head and looks at us, and we give the rebel yell and shout and cry and wave our flags and look at him once more. For a wave of sentiment—something like what came a year later at Appomattox, when he rode back from his meeting with Grant,—seemed to sweep over the field. All felt the bond which held them together. There was no speaking, but the effect was as of a military sacrament."

Many changes had occurred both in the artillery officers and the batteries in the Army during the winter and spring. Besides Griffin's 2d Maryland Horse Battery, Dement's and Brown's 1st and 4th Maryland batteries, the latter now under Lieut. W. S. Chew, had also been transferred to the Maryland line. Blount's, Caskie's, Macon's, and the Fauquier Battery, the latter now commanded by Marshall, had been transferred under Maj. J. P. W. Read to Whiting's Division, and Owen's Washington Artillery Battalion to Colquitt's Division, both on duty in the Department of North Carolina. Early in May, Col. H. P. Jones was assigned to the command of these two battalions. The remnants of the Louisiana Guard Battery had been sent to Richmond for reorganization.

On the 1st of May, the Artillery with the Army on the Rapidan was organized as follows:

1st CORPS

Brig.-Gen. Edward Porter Alexander, Chief of Artillery

HUGER'S BATTALION

Lieut.-Col. Frank Huger
Maj. Tyler C. Jordan

Brooks' (S. C.) Battery,	Capt. William W. Fickling.
Madison (La.) Battery,	Capt. Geo. V. Moody.
Richmond Battery,	Capt. William W. Parker.
Bedford Battery,	Capt. J. D. Smith.
Bath Battery,	Capt. Esmond B. Taylor.
Ashland Battery,	Capt. Pichegru Woolfolk, Jr.

HASKELL'S BATTALION

Maj. John C. Haskell
Maj. James Reilly

Rowan (N. C.) Battery,	Capt. John A. Ramsey.
Palmetto (S. C.) Battery,	Capt. Hugh R. Garden.
Nelson (Va.) Battery,	Capt. James N. Lamkin.
Branch (N. C.) Battery,	Capt. John R. Potts.

CABELL'S BATTALION

Col. Henry Coalter Cabell
Maj. S. P. Hamilton

Battery "A", 1st N. C. Reg't,	Capt. Basil C. Manly
1st Co. Richmond Howitzers,	Capt. Edward S. McCarthy.
Pulaski (Ga.) Battery,	Lieut. Morgan Callaway.
Troup (Ga.) Battery,	Capt. Henry H. Carlton.

2D CORPS

Brig.-Gen. Armistead Lindsay Long, Chief of Artillery
Col. John Thompson Brown, Chief of First Division

HARDAWAY'S BATTALION

Lieut.-Col. Robert Archelaus Hardaway

Powhatan Battery,	Capt. Willis J. Dance.
1st Rockbridge Battery,	Capt. Archibald Graham.
Salem Battery,	Capt. Charles B. Griffin.
2d Co. Richmond Howitzers,	Capt. Lorraine F. Jones.
3d Co. Richmond Howitzers,	Capt. Benj. H. Smith, Jr.

NELSON'S BATTALION

Lieut.-Col. William Nelson
Maj. David Watson

Amherst Battery,	Capt. Thomas J. Kirkpatrick.
Fluvanna Battery,	Capt. John L. Massie.
Georgia Battery,	Capt. John Milledge.

BRAXTON'S BATTALION

Lieut.-Col. Carter M. Braxton
Maj. Marcellus N. Moorman

Alleghany Battery,	Capt. John C. Carpenter.
Stafford Battery,	Capt. Raleigh L. Cooper.
Lee Battery,	Capt. William W. Hardwicke.

Col. Thomas H. Carter, Chief of Second Division

CUTSHAW'S BATTALION

Maj. Wilfred E. Cutshaw
Maj. Robert M. Stribling

Charlottesville Battery,	Capt. James McD. Carrington.
Staunton Battery,	Capt. Asher W. Garber.
Richmond Courtney Battery,	Capt. Wm. A. Tanner.

PAGE'S BATTALION

Maj. Richard Channing Moore Page

King William Battery,	Capt. William P. Carter.
Jeff Davis Alabama Battery,	Capt. William J. Reese.
Louisa Morris Battery,	Lieut. ——————————.
Richmond Orange Battery,	Capt. Charles W. Fry.

3D CORPS

Col. Reuben Lindsay Walker, Chief of Artillery

POAGUE'S BATTALION

Lieut.-Col. William T. Poague
Maj. George Ward

Madison (Miss.) Battery,	Capt. Thomas J. Richards.
Warrenton Battery,	Capt. Addison W. Utterback.
"C" Battery, 1st N. C. Reg't,	Capt. Joseph Graham.
Albemarle Battery,	Capt. James W. Wyatt.

McINTOSH'S BATTALION

Lieut.-Col. David Gregg McIntosh
Maj. Marmaduke Johnson

Richmond Battery (Johnson's),	Capt. Valentine J. Chilton.
Danville Battery,	Capt. Berryman Z. Price.
2d Rockbridge Battery,	Capt. Wm. K. Donald.
Hardaway's Alabama Battery,	Capt. Wm. B. Hurt.

PEGRAM'S BATTALION

Lieut.-Col. Wm. Johnson Pegram
Maj. Jos. McGraw

Richmond Letcher Battery,	Capt. Thomas A. Brander.
Richmond Purcell Battery,	Capt. George M. Cayce.
Richmond Crenshaw Battery,	Capt. Thomas Ellett.

Pee Dee (S. C.) Battery,	Capt. Wm. E. Zimmerman.
Fredericksburg Battery,	Capt. Edward A. Marye.

CUTTS' BATTALION

Col. Allen S. Cutts
Maj. John Lane

"B" Battery, Sumter (Ga.) Batt.,	Capt. Geo. M. Patterson.
"A" Battery, Sumter (Ga.) Batt.,	Capt. Hugh M. Ross.
"C" Battery, Sumter (Ga.) Batt.,	Capt. John T. Wingfield.

RICHARDSON'S BATTALION

Maj. Charles Richardson
Maj. M. B. Miller

Norfolk L. A. Blues,	Capt. Chas. R. Grandy.
Donaldsonville (La.) Battery,	Capt. R. Prosper Landry.
Norfolk Battery,	Capt. Jos. D. Moore.
Pittsylvania Battery,	Capt. Nathan Penick.

HORSE ARTILLERY

Maj. Robert Preston Chew, Chief of Artillery

BREATHED'S BATTALION
Maj. James Breathed

Washington (S. C.) Battery,	Capt. James F. Hart.
1st Stuart H. A. Battery,	Capt. Philip Preston Johnston.
2d Stuart H. A. Battery,	Capt. Wm. M. McGregor.
Lynchburg Beauregards,	Capt. J. J. Shoemaker.
Ashby Battery,	Capt. James W. Thomson.

With Ransom's Division near Petersburg was Lieut.-Col. C. E. Lightfoot's Battalion, consisting of Hankins' Surry, Rives' Nelson, and Thornton's Caroline batteries; with Hoke was Eshleman's Battalion consisting of Martin's, Owen's, and Payne's batteries; and at Chaffin's farm was Maj. A. W. Stark's Battalion, consisting of Armistead's Mathews, and French's Giles batteries, Lieut.-Col. E. F. Moseley's Battalion of Cumming's and Miller's North Carolina, Staten's Georgia, and Young's Yorktown batteries, and Maj. J. C. Coit's Battalion of Bradford's Mississippi, Kelly's South Carolina, Pegram's Petersburg, and Wright's Halifax batteries. Including the eight batteries of

Owen and Eshleman, with Colquitt and Whiting, and
Green's Louisiana and Sturdivant's Albemarle batteries,
unassigned, there were then not less than 26 field batteries in the neighborhood of Richmond and Petersburg,
while there were 52 light and 5 horse, or a total of 57
field batteries with the Army on the Rapidan.   With
this army there were exactly 213 guns.*   The artillery
personnel numbered May 1st about 4,800 effectives.
Deducting this number from the effective strength of
the Army, and we have 213 guns for 57,000 infantry
and cavalry, or a proportion of nearly 4 guns per thousand men of the other arms.   The proportion of horse
guns to cavalry was exactly 2.5 per thousand, there being 8,000 troopers and 5 horse batteries of 4 guns each.
At this time the effective strength of the Federal Army
under Grant was about 119,000, including an artillery
personnel of 10,210 and 318 guns, or a proportion of
about 3 guns per 1,000 of the other arms.   One must
admire the ability of Lee to maintain so high a proportion of artillery in spite of the seemingly insurmountable difficulties in his way.   Yet his field army
was outnumbered in guns by the enemy by nearly a
third.

---

*Rebellion Records, Vol. XXXVI, Part I, p. 1036.   Gens. Humphreys and
Alexander estimated that there were 224.

CHAPTER XXXVI

BEFORE taking up the narrative of the next campaign, it may be interesting to glance once more at the four senior artillery officers of the Army at the time the Artillery arm had attained its maximum efficiency in personnel, material, and organization. At the close of its third year, it was truly a formidable corps, though somewhat reduced in the number of its guns. With the purely military record of its commanders, we are already quite familiar, but what was the contemporary and what is a fair estimate of them at this time?

Gen. William Nelson Pendleton, by far the senior in age as well as in rank among the officers of this arm, like Bishop Polk of the Western Army, entered the service of the Confederacy, as we have seen, from the service of the church. Born at Lexington, Virginia, December 23d, 1809, he was appointed a cadet at the United States Military Academy in 1826, graduating with his class. While at West Point he formed a lasting friendship with Robert E. Lee and Jefferson Davis. Assigned to the Artillery, he served one year in the garrison of Augusta, Ga., with the rank of second lieutenant, and was then ordered back to the Academy as assistant professor of mathematics. Subsequent to this duty, he served with troops at Fort Hamilton, where he resigned in 1833 to accept the chair of mathematics at Bristol College, Pennsylvania, later becoming connected with the faculty of Delaware College. In 1837, he became a clergyman in the Episcopal Church, influenced to enter the ministry by the spirit of revival, which reigned at West Point while he was a cadet, many of his school-day companions doing the same. When the war broke out, he was serving as rector of the Lexington parish. His entrance into the Confederate military service as the original commander of the Rockbridge Artillery has already been mentioned.

While Gen. Pendleton possessed many virtues as an administrator, he lacked the dash requisite to popularity as a soldier. The officers and men of the Army knew little about his ceaseless activity in matters pertaining to the equipment and arming of his command. His constant attention to the care and preservation of the material and horses was practically unknown to them, nor are such things of a nature calculated to add to the reputation of a soldier. They are regarded as matters of course, and little interest is shown by the troops in them. Boldness and dash in the presence of the enemy appeal to the soldiery of an army. With such qualities an officer, entirely lacking in administrative ability and skill as an organizer, will acquire repute quite incommensurate with his true merit. The faithful performance of the drudgery of the service adds little to the lustre of a military name.

Pendleton was never conspicuous as a leader in battle, though, as we have shown, he was by no means lacking in courage. He was regarded from the first as slow and lacking in aggressive spirit, and his natural caution due to his age led to unfounded accusations. His name was unjustly coupled with the midnight route at Shepherdstown, after the battle of Sharpsburg, in an unpleasant way. Notwithstanding a court of inquiry, appointed to investigate the incident, clearly established the fact that no blame attached to him for his conduct on that occasion, yet a military reputation is bound to suffer, even when unjustly involved in such an incident. In this case, the tongue of the scandal monger was simply set to wagging all the more. Unfortunately, Pendleton was again present and in command when the Artillery was withdrawn from the heights of Fredericksburg before Sedgwick's advance. Not only was he absolutely free of blame on this occasion, but as has been shown and testified to by Gen. Early, who was with him, the guns were removed over the protest of the Chief of Artillery. The withdrawal on this occasion was the result of a serious mistake on the part of one of Gen. Lee's own staff officers. Pendleton's critics entirely overlooked the fact that Early, who was really in command at Fredericksburg, withdrew his troops at the same time, yet no question ever arose over the conduct of Early. The readiness with which Pendleton's action was taken up and adversely discussed shows the sentiment in the Army with respect to him. The feeling was not unknown to Pendleton. His staff officers got wind of the calumnies that were being circulated and very promptly informed him, in order that he might defend himself against such gross injustice. Gen. Pendleton at once addressed Gen. Lee upon the subject, with the result that he received the following letter from the Commander-in-Chief, which should for all time dispose of any doubts as to the propriety of his conduct on this occasion.

"ORANGE, September 15, 1863.

"GENERAL—Your letter of 8th inst., inclosing one from Maj. Page, reached me at a time when I was pressed by business that had accumulated during my absence. I cannot now give the matter much attention, and have only been able to read partially Maj. Page's letter. I think the report of my dissatisfaction at your conduct is given upon small grounds, the statement apparently of your courier, upon whom I turned my back. I must acknowledge I have no recollection of the circumstances, or of anything upon which it could have been based. The guns were withdrawn from the heights of Fredericksburg under general instructions given by me. It is difficult now to say, with the after-knowledge of events, whether these instructions could, at the time, have been better executed, or whether if all the guns had remained in position, as you state there was not enough infantry supports for those retained, more might not have been captured.

"I am, very respectfully, your obedient servant,

"R. E. LEE,
"*General.*"

It would seem that Pendleton's critics did not know that some of the batteries, which were withdrawn in obedience to the order which Chilton transmitted erroneously, had proceeded too far towards the rear to return in time to take part in the final action. They only knew a part of the story—that is, that all the Artillery was withdrawn, and that some of it did not return.* What was known was sufficient, however, for those who were willing enough to put the worst construction on the affair. They took full account of Pendleton's haste to withdraw his guns, in obedience to the peremptory order he received, the tenor of which order they did not know, but they overlooked the haste with which he returned to his position when the error in that order was discovered.

The fact that Gen. Lee suggested the permanent retention of his Chief of Artillery in the West by Gen. Johnston while it certainly proves Pendleton was not indispensable to the Army of Northern Virginia, does not prove his services were not valued. The Artillery had gradually attained a corps organization under three most competent corps chiefs. These officers were not only administrative, but tactical commanders, and under their immediate control fell all the artillery of the Army. Very naturally Pendleton, whose duties had become in the process of evolution purely administrative, could be better spared than Alexander, who was applied for by Johnston, or either of the other two tactical commanders, Long and Walker. It must not be thought, however, that Pendleton had become superfluous because no tactical command remained to him. One only need recall the splendid service he rendered the Artillery by that general supervision, which led in one instance to the creation of the remount department, and in another to the establishment of forage districts in the winter of 1863-64. The Artillery, in fact the Army, owed much to his foresight in innumerable matters of this character, which were quite beyond the province of the corps commanders and their chiefs of artillery.

After everything is said in his favor that can be said, the fact remains that Gen. Pendleton, though admired

---

*For foregoing incident see chapter on battle of Chancellorsville.

by those who knew him for the integrity of his character, was not rated by the officers and men of the Army of Northern Virginia as an efficient field soldier. We believe, however, that it has been shown that he was far more efficient than he was thought to be by his contemporaries, who were generally ignorant of his true worth and services. In the popular and contemporary estimate of Pendleton, an element entered, the influence of which we can now fully appreciate. The delicate task of the various reorganizations of the Artillery from the beginning to the end of the war fell solely upon his shoulders. Promotion was necessarily very slow, and much discontent existed among officers really entitled by their services to reward, but for whom the number of vacancies at no time afforded promotion. Under such circumstances, dissatisfaction was as general as it was inevitable, and to Pendleton, whose recommendations were final, the malcontents of course attributed the fact that their merits were not recognized. His position was not an enviable one, and, lacking those qualities which enable a commander to silence the voice of the malcontents under him by the brilliancy of his achievements, it was not strange that Pendleton's popularity as a soldier suffered. The old officer fully appreciated the unenviable character of the duty he was called upon to perform, but never once did he complain. He set about his task with the utmost resolution to perform it as best he could, and relieve Gen. Lee of as much of the burden of command as he could take upon himself. His recommendations, as we have seen, were invariably the result of the most careful consultation of the wishes of the corps and division commanders of the Army, and were never submitted until he had brought to bear upon the claims of all the most mature deliberation, with the result that the selections of the Chief of Artillery were quite generally believed by unprejudiced parties to be judicious and eminently fair in every respect. The knowledge on the part of Gen. Lee that Pendleton would allow no political or personal considerations to influence him in making his recommendations, was alone a sufficient reason for his retention as Chief of Artillery, especially since there was no necessity for his exercising a tactical command. It would indeed have been difficult to find another as conscientious and as free of all bias as was Pendleton.

Personally Gen. Pendleton, so much like Gen. Lee in appearance, was a most lovable man. His influence for good in the Army was great, and never once, despite the asperities of war, did he lose sight of his mission as a minister of the gospel, for he was a Christian of the highest order, in fact as well as by profession. It is a well-authenticated fact that on more than one occasion his entrance into battle was preceded by an invocation of a blessing upon the enemy. It is related that at Haynesville, his first engagement, before giving the word of command to open fire he raised his hand aloft and in a loud voice, so that his men might hear, exclaimed: "May God have mercy upon their souls."*

After the war, Gen. Pendleton, who had made a noble sacrifice to the cause in the loss of his only son, Col. A. S. Pendleton, returned to his pulpit in Lexington, where he spent a part of his remaining years in close and constant companionship with his immortal leader. Together Pendleton and Lee ceaselessly labored, the one as rector, the other as a vestryman, in building up the Episcopal Parish of their community. Outliving Gen. Lee some years, Pendleton died January 25, 1883, and, like his former commander and devoted friend, is buried in Lexington, beside his son, and within the shadow of Jackson's monument.

Brig.-Gen. Armistead Lindsay Long, next in order of seniority to Pendleton in the Artillery, was an officer of exceptional merit and high accomplishments. Born in Campbell County, Virginia, September 3, 1825, he was graduated from the United States Mili-

---

*When asked if this were true by a brother minister, the Rev. Mr. Royce, now rector of New Windsor Parish on the Hudson, Gen. Pendleton admitted that it was. Thus the incident seems to be without the vale of mere tradition. The Rev. W. N. Pendleton was granted the degree of Doctor of Divinity in 1868.

tary Academy in the Class of 1850. On duty as a second lieutenant in the 2d Artillery at Fort Moultrie for two years, he was then promoted first lieutenant, serving for the next nine years on the frontier of New Mexico, at Barrancas Barracks, Fort McHenry, Fort Monroe, and taking part in the various Indian campaigns in Indian Territory, Kansas, and Nebraska. When the crisis between the States arrived, he was on duty at Augusta, Georgia, from which point he was transferred to the National Capital, where he resigned his commission June 10, 1861, after 11 years of service. While in the Old Army, he had been placed under Capt. Hunt, later Chief of Artillery Army of the Potomac, for special instruction, and under the tutelage of that able artillerist he had acquired an exceptional knowledge of the theory as well as the practice of gunnery. He also served, in 1860, as aide on Gen. E. V. Sumner's staff.

An interesting anecdote concerning Gen. Hunt and Long may here be recounted. At Appomattox Gen. Hunt sought out Gen. Long to render him such services as he could. In the course of their conversation, Hunt told his old friend that he was not satisfied with the artillery preparation at Gettysburg, inasmuch as he, Long, had not done justice to his instruction; that the Confederate batteries, instead of concentrating their fire on the point of attack, were scattered over the whole field. Long was much amused at the criticism of his former tutor and said: "I remembered my lessons at the time, and when the fire became so scattered wondered what you would think about it."

Repairing to Richmond immediately after resigning from the Old Army, he accepted a commission as Maj. of Artillery in the Confederate service, and soon accompanied Gen. Loring in the capacity of Chief of Artillery to West Virginia.* After this service in the Trans-Alleghany Department, he was assigned in the

*Resigned June 1, 1861; reached Richmond July 18, on which day he was appointed Major of Artillery.

fall of 1861 to duty under Gen. Lee as chief-of-staff in the Department of South Carolina, Georgia, and Florida. When Gen. Lee was given command of the Army of Northern Virginia Long was appointed his military secretary with the rank of colonel. In this capacity he was recognized as the artillery expert of Gen. Lee's staff, and rendered valuable service in connection with the Artillery at Fredericksburg, Chancellorsville, and Gettysburg. In his professional ability and special knowledge of artillery Gen. Lee reposed great confidence, and it is readily seen that his assignment to tactical command was most acceptable to Army Headquarters. His preferment over Col. Brown as Chief of Artillery of the 2d Corps was not viewed at headquarters as a slight in any sense to that officer, and as he ranked Alexander and Walker, and held his commission in the Artillery, his prior appointment to them as brigadier-general was not a technical promotion over their heads. Yet, in a sense, his preferment over Alexander, Walker, and Brown especially, was felt to be at the time not wholly justifiable, in spite of his eminent ability and long service. This was most natural, since he had not been so thoroughly identified with the Artillery as they and others had been. It was the old story of the claims of line officers and staff officers. The former always feel that active duty with troops entitles them to more consideration than officers, even superior in rank, whose service has been principally on the staff.

In the selection of Long for Chief of Artillery of the 2d Corps, the personal equation undoubtedly entered, and such influences must never be lost sight of in the consideration of army, as well as other appointments. It must also be remembered that his service in the Old Army had been longer than that of any other artillery officer of the Confederate Army.

Thirty-nine years of age at the time of his appointment as brigadier-general, he was six feet tall and of handsome and commanding presence. His hair was dark, and his complexion swarthy. A small military mustache gave him a decided French appearance. In manner Gen. Long was most affable, even gentle, but beneath his pleasing exterior there lay a sternness of character apparent to all. Of wide intellectual attainments and rare culture, he was perhaps one of the most profound military scholars in the Army. He certainly had no superior in the Confederacy in the theoretical knowledge of his special arm, and beside was a tactician of exceptional merit. As an organizer, he was superior to Alexander, and probably the equal of Walker, but he lacked the unusual dash of the former. We believe it is a fair estimate of Gen. Long to say that taken all in all he was one of the most accomplished officers in the Army of Northern Virginia.

As to his personal character, no one who has read his *Memoirs of Gen. Lee,* the best military historial work of the kind yet written, can entertain a doubt. Bereft of his eyesight after the war and at the time this splendid work was written, he displayed in its preparation the most remarkable patience and persistence, and evidenced a lack of bias and prejudice equalled by few writers on the war. It also testifies to the careful mental training of the author, and his wide knowledge of the military science in all its branches.* Gen. Lee entertained a high regard for him as evidenced by the following testimonial written after the war: "Gen. A. L. Long entered the Confederate service in 1861, and has served continuously till the surrender of the Army of Northern Virginia, April 9, 1865. His conduct during that time has been marked by zeal and gallantry. . . ."

Reuben Lindsay Walker, Chief of Artillery 3d Corps, was the last to attain the rank of brigadier-

---

*After the war closed, Gen. Long was appointed Chief Engineer of the James River and Kanawha Canal Company. In 1869 he lost his eyesight from injuries received from the explosion of a caisson in the service, and subsequent exposure. He then removed to Charlottesville, where he resided until his death, April 29, 1891. It was during the last twenty years of his life that he wrote his *Memoirs of General Lee,* which were published in 1886. He also wrote reminiscences of his own career, a comparative sketch of Stonewall and Andrew Jackson, and a *History of America in the Seventeenth Century.* By reason of his infirmity, he was compelled to use a slate prepared for the use of the blind, and to depend upon the members of his family and on his friends for much assistance. Under all these disadvantages he labored on uncomplainingly, recording the history of his immortal leader of whom he was a most devoted admirer, cheerful and courageous to the end.

general in Lee's Artillery. He was born on his paternal
estate, Logan, Albemarle County, Virginia, May 29,
1827, and was therefore about the same age as his kinsman, Gen. Long. In his veins flowed the best blood of
the Old Dominion, being a son of Capt. Lewis Walker,
and a descendant of forebears who had been prominent
in the early settlement of the western part of the State.
By every influence of blood, environment, and tradition, he was trained to be a leader of his fellows, and
was perhaps the most picturesque figure in Lee's
Army. Of immense frame and exceptionally broad
shoulders, he was as handsome in figure as in countenance. Six feet four inches or more in height, his hair
was long and dark, and a sweeping mustache and imperial beard added to his soldierly appearance. Above
all he was a superb horseman and seemed to have been
born to the saddle in spite of his immense stature. In
repose his face wore a grave expression, and a piercing
black eye, capable of great intensity, enhanced the individuality of his features. His brow was massive and
his head sat gracefully upon his shoulders. Looking
into his handsome face, no man could doubt the determination and the will-power which animated and characterized his being. In manner Walker was not particularly alert, and while by no means dull, his mind was
not an active one. In physical hardihood, fixity of purpose, dogged determination, and dauntless courage, he
was unexcelled by any officer in the Army. But while
he was bold, he cannot be said to have possessed the dash
of Alexander, Pelham, Pegram, Chew, or Breathed, or
the intellectual brilliance of Long and Alexander. His
forte was organization, and it was generally conceded
that he had throughout the war the best organized artillery in the Army, whether it were a battery, a battalion, or a corps division under his command. His
character was distinguished by great integrity, resolution and devotion to duty. His admiration for and
confidence in Gen. Lee were unbounded, and few
soldiers were ever as much beloved by officers and men

under their command as was Reuben Lindsay Walker. Upon being asked to give his estimate of Walker as a soldier, his old adjutant, Capt. William W. Chamberlaine, declared that in addition to Gen. Walker's ability as an organizer, his most striking characteristics were his intuitive knowledge of country, his appreciation of terrain, and his ability to select and occupy the best available positions for his guns and then to hold them with great pertinacity. From this, one sees how his experience as an engineer stood him in good stead as a soldier.

The following incident well illustrates Walker's character. As a cadet at the Virginia Military Institute, where he was graduated with the Class of 1845, he had for three years committed every offense, short of one which would have resulted in his dismissal. Gen. Smith, the Superintendent, narrates that he sought to reduce him to good order and submission in many ways. Threats, penalties, and punishments of the severest nature only sufficed to confirm the imperious youth in his course of utter disregard of all regulations. Admiring the young man for his lovable nature, his superb physique, and his unflinching courage in adversity, the Superintendent at last sought to appeal to his pride by appointing him a lieutenant in his first class year. From that time on, Cadet Walker was an example of all that was conscientious, dutiful and soldierly. Never once did he prove derelict in the discharge of the trust reposed in him. And this may be said of his career as an officer in the Army.

Walker followed the profession of Civil Engineering until the outbreak of the war. Visiting Richmond in February, 1861, he was promptly seized upon by Mr. Purcell, a patriotic citizen, who had undertaken to recruit and equip a light battery at his own expense, and placed in command of it. Not even was Capt. Walker permitted to return to his home, then at New Kent Courthouse, but he was hustled off with the famous Purcell Battery to Aquia Creek, without even bidding his wife farewell. From the day of this unceremonious departure for the front, he had never had a day's leave of absence from his command, and when next he met his wife he was introduced to a child nearly a year old which had been born to his wife in his absence. Such was the fortitude of both men and women in those days. But this particular mother had suffered separation enough from her husband. From thenceforth she accompanied her soldier husband in the field. Mrs. Walker's ambulance and mules, driven by a faithful white retainer, was a familiar sight to the men of the Army of Northern Virginia. From battlefield to battlefield she moved with the ammunition trains, often bivouacking with her children along the roadsides in her improvised house on wheels, when the neighborhood afforded no shelter in the homes of friends and relatives. In her determination to remain close to her husband's side, not only did she accept all the hardships of campaign, but she also added a new member to her family. For a brief space only did this Spartan mother desert her husband in the midst of the perils of war. She followed him to the end, ready to carry his stricken body from the field, or minister to him in sickness and disease. On one occasion while her driver was absent Mrs. Walker's team of horses was impressed by a not-overscrupulous Confederate teamster. Other horses could not be purchased, but so insistent was the good lady that means of transport be secured for her ambulance, that soon her faithful retainer appeared with a fine pair of mules branded with the familiar "U. S." It has never been explained whence they came.

Strange to say that with all this loving care and constant attendance on the part of his wife, Walker was never once wounded, in the sixty-three engagements in which he participated during the war, nor was he invalided at any time. In latter years he even grew sensitive to the inquiry. "Why General, not wounded in the war?" Invariably he would draw himself up to

the full height of the giant that he was, and, squaring his
massive shoulders, reply, "No, sir, and it was not my
fault."*

And now we come to Alexander, who among the
senior officers was the artilleryman *par excellence* of
Lee's Army, though third in rank in his arm. A
graduate of West Point in the Class of 1857, his service
in the Engineer Corps, then as Commandant of the
Corps of Cadets and instructor of gunnery, his service
on the plains and in connection with the development
of the Myer signal system, we are already familiar with,
as well as with his early service in the Confederacy, first
as artillery instructor, then as signal officer on Beauregard's staff, and then as Chief of Ordnance of the Army
of Northern Virginia. To repeat, entering the Confederate service April 3, 1861, as a captain, at the age
of 24 years, he was commissioned lieutenant-colonel of
artillery in December, 1861, and colonel a year later.
After the most distinguished service in every battle from
Fredericksburg to date, he was commissioned brigadier-
general of artillery February 26, 1864.

Although Alexander had accompanied Longstreet to
Tennessee, and served in the capacity of his Chief of
Artillery in the Knoxville campaign, not having reached
Chickamauga with his battalion in time to participate
in the battle, he was in fact, up to the time of his promotion, the inferior in rank of Colonels Walton and
Cabell, though of the same grade with them. But while
their inferior, he had for some time practically directed
the tactical employment of the artillery of his corps.

---

*Surrendering with the army at Appomattox, Walker, who was promoted
Brigadier-General of Artillery in January, 1865, retired to private life as a
farmer, with a record of having participated in sixty-three engagements during
the four years of his military service. In 1872 he removed to Selma, Ala.,
where he was Superintendent of the Marine and Selma Railroad. In 1876 he
returned to Virginia in the employment of the Richmond and Danville Railroad,
and was later Superintendent of the Richmond Street Railway Company. Soon
he was engaged as constructing engineer of the Richmond and Alleghany Railroad, or the present James River Division of the Chesapeake and Ohio Railway.
In 1884 he became superintendent of construction of the Texas State Capitol, and
resided at Austin until 1888. Much scandal in connection with the previous
management of the work led the authorities to place it in his hands, by reason
of his known integrity. He was handsomely rewarded for the faithfulness and
efficiency with which he discharged the trust. He died at his home, "Point of
Forks," on the James River, June 7, 1890, where he spent the last two years of
his life as a farmer.

At Fredericksburg, he was the directing genius of Longstreet's defense. It was there, in referring to the positions of his guns on Marye's Hill, that he remarked to his corps commander: "We cover that ground so well, that we will comb it as with a fine-tooth comb. A chicken could not live on that field when we open on it." And as has been seen, Alexander's forecast was quite fulfilled. Again at Gettysburg where Col. Walton, his senior, and the nominal Chief of Artillery, was present, Alexander was in complete control of the Artillery in the fight. On former occasions, his recognized ability had merely enabled him to influence the disposition of the artillery under Walton's immediate control, but at Gettysburg we find him as a junior officer actually in command, while his senior was present and participating in the battle. This has always seemed a remarkable anomaly, not so much as to the wisdom of it, but that Walton would consent to it. A careful investigation and study of the matter discloses that it came about in the following way: Col. Walton was old, and physically unequal to the exertions of the campaign. Though a meritorious officer, of dauntless courage, and with a fine military record, he now lacked the energy to keep pace with events. Already one of his former battery commanders, Eshleman, had supplanted him as active leader of the celebrated Washington Artillery Battalion. Longstreet knew Walton's capabilities full well, and while he retained the gallant old officer as Chief of Artillery of his corps, both for political and personal reasons, he did not feel that he would be justified in committing the tactical leadership of the artillery to his hands, for those or any other considerations. In the movement upon Gettysburg, Walton's Battalion was held back, whether intentionally or not cannot be determined, but at any rate, Alexander arrived on the field some time in advance of Walton and was placed in charge of the artillery already up. An important mission was entrusted to him, and upon its discharge the young officer had already entered when his senior arrived. The situation was such that when Walton did come up, no consideration of rank could be allowed to jeopardize the success of the battle already under way. Such arguments were unanswerable, and however chagrined Col. Walton may have felt, he was powerless to deny the force of the circumstances which debarred him from the exercise of the tactical command to which his rank entitled him. That he was chagrined is quite well established by the verbal testimony of his contemporaries and his own letters, and it was not long before he expressed the desire to be transferred to service at Mobile. In justice to the old officer, his wish should have been instantly complied with. In fact, he should have been given the opportunity to transfer, before being publicly overslaughed. But he was retained on the roll of the 1st Corps, and after being gradually sidetracked by being assigned to duty as Inspector-General of Artillery at Large and placed on detached duty, relinquished his commission in the 1st Corps July 8, 1864.

From the time of his first appearance in the Artillery, in fact in the Army, young Alexander was a marked man and one destined to attain preëminence in his arm. Rapidly he acquired a reputation which extended far beyond the Army in which he was actually serving. First Jackson sought to have him appointed a general officer in the infantry, then Johnston urged his transfer to the Western Army, with advanced rank. But he was too well appreciated in the Army of Northern Virginia to permit of his loss. Stephen D. Lee might be spared to the far South, but not Alexander to the West. The young Georgian was needed in Virginia.

In appearance, Alexander did not present so fine a military figure as did Long and Walker. Of about the average height, and of muscular build, yet he was by no means a handsome man. In fact, his features were rather irregular, and the scraggly, ill-shapen beard, which his youth afforded, failed to hide a decidedly ugly mouth. But his eye was bright and penetrating, and about the man, both in his general appearance and carriage, was the unmistakable evidence of high breeding and exceptional intellect, and these appearances did not belie the facts, for he was the scion of a noble stock, and brilliant beyond his years. To the latter fact, his whole career at West Point and in the Old Army testifies. No man becomes an engineer officer and the Commandant of the Corps of Cadets at the United States Military Academy unless he possesses rare qualities of mind and heart combined.

In manner, Alexander was active and alert, and his whole character was vibrant with intenseness. Strong in likes and prejudices, he was yet most amiable and possessed the traits which make men socially popular. As an officer, he was quick to estimate the situation before him, prompt to direct, and inexorably firm in holding his subordinates to their duty. He possessed wonderful personal magnetism, and transmitted much of his own enthusiasm and spirit to his subordinates. Above all things, he detested delay. Full of dash and the love of responsibility, he perhaps expected too much of others, in this respect forgetting that few men possessed that *élan* which characterized himself. His was a nature which loved prompt action; he liked rapidity of motion; anything that savoured of slowness, of lack of energy, of excessive deliberation, provoked him sorely. His mind was the kind that had figured out and matured the plans in advance which most men pause to consider when the time for action comes. He courted favor from no one, and while immensely energetic and ambitious he was yet able to forego an offered advancement in another arm in the evident knowledge that he was needed in his own. Endowed with such a nature and exuberant with vigorous youth, it was natural that he should have chafed at the shortcomings of others, for in his genuine lack of vanity he was unable to appreciate the fact that he himself was not like other men. He invariably measured others by his own standard, and few came up to it. This habit made him rather critical, and he never hesitated to express his views, hit whom they did, but he was never disloyal to Gen. Lee, nor to the memory of Gen. Longstreet. In fact, his devotion to the latter carried him, in an attempt to defend his old corps commander, beyond the limits of sound reasoning, as one who studies his book, in other respects a masterpiece of critical analysis, will discover.* Like Long, his writings prove him to be a man of exceptional intellect, a wide student of war and human nature, and to have possessed a remarkable lack of bias. In his memoirs, much after-acquired information was of course brought to bear upon the solution of the military problems of the war, however conscientiously he may have sought to view things from a contemporary standpoint. The author was a much wiser man when he wrote his book than when he was actually confronted by the problems which others were called upon to solve, but no one is misled by his sagacity after the event, for it is not difficult to distinguish between his contemporaneous foresights, and the maturer reflections of the author, or his hindsights.

Brig.-Gen. Edward Porter Alexander, age 27 years, was a soldier, who, had he served Napoleon, would have been rewarded by a baton, for he possessed those soldierly characteristics so dear to the Emperor. He was far and away the superior of all others in his arm, whose opportunity was equal to his own. Like Gen. Hunt of the Federal Army, he was preëminent in the Artillery of his army. His opportunities were never equal to those of Senarmont and Drouot, for even Gettysburg cannot properly be compared to Friedland and Wagram; the tactical combinations were so different that the number of guns engaged forms no basis for comparison. Nevertheless, as written by Maj. May, R. H. A., the names of Hunt and Alexander are as worthy of remembrance as are those of the two great artillerists of the Grand Army. Then, too, it must be remembered

---

*Military Memoirs of a Confederate, published by Charles Scribner's Sons in 1908.

that Alexander had no leader who held him always in hand, prepared to throw his masses of guns into action, as did Napoleon at the crisis of the combat, thus enabling the Artillery to reap the fame of victory, when the way to inevitable success had been carefully paved. On the contrary he, like the other artillery commanders, while given a free hand, was always expected to shoulder a burden from the first, which precluded the more brilliant maneuvers of the battlefields of the French. Their services were none the less valuable; they simply show in a different light.   The issue largely depended on the efforts of the Confederate artillerymen, but no great reserve masses existed to be employed at the psychological instant, and win for their leaders the credit of having capped the climax, so to speak.*

From now on, the historical narrative of events will trace the military careers of Lee's senior artillerymen subsequent to the period of which we write.   The foregoing discussion of their characters should give a better insight into the affairs of the Artillery in general.

*General Alexander, as we shall see, played a leading rôle in the Artillery until the close of the War.   After the Surrender at Appomattox, he became Professor of Mathematics and of Civil and Military Engineering at the University of South Carolina, in which position he served from January, 1866, to October, 1869.   He then became President of the Columbia Oil Company.   In May, 1871, he became Superintendent of the Charlotte and Augusta Railroad, and in October, 1871, President of the Savannah and Memphis Railroad.   In 1875 he became President and General Manager of the Western Railroad of Alabama, and of the Georgian Railroad and Banking Company.   He was Vice-President of the Louisville and Nashville Railroad from 1880 to 1882, Capital Commissioner of the State of Georgia from 1883 to 1888, and from 1887 to 1893 President of the Central Railroad and Banking Company, and the Ocean Steamship Company.   He wrote a valuable treatise on *Railroad Practice.*   His death occurred in 1911.

CHAPTER XXXVII

THE WILDERNESS

For six months the hostile armies had confronted each other along the Rapidan, and every man in both knew that the next campaign was to be the most serious one yet conducted. Gen. Ulysses S. Grant, who had been called from the West to take supreme command of the Federal forces, arrived in Virginia in March, establishing his headquarters at Culpeper Courthouse on the 26th. He had been by far the most successful Federal commander up to that time, and possessed an iron determination, which, coupled with the unlimited military resources placed at his disposal, served to revive the spirits of the North. Furthermore, his selection was a guarantee to those who knew him that military operations would be conducted from Army headquarters and not by the President, his cabinet, the press, and the politicians of the North.

Grant's strategy cannot be discussed here. Suffice it to say that his general plan was well formulated and it contemplated the thorough coöperation of the various Federal armies under his control, with a definite end in view. While that end was the subjugation of the South in the shortest possible time, the objective of the Army of the Potomac, under the immediate command of Meade, was the Army of Northern Virginia, and indirectly Richmond, since the two were by circumstances almost inseparably identified. Previous commanders had failed to appreciate the fundamental strategic principle that an enemy's capital must fall with the army which defends it, wherever that army may be. This fact was not ignored by Grant.

When Grant took charge the situation in Virginia was as follows: West Virginia was in the hands of the North, and all that part of old Virginia north of the Rapidan and east of the Blue Ridge. On the sea-coast,

Butler with the Army of the James, numbering about 30,000 men, held Fort Monroe and Norfolk. In North Carolina, the Federals held Plymouth, Washington, and New Berne, from which points Richmond could also be threatened. The 9th Corps under Burnside, 20,000 strong, was soon rendezvoused at Annapolis, Maryland, from which point it could reinforce Meade or operate independently along the coast.

Longstreet's Corps was at Gordonsville, Ewell's along the south bank of the Rapidan above Mine Run, and Hill's on his left, and higher up the river. The Confederate line was partially intrenched in position. Gen. Lee's headquarters were two miles northeast of Orange Courthouse. Meade's Army, consisting of Hancock's, Warren's, and Sedgwick's, or the 2d, 5th and 6th Corps, lay along the north bank of the Rapidan. The Army of the Potomac had never been so thoroughly equipped before, nor as powerful as a fighting machine. It was lavishly supplied with all a rich country could give it. The Army of Northern Virginia, on the other hand, little more than half as large as its persistent antagonist, was practically devoid of everything in the way of clothing and supplies. Its arms and the temper of the veterans which wielded them were, however, perhaps never better. Such was the situation on the 2d of May, when Gen. Lee with the utmost confidence examined with his glasses from Clark's Mountain on the south side of the Rapidan the Federal lines on the opposite bank.

Meade's activity in the direction of the upper fords had not deceived Lee for an instant, and on the 3d of May the Federals were discovered moving to his right, just as he had predicted they would be. He at once prepared to move upon Meade's flank with his whole force as soon as the enemy crossed the Rapidan and became entangled in the Spotsylvania Wilderness, through which the route selected by Grant lay. Again was Lee willing to forego the defense of a natural obstacle, which could in time be turned by superior numbers, in order to avail himself of the great advantage of a most difficult terrain, which he knew to be a *terra incognita* to his adversary. And again did the Federals play into his hands by entangling themselves in the gloomy wilderness, thus, in a measure, at least, neutralizing their numerical superiority.

The Army of the Potomac began to cross the Rapidan at noon, May 3, its way having been prepared by Sheridan's Cavalry. Bridges were laid in advance at Germanna, Ely's, and at Culpeper Mine fords, covering a front of about seven miles. Hancock, preceded by Gregg's Cavalry, crossed at Ely's Ford, and moved to Chancellorsville, which placed him on the left; Warren, with Wilson's Cavalry in front, followed by Sedgwick, crossed at Germanna Ford and followed the Germanna Plank Road, due southeast, to Wilderness Tavern. Sedgwick encamped for the night three miles south of the river. In these positions Meade's corps remained until 2 P. M. of the 5th, while the 65 miles of trains were crossing at Germanna and Culpeper Mine fords, the movement of which was more difficult than anticipated, and to which fact the unexpected delay in the advance was attributed. The situation was now about as follows: Near the Lacy house, where Grant, Meade, and Warren had established their headquarters, there were two roads, the Orange Turnpike on the right or south, and the Orange Plank Road on the north or left, both following the general direction of the river from Orange Courthouse to Fredericksburg and nearly parallel to each other. The route of the Federal Army lay directly across the two roads along the western border of the Spotsylvania Wilderness. When the Confederates gained contact with the Federal advance, Sedgwick's Corps in general occupied the Germanna, and Hancock's the Brock Road, while Warren's occupied the space within the obtuse angle made by the two.

About noon on the 4th of May, Lee put Ewell's Corps in motion along the Orange Turnpike, while

A. P. Hill with two divisions moved along the Orange Plank Road. The two divisions of Longstreet's Corps, in camp near Gordonsville, were ordered to move rapidly across the country and follow Hill's advance.

It was apparent from the first that the terrain selected by Lee for his initial operations would afford no opportunity for the effective employment of the Artillery, but instant steps were taken to bring it up and assemble it from its widely dispersed camps.

In the 1st Corps, Huger's Battalion which was recruiting at Cobham Depot, Haskell's Battalion, also in camp at that point, and Cabell's Battalion at Morton's Ford, where it had been on picket duty during the winter, were ordered on the 4th to rendezvous at Richard's Shop, where they arrived late in the night on the 5th, and at 3 A. M. on the 6th they marched for Parker's Store on the Plank Road in rear of the Army. Gen. Long's five battalions which had wintered at Frederick Hall, and which later in the spring had been moved to grazing camps near Liberty Mills in Orange County, also received orders to march on the 4th, and were concentrated early on the 5th at Locust Grove on the turnpike in rear of Ewell's Infantry. Walker, with four battalions of the 3d Corps, left Cobham and Lindsay depots on the 4th, and bivouacked that night near Verdierville, joining Hill on the 5th and accompanying Heth and Wilcox down the Plank Road. Cutts' Battalion of this corps, which had been on picket duty during the winter in the neighborhood of Rapidan Station, was directed to remain with Anderson's Division, which constituted the rear guard of the Army. The five batteries of the Horse Artillery which had wintered at Charlottesville and then moved to Gordonsville, were now operating with Stuart on Lee's right, and were constantly engaged in harassing the enemy's advance. The batteries had been ordered up from camp on the 4th, and most of them were engaged the next day with Rosser on the Catharpin Road.

The rapid concentration of the Artillery at the front was effected in a most creditable manner, and is sufficient evidence of the high state of efficiency of the arm at this time. Nothing so tests the metal of field artillery as long and rapid marching. In this instance it was assembled without a hitch of any kind, every battalion moving as if by clockwork. One need only measure on the map the distances covered by the various batteries between the 4th and 5th of May to appreciate the celerity of their movements. Suffice it to say that many of the batteries covered 30 miles or more in less than 24 hours, all finding their appointed positions without mishap of any kind.

Ewell's Corps was the first to gain close contact with the enemy. As it advanced along the turnpike on the morning of the 5th, the Federal column was seen crossing the road from the direction of Germanna Ford. Ewell had been instructed to regulate his advance by the head of Hill's column, which Stuart was to lead to the south of him, and not to bring on a general engagement until Longstreet arrived. Promptly forming Johnson's Division across the road, he refrained from provoking the enemy, and communicated with Lee, who was still with Hill, but the position he occupied was on the flank of the Federal line of march, and very naturally such a collision soon led to active hostilities. Warren, whose troops were passing when Ewell came upon them, halted them and, turning to the right, made a vigorous attack upon Johnson's Division, with which Nelson's Battalion of artillery had been deployed. Milledge's Battery in front of Jones' Brigade on the right of the road was soon withdrawn when the infantry support was forced to fall back about two miles to the Flat Run Road, where it intersects the turnpike. Jones was roughly handled, but Steuart's Brigade was pushed forward and Rodes' Division was thrown in on its right, south of the road. When the line was thus reëstablished, the Confederates pressed forward vigorously and, after desperate fighting in the dense woods which hid friends and foe alike, drove back the enemy. Ewell's entire corps had now come up, Johnson's Division across the turnpike, Rodes on his right, and Early in reserve. Few practicable positions were available for artillery, but Nelson had placed some of his guns on a commanding ridge with a small field in their front on the right and about a mile from the Lacy house. Two of his guns were also placed on the road leading to the Germanna Road to operate with the infantry of the left wing. In these positions the Artillery rendered such aid as it could in repelling the attacks of the Federals during the afternoon.

Soon after Warren's repulse, Sedgwick moved up to his right to oppose Early, who moved into the front line and, supported by several of Nelson's guns, clung to his position on the Federal flank, in spite of every effort to dislodge him. The Federal efforts continued until nightfall.

The collision with Ewell at first led Meade to believe Lee had only left a division to oppose his progress, and to impose upon him while the main army was being concentrated across his path on the North Anna, but when Hill's advance was also discovered on the Plank Road, Meade abandoned his original view. It was but a short time after Ewell became engaged when Hill struck the Federal outposts near Parker's Store, just at the edge of the Wilderness, and drove them in upon Sedgwick's column which was moving along the Stevensburg and Brock roads to Spotsylvania Courthouse. Heth's Division, followed by the corps artillery with Poague's Battalion in the lead, first encountered the enemy's cavalry, whereupon Richards' Battery was thrown forward and assisted in driving in the outposts. The head of Hill's column reached an opening on the left of the Plank Road at midday, at a point about two miles from its intersection with the Brock Road, and was halted. From the ridge occupied by Heth, the enemy was seen in force to the north and dispositions were at once made for an encounter. The small clearing on the ridge afforded the only practicable position for artillery. There, near the Widow Tabb's house, Gen. Pendleton, after consultation with the Commander-in-Chief, established Poague's Battalion. Poague moved one of his pieces down the road a few hundred yards and placed it in line with Heth's Infantry. This, as will be seen later, was most fortunate for the Confederates.

Immediately upon discovering Hill's presence, Meade recalled Hancock's Corps, which was marching from Chancellorsville to Spotsylvania Courthouse, and at 4 P. M. Hancock was ordered to drive Hill "out of the Wilderness," which he had entered. Wilcox was brought up to Heth's support and then ensued a desperate encounter between the individuals of both sides. Division, brigade, regimental, and even company leading was out of the question. At no time were more than a handful of men in sight from any one point, and the troops simply fell upon each other and locked in a death embrace, as chance directed their steps. As darkness approached, the flashing muskets alone marked the contending and intermingled lines. But never once was the road occupied in force by the enemy, for Poague's single piece, with the gallant battalion commander himself beside it, swept the approach and completely dominated it from first to last. The battalion from its position on the ridge was practically debarred from participating in the struggle, as its fire would have been as dangerous to friend as to foe in that seething cauldron which boiled beneath its muzzles. Meanwhile the other battalions of the 3d Corps were held in the immediate rear of Hill's Infantry.

When the battle closed at 8 o'clock, Ewell's and Hill's Corps had already formed a junction at a point about halfway between Parker's Store and the Orange Turnpike. Longstreet was now ordered to make a forced march during the night and arrive upon the field before dawn. Moving at 1 A. M. of the 6th, it was daylight when he reached Parker's Store on the Plank Road, three miles in rear of Heth and Wilcox.

All night Hill's advanced troops, who had maintained themselves so resolutely and successfully against Hancock's six divisions, heard the Federals preparing to renew the attack in the morning. Worn and much cut up by the fighting of the previous afternoon and expecting relief during the night, the infantry failed to prepare to meet the inevitable attack. The lines were much disordered, and commands were mixed. But not so with Poague's Battalion on the ridge in the clearing.

At 5 A. M. Hancock's troops swept forward and soon overlapped Wilcox's Division south of the road, rolling it up and compelling Hill's whole line to retire in confusion past the single battalion of artillery, which stood alone like a wall of flame across the enemy's path. Not until the great masses of Hancock's troops came face to face with the artillery did they cease to press forward, but no troops could pass through such a storm of fire as that which Poague now opened upon them. The gunners worked with almost superhuman energy, the muzzles belched their withering blasts, the twelve pieces blended their discharges in one continuous roar, and there among them stood beneath the dense canopy of smoke, which hovered above the four batteries, Lee himself as if with a halo of war above his head. The great commander knew then full well that between him and disaster Poague's Battalion stood alone. What glory for a soldier! This single incident brought more of honor to the little colonel of artillery than most soldiers attain in a life of service. It would be hard for some to imagine in those soft, mild eyes, so familiar to the writer, the light which must have radiated from them as he stood among his guns on the 6th of May, 1864, the bulwark of Lee's defense, and in the very presence of his immortal commander. But one who has been thrown with him, who has learned to know the quality of the man, must feel that no heroism could transcend the limits of his soul. And yet the incident is not referred to by the historians of our time. We read that Poague's Battalion was present in the battle of the Wilderness. No more. Even Morris Schaff, whose writings are inspired with the noblest sentiments of appreciation, and whose studious work on the battle of the Wilderness is by far the best yet written, overlooks the heroic deeds of Poague, though no more ready hand than his ever brought the pen to bear with sweeter touch for friend and foe alike. In the saving of such incidents to posterity, of deeds unrecorded by contemporaries, almost unknown even to the present generation, one must feel thankful to the Goddess of Fame, nay, more, to the Almighty that it may be done.

For awhile as Gen. Lee stood among Poague's unsupported guns, matters were indeed in a critical condition for the Confederates. After sending a courier to hasten the advance of the 1st Corps, and another to prepare the trains to be moved to the rear, he at last discerned the dust thrown up by the hurrying feet of Longstreet's men. In perfect order, with ranks well closed and no stragglers, the double column swung down the road at a trot, and, regardless of the confusion which beset their path, these splendid troops pressed on to the point of danger. At their head rode Longstreet at his best, ardent for the fray, as if but now he had slipped the leash which held his tugging columns in check. Rapidly deploying into line on the right of the road, Kershaw's Division obliqued to the right under a withering fire to meet the Federal left which had all but outflanked Poague's batteries, and which was working havoc among them. On the left of the road, Field's Division also deployed and swept past the guns, among which the men detected Gen. Lee, whom they cheered lustily. When they perceived that "Marse Robert" contemplated leading them in the charge, they cried loudly for him to forego his intention. "We won't go unless you go back," shouted the Texans, while one of the gallant fellows seized his bridle rein and turned Traveller to the rear. Gen. Gregg then urged Gen. Lee to do as the men desired him to do, but it was with evident disappointment that Lee turned off and joined Gen. Longstreet.

As Longstreet's men swept onward, McIntosh's Battalion was thrown into position by Walker on Poague's left, while three of the guns of Price's Battery advanced along the Plank Road with the infantry. Pegram's Battalion soon went into action on the ridge, half a mile to the left of McIntosh's, to oppose the efforts of the enemy to penetrate between Ewell and Hill. Later on Cutts moved up to the support of Pegram, while Richardson's Battalion and Alexander's entire corps artillery were held in reserve at Parker's Store.

Longstreet's charge was irresistible; the Federals were first checked in their advance and then driven back past their first line of log works. Back and forth for two hours the lines of battle surged, settling down at length almost where they had rested during the night before.

Simultaneously with these events on the Confederate right, the Federals had made an unsuccessful effort to turn Ewell's left next the river, the brunt of the attack falling upon Early's Division, behind the flank of which Col. Carter had massed a number of his guns. The batteries there posted were heavily engaged and rendered splendid service in repelling the attack upon Gordon's Brigade. Cutshaw's Battalion was placed by Gen. Long on the right of the turnpike, relieving Nelson's batteries in their old position, while Hardaway's Battalion relieved those guns of Nelson's Battalion on the Germanna Road. Braxton's Battalion occupied a position further to the right, about midway between the turnpike and the Plank Road, from which point it was able to cross fire to a certain extent with Pegram's guns behind Hill's left. While seeking an advanced and much exposed position for the three battalions of his division early in the morning, the veteran artillery officer, Col. John Thompson Brown, fell, instantly killed by the bullet of a sharpshooter, adding another illustrious name to the list of artillery officers lost in battle. Little can be added concerning Col. Brown to what his superiors in his own arm have written of him.

In his report, Pendleton wrote of this much lamented officer: "To the fine qualities of a Christian gentleman of superior and cultivated intellect were added in Col. Brown very high excellencies as a soldier. Judicious, prompt, energetic and of dauntless gallantry, he had rendered conspicuous service in every campaign of the war. His example will not be forgotten in the arm to which he was an ornament, nor his memory be uncherished by a grateful country." And, of him Gen. Long, whose senior artillery division commander he was, wrote: "His loss was deeply felt throughout the whole army. He not only exhibited the highest social qualities, but was endowed with the first order of military talents. On every field where he was called to act he was distinguished for gallantry and skill. The Artillery will ever remember him as one of its brightest ornaments."*

By 8 A. M. Anderson's Division had rejoined Hill's Corps. Meanwhile, it had been discovered by Gen. Lee's engineer that the Federal left flank rested in the air only a short distance south of the Plank Road, near the unfinished railroad. When this was reported to Longstreet about 10 A. M. he at once organized a column of four brigades, G. B. Anderson's and Wofford's of his own, and Mahone's and Davis' of Hill's Corps, for the purpose of turning the Federal flank. Moving rapidly to the right and then forward, the column was deployed along the railroad at right angles to the hostile line. About 11 A. M. the four brigades, led by Col. Sorrell in person, Longstreet's Adjutant-General, advanced, striking the flank of the Federal line in reverse, while a general attack was instituted along the Confederate front. The success of Longstreet's brilliant movement was complete. From a tactical point of view no more beautiful movement was executed during the war, and it only serves to show the remarkable ability of Longstreet as a tactician when his was the plan that was

*For full and accurate account of the life and military career of this superb officer, see *The University Memorial,* p. 560.

being executed. Brigade after brigade of the enemy was rolled up and routed. Hancock, totally unable, in spite of the noted influence he exercised over his men, to stay their flight, was compelled to content himself with reforming them along the Brock Road, where luckily he had thrown up hasty intrenchments the preceding day. Panic had seized upon two whole Federal corps, and a great Confederate victory seemed assured when Longstreet, who rode forward south of the Plank Road, at the head of five fresh brigades to press his advantage, fell before a volley from one of Mahone's regiments advancing at right angles to his own course, and which mistook Longstreet and the group of officers about him for Federals. But Longstreet was not so seriously wounded that he could not place Gen. Field in command and direct him how to proceed. He explained that one of his columns should continue the direct attack, while the other moved further around Hancock's left by a route which Gen. Smith had reconnoitered and was thoroughly familiar with. If this were done, the already-broken enemy would be forced to surrender or be destroyed. Before Field, however, got under way, Gen. R. H. Anderson, his senior, then Gen. Lee himself, arrived. Longstreet's knowledge of the situation was of course not possessed by either Lee or Anderson. They only found the lines much disordered, and before the realignment which the former directed to be made could be effected, much delay had ensued. It was 4:15 p. m. before Field's and Anderson's divisions renewed the attack. Thus at the very crisis of the battle, when the enemy was not only already defeated, but an appalling disaster stared Meade in the face, Lee's second great lieutenant was smitten and this almost within gunshot of the field where Jackson fell just twelve months before. In fact part of the enemy's forces occupied the old Chancellorsville battlefield at the time.

It would almost seem that Providence was fighting against the Confederates. Certain it is that Fate was against them, for in the battle of the Wilderness even another ill-fortune had fallen upon Lee's Army. Before 9 A. M. Gordon had discovered the exposed character of the Federal right wing, and had later verified the reports of his patrols by personal reconnaissance in its rear. He at once reported the fact to Early, and begged to be allowed to attack Sedgwick, with a view to rolling up his line. But Early objected on the ground that Burnside, whose troops were arriving on the field, would be found behind Sedgwick. Gordon knew from personal observation that Burnside was not there, and in vain he appealed, first to his division commander, then to Ewell, to be allowed to attack, urging them both to verify his own information. Ewell was completely dominated, however, by Early, and neither went himself nor sent any one to investigate the situation for him. About 5:30 P. M. Gen. Lee, astounded by the inactivity on the left, rode over from the right where Longstreet and Hill had been so heavily engaged, to discover the cause of Ewell's silence. Gordon, in the presence of both Ewell and Early, explained the situation to Gen. Lee as he knew it to be, with the result that he was ordered to attack at once. The attack took place just as the sun went down, too late to reap the fruits of a surprise which to Sedgwick was as great as Longstreet's flanking attack had been to Hancock. Moving around to their rear, Gordon alone drove the Federals from a large portion of their works and took 600 prisoners, and among them two general officers. But darkness intervened to save Sedgwick just as a bullet had saved Hancock and Warren, and so Grant's army was saved from destruction and enabled to fall back and establish a new line for the defense of which Burnside's entire and almost wholly fresh corps was now available.

Viewing Meade's precarious situation throughout the 6th, it seems certain that had Gordon been permitted to attack when he desired to, his effort, which would have been closely connected in time with Longstreet's success on the right, would surely have brought complete disaster to the Army of the Potomac. What he accomplished at 6 P. M. could have been done at 11 A. M., and with an enemy in his front and in rear of both flanks, it is inconceivable that Meade could have successfully withdrawn his army, even had the terrain favored him instead of practically eliminating all possibility of the movement of broken troops.

During the day, Stuart had persistently sought to penetrate to the left rear of Meade's Army, but found Sheridan confronting him at all points. The conflict between the cavalry of the two armies was continuous, and in the various more or less disjointed affairs between Stuart's brigades and those of Sheridan, the Horse Artillery was actively engaged. Johnston's Battery remained in position near Shady Grove, Thomson's and Shoemaker's being heavily engaged near Rowe's farm, and Hart's not far from Todd's Tavern. McGregor's Battery remained at Orange Courthouse, with W. H. F. Lee's Brigade. The nature of the cavalry operations in the dense country was such, of course, as to preclude the possibility of Chew's handling the battalion as a unit. On the 6th, when with Rosser, who was engaging Wilson on the Catharpin Road, Chew personally led Thomson's Battery in the charge of the cavalry brigade, and, throwing the guns into action just before the troopers struck the enemy, did fine execution with them. The next day at Rose's farm, where Stuart was in command, he again accompanied the cavalry in a charge with his old battery, much to the delight of Stuart, who now seems to have realized for the first time that in Maj. Chew, Pelham had a worthy successor.* Stuart's previous lack of appreciation of Chew was most natural, for the two had scarcely ever been thrown together before this time. It seems unfortunate that the association of such bold and congenial spirits was so brief. But the wide recognition of this artilleryman's

*"Gen. W. N. Pendleton—Your note concerning Dearing is just received. Maj. Chew, the officer now in charge of the Stuart Horse Artillery, is doing so well that I am disinclined to put any one over him, although I have a high appreciation of the officer you propose. I think Chew will answer as the permanent commander, and, being identified with the Horse Artillery, is therefore preferable to others.
"J. E. B. Stuart, *Major-General*, April 6, 1864."

ability and the reputation as an unexcelled leader of horse artillery which he had established for himself were all the more to his credit since he owed nothing to the great Stuart for them. Indeed, his service since Ashby's death had been quite independent of illustrious commanders, and he therefore reflected none of the lustre of others. He was a self-made soldier in the highest sense of the word, and the fact that he could by his own merit acquire precedence over such an officer as Breathed, so long and so familiarly associated with Stuart, may seem remarkable to those who have never known the man. Slight personal contact with him is sufficient, however, to brush away all surprise. Near seventy years old at the time this is written, Col. Robert Preston Chew retains the mental activity and much of the physical hardihood of youth. Erect, of full muscular development and above the average height, with a handsome face upon which character has delineated its unmistakable features, in appearance he is the ideal soldier, and he is as much beloved by those with whom he is now associated in his peaceful pursuits, as he was by the splendid men of the Confederate Horse Artillery during the war.*

---

*Col. Chew now resides in Charles Town, West Virginia. He tells the writer that he is engaged in writing the history of the Horse Artillery. May God spare him until he has completed the priceless record he alone is now capable of preparing, and for many years to come.

CHAPTER XXXVIII

SPOTSYLVANIA

GRANT had utterly failed on the 5th and 6th of May to carry out his plan of "swinging past" Lee's Army and placing himself between it and Richmond, and while Lee had delivered the Federal Army a stunning blow, it still remained on its route, now secure behind strong works, and with Hunt's tremendous force of artillery established in position with the usual skill of its commander. It was impracticable for the Confederates, who had established themselves upon the flank of Grant's line of operations, to attack Meade's Army. Whatever the conditions may have been in the Federal Infantry, which had been so roughly handled, and which had escaped complete disaster by the merest chance, Lee knew that Hunt was undismayed and that no troops could sweep over that superb line of guns in the Wilderness. So both armies lay behind their intrenchments on the 7th, contenting themselves with skirmishing along the front. Meanwhile, Lee kept a close lookout for a movement of the enemy to his right and directed the Chief of Artillery to open roads for the movement of the artillery in that direction, should it be needed there. The work was quickly accomplished by working parties from the various batteries of the 3d Corps, under the immediate direction of Col. Walker. At the same time, Gen. Long made a reconnaissance under orders from Gen. Ewell on the extreme left. Taking Jones' infantry brigade and W. P. Carter's Battery, Long moved around to Beale's house on the Germanna Road, where he struck several regiments of Federal cavalry, which were quickly dispersed by the battery. No other hostile troops being found, it was evident that the enemy was withdrawing from before the Confederate left, for the dead and wounded still lay upon the field in that quarter. Soon after Long made the report of his reconnaissance to Lee, Stuart, about 3 P. M., discovered Meade's trains moving to the Confederate right, and later the unmistakable rumble of moving columns along the Brock Road was heard.

With roads clear of the trains, Meade had been ordered by Grant to move his troops at 8:30 P. M., and to establish one of his corps at the Courthouse, twelve miles distant, one at the crossroads known as the Brock House, and one at Todd's Tavern.

About dusk, Gen. Lee directed Pendleton to send a staff officer to Anderson, who had succeeded Longstreet in command of the 1st Corps, to guide him over the roads cut through the woods. Without a doubt in his mind as to Grant's intention, Lee had taken up the race for position at Spotsylvania. Going himself to Anderson, Pendleton described the route and left with him a competent staff officer to lead the column. Anderson's orders were to start at 3 A. M., but he knew the route he would have to follow to the Courthouse was longer than that pursued by the Federals, so he set his troops in motion at 11 P. M., four hours earlier than ordered. We shall see later how fortunate was the exercise of this initiative on his part. The Artillery of the 1st Corps, which had not been engaged the two preceding days, was ordered to follow the infantry column from Parker's Store.

Anderson's two divisions, with Alexander's Artillery, had about 15 miles to travel, but Fitz Lee and Hampton kept the road open and held back the cavalry during the night in front of Spotsylvania and at Corbin's Bridge, by blockading the narrow avenues of approach through the forest with felled timber. Alexander moved during the night by way of the Shady Grove Road and Corbin's Bridge, rejoining the infantry about daylight near the Po River, where the 1st Corps rested and prepared breakfast. Already the efforts of the Federals to brush the cavalry from their front could be heard in the heavy firing to the left. Grant and Meade, as was their

entire army, were sure the race had been won by them,
and heavy attacks were being made by Wilson's
Cavalry, on Rosser at the Courthouse, and by Warren's Corps on Fitz Lee at the Spindler farm on the
Brock Road.   Reaching the Brock House at 7 A. M.,
Anderson sent Kennedy's and Humphreys' brigades,
with two batteries of Haskell's Battalion, to the assistance of Fitz Lee about a mile away, and Wofford's
and Bryan's brigades with the rest of the Artillery to
Rosser half a mile further to the front.   Haskell's two
batteries at once became involved in a desperate conflict, in which Capt. Potts was mortally wounded.
After two hours they exhausted their ammunition, but
not until they had rendered most effective service in repulsing a charge of three of Warren's brigades.   Field's
Division now came up to the support of Kershaw's two
brigades, and extended his line to the left.   Five batteries of Huger's Battalion were then posted by Alexander
on a ridge in the edge of the pine thicket on the Todd's
Tavern Road, where the cavalry had made its stand,
and Cabell's Battalion was held in reserve.   Fitz Lee
when thus relieved joined Rosser at the Courthouse
and together they compelled Wilson to retire before
them.   This enabled Wofford and Bryan to rejoin Kershaw.

After Robinson's repulse, Griffin's Division rendered
two assaults, the first suffering a complete repulse, the
second enabling the Federals to establish themselves
under cover about 400 yards to the right front of the
Confederate line, where they began to intrench.   Crawford's Division next came up and extended Griffin's
line to the left, and then Cutler's Division attacked the
Confederate left without success, and prolonged
Griffin's line of intrenchments to the right.   During the
latter's attack, all five of Cabell's batteries under Maj.
Hamilton were brought into action.   Meantime
Haskell's two batteries, which had suffered severely on
the Todd's Tavern Road under a reverse fire from a
horse battery near the Courthouse, were withdrawn.

Anderson had won his race and Warren's whole corps had been halted over a mile short of its goal by two small Confederate divisions, and the bold use of the artillery, which in places had been brought into action within 400 yards of the enemy, and not over 100 yards from their skirmishers. Instead of being in position waiting for Lee at Spotsylvania Courthouse, the advance of Meade's Army was completely cut off from it and the direct routes thereto.

Both Lee and Meade now began to hurry forward their troops. Ewell had left the Wilderness at dawn and arrived in position on Anderson's right just in time to assist in severely repulsing the combined attack about 5:30 P. M., of Warren's and Sedgwick's corps upon Anderson's line. In this affair nearly every gun of Alexander's command was actually engaged, but only a few of Long's that were in position in front of the Courthouse took part, the bulk of the 2d Corps Artillery arriving later and going into park near the Courthouse for the night. The 3d Corps, under Early, which had been left behind as a rear guard, did not leave its old position until late on the 8th, bivouacking for the night near Shady Grove. During the day a single section of McIntosh's Battalion was engaged with the enemy's cavalry, which pressed upon the flanks of the 3d Corps as it advanced.

Upon arriving at Spotsylvania, early on the 9th, the 3d Corps, with the exception of Mahone's Division, extended Ewell's line of intrenchments to the right, while Mahone moved to a commanding position on Anderson's left, overlooking the Po. The Confederates had now established a line covering Spotsylvania Courthouse, with the 1st Corps on the left resting across the Po River, the 2d Corps in the center north of the Courthouse, and the 3d on the right crossing the Fredericksburg Road. While the brigades and divisions were frequently shifted, these positions were generally maintained during the battles that ensued.

During the 9th, while no attack was made by either side, an incessant sharpshooting was kept up, resulting in many losses to both sides, including the gallant Gen. Sedgwick, who was killed on the Brock Road. The day was largely devoted to the strengthening of old and the construction of new breastworks. The Confederate batteries were extended along the entire front of the line, and most of the guns placed in pits or behind slight epaulments. Cabell's Battalion occupied an elevation in rear of and slightly above Anderson's left, with four guns under Maj. Gibbes on the extreme left of the infantry line. On Cabell's right and in the second line were posted Haskell's Battalion, and Woolfolk's Battery. Huger's remaining five batteries were placed in the infantry line. Beyond them and also with the infantry, Page's and Braxton's battalions were in position with the 2d Corps. The field of fire for the guns at this point, as at the Wilderness, was very limited and the terrain afforded little opportunity for the effective use of artillery. Further to the right and on the left of the Courthouse clearing, Long posted Hardaway's and Nelson's battalions, while Cutshaw's was held in reserve on the road behind them. In the 3d Corps, Walker, upon arriving, dispatched McIntosh's Battalion to the extreme left, where it went into position behind Mahone at a point where the Shady Grove Road crosses the Po River. Poague's Battalion occupied the infantry works on the left of the 3d Corps line, Pegram's the line where it crossed the Fredericksburg Road several hundred yards from the Courthouse, and Cutts' a position on the extreme right in advance of the road to Massaponax Church. Richardson's Battalion was held in reserve behind the center. Thus it is seen that nearly every gun in Lee's Army was in position either in the advanced line, or in works close behind. The nature of the terrain absolutely forbade the effective massing of guns for the more effective command of a given field of fire. The situation demanded, if artillery were to be employed at all, that it should fight with the infantry, and simply endeavor to sweep the field in its immediate front, and thus supplement the musketry fire. Truly the Artillery was to fight as infantry at Spotsylvania. There was to be no such thing as artillery tactics there. It was simply a question of how much it could increase the intensity of the fire of the defense. No question of the time and the manner in which that fire was to be delivered was open to discussion, for tactics were ruled out in favor of the knock-down-and-drag-out method, which the topography imposed upon the Artillery. Never in all the war was the Confederate Artillery called upon to serve in such a manner as in the days of Spotsylvania.

The principal activity of the enemy on the 9th was in front of the Confederate left and center, but the Artillery fired only a few rounds and those principally at the enemy's sharpshooters whenever they were seen to gather in sufficient numbers to afford a reasonable target.

Hancock crossed his three divisions over the Po on the afternoon of the 9th and occupied the Shady Grove Road, thus threatening the Confederate rear and endangering the trains which were parked on the road leading by the old Courthouse to Louisa Courthouse. Lee's main line was north of the Po, with its left, Field's Division of the 1st Corps, resting on the stream at a point just above the crossing of the Shady Grove Road. Mahone, as we have seen, had been posted with McIntosh's Battalion on the other side of the stream to protect the flank. Lee ordered Early on the morning of the 10th to move around Mahone's left and strike Hancock's right. Taking Heth's Division, Richardson's Battalion and Ellett's Battery of Pegram's Battalion, Early moved to the rear and then followed the Louisa Courthouse Road across the Po until he reached a road coming in from Waite's Shop on the Shady Grove Road. Moving about a mile along this road, he met Hampton's Cavalry falling back before Hancock, who had pushed out a column of infantry somewhat to the rear of the Confederate line. After driving the Federal advance back to the Shady Grove Road, Early reached Waite's Shop, from which point Heth attacked in earnest, but he was twice repulsed in his effort to gain the ridge upon which only two of Barlow's brigades were posted with artillery, for Hancock had already withdrawn his other divisions. In this attack, Richardson's Battalion came under a heavy artillery fire, and was suffering severely, when Pendleton caused Cabell's Battalion, from its elevated position behind Anderson's left, to concentrate upon the enemy's guns. The effect was instant and Richardson was relieved from a nasty situation. A fire now broke out in the woods, and although Barlow had not been driven from his ridge by Early, Meade ordered him to withdraw to the north side of the stream. Mahone's Division now crossed from the east bank, as the road was clear, with several of McIntosh's batteries, and inflicted some loss upon the retiring Federals, who were compelled to abandon a gun which had been wedged between two trees by its affrighted team. Night was now approaching, and as the enemy was found with artillery well intrenched on the north bank, Early refrained from further attempts and soon Heth returned to the right, leaving Mahone in possession of the position on the Shady Grove Road, from which Barlow had been driven. To this point, all of McIntosh's guns were brought up during the night and intrenched.

During the fighting on the extreme left, Meade had made a tremendous effort to break Lee's line. First a demonstration was made against the right immediately in front of Spotsylvania Courthouse, but the attacking infantry was roughly handled and driven back to their trenches by Cutts' and Pegram's battalions. The main attack was directed against Field's Division on the left, and meeting with a bloody repulse was renewed at 3 P. M. with the same result. In these affairs Cabell, Huger, and Haskell were all heavily engaged. Alexander had posted their guns in such a way that they partially enfiladed the approaches to the infantry line, and as Warren's troops advanced through the dense thickets in Anderson's front, the woods were riddled with canister, which effectually broke the enemy's formation. As the Federals emerged in bad order, unable to reform under the Confederate musketry fire, but few of them were able to press home, and these were cared for by the infantry, many of the men of which were double armed with the muskets previously abandoned in front of the works by the enemy earlier in the day. The intensity of the Confederate musketry fire, thus increased, was unusual. A lull of several hours now ensued. About 7 P. M. Hancock made the third assault on Anderson's line with Birney's and Gibbon's divisions supported by the 5th Corps. Near sunset, Anderson's skirmishers were suddenly swept back, and almost without warning the successive lines of the enemy were soon seen surging forward at the trot. Rushing forward, the front line dissolved, but on came the determined supports, driving the Confederates from their works, but failing to break their resistance. The line of the defenders was nearly bent back by the pressure and the fight continued in the rear of the breastworks until Anderson's Brigade, which had cleared its front, was able to turn upon the flank of the assailants and drive them over and beyond the works which they had so gallantly taken.

As to the character of the work the Artillery performed in these attacks, a vivid description of the foregoing affair by the adjutant of Cabell's Battalion is here inserted:*

"The troops supporting the two Napoleon guns of the Howitzers (1st company) were, as I remember, the Seventh (or Eighth) Georgia and the First Texas. Toward the close of the day, everything seemed to have quieted down, in a sort of implied truce. There was absolutely no fire, either of musketry or cannon. Our weary, hungry infantry stacked arms and were cooking their mean and meager little rations. Some one rose up and looking over the works—it was shading down a little toward the dark—cried out:

*Four Years under Marse Robert, Stiles, p. 254.

'Hello! what's this? Why, here come our men on the run, from—
no, by Heavens! it's the Yankees!' And before any one could
realize the situation or even start towards the stacked muskets, the
Federal column broke over the little works, between our troops and
their arms, bayoneted or shot two or three who were asleep, before
they could awake, and dashed upon the men who were at their
low fires,—with cooking utensils instead of weapons in their hands.
Of course they ran. What else could they do?

"The Howitzers—only the left, or Napoleon section was there—
sprang to their guns, swinging them around to bear inside our
lines, double shotted them with canister, and fairly spouted it into
the Federals, whose formation had been broken in the rush and
plunge over the works, and who seemed to be somewhat massed
and huddled and hesitating, but only a few rods away. Quicker
almost than I can tell it, our infantry supports, than whom there
were not two better regiments in the army, had rallied and gotten
to their arms, and then they opened out into a V shape and fairly
tore the head of the Federal columns to pieces. In an incredibly
short time those who were able to do so turned to fly and our
infantry were following them over the intrenchments; but it is
doubtful whether this would have been the result had it not been
for the prompt and gallant action of the artillery.

"There was an old Capt. Hunter,—it seems difficult to determine
whether of the Texas or the Georgia Regiment,—who had the
handle of his frying-pan in his hand, holding the pan over the coals,
with his little slice of meat sizzling in it, when the enemy broke
over. He had his back to them, and the first thing he knew his
men were scampering past him like frightened sheep. He had not
been accustomed to that style of movement among them, and he
sprang up and tore after them, showering them with hot grease and
hotter profanity, but never letting go his pan. On the contrary,
he slapped right and left with his sooty, burning bottom, distributing his favors impartially on Federal and Confederate alike—
several of his own men bearing the black and ugly brand on their
cheeks for a long time after, and occasionally having to bear also
the captain's curses for having made him lose his meat that evening.
He actually led the counter-charge, leaping the works, wielding and
waving his frying-pan, at once a sword and a banner."

Now exactly how accurate this interesting account
is, the writer cannot pretend to say, but it is valuable
as is the following incident from the same pen:

"There were two men in the First Howitzers older than most
of us, of exceptionally high character and courage, who, because
of the deafness of the one, and the lack of certain physical
flexibility and adaptation in the other, were not well fitted for

regular places in the detachment, or service about the gun. For a time, one or both of them took the position of driver, but this scarcely seemed fitting, and one or both were finally classed as 'supernumeraries,' but with special duties under the surgeon of the battalion, as bearers of our camping litters and our other simple medical and surgical outfit. For this and other reasons the elder of these two good and gritty soldiers was always called 'Doctor.'

"When the break occurred these two men, always at the front, were overwhelmed with amazement, not so much at the irruption of the enemy, as at what seemed to be the demoralized route of the Georgians and Texans. They ran in among them asking explanation of their conduct, then appealing to them and exhorting them, the Doctor in most courteous and lofty phrase: 'Gentlemen, what does this mean? You certainly are not flying before the enemy! Turn, for God's sake; turn, and drive them out!' Then with indignant outburst: 'Halt, you infernal cowards!' and suiting the action to the words, these choleric cannoneers tore the carrying poles out of their litters, and sprang among and in front of the fugitives, belaboring them right and left, till they turned, and then turned with them, following up the retreating enemy with their wooden spears.

"Some weeks later, after we had reached Petersburg in the nick of time to keep Burnside out of the town, and had taken up what promised to be a permanent position and were just dozing off into our first nap in forty-eight hours, an infantry command passing by, in the darkness, stumbled over the trail handspikes of our guns, and broke out in the usual style: 'Oh, of course! Here's that infernal artillery again; always in the way, blocking the roads by day and tripping us up at night. What battery is this anyway?' Some fellow, not yet clean gone in slumber, grunted out: 'First Company Richmond Howitzers.' What a change! Instantly there was a perfect chorus of greetings from the warm-hearted Texans. 'Boys, here are the Howitzers! Where's your old deaf man? Trot out your old Doctor. They're the jockeys for us. We are going to stay right here. We won't get a chance to run if these plucky Howitzer boys are with us.' "*

Clearly Meade could not break Anderson's line. But he met with better success in the center, where he had massed about 40,000 of his men against Ewell's line. With the eye of an engineer, he had detected the weak point, where a long salient jutted out in advance of the

*The Richmond Howitzers had a splendid reputation throughout the Army. The personnel was unusual. Stiles and others tell us that it included many professional and college men, and that one of the privates actually kept a diary throughout the war in Greek. There was a law club in the battery, a trained Glee Club, and orations were frequently delivered in Latin at the gatherings of the men, as well as Greek odes.

general line, and in front of which there was a most
limited field of fire.   He saw that an overwhelming
force massed near the enemy's line could by sheer weight
break it at that point.   In the hasty extension of the
Confederate line on the 8th, Ewell, to keep on high
ground, had occupied with his left and center an elevation running nearly a mile in advance of Anderson's
line, then bending back so abruptly that the gorge of
the immense salient was but three-fourths of a mile
wide.   The forward angle of this salient was occupied
by Doles' Brigade, of Rodes' Division, and Smith's
Howitzer Battery of Hardaway's Battalion.   It has
since the events of the 10th been known as the "Bloody
Angle."

From the first, Meade had been reconnoitering and
feeling Ewell's weak point.   The Confederates behind
the works had thrown up traverses on both sides of the
salient at close intervals to protect themselves against
the enfilade fire of the Federal skirmishers, and other
than this no effort had been made to correct the evils of
the position.   On the morning of the 10th, Long had
relieved Braxton's and Page's battalions, substituting
Nelson's and Hardaway's battalions for them.   Nelson
now occupied Johnson's and Hardaway Rodes' front.

At 5 P. M. Col. Emory Upton silently led twelve regiments with fixed bayonets and loaded muskets through
the thicket in Doles' front, after carefully explaining
the part each was to play.   Upon reaching the works,
half the leading column of attack was to sweep to the
right and half to the left down the faces of the salient,
while a second line was to remain in position at the angle
and open fire to the front.

Upton's men succeeded in rushing the works at the
angle, and after a desperate hand-to-hand encounter,
swept the Confederates from behind their traverses;
many combatants on both sides were killed and
wounded.   But as the Federals swept through the gap
thus made, Daniels' Brigade on one side, and Steuart's
on the other drew back from their lines and fell upon

the flanks of the enemy, while Battle's and Johnson's brigades were hurried up from the left and thrown across the gorge. Mott's Division was to have supported Upton on the left, but upon forming for the advance, found itself the target of Hardaway's and Nelson's batteries on Ewell's right, and were compelled to abandon the task assigned it. In fact, Mott's brigades were broken by the Confederate Artillery, and driven back in confusion to the cover of their works at the base of the hill in Ewell's front. Assailed on three sides at once and unsupported, Upton's men were first forced back into the angle, in turn seeking cover behind the traverses, and then over the works, retiring in disorder to their own lines, after a loss of 1,000 men, or 20 per cent of the number engaged in the assault, while Ewell lost 650 men, 350 of whom were captured.

In the mêlée following upon the irruption of the Federals into Ewell's works, Smith's Richmond Howitzer Battery at the angle was seized by the enemy, but later recovered, the battery commander maintaining his fire until he with a number of his cannoneers was actually snatched from among the guns by the assailants. In the subsequent repulse of the Federals, Hardaway's remaining batteries were alone engaged. Thrown into position on the right of the salient, these four batteries had relentlessly poured canister into Upton's huddled troops and pursued them with their fire until they left the works. Two of Cutshaw's batteries which had been held in reserve near the Courthouse were rushed to the gorge, but were too late to assist in the repulse. As the Federals withdrew, some of the men of Garber's Battery of Cutshaw's Battalion, under their captain, entered the works and turned two of Smith's guns, for which no cannoneers remained, upon the fleeing masses. Both Lieut-Col. Hardaway, and his field-officer, Maj. David Watson, were wounded, the former slightly, the latter mortally, but in spite of a painful wound, Hardaway with his clothes riddled with bullets remained at his post and directed the fire of his batteries. The loss of Maj. David Watson was a serious one. In the words of the Chief of Artillery, this veteran artilleryman who had served from the very first of the war as a lieutenant at Yorktown with Magruder, then as captain of the 2d Company of Richmond Howitzers until his recent promotion, was "an accomplished gentleman, a faithful, patriot, and gallant soldier."*

Grant attributed the failure of Upton's attempt of the 10th to Mott's inability to advance, and on the 11th planned a much more powerful attack to be made by the whole of the 2d and 9th Corps. The angle was again selected for the focus of the assault.

A much exaggerated report of Federal activity on the Confederate left led Lee to believe that Meade would attempt to move in that direction during the night, so the chiefs of artillery were ordered to withdraw all their guns from the front line, in order that the Confederates might move under cover of darkness without being heard. Mahone's Division on the extreme left was ordered to march during the night and occupy Shady Grove before daylight. Gen. Long had in the morning placed Cutshaw's and Page's battalions in position along Johnson's front, the weakest part of Ewell's line, relieving some of Hardaway's batteries. Late in the afternoon the orders came to him to have "all of his batteries which were difficult of access" prepared to be removed before dark and was informed that the projected movement required him to be ready to take up the march at a minute's notice. He immediately ordered all the artillery on Johnson's front, except two of Cutshaw's batteries, to be withdrawn, as it had to pass through a wood by a narrow and difficult road, and the night bid fair to be very dark. Alexander showed more foresight on this occasion than Long, for he ventured to accomplish the intent of the order without

---

*For full and accurate account of his life and military career, see *The University Memorial*, p. 570. He was the devoted friend and companion of Col. Brown, who fell but four days before him. The sad coincidence of their deaths and the similar features of their characters and careers lead us to paraphrase what Tacitus wrote of Agricola, *"Similes non vitœ tantum claritate, sed etiam opportunitate mortis."*

literal compliance with it.   Thus while Long withdrew twenty-two guns of Page's and Cutshaw's battalions from the salient, Alexander visited every one of his batteries in person, had their ammunition chests placed on the limbers (they were usually dismounted and placed beside the guns in the pits), and the carriages so placed and the roads leading from the works so marked and prepared that they could easily withdraw without making the slightest noise.   All of Longstreet's guns, therefore, remained in position.

About 3 A. M., Lee discovered that Meade was massing for an assault upon Ewell instead of withdrawing from his lines, and the orders to the Artillery were at once countermanded.   But already Ewell's line, which had been caused to conform to the terrain for the sole purpose of affording the Artillery good positions, was practically stripped of its guns and now remained a dangerously weak projection, with a very poor field for musketry fire.   Naturally defective, yet with artillery so posted as to sweep its faces, many of the objections to the salient line had been overcome.   Now the line was totally lacking in defensive qualities, with the exception that a hasty line of intrenchment had been partially completed across the gorge.

All night Meade was engaged in massing Barlow's, Birney's, Mott's, and Gibbon's divisions in front of Johnson.   The charge was ordered for 4 A. M., but owing to a fog Hancock, who was to direct the attack, delayed until 4:35.   The distance to the Confederate works was about 1,200 yards.   The Federal masses were very compactly arranged, too much so for freedom of action over the ground to be traversed.   Moving off quietly and slowly, it was not until the Confederate pickets gave the alarm that the Federals broke into a run and commenced to cheer.

Johnson's men had heard the enemy's column forming, and repeated calls had been sent for the Artillery. Long had already received orders to return the guns to the works, and Cutshaw and Page were hastening back by separate routes.

The Federals came on, to use Gen. Johnson's words, "in great disorder, with a narrow front, but extending back as far as I could see." But there was hardly a gun to fire upon the seething, confused mass of Federals. Truly a great opportunity had been sacrificed, for it is dreadful to contemplate what the effect of Long's twenty-two guns would have been had they opened a concentrated fire on the Federal column. It is not difficult to picture the result, however, for that dense, overcrowded column would never have reached the Confederate works. What an opportunity was this for the artillery! Never since Pope uncovered Porter's flank at Second Manassas to Reilly's guns had the breast of the Federal Infantry been so bared. "Nowhere else in the whole history of the war was such a target presented to so large a force of artillery. Ranks had already been lost in the crowd, and officers could neither show example nor exercise authority. A few discharges would have made of it a mob, which could not have been rallied. There was a thick abattis of felled trees in front, and 'chevaux de frise,' which, Barlow says, 'would have been difficult to get through under a cool fire.' For the mob, which his division would have soon formed, there would have been no escape but flight, with phenomenal loss for the time exposed to fire.'*

"Had the Artillery been in position the result might have been different, or had the weather been favorable, the disaster might have been avoided; but the morning was so dark and foggy that it was with difficulty that we could distinguish friend from foe." These are the comments and explanations of Gen. Long, himself, but his guns were not there and he had lost his great chance. And here it may be said that nothing so well illustrates the difference between Alexander and Long as the manner in which they both complied with their orders on this occasion. We sometimes hear that great soldiers have often been the product of opportunity. But this is not generally true. The casual observer fails to de-

*Military Memoirs of a Confederate, Alexander, p. 520.

tect the fact that it is preparedness to profit by opportunity, and not merely the favor of fortune that enables
soldiers to win great reputations. Take for instance the
case just considered. Alexander sized up the situation
at a glance, and stood prepared to grasp what he foresaw
as a great opportunity, should it be presented to him.
Long failed utterly to realize what might be in store for
him, and neglecting to prearrange therefor, the greatest opportunity of his military career passed him by.
True he obeyed his orders and cannot be censured. The
point made is not one of blame, nor does opportunity
weigh orders.

The two leading guns of Page's Battalion only arrived in time to unlimber and fire three rounds between
them into the Federal masses before they were surrounded and seized. Twelve of Page's, and eight of Cutshaw's guns were then captured along with two-thirds
of Johnson's Division, including the division commander and Brig.-Gen. Steuart. Only the two rearmost
guns of Montgomery's Louisa Battery of Page's Battalion escaped.

The Confederate Infantry in the salient, deprived of
their artillery, had done all it could to check the onward
rush of the Federals. The whole thing happened so
quickly that neither Hancock nor Ewell at first realized
the extent of the disaster to the Confederates. After
their first success, the disordered Federals paused in the
advance to reform; as the fugitives from the salient
streamed to the rear, they met reinforcements from
the brigades of Johnston and Gordon on the right, and
from those of Daniel and Ramseur on the left, who
promptly checked the disorganized pursuers. The situation was indeed a critical one for the Confederates, and
Gordon's (Early's) Division had only arrived in the
nick of time to establish the new line. Again Gen. Lee
had placed himself at the head of his troops to lead them
forward, and again the men had insisted on his retiring
before they charged the enemy and pressed them back
to the head of the salient.

Upon learning that Hancock's advance was being checked, Grant ordered eight brigades of the 6th Corps to reinforce him, and about 8 A. M. these additional troops increased the confusion and crowding in the limited space within the salient. Burnside had also been ordered to assault the Confederate lines and about 5 A. M. fell upon A. P. Hill on the right. On Hill's left center, Burnside met with no success whatever, Nelson's, Poague's, and Pegram's battalions simply tearing the dense attacking columns to pieces as they appeared in the open, but on the extreme right Potter's Division swept Lane's Brigade from its trenches and seized two guns of Cutts' Battalion. But Lane reformed his men some distance to the rear and recovered both his works and the guns, driving Potter off. Failing in his attack, Burnside was then ordered to move to his right and connect with Hancock's line, which he did by 9:15 A. M. Meanwhile both sides had moved up artillery to bear on the salient space, across the gorge of which the Confederates had formed behind the uncompleted breastworks. About this time a most gallant act occurred. Unable to draw off two guns of the Staunton Battery, which they had seized, the Federals had left them between the lines. Cutshaw and Garber, the latter the battery commander, now saw these guns standing idle in the lead-swept space. Not a moment did they hesitate, but, followed by those men of the battery who had escaped capture, rushed to the pieces, turned them upon the enemy and maintained their fire until the Federal line again swept forward. There between the struggling lines they plied the guns with many thousand eyes upon them, and not a cannoneer faltered at his post. But if this exploit was superb what of that of the gallant Capt. Charles R. Montgomery, who had saved two of his pieces when the other guns of Page's Battalion were captured? Appreciating the seriousness of the situation he had moved without a word of direction one of his guns with great labor down a small ravine on the right of the Harris house to a point within two hundred yards of the enemy, and from that position maintained his fire against all odds until three full caissons had been exhausted.

The conspicuous gallantry of Cutshaw, Garber, and Montgomery on this occasion won the plaudits of two armies, but alone they could not resist the increasing pressure on their front. Braxton's, Nelson's, and a part of Hardaway's Battalion had been promptly posted by Col. Carter under the direction of Gen. Long on a second line in rear of them at the gorge, and to the left of the Courthouse. From this group, therefore, Capt. Dance with Hardaway's batteries now moved forward to the gorge, but by noon Long was compelled to call for artillery reinforcements from the other corps. Accordingly Col. Cabell with the 1st Company of Richmond Howitzers was ordered to Ewell's line from the left and went into action at the left base of the salient just to the left of Dance's batteries while McIntosh, with two batteries, also arrived, going into position at the Harris house, and posting two guns above the McCool house.

A tremendous infantry combat had been raging for some time before the artillery reinforcements arrived. Lee had brought up Perrin's, Harris' and McGowan's brigades from his left, and Grant had assembled twenty-four brigades in and about the angle of the salient. He had also posted field batteries to rake its faces, while eight 24-pounder Coehorn mortars from the reserve were placed so as to drop shells behind the work at the gorge and behind the traverses along the western face. Before 10 o'clock, Gen. Lee had brought up every man and gun to the salient that could be spared for the defense of his broken center. From then on, it was but a question of endurance, for all day long the struggle continued, neither side being able to make a successful advance. During the day diversions were made on both sides in favor of the center, the most serious fighting being that between Warren and Anderson west of the salient.

At dawn, Warren had opened all his guns and sent forward skirmishers to prevent Anderson from detaching troops to Ewell's support. Alexander's guns, all in position, replied slowly to those of Warren, their presence seeming to deter him in his attack. Finally, at 9:15 A. M., Grant ordered him to attack at once, and about 10 A. M. his men appeared in the open. By common consent, Anderson's Infantry and the Artillery in the trenches both held their fire until the Federal lines were within 100 yards, then opened, while the guns which Alexander held in his second line engaged the enemy's batteries and diverted their fire from the works. No sooner did the blizzard of Confederate fire burst upon them than Warren's men turned and fled in such utter consternation that it would seem two of his divisions lost their bearings in retiring, and engaged in a fire fight with each other for some time, in which both lost heavily, while the amazed Confederates merely listened as at Chancellorsville during Sickles' attack. The havoc worked with Warren's assaulting columns, not half so dense as those of Hancock, gives some indication of what would have happened to the latter had Long's Artillery, like Alexander's, been in position.

Soon after Warren's failure, his corps, with the exception of four brigades, was transferred to the angle, adding eight more brigades to the twenty-four already massed there for a fresh attack, but Grant abandoned his determination when it was discovered that Lee had greatly strengthened the gorge line and brought many batteries to bear on the space in front, in addition to having reinforced his infantry. The Federals for the rest of the day simply contented themselves by keeping up a heavy infantry and artillery fire to which the Confederate Infantry replied, while the Artillery maintained only a desultory fire in order to save ammunition.

When night fell, Grant had lost in his great assault, 6,820 men; Lee 9,000, of which 4,000 were prisoners, and twenty guns. Hancock's attack had failed by reason of the excessive number of men required to maneu-

ver over so limited a space, and nothing of importance
had been accomplished but the compelling of Lee to
correct a faulty line, and a certain advance in the relentless process of attrition, which comprised the major
part of the Federal strategy.

During the night, the remnant of Ewell's Corps
abandoned the faces of the salient, the rear portions of
which it held throughout the day, and established itself
behind and improved the works at the gorge. Before
morning, Long's Artillery, with the batteries sent to its
assistance, was well intrenched in strong positions, completely dominating the space within the abandoned faces
of the salient. The 13th, therefore, proved a day of rest
since Grant wisely gave up his efforts to break Lee's
new line. In fact, his troops themselves rendered the
verdict, for while as brave as any that ever lived, they
were after all human, and conscious of the futility of
further assaults.

On this day, Maj. Cutshaw was assigned to the command of Hardaway's Battalion, Hardaway having at
last been compelled by his wounds to relinquish active
command. The remnants of Cutshaw's and Page's battalions were united under Maj. Page.

The losses in the 2d Corps Artillery had been unusually heavy, but in the other corps little damage had
been received. First Lieut. Dent Burroughs, commanding Moody's Battery, Huger's Battalion, had been
killed by a shot which penetrated the works. He was
said by Alexander to have been a superb young officer.
Several of the 1st Corps guns in the infantry trenches
had been struck and disabled in the repulse of Warren's
assault.

While the Light Artillery was engaged at Spotsylvania, the Horse Artillery was winning laurels on
other fields. Pelham's and Breathed's old battery,
now under Capt. P. P. Johnston, had again distinguished itself while operating with Fitz Lee on the
8th. On that occasion, the battery was near the Courthouse, and well to the front of a portion of Anderson's

Corps. A strong line of the enemy suddenly advanced against Johnston's unsupported guns, which he held in position, firing rapidly, while the led horses and dismounted men were retired. The Federals were so numerous that four guns were unequal to the task of holding them back, and on they pressed, bent on seizing the battery. Maj. Breathed, who was present, finally ordered Johnston to retire his left section, leaving the other with him to cover the withdrawal, but the captain declined to leave any of his guns while in action, and undertook to withdraw them piece by piece. When the enemy had begun to cry for their surrender, and while he was preparing to move off the last piece, Johnston was shot through the shoulder, and before the gun could be limbered the drivers and horses of the lead and swing teams were struck down, and the arm of the driver of the wheel team was shattered. As if unconscious of the presence of the enemy, Maj. Breathed sprang from his horse, cut loose the disabled teams that were struggling on the ground, mounted a wheel horse, and brought off the gun almost as if by a miracle, while the surging enemy mingled their cheers with those of Anderson's men, who now crossed the crest in rear of the battery, and stopped the pursuit. Breathed, Breathed, what a name is thine! How justly are thy praises sung by comrades and the erstwhile foe alike. It was you of whom Wade Hampton wrote, "A braver and more gallant soldier never lived"; whom Fitz Lee characterized as "one of the bravest and best soldiers the Confederacy produced"; of whom Wickman said, "Capt. Breathed is the best man for the management of a battery of horse artillery that I have ever known"; whom Rosser declared to be "one of the most noted officers in the Confederacy for fighting qualities," and whom Munford claimed to be "as brave an officer and as hard a fighter as appeared in the war." Of him Fitzhugh Lee, years after the war, also wrote, "Should I, for any reason, go to the field again, and get in the saddle once more, no one would I rather have by my side, were he living, than the gallant

Breathed." Stuart's opinion of Breathed is amply testified to by the following letter from him to Lee concerning him: "I will never consent for Capt. Breathed to
quit the Horse Artillery, with which he has rendered
such distinguished service, except for certain promotion,
which he has well earned."

But, see what the Commander-in-Chief, himself,
is said to have written of this young officer—"With an
army of Breathed's, I could have conquered the world."

During the 8th, Sheridan concentrated his cavalry
in rear of the Federal Army, and moved to the vicinity
of Fredericksburg. On the morning of the 9th, with
about 12,000 troops and a large body of horse artillery,
he struck the Telegraph Road, *via* Hamilton's Crossing,
and advanced upon Richmond. At Mitchell's Station,
he was resisted by Wickham, who was then reinforced by
Stuart with Fitz Lee's and Gordon's brigades, Johnston's, Griffin's, and a section of Hart's batteries. Again
the Confederate Cavalry sought to check Sheridan's
column at Beaver Dam, but failed. After resting his
exhausted men for a few hours, Stuart moved rapidly
to Yellow Tavern, which he reached at 10 A. M., on the
10th, in advance of Sheridan, and there posted Wickham on his right and Lomax on the left. The latter's
line followed the Telegraph Road a short distance, then
crossed it to a hill on which Breathed had placed a single
piece of Hart's Battery, a section of which also occupied the road, while Johnston's Battery was posted
on an elevation in rear of the line.

About 4 P. M., the enemy suddenly attacked, capturing most of the men and horses of Griffin's Battery on
the left, but no guns, and driving back Lomax's line.
Stuart assembled a handful of men on the road where
Hart with two guns remained undaunted, firing into
the flank of the enemy as they swept by. The Federals
were soon checked by a charge of the 1st Virginia
Cavalry and driven past the guns, which continued to
fire upon the surging masses. As the enemy's line retired, a dismounted trooper turned as he passed and dis-

charged his pistol at Stuart. Thus was the fatal wound inflicted upon the great cavalry leader while he stood mounted among his guns, seeking by his example to rally his cavalry. He died two days later in Richmond.

The Confederate Cavalry was now badly broken up, and Hart almost alone remained between the fallen chieftain and the enemy. On this occasion, Hart's conduct was as heroic as Poague's had been at the Wilderness. The result of the battle is known. The Confederate Cavalry certainly met with defeat, but Sheridan had been delayed and failed to enter Richmond. We search in vain, however, for reference to the leading part which the Horse Artillery took in this delaying action, notwithstanding the fact that it bore the brunt of the Federal attack, saved the Cavalry from a complete rout, and remained alone in action long enough for the bulk of the Cavalry to rally and retire in order. One cavalry regiment, the 1st Virginia, kept its organization and supported the batteries after the enemy was checked.

Meanwhile, Shoemaker's Battery remained with W. H. F. Lee, near the Army, while Thomson's and McGregor's under Chew were operating with Hampton and Rosser on the left.

No account of the Artillery at Spotsylvania would be complete without a brief mention, at least, of Maj. Joseph McGraw of Pegram's Battalion.

This remarkable soldier had been discovered by Pegram, who rapidly caused his advancement from a teamster, through the lower grades. He was a man of enormous stature and unusual ability, possessing those rare qualities which distinguish the born commander. His courage was proverbial; the character of the man is well illustrated by the following anecdotes related to the writer by Capt. W. Gordon McCabe, Adjutant of Pegram's Battalion.

While sitting on his horse at Spotsylvania a solid shot tore Maj. McGraw's left arm from his body, leaving only a stump in the shoulder socket. For an instant his officers and men hesitated in their work to proffer aid to their much beloved field-officer. "Don't mind me, men," he cried, "I'm all right—give it to 'em," and with such words on his lips he fell forward from the saddle without a cry of pain.

Upon regaining consciousness, McGraw refused to receive the usual anæsthetic, and exercising the prerogative of his authority as senior officer to the surgeon in attendance, commanded the latter to remove the shattered remains of his arm, which was done without eliciting a groan from the patient or a blink from his marvelous blue eyes.

One of his officers undertook to commiserate with the Major over his wound. "Pretty bad," replied Mc-Graw, "I reckon I'll be off duty thirty days."

Sometime after McGraw's wounding, Col. Pegram and his adjutant, who like Damon and Pythias were inseparable, were sitting in their tents in the lines at Petersburg. Orders had been given that no one should approach the lines mounted, as the danger from Federal sharpshooters was very great. The hoof falls of a horse were heard approaching, and running to the tent door to see who the reckless equestrian might be Col. Pegram was confronted by McGraw, who calmly and in the most soldierly manner saluted with his right hand and reported, "Sir, Maj. Joseph McGraw returns to duty."

Just before the withdrawal of the Army from the Petersburg lines McGraw was promoted lieutenant-colonel and placed in charge of 24 guns with their horses. A few days later on the retreat he jocularly declared that he held an unparalleled military record in that he had lost 23 guns in 24 days! McGraw knew that the man did not live who could justly criticize the rectitude of his conduct in battle.

CHAPTER XXXIX

THE NORTH ANNA

In the interval between the 12th and 18th of May, Lee gradually moved his army eastward to meet corresponding movements of the enemy. The first Corps was shifted on the night of the 15th, from the extreme left to the extreme right beyond the Fredericksburg Road and extending to the Po. Huger's and Haskell's battalions were placed in position along the new line, while Cabell's was held in reserve. On the morning of the 18th, Meade again attempted to break Lee's line at the salient where Ewell remained in position with thirty pieces of artillery well posted. Long withheld his fire until the dense attacking column came within short range, when Col. Carter in command of Page's reorganized battalion gave the word to fire. The murderous fire of canister and spherical case at once arrested the advance, threw the enemy into confusion, and hurled them back in disorder, and this before they entered the zone of effective musketry fire. Indeed before emerging from the woods, the attacking infantry was much shaken; some of the enemy's brigades were almost at once eliminated by the furious fire of the hostile artillery. Only a few of the assailants reached the abattis, none penetrated it, and the attack over the identical ground, which had formed the battlefield of the 12th, was not renewed. Few of the Confederate infantrymen discharged their muskets, and practically no loss was sustained either by the Confederate Artillery or Infantry. The Federal medical returns state that "five hundred and fifty-two wounded was the result, and the character of the wounds were unusually severe, a large portion being caused by shell and canister." Thus did the twenty-nine guns actually engaged by Carter overthrow 12,000 picked infantry. One pauses to contemplate what might have been the result on the 12th had Long been prepared to meet Hancock's attack. When we consider the effect of Alexander's Artillery on that same day, and of Carter's guns on the 18th, the contention that Hancock's crowded masses would never have reached the Bloody Angle on the 12th, had the artillery been in position, seems well supported.

During the afternoon, and after the failure of the Federal assault, Ewell determined to make a flank movement around Meade's right. Braxton, with six guns of select caliber, was ordered to accompany the column, but the roads proving impassable, due to the heavy rains of the past week, he was soon compelled to return to the lines. Simultaneously with his attack on Ewell, Meade had assailed Hill's line in front of the Courthouse. Placing a number of batteries in a position from which they could partially enfilade the works of the 3d Corps, Meade attempted to advance a large number of guns under cover of their fire, and with them prepare the way for a large infantry assault in force. Pegram's and Cutts' batteries bore the brunt of the furious cannonade, which ensued during the next hour, and succeeded in silencing the more advanced batteries of the enemy, which caused the attack to be abandoned. In the artillery duel Maj. Joseph McGraw, of Pegram's Battalion, was severely wounded, as were several other officers. Richardson's Battalion further to the right and Alexander's Artillery beyond were not engaged.

Unsupported by artillery, Ewell had lost 900 men, but he learned on the 19th that the enemy had not only moved from Anderson's front, leaving his dead and wounded on the ground, but was also preparing to move from his own front. Early on the 21st he discovered that he was unopposed, so the 2d Corps, with all its artillery, was moved to the right, passing by the other corps to the Telegraph Road south of the Po, and then by that road toward Hanover Junction. Later in the day, the 1st Corps, with its artillery and some of Walker's battalions, followed Ewell. That night the

3d Corps with its remaining artillery brought up the rear after a collision with Warren's troops, in which sharp skirmishing occurred. A. P. Hill then moved upon Hanover Junction by a road slightly west of and almost parallel to the Telegraph Road. About noon on the 22d, after a march of thirty miles, the head of Lee's column reached the North Anna, and before night the whole army was in position on the south bank, having moved over the chord of the arc which Grant had been compelled to follow.

In the new position near Hanover Junction, the 1st Corps occupied the center at the Telegraph Road bridge, the 2d extending down and the 3d up the river on the right and left, respectively. The small works at the crossing, which had been prepared in advance, were now greatly strengthened and every available gun was placed in position, the Artillery with an extensive and unrestricted field of fire completely commanding every approach.

Breckinridge's Division from the Valley joined the Army here with two battalions of artillery under Maj. William McLaughlin; these troops were held in reserve at Hanover Junction.

The reinforcement which Breckinridge brought to Lee did not number over 3,500 men, but they were seasoned troops and the additional artillery more than made up for the loss in guns at Spotsylvania. Breckinridge had fought one of the most brilliant small engagements of the war on the 15th at New Market in the Valley, where with about 4,500 men of all arms, he had defeated Sigel with not less than 6,000 men and 28 guns, thus preventing him from seizing the upper Valley and moving around Lee's flank. It was in this interesting battle, of far more importance than the numbers engaged would seem to indicate, that the Corps of Cadets of the Virginia Military Institute with four companies under its commandant and a section of artillery under Cadet Capt. C. H. Minge, aggregating about 250, saved the

Confederates from defeat by a brilliant charge at the crisis of the combat, losing 9 killed and 48 wounded, or over twenty per cent of the Corps.*   But the charge of the cadets was not the only brilliant incident of the battle, for Maj. William McLaughlin, formerly captain of the 1st Rockbridge Battery, in command of Breckinridge's Artillery, there won fresh laurels for his arm of the service.   His command consisted of Chapman's, Jackson's, and McClannahan's batteries, with six, four, and six guns, respectively, and a total personnel of about 250 men, to which was added in the battle, the cadet section of two rifles and thirty men. This battalion of artillery was one of those which Breckinridge now brought to the Army. The most careful research fails to disclose with certainty the composition of the other battalion at this time under McLaughlin's command.   It will be recalled, however, that Pendleton had urged Alexander to endeavor to secure two batteries of Col. J. Floyd King's Battalion for the 1st Corps, but before January this battalion was transferred from the south, where it had been operating, to Gen. Samuel Jones' command in the Department of Western Virginia with the following organization:

Capt. George L. Davidson

Davidson's Lynchburg Battery,	Lieut. John T. Johnson.
Lowry's Wise Legion Battery,	Lieut. J. H. Pence.
Richmond Otey Battery,	Capt. David N. Walker.
Danville Ringgold Battery,	Capt. Crispen Dickenson.

But on May 1, the return of Breckinridge's Division shows the following batteries:

Monroe Virginia Battery,	Capt. George B. Chapman.
Lewisburg Battery,	Capt. Thomas A. Bryan.
Roanoke Battery,	Capt. Warren S. Lurty.
Botetourt Battery.	Capt. Henry C. Douthat.
Rhett (Tenn.) Battery,	Capt. William H. Burroughs.
Tennessee Battery,	Capt. Hugh L. W. McClung.
Charlottesville Battery,	Capt. Thomas E. Jackson.

*For full account of this heroic incident, see *The Military History of the V. M. I.*, J. C. Wise, and *The Battle of New Market*, John S. Wise.

The effective personnel of these seven batteries numbered 30 officers and 597 men. Before Breckinridge joined Lee, he himself was joined by Imboden with McClannahan's Battery, which as we have seen with Chapman's and Jackson's batteries comprised McLaughlin's Battalion. On May 5th, Breckinridge was ordered to send Col. King with two of his four batteries to the Army of Northern Virginia for assignment to the 1st Corps, and the other two were to remain with Breckinridge. According to statements in the history of the Washington Artillery, by Maj. Wm. M. Owen, pp. 328, 347, the 13th Virginia Battalion which he had commanded in East Tennessee was in the trenches with Breckinridge at Cold Harbor on June 6, and was commanded by Lieut.-Col. King, himself, and when he was reassigned to its command July 31 it consisted of Davidson's, Dickenson's and Walker's batteries.

Exclusive of these two battalions, Lee's Artillery personnel now numbered:

1st Corps, 465; 2d Corps, 1,977; and 3d Corps, 2,632; total 4,074, with an aggregate present and absent of 6,563.* The twenty pieces lost at Spotsylvania and the casualties in personnel, were more than compensated for by the reinforcement with Breckinridge, so that at the North Anna, Lee had in the strongest position he had yet occupied in this campaign, and by far the most favorable one for artillery, not less than 225 guns manned by the most numerous artillery personnel ever brought by him into action.

At this time, the Federal Army, with the reinforcements it had received, numbered about 100,000 men with an undiminished force of artillery, while the entire Confederate force, including an additional reinforcement which soon arrived under Pickett, did not exceed 40,000 men, or about 35,000 infantry and 5,000 artillery. According to Col. Taylor's estimate, the reinforcement received by the Confederates from the Wilderness to Cold

---

*See *Rebellion Records,* Series I, Vol. XXXIII, p. 1136.
Horse Artillery, 473 present for duty. Aggregate present and absent, 674.

Harbor, was about 14,400 men, while during the same time Grant brought up 50,000 fresh troops. Thus it is seen that the proportion of artillery to infantry continued to increase as the infantry failed in numbers, being now nearly seven guns per thousand infantry, with the artillery personnel comprising about one-seventh of the field army. Truly were the precedents of Frederick and Napoleon being followed.

The Confederates had hardly commenced intrenching on the 23d, when the enemy appeared on the north bank in the forenoon, and opened fire with artillery upon the bridge-head works at the north ends of the railroad and Telegraph Road bridges, which had been constructed the year before. Eight guns of Huger's and a like number of Haskell's Battalion were quickly placed in position near the river by Alexander for the defense of these works, while the Chief of Artillery reconnoitered the defensive line above and below them. The fords on the right were soon protected by the Artillery of the 2d Corps, Braxton's Battalion being posted well in advance near the Doswell house. About 4:30 P. M. Warren's Corps crossed the river without opposition at Jericho Ford, four miles above the Chesterfield bridge on the Telegraph Road, while Hancock advanced along the Telegraph Road, and Burnside on his right moved towards Ox Ford Crossing. Burnside was unable to cross and Hancock was held back in reserve. From the 3d Corps, Heth's Division with Poague's Battalion, and Wilcox's Division with Pegram's Battalion, were now sent to oppose Warren, while McIntosh's Battalion was placed in position to cover Anderson's Ford on Hill's right, and below him near the center of the position Maj. Lane with six rifles of Cutts' Battalion was posted on a bluff back of the Montgomery house, which commanded both the Chesterfield bridge and Anderson's Ford above.

Warren had formed line of battle in a very favorable position with his front concealed within the edge of a wood. His left rested on the river, which made a large concave bend in his rear, and again drew near his right.

The open ground in front of his right flank was commanded by his artillery. But, while his position was a strong one, his situation in relation to the rest of Meade's Army was precarious, for a river lay between him and his supports. As Hill's two divisions formed for attack, Poague and Pegram advanced under cover of rising ground behind the right of the line, until within good supporting distance of the infantry, and as the Confederates moved out to attack, their batteries, hitherto unseen, galloped to the crest in their front and opened with destructive effect upon the enemy's reserves at the ford. Cutler's Division on the Federal right was broken and pursued by Hill's troops, but the Federal artillery on that flank first checked the Confederates and then engaged in a duel with Pegram and Poague, who had meanwhile thrown the Federal reserves massed near the left into great disorder. In the Federal center, Griffin's Division in the woods maintained itself with great resolution, and Hill was compelled to forego the attack. In the artillery duel which ensued, Maj. Ward, a most valuable officer of Poague's Battalion, was killed by a cannon shot. Meanwhile, McIntosh had also become engaged with the enemy's artillery, losing Lieutenant Pearce, in command of Clutter's Battery, and a limber by explosion. In the center, Haskell and Huger had held the bridges in their front, but the small infantry line in the works on the north bank had either been captured or forced to retire, leaving the works in the hands of the enemy, who had aproached under cover of the ravines leading to the river and which the Confederate batteries were unable to search effectively. At nightfall, the south end of the railroad bridge was burned, and soon the Confederate center and right was moved back to a line further from the river and on more advantageous ground. This line, according to Gen. Alexander, was too good, for its apparent strength defeated Lee's object, which was to induce the enemy, by withdrawing, to attack him. Its center rested on the river half a mile above the Ox Ford bridge, and thence, leaving the

North Anna, it ran across the narrow peninsula formed by the bend in the river, one and a half miles to Little River, where its left rested. From the center on the river the line ran southeast across another bend of the river and rested three miles below near Morris' Bridge. Along the center and right, the batteries of the 1st and 2d Corps were posted with their infantry while the 3d Corps held the left.

On the morning of the 24th, the enemy's 5th and 6th Corps formed in front of Lee's left wing, while the 2d and part of the 9th crossed to the south bank and appeared in front of his right. Occasional skirmishing and artillery firing broke out during the morning, but while Meade's troops were massing nothing serious occurred. Demonstrations on the Confederate left caused Poague's Battalion to be sent to the extreme flank at Little River, Pegram's, McIntosh's, and Lane's battalions retaining their positions of the previous day, while Richardson's with Mahone's Division occupied a second line near the Anderson house. Gordon's Division, with Braxton's Battalion, soon joined Mahone, and Breckinridge's Division with its two artillery battalions was moved up to take Gordon's place on the right.

One need only look at the map to appreciate the peculiar situation of Meade's Army. To say the least, it was a dangerous one, affording a tactical opportunity to the Confederates, which eluded them by reason of the illness of Gen. Lee. The point cannot here be discussed further. The possibilities of the situation belong to the realm of speculation, for the only activity was on the part of the Federals. Burnside was first ordered to attack and carry Ox Ford, which, if done, would at once unite the Federal wings and correct the evils of Meade's position. If successful, the attack would also divide Lee's wings. But Burnside pronounced the task assigned to him impossible, and did not even attempt it. Hancock, on his left and Warren, on his right, each advanced skirmishers and felt Lee's lines, but both reported against a serious attack, for they had acquired from their recent experiences the utmost respect for the defensive abilities of the Confederates. Furthermore, they now saw the Confederate Artillery well intrenched and bearing upon every portion of the field over which they would have to advance, and well knew the power of its guns in such a position. The lesson of Fredericksburg had not been forgotten to say nothing of recent events at Spotsylvania, where artillery alone had hurled their splendid columns back on several occasions, almost without the aid of infantry. They saw here these same guns in the most favorable position they had yet occupied, with a clear field of fire unbroken by covered approaches of any kind, and they knew that to pass through the zone of artillery fire was but the first stage of the attack, for those guns could not be silenced and would remain in the front line to add their canister to the musketry effect of an infantry, never yet driven from its works. Thus Lee, who, in spite of his physical condition, was seeking to impress his army with the necessity of striking the enemy a crushing blow when the opportunity arrived, was deprived of his chance by the forbidding aspect of his position. Nor was Lee capable at the psychological moment of supplying his army with the necessary energy to enable it to assume the offensive. His subordinates assigned the same objections to an attack on the Federals that the latter had advanced against the plan to assault Lee's position. The country occupied by the Federals on both flanks, and especially on their left, was flat and open, allowing the most effective use of their artillery and infantry behind well prepared intrenchments, and the Confederates knew full well that Hunt was in command of Meade's Artillery. Others might blunder, but they were satisfied that Hunt would make the most of any natural or artificial aid afforded by the terrain, and that as at Malvern Hill, Sharpsburg, and Gettysburg, the Federal Artillery would prove a bulk-head, which could not be battered in, even after the infantry had been driven to cover. If the Federals had learned to respect Lee's

Artillery, none the less had the Confederates learned to respect Hunt. They never entertained the least misgiving as to their ability to drive the enemy's infantry, nor were they especially mindful of the Federal guns in other hands, but there was not a man in Lee's Army who had not been impressed by the splendid abilities of Hunt as an artillerist, and they never counted on his making a mistake. A close study of the struggle between the Army of Northern Virginia and the Army of the Potomac will satisfy the student that no officer in the Federal Army, from first to last, commanded the same respect from his enemy that Henry J. Hunt did.

Had Lee been entirely invalided and absent from his army, as it lay in position on the North Anna, with the Federals in a dilemma before it, it is possible something might have been attempted by the Confederates. Some strong will might have improved the opportunity which Meade's position afforded. But, with Lee present, neither the collective nor any individual will was capable of asserting itself. It was impossible for the Army to realize that he was really incapacitated, and the most natural inertia of his subordinates under the circumstances was heightened by a confidence in his genius, almost sublime. Such is the effect of a master mind upon mediocrity. It may be frequently noted in the history of war. Who would have dared take the lead in Italy with Hannibal present? And in the whole list of Napoleon's marshals, however brilliant as fighting lieutenants they may have been, we fail to detect a single captain. The one man beside Lee in the Army of Northern Virginia, who may be classed as a captain, had fallen at Chancellorsville. Had he been present, even Lee no doubt would have temporarily surrendered the reins of control with a confidence born of experience, impossible in the case of Ewell, A. P. Hill, or Anderson, his corps commanders. This is an assertion which must not be taken as a reflection upon any of the three gallant lieutenants then leading the Confederate Corps, for we are not discussing their potentialities as captains, but conditions as they actually were. We are projecting our view deep into the human side of the situation, which is the only way a true understanding of many military problems may be had, and the more the historian cultivates this habit, the more correctly will history be written. When Napoleon declared that history was essentially false, he did so in the full knowledge that the historian commonly reasoned from effect to cause, and not from cause to effect. Conscious of the motives which guided his own career and the circumstances which dictated his military maneuvers, his faith in the history of his time based, as it was, upon the imperfect perceptions of his critics, was entirely destroyed, and he realized that what was true in his own case was true in the case of others. With what scorn must he have viewed historians who insisted upon logic for the satisfaction of their formulæ! "Here is a result," said the military critic; "give us that orderly process of reasoning and events which led to it, and in such a way that the science of war as propounded in our manuals will be exemplified." And, so to meet their demands and to discourage his opponents, who invariably sought to observe every rule of war, failing of course in the attempt, he caused Berthier to manufacture what they required. Thus was the world misled, and yet it still continues in the attempt to formulate the operations of one who was neither guided by, nor observed, any rule. All this is true of every great soldier, and never until this fact is grasped will the world appreciate the loss it suffered when Lee died without writing the history of his military career. In that work, had it been written, the mist which enshrouds the science of war, especially the leading of an army, would have been dissipated, for free as he was of all vanity, deceit, and personal interest, he would have set forth no false formulæ as the guiding principles of Chancellorsville, and the Wilderness, and he would have acknowledged many blunders which proved both successful and unsuccessful, and for the commis-

sion of which science has been called upon to supply
the reasons. An account of his military operations
would have set forth the human side of war as never before or since disclosed, and the full truth of Moltke's
definition of war as "the practical adaptation of the
means at hand to the accomplishment of the end in
view" would have dawned upon every reader. The
usual manual of military field engineering prescribes
in detail the kind of intrenchments suited to a given
position, and even declares how many men are required,
and how long it will take them, to erect these works.
But suppose the first blow of the mattock uncovers
stone instead of sinking the tool in unresisting earth?
What then of position and time? Shall the troops lay
exposed on the rugged slope simply because the position is the correct one according to formulæ and Kriegspiel? Will the enemy lie dormant, while dynamite is
brought forward to supply the place of pick and spade?
How better, than by these queries, can the real meaning
of the science of war be illustrated, or the tactics of
Second Manassas, Chancellorsville, and the Wilderness be explained? The leader of troops is but a military engineer by whom every expedient must be employed. In the solution of the problem, if the human,
the psychological element, is ignored, the troops will
be exposed on the prescribed position.

The foregoing disgression may appear at first sight
to have little bearing upon the situation at Hanover
Junction. In truth it has all to do with it, for in the
problem the human element is the unknown factor to
the ordinary critic, which, when introduced into the
equation, solves it.

Before Lee recovered his motive power sufficiently to
take advantage of his opportunity at the North Anna,
Grant removed the temptation by withdrawing his
troops across the river and setting them in motion for the
Pamunkey. During the last two days of his presence
before the Confederates, Lee's Artillery had been little
engaged. But two incidents in connection with the use

of the guns should be preserved.   On the 24th, Lane's Battalion had been actively employed in harassing the enemy near the Telegraph Road bridge, and in doing so had drawn upon itself a heavy fire from the hostile batteries across the river, which caused some loss. Bursting in one of Lane's pits, where several detachments of men were under cover, a shell ignited the tow in a dismounted ammunition chest, which it shattered. The explosion of the ammunition, which was momentarily expected, would probably have killed every man in the pit. Seeing the danger, Capt. John R. Wingfield and private Hemington, without thought for their own safety, sprang to the chest and extinguished the blaze with their hands. The other incident also concerns a battery of this (Cutts' or Lane's) battalion. Battery "A," in command of Lieut. Lucius G. Rees, had been left with McGowan's Brigade as the rear guard of the 3d Corps in the movement from Spotsylvania to the North Anna. It was, therefore, at the very rear of the whole army. When Hill collided with the enemy, Rees with his four guns was cut off by a large force of infantry, and with unusual presence of mind dashed past them to prevent the capture of his battery.   This brought him in the enemy's rear, but he unlimbered and, firing a piece at a time, while the others withdrew, he managed to elude his pursuers with the loss of but one man mortally wounded. Moving by a long circuit to the west and south, he then passed around the enemy's right at Little River, and rejoined his battalion on the 24th, after two days of separation, most of which time he was in the enemy's rear.

Pickett's Division of about 3,300 men rejoined from Petersburg about this time.

CHAPTER XL

At noon on the 26th, Grant sent Sheridan, who had rejoined the Army with the cavalry after a raid to the James River, with the pontoon train to Hanover Town on the Pamunkey River, under orders to prepare the crossing, and after dark the infantry followed. Screened by cavalry pickets, the withdrawal of the enemy was not discovered by the Confederates until the morning of the 27th, when Lee again took up the race. Moving by the Telegraph and parallel roads, towards Ashland, thence towards Atlee's Station, the Army bivouacked for the night after an exhausting march of about fifteen miles near Half Sink and Hughes' Shop. While the Army was covering the remaining thirteen miles to the Totopotomoy on the 28th, Hampton and Fitz Lee, with all the Horse Artillery, were opposing Sheridan's advance at Hawe's Shop on the road from Hanover Town to Atlee's Station. This affair was one of the severest cavalry engagements of the war, and was only broken off by both armies arriving and taking up positions confronting each other. As the Confederates arrived, Breckinridge's Division with McLaughlin's Battalion of artillery occupied the southwest bank of Totopotomoy Creek on the left of Lee's line, at the Hanover Town Road. Next came the 1st Corps, Alexander promptly placing every available gun in position on Anderson's right, then the 2d Corps now under Early, with Long's batteries well placed. The right of the line near and beyond Pole Green Church was occupied by the 3d Corps, while Walker's battalions were parked in reserve behind Breckinridge's Division on the left. Again had Lee won the race, in which at one time the Federals were eight miles nearer Richmond than the Confederates.

The next morning, Walker posted McIntosh's Battalion on the left of the Hanover Town Road to support Breckinridge, before whom the enemy had appeared in force, and the following day some of Lane's batteries were placed in position between McIntosh and McLaughlin.   Alexander had skillfully placed batteries from Cabell's and Huger's battalions on Breckinridge's right, so as to secure for them an enfilade fire down his front and a cross-fire with Walker's batteries, and during the 30th and 31st all these guns were constantly and most effectively engaged against the enemy's infantry and artillery.   While the enemy demonstrated throughout these two days against Lee's left, active efforts were also directed upon the 2d Corps, the Artillery of which now under Carter, Gen. Long having been incapacitated by a severe illness, proved most effective.   Nelson's Battalion on the evening of the 30th accompanied Rodes' Division on the Old Church Road and took a prominent part in the attack which drove the enemy's left from Johnson's farm to Bethesda Church.   In this affair, First Lieut. Ancell, of the Fluvanna Battery, a meritorious officer, was killed.   Returning to the lines that night with the infantry division, Nelson's Battalion resumed its old position, while Hardaway who had recovered from his wound and rejoined his battalion on the 21st, posted his guns on Nelson's left.   Braxton, Cutshaw, and Page held their battalions in reserve.

Though maintaining the greatest activity in Lee's front along the Totopotomoy, Meade could not bring himself to the point of a real assault on the Confederate lines.   Again he found Lee well intrenched; the activity of the Confederate artillery alone sufficed to give the warning, for here as before the Confederate batteries held the Federals at arm's length, while the infantry for the most part rested in the trenches.   With the exception of Rodes' brilliant attack on the Federal left, the infantry was not called upon to exert itself.   On the left where the threat was the most serious, the front was so thoroughly dominated by McIntosh, McLaughlin, Lane, Cabell and Huger, with upwards of fifty guns, that the Federal Infantry hardly disturbed the men in the trenches. Verily was the Artillery doing its part by its sister arm in this campaign. Shoulder to shoulder it stood with the Infantry and watched and fought while the latter conserved its strength.

On May 30, Hoke's Division with Dearing's old battalion, now commanded by Maj. J. P. W. Read, was ordered to march from Drewry's Bluff and join the Army. The battalion still consisted of Blount's, Caskie's, Macon's, and Marshall's (Stribling's) batteries, with a personnel of 17 officers and 355 men present for duty, and 16 guns.* But one battalion remained absent from the 1st Corps, and that, the Washington Artillery now under Maj. Owen, was stationed near Drewry's Bluff, having rendered distinguished service in the operations against Butler, south of the James.

Before resuming the narrative, it seems proper to give a brief account of the operations of Read's or Dearing's old battalion while detached from the Army with Pickett, especially as no history of the Artillery of the Army of Northern Virginia would be complete without reference to the heroic service rendered by one of the batteries in particular.

On the 1st of February, Pickett with Hoke's, Clingman's, and a part of Corse's Brigade, and Read's Battalion, had moved from Kinston, N. C., to threaten Newberne, while Dearing in command of the cavalry covered the front. Barton's three brigades and a naval force on the Neuse were to coöperate with Pickett.

Dearings movement towards the north was successful in diverting the attention of the Federals from Pickett's columns, and Col. R. Taylor Wood, with his small flotilla, effected a complete surprise, capturing a gunboat under the very walls of the fort at Newberne. By 2 o'clock in the morning Pickett reached Bache-

---

*Now designated 38th Battalion Virginia Artillery.

lor's Creek, seven miles distant, where he struck the enemy's troops whose pickets were captured, but being reinforced the Federal force checked the Confederate advance, after the outer defenses had been lost. Pickett now impatiently awaited the result of Barton's flank movement, which was to open his way to Newberne, but Barton failed to coöperate as planned and after remaining in position all the next day, Pickett was compelled to retire to Kinston after inflicting some damage upon the enemy, including the capture of a section of artillery and a large number of horses, wagons, etc. In Pickett's assault upon the enemy, in front of Newberne, Capt. William H. Caskie in command of the Richmond Hampden Battery, with his teams in a gallop actually led the charge of the infantry. Almost instantly his horse was wounded, but the gallant young officer seized a musket and continued on foot at the head of his battery. Seeing that he was dismounted, Gen. Pickett sent him a fresh horse, upon which he continued in the fight, not halting to unlimber his guns until within a stone's throw of the enemy's infantry. For his superb conduct on this occasion, he was soon promoted, Capt. J. E. Sullivan succeeding to the command of his battery.

The oldest of Read's batteries was the Richmond Fayette, named as we have seen in honor of LaFayette, who was visiting Richmond when it was formed, May 27, 1824. In acknowledgement of the compliment, the distinguished Frenchman presented the battery with two brass 6-pounders, which he had brought to this country during the Revolution. Col. John Rutherford was its first commander, Col. Henry Coalter Cabell commanding it in April, 1861, when it volunteered for duty, soon being assigned to Magruder at Yorktown, from which time it had served in every great battle of Lee's Army.

The Fauquier, or Stribling's original battery, had also served with great distinction from the first, having been specially mentioned in the Federal reports of the fighting at Turkey Island just after Malvern Hill, where without support it repulsed a cavalry charge. It was one of the few batteries to pursue the enemy on their retreat from Second Manassas. Later it accompanied Longstreet on the Suffolk campaign, in which it was surrounded by an overwhelming force and lost its guns and officers. After the latter were exchanged the battery was reorganized and rearmed with six Napoleons at Richmond, and took part in the Gettysburg campaign as we have seen. Stribling was soon thereafter promoted and succeeded by Lieut. William C. Marshall, who in command of the battery escaped with it from Appomattox, disbanded his men and destroyed his guns at Lynchburg.

The remaining or the Latham-Dearing-Blount Battery was organized in Lynchburg in April, 1861, and served under its first commander at First Manassas. It is said by some to have fired the first Confederate gun on that day. Serving throughout the war with great distinction, it also escaped the Surrender and disbanded at Lynchburg, after destroying its guns. After Latham transferred to the Branch, N. C., Battery, Dearing established his brilliant reputation as an artillerist with this Lynchburg battery.

Such was the record of this battalion, which more than any other had served apart from the army to which it belonged. The foregoing facts have been given lest its detached service on other fields might be thought to have injured its record.

On the 31st, Sheridan took possession of Cold Harbor, to which point Meade at once sent the 6th Corps. The sidling movement was again met by Lee, who dispatched the 1st Corps, a part of the 3d, and Breckinridge's and Hoke's divisions, the last having just arrived from Petersburg, with Read's Battalion of artillery, to his right with a view towards turning and attacking Meade's left. Cabell's, Huger's, Haskell's, and Read's battalions were to coöperate with Kershaw's,

Pickett's, Field's, and Hoke's divisions, respectively, while McLaughlin operated with Breckinridge.

Grant had also ordered Gen. W. F. Smith with the 18th Corps, just landed at the White House with 10,-000 men and 16 guns, to Cold Harbor. With but fifteen miles to march, Smith lost his way and it was 4 p. m. of the 1st when the 18th united with the 6th Corps, which arrived about 10 a. m., after a distressing night march.

Kershaw had arrived and attacked Sheridan about 6 a. m., but putting in only two brigades, they were repulsed by the Federal troopers with their magazine carbines. Hoke, on Kershaw's right, who had not been placed under Anderson's command, failed to attack, and the remainder of the long column with practically all the Artillery remained halted in rear on the roads, while the 6th Corps was arriving in support of Sheridan. The whole movement was a distinct failure, and through lack of leadership and clear orders a brilliant opportunity to strike the 6th Corps en route, which was well assembled by 1 p. m., was lost. Meantime, the Confederate column had been ordered to intrench as it stood, and the guns were ordered up and placed along the line. The works were no more than kneeling intrenchments, however, when Grant about 5 p. m. ordered the 6th and 18th corps to assault the Confederate line over an intervening space of about 1,400 yards. Between Kershaw's and Hoke's divisions was an interval of about 50 yards occupied by a strip of marshy ground. The Confederates had given up all ideas of an attack that evening, when a sudden increase of fire along the picket line 300 yards in front of the main line and the opening of the enemy's guns interrupted their digging. It was soon learned that the enemy had been successfully resisted by Hoke, Kershaw, and Pickett, upon whose divisions the attack had fallen, except at the gap, from which a thicket extended well forward, allowing the Federals as at Second Manassas and Fredericksburg to approach the line unobserved. A large Fed-

eral force had worked through this interval to the rear
of the Confederate line, and soon compelled Kershaw
and Hoke to refuse their adjacent brigades and extend
across the gap in its rear. This action, which should have
been taken long before, checked the enemy after they
had taken several hundred prisoners. Hinton's and
Gregg's brigades of the 1st Corps were now hurried to
the spot and driving back the enemy reëstablished the
line, while the Federals intrenched themselves about 300
yards in its front. Darkness put an end to the fight.
The Artillery had hardly fired a shot, for so dense were
the woods that no position was available for its use.
During the night a Napoleon gun of Cabell's Battalion,
under Lieut. Falligant, was posted in the rear of the
gap in a position much exposed to the enemy's sharpshooters, and not more than 50 yards distant from them.
The other pieces of Cabell's Battalion were now posted
along Kershaw's, while Huger's and Haskell's batteries occupied Pickett's and Field's line extending to the
left.

Meade had also made a serious attempt against the
3d Corps on Anderson's left, but the assault fell upon
Heth's position, where Hardaway's Battalion had by
merest good fortune been posted near the Mander
house. Under cover of a skirt of woods, the Federals
advanced to within 50 yards of the Confederate intrenchments, but at that point were overwhelmed by
Hardaway's canister fire. Having very little protection, Hardaway's batteries suffered severely and were
relieved during the night by Poague's Battalion.

By the morning of the 2d of June, the opposing lines
had settled down in their intrenchments closer to each
other than ever before, the hostile troops so close that
every exposed movement was plainly discernible. Three
Federal corps now confronted Lee's right at Cold Harbor, while the other two lay opposite Early's or the 2d
Corps, at Bethesda Church. The fighting opened with a
renewed effort on the part of the Federals to force the
gap in Anderson's line, but Falligant's single piece was

kept constantly in action, and by the expenditure of an enormous amount of canister passed along the line by hand to it for several hundred yards, kept the swampy space clear of the enemy while his gallant detachment was relieved from time to time from the batteries nearby.

In the afternoon, Gen. Early, perceiving a movement that indicated a withdrawal of the enemy from his front, advanced against Burnside's right flank, making a half wheel with the Johnson house position as his pivot. Gen. Long, though still ill, had returned to duty the day before. Cutshaw moved his battalion out of its works and posted it in line with Garber's Battery on the right just beyond the old Church Road.

This was a most fortunate disposition, and one which enabled Garber with canister to check the pursuit of one of Gordon's brigades, which pursuit was repulsed and driven back by the guns. But Early's movement was as a whole most successful. Striking Burnside's Corps while in motion and sweeping down on Warren's right, he not only took a number of prisoners with small loss to himself, but prevented two entire corps from taking part in the attack at Cold Harbor, which had been planned by Grant. Long's Artillery had been greatly assisted by Haskell's Battalion on Field's front, which Alexander had moved out in front of the works in order to get an enfilade fire. This battalion kept up a constant fire upon Warren's line and prevented it from changing front. All day the sharpshooting and artillery practice were incessant. During this day a number of Alexander's gun carriages in Pickett's and Kershaw's front were actually disabled by bullets which passed through the embrasures and cut the spokes of the wheels. The terrain behind the intrenchments was so flat that it was fully exposed to even the frontal fire of the enemy, which prevented all movements of men and horses.

During the day, Grant received a fresh reinforcement of 5,000 troops, who were to take part with Wilson's

Cavalry in a flank attack on Early in the morning, while Burnside and Warren made a frontal assault. Meanwhile, Lee had by marching Breckinridge's, Wilcox's, and Mahone's divisions across his rear, extended Hoke's line to the Chickahominy, picketing the south bank of the river with Fitz Lee's Cavalry and Johnston's and Shoemaker's batteries. During the night, Cutshaw was relieved by Hardaway, and the position of Kershaw's left at the gap was slightly changed and greatly strengthened by placing there four guns of Cabell's Battalion, behind good epaulments, to one of which Falligant's gun was noiselessly withdrawn after the old works were levelled to the ground. Law's Brigade was also moved up as a support and intrenched in rear of the line at this point, for the massing of the enemy's columns opposite had been plainly heard.

The Confederates in the best of spirits and utmost confidence were waiting under arms for the attack, when at the first blush of dawn the fire of the pickets in the gap announced the appearance of the enemy. As the Federals burst from the thickets, not over 100 yards away, wildly cheering and with bands playing in their rear, the Confederates, who for several hours had been fearful less the attack would not come off, set their teeth and took a firmer hold of their muskets. Pushing forward to the point where the Confederate works stood in the gap the night before, for a moment it seemed to the Federals as if they had succeeded, but not so. Cabell's four pieces under Lieut. Callaway, concealed in their individual works, two on either flank of the infantry trench, which traversed the gap somewhat in rear of the old line, burst forth as if but one gun with doubled charges of canister, partially enfilading the enemy and crossing their fire at the deserted line. Of course, the repulse of the enemy at this point was immediate and bloody, and though Callaway's men suffered from musketry fire at the closest range, alone he would have been able to clear his front. For his superb conduct on this occasion, he was specially mentioned in orders.

Read's guns along Hoke's and those of Cabell on Kershaw's line were equally active, the approach of the Federals generally being arrested about 50 yards from the works. From Kershaw's right, Huger's Battalion delivered a withering enfilade fire upon the space over which the assault was rendered, while Pickett sent forward a line of skirmishers to fire upon the flank of the attacking column. Haskell also opened to aid the troops on his left.

On Early's front, Hardaway secured a most effective oblique fire on the enemy and Cutshaw from his position in reserve moved rapidly to the front of the line and to the left of Hardaway, when the attack developed and from a most exposed point opened a terrific enfilade fire upon the column which assaulted Rodes' works. Heth's Division held the extreme left of Early's advanced line, and to it Poague's Battalion had been assigned. The division commander directed Col. Poague to post two batteries, Wyatt's and Richards', on the left, but after a rapid reconnaissance, Col. Poague reported in favor of a better position, as the one indicated was plainly untenable. Heth, however, reiterated his orders, and nothing was left the gallant Poague but to obey them. As the batteries galloped forward, the heavy line of skirmishers, with artillery in support, which Poague had discovered not over 250 yards away, simply riddled the teams and shot down many of the cannoneers. After firing but a few rounds, the two batteries were so badly crippled that they were no longer able to remain in action. Poague was struck by a fragment of a shell, narrowly escaping death. Capt. Wyatt and Lieut. Rives were killed, many men and horses were killed or disabled, and nothing but the most heroic efforts of the survivors saved the guns from capture. Thus did an infantry commander usurp the function of his artillery leader, and by disregarding the advice and experience of one of the most competent and daring artillerymen in the Army, uselessly sacrifice two superb batteries, which might have rendered valuable service under the direction of their proper leader. It was such ignorance that had long since caused the Artillery to be given a more independent organization, for the experiences of the first year of the war had taught that division and brigade commanders as a rule neither understood nor were capable of handling artillery in camp, on the march, or in action. The employment of the artillery as a whole at Cold Harbor, and in the entire campaign, was marked by a degree of independence of the infantry hitherto unknown. Frequently we have found a battalion of one corps in the line of another corps. It was a fatal mistake to turn Poague over to Heth's mercies, but the error had its good effects, as it simply emphasized the impracticability of the repetition of such a practice, for Col. Walker's protest was prompt and forceful.

On the right, Breckinridge's Division and the 3d Corps, minus Heth's Division and Poague's Battalion, had taken position about Gaines' farm, with the flank of their line resting on the Chickahominy. Pegram's Battalion, to which Dement's and Chew's Maryland batteries from Richmond had now been added, occupied a fine position on Turkey Ridge, with McIntosh's, Richardson's, and Lane's battalions in order on its left. In the rear of his batteries, McIntosh posted a 24-pounder howitzer, which he had adjusted for high angle fire over the ridge, and which he successfully employed with indirect fire against the enemy's working parties in his front. On this part of the field the Federals were generally held at arm's length by the Artillery which was most actively employed. The action proper lasted but about one hour, though at isolated points small attacks reoccurred, and long-range artillery fire was kept up by the enemy until noon. At one point only was the Confederate parapet carried, and this on the right by Barlow's Division, which approaching under cover to within 75 yards of the works swept over them and seized three pieces of artillery. But here Finnegan's Brigade succeeded in driving out the enemy and recovering the guns.

By 7 A. M., Grant had authorized Meade to discontinue his efforts, and gradually the futility of further attack became apparent even to Meade, who had lost over 7,000 men during the morning, while the Confederate casualties did not exceed 1,500, including several hundred captured.

The bulk of the Federal casualties was due to the Artillery which had been superbly handled throughout the day, as testified to by the complaints in the reports of every Federal corps. At many points the enemy had either been enfiladed, as by Cutshaw and Huger, or had met with destructive oblique and cross fires, which, according to Gen. Humphreys, swept through the ranks "from the right of Smith to the left of Hancock." Again he states, "The assault on the 2d Corps could not be renewed unless the enemy's enfilade artillery fire could be silenced," and of the 6th Corps he writes: "During all this time, besides the direct fire, there was an enfilade artillery fire that swept though the ranks from right to left." Here he undoubtedly refers to the effect of Hardaway's, Cabell's, Haskell's, and Huger's guns, which literally tore the assaulting column to pieces. In writing of Smith's attack, he also says: "The fire from the right came from a part of the enemy's works against which no part of our attack was directed, and Gen. Smith was unable to keep it down with his artillery," which is but another reference to the 24 guns which Huger pushed out in front of Pickett and Field. After reading such statements, is it any wonder that when Meade attempted to renew the assault his troops laid down? The order for this fresh effort did not come from Grant, who as we have seen had had enough early in the morning. Meade's was the unconquerable will. He desired to try conclusions again, and would have done so had he been able, but "His immobile lines pronounced a verdict against further slaughter," declared Swinton. Gen. Alexander denies this. He asserts that no such mute protest on the part of Meade's men occurred, and that they lay down merely pending the organization of a fresh attack, in order to find cover while the arrangements which necessarily consumed much time were being made. This may be true, and as it is more in consonance with the conduct of the Federal Infantry on many other occasions, it probably is. Swinton did not like Grant. He had been caught, it is said, eavesdropping about Grant's headquarters, and reproved by the stern soldier in no gentle terms. Besides he was writing for home consumption, for already deputations were calling upon Lincoln for the removal of "that butcher Grant." Just as he erred in imputing the order for the renewal of the assault to Grant, so may Swinton have been mistaken in other respects. A good authority declares that Meade's troops, as if by general agreement, after their bloody repulse in the early morning, pinned white badges on their breasts bearing their names and addresses, in order that they might be identified by the enemy since they felt certain that they could not successfully cross the Confederate fire zone. This circumstance, if true, does not indicate that the troops were unwilling and did not intend to renew their efforts, for in no way can that badge be likened to a white feather. On the contrary, it showed that the men who wore it were resolved to do or die, and rather expected to die. That many of his officers and men criticised Grant for what they ignorantly styled the merciless slaughter of his troops cannot be denied. They failed to see that in no other way could he defeat Lee except by fighting, and that to attack the Army of Northern Virginia behind breastworks, under the most favorable conditions, meant heavy losses. If their lack of faith in Grant, coupled with the devotion of the Confederates in Lee, enhanced the chances of Federal losses, that was not Grant's fault, as a general. His was not the character, however, which could make a veteran on the battlefield cry out: "God bless Marse Robert. I wish you were Emperor of this country, and I were your carriage driver."

After all criticism has been passed upon Grant and Meade, the latter a soldier whose great ability was unfortunately overshadowed by the presence of Grant, and who grows in stature with the passing of time, Cold Harbor was but the exemplification of Jackson's statement two years before: "We sometimes fail to drive the Federals from their intrenchments, but they always fail to drive the Confederates out." Let it be asked then, who had succeeded before Grant failed?

To return to our narrative. On June 3 and 4, the Chief of Artillery made a thorough reconnaissance of the Chickahominy fords below Hill's right. On the 2d, Maj. Owen with the 2d, 3d, and 4th companies of Washington Artillery, had been ordered to report to Gen. Ransom at Bolton's Bridge, and to leave the 1st Company at Drewry's Bluff where the battalion had been engaged on the 21st of May with Butler's troops and the Federal gunboats. At 10 A. M. on the 3d the batteries reached Bolton's Bridge, during the fighting at Cold Harbor, and were the next day posted at the fords as far down as the York River railroad bridge by Pendleton. Col. Eshleman now arrived and assumed command. In the meantime, Lieut.-Col. Pemberton, of Vicksburg fame, arrived with the Richmond Defense Battalion, in command of Lieut.-Col. C. E. Lightfoot. This battalion, with Fitz Lee's Division and Shoemaker's and Johnston's batteries, were held in Bottom's Ford to guard Lee's right flank. During the 4th, the enemy appeared, and made strong demonstrations as if to cross the river, but the fire of the Artillery prevented their near approach to the ford.

After several days of inactivity, Lee assumed the offensive. On the 6th, he endeavored to turn Meade's right flank by sending Early to the north of Matadequin Creek, and again on the 7th by a movement south of that stream, but the swampy and impassable character of the terrain prevented any success on both occasions.

When it was discovered on the 7th that the enemy had withdrawn from Field's front, Haskell's Battalion was transferred to the south bank of the Chickahominy, and posted at the Grape Vine and Federal bridges. During the better part of the next week, skirmishing at short range all along the lines from Pickett's front to the river was incessant, and the Artillery was constantly engaged, though in a desultory way. So close were the lines that the guns had to be thoroughly covered, in spite of which many casualties were incurred, especially in Cabell's Battalion, which lost the veteran battery commander of the 1st Richmond howitzers. No officer in the Artillery had seen more service than Capt. Edward S. McCarthy, who was shot in the head and killed on the 4th.

One matter of particular interest in connection with this random fighting was the employment and development of McIntosh's high angle fire with howitzers adjusted as mortars, a practice which was the outgrowth of the conditions. This indirect method of fire, extensively employed here for the first time, offered many advantages inasmuch as it could be delivered without the exposure of the cannoneers to the vigilant sharpshooters of the enemy. Exceptionally good effect seems to have been obtained by McIntosh with his first howitzer, which led to the use of others, and this is the only instance of indirect fire met with so far, except Alexander's cannonade of Bank's Ford the preceding year. It was subsequently used quite extensively at Petersburg, where it was also necessary to screen the guns and detachments, but never fully appreciated, nor did it attract the attention it warranted. It was to be many years before Gen. Langlois was to give to the world indirect fire in its modern stage of perfection.

It was in connection with McIntosh's experiments with his howitzers that Pendleton sought the assistance of the Chief of Ordnance in the preparation of "stink-shells." In other words he desired to secure a projectile from the bursting of which in the enemy's works a suffocating effect would be obtained. "It seems at least worth a trial," he wrote. He also urged that hand grenades be provided the Confederate troops to be used by them in assaulting the enemy's works.* The grenades were reported to be available for issue, but no "stink-shells" were made and nothing seems to have come of the proposal.

On June 5th, Hunter, who had succeeded Milroy, defeated Jones, who had succeeded Breckinridge, and on the 12th Breckinridge was ordered to return to the Valley with his division, and McLaughlin's Battalion of artillery, to the command of which Lieut.-Col. King was now assigned, while Maj. Gibbes was transferred from Cabell's to the command of King's Battalion. Three days later, when it was discovered that Meade had again moved towards the Confederate right, Lee also detached Early's Corps with Nelson's and Braxton's battalions under Gen. Long, and dispatched the force *via* Charlottesville to the Valley. Early's instructions were to attack Hunter in the rear, and after uniting with Breckinridge to move down the Valley, cross the Potomac, and threaten Washington. These orders were given in the hope that the movement might result in Grant's recall for the defense of the Capital.

While the main army was engaged with Meade, the Horse Artillery had been actively employed with the cavalry divisions. McGregor's Battery, after being sharply engaged at Stanard's Mill on the Po, from the 16th of May to the 19th, accompanied W. H. F. Lee's Division as rear guard of the Army to Hanover Junction, and from there to Hanover Courthouse, where on the 31st it had again been heavily engaged. In this last action, Lieut. Ford, conspicuous for his gallantry, was killed. Hart's Battery participated in a small affair at Ashland on the 1st, and on the same day Shoemaker's and Johnston's batteries under Breathed were warmly engaged at Bottom's Bridge, and Cold Harbor, where three years before Pelham had won such undying laurels. The story of the service of these batteries is one in itself, and at the time of which we write perhaps no

---

Rebellion Records, Series I, Vol. XXXVI, Part III, pp. 888-889.

organization in the Army commanded the admiration and appealed to the pride of the Army as a whole as did Chew's Battalion of Horse Artillery.* Its record in marching and fighting is not excelled by that of any artillery battalion that ever took the field.

During the fighting of the first few days of June, Sheridan had drawn off around Meade's rear and attempted another raid on Lynchburg, *via* Gordonsville, in coöperation with Hunter's movement up the Valley. Accordingly on the 8th, Col. Chew and Maj. Breathed with Hart's, Thomson's, Johnston's, McGregor's, and Shoemaker's batteries, moved with Hampton's and Fitz Lee's divisions to intercept the Federal Cavalry, which they did at Trevillian Depot, on the Virginia Central Railroad.   In this affair, Hart's, Thomson's, and Johnston's batteries only were engaged, and ably maintained themselves against Pennington's four horse batteries.   Next to Brandy Station, this was the largest purely cavalry combat fought in Virginia, and Chew's handling of the horse batteries on this occasion was especially brilliant.

It may prove interesting to note the condition of the Horse Artillery at this time. The report of Capt. John Esten Cooke, Assistant Inspector General of Artillery on Pendleton's staff, dated May 25, fully sets forth the facts.

Johnston's Battery had lost 33 horses since the first of the month, most of them in action, and many others were badly broken down. Two guns had teams of but five and two of but four horses. Shoemaker's Battery, while it had lost fewer horses in action, was in a worse plight than Johnston's as to the condition of its teams. These batteries each required a minimum of 30 horses to make them fully effective. The five batteries had lost in all 99 animals and many of the cannoneers had been relegated to Battery "Q," in order to supply draught teams.

---

*Let us hope for the promised history of his battalion, by its commander, before referred to.

Requisition was immediately made by Pendleton on the receipt of the report for 100 fresh horses, and he endorsed Col. Chew's request that McClannahan's and Jackson's horse batteries of McLaughlin's Battalion be assigned to his command. Capt. Cooke reported that every care was being taken of the animals, which were being grazed whenever possible, in addition to receiving eight pounds of corn daily.* On the 8th of June, Cooke inspected Thomson's and Hart's batteries under the immediate command of Chew, in camp with Hampton's Division on the Brooke Turnpike above Meadow Bridge. Their condition he reported as exceptionally good under the circumstances, especially Thomson's, as a result of that officer's efficiency and ceaseless care. At this time, Thomson had 98 and Hart 112 men. The limbers and caissons were full and the ordnance wagons well supplied, except with Blakely ammunition, but mules were needed by the train. The requisition for horses for the battalion had been filled. So that in spite of its service and an enormous loss of horses and casualties aggregating about 100 men for the past month, the Horse Artillery was in fine fettle, when it encountered Sheridan at Trevillian's a few days later.†

Griffin's Horse Battery with Chew's and Dement's 4th and 1st Maryland batteries had been detached from the cavalry in the field and attached to the Maryland Line, stationed at Richmond under command of Gen. Bradley T. Johnston.

Notwithstanding the demands upon him incident to the field operations of the campaign, the Chief of Artillery had not only hastened forward the refitting of the Horse Artillery, but he had also found time to urge legislation upon the President for the more complete organization of the entire artillery arm. In conference with Long, Alexander, and Walker, on the 3d of May, he had accepted certain radical proposals drawn up by Long and at once forwarded them to Gen. Lee. But hearing nothing from them, he addressed the President

---

*Rebellion Records, Series I, Vol. XXXVI, Part III, pp. 831-847.
†Ibid., pp. 883, 884, and Part I, p. 1053.

direct concerning them on June 8, urging that a more just rule be adopted by Congress with respect to the authorized quota of artillery officers. The abstract of the proposed bill follows:

"A battery of field artillery to consist of 4 guns. For such a battery 100 to 125 effective privates, 4 sergeants, 8 corporals, 1 sergeant-major, 1 quartermaster sergeant, 2 buglers, 2 artificers, 1 guidon, 1 captain, 2 first lieutenants, and one second lieutenant. Six gun batteries now existing may so remain till their number of men is reduced to the above standard. The batteries shall be organized into battalions of 3 or 4 batteries, and whenever it can be done without detriment to the service, batteries from the same state shall be thrown together. To each battalion of 4 batteries there should be a lieutenant-colonel and major; 1 adjutant, with the rank of first lieutenant; assistant quartermaster, with the rank of captain; a chaplain, surgeon, and assistant surgeon. Battalions of 3 batteries may have officers of each grade, or fewer and of less rank, as commanding generals may recommend. Two or three battalions may constitute a regimental group, to be commanded by a colonel, entitled to 1 adjutant, with the rank of captain, and 1 aide with the rank of first lieutenant. Two regimental groups to form a brigade, to be commanded by a brigadier-general. Staff of a brigade to be 1 adjutant-general, rank of captain; 1 aide-de-camp, rank of first lieutenant; 1 quartermaster, rank of major; 1 commissary, rank of major; and 1 chief surgeon. The artillery of an army, provided it consists of two or more brigades, to constitute a corps of artillery, to be commanded by a general of superior rank to a brigadier-general, with a staff as designated by law for generals of like grade. All appointments above the rank of captain to be made by selection."

These indeed were radical proposals, but certainly very wise ones. The contemplated reorganization would have provided for many promotions in the arm, and relieved a situation which was fraught with many difficulties. It would not only have greatly enhanced the efficiency of the arm, but would have enabled many deserving officers to be awarded well earned promotions. Again, it would have ruled out politics to a large extent, for Congress would have been restricted to the appointment of junior officers only, all others depending upon their military records for preferment.

Pendleton's communication was referred by Mr. Davis to Gen. Bragg, his military adviser, who disapproved the proposed method of determining the number of officers in the arm, and declared the gun to be the proper unit upon which to base the strength of the commissioned personnel. But he very justly said that the present proportion of officers to guns was inadequate, and that he saw no valid reason for restricting the senior artillery grade to that of brigadier-general. "The Artillery of an army of three corps like Gen. Lee's is equivalent in importance to either corps of infantry," wrote Bragg. Gen. Lee also declared in favor of the gun as the proper unit. Every battalion should have two field officers, and his army was entitled to a major-general of artillery, while each corps chief, whose command was far more important than that of a brigade of infantry, should bear the rank of brigadier-general, he thought.

The matter was referred in September by the President to the Secretary of War for conference with the Committee of Military Affairs, as to the legislation recommended in his annual message, and in the report of the Secretary of War advocating an increase in the commissioned personnel of the Artillery.

At the end of June, the artillery material of the three corps proper consisted of ninety-four Napoleons, four 24-pounder and six 12-pounder howitzers, twelve 20-pounder and forty-eight 10-pounder Parrotts, and thirty-two 3-inch rifles, or a total of 196 pieces including those of Gibbes', or King's old battalion, which had been assigned to the 1st Corps in lieu of the Washington Artillery, and not including those of Read's Battalion. The 2d Corps also had then but four battalions, Cutshaw having been assigned to the command of the one formed by the consolidation of the remnants of his own, and Page's upon Hardaway's return to duty, Page being relieved from command. If we take King's Battalion as counterbalancing the loss of Page's 20 guns, it will be seen that Lee had 16 more guns, not including McLaughlin's, Eshleman's, Lightfoot's, and Owen's, at Cold Harbor than he started with, and allowing four pieces for each of the 15 batteries of those four battalions he must have had, exclusive of the Horse Artillery, at Cold Harbor, not less than 275 pieces of artillery, while his infantry had diminished in numbers in spite of reinforcements by at least 10,000 men. His proportion of guns to infantry had therefore risen to nearly nine guns per thousand infantry before he reached Petersburg. In the meantime, Meade had lost near 60,000 men, killed, wounded and missing, but had gained fully 40,000 by reinforcement. His original proportion of artillery had diminished, however, for nearly one hundred guns had been returned to the base.

Little remains to be said concerning the Artillery in the campaign from the Wilderness to Cold Harbor, which included a rapid series of tremendous combats. The narrative has traced the movement of the various commands in detail, and those movements fully expose the tactics of the arm. It can only be added that nothing is so accurate a test of efficiency as results, and even the casual reader must have been impressed by the wonderful results obtained by Alexander, Long, and Walker. It is inconceivable that Lee's Infantry, however superb it was, could have withstood the shock of the blows which Grant and Meade aimed at it, had there not been mingled with its men in the foremost line, and shoulder to shoulder with them, willing toilers at the muzzles and the lanyards of the guns. As has been said before, little opportunity was found to employ artillery in masses, and it was understood by the gunners from the first that their part lay in taking the brunt of the Federal attacks from the shoulders of the Infantry by ceaseless vigilance and instant readiness to stem the tide of assault before it washed up against the Infantry lines. They were called upon to do this over and over again, always, except at North Anna, where no great effort was made by the enemy, under the most adverse circumstances, for they found neither commanding positions nor extensive fields of fire. For the time being, one might say, they simply took the place of the Infantry,

and only once, at the Bloody Angle, did they allow the
enemy to cross bayonets with their sister arm. What a
record indeed is this!

To one more point must attention be called. From
the day of the rapid concentration of the Artillery along
the Rapidan on the 5th of May, there was never an hour
when every battery of Lee's Army was not either in
position, in immediate support, or on the march and
actually with the infantry divisions. Not one single
instance of delay in the movement of the Artillery, or
of a single battery, has been encountered, for the simple
reason that the wonderful organization it had been given
and the remarkable artillery leaders the war had developed, always enabled the batteries to be in the first
line. One may search military history in vain for a
parallel. It will not be found in the Napoleonic campaigns, nor will it be found in the French War of 1859,
the Danish War of 1864, the Austro-Prussian War of
1866, or in the Franco-German War of 1870-71. Read
Hohenlohe, who never fails to present the record of the
Prussian Artillery in its best garb, and see how great
masses of artillery remained idle at the critical moment;
how the unwieldy columns blocked the roads in the rear
of the armies, and then remember that the beautiful
countries of Bohemia and France, with their wide
chausses and rolling hills afforded ideal artillery terrain
as compared to the Wilderness of Spotsylvania, and the
almost pathless forests of Hanover, where scarce a clearing a mile wide or a commanding position is to be found.
Then pursue the investigation further and study the
operations of the Federal Artillery with Grant, and it
will be found that near 100 of his guns were returned
to Washington because no adequate use could be made
of them, nor were those which he retained wholly employed at any one time. As a matter of fact, fewer
were engaged in any one battle than remained idle, and
this in spite of Hunt with all his skill and ability.

CHAPTER XLI

AFTER dispatching the 2d Corps to the Valley, Gen. Lee moved the 1st and 3d Corps across White Oak Swamp to the neighborhood of Riddles Shop, at which point Wilcox's Division and Pegram's and McIntosh's battalions relieved the Cavalry and pressed back the enemy's advance. In this affair, Pegram with his old battery, now commanded by Capt. Cayce, made a most superb attack upon the enemy's leading troops, displaying all the dash and strength of his character. During the past campaign, he had, though constantly engaged, found little opportunity to exhibit his rarest quality, which was rapidity of action, but nevertheless his services had been distinguished and his reputation as a fighter was unsurpassed by that of any artilleryman in the Army. Very small, slight of figure, and only about twenty-four years old, he had the heart of a lion and, as the men said, "was always itching for a fight." Fortunate indeed is the officer who acquires such a reputation, for it is such men that instill in those under their command the *élan* which carries them on to victory. Illustrative of the feeling of the soldiers who knew him towards this youthful and dashing artilleryman, the following anecdote is recounted. On a certain occasion when it was doubtful if there was to be a fight, Pegram was seen galloping down the line of the infantry from position to position occupied by his batteries, followed by Capt. W. Gordon McCabe, his adjutant, who, like Pegram, was a veritable game-cock. The troops were in the humor for fighting, and as an old veteran spied the pair of artillerymen approaching, he rose from the trenches, waved his hat aloft and cried, "Come on, boys! Here comes that d——n little man with the glasses. We're going to fight 'em now."

On the 12th, Read's Battalion, accompanying Hoke's Division, marched from Cold Harbor to Petersburg, ar-

riving there on the 15th, and was immediately thrown
into position near the Hare house to repel the threatened
attack. During the 14th, 15th, and 16th, the 1st and 3d
corps remained in observation of the enemy near Malvern Hill, while part of Lee's Army opposed Butler
on the south side of the river. It was from their
present position that Lee expected the enemy to attempt
an advance against Richmond, but Grant had determined to cross the James at Wilcox's Landing, ten
miles below City Point and entirely out of Lee observation, and to move thence directly upon Petersburg
with his whole army. This movement had been suggested to him by Halleck some days before, and Grant
was also, no doubt, familiar with McClellan's intention
to do the same thing just three years before. His proposed line of operations would lead him in the rear of
Butler and enable him to fall on the extreme right of
the Confederate defensive line, which now rested at
Petersburg, for the defense of which only a part of the
troops of the Department of North Carolina and Southern Virginia under Gen. Beauregard were immediately
available, in addition to Lee's Army, which he hoped to
elude and outmarch. This was all but accomplished,
for while Lee remained on the north bank of the James,
watching what he believed to be the entire Federal force,
Grant had performed a feat unheard of before, and with
secrecy and celerity transferred nearly his entire army
across the river. On the 15th, 16th, and 17th, part of
his troops were actually arriving at Petersburg and endeavoring to take the city, and were only prevented
from doing it, on the 15th, by Wise's Brigade, not more
than 1,200 strong, two small regiments of cavalry under
Dearing, Moseley's Battalion and Sturdivant's and
Martin's batteries with 22 guns, and some old men and
boys called Local Reserves, or a total force of less than
3,000 of all arms and conditions. The resistance of these
troops was grandly heroic and they have never received
the credit their conduct deserved, for they stood between
Lee and disaster, against odds perhaps never before

paralleled. It was only upon the most urgent representations that Lee was persuaded by Beauregard to send reinforcements to Petersburg, for the great soldier could not believe that the Federals had crossed the river. He finally sent Hoke's Division and Read's Battalion of artillery from Drewry's Bluff on the morning of the 18th. With 18 miles to go, the head of Hoke's column reached Petersburg at sunset, having traveled partly by rail; the bulk of the division by forced marching, at 9 P. M. All that day, while Wise and Dearing were resisting the ever-increasing pressure at Petersburg, Lee remained near Malvern Hill, his attention occupied by the Federal Cavalry, but when on the morrow he finally concluded that a part of Grant's troops had crossed the James, he set the 1st Corps in motion for the south side of the river.

Early in the morning, Pickett's and Field's divisions with Huger's, Haskell's, and Gibbes' battalions, crossed the pontoon bridge near Drewry's Bluff and advanced towards the Bermuda Hundred lines, from which Beauregard had been compelled to withdraw Bushrod Johnson's Division on the night of the 15th for the support of Wise at Petersburg.

Kershaw's Division was halted near Drewry's Bluff. The next day Pickett and Field, after a skirmish with Butler's troops near Port Walthall, in which Alexander's two battalions were engaged, recovered Beauregard's abandoned lines. On that same day, Kershaw's Division, with Cabell's Battalion, and the 3d Corps with its artillery, which had encamped the previous day near Chaffin's Bluff, also crossed the river upon the bridge near Drewry's Bluff, and was ordered to Bermuda Hundred. On the 18th, Pickett's Division, with Huger's Battalion, established itself on a line fronting Bermuda Hundred from Howlett's on the James River, to the confluence of Swift Creek with the Appomattox.

During the 15th, 16th, and 17th, Beauregard had made a grand fight against the head of Grant's Army,

but at last was compelled to request reinforcements or
instructions for his retreat. The fighting at Petersburg
had lasted until midnight on the 17th, and he knew that
his small force, now consisting of Wise's, Elliott's, and
Johnson's brigades of Bushrod Johnson's Division, and
Hoke's Division, a total of about 14,000 infantry, could
no longer maintain the lines. Already he had been
forced to relinquish the outer works of the eastern defenses and fall back upon a new line hastily laid off from
the river and running from the Hare house and Bland-
ford Cemetery to the Rives house.

After the receipt of Beauregard's dispatch on the
night of the 17th, Kershaw was ordered to march to
Petersburg, though Lee was not yet convinced that
Beauregard was correctly informed about the enemy.
It was not until a third staff officer arrived from Beau-
regard at 3 A. M. on the 18th, that Lee was convinced
that Grant's entire army was massing in front of Peters-
burg. He now sent orders to Anderson to march with
Field's and Pickett's divisions for Petersburg, where
Kershaw arrived about 7:30 A. M.

Upon his new line, Beauregard had skillfully posted
his artillery under Col. Hilary P. Jones. It consisted
of Read's, Moseley's, Coit's, and Boggs' battalions.
This large artillery force of sixteen batteries and 53
guns had proved of inestimable value to him in his
defense of Petersburg. Without it he could never have
maintained the front he did from the 15th to the 17th.
As it was now merged into Lee's Army, let us examine
its organization. With the organization of Read's Battalion, we are already familiar. That of the other battalions was as follows:

MOSELEY'S BATTALION

Maj. Edgar F. Moseley

Yorktown Battery,	Capt. Edward R. Young.
Macon (Ga.) Battery,	Capt. C. W. Staten.
Battery "E", 1st N. C. Reg't,	Capt. John O. Miller.
Battery "C", 13th N. C. Batt.,	Capt. James D. Cumming.

COIT'S BATTALION

Maj. James C. Coit

Halifax Battery,	Capt. Samuel T. Wright.
Petersburg Battery,	Capt. Richard G. Pegram.
S. C. "Chesterfield" Battery,	Capt. James I. Kelly.
Miss. Confederate Guards Battery,	Capt. William D. Bradford.

BOGGS' BATTALION

Maj. Francis J. Boggs

Albemarle Battery,	Capt. N. C. Sturdivant.
Richmond Battery,	Capt. S. Taylor Martin.

Read's Battalion after being engaged at Cold Harbor on the 1st, 2d, and 3d of June, had reached Petersburg on the afternoon of the 17th in time to materially assist in the defense. Moseley's Battalion which had been organized about the time of Butler's advance, had been engaged in the fighting at Drewry's Bluff, and on the Bermuda Hundred lines, when Beauregard bottled up the Army of the James so successfully. Its commander had formerly served as a field officer in the 1st Virginia Regiment of Artillery, after its organization by Col. John Thompson Brown as part of Magruder's Army in 1861. Coit's Battalion had been organized for service in North Carolina in the early spring, later operating with Beauregard against Butler. Both Moseley's and Coit's battalions had rendered excellent service. Boggs' Battalion had only been organized on the 17th as such. Hitherto its two batteries had operated independently in the vicinity of Petersburg, and had been engaged against Butler. On June 5, Capt. Sturdivant and two of his guns had been captured.

The batteries of these battalions averaged about four guns and 90 men, and therefore comprised a valuable addition to Pendleton's command, depleted by the detaching of Long's two battalions, especially since Lee was now called upon to defend so extensive a line.

On the morning of the 18th, before Lee's troops arrived, Bradford's three 20-pounder Parrotts and

Wright's five Napoleons of Coit's Battalion were placed in position on the north bank of the Appomattox to enfilade the approaches to Beauregard's left. The rest of Jones' Artillery was either placed along or in rear of the infantry trenches of the new line, and all of it was most effectively employed during the day.

At 4 A. M., the 18th, Grant made a general advance with the 2d, 5th, and 7th Corps, while the 6th and 18th were held in reserve. He learned during the morning with the utmost surprise that Beauregard's whole force during the preceding days consisted of but two small divisions, and very much chagrined he now urged his corps commanders to press forward with energy and carry the new line before it could be materially strengthened. Meade himself fixed noon as the hour of attack. By that time, Kershaw had relieved Johnson, and Jones' guns had been skillfully disposed. Field's Division had also begun to arrive and occupy the trenches on Kershaw's left, while Hoke and Wise remained in position.

About midday the assault commenced, falling principally on Wise and Hoke next to the river, but was repulsed with loss, Wright and Bradford simply tearing the Federal ranks to shreds with their enfilade fire, while the other batteries of Beauregard's command swept the approaches with a most destructive frontal fire. So successfully did Jones' battalions perform their task that a variance occurs in the reports of the fighting this day, which can only be attributed to the effect of the "long arm." Humphreys states that every Federal Corps assaulted in force and that they were repulsed with loss, while on the Confederate side the day was not considered as one of general battle by the infantry, but as one of artillery fighting alone.

"It was necessary to wait until night before Beauregard's artillery could receive its plaudit of 'Well done, good and faithful servant,' and be relieved by fresh battalions of Longstreet's Corps. Of all the moonlight nights I can remember, I recall that Saturday night as perhaps the most brilliant and beautiful. The weather was exceedingly dry, the air perfectly calm, with an exhilarating electrical quality in it. The dust rose with every movement and hung in the air. The whole landscape was bathed and saturated in silver, and sounds were unusually distinct and seemed to be alive and to travel everywhere. It was not a night for sleep in the trenches. There was a great deal to be done at all points to strengthen and improve them, and every man was personally interested in working at his immediate location.

"In spite of all pains, the drawing out of old guns and approach of new was attended with sounds which wandered far, and with luminous clouds of dust gradually rising in the air. Then the enemy would know we were moving, and there would come crashes of musketry at random and volleys of artillery from their lines. Then our infantry would imagine themselves attacked, and would respond in like fashion, and the fire would run along the parapet to right and left, and gradually subside for a while, to break out presently somewhere else."

Such is Gen. Alexander's graphic description of the night of the 18th of June, when with his accustomed energy and bravery he was engaged with Lieut.-Col. Branch of Beauregard's Artillery in replacing the latter's guns with his own. All through this work, his exposure was constant and to the verge of recklessness, but there was work to be done, and in spite of the protests of his men he galloped back and forth, ordering here, suggesting there, and utterly regardless of his own safety until all was done that the exigencies of the situation required. As the 1st Corps arrived, it had taken position on Beauregard's right. After substituting Huger's guns for Jones' along Hoke's and Wise's front, Alexander then placed two batteries of Haskell's and Gibbes' Battalion in the trenches between the Baxter Road and the Rives house. Haskell's remaining batteries were then posted on elevated positions in the second line.

Beginning at the salient formed by the junction of the new with the old works, known as the Rives salient, where he posted Richardson's Battalion, Col. Walker, to whose command the Washington Artillery had now been assigned, occupied the line with the batteries of the 3d Corps on Alexander's right, and extending around to the south and west as far as the Weldon Railroad.

The works comprising the line of defense at Petersburg were by far the most pretentious which the Confederates had yet occupied. With the exception of the
portion of the line recently established by Beauregard
when forced back on the 17th, they had been laid out by
engineer officers and constructed in advance by slave
labor. Every advantage of terrain had been taken and
a broad field of fire for artillery cleared in front of the
line. Of course there were defects, but to a large extent these were corrected as they developed, and the
works throughout were rapidly extended and improved.
The trenches at Cold Harbor had barely afforded cover
for the infantry, and the epaulments for the guns
were there of the crudest kind, but now the artillery was
to fight behind real cover and placed to the best advantage after careful reconnaissance of the approaches.

The morning after Pendleton's Artillery arrived, the
Chief of Artillery accompanied by Gen. Beauregard
visited the north bank of the river and, after a rapid inspection of the terrain, ordered Lane's Battalion and
Penick's Battery of Richardson's to move over and
fortify the commanding eminence at the Archer House,
while Chew's and Clutter's batteries of McIntosh's Battalion, under Maj. Marmaduke Johnson, were ordered
to be intrenched on a lower elevation half a mile higher
up the river. Poague's Battalion under Capt. Utterback joined Bradford's and Wright's batteries immediately opposite the point where the main line rested
on the south bank of the river. There were now, therefore, about fifty guns placed to enfilade the approaches
to the Confederate left. But Grant did not renew his
assaults on the 19th, and his troops occupied themselves
intrenching where they had bivouacked during the night
in close proximity to the Confederate works. The opposing lines thus established by accident in a measure
remained substantially unchanged until Lee's evacuation ten months later.*

---

*For a detailed account of the Richmond Artillery defenses at this time,
see *Rebellion Records,* Series I, Vol. XXXVI, Part III, pp. 809-11. There were
38 pieces of position on the lines, with a force of Heavy Artillery aggregating
2,893 present for duty, and the 1st, 2d, and 4th Maryland field batteries with
232 men and 10 guns. Ibid., p. 861.

CHAPTER XLII

FROM the day the two armies confronted each other, sharpshooting and artillery practice were incessant, while both sides labored constantly, improving their works. The great enfilading group of guns north of the river to the command of which Col. Cutts had been assigned, and to which several 30-pounder Parrotts and 12-pounder Whitworths were added and placed in position at the Archer house, at once attracted the attention of the Federal Artillery. When Cutts opened on the enemy's line on the 20th, the effect of his fire, enfilade, and on some points of the opposing line reverse, was so overwhelming as to cause great confusion among the Federals, and lead to an almost immediate change of position. A great effort was now made by Hunt to silence the Confederate group. During the next few days, Abbott's reserve artillery regiment of 1,700 men with 60 mortars, ranging from 24-pounder Coehorns to 10-inch sea coast pieces, was brought up and undertook to subdue Cutts' fire, but all in vain. His men toiled all the harder at their fortifications and soon protected themselves and their guns with bomb proofs and works of the most substantial character. In the meantime, however, they had suffered many casualties from Abbott's terrific mortar fire, including Lieut. Lucius G. Rees, of Cutts' Battalion, who had so distinguished himself on the North Anna, killed, and Lieut. James of the same battery, wounded.

The effect of the Federal mortar fire was also felt at other points of the line, and steps were now taken by Gen. Alexander to counteract it. Fortunately, he had ordered some 12-pounder mortars constructed in Richmond several weeks before, and these began to arrive on the 24th. They were light and convenient to handle, and with characteristic energy and skill Alexander placed them at points where they could best assist in the defense of the weaker salients of the line, up against which the enemy had pressed to short range. The number of these mortars was gradually increased until twenty-seven 12-pounder, 24-pounder, and 8-inch mortars were in position along Beauregard's line, and thirteen of like caliber beyond the Rives salient. Interior lines were now constructed at the gorges of the salients, a number of heavy pieces of position from Richmond placed therein to reply to six 100-pounder and forty 30-pounder Parrotts, which Abbott had drawn from his seige train and mounted in the permanent works along Beauregard's abandoned line. These redoubts, with the infantry trenches which connected them, formed a veritable citadel, behind which a small force of defenders were secure against assault, and enabled Grant to constantly extend his lines to the west, while a system of redans and infantry trenches in their front and pushed close up to the Confederate works made detachment of the Confederate troops from their front extremely risky. But the weakest part of the Confederate line was Elliott's salient, named from the brigade assigned to its defense. Here the edge of the deep valley of Poor Creek, which ran nearly parallel to the Confederate line of works, was but 133 yards distant, while the depression afforded ample space and perfect cover for the massing of a large body of infantry. Along the rear edge of this valley, the Federals threw up strong rifle pits with elaborate head-logs and loop-holes from which an incessant fire was kept up upon the Confederates. At this point, Col. Walker posted Cayce's Battery of Pegram's Battalion, and under cover of night the men managed to place obstructions in front of the parapet.

On the 20th, Thomson's, Hart's, Shoemaker's and Johnston's batteries were engaged the entire day at the White House with Fitz Lee and Hampton, who had returned from Trevillian's, and underwent the unusual experience of horse artillery fighting both field artillery

and gunboats at the same time.* Two days later, Mc-
Gregor's Battery was engaged with W. H. F. Lee in
an affair with Wilson's and Kautz's Cavalry at the
Davis house on the Weldon Railroad. The Federal
Cavalry was followed by W. H. F. Lee to the Staunton
River, where its progress was barred by local militia and
a force of artillery at the bridge. Attacked in rear by
the Confederate Cavalry, with an impassable stream in
their front, Wilson and Kautz decided after having done
much damage to the railroads to return to Petersburg,
and in doing so were assailed by Hampton's, Fitz Lee's,
and W. H. F. Lee's brigades, two brigades of infantry
under Mahone, Cayce's Battery under Pegram and the
entire Horse Battalion under Chew and Breathed at
Reams Station, where they were completely routed,
losing 1,500 men, two horse batteries complete with
twelve guns, and their wagon trains. In this affair, Pegram, Chew, and Breathed were in their glory, and in no
engagement of the war did the Horse Artillery display
greater dash, notwithstanding the preceding weeks of
constant marching and fighting.

Another affair in which the Artillery shone with particular brilliance had, meantime, occurred at Petersburg,
in which McIntosh was the bright star.

Advised on the 22d of a movement by the 2d and 6th
Federal Corps from their works opposite Hill, against
the railroads on his right, Lee sent Hill with Wilcox's
and Mahone's divisions, supported by Johnson's, to
meet it. McIntosh with the 1st Maryland Battery
under Lieut. Gale was to move out with the infantry.
Hill's orders were to strike the enemy while stretched
out to the left, while Col. Walker's Artillery coöperated
with him from the lines. When all was ready, Mc-
Intosh with Gale's section of Clutter's Battery galloped
forward to within a few hundred yards of the enemy's
intrenchments and opened upon their columns, instantly
causing confusion among them, while the infantry

---

*It will be recalled that the artillery had engaged gunboats on the Rappa-
hannock in 1862. Forrest also attacked gunboats on the Tennessee River with
Morton's horse batteries.

rushed forward under cover of his fire and carried the
Federal line.   Lieut. Wilkes' section of Capt. Valentine
J. Clutter's Richmond Battery, recently added to Mc-
Intosh's Battalion, now moved out and supported Gale.
While Wilcox obstructed the advance of the 6th Corps,
Mahone and Johnson passed through a gap between it
and the 2d Corps, and struck Barlow's Division, which
was moving around the 6th Corps, in the rear, capturing
1,700 prisoners and four guns, which were successfully
brought off during the night by Hill after also routing
Mott's Division.   The conduct of McIntosh, Gale, and
Wilkes on this occasion elicited the highest praise from
all arms, and gives us a rare instance of light batteries
actually maneuvering between intrenchments.   One is
almost compelled to inquire if there were any limitation
upon what the artillerymen would attempt.

Lee now planned an attack on Meade's right to be
preceded by a great artillery preparation.   It was hoped
that the infantry under cover of Cutts' enfilading and
Alexander's frontal fire might reach the Federal mortar
batteries and recover the outer line.   Promptly on the
morning of the 24th, the Artillery opened the greatest
cannonade which the siege had yet seen, but for some
reason no infantry assault occurred.   The cannonade was
not without its effect, however, for the enemy was impressed with the futility of making subsequent attempts
in that quarter, by the tremendous power which the Artillery developed.

During the next few days, Gen. Alexander's attention was especially attracted by the enemy's activity in
front of the Elliott salient.   Having been an engineer
officer of some experience, he detected signs, which convinced him that underground work was going on.   He
had confidently expected each morning to see a "Flying
Dutchman" in that quarter, or some other evidence of
the opening of approaches across the narrow space in
front of the salient, but instead he had noted an increase
of musketry fire from the Federal works there, and a
diminishment of alertness among the enemy's sharp-

shooters on either side. Each day he visited the salient
and carefully watched what was going on. On his way
back to his headquarters on the 30th, he was slightly
wounded by a sharpshooter, and before leaving the
Army the next day, for six weeks, to visit his home in
Georgia, he called at Gen. Lee's headquarters in person and reported his views about the mine. Mr. Law-
ley, an English war correspondent of the *London
Times,* was present and inquired how far it would be
necessary for the Federals to mine, and when told by
Alexander the distance was 500 feet, he replied that
the tunnel at the Siege of Delhi, the longest ever dug,
was but 400 feet, and that it was found impossible to
ventilate a longer gallery. Alexander replied that there
were many Pennsylvania miners in Meade's Army, and
that military precedents would not deter them from
making the attempt. It so happened that upon the
advice of Lieut.-Col. Pleasants, of the 48th Pennsylvania Regiment, a coal miner, against the advice of
every engineer in Meade's Army, the Federals had
opened a gallery on the 27th of June, just two days before Alexander called Lee's attention to the danger.

Alexander did not return to the Army until August
18, Cabell commanding the Artillery of the 1st Corps
in his absence, but upon his advice Huger was assigned
to the command of the guns and mortars near the
salient. The day after his departure Gen. Lee directed
his engineers to open countermines. Shafts with listening galleries were promptly sunk, unfortunately, on the
flanks of the salient, for the Federals were tunneling
straight for its apex and their operations were not
heard. Had Alexander been present, it is safe to say
the battle of the Crater would never have been fought,
for having devoted so much attention to the salient, he
would most certainly have been placed in charge of the
countermines and would have caused the first one to be
opened at the apex. From that point the enemy's mining
20 feet below the surface would readily have been detected and their gallery destroyed by the explosion of a
camouflet, or smothered mine.

CHAPTER XLIII

THE strength of the Artillery about Richmond and Petersburg had been greatly enhanced during the past month while the Infantry composed of Johnson's and Hoke's divisions of Beauregard's Army, Pickett's, Field's, and Kershaw's divisions of the 1st Corps, Anderson's, Heth's, and Wilcox's divisions of the 3d Corps, showed a marked diminishment. In fact, recruiting for the Infantry had almost come to a standstill, and on July 10, while the paper strength of the foregoing commands aggregated 103,178 men, there were but 51,867 present for duty. In the Cavalry Corps composed of Hampton's, Fitz Lee's, and W. H. F. Lee's divisions, with 23,180 men on the rolls, there were but 10,493 effectives in the field. In marked contrast to these figures are those of the Artillery which, not including Long's command in the Valley, numbered 6,472 present for duty, with an aggregate present and absent of 9,435. In other words, while Lee was able to muster but half his infantry and cavalry in the field, but one-third of his artillery personnel was absent, a fact which seems to testify to a comparatively high state of discipline in the artillery arm.

To the work of maintaining his corps, Pendleton constantly addressed himself. Furthermore, he now sought to bring order in his arm out of the chaos into which the recent campaign, with its heavy losses, had necessarily thrown the Army.

It will be recalled that when Longstreet moved to Petersburg *en route* to Tennessee, he had started from the Rapidan with Alexander's, Walton's, and Dearing's battalions, but that the first only through a change of plans accompanied him to the West, the Washington Artillery and Dearing's Battalion remaining throughout the winter in the Department of North Carolina and Southern Virginia with Pickett. Since that time, these two battalions had considered themselves no longer an integral part of the 1st Corps to which they had been assigned by *G. O. No. 19, June 4, 1863.* True, they had rejoined the Army at Cold Harbor in June, but they had not fallen under Alexander's immediate control. In fact, Dearing's old command under Read had again been detached to Petersburg with Hoke's Division, and the Washington Artillery, to the command of which Lieut.-Col. Eshleman had been assigned, after his provisional battalion had been broken up, later accompanied the 3d Corps to Petersburg.

Since the battle of Gettysburg, where Walton was so rudely displaced by his junior, the Washington Artillery had not been well disposed towards Alexander. These troops were serving in a foreign land and were naturally sensitive to anything in the nature of a slight to their old commander, so they had welcomed their separation from the 1st Corps Artillery to the command of which Alexander had been assigned, March 1, 1864, with advanced rank from February 26. And so, when on June 13, Lee commenced his movement from Cold Harbor, the Washington Artillery applied direct to the President to be allowed to attach itself to the 3d Corps. * This was of course a violation of army regulations, but it must be remembered that state politics entered into the affairs of the Army of Northern Virginia, as in the case of all other armies that have ever taken the field. Dissatisfaction on the part of these troops with the persistent disregard of Walton's claims was now open, and as his case was undoubtedly the principal matter in the politics of the Artillery Corps, the facts should be cited.

On coming into the field in May, 1861, Maj. Walton was the senior artillery officer in the Army and commanded the largest artillery organization. After First Manassas, an act of Congress was passed at the instance of Beauregard to authorize the promotion of artillery

---

*In Camp and Battle With the Washington Artillery Battalion, Owen, p. 329.

officers, Walton's case being especially mentioned as a
deserving one. Under this provision, Walton was promoted Colonel and assigned to duty as Chief of Artillery of the Army of the Potomac, retaining immediate
command of the Louisiana Battalion. Soon after this,
Pendleton, who had been advanced from the grade of
captain, subsequent to Walton's arrival in Virginia,
was promoted to the grade of colonel with temporary
rank, under the law authorizing the President to confer such rank. Though still Walton's junior, he was
again promoted and made brigadier-general and
chief of artillery, when the reorganization in the
winter occurred, and Col. Walton was assigned to duty
as chief of artillery of the 1st Corps. In the meantime, Beauregard and Longstreet repeatedly recommended the promotion of Walton, who was by service
the senior artillery officer in the Confederate armies,
but it was announced that no more brigadier-generals
of artillery would be appointed. All this, and his dis-
placement at Gettysburg was taken by Walton with
commendable grace, though naturally he was much
chagrined. Beauregard had, just after the reorganization, written him as follows: "I regret to hear that you
have not been promoted to the rank of brigadier-
general of artillery, which in the estimation of your
friends you have won by your efficient services on so
many glorious battlefields, commencing with Bull Run.
If my testimony to your efficiency, zeal and capacity,
whilst commanding the Battalion of Washington Artillery in the Army of the Potomac and acting as chief
of artillery of the First Corps of that Army, can be
of any service to you I will willingly give it to you, not
as a favor, but as a right to which you are entitled."
And Longstreet, before the reorganization, wrote him:
"I have on three occasions and several times in conversation expressed my opinion and wishes in favor of having you promoted to the rank of brigadier-general. I
still think your services give you the best claim to the
promotion of any officer in the service, and I am quite

satisfied you are as well qualified to fill the office. I still hope your promotion may soon come." But it will be recalled that these letters were written early in the war and before experience showed the necessity of trained artillery leaders. Beauregard was from Louisiana himself, and Longstreet from Georgia, and it is a fact that before the tremendous campaigns of 1862 welded the Army of Northern Virginia into a thoroughly organized and disciplined fighting machine, state prejudices were rife and entered into every appointment. In fact, Longstreet, above all others, persisted to the end in harping on the favoritism he imagined was shown Virginians. But it must be recalled that Pendleton owed his preferment over Walton largely to Mr. Davis' influence, with whom he had been a cadet at West Point, and besides the day was one when graduates of the United States Military Academy were in the ascendant.

Though a veteran of the Mexican War, Walton was not a West Pointer. To soothe his disappointment, he was now offered the command of a Louisiana Brigade with advanced rank in the infantry, but this he refused, as he could not see how assignment to the command of an infantry brigade of 1,000 men, in lieu of that over 80 guns, was really a promotion. The next affronts to Walton were the appointment of Long as brigadier-general September 21, 1863, Shoup during the winter in the Western Army, and Alexander, his second ranking battalion commander, March 1, 1864, with rank from February 26. In the meantime, Col. Stephen D. Lee, of the Artillery, had been promoted and assigned to the command of an infantry brigade in the West, November 6, 1862, soon to be again promoted August 3, 1863. Whatever Longstreet's early views about Walton may have been, it would not seem that he had long retained them, for he supplanted him, as we have seen, at Gettysburg by Alexander and intentionally left him behind when he made his expedition to Tennessee. One thing seems certain. If Longstreet still, in

1863, professed the advocacy of Walton's promotion, he was not acting in good faith or was doing so to secure his transfer from the 1st Corps.

In the meantime, Walton was not the only artillery officer sidetracked. Col. Cabell had been persistently overslaughed because of his age. His own adjutant has recorded that this distinguished member of a proud and historic family "lacked self-assertion and aggression; to some extent, too, he lacked the manner and bearing of a soldier, and he never maneuvered for position for himself or his battalion."* "His essential characteristics were a pure and unselfish nature, tender and affectionate heart, gentle and unfailing courtesy, single-hearted and devoted partiotism, quiet but indomitable courage." "He was a man of intellect and culture, as well as character." But all these virtures together did not spell fitness for high command in the Artillery and their very enumeration points to the fact that his military *confidante* knew he lacked the dash and ability requisite for successful leadership and confirms the estimate of him entertained at headquarters which has been previously stated. A serious effort, it will be recalled, was made to sidetrack Cabell by transferring him to the defenses of Richmond, and there was even the suggestion that he be given advanced rank in order that it might be accomplished. Upon learning from his friends of this suggested promotion, the gallant old soldier was much gratified, until by accident he discovered the motive, when he flamed into an ungovernable rage and demanded to know if he was taken for a "damned sneak and coward and fool." He surrendered his old battalion, it is true, but not until Appomattox.

We have seen how Col. Brown was overslaughed in the interest of Long, not by reason of lack of ability, for he was an exceptionally fine officer, competent and successful, but because Long's claims were more acceptable at headquarters. Cabell and Brown, like Walton, were not West Pointers. From the foregoing

---

*Four Years Under Marse Robert, Stiles, p. 155.

facts, it does not appear that Walton was the only one who was overslaughed, whether justly or not, or that state politics alone controlled in his case.   Indeed, we can go still further in tracing the effort to hand the tactical reins of the Artillery over to young and trained soldiers, for was not Pendleton himself, at first seized upon with such avidity as the senior artilleryman, gradually displaced from tactical command?   The effort to dispose of him on the battlefield has been clearly perceptible in every reorganization of the arm.   In fact, except with regard to his actual rank, his case was not dissimilar to that of Walton's, and an unprejudiced student of the Army of Northern Virginia will be compelled to admit that all these unfortunate maneuvers, disappointing as they were to certain faithful soldiers and their friends, were in the interest of artillery efficiency.   Of course Walton and Cabell could not appreciate this.   Soon after Alexander's promotion, Walton had applied to be relived from duty with the Army of Northern Virginia, and at his own suggestion was assigned to duty as Inspector of Field Artillery at Large.   During his absence, a strong effort developed in the Artillery arm to declare all positions not actually filled in the mobile army vacant, in order that adequate promotion might be given officers present in the field. In pursuance of this hard plan, concerning which much is to be said on both sides, Maj. S. F. Pierson, who had not served with the Army in the field for several years, but who still held his commission therein, was transferred to the Virginia Reserves on July 21, and Lieut.-Col. John S. Saunders was transferred to the Inspector Generals Department.*   But Walton had a friend at court in Gen. Bragg, who had him ordered back to the Army to prevent his elimination.   Returning to the Army after an arduous tour of duty in the South, Walton now found it necessary to accept service under those formerly his juniors, or resign.   While he did not disparage the ability of Long and Alexander, yet he did

---

*Rebellion Records, Series I, Vol. XL, Part III, pp. 790, 797.

not feel that such a course was consistent with his dignity. Furthermore, he was forced to the conclusion upon a review of events than his services were no longer valued. Accordingly on July 18, he tendered his resignation and addressed a remarkable and pathetic communication to his gallant command, in which much of the foregoing matter is included. "It is with reluctance," wrote he, "that I have been forced from the service, with grief that I find myself separated from you, with whom, I had hoped, should Providence permit, to return to the city of our home. Circumstances have denied me this privilege; but harsh as may be their decree, they cannot rob me of the consolatory conviction that while with you I tried to deserve your affection and esteem, nor of the hope that while absent I may retain them."

In the diary of the Washington Artillery as an entry of July 20, the following is found: "The resignation of our gallant old chief, Col. Walton, has been accepted. We shall never cease to regret the circumstances that have induced this action. All our hearts are so attached to him, that no one, no matter how capable he may prove himself, can command the Washington Artillery as he has done, in peace as well as in war." Such were the sentiments which animated the men of that splendid command, whose services in Virginia were so heroic and so unselfish from first to last. But it is not difficult to see in the pages of the diary quoted from that the circumstances which entailed the resignation of Walton were appreciated in their proper light, as well as lamented. The devotion of his officers and men to Walton could not blind them to the fact that his age (54 years) and physical strength had rendered him unsuited to further activity in the field.

On the day of Walton's resignation, the Washington Artillery was ordered to rejoin the 1st Corps, and regularly report through its chief. This order of Gen. Pendleton's no doubt precipitated Walton's final action. But special authority was obtained from the President overruling Pendleton's order, and the battalion was assigned to Col. Walker's 3d Corps Artillery, although desirous of being attached to Beauregard's command. This transfer met with Pendleton's approval, provided another battalion were assigned to the 1st Corps in its place. On July 31, however, Maj. Owen was again assigned to the command of the 13th Virginia Battalion, which he had previously commanded in Tennessee, relieving Maj. Gibbes and reporting to Lieut.-Col. Frank Huger, Acting Chief of Artillery 1st Corps, in the absence of Alexander. The 13th Virginia Battalion then consisted of Davidson's, Walker's "Otey," and Dickenson's batteries, with 12 guns and 450 men.

Another matter affecting the artillery organization now came up for final adjustment. During the month of July, Maj. Edgar F. Moseley, who, though holding his commission in the 1st Virginia Regiment of Artillery, had for some time commanded a battalion under Beauregard, was promoted lieutenant-colonel and reassigned to the same battalion. From the first it had appeared an incongruity to allow officers of a single independent regiment to be promoted without reference to other commands and to command battalions while holding a commission in this regiment. Before Col. Brown's death, he had sought to have Maj. Moseley promoted in the 1st Regiment vice Lieut.-Col. Coleman, but met with Pendleton's opposition on the ground that there could be no such independent regimental promotion. But at last Moseley was promoted without reference to Pendleton's views, whereupon the Chief of Artillery strenuously protested against the disregard of the claims of other officers in the arm, senior in rank, and with infinitely more service than Moseley had to his credit. Furthermore, Pendleton now sought to have the old regimental organization of the 1st Virginia Artillery abolished as inconsistent with the general scheme of artillery organization.

This regiment was organized under state authority in 1861, in the Army of the Peninsula under Magruder,

and turned over to the Confederacy as such by Virginia. Magruder, it will be recalled, was an artilleryman
himself, and had with Alexander, from the first urged
the organization of artillery in large groups, and this
he proceeded to do in his own army. The original officers elected in the regiment were Col. George W.
Randolph, afterwards Brigadier-General and Secretary of War, Lieut.-Col. Henry Coalter Cabell, and
Maj. John Thompson Brown. When Randolph was
promoted, Cabell became colonel and Brown lieutenant-
colonel, but the majority remained vacant for some time.
The companies associated to form the regiment were
the Richmond Fayette, originally commanded by
Randolph, then Cabell; the 2d Richmond Howitzers,
originally commanded by Brown; the 3d Richmond
Howitzers, orginally commanded by Robert Stanard;
Sands' or Ritter's Henrico; Southall's or Wyatt's
Albemarle; and Allen's Hampton; Cosnahan's Peninsula; Coke's Williamsburg; Young's Yorktown; and
Richardson's James City, batteries. Of these Allen's
was soon detached from the Army of Northern Virginia, being brigaded with another to form Allen's Battalion, while Cosnahan's and Coke's were merged in
the spring of 1862 under Capt. John Coke. In October,
Coke's and Ritter's batteries were broken up and the
men and guns distributed among other batteries, so that
but six of its original batteries remained in the Army
after the reorganization, the Fayette being sooner or
later assigned to Dearing's, then Read's, the 2d and 3d
Howitzers to the 1st Virginia Regiment under Brown,
and Wyatt's to Poague's Battalion, while Young's and
Richardson's only remained with Moseley when elected
major of the regiment in the summer of 1862.

In July, 1864, Young's Battery alone remained in
Moseley's Battalion, Richardson's being on detached
duty at Chaffin's Bluff, so that the original regiment
was virtually defunct and was entitled to no field-
officers.

Pendleton's recommendation for the official disband-
ment of the regiment was forwarded approved by Gen.
Lee and referred to Gen. Bragg by the Secretary of
War, who endorsed the views of the Chief of Artillery.
The upshot of the whole matter was the official dis-
bandment of the regiment on August 29, 1864, and its
recognition as a battalion of six companies to which no
extraordinary rule of promotion should apply.

Having taken steps to accomplish this end, though
failing in having the Washington Artillery reassigned
to the 1st Corps, Pendleton now called on Col. Jones
for the return of Read's Battalion to Pickett's Division,
from which it had been detached to operate with Hoke.

When Lee crossed the James on June 17 and 18, he
had left behind near Malvern Hill Cutshaw's and
Hardaway's battalions of the 2d Corps under Col.
Carter to patrol the river and resist the approach of
transports and gunboats. On the 13th of July, Col.
Carter, with Cutshaw's Battalion, had moved to
Walker's farm, while a small Confederate cavalry
force advanced towards Rowland's Mill and a regiment
to the vicinity of Charles City Court House. Carter's
scouts along the river reported that no vessels of any
kind had passed down the river since the 11th, but about
4 P. M. he discerned two vessels, one a passenger and
the other a freight steamer, moving up stream. Throwing Cutshaw's guns into action on the bank, among
them a Whitworth rifle, Carter opened fire on these
vessels, injuring the freighter to some extent and striking the transport, which caused it to turn back to Fort
Powhatan before reaching the channel nearest the guns.
That night the battalion withdrew to Phillip's Farm,
six miles back from the river, and went into camp. On
the 14th, Carter reappeared at Malvern Hill and with
the Whitworth drove off a picket gunboat opposite
Turkey Island House. Two days later the Whitworth
successfully drove back down the river three small gunboats which had steamed up stream to clear the river of
the Confederate artillery, while Graham's Battery of

Hardaway's Battalion, with four 20-pounder Parrotts opened from Tilghman's Gate upon the pontoon bridge, a gunboat, and the Federal camp at Deep Bottom. The gunboat was struck several times and finally retired to the cover of the river bank and the camp was thrown into such a commotion that an entire brigade left the woods near Four-Mile Creek at a double-quick and took shelter in the trenches. Carter also employed his cannoneers in these expeditions as sharpshooters, having armed them with captured cavalry carbines, and proposed thereafter to operate with a single battery fully mounted. Again it may be said, this was remarkable service for field artillery, but it showed the ready adaptability of that arm to meet the exigencies of any situation.

Carter's activity along the James shelling the Federal transports, gunboats, and landings, kept Butler in such a constant state of alarm, that soon Grant's attention was directed to this quarter. On the 26th, Hancock with 20,000 infantry and 22 pieces of artillery, and Sheridan with 6,000 cavalry, were started for Deep Bottom to coöperate with Butler in surprising the Confederates, and making a dash upon Richmond. Wilcox's Division was already at Drewry's Bluff, for noting a movement among the enemy towards the James, Lee had sent it and Kershaw's Division on the 24th to reenforce Conner's Brigade and Carter's artillery force on the north bank of the river. During the night of the 26th, Hancock and Sheridan crossed the river and at dawn advanced. Kershaw's Infantry almost at once fell back, leaving Graham's 1st Rockbridge Battery without supports in an advanced position, where after defending itself with superb coolness for some time its four large Parrotts were captured. On hearing of Hancock's crossing, Lee immediately sent over W. H. F. Lee's Division of cavalry with McGregor's Battery, and Heth's Division of the 2d Corps, while on the night of the 28th, Poague's Battalion and Penick's Battery were ordered from their positions north of the Appomattox to join Col. Carter. When Grant found that his movement had been anticipated, he ordered Hancock to recross the river on the night of the 29th. Col. Poague was now directed to take position on the left of Pickett's line, and guard that flank against the approach of the enemy from Dutch Gap, where he remained throughout the winter shelling Butler's working parties along the canal with guns and mortars.

On the north side of the river, the Confederate line extended from New Market toward White Oak Swamp, the right resting near the Chaffin farm. When Hancock first appeared before this line, Gen. Ewell, who commanded the Richmond defenses, had urged the turning out of the Local Defense troops, but to this the Secretary of War had objected on account of the inconvenience and interruption it caused the government departments, from which the men were mostly drawn. The dispatch of Anderson to the James by Gen. Lee, with Wilcox's and Kershaw's divisions, had rendered the step unnecessary, but Lieut.-Col. Pemberton, in charge of the Artillery defenses of the city, had on the 27th posted two batteries of Lightfoot's Battalion at the intersection of the Mill and Varina Roads, behind Conner's right, and the other battery near the New Market Road, all on the exterior line of works, while Maj. Stark's Battalion, composed of the Mathews and Giles batteries under Capts. Andrew D. Armistead and David A. French, respectively, were posted near the Barton house. Pemberton's two battalions numbered 700 men with 22 guns, or about 100 men per battery. Soon the Louisiana Guard Battery, Capt. Charles A. Green, Jr., which had been on duty in Richmond since its misfortune on the Rapidan, joined Stark's Battalion.

CHAPTER XLIV

THE CRATER

WE have seen that Gen. Alexander had detected signs of the enemy's mining operations, and that on July 1 the Confederate engineers had opened counter-mines. By July 10, the Confederates had done enough work, had it been done at the salient, to have heard the enemy, who would have been directly beneath them. Besides those on the flanks of the salient, two other shafts farther to the left near Colquitt's and Gracie's salients were opened on the 10th and 19th, respectively, and were being vigorously pushed. A perfect mania for tunneling seemed to have broken out among the Confederates. On the 11th, Bushrod Johnson urged that listening galleries be constructed along his lines, all of which goes to show that no one but Alexander had really perceived the enemy's objective. On the 12th, the enemy opened upon Wise's Brigade an un-usually heavy mortar fire, which not only necessitated night work on the bomb-proofs, but caused Johnson to order greater efforts on Maj. Moseley's part to sub-due this fire.

Before leaving the Army, Alexander had placed about half a dozen Coehorn mortars in the ravines im-mediately in rear of Elliott's salient, and on June 20 he had posted the 16 guns of Haskell's Battalion in the sunken Jerusalem Road, 600 yards in its rear, all under Col. Haskell. Though somewhat exposed to the enemy's fire, which overshot the works in their front, Haskell's batteries were not permitted to break ground or show any sign of their presence. This disposition of these guns was a foresight for which the entire Army, as we shall see, should have been grateful to Alexander.

On the 27th, Alexander, before being ordered to the north of the James River, carefully inspected his lines and was by no means satisfied with the protection Col.

Huger had provided for the 1st Corps guns. The works of Huger's and Cabell's battalions were in his opinion entirely too slight to withstand the fire of the heavy pieces, which he expected the enemy to bring to bear on them. Accordingly Huger was directed to employ his cannoneers in strengthening these works, as no infantry or other labor was available.

The next day, Col. Walker, who still had Pegram's, McIntosh's, and Richardson's battalions less Penick's Battery, in position on Huger's right, reported that the enemy were strengthening their works in his front, and increasing the number of their guns to such an extent that he was working his cannoneers in reliefs of from 40 to 100 men day and night, while Mahone's Division of the 3d Corps alone remained in the trenches in support of his guns. On the night of the 28th, Colquitt's Brigade of Hoke's Division, and Wise's of Johnson's Division were secretly transferred to the portion of the line which had been held by Field's Division before it was moved across the James River with Anderson to oppose Hancock, while Gracie's Division was placed in the works on Johnson's left. The utmost caution and silence was enjoined upon the troops. Capt. Richard G. Pegram's Petersburg Battery, of Coit's Battalion, still occupied Elliott's salient.

Having practically completed his mine, Grant had sought, as we have seen, to draw off a large portion of the Confederates to the north side of the river, before springing it. A gallery 511 feet long, with two branch galleries at the end, to the right and left, each 37 feet long, had been successfully dug. Col. Pleasants' method of ventilation was a simple one. "When the tunnel had penetrated the hill far enough to need it, a close partition was built across it near the entrance with a close-fitting door. Through the partition on the side of this door was passed the open end of a large square box, or closed trough, which was built along on the floor of the tunnel, conveying the fresh outside air to the far end of the tunnel, where the men extending it were at work.

"To create a draught through the air box, a fireplace was excavated in the side of the tunnel, within the partition, and a chimney was pierced through the hill above it. A small fire in this chimney place, and the outside air would pass through the air-box to the far end of the tunnel, whence it would return and escape up the chimney, taking with it the foul air of the tunnel." This gallery was finished July 17th, the flank galleries on the 23d, and on the 28th, the very day Lee was moving his troops from his line to oppose Grant's feint to the north, each gallery was charged with 4,000 pounds of gunpowder.

The Federals knew that Lee had detected their operations, for they themselves could hear the Confederates at work in the countermines. Nevertheless, they determined to delay the explosion until preparations for a grand charge to succeed it could be completed. For the assault a large force of infantry was to be employed, which was to rush forward under cover of the concentrated fire of many batteries. From their signal towers, the Federal lookouts had located the position of nearly every gun in the Confederate lines, and 81 heavy guns and mortars, and about as many field pieces were brought up and placed in position to bear on them. But Haskell's Battalion was overlooked, thanks to Alexander.

Having failed in his effort against Ewell's outer line, Grant at Deep Bottom on the 28th gave orders for the explosion of the mine on the morning of the 30th. "The explosion might have been arranged for the afternoon of the 29th, but the morning of the 30th was chosen, as it permitted the placing of more heavy guns and mortars for the bombardment, which would follow the explosion as well as preliminary arrangements, such as massing the troops, removing parapets and abattis to make passages for the assaulting columns, and posting of pioneers to remove our abattis and open passages for artillery through our lines. Depots of intrenching tools, with sand bags, gabions, fascines, etc., were established, that lodgments might be more quickly made, though the pioneers of all regiments were already supplied with tools." Engineer officers were detailed to accompany each corps, and the Chief Engineer was directed to park his pontoon trains at a convenient point, ready to move at a moment's warning, for Meade having assured himself that the Confederates had no second line on Cemetery Hill, as he had formerly supposed, and as had been positively reported to him, was now sanguine of success, and made these preparations to meet the contingency of the meagre Confederate force retiring beyond the Appomattox and burning the bridges. In such an event, he proposed to push immediately across the river and Swift Creek and open up communications with Butler at Bermuda Hundred, before Lee could send any reinforcements from his five divisions north of the James.

On the afternoon of the 29th, when Meade issued his orders for the attack, Lee had but three small divisions, Johnson's, Hoke's, and Mahone's behind his works, and Alexander's, Jones', and three battalions of Walker's Artillery. As soon as it was dark, Burnside was to mass his troops in the valley opposite Elliott's salient and remove the abattis in his front, so that the columns of assault might debouch rapidly. He was to spring the mine at about 3:30 A. M., and, moving rapidly through the breach, seize the crest of Cemetery Hill, a ridge four hundred yards in rear of the Confederate lines.

Ord was to mass the 18th Corps in rear of the 9th, and to follow and support Burnside's right.

Warren was to reduce the number of men holding his front to the minimum, concentrate heavily on the right of his corps, and support Burnside's left. Hancock was to mass the 2d Corps in rear of Ord's trenches, and be prepared to support the assault as developments might dictate, while Hunt was to concentrate his artillery on the hostile guns in, and commanding the salient. Thus did Grant mass 60,000 men to fall upon a single point of Lee's ten miles of line, behind the whole of which there was hardly one man for every six in the assaulting column. Now let another describe what occurred:*

"Long before dawn of the 30th the troops were in position, and at half past three, punctually to the minute, the mine was fired. Then the news passed swiftly down the lines, and the dark columns, standing in serried masses, waited in dread suspense the signal, knowing that death awaited many of them on yonder crest, yet not animated by the stern joy of coming fight, nor yet rosolved that though death stalked forth with horrid mien from the dreadful breach, it should be but to greet victory.

"Minute followed minute of anxious waiting,—a trial to even the most determined veterans,—and now the east was streaked with gray, yet the tender beauty of the dim tranquillity remained unvexed of any sound of war, save one might hear a low hum amid the darkling swarm as grew the wonder at delay. Nor was the cause of hindrance easy to ascertain, for should it prove that the fuse was still alight, burning but slowly, to enter the mine was certain death. Thus time dragged slowly on, telegram upon telegram of inquiry meanwhile pouring in from Meade, who, unmindful of the dictum of Napoleon, that 'in assaults a general should be with his troops,' had fixed his headquarters full a mile away. But these were all unheeded, for Burnside knew not what to answer.

"Then it was that two brave men, whose names should be mentioned with respect whenever courage is honored, Lieut. Jacob Douty and Sergt. Henry Rees, both of the Forty-eighth Pennsylvania, volunteered for the peculiar service and entered the mine. Crawling on their hands and knees, groping in utter darkness, they found that the fuse had gone out about 50 feet from the mouth of the main gallery, relighted it and retired.

"'In eleven minutes now the mine will explode,' Pleasants reports to Burnside at thirty-three minutes past four, and a small group of officers of the Forty-eighth, standing upon the slope of the main parapet, anxiously await the result.

"'It lacks a minute yet,' says Pleasants, looking at his watch.

"'Not a second,' cried Douty, 'for there she goes.'

"A slight tremor of the earth for a second, then the rocking as of an earthquake, and with a tremendous burst which rent the sleeping hills beyond, a vast column of earth and smoke shoots upward to a great height, its dark sides flashing out sparks of fire, hangs poised for a moment in mid-air, and then hurtling downward with a roaring sound, showers of stones, broken timbers, and blackened human limbs, subsides—the gloomy pall of darkening smoke flushing to an angry crimson as it floats away to meet the morning sun. Pleasants has done his work with terrible completeness, for now the site of the Elliott Salient is marked by a horrid chasm, 135 feet in length, 97 feet in breadth, and 30 feet deep, and its brave garrison all asleep, save the guards, when thus surprised by sudden death, lie buried beneath the jagged blocks of blackened clay—in all, 256 officers and men of the 18th and 22d South Carolina,—2 officers and 20 men of Pegram's Petersburg Battery."

Two of Pegram's guns were hurled through the air to a great distance. Of the two Confederate galleries on the flanks of the mine, one, which was unoccupied, was destroyed by the explosion, while the miners at work in the other were badly shaken up but climbed out and escaped as the gallery was not crushed in.

"The dread upheaval has rent in twain Elliott's Brigade, and the men to the right and left of the large abyss recoil in terror and dismay. Nor shall we censure them, for so terrible was the explosion that even the assaulting column sunk back aghast, and nearly ten minutes elapsed before it could be reformed.

"Now a storm of fire bursts in red fury from the Federal front, and in an instant all the valley between the hostile lines lies shrouded in bellowing smoke. Then Marshall, putting himself at the head of the stormers, sword in hand, bids his men to follow.

"But there comes no response befitting the stern grandeur of the scene—no trampling charge—no rolling drums of austerity—no fierce shouts of warlike joy as burst from men of the 'Light Division' when they mounted the breach of Badajos, or from Frazier's Royals, as they crowned the crimson slopes of Saint Sebastian.

"No, none of this there. But a straggling line of men of the Second Brigade, First Division, uttering a mechanical cheer, slowly mounts the crest, passes unmolested across the intervening space, and true to the instinct, fostered by long service in the trenches, plunges into the Crater, courting the friendly shelter of its crumbling sides.

"Yonder lies Cemetery Hill in plain view, naked of men, and hard beyond the brave old town, nestling whitely in its wealth of green.

"Silence still reigned along the Confederate lines, yet Ledlie's men did not advance, and now the supporting brigade of the same division running forward over the same crest, and with an incredible folly crowding in upon their comrades, already huddled together in the shelving pit, all regimental and company organization was lost, and the men speedily passed from the control of their officers.

"If we except Elliott, who with the remnant of his brigade was occupying the ravine to the left and rear of the Crater, no officer of rank was present on the Confederate side to assume immediate direction of affairs, and a considerable time elapsed before Beauregard and Lee,—both beyond the Appomattox,—were informed by Col. Paul, of Beauregard's staff, of the nature and locality of the disaster.

"But almost on the moment, John Haskell, of South Carolina, a glorious young battalion commander, whose name will be forever associated with the Artillery Corps of the Army of Northern Virginia, galloped to the front, followed by two light batteries, and having disposed these pieces along the Plank Road, and opened Flanner's light guns from the Gee house, passed to his left to speak a word of cheery commendation to Lamkin of his battalion, who was already annoying the swarming masses of the enemy with his Virginia Battery of eight-inch mortars. Passing through the covered way, Haskell sought Elliott, and, pointing out to him the defenseless position of the guns on the Plank Road, urged him to make such dispositions as would afford them protection. Essaying this, Elliott sprang forward, followed by a mere handful of brave fellows, but, almost on the instant, fell stricken by a grievous hurt and was borne from his last field of battle.

"The fire of the enemy's artillery was now very severe, owing to their superior weight of metal, and the guns of the Plank Road, exposed in addition to the fire of the sharpshooters, were suffering such loss that it was determined to retire all but six pieces, and, as the situation seemed rather hopeless, to call for volunteers to man these. To Haskell's proud delight every gun detachment volunteered to remain.

"Nor did the artillery to the right and left fail to bear themselves with the resolution of men conscious that, for the time, the hope of the Army was centered in their steadiness, and that their guns alone barred the road to Petersburg; for, let me repeat, Cemetery Hill was naked of men."

With the superb Haskell encouraging them to every effort, his cannoneers labored at their pieces like fiends. He actually moved two detachments with their mortars forward to the trenches within fifty yards of the Crater, into which they burst their shell at a surprising rate. No less active was Maj. Hampton Gibbes, whose battalion, on the right of the Crater, opened as soon as the pieces could be brought to bear on the

enemy's massed troops. At first the left gun of Davidson's Battery alone had an effective command of the
Crater, and it was left for a time unserved through the
misbehavior of the acting battery commander, Lieut.
James C. Otey, who, owing to a combination of circumstances, was the only officer at the time present
with the battery. This unfortunate young officer, the
first and the last in the whole career of Lee's Artillery
Corps to abandon his guns in cowardice, seems to have
been entirely unmanned by the awfulness of the cata-
clysm, in which he and his men had all but been en-
gulfed. Let us not be too harsh in our judgment of
him. Let us imagine ourselves in his position and ask
if the mere thought of such an experience as that
through which he had passed does not shake our resolution. If poor Otey were at fault, then he has long
since atoned for his misdoing. To the writer he is more
to be pitied, and demands more of charity than any
other soldier in that grand artillery corps of Lee's
Army. Would that his name might not be mentioned,
but there it is in black and white in the record for all
time. The hand of mortal cannot obliterate it, the stain
is indelible. The incident is not recounted here to hold
Otey up to scorn, but to show that misconduct before
the enemy was so rare, so unheard of in Lee's Artillery,
that even on the part of a miserable, insignificant youth,
it attracted the attention of an army.

If Otey allowed his guns to remain inactive, it was
not to be for long, for Gibbes and Maj. Samuel Preston, of Wise's Brigade, personally manned one of the
pieces and worked them with excellent effect, until they
both fell desperately wounded, thus making glorious
the spot of Otey's defection. Again the guns became
silent, and again a number of artillery officers, heedless
of all personal danger, rushed to the position to man the
pieces. This time it was Lieut.-Col. Huger, Acting
Chief of Artillery of the 1st Corps, with Capts. Winthrop, Mason, and Haskell, of Gen. Alexander's staff,
that reopened the fire, soon joined by Private L. T.

Covington, of Pegram's destroyed battery. "Frank Huger, who like Edward Freer of the Forty-third had seen more combats than he could count years, was, as always, to the fore, working as a simple cannoneer at his heated Napoleons, cheering and encouraging his men by joyful voice and valiant example." Thus did Gibbes, Preston, Huger, and the other gallant artillerymen maintain their fire at the critical moment in spite of the concentration of the enemy's guns upon them until, spurring hard from the hospital, with the fever still upon him, came Lieut. John Hampden Chamberlayne, of the 3d Corps Artillery, who with volunteers from other batteries and Wise's infantrymen, so handled the guns which had been abandoned by their men and until then only manned by a few officers, that from that day the battery bore his name, and he wore another bar upon his collar.

The left gun of Davidson's Battery in the next salient on the right of the Crater, which in the hands of those we have mentioned did such fearful execution, was so well protected that it could never be kept silent by Hunt's concentrated fire. Whenever the Federals showed themselves it reopened. Gibbes alone fired forty or more rounds, at a range of less than 400 yards, with it, before he was wounded. Five hundred yards to the left was Wright's Halifax Battery of Coit's Battalion. These guns, which had a flanking fire on the left of the destroyed salient and across all the approaches thereto, were posted in the depression behind the infantry line and thoroughly masked from the hostile artillery fire not only by the ground in their front, but by a heavy fringe of pines in advance of the Federal line, which the enemy had carelessly neglected to level. Wright's fire was rapid, incessant, and accurate, causing great loss. The Federal Artillery made vain efforts to locate him with their mortar shells, which tore up the ground all around, but could never hit him or silence his four guns. Besides these, a half dozen or more of Haskell's 8-inch Coehorn mortars, from two or three ra-

vines in the rear, threw shell aimed at the Crater, and
Langhorne's 10-inch mortars along the Baxter Road
also took part in the work of destruction. It was now,
too, that Alexander's foresight was to yield such fine results, for Haskell's sixteen guns which he had so long
kept concealed in the sunken Jerusalem Plank Road
were in position 600 yards directly in rear of the Crater.
The group simply swept the front from first to last.

As soon as the Federal attack developed, Cutts' great
group of guns north of the Appomattox opposite the
enemy's right, and Jones' batteries along Beauregard's
front near the river, opened upon the hostile artillery
and kept up a furious cannonade to prevent Hunt from
concentrating his fire upon the point to be assaulted, and
on the Confederate right Walker's batteries also sought
to divert the enemy's fire.*

"On the Federal side, Griffin of Potter's Division, not waiting
for Wilcox, pushed forward his brigade, and gained ground to the
north of the Crater, and Bliss's Brigade of the same division,
coming to his support, still further ground was gained in that
direction. But his leading regiments, deflected by the hostile fire,
bore to their left, and, mingling with Ledlie's men swarming along
the sides of the great pit, added to the confusion. Wilcox now
threw forward a portion of his division and succeeded in occupying
about one hundred and fifty yards of the works south of the Crater,
but stopped by the fire of Chamberlayne's guns, and, whenever
occasion offered, by the fire of the infantry, his men on the exposed
flank gave ground, and, pushing the right regiment into the Crater,
the confusion grew worse confounded. Some of the men, indeed,
from fear of suffocation, had already emerged from the pit and
spread themselves to the right and left, but this was a matter
of danger and difficulty, for the ground was scored with covered
ways and traverses, honeycombed with bomb-proofs, and swept by
the artillery. Others of them pressed forward and got into the
ditch of the unfinished gorge lines, while not a few creeping along
the glacis of the exterior line, made their way over the parapet into
the main trench. In all this there was much hand-to-hand fighting,
for many men belonging to the dismembered brigades still found
shelter behind the traverses and bomb-proofs and did not easily
yield.

---

*As regards the execution of Chamberlayne's guns, see especially statement
of Gen. Warren, *Report of Conduct of the War* (1865), Vol. I, p. 166; Gen.
Hunt, pp. 98, 184; Duane, p. 100.
    For the efficiency of the Confederate artillery fire, see Meade's report, Ibid.,
p. 31; Col. Loring's statement, p. 95; Gen. Potter, pp. 87, 177.

"Meanwhile, Gen. Meade, 'groping in the dark,' to use his own phrase, sent telegram upon telegram to Burnside to know how fared the day, but received answer to none. At fifteen minutes to six, however, one hour after Ledlie's men had occupied the breach, an orderly delivered him a note in pencil, written from the Crater by Gen. Loring, Inspector General of the 9th Corps, and addressed to Gen. Burnside. This was Meade's first information from the front and was little cheer, for Loring stated briefly that Ledlie's men were in confusion and would not go forward.

"Ord was now directed to push forward the 18th Corps, and the following dispatch was sent to Richmond:

" 'HEADQUARTERS, ARMY OF THE POTOMAC,
" 'July 30, 1864, 6 A. M.

" 'MAJ.-GEN. BURNSIDE—Prisoners taken say that there is no line in their rear, and that their men were falling back when ours advanced, that none of their troops have returned from the James. Our chance is now. Push your men forward at all hazards, white and black, and don't lose time in making formations, but rush for the crest.

" 'GEORGE G. MEADE,
" 'Major-General, Commanding.'

"But Ord could not advance, for the narrow debouches were still choked up by the men of the 9th Corps and by the wounded borne from the front, and although Burnside promptly transmitted the order to his subordinates, the troops in rear moved with reluctant step, while no general of division was present with those in front to urge them forward.

"Again did Meade telegraph to Burnside: 'Every moment is most precious; the enemy are undoubtedly concentrating to meet you on the crest.' But not until 20 minutes past seven did he receive a reply to the effect that Burnside 'hoped to carry the crest, but it was hard work.'

"Then Meade's patience seems fairly to have broken down. 'What do you mean by hard work to take the crest?' he asks. 'I understand not a man has advanced beyond the enemy's line, which you occupied immediately after exploding the mine. Do you mean to say your officers and men will not obey your orders to advance? If not, what is the obstacle? I wish to know the truth, and desire an immediate answer.

" 'GEORGE G. MEADE, Major-General.'

"To which Burnside, in hot wrath, straightway replied:

" 'HEADQUARTERS, NINTH CORPS,
" '7:35 A. M.

" 'GEN. MEADE—Your dispatch by Capt. Jay received. The main body of Gen. Potter's Division is beyond the Crater.

" 'I do not mean to say that my officers and men will not obey my orders to advance. I mean to say that it is very hard to advance to the crest. I have never in any report said anything different from what I conceived to be the truth. Were it not insubordinate, I would say that the latter remark of your note was unofficerlike and ungentlemanly.

" 'A. E. BURNSIDE, *Major-General.'*

"Griffin, it is true, in obedience to orders to advance straight for Cemetery Hill, had during this time attempted several charges from his position north of the Crater, but his men displayed little spirit, and, breaking speedily under the fire of the artillery, sought their old shelter behind the traverses and covered ways. The rest of Potter's Division moved out slowly and it was fully eight o'clock, more than three hours after the explosion, when Ferrero's negro division, the men beyond question inflamed with drink, burst from the advance line, cheering vehemently, passed at a double quick over the crest under a heavy fire, and, rushing with scarce a check over the heads of the white troops in the Crater, spread to their right, capturing more than two hundred prisoners, and one stand of colors."

The negroes, however, could not traverse the space which Haskell's guns dominated. No troops with their formation could have done so. As the dense mass came in sight, partly emerging from the Crater, the sixteen guns concentrated upon it and drove the assailants to cover without the aid of a hundred muskets. A single negro private, with his musket at support arms, charged home to the guns and was felled with a rammer staff, as he sprung into the sunken road among the pieces.

At the same time that Ferrero made his effort, Turner, of the 10th Corps, pushed forward a brigade over the 9th Corps parapets, seized the Confederate line further to the north, and quickly disposed the remaining brigades of his division to confirm his success.

"Now was the crisis of the day, and fortunate was it for maiden and matron of Petersburg, that even at this moment there was filing into the ravine, between Cemetery Hill and the drunken battalions of Ferrero, a stern array of silent men, clad in faded gray, resolved with grim resolve to avert from the mother town a fate as dreadful as that which marked the three days' sack of Badajos.

"Lee, informed of the disaster at 6:10 A. M., had bidden his aide, Col. Charles Venable, to ride quickly to the right of the army and bring up two brigades of Anderson's old division, commanded by Mahone, for time was too precious to observe military etiquette, and send the orders through Hill. Shortly after the General in Chief reached the front in person, and all men took heart when they descried the grave and gracious face, and 'Traveller' stepping proudly, as if conscious that he bore upon his back the weight of a nation. Beauregard was already at the Gee house, a commanding position five hundred yards in rear of the Crater, and Hill had galloped to the right to organize an attacking column, and had ordered down Pegram, and even now the light batteries of Brander and Ellett were rattling through the town at a sharp trot, with cannoneers mounted, the sweet, serene face of their boy-colonel lit up with that glow which to his men meant hotly impending fight.

"Venable had sped upon his mission and found Mahone's men already standing to their arms; but the Federals from their lofty lookouts were busily interchanging signals, and to uncover such a length of front without exciting observation demanded the nicest precaution. Yet was the difficulty overcome by a single device, for the men being ordered to drop back one by one, as if going for water, obeyed with such intelligence that Warren continued to report to Meade that not a man had left his front.

"Then forming in the ravine in rear, the men of the Virginia and Georgia brigades came pressing down the Valley with swift, swinging stride,—not with the discontented bearing of soldiers whose discipline alone carries them to what they feel to be a scene of fruitless sacrifice, but with the glad alacrity and aggressive ardor of men impatient for battle, and who, from long knowledge of war, are conscious that Fortune has placed within their grasp an opportunity which, by the magic touch of veteran steel, may be transformed to 'swift-winged' victory.

"Halting for a moment in rear of the 'Ragland House,' Mahone bade his men strip off blankets and knapsacks, and prepare for battle.

"Then riding quickly to the front, while the troops marched in single file along the covered way, he drew rein at Bushrod Johnson's headquarters and reported in person to Beauregard. Informed that Johnson would assist in the attack with the outlying troops about the Crater, he rode still further to the front, dismounted, and, pushing along the covered way from the Plank Road, came out into the ravine in which he formed his men. Mounting the embankment at the head of the covered way, he descried within one hundred and sixty yards a forest of glittering bayonets, and beyond, floating proudly from the captured works, eleven Union flags. Estimating rapidly from the hostile colors the probable force in his front, he at once despatched his courier to bring up the

Alabama Brigade from the right, assuming thereby a grave responsibility, yet was the wisdom of the decision vindicated by the event.*

"Scarcely had the order been given when the head of the Virginia Brigade began to debouch from the covered way. Directing Col. Weisiger, its commanding officer, to file to the right and form line of battle, Mahone stood at the angle, speaking quietly and cheerily to the men. Silently and quickly they moved out and formed with that precision dear to every soldier's eyes—the sharpshooters leading, followed by the 6th, 16th, 61st, 41st, and 12th Virginia—the men of Second Manassas and Crampton Gap!

"But one caution was given,—to reserve their fire until they reached the brink of the ditch; but one exhortation, that they were counted on to do this work, and do it quickly.

"Now the leading regiment of the Georgia Brigade began to move out, when suddenly a brave Federal officer, seizing the colors, called on his men to charge. Descrying this hostile movement on the instant, Weisiger, a veteran of stern countenance, which did not belie the personal intrepidity of the man, uttered to the Virginians the single word, 'Forward.'

"Then the sharpshooters and the men of the 6th on the right, running swiftly forward, for theirs was the greater distance to traverse, the whole line sprang along the crest and there burst from more than eight hundred warlike voices that fierce yell, which no man ever yet heard unmoved on field of battle. Storms of case shot from the right mingled with the tempest of bullets which smote upon them from the front, yet was there no answering volley, for these were veterans, whose fiery enthusiasm had been wrought to a finer temper by the stern code of discipline, and even in the tumult the men did not forget their orders. Still pressing forward with steady fury, while the enemy, appalled by the inexorable advance, gave ground, they reached the ditch of the inner works— then one volley crashed from the whole line, and the 6th and 16th, with the sharpshooters clutching their empty guns and redoubling their fierce cries, leaped over the retrenched cavalier, and all down the line the dreadful work of the bayonet began.

"How long it lasted none may say with certainty, for in those fierce moments no man heeded time, no man asked, no man gave quarter; but in an incredibly brief space, as seemed to those who looked on, the whole of the advanced line north of the Crater was taken, the enemy in headlong flight, while the tattered battle flags planted along the parapets from left to right told Lee, at the Gee house, that from this nettle danger, valor had plucked the flower, safety for an army.

---

*The young courier by whom this order was transmitted was Jimmy Blakemore, an ex-cadet of the Virginia Military Institute, to whom Mahone constantly entrusted the most important missions. Mahone, it will be recalled, was himself an old cadet.

"Redoubling the sharpshooters on his right, Mahone kept down all fire from the Crater, the vast rim of which frowned down upon the lower line occupied by his troops.

"And now the scene within the horrid pit was as might be fitly portrayed only by the pencil of Dante, after he had trod 'nine-circle Hell.' From the great mortars to the right and left, huge missiles, describing graceful curves, fell at regular intervals with dreadful accuracy and burst among the helpless masses huddled together, and every explosion was followed by piteous cries, and oftentimes the very air seemed darkened by flying human limbs. Haskell, too, had moved up his Eprouvette mortars among the men of the 16th Virginia, so close, indeed, that his powder charge was but one ounce and a half—and, without intermission, the storm of fire beat upon the hapless mass imprisoned within.

"Mahone's men watched with great interest this easy method of reaching troops behind cover, and then, with the initiative ingenuity of soldiers, gleefully gathered up the countless muskets with bayonets fixed, which had been abandoned by the enemy, and propelled them with such nice skill that they came down upon Ledlie's men like the rain of the Norman arrows at Hastings.

"At half past ten the Georgia Brigade advanced and attempted to dislodge Wilcox's men, who still held a portion of the line south of the Crater, but so closely was every inch of the ground searched by artillery, so biting was the fire of musketry, that obliquing to their left, they sought cover behind the cavalier trench won by the Virginia Brigade,—many officers and men testifying by their blood how gallantly the venture had been essayed.

"Half an hour later the Alabamians under Saunders arrived, but further attack was postponed until after 1 P. M., in order to arrange for coöperation from Colquitt on the right. Sharply to the minute agreed upon, the assaulting line moved forward, and with such astonishing rapidity did these glorious soldiers rush across the intervening space that ere their first wild cries subsided their battle flags had crowned the works. The Confederate batteries were now ordered to cease firing, and forty volunteers were called for to assault the Crater, but so many of the Alabamians offered themselves for the service that the ordinary system of detail was necessary. Happily, before the assaulting party could be formed, a white handkerchief, made fast to a ramrod, was projected above the edge of the Crater, and, after a brief pause, a motley mass of prisoners poured over the side and ran for their lives to the rear.

"In this grand assault on Lee's line for which Meade had massed 65,000 troops, the enemy suffered a loss of above 5,000 men, including 1,101 prisoners, among whom were two brigade commanders, while vast quantities of small arms and twenty-one standards fell into the hands of the victors.

"Yet many brave men perished on the Confederate side. Elliott's Brigade lost severely in killed and prisoners. The Virginia Brigade, too, paid the price which glory ever exacts. The 6th carried in 98 men and lost 88, one company 'the dandies,' of course,—'Old Company F' of Norfolk, losing every man killed or wounded. Scarcely less was the loss in other regiments.

.   .   .   .

"Such was the battle of the Crater, which excited the liveliest satisfaction throughout the Army and the country. Mahone was created major-general from that date; Weisiger, who was wounded, brigadier-general; Capt. Girardey, of Mahone's staff, also brigadier, the latter an extraordinary but just promotion, for he was a young officer whose talents and decisive vigor qualified him to conduct enterprises of the highest movement. Yet, fate willed that his career should be brief, for within a fortnight he fell in battle north of the James, his death dimming the joy of victory."

We search in vain for any such recognition of those dauntless gunners, who alone stood between the enemy and Petersburg after the explosion of the mine. "Ham" Chamberlayne became a captain, but glory was the only reward Gibbes and Haskell and Huger, and the others received. Such was the lot of the artillerymen. Indeed no one seemed to think promotion, in an arm whose officers distinguished themselves on every occasion, was necessary. It would seem that the Army had come to regard deeds of heroism and feats of extraordinary valor as matters to be expected and not rewarded, in the Artillery.

"On the Federal side, crimination and recrimination followed what Gen. Grant styled 'this miserable failure.' There was a Court of Inquiry, and a vast array of dismal testimony, which disclosed the fact that of four generals of division belonging to the assaulting Corps, not *one had followed his men into the Confederate lines*. Nay, that the very commander of the storming division, finding, like honest Nym, 'the humor of the breach too hot,' was at the crisis of the fight palpitating in a bomb-proof, beguiling a Michigan surgeon into giving him a drink of rum, on the plea that 'he had malaria, and that he had been struck by a spent ball,'—

legends of a hoary antiquity, whereof, let us humbly confess, we ourselves have heard."

Although few promotions in the arm resulted from the conduct of the Artillery in the Crater fight, the Army, Petersburg, and the whole South knew that the gunners had saved the day. They knew that the batteries had stood their ground without infantry supports, and hurled back the enemy in their front. They knew how Haskell, and Pegram, and Coit, from rear, from right, and from left had formed a circle of fire about the threatened point and, unaided, denied the enemy's advance to the town, while Mahone was bringing his men up from the right just in time to prevent Ayres' Division of Warren's Corps from charging Chamberlayne's "one-gun battery," as the enemy called the piece which Gibbes and Huger and the other gallant officers had heroically kept in action. The deeds of the artillerymen were upon every tongue. Indeed, even in the Federal accounts of the affair, a large part of every report is devoted to the overwhelming and destructive effect of the Confederate Artillery and never once did the enemy thereafter forget the power of the guns which occupied the works in their front.

CHAPTER XLV

WHILE the Federals were mining, and the Confederates countermining, many things of interest to the Artillery were occurring besides the gathering of unexploded Federal shells from in front of the lines by night, and the incessant artillery practice by day.

Between July 6 and 9, Grant had detached three divisions of the 6th Corps to Washington to oppose Early and Breckinridge, who had reached Lynchburg ahead of Hunter and without a fight sent him whirling back through West Virginia, after he had devastated the Valley and destroyed much private property usually exempt from destruction, against both Lincoln's and Grant's orders. Perhaps the greatest feat of Hunter's ruthless campaign was the demolition of the Virginia Military Institute. As a measure of military necessity, this was of course justified, in so far as the burning of its buildings and military equipment was concerned, but the wanton burning of its valuable library, its scientific apparatus, and the private houses and property of its professors, over the protest of his officers, was an act for which Hunter's government will yet have to pay.*

Nelson's and Braxton's battalions of artillery which under Gen. Long were alone detached from the Army with the 2d Corps, though marching continuously and with great speed, failed to reach Lynchburg before Hunter decamped. On June 22, however, these two battalions were united with Breckinridge's Artillery near Salem. Thence the Army of the Valley moved by the direct route to Staunton. During the halt of two days at that point, Gen. Long organized his entire force

*At the time this is written, a bill is pending in the United States Senate, providing for an indemnity to the Institution for $214,000, which includes no interest. This bill was drawn and introduced by Senator Henry A. Du Pont, of Delaware, who like William McKinley was an officer in Hunter's army, and both of whom protested against the destruction of the school. Senator Du Pont was Hunter's Chief of Artillery and commanded the 5th United States Battery, solid shot from the guns of which still remain in the walls of the barrack.

of artillery. The least efficient batteries of Breckinridge's Division were to be left in a reserve artillery
camp at Staunton, in command of Maj. Leyden, while
Nelson's, Braxton's, and McLaughlin's battalions were
fully horsed, armed, and equipped. The three battalions thus organized, with forty pieces, were placed
under the immediate command of Col. J. Floyd King,
while Jackson's, Lurty's, and McClannahan's horse batteries with ten guns were organized into another battalion to operate with McCausland's force of 1,500
cavalry. The 2d Corps and Breckinridge's Division together numbered 8,000 infantry.

Hunter's retreat to the Ohio, or flight, it might be
more properly styled, left the Valley open to Early, who
promptly moved down it, and after encountering little
resistance crossed the Potomac at Shepherdstown July
5 and 6. On the 9th, he advanced upon Fredericks-
town, whereupon Gen. Wallace withdrew his force of
about 5,000 men and placed them in line of battle along
the Monocacy a mile or two east of the town.

When Early determined to attack that portion of the
line opposite the railroad bridge, the ford, and across
the Georgetown Road, Gen. Long skillfully posted a
number of guns on the west bank which soon effectively
prepared the way for McCausland and Gordon to cross
the stream. These troops were soon assailed by the
enemy, whose line of battle was formed at right angles
to the river, presenting an opportunity to Long, of
which he immediately availed himself. Gordon hardly
became engaged before the supporting artillery raked
the Federal line from flank and in reverse, immediately
crushing it and driving the enemy in a route from the
ford and bridge. Never was victory more complete,
and seldom has one of equal magnitude been attained
with so little effort and cost to the assailants. The result was due entirely to the skillful employment by
Long of his artillery in the operations of which the
most thorough coöperation between Nelson, Braxton,
and McLaughlin was obtained. On this occasion a

few batteries only were used to clear the crossings, the others being held in readiness under cover while the infantry and cavalry tempted Wallace to assail them. The plan worked to perfection, and no sooner had the Federal line advanced and exposed its flank, than Long and King threw every gun into action with decisive effect, with the loss of but a score of men and two officers. Lieut. Hobson, of the Amherst Battery, fell mortally, and Lieut. Southall, Acting Assistant Adjutant-General on Long's staff, severely wounded.

The conduct of the brave old Col. Nelson on this occasion and throughout the succeeding campaign, as well as that of McLaughlin and Braxton, was highly commendable. William Nelson, closely connected by blood with Lee, Pendleton, Page, Braxton, Carter, and many other officers of the Artillery, was a picturesque character. Among the first to raise a battery in the spring of 1861, he had gradually risen to high rank. Like Cabell, he was not noted for dash, nor was he by training a soldier. But he possessed an unblemished character, was sternly courageous, as dependable as any officer in the Army, and was adored by his men who regarded him as a father. The young farmer boys of Hanover, and Louisa counties, flocked by hundreds to his standard, and followed him from first to last with a devotion which military prowess alone could not have commanded. In appearance, the "Old Colonel," as his men affectionately styled him, was truly a remarkable figure. Gen. Bushrod Johnson commonly wore a linen duster and straw hat, Gen. William Smith, ex-Governor of Virginia and known as "Extra Billy," usually carried an umbrella on the march, Gen. Mahone a cow in his headquarters train, but Col. Nelson alone adorned himself with a high silk hat! On many occasions as he rode past strange troops, the men with shouts of merriment cried after him, "Old man, come out of that hat!" and similar humorous gibes. This eccentricity of dress, however, was not abandoned by him in spite of the derisive comments of the soldiery. His own men knew

and loved him, for after all it was the head and heart
and not the helmet of their leader that mattered.

On the 10th, Early advanced rapidly against Washington, which beside its garrison of near 20,000 troops
was now defended by the two divisions of the 6th Corps
detached from Petersburg, and 6,000 men of the 19th
just arrived from New Orleans. After creating great
alarm in the north, Early withdrew from before the
Capital on the night of the 12th, conscious of his inability
to carry the strong Federal works by storm, recrossed the Potomac at White's Ford on the 14th, encamped for a few days at Leesburg, and then moved
through Snicker's Gap to Berryville, picketing the adjacent fords of the Shenandoah River with his artillery.

McLaughlin at Castleman's Ferry was soon heavily
engaged in repelling an attempt of the enemy's advance
guard to cross, but as the main column began to arrive
Early retired from Berryville *via* White Post to Newtown. Col. Nelson with two batteries then accompanied
Ramseur's Division to Winchester where they made an
unsuccessful attack upon the enemy, losing the guns of
Kirkpatrick's Amherst Battery. Nelson had advanced
his guns so close to the Federal line that when Ramseur's troops met with a severe reverse and fell back
in confusion, the battalion commander, whose conduct
was heroic on this occasion, was unable to save Kirkpatrick's guns. The battery was rearmed, however,
August 20.

After retiring to Strasburg and allowing the enemy
to occupy Winchester and push their advance to Newtown, Early turned upon them a few days later and
drove them in great haste through Winchester toward
Martinsburg. The Federal retreat was so rapid that although it was followed across the Potomac at Williamsport, no punishment could be inflicted upon the enemy,
and Early resumed his position at Strasburg. During
these operations the Artillery, while little engaged, was
called upon for the most tremendous exertions in marching and countermarching.

At this juncture, Sheridan assumed command of a large Federal force in the Valley, and Early fell back before him to Fisher's Hill. Before the end of July, Early's command had marched by road over 400 miles, losing less than 3,000 men, and dispersing two armies of an aggregate strength of double his own. During this period, the Artillery was constantly with the infantry column and with the exception of the physical breakdown of Gen. Long, was in as good order as when it left Cold Harbor. As a record of field artillery marching this campaign is worthy of the most careful study, for in that respect it excelled all others of the war and shows to what a high degree of mobility field batteries may be brought. Horses now are just as capable of performing such work as they were in 1864, and yet it is doubtful if a single battery in our army could march 400 miles on short provender, in less than 60 days, and engage in a pitched battle with any degree of effect.*

Meanwhile Anderson with Kershaw's Division and Cutshaw's Battalion of artillery had joined Early, and on the 14th of August, Fitz Lee's Division of cavalry with Johnston's and Shoemakers's horse batteries arrived at Front Royal. Early again drove the enemy out of Winchester. On the 19th, Gen. Long was compelled to relinquish his command, placing Col. Nelson in charge of the Artillery, while Capt. Kirkpatrick assumed command of Nelson's Battalion.

After much marching and skirmishing, in all of which the Artillery was constantly engaged, the enemy retired to Harper's Ferry on the 21st. Early remained in the neighborhood of Charles Town until the 25th, moving thence to Shepherdstown, and then into camp at Bunker Hill. On the 31st, Milledge's and Massie's batteries accompanied Rodes' Division to Martinsburg, where the latter battery was heavily engaged. Early then concentrated his army near Stephenson's Depot.

Col. Carter had been relieved from his more or less amphibious duties along the James on August 2, and

---

*Early made enforced requisition upon the Maryland farmers for horses, but only a few were assigned to the artillery. See his *Memoirs,* p. 395.

ordered to join Early as Chief of Artillery. He reported for duty September 9. His selection to fill Gen. Long's place was as wise as it was merited. In all that great army, there was not a more gallant artilleryman than Tom Carter, of Pampatyke, devoted friend and near kinsman of Lee. Graduating from the Virginia Military Institute in the Class of 1849, he studied medicine at the University of Virginia. He soon forsook his profession, however, and settled upon his fine estate in King William County. There during the years immediately preceding the war, he reigned in lordly state among his kinsmen and people, as his father had done before him. Noted for the purity and strength of his character, beloved and respected by all, dispensing hospitality to his friends and charity to the poor and needy of the country-side, he peacefully awaited the call to arms, ready to repay with blood and valor his State for the education it had given him. No sooner was the summons issued than he called together his slaves, admonished them to be faithful in his absence, and committing them to the care of a young and beautiful wife, saddled his thoroughbred charger and rode proudly to the Court House where the guidon of his battery was planted, and assumed command as if by inherited right. A few days, nay hours, saw the King William Artillery ready to receive its guns, for a hundred feminine hands had toiled ceaselessly with needle and thread upon the uniforms for his men. With a score of young kinsmen of the country-side, consumed with martial ardor, there was no lack of material for the officers and noncommissioned officers of the battery, mounted as they were upon the best blooded animals which Virginia could boast. There was no need to teach these men horsemanship, and the influence a century of association among their projenitors and a lifetime spent with their captain supplied the discipline of regular troops. A cousin of Robert E. Lee, Tom Carter combined more of the modesty, simplicity, and valor of his great kinsman than any other man in Virginia. It is recounted that at Seven Pines, while he sat with one foot in his stirrup and the other thrown across the pommel of his saddle, coolly directing under a hail of fire the remaining fragment of his battery, up rode D. H. Hill, of iron nerve, and in the midst of the carnage about him, rose in his stirrups and after saluting Carter declared that he would rather be the captain of the King William Artillery than President of the Confederate States.

From that day when Carter first fought under the eye of Lee, his name was the very synonym of valor. Promotion meant nothing to him. It came it is true, and was well earned, but his sole desire was to serve Lee and Virginia faithfully and well. On several occasions he was not rewarded by increased rank when it should have been given him, but he was the kinsman of Lee and knew that in spite of his merit his claims must not be pressed. So it was that when Shoup was promoted in the Western Army, Carter preferred to remain in Virginia, to the soil of which every tie of blood and duty bound him. It was in Virginia that he belonged and there he remained. As the great invading host swept around Lee's Army, trampling Carter's crops, driving off his horses and cattle, demolishing his barns and fences, it was there on the very lawns of his ancestral estate that he planted his guns while a devoted wife, with the sublime courage of womanhood, ministered tenderly to the victims of his fire. Soon the crash of the guns ceased to disturb the peace of Pampatyke, but not until it lay a rent and bleeding wreck in the path of the great armies. But still at her post its mistress remained, surrounded only by a score of faithful blacks, who looked upon the tragic scenes of war, and bewildered could not understand. Hardly a week that the cavalry patrols of one army or the other did not pass and repass, or that the heroic wife of the absent artilleryman did not like a sainted creature beckon some ambulance with its woeful burden through the gates of Pampatyke. Friend and foe alike there found relief, for while the lips of Sue Roy bade her soldier husband struggle on to

the last, her angelic hands and heart were animated
only by the spirit of Christ in the alleviation of the suffering about her.   Her deeds were known to all—to both
armies,—and so when her gallant husband returned
from Appomattox, he was able to receive into his home,
wrecked but not wholly destroyed, the weary chieftain
whom he had followed on a hundred battlefields.   Ah!
who can say what were the emotions of Robert E. Lee,
and Tom Carter, and Sue Roy during those bitter days
after Appomattox.   Let us not profane the sanctity of
their haven of retreat.   Let us avert our eyes after seeing the great master of war dismount at the doorway,
and grasp in silence the outstretched hand of the kinsman whose blood had proved his devotion.   More of the
sacred scene is not for us.   Let us leave them, as an
ancient negro respectfully slips the martial trappings
from the back of old Traveller, and turns him out to
rest and graze beneath the patriarchal oaks of Pampatyke, where no longer the manger is full, where no
longer the grain bins are laden with the golden freight
of yore, where no longer the fields are flooded by a sea
of tasseled wheat.   But leaving them, how can it be
otherwise than with regret that ours is not the brush
to place on canvas this scene, so sweetly pathetic, and
yet so fraught with lessons of fortitude and courage that
no man might look thereon without seeing through his
tears a flash of the unconquerable spirit of Lee and Virginia.

Such as we have described him, was Col. Thomas H.
Carter, the man who now succeeded Gen. Long in command of Early's Artillery.   He came to this important
post just as he did to the county courthouse in the spring
of 1861, received by all not only with respect, but with
affectionate regard.   He did not come to displace Nelson.   He merely received his long deferred due.*

At daylight on the 19th of September, the Confederate cavalry pickets at the crossing of the Opequon
and Berryville Road, were driven in, and information

*After the war Col. Carter became Rector of the University of Virginia.

having been received by Early of the fact, he immediately ordered all the troops at Stephenson's Depot to be in readiness to move, while Gordon, who had arrived from Bunker Hill, was directed to move at once. By some mistake, Gordon failed to receive his orders. Ramseur was already in position across the Berryville Road skirmishing with the enemy, when Early reached him and learned that Gordon was not moving up. He at once directed Breckinridge and Rodes to hasten forward as rapidly as possible. The position occupied by Ramseur was about one mile and a half out from Winchester on an elevated plateau between Abraham's Creek and Red Bud Run, in the angle formed by the Martinsburg and Front Royal roads. In his right front the country was open, while to his left the ground sloped off to Red Bud Run along which there were some patches of woods which afforded cover for troops. In his front and towards the Opequon ran the Berryville Road with hills and woods on both sides, which also afforded admirable cover for the approach of the enemy.

Nelson's Battalion was posted on Ramseur's line, covering the approaches as far as practicable, and Lomax with Jackson's Cavalry and part of Johnson's was on the right, watching the valley of Abraham's Creek and the Front Royal Road beyond, while Fitz Lee was on the left, across the Red Bud, with his cavalry and Johnston's Horse Battery.

Gordon's Division reached the field a little after 10 A. M. and was placed under cover in rear of a wood behind the interval between Ramseur and the Red Bud. Knowing that it would not do to await the shock of the heavy assaulting columns, which were being formed, Early ordered Gordon to examine the ground on his left with a view to making an attack himself, and placed Rodes' three brigades as they came up on Gordon's right, also in some woods. The enemy was now discovered moving in great force both against Ramseur's front and left. Already Ramseur's men were falling

back behind Nelson's batteries, which remained steadfast, however, and single-handed checked the advance
while Early made his dispositions to hurl Gordon and
Rodes on the right of the Federal column. Meanwhile,
Nelson's batteries were being severely punished, but
gallantly continued to pour a most destructive fire into
the enemy's ranks, while Braxton's Battalion galloped
into position in front of Gordon and also opened fire
upon the Federal flank. Evans' Brigade of Gordon's
Division, passing beyond the guns, was soon overcome
and followed by the enemy, who rolled back the Confederate left wing until it rested at right angles to Ramseur's line with seven of Braxton's guns at the salient.
The onrushing enemy actually approached to within
musket range of these pieces, which were totally unsupported, but could not drive the gunners from their position. Of the situation at this juncture Early wrote:
"This caused a pause in our advance and the position
was most critical, for it was apparent that unless this
force was driven back the day was lost. Braxton's guns,
in which now was our only hope, resolutely stood their
ground, and under the personal superintendence of
Lieut.-Col. Braxton, and Col. T. H. Carter, my then
Chief of Artillery, opened with canister on the enemy.
This fire was so rapid and well directed that the enemy,
staggered, halted, and commenced falling back, leaving
a battle flag on the ground whose bearer was cut down
by a canister shot. Just then, Battle's Brigade of
Rodes' Division, which had arrived and had been formed
in line for the purpose of advancing to the support of
the rest of the division, moved forward and swept
through the woods, driving the enemy before it, while
Evans' Brigade was rallied and brought back to the
charge."

Ramseur's Division, which with Nelson's batteries always in front bore the brunt of the attack, was at first
forced back a little, but rallying behind the guns soon
recovered itself. Lomax on the right had greatly assisted Ramseur by making a gallant charge against the

left flank of the attacking infantry, and Breathed's batteries with Fitz Lee managed to secure a destructive
flank fire across the Red Bud on the left, while in the
words of Early, "Nelson's and Braxton's battalions had
performed wonders."

Although the Confederates had before noon won a
splendid victory, it was not without paying a high price,
for the superb Rodes had been killed at the very moment of success. Thus one by one were Jackson's
veterans falling, and who should take their places was
already becoming a problem.

The attack so far had been rendered by the Federal
6th and 19th Corps, but another remained. Early's
lines were now formed from Abraham's Creek across to
the Red Bud and were much attenuated.

About 2 o'clock, Breckinridge's and Wharton's divisions, and McLaughlin's Battalion reached the field
after a heavy engagement during the morning with the
enemy's cavalry on the Charles Town Road. Patton's
Brigade of Wharton's Division was then sent to reenforce Fitz Lee, while Col. King placed his batteries
on a hill in rear of Breckinridge's line, which now faced
to the left. Later in the afternoon two divisions of the
enemy's cavalry drove in the pickets north of the Rose
Bud and Crook's infantry corps, which had not been
engaged, forced back Patton and Fitz Lee. The Federal Cavalry then swept around Early's left flank to oppose which Wharton's other two brigades, King's Artillery, and one of Braxton's guns were double-timed to
the rear. Breckinridge, after driving back the enemy,
formed his division in line in rear of Early's left and at
right angles to the Martinsburg Road, again repulsing
the enemy. But many of the men on Early's front line
hearing Breckinridge's fire in their rear, and thinking
they were flanked and about to be cut off, commenced
falling back, thus producing great confusion. At the
same time, Crook advanced against Gordon and struck
his line while in confusion. The whole front line now
gave way, but a large number of the men were rallied

behind a line of breastworks, which had been thrown up just outside of Winchester during the first year of the war. At this point, the Artillery was gradually massed and checked all pursuit. Of this movement of the Artillery, Col. Carter wrote in his report: "Fortunately the Artillery was under perfect control to the last, and maneuvered and fought with untiring courage. The guns retired from point to point, halting, unlimbering, and firing, while efforts were made by general officers to rally the infantry."

Wharton's Division maintained its organization on the left, and Ramseur fell back in good order on the right. But, again, the Federal Cavalry got around Early's left and he was compelled to retire through the town under cover of Wickham's Brigade of cavalry, and Breathed's guns on Fort Hill. A new line was formed east of the town, which was maintained until nightfall, when Early retired without serious molestation to Newtown.

Near the close of the day, Col. Carter received a painful wound from a fragment of shell, which compelled him to turn over the command of the Artillery to Nelson, but he was not permanently disabled.

While many recriminations followed upon this affair, the whole army testified to the stout resistance made by the Artillery in the long and exhausting struggle which lasted from dawn to dark. The ultimate loss of the battle was due to the Federal superiority in cavalry, which was free to encircle the left flank, gradually compelling Early's line to fall back before the infantry in its front. Had Carter had sufficient artillery to crown the heights northwest of the town, he might have prevented the movement of the enemy's cavalry in that direction. Unfortunately Cutshaw was off with Kershaw's Division on an expedition east of the Blue Ridge.

Three guns of King's Battalion were lost in this battle, two of which were loaned the cavalry, and one of which was abandoned on the retreat, after its teams were shot down.

After Early's reverse at Winchester, he retreated during the night with all his trains secure to Fisher's Hill, and formed line of battle on the morning of the 20th, with McLaughlin's Battalion on the right, Braxton's in the center, and Nelson's on the left. The afternoon of the 20th, Sheridan appeared on the banks of Cedar Creek, about four miles from Fisher's Hill, and for the greater part of the next two days was engaged in reconnoitering Early's line. After some sharp skirmishing the enemy began to fortify in Early's front, but it was soon discovered that an attack was intended on the Confederate left. Early now gave orders to retire, but just before sunset Crook's infantry drove back Lomax's dismounted cavalry and involved Ramseur's left before the withdrawal could be effected. Ramseur made an attempt to meet this movement by throwing his brigades successively into line to the left, and Wharton's Division was sent for from the right, but it did not arrive. Pegram's brigades were also thrown into line in the same manner as Ramseur's, but the movement resulted in confusion in both divisions and as soon as this was noticed by the enemy, a general advance along the whole Federal line was ordered. After very little resistance the Confederate Infantry made for the rear in confusion, leaving the Artillery in the lurch, as it had never done before. Of this incident Early wrote, "The men and officers of the Artillery behaved with great coolness, fighting to the very last, and I had to ride to some of the officers and order them to withdraw their guns, before they would move. In some cases, they had held out so long, and the roads leading from their positions into the pike were so rugged, that eleven guns fell into the hands of the enemy."*

Early is in error as to the number of guns. There were fourteen lost, four of Nelson's, two of Lomax's Horse Artillery, seven of Braxton's and one of King's taken by the enemy on this occasion. Again Col. Nelson's conduct was conspicuously gallant as he withdrew

*Gen. Jubal A. Early, etc., p. 430.

his pieces in small groups, alternately unlimbering and
firing and entirely without infantry support.

From near Fisher's Hill, Early fell back on the 26th,
in line of battle beyond New Market, Nelson, Braxton,
and McLaughlin in the rear guard occupying every
practicable position from which to retard the pursuers.
In this retreat in which Nelson led the Artillery
with consummate skill, Capt. John L. Massie, of the
Fluvanna Battery, fell mortally, and Lieut. N. B.
Cooke, of Braxton's Battalion severely, wounded.
Early then moved toward Port Republic, arriving at
Brown's Gap on the 25th, where he was rejoined by
Kershaw's Division, and Cutshaw's Battalion. On the
same day, Col. Carter resumed command of the Ar-
tillery, of which Carpenter's and Hardwicke's batteries
were engaged on the 26th and 27th.

On the 28th, Early again put his army in motion down
the Valley, marching *via* Waynesborough to Mount
Sidney, and thence by slow stages to Hupp's Hill below Strasburg, which position he reached October 13th.
Here an affair occurred in which Fry's Richmond
Orange Battery participated with great credit and in
which Lieut. S. S. French, adjutant on Carter's staff,
was severely wounded.

The Cavalry had meanwhile been moving by the back
road, and on the morning of the 8th had encountered
the enemy. In this affair the Cavalry broke badly, leaving Thomson's and Johnston's batteries entirely isolated, but the gunners managed to cut their way to
the rear, not, however, without the loss of six pieces.
The very next day Shoemaker's Battery and the remaining section of Thomson's, which were serving with
Lomax's Cavalry as a guard to Early's wagon trains
near Woodstock, were again deserted by the Cavalry,
which fled precipitately to the rear. With the exception of one of Thomson's, all the guns were saved
by the extraordinary heroism of the horse artillerymen. On this occasion Capt. Carpenter of the Alleghany Battery, a classmate and devoted friend of

Jimmie Thomson's at the Institute, particularly distinguished himself. Observing the danger to which his comrades were exposed, he quickly rallied a number of the fugitive troopers and again and again formed them across the Valley Pike to check the pursuers. In this way he contributed materially towards saving the guns and trains, losing an arm as a result of his reckless exposure. But what was an arm to Carpenter, if by losing it he could save the gallant Jimmie Thomson!

The following extract from the diary of a horse artilleryman of Thomson's Battery throws some light on the affair of October 9th: "The shameful way that our Cavalry, especially that portion that tried to operate on the North Mountain Road, fought, bled, and died, a running rearward, was enough to make its old commander, Gen. J. E. B. Stuart, weep in his grave. Ring down the curtain on that scene, for the Cavalry played a regular exeunt act."

This was the famous battle of Tom's Brook, sometimes called by the Federals in a spirit of derision, "The Woodstock Races." At any rate, like the one the preceding day, it was a disgraceful affair on the part of the Confederate Cavalry. Soon after a Washington paper contained a card signed by Gen. Custer to the effect that he had captured all the guns of the Stuart Horse Artillery but one, and offering a reward of $1,000.00 for that. The reward was never claimed.

On October 19, at a very early hour, Early moved forward to attack the enemy beyond Cedar Creek, and by 10 A. M. not only had he routed two Federal Corps, seized their camps with twenty-four pieces of artillery, but Carter's battalions almost unaided by the Infantry had dislodged the 6th Corps near Middletown. It was here that a fatal halt by Early occurred in spite of Gordon's and Carter's urgent requests to be allowed to follow up the success of the morning. Carter even went so far as to declare that with his guns alone he could crush out all resistance of the enemy and begged that he be allowed to follow the Federals up, but Early de-

layed to reform the disordered troops which he found in
the captured trains, and gave Sheridan time to stay the
route of his army and lead part of it back to the field
of battle. Early then formed his line across the pike
north of Middletown and at right angles thereto with
Wofford's Brigade on the right, then Wharton's Division, then Pegram's Division across the road, then Ramseur considerably in advance, with Kershaw and Gordon
in order to the left. Between Gordon and Rosser's
Cavalry, with Thomson's Battery on the extreme Confederate left, was an interval of about a mile in which
about 3 P. M. Carter, of his own accord, placed six of
Cutshaw's and two of Jones' guns. Shortly after, about
3:30 P. M., the enemy assailed Gordon in force and again
the Infantry gave way while the guns were retired only
upon Gordon's order. Nelson's, Braxton's and Mc-
Laughlin's battalions and the other batteries of Cutshaw's, posted from right to left along the infantry line,
resolutely held their positions until the left began to
roll up, whereupon Carter withdrew them to a commanding elevation several hundred yards in rear of the
infantry line. Soon the Infantry began to break and
move to the rear, but the Artillery maintained its fire,
holding the Federals for over an hour, and not until
its ammunition was exhausted was the order to retire
given. Meantime, Carter had placed a small group of
guns on the heights south of Cedar Creek to cover the
withdrawal of the Infantry and Artillery.

Again Early's Infantry had failed him after winning
a splendid victory, the Artillery as at Winchester alone
saving the retreat from becoming a rout. Night at
last came and under cover of darkness and the fire of
Carter's rearmost guns, the Army was falling back in
apparent safety. While the main body of the Artillery
was marching in column towards Hupp's Hill, a small
body of Federal cavalry burst into the fields on the right
of the turnpike and charged the column and trains in
rear. The bugle blasts, cheers, the rush of horses' feet,
and pistol shots in the darkness, at once created a panic

in the infantry support, already much disorganized. The artillery officers and men appealed in vain to the panic-stricken infantrymen for muskets to defend the trains, but could not secure them, and as the cannoneers were totally unarmed they were compelled to abandon a large number of guns and wagons. Not only did the enemy recover all the guns captured from them in the morning, but twenty-three others besides. "One hundred men in an organized state, with muskets, could have saved the train," wrote Col. Carter.

This incident was as disgraceful to the Confederates as it was pleasing to Sheridan. It was not, however, the fault of the Artillery. The attack, in the nature of an ambush, occurred at a very narrow passage south of Strasburg, between the precipitous bank of the river on the one side and bluffs for the most part on the other. A bridge on the turnpike had failed and caused the road to become congested with ordnance and medical trains, and a long column of over 1,400 prisoners. There was absolutely no chance, therefore, for escape, and the cannoneers could not be expected to engage with fence rails or stones, even had they been available, in a night conflict with armed troopers. That their conduct was in every way commendable is attested by Col. Carter, who declared that throughout the night, with confusion and disorder all about them, the artillerymen remained cool and thoroughly under control, and as a guarantee against the repetition of such occurrences, he took occasion to recommend at once that a certain proportion of artillerymen be armed with carbines.

After this misfortune, Early retreated to New Market, in the neighborhood of which he remained until the last of November, when the Army proceeded to Harrisonburg, the Artillery going into winter quarters near Staunton. Thus did Early's Valley Campaign of 1864 come to a close, brilliant in many respects yet, in the main, ill-fated. With the exception of the Artillery it hardly seemed possible that the troops which broke so badly at Winchester, at Fisher's Hill, at Woodstock, and on several other occasions were the men which had fought under Longstreet, Jackson, Stuart, and Lee himself. It has been attempted to explain the poor conduct of Early's troops by saying that these men were simply fought out, that they had reached the limit of physical endurance, and that with a failure of physical stamina came their demoralization as a natural consequence. This explanation is on a par with that which makes of Jackson a religious fanatic at Gaines' Mill and White Oak Swamp. Neither are satisfactory. Why, if Early's Infantry was exhausted, was the Artillery still capable of performing deeds of unsurpassed valor on the field of battle, as well as the same marches which fell to the Infantry? No. Some other explanation is necessary and the correct one would seem to concern the discipline of the several arms. Is it too much to suggest a comparison of the field-officers and battery commanders of the Artillery with the officers of equal rank in the Infantry and Cavalry? Is it too much to say that in the comparatively long service and training of the junior officers of the Artillery, many of whom had served in the lower grades of their arm since the beginning of the war, lies the explanation? Is it too much to say that in the artillery enlisted personnel, there may be found a further cause for the superior conduct of the gunners over that of the other troops, large numbers of whose best men had fallen in battle, while an ever-increasing number of conscripts, and inferior material filled their places? Some such explanation seems reasonable, for certain it is that there was a marked difference which Early fully recognized. It is well known that he made some harsh criticisms of his troops, and in this connection an incident concerning the Artillery should be recorded.

On a certain occasion it was reported that Early, in his natural disappointment over the result of his campaign, had impugned the fighting qualities of his army. Whereupon, Col. Carter, politely but firmly, demanded a retraction in favor of the Artillery and got it. It is not difficult in reading Early's memoirs to see that such a discrimination was sincere on his part. Again and again he bears tribute to the Artillery of his command, when only veiled reproaches are found for the others.

The principal artillery lessons to be drawn from Early's operations in the Valley are as to the endurance of artillery, and what may be exacted of it in rear guard actions, in the face of a superior force—superior not only in point of numbers, but moral as well. Carter's Artillery formed the very backbone of Early's Army from Winchester to the end of the campaign. Without it, on more than one occasion, withdrawals from before the enemy would have been decisive defeats, and retreats would have become disgraceful routs. It was always at hand, as we have shown, in the forefront of the advance, and on every hilltop on the retreat, either to open the battle with encouragement to the Infantry, or to deny Sheridan's superb and overwhelming force of cavalry the full fruits of victory.

CHAPTER XLVI

GRANT had learned a lesson, and for three weeks after the Crater fight comparative quiet reigned at Petersburg, though many brave men perished in the trenches. Picket firing and artillery practice was continuous, "while the fiery curves of mortar-shell by night, told that the portentous game of war still went on."

About August 10th, Fitz Lee's Division of cavalry, with Johnston's and Shoemaker's batteries under Capt. Johnston, received orders to join Early in the Valley. Maj. Breathed had been wounded in a skirmish on June 29. This force reached Front Royal on August 14, and thenceforth participated in all of Early's operations in the Valley.

Upon Alexander's return to the Army August 18, he at once examined the Artillery defenses with the Chief of Artillery, and steps were instantly taken by the latter to have the works in rear of the Crater greatly strengthened. A number of Blakelys, Columbiads, and 30-pounder Parrotts were issued to the 3d Corps and caused to be mounted and manned by the cannoneers of Penick's Battery, while more careful instructions were drawn up for the Artillery in general, in order to secure the most systematic routine of duty possible and guard against all surprises. In connection with this work, Gen. Pendleton was constantly in the works and trenches.

About this time Lieut.-Col. Pemberton renewed Carter's proposal to organize a special body of horse artillery for the purpose of harassing the enemy along the river, a duty which required great mobility, but nothing was accomplished in that direction. Towards the end of the month, Col. Hilary P. Jones was ordered to Wilmington to organize the Artillery of the 3d Military District on the same basis as that of the Army in

Virginia, leaving Lieut.-Col. Moseley in command of Beauregard's Artillery.

Grant's next move after the Crater was an attempt to seize the Weldon Railroad by gradually extending his left. To meet this threat, Heth's Division and Brander's Battery of Pegram's Battalion moved out on the 18th and attacked the enemy at the Davis house on the railroad, the affair resulting successfully for the Confederates. The next day, Mahone's Division and Pegram, with the rest of his battalion, joined Heth and Brander and renewed the attack. In this engagement in which the Federals lost nearly 3,000 prisoners, Pegram greatly distinguished himself, and together with a part of Heth's Division bore the brunt of the battle. Again on the 21st, Pegram with twelve guns was heavily engaged at Poplar Spring Church, where Mahone, attacking with six small brigades, failed to dislodge the enemy. On this occasion instead of encountering a small force as expected, he found an army corps well entrenched with every approach to the hostile works swept by a powerful array of artillery. On the 24th, Pegram was directed, with Brander's and Cayce's batteries of his own battalion, Ross's of Lane's, and sections of Hurt's and Clutter's of McIntosh's, to accompany Heth's column in its attack upon the enemy at Reams Station. The following day Heth made a splendid effort capturing twelve stands of colors, nine pieces of artillery, ten caissons, 2,150 prisoners, and 3,100 muskets, losing himself but 720 men. In this brilliant affair Pegram, with characteristic dash and skill, prepared the way to victory. While the conduct of the North Carolina troops was superb and won fresh laurels for the old North State, Heth himself declared that he did not believe any troops could have carried the works of the enemy without such assistance as Pegram rendered the North Carolinians, by first shaking the hostile line with the fire of his guns.

By the end of August, however, Grant was firmly established across the Weldon Road and had thus taken

another important line of communication from Lee. To
seize it had cost him in the four engagements of August
not less than 8,500 men, as opposed to a loss of one-
fourth that number to his adversary, but the advantage
was worth the cost. He knew that similar successes,
even at such disproportionate losses, would soon enable
him to accomplish his purpose.

In the severe fighting of August on the right, Hampton had also won fresh laurels for the Cavalry, eliciting
high praise for his regiments and Hart's and Mc-
Gregor's batteries from Lee himself. From September
14 to 30, these two batteries with Edward Graham's
Petersburg Battery of Beauregard's Artillery, now converted from light to horse artillery, rendered service
of the most brilliant character, in coöperation with the
Cavalry.

On the 29th of September, the enemy succeeded in
carrying by surprise, a commanding salient of the Con-
federate works, known as Fort Harrison, near
Chaffin's Bluff. To meet this threat against Richmond,
Gen. Alexander, who had rejoined his command in
August, accompanied Field's Division that night with
Clutter's Battery of McIntosh's Battalion, and Marye's
Battery of Pegram's Battalion, both under Maj. Mar-
maduke Johnson. The next morning Haskell's Bat-
talion joined Alexander north of the James, and Lieut.-
Col. Hardaway, who had been placed in command of the
Artillery on the James when Carter was ordered to join
Early, September 2, reported to Alexander with his
own and Stark's Battalion.

Immediately an effort was made to recover Fort
Harrison. Hardaway's and Stark's battalions co-
operated as far as practicable with Johnson's and
Haskell's in the unsuccessful effort of the 30th to recover the fort from Butler, but the nature of the terrain
and the advantageous position of the enemy placed
Alexander at a great disadvantage. When the attack
was resumed October 1, Haskell's Battalion was united
with Hardaway's and Stark's on the right near the

river, and Lamkin's Battery, which had gained much experience with high angle fire in the trenches at Petersburg, was assigned the task of shelling the hostile works with a number of mortars. But again the attempt to drive Butler out of Fort Harrison proved unsuccessful, and the Artillery was withdrawn to the defensive lines with the exception of Lamkin's Battery, which remained in the advanced position with the mortars.

While the Confederates were thus opposing Butler on their extreme left, heavy fighting was also taking place on the right, brought on by the continuous extension of the enemy in that direction. In the affairs of September 30 and October 1, known as the "Battles of the Jones House," Pegram with Brander's and Ellett's batteries on the first day operated with Heth in his attack on the Federal left, and on the second day with Brander's and Cayce's batteries in the combined attack of Heth and Wilcox. On the 2d, Pegram with Ellett's, Cayce's under command of Lieut. Hollis, who greatly distinguished himself the preceding day, and Gregg's batteries, took a prominent part in repulsing the Federal assault on Heth's position. In these affairs, the Federals again lost heavily and again the reports teem with references to the extraordinary effectiveness of the Confederate Artillery.

Repeatedly during the siege was Pegram praised by the generals of the divisions with which he served, as well as by his corps commander. In the action of September 30, when Heth's and Wilcox's divisions were assigned the task of recovering the extension of the line of rifle-pits to the right of Petersburg, he shone with especial brilliance. On this occasion McGowan's Brigade after a gallant resistance was borne back by sheer weight of opposing numbers. Seeing that the South Carolinans were giving ground, Pegram, who had gone forward with them in their initial advance, rode through the line of battle, snatched the colors from the ensign and rode with them straight toward the enemy. "When forty or fifty yards in advance of the whole line, placing the color-staff on his stirrup and turning halfway round in his saddle, he dropped the reins on his horse's neck, raised his hat and shouted out in tones sweet and clear as a bugle, 'Follow me, men!' It was a scene never to be forgotten—the glorious sunset, the lithe, boyish form, now sharply cut against the crimson western sky, then hid for a moment by the smoke of battle, the tattered colors, the cheering lines of men. With a rousing yell, the sturdy brigade closed up, and never after gave back a single inch. The color-bearer ran out to him, the tears standing in his eyes, and cried out: 'Give me back my colors, Colonel! I'll carry them wherever you say!' 'Oh! I'm sure of that,' he answered cheerily, 'it was necessary to let the whole line see the colors; that's the only reason I took them.' "*

On the 7th, Haskell's and Johnson's battalions shared in the repulse of the enemy by Field's Division, along the New Market and Darbytown roads north of the James and were particularly effective, the gallant Haskell being struck in the head by a bullet and Lieut. McQueen of Garden's Battery also falling severely wounded. Haskell's Battalion was again engaged on the 13th under Capt. Garden, in an affair memorable in the Artillery for the heroic conduct of Corporal Fulcher, of Flanner's Battery. A Federal shell bursting among the ammunition, wounded six men and ignited the fuses of a number of shell, which had been improperly exposed. Though himself wounded, Fulcher seized the shells and carrying them under fire to a nearby pool extinguished the burning fuses.

The Presidential election in the North was now near at hand, and before settling down into winter quarters, Gen. Grant determined to make one more vigorous effort to turn Lee's right, seize the southside road, and compel the evacuation of Petersburg. For this purpose, he concentrated on his left the greater portion of three army corps, at the same time directing pressure to be exerted all along the line, and especially north of the

*See W. Gordon McCabe's sketch of Pegram in *The University Memorial*.

James.   On the 27th, a simultaneous attack was made
on the lines below Richmond, and on Lee's right flank,
resulting in the latter quarter in the battle of Hatcher's
Run.

The Federal advance below Richmond, though general and in considerable force, was easily repelled.
While the enemy delivered a frontal attack upon the
Confederates in position, with Hardaway's and Stark's
battalions between the Darbytown Road and Fort
Harrison, Haskell's and Johnson's battalions moved out
around the extreme left of Field's Division and secured
a most destructive flank fire upon the attacking columns,
literally sweeping the approaches along the Williamsburg, and Nine Mile Roads, and even as far as the
Charles City Road. The entire shock of the assault was
in this way diverted from the Infantry and the attack
was abandoned before it developed serious proportions.
Lieut. Wilkes, commanding Clutter's Battery, a young
officer of distinction, fell mortally wounded.

In connection with this affair it is to be noted what
might have been accomplished with artillery in June,
1861, on the same ground had it been in the same hands.
But at that time, there were no Alexanders, Haskells,
and Hardaways, but only a great mass of disintegrated
artillery, without organization and operating solely as
individual batteries.   It was the experience of four
years of constant fighting that now enabled the Artillery
to maneuver in large groups over country which had
formerly precluded the movement of a single battery.
The time had come when the modern belief that artillery
can go with the infantry was everywhere entertained,
and it seems surprising that so soon as Lee's Artillery
surrendered its guns, or buried them, that the world
should have ignored the lessons which it had been taught
by Alexander, Long, and Walker, only after nearly
half a century to be retaught by Langlois, the father of
modern field artillery.

On the extreme right, the Federal attack was no more
successful than below Richmond.   Advancing through

the most densely wooded region, confusion added to the resolute resistance of the Confederates, brought failure to the movement. At first the enemy advanced, gradually forcing Hampton back to and across the Boydton Plank Road. While rendering splendid service with the advanced line, Capt. Hart fell at the head of his battery with a severe wound.

After the enemy had crossed Hatcher's Run and pressed forward to Burgess's Mill, Lee hurled a part of Hill's Corps upon Hancock's isolated column, determined to recover the Boydton Road which was now of so much importance to him, since the Weldon Railroad had been lost. Here Pegram, with Ellett's Battery under Lieut. Hollis, and Gregg's Battery, again fought his guns with the most desperate courage. In action the mild appearing youth seemed to have become a fiend incarnate, and innumerable tales of his reckless daring and total disregard of danger to himself and his men might be recounted. In the fighting around Petersburg he had become one of the foremost figures in the Artillery and such a reputation had he acquired for valor that in all that splendid artillery corps, no name was more prominently before the Army.

At the same time that Hill's troops and Pegram hurled themselves upon the head of Hancock's column, Hampton's cavalry division which with Hart's, McGregor's, and Graham's batteries had worked its way around to the right, fell upon the Federal left and rear, with the result that Hancock was compelled to withdraw in confusion after losing about 1,500 men.

After these signal reverses Grant refrained for some time from further attempts on Lee's flanks, contenting himself with a ceaseless cannonade and redoubling the activity of the sharpshooters. And so the inexorable process of attrition wore on, every loss of life in the trenches placing the Federals that much nearer the inevitable issue.

On the 12th of October, orders were received to arm all cannoneers that could be spared from the guns with muskets for the defense of the trenches. In this way only could the rapidly failing infantry lines be reinforced. In the Washington Artillery Battalion alone one-half of the drivers were thus armed and organized as an infantry garrison for Fort Gregg. After six months of service in the trenches, exposed day and night to hostile fire, this battalion was at last relieved by that of Lieut.-Col. Moseley, and ordered to the extreme right to serve thereafter with the 3d Corps. It would seem certain that Longstreet's recent return to the command of his corps had something to do with the transfer. Not only was Eshleman's Battalion transferred, but Gibbes' old battalion, now commanded by Maj. Owen, formerly of the Washington Artillery, was transferred November 3, from the 1st to Beauregard's old command, or Anderson's Corps. But on the 15th, Owen's Battalion was again transferred, this time to the 3d Corps.

On November 4, an order was published permanently assigning assistant adjutant-generals in the Artillery Corps, as follows:

STAFF OF CHIEF OF ARTILLERY

Capt. Dudley D. Pendleton

1st Corps, Capt. S. Winthrow, and Capt. J. C. Haskell.
2d Corps, Capt. W. A. Percy.
3d Corps, Capt. William W. Chamberlaine and Capt. Richard Walke.

Pendleton now again sought to have the measure proposed in May, in the form of a bill for the increase of the commissioned personnel, adopted. With this end in view he addressed the Secretary of War, November 8, but soon received a reply from Mr. Sedden, in which it was apparent that with the exception of allowing increased rank to general officers in the Artillery Corps, no help from the War Department need be expected.* This was not what Pendleton wanted. His efforts were not in the interest of himself but for the welfare of the Corps, and he promptly pointed out to the Secretary the injustice being done artillery officers by the Government

---

*Rebellion Records, Series I, Vol. XLII, Part III, pp. 1205, 1211.

continuing the old system. In arguing the case of his corps, Pendleton wrote on the 15th to the Secretary of War as follows:

"DEAR SIR—Permit me, in acknowledging your kind favor of the 12th instant, to submit additional considerations in reply to your objections to our proposed bill.

"*First.* You regard such legislation as objectionable, because in the main unnecessary, since the organization asked for virtually exists in this army by regulation and can be similarly introduced in any other.

"*Second.* It will prove, you apprehend, embarrassing in several respects: First, a system fixed by law allows to the commanding general less freedom in adapting his resources to emergencies; second, a plan suitable for a large army may not be adapted to smaller commands; third, officers attached under law cannot be as freely transferred as the commanding general may desire.

"The considerations in reply to both of these objections seem to me to be really decisive. First, as to the necessity of the case; although we have artillery battalions formed under orders of the commanding general, sanctioned by the Department, and although this organization has proved one of the most efficient instrumentalities in our great struggle, the result is attained at the cost of very serious injustice to a large class of most deserving officers; is attended by inconveniences which experience satisfied us ought to be obviated, and is liable to depreciate in the future, if remedial measures be not adopted. The injustice of which I speak results partly from the fact that the status of artillery officers as now determined by number of guns, 80 for a brigadier, 40 for a colonel, 24 for a lieutenant-colonel, and 16 for a major, is entirely disproportioned to their merit and services. A single case may illustrate: The Chief of Artillery of one of our Army Corps, although his command in extent, importance, and responsibility greatly exceeds that of any infantry brigadier, must remain a colonel, as our roll already has 3 brigadiers of artillery, and we have not four times 80 guns.* In like manner, battalion commanders, whose commands, admirably managed, in difficulty and importance far surpass ordinary infantry regiments, must remain lieutenant-colonels, or majors, because we have not a sufficient number of times 40 or 24 guns to allow of their being rewarded with another grade. In truth, my dear sir, there ought to be more scope for promotion in this arm. Officers painfully feel that they are not fairly estimated, that in spite of noblest service they are often needlessly far behind their brethren of other arms. This might, indeed, be remedied in part by reducing the number of guns required for the several

---

*Pendleton here, of course, refers to Col. Walker of the 3d Corps.

grades. But this is not the whole case,—our artillery field officers feel that in the present plan they occupy rather a false position; it seems to regard them somewhat as exceptional and almost superfluous, instead of as an essential element of the structure and efficiency of the army. Their arm they know to be of eminent value. Their power they are equally satisfied is greatly enhanced by combination, the significance of its extensive organization they have seen fully proved, and to leave them nearly unrecognized by legal sanction, appears to them something like a degradation of their branch of the service. There are, besides, others on whom the present plan operates hardly. Every regiment of infantry or cavalry has its own non-commissioned staff provided by law; our artillery battalion as now existing, though imperatively needing such officers, are not allowed them except by temporary detail, without recognized authority. The service cannot but suffer from these things, and especially from the insufficient number of field officers. It not unfrequently now occurs that instead of two field officers to a battalion, we cannot under the casualties of service get one; and if, as is sometimes the case, the eldest captain be not efficient for larger command, hazard may ensue, which ought not to be permitted.

"These, my dear sir, are not matters of speculation, or fancy; they are realities seriously felt by some of the best men we have in service, and they seem conclusively to show that some such legislation as that proposed is really called for in justice to our arm, and with a view to the best interests of the service. With regard, in the second place, to embarrassments involved in applying law to this organization, first that the general cannot arrange detachments as readily as he may wish, the breaking of batteries has rarely been found necessary during the past two years, nor could there be difficulty in doing it if necessary, were batteries fully legalized. The same great principle of military control under which commanding generals can send infantry or cavalry companies, regiments, brigades, etc., where he deems it necessary, must, of course, apply to artillery organizations of whatever kind, and, besides, as you observe, we expressly guard that point in our bill. Gen. Lee would undoubtedly have commented unfavorably on this feature of the plan had it constituted in his judgment a real objection. Second, that which may suit a large army may not be adapted to smaller commands. This the bill also provides for; it is not mandatory, only permissive, each case can be arranged according to its own conditions. Third, officers assigned under the law become inconvenient fixtures. There is undoubtedly an evil here, though we guard against it by a clause in the bill, and besides, whatever be the evil, it pertains equally to the infantry and cavalry regiments, brigades, etc., yet the advantages of a definite legal

system for these have been found greatly to overbear the disadvantages suggested; and so it would prove for similar reasons
in the artillery.

"These views, my dear sir, I submit with kind candor, yet
with sincere deference. Impartial observers like yourself, surveying processes from a position allowing wide range of view, can
often detect errors which escape the notice of those more occupied
with details; but in a case of this nature, where all the chief
officers of an arm, under frequent appeals from those of highest
authority associated with them, concur in recommending a specific
as well tested by experience and approved in their judgment; and
when that recommendation is enforced by the deliberate approval
of so rigidly careful a judge as Gen. Lee, I feel that there can be
little danger of mistake in asking for the legislation in question, as
really needed and likely to promote the best interests of the
service."

The foregoing communication from the Chief of Artillery is given in full, for to the careful reader, it is a
history of the conditions in the Artillery arm as they
existed at the time of its writing. Not only did Pendleton decline to be brushed aside, but he made bold to put
the matter squarely up to the Department, in such a way
that to disapprove meant to accept full responsibility
for further neglect of the claims of artillery officers.

December 7, the enemy's cavalry set out in force upon
a raid toward Belfield and beyond, which movement
called forth Hampton's Division and his horse batteries.
At Hicksford, Hampton met the raiding column and repelled it. An infantry column accompanied by Pegram's Battalion and the Washington Artillery was unable to overtake the main body of the enemy, and after
seven arduous days of marching and some skirmishing
with the rear guards, returned to the lines worn out by
the incessant toil over frozen and all but impassable
roads.

Both armies now settled down for the winter, but with
ever-watchful eyes upon each other. The Confederate
Artillery had indeed borne its share of the struggle.
The weeks which followed witnessed privations un-
dreamed of before. The awful monotony of life in the
trenches was occasionally broken, however, by the ex-

citement of Hill's activities during January and February on the right. On several occasions the Washington Artillery was called upon to march and countermarch in that quarter, finally going into cantonments near Burgess's Mill.

Again did the spirit of revival sweep over the Army, and serve in a great measure to hold the weary troops steadfast. In the diary of the Washington Artillery is found the following significant passage: "January 29—The men have built a chapel just behind my tent, and have prayer-meetings nightly. The whole army has taken to praying, and if prayer accomplish anything, we should whip the fight yet. Peace commissioners started for Washington yesterday. No good is expected from the mission. We will certainly have a campaign in the spring of some sort or other." The men who were now "praying nightly" were the gay Louisianians, who but a short while before enlivened the camps with their music and dancing. Thus had time, adversity, and starvation wrought a change in the spirit of the troops. But with the love and fear of God had come an unconquerable resolve to die at their posts, a resolve unknown in the earlier stages of the war. Then it was the joy of victory which inspirited the troops to deeds of valor. Now it was a sacred devotion to duty, to a cause, to God, that animated the Confederate soldier and enabled him to bear the travail of war and slow death in the trenches, without even the hope of eventual success. Before it was the innate bravery of the race; in the winter of 1864-65, as at Fredericksburg, it was a sterner God-given courage which held the men to their colors.

To foster the spirit of sacrifice among the men of his command Gen. Pendleton was constantly at work. His love for them was great, and he watched over them with the spirit of one personally responsible for their future state. Of his command at this time he wrote: "In the whole of the eventful campaign of 1864, the Artillery of the Army of Northern Virginia bore a distinguished part, and in every portion of the widely-extended field of operation rendered signal service. It was everywhere and at all times proved reliable, howsoever great the emergency. In the wildest fury of battle and ceaseless harassment and exposure from sharpshooters and shelling on the lines, on the toilsome march, amid all the hardships of the trenches, through summer, fall, and winter, and when steadily breasting the tide of reverse against friends unnerved or overpowered, and foe flushed with triumph, the brave officers and men of this branch of our army have almost without exception exemplified the very highest virtues of Christian soldiers battling for their faith, their honor, and their homes."

At this time the staff of the Chief of Artillery was as follows: Capt. Dudley D. Pendleton, Assistant Adjutant-General; Lieut. George W. Peterkin, and Acting Lieut. Charles Hatcher, aides-de-camp; Capt. John Esten Cooke, and Lieut. E. P. Dandridge, Assistant Inspector Generals; Maj. John C. Barnwell, Ordnance Officer; Dr. John Graham, Surgeon; Maj. John Page, Quartermaster; and of them their chief reported, "It is but just that I should say they have uniformly discharged their duties with faithful alacrity and to my entire satisfaction."

Artillery headquarters were located during the winter near the railroad cut on the extension of Halifax Street, and about this center the most ceaseless activity reigned. The labors of the Chief and his staff and of the artillery corps commanders were incessant in the effort to secure and care for the horses and maintain the material in serviceable condition. Then, too, there were many vacancies to fill and where so many were deserving of reward the problem of promotion imposed no light task.

The difficulty of securing needed supplies at this time can be illustrated in no better way than by giving the following extract from the record of purchases, with

Confederate money, by an artillery officer traveling from Augusta, Ga., to Petersburg, in the early days of 1865.

1 curry comb	$ 10.00
Mending pants	20.00
Hair cutting and shave	10.00
Meal on road	20.00
Cigars and bitters	60.00
Pair of eyeglasses	135.00
Candles	50.00
Coat, vest, and pants	2,700.00
1 gallon whiskey	400.00
1 pair pants	700.00
6-yd. linen, 2¾ ft. wide	1,200.00
1 oz. sulphate quinine	1,700.00
2 weeks' board	700.00
1 doz. Catawba wine	900.00
Shad and sundries	75.00
Matches	25.00
Penknife	125.00
1 package brown Windsor soap	50.00

Army boots were selling in Richmond at this time for from $500.00 to $600.00 a pair, and artillery officers commonly paid $175.00 for the leather and $75.00 for the fabrication of the coarsest kind of military boots. One may easily imagine the difficulty encountered in replacing and repairing artillery harness, equipments, etc., the price of leather being $5.30 per pound. The matter of securing draught animals was even more serious. The schedule of prices established by the War Department in August, 1864, which provided for the impressment of animals, fixed the value of first-class artillery horses and mules at $500.00.* The price was bad enough. The main difficulty was to find the animals and to feed those already on hand. The schedule prices for feed at this time were as follows:

Corn, per bu. 56 lbs.	$4.00
Unshelled corn	3.95
Cleaned oats, per bu. 32 lbs.	2.50

*Rebellion Records, Series I, Vol. XLII, Part II, p. 1153.

Wheat bran, per bu. 17 lbs._____$ .50
Hay, unbaled, per 100 lbs._____ 3.00
Sheaf oats, baled_____ 4.40
Sheaf oats, unbaled_____ 3.50
Blade fodder, baled_____ 3.90
Shucks, baled _____ 2.60
Wheat straw, baled, per 100 lbs._____ 2.20

We have followed its trials and tribulations in some detail, but nothing can so impress one with the severity of the ordeal through which the Artillery had passed since the first of May, as a summary of its losses, which itemized by corps and battalions were as follows:

Huger's Battalion_____ 37
Cabell's Battalion_____ 47
Haskell's Battalion_____ 68
Hardaway's Battalion_____ 4
Stark's Battalion _____ 2
Gibbes' Battalion _____ 20
Johnson's Battalion_____ 19
                                                ———
    Total 1st Corps_____ 197

Field and Staff_____ 3
Page's Battalion_____ 177
Cutshaw's Battalion_____ 191
Hardaway's Battalion _____ 74
Nelson's Battalion _____ 116
Braxton's Battalion_____ 128
McLaughlin's Battalion_____ 103
                                                ———
    Total 2d Corps_____ 788

Pegram's Battalion_____ 78
Poague's Battalion_____ 82
McIntosh's Battalion_____ 84
Richardson's Battalion_____ 51
Lane's Battalion_____ 64
Owen's Battalion _____ 33
Washington Artillery_____ 18
                                                ———
    Total 3d Corps_____ 370

Stribling's Battalion _____ 132
12th Virginia Battalion_____ 41

Moseley's Battalion_____ 87
Coit's Battalion _____ 58

Total Anderson's Corps (Beauregard)_____ 318
Horse Artillery_____ 79

RECAPITULATION

1st Army Corps_____ 197
2d Army Corps_____ 788
3d Army Corps_____ 370
Anderson's Corps_____ 318
Horse Artillery_____ 79

Aggregate _____ 1,752

Of this number, exactly 500 were reported as missing, principally in the 2d Corps, due to captures at Spotsylvania, where 7 officers and 137 men of Page's, and 4 officers and 128 men of Cutshaw's Battalion were taken by the enemy. Deducting 17 officers and 483 men missing from the aggregate loss and the casualties in battle are found to be 1,252, of which number 72 were officers. In the 3d Corps alone 7 officers were killed and 25 wounded, Poague's Battalion losing 12 of the number, Lane's 8, McIntosh's 6, and Pegram's 4. In the 2d Corps there were 9 officers killed, 18 wounded, and 16 missing.

If we take the aggregate loss at 1,752, we find the loss of the Artillery Corps to have been over thirty per cent of its original strength, with a total loss in killed and wounded of over twenty-eight per cent! It is small wonder that Lee's Artillery was so highly regarded by both friend and foe. The writer knows of no such figures as these as applicable to any other artillery.*

In spite of the great drain on the personnel incident to such a list of casualties, never was the Artillery Corps allowed to become depleted to the point of ineffectiveness. The total artillery personnel of the 1st, 3d, and Anderson's Corps, as stated in the returns of October 20, 31, November 10, and December 10, being 5,339,

*Rebellion Records, Series I, Vol. XXXVI, Part I, p. 1052.

6,167, 6,277, and 6,179, respectively. It was not until after the opening of spring that disintegration began to set in.

On December 28, 1864, the distribution and armament of the Artillery was as follows:

1st CORPS

Brig.-Gen. Edward Porter Alexander

CABELL'S BATTALION

Col. Henry Coalter Cabell

1st Co. Richmond Howitzers,   Capt. Robert M. Anderson.
     4 Napoleons.
Troup (Ga.) Battery,   Capt. Henry H. Carlton.
     4 10-pounder Parrotts.
Battery "A", 1st N. C. Reg't,   Capt. Basil C. Manly.
     2 Napoleons, 2 3-inch rifles.
Pulaski (Ga.) Battery,   Lieut. Morgan Callaway.
     4 Napoleons.

HUGER'S BATTALION

Lieut.-Col. Frank Huger
Maj. Tyler C. Jordan

Brooks' (S. C.) Battery,   Capt. William W. Fickling.
     14 12-pounder howitzers.
Madison (La.) Battery,   Lieut. Jordan C. Parkinson.
     2 12-pounder, 4 24-pounder howitzers.
Richmond Battery,   Capt. William W. Parker.
     4 3-inch rifles.
Bedford Battery,   Capt. John D. Smith.
     4 3-inch rifles.
Bath Battery,   Capt. Esmond B. Taylor.
     4 Napoleons.
Ashland Battery,   Lieut. James Woolfolk.
     2 Napoleons, 2 20-pounder Parrotts.

HASKELL'S BATTALION

Maj. John C. Haskell

Branch (N. C.) Battery,   Capt. Henry G. Flanner.
     4 Napoleons.
Palmetto (S. C.) Battery,   Capt. Hugh R. Garden.
     3 Napoleons, 1 10-pounder Parrott.

Nelson Battery,   Capt. James N. Lamkin.
    26 mortars.
Rowan (N. C.) Battery,   Capt. John A. Ramsey.
    1 12-pounder Whitworth, 2 8-pounder Armstrongs.

HARDAWAY'S BATTALION

Lieut.-Col. Richard A. Hardaway

Powhatan Battery,   Capt. Willis J. Dance.
    4 3-inch rifles.
3d Co. Richmond Howitzers,   Capt. Benj. H. Smith, Jr.
    4 Napoleons.
1st Rockbridge Battery,   Capt. Archibald Graham.
    2 3-inch rifles, 2 10-pounder Parrotts.
Salem Battery,   Capt. Charles B. Griffin.
    4 Napoleons.

STARK'S BATTALION

Maj. Alexander W. Stark

Mathews Battery,   Capt. Andrew D. Armistead.
    4 Napoleons.
Louisiana Guard Battery,   Capt. Charles A. Green.
    4 Napoleons.
Giles Battery,   Capt. David A. French.
    4 Napoleons.

JOHNSON'S BATTALION (Improvised)

Maj. Marmaduke Johnson

Clutter's Richmond Battery,   Lieut. Lucas McIntosh.
    2 Napoleons, 2 3-inch rifles.
Fredericksburg Battery,   Lieut. John G. Pollock.
    4 Napoleons.

2D CORPS

Col. Thomas Hill Carter

NELSON'S BATTALION

Lieut.-Col. William Nelson

Amherst Battery,   Capt. Thomas J. Kirkpatrick.
    2 Napoleons, 1 3-inch rifle.
Georgia Regular Battery,   Capt. John Milledge, Jr.
    3 3-inch rifles.
Fluvanna Battery,   Capt. Charles G. Snead.
    2 12-pounder howitzers.

BRAXTON'S BATTALION

Lieut.-Col. Carter M. Braxton
Maj. Marcellus N. Moorman

Alleghany Battery,	Capt. John C. Carpenter.
2 Napoleons.	
Stafford Battery,	Capt. R. L. Cooper.
2 10-pounder Parrotts.	
Lee Battery,	Capt. William W. Hardwicke.
2 Napoleons.	

CUTSHAW'S BATTALION

Maj. Wilfred Emmet Cutshaw

Richmond Orange Battery,	Capt. Chas. W. Fry.
2 12-pounder howitzers.	
Staunton Battery,	Capt. Asher W. Garber.
2 3-inch rifles.	
2d Co. Richmond Howitzers,	Capt. Lorraine F. Jones.
2 Napoleons, 2 10-pounder Parrotts.	

KING'S BATTALION

Lieut.-Col. J. Floyd King
Maj. William McLaughlin

Lewisburg (W. Va.) Battery,	Capt. Thomas A. Bryan.
2 3-inch rifles.	
Monroe Battery,	Capt. George B. Chapman.
2 Napoleons.	
Wise Legion Battery,	Capt. William M. Lowry.
2 Napoleons.	

3D CORPS

Col. Reuben Lindsay Walker

McINTOSH'S BATTALION

Lieut.-Col. David Gregg McIntosh
Maj. Marmaduke Johnson

1st Maryland Battery,	Capt. William F. Dement.
4 Napoleons.	
4th Maryland Battery,	Capt. Walter S. Chew.
1 10-pounder Parrott, 2 3-inch rifles.	
2d Rockbridge Battery,	Capt. William K. Donald.
3 24-pounder Parrotts.	
Hardaway's Alabama Battery,	Capt. William B. Hurt.
2 3-inch rifles, 1 12-pounder Whitworth.	
Danville Battery,	Capt. Berryman Z. Price.
4 Napoleons.	

PEGRAM'S BATTALION

Lieut.-Col. William J. Pegram
Maj. Joseph McGraw

Richmond Letcher Battery,   Capt. Thomas A. Brander.
    4 Napoleons.
Richmond Crenshaw Battery,   Capt. Thomas Ellett.
    4 3-inch rifles.
Richmond Purcell Battery,   Capt. George M. Cayce.
    4 Napoleons.
Fredericksburg Battery,   Lieut. John G. Pollock.
    4 Napoleons.
Battery "B", 1st N. C. Reg't,   Capt. Thomas E. Gregg.
    4 Napoleons.

POAGUE'S BATTALION

Lieut.-Col. William T. Poague

Albemarle Battery,   Capt. Charles F. Johnston.
    1 Napoleon, 2 10-pounder Parrotts.
Madison (Miss.) Battery,   Capt. Thomas J. Kirkpatrick.
    4 Napoleons.
Pittsylvania Battery,   Capt. Nathan Penick.
    2 10-pounder Parrotts, 2 3-inch rifles.
Warrenton Battery,   Capt. Addison W. Utterback.
    4 Napoleons.
Graham's N. C. Battery,   Capt. Arthur B. Williams.
    2 Napoleons, 1 3-inch rifle.

RICHARDSON'S BATTALION

Lieut.-Col. Charles Richardson
Maj. Victor Maurin

Norfolk Blues Battery,   Capt. Charles R. Grandy.
    2 Napoleons, 2 3-inch rifles.
Donaldsonville (La.) Battery,   Capt. R. Prosper Landry.
    2 Napoleons, 2 10-pounder Parrotts.
Norfolk Battery,   Capt. Jos. D. Moore.
    4 Napoleons.

CUTTS' BATTALION

Col. Allen S. Cutts
Maj. John Lane

Battery "A", Sumter (Ga.) Batt.,   Capt. Hugh M. Ross.
    4 Napoleons, 2 10-pounder Parrotts.
Battery "B", Sumter (Ga.) Batt.,   Capt. George M. Patterson.
    6 Napoleons.

Battery "C", Sumter (Ga.) Batt.,   Capt. John T. Wingfield.
   4 Napoleons, 2 10-pounder Parrotts, 2 3-inch rifles.

ESHLEMAN'S BATTALION

Lieut.-Col. Benj. F. Eshleman
Maj. M. B. Miller

1st Co. Washington Artillery,   Capt. Edward Owen.
   1 10-pounder Parrott, 3 3-inch rifles.
2d Co. Washington Artillery,   Capt. J. B. Richardson.
   4 Napoleons.
3d Co. Washington Artillery,   Capt. Andrew Hero, Jr.
   4 Napoleons.
4th Co. Washington Artillery,   Capt. Joe Norcom.
   3 Napoleons, 1 10-pounder Parrott.

GIBBES' BATTALION

Maj. William W. Owen

Lynchburg Battery,   Capt. John Hampden Chamberlayne.
   4 Napoleons.
Ringgold Battery,   Capt. Crispen Dickenson.
   4 Napoleons.
Richmond Otey Battery,   Capt. David N. Walker.
   4 Napoleons.

ANDERSON'S CORPS

Col. Hilary P. Jones

MOSELEY'S BATTALION

Maj. William H. Caskie

Battery "C", 13th N. C. Battalion, Capt. James D. Cumming.
   2 Napoleons.
Battery "E", 1st N. C. Reg't,   Capt. John O. Miller.
   4 10-pounder Parrotts.
Macon (Ga.) Battery,   Capt. C. W. Staten.
   4 Napoleons.
Yorktown Battery,   Capt. Edward R. Young.
   4 Napoleons.

BRANCH'S BATTALION

Lieut.-Col. James R. Branch
Maj. James C. Coit

Confederate Guards, Miss. Battery, Capt. William D. Bradford.
   2 12-pounder, 3 20-pounder Parrotts.
Petersburg Battery,   Capt. Richard G. Pegram.
   4 Napoleons.

Halifax Battery,   Capt. Samuel T. Wright.
    4 Napoleons.
S. C. "Chesterfield" Battery,   Capt. James I. Kelly.
    2 Napoleons.

STRIBLING'S BATTALION

Maj. Robert M. Stribling
Maj. Joseph G. Blount

Lynchburg Battery,   Capt. James M. Dickerson.
    4 Napoleons.
Fauquier Battery,   Capt. William C. Marshall.
    4 Napoleons.
Richmond Fayette Battery,   Capt. Miles C. Macon.
    2 10-pounder Parrotts, 2 3-inch rifles.
Richmond Hampden Battery,   Capt. J. E. Sullivan.
    4 Napoleons.

BOGGS' BATTALION

Maj. Francis J. Boggs

Martin's Richmond Battery,   Lieut. Samuel H. Pulliam.
    3 Napoleons, 1 12-pounder howitzer.
Albemarle Battery,   Lieut. William H. Weisiger.
    4 Napoleons.

HORSE ARTILLERY

Lieut.-Col. Robert Preston Chew

CHEW'S BATTALION

Lieut.-Col. Robert Preston Chew

Petersburg Battery,   Capt. Edward Graham.
    2 3-inch rifles, 2 12-pounder howitzers.
Washington (S. C.) Battery,   Lieut. E. Lindsay Halsey.
    4 3-inch rifles.
2d Stuart H. A. Battery,   Capt. William M. McGregor.
    4 3-inch rifles.

BREATHED'S BATTALION

Maj. James Breathed

1st Stuart H. A. Battery,   Capt. Philipp P. Johnston.
Lynchburg Battery,   Capt. John J. Shoemaker.
Ashby Battery,   Capt. James W. Thomson.
Roanoke Battery,   Capt. Warren S. Lurty.

HORSE ARTILLERY BATTALION OF LOMAX'S DIVISION

2d Maryland Battery,   Capt. William H. Griffin.
Charlottesville Battery,   Capt. Thomas E. Jackson.
Staunton Battery,   Capt. John H. McClannahan.

Chew's own battalion was serving with Hampton near Petersburg and Breathed's with Rosser and Fitz Lee in the Valley. The Horse Artillery had gradually been increased to ten batteries.

At the beginning of the New Year, Haskell's, Hardaway's, Johnson's and Stark's battalions under Gen. Alexander were still north of the James and had been recently joined by Poague's Battalion. Cutts' and Richardson's battalions remained in position north of the Appomattox, with the exception of Penick's Battery, which had been attached to Poague's Battalion. The 2d Corps Artillery was in the Valley, while Cabell's and Huger's battalions of the 1st Corps, Jones' battalions of Anderson's, and Pegram's, McIntosh's and Gibbes' remained in the trenches, and Eshleman's near Burgess's Mill.

In addition to the twenty-six mortars manned by Lamkin's Battery, Poague manned four, McIntosh two 8-inch howitzers and two 8-inch mortars, Pegram two 8-inch and two 24-pounder mortars, Cutts one 8-inch columbiad and seven 24-pounder mortars. In Anderson's Corps, Coit, Blount, and Caskie manned four 30-pounder Parrotts, one 8-inch Columbiad, four 8-inch, twelve 24-pounder, nine 12-pounder mortars, and about 25 howitzers of various calibers. Exclusive of the heavy guns and pieces of position, and the guns of the Horse Artillery there were in the four corps of Lee's Army, January 1, 1865, 282 field guns, including 192 Napoleons and howitzers, and 90 rifled pieces.*

Of the field-officers, Col. Moseley had been killed December 16, Gibbes had been wounded on July 30, Caskie was absent on indefinite sick leave, Boggs was on duty in Richmond, Maurin at High Bridge, and Branch was absent on leave. Maj. Miller was therefore assigned to duty with Richardson's Battalion in the absence of Maurin, while Maj. Blount had succeeded to the command of Dearing's, or Read's, and Maj. Owen

---

*For tabular report showing heavy artillery in position and manned by field artillery at Richmond and Petersburg, see *Rebellion Records*, Series I, Vol. XLII, Part III, p. 1354.

to Gibbes' Battalion.   Dement's Battery, leaving its guns in the trenches at Petersburg, was on duty at Drewry's Bluff.

Notwithstanding the strenuous service which it had rendered and losses which almost seem to have been annihilating, the condition of the Artillery at the close of the year 1864 was actually better than when it left winter quarters the preceding spring.   On this point, Pendleton, in his report, wrote February 28, 1865: "In conclusion I am able to report that our artillery remains at the close of this arduous campaign in a condition of most encouraging efficiency, and that with reasonable effort toward supplying it with a few guns to replace some lost in unfortunate affairs that have been described (here he refers to loss in the Valley), and with horses to reëstablish a number of teams disabled in action or worn down by hard service, it will be in full strength for the campaign of the ensuing spring.   It may be confidently relied upon to accomplish, by the Divine blessing during the next season, as it has so well done through the last, its entire share in the defense of our country."*

*For condition of Walker's Artillery of the 3d Corps, September 30, 1864, see *Rebellion Records,* Series I, Vol. XLII, Part II, p. 1309.

CHAPTER XLVII

WHEN Longstreet rejoined the Army and was assigned to the command of the troops north of the James, he found the outer artillery defenses in a state not altogether satisfactory, and, it would seem, held Lieut.-Col. J. C. Pemberton responsible for the condition of affairs. But in this Longstreet was in error, for whatever may have been Pemberton's shortcomings at Vicksburg, he had labored incessantly upon the works below Richmond, and had with little encouragement greatly improved them. Longstreet's criticisms, however, soon led to dissatisfaction, and on January 7, Pemberton was relieved from his former duties and assigned to duty as Inspector General of Artillery and Ordnance with Capt. L. S. Marye as his assistant. Alexander was now placed in entire charge of the artillery defenses north of the river, while Col. Stapleton Crutchfield, still quite unfit to perform active field service, was assigned to the command of the garrison at Chaffin's Bluff, where Hardaway had for some time been stationed with his battalion. On January 16, Alexander was again compelled to rest from his duties for a brief space, leaving Col. Cabell in control as Acting Chief of Artillery of the 1st Corps.

At the close of January, the entire effective strength of Carter's four battalions of artillery in the Valley was but 35 officers and 538 men present for duty, with an aggregate present and absent of 2,082. Of the latter number, 16 officers and 383 men were carried as prisoners of war. The rolls showed 32 guns in service.

The condition of Early's command in camp near Staunton was most unsatisfactory, particularly with respect to the artillery horses, for which on account of Sheridan's activities and long droughts during the past summer sufficient forage could not be secured.

After sending Fitz Lee's Cavalry Division to Petersburg, Lomax's Brigade to the pasture lands in the Alleghanies, and temporarily disbanding Rosser's Brigade, the men of which were allowed to return to their homes with their horses, the situation was still serious. Accordingly the men and horses of King's or McLaughlin's artillery battalion were sent to southwestern Virginia to be wintered, while the officers and men of Braxton's and Cutshaw's battalions under Col. Carter were ordered to report to Gen. Lee to man the works about Richmond. Col. Nelson with six pieces of his battalion remained with Early. · About this time Gen. Long again reported to Early for duty, and caused the guns of the 2d Corps, from which the men and horses had been taken, to be shipped by rail to Lynchburg. This was a deplorable state of affairs, but it could not be avoided, as the horses of the Cavalry and Artillery would have perished had they been kept in the Valley.

Two very small brigades of Wharton's Division, and Nelson's artillery command now comprised Early's whole force, which was placed in camp near Fishersville between Staunton and Waynesborough.

At the time Braxton and Cutshaw were ordered to Richmond, there were Lieut.-Col. Atkinson's four battalions of heavy artillery under Majs. Hensley, Hardin, Cary, and Robertson, respectively, and Lightfoot's Local Defense Battalion and Leyden's 9th Georgia Battalion of light artillery manning the lines, with a total of 68 officers and 1,517 men present for duty. Other forces of heavy artillery were assigned to the defenses of Petersburg, and the Richmond and Danville Railroad under Lieut.-Col. Howard and Maj. Boggs, respectively.*

Genls. Lee and Pendleton were now making every effort to secure horses for the artillery in order that it might be placed in condition before spring to take the field. On the 1st of February, it was estimated that

---

*For detailed distribution of this force and that at Petersburg along the Richmond and Danville Railroad, see *Rebellion Records,* Series I, Vol. XLVI, Part II, pp. 1196-97-98 and 1185.

6,000 horses and 4,000 mules were needed for the armies of the Confederacy, and that the number which could possibly be secured before spring was 5,000; 3,000 from Mississippi and 2,000 in Virginia. The Inspector General of Transportation estimated that with ample funds 15,000 animals might sooner or later be secured in Mexico and Texas, at $70.00 gold per head, but these animals were totally unsuited to artillery service. In Mississippi the animals would have to be purchased from within the enemy's lines at a vastly greater cost, while in Virginia the available supply would only be forthcoming for cash payments in gold.* Such was the condition of affairs and well might Pendleton have despaired of remounting his batteries.

A suggestion was now made by Col. Carter to drive the unserviceable animals of the Artillery west to the counties of Augusta and Rockbridge, where they could be exchanged with the farmers for fresh ones, should authority to that effect be granted. He reported that a fairly large supply of horses could be had in this section, calling attention to the fact that Sheridan had but recently taken therefrom over 1,700 animals in spite of the drain of the war. This plan was promptly proposed to the Inspector General of Transportation, and again Pendleton protested against the practice of herding the condemned artillery horses in great droves only to perish from neglect, and consume forage, when they might be distributed among the farmers for purposes both of recuperation and aid to agriculture.

In a report dated February 14, Maj. Cole states that 2,482 horses and 1,370 mules were immediately required by the Army at Petersburg, and a grand total of 3,270 horses and 2,409 mules for all the forces in Virginia. Having been provided with $100,000 in gold and $3,-000,000 in treasury notes, he was hopeful of securing 2,500 animals in Virginia and North Carolina, provided he was allowed to impress and pay for them at

*Letter of Inspector General of Transportation, February ⌐, 1865, *Rebellion Records*, Series I, Vol. XLVI, Part II, p. 1190.

local appraisements. In addition to this number, he reported that 700 artillery horses would be returned from the infirmaries before April 1.*

The horse depots which had been established at Pendleton's suggestion had proved of great benefit to the service, for by means of them large numbers of exhausted animals had been rendered serviceable and reissued. But the losses in the field continued to be greater than the supply, especially in the tidewater section of Virginia. Many of the animals were bred and raised in the mountainous regions of the west, and were not acclimated to the lowlands about Petersburg, nor could they be made to flourish, in spite of every effort, when taken from their accustomed pastures and placed on army forage. Glanders and farcy, the most dreaded equine diseases, became prevalent in the corrals at Petersburg, and Owen's 13th Virginia Battalion was almost dismounted before the close of the winter from these maladies of the horses.†

So vehemently had Braxton and Cutshaw protested against the unhorsing of their commands, that early in March it was decided to issue horses and new guns to the former, and it was ordered to relieve Poague's Battalion on duty under Alexander. But after issuing the horses, and before the guns arrived from Richmond, the issue of forage became so scarce that many of the animals perished. About this time Cutshaw applied to have his battalion converted into cavalry for more active service than that which he was performing as heavy artillery. Both the officers and men of his command, he declared, were desirous of this change and were willing to repair to the Valley, where in small groups they would secure their own mounts.

Conditions were indeed becoming desperate. Even the Horse Artillery which Pendleton was endeavoring to reorganize and place upon a more efficient footing for the anticipated campaign, was in urgent need of guns

---

*Rebellion Records, Series I, Vol. XLVI, Part II, p. 1232.
†Ibid, p. 1305.

and equipment, necessitating a call upon Alexander for rifles for its armament.   But to this Alexander objected, urging that howitzers be issued the horse batteries, instead of his much-needed rifle pieces, of which he already had too few.   He was even now compelled to strengthen the line he was defending by planting sensitive shell among the abattis in his front, illuminating his field of fire by night with fire balls, etc., and to take from him his best ordnance was an act of folly, which he strenuously opposed.

As spring approached conditions in the Army in general grew worse and worse.   From the trials of the late winter, "history would fain avert her eyes."   They were such as can never be forgotten by those who watched and waited; such as can never be credited by those who read the story in peace and plenty.   To guard the long line of intrenchments from the Chickahominy to Hatcher's Run, there was now left but a gaunt remnant of that valiant host which had hurled back nearly thrice its number at Cold Harbor, and wrought humiliation to the Army of the Potomac on a score of fields in this vigorous campaign.

"Living on one-sixth of a ration of cornmeal and rancid pork, thinly clad, their bodies indeed shivered under the freezing blasts of heaven, but their dauntless spirits cowered not under the fiery blasts of war.   But there was to be added a pang deeper than the pang of hunger; sharper than the rigor of the elements or hurt of shot and steel.   For now from the cotton lands of Georgia and the rice fields of Carolina, came borne on every blast the despairing cry, which wives with little ones raised to wintry skies, lit by the glare of burning homes, and the men of the 'Old North State' bethought them of the happy homesteads which lay in the path of the ruthless conqueror, who was waging war with an audacious cruelty, capable of destroying a whole nation. A subtle enemy, till then well-nigh unknown, attacked in rear the Army which still haughtily held its front, and men, with bated breath and cheeks flushing through their bronze, whispered the dread word 'desertion.' "

On the 28th of February, Gen. Lee reported to the Secretary of War a total of 1,094 desertions between the 15th and 25th of the month! Of this number, 586 were in Hill's and 217 in Anderson's Corps. During the ten days ending March 8, 779 men abandoned their colors, 450 from these same corps.

"The historian, far removed from the passions of the time, may coldly measure out his censure; but we, comrades, bound to these men by countless proud traditions, can only cry with the old Hebrew prophet, 'Alas! my brother!' and remember that these were valiant souls, too sorely tried."*

In response to a circular of March 7, calling for suggestions as to how to cure the dread malady which now unabated threatened to destroy the Army of Northern Virginia, Gen. Alexander promptly proposed the classification of offenses with appropriate punishments and an increase of the authority of regimental courts, to be employed in lieu of the cumbersome system of Corps Courts hitherto in use. The proceedings under the proposed system were to be more summary and the death penalty more frequent.† But it is exceedingly doubtful if desertion could have been checked by more drastic punishment, or in any way. The Army of Northern Virginia was doomed—the Confederacy had long since shown the hectic flush upon its check.

Gen. Lee had already disclosed his plans to Gen. Pendleton and given him confidential instructions regarding the proposed withdrawal of the Army. In accordance with these plans Pendleton redoubled his efforts to place the Artillery on the most efficient footing possible, and at last, with the support of Gen. Lee, he succeeded in securing the many needed promotions in his corps, for which he had so long struggled, and authority

*Address of W. Gordon McCabe on the Siege of Petersburg, *Army of Northern Virginia Memorial*, p. 169.

†A careful study of Gen. Alexander's plan will repay the student, *Rebellion Records*, Series I, Vol. XLVI, Part II, pp. 1300, 1301.

to reorganize his battalions. On March 1, the following promotions were announced, with rank from February 18.

To be Brigadier-General—Col. Reuben Lindsay Walker.
To be Colonels—Lieut.-Col. William Nelson, D. G. McIntosh, Frank Huger, and W. J. Pegram.
To be Lieutenant-Colonels—Majs. John C. Haskell, W. M. Owen, John Lane, R. P. Chew, W. E. Cutshaw, Marmaduke Johnson, and R. M. Stribling.
To be Majors—Capts. H. W. Ross, T. J. Kirkpatrick, W. J. Dance, B. C. Manly, T. O. Brander, S. T. Wright, N. V. Sturdivant, J. F. Hart, P. P. Johnston, J. A. Thomson, and W. G. McGregor.

Never in its history was the Artillery Corps so well provided with field-officers as now. It seems too bad that Pendleton's insistence could not have been rewarded before. He now set about the task of reorganization with renewed energy, and everywhere found the greatest encouragement reigning among his officers. But there had as usual been some oversights. Hardaway, who well deserved promotion, was left out and Alexander, calling attention to his merits, suggested the consolidation of Johnson's Battalion with Leyden's in order that the necessary vacancy in the grade of colonel might be created. He also recommended Garden, Parker, Lamkin, Woolfolk, and Moody to be promoted majors, and Leyden a lieutenant-colonel.

Pendleton himself was not promoted, but it is probable he would have been had time permitted. From a confidential communication from Gen. Pendleton written some years after the war the following extract is taken.

"On the ground, probably, that this arm of the service, all essential as it is, can never be independent, but always only coöperative with others, Confederate law allowed in it no grade above that of Brigadier-General. Only such, therefore, was I to the last, though having under me three other Brigadier-Generals, and, consequently serving in fact as a Major-General. But no exaltation of name was, so far as I know myself, a ruling motive with me, the incongruity never disturbed me. It was about to be corrected on Gen. Lee's recommendation when irremediable reverse befell our army and cause."

Instead of consenting to the conversion of Cutshaw's Battalion, Pendleton at once addressed himself to the task of reorganizing the entire Artillery of the 2d Corps. Sending Col. Carter to Gen. Long, he proposed through him to fully remount Nelson's, Braxton's, and Cutshaw's battalions, and place them on the most effective basis. For this purpose, McLaughlin's Battalion was to be ordered East, dismounted, placed in the stationary batteries, and its horses, guns, and equipment used for the other battalions. Gen. Long promptly assented to the plan, and at once Cutshaw was withdrawn from Fort Clifton, Braxton from Chaffin's Bluff, Nelson ordered to Lynchburg and the work undertaken. Cutshaw's Battalion at this time consisted of Fry's, Montgomery's, Reese's, Carter's, Garber's, Carrington's, Tanner's, and Jones' batteries, with 674 officers and men present for duty and 1,047 on the rolls. It, therefore, afforded a surplus which was to be used in completing the personnel of Nelson's and Braxton's battalions. Accordingly, on March 17, McLaughlin was ordered to report to Col. Carter at Lynchburg, turn over his horses and material to Nelson, and proceed by the canal with his men to Richmond.

Other changes in the Artillery were also now necessary. In the 3d Corps, Chew's 1st Maryland Battery, in which there were but 36 men present for duty, was recommended to be consolidated with Griffin's horse, or the 2d Maryland Battery, of Breathed's Battalion.

Martin's and Dickenson's batteries of Sturdivant's and Owen's battalions, respectively, were relieved of their guns and formed into a battalion with Douthat's Battery, which was brought from the southwest with McLaughlin's Battalion. This new battalion under command of King was assigned to duty in the stationary batteries of Alexander's line. Walker's Battery of Owen's Battalion was assigned to Sturdivant's Battalion, in place of Martin's, and Chamberlayne's to McIntosh's Battalion in place of Chew's, while Maj. Owen was assigned to duty under McIntosh. Thus was the

13th Virginia Battalion disbanded and sufficient material from Martin's, Dickenson's, and Chew's batteries secured in addition to that of McLaughlin's Battalion to fully rearm and equip Nelson's, Cutshaw's, and Braxton's veteran battalions.* These changes were officially promulgated March 20, and on that same day the Horse Artillery, with Chew as Chief, was reorganized, as follows:

Maj. Hart's Battalion:
  Hart's Battery and Graham's Battery, to serve with Gen. Butler's Division.

Maj. McGregor's Battalion:
  McGregor's Battery and McClannahan's Battery, to serve with Gen. W. H. C. Lee's Division.

Maj. Breathed's Battalion:
  Shoemaker's Battery and Griffin's Battery, to serve with Gen. Fitz Lee's Division.

Maj. Johnston's Battalion:
  Johnston's Battery and Jackson's Battery, to serve with Gen. Lomax's Division.

Maj. Thomson's Battalion:
  Thomson's Battery and Lurty's Battery, to serve with Gen. Rosser's Division.

Col. Chew, like all the other artillery commanders, was now admonished to be prepared for active operations, however early or unexpectedly the call might come.

Rebellion Records, Series I, Vol. XLVI, Part III, pp. 1316-17-19-21-22-23-27-28 and 1333.

CHAPTER XLVIII

"LE DEBACLE"

WELL might Pendleton caution his subordinates that their measures should be prompt, for already the evacuation had been too long deferred. How Lee was overruled and compelled to remain in the Petersburg lines against his will cannot be discussed here. Nor how, when the object of the peace conference failed, the Army, although bitterly disappointed, set its teeth, once more resolved to struggle on to the end, whatever that might be. We must content ourselves solely with tracing the events which concerned the Artillery.

Sheridan's cavalry divisions were circling about Lee's Army like great vultures impatient for their prey. One of his columns was marching upon Lynchburg, and to meet the danger Pendleton was directed to send enough of his men there to man the field guns which Early had turned in during the winter. Accordingly, Garber's, Jones', and Carrington's batteries were dispatched to Col. Carter, who with his usual energy and skill prepared to meet the raiders.

On the morning of March 25, the Chief of Artillery was summoned to meet the commanding general at the headquarters of Gen. Gordon at 5 A. M. Gen. Lee had decided to make a daring attempt to break Grant's line near the center by an attack upon Fort Steadman, which, it was believed, could be carried by surprise. How Gordon's sudden blow was at first crowned with success; how his guides ran away and left his storming columns groping in ignorance; how his supports failed to reach him, must be read elsewhere. Suffice it here to say that what bid fair to be a brilliant success through unwonted misfortune, dereliction, or what not, resulted in miserable failure.

This unsuccessful effort, in which, however, the Artillery fully performed its allotted task, was quickly fol-

lowed by a vigorous advance on the part of Grant.
Early on the morning of the 29th, the corps of Warren
and Humphreys moved toward Lee's intrenchments
on the extreme right, while the inexorable Sheridan
swept around the flank and occupied Dinwiddie Courthouse, six miles southwest of the infantry column. Lee,
quickly divining the intention of the enemy, moved out
along the White Oak Road with 15,000 infantry and
2,000 cavalry, leaving Longstreet north of the James
and Gordon alone in front of Petersburg. On the 31st,
he attacked the Federals in flank, but after pursuing
as far as the nature of the country permitted, was compelled to return to his works. On the same day, Sheridan advanced to Five Forks, driving Fitz Lee and part
of Pickett's command before him. The following morning, Sheridan was reinforced by Warren and Humphreys, and in the evening defeated the 3d Corps. Perceiving that his forces were too weak to combat successfully with the enemy, Lee ordered Longstreet on the
evening of the 1st to move rapidly across the river to
Petersburg.

In the battle of Five Forks, the Artillery suffered a
loss indeed irreparable, a loss directly due to Gen.
Pickett's orders. On this occasion Gen. Pickett assumed to designate the position for Pegram's guns—a
position with every defect known to artillerymen. But
Pegram with that spirit of blind obedience which constituted his sole fault did not question his orders and
died like a rat in the trap to which he was assigned.

No finer tribute to Pegram can be penned than that
which his gallant adjutant and comrade has already
given to the world, and so those eloquent lines are quoted
here: "Of him I almost fear to speak, lest I should do
hurt to that memory which I would honor. For to those
who knew him not, the simplest outline of a character so
finely tempered by stern and gentle virtues would seem
but an ideal picture touched with the tender exaggeration of retrospective grief; while to so many of you who
knew him, as he was, the gentle comrade and the

brilliant fighter, any portrait must prove, at best, but a blurred semblance of the young soldier, whose simple, heroic, godly life rejects, as it were, all human panegyric. Yet even the coldest must allow that it was a life which afforded a notable example of how great a career may be crowded within the compass of a few years. In the spring of '61, a youth of modest demeanor, he entered the military service as a private soldier; in the spring of '65, still a mere lad, he fell in action, Colonel of Artillery, mourned by an Army.

"More than once in desperate and critical events were grave trusts confided to his prudence, skill and courage; more than once did he win emphatic praise from Hill, from Jackson and from Lee. Thus it was his lot to be tried in great events, and his fortune to be equal to the trial, and having filled the measure of perfect knighthood, 'chaste in his thoughts, modest in his words, liberal and valiant in deeds,' there was at last awarded him on field of battle the death counted 'sweet and honorable.'

"Such was William Johnson Pegram, of the Third Corps, who at the early age of twenty-two died, sword in hand, at the head of his men, with all his 'honor owing wounds' in front 'to make a soldier's passage for his soul.' " And may the author add, such was the soldier who was sacrificed by the ignorance of his division commander—an infantry officer who undertook to direct the placing of his artillery without discretion on the part of his artillery commander.

Had Col. Pegram lived and the war continued he would have attained to high command. Already Gen. Lee had expressed his intention to give the young soldier a brigade at the first opportunity which presented, but it is doubtful if the gallant artilleryman would have exchanged his sixteen guns for such a command.

Early on the morning of the 2d, the Federals renewed the attack, breaking the lines of the Confederates and forcing them from their position covering the Boyd-

ton Plank Road, and Gibbon's Division of Ord's Corps
boldly essayed to break through into the town. The
morning of the 1st, Pendleton had ordered seven guns
of Poague's command, which had been held in reserve
near Howlett's, to march for Petersburg, and that night
the whole battalion was directed to follow. When the
first two batteries arrived they were ordered to proceed
to the right and conceal themselves before dawn near
the Turnbull house.

After capturing all the works to the south and west,
Grant found a more difficult task before him at the town,
for Ord's way was barred by two open profiles, known
as Battery Gregg and Fort Whitworth, the latter from
the character of a gun mounted therein. These works
were about 200 yards apart and 1,000 in front of the
main line of intrenchments. The gorge of Battery
Gregg was closed by a palisade and its ditch was generally impassable. On the right flank, however, a line to
connect with Whitworth had been started, and here the
unfinished ditch and parapet gave a narrow access to
the parapet of Gregg. It was by this route that the
enemy finally reached it. It was defended by two guns
of the Washington Artillery, under Lieut. McElroy,
and the 12th and 16th Mississippi, 214 men in all. Fort
Whitworth was open at the gorge and was held by
three guns of the Washington Artillery, under Lieut.
Battles, and two Mississippi regiments.

Thrice Gibbon's columns, above 5,000 strong, surged
against Gregg and each time were repulsed by the devoted garrison, McElroy fighting his guns with great
valor while his drivers armed with muskets aided the
infantry. The day was an eventful one for the Washington Artillery, for early in the morning when Battles
was ordered to withdraw from the outer line, before his
horses could be brought up the enemy rushed to the
works and seized his guns. But, McElroy in the fort,
seeing Battles surrounded and cut off led a charge of
his pseudo-infantry, and recovered the pieces.

Shortly before noon, Gibbon, reinforced by two brigades of Turner's Division, while the third advanced against Whitworth, again assailed Gregg, and this time his men swarmed over the parapet and captured McElroy's guns. Of the garrison 55 were killed, 129 were wounded, and only 30 were found uninjured, while Gibbon lost 122 killed and 592 wounded in the four assaults.

McElroy had again performed a splendid feat of arms. Surely he felt no shame over the loss of those two guns, which "taught prudence to the enemy for the rest of the day." It was the unflinching character of Lee's artillerymen as exemplified by McElroy that prompted Meade in July to telegraph Grant, "I cannot advise an assault. . . . It is not the number of the enemy, which oppose our taking Petersburg; it is their artillery and their works, which can be held by reduced numbers against direct assault."*

The seven guns of Poague's Battalion from near the Turnbull house assisted Eshleman's other batteries on the Boydton Road in checking the enemy's pursuit, and while heavily engaged had been joined by Poague with the remainder of his command. Maj. Brander had also posted three guns on the north bank of the Appomattox, from whence they were able to enfilade the Federal left as it swung towards the river, while Chew threw four pieces into action on the right of the Cox Road. But by noon the Federals had seized Gregg and Whitworth, and fully established their line from these works to the river. Nevertheless, McElroy, Poague, Brander, and Chew had checked the enemy and given Field's Division time to reach Petersburg before the outer line fell. Kershaw now alone remained north of the James to confront Weitzel. A. P. Hill, veteran of many fields, a knight *sans peur et sans reproche,* had fallen. But all was not yet lost.

During the day, the artillery fire on the east of the city had been unusually severe. Beginning the previous

*Written July 26.

night, the enemy's mortars and guns had been kept
incessantly at work.

Lee and Longstreet had watched the defense of Fort
Gregg, with the utmost admiration, fully expecting the
compact Federal masses to assail the inner works, behind which Field had been placed. Early in the morning, Lee had advised the President that he must abandon the lines that night, and having noted Grant's
pause, about 3 P. M., issued the formal orders for the
evacuation in time to begin the move by dark, and the
troops north of the James were directed to march
through Richmond and join the Army on the roads
leading westward. While Alexander stood at the north
end of the pontoon bridge, near Drewry's Bluff, watching his batteries file by, Walker and Jones withdrew
their battalions from the Petersburg lines. Pendleton
had ordered all the guns to move out at 8 P. M. This
was accomplished with great success in spite of the
enemy's ceaseless cannonade. But ten pieces had to be
abandoned and these by Jones for lack of teams, all
being disabled. Even a number of mortars were saved,
and by 2 A. M. all the field artillery had crossed the
Appomattox and commenced the march westward along
the Hickory Road. Thus did Lee evacuate the forty
miles of intrenchments which for nine months had been
"clothed in thunder," and for the defense of which the
line of defenders had at last been overstretched.

Along the north bank of the Appomattox moved the
long lines of artillery and dark silent columns of infantry through the gloom of the night towards Amelia
Courthouse, where rations had been ordered to be collected for the Army. "As the troops moved noiselessly
onward in the darkness that just precedes the dawn, a
bright light like a broad flash of lightning illumined the
heavens for an instant, then followed a tremendous explosion. 'The magazine at Ft. Drewry is blown up,'
ran whispers through the ranks, and again silence
reigned." All knew now that Alexander and Kershaw had spiked their heavy guns and were on the way

to join the main column. Passing through Manchester at daybreak, Alexander's column marched 24 miles on the 3d, going into camp that night near Tomahawk Church, while the main column halted about nine miles from Goode's Bridge after a distressing night and day of toil, broken only by a brief halt at Chesterfield Courthouse, about dawn that morning.

At 8:15 A. M. Richmond in flames had been surrendered to Weitzel, and the sun was hardly up before Meade's troops entered the works about Petersburg.

Alexander's command had just gone into bivouac when he was ordered to accompany some engineer officers to prepare a wagon route for the Artillery and trains to an overhead railroad bridge across the Appomattox River. Marching all night in the mud, the entire column was safely gotten across during the 4th and went into camp near sundown about three miles from Amelia Courthouse. During the day, Pendleton was busily engaged making arrangements for the reduction of the Artillery to a basis proportionate to the other troops, and to dispose of the surplus. Only the best equipped battalions were to remain with the Army, while all the rest were to be taken by Gen. Walker to Lynchburg.

The morning of the 5th, Walker set out by a road to the right and west of the main column after destroying ninety-five caissons with a great quantity of ammunition, which had early in the winter been sent to Amelia from Petersburg.

As soon as Grant learned of Lee's line of retreat, he pushed forward his whole available force, numbering near 80,000 men, in order to intercept him on the Richmond and Danville Railroad. The Federal pursuit was as rapid as the progress of Lee's Army was slow. The heavy rains, bottomless roads, and utter lack of forage soon reduced the artillery teams and transport to a most distressing state of exhaustion, and hundreds of men were forced to leave the ranks from hunger. The long wagon trains with their broken-down teams encumbered the roads at every turn, the men cheered on at first by the promise of food at Amelia Courthouse. But, disappointment there awaited them, for Lee's orders had miscarried and the rations and forage intended for the Army lay in the storehouses in Richmond. Nothing remained but the wide dispersion of the troops for foraging purposes, and dissolution under these conditions was inevitable.   The delay at Amelia entailed by the necessity of collecting food was fatal, for already Sheridan's troopers were harassing the flank and even the head of the column, while Grant's whole force well fed and carried forward by the stimulating hope of early victory was marching on nearly parallel roads.

In the words of one of Pendleton's staff officers, "It was a period in which no note was taken of day or night; one long, confused, dreadful day.   There seemed to be no front, no rear, for firing might be heard ahead and behind, and on both sides at once.   There were no headquarters, except where the ambulance happened to be." Small wonder that the brave men and their horses fell by the roadside exhausted by want and weariness.

Such was the condition when it was learned that Sheridan was across Lee's path at Jetersville, whereupon the Army was formed into line of battle to attack him.   But it was now reported that the 2d and 6th Corps were in front of the Army, and in order to pass them the column was countermarched a short distance, turned off to the right through Amelia Springs, and after marching all night reached Rice's Station six miles west of Burkeville at daylight.

During the night a serious panic was started by a large black stallion carrying a fence rail swinging to his bridle, and running through the column.   In the long continued firing which broke out, many officers and men were killed, among them Maj. Smith, who was in command of the detachment of heavy artillerymen from Drewry's Bluff.

At Rice's Station, Alexander was directed to select a line of battle upon which Lee soon formed his army, now reduced to about 10,000 men, while Pendleton placed his battalions in positions commanding the Burkeville Road and from which they could sweep the approaches on the left.

All day the 2d Corps had closely pressed Lee's rear, while the cavalry and the 6th Corps struck Ewell's column at Sailor's Creek. The latter force of about 8,000 men consisted of Kershaw's Division, a number of departmental employees under Gen. Custis Lee, the marines and sailors of the fleet under Admiral Tucker, and the heavy artillery from Drewry's and Chaffin's bluffs, under Col. Crutchfield and Maj. Stiles. After a most desperate conflict in which Ewell's nondescript force first repulsed, then charged the enemy, it was overborne by numbers and captured. Gen. Lee had gone in person to try to save Ewell's command, but now returned to the other troops, and told Gen. Pendleton on coming up with him, "General, half of our army is destroyed."

Toward noon, the enemy began to appear in Lee's front at Rice's Station, but were easily held off by Pendleton and Alexander with the Artillery. During the day Dearing's and Rosser's cavalry had met and captured a small mixed force of the enemy which had been sent forward to destroy the High Bridge on the Lynchburg Road. In this affair, both Gen. Dearing and Maj. James W. Thomson were killed. Thus two more officers, whose names will be remembered as long as any others in Lee's Artillery, laid down their lives.

The combat was short and bloody, the Confederate victory complete, and Dearing and the gallant Col. Boston of the Cavalry both fell in the first flush of victory. Opposite the Confederate center and left, the enemy sent up the white flag. But on the extreme right, Thomson, in ignorance of the surrender, pressed forward with his mounted cannoneers. As he did so, he caught sight of the white flag away down the line and gave a shout of joy. At that very moment he was struck with two balls, either of which would have proved fatal. With a deep groan he reeled from his saddle and fell dead. A moment later not a shot was to be heard. About the stricken body of the youthful major, his gunners grouped themselves in silence, among them his devoted friend and comrade, Maj. James Breathed, who, as he sighed and turned away, said, "With ten thousand such men as Jimmie Thomson, I could whip Grant's Army."

So died this martial youth, who from the day he entered the Virginia Military Institute in September, 1860, until the hour of his death, personified all that was valiant, all that was noble. No space here to tell of the many fields upon which he had won fame. But a lad of eighteen when as a lieutenant he helped Chew organize Ashby's Horse Battery, but twenty when captain of that battery, and but twenty-one when he became a battalion commander in the Horse Artillery, yet he was a veteran when he died, and was able to boast continuous service from the very beginning to the very end of the war. With Ashby, Jackson, and Stuart, he had fought upon every field made famous by their names, and on many an unknown field he had followed Chew who fought while others rested.

There beside Dearing and Boston he lay, all of them covered by their rubber blankets, suggestive of the curtain which had fallen upon these heroic lives. But another scene in the tragedy remained. An officer quickly searches the field. It is Jimmie Thomson's roommate at the Institute, the son of Admiral Smith Lee, who has heard of his death and is looking for his body, and more,—for the letter and the picture which he knows will be found in the breast pocket of that stained gray jacket. And on another portion of the field is found by a Confederate officer, in the haversack of a Federal soldier, a slip of paper containing a description of Thomson's death, and on it is written the following verse:

"His life burned not to ashes, white with doubt,
 But flaring up in battles' breath went out,
 His young blood pulsing years in a wild route,
     Then halting at high tide.

"In the loud trumpet blast, in the grand rush of lifted banners met,
 With his cheeks flushing and his saber wet,
 His young eyes flashing and his young lips set;
     So his rich spirit passed.

"Just when the field was won,
 When the clouds broke from off the hard-won fight,
 And the pierced flag leaped out upon our sight,
 In victory upspringing from the right,
     His brave young soul went out."*

During the afternoon Lee received information of an attack by the Federal Cavalry on his wagon train two miles in rear, whereupon he requested Gen. Pendleton to go back and see what could be done to save further loss. Meeting the remnants of Harris' Brigade, Pendleton gathered together about twenty volunteers and soon joined by a regiment of Cooke's Cavalry moved back to the train on which the enemy had fired. Pendleton and Cooke attacked the hostile cavalry, but were soon compelled to fall back, unable to save the wagons, and pursued for some distance by the enemy.

About sundown the Federals began massing in front of the line at Rice's Station for an attack in force, and Lee gave orders to resume the retreat. The Army, now cut off from Danville, marched towards Lynchburg, reaching Farmville at sunrise, after great hardships. During the entire night but six miles were covered. At Farmville, the weary column crossed to the north side of the Appomattox, and received a small supply of rations. As the Artillery began crossing the bridges at Farmville, the enemy pressed closely upon the rear guard, whereupon Pendleton placed several batteries in position on the heights on the north bank to cover the crossing.

*The finder of this paper was the Hon. W. L. Wilson, Member United States Congress from West Virginia, and later President of Washington and Lee University.
For a beautiful and most interesting account of Maj. Thomson's career, see "A Modern Greek," by John S. Wise, *Bob Taylor's Magazine,* December, 1906.

Gen. Lee now sent for Alexander, and with his map explained to him that the enemy had taken a highway bridge across the Appomattox near the High Bridge, were crossing on it and would come in upon his road about three miles ahead of him. Directing Alexander to send artillery to cover this passage, he placed the two bridges at Farmville under the latter's personal charge with orders to destroy them after the troops had all crossed. After pointing out on the map a shorter route to Lynchburg than that which Lee was following, and producing a resident of the section to confirm the map, Gen. Alexander retired and immediately set fire to the railroad bridge as the enemy was already in sight.

Poague's Battalion of artillery had been sent ahead to the point indicated by Lee, and Mahone's Division supported by Poague's guns took up a good position and began to intrench. Persistently assailed by Miles' Division throughout the day, Mahone held his own, while Poague fought his guns with desperate determination, losing then recovering one of his pieces. The service which the stern and indomitable Poague here rendered fully satisfied the confidence reposed in him by Pendleton, who selected the gallant little hero of the Wilderness in preference to all others for the delicate task of opening the way for the Army.

At midnight, the main column moved on the road toward Buckingham Courthouse, with Mahone and Poague forming the rear guard. During a truce, after sundown on the 7th, which Mahone secured for the removal of his wounded, a letter from Grant was transmitted to Lee through him, in which Grant first suggested the surrender of the Army of Northern Virginia, to which Lee promptly replied, inquiring what terms would be offered.

In spite of the roads, a long march was made during the night, and the morning of the 8th found the head of the Confederate column near Appomattox Courthouse.

During the march on the 8th, as Pendleton and Alexander rode together, the Chief of Artillery mentioned the fact that a number of the senior officers of the Army had conferred together and concluded it should be represented to Lee that in their opinion further resistance was futile, in order that he might surrender without incurring the odium of first proposing the step.

According to Alexander, Pendleton's contemporary account was about as follows:

It being the concensus of opinion among certain officers that Longstreet should approach the Commander-in-Chief on the subject, he, Pendleton, had suggested such action to Longstreet, but his proposal had been indignantly rejected, with the emphatic remark that it was his duty to support and not hamper his superior in the execution of his trust; that his, the 1st Corps, could still whip twice its number, and that as long as that was so, he would never suggest surrender. Failing to enlist Longstreet's services for the purpose proposed, he, Pendleton, had himself made bold to suggest a surrender to Gen. Lee, but was snubbed by the Commander-in-Chief, who coldly declared that "There are too many men here to talk of laying down their arms without fighting."

Gen. Alexander further asserted that in recounting these events, Pendleton was plainly embarrassed by the reception he had been given by Gen. Lee, which he, Alexander, at the time inferred to have been much in the nature of a rebuke. Concerning this whole incident, however, there are many recorded discrepancies.

In later years, Pendleton, always loth to discuss the sad circumstances connected with the retreat and surrender of the Army, gave the following account of his discharge of the mission upon which he was deputed by his fellow officers.

"Fighting was going on, but not very severely, so that conversation was practicable. Gen. Gordon had an interview with me; told me of discouraging intelligence from the South, and of a conference which had been held between other responsible officers and himself, and announced their joint wish that, if my views agreed with theirs, I should convey to Gen. Longstreet, as second in command, and then, if he agreed, to Gen. Lee, our united judgment that the cause had become hopeless, so we thought it wrong longer to have men killed on either side, and not right, moreover, that our beloved commander should be left to bear the entire trial of initiating the idea of terms with the enemy. My judgment not conflicting with those expressed, it seemed to me to be my duty to convey them to Gen. Lee. At first, Gen. Longstreet dissented, but on second thought preferred that he himself should be represented with the rest. Gen. Lee was lying alone, resting, at the base of a large pine tree. I approached and sat by him. To a statement of the case he quietly listened, and then, courteously expressing thanks for the consideration of his subordinates in desiring to relieve him in part of existing burdens, spoke in about these words: 'I trust it has not come to that. We certainly have too many brave men to think of laying down our arms. They still fight with great spirit, whereas the enemy do not. And, besides, if I were to intimate to Gen. Grant that I would listen to terms, he would at once regard it as such an evidence of weakness that he would demand unconditional surrender, and sooner than that I am resolved to die. Indeed, we must all determine to die at our posts.' My reply could only be that every man would no doubt cheerfully meet death with him in the discharge of duty, and that we were perfectly willing that he should decide the question."

This account differs widely from Alexander's. It may be that as time wore on, Gen. Pendleton saw matters in a softer light, and felt that what had at first appeared as a rebuke to him, was in fact the result of overwrought nerves.

After Pendleton's conversation on the march with Gen. Alexander, he pushed on to communicate in person with Gen. Walker, whose column he found about two miles beyond the Courthouse on the road to Appomattox Station. While he was conversing with Walker, whose batteries were parked and who himself was engaged in the duty of shaving, a large force of Federal cavalry burst upon the camp and began firing upon the defenseless men and their horses. The situation was desperate, but with great coolness, and the utmost presence of mind, Gen. Walker remained master of the situation. Almost instantly Walker's and Dickenson's batteries, which had been relieved of their guns and armed as a guard with muskets, formed line in a fringe of pines, and held the enemy at bay until a number of guns could be thrown into action, while the train was withdrawn. Thus did Walker's Artillery, entirely unsupported, maintain itself against the enemy. There was no panic whatever among these brave gunners. The following interesting account of this affair is taken from the diary of the Washington Artillery, written by Maj. W. M. Owen.

"After we went into bivouac this evening, the artillery firing we had heard in front late in the afternoon seemed to be approaching nearer. It was not a great while before long trains of wagons came tearing down the road from the front, the drivers whipping up their mules and shouting lustily. I mounted my horse and rode forward to see what was the matter. I had not gone far before I came up to a force of infantry that were being aligned across the road and preparing for defense.* Here I met some officers and men of the Washington Artillery, from whom I learned that Gen. Walker's column of artillery (about sixty pieces) had been marching in front of the Army all day, and at about 4 p. m. had halted in a grove just before reaching Appomattox station, on the Lynchburg railroad. Everything had been so quiet that they concluded to have a good rest, the officers and men taking advantage of the time to wash up and refresh themselves. It was not thought necessary to put out pickets, as the enemy was supposed to be pushing only our rear. While enjoying this supposed security, all of a sudden a bugle call rang out upon the air, and a squadron of Federal cavalry was seen preparing to charge. Men rushed to their guns in a hurry, horses were hitched up, and as the enemy advanced they were met by a raking fire of canister, which repulsed them. But again and again the enemy, reinforced, charged. They were Sheridan's cavalry.† The guns that could be gotten off fired retiring, and fell back to Appomattox Courthouse, where in the streets of the town they met infantry coming to their support, who in turn drove the enemy's cavalry back with loss. But the Washington Artillery, fighting to the last and evading capture with difficulty, destroyed their gun carriages, buried their guns in the woods, and nearly all the officers and men went to the mountains. They fired their last shot to-day, after three years and nine months of service in the field, since Bull Run, July, 1861."

This account explains the fact that some of the Artillery known to have been with Walker's column surrendered the following day with Pendleton's command.

---

*These were Walker's dismounted cannoneers.—Author's note.
†Custer's command.—Author's note.

While with Walker, and after the repulse of the enemy's cavalry, Pendleton received a summons from Gen. Lee, and setting out to rejoin the main column narrowly eluded a hostile force of cavalry, which was sweeping through the village, by leaping his horse over a fence and skirting the fields. When he reported to the Commander-in-Chief about 1 A. M. of the 9th, he found him "dressed in his neatest style, new uniform, snowy linen, etc." To Gen. Pendleton's expression of surprise, Gen. Lee explained, "I have probably to be Gen. Grant's prisoner, and thought I must make my best appearance."

Here the question suggests itself, was Lee really preparing to meet his victorious adversary, or was he, prompted by that spirit, the flash of which Pendleton has described, resolved to die at the head of his army in the event Grant failed to grant him honorable terms? He had placed himself on several occasions at the head of his troops, with the evident determination to die at their head if need be. It would almost seem that he was now clothing himself for the final sacrament in the cause which he held to be holy.

Grant was now hurrying forward his troops and massing a large force in Lee's front, having despatched a column by the short route pointed out to Lee by Gen. Alexander. Almost before Pendleton rejoined Lee, he heard the firing of artillery beyond the Courthouse, which could only mean the capture of Walker's Artillery column. Against cavalry alone, the sturdy gunners could contend, but not against the infantry, which was soon brought up by the defeated troopers.

Late in the afternoon of the 8th, Lee had received Grant's reply to his note of the evening before, and again he addressed the Federal commander, proposing a meeting between them at 10 A. M. the next day, this communication being delivered to Grant about midnight. But as the terms of Lee's note rather suggested a discussion of political character, Grant in a third note declined the interview.

At daylight, it was discovered that the enemy was in great force astride the Confederate line of retreat, and that Walker's command had been captured. A collision was unavoidable. Indeed Gordon, now in command of the 2d Corps, and leading the column, had been directed to clear the road at dawn.

At three o'clock on the morning of the 9th of April, the Confederates moved silently forward. Reaching the heights a little beyond the Courthouse Gordon found the enemy disposed to dispute his way, and at once deployed the 2,000 men of his corps, while Gen. Long brought forward the thirty pieces of artillery which were all that were left of Carter's, Poague's, Johnson's, and Stark's battalions. A well directed fire from the Artillery and an attack by Fitz Lee quickly dislodged the force immediately in Gordon's front, but beyond he could already discover the dark masses of the enemy's infantry, and knew further effort unaided was useless. In this affair Fitz Lee actually took a number of prisoners, and two 12-pounder Napoleons, but it was apparent to all that the sacrifice of life incident to further fighting would be as useless as it would be culpable.

Though Gordon, Long, and Fitz Lee fought with great spirit, still at noon the main column had not advanced beyond the Courthouse. When Lee early in the morning inquired of Gordon how he was progressing, the answer was that nothing could be accomplished without heavy reinforcements from Longstreet. Whereupon Lee took immediate steps to bring the fighting to an end and reopened negotiations with Grant. This was the only thing left, for Field's and Mahone's divisions and Alexander's Artillery were holding Meade back in the rear and could not be spared for an attack in the front.

Meanwhile, the march of the Army had been brought to a halt by Gordon's inability to advance, and the rear was closing up. Longstreet directed Alexander to form a line of battle, on which Mahone's and Field's divisions were to be rallied for a last stand. Alexander at once

placed all his artillery and all the organized infantry
in position behind the North Fork of the Appomattox.
While the enemy were extending their lines to the left
the battery commanders begged to be allowed to open
upon them, but this Alexander would not permit.

A flag of truce was now sent Grant, requesting a
suspension of hostilities pending negotiations for surrender, and an order to Gordon's troops to suspend their
fire.   This order, when received by Gen. Long, was
sent by him through Majs. Southall, Parker, and other
members of his staff to the different batteries, while he,
himself, proceeded to the Courthouse.   On reaching
that point he discovered that the order had not carried
to Clutter's Battery under Lieut. McIntosh, a brother
of the battalion commander.   This battery occupied a
hill immediately above the village, and continued to fire
rapidly upon an advancing line of the enemy's infantry.
Gen. Long at once rode in person to the battery, and
ordered the captain to cease firing and to withdraw his
battery to a small valley east of the village, where the
Artillery was being parked.

According to Gen. Long, the shots which Lieut.
Wright's section of Clutter's Battery fired were the
last fired in battle by the Army of Northern Virginia.

Some time before the order to cease firing was given,
as Alexander came upon Lee and his staff by the roadside at the top of the hill, the General called him aside
and again laid the map before him saying that the Army
had come to the junction and inquired, "What have
we got to do to-day?"

After talking with Gen. Pendleton, Alexander had
formulated a plan in his own mind and now proceeded
to present it.   His own words are here quoted:

"My command having been north of the James had had no share
in the fighting about Petersburg, and but little in the retreat.   They
had now begun to hear of a surrender, and would hint their sentiments in loud voices when I rode by.

" 'We don't want to surrender any ammunition.   We've been
saving ammunition all this war.   Hope we are not saving it for a
surrender.'

"I told the general of this, and said that if he saw fit to try to cut our way out, my command would do as well as they had ever done.

"He answered:

"'I have left only two divisions, Field's and Mahone's, sufficiently organized to be relied upon. All the rest have been broken and routed and can do little good. Those divisions are now scarcely 4,000 apiece, and that is far too little to meet the force now in front of us.'

"This was just the opportunity I wished, and I hastened to lay my plans before him. I said:

"'Then we have only choice of two courses. Either to surrender, or take to the woods and bush, with orders either to rally on Johnston, or perhaps, better, on the Governors of the respective States. If we surrender this army, it is the end of the Confederacy. I think our best course would be to order each man to go to the Governor of his own State with his arms.'

"'What would you hope to accomplish by that?' said he.

"'In the first place,' said I, 'to stand the chances. If we surrender this army every other army will have to follow suit. All will go like a row of bricks, and if the rumors of help from France have any foundation the news of our surrender will put an end to them.

"'But the only thing which may be possible in our present situation is to get some kind of terms. None of our armies are likely to be able to get them, and that is why we should try with the different States. Already it has been said that Vance can make terms with North Carolina, and Jo Brown with Georgia. Let the Governor of each State make some sort of a show of force and then surrender on terms, which may save us from trial for treason and confiscation.'

"As I talked it all looked to me so reasonable that I hoped he was convinced, for he listened in silence. So I went on more confidently:

"'But, General, apart from all that—if all fails and there is no hope—the men who have fought under you for four years have got the right this morning to ask one favor of you. We know that you do not care for military glory. But we are proud of the record of this army. We want to leave it untarnished to our children. It is a clear record so far, and now is about to be closed. A little blood more or less now makes no difference, and we have the right to ask of you to spare us the mortification of having you ask Grant for terms, and have him answer that he has no terms to offer. That it is "U. S.—Unconditional Surrender." That was his reply to Buckner at Fort Donelson, and to Pemberton at

Vicksburg, and that is what threatens us. General, spare us the mortification of asking terms and getting that reply.'

"He heard it all so quietly and it was all so true, it seemed to me, and so undeniable, that I felt sure that I had him convinced. His first words were:

" 'If I should take your advice, how many men do you suppose would get away?'

" 'Two-thirds of us,' I answered. 'We would be like rabbits and partridges in the bushes, and they could not scatter to follow us.'

"He said: 'I have only 15,000 muskets left. Two-thirds of them divided among the States, even if all could be collected, would be too small a force to accomplish anything. All could not be collected. Their homes have been overrun, and many would go to look after their families.

" 'Then, General, you and I as Christian men have no right to consider only how this would affect us. We must consider the effect on the country as a whole. Already it is demoralized by four years of war. If I took your advice, the men would be without rations and under no control of officers. They would be compelled to rob and steal in order to live. They would become mere bands of marauders, and the enemy's cavalry would pursue them and over-run many wide sections they may never have occasion to visit. We would bring on a state of affairs it would take the country years to recover from.

" 'And as for myself, you young fellows might go to bush-whacking, but the only dignified course for me would be to go to Gen. Grant and surrender myself and take the consequences of my acts.'

"He paused for only a moment and then went on.

" 'But I can tell you one thing for your comfort. Grant will not demand an unconditional surrender. He will give us as good terms as this army has a right to demand, and I am going to meet him in the rear at 10 A. M. and surrender the army on condition of not fighting again until exchanged.'

"I had not a single word to say in reply. He had answered my suggestion from a plane so far above it that I was ashamed of having made it. With several friends I had planned to make an escape on seeing a flag of truce, but that idea was at once abandoned by all of them on hearing my report."

Thus did the plan upon which the bold young Alexander had cogitated during the preceding days come to naught, dissipated like thin smoke in the air of Lee's nobility of soul. In maturer years, Gen. Alexander came to see the folly of his proposals, and magnanimously acknowledged the error of his hot youth, accepting the inevitable in the same spirit it was received by Lee. Let us not censure him if in the enthusiasm of his youth he failed to perceive that in defeat there was a greater courage than prolonged resistance with the useless sacrifice of brave lives. Such an end to a struggle for liberty may have been suited to Cronge and de Wett, but it was beneath a Lee, from whose view that higher duty to God was not obscured by any false sense of obligation to his army and his people.

About 8:30 A. M., Gen. Lee, in his full new uniform, begirt with sword and sash, rode to the rear to meet Grant, and soon received the communication from the latter before mentioned. He at once wrote the Federal chieftain, again requesting an interview, but in terms which suggested fuller compliance with the original proposal. While this last message was being prepared, a messenger riding like the wind dashed around a curve and, seeing Lee, brought his superb charger to a halt. It was the gallant, one-armed John Haskell of artillery fame at Petersburg, nay, more, of world fame. All recognized the rider, who with his good arm only succeeded in drawing up his lathered steed one hundred yards or more beyond the group. Gen. Lee went to meet him, exclaiming: "What is it? What is it?" and then seeing the sad plight of Col. Haskell's magnificent animal so well known to the Army, without waiting for a reply, sorrowfully said: "Oh, why did you do it? You have killed your beautiful horse!"*

Col. Haskell explained that Fitz Lee had sent in a report that he had found a road by which the Army could escape, and that Longstreet had ordered him to overtake Lee, before he could send a note to Grant, and to kill his horse if necessary to do it.

Lee, however, did not credit the report, which later proved to be a mistake.

---

*This animal was noted for its beauty and speed. It had been led all the way from Richmond on the retreat, with a view to making an escape in case of surrender. The horse recovered and was sold to a Federal officer for a handsome sum in gold.

What need to describe the sad rites which now ensued? Or to tell of the anguish which showed in the
eyes of those heroic men that had for four horror-laden
years toiled wearily on to Appomattox, whither the inexorable sign posts of Fate had led them—to which we
now know the fickle dame, ofttimes disguising the
route with cajoling flatteries, had guided them from the
first? Was it another trick of Fate that the very roof
which shielded the proud Lee from the gaze of the
curious, as he conferred with Grant, was the haven in
which its owner had sought refuge from the stricken
field of First Manassas? Well may it be said that no
home in all that bleeding Southland was free from the
merciless intrusions of war?*

After the formal surrender of his army, Gen. Lee
appointed Gens. Longstreet, Gordon, and Pendleton
to conduct the transfer of property, and to supervise the
paroling of the officers and men. In accordance with
the stipulations of the agreement the guns and troops
were withdrawn from the lines, and the work was
promptly undertaken.

The return of the Chief of Ordnance for the morning
of April 9 showed 7,892 organized infantry, with 75
rounds of ammunition each, and 63 field guns with an
average of 93 rounds. But 61 guns and 13 caissons,
however, remained, for two pieces had been destroyed
during the morning.

The infantry were first massed near the Courthouse,
and after stacking arms were directed to retire, while
the Federal officers took charge. Alexander was directed to form all the guns and caissons in a single
column along the road, that the Federal ordnance officers might conduct them into their lines. The animals
had been practically without forage of any kind for several days. Alexander writes: "With a heart full of sympathy for the poor brutes, I formed the column on
Tuesday, April 11, and left them standing in the road,

---

*The house in which the articles of surrender were signed was the residence
of Maj. McLean, to which he had removed after his home at Manassas was
destroyed in the battle of Bull Run, July 21, 1861.

which they filled for about a mile. The next morning I bade good-bye to Appomattox, and as I rode off from the scene I saw the mournful column of artillery still standing in the road unattended, but with many of its poor horses now down in the mud and unable to rise."

Let us avert our eyes from the sad picture and be thankful that a large number of the artillery horses, including all the mounts, had been claimed by the officers and men.

Many batteries had escaped the surrender, both from Walker's column on the 8th, and from the Army at Appomattox the following day. Some made their way to Lynchburg, where the guns were destroyed, and others buried their guns by the roadside and disbanded. Of all that great corps of near three hundred pieces, little more than half a hundred were surrendered. Many of the artillerymen joined Johnston, among them a large detachment of horse artillery under Col. Chew, who escaped with Rosser's Cavalry Division and reported at Greensboro, N. C., April 30. They were not allowed to engage in hostilities against Sherman, for the view was taken that they were an integral part of Lee's Army, and therefore embraced in the surrender. Later they were paroled with Johnston's troops.

The total number of officers and men of the Army of Northern Virginia paroled by Grant during the 10th and 11th of April was 28,231, for large numbers of stragglers soon joined the organized force which stacked arms on the 9th.

It is difficult to determine with certainty the exact composition of the Artillery present at the Surrender. The parole lists indicate that the remaining organizations were as follows:*

Stark's Battalion_____ { Giles Battery
Louisiana Guard Battery
Richmond Hampden Battery

*See Vol. XV, Southern Historical Papers. In this valuable volume the names of the artillery officers who surrendered, as well as of the enlisted men, are given.

Cutshaw's Battalion
- 2d Richmond Howitzers
- Staunton Battery
- King William Battery
- Richmond Orange Battery
- Reese's Alabama Battery
- Louisa Morris Battery

Lightfoot's Battalion
- Caroline Battery
- Surry Battery

Hardaway's Battalion
- 3d Richmond Howitzers
- 1st Richmond Howitzers
- Norfolk Blues Battery
- Salem Battery
- 1st Rockbridge Battery
- Powhatan Battery

Johnson's Battalion
- Fredericksburg Battery
- Clutter's Battery
- 1st Maryland Battery
- Southside Battery

Haskell's Battalion
- Lamkin's Nelson Battery
- Palmetto (S. C.) Battery
- Rowan (N. C.) Battery
- Branch's (N. C.) Battery

Huger's Battalion
- Bedford Battery
- Madison (La.) Battery
- Ashland Battery
- Parker's Richmond Battery
- Bath Battery

McIntosh's Battalion
- 4th Maryland Battery
- Danville Battery (Price's)
- Lynchburg Battery (Chamberlayne's)
- 2d Rockbridge Battery
- Ringgold Danville Battery
- Graham's Petersburg Battery
- Jeff Davis (Ala.) Battery

Richardson's Battalion——Donaldsonville (La.) Battery

Poague's Battalion
- Manly's N. C. Battery
- Pittsylvania Battery
- Warrenton Battery
- Williams' N. C. Battery
- Albemarle Everett Battery
- N. C. Battery (?)

Braxton's Battalion——Lynchburg Lee Battery

With the Army were fragments of other batteries, including men from the four companies of the Washington Artillery Battalion who attached themselves, after escaping from Walker's column, to Alexander's and Long's commands. Some of the batteries enumerated as present with the Army at the Surrender numbered but a mere handful of men. The strength of the various battalions may be determined from the following enumeration:

ARTILLERY PAROLE ROLLS, DATED APRIL 9, 1865

	Officers	Enlisted Men	Total
General Headquarters, Brig.-Gen. Pendleton and Staff	12	13	25
First Army Corps, Brig.-Gen. E. P. Alexander and Staff	11	36	47
Haskell's Battalion, Lieut.-Col. J. C. Haskell	15	139	154
Huger's Battalion, Maj. Tyler C. Jordan	21	307	328
McIntosh's Battalion, Lieut.-Col. Wm. M. Owen	14	268	282
Poague's Battalion, Lieut.-Col. Wm. T. Poague	17	279	296
13th Virginia Battalion, Capt. D. N. Walker	2	10	12
Richardson's Battalion, Capt. R. Prosper Landry	4	77	81
Total First Army Corps	84	1,116	1,200
Second Army Corps, Brig.-Gen. A. L. Long and Staff	8	22	30
Carter's Command, Col. Thomas H. Carter	2	4	6
Braxton's Battalion, Lieut.-Col. Carter M. Braxton	7	19	26
Cutshaw's Battalion, Capt. C. W. Fry	12	199	211
Hardaway's Battalion, Lieut.-Col. R. A. Hardaway	19	382	401
Johnson's Battalion, Lieut.-Col. Marmaduke Johnson	8	135	143
Lightfoot's Battalion, Asst. Surg. J. B. Coakley	1	29	30
Stark's Battalion, Lieut.-Col. Alex. W. Stark	11	154	165
Total Second Army Corps	68	944	1,012
Anderson's Corps, Col. Hilary P. Jones	2	1	3
Blount's Battalion	3	21	24
Coit's Battalion		37	37
Stribling's Battalion	2	8	10
Total Anderson's Corps	7	67	74
Smith's Battalion, Capt. W. F. Dement	13	252	265
Total Artillery	184	2,392	2,676

The foregoing rolls partially disclose the organization of the Artillery as effected by Pendleton at Amelia Courthouse, when the reduction in the force with the Army became necessary, and at which time parts of Coit's, Eshleman's, Cabell's, King's, Nelson's, Pegram's, and Sturdivant's battalions were placed under Gen. Walker to be taken to Lynchburg. According to Custer, there were over thirty pieces of artillery with Walker, besides a large train, and twenty-four of these guns and many prisoners were captured, but Sheridan places the number of guns captured by Custer from Walker at twenty-five. Custer claims that during the ten days preceding the Surrender his command captured forty-six guns.*

The exact composition of the various artillery commands after leaving Amelia is difficult to determine, but the following order, the last issued by Gen. Walker, and for which the author is indebted to Gen. Walker's Assistant Adjutant-General, Capt. William W. Chamberlayne, throws some light on the subject.

"Hd. Qrs. Reserve Arty, A. N. Virginia,

"April 7, 1865.

"Circular.

"This command will move at 1 o'clock A. M., in the following order:

"Lightfoot's Battalion,
"Coit's Division,
"Eshleman's Division,
"Cabell's Division,
"Walker's Battalion, ⎱ Rear Guard.
"Leyden's Battalion, ⎰

"Col. Cabell will furnish a section of Napoleons to march with the Rear Guard.

"The wagons in rear of their respective Battalions.

"By command of Gen. Walker.

"Wm. W. Chamberlayne,
"A. A.-General."

[Receipted on the back.]

*It will be recalled that some of Walker's batteries had buried their guns, others joined the main column, and others dispersed before Custer's final attack.

Hd. Qrs. Cabell's Batt.,
Received by WALTER B. CARR,
April 7, '65.   *Sergeant Major.*

Hd. Qrs. Reserve Arty 3d Corps,
April 7, '65.   B. F. ESHLEMAN,
               Lt.-Col. Commanding.

Received by JAS. C. COIT,
          Maj. Commanding Batt.

[Other receipts torn off.]

If we allow Walker a force of 500 men, and the various batteries which escaped to Lynchburg and the ten batteries of horse artillery 800, it will be seen that the Artillery personnel numbered not less than 3,800 officers and men April 8, 1865. Thus, whatever may be said of the state of disorganization of the Infantry and Cavalry, there being not more than 2,000 of the latter towards the end of the retreat, it is apparent that the Artillery maintained its organization in a comparatively high state of efficiency to the end, with its personnel only slightly reduced since its departure from Petersburg.* No higher tribute can be paid its commanders than this fact, for the Artillery in the nature of things should have been the first to show signs of dissolution.

Grant's terms were honorable. The arms, artillery, such of it as was left, and all public property were to be turned over to the victors, all officers retaining their sidearms, private horses and baggage. In addition to this and in the interest of the desolate Southern people, every soldier in the Confederate Army who claimed to own a horse or mule was to be permitted to retain it for farming purposes. And so many of the artillery teams, for the preservation and care of which Pendleton had labored so incessantly, were now to exchange the gun and the caisson for the plow and the harrow, the implements in that struggle for existence, which for

---

*Shoemaker's Horse Battery contained 90 men when it surrendered. There is no reason to suppose the other horse batteries were not as strong, so the foregoing estimate is extremely conservative. Three full batteries of Blount's Battalion with certainly 50 men each escaped to Lynchburg.

the next decade proved to be far more cruel and distressing than the mere war for liberty, through which
the South had passed. Who can tell what were the
emotions of those gallant gunners when first they struck
the plowshare of peace into the poverty-stricken soil
of their native fields? Did not the war-stained harness,
which still hung from the backs of those weary, worn
animals, recall to mind the charger and the martial
trappings of a hundred battlefields? Did not the dumb
patience of those faithful brutes, bearing like their
masters the wounds and scars of battle, hold for Lee's
men a lesson of fortitude and admonish them
that together the old war horse and the veteran must
labor on for the salvation of the land? Ah! it is sweet to
believe that these brave gunners, often as at dawn they
led their old artillery teams from the leaky shelters that
stabled them, recalled the reveille of other days, and perhaps with a manly tear in their eyes gently stroked the
muzzles of those faithful steeds. Or perhaps, as they
rested together, man and beast, in the heat of noon-tide,
'neath the generous shade of some ancient oak, the sighing of the nearby pines recalled to their minds the rush
of the guns, the hastening feet, the roar of battle, of another day, and admonished them to be brave so that
when the final Appomattox came upon them they
might be released from the plow of life with the same
consciousness of duty, well performed, that filled their
souls on that April day in 1865—that day when nature
with her sweet scented fields and budding trees sought
to sweeten the bitterness of defeat, and soothe with her
beauties the fevered brow of a vanquished army.

It has been said that the shots fired by Lieut. Wright
were the last, but let us accept Page's beautiful story as
one of fact. Two weeks before the Surrender an old artillery officer had been sent with a small column and
a battery to guard an important pass in the Blue
Ridge, through which a Federal column from Southwest Virginia was expected to attempt to move upon
Lee's rear.

The "Old Colonel" had seized and held the crossing. The position for his guns had been carefully selected. It was at the highest point of the pass just where the road crawled over the shoulders of the mountain along the limestone cliff, a hundred feet sheer above the deep river, where its waters had cut their way in ages past, and now lay deep and silent as if resting after their arduous toil before they began to boil over the great bowlders which filled the bed of the stream. The position was impregnable, and the "Old Colonel" had been ordered to hold it until relieved.

Late on the 10th, the enemy assailed the battery, but all in vain. Numbers counted for little in that wild eyrie, where a single gun could hold out against a host. On the 11th, the Federals attempted under a flag of truce to convince the "Old Colonel" that Lee had surrendered, but still he remained at his post, awaiting some order to withdraw. No order came, but soon undoubted news arrived of the sad event. At last, as the sun set in all its glory, throwing the great western peaks in dark relief against the golden sky, and the shades of night spread through the silent vales, the pickets were called in and the old battery formed as if for parade. Once more the men were to be allowed to make the mountains echo with the crash of their guns.

The embers of the sinking camp-fires threw a faint light on the guns, standing so grim and silent in the embrasures of the little work; nearby stood the caissons with the harness hanging limply from the poles. Not a word was spoken, except that of command. "At the order each detachment went to its piece; the guns were run back, and the men with their own hands ran them upon the edge of the perpendicular bluff above the river, where, sheer below, the waters washed its base. The pieces stood ranged in the order in which they had so often stood in battle, and the gray, thin fog rising slowly and silently from the river deep down between the cliffs, and wreathing the mountain side above, might have been the smoke from some unearthly battle fought by ghostly guns, posted there in the darkness and manned by phantom cannoneers. At the word the gunners drew their lanyards taut—as if a single piece the six guns belched forth a sheet of flame, roared a last challenge on the misty night, and sent their thunder reverberating through the darkening mountain tops, while startling alike the blue-coated warriors in their camp below, the browsing deer and the prowling fox."

A deadly silence now fell upon the scene, broken only by the sighing of the tree-tops above and the rushing torrent. Then came another command—"Let them go, and God be our helper. Amen!"

For a few moments there was utter silence; then one prolonged, deep, resounding splash, as the war-worn guns plunged into the pool, spreading over its once-placid surface a spray, as if some titan hand had lain a floral tribute upon the abysmal tomb of Lee's Artillery. Such was the final sacrament of those men, whose record is enshrined in the names of Pendleton, Long, Alexander, Walker, Walton, Crutchfield, Brown, Pelham, Pegram, Chew, Breathed, Latimer, Thomson, Landry, Cutshaw, McIntosh, Poague, Carter, Braxton, Haskell, Huger, Hardaway, Cabell, Gibbes, Watson, McGregor, McGraw, McCarthy, Nelson, Chamberlayne, Caskie, and a host of their peers too numerous to mention, the like of whom the world has never known before or since their time. Such was the hallowed rite that marked the "Burial of Lee's Guns" and the end of that strife in which Sumter was the primer that discharged the explosive compounded of political antagonism. An apparent motive only had been needed, both north and south, for the pulling of the lanyard to expand an energy stored up through years of cherished animosity. But now, the end had come and once more the placid waters settled over a cause, buried but not forgotten.

If in its record there is a single incident to inspire other generations to emulate the devotion to duty, the valor, the Christian fortitude, of the men who fought its guns, then the "Long Arm of Lee" did not exist, struggle, and perish in vain.

GENERAL INDEX

Battery and battalion organizations are not included in the General Index, but in the "Battery Index" and the "Battalion Index," which follow. The records of the batteries and battalions are the records of their commanders, who are referred to in the General Index in their individual capacity only. Thus, if it be desired to trace the record of Captain, later Colonel, Thomas H. Carter, the references to Carter's Battery and Carter's Battalion should be consulted, as well as the item, "Carter, Col. T. H.," in the General Index. Statistics, such as numbers engaged, organization, personnel, material, captures, losses, ammunition expenditure, tactical features and dispositions, topography, Confederate and Federal, are not generally indexed, but will readily be found in the appropriate chronological chapter of the text.

	PAGE
Administrative Regulations for Artillery	199
Alburtis, Capt.	335
Aldie, action at	218
Alexander, E. P., appointed Col. and Chief of Ordnance	72
his former record	73
mentioned, 115, 130, 136, 140, 141, 155	
criticisms of	193, 194, 195
quoted	218, 226, 227, 239
his attack on Pendleton,	227, 231, 232
referred to..288, 292, 293, 319, 337, 343, 351, 363, 372, 376, 378, 387, 400, 413, 416, 424, 440, 445, 490, 494, 505, 507, 508, 509, 511, 534, 536, 537, 539, 545, 549, 551, 553, 554, 564, 565, 570, 572, 635, 642, 645, 646, 647, 658, 664, 667, 670, 671, 672, 674, 676, 680, 681, 682, 684, 686, 688, 689, 695, 696, 697, 704, 720, 731, 736, 754, 776, 781, 787, 789, 793, 823, 840, 842, 845, 850, 868, 895, 897, 900, 919, 923, 924, 933, 934, 936, 939, 940, 944, 945, 947,	949
Allan, Col. William, quoted	195
mentioned	564
Alphabetical designation for battalions	415
Altercation over use of land torpedoes	178
Ambuscade of artillery column,	891, 892
American tactics	160, 161
"American Artillerist's Companion"	149
Ammunition, fixed, introduction of	32
purchased in Europe, 1861..	37
seized with Baton Rouge arsenal	38
laboratories	40
manufacture of	42
capacity of laboratories...45,	46
purchased up to 1863	55
amount made	56
furnished by West Point Foundry	64
lack of in 1861......76, 139,	140
expenditure of at Coggin's Point	234
supply of	243
expenditures compared ..269,	274
expenditure	326
improved in 1862	340
report on	424
poor quality at Chancellorsville	509
influence of	548
Board for study of	564
expenditures	597
Federal reserve at Gettysburg	637, 638
Anderson, Jos. R. & Co., proprietors of Richmond Tredegar Works, the Confederate "Krupps"	51
mentioned	341
Anderson, Lieut. R. M.	657
Anderson, Capt. Robt., his manual	154
Andrews, Lt.-Col. R. Snowden, 244, 414, 416, 515, 516, 551, 605, 704,	720
Anecdote, concerning cavalry trooper	196

PAGE

Antietam, Battle of 294
Antimony, sulphuret of 47
Appropriations for ordnance
   work 36, 37
Archer, Dr. Junius L., manu-
   facturer of guns........... 68
Archer Projectiles, defects of.. 128
Armament of batteries on the
   Peninsula 201
   of army in 1862, tabulated.. 284
Armored car 216
Armistead, Capt. George...... 90
Arms, captured, regulations
   concerning 39, 59
   purchased abroad 55
   destroyed at Harper's Ferry 68
Armstrong, Sir William, devel-
   opes breech-loader 29
Armstrong Guns 243
Arsenals, seizure of Federal
   by Confederates 24, 41
   U. S., created.............. 26
   erected by C. S. A........35, 36
   material seized with Federal 38
   location of Confederate..... 40
Articles of War, C. S. A...... 109
Artificers, pay of........... 108
Artillery, American, reputation
   of in 1861.............. 31
   amount of Confederate originally proposed 42
   officers detailed for ordnance
   work 39, 52, 53
   of Virginia, armament of..62, 67
   early American 85
   early instruction 85, 91
   in Mexican War........... 93
   merged with Engineer Corps 89
   status of in 1808........... 88
   in 1815 90
   in 1837 91
   in 1860 94
   officers in from West Point.. 95
   Corps of, C. S. A...108, 109, 117
   law creating officers.108, 109, 117
   pay of officers in........... 108
   Provisional, C. S. A., created 107
   of Virginia 112, 115
   strength of in 1861........ 140
   French Schools 152
   mass tactics 152, 153
   proportion of to infantry 151, 153
   Federal organization 156
   administration of Confederate 199
   nature of the arm.......... 209
   efficiency of 277, 278
   reorganization of C. S. A... 279

PAGE

   organization at Sharpsburg,
                     282, 283
   reorganization of 1862...... 332
   reduction of in 1862........ 337
   strength of in Oct., 1862.339, 346
   assignment of in 1862...... 345
   strength of in Dec., 1862.... 411
   organization of in April, 1863. 419
   organization of in May, 1863. 442
   error of at Chancellorsville.. 490
   mobility of at Chancellors-
    ville 491
   fire effect of at Chancellors-
    ville 511
   status of Federal in 1863,
                    546, 550
   Confederate and Federal com-
    pared 547, 548, 573
   number and grades of officers
    in 1863 565
   reorganization of 1863...... 565
   organization of in 1863.... 567
   strength of in July, 1863... 575
   of Western Army, inspected
    by Pendleton 583
   charged by cavalry,
         585, 587, 591, 596
   movement of to Gettysburg.. 599
   reconnaissances,
       623, 631, 639, 643, 658
   resisting power of........ 649
   faulty disposition of at
    Gettysburg 666
   efforts to secure promotion
    for officers in....719, 723, 724
   divisions created 722, 725
   of Western Army reorganized 731
   character of C. S. A. com-
    manders 742
   proposed organization of in
    1864 830
   superior personnel of in 1864. 893
   proposed increase of C. S. A.
    Corps in 1864............ 902
   Pendleton's tribute to his... 906
   headquarters of at Peters-
    burg 907
   staff of in 1864........902, 907
   losses of at Petersburg..... 909
   heavy batteries about Rich-
    mond 920
   promotions in, in 1865...... 925
Ashby, Gen. Turner.......162, 163
Atkinson, Lt.-Col. 920
Atlanta Arsenal 57
Augusta Arsenal 40
Augusta Powder Mills........ 40

PAGE

erected 43
site and capacity of........ 45
Superintendent of 57
Austerlitz, Battle of.......... 153
Austrian, guns purchased....37, 55
    artillery 155
    tactics in 1859............. 172
    ammunition expenditure 274
Auxonne, Artillery School..152, 159
Badajos 864
Baggage allowance....428, 708, 709
Balaclava, charge of Light
    Brigade at, compared to
    Brandy Station 587
Balck, quoted 106
Baldwin, Col. J. B........... 116
Baldwin, Col. Briscoe G., Chief
    of Ordnance......341, 351, 570
Balloons, Federal observation,
                    234, 366, 376
Barefooted gunners 355, 356
Barksdale, Lieut. 526
Barnwell, Maj. J. C...198, 319,
    380, 387, 388, 417, 423, 907
Barry, Lieut. 216
Barry, Col. Wm. F., Chief of
    Artillery 133, 157
Baton Rouge Arsenal.......37, 40
    powder seized with......... 38
Battalions, organization of pro-
    posed 141
    created 155
    use of 344
    organization of 413, 415
    no longer part of infantry
    commands 556
    proposed composition of in
    1864 830
Battery, the organization of a,
                    109, 110
    material of a.............. 110
    complement of horses....... 111
    authority to raise.......... 144
    strength of a Va. militia... 144
    mobility of 165
    Lee discourages raising of
    additional 197
    those disbanded in 1862.... 284
    proposed organization of a,
    in 1864 830
Battles, Lieut...684, 685, 931, 932
Bautzen, Battle of........... 153
Bayard, Gen. Geo. D., killed by
    shell 350
Bayne, Maj. T. L., command-
    ing Blockade Service..... 56
Beauregard, Gen., at Petersburg 836
Beaver Dam, Battle of....207, 211

PAGE

Beckham, Col. R. F..128, 162,
    597, 733, 720, 722, 725
    (See Beckham's Battery and
    Beckham's Battalion)
Beef, issued in 1862.......... 374
    cattle 427
Bellona Arsenal, created...... 26
    mentioned 51
    guns seized at............. 68
Bercier's Orleans French Bat-
    tery of La.............. 93
Bermuda Agency 56
Bernadotte, his proud boast
    that he had never lost a
    gun 525
Bernard, Col. Simon.......... 97
Besancon, Artillery School.... 152
Best, Capt. 550, 554
Bethesda Church, Battle of.... 207
Beverly Ford 259
Big Bethel, Battle of, rifle guns
    used in 64
    described 118
Blackburn's Ford 127
Blacksmiths, pay of.......... 108
Blakely guns, purchased...... 55
    mentioned 243
    in Horse Artillery.......... 346
Blankets 115
Blockade Running Service..... 56
Blount, Maj. J. G.........564, 917
    (See Blount's Battery)
Blücher, calls for more guns.. 153
Blumenau, Battle of.......... 274
Board of War, 1776.......... 25
Boggs, Maj. Francis J., 838, 917, 920
    (See Boggs' Battalion)
Bombardment of Fredericksburg 362
Bomford, Col. George, Chief of
    Ordnance 26, 91
Boonsboro, Battle of.......... 292
Boots, price of in 1864........ 908
Borman fuses, defective...... 122
Boston, Col. 936
Bourcet 160
Bowen & Co., of Pendleton,
    S. C., powder contractors.. 43
    saltpetre contractors 44
Bowling Green, Artillery Camp
    at 410, 556
Bragg's Battery (Horse Artil-
    lery) 164
Bran, price of in 1864........ 909
Branch, Col. James R....840, 917
    (See Branch's Petersburg
    Battery and Branch's Bat-
    talion)
Brander, Maj. 932

PAGE

Brandy Station 434, 584
Braxton, Lt.-Col. Carter M.,
    416, 421, 509, 720, 878, 885
    (See Braxton's Battery and
    Braxton's Battalion)
Breathed, Maj. James..162, 338,
    346, 440, 577, 720, 795, 937
    (See Breathed's Battery and
    Breathed's Battalion)
Breech-loading gun, develop-
    ment of 29
    origin of 31
    varieties of 32
Brenizer, Capt. A. C., Supt.
    Salisbury Foundry 57
Bridge, gallant defense of a, at
    Stephenson's Depot 607
Bridles, number issued.....56, 114
Brigade groups, proposed in
    1864 830
Brockenbrough, Maj. J. P.,
    380, 382, 383, 384, 408, 417,
    421, 423, 720
    (See Brockenbrough's Bat-
    tery and Brockenbrough's
    Battalion)
Brooke, Capt. John Mercer,
    invents gun 67
Brooke gun, invention of...... 51
Brown, Capt. J. S............ 335
Brown, Lieut. J. Thompson, Jr. 454
Brown, Col. John Thompson,
    114, 118, 226, 338, 417, 469,
    470, 494, 545, 549, 551, 552,
    556, 562, 568, 624, 625, 636,
    637, 658, 665, 666, 673, 696,
    697, 701, 704, 713, 769, 851, 855
    (See Brown's Battery, Brown's
    Battalion, and Brown's
    Division)
Broun, Lieut.-Col. W. LeRoy,
    Supt. Richmond Arsenal.52, 57
Buddecke's Battle Orders.... 229
Bull Run, Battle of.......127, 130
    reason for victory of........ 99
Bullet, the perfect expansion,
    origin of 28
Bülow, quoted 106
Bunker Hill, camp at........ 327
Bureau of Artillery and
    Ordnance, proposed 38
Bureau of Foreign Supplies,
    created 35
    work of 55, 56
Bureau of Mining and Niter,
    created 35, 44, 49
    officers of 53

PAGE

Bureau of Ordnance, C. S. A.,
    organized 34, 38
    officers of 39, 52, 53, 54
    work of 40
    laborers impressed 44
    organization and operations,
        52, 54, 55
    expenditures of 54, 55
    its fleet of blockade runners 56
    credits allowed 56
    gradual restriction of its
        field of operations........ 59
"Burial of the Guns"......... 956
Burnside, his escape from
    Fredericksburg 402
    his "Mud March".......... 445
Burroughs, Lieut. Dent....... 794
Burton, Supt. J. H., Macon
    armory 57
Burton Projectiles, defects of.. 128
Burwell, Lieut. 460, 461
Cabell, Col. Henry Coalter,
    280, 372, 386, 387, 391, 396,
    415, 517, 523, 556, 720, 722,
    846, 851, 852, 855, 919
    (See Cabell's Richmond
    "Fayette" Battery, and
    Cabell's Battalion)
Cadets, of V. M. I., as in-
    structors 99, 115
Cadets, Richmond School..... 731
Cæsar 431
Caisson, of Cadet Battery,
    Jackson's hearse 560
Caissons, number made....... 56
Callaway, Lieut. Morgan..820, 911
    (See Pulaski, Ga., Battery)
Camp Meetings, Religious..... 430
Camps, Artillery, in 1863,
        556, 716, 717
Cantonments, Artillery, winter
    of 1861-2 145
Cape Fear River, fishery estab-
    lished on 48
Captured arms, regulations con-
    cerning 39, 59
Carbines, for cannoneers recom-
    mended 892
Carpenter, Capt. John C.,
        337, 338, 440, 889, 890
    (See Carpenter's Alleghany
    Battery)
Carpenter, Capt. Joseph,
        337, 338, 440
    (See Carpenter's Alleghany
    Battery)

PAGE

Carter, Capt. J. W.,
347, 588, 589, 594
(See Carter's "Ashby" Bat-
tery)
Carter, Col. Thomas Hill,
326, 337, 379, 380, 399, 416,
440, 507, 508, 509, 551, 720,
733, 769, 799, 813, 856, 857,
880, 881, 882, 883, 885, 887,
889, 890, 891, 892, 893, 895,
897, 920, 921, 926, 928, 944
(See Carter's King William
Battery, Carter's Battalion,
and Carter's Division)
Carthaginian Army 431
Cary, Maj. 920
Caskie, Maj. William H...440, 815
(See C a s k i e ' s Richmond
"Hampden" Battery)
Cavalli, designs breech-loader.. 29
Cavalry, ordered to help bat-
teries 195
anecdote concerning 196
Cavalry charges vs. Artillery,
585, 587, 591, 596
Cavalry tactics, proper........ 404
Cayce, Capt. 834
(See Richmond "Purcell"
Battery)
Cedar Mountain, Battle of.... 241
Chalons, school at........... 152
Chamberlaine, Capt. W. W., 717, 902
Chamberlayne, Capt. J o h n
Hampden...493, 506, 867, 874
(See Chamberlayne's Battery)
Chancellorsville, Battle of..... 442
May 3 ....505, 515
May 4 530
Chaplains, inadequate number
of 430
Charcoal, how procured....... 42
Charges, made by horse bat-
teries 166, 168
of Cavalry vs. Artillery.
585, 587, 591, 596
Charleston Arsenal 40, 57
Charlotte Chemical Works.... 40
Charlottesville, Horse Artillery
saves 726
resolutions of thanks of town 728
Chateaudun, Prussian battery
at 525
Chatham Artillery of Savannah 88
Chemists, Ordnance, discov-
eries of 43, 45, 47
Chesterfield Depot, Artillery
Headquarters, in 1863.... 450

PAGE

Chew, Lt.-Col. Robert Preston,
162, 326, 337, 349, 423, 440,
720, 727, 773, 774, 927, 937, 950
(See Chew's "Ashby" Battery
and Chew's Battalion)
Chew, Capt. Walter E........
(See 4th Md. Battery)
Chief of Artillery, proper rela-
tions of a, with his com-
mander 560
Childs, Maj. F. L., Supt.
Fayetteville Arsenal 57
Childsburg, Artillery Camp at. 410
Chinese multiple firing guns.. 31
Christ, in the camp........... 430
Cigars and tobacco, price of in
1864 908
Clarksville Harness Shops..... 57
Clausewitz, quoted....106, 183, 238
Cleveland, Tenn., manufactured
copper found at.......... 47
Clothing, men without reported
sick 425
condition of in 1863........ 425
anecdote concerning 426
cost of in 1864-5........... 908
Clutter, Capt. Valentine C..... 378
(See Clutter's R i c h m o n d
Battery)
Cocke, Gen. Philip St. George 115
Coggin's Point, bombardment at 234
Coit, Maj. James C........... 838
(See Coit's Battery and
Coit's Battalion)
Cold Harbor, 1st Battle of.211, 212
Cold Harbor, 2d Battle of.... 812
Cold Harbor to Petersburg.... 834
Coleman, Lt. Col. Lewis M..204 392
Colonial Artillery 85
Colston, Gen. R. E........... 105
Columbus Arsenal 57
Combat unit, the............. 344
the battalion as the........ 413
Commanders, artillery, char-
acter of 742
Commissioner of Artillery, 1776 25
Company "Q" 727
Confederacy formed 107
Confederate Powder Mills..... 40
site and capacity of........ 45
Contee, Lieut. 607, 608
Contractors for sulphur....... 42
Contribution from Washington
Artillery for people of
Fredericksburg 410
Cooke, John Esten, his tribute
to Pelham 434, 435
mentioned 828, 907

PAGE

Cooke, Lieut. N. B............ 889
Copper, how obtained......... 47
Corn, ration of.............. 428
   price of in 1864............ 908
Cornmeal, component of ration 374
Corps artillery, use of,
          160, 284, 285, 287, 568
Corps Reserve....284, 285, 287, 568
Corps Chief of Artillery, pro-
   posed 415
Corps Groups, proposed in 1864, 830
Court of Inquiry for Artillery 341
Courtney, Maj. A. R..244, 281, 654
   (See Courtney's Battery and
      Courtney's Battalion)
Covington, Private L. T....866, 867
Cowardice, case of............ 866
Crater at Petersburg,
          846, 847, 859, 863
Creeping, practice in artillery.. 605
Cross Keys, Battle of......... 173
Crozet, Col. Claudius......... 96
Crutchfield, Col. Stapleton,
          105, 170, 246, 258, 264, 267,
          272, 276, 278, 281, 290, 291,
          293, 298, 325, 326, 327, 328,
          337, 358, 377, 378, 379, 381,
          384, 385, 391, 392, 410, 413,
          420, 423, 424, 428, 440, 450,
          468, 489, 490, 491, 493, 494,
          549, 551, 560, 561, 712, 713,
                    719, 919, 936
Culpeper, Artillery cantonments
   near 145
Cummings, Col. A. C......... 133
Curry combs, number issued, 56, 114
   price of in 1864............ 908
Custer, Gen., advertises for
   Confederate guns 890
Cutshaw, Lt.-Col. Wilfred Em-
   met 337, 440, 720, 791
   (See Cutshaw's Battery and
      Cutshaw's Battalion)
Cutts, Col. Allan S.,
          417, 427, 704, 720, 842
   (See Cutts' Battery and
      Cutts' Sumter, Ga., Bat-
      talion)
Cuyler, Lt.-Col. R. M., Supt.
   Macon Arsenal 57
Dabney, Lieut., of King Wil-
   liam Battery............ 322
Dahlgren's Raid 729
Dance, Capt. Willis J.,
          510, 568, 600, 792
   (See Dance's Powhatan Bat-
      tery and Dance's Battalion)

PAGE

Dandridge, Capt. Edward P.,
          198, 412, 424, 718, 907
Danville Depot 57
Daum, Lieut.-Col. Philip...... 169
Davidson, Capt. Geo. L....... 802
   (See Lynchburg Battery)
Davidson, Capt. Greenlee,
          380, 382, 383, 384, 393, 511
   (See Richmond "Letcher"
      Battery)
Davis, Gen., manufactures
   powder 43
Davis, Jefferson, false accusa-
   tion against 24
Dearing, Col. James,
          415, 564, 565, 572, 646, 647,
          658, 720, 722, 725, 816, 936
   (See Dearing's Lynchburg
      Battery, Dearing's Light
      Battalion, and Dearing's
      Horse Artillery Battalion)
Deflection marks, used at
   Banks' Ford 539
De Lisle, Maj. Roman........ 87
Depots, horse 710
De Russy, Lieut., killed...... 525
Desertion, becomes prevalent.. 923
   proposals to stop.......... 924
Deshler, Col. James......202, 205
   (See Deshler's Battery and
      Deshler's Battalion)
Dilger, Capt. Hubert, his ex-
   ploits 475, 480,
          481, 482, 484, 550
   (See Dilger's Federal Bat-
      tery)
Dimmock, Col. Charles, Chief
   of Ordnance of Va....... 69
   his efforts 70
Disbanded, organizations, in
   1862 284
Diseases of horses, 332, 709, 710, 922
Divisions of artillery created,
          570, 722, 725
Divisional reserves created.... 200
Downer, Supt. W. S., Rich-
   mond Armory and Clarks-
   ville Harness Shops....... 57
Douay, Artillery School...... 152
Drivers, experience of........ 331
Drouot 159, 230
Drunken negro troops........ 870
Ducktown, Tenn., copper smelt-
   ing at 47
Duel, artillery, only one on
   Peninsula 237
   at Cedar Mountain......... 250

PAGE

Du Teil, original exponent of
masses 159
Early's Valley Campaign, 827, 876
Ellett, Capt. Thomas......... 378
(See Ellett's Richmond Bat-
tery)
Elliott, Lieut., of Maurin's Bat-
tery 311
Employees of Bureau of Ord-
nance, number of........ 57
organized as armed guards.. 58
Engineer Corps, merged with
Artillery 89
Entente Cordiale, between Ar-
tillery and Infantry...... 406
Epaulments, use of.......... 545
Eshleman, Lt.-Col. Benj. F.,
129, 356, 519, 565, 720
(See Eshleman's Battery and
Eshleman's Battalion)
Eubank, Cadet Hill Carter.... 657
"Eugenia," blockade runner... 56
European agent of Bureau of
Ordnance appointed 35, 37
Evelington Heights, Pelham's
and Stuart's blunder at... 233
Exemptions of mechanics....48, 57
Explosion of Parrotts......... 388
Fair Oaks or Seven Pines,
Battle of 192
Fallagant, Lieut. 820
Farcy, disease of............ 922
Farriers, pay of............. 108
Fayetteville Arsenal and
Armory 40, 57
Federal Artillery, organization
of 156
sorry condition of in 1863... 573
its status in 1863.......546, 550
Infantry, immobile at Cold
Harbor 823, 824
Ferrell, Lieut................. 538
Field Officers for battalions... 570
Artillery, in 1863, list of... 719
assignment of 720
in 1865 925
Fishery, established for oil
supply 48
Fire balls used at Petersburg.. 923
"First American" Regiment, 89, 93
Fleet, of Bureau of Ordnance.. 56
Fleetwood, affair at.......... 349
Floyd, Mr., Secretary of State,
accusation against 24
Fodder, price of in 1864...... 909
Forage, hauled by batteries... 425
where secured 425, 426
how collected 428

PAGE

measures to procure in 1863, 718
price of in 1864-5.......... 908
lack of in 1864-5.......919, 920
Ford, Lieut. 827
Forges, number made......... 56
Forno, Capt. Henry, of La.... 93
Fort Drewry, blown up....... 933
Fort Gregg, action of.....902, 931
Fort Harrison, action of...... 897
Fort Pulaski, rifled guns used
in defense of............. 66
Fort Steadman, action of...... 928
Fort Whitworth, action of..... 931
Fortress Monroe 91
Foundries, created 40
Franco-German War, artillery
experience of 239
Fraser, Capt. 564, 694
(See Pulaski, Ga., Battery)
Frazier's Farm, Battle of...... 215
Friedland, Battle of.......... 153
Friction-tubes, purchased in
Europe in 1861.......... 37
manufactured 47
purchased abroad 55
number made 56
Frobel, Maj. B. W........257, 280
(See Frobel's Battalion)
Fry, Capt. 334
Frederick the Great, his artil-
lery 150, 153
mentioned 432, 707
Fredericksburg, Battle of...... 362
Freemantle, Col., witnesses
Gettysburg 687
French, Lieut. S. S............ 889
French, influence of the on
American system....87, 88, 89
French Artillery, organization of 150
in 1859 190
Artillery Schools 152
"French Detachment," of
Henry's Battery 352
French Gunners of Louisiana,
heroism of 389
Fuel, in 1862................ 373
Fuentes de Onoro, horse artil-
tery at 166
Fulcher, Corporal, his gallantry 899
Fulminate of mercury, sub-
stitute for 47
Fuzes, time, new invented..... 47
purchased abroad 55
number made 56
Borman type defective..... 122
igniter attachment fails to
work 538
Gaines' Mill, Battle of........ 210

PAGE

Gainesville, Battle of......... 255
Gale, Lieut. 844, 845
Garber, Capt. Asher W....383, 791
(See Garber's Staunton Battery)
"Garde Royale," manual of... 154
Garden, Capt. Hugh R....... 899
(See Palmetto, S. C., Battery)
Garnett, Maj. John J., Inspector of Ordnance,
355, 415, 565, 704, 720, 722
(See Garnett's Battalion)
Garnett, Lieut. J. M.......... 164
Gatling, Dr. R. J., his gun first
used 32, 33
General Chief of Artillery.... 415
Georgia, supplies and provisions in 427
German artillery experience in
1870 191
Getty, Capt. C. T., Supt. Lynchburg Depot 57
Gettysburg, Battle of........ 221
movement of army upon.... 598
errors in campaign of....... 611
faulty artillery positions of 667
strategic situation of town.. 613
tactical features of battlefield 614
disposition of troops at.... 615
action of July 1........... 616
action of July 2........... 635
action of July 3........... 660
retreat from 695
Gibbes, Maj. J. Hampton,
779, 865, 866, 867, 874, 902
(See Gibbes' Battalion)
Gibbon's Artillerist's Manual,
1859 29
Gilham, Col. William........96, 98
his manual..............99, 154
referred to................ 337
Girths 115
Gitschin 238
Glanders, disease of.......... 922
Glendale, Battle of.......... 216
Gneisenau 238
Golly, Maj., of Louisiana...... 93
Gorey, Lieut., his gallantry at
Sharpsburg 301
Gorgas, Brig.-Gen. Josiah, appointed Chief of Ordnance 34
his character and work....35, 36
statement of..............39, 40
recommendations of.......35, 54
referred to................ 564
Graham, Dr. John............ 907
Graham, Lieut................ 385
Grain, where secured......425, 426

PAGE

Grant, Gen. U. S., remarks of
on artillery.............. 190
discussion of his character,
823, 824
Gravellotte, Battle of........ 274
Greased Heel, horse disease.... 348
Greble, Lieut. John T., killed.. 118
Greener, William, C. E., his
treatise on arms........ 28
inventions 28
Grenades, proposed use of..... 827
Grenoble, Artillery School..... 152
Gribeauval's system........... 150
Gridley, Col. Richard......... 86
Grimes, Capt. Cary F......... 92
(See Grimes' Portsmouth Battery)
Grooved-guns, origin of......28, 29
experiments with........... 31
Groveton, Battle of........... 255
Gunboats, artillery encounters
with 844, 857
Gun carriages, manufacture of 48
number made 56
made in Va. in 1861......78, 79
Guns, manufacture of........ 51
Austrian purchased 37, 55
Blakely purchased.......... 55
number made at Tredegar
Works 56
furnished by West Point
Foundry 64
brought by Washington Artillery 71
captured at First Manassas 71
list of those made in 1861... 78
number of Federal and Confederate in 1862.....148, 286
number and proportion of at
Sharpsburg 286, 325
kinds favored by Gen. Lee... 340
mortification over loss of.... 524
proper spirit over loss of.... 525
Prussian rule as to withdrawal from action....... 525
Gunners defend their pieces,
585, 587, 591, 597
Gunnery, theory of, provision
for study of in 1863...... 564
Board of, appointed in 1863 564
Guibert 160
Guidon, pay of............... 110
Gustavus, his artillery proportion 153
Gwynn, Maj.-Gen. Walter..... 113
Hainesville, Battle of......66, 125
Halters, number issued.....56, 114

PAGE

Hamburg, ordnance material shipped from............ 37
Hamilton, Gen. Alexander, his drill regulations.......... 149
Hamilton, Maj. S. P., 280, 370, 386, 391, 396, 415, 419, 450, 451, 466, 468, 528, 777
(See Hamilton's Battalion)
Hardaway, Lieut.-Col. Robert Archelaus, 319, 380, 417, 421, 423, 468, 469, 510, 513, 535, 536, 537, 538, 540, 549, 704, 720, 786, 813, 897, 900, 919, 925
(See Hardaway's Ala. Battery and Hardaway's Battalion)
Hardin, Maj. M. B........... 920
Hardwicke, Capt.............. 636
(See Hardwicke's Lynchburg "Lee" Battery)
Harness, purchased in Europe 1861 37
leather for manufacture of.. 47
made from oiled canvas..... 48
purchased abroad.......... 55
number of sets made........ 56
Clarksville shops 57
condition of............... 424
price of in 1864............ 908
Harper, Maj.-Gen. Kenton, relieved 113
Harper's Ferry Arsenal, created 26
value of 68
destroyed by Federals....... 68
reconstructed 70, 71
Harper's Ferry, Battle of..... 288
Harrison, Col. Charles....... 87
Harrison's Landing.......... 233
Hart, Maj. James F.......332, 901
(See Hart's Battery and Hart's Battalion)
Harvie, Col. E. J., Inspector-General 355
Haskell, Col. J. C., 440, 684, 685, 704, 865, 866, 873, 874, 899, 900, 902, 948
(See Haskell's Battalion)
Haskell, Capt. J. C.......... 907
Hatcher, Lieut. Charles, 198, 732, 907
Hatcher's Run, Battle of...... 900
Havana Agency.............. 56
Hawes, Lieut. S. H.......... 334
Hay, where and how secured, 425, 426
price of in 1864............ 909

Hazard, Capt................. 670
(See Hazard's Federal Battery)
Heavy Artillery, in defenses of Richmond 920
Hemington, Private, his gallantry 811
Henderson, Col. G. F. R., quoted 106, 219
his error 378
Henry, Capt. M. W...346, 564, 712
(See Henry's Battery and Henry's Battalion)
Hensley, Maj................. 920
(See Hensley's Battery)
High angle fire at Cold Harbor, 822, 826
High Bridge, action at....... 936
Hill, A. P., erroneous use of artillery by.....208, 211, 213
his fatal error at Gettysburg 615
Hill, Gen. D. H.............. 122
Hindman, Col., Saltpetre contractor 44
Hobson, Lieut. 878
Hohenlohe, Prince Kraft...... 160
quoted 238
Hollinguist, Lieut.-Col........ 733
Hollis, Lieut. 901
Holman, Maj. Christian....... 87
Hooker, Gen., his movements discussed 455, 472
destroys artillery organization 547, 550, 574
Horse Artillery, origin of..150, 151
C. S. A. created........... 162
charges made by........166, 168
operations of in 1862....... 347
operations of in 1863....446, 448
at Chancellorsville, 460, 467, 471
at Brandy Station.......... 585
organization and status of in 1863 576
reviews of in 1863......580, 581
organization, 1863 ......706, 725
camp of in 1863............ 717
fight of at Charlottesville... 726
receives thanks of town..... 728
criticism of 773, 774
condition of in 1864........ 828
proposed increase of........ 895
reorganization of in 1864, 922, 923, 927
Horses, complement of a battery 111
efforts to secure............ 114
taken from cavalry for guns 178
extra for batteries......... 214
scarcity of in 1862......327, 328

PAGE

number per battery......328, 333
regulations concerning 330
experience of artillerymen
with 331
character of animals....331, 332
purchased in Texas......... 332
diseases of 332, 348
shelters for 356
for artillery secured in
Georgia 418
care of demanded of officers 423
reported condition of....... 424
number required in 1863..... 427
sickness among 427, 428
deficiency of 412
condition of in May, 1863,
556, 562, 563
sale of condemned to farmers 563
number distributed in 1863.. 563
mentioned 574
requisitioned 697
"pressing for shorts"....... 698
provisions for care of....... 709
diseases of................. 710
price of in 1863............ 710
where obtained............. 711
condition of in 1864......... 829
price of in 1864........908, 921
great effort to procure...921, 922
care of in depots........... 922
fate of the artillery horses,
949, 954, 955
Horseshoes, manufacture of.... 48
supply of 49, 115
Horse brushes, number issued 56
Horse equipment, deficiency of
in 1862.................. 412
Horsemen, artillerymen as..... 331
Hotchkiss Guns 243
Howard, Lieut. James........ 277
Huckstep, Capt.............. 334
(See Huckstep's 1st Flu-
vanna Battery)
Huger, Benj., Col. U. S. Ord-
nance Corps 26
appointed Inspector General
Artillery and Ordnance, C.
S. A.................... 53
Huger, Lieut.-Col. Frank,
338, 420, 508, 534, 537, 541,
549, 636, 645, 646, 664, 720,
846, 866, 867, 874
(See Huger's Norfolk Battery
and Huger's Battalion)
Huger, Capt. Francis K....... 90
Humphreys, Maj. F. C., Supt.
Columbus Arsenal........ 57

Hunt, Gen. Henry J.,
222, 230, 233, 243, 276, 298,
546, 629, 638, 641, 675, 678,
748, 775
Huse, Caleb, Foreign Purchas-
ing Agent 37
purchases Austrian batteries 37
inspects Armstrong and
Blakely plants 37
his purchases abroad........ 55
Hutter, Capt. E. S., Supt. Dan-
ville Depot 57
Illuminators, at Petersburg.... 923
Incendiary shells, prepared by
Pendleton 398
Indirect fire, first instance of.. 539
employed at Cold Harbor by
McIntosh 822, 826
Infantry supports for artillery 177
Initiative, opportunity for..... 482
Inspection, of batteries....354, 355
of artillery, Jan., 1863...... 412
results of................. 413
of Johnston's Artillery by
Pendleton in 1864........ 732
Inspector General Artillery and
Ordnance 53
Inspector of Ordnance and Ar-
tillery 355
Instruction, Artillery, Early,
85, 86, 89, 91
in the South........98, 101, 149
Intrenchments, constructed at
Fredericksburg...369, 372, 429
constructed by gunners..... 537
Iron Clads, armor for, made... 51
Iron Mines and Ores.......... 50
Iron Pyrites, of Louisiana and
Alabama used in produc-
tion of sulphur........... 42
Izard, Capt. George.......... 90
Jackson, Gen. T. J., referred to 30
tests Parrott gun.......... 64
favors rifled guns........... 65
element of his success....... 103
anecdote concerning 106
appointed Colonel 113
mentioned 114, 123, 126
at Bull Run............... 134
his failure on Peninsula..... 218
himself again 246
congratulates Beckham on
field 481
death of described......... 557
his wife arrives at his death-
bed 558
Cadet caisson his hearse.... 560
affection for in artillery.... 560

PAGE

James, Lieut. 842
James rifles, c a p t u r e d at
    Manassas 72
Jealousy, caste, in service. . . . 405
Johnson, Capt. John R. 339
    (See Johnson Bedford Bat-
    tery)
Johnson, Maj. Marmaduke,
                720, 897, 898
    (S e e Johnson's Richmond
    Battery and Johnson's Bat-
    talion)
Johnston, Jos. E., his inability
    to advance on Washington,
                24, 76, 139
    knew little of rifling. 64
    preferred smooth bores. . . .65, 75
    lacked ammunition in 1861. . 76
    appointed Major-General. . . . 113
Jomini, quoted. 106
Jones, Col. Hilary P.,
    416, 423, 508, 549, 720, 725,
                737, 837, 895, 933
    (See Jones' Battalion)
Jones' House, Battles of the. . . 898
Jordan, Maj. Tyler C. 720
    (See Bedford Battery)
Kelly's Ford, Battle of. . . .432, 714
Kellysville 432
Kemper, Maj. Del. 415
    (See Kemper's Alexandria
    Battery)
Kernstown, Battle of. 169
King, Col. J. Floyd. . .802, 803, 877
    (See King's Battalion)
Kirkpatrick, Capt. T. J. 880
    (See Amherst Battery and
    "Madison," M i s s., Bat-
    tery)
Knox, Col. Henry, recommends
    artillery schools, etc. 86, 89
Königgrätz, Battle of, 221, 238, 274
Kosciusko, Gen., his manual for
    artillery 149
Kostenetski, at Austerlitz. 168
Kuropatkin's Cavalry tactics. . 404
Labor, skilled and unskilled. .48, 57
    training of 58
Ladies, visit Cavalry Camp. . . . 580
"Lady Davis," blockade runner 56
La Fere, Artillery School. 152
Lahitte system of rifling. 30
Laidley, Maj., revises Ordnance
    Manual 26
Lallemand's treatise 149
Lambie, Lieut. W. T. 600, 607

PAGE

Lamkin, Capt. 925
    (See Amherst-Nelson Bat-
    tery)
Lancaster grooved gun. 29
Landry, Capt., heroism of. 389
    (See Donaldsonville, La., Bat-
    tery)
Lane, Maj. John. 417, 422
    (See Lane's Ga. Battery and
    Lane's Battalion)
Lantz, Corporal Joseph T. V. . . 657
    his gallantry. 423
Latham, Capt. A. C. 816
    (See Latham's Battery)
Latimer, Maj. Joseph White,
    337, 379, 380, 384, 393, 399,
    416, 421, 440, 453, 568, 601,
                610, 636, 651, 653, 694
    (See Richmond "Courtney"
    Battery and Latimer's Bat-
    talion)
Latrobe, Capt. O., his gallantry 389
Lead, supply and price of. 49
    purchased abroad. 55
Leather, supply and curing of. . 47
    contracts for. 48
    purchased abroad. 55
    price of in 1864. 908
"R. E. Lee," blockade runner. . 56
Lee, Gen. Charles. 87
Lee, Lieut. H. H. 164
Lee, Gen. Robert E., assists in
    ordnance work of Va. 70
    appointed Maj.-Gen. 113, 116
    his policy respecting promo-
    tion 413, 418
    his boldness at Chancellors-
    ville 542
    his dispatch on Jackson's
    death 562
    his Gettysburg plans. 598
    his conduct after Pickett's
    charge 688
    his lost opportunity at the
    North Anna. 799
Lee, Robert E., Jr., Private, in-
    cident concerning. 310
Lee, Col. Stephen Dill,
    201, 278, 299, 312, 313, 323,
                326, 337, 338, 351
    (See Lee's Battalion)
Leipzig, Battle of. 153, 274
Leonard and Riddle, Saltpetre
    contractors 43
Letcher, Gov. John, of Va. 63
Lewis, Maj. J. R. C. 416, 572
Lewisburg, Va., powder manu-
    factured in 43

PAGE

Leyden, Maj................... 877
  (See Leyden's Battalion)
Liaoyang, Battle of........... 274
Lichtenstein 230
Light batteries mistaken for
  horse 550
Lightfoot, Lieut.-Col. C. E.,
               277, 720
  (See Lightfoot's Battalion)
Linseed oil, used in manufac-
  ture of harness........... 48
Little Rock Arsenal........... 40
Local Reserves 835
Lombardy Campaign of 1859.. 190
L o n g, Brig.-Gen. Armistead
  Lindsay......95, 712, 716,
  719, 729, 731, 736, 747, 770,
  775, 785, 787, 788, 789, 792,
  793, 813, 819, 827, 852, 876,
  877, 880, 881, 900, 920, 926, 945
Longstreet, Gen., detaches valu-
  able artillery force........ 443
  difference between him and
    Jackson 444
  Alexander's defense of...... 445
  at Gettysburg.........630, et seq.
  his orders to artillery...... 635
  his Tennessee Campaign..... 711
  his N. C. Campaign........ 814
"Long Toms," or 30-pounder
  Parrotts 370
Losses, no test of artillery efficiency 267
  of artillery at Petersburg... 909
Louisiana batteries in Mexican
  War 93
Lützen, Battle of............. 153
Lynchburg Depot............. 57
Machine Guns, first use of...32, 33
Machinery, imported for powder
  mills 46
  made at Richmond Tredegar
    Works 46
  loss and destruction of..... 58
  saved at Harper's Ferry..... 69
Macon Armory............... 57
Macon Arsenal............... 57
Macon Ammunition Labora-
  tories, nature and capacity
  of 45, 57
  erected 46
Maddox, Lieut............... 319
Magruder, Gen. J. B., 114, 118, 337
Magruder, Lieut.............. 336
Mahone, Gen. William, at the
  Crater 871
Mallet, Col. Jno. W., Supt. of
  Laboratories 45
  his work and character....45, 46

PAGE

Malvern Hill, instance of cited 191
  battle of.................. 221
Manassas, First, Battle of..... 127
Manassas, Second, Battle of... 266
  great artillery victory...... 267
Manuals for artillery......... 149
Marceau, Pelham likened to... 440
March, remarkable, by artillery 261
Markham's, affair at......... 352
Marching, ability of batteries.. 165
"Marseillaise Hymn," gunners
  sing 353
Martinsburg, 1863............ 600
Marye, Capt. E. A........311, 378
  (See Fredericksburg Battery)
Marye, Capt. L. S............ 919
  (See Richmond "Hampden"
    Battery)
Marye's Hill, remarkable artil-
  lery position............. 397
Maryland Invasion, First..... 277
Maryland, preparation for sec-
  ond invasion of.......... 556
Masked Batteries, caution as to 138
Mason, Capt................. 866
Masses, use of artillery....... 141
  used by Napoleon.......152, 153
  originated 159
  effect of 160
  employed by Porter.....208, 212
  why not employed at first... 237
  employed at Second Manassas 275
  Hunt's, at Sharpsburg...... 324
Massie, Capt. J. L...125, 334, 889
  (See Massie's Fluvanna Bat-
    tery)
Material, of a battery.....110, 111
  captured at Manassas....71, 136
  defects of at Big Bethel.... 123
  Confederate at Manassas.... 136
  number of guns comprising
    in 1861.................. 115
  at Sharpsburg 284
  on Peninsula............. 201
  in Oct., 1862............. 340
  condition of in 1863,
          556, 562, 563, 564
  distribution of by battalions 570
  of horse artillery in 1863... 579
  character of in 1863....706, 707
  in June, 1864............. 831
  siege issued at Petersburg... 895
  number of guns in 1864..... 917
  (See also Ordnance Material)
Maurin, Maj. Victor......720, 917
  (See Maurin's Donaldsonville,
    La., Battery)

PAGE

May, Maj., quoted........... 221
McCabe, Capt. W. Gordon,
  quoted 250
  referred to 344, 440
  quoted 797, 798,
    834, 863, 864, 865, 866, 899, 929
McCarthy, Capt. Edward S.... 826
  (See 1st Co. Richmond How-
    itzers)
McClellan, reorganizes artillery 156
McCorkle, Lieut.............. 392
McDowell, Battle of.......... 170
McElroy, Lieut............931, 932
McGilvery Artillery Brigade, at
  Gettysburg,
    642, 647, 670, 678, 686
McGraw, Maj. Joseph,
    440, 720, 797, 798, 800
  (See Richmond "Purcell"
    Battery)
McGregor, Capt. Wm. M....... 577
  (See McGregor's Battery and
    McGregor's Battalion)
McIntosh, Col. David Gregg,
    423, 440, 508, 549, 720, 822, 912
  (See McIntosh's Battery and
    McIntosh's Battalion)
McKim, Lieut. Randolph H.,
  his gallantry............. 608
McLaughlin, Maj. William,
    801, 802, 878
  (See McLaughlin's Battery
    and McLaughlin's Battal-
    ion)
McQueen, Lieut.............. 899
Meade, Gen., his plan at Get-
  tysburg 613
Meade, Capt. William........ 198
Meade, Lieut. R. H........... 164
Mechanics, exemptions of those
  employed 48
  number of employed....... 57
Mechanicsville, Battle of..... 206
Medical supplies 709
Medicine, price of in 1864..... 908
Memphis Depot 41
Mercury, imported........... 47
Metals, how obtained........ 49
Metz, Artillery School.....152, 154
Mexican War, Southern artil-
  lery in 93
Mexico, purchases of material
  and powder in..........38, 43
  mercury imported from..... 47
  leather supply from cut off.. 48
  lead purchased in.......... 49
  horses from.............. 921
Middleburg, affair at......353, 610

PAGE

Middletown, Battle of, 1864... 890
Militia, of Virginia, provisions
  for 61
  armament of 62, 67
  artillery, early............. 89
  organization of in 1792..... 91
Miller, Maj. M. B.........720, 917
  (See 3d Co. Washington Ar-
    tillery)
Mine Run Campaign.......... 715
Mining Bureau, created..35, 44, 49
  remarkable work of.......49, 50
  officers of................. 53
Mining at Petersburg, 845, 846, 860
Mobility, of artillery, instances,
    165, 261, 548, 549, 832, 833,
    894, 900
Monocacy, Battle of.......... 877
Montgomery Depot 40
Montgomery, Capt. Chas. R.... 791
  (See Louisa "Morris" Bat-
    tery)
Moody, Capt............... 925
  (See Moody's "Madison,"
    La., Battery)
Moore, David, gunner......... 125
Moorman, Maj. Marcellus N.,
    308, 346, 720, 726, 729
  (See Moorman's Battery and
    Moorman's Battalion)
Morel, Corporal, heroism of... 389
Mordecai, Capt. Alfred, Ord-
  nance Corps............26, 91
Morgan, S. D., of Nashville,
  Tenn., powder contractor.. 43
Mortars, at Petersburg and
  Crater 868, 873
Moseley, Lieut.-Col. E. F.,
    120, 121, 838, 854, 896, 902
  (See Moseley's Battery and
    Moseley's Battalion)
Motes, Lieut.............658, 684
Motienling, Battle of.......... 482
Mount Vernon Arsenal........ 40
Mountain rifles.............. 27
Mountain howitzers, at Port
  Republic 174
Mt. Carmel Church, Artillery
  Camp in '63............ 450
Mukden, Battle of............ 221
Mules, conduct of in battery at
  Port Republic........... 175
  supply of for trains....... 332
  amusing incident concerning
    in Stuart's Cavalry review 582
Munchengratz 238
Munford, Gen. T. T.......... 105
Murat, Pelham likened to..... 440

PAGE

Murray, Lieut. Thomas A., his
   coolness 524
Musicians, pay of 108
Muskets for gunners, recom-
   mended 892
Nachod 238
Napoleon, remarks on artillery,
   152, 153
   his principles 159
   cited 238, 310, 362, 365, 707
   his rules of war............ 809
Napoleons, 12-pounder, demand
   for 340
   substituted for howitzers.... 719
Nash, Maj. Herbert N......... 717
Nashville Arsenal 41
Nassau Agency............... 56
"Native American" Artillery of
   Louisiana 93
Negro, misleads Dahlgren..730, 731
Negro Troops at the Crater... 870
Nelson, Capt. G. W.,
   335, 380, 387, 388, 412
   (See Hanover Battery)
Nelson, Col. William......417,
   878, 880, 883, 885, 888, 889, 920
   (See Hanover Battery and
   Nelson's Battalion)
New Berne Campaign......... 814
New Cold Harbor, battle near 211
New Market, Battle of....801, 802
New Orleans Depot........... 41
New York, 71st Reg. Battery,
   132, 136
Night Attack, by artillery..... 234
Nimmo, Lieut. John.......... 657
Niter, secured in Alabama and
   Tennessee 42, 44
   purification of 43
   supply of in 1864.......... 44
Niter Bureau created....35, 44, 49
   officers of 44, 53
Nitric acid, made.......|.... 47
Non-commissioned staff, pro-
   posed in 1864............ 830
Norfolk Navy Yard, destruc-
   tion of 69
North Anna, Battle of........ 799
   Artillery Camp on the...... 410
Norton, Capt., inventor of ex-
   plosive lead shell......... 28
Oats, price of in 1864,
   803, 908, 909, 942
Observers, Federal aerial...... 234
Officers, furnished Confederacy
   by West Point........... 95
   to artillery by West Point
   and V. M. I.............. 101

PAGE

artillery, rank and pay of... 108
proportion of based on guns,
   145, 423
efficiency of................ 337
proportion of from Virginia,
   413, 418
Jackson on appointment of.. 423
authorized number 423
Lee's estimate of artillery... 424
inefficient culled out........ 430
individuality of artillery.... 440
number and distribution of
   artillery in 1863......... 565
promotion of in 1863....... 565
slowness in promotion of.... 572
few transfers among........ 572
supply drawn from........ 573
authorized number of and
   grades 719, 722
list of artillery field officers in
   1863 719
assignments of..........720, 724
increase of proposed in 1864,
   830, 902
conditions concerning 903
Old Point Comfort Arsenal,
   created 26
Orders, error in transmitting at
   Fredericksburg...516, 517, 522
Ordnance Department, U. S. A.,
   created, ... 25
   developed 26
Ordnance Material, character of
   in 1861 ....27, 28
   purchase of foreign......... 27
   rifled employed by French in
   Italy 30
   employed by Prussians in
   1864 30
   multiple firing guns......31, 32
   material (C. S. A.) on hand
   1861 37
   purchased in Europe in 1861 37
   seized with Federal arsenals,
   37, 41
   first made at.............41, 42
   most important plant for
   manufacture of.......... 51
   amount procured up to 1863 55
   statement of amount made.. 56
   obtained by capture........ 59
   of Virginia in 1861........ 67
   issued in Virginia in 1861... 70
   in possession of Washington
   artillery 71
   captured at 1st Manassas... 71
   list of that secured in Virginia in 1861...........78, 79

PAGE

character of in 1862........ 284
captured at Harper's Ferry.. 291
demand for in 1862........ 340
types made in 1862....340, 341
heavy demanded by Gen. Lee 411
new issued............426, 427
Ordnance Manuals, U. S. A.... 26
C. S. A................... 26
Ordnance Officers, proposals
concerning 38
regulations concerning 39
improved processes developed
by 46
discoveries of 47
authorized and rank of....52, 53
educational requisites and
promotion 52, 53
recommendations concerning
rank of................. 54
mentioned 109, 110
efforts of 288
Ordnance Operations, field, successful in 1863........... 564
Ordnance Regulations, U. S. A.,
26, 27
C. S. A. adopted...38, 52, 53, 54
Ordnance Rifles, 3-inch, demand
for 340
Ordnance Storekeepers, pay and
rank of 57
Ordnance Train, Reserve...243, 292
Organization, of Artillery
Corps 108
of field batteries........... 109
of Virginia troops.......... 116
of artillery in Dec., '61..... 142
of artillery in 1864, 903, 905, 927
at surrender.......950, 951, 952
Orleans Artillery, in Mexican
War 93
Osborn, Maj.....550, 554, 623, 668
Ostendorff & Co., J. M., of Wal-
halla, S. C., powder con-
tractors 43
Otey, Lieut. James C......... 866
Owen, Maj. W.............. 917
(See 1st Co. Washington Ar-
tillery and Owen's Bat-
talion)
Page, Maj. John, 198, 427, 718, 907
Page, Maj. R. C. M...506, 718, 720
(See Louisa "Morris" Bat-
tery and Page's Battalion)
Page, Maj. T. J., Jr.,
336, 380, 415, 422, 718
(See Page's Yorktown "Ma-
gruder" Battery)
Page, Dr. Isham Randolph.... 198

PAGE

Paris, affair at.............. 348
Parker, Capt. W. W......... 925
(See Richmond Battery)
Parkinson, Lieut. Jordan C.... 911
Parole lists.................. 952
Parrott, Capt. R. P., his rifled
gun 30, 63
Parrott Rifles, tested at V. M. I.,
63, 64, 80
captured at Manassas....... 71
number furnished during war 64
first used at Big Bethel..... 64
mentioned 119, 197
demand for................ 340
20-pounders 344
explosion of 30-pounders.... 388
Patchenko's Russian Battery.. 274
Paxton, Maj., Horse Agent.... 711
Pay of Artillery Officers...... 108
Pearce, Lieutenant........... 805
Peas, black-eye, component of
ration 374
Pegram, Col. William Johnson,
249, 250, 278, 366, 416, 420,
440, 461, 489, 494, 506, 507,
508, 511, 540, 549, 554, 704,
720, 798, 834, 896, 898, 899,
901, 929, 930
(See Pegram's Richmond
"Purcell" Battery and
Pegram's Battalion)
Pegram, Capt. R. G.......... 691
(See Pegram's Petersburg
Battery)
Peet, Lieut. W. T............. 459
Pelham, Col. John,
162, 178, 233, 298, 299, 326,
337, 346, 349, 350, 352, 354,
382, 383, 384, 385, 392, 403,
404, 433, 434, 435, 439, 577, 773
(See Pelham's Battery and
Pelham's Battalion)
Pemberton, Lieut.-Col. J. C.,
726, 895, 919
Pendleton, Gen. Wm. N., favors
rifled guns 64, 65
sent to Richmond to procure
ordnance 75
his splendid work 76, 77, 78
mentioned 95, 124,
125, 127, 134, 137, 140, 143,
146, 147, 155, 182, 192, 193,
194, 195, 198, 200, 225, 234,
239, 243, 255, 257, 277, 278,
318, 319, 333, 338, 341, 343,
346, 372, 373, 410, 413, 425,
430, 450, 451, 454, 515, 516-
24, 530, 551, 557, 563-74,

PAGE

583, 610, 622, 623, 630, 631,
632, 639, 643, 653, 658, 664,
666, 668, 677, 701, 703, 704,
709, 718, 719, 722, 731, 734,
735, 742, 766, 770, 776, 826,
829, 847, 849, 850, 853, 854,
895, 902, 903, 906, 918, 920,
922, 925, 928, 934, 938, 939,
940, 942, 945, 949
Pendleton, Maj. A. S., his letter 429
Pendleton, Capt. Dudley D.,
198, 334, 902, 907
Peninsula Campaign.......... 176
summary of................ 239
Penick, Capt. Nathan......... 521
(See Pittsylvania Battery)
Percussion Caps, manufactured 47
Percy, Capt. W. A............ 902
Personnel, character of artillery 165
of Confederate Artillery su-
perior 572
Henderson's error as to
character of 572
Peterkin, Lieut. George W.,
198, 718, 732, 907
Petersburg, Grant's movement
upon 835
siege of.................... 842
winter of 1864 at.......... 895
Petersburg Smelting W o r k s
created 40
erection of................. 49
Peyton, Capt. T. J............ 334
(See Richmond "Orange"
Battery)
Phelps, Lieut................. 448
Pickens' Heavy Artillery...... 135
Picket ropes 114
Pickett, his interference with
the artillery 821
his charge................. 683
Pierson, Maj. S. F............ 852
(See Pierson's Battalion)
Pigott, Dr., lead-smelting proc-
ess of 49
Pinckney, Gen., his drill regu-
lations 149
Plater, Lieut................. 384
Pleasants, Lieut.-Col., designs
mine at Petersburg,
846, 860, 863
Pleasants, Lieut.............. 385
Pleasonton, Gen., his misstate-
ments.......486, 487, 496, 593
Plevna, Battle of............. 221

PAGE

Poague, Col. William Thomas,
326, 344, 417, 421, 440, 508,
549, 720, 767, 768, 939
(See Poague's Battery and
Poague's Battalion)
Pollock, Lieut. John G........ 912
Poplar Spring Church, action of 896
Pork Packeries.............. 51
Port fires, number made...... 56
Port Republic, Battle of....... 173
Position, artillery, at Second
Manassas 264
Potash, chloral.............. 47
Potts, Capt..............378, 777
(See N. C. Battery)
Powder, purchase of in Europe,
1861 37
amount ordered in 1861.... 37
Confederate mills 40
amount on hand in 1861.... 41
amount required in 1861.... 42
manufacture of, and mills,
42, 43, 45, 46
contracts for.............. 43
Powder Mills, created........ 40
necessity for.............. 42
location of private........42, 43
Preparation, lack of artillery,
208, 213
at White Oak Swamp....... 219
plan for at Malvern Hill.... 224
utter lack of at Malvern Hill,
225, 226, 230, 237
by artillery............... 324
lack of at Fredericksburg... 397
splendid artillery at Winchester, 1863 ....602, 603
Preston, Col. John T. L......96, 97
Preston, Maj. Samuel.....866, 867
Prices, for articles in 1864.... 908
Pringle, Lieut., of Garden's
Battery 322
Projectiles, defects of........ 128
for Whitworth guns........ 564
Promotion, in continental artillery 88
discussed 413, 418
slowness of in C. S. Artillery 572
proposed regulation of in
1864 830
for artillery officers urged... 902
granted March 1, 1865...... 925
Proportion of field officers to
guns 423
Provisional Army C. S. A.
created 107
Prussian Artillery........... 155
tactics 160, 161

PAGE

in 1866.................... 171
lack of masses in 1866...... 238
ammunition expenditure of.. 274
experiences of 1866 and 1870 287
Prussian Horse Artillery..166, 168
Railroad battery..........197, 216
Raine, Maj. Chas. J........... 720
(See Lynchburg "Lee" Battery)
Rains, Gen. G. W., Bureau of
Ordnance 43
invents new powder process.. 47
Ramsey, Capt................ 309
(See Rowan, N. C., Battery)
Ramsey's Horse Battery (British) 166
Randolph, Geo. W.,
114, 118, 123, 141
Randolph, Capt.............. 641
Randolph, Lieut. Thos. N...... 198
Ranging, difficulty of with poor
shell 510
Rapidity of fire, at Cold Harbor 212
Rappahannock Bridge, Battle of 714
Rations in 1862............. 374
Read, Maj. J. P. W........415, 420
(See Read's Ga. Battery and
Read's Battalion)
Reconnaissance, lack of,
208, 213, 219, 224, 225, 226
at Sharpsburg by Col. Lee,
312, 316
mentioned 505
Reduction, of Artillery Corps.. 337
Reed, Dr., invents shell for
rifled guns 32, 66
manufacture of his shell.... 47
Rees, Lieut. Lucius G......811, 842
Regimental Groups, proposed in
1864 830
Regimental promotion 88
Regulations, for Federal Artillery 157
for artillery administration.. 199
for Artillery Corps......... 330
Reilly, Maj. James........... 564
(See Reilly's Rowan, N. C.,
Battery)
Religious, interest, in artillery 430
spirit, at Petersburg........ 906
Remedies, proposed to overcome
evils of the artillery...... 414
Remount depots 574, 710
Reorganization, of artillery,
278, 279
in 1862.................... 327

PAGE

in 1863.................... 413
proposed in 1863........... 565
in Aug., 1863.............. 906
in Dec., 1864.............. 911
Reserve Artillery, winter quarters of 146
use of as tactical unit discussed 160
movements of on Peninsula,
178, 192, 193, 237
divisional, created......... 200
composition of..........242, 255
referred to.....277, 278, 287, 292
use of as tactical unit...... 287
involved in investigation.... 341
composition of in 1862-3.... 345
camp of in 1862............ 354
strength of in 1862......... 361
mentioned 370, 371
lack of at Chancellorsville
keenly felt by Lee,
455, 467, 528, 550
corps, in 1863.............. 568
at Gettysburg.............. 616
captured in April, 1865..942, 944
Reserve Ordnance Train,
292, 293, 327
Respect, mutual, between artillery and infantry......... 406
Retreat, The................ 933
Reviews, of Stuart's Cavalry
and Horse Artillery in 1863 580
of army at Culpeper in 1863 717
of artillery of Western Army,
733, 734
of Longstreet's Corps....... 736
Revival Meetings, in Camp.... 430
Reynolds, Gen., nobility of.... 617
Rhett, Col. T. S......52, 277, 707
Rhode Island, Colonial battery 86
Rice's Station, action at...936, 938
Richardson, Gen. W. H., of Va. 97
Richardson, Lieut.-Col. Charles,
327, 415, 419, 574, 636, 651,
664, 676, 699, 720
(See Richardson's Battalion)
Richmond, Armory and Arsenal,
40, 62
issues of during war........ 56
superintendents of......... 57
Richmond Artillery defenses... 841
Richmond Tredegar Works.... 341
Rifling, knowledge of in 1861.. 28
Napoleon's experiments with 29
Lahitte System............. 30
experiments with rifling..... 31
of ordnance recommended... 63

PAGE

slight knowledge of in America 64, 65, 66
sudden developments of..... 80
Ringold, Maj., his manual..... 154
Rives, Lieut................. 821
Roads, condition of on Peninsula 177, 190, 191
Roberts, Lieut.-Col. Owen..... 87
Robertson, Maj.............. 920
Robertson, Lieut.............. 334
Rockets, number issued....... 56
Rodes, Gen. R. E............. 105
Rodman guns, reputation of... 31
Rogers, Maj. A. L............. 417
  (See Loudoun Battery)
Rolling mills created 40
Rome, Ga., guns cast at...... 42
Romney, loss of guns at...... 164
Ross, Richard, Saltpetre contractor 44
Rosser, Gen. Thos. L.......... 565
Rouse, Lieut. Milton......162, 338
Rubber, India, lack of........ 48
Ruggles, Gen................. 115
Russian ammunition expenditure 274
Sacrament, the final.......... 956
Saddles, number issued...... 56
  how made................. 114
Sailor's Creek, Battle of...... 936
Saint Privat, Battle of....274, 287
Saint Sebastian 864
Salisbury Foundry 57
Saltpetre, contracts for....... 43
  supplies of................. 44
  yield of Tennessee beds..... 44
  price of 44
  location of beds........... 44
  purchased abroad.......... 55
San Antonio Arsenal 40
Saunders, Maj. J. S......280, 852
  (See Saunders' Battalion)
Savage's Station, Battle of.... 215
Savannah Depot.............. 40
Saye, Private Richard W., his gallantry 524
Scarlett's charge at Balaclava 587
Scharnhorst 238
School of Fire, Fortress Monroe 91
School, training for officers of C. S. A.................. 99
Schools, French Artillery...... 152
Schoolfield's Battery uses machine gun................ 32
Scoffern, his treatise on warfare and. arms................ 29
Scott, Gen. Winfield....89, 90, 149
Second Manassas, Battle of.... 266

PAGE

Sedan, instance of cited...191, 221
Prussian Artillery at....... 287
compared with Harper's Ferry 291
compared with Fredericksburg 402
Sedden, Mr., Secretary of War 731
Selma Arsenal 57
Senarmont 153, 159, 230
Sensitive shell, used at Petersburg 923
Seven Days' fighting......197, 235
Seven Pines or Fair Oaks, Battle of 192
Sha-ho, Battle of............. 274
Sham battles 580, 583
Sharpsburg, Battle of......... 294
Shell, with copper band, invented 32, 47
  polygonal cavity invented... 47
  purchased abroad.......... 55
  number issued 56
  fail to explode.........509, 538
  burst at muzzle........... 564
Shelters, for horses.......... 356
  for men 373
Sherman's Artillery 191
Shepherdstown, affair at...... 341
Shields, Capt. J. C............. 114
  (See 1st Co. Richmond Howitzer Battalion)
Ships, owned and operated by Bureau of Ordnance...... 56
Shoemaker, Capt. J. J.....449, 729
  (See Shoemaker's Lynchburg Battery)
Shoes, men without reported sick 425
  lack of 355
Shoup, Brig.-Gen. 734
Shrapnel, purchased abroad.... 55
Shumaker, Maj. L. M......257, 258
  (See Shumaker's Danville Battery and Shumaker's Battalion)
Sickness, in the artillery...... 425
Sloan, Capt. Benj., Ordnance Corps 53
Smith, Lieut. J. D............. 545
Smith, Capt. B. H., Jr., his gallantry 347
  (See 3d Co. Richmond Howitzer Battalion)
Smith, Gen. Francis H........ 98
Smith, Maj. F. W............. 935
Smith, Col. Persifer F........ 93
Soft Hoof, horse disease...... 332
Sor, Battle of................. 238

PAGE

Sore Tongue, disease of horses 332
South Carolina, early artillery
  of 87
South Mountain, Battle of..... 292
Southern Artillery, early....85, 92
  in Mexican War............ 93
Spotsylvania, Battle of........ 775
Spurs, number pairs issued.... 56
Squires, Capt................. 129
Staff, of Chief of Artillery.... 198
  proposed for artillery....... 830
  of Artillery Corps in 1864,
    902, 907
"*Stag*," blockade runner....... 56
Stanard's Farm, Artillery Camp
  at in 1863............... 556
Stansbury, Maj. S., Ordnance
  Corps 53
Steaming, improved process... 46
  invented by Gen. Rains..... 47
Stephenson's Depot, 1863...... 606
Stevens, Capt., his book of tactics 149
Stink-shells, proposed......... 826
Stiles, Maj. Robert, quoted, 782, 783
  mentioned 936
Stockton, Capt. Isaac F., of La. 93
Strasburg, Artillery School.... 152
Strategy, of Lee at Fredericksburg 364
Straw, price of in 1864....... 909
Stribling, Maj............... 720
Stuart, Gen. J. E. B., his tribute to Pelham........... 233
  his reviews and sham battles 580
  amusing incident concerning 582
  effect of his absence from
    Gettysburg 611
Subterfuges, artillery, in use.. 516
Suffocating Projectile, proposed 826
Sulphur, secured in Louisiana 42
  contracts for supply of..... 42
Superintendents of armories,
  rank and pay of........... 57
Supplies, lack of at Petersburg 907
Surrender, proposed 939
  the 948
"Swamp Angel," rifled gun used
  at Sumter 66
Tactics, for use of horses of
  battery 111
  of light artillery.......... 141
  early American 149
  of Federal Artillery........ 156
  originated by Chew.....166, 168
  for divisional reserves....... 200
  erroneous 208, 213
  improvement of execution of 275

PAGE

peculiar at Sharpsburg..... 324
at Fredericksburg ..372, 402, 404
at Chancellorsville, discussed,
  542, 548
in 1864............832, 833, 900
Talcott, Col., Chief of Ordnance,
  U. S. A................... 26
Talcott, Capt................. 91
Tashichiao, Battle of......... 274
Taylor, Capt. E. B........458, 544
  (See Eubank's Bath Battery)
Taylor, Capt. J. S....281, 300, 322
Teamsters, character of....... 331
Tennessee Campaign of Longstreet 711
Tentage, allowance of......... 429
Terry, Lieut. Nathaniel....... 247
Texas, horses for artillery..332, 921
Texas Arsenal................. 40
Thomas, Lieut., "A", 4th U. S.
  F. A.................... 305
Thomson, Maj. James Walton,
  162, 338, 440, 890, 891, 936,
  937, 938
  (See Thomson's "Ashby" Battery and Thomson's Battalion)
Thurmond, Lieut.............. 334
Tin, how obtained........... 49
  purchased abroad.......... 55
Tobacco, price of in 1864-5.... 908
Tom's Brook, Battle of....889, 890
Torpedoes, first manufactured 51
  explosive for land use...... 178
  altercation over 179
  invented by Gen. Rains..... 180
Torres Vedras................. 429
Torstenson 153
Toulouse, Artillery School..... 152
Tousard, Col. Louis de, his
  manual 149
Tracy, Gen. E. L., of Louisiana 93
Trains, Reserve Ordnance..... 243
  regulations for wagon 429
Transfers, few among Artillery
  Officers 572
Transportation, Field Artillery,
  428, 708
Trautenau, Battle of.......... 238
Tredegar Works, Richmond,
  makes machine gun....... 32
  referred to............36, 41, 46
  sketch of; its work........ 50
  immense importance of...... 51
  work of during war........ 56
  military organization of employees 58
  troops of called out......... 731

PAGE

Trevillian Depot, Battle of.... 828
Trezevant, Maj. T. J., Supt.
    Charleston Arsenal 57
Truehart, Maj. Daniel.....164, 337
Tunis, Lieut. 452, 453, 516, 534
Tyler, Lieut., sent to Metz.... 154
Tyler, Col. Robert O.......... 223
Ullmann, Dr., sulphur con-
    tractor 42
Upperville, Battle at.......... 348
    action at 610
Utterback, Capt. 841
Utz, Lieut................... 385
Valley Campaign of 1864..827, 876
Valley Campaign, Artillery in
    Jackson's 162
Vessels, operated by Bureau of
    Ordnance 56
Vionville, Battle of........... 274
Virginia, Commission for the
    Public Defense 63
appropriations of for defense,
                   62, 69
officers in Colonial Artillery,
                   87, 88
early artillery of.........87, 88
volunteer artillery of....112, 113
strength of batteries........ 145
proportion of Artillery Of-
    ficers 413, 418
Virginia Military Institute,
    rifled gun sent to for test   64
ordnance material at....... 67
mentioned 80
as a school of arms........ 95
its influence 100, 155, 170
Jackson at the............. 246
mentioned 337, 351
graduates of at Chancellors-
    ville 477
burial of Jackson at........ 560
mentioned 573
demolished by Hunter....... 876
Von Caemmerer, quoted....... 159
Von der Goltz, quoted........ 106
his battery at Königgrätz... 525
Von Hindersin, Inspector Gen-
    eral of Artillery.......... 30
compared with Jackson..... 30
referred to................ 161
Von Kiesling's Battle Orders.. 229
Von Moltke, quoted......106, 365
"Wacht am Rhine," Prussian
    gunners sing when out of
    ammunition 525
Wagner, Col., quoted......... 230
Wagons, transport, manufac-
    ture of................. 48

PAGE

shortage of in 1862........ 327
regulations concerning 330
number of per battery...... 425
allowance of............428, 429
field 708, 709
Wagram, Battle of........... 153
Wahrendorff gun 29
Wainwright, Col., commands
    Federal Artillery,
        547, 622, 623, 668
Walke, Capt. Richard.....717, 902
Walker, Brig.-Gen. Reuben
    Lindsay......95, 113, 246,
    248, 251, 252, 253, 278, 281,
    289, 290, 291, 293, 311, 321,
    326, 337, 378, 379, 380, 383,
    384, 391, 416, 440, 511, 549,
    551, 569, 571, 623, 630, 636,
    643, 658, 664, 669, 673, 684,
    686, 696, 704, 719, 750, 775,
    900, 918, 925, 933, 934, 941,
                   942, 953
(See Walker's "Purcell" Bat-
    tery and Walker's Bat-
    talion)
Wallace, Lieut................ 619
Walton, Col. James Birge,
    93, 94, 117, 127, 130, 135,
    143, 146, 155, 258, 281, 326,
    338, 377, 379, 410, 523, 556,
    560, 677, 704, 719, 722, 755,
    848, 849, 850, 851, 852, 853
(See Walton's Battalion and
    Washington Artillery of
    La.)
Ward, Maj. Geo...........720, 805
(See Mississippi Battery)
Washington Regiment, of Louisi-
    ana 93, 94
Waterloo Bridge (Va.),
            259, 260, 261
Watson, Maj. David,
        508, 720, 786, 787
(See 2d Co. Richmond Howit-
    zer Battalion)
Weed, Capt.................. 550
West Point Foundry.......... 63
guns furnished by during war   64
"West Point of the Confeder-
    acy" 96
West Pointers, number of in
    Confederate Artillery...95, 101
influence of upon promotion,
           713, 734, 851
Western Army, artillery of in-
    spected by Pendleton..... 583
Westover 234
Wheat, price of in 1864....... 909

PAGE

White, Lieut.-Col. J. L., Supt.
    Selma Arsenal 57
White Oak Swamp, Battle of,
    215, 216
Whiskey, price of in 1864 708
Whitworth Guns,
    243, 344, 389, 452, 453, 454,
        516, 534, 538, 540, 564
Wilderness, Battle of the 760
Wilkes, Lieut. 845, 900
Wilkinson, Gen. James, his
    drill regulations 149
Williams, Lieut. 692
Williams, Capt. R. S., his in-
    vention antedates that of
    Gatling 32
    his gun used at Seven Pines 32
    specifications of his gun 32
Willis, Lieut. Ed. 164
Willisen, quoted 106
Winchester, First Battle of . . . 171
    Battle of, 1863 600
Wingfield, Capt. John R. 811
    (See Georgia Battery)
Winter quarters for 1863 410
Winthrop, Capt. S. 866, 902

PAGE

Wise, Gen. H. A., his defense of
    Petersburg 731, 835
Withdrawal of guns, Prussian
    practice 525
Wolffe, Maj. B. L. 198, 718
Wooding, Capt. 384
    (See Danville Battery)
"Woodstock Races" 890
Woolfolk, Capt. Pichegru 925
    (See Ashland Battery)
Woolfolk, Lieut. James, his gal-
    lantry 458
Woolwich, Artillery School 86
Worley, William, Saltpetre
    contractor 44
Wright, Col. M. H., Supt. At-
    lanta Arsenal 57
Wright, Capt. S. T. . . . 277, 945, 955
    (See Halifax Battery)
Wyatt, Capt. J. W. 821
    (See Albemarle "Everett"
        Battery)
Yale, C. D., of Virginia, powder
    contractor 43
Yellow Tavern, Battle of 796

BATTERY INDEX

The battery organizations of the Army of Northern Virginia always bore two, and sometimes three names, a fact which leads to much confusion in the study of the Artillery records. The following index is arranged under two heads: "A", according to the locality in which the batteries were recruited; "B", according to the names of the battery commanders. Text references will be found under heading "A" only.

Thus the references to Pegram's Richmond "Purcell" Battery will be found under "A", opposite *Richmond*, while Chew's "Ashby" Battery, and Brown's "Wise" Battery, which were not local organizations, will be found under "A", opposite *"Ashby"* and *"Wise"*, respectively. In order to trace the complete record of a particular battery it is essential to know to what battalion it belonged at various periods, as the Artillery was frequently referred to in the records by battalions, especially during the latter years of the War when the battalion was the tactical unit. The record of a battalion embraces the record of the constituent batteries.

Federal batteries are indexed under index "B" only.

BATTERY INDEX "A"

PAGE

Alabama Battery (Hardaway, Hurt)....202, 203, 282, 285, 297, 350, 352, 358, 380, 410, 421, 510, 514, 538, 540, 569, 618, 619, 664, 691, 739, 896, 913

Alabama Battery (Bondurant, Reese, "Jeff Davis"), 142, 184, 189, 202, 203, 211, 212, 282, 285, 298, 336, 358, 421, 508, 568, 619, 620, 739, 926

Albemarle Battery (Southall, Wyatt, "Everett"), 241, 242, 334, 569, 665, 739, 821, 855

Albemarle Battery (Sturdivant, W. H. Weisiger, C. F. Johnston)........707, 741, 835, 838, 914, 916

Alexandria Battery (Kemper, Smoot)........130, 131, 132, 134, 142, 184, 189, 201, 203, 215, 707

Alleghany Battery (Jos. Carpenter, J. C. Carpenter), 143, 164, 169, 170, 171, 172, 173, 174, 203, 230, 244, 245, 248, 258, 262, 266, 270, 282, 284, 285, 290, 327, 329, 358, 378, 408, 410, 421, 520, 568, 600, 601, 606, 607, 636, 651, 738, 889, 913

Amherst Battery (T. J. Kirkpatrick).......143, 205, 242, 283, 285, 293, 319, 335, 360, 380, 422, 454, 568, 738, 878, 879, 912

Amherst-Nelson Battery (W. G. Latham, Lamkin), 712, 738, 865, 898, 912, 917

Andrews' Battery, Co. "A", Stark's Batt. Heavy Artillery 205

Ashland Battery (Woolfolk), 143, 202, 205, 242, 281, 284, 299, 300, 303, 322, 335, 336, 358, 371, 396, 397, 420, 452, 508, 534, 545, 567, 646, 737, 779, 911

"Ashby" Horse Battery (Chew, Thomson, J. W. Carter), 143, 162, 163, 164, 166, 167, 170, 173, 205, 259, 283, 296, 346, 347, 422, 446, 576, 578, 580, 584, 588, 594, 595, 597, 610, 691, 701, 725, 740, 773, 796, 828, 829, 845, 889, 890, 891, 916, 927, 937

Baltimore, 2d Battery (See Maryland Horse Battery)

Bath Battery (Eubank, Taylor), 256, 257, 271, 281, 285, 296, 303, 309, 310, 358, 371, 420, 452, 458, 509, 534, 544, 567, 645, 657, 737, 911

"Beauregard Rifles" Battery (See Lynchburg Battery)

PAGE

Bedford Battery (Jordan, Hensley, Claytor, J. D. Smith), 201, 256, 257, 271, 281, 285, 296, 300, 303, 308, 321, 338, 358, 371, 396, 397, 420, 450, 452, 458, 459, 466, 469, 510, 513, 535, 536, 537, 539, 545, 567, 646, 737, 911

Bedford Battery (Bowyer, J. R. Johnson). Disbanded Oct., 1862 and merged with Dearing's and Stribling's batteries, 142, 204, 211, 244, 245, 247, 259, 270, 281, 284, 335

Botetourt Battery (Douthat, Anderson). Converted into heavy artillery in 1865..802, 926

Cadet Battery (See Va. Mil. Inst. Battery)

Campbell Battery (Clarke, Wimbish, "Long Island"). Mustered out Oct., 1862, 202, 203, 205, 242, 282, 284, 334

Cape Fear Battery (See North Carolina)

Caroline Battery (Thornton), 707, 740

Charleston Battery (See South Carolina Battery)

Charlotte Battery (Bruce, "Staunton Hill Artillery")

Charlotte Battery (See North Carolina Battery)

Charlottesville Battery (Carrington)......173, 174, 203, 211, 242, 244, 281, 285, 358, 421, 508, 568, 602, 603, 621

Charlottesville Horse Battery (Jackson).....691, 699, 706, 802, 803, 829, 877, 916, 927

"Chesapeake" Battery (See 4th Maryland Battery)

Chesterfield Battery (Epes, "Johnston")

Chesterfield Battery (See South Carolina)

"Cockade Artillery" (See Petersburg Battery)

"Confederate Guards" Battery (See Mississippi Battery)

"Courtney" Battery (See Richmond Battery)

Danville Battery (Stamps, Dickenson, "Ringgold"). Converted into heavy artillery in 1865...282, 284, 285, 327, 329, 358, 378, 384, 421, 508, 802, 803, 854, 915, 926, 941

PAGE

Danville Battery (Shumaker, Wooding, B. Z. Price), 170, 173, 174, 203, 218, 258, 262, 270, 569, 618, 739, 769, 913

"Dixie Artillery" (See Monroe Battery)

Donaldsonville Battery (See Louisiana Battery)

"Eighth Star" Battery (See Page-Shenandoah Battery)

"Everett Artillery" (See Albemarle Battery)

Fairfax Battery (Young). Became Co. "G", 14th Va. Infty. in Oct., 1862, but later served as a light battery.

Fauquier Battery (Stribling, Marshall).....142, 184, 188, 202, 204, 258, 273, 280, 285, 336, 358, 370, 410, 420, 445, 567, 700, 737, 814, 815, 916

"Fayette Artillery" (See Richmond Battery)

Fluvanna, 1st Battery (Cocke, Huckstep). Merged with 2d Fluvanna to form Massie's Fluvanna Battery, Oct. 4, 1862.....143, 205, 242, 283, 294, 319, 320, 322, 336

Fluvanna, 2d Battery (Holman, Ancell). Merged with 1st Fluvanna Battery to form Massie's Fluvanna Battery, Oct. 4, 1862....143, 205, 242, 283, 294, 319, 320, 322, 334, 336

Fluvanna Battery (Massie, Snead)....285, 360, 380, 422, 454, 568, 715, 738, 813, 880, 912

Fredericksburg Battery (Braxton, E. A. Marye), 142, 164, 185, 188, 204, 211, 245, 258, 267, 281, 285, 289, 311, 312, 319, 358, 378, 420, 506, 508, 513, 538, 569, 730, 740, 897, 912, 914

Georgia Battery, "A", Sumter Battalion (Cutts, Ross), 143, 205, 242, 282, 285, 298, 334, 360, 373, 380, 422, 454, 533, 569, 651, 740, 896, 914

Georgia Battery, "B", Sumter Battalion (Price, Patterson), 205, 242, 282, 285, 298, 334, 360, 380, 422, 454, 516, 522, 524, 525, 569, 740, 915

Georgia Battery, "C", Sumter Battalion (Crawford, Wingfield).........241, 242, 282,

PAGE

285, 298, 360, 422, 569, 651,
740, 811, 914, 915
Georgia Battery, "D", Sumter
B a t t a l i o n (Blackshear).
Mustered out Oct., 1862,
205, 242, 282, 284, 298, 334
Georgia Battery, "E", Sumter
Battalion (Lane),
143, 201, 205, 242, 334, 363,
369, 380, 388, 410, 450, 454
Georgia B a t t e r y (Carlton,
"Troup")...,....201, 203, 280,
284, 289, 321, 357, 369, 419,
450, 451, 454, 516, 517, 518,
522, 523, 525, 533, 563, 567,
657, 684, 701, 722, 738, 911
Georgia Battery, Regular (Milledge)........125, 205, 234,
242, 283, 285, 293, 319, 320,
322, 360, 366, 422, 454, 568,
668, 738, 764, 850, 912
Georgia B a t t e r y, Regular
(Hamilton) 143, 205
Georgia Battery (Read, Fraser,
"Pulaski")....184, 189, 201,
203, 280, 284, 289, 304, 321,
357, 369, 410, 419, 450, 451,
454, 516, 522, 523, 525, 533,
539, 563, 567, 657, 722, 738,
820, 911
Georgia Battery (Blodget).... 142
Georgia Battery (Ells, Staten,
Macon).......360, 370, 380,
708, 740, 837, 915
"German Artillery" (See South
Carolina Battery)
Giles Battery (McComas, D. A.
French).......202, 205, 280,
708, 740, 858, 912, 950
Gloucester Battery (Montague,
Yeatman). Heavy artillery
company but served as light
battery. Became Co. "A",
34th Va. Infty., in 1864.
Goochland Battery (Roemer,
Turner, Leake). Mustered
out Oct., 1862, and merged
with King William Battery,
202, 204, 242, 258, 280, 282,
284, 333, 334, 336
Goochland Battery (Guy, Tal-
ley) 707
Halifax Battery (Wright),
708, 740, 838, 839, 867, 916
"H a m p d e n Artillery" (See
Richmond Battery)
Hampton Battery (Allen)..... 855

PAGE

Hanover Battery (W. Nelson,
G. W. Nelson). Mustered
out Oct., 1862, and merged
with Amherst and Ashland
batteries.......202, 203, 335, 360
"Harbor Guards" (See Norfolk
Battery)
Henrico Battery (Sands, Rit-
ter). Mustered out Oct., 1862,
184, 189, 202, 242, 334, 855
Irwin Battery (See Georgia
Battery. Wingfield)
James City Battery (Hankins,
Richardson),
202, 203, 242, 707, 853
"Jeff Davis Artillery" (See
Alabama Battery)
"Johnston Artillery" (See Ches-
terfield Battery)
King and Queen B a t t e r y
(Groves, "Newtown")...128, 134
King William Battery (T. H.
Carter, W. P. Carter),
111, 142, 184, 189, 202, 203,
282, 285, 298, 309, 310, 312,
322, 323, 336, 358, 421, 425,
489, 507, 508, 513, 537, 539,
568, 619, 620, 739, 775, 881,
882, 926
"Lee Artillery" (See Lynchburg
Battery)
"Letcher" Battery (See Rich-
mond Battery)
Lewisburg (W. Va.) Battery
(Bryan) 802, 913
"Long Island" Battery (See
Campbell Battery)
Loudoun Battery (Rogers).
Mustered out Oct., 1862, and
merged with the Fauquier
Battery.......130, 131, 135,
142, 187, 188, 202, 203, 258,
280, 284, 336
Louisa Battery (Coleman, R.
C. M. Page, Montgomery,
"Morris").....143, 184, 189,
205, 242, 282, 285, 358, 421,
506, 511, 513, 568, 619, 620,
739, 790, 791, 926
Louisiana B a t t e r y, 1st Co.
Washington Artillery Bat-
talion (Squires, Owen),
143, 204, 258, 273, 280, 285,
297, 303, 308, 310, 319, 358,
371, 420, 425, 567, 915
Louisiana B a t t e r y, 2d Co.
Washington Artillery Bat-

PAGE

talion (Rosser, J. B. Richardson) 143, 204, 257, 273,
281, 285, 296, 309, 310, 319,
358, 371, 420, 454, 519, 522,
525, 567, 915
Louisiana B a t t e r y, 3d Co.
Washington Artillery Bat-
talion (M. B. Miller, Hero),
143, 204, 258, 273, 280, 285,
307, 310, 319, 358, 371, 396,
420, 519, 522, 525, 567, 677,
684, 915
Louisiana B a t t e r y, 4th Co.
Washington Artillery Bat-
talion (Eshleman, Norcom),
143, 257, 280, 204, 285, 309,
310, 319, 358, 371, 420, 525,
567, 684, 915
Louisiana Battery (Girardey,
D'Aquin, Thompson, Green,
"Louisiana Guard"),
241, 245, 248, 258, 259, 270,
281, 285, 358, 385, 414, 421,
443, 508, 568, 637, 696, 714,
715, 737, 741, 858, 912, 950
Louisiana Battery (Maurin,
Landry, "Donaldsonville"),
204, 258, 273, 280, 284, 312,
319, 320, 322, 357, 370, 371,
377, 379, 386, 387, 388, 397,
419, 447, 914
Louisiana Battery (M o o d y,
"Madison") 185, 188, 202,
281, 285, 300, 303, 308, 321,
327, 358, 371, 386, 387, 396,
397, 400, 420, 452, 458, 508,
534, 545, 567, 645, 737, 794, 911
Lynchburg Battery (G. S. Davidson, Chamberlayne),
802, 854, 866, 867, 926
Lynchburg Horse B a t t e r y
(S h o e m a k e r, Moorman,
"Beauregard Rifles"),
204, 230, 258, 280, 284, 285,
322, 335, 336, 346, 370, 422,
446, 448, 449, 460, 467, 471,
480, 481, 577, 578, 584, 587,
591, 596, 610, 691, 701, 726,
729, 740, 773, 796, 823, 828,
845, 880, 889, 895, 916, 927
Lynchburg Battery (Deshler,
Raine, Hardwicke, "Lee"),
170, 173, 174, 258, 282, 285,
299, 300, 328, 378, 384, 421,
568, 605, 636, 665, 738, 889, 913
Lynchburg Battery (H. G.
Latham, Dearing, Blount,

PAGE

Dickerson) 114, 130, 142,
184, 188, 189, 202, 204, 420,
445, 567, 737, 803, 814, 815,
915, 916, 926, 941
"Macbeth Artillery" (See South
Carolina Battery)
Macon Battery (See Georgia
Battery)
"Madison" Battery (See Louisiana Battery)
"Madison" Battery (See Mississippi Battery)
"Magruder Artillery" (S e e
Yorktown Battery)
Manchester Battery (Weisiger) 244
Maryland Battery (Brockenbrough, W. H. Griffin, 2d
Baltimore L. A.). Converted
into horse artillery in 1863,
142, 170, 173, 174, 203, 211,
244, 258, 262, 266, 270, 282,
285, 327, 446, 578, 600, 602,
612, 691, 701, 737, 796, 829,
841, 916, 926, 927
Maryland, 1st Battery (R. S.
Andrews, Dement),
185, 188, 204, 205, 211, 245,
248, 259, 262, 266, 281, 285,
289, 293, 298, 414, 421, 568,
600, 605, 606, 607, 608, 636,
651, 737, 822, 829, 841, 913,
918, 926
Maryland, 4th Battery (W. D.
Brown, W. F. Chew, "Chesapeake"). Converted i n t o
heavy artillery in 1865,
204, 211, 244, 245, 248, 259,
281, 284, 285, 290, 293, 298,
309, 310, 358, 384, 410, 421,
515, 519, 568, 636, 651, 737,
822, 829, 841, 913
Masters' Battery (Masters).
Heavy siege battery employed
as field artillery in Peninsula
Campaign 204
Mathews Battery (Armistead),
185, 708, 740, 858, 912
"McComas Artillery" (See Giles
Battery)
Mercer (W. Va.) Battery (N.
B. French)
Mississippi Battery (Richards,
Ward, T. J. Kirkpatrick,
"Madison"),
569, 651, 739, 765, 821, 914
Mississippi Battery (Bradford,
"Confederate Guards"),
708, 740, 838, 915

PAGE

Middlesex B a t t e r y (Fleet, Hardy). Mustered out Oct., 1862, and distributed among Ashland, 2d Fluvanna, and Johnson's Richmond batteries, 241, 246, 248, 258, 281, 284, 336

Monroe Battery (Booton, Chapman, "Dixie"), 202, 204, 257, 273, 283, 284, 319, 335, 802, 913

"Morris Artillery" (See Louisa Battery) ·

Nelson Battery (Rives), 205, 284, 707, 740

Nelson-Amherst Battery (See Amherst-Nelson Battery)

"Newtown" Battery (See King and Queen Battery)

Norfolk Battery (J. J. Young, "Harbor Guards"), 183, 202, 242, 334

Norfolk B a t t e r y (Vickery, G r a n d y, "Light Artillery Blues") 92, 112, 113, 202, 257, 284, 369, 419, 447, 452, 459, 569, 740, 914

Norfolk Battery (Huger, J. D. Moore) 113, 202, 204, 258, 280, 284, 335, 357, 370, 371, 419, 447, 521, 526, 527, 569, 578, 700, 740, 914

North Carolina Battery, "C", 13th N. C. Batt. (Cumming), 740, 837, 915

North Carolina Battery, "F", 13th N. C. Batt. (Branch, H. G. Latham, Potts, Flanner) 202, 205, 245, 258, 267, 280, 281, 285, 358, 414, 420, 425, 445, 567, 643, 684, 738, 899, 911

North Carolina Battery, "A", 1st N. C. Reg. (Manly), 184, 189, 202, 203, 280, 284, 335, 357, 369, 419, 450, 451, 452, 466, 528, 534, 535, 563, 567, 657, 722, 738, 911

North Carolina Battery, "B", 1st N. C. Reg. (Gregg) . . 901, 914

North Carolina Battery, "C", 1st N. C. Reg. (Brem, J. Graham, Williams, Charlotte), 202, 205, 241, 569, 739, 914

North Carolina Battery, "D", 1st N. C. Reg. (Reilly, Ramsey, Rowan), 142, 185, 203, 237, 269, 272,

PAGE

280, 285, 296, 300, 309, 310, 335, 355, 358, 370, 410, 420, 445, 567, 643, 658, 683, 737, 789, 912

North Carolina Battery, "E", 1st N. C. Reg. (Moore, J. O. Miller, Wilmington, "Cape Fear") 708, 740, 837, 915

N o r t h C a r o l i n a Battery (Lloyd). Mustered out Oct., 1862, and merged with Manly's and Reilly's N. C. batteries, 202, 282, 284, 298, 321, 335

North Carolina Battery (Webb) 707

"Orange" Battery (See Richmond Battery)

"Otey" Battery (See Richmond Battery)

Page-Shenandoah Battery (Rice, 8th Star). Merged with Wooding's Danville Battery, Sept. 26, 1862, 170, 173, 244, 258, 270, 283, 284, 327, 329

"Palmetto Artillery" (S e e South Carolina Battery)

"Pee Dee Artillery" (See South Carolina Battery)

"Peninsula" Battery (Cosnahan, W. B. Jones). Merged with Williamsburg Battery in April, 1862, 184, 189, 201, 282, 322, 855

Petersburg Battery (Rambout, Stoope, "Cockade Artillery")

Petersburg Battery (J. R. Branch, R. G. Pegram). Converted into horse artillery in 1864 . . . . 202, 205, 280, 285, 296, 303, 358, 369, 370, 377, 708, 740, 838, 860, 864, 875, 901, 915

Petersburg Battery (Nichols, E. Graham). Converted into horse battery in 1864, 202, 205, 378, 569, 897, 901, 916, 927

Pittsylvania Battery (Lewis, Penick) 284, 357, 362, 369, 377, 379, 410, 419, 447, 452, 461, 520, 526, 527, 537, 550, 569, 740, 841, 857, 895, 914, 917

Portsmouth Battery (Grimes, Thompson, "Light Artillery"). Mustered out Oct., 1862, and merged w i t h Moorman's

Lynchburg and Huger's Norfolk batteries,
92, 112, 202, 204, 230, 256, 257, 280, 284, 335, 377
Powhatan Battery (Dance),
143, 241, 242, 282, 285, 360, 385, 392, 421, 510, 568, 637, 665, 714, 715, 738, 912
"Pulaski" Battery (See Georgia Battery)
"Purcell" Battery (See Richmond Battery)
Richmond Battery, 1st Co. Howitzers (J. C. Shields, Palmer, McCarthy, R. M. Anderson).....114, 130, 142, 184, 189, 203, 280, 284, 304, 357, 370, 419, 450, 451, 452, 466, 528, 537, 538, 563, 567, 657, 692, 713, 722, 738, 782, 783, 784, 792, 826, 911
Richmond Battery, 2d Co. Howitzers (J. T. Brown, Hudnall, Watson, L. F. Jones)........118, 202, 205, 242, 282, 285, 293, 360, 385, 421, 508, 568, 637, 665, 738, 785, 787, 855, 913
Richmond Battery, 3d Co. Howitzers (R. Stanard, Moseley, B. H. Smith, Jr.),
114, 134, 141, 187, 188, 202, 204, 242, 282, 285, 347, 360, 385, 421, 508, 568, 637, 665, 738, 785, 786, 855, 912, 926, 928
Richmond "Purcell" Battery (R. L. Walker, W. J. Pegram, McGraw, Cayce),
113, 131, 132, 133, 134, 142, 204, 211, 230, 236, 245, 248, 249, 250, 258, 266, 281, 285, 289, 290, 291, 311, 312, 335, 358, 378, 395, 420, 425, 466, 507, 511, 569, 739, 834, 843, 844, 896, 898, 914
Richmond "Hampden" Battery (Caskie, L. S. Marye, Sullivan)..........170, 173, 203, 244, 245, 248, 258, 282, 285, 327, 336, 358, 378, 420, 445, 567, 569, 730, 737, 814, 815, 916, 950
Richmond "Letcher" Battery (G. Davidson, Brander),
204, 230, 236, 258, 281, 285, 289, 293, 378, 420, 466, 507, 511, 569, 739, 780, 871, 891, 896, 898, 914

Richmond "Thomas" Battery (P. Stanard, E. J. Anderson). Merged with "Hampden" Battery in 1862,
128, 142, 202, 203, 204, 230, 257, 258, 267, 281, 283, 284, 333, 336
Richmond "Otey" Battery (Otey, D. N. Walker),
802, 854, 915, 941
Richmond "Orange" Battery (Peyton, Fry),
202, 203, 205, 242, 282, 285, 334, 358, 421, 508, 513, 537, 568, 619, 620, 739, 889, 913, 926
Richmond "Fayette" Battery (Cabell, Macon, Fleming),
114, 184, 188, 202, 205, 242, 280, 285, 357, 370, 420, 445, 567, 700, 737, 814, 815, 855, 916
Richmond "Courtney" Battery (Courtney, Latimer, Tanner),
142, 170, 173, 174, 203, 211, 244, 245, 247, 259, 262, 270, 281, 285, 289, 293, 298, 358, 421, 508, 509, 568, 637, 691, 926
Richmond Battery (Parker, J. T. Brown, Jr.),
241, 256, 257, 271, 281, 285, 296, 299, 300, 303, 308, 321, 358, 371, 378, 387, 396, 420, 452, 454, 458, 508, 516, 522, 525, 536, 537, 545, 567, 645, 737, 911
Richmond Battery (Crenshaw, Ellett)........204, 211, 258, 267, 281, 285, 289, 290, 311, 312, 358, 420, 466, 569, 739, 871, 901, 914
Richmond Battery (M. Johnson, Clutter, Chilton),
283, 285, 294, 319, 320, 322, 336, 358, 377, 421, 569, 618, 622, 739, 805, 840, 845, 912, 945
Richmond Battery (Martin). Converted into heavy artillery in 1865,
707, 740, 838, 844, 916, 926
Richmond Battery (Dabney).. 707
"Ringgold Artillery" (See Danville Battery)
Roanoke Battery (Lurty). Converted into horse artillery in 1864.........802, 877, 916, 927
Rockbridge, 1st Battery (Pendleton, McLaughlin, Poague, A. Graham),
116, 124, 126, 127, 141, 143,

PAGE

164, 169, 170, 171, 172, 173,
174, 175, 202, 203, 205, 230,
244, 245, 246, 248, 258, 263,
266, 270, 279, 282, 285, 297,
298, 300, 301, 310, 323, 327,
360, 366, 385, 391, 401, 408,
410, 421, 453, 515, 516, 519,
530, 531, 568, 636, 665, 714,
715, 738, 856, 912

Rockbridge, 2d Battery (Miller,
Lusk, Donald),
170, 173, 174, 244, 285, 358,
421, 508, 569, 618, 739, 913

Rowan Battery (See North
Carolina Battery)

Salem Battery (Hupp, C. B.
Griffin, "Flying Artillery"),
241, 242, 282, 285, 360, 395,
421, 510, 536, 568, 637, 664,
738, 912

Shenandoah-Page Battery (See
Page-Shenandoah Battery)

South Carolina Battery (Bachman, "Charleston German
Artillery") 204, 257, 269,
272, 280, 285, 296, 297, 300,
303, 308, 309, 310, 322, 355,
358, 370, 420, 445, 567, 642,
643, 683

South Carolina Battery (Boyce,
"Macbeth"),
258, 280, 284, 307, 308, 310

South Carolina Battery (Coit),
241, 708

South Carolina Battery (Rives) 142

South Carolina Battery (Rhett,
Brooks, Ficklin),
203, 205, 236, 242, 256, 257,
271, 281, 285, 296, 299, 300,
303, 308, 321, 358, 371, 378,
380, 387, 410, 420, 454, 458,
516, 567, 645, 737, 911

South Carolina Battery (Garden, "Palmetto"),
257, 269, 280, 355, 358, 370,
420, 445, 567, 643, 684, 738,
899, 911

South Carolina Horse Battery
(Hart, "Washington"),
203, 215, 283, 346, 422, 446,
449, 577, 578, 584, 585, 586,
589, 590, 591, 596, 610, 683,
691, 699, 700, 703, 726, 740,
773, 796, 797, 827, 828, 829,
897, 901, 916, 927

PAGE

South Carolina Battery (McIntosh, Brunson, Zimmer-
man, "Pee Dee"),
204, 211, 258, 281, 285, 289,
311, 358, 378, 395, 420, 466,
506, 569, 740

South Carolina Battery (Kelly,
"Chesterfield") 740, 838, 916

Stafford Battery (Cooke, T. B.
French, Cooper),
142, 202, 205, 280, 285, 296,
303, 358, 360, 370, 377, 410,
738, 913

Staunton Battery (Balthis,
Garber) 128, 132, 175,
185, 188, 203, 230, 244, 259,
262, 266, 281, 285, 288, 289,
293, 298, 358, 385, 421, 568,
913, 926

Staunton Battery (Imboden,
McClannahan). Light, 1861,
Mountain, 1862, Horse, 1863-
5 . . . . 128, 132, 142,
175, 185, 188, 578, 691, 699,
700, 706, 803, 829, 877, 916, 927

"Staunton Hill Artillery" (See
Charlotte Battery)

"Stonewall Artillery" (See Alleghany and 1st Rockbridge
batteries)

Stuart Horse Artillery, 1st Battery (Pelham, Breathed, Mc-
Gregor, P. P. Johnston),
178, 185, 186, 187, 189, 205,
211, 233, 256, 259, 262, 283,
296, 346, 348, 422, 424, 448,
460, 467, 471, 477, 478, 480,
483, 577, 578, 586, 610, 691,
701, 725, 740, 773, 794, 796,
825, 827, 843, 880, 884, 889,
895, 916, 927

Stuart Horse Artillery, 2d Battery (Henry, McGregor),
346, 348, 352, 353, 422, 448,
460, 471, 483, 577, 578, 584,
590, 591, 596, 610, 691, 701,
726, 740, 773, 796, 827, 828,
843, 857, 897, 901, 916, 927

Sumter Battery (See Georgia
Battery)

Surry Battery (Ruffin),
241, 707, 746

Tennessee Battery (Rhett, Bur-
roughs) 802

Tennessee Battery (McClung) . . 802

"Thomas" Battery (See Richmond Battery)

PAGE

"Troup Artillery" (See Georgia Battery)

Va. Mil. Inst. Battery (Minge), 114, 124, 320, 801

Warrenton Battery (Utterback, Brooke) 285, 360, 421, 508, 569, 651, 739, 914

"Washington" Battery (See South Carolina Battery)

"Washington Artillery" (See Louisiana batteries)

"West Augusta" Battery (Waters) 164, 169

Williamsburg Battery (Garrett, Coke). Mustered out Oct., 1862..............183, 188, 202, 205, 242, 282, 284, 334, 855

Wilmington Battery (See North Carolina)

PAGE

Winchester Battery (Cutshaw). Mustered out and merged with Carpenter's Alleghany Battery Sept. 26, 1862, 164, 169, 170, 171, 172, 173, 258, 283, 284, 327, 329, 380

"Wise Artillery" (Alburtis, J. S. Brown). Mustered out and merged with Lynchburg "Lee" Battery Oct., 1862, 128, 141, 142, 201, 203, 280, 284, 285, 335, 377, 577

"Wise Legion" Battery (Lowry) 802, 913

Yorktown Battery (E. R. Young)...707, 740, 837, 853, 915

Yorktown Battery (T J. Page, "Magruder Artillery"). Mustered out and distributed among Lee's Battalion Oct., 1862..202, 203, 283, 284, 336, 787

BATTERY INDEX "B"

CONFEDERATE

Aiken's Battery (Henrico "Varina")

Alburtis' Battery ("Wise Artillery")

Allen's Battery (Hampton)

Ancell's Battery (2d Fluvanna)

Anderson's Battery (1st Richmond Howitzers)

Anderson's Battery (Botetourt)

Anderson's Battery (Richmond "Thomas")

Andrews' Battery (1st Maryland)

Andrews' Battery (Co. "A", Stark's Battalion Heavy Artillery, 1861. This battery was detached from the defenses at Drewry's Bluff and served with the Light Artillery in the Peninsula Campaign)

Armistead's Battery (Mathews)

Bachman's Battery (Charleston, "German," S. C.)

Balthis' Battery (Staunton)

Beckham's Battery (Groves' King and Queen. Improvised)

Blackshear's Battery ("D" Sumter, Ga. Disbanded Oct., 1862)

Blodget's Battery (Georgia)

Blount's Battery (Lynchburg)

Bondurant's Battery ("Jeff Davis," Ala.)

Booton's Battery (Dixie or Monroe)

Bowyer's Battery (Bedford)

Boyce's Battery ("Macbeth," S. C.)

Bradford's Battery (Confederate Guards, Miss.)

Branch's Battery (Petersburg)

Branch's Battery (H. C. Latham's, N. C.)

Brander's Battery (Richmond Letcher)

Braxton's Battery (Fredericksburg)

Breathed's Battery (1st Stuart Horse Artillery)

Brem's Battery (North Carolina)

Brockenbrough's Battery (Baltimore Light Artillery or 2d Baltimore)

Brooks' Battery (Rhett's, S. C.)

Brooke's Battery (Warrenton)

Brown's Battery (Wise Artillery)

Brown's Battery (Parker's Richmond)

Brown's Battery (4th Md. or "Chesapeake")

Brown's Battery (2d Richmond Howitzers)

Bruce's Battery (Charlotte or "Staunton Hill")

Bryan's Battery (Lewisburg, W. Va.)

Burroughs' Battery (Tennessee)

Cabell's Battery (Richmond "Fayette")

Carlton's Battery ("Troup," Ga.)

Carter's Battery (King William)

Carter's Battery ("Ashby" Horse Artillery)
Carpenter's Battery (Alleghany)
Carrington's Battery (Charlottesville)
Caskie's Battery (R i c h m o n d, "Hampden")
Cayce's Battery (Richmond "Purcell")
Chamberlayne's Battery (Lynchburg)
Chapman's Battery ("Dixie" or Monroe)
Chew's Battery ("Ashby" Horse Artillery)
Chew's Battery (4th Md. or "Chesapeake")
Chilton's Battery (Richmond)
Clarke's Battery ("Long Island," Campbell)
Claytor's Battery (Bedford)
Clutter's Battery (Richmond)
Cocke's Battery (1st Fluvanna)
Coit's Battery (South Carolina)
Coke's Battery (Williamsburg)
Coleman's Battery (Louisa, "Morris")
Cooke's Battery (Stafford)
Cooper's Battery (Stafford)
Cosnahan's Battery (Peninsula)
Courtney's Battery (Richmond)
Crawford's Battery ("C", Sumter, Ga.)
Crenshaw's Battery (Richmond)
Cumming's Battery ("C", 13th N. C. Battalion)
Cutshaw's Battery (Winchester. Merged with Carpenter's Alleghany Battery in 1862)
Cutts' Battery (Sumter, Ga.)
Dabney's Battery (Richmond)
Dance's Battery (Powhatan)
D'Aquin's B a t t e r y ("Louisiana Guard")
Davidson's B a t t e r y (Richmond "Letcher")
Davidson's Battery (Lynchburg)
Dearing's Battery (Lynchburg)
Dement's Battery (1st Maryland)
Deshler's B a t t e r y (Lynchburg "Lee")
Dickenson's Battery (D a n v i l l e "Ringgold")
Dickerson's Battery (Lynchburg)
Donald's Battery (2d Rockbridge)
Douthat's Battery (Botetourt)
Drewry's Battery ("South Side")
Ellett's Battery (Richmond "Crenshaw")

Ellett's Battery ("Pamunkey")
Ells' Battery (Macon, Ga.)
Epes' Battery (Chesterfield)
Eshleman's Battery (4th Co. Washington Artillery, La.)
Eubank's Battery (Bath)
Ficklin's Battery (Brooks', S. C.)
Flanner's Battery ("F", 13th N. C. Battalion)
Fleet's Battery (Middlesex)
Fleming's Battery (Richmond "Fayette")
Fraser's Battery (Pulaski, Ga.)
French's Battery (Stafford)
French's Battery (Mercer, W. Va.)
French's Battery (Giles)
Fry's Battery (Richmond "Orange")
Garber's Battery (Staunton)
Garden's Battery (Palmetto, S. C.)
Garrett's Battery (Williamsburg)
Girardey's Battery ("Louisiana Guard")
Graham's Battery (North Carolina)
Graham's Battery (1st Rockbridge)
Graham's Battery (Petersburg)
Grandy's Battery (Norfolk L. A. Blues)
Green's Battery ("L o u i s i a n a Guard")
Griffin's Battery (Salem "Flying")
Griffin's Battery (2d Baltimore Light Artillery)
Gregg's Battery ("B", 1st N. C. Reg.)
Grimes' Battery (Portsmouth Light Artillery)
Groves' Battery ("Newtown," King and Queen)
Guy's Battery (Goochland)
Hamilton's Battery (Georgia Regular)
Hankins' Battery (James City)
Hardaway's Battery (Alabama)
Hardwicke's Battery (Lynchburg "Lee")
Hart's Battery ("Washington," S. C.)
Henry's Battery (2d Stuart Horse Artillery)
Hensley's Battery (Bedford)
Hero's Battery (3d Co. Washington Artillery, La.)
Holman's Battery (2d Fluvanna)
Huckstep's Battery (1st Fluvanna)
Hudnall's Battery (2d Richmond Howitzers)
Huger's Battery (Norfolk. Formed from Norfolk L. A. Blues 1861)
Hupp's Battery (Salem)

Hurt's Battery (Alabama)
Imboden's Battery (Staunton)
Jackson's Battery (Charlottesville)
Johnson's Battery (Bedford)
Johnson's Battery (Richmond)
Johnston's Battery (1st Stuart Horse Artillery)
Johnston's Battery (Albemarle)
Jones' Battery ("Peninsula") .
Jones' Battery ("Pamunkey")
Jones' Battery (2d Richmond Howitzers)
Jordan's Battery (Bedford)
Kelly's Battery (South Carolina)
Kemper's Battery (Alexandria)
Kirkpatrick's Battery (Amherst)
Lamkin's Battery (Amherst-Nelson)
Landry's Battery (Donaldsonville, La.)
Lane's Battery ("E", Sumter, Ga.)
Latham's Battery (Nelson-Amherst)
Latham's Battery (Lynchburg)
Latham's Battery (Branch's, N. C.)
Latimer's Battery (Richmond)
Leake's Battery (Goochland)
Lewis' Battery (Pittsylvania)
Lloyd's Battery (N. C.)
Lowry's Battery ("Wise Legion")
Lusk's Battery (2d Rockbridge)
Lurty's Battery (Roanoke)
Macon's Battery (Richmond "Fayette")
Manly's Battery ("A", 1st N. C. Reg.)
Marshall's Battery (Fauquier)
Martin's Battery (Richmond)
Marye's Battery (Fredericksburg)
Marye's Battery (Richmond "Hampden")
Massie's Battery (Fluvanna Consolidated)
Masters' Battery (Erroneously referred to in Rebellion Records as a Virginian Light Battery. It was composed of 4 siege guns and was commanded by Captain L. Masters, Assistant Inspector, General A. P. Hill's Staff, Captain Artillery, Provisional Army, C. S. A.)
Maurin's Battery (Donaldsonville, La.)
McCarthy's Battery (1st Richmond Howitzers)
McClannahan's Battery (Staunton)
McClung's Battery (Tennessee)
McComas' Battery (Giles)
McGregor's Battery (2d Stuart Horse Artillery)

McIntosh's Battery ("Pee Dee," S. C.)
McLaughlin's Battery (1st Rockbridge)
Milledge's Battery (Georgia Regular)
Miller's Battery (2d Rockbridge)
Miller's Battery (3d Co. Washington Artillery)
Miller's Battery ("E", 1st N. C. Reg.)
Minge's Battery (V. M. I. Cadet)
Montague's Battery (Gloucester. Transformed into Co. "A", 34th Va. Infantry, in 1864)
Montgomery's Battery (Louisa "Morris")
Moody's Battery ("Madison," La.)
Moore's Battery ("E", 1st N. C. Reg.)
Moore's Battery (Norfolk)
Moorman's Battery (Lynchburg)
Moseley's Battery (3d Richmond Howitzers)
Nelson's Battery (Hanover)
Nichols' Battery (Petersburg)
Norcom's Battery (4th Co. Washington Artillery)
Otey's Battery (Richmond)
Owen's Battery (1st Co. Washington Artillery, La.)
Page's Battery (Yorktown "Magruder")
Page's Battery (Louisa "Morris")
Palmer's Battery (1st Richmond Howitzers)
Parker's Battery (Richmond)
Patterson's Battery ("B", Sumter, Ga., Batt.)
Pegram's Battery (Richmond "Purcell")
Pegram's Battery (Petersburg)
Pelham's Battery (1st Stuart Horse Artillery)
Pendleton's Battery (1st Rockbridge)
Penick's Battery (Pittsylvania)
Peyton's Battery (Richmond "Orange")
Poague's Battery (1st Rockbridge)
Potts' Battery (North Carolina)
Price's Battery (Danville)
Price's Battery ("B", Sumter, Ga.)
Raine's Battery (Lynchburg "Lee")
Rambout's Battery (Petersburg "Cockade")
Ramsey's Battery (Rowan or "D", 1st N. C. Reg.)
Read's Battery (Pulaski, Ga.)

Reese's Battery ("Jeff Davis," Ala.)
Reilly's Battery (Rowan, N. C.)
Rhett's Battery (South Carolina)
Rhett's Battery (Tennessee)
Rice's Battery ("8th Star" or Shenandoah-Page. Merged with Wooding's Danville Battery in 1862)
Richards' Battery ("Madison," Miss.)
Richardson's Battery (2d Co. Washington Artillery, La.)
Richardson's Battery (James City)
Ritter's Battery (Henrico)
Rives' Battery (South Carolina)
Rives' Battery (Nelson)
Robertson's Battery ("Appomattox Invincibles")
Roemer's Battery (Goochland)
Rogers' Battery (Loudoun. Disbanded Oct., 1862)
Ross's Battery ("A", Sumter, Ga.)
Rosser's Battery (2d Co. Washington Artillery, La.)
Ruffin's Battery (Surry)
Sands' Battery (Henrico)
Shields' Battery (1st Richmond Howitzers)
Shoemaker's Battery (Lynchburg)
Shumaker's Battery (Danville)
Smith's Battery (Bedford)
Smith's Battery (3d Richmond Howitzers)
Smoot's Battery (Alexandria)
Snead's Battery (Fluvanna)
Southall's Battery (Albemarle "Everett")
Squires' Battery (1st Co. Washington Artillery, La.)
Stamps' Battery (Danville "Ringgold")
Stanard's Battery (Richmond "Thomas")
Stanard's Battery (3d Richmond Howitzers)
Staten's Battery (Macon, Ga.)
Stoope's Battery (Petersburg "Cockade")
Stribling's Battery (Fauquier)
Sturdivant's Battery (Albemarle)

Sullivan's Battery (Richmond "Hampden")
Talley's Battery (Goochland)
Tanner's Battery (Richmond)
Taylor's Battery (Bath)
Thompson's Battery ("Louisiana Guard")
Thompson's Battery (Portsmouth. Mustered out Oct., 1862)
Thomson's Battery ("Ashby" Horse Artillery)
Thornton's Battery (Caroline)
Turner's Battery (Goochland)
Utterback's Battery (Warrenton)
Vickery's Battery (Norfolk L. A. Blues)
Walker's Battery (Richmond "Purcell")
Walker's Battery (Richmond "Otey")
Ward's Battery ("Madison," Miss.)
Waters' Battery (West Augusta)
Watson's Battery (2d Richmond Howitzers)
Webb's Battery (North Carolina)
Weisiger's Battery (Manchester)
Weisiger's Battery (Albemarle)
Williams' Battery ("C", 1st N. C. Reg., Charlotte)
Wimbish's Battery ("Long Island," Campbell. Disbanded Oct., 1862)
Winfield's Battery ("C", Sumter Batt., Irwin, Ga.)
Wooding's Battery (Danville)
Woolfolk's Battery (Ashland)
Wright's Battery (Halifax)
Wyatt's Battery (Albemarle, "Everett")
Yeatman's Battery (Gloucester)
Young's Battery (Norfolk "Harbor Guards")
Young's Battery (Yorktown)
Young's Battery (Fairfax. Became Co. "G", 14th Va. Infty., in Oct., 1862, but later transformed into a light battery)
Zimmerman's Battery ("Pee Dee," S. C.)

FEDERAL

PAGE

Arnold's Battery, 132, 136, 388, 670, 683
Ayres' Battery 136
Bigelow's Battery 642, 647
Benjamin's Battery 298, 310
Best's Battery 171

PAGE

Brady's Battery.............. 194
Brown's Battery 647, 670, 685
Calef's Battery 617, 618
Campbell's Battery 299
Carlisle's Battery 136
Cothran's Battery........ 171, 305

PAGE

Clark's Battery..169, 310, 468, 641
Cook's Battery.............. 310
Cooper's Battery............. 618
Cowan's Battery.........305, 686
Cushing's Battery............ 670
Daniel's Battery.............. 670
Dickenson's Battery.......... 387
Dieckmann's Battery......... 479
Dilger's Battery......475, 479, 619
Dimick's Battery............. 505
Dow's Maine Battery......... 647
Durrell's Battery............. 310
Edwards' Battery............ 136
Fitzhugh's Battery........... 685
Frank's Battery.............. 305
Gibson's Battery............. 319
Graham's Battery............ 308
Greene's Battery............. 136
Griffin's Battery..132, 133, 136, 223
Hall's 2d Maine Battery...617, 618
Hampton's Battery.......... 171
Hart's Battery............... 642
Hazlett's Battery............. 650
Hazzard's Battery,
              215, 391, 395, 686
Heckman's Battery........... 621
Hill's Battery............393, 480
Hunt's Battery.............. 136
Kirby's Battery.............. 194
Knapp's Battery 171, 249, 305
Martin's Battery............. 596
Muhlenberg's Battery........ 310
McMullen's Battery.......... 310

PAGE

Osborn's Battery 215
Parson's Battery 685
Pendleton's Battery........... 348
Pennington's Battery 589
Pettit's Battery 215, 363
Phillips' Battery 642
Randall's Battery 395
Randolph's Battery........... 216
Reynolds' Battery 618
Rhode Island Battery.....132, 136
Rickett's Battery, 132, 133, 136, 655
Robertson's Battery,
        210, 308, 309, 319, 585
Roity's Battery 670
Seeley's Battery.............. 641
Simmon's Battery............ 310
Smith's Battery..641, 645, 646, 657
Stevens' Battery.............. 655
Stewart's Battery 622
Taft's Battery............310, 669
Thompson's Battery.......393, 642
Tidball's Battery,
      136, 210, 309, 319, 350
Von Kleiser's Battery......... 310
Weeden's Battery............ 223
Weed's Battery..........310, 459
Weidrick's Battery.......479, 480
Weir's Battery............... 685
Wheeler's Battery....479, 480, 619
Wilkerson's Battery.......620, 621
Winslow's Battery............ 641
Woodruff's Battery.......... 670

BATTALION INDEX

The battalion organizations of the Army of Northern Virginia always bore two, and sometimes three names, a fact which leads to much confusion in the study of the Artillery records. The records of the battalions, which were referred to as such in the latter part of the War, embrace the records of the constituent batteries. It is, therefore, essential for the student to know to what battalion a particular battery belonged in order to trace the complete record of the latter. The battalion organizations are frequently included in the text in order to simplify a study of the various batteries.

PAGE

Alexander's Battalion (Lee's old battalion),
358, 361, 371, 374, 377, 388, 396, 416, 420, 442, 450, 452, 467, 507, 509, 528, 535, 549, 563, 567, 575, 599, 635, 636, 644, 647, 656, 657, 664, 689, 693, 696, 701, 704, 712

Andrews' Battalion,
244, 245, 248, 345, 358, 379, 393, 399, 408, 421, 442, 451, 453, 454, 458, 515, 516, 519, 520, 530, 534, 535, 541, 545, 562, 563, 568, 600, 601, 606, 608, 610, 624, 625, 630, 636, 651, 665, 666, 696, 704

Beckham's Battalion (Pelham's old battalion. See Horse Artillery Battalion)

Boggs' Battalion..707, 837, 909, 916

Branch's Battalion........708, 915

Braxton's Battalion (Andrews' old battalion),
724, 730, 738, 769, 779, 785, 792, 800, 804, 806, 813, 827, 876, 885, 886, 888, 889, 891, 909, 913, 917, 920, 922, 926, 944

Breathed's Battalion (Horse Artillery) 916, 917, 927

Brockenbrough's Battalion, 345, 358

Brown's Division (Nelson's and Hardaway's battalions),
725, 726, 730, 738

Brown's Battalion (See First Virginia Regiment)

Brunson's Battalion (See Pegram's Battalion)

Cabell's Battalion (See also Hamilton's Battalion),
189, 199, 304, 305, 321, 328, 357, 369, 370, 371, 377, 379, 380, 391, 396, 408, 409, 419, 442, 450, 451, 452, 518, 545, 563, 567, 609, 635, 636, 643, 646, 657, 658, 664, 701, 704, 712, 714, 722, 738, 763, 777, 779, 781, 782, 792, 799, 813, 816, 818, 820, 821, 823, 825, 836, 860, 865, 909, 911, 917

Carter's Division (Cutshaw's and Page's battalions),
725, 726, 730, 739

Carter's Battalion,
421, 442, 489, 490, 493, 494, 506, 507, 509, 510, 512, 513, 545, 562, 563, 568, 599, 600, 610, 619, 620, 630, 636, 651, 664, 696, 697, 701, 703, 709

Chew's Battalion (Pelham's old battalion. See Horse Artillery)

Coit's Battalion,
740, 837, 860, 867, 875, 909

Courtney's Battalion,
244, 245, 258, 259, 281, 328, 329, 358

Cutshaw's Battalion (Original battalion).....725, 730, 739, 769, 779, 786, 787, 788, 790, 792, 813, 819, 820, 821, 823, 831, 856, 889, 909, 913, 917, 920, 922, 926, 944

Cutshaw's Battalion (Page's and Cutshaw's consolidated)

Cutts' Battalion (See Sumter Battalion)

Dance's Battalion (See First Virginia Regiment)

Dearing's Battalion (See also Jones' Battalion and Read's Battalion).....358, 411, 420, 442, 445, 455, 567, 575, 577, 609, 635, 636, 646, 647, 658, 664, 701, 704, 712, 722, 723, 814, 847, 855

PAGE

Dearing's Battalion (Pelham's old battalion. See Horse Artillery) 725

De Lagnel's Battalion 204

Deshler's Battalion ...205, 831, 909

Eshleman's Battalion (See Washington Artillery)

Eshleman's Battalion (Improvised),
722, 726, 740, 848, 902, 909

First Virginia Regiment (Brown's, Dance's, Hardaway's) 205, 234, 236, 242, 280, 282, 287, 292, 293, 325, 333, 339, 345, 346, 360, 374, 379, 385, 395, 408, 421, 442, 466, 469, 507, 540, 545, 562, 563, 568, 600, 602, 610, 624, 630, 636, 696, 697, 704, 854, 909

Frobel's Battalion, 257, 269, 272, 280, 297, 300, 309, 322, 328, 333, 370, 377

Garnett's Battalion (See Richardson's Battalion), 419, 442, 450, 452, 467, 545, 569, 575, 609, 618, 622, 623, 630, 636, 651, 664, 677, 699, 701, 703, 704

Gibbes' Battalion (King's old battalion) 827, 831, 836, 840, 854, 865, 902, 909, 915, 917

Hamilton's Battalion (See also Cabell's Battalion), 280, 289, 380

Hart's Battalion (Horse Artillery) 927

Hardaway's Battalion (Brown's old battalion), 725, 736, 738, 769, 779, 785, 786, 787, 813, 818, 820, 821, 823, 831, 856, 897, 909, 912, 917, 919

Haskell's Battalion (Henry's old battalion), 712, 714, 722, 725, 738, 763, 777, 779, 781, 799, 804, 805, 816, 818, 819, 821, 823, 825, 836, 840, 859, 861, 868, 875, 897, 900, 909, 911, 917

Henry's Battalion (See also Haskell's Battalion), 411, 420, 442, 445, 453, 557, 567, 609, 635, 636, 642, 643, 645, 658, 664, 696, 701, 703, 704, 712

PAGE

Horse Artillery Battalion (Pelham, Beckham, Dearing, Chew) 298, 299, 300, 301, 302, 303, 305, 310, 312, 317, 323, 346, 347, 349, 350, 352, 354, 366, 373, 379, 380, 408, 422, 434, 442, 460, 461, 468, 480, 494, 550, 576, 578, 583, 584, 585, 586, 587, 590, 591, 592, 594, 595, 706, 717, 747, 763, 773, 794, 828, 829, 904, 909, 916, 917, 932

Huger's Battalion (Alexander's old battalion), 724, 736, 737, 763, 777, 787, 794, 799, 804, 805, 813, 816, 818, 821, 823, 836, 840, 859, 860, 909, 911, 917

Johnson's Battalion (Improvised) 897, 898, 900, 909, 912, 917, 925, 944

Johnston's Battalion (Horse Artillery) 927

Jones' Division (Read's and Owen's battalions) 737

Jones' Battalion (See also Cutshaw's Battalion), 203, 205, 236, 242, 279, 282, 297, 306, 307, 328, 334, 339, 345, 358, 391, 421, 442, 467, 494, 507, 512, 545, 562, 563, 568, 600, 602, 603, 604, 605, 610, 621, 630, 637, 651, 665, 666, 697, 704, 715, 891, 909

King's Battalion (13th Va. Batt.) 736, 801, 802, 806, 826, 827, 831, 854, 887, 909

King's Battalion (McLaughlin's old battalion), 887, 909, 913, 917, 920

King's Battalion (Improvised. Dismounted) ...913, 917, 920, 926

Lane's Battalion (See Sumter Battalion)

Latimer's Battalion (See Andrews' Battalion)

Lee's Battalion (See also Alexander's Battalion), 204, 257, 269, 270, 271, 272, 275, 276, 281, 287, 292, 297, 300, 303, 306, 307, 328, 335, 336, 339

Leyden's Battalion (9th Georgia Battalion) 920, 925

PAGE

Lightfoot's Battalion (Richmond Defense Battalion),
825, 707, 740, 825, 831, 858,
909, 920

McGregor's Battalion (Horse Artillery) 927

McIntosh's Battalion,
421, 442, 467, 494, 507, 510,
512, 540, 545, 562, 563, 569,
609, 616, 618, 620, 621, 630,
651, 701, 704, 739, 769, 778,
779, 780, 781, 792, 804, 805,
806, 813, 822, 826, 834, 844,
845, 860, 896, 897, 899, 909,
910, 913, 917, 926

McLaughlin's Battalion (See also King's Battalion),
801, 802, 877, 879, 886, 888,
891, 909, 926, 927

Moore's Battalion (3d North Carolina Battalion)..... 335, 361

Moseley's Battalion,
707, 740, 805, 837, 838, 859, 915

Nelson's Battalion,
199, 205, 234 237, 242, 283,
292, 293, 318, 325, 335, 339,
345, 346, 360, 380, 397, 422,
442, 450, 454, 516, 528, 546,
568, 610, 624, 630, 637, 651,
666, 696, 701, 704, 715, 716,
717, 738, 764, 765, 769, 779,
785, 792, 813, 827, 876, 879,
880, 885, 886, 888, 891, 909,
912, 917, 920, 926

Owen's Battalion (King's old battalion, 13th Va. Batt.),
722, 737, 814, 825, 831, 854,
902, 909, 922, 926

Owen's Battalion (See Washington Artillery)

Page's Battalion (Carter's old battalion)..... 779, 785, 787,
788, 790, 791, 799, 813, 831, 909

Page's Battalion (Page's and Cutshaw's consolidated)

Pegram's Battalion (Walker's old battalion),
564, 609, 616, 618, 619, 620,
622, 630, 651, 701, 704, 739,
769, 779, 780, 781, 791, 797,
800, 804, 805, 806, 822, 834,
841, 871, 875, 896, 905, 906,
909, 910, 914, 917, 929

Pelham's Battalion (See Horse Artillery Battalion)

PAGE

Pendleton's Battalion (Reserve Battalion).....143, 185, 189, 205

Pierson's Battalion........203,
279, 282, 297, 303, 307, 322, 327

Poague's Battalion,
569, 609, 618, 622, 630, 636,
651, 665, 701, 704, 739, 767,
768, 769, 791, 804, 805, 818,
821, 822, 857, 858, 909, 910,
914, 917, 931, 932, 939, 944

Read's Battalion (Dearing's old battalion),
737, 814, 816, 821, 831, 834,
837, 838, 848, 855, 856, 909

Richardson's Battalion (Original)..........199, 205, 237, 242

Richardson's Battalion (Garnett's old battalion),
740, 769, 779, 780, 781, 800,
806, 840, 860, 909, 914, 917

Richmond Howitzer Battalion (See also Richmond Batteries),
114, 115, 118, 130, 141, 142,
184, 188, 189, 202, 204, 242, 280

Saunders' Battalion...280, 289, 380

Shumaker's Battalion,
257, 258, 266, 282, 327

Stark's Battalion,
708, 740, 858, 897, 912, 917, 944

Stribling's Battalion 909, 916

Sturdivant's Battalion 926

Sumter Battalion (11th Georgia Artillery Battalion, Cutts', Lane's. See also Georgia Batteries).....143, 184, 199,
201, 205, 234, 237, 241, 242,
282, 283, 292, 297, 303, 306,
307, 328, 334, 335, 339, 345,
346, 360, 380, 422, 442, 450,
454, 528, 546, 569, 609, 618,
622, 630, 651, 701, 703, 704,
717, 740, 763, 781, 791, 800,
804, 806, 842, 845, 909, 910,
914, 917

Thomson's Battalion (Horse Artillery) 927

Walker's Battalion (See also Pegram's Battalion),
204, 245, 254, 258, 281, 311,
323, 328, 335, 345, 358, 379,
399, 408, 420, 442, 461, 466,
467, 489, 494, 506, 507, 510,
513, 540, 545, 562, 563

PAGE

Walton's Division (Eshleman's
and Dearing's battalions)... 722
Walton's Battalion (See Washington Artillery)
Washington Artillery Battalion
of Louisiana (Walton's, Eshleman's, Owen's. See also
Louisiana Batteries),
38, 71, 94, 116, 128, 130, 135,
141, 143, 185, 189, 199, 204,
205, 258, 273, 281, 285, 287,
296, 297, 300, 303, 306, 307,

PAGE

309, 310, 319, 321, 322, 328,
333, 336, 339, 355, 356, 357,
358, 361, 370, 374, 377, 386,
387, 388, 390, 396, 397, 409,
410, 414, 415, 420, 442, 450,
451, 454, 515, 516, 518, 522,
524, 525, 532, 545, 563, 567,
609, 635, 636, 664, 670, 677,
684, 685, 691, 699, 700, 704,
712, 722, 726, 737, 814, 825,
831, 840, 847, 848, 853, 902,
905, 909, 915, 931